LOWNDES AND RUDOLF

The Law of General Average and The York-Antwerp Rules

BRITISH SHIPPING LAWS

LOWNDES AND RUDOLF

The Law of General Average and The York-Antwerp Rules

FOURTEENTH EDITION

By

R. R. CORNAH
Fellow of the Association of Average Adjusters

J. REEDER QC
of Stone Chambers

SWEET & MAXWELL

THOMSON REUTERS

Published in 2013 by
Sweet & Maxwell Limited of 100 Avenue Road,
http://www.sweetandmaxwell.co.uk
Typeset by LBJ Typesetting Ltd of Kingsclere
Printed and bound in Great Britain by
Athanaeum Press Ltd, Gateshead

No natural forests were destroyed to make this product;
only farmed timber was used and re-planted.

British Library Cataloguing in Publication Data

A CIP catalogue record for this book is available from the British Library

ISBN 9780414028463

THE LAW OF GENERAL AVERAGE

First Edition	(1873) By Richard Lowndes
Second Edition	(1874)
Third Edition	(1878)
Fourth Edition	(1888)
Fifth Edition	(1912) By Edward L. de Hart and George Rupert Rudolf
Sixth Edition	(1922)

THE YORK-ANTWERP RULES

First Edition	(1926) By George Rupert Rudolf

LOWNDES & RUDOLF: THE LAW OF GENERAL AVERAGE AND THE YORK-ANTWERP RULES

Seventh Edition	(1948) By A. J. Hodgson and George Rupert Rudolf
Eighth Edition	(1955) By J. F. Donaldson and C. T. Ellis
Ninth Edition	(1964) By J. F. Donaldson, C. T. Ellis and C. S. Staughton
Tenth Edition	(1975) By Sir John Donaldson, C. S. Staughton and D. J. Wilson
Eleventh Edition	(1990) By D. J. Wilson and J. H. S. Cooke
Twelfth Edition	(1997) By D. J. Wilson and J. H. S. Cooke
Thirteenth Edition	(2008) By J. H. S. Cooke and R. R. Cornah
Fourteenth Edition	(2013) By R. R. Cornah and J. Reeder

PREFACE TO THE FOURTEENTH EDITION

In 1873, the original year of publication of this work, Richard Lowndes was the first Chairman of the Association of Average Adjusters to deliver a formal Address. He noted that "we live in times in which it is hardly possible to stand still". The law of insurance and general average was becoming "every year more of a science", relying on the increasing number of Court judgements that were supplanting the somewhat haphazard Customs of Lloyd's. From this Address and a subsequent one given at the first meeting of the Liverpool Association of Average Adjusters in 1883, it is clear that he recognised and embraced change, welcoming the closer involvement of insurers and shipowners and the opportunities to define new principles that met the needs of a rapidly evolving commercial world.

He would undoubtedly have been delighted to see that his "bible" on General Average was also continuing to evolve, with this 14th Edition being the first to be available to subscribers online. The idea of hyper-links in the text that take you to statutes and judgements might have taken him a little getting used to but, once understood, he would have applauded the obvious usefulness to busy commercial people.

He would also have approved of the constructive dialogue now taking place internationally that is directed towards restoring the broad consensus that existed for so many years prior to the appearance of the 2004 York-Antwerp Rules. The recent meetings of the Comite Maritime International, the custodians of the Rules, are summarised in Section 3 and the outcome is expected to be a new version of the Rules in 2016 which, it is to be hoped, will enjoy the support of all practitioners and commercial interests.

By that time it is likely that the fate of the Rotterdam Rules will have become clearer and General Average procedures will need to take account of the practical implications of their "presumed fault" regime. The provisions of the Rotterdam Rules relevant to general average are therefore reviewed in Section 2.

Piracy has continued to trouble sea-farers in many parts of the world and it has therefore seemed appropriate to extend further the comments made in the last edition. The "Bunga Melati Dua", a cargo case, touched on the difficult relationship between public policy and the payment of ransoms to pirates. There has been limited new case law of direct relevant to general average but the "Lehman

Timber" has shed useful light on matters relating to general average security documents and the cost of exercising lines.

Recent changes in Lloyd's Open Form relating to large container vessels have been welcomed by lawyers and average adjusters alike, and are duly summarised in the Chapter on Rule VI.

We gratefully acknowledge the kind permission granted by the Association of Average Adjusters to copy a selection of their rules of Practice; the United States Association of Average Adjusters to copy their Notes on the Rule of Practice dealing with airfreight; and the Corporation of Lloyd's, BIMCO and the International Salvage Union in respect of their documentation reproduced in Appendix 4.

R.R.C.
Royal Liver Building,
Liverpool, L3 1JR

J.R.
Stone Chambers,
London, WC1R 5EF

TABLE OF CONTENTS

SECTION 1
HISTORICAL INTRODUCTION

SECTION 2
SOME PRINCIPLES OF THE LAW OF CARRIAGE BY SEA

SECTION 3
HISTORY AND DEVELOPMENT OF THE YORK-ANTWERP RULES

SECTION 4
THE YORK-ANTWERP RULES 1994 AND 2004

SECTION 7
GENERAL AVERAGE, INSURANCE AND RECOVERIES

APPENDICES

Table of Cases

Table of Statutes

SECTION 1

HISTORICAL INTRODUCTION

1. ORIGINS OF THE LAW OF GENERAL AVERAGE

The Rhodians

The first known statement of the law of general average is a small fragment of ancient Greek legislation, which forms the text for a chapter in the Digest of Justinian: "*Lege Rhodia cavetur ut si levandae navis gratia jactus mercium factus est, omnium contributione sarciatur quod pro omnibus datum est.*"[1] "The Rhodian law decrees that if in order to lighten a ship merchandise has been thrown overboard, that which has been given for all should be replaced by the contribution of all." This short sentence contains both the principle and a perfect example of the peculiar communism to which seafaring men are brought in extremities. What is given, or sacrificed, in time of danger, for the sake of all, is to be replaced by a general contribution on the part of all who have been thereby brought to safety. This is a rule which from the oldest recorded times has been universal amongst seafaring men, no matter to what country they belonged, being obviously founded upon the necessities of their position. **00.01**

The emergence of Rhodes as a maritime state is described as follows by Pardessus: **00.02**

> "While the Phoenicians and the Carthaginians were making a commerce truly universal, a career less vast, but yet not without importance, was opening itself to the navigation of the Greeks, and especially the Greek colonies in Asia Minor and the adjacent islands. These, surrounded by fertile lands, intersected with bays and rivers, not far off from one another, and yet very diversified in their agricultural products, early profited by the facilities their position gave them, to exchange their commodities, and to carry them into Phoenicia, which was a sort of entrepôt."[2]

Thus sprung up a commerce which appears to have been of some importance, though perhaps not extending very far beyond the limits of the Aegean Sea.

[1] Digest XIV, 2.1.
[2] J.M. Pardessus, *Collection des Lois Maritimes* (1837), Intr. xxvi, xxvii.

Rhodes is one of the cities decorated by the title of "mistress of the sea". In the Punic wars, according to Polybius, Rhodes took the Roman side, and did good service in attacking the war-vessels of the Carthaginians.[3] Cicero says of the Rhodians that they were a people whose naval power and discipline remained even to times within his own memory.[4] Pardessus considers it probable that the Rhodians borrowed their maritime laws from the Phoenicians, though he hardly offers any particular reasons for the conjecture.[5]

00.03 However, to say that Greeks from Rhodes were the first to express the principle of general average in words, and so give it currency, throws very little light on its true origin. It must have been already very ancient and very widespread as a practice before it became so neatly formulated. It must be remembered that for perhaps thousands of years, the merchants or owners of cargo used, to sail with their wares from port to port like pedlars. In these little vessels, mostly navigating the Mediterranean or Aegean Sea where storms quickly spring up and subside, occasions would be frequent where shipwreck could only be averted by lightening the ship of portions of her cargo, a measure which, however beneficial to the rest, might to one man on board mean ruin. His consent to such a sacrifice could only be bought by a promise–first express, then customary and taken for granted–that when, or if, the ship came safe to shore, all who had profited by his loss would pay their share to make it good.

The Romans

00.04 The Romans, the great improvers of other people's inventions, have given us a good illustration in the chapter of the Digest of Justinian headed De Lege Rhodia de Jactu. The sentence quoted above takes the place of honour, as a sort of text, and is followed by a fragmentary collection of short judgments or opinions. It is not easy to trace the principle of arrangement,[6] unless it be, first, to show by examples (such as the cutting away of a mast) that the case of throwing cargo overboard is only to be treated as an illustration of some more general principle; secondly, to establish that this rule of contribution is to be restricted to such sea-losses as flow from a voluntary sacrifice for the sake of all, leaving every loss, whether of ship or cargo, which is the result of pure accident, to lie where it falls; and thirdly, when these two points are made clear, to determine some of the more complicated questions which arise in carrying the principle consistently into operation.

For an example under the third head, in the opinion of Julianus a claim for contribution to the cost of temporary repairs at a port of refuge (Hippo) failed, since the expenditure was incurred rather to fit out the ship than to save the cargo (*sumptus instruendae magis navis, quam conservandarum mercium gratia factus est*).[7] Some of the texts are not concerned with general average at all,

[3] Park. Ins. Intr. xlvii.
[4] Pro. leg. Manil. c.13.
[5] 1 Pard. Intr. xxix.
[6] But see Buckland's *Manual of Roman Private Law*, p.23.
[7] Digest XIV, 2.6. See now r.XIV of the York-Antwerp Rules.

the last in the chapter being an explanation of the difference between lump-sum freight and freight calculated on the quantity of cargo carried or discharged.[8] Another records a case of shipwrecked seamen who "were plundered by the tax-farmers who live in the Cyclades Islands". The rescript of the Emperor Antoninus ran:

> "Let it be judged by the Rhodian law which deals with nautical matters, so far as that is not directly contrary to our own law. For I am lord of the whole world, but the law is lord of the sea."[9]

This may have been an early recognition of the difficulties encountered even by the most powerful nations in seeking to regulate the international transactions of merchants exclusively by their own laws.[10]

The Middle Ages

After the fall of the Roman Empire, its laws fell into oblivion. In the recollection of seafaring men, however, or as tradition, or as a rule commending itself on account of its utility, the outlines of this chapter *de jactu* retained a hold in some degree over the seafaring population of Europe, and were reproduced, in a simpler form, in the several collections of sea laws which belong to a later period. **00.05**

The Rolls of Oleron

Of the codes or collections of customs here spoken of, perhaps the most important, as that which had the most extended authority, is one called the *Rolls* or *Judgments of Oleron*. Their origin is lost in obscurity, but from internal evidence we may conclude that they were a collection of judgments, probably delivered in some court of Bordeaux, and having reference to the commerce in wine which had its centre in that city. According to Selden these rolls were revised by Richard I on his return from the Holy Land during his stay at the Isle of Oleron, and were declared to be the law of the sea, under the title of la ley Olyroun.[11] Be that as it may, for some reason or other these judgments obtained, and held for some centuries, over the greater part of Europe a very considerable authority. They were copied into the Black Book of the Admiralty.[12] In 1402 Parliament petitioned Henry IV to require the Admirals to govern their decisions exclusively by the laws of Oleron, the ancient laws of the sea, and the common law of England.[13] The old **00.06**

[8] Digest XIV, 2.10.

[9] Digest XIV, 2.9.

[10] In 1935 a translation of The York-Antwerp Rules 1924 by G.R. Rudolf (a constituent part of this present work) was published in the Soviet Union. The foreword commended the book for its utility, but added: "It can be definitely stated that with the evolution of a socialist society there will be no need of any general average rules".

[11] Selden, *Mare Clausum*, lib. 2, cap. 24; 1 Pard. 289.

[12] 1 Pard. 309; Twiss, *Black Book*, p.97.

[13] *Rotuli Parliamentorum*, Vol.3, p.498; 4 Pard. 197, where it is erroneously treated as an Act of Parliament.

laws of Flanders,[14] of Catalonia,[15] of Genoa,[16] and of Holland,[17] in like manner contain clauses literally copied from the *Judgments of Oleron*.

00.07 So far as concerns general average, all that is said in the Rolls of Oleron is the following:

> "ART.8. A ship leaves Bordeaux or elsewhere, and it happens that a storm takes it at sea and the ship cannot escape without throwing out goods from within. The master is bound to say to the merchants: "Signors, we cannot escape without throwing out the wines and the goods." The merchants, if there are any, shall signify their good will who shall agree to this jettison, and that the master's reasons are most clear; and if they do not agree, the master ought, nevertheless, not to fear to throw out as much as shall seem to him good, swearing himself and the third of his crew on the Holy Gospels, when he shall have come safe ashore, that he did it of no malice, but to save their lives, the ship, the goods, and the wines. Those which have been thrown out ought to be appraised at the rate of those which shall come safe, and shall be divided pound by pound amongst the merchants; and the master ought to share on account of the ship or his freight, at his choice, to restore the damage. The mariners ought to have each a ton (tonnel) free, and the rest shall contribute to the jettison according to what he has, if he defends himself on the sea like a man; and if he does not defend himself, he shall have nothing free; and the master shall be believed upon his oath. And this is the judgment in this case.[18]
>
> ART. 9. It occurs that the master of a ship must cut away his mast by force of tempest; he ought to call the merchants and show them that it is fitting to cut the mast to save the ship and the wares; and sometimes it occurs that one cuts cables and the anchors to save the ship and the wares. These ought to be counted pound by pound like jettison; and the merchants ought to share and pay without delay before their goods are put out of the ship; and if the ship was held fast (en dur siege) and the master was delayed by their debate, and there was collusion, the master ought not to suffer, but he ought to have his freight on those wines as he will take for the others. And this is the judgment in this case.[19]
>
> ART. 35. It is ordered and established for custom of the sea that, when it occurs that one makes jettison from a ship, it is well written at Rome that all the merchandise and effects contained in the ship should share in the jettison, pound for pound; and if there are cups of silver more than one in the ship, they ought to contribute to the jettison [ou faire gré], and one cup also, if it is not borne at table for the service of the mariners; robes and linen if they are not yet cut, or have not yet been worn, all shall contribute to the jettison. And this is the judgment in this case."[20]

Other Old Sea-laws of Europe

00.08 Most of the other old sea-laws of Europe, such as the law of Wisbuy,[21] the laws of Amsterdam, of the Hanseatic League, of Flanders, of Genoa, and Catalonia,

[14] 1 Pard. 375.
[15] 5 Pard. 362.
[16] 4 Pard. 521.
[17] 1 Pard. 406.
[18] *Rolls of Oleron*, Art.8; 1 Pard. 328. In explanation of this franchise allowed to the sailors, it may be mentioned that by Art.31, those seamen who have agreed to be paid as wages a certain proportion of the freight shall each be allowed one ton free of freight. This ton was likewise, it appears, free of contribution to average if its owner behaved well.
[19] *Rolls of Oleron*, Art.9; 1 Pard. 329.
[20] *Rolls of Oleron*, Art.35; 1 Pard. 329. This article is No.32 in the manuscript of the English Admiralty. It is not found in any other copy, printed or MS. (1 Pard. 329, fn.1).
[21] Tradition ascribes the origin of the law of Wisbuy to a convention of mariners and merchants from all parts of Europe, meeting on the occasion of some great fair or mart at Wisbuy in the Baltic.

either set forth literal translations of these three articles, or reproduce their substance, albeit with less drama and vivacity. Everywhere jettison and the cutting away of a mast and slipping a cable are the first examples of a general contribution; to which are gradually added, in later codes, some instances of extraordinary expenditure for the common safety, such as the expense incurred in lightening a stranded ship.

English Origins

England was almost the only maritime country which did not possess a code of sea-law. Its early commercial law appears to have been regulated by the merchants themselves. The name of Lombard Street[22] attests the tradition which attributes to settlers from the Lombard cities, probably in the times of the Medici, the introduction to England of the practice of marine insurance. Pardessus gives the text of a statute of the time of William I concerning jettison, which, however, is not to be found in the Statute Book, and cannot be safely treated as authentic.[23] A statute of Elizabeth I recorded that questions of insurance and trade had theretofore been dealt with by certain older merchants, "grave and discreet persons", appointed by the Lord Mayor of London, "as men by reason of their experience fittest to understand such matters".[24] This statute constituted a special mercantile tribunal to take their place; but the tribunal never found much favour amongst the merchants.[25] In the meanwhile, according to such books as Beawes, Magens and others, published by mercantile men for use among themselves, the rules followed in these matters consisted of a body of customs, in which were embedded provisions borrowed without visible discrimination from the various codes and sea-laws of all the countries of Europe. When, in London, Lloyd's coffee-house came to be the headquarters of the business of marine insurance, it became also, naturally, the headquarters of information as to these customs, which hence acquired the title of "the Customs of Lloyd's". **00.09**

What is almost certainly the earliest recorded instance of a dispute concerning contribution towards a jettison in the English courts was heard in the Court of King's Bench in 1285, about 20 years after the promulgation of the Rolls of Oleron, and was a successful attempt to prevent the modification of existing customs to accord with the law as there stated. The dispute was between, on the one side, the barons of the Cinque Ports and sailors, and, on the other, various merchants, principally importers of wine from Gascony, led by Gregory de Rokesley and Henry le Waleys. The complaint of the former was that, when cargo was jettisoned, although it had been conceded to them since time immemorial that the ship should be free of any obligation to contribute, the merchants were compelling them to "appraise their ships . . . in order to make acquittance for the wines or **00.10**

[22] The policy which is set out in the first schedule to the Marine Insurance Act 1906 includes these words: "And it is agreed by us, the insurers, that this writing or policy of insurance shall be of as much force and effect as the surest writing or policy of assurance heretofore made in Lombard Street . . .".

[23] 4 Pard. 203.

[24] 1 Marshall, *Insurance*, p.25.

[25] 1 Marshall, *Insurance*, p.26.

goods thrown in this way into the sea . . . to the most grievous loss of those barons and sailors . . . and in defiance of the liberties granted to those same barons etc.". The report continues[26]:

> "And the aforesaid Gregory and Henry came along with many merchants of England and Gascony. And, after hearing the arguments of those merchants as well as those of the aforesaid barons and sailors, it is decreed, granted, and definitively adjudged by the Lord King and his council that, in the first place, henceforth the ship in which the wares or wines were with all its apparatus, the ring carried on the finger of the ship's captain, the sailors' victuals, the implements used in making their meals, the jewelry, belt and silver cup from which the ship's captain drinks, if he possesses any, shall be freed from contributing to any aid for the aforesaid jettisoning into the sea. And also the sailors shall keep the freightage of the wines and other goods on board ship which have been saved. And the ship's captain shall lose his freightage for the barrels or goods thus thrown into the sea. And all other goods on board ship, of the sailors as well as of the merchants, such as wines, merchandise, money in gross, beds and other goods and wares, with the exception of the aforesaid apparatus and tackle for the ship, the sailors' victuals, the implements for making their meals, the jewelry, belt and silver cup, the ring and the freightage for goods which have been saved, as aforesaid ought henceforth to be appraised for the purposes of making an aid in acquittance for the wines or goods thrown out of the ship into the sea through a storm at sea."

2. Origin of the Word "Average"

Early References

00.11 The word "average" is of much later origin than the thing. However, there are to be found in the Constitutum Usus of the City of Pisa, a code dating from about A.D. 1160, some faint traces of the growth of a technical term out of the common Italian word avere, the having of property. The code is written in a sort of Italianised or mongrel Latin; the captain, for example, is called capitaneus, the sailors marinarii, and so forth. The word avere is used throughout the code to denote the basis of contribution or contributory value: thus, the jettison and damage through jettison, it says, shall be equalised over "totum avere", all the property remaining in the ship. In another place it speaks of those whose avere (property) has been cast out, and those whose avere is safe.[27] In a later Pisan code, A.D. 1298, a regulation concerning jettison is headed, "de divisione haveris projecti".[28] In a Genoese code, A.D. 1341, the word averia, or avaria, for it is spelt both ways, has come to mean expenses or losses for the common good, and as such forming charges upon the avere or entire property.[29] In a statute of Ancona of 1397, the word varea is used to

[26] Sayles, *Select Cases in the Court of King's Bench*, Vol.1. (Selden Society Publications, Vol.55, pp.156–157, 1936) reproduced by kind permission of the Society.

[27] 4 Pard. 580–581.

[28] 4 Pard. 593.

[29] 4 Pard. 521.

denote the contribution itself.[30] And in a Venetian code of the fourteenth century we find the phrase dividatur per avariam used to express a general contribution.[31] All sorts of theories have been propounded as to the origin of the word "average", which in this sense is universal in all the languages of Europe under various thin disguises, as avarie, haverei, and the like.[32] These theories, however, are purely conjectural, whereas here we have something like the vestiges of the actual growth of this peculiar technical expression.

Guidon de la Mer, 1556–1584

Coming now to a much later period, between the years 1556 and 1584, we find, in the remarkable treatise called the *Guidon de la Mer*,[33] the first express definition of general average. The work is a digest, or authoritative code, of the law of insurance, apparently intended for the use of the then newly constituted consular court of Rouen. Incidentally, however, it touches on other branches of maritime law such as affreightment, bottomry and general average: 00.12

> "The insurer is bound to indemnify his merchant for the expenses, losses (mises), average, and damage which occur to the merchandise from the time of loading, the whole of which is comprised in this word average, which receives several divisions. The first is called common or gross average, that which arises by jettison, for ransom or composition, for cables, sails, or mast cut for the saving of the ship and merchandise, the compensation for which is levied upon (se prend sur) the ship and merchandise; for which reason it is called common."[34]

Ordonnance of Louis XIV, 1681

The Ordonnance of Louis XIV, in 1681, gave the force of law to a definition of general average, evidently modelled upon this of the Guidon: 00.13

> "Every extraordinary expense which is made for the ship and merchandise conjointly or separately, and every damage that shall occur to them from their loading and departure until their return and discharge, shall be reputed average. Extraordinary expenses for the ship alone, or for the merchandise alone, and damage which occurs to them in particular, are simple and particular average; and extraordinary expenses incurred and damage suffered, for the common good and safely of the merchandise and the vessel, are gross and common average. Simple averages are borne and paid by the thing which shall have suffered the damage or caused the expense, and the

[30] 5 Pard. 139.

[31] 5 Pard. 97.

[32] See Manley Hopkins, *Handbook of Average*, 4th edn, pp.3 et seq., where the different meanings and the derivation of the word are discussed at length. See also "Average", in Professor Skeat, Etymological Dictionary. The learned professor, one of the greatest authorities on the etymology of the English language, says that the word is a Mediterranean maritime term of unknown origin. In the New English Dictionary, edited by Sir James Murray, its derivation is also stated to be uncertain.

[33] For a fuller account of the Guidon, see Lowndes, *Marine Insurance*, Intr. xxiv.

[34] 2 Pard. 387. Examples of general average are afterwards given (2 Pard. 392–396), some of them evidently taken from the Digest of Justinian.

gross and common shall fall as well upon the vessel as upon the merchandise, and shall be equalised over the whole at the shilling in the pound (au sol la livre)."[35]

00.14 The Ordonnance set an example which was followed throughout Europe. By 1750, codes had been published in Hamburg, Prussia, Denmark Sweden and Spain, together with ordinances in Amsterdam, Rotterdam and Middleburg, and the definition found in the French Ordonnance was followed elsewhere in similar terms. Although the introduction of Napoleon's "Code de Commerce" resulted in a partial change in France, the pattern throughout Europe had been set, as was the general practice of allowing all or most expenses at a port of refuge as general average. In many countries this latter practice was implied rather than set out in detail, although there were some exceptions, for example the Prussian:

> "If a vessel, having sprung a leak or sustained any other damage, be forced to go into a port, all the charges inwards and outwards, and the charges of unloading and re-loading, if the cargo has to be discharged in port in order to repair the vessel, or for other sufficient reasons, and, also the maintenance of the crew in port and their wages during the delay, shall be general average."

Some minor distinctions were made; for example the Spanish code allowed wages while detained in a port of refuge if the vessel was under time charter, but not if engaged on a voyage freight basis. The Napoleonic code changed French law to the extent that if resort to a port of refuge was due to particular average (accidental) damage, no general average allowances were permitted. Otherwise the European practice remained that costs at a port of refuge would be general average whether the damage in question was due to a general average sacrifice or an accident on the voyage.

The law and practice of the United States developed on similar lines, embracing the principle of common benefit rather than restricting general average allowances to sacrifices and expenditure incurred for the common safety. Thus expenditure incurred at a port of refuge to enable the vessel to be repaired so that she could complete the voyage were allowable in general average.

English Origins

00.15 It is not till the year 1799 that any trace can be found of the actual term "general average" in the English courts of law. "General average", said Lord Stowell, in the Court of Admiralty, "is for a loss incurred, towards which the whole concern is bound to contribute pro rata, because it was undergone for the general benefit and preservation of the whole."[36] This definition was practically superseded by one laid down two

[35] Ordonnance. tit. 7, arts 2, 3; 4 Pard. 380.

[36] *The Copenhagen* (1799) 1 C.Rob. 289. The first reference to general average in an American court occurred one year earlier: *Campbell v The Alknomac* (1798) Bee 124; Fed. Cas. 2350. The word "average" to denote a general average contribution is, however, found in the report of *Hicks v Palington* (1590) Moore 297, and of *Marsham v Dutrey* (1719) *Select Cases of Evidence 58*. See also *Sheppard v Wright* (1698) Show. P.C. 18. MacKinnon L.J. in his presidential address to the Association of Average Adjusters on May 10, 1935, referred to the Select Pleas in the Court of Admiralty published by the Selden Society, and edited by the late R.G. Marsden. He instanced several earlier cases in which

years later in the Court of King's Bench by Lawrence J., in the case of *Birkley v Presgrave*,[37] on which the English law of general average has been constructed.

The first statutory mention of the profession of "average adjuster" is to be found in the Compensation (Defence) Act 1939, which by s.8 enacted that the third member of the Shipping Claims Tribunal shall be "a person appearing to the Lord Chancellor to have special qualifications as an average adjuster or accountant". Thus 140 years after Lord Stowell's recognition of general average as a legal conception, the average adjuster as an individual appears in the Statute Book.

3. Basis of the Right to General Average

Is the right to general average founded on authority merely, no matter whether that of the Rhodian, or Roman, or any later positive law, or of immemorial custom, or on some more primary grounds? And, if the latter, are they grounds of natural equity or utility, or do they rest on some contract between the parties, originally perhaps express, but which in course of time has come to be constantly implied, or on some theory as to agency? **00.16**

At first sight there is little to be gained in seeking to lay down the precise basis of the right. The same could be said of the doctrine of frustration, whereby a contract is held to be dissolved by supervening events. Arguments as to whether this results from an implied term in the contract, or from the construction of the contract, or from an independent rule imposed by law[38] are of little practical interest, unless they have a bearing on the test to be applied in order to establish frustration, or on the consequences which flow from it. Otherwise they merely provide an interesting reflection of changing judicial views as to the force of the doctrine of freedom of contract. However, this is unfortunately not always the case with the right to general average contribution. It may be important to determine the nature of the right, for example, in order to select the appropriate rule on which to found jurisdiction,[39] or to consider whether a claim to contribution is barred by some statutory or contractual period of limitation.[40] **00.17**

Bargain Made on the Spot

In the Judgments of Oleron, as in all the sea-laws of Europe which adopted and developed those judgments, the idea which lies at the foundation of this **00.18**

general average is mentioned; in a charterparty of the Jesus, dated 1562, in a claim settled by arbitration in 1540 arising out of the voyage of the Trinity James from Normandy to the Thames and in an arbitration award in 1575 for "contribution or average every man according to the rate of his goods", where part of the cargo of the Elizabeth had been seized to satisfy the demands of the tolner of the King of Denmark in lieu of the arrest of the ship.

[37] *Birkley v Presgrave* (1801) 1 East 220 at 228. Lawrence J.'s definition is quoted at para.A.02, below.

[38] See, e.g. *Davis Contractors Ltd v Fareham Urban DC* [1956] A.C. 696.

[39] See paras 30.65 et seq., below.

[40] See paras 23.01–23.09, below.

contribution is that of a bargain or agreement made between the captain and the owners of the cargo at the moment of danger: on the part of the latter a consent to part with their goods; on the part of the former, and likewise of the latter as amongst themselves, an undertaking to make rateable compensation in case safety shall be attained. Of this idea there is no trace in the Roman law, the terms of which would rather lead one to suppose that the rule was laid down as obligatory on grounds of natural equity.

Delegation to master

00.19 The older English law writers on average, probably following Emerigon and other French lawyers, based the right to contribution simply on natural justice:

> "This obligation . . . is founded on the great principle of distributive justice; for it would be hard that one man should suffer by an act which the common safety rendered necessary, and that those who received a benefit from that act should make no satisfaction to him who had sustained the loss."[41]

However, as the subject of general average came to be more familiar, it seems to have been felt to be more consonant with the spirit of the English common law that, in seeking to place this right of contribution on a secure basis, some implied contract or implied agency should, if possible, be found for it to rest on. Several such easily presented themselves. It might be supposed, for instance, that, at the time of shipping or entering into the contract for shipping the goods, all shippers impliedly contract with the shipowner and with each other, that the master shall have authority in case of danger to make all needful sacrifices, to the expense of which they, the shippers, will contribute their share; or it may be supposed artificially in modern conditions, that a similar engagement is made between the parties, at the moment of danger, treating them as if on the spot, as they originally were; or, again, if an implied agency is preferred, the master may be supposed to have, in virtue of his office, an authority to do for each cargo-owner, as well as for the shipowner, whatever any one of those parties would have had the duty or the power to do had he been on the spot; so that the master's act should on each occasion be taken to be the act of his appropriate principal. It will be noted that under each of these theories, the right to contribution is based in part on the agency of the master (or in modern conditions frequently the shipowner), and this feature has gained widespread acknowledgement in the decided cases.[42] It has been suggested that the decision of the majority of the House of Lords in *Morrison S.S. Co v Greystoke Castle*[43] takes the principles of agency, in the context of general

[41] Park, *Insurance*, 8th edn, p.277. See also Abbott, *Shipping*, 5th edn, p.344, and *The Star of Hope* (1869) 9 Wall. 203 at 230.

[42] *The Gratitudine* (1801) 3 C.Rob. 240 per Lord Stowell at 257 (approved by Lord Roche in *Morrison S.S. Co v Grevstoke Castle*; *The Cheldale* [1947] A.C. 265); *The Hamburg* (1864) 2 Moo. P.C. (N.S.) 289 at 321; 33 L.J. Adm. 116 at 118, per Lord Kingsdown; *Morrison S.S. Co v Greystoke Castle*; *The Cheldale* [1947] A.C. 265 per Lord Roche at 281–283, Lord Porter at 294, and Lord Uthwatt at 311–312.

[43] *Morrison S.S. Co v Greystoke Castle*; *The Cheldale* [1947] A.C. 265.

average, to their logical conclusion and may therefore lead to the result that the cargo-owner is directly liable, as co-principal, to third parties for general average expenditure incurred by the master or shipowners, for example the costs of entering a port of refuge.[44] However, the speeches of the majority clearly disavow this conclusion,[45] and the position therefore seems to be, at any rate where expenditure is concerned, that although the expenditure is incurred on behalf of all the parties to the adventure, rather than simply for their benefit, nevertheless the master or shipowner pledges only his own credit in contracting with third parties, and does not create contractual relations between them and the cargo interests. He will only create contractual relations where he has the authority to and does enter into the contract as agent for cargo interests, as in the case, for example, of no cure no pay salvage contracts.[46]

Contract, or Rule Imposed by Law

However, while the concept of agency, in the special or limited sense described above, forms an important element in the legal basis of general average, it cannot of itself explain its entire basis, for the question remains whether the agency arises as a result of the express or implied contract or consent of the parties, or simply by operation of law. As demonstrated below, the preponderance of judicial opinion favours the latter view, although the implied contract theory does not wholly lack support. **00.20**

Some judicial opinions

In *Simonds v White*[47] Abbott C.J. said: **00.21**

> "The principle of general average . . . is of very ancient date, and of universal reception among commercial nations. The obligation to contribute, therefore, depends not so much upon the terms of any particular instrument as upon a general rule of maritime law. The obligation may be limited, qualified, or even excluded by the special terms of the contract as between the parties to the contract."

In *Pirie v Middle Dock Co*[48] Watkin Williams J. said:

> "It is a law founded upon justice, public policy, and convenience, and rests . . . upon reasons which are so obvious that it is not surprising to find that it is older than any other law or rule in force . . . This principle of law must, in my judgment, be regarded as incorporated in and forming part of the unwritten common law of England."

[44] See *Scrutton on Charterparties*, 20th edn, p.272, fn.23.

[45] *Morrison S.S. Co v Greystoke Castle; The Cheldale* [1947] A.C. 265 at 281 (Lord Roche), 294–295 (Lord Porter) and 311–312 (Lord Uthwatt).

[46] As to the master's authority to enter into salvage contracts as agent for cargo see para.6.01, below.

[47] *Simonds v White* (1824) 2 B. & C. 805 at 811.

[48] *Pirie v Middle Dock Co* (1881) 4 Asp. Mar. Law Cas. 388 at 390; 44 L.T. 426.

00.22 Bramwell L.J., delivering the judgment of the Court of Appeal in *Wright v Marwood*,[49] said:

> "When such sacrifice is made, as was here, for the common good, as a rule it comes within general average, and must be borne proportionally by those interested. It is not necessary to say what is the origin or principle of the rule, but, to judge from the way it is claimed in England, it would seem to arise from an implied contract inter se to contribute by those interested."[50]

The way that general average was then claimed may be ascertained by reference to the record in *Anderson v Ocean S.S. Co*.[51] The statement of claim there alleged that:

> "the Defendants promised that they would contribute and pay their just share and proportion in respect of the said goods of any general average loss that might arise or happen to the said ship during the said voyage."

Lord Blackburn said:

> "I think that the promise stated in the first paragraph of the Statement of Claim is one that would be implied by law in every contract for the carriage of goods."[52]

This was the zenith of the contract theory, which has subsequently been in retreat, although not entirely moribund, as indicated in para.00.28, below.

00.23 A year earlier the rule of law theory had begun to gain support with the judgment of Brett M.R. in *Burton v English*[53]:

> "How does such a claim [for jettison of cargo] arise? In theory it arises from an act done by the master of a ship, not as the servant of the ship-owner, but as the servant of the cargo-owner, a relation which is imposed on him by the necessity of the case. It arises by reason of a voluntary sacrifice by the cargo-owner for the benefit of the ship and cargo, and not from any act done for the ship-owner at all. By what law does the right arise to general average contribution? Lord Bramwell in his judgment in Wright v Marwood,[54] considers it to arise from an implied contract; but although I always have great doubt when I differ from Lord Bramwell, I do not think that it forms any part of the contract to carry, and that it does not arise from any contract at all, but from the old Rhodian laws, and has become incorporated into the law of England as the law of the ocean. It is not as a matter of contract, but in consequence of a common danger, where natural justice requires that all should contribute to indemnify for the loss of property which is sacrificed by one in order that the whole adventure may be saved. . . . The acts of the captain with reference to properly or improperly jettisoning part of the cargo are not both done by him in the same capacity; one is done by him as the agent of the cargo-owner, and the other as the servant of the shipowner."[55]

[49] *Wright v Marwood* (1881) 7 Q.B.D. 62 at 67.
[50] See to the same effect, Maclachlan, *Merchant Shipping*, 5th edn, p.734n.
[51] *Anderson v Ocean S.S. Co* (1884) 10 A.C. 107.
[52] *Anderson v Ocean S.S. Co* (1884) 10 A.C. 107 at 115.
[53] *Burton v English* (1883) 12 Q.B.D. 218.
[54] *Wright v Marwood* (1881) 7 Q.B.D. 62.
[55] *Burton v English* (1883) 12 Q.B.D. 218 at 220–221, cited by Bailhache J. in *Austin Friars S.S. Co v Spillers and Bakers* [1915] 1 K.B. 833 at 837, and by Greer L.J. in *Tate & Lyle Ltd v Hain Shipping Co* (1934) 39 Com. Cas. 259 at 280.

Bowen L.J. in the same case summed up the matter so as quietly to indicate that we were not, after all, to suppose it to be of any great practical importance. He said:

> "In the investigation of legal principles, the question whether they arise by way of implied contract or not often ends by being a mere question of words. General average contribution is a principle which comes down to us from an anterior period of our history, and from the law of commerce and the sea. When, however, it is once established as part of the law, and as a portion of the risks which those who embark their property upon ships are willing to take, you may, if you like, imagine that those who place their property on board a ship on one side, and the shipowner who puts his ship by the quay to receive the cargo on the other side, bind themselves by an implied contract which embodies this principle; just as it may be said that those who contract with reference to a custom impliedly make it a part of the contract. But that way, although legally it may be a sound way, nevertheless is a technical way of looking at it. This claim for average contribution, at all events, is part of the law of the sea, and it certainly arises in consequence of an act done by the captain as agent, not for the shipowner alone, but also of the cargo-owner, by which act he jettisons part of the cargo on the implied basis that contribution will be made by the ship and by the other owners of cargo."[56]

In *Strang, Steel & Co v A. Scott & Co*[57] Lord Watson, after referring to the Rhodian law[58] and the judgments in *Wright v Marwood and Burton v English*,[59] said: **00.24**

> "Whether the rule ought to be regarded as a matter of implied contract, or as a canon of positive law resting upon the dictates of natural justice, is a question which their Lordships do not consider it necessary to determine. The principle upon which contribution becomes due does not appear to them to differ from that upon which claims of recompense for salvage services are founded. But, in any aspect of it, the rule of contribution has its foundation in the plainest equity. In jettison, the rights of those entitled to contribution, and the corresponding obligations of the contributors, have their origin in the fact of a common danger which threatens to destroy the property of them all; and these rights and obligations are mutually perfected whenever the goods of some of the shippers have been advisedly sacrificed, and the property of the others has been thereby preserved."

In *Milburn v Jamaica Fruit Importing Co*,[60] where the York-Antwerp Rules 1890 applied, A.L. Smith L.J. expressed views on this point which agree with that of Lord Esher, saying:

> "The foundation of a general average claim is ordinarily not that of contract, but is founded upon a loss which arises in consequence of extraordinary sacrifices made or expenses incurred for the preservation of the ship and cargo in the time of peril, and which must be borne proportionately by all who are interested."

[56] *Burton v English* (1883) 12 Q.B.D. 218 at 223.

[57] *Strang, Steel & Co v A. Scott & Co* (1899) 14 App. Cas. 601 at 607–608. The advice was that of Lords Watson, Fitzgerald, Hobhouse and MacNaghten.

[58] See para.00.01, above.

[59] See paras 0.22–0.23, above.

[60] *Milburn v Jamaica Fruit Importing Co* [1900] 2 Q.B. 540 at 546, 550.

Similarly, Vaughan Williams L.J. says:

> "The liability to contribute in no sense results from the contract of carriage, but exists wholly independently of the contract of carriage, by virtue of the equitable doctrine of the Rhodian law, which as part of the law maritime has been incorporated in the municipal law of England."[61]

00.25 Two brief references to the point may be found in the speeches of the House of Lords in *Hain S.S. Co v Tate & Lyle*.[62] Lord Atkin, speaking of a claim for contribution, said: "No doubt the claim does not arise as a term of the contract".[63] Lord Maugham described the lien for contribution as "a right resting not on the charterparty but on the general maritime law".[64]

In *Morrison S.S. Co v Greystoke Castle; The Cheldale*,[65] when the carriage was under the York-Antwerp Rules 1924, Scott L.J. said:

> "The common law of the sea in regard to general average imposes the duty to disburse on the master of the ship, and equally imposes the duty to contribute on the other parties to the adventure, whenever an event causes danger of loss to the whole adventure."

Where the York-Antwerp Rules apply

00.26 In the cases referred to above, even though in some of them the York-Antwerp Rules were incorporated into the contract, the court was considering the basis of the right to contribution independently of the Rules. The question whether the position is different where the contract of carriage incorporates the Rules was considered in *Alma Shipping Corp v Union of India*[66] where it had been agreed that any dispute arising "under" the contract of carriage should be referred to arbitration, and that any claim should be deemed to be waived unless made within 12 months of discharge. The York-Antwerp Rules 1950 applied, and made some slight difference to the shipowners' claim for general average contribution, if only in respect of commission and interest. Likewise it was alleged that the shipowners were at fault in the events which led to the general average act, from which fault they could only claim exemption (and thus recover contribution) by relying on exceptions in the contract of carriage. In giving judgment Roskill J. said that, since the York-Antwerp Rules were incorporated by contract, and since the shipowners would need to rely on the exception of negligent navigation in the contract "... the present claim is clearly a dispute arising under this charterparty ...".

[61] The same view has been expressed in several decisions of the American Courts: see *The Roanoke* (1893) 59 Fed. Rep.161; *Marwick v Rogers* (1895) 163 Mas. 50; *The Eliza Lines* (1896) 61 Fed. Rep. 308 at 325. "The principle on which this contribution is founded is not the result of a contract, but has its origin in the plain dictates of natural law." Story, *Equity Jurisprudence*, p.490. In *Marwick v Rogers* it was held that the cesser clause in a charterparty could not relieve the owner of cargo, who was also the charterer, from liability to contribute.

[62] *Hain S.S. Co v Tate & Lyle* (1936) 41 Com. Cas 350.

[63] *Hain S.S. Co v Tate & Lyle* (1936) 41 Com. Cas 350 at 357.

[64] *Hain S.S. Co v Tate & Lyle* (1936) 41 Com. Cas 350 at 372.

[65] *Morrison S.S. Co v Greystoke Castle; The Cheldale* [1945] P. 10 at 14.

[66] *Alma Shipping Corp v Union of India* [1971] 2 Lloyd's Rep. 494.

This decision was approved by the House of Lords in *Union of India v E.B. Aaby's Rederi A/S*,[67] where the relevant circumstances were similar except that, in order to release the cargo from lien, the cargo-owners had given a written undertaking to pay such general average as might be legally due. Lord Morris, who delivered the leading judgment, first considered what the position would have been if no undertaking had been given: 00.27

> "Though claims for general average contribution have their origin in the common law so that they need not necessarily be the creature of contract I feel satisfied that in the present case (leaving aside the [undertaking]) a claim for general average contribution relating to events during the operation of the charterparty would have been a claim arising out of the charterparty. The term that general average should be payable was contractual as was the further term that the York-Antwerp Rules 1950 were to apply–as was the further term 'to be settled in London'–as was the inclusion . . . of the Jason clause."

Thus in the absence of the undertaking, the claim would have fallen within the arbitration clause, as a dispute "arising out of" the charterparty, and accordingly have been time-barred. Lord Morris went on to hold, however, that neither the time limit nor the arbitration provision in the contract of carriage provided an answer to a claim brought upon the undertaking.

The view that rights and obligations in general average may arise independently of contract, express or implied, was reaffirmed by Lord Diplock in *Castle Insurance v Hong Kong Shipping Co*,[68] but he also pointed out that a claim for general average will in practice almost invariably be contractual: 00.28

> "Under that branch of English common law into which the lex mercatoria has long ago become absorbed, the personal liability to pay the general average contribution due in respect of any particular consignment of cargo that had been preserved in consequence of a general average sacrifice or expenditure lies, in legal theory, upon the person who was owner of the consignment at the time when the sacrifice was made or the liability for the expenditure incurred. In practice, however, the personal liability at common law of whoever was the owner of the contributing consignment of cargo at the time of the general average act is hardly ever relied upon. There are two reasons for this. The first is that the contract of carriage between the shipowner and the owner of the consignment, whether the contract be contained in a charterparty or a bill of lading, invariably nowadays (so far as the decided cases show) contains an express clause dealing with general average and so brings the claim to contribution into the field of contract law."

Similar views were expressed by Staughton L.J. in *Sameon Co SA v NV Petrofina SA*,[69] (York-Antwerp Rules 1974) although he left open the question whether, even in the absence of express contractual provisions, the claim is nevertheless contractual in its nature, being founded on implied contract[70]:

[67] *Union of India v E.B. Aaby's Rederi A/S* [1975] A.C. 797, affirming [1973] 1 Lloyd's Rep. 509; [1972] 2 Lloyd's Rep. 129.

[68] *Castle Insurance v Hong Kong Shipping Co* [1984] A.C. 226 at 233, PC. The decision is discussed at para.30.43 et seq., below.

[69] *Sameon Co SA v NV Petrofina SA* Unreported April 30, 1997, CA.

[70] See also the similar views expressed by the same judge in (1998) 114 L.Q.R. 677, 678.

> "Although there is room for argument whether an obligation to contribute in general average is by its nature contractual, it is very commonly, almost invariably, regulated by contract, and it is beyond dispute that the obligation is contractual in the present case."

Principles Established by the Cases

00.29 The preponderance of judicial authority favours the view that, in the absence of express contractual provisions governing the adjustment of general average in the contract of carriage, a claim for general average contribution is not based upon contract, express or implied, but arises under the general law. This view is shared by most textbook and academic writers.[71] However, if there is a contract between the parties which incorporates the York-Antwerp Rules, or makes other provision relating to general average, the claim is contractual. A slightly different view of the effect of the authorities is that the claim is not contractual, even where the York-Antwerp Rules are incorporated, if the same claim could be made without the aid of the York-Antwerp Rules and in accordance with the law and practice of the port of discharge. The distinction is probably of no more than academic interest, since it is difficult to imagine a case in which the York-Antwerp Rules will have no effect whatsoever on the adjustment, if only in terms of contributory values, commission or interest. Even if the claim itself is not founded on contract, it may give rise to a dispute which arises out of the contract owing to the nature of the defence to the claim.[72]

Where two shippers have each agreed with the shipowner that the same version of the rules shall apply, and one shipper claims general average contribution from the other shipper, it is submitted that those rules apply as a matter of contract between them, for the reasons discussed in para.30.24, below.[73]

4. Continuing Need for General Average

00.30 Lowndes raised the question whether, when merchants began to live ashore, and the institution of marine insurance began to evolve, the abolition of the system of contribution towards sacrifices for the common safety may not have been considered. There is no evidence that it was, but during the last 100 years or more there have been intermittent calls for abolition on various grounds. Earlier

[71] *British Shipping Laws*, Vol.3; Carver, Carriage by Sea, para.1349; Goff and Jones, *Law of Restitution*, 6th edn, paras 13.003, 14.042b; Rose, *General Average Law and Practice*, 2nd edn, paras 1.14–1.20. Rose regards general average as part of the law of restitution of unjust enrichment (see also F.D. Rose "General Average as Restitution" (1997) 113 L.Q.R. 569, whereas Goff and Jones prefer to regard it as sui generis).

[72] See the cases referred to in paras 00.26 and 00.27, above.

[73] In *British Shipping Law*, Vol.3: Carver, paras 1349–1350, the view is preferred that the obligation to contribute is one imposed by law. As to the case of a claim by one shipper on another, it is there suggested (citing *Thomson v Micks Lambert* (1933) 39 Com. Cas. 40, *Grange v Taylor* (1904) 9 Com. Cas. 223 and *United States Shipping Board v Durrell* [1923] 2 K.B. 739) that either the rules apply by reason of implied contract or agency, or they are not applicable at all to such a claim.

editions of this work dealt at some length with arguments for and against abolition.[74] However, for present purposes it may be sufficient to state the principal points only.

The case for abolition was based on the premise that the cost and trouble of redistributing losses in this manner was disappropriate to any benefits the system might bring; further, such an archaic institution was no longer appropriate for modern commerce in which the distribution was largely between insurers rather than private merchants. The abolitionists recognised the difficulty of eradicating a concept that was so deeply embedded in the law of all maritime countries that the express agreement of all parties to each adventure would be required to preclude the possibility of contribution. It was also generally conceded that the system was important in that it gave the master freedom of action in a crisis, knowing that any losses would be met by equitable contribution, whichever course he might choose. Nonetheless, concerns regarding the cost-effectiveness of the system continued to be voiced, particularly by representatives of the International Union of Marine Insurers who produced statistics showing the high costs of the adjustment process, (which often involved lawyers, consultants and average agents in addition to the adjusters themselves) relative to the amounts at issue and questioned the benefits of sharing losses in this manner.

A partial solution has emerged that continued to use the general average system **00.31**
(or more particularly the York-Antwerp Rules) to define certain categories of loss or expense but dispensed with the contribution to those losses or expenses by the different parties to the adventure. Rather, such losses lay where they fell, on the shipowners, and were paid by his hull and machinery insurers up to a specified limit. This was achieved by the insertion of general average "Absorption Clauses" into hull and machinery policies and these are discussed in more detail below in Section 7 at paras 50.33 et seq.

The number of general average situations that result in the collection of security and then contributions from cargo has therefore been significantly reduced and the trend is for the Absorption Clause limits to increase. In the container trades the amounts recoverable directly from the Hull Insurers may be supplemented by a special insurance that provides an additional layer of cover for what would otherwise be cargo's proportion of any general average; the process of contribution between the parties, with its attendant additional costs, therefore only occurs in the case of the more serious casualties.

A frequent and pragmatic response to the arguments for an abolition or signifi- **00.32**
cant restriction of general average was founded on the realisation that general average losses and expenses would not go away simply because the historical concept that had been used to identify and distribute them was extinguished or curtailed. The same risks would continue to exist and would need to be allocated between the parties under the contract of affreightment and arrangements then made for insurance of that exposure.

[74] 9th edn, para.11 and Appendix 4.

The principles of general average, as now embodied in the York-Antwerp Rules, also continue to perform a useful function in patrolling two important borders that lie between:

- Matters that form part of the shipowners' reasonable obligations to carry out the contracted voyage, and those losses and expenses that arise in exceptional circumstances.
- Property and liability insurers as their differing responsibilities meet and sometimes merge, in the context of a serious casualty.

Both of these difficult areas benefit from the reservoir of established law and practice that general average provides, helping to secure a degree of certainly that is always the objective of commercial interests. However, practitioners must be aware that such commercial interests will have little patience with any system that becomes inflexible or too demanding of time and money, and the principles and practice of general average will continue to need to be kept under review.[75]

[75] See also para.00112 below. It is interesting to note that none of the 26 respondents to CMI's 2013 questionnaire were interested in re-starting the abolition debate.

SECTION 2

SOME PRINCIPLES OF THE LAW OF CARRIAGE BY SEA

Although the law of carriage by sea lies outside the scope of this work and reference should in case of need be made to the specialised works on the subject,[1] a brief reference to the general principles may not be out of place. The main importance of these principles in the context of general average is that the question may arise whether the accident which gave rise to the sacrifice or expenditure was caused by the actionable fault of one of the parties to the adventure, with the consequences described later in this work.[2] Another question which frequently arises in the adjustment of general average is whether the common maritime adventure has been or might be frustrated by damage to the ship or cargo, or by delay.[3] **00.33**

1. THE CONTRACT OF CARRIAGE

Carrier's Obligations under English law

The shipowner usually engages by his contract to deliver the goods entrusted to his care, subject to certain excepted causes of loss or damage. But the 'shipowner's obligations may not be confined to what appears on the face of the contract, for obligations may be implied by law, of which the most important are (1) that the vessel is seaworthy, and (2) that the carrier will take reasonable care of the goods. **00.34**

Warranty of seaworthiness

The shipowner impliedly warrants that, at the commencement of the voyage, the ship is seaworthy.[4] Seaworthiness involves firstly that the ship's hull, machinery **00.35**

[1] See, e.g. *British Shipping Laws*, Vols 2 and 3; Carver, *Carriage by Sea*, 13th edn (1982); *Scrutton on Charterparties*, 20th edn (1996).
[2] See paras D.01 et seq., below.
[3] See paras 00.41-00.45, below.
[4] *Kopitoff v Wilson* (1876) 1 Q.B.D. 377; *Cohn v Davidson* (1877) 2 Q.B.D. 455; *Steel v Slate Line* (1877) 3 App. Cas. 72; *The Glenfruin* (1885) 10 P.D. 103. As to cargo-worthiness see *Tattersall v National S.S. Co* (1884) 12 Q.B.D. 297; *McFadden v Blue Star Line* [1905] 1 K.B. 697.

and equipment are in a fit condition to undertake the voyage and withstand the marine perils which may foreseeably be encountered, secondly that she is properly equipped and supplied, and manned with a competent crew, and thirdly that the ship is cargo-worthy, that is to say that her holds are in a suitable condition to receive the cargo and to care for it during the voyage, and that any special equipment necessary for the proper carriage of the contemplated cargo, such as refrigeration machinery, heating coils or ventilators, are in good working order. Bad stowage which endangers the safety of the ship may also amount to unseaworthiness.

The standard of seaworthiness required is one of reasonable fitness, not perfection; the test is whether a prudent shipowner, with full knowledge of the actual condition of the ship, would have sent her on the voyage in question, and with the cargo in question.[5]

However, while the standard of seaworthiness required is not absolute, at common law the obligation itself is strict; that is to say it is no defence for the shipowner to demonstrate that he and his representatives took all reasonable care to ensure the ship's seaworthiness. However, the strict obligation is almost invariably modified by the terms of the contract of carriage, most commonly by a provision that the shipowner is not liable for unseaworthiness unless it results from his failure to exercise due diligence to make the ship seaworthy.

Obligation to take reasonable care of the goods

00.36 The shipowner also impliedly undertakes to exercise reasonable care in the carriage and custody of the goods, and in such operations as loading, stowage and discharging, to the extent that these operations are performed by him. He is also obliged to carry and care for the goods in accordance with a sound system, having regard to the practice prevailing in the trade, and such knowledge as the shipowner has, or ought to have, as to the nature of the goods and any special precautions to be adopted in their carriage. At common law the obligation extends to the proper navigation and management of the ship,[6] although this aspect of it is frequently excluded by the terms of the contract.

Effect of negligence or breach of warranty of seaworthiness

00.37 The effect of a breach by the shipowner of his obligations described above is that he is liable for any loss of or damage to the cargo thereby caused, and this liability will extend to the case where the immediate cause of the loss or damage was an excepted peril. Thus if "fire" is an excepted peril and a fire breaks out on the voyage and damages the cargo, the shipowner will be liable for the damage if the fire resulted from the unseaworthiness of the ship at the commencement of the

[5] *Bradley v Federal Steam Navigation Co* (1926) 24 Ll. L. Rep. 446; *M.D.C. Ltd v N.V.Z.M. "Beurstraat"* [1962] 1 Lloyd's Rep. 180.

[6] *Wilson v Owners of Cargo per Xantho* (1887) 12 App. Cas. 503, 513.

voyage, or the negligence of the master or crew, unless the unseaworthiness or negligence are themselves also covered by an exclusion clause.

Exclusion of liability for negligence or unseaworthiness

It used to be common for contracts of carriage to attempt to exclude all liability for unseaworthiness, or for negligence. Such exclusions, except where the Hague Rules apply (as to which see paras 00.46-00.47 below) are perfectly valid, but they are interpreted restrictively, and will therefore not exclude liability unless they clearly so provide. Thus an exception of "negligence"[7] or "breakdown of machinery"[8] has been held to apply only to events occurring on the voyage, and to have no effect on the shipowner's implied obligation to provide a ship which is seaworthy at its commencement. Since the introduction of the Hague Rules attempts to exclude the obligations completely have become rare and most exclusion clauses, even in charterparties, mirror the provisions of the Rules, which modify, but do not exclude the implied obligations. **00.38**

Deviation

The shipowner further impliedly engages in every contract of affreightment that the ship shall proceed on the voyage without departure from her proper route, and without unreasonable delay. Any departure from the proper route, except in cases of necessity, such as to effect essential repairs or to save life, is called a deviation. Delay which is of such length as to "substitute an entirely different voyage for that contemplated by the bill of lading" is, unless excused by an exceptions clause, also a deviation.[9] **00.39**

In considering whether there has been a deviation in any particular case, it must not be forgotten that the contract of affreightment may, and usually does, contain a wide clause giving liberty to deviate.[10]

Effect of unjustifiable deviation

The legal effects of a deviation are more far reaching than those of any other breach of the contract of affreightment.[11] Deviation is a fundamental breach of the contract of carriage which gives the cargo-owner the right to elect whether (1) to waive the breach and affirm the contract, or (2) to terminate the contract. If he affirms, all the terms of the contract continue to apply to the adventure, but the cargo-owner can claim damages (or exercise his rights and remedies in relation to **00.40**

[7] *Steel v State Line* (1877) 3 App. Cas. 72; *Thin v Richards* [1892] 2 Q.B. 141.

[8] *Cargo Ex Maori King v Hughes* [1895] 2 Q.B. 550.

[9] *Brandt v Liverpool S.N. Co* [1924] 1 K.B. 575.

[10] See *British Shipping Laws*, Vol.3; Carver, *Carriage by Sea*, 13th edn, paras 1176–1186; *Scrutton on Charterparties*, 20th edn, pp.261–264.

[11] See *British Shipping Laws*, Vol.3; Carver, *Carriage by Sea*, 13th edn, paras 1187–1204; *Scrutton on Charterparties*, 20th edn, pp.258–261; *Hain S.S. Co v Tate & Lyle* (1934) 49 Ll.L. Rep.123, CA; (1936) 41 Com. Cas. 350, HL.

actionable fault[12]) in respect of any loss or liability to contribute caused by the deviation.[13] If he terminates the contract, it ceases to apply, and the shipowner thereafter holds the goods as a common carrier—that is to say he is strictly liable for any loss or damage unless caused by act of God, the Queen's enemies or inherent vice,[14] and he can prove that the loss would have occurred even if there had been no deviation.

So far as general average contribution is concerned, unjustified deviation, unless the contract be affirmed, has the following effect:

(a) The shipowner's contractual right to contribution under the contract of carriage[15] ceases to exist; he will thus lose any right to claim under the provisions of that contract, for example to claim contribution in accordance with the York-Antwerp Rules or to hold liable a consignee (not being the owner of the goods at the time of the general average) who would otherwise have been liable under the terms of the bill of lading.[16] The position of the consignee who has entered into an average bond or agreement is considered in Section 5.[17]

(b) It is an unresolved question whether the shipowner's right to contribution at common law is likewise destroyed. In *Hain S.S. Co v Tate & Lyle*[18] Scrutton L.J. expressed the view that all rights of contribution of all parties (including innocent cargo-owners) were destroyed, because:

> "they were not parties by agreement to the adventure after the deviation. The basis of general average contribution, the 'common adventure' had been destroyed by the deviation . . ."

However, while there is undoubtedly much to be said for this point of view, there remains room for debate on the question, since general average at common law does not depend on agreement, and a deviation does not render unlawful the shipowner's possession of the goods during the remainder of the voyage,[19] which may therefore be said still to retain the essential features of a common adventure.[20] In practice, because of the strict liability of a shipowner for loss or damage after

[12] See paras D.01 et seq., below.

[13] See *Hain S.S. Co v Tale & Lyle* at 371, HL, per Lord Maugham. As to whether a loss is caused by a deviation see paras 30.59 et seq., below.

[14] Possibly also subject to statutory exceptions, such as that of fire under the Merchant Shipping Act 1995; see Carver, *Carriage by Sea*, 13th edn, para.1196.

[15] See *Hain S.S. Co v Tate & Lyle*. In *Drew Brown v The Orient Trader* [1973] 2 Lloyd's Rep. 174 the Canadian Supreme Court, applying US law, held that the effect of the New Jason Clause in the bill of lading was that the carrier could recover general average loss caused by a fire which broke out after a deviation, it not being shown that the fire was caused by the deviation. It is clear, however, that English law is to the opposite effect.

[16] See paras 30.56 et seq., below, as to the persons against whom proceedings for contribution will lie.

[17] Paras 30.59 et seq., below.

[18] *Hain S.S. Co v Tate & Lyle* at 131. See also in HL per Lord Atkin at 357, and the dissenting judgment of Spence J. in *Drew Brown v The Orient Trader*.

[19] *Hain S.S. Co v Tate & Lyle* at 371, HL, per Lord Maugham.

[20] See also *British Shipping Laws*, Vol.3; Carver, *Carriage by Sea*, 13th edn, para.1198.

deviation, there would be few cases in which a cargo-owner would be unable to defend the shipowner's claim for contribution on the ground of actionable fault,[21] but the same would not apply to claims for contribution by other cargo-owners.

(c) The cargo-owner who claims contribution from the shipowner may elect to waive the deviation and claim in accordance with the provisions of the contract of carriage. However, it will usually be more advantageous to him to rescind the contract and to hold the shipowner strictly liable, as a common carrier, for the whole loss.

(d) The rights of cargo-owners inter se are a difficult question. Where there is a contract between one cargo-owner and another governing contribution to general average,[22] it is not obvious that a deviation by the shipowner should entitle either cargo-owner to rescind that contract, and refuse to contribute, according to its terms, to a general average loss incurred by the other. The question whether any rights of contribution survive at common law has already been discussed in head (b) above. There seems little justification for depriving a cargo-owner of his contractual or common law right of contribution from another cargo-owner as a result of a deviation by the shipowner.

It is an unresolved question whether, if the cargo-owner elects to rescind the contract of carriage, the rescission brings an end to the contract as from the beginning, or whether the contract continues to apply up to the moment of deviation, or even up to the date of the rescission.[23] It is submitted that the better view is that it applies up to the date of the deviation.

In *The Kapitan Petko Voivoda*[24] the court rejected an attempt by cargo-owners to equate unauthorised deck carriage with deviation.

Effect of Frustration

Frustration is the main exception to the basic rule that contracts are absolute— **00.41**
that is, they must be fulfilled however difficult, inconvenient or expensive performance may become. It occurs when, as a result of some extraneous event outside the control of either party, further performance of the contract becomes

[21] See paras D.01 et seq., below.

[22] The circumstances in which, and the grounds upon which, such a contract may arise are discussed at paras 30.24 et seq., below.

[23] cf. *British Shipping Laws*, Vol.3; Carver, *Carriage by Sea*, 13th edn, para.1200; *Scrutton on Charterparties*, 20th edn, p.259. The ordinary contractual rule is that the rescission of a contract by the innocent party does not operate retrospectively, but takes effect only from the date of rescission: *Photo Production v Securicor* [1980] A.C. 827. However, in *Hain S.S. Co v Tate & Lyle* it was said that it "displaces" (Lord Atkin) or "abrogates" (Lord Wright) the contract. In *Thiess v Australian S.S. Co* [1955] 1 Lloyd's Rep. 459 the termination was held to take effect from the date of the deviation. See also *Suisse Atlantique Soc. d'Armement v Rotterdamsche Kolen Centrale* [1967] 1 A.C. 361.

[24] *Daewoo Heavy Industries Ltd v Klipriver Shipping Ltd (The Kapitan Petko Voivoda)* [2003] 2 Lloyd's Rep. 1, CA, overruling *Kenya Ry v Antares* [1987] 2 Lloyd's Rep. 424.

physically impossible, or illegal,[25] or "something radically different from that which was undertaken by the contract".[26]

In the absence of frustration, or some express provision in the contract, the adventure can only be lawfully[27] terminated by carriage to the contractual destination or by express agreement between the carrier and cargo interests.

Frustration of the adventure does not bring to an end accrued rights to contribution in general average.[28] Its importance in matters of general average is that when it occurs it will usually cause the common adventure to end before arrival at the contractual destination and this premature termination of the adventure may affect the valuation of the contributing interests, the law governing the adjustment and the period over which port of refuge expenses are allowable.

Frustration of the adventure at a port or place of refuge

00.42 Frustration may result from many types of event, such as war, ice, or total loss of ship or cargo, but in the context of general average the issue most likely to arise is whether damage to the ship or the cargo suffered as a result of an accident on the voyage, or the delay consequent thereon, is sufficiently serious to frustrate the contract and thus to terminate the adventure at a port or place of refuge. In essence, the test to be applied in such a case is the same as in any other. In *Hill v Wilson*[29] where both ship and cargo were damaged on a voyage to Hull and the ship put into Copenhagen as a port of refuge, Lindley J. stated that in order to uphold an adjustment made at Copenhagen, in accordance with Danish law, against the cargo-owners the shipowner would have to prove that the voyage terminated there:

> "either by agreement or by necessity, i.e. the occurrence of circumstances beyond the control of the [shipowner], and such as rendered the completion of the voyage on the terms originally agreed upon physically impossible, or so clearly unreasonable as to be impossible in a business point of view."

The circumstances in which this test is likely to be fulfilled are investigated in more detail below.

00.43 (1) *Damage to the ship.* If the ship sustains such serious damage that the cost of repairs will exceed the value of the ship when repaired plus the

[25] In general, supervening illegality by the proper law of the contract or by the law of the place of performance will bring about frustration.

[26] See *Davis Contractors v Fareham Urban DC* [1956] A.C. 696 at 729, per Lord Radcliffe.

[27] It may also be terminated by a breach of contract which the innocent party is entitled to, and does, treat as a repudiation of the contract.

[28] One reason is that, although the obligation to contribute will normally arise out of the contract (see paras 00.26 et seq., above) the Law Reform (Frustrated Contracts) Act 1943, does not apply to contracts for the carriage of goods by sea other than time charterparties or charterparties by demise. In any event, it is submitted that a provision regarding general average is severable from the remainder of the contract of carriage and is intended to apply to all general averages, including those which occur in circumstances which bring about the frustration of the adventure (cf. *Heyman v Darwins* [1942] A.C. 356). Where the Act does apply, see s.2(3).

[29] *Hill v Wilson* (1879) 4 C.P.D. 329 at 333. The passage quoted here was relied upon in *Assicurazioni Generali v The Bessie Morris S.S. Co* [1892] 1 Q.B. 571; [1892] 2 Q.B. 652, CA.

value of freight still at risk,[30] or if the time required to effect the repairs will be so great that the delay would frustrate the adventure, the shipowner is entitled to abandon the voyage, and, unless he exercises his option to tranship, as to which see para.00.45, below, the adventure is frustrated. In all such cases, it is the cost and the duration of such repairs as are necessary to complete the voyage, and not of permanent repairs (if temporary repairs are possible), which are the relevant consideration.[31]

(2) *Damage to the cargo*. Damage to the cargo will frustrate a contract when the cargo is rendered unfit for onward carriage from the port of refuge, and cannot be reconditioned without frustrating delay or without such expenditure as would render it commercially "impossible" in the sense described above.

(3) *Delay.* Unavoidable delay in prosecuting the voyage from the port of refuge will give rise to frustration if it is so great as to destroy the commercial purpose of the voyage. It is impossible to lay down any general rule as to the length of delay which will have this result, but the following factors are relevant:

(a) The length of time which the voyage would normally be expected to last. A delay of one month on a voyage which would normally last one week would be more likely to give rise to frustration than if the normal length of the voyage were six weeks.

(b) The nature of the cargo—for instance, a cargo of bananas could not survive a long delay whereas a cargo of iron ore could remain indefinitely in a vessel. The likelihood of minor damage to the cargo resulting from the delay will not give rise to frustration, but where the damage is likely to be significant, or even where it is unpredictable and might be significant, the adventure is frustrated.[32]

(c) Whether the cargo is intended for a particular market or a particular use which makes it of fundamental importance that it should arrive promptly.

Frustration will occur as soon as it is possible to make a reasonably reliable and well-informed estimate that the damage to ship or cargo is so great, or the delay is likely to be so long, as to be sufficient to frustrate the adventure under the principles described above. It is not necessary to wait until the facts are known with absolute certainty. In *Bank Line v Capel*,[33] where the issue was whether delay caused by a requisition of the ship had frustrated a time charter, Lord Sumner explained the correct approach as follows: **00.44**

[30] *Moss v Smith* (1850) 9 C.B. 94; *Jackson v Union Marine Insurance* (1874) L.R. 10 C.P. 125; *Assicurazioni Generali v The S.S. Bessie Morris Co; Carras v London & Scottish Assurance* [1936] 1 K.B. 291.

[31] *Kulukundis v Norwich Union Fire Insurance Co* [1937] 1 K.B. 1.

[32] *The Fjord Wind* [1999] 1 Lloyd's Rep. 307, 332-333. The point did not arise in the Court of Appeal [2000] 2 Lloyd's Rep. 191.

[33] *Bank Line v Capel* [1919] A.C. 435 at 454.

> "The probabilities as to the length of the deprivation and not the certainty arrived at after the event are also material. The question must be considered at the trial as it had to be considered by the parties, when they came to know of the cause and the probabilities of the delay and had to decide what to do. Rights ought not to be left in suspense or to hang on the chances of subsequent events. The contract binds or it does not bind, and the law ought to be that the parties can gather their fate then and there."

The Shipowner's Right to Tranship

00.45 The general rule is that frustration occurs automatically once the frustrating event has happened and its effect on further performance of the contract is known or can be predicted with sufficient certainty; the cargo interests are thereupon bound and entitled to take possession of their cargo at the port of refuge, unless some new agreement is entered into between the parties.

To this rule there is one important exception, namely that the shipowner has an implied right to tranship the cargo and complete the voyage in another ship, provided that the cargo is fit to stand the voyage and that the voyage can be completed without unreasonable delay. The shipowner is under no obligation to exercise this right[34] but if he wishes to do so he must act promptly. Similar considerations apply to towage to destination. It has been held that the shipowner is entitled but not obliged to take this course,[35] although in the case of a breakdown very near the port of destination the result might be different.

Many bills of lading, especially in the liner trade, and some charterparties, contain an express right of transhipment, or substitution, at any time before or during the voyage. Whilst the effect of each of these clauses will depend upon its precise wording, some may produce the result that the shipowner cannot claim that the adventure is frustrated if further performance in the carrying ship becomes impossible, and must exercise his rights under the clause. In one such case[36] where the charter conferred on the owners "the liberty of substituting. . . . a vessel . . . at any time before or during this charter-party", Devlin J. said:

> "It might well be that the charterers in this case could say, if they so desired, 'You have an option to perform the charter-party in some other way and you do not excuse yourself from further performance . . . merely by saying that the named ship has been sunk. You must show that you have no other ship available with which you can perform the charter-party.'."

Thus in *The Super Servant Two*,[37] where the carrier had the right to perform the transportation of a drilling rig with either of two transportation units, the loss of one unit, which the carrier had scheduled the perform the contract, did not lead to

[34] The shipowner may be obliged to tranship where the ocean voyage is effectively at an end so that e.g. the voyage could be completed by transhipment into lighters: see *Kulukundis v Norwich Union Fire Insurance Co* at 16-17, per Greer L.J. cf. *Western Sealanes Corp v Unimarine* [1982] 2 Lloyd's Rep. 160 at 166–167.

[35] *The Fjord Wind* [1999] 1 Lloyd's Rep. 307, 334. The point did not arise in the Court of Appeal [2000] 2 Lloyd's Rep. 191.

[36] *SA Maritime & Commerciale v Anglo Iranian Oil* [1953] 1 Lloyd's Rep. 229, 234.

[37] *The Super Servant Two* [1990] 1 Lloyd's Rep. 1, affirming [1989] 1 Lloyd's Rep. 148.

the frustration of the contract, although he could not have performed it without breaching other contracts.

2. Hague Rules and Similar Legislation

Exceptions Clauses and the Hague Rules

A contract for the carriage of goods by sea covered by a bill of lading (including any bill of lading issued under charterparty if and when the holder of the bill of lading is a person other than the charterer) is by force of legislation almost invariably subject, both in this country and in most maritime countries, to the provisions of the Hague Rules as applied by various statutes. These Rules do not apply by force of law to charterparties, but they may be incorporated in a charterparty, or in a bill of lading to which they would not otherwise apply, by the agreement of the parties, and this is frequently done. **00.46**

In the United Kingdom the Hague Rules were first given statutory effect by the Carriage of Goods by Sea Act 1924. Amendments to the Rules were formulated in the Brussels Protocol of 1968, and the amended Rules form the Schedule to the Carriage of Goods by Sea Act 1971,[38] which applies to bills of lading issued on or after June 23, 1977.[39] Further amendment to the financial limits of the carrier's liability for loss or damage, was made by the Protocol of 1979, which was given statutory force by the Merchant Shipping Act 1981.[40] **00.47**

Whether or not the Rules apply to a contract of carriage, where not incorporated by express agreement, will depend on the proper law of the contract and the extent to which the courts in which the action is brought will give effect to that law.[41] Where English law applies, the effect of the Carriage of Goods by Sea Act 1971, and of the amended Rules, is that the Rules apply:

(1) where the port of shipment is in the United Kingdom;
(2) where the bill of lading provides that the Rules are to govern the contract; or
(3) where the bill of lading relates to carriage between different states; and
  (a) the bill of lading is issued in a contracting state,[42] or
  (b) the carriage is from a port in a contracting state,[43] or
  (c) the contract provides that the amended Rules or legislation giving effect to them is to govern the contract.[44]

[38] Carriage of Goods by Sea Act 1971 c.19.
[39] The Carriage of Goods by Sea Act 1971 (Commencement) Order 1977 (SI 1977/ 981).
[40] See now the Merchant Shipping Act 1995 Sch.13 para.5.
[41] See *Vita Food Products v Unus Shipping Co* [1939] A.C. 277.
[42] A contracting state is a state which is a party to the Protocol of 1968, whether or not a party to the Protocol of 1979: see the Merchant Shipping Act 1981 s.2(6).
[43] For a list of contracting states, see the Carriage of Goods by Sea (Parties to Convention) Order 1985 (SI 1985/443).
[44] See the Carriage of Goods by Sea Act 1971 s.l(3) (6), and Art.X of the amended Rules.

There are many countries, including the United States, which have not adopted the amended Rules. As a result, it is frequently the unamended Rules which will apply.[45] References to the Hague Rules in the remainder of this section apply equally to either version unless the contrary is stated.

00.48 The main reason for the introduction of the Hague Rules was to restrict the right of carriers by sea to exclude liability for loss of or damage to cargo caused by unseaworthiness of the ship or the negligence of their servants. This is achieved by imposing on the carrier specific obligations, described in more detail below, relating to seaworthiness and to the care of the goods, and prohibiting the carrier from excluding his liability for breach of those obligations, or limiting his liability to a lower sum than that provided for in the Rules. Under the Rules the carrier is entitled to the benefit of a number of rights and immunities, unless the contract expressly provides to the contrary, and these rights and immunities operate in effect as exceptions clauses. The detailed application of these obligations, rights and immunities lies outside the scope of this work, but brief mention must be made of one or two of the more important effects of the Rules.

Effect of Hague Rules on Obligation to make Ship Seaworthy

00.49 Section 2 of the 1924 Act (s.3 of the 1971 Act) excludes the implied absolute warranty of seaworthiness, described at para.00.35, above, and replaces it with an undertaking that the carrier, including any servants or sub-contractors employed by him, will use due diligence before and at the beginning of the voyage to secure that his ship is seaworthy, properly manned, equipped and supplied, and fit to carry the cargo. Thus where loss or damage results from unseaworthiness, the carrier is liable if the unseaworthiness resulted from failure to exercise due diligence, but not otherwise.

Effect of Hague Rules on Duty to Care for the Goods

00.50 Article III r.2 of the Hague Rules provides that the carrier shall "properly and carefully load, stow, carry, keep, care for and discharge the goods". This reflects the duty at common law, described at para.00.35, above, to exercise reasonable care in the carriage of the goods. However, the Rules also contain (art.IV r.2) an important exception of "act, neglect or default of the master, mariner, pilot, or the servants of the carrier in the navigation or in the management of the ship". In order to reconcile these provisions, it is necessary to draw what is often a narrow distinction between negligence in the care of the cargo, and negligence in the management of the ship as a whole. Thus a failure to close the hatches when in port has been held to be negligence towards the cargo rather then the ship,[46] as has a failure correctly to operate the refrigeration machinery used for cooling the

[45] For the application of the unamended Rules see British Shipping Laws, Vol.2: Carver, Carriage by Sea, 13th edn, paras 571–578.

[46] *Gosse Millerd v Canadian Govt Merchant Marine* [1929] A.C. 223.

cargo.[47] On the other hand, a failure properly to secure the tarpaulins on the hatch covers, with the result that seawater entered the holds on the voyage, was held to be negligence in the management of the ship.[48]

Effect of the Hague Rules on Deviation

00.51 So far as deviation is concerned the Rules have made little difference. The provisions of art.IV r.4, provide:

> "Any deviation in saving or attempting to save life or property at sea or any reasonable deviation shall not be deemed to be an infringement or breach of these Rules or of the contract of carriage, and the carrier shall not be liable for any loss or damage resulting therefrom."

What is a reasonable deviation was described as follows in *Stag Line v Foscolo Mango & Co*[49] :

> "The true test seems to be what departure from the contract voyage might a prudent person controlling the voyage at the time make and maintain, having in mind all the relevant circumstances existing at the time, including the terms of the contract and the interests of all parties concerned, but without obligation to consider the interests of anyone as conclusive."

Negligent navigation in the course of an otherwise reasonable deviation does not render it unreasonable.[50]

The rule does not restrict the operation of liberty clauses which provide for substituted performance in specific events, such as strikes,[51] and probably has no restrictive effect on other deviation clauses, so long as they are not inconsistent with the carrier's obligation to care for the goods.[52]

Effect of Hague Rules on Provisions regarding General Average

00.52 It is uncertain to what extent the Hague Rules affect the parties' freedom to contract on such terms as they wish with regard to general average. The rules contain the following provisions relevant to this question:

[47] *Foreman & Ellams v Federal S.N. Co* [1928] 2 K.B. 424.

[48] *International Packers v Ocean S.S. Co* [1955] 2 Lloyd's Rep. 218.

[49] *Stag Line v Foscolo Mango & Co* [1932] A.C. 328 per Lord Atkin. See also *Danae Shipping v T.P.A.O.* [1983] 1 Lloyd's Rep. 498; *Lyric Shipping v Intermetals Ltd (The Al Taha)* [1990] 2 Lloyd's Rep. 117. For a detailed discussion of the effect of art.IV r.4, see *British Shipping Laws*, Vol.2; Carver, *Carriage by Sea*, 13th edn, paras 546–550; and *Scrutton on Charterparties*, 20th edn, pp.447-449.

[50] *The Al Taha* [1990] 2 Lloyd's Rep. 117; *Rey Banano del Pacifico v Transportes Nav. Ecatorianos (The Isla Fernanda)* [2000] 2 Lloyd's Rep. 15.

[51] *Renton v Palmyra Trading Corp* [1957] A.C. 149.

[52] *Renton v Palmyra Trading Corp* in Court of Appeal [1956] 1 Q.B. 462, 505. The House of Lords expressed no view on the point.

Article III Rule 8

Any clause, covenant or agreement in a contract of carriage relieving the carrier or the ship from liability for loss or damage to or in connection with goods arising from negligence, fault or failure in the duties and obligations provided in this Article or lessening such liability otherwise than as provided in these Rules, shall be null and void and of no effect.

A benefit of insurance in favour of the carrier or similar clause shall be deemed to be a clause relieving the carrier from liability.

Article IV Rule 3

The shipper shall not be responsible for loss or damage sustained by the carrier or the ship arising or resulting from any cause without the act, fault or neglect of the shipper, his agents or his servants.

Article V

Nothing in these Rules shall be held to prevent the insertion in a bill of lading of any lawful provision regarding general average.

00.53 It is clear that art.V overrides art.IV r.3, with the result that the shipper's liability to contribute in general average is not affected by absence of fault on his part. However, it seems unlikely that art.V was intended to override art.III r.8, so as to allow wider exemption clauses to operate in respect of claims in general average.

Whether this intention has been achieved is doubtful. Although the purport of the word "lawful" in Art.V is unclear, if the words of the Article are given their ordinary meaning it is difficult to resist the conclusion that no provision of the Rules, including art.III r.8, may be invoked in order to invalidate a "provision regarding general average" which would otherwise be lawful. Moreover, in *Goulandris Bros Ltd v B. Goldman & Sons Ltd*[53] it was held by Pearson J. that the words "loss or damage" in the 1924 version of art.III r.6 (which provides that the carrier shall be discharged from liability unless suit is brought within one year) do not include liability to contribute in general average. If that is so, the words "loss or damage to, or in connection with, goods" in art.III r.8 can scarcely include liability to contribute.[54]

00.54 Hence the effect of art.III r.8 and art.5 appears to be that a contract of affreightment which was subject to the Rules could lawfully provide that the shipowner should be entitled to general average contribution, notwithstanding any breach of the obligations imposed by art.III rr.1 and 2. Such provisions though not unknown[55] are rare, and the result is one which the courts might be reluctant to reach; but it is submitted that it must follow, unless the decision of Pearson J. in *Goulandris Bros Ltd v B. Goldman & Sons Ltd*[56] as to the meaning of "loss or damage" is

[53] *Goulandris Bros Ltd v B. Goldman & Sons Ltd* [1958] 1 Q.B. 74.

[54] Although they are not limited to physical loss or damage: *G.H. Renton & Co Ltd v Palmyra Trading Corp* [1957] A.C. 149; cf. *Adamastos Shipping Co Ltd v Anglo-Saxon Petroleum Co Ltd* [1959] A.C. 133.

[55] Both the 1978 and the 1994 editions of the widely-used Congenbill contain, in addition to a clause paramount and a New Jason Clause, the following provision: "Cargo's contribution to General Average shall be paid to the Carrier even when such average is the result of a fault neglect or error of the Master, Pilot or Crew." On the face of it, this provision entitles the carrier to general average contribution even where the fault or neglect is in the care of the cargo rather than in the navigation or management of the ship and would therefore involve a breach of the Hague Rules: see para.00.50, above.

[56] See fn.53, above.

reconsidered,[57] and unless the court is prepared to give a very restrictive interpretation to art.V.

The Harter Act

Contracts for the carriage of goods on Atlantic voyages sometimes contain a clause incorporating the provisions of the "Harter" Act, a statute of the United States, passed in 1893, to regulate the trade between the United States and foreign ports. Sections 1 and 2 of the Act prohibit and avoid clauses which relieve the shipowner from the duty to take care of the cargo and provide a seaworthy ship; but s.3 enacts that if the shipowner has exercised due care to make the vessel seaworthy, neither he, the vessel, her agent, nor her charterers shall be liable for damage or loss arising from (inter alia) faults or errors in navigation, or in the management of the vessel.[58] It was held by the Supreme Court of the United States in The Irawaddy[59] that this exemption in the Act has not the effect of entitling the shipowner to claim a contribution for a general average loss due to the negligence of his servants. However, under an English contract incorporating the Act, the shipowner would not be precluded by the decision of the Supreme Court from claiming contribution; the incorporation of the Act is only equivalent to the insertion into the contract of an exclusion clause in the terms of the Act, the effect of which falls to be determined by English law.[60] Under English law, since the negligence of the shipowner's servants in the navigation or management of the ship would not be actionable fault, contribution would be recoverable.[61] **00.55**

[57] The decision on the effect of art.III r.6, was not essential to the result, and was reached without the benefit of the decision of the House of Lords in *Adamastos Shipping Co Ltd v Anglo Saxon Petroleum Co Ltd* (above). However, it has been said that the incurring of a liability to contribute is not "loss" within the meaning of the Merchant Shipping Act 1894 s.503: see *Greenshields, Cowie and Co v Stephen and Sons Ltd* [1908] A.C. 431, HL; *Louis Dreyfus v Tempus Shipping* [1931] A.C. 726 at 739, per Lord Dunedin.

[58] For a consideration of this Act and the effect of its incorporation into an English bill of lading, see *Dobell v S.S. Rossmore Co* [1895] 2 Q.B. 408.

[59] *The Irawaddy* (1898) 171 U.S. 187. Before the Act any clause in a bill of lading which exempted the shipowner from liability for the negligence of himself or his servants was considered by the US courts to be contrary to public policy and void. Section 3 only provides a defence where none existed previously; it does not entitle a shipowner to claim general average contribution consequent upon negligence, since it does not mention general average. Equally (or perhaps a fortiori) the section does not exonerate the shipowner from liability to contribute in general average to the loss of cargo; for otherwise he might be in a better position if his servants had been negligent than if they had not: *The Jason* 225 U.S. 32 (1910); *The Ernestina* 259 Fed. Rep. 772 (1919). And the shipowner's sacrifices and expenditure must be taken into account in any claim by cargo for contribution, notwithstanding his negligence or that of his servants; in this manner such a claim may be reduced or wholly extinguished: *The Strathdon* 94 Fed. Rep. 206 (1899); 10 Fed. Rep. 600 (1900).

[60] *Dobell v S.S. Rossmore Co* [1895] 2 Q.B. 408, CA, "They then introduce into their bill of lading the words of the Harter Act, which I decline to construe as an Act, but which we must construe simply as words occurring in this bill of lading": per Lord Esher. See also *Rowson v Atlantic Transport Co* [1903] 2 K.B. 666, CA.

[61] See para.D.02 et seq., below.

The Jason Clause and the New Jason Clause

00.56 In consequence of the decision in *The Irrawaddy*[62] a negligence general average clause is almost invariably included in bills of lading under which general average is likely to be adjusted in the United States. If this be the Jason Clause,[63] the shipowner's right to general average contribution is expressed to be subject to the condition that he shall have exercised due diligence to make the ship seaworthy and properly manned, equipped and supplied; if he has not, it matters not that there was no causal connection between his failure and the casualty.[64] In the New Jason Clause, on the other hand, the right is subject only to the condition that the casualty shall not have resulted from a cause for which the shipowner is responsible by statute, contract or otherwise.[65]

00.57 Despite the provenance of the Jason Clause and the New Jason Clause, one or other of them (and sometimes both) is from time to time included in a contract of carriage where general average is to be adjusted elsewhere than in the United States. The question has been raised whether this has the result of reducing the shipowner's rights.[66]

Thus in *Goulandris Bros Ltd v B. Goldman and Sons Ltd*,[67] it was argued that, whatever the effect of r.D of the York-Antwerp Rules, the result of incorporating a New Jason Clause in the bill of lading was that the cargo-owner had a pure defence to a claim for general average whenever the danger arose from the actionable fault of the shipowner. However, since Pearson J. decided the issue in favour of the cargo-owner on the construction of r.D itself, he did not deal with this question.

In *E.B. Aaby's Rederi v Union of India (No.2)*,[68] it was argued that the effect of the incorporation of a Jason Clause in the bill of lading was to deprive the shipowner, who had failed to exercise due diligence to make the ship seaworthy, of a right to contribution, even if the unseaworthiness in question was not the cause of the casualty. The bill of lading incorporated the Hague Rules, and references to the Harter Act had been deleted. Donaldson J. rejected this argument, holding that the effect of the clause did not detract from the ordinary right of the shipowner under English law or under the York-Antwerp Rules to recover contribution unless his actionable fault was the cause of the peril. The same issue was argued afresh in *The Kamsar Voyager*[69] and Judge Dean QC reached the same conclusion as Donaldson J.

[62] See para.00.55, above.

[63] *The Jason* 225 U.S. 32 (1910).

[64] *The Isis* (1934) 48 Ll.L.R. 35. In one case the general average clause has been held itself to determine the shipowners' duties under the contract, as far as concerned general average: *Schade v National Surety Corp* (1961) A.M.C. 1225.

[65] For a discussion of the history of these clauses, see *Drew Brown Ltd v The Orient Trader* [1972] 1 Lloyd's Rep. 35 at 47-48; [1973] 2 Lloyd's Rep. 174.

[66] See below. See also *The Makedonia* [1962] 1 Lloyd's Rep 316 at 341.

[67] [1958] 1 Q.B. 74 at 106. For the decision in this case on r.D, see paras D.31-D.32, below.

[68] [1976] 2 Lloyd's Rep. 714. The argument was not pursued in the Court of Appeal [1978] 1 Lloyd's Rep. 351.

[69] *Guinomar of Conakry v Samsung Fire and Marine Insurance (the Kamsar Voyager)* [2002] 2 Lloyd's Rep. 57.

The Hague Rules in the United States

The Carriage of Goods by Sea Act 1936 gave effect with slight modifications to the Hague Rules[70] and enacted (s.13) that it should apply to all foreign trade to and from the ports of the United States. By s.12, however, the Harter Act remained applicable before loading and after discharging cargo. It would therefore appear that so far as general average is concerned, the decisions under the Harter Act are of academic interest only, except on the point mentioned in para.00.55, above. **00.58**

The Hamburg Rules 1978

The Hamburg Rules, contained in the UN Convention on the Carriage of Goods by Sea concluded at Hamburg in 1978, were intended to replace the Hague Rules as an internationally adopted code, applying compulsorily to contracts for carriage of goods by sea other than charterparties. The United Kingdom has ratified the Convention, but it has taken no steps to introduce legislation to give legal effect to the Rules. A small number of states, mainly non-maritime, have given legal effect to the Hamburg Rules, but in view of the work now in progress on the project described in the next paragraph, there is no real prospect that they will gain international acceptance and become an effective replacement for the Hague Rules. **00.59**

Where the Hamburg Rules do apply, they render the carrier prima facie liable for loss, damage or delay while the goods are in his charge during the voyage or at the port of loading or discharge. In order to avoid liability the carrier must prove "that he, his servants or agents took all measures that could reasonably be required to avoid the occurrence and its consequences". The most important difference in practical terms between the Hamburg Rules and the Hague Rules is that under the Hamburg Rules the carrier will always incur liability for loss, damage or delay caused by negligence, and that there is no exception of "act, neglect or default . . . in the navigation or in the management of the ship".

The Uncitral Draft Contract of Carriage

Rotterdam Rules

For some years, prompted in part by the Uncitral Draft Contract of Carriage, work was in progress to provide an effective replacement to the Hague Rules. It appeared to be generally accepted that the carrier's protection in respect of casualties arising from faults in navigation or management of the ship was no longer appropriate, and that the multi-model nature of modern maritime transport needed to be recognised. **00.60**

The Rotterdam Rules were adopted by the United Nations Commission on International Trade Law on 11 December 2008. A significant number of leading

[70] In the US the Brussels Protocol of 1968 (see para.00.47, above) has not yet been enacted or brought into force.

maritime nations were signatories but to date only two countries, Spain and Togo, have ratified the Convention. However, when or if countries such as the United States also ratify the Rules it is expected that others will follow suit rapidly; a brief overview of the Rules is therefore given below, together with comments on practical implications relevant to general average.

The basis of liability is set out in Article 17 as follows:

> *"Article 17*
> *Basis of liability*
>
> 1. *The carrier is liable for loss of or damage to the goods, as well as for delay in delivery, if the claimant proves that the loss, damage, or delay, or the event or circumstance that caused or contributed to it took place during the period of the carrier's responsibility as defined in chapter 4.*
> 2. *The carrier is relieved of all or part of its liability pursuant to paragraph 1 of this article if it proves that the cause or one of the causes of the loss, damage, or delay is not attributable to its fault or to the fault of any person referred to in article 18.*
> 3. *The carrier is also relieved of all or part of its liability pursuant to paragraph 1 of this article if, alternatively to proving the absence of fault as provided in paragraph 2 of this article, it proves that one or more of the following events or circumstances caused or contributed to the loss, damage, or delay:*
>
> (a) *Act of God;*
> (b) *Perils, dangers, and accidents of the sea or other navigable waters;*
> (c) *War, hostilities, armed conflict, piracy, terrorism, riots and civil commotions;*
> (d) *Quarantine restrictions; interference by or impediments created by governments, public authorities, rulers, or people including detention, arrest, or seizure not attributable to the carrier or any person referred to in article 18;*
> (e) *Strikes, lockouts, stoppages, or restrains of labour;*
> (f) *Fire of the ship;*
> (g) *Latent defects not discoverable by due diligence;*
> (h) *Act or omission of the shipper, the documentary shipper, the controlling party, or any other person for whose acts the shipper or the documentary shipper is liable pursuant to article 33 or 34;*
> (i) *Loading, handling, stowing, or unloading of the goods performed pursuant to an agreement in accordance with article 13, paragraph 2, unless the carrier or a performing party performs such activity on behalf of the shipper, the documentary shipper or the consignee;*
> (j) *Wastage in bulk or weight or any other loss or damage arising from inherent defect, quality, or vice of the goods;*
> (k) *Insufficiency or defective condition of packing or marking not performed by or on behalf of the carrier;*
> (l) *Saving or attempting to save life at sea;*
> (m) *Reasonable measures to save or attempt to save property at sea;*
> (n) *Reasonable measures to avoid or attempt to avoid damage to the environment, or*
> (o) *Acts of the carrier in pursuance of the powers conferred by article 15 and 16"*

Specific references to general average consist of the following:
Article 84 deals with the topic in general terms:

> *"Nothing in this Convention affects the application of terms in the contract of carriage or provisions of national law regarding the adjustment of general average."*

Two earlier Articles deal with the specific points of dangerous goods and cargo sacrifices.

> *"Article 15*
> *Goods that may become a danger*
>
> *Notwithstanding articles 11 and 13, the carrier or a performing party may decline to receive or to load, and may take such other measurers as are reasonable, including unloading, destroying, or rendering goods harmless, if the goods are, or reasonably appear likely to become during the carrier's period of responsibility, an actual danger to persons, property or the environment."*
>
> *"Article 16*
> *Sacrifice of the goods during the voyage by sea*
>
> *Notwithstanding articles 11, 13, and 14, the carrier or a performing party may sacrifice goods at sea when the sacrifice is reasonably made for the common safety or for the purpose of preserving from peril human life or other property involved in the common adventure."*

A variety of views have been expressed as to how the mechanism for establishing liability will work in practice, discussion of which is outside the scope of this book. However, it is suggested that some practical issues relating to general average may need to be considered. While hull insurers would not be greatly affected (except in the relatively rare cases of ship sacrifice), the P&I Clubs would clearly be paying cargo's proportion of general average more frequently, as cargo declines to pay on the grounds of a breach of the contract of affreightment in cases where the "nautical fault" exceptions no longer apply.

An immediate practical implication would be that the increased likelihood of cargo having a defence to contribution would make it unwise to automatically incur the costs of an expensive security collection from a multi-interest cargo. However, deciding not to collect security is not a judgement the shipowner should make without consulting the P&I Club, whose cover is likely to be conditional on proper security having been collected and a demonstrable breach of contract having occurred.

In most salvage cases (see Article 13.2 Salvage Convention 1989), cargo will still have a direct liability to provide security to salvors and pay their proportion of the award, before seeking recovery from the carrier, albeit with a much greater chance of success under the Rotterdam Rules. Counter-security in respect of cargo's rights to recover salvage paid to salvors may therefore become a more contentious issue. It is possible that Owners and their P&I Clubs may sometimes agree to provide security on behalf of cargo and pay 100% of the salvage in order to reduce costs and achieve a quick negotiated settlement, but the bigger the exposure the greater the pressure will be to let matters run their normal course.

That pressure can only be increased by the Rotterdam Rules' repeated reference in Article 17 to "all or part" of a liability for a loss and the concept of a loss being apportioned somehow if the carrier can partly disprove his fault. In a collision where it seems likely that both ships are equally to blame, the owner knows that he is no longer protected by the "nautical fault" exception, but equally he is not at fault in respect of the blame attaching to the other vessel. On that basis could he not recover 50% of any general average contribution due from his cargo? That would seem to be the case.

Many of the most serious casualties in recent years have involved containership fires originating in cargo. These have given rise to complex legal disputes, particularly on factual issues with the shipper alleging poor stowage (perhaps over a heated bunker tank) and the carrier pointing to the (undeclared) dangerous nature of the cargo. This situation arose in the recent High Court judgment in the "Aconcagua" [2010] 1 Lloyds Rep 1. The carrier (actually the charterer seeking indemnity for US$27 million paid to the shipowner) won the day on the basis that it was a rogue cargo and the shipper could not prove that the heating of the bunker tank was causative. However if the heating of the tank had been causative the Court indicated that this would have constituted negligence in the management of the ship – an excepted peril under the Hague Rules. Under the Rotterdam Rules the carrier will lose the protection of that excepted peril but this would surely be a case in which the point about contributing causes (rogue cargo/fault of crew) would be at issue.

Whilst under the Rotterdam Rules it is highly likely the carrier will usually have to accept some degree of fault, there will remain a considerable incentive to allege partial fault of others. Some difficult decisions will need to be made very quickly about whether to collect general average and/or salvage security in such cases, when multiple interests are involved.

3. The Carrier's Obligation to Incur General Average Expenditure

00.61 The shipowner is not released from his duty to care for the cargo merely because an accident occurs which necessitates extraordinary measures, involving either sacrifice or expenditure. If the carrier ought reasonably to have taken such measures, he will be liable to the owner of the cargo which is damaged by his failure to do so.

In *Notara v Henderson*[71] a cargo of beans, wetted by seawater when the ship was involved in a collision, was discharged at a port of refuge. The shipowner failed to take any steps to dry the beans, as a result of which they suffered much greater damage than would otherwise have been incurred. It was held that the shipowner was liable for this damage. Although not responsible for the collision, the shipowner was under a duty to care for the cargo after the collision and he ought reasonably to have arranged for the beans to be dried. If he had done so, the costs of drying the beans could have been recovered from the shipper as a particular charge.[72]

[71] *Notara v Henderson* (1870) L.R. 5 Q.B. 346; (1872) L.R. 7 Q.B. 225.

[72] See *Notara v Henderson* at 354, per Lord Cockburn C.J., and at 233, 235, per Willes J.

The principle in *Notara v Henderson*[73] is equally applicable to the case of general, as well as particular, average, and it exposes the fallacy of an assertion which is sometimes advanced, namely that the making of a sacrifice or the incurring of expenditure cannot be a general average act if the shipowner is under a duty under the contract of carriage to make or to incur it. The proper inquiry is whether the shipowner is obliged to make the sacrifice or incur the expenditure and to bear the whole burden thereof himself as part of the cost of performing his contractual obligations. In a case concerned with temporary repairs,[74] after pointing out that it was the shipowner's obligation under the contract of carriage to effect the repairs and complete the voyage, Hobhouse J. continued: 00.62

> "The existence of the obligation is not decisive of the question before me. Many types of general average expenditure are incurred by the master in the fulfilment of his duties to the interests involved in the common adventure, including to the cargo-owners, and the function of general average is to provide a superimposed scheme for the sharing of the burden of that expenditure in an equitable fashion."

In the Court of Appeal, Hoffman L.J. made the same point, although slightly more circumspectly[75]:

> ". . . there seems to be no rigid principle that sacrifice or expenditure cannot qualify general average because the owner was under a contractual duty to make it."

Thus if, under the principles examined in this work, the shipowner is entitled to contribution in general average toward his sacrifice or expenditure from the other parties to the adventure, he is not to be deprived of that entitlement on the ground that he would have been in breach of his obligations toward those other parties if the master had failed to act as he did. However, slightly different considerations may apply when the claim is for substituted expenses, and these are discussed in commentary on r.F of the York-Antwerp Rules.

4. Obligations of Charterer or Shipper

The contract of carriage usually imposes on the charterer or shipper certain obligations with regard to the nature of the goods shipped. If goods shipped in breach of those obligations are sacrificed because they had become a danger to the ship or to other cargo on board, the shipper will be precluded from claiming contribution in general average on the grounds that the peril arose by his actionable fault. 00.63

[73] See fn.71, above.

[74] *Marida v Oswal Steel; The Bijela* [1992] 1 Lloyd's Rep. 636 at 643 (reversed on another point [1994] 2 Lloyd's Rep 1, HL). The claim was for the cost of temporary repairs of accidental damage under r.XIV of the York-Antwerp Rules, and the case is discussed in the context of that rule.

[75] [1993] 1 Lloyd's Rep. 411, 420.

Dangerous goods

00.64 In addition to any express terms of the contract, which may prohibit the shipment of certain types of goods, there is at common law an implied warranty on the part of the shipper that he will not ship dangerous goods without giving notice to the shipowner of their dangerous character.[76] If the dangerous character is obvious from the description given to the shipowner, the shipowner is deemed to have notice, and no further warning is necessary[77] unless the goods possess some special characteristic which gives rise to special risks, or requires the use of special precautions during the voyage.[78] The implied obligation of the shipper is absolute. It is not merely to give notice of those dangerous characteristics of which he was, or ought to have been, aware.[79] An absolute obligation is also frequently imposed by the express terms of the contract.

00.65 Where the Hague Rules apply, art.IV r.6 provides:

> "Goods of an inflammable, explosive or dangerous nature to the shipment whereof the carrier, master or agent of the carrier, has not consented, with knowledge of their nature and character, may at any time before discharge be landed at any place or destroyed or rendered innocuous by the carrier without compensation, and the shipper of such goods shall be liable for all damages and expenses directly or indirectly arising out of or resulting from such shipment.
>
> If any such goods shipped with such knowledge and consent shall become a danger to the ship or cargo, they may in like manner be landed at any place or destroyed or rendered innocuous by the carrier without liability on the part of the carrier except to general average, if any."

The effect of the first paragraph is that the liability of the shipper is absolute, and it is not qualified by the provisions of art.IV r.3.[80] All that the carrier need prove is that (1) the goods were of an inflammable, explosive or dangerous nature, and (2) he did not consent to their shipment with knowledge of their nature and character. In these circumstances, the shipper is liable to compensate the carrier for all losses resulting from the shipment. Also he is denied any right of contribution in general average, since the words "without compensation" are, it is submitted, wide enough to apply to contribution.

Position of consignee when dangerous goods are shipped

00.66 Under both the common law and the Hague Rules, it is the shipper upon whom the obligations relevant to the shipment of dangerous goods are imposed. It is an

[76] *Brass v Maitland* (1856) 26 L.J.Q.B. 49; 6 E. & B. 470; *Bamfield v Goole & Sheffield Transport Co* [1910] 2 K.B. 94; *Ministry of Food v Lamport & Holt* [1952] 2 Lloyd's Rep. 371; *Atlantic Oil Carriers v British Petroleum* [1957] 2 Lloyd's Rep. 55 at 95.

[77] *Acatos v Burns* (1878) 3 Ex.D. 282; *Greenshields Cowie & Co v Stephen & Sons* [1908] A.C. 431.

[78] *Atlantic Oil Carriers v British Petroleum* (above).

[79] *Effort Shipping v Linden Management* [2008] A.C. 605, HL, affirming [1996] 1 Lloyd's Rep. 577, affirming [1994] 2 Lloyd's Rep. 171.

[80] *Effort Shipping v Linden Management* (above).

unresolved question whether the common law obligations are transferred to a subsequent holder of the bill of lading by virtue of the Carriage of Goods by Sea Act 1992,[81] but there seems little reason to doubt that the shipper's obligations under art.IV r.6 of the Hague Rules are transferred.[82] The transfer has no effect upon the liability of the shipper, who remains liable for any breach of the obligation[83] ; intermediate holders of the bill of lading, by contrast, are divested of their liability when they transfer the bill of lading to an intermediate holder.[84]

The question whether the shipper's liabilities are transferred might be of importance in the context of a claim for general average if dangerous goods, shipped without notice or consent, are sacrificed after property has passed from the shipper to the consignee. If the contractual obligations are also transferred, the shipowner will be able to establish actionable fault on the part of the consignee, and avoid liability to contribute on that ground,[85] whereas otherwise he would have to pursue a separate action against the shipper. However, where the Hague Rules apply, it will be irrelevant whether the claim for contribution is brought by the shipper or by the consignee, since the effect of the first paragraph of art.IV r.6[86] of the Hague Rules is that no claim in general average arises out of the sacrifice of dangerous goods shipped without the carrier's consent.

5. General Average Sacrifice as a Defence

The character of a defence that exists in general average sacrifices has long been recognised, and has its basis in the theory that the master, when making the sacrifice, is acting on behalf of all the parties to the adventure.[87] The effect of this is that if, for example, the master decides to jettison cargo for the common safety, he does so as agent for all the parties, including the owner of the cargo jettisoned. Thus his jettison of the cargo involves no breach of duty to its owner, and the only liability incurred by the shipowner in consequence is to contribute in general average. **00.67**

However, whilst this feature does not relieve the shipowner or master of their duty, as bailees of the cargo, to take reasonable care in the carrying out of the general average act. As Hobhouse J. said in The Alpha:

[81] See *Ministry of Food v Lamport & Holt* [1952] 2 Lloyd's Rep. 371 at 382; *British Shipping Laws*, Vol.2; Carver, *Carriage by Sea*, 13th edn, para.95; *Scrutton on Charterparties*, 20th edn, p.40.

[82] This seems to have been assumed in *Effort Shipping v Linden Management* (above) (decided under the Bills of Lading Act 1855) and *Borealis v Stargas Ltd (The Berge Sisar)* [2001] 1 Lloyd's Rep. 663.

[83] Carriage of Goods by Sea Act 1992 s.3(3). The position was the same under the Bills of Lading Act 1855: *see Effort Shipping v Linden Management*.

[84] *The Berge Sisar* (above).

[85] See paras D.01 et seq., below.

[86] See para.00.65, above.

[87] See, e.g. the judgment of Lord Stowell in *The Gratitudine* (1801) 3 C.Rob. 240 at 257; quoted para.1.02, below.

"The fact that the master was acting as an agent of necessity in the interests of the joint adventure does not relieve him of his duty to exercise reasonable care in the preservation of the cargo."[88]

The failure to exercise reasonable care may, of course, be covered by an exception clause, in which case it will not be actionable, as was the case in *The Alpha*. However, in the absence of an exception clause, the shipowner will be liable if the general average act is carried out with a lack of reasonable care and skill which causes, or exacerbates, damage to the cargo.

00.68 In *Federal Commerce and Navigation Co Ltd v Eisenerz GmbH*,[89] a case decided in the Supreme Court of Canada, the shipowners were held to be in breach of this duty. The vessel Oak Hill, owned by the appellants, loaded two part cargoes of pig iron at Sorel, P.Q., for carriage to Genoa. Owing to the negligence of the pilot, for which the appellants were by contract not responsible, the vessel stranded in the St Lawrence River and put into the port of Levis, P.Q., as a port of refuge for repairs. It was necessary to discharge and subsequently reload the pig iron in order that repairs could be carried out and, during the course of these operations, the cargoes became intermingled and to a limited extent lost and destroyed. The respondent, as owner of the cargo, claimed for the full amount of the loss and damage. The appellants relied on r.XII of the York-Antwerp Rules 1950 as a defence.

If the facts had stopped there, the appellants would (as the Supreme Court evidently considered) have had a defence to the claim. It is submitted that this defence would not have rested on r.XII which affords the owner of cargo lost or damaged at a port of refuge a right to general average contribution; it would have rested on the inherent characteristic of all general average sacrifices, that the shipowner is not liable for loss of or damage to cargo resulting from a general average act, except to the extent of his contribution.

It was found, however, that the loss and damage was caused by the negligence of the master and of general average surveyors appointed by the shipowners. The appellants contended that the port of Levis was so ill-equipped for the reception of pig iron that the mixing and breaking might have taken place without anybody's negligence, but this contention was rejected. The Supreme Court held the shipowners liable. Ritchie J. said:

"In entering upon the general average act and in making all reasonable and necessary expenditures consequent thereon, the master is to be taken as acting with the implied authority of the cargo-owners as well as the ship, but this authority does not extend so as to identify the cargo-owners with the negligence of the master or those employed by him in carrying out the general average procedure or to derogate from his overriding responsibility to care for the cargo in his capacity as the servant of the shipowner."[90]

[88] *Corfu Navigation Co v Mobil Shipping* [1991] 2 Lloyd's Rep. 515, 522. The case is discussed in the context of r.VII. See also per Brett M.R. in *Burton v English* (quoted at para.00.23, above) for the case where the master improperly jettisoned cargo.

[89] *Federal Commerce and Navigation Co Ltd v Eisenerz GmbH* [1970] 2 Lloyd's Rep. 332; [1975] 1 Lloyd's Rep. 105.

[90] [1975] 1 Lloyd's Rep. 105 at 114.

The court's reasoning whereby the shipowners were held liable was that, since the negligence broke the chain of causation between the cargo handling operations and the damage, the damage to the cargo was not, after all, a general average loss.[91] However, the logical consequence of the court's conclusions in the passage quoted above is, it is submitted, that whether or not the damage was general average, the defendants were liable for it in full, as damages for breach of contract, since it resulted directly and foreseeably from their breach. On the court's reasoning, if the negligent handling had been covered by an exception with the result that the shipowners were not liable in damages, the cargo-owners would be deprived of any remedy, even by way of contribution in general average. This could lead to the unfortunate conclusion that the shipowners would be financially better off if the damage resulted from their negligence than if it resulted from difficult conditions at the port of refuge. **00.69**

[91] It is submitted that whilst the court's reasoning might have been correct if causation had been governed by r.C, it was not correct under r.XII. See paras C.28 et seq. and 12.14, below.

SECTION 3

THE HISTORY AND DEVELOPMENT OF THE YORK-ANTWERP RULES

INTRODUCTION

The York-Antwerp Rules have recognised two main types of allowance: 00.70

(1) "Common safety" allowances: sacrifice of property (such as flooding a cargo hold to fight a fire) or expenditure (such as salvage or lightening a vessel) that was made or incurred while the ship and cargo were actually in the grip of peril. Since the early 19th century, English law and practice has largely recognised only this category of general average.

(2) "Common benefit" allowances: once a vessel was at a port of refuge, European countries and the United States generally viewed expenses necessary to enable the ship to resume the voyage safely (but not the cost of repairing accidental damage to the ship) as also being general average; for example, the cost of discharging, storing and reloading cargo as necessary to carry out repairs, port charges, and wages etc. during detention for repairs and outward port charges.

Continental and American law therefore took the view that attaining a position of safety was only the first stage in completing the original aim of the common adventure, which was not merely that of achieving safety at an intermediate place, but of reaching destination. To the merchant, it is completing the voyage that is important; cargo that is safe but thousands of miles away from the intended market is as good as lost. It was therefore considered that general average should continue after immediate safety had been achieved, while expenses were being incurred to get ship and cargo to destination–hence the "common benefit" approach.

At the time of the Glasgow Resolutions in 1860, when the groundwork for the first York-Antwerp Rules was being prepared, the vote was 24 to 5 in favour of going beyond the English law approach, and since that time the York-Antwerp Rules have included "common benefit" expenses.

In practice, the agreed framework for dealing with common benefit expenditure has increased the likelihood that the voyage will be prosecuted without lengthy legal wrangling and delay; the ability to allow transhipment costs, for example, as substituted expenses will often bring the cargo forward very rapidly indeed. When a very serious casualty has occurred, the existence of a system for sharing certain costs (i.e. discharging, storing and reloading cargo in order to effect repairs) often prevents the premature and disputed abandonment of the voyage, without prejudicing the parties' rights and liabilities under the contract of affreightment.

In addition to addressing various minor differences in practice between maritime nations, the main thrust of the York-Antwerp Rules has therefore been to unite these two strands.

More recently, the need to deal with the effect of marine casualties on the environment came to the forefront with international conventions imposing strict liability for many types of oil pollution, giving coastal states extensive powers of intervention and changing the basis for salvage remuneration in certain circumstances. The compromises reached between property and liability insurers with regard to environmental liabilities and costs were reflected initially in the 1990 amendment to the 1974 Rules and then more fully in the 1994 and 2004 Rules.

1. Glasgow Resolutions 1860

00.71 The movement for attaining international uniformity may be dated from the year 1860. Early in that year an appeal was made to the National Association for the Promotion of Social Science, London, by Lloyd's, the Underwriters' Association of Liverpool, and several other important commercial bodies, to take up this work. In response to this appeal the National Association issued a circular letter, dated May 3, 1860, which was addressed to all the maritime countries of Europe, and to the United States. This letter read as follows:

> "The system of general average is one which, to prevent confusion and injustice, preeminently requires that the same principles should be acknowledged amongst the chief maritime nations. So far is this from being the case, however, that some of the most important rules vary not only in the same country, but in the same port. Uncertainty in law is always an evil: and, in regard to general average, the evil is peculiarly felt. The ship may be owned in one country, insured in another, her cargo owned and insured in several, and the port of destination, where the general average is made up, may be in a country which has different rules to any of the others. What is considered to be particular average on ship in one port is held to be general average in another, so that the owner of an outward-bound ship may find himself unable to recover his loss either from his underwriters at home, or as general average abroad; or on the other hand, he may be in a position to indemnify himself fraudulently twice over. A similar remark would apply to special charges on freight and on cargo. A very large portion of the most important questions rest in England nominally upon the decision of that extremely vague authority, 'the custom of Lloyd's', but really depends upon the idiosyncrasy of the particular adjuster who may be entrusted

with the papers. Hence arise many cases where apparently injustice must be done to assurer or assured. Either the assured finds himself saddled with a loss against which he believed himself insured, or the underwriter pays one which was not considered in the premium.

Much loss is occasioned to the mercantile community and to the country at large, and much valuable time is worse than wasted through business being impeded by misunderstandings and irritated feelings.

A still more crying evil, resulting from the present uncertainty of law and custom, is the opening which it leaves for every sort of abuse. Attempts are daily being made to introduce charges of the most outrageous description, which do not even go into the pocket of the shipowner, but which he feels himself helpless to resist from want of a law to appeal to; and he naturally considers himself hardly used should charges which he himself has paid be refused by his underwriters, though these last are obliged to refuse in justice to themselves and to prevent the innovation becoming a precedent.

The evils of such a state of things are notorious and unquestioned, though it may be doubted whether many which are distinctly traceable to it, and are therefore removable, are clearly realised as proceeding from this source. Probably the chief reason which has hitherto prevented any general movement in favour of this reform is an exaggerated estimate of the difficulties in the way of carrying it out. The difficulties are, no doubt, considerable, but they are far from being insuperable, and the importance of the end amply justifies an attempt to grapple with them.

Both the assured and the underwriter are interested in placing their mutual relations upon a footing which would effect a saving of time and temper, and would secure them against the annoying pecuniary loss to which they are at present exposed. It is not of so much importance how the disputed points of general average are settled, as that they should be settled. Most of the questions are in the end merely matters of account between one set of underwriters and another, and it would make little difference to any underwriter upon which interest it might be determined the charge should fall. It is true that there are points, such as the allowance of wages and provisions in a port of refuge, which would raise questions between shipowner and underwriter, but for the sake of both it is to the last degree desirable that these should not be left as a bone of contention between assurer and assured, as they are at present, e.g. when goods to America are insured in England.

The evils of the present system have already caused much dissatisfaction in America as well as in this country, and will become more and more intolerable as the commerce of the world increases, which it seems likely to do with a rapidly hitherto unexampled. The time then would seem to have come, when an attempt should be made to remove this most unnecessary element of irritation between assured and underwriter.

In the hope of coming to an understanding upon this question, the Council of the National Association for the Promotion of Social Science have determined that it shall be brought forward for discussion at their next meeting at Glasgow on Monday, September 24 next, and the following days; and we earnestly trust that you will find it in your power to send representatives of your body to that meeting, as it is very desirable that delegates from the commercial bodies in different parts of the world which are chiefly interested should be present."

A few days before the Conference assembled at Glasgow, the following memorandum was issued: **00.72**

"The adjustment of a general average is governed by the laws and customs of the State in which it is adjusted. The laws and customs of different States vary materially, and that which is general average in one country is not general average in another. It is admitted that this is a great practical grievance, and the object of this meeting is to put an end to it.

The following are the principal points on which differences exist:

1. Damage done to ship and cargo by voluntary stranding.
2. Damage done to ship and cargo in extinguishing a fire.
3. Chafage and breakage of cargo after jettison.
4. Damage done to cargo by discharging it at a port of refuge.
5. Cutting away the wreck of masts accidentally carried away.
6. Expenses of warehouse rent on cargo, re-shipping it, and outward port charges, at a port of refuge, when the original ship carried on the cargo from that port.
7. Carrying a press of sail.
8. Wages and provisions for the crew during the delay caused by putting into port.
9. Contributing values of ship, freight, and cargo.

The opinion of the meeting will be taken on each of these points:

1st. As to the principle which should govern it–i.e. whether the loss is, or is not, in principle, allowable in general average.

2nd. As to the expediency of adopting a practical rule to modify or prevent abuse of that principle."

00.73 The Conference was opened on September 25, 1860, under the presidency of Lord Brougham. The proceedings lasted for three days, during which papers were read and discussions ensued, and finally the following resolutions were adopted:

"1. That the meeting hereby requests the Council of the Association to assist by their counsels such person or persons as may be approved of by them, in drawing up a Bill, with a view to its being enacted into a law by the legislative authorities of the several nations of the world, which Bill shall define, as clearly as may be, the term 'general average.' and describe more or less fully the cases intended to be included within the definition, and which shall also specify the nature of the loss, damage, or expense allowable in general average, and the principle on which the amount of the loss, damage, or expense shall be ascertained: also, furnish a rule or rules for ascertaining the contributory values of the interests concerned, and which shall contain such matters as the person or persons drawing up the Bill may think it advisable to insert. That upon such Bill being drawn up and printed, copies thereof shall be transmitted to the several Chambers of Commerce, Boards of Underwriters, Shipowners' Associations, and other commercial societies in different parts of the world, accompanied by a copy of this resolution, and a request to them to examine and return the said copies, with such alterations or amendments as they may think proper to make therein, within six months from the time of the receipt thereof. That, upon the return of the said copies, or upon the expiration of the said six months, the said Bill shall be revised by the person or persons drawing up the same, enlightened by the information acquired as aforesaid. That, upon the Bill being perfected in the manner aforesaid, it be recommended to the legislative authorities of all commercial nations to enact the same into a law.

2. That, in the meantime, the meeting resolves to circulate as widely as possible, for general information, the rules embodied in the resolutions which have been passed by the meeting, as those which, under a uniform system, it might be desirable to consider."

Eleven working rules, largely on the subjects detailed in para.00.72 above, were passed and embodied in the Glasgow Resolutions, and the full text of each is quoted in Appendix 2A.

2. York Rules 1864

It will be seen from the first of the two general resolutions quoted above that the Glasgow Conference decided to proceed on the lines of legislation rather than by the path of voluntary agreement. The terms of the resolution indicate that the ultimate aim was uniform legislation in the various countries concerned, but by committing itself to the drafting of a Bill, which by its terms clearly indicated that it was a draft of a Bill to be introduced into Parliament, the Conference ran a grave risk of being misunderstood as to its real aim and intention. **00.74**

Unexpected delays took place in drafting and instead of the six months which the Glasgow Conference, it appears, had allotted to the task of translating their 11 resolutions into a parliamentary draft, some two years elapsed before the draft Bill made its appearance. It was entitled "Draft of a Bill entitled An Act to Consolidate and Amend the Laws relating to General Average Sacrifices and General Average Contributions", and consisted of 126 sections. Those who may wish to study its provisions are referred to Wendt's Maritime Legislation, in which it is printed in full.[1] The Bill was subjected to severe criticism by experts, and after careful scrutiny a committee appointed by the National Association for the Promotion of Social Science reported that of the 126 sections:

- 29 sections could not be agreed upon and were left open for public discussion;
- 22 sections were recommended for amendment;
- 30 sections were recommended to be struck out altogether;
- 5 sections should be altered by the draftsmen of the Bill as instructed;
- and only 40 sections were passed as originally drafted.

This report was presented to a conference held at the Guildhall, London, in June 1862. No public discussion took place on the Bill. The delegates proceeded to consider its terms in private and various amendments were suggested, but in the end it was decided to proceed no further with the onerous work of remodelling the Bill, but to leave to a committee the task of deciding upon and drafting "a Bill, or series of resolutions, having for object the establishing of one uniform system of general average throughout the mercantile world". This committee, which consisted of 16 members, had for its chairman Dr E.E. Wendt, and for its secretary Mr Richard Lowndes, and was composed of representatives from the United States, Holland, Belgium, Denmark, as well as from Great Britain. As a start, this committee drew up a statement of the various arguments on each side of what were regarded as the principal questions of general average in dispute, which was issued in 1863 to all the members of the committee, together with a "Projet de Code" submitted by Messrs Engels and van Peborgh of Antwerp, a compilation of the Danish law on general average and a translation of the German Code of 1862. Opinions and criticisms were invited, and these, together with the documents **00.75**

[1] Wendt, *Maritime Legislation*, 3rd edn, pp.71–94.

referred to, were published in January 1864, under the title of "Transactions of the International General Average Committee".

Shortly afterwards, it was decided that the Third International General Average Congress should meet at York on September 26, 1864, and a draft Bill[2] was circulated in advance as a basis for discussion at the Congress with a view to recommending a draft Bill to the English Legislature and the legislative authorities of all commercial nations.

00.76 The Congress continued its labours for three days and at its conclusion 11 rules (The York Rules[3]) were agreed to. On the motion of Lowndes the following resolutions, among others, were carried as to the future procedure to be adopted:

> "That the draft Bill as now amended in Congress, ought, in the opinion of this Congress, to be the basis of International General Average Law.
>
> That in order to carry out this object, associations should be formed, or other measures taken, in each of the countries represented in Congress, and in other countries where practicable, for the purpose of causing this Bill to become the law and practice of such country.
>
> That this end should be pursued through the Legislatures of each country where applicable, and also, pending legislation, by means of clauses to be introduced into bills of lading and charter parties.
>
> That the clauses recommended for this purpose be the following: 'All claims for general average to be settled in conformity with the International General Average Rules, framed at York in 1864'.
>
> That the representative or representatives of each country or place, as named above, shall charge himself or themselves with the task of organising an association or committee for such place, or taking such other measures as in his judgment shall be best conducive to the carrying out of the purposes laid down in the foregoing resolutions."

3. York and Antwerp Rules 1877

00.77 In accordance with the last-quoted resolution, many of the delegates to the York Conference published reports on the subject, which led to public discussions on the new rules. Repeated attempts were also made through the Associated Chambers of Commerce to obtain legislation on the basis of the York Rules, but these led to no practical results, and no doubt the indifference, if not the opposition, of Lloyd's to legislation on these lines had considerable influence on the attitude of the government authorities. The movement for international uniformity, launched with such vigour and hope in 1860, languished for more than 10 years, although it is recorded by Lowndes[4] that in 1871 the Italian Government proposed a Congress at Naples for the discussion, among other things, of the practicability of establishing a uniform code of general average in all countries.

[2] See Wendt, *Maritime Legislation*, 3rd edn, pp.126–128.
[3] See Appendix 2A, below.
[4] 4th edn, p.669.

In 1875, however, the subject was brought to notice again at the third annual Congress of the Association for the Reform and Codification of the Law of Nations, held at The Hague in that year, when one of the members drew attention to the desirability of reviewing the laws of general average. In 1876, at the next Congress of the Association, a paper was read by Mr Hach of Bremen, reviewing the history of the movement and proposing that it should be continued on the lines of considering the practicability of a code, which, it is to be noted, should contain a definition of general average. After discussion, a committee was appointed "to consider the subject of general average".

As a result, a meeting was called for August 30, 1877, at Antwerp, for the purpose of making a further and serious attempt to obtain international agreement on the subject. The meeting was presided over by Sir Travers Twiss and was attended by 68 delegates. The delegates from Lloyd's protested against the York Rules being adopted as a basis for discussion, and proposed that uniformity could best be achieved by the abolition of general average; but the expressed feeling of the meeting was clearly against such an expedient and the consideration of the York Rules was then proceeded with.

After three days' discussion these rules were finally approved with certain modifications, of which the most important were: **00.78**

> "1. In the first, the exception in favour of timber or deals jettisoned from deck was deleted, so that no jettison of deck cargo should be allowed in general average.
> 2. To the third rule, the provision was added that no compensation was to be allowed to packages which had been on fire.
> 3. In the seventh and eighth rules, the clauses relating to the exemption from contribution to port of refuge expenses of cargo left at such port, were deleted.
> 4. In the tenth rule, the basis for the contributing value of freight was altered from three-fifths of the gross amount to the gross freight less port charges and crew's wages, incurred after the general average act."

A 12th rule was also added, reading as follows:

> "The value to be allowed for goods sacrificed shall be that value which the owner would have received if such goods had not been sacrificed."

A proposal to preface the rules with a definition of general average met with no favour.[5]

The delegates from Lloyd's joined in the discussions at the Conference, but expressly dissociated themselves from the general approval of the new rules that was given by the meeting. At the conclusion of the proceedings, it was resolved that local committees should immediately take steps to ensure consideration of the revised rules "and the favourable attention and action of their respective governments". Vigorous steps to this end were undoubtedly taken; and in Britain, in 1878, the General Shipowners' Association convened a meeting in London of shipowners, underwriters and others, which resolved that the York

[5] For full details of the York and Antwerp Rules, see Appendix 2A, below.

and Antwerp Rules should be bought into operation and that the most expedient way of achieving this was by incorporation of appropriate wording into bills of lading.

00.79 At the next Conference of the Association for the Reform and Codification of the Law of Nations, held at Guildhall, London, in 1879, it was reported that the owners of more than two-fifths of the registered tonnage of Great Britain had agreed to include the rules in their bills of lading and charterparties, that a large number of the mutual insurance associations had adopted them, and that underwriters generally, despite the continued opposition of Lloyd's, were agreeing to the inclusion of the new foreign general average clause without additional premium. This general approval of the rules was, no doubt, facilitated by certain decisions in the English courts, which gave effect to the principles underlying several of the rules, even though the practice of average adjusters in this country had up to then been to a contrary effect. It was stated by Lowndes at the general meeting of the Association of Average Adjusters in 1880 that all except two of the York Rules had been adopted into the law and practice of this country. Encouraging figures were also given at the 1879 Conference of the progress which had been made in other countries, and it appeared that almost without exception shipowning and underwriting bodies, and indeed all the great mercantile communities, in the United States, the British Colonies and on the European Continent, had approved the new rules and given effect to them in contracts of affreightment and policies of insurance.

4. York-Antwerp Rules 1890

00.80 After the rules had undergone the practical test of some 10 years' operation, it was recognised that they did not entirely conform to the changing needs of commerce and that some revision was desirable. The Association of Average Adjusters drafted a report suggesting various amendments in and additions to the rules for submission to the Conference of the Association for the Reform and Codification of the Law of Nations, held at Liverpool in 1890. The proceedings lasted for four days, during which the report presented by the Association of Average Adjusters was very fully discussed and criticised, as a result of which certain amendments to the existing rules were agreed and a few entirely new rules were adopted. The resulting group of 18 rules was entitled the York-Antwerp Rules 1890,[6] and adopted almost universally throughout the world.

It may be added here that at the Antwerp Conference of 1903 a further rule was recommended for adoption entitled "Antwerp Rule 1903", which read as follows:

> "Rights to contribution in general average shall not be affected though the danger which gave rise to the sacrifice, or expenditure, may have been due to default of one

[6] See Appendix 2B, below.

> of the parties to the adventure; but this shall not prejudice any remedies which may be open against that party for such default."

This rule embodied the law of most countries on the particular point, but was never very generally adopted in contracts of affreightment.

The 1890 Rules consisted of a group of rules dealing with certain specific points upon which the law or practice was known to differ at the time when the first conferences on the subject were held, and which had been added to or amended at succeeding conferences in the light of further experience of their working or the development of commercial requirements. This lack of guiding principles underlying the rules had practical consequences of a far-reaching nature. Commerce was constantly developing in directions and by means which it was impossible to prophesy from year to year. With these conditions of change ever present, any code of rules confined to certain limited points of practical importance at any given date must continue to grow out of date and to lose its value for use in commercial contracts. The movement for international uniformity therefore did not cease after 1890. **00.81**

In 1895 an article appeared in the January issue of the *Law Quarterly Review* by Mr (later His Honour Judge) Dowdall QC in which he revived the idea of a code for international adoption, and proceeded to state the terms of such a code, consisting of 32 sections, which dealt with the definition of general average, the calculation of general average losses, the method of contribution thereto, and the means of enforcing payment. **00.82**

The Conference of the International Law Association, held in London in 1910, was the occasion of an important development in the movement towards uniformity. Mr Dowdall returned to the subject which he had made peculiarly his own, and read a paper on the "Codification of the Law of General Average". In this he submitted: **00.83**

> ". . . that a great service would be rendered to the commercial community and a great advance made if it were possible to effect a systematic and comprehensive survey of all the various contemporary laws and practice of average adjustment as regarded in the light of intelligible principles, pointing out those considerations of expediency which in special circumstances make it necessary to depart from those principles or to raise presumptions of fact by which those principles should on occasion be superseded."

As a result, a resolution was passed to form a committee to collate details of the law of general average amongst maritime nations. The report of the committee was presented to the Paris Conference in 1912.

On the motion of Kennedy L.J., it was decided to refer the matter back to the committee, with the instruction to prepare upon the basis of the report an avant projet, or model form of the law of general average. At the Madrid Conference held in 1913, the avant projet prepared by the committee was presented. A resolution was passed at the Conference provisionally accepting the avant projet, and the convenor of the committee (Mr Dowdall) was subsequently authorised to obtain the opinions of those interested, in order that the matter might **00.84** be widely discussed before the next Conference of the International Law Association, which was to be held at The Hague in September, 1914. The avant projet, with some minor alterations, was thereupon printed and circulated under the title of a "Draft International Code relating to General Average" in the spring of 1914.

00.85 The reception of the draft Code by the mercantile community was mixed. Certain bodies, notably the Liverpool Steamship Owners' Association, which expressed its approval of the Code subject to certain minor amendments, and the Liverpool Underwriters' Association, which passed a resolution in favour of the principle of codification, gave encouragement to the project, but it was clear from the reports which were received that the business community as a whole did not welcome the idea of codification and preferred to retain the York-Antwerp Rules, possibly in an amended form, as the common basis for the regulation of general average.

00.86 A committee of the Newcastle Chamber of Commerce reported in favour of a revision of the York-Antwerp Rules and a combination of them with sections embodying general principles, the germ of an idea which found development in the York-Antwerp Rules of 1924, as will be seen later. Further consideration of the draft Code, however, and indeed of all other attempts towards international agreement, was suddenly suspended by the outbreak of the First World War. Needless to say, nothing further was heard of the project until after peace was declared and the citizens of the world had had an opportunity of re-establishing some degree of order in their affairs, both political and social, which hostilities had so rudely interrupted.

5. York-Antwerp Rules 1924

00.87 Invitations were issued by the International Law Association to a meeting to be held at Gray's Inn on January 16, 1924, for the purpose of considering the best means of procedure to be adopted to attain some practical result which would commend itself to the mercantile community. The meeting was held under the chairmanship of Sir Henry Duke (later Lord Merrivale) and was attended by representatives of shipowning and underwriting bodies, average adjusters and others interested in the subject, as well as by certain representatives from the Continent. As a result of a long discussion the following resolution was carried unanimously:

> "That a settlement of the difference which exist with regard to general average will be aided by co-operation among the business interests concerned with a view to:
> (a) Formulation of Rules of Practice so far as the same are not now expressed or are insufficiently expressed in the York-Antwerp Rules, and in due course:–
> (b) The ascertainment and authoritative statement of the law of general average so far as international agreement thereon exists or can be obtained, and
> That this meeting agrees that it will be of public advantage that the International Law Association shall continue its action with a view to promoting these objects."

In May 1924 Sir Norman Hill, at the International Conference of Shipowners held in London, moved the following resolution, which was carried unanimously: 00.88

"That this Conference takes note of the movement of the International Law Association to secure greater international uniformity and certainty in general average law and practice throughout the world and is of the opinion that the object in view can best be obtained by:

(1) A revision of the York-Antwerp Rules to bring them into line with modern requirements.

(2) The embodiment in the revised rules of a general declaration of the principles underlying the rules of practice therein contained, so that such principles may be accepted and applied in those cases which are not provided for in such rules."

This was shortly followed by the summoning of a meeting of the General Average Committee of the International Law Association at Gray's Inn, which was held under the chairmanship of the Right Hon. Lord Phillimore on June 16, 1924. The position which had now been reached was put before the meeting by Sir Norman Hill, and after a lengthy discussion on the whole question of how uniformity could best be attained, the following resolution was adopted: 00.89

"That it is desirable that a draft be prepared for consideration of the Conference at Stockholm, embodying:

(1) A revision of the York-Antwerp Rules, and therein

(2) A declaration of the general principles applicable to general average.

And that, in preparing No.1, the drafting committee take for its guidance the revision made by the Average Adjusters' Association of the United Kingdom with the modifications suggested by the French, Dutch, German, Swedish, Norwegian and Belgian committees and any further reports which national committees may send in.

And that, in preparing No.2, the drafting committee do take into consideration the draft code prepared by His Honour Judge Dowdall, K.C, and the Avant Projet of Monsieur Dor."

The drafting committee appointed by the meeting in accordance with the above resolution consisted of Sir Norman Hill, Bart., His Honour Judge Dowdall K.C., Maître Léopold Dor, and Mr G.R. Rudolf, with Mr A.F. Greenwood as secretary. Its report was issued on July 24, 1924. The committee's draft revision contained a definition of principles (lettered rules), followed by the rules (numbered) dealing with points of practice, which were simply the 1890 Rules amended (r.XVIII being omitted) with the addition of six new rules. 00.90

The 33rd Conference of the International Law Association was opened at Stockholm in the presence of His Majesty the King of Sweden on September 8, 1924. The consideration of the drafting committee's report was undertaken by the general average section of the Conference, and the international character of the meetings may be gauged from the fact that delegates attended from the United States, Great Britain (including the vice-chairman of Lloyd's), France, Germany, Holland, Belgium, Norway, Sweden, Denmark, and Japan. The proceedings were presided over by Sir Norman Hill, and lasted for four days, at the end of which the new rules were finally agreed, under the title of the York-Antwerp Rules 1924, 00.91

and were adopted on the following day by the general Conference.[7] The report accompanying the draft of the 1924 Rules, as presented to the Conference, contained the following clauses:

> "4. In the opinion of this Conference the draft as so amended will attain the objects to which the International Shipping Conference directed its attention, viz.:
> First, Bring the York-Antwerp Rules 1890 into line with modern requirements.
> Second. Establish principles which may be accepted and applied in those cases which are not provided for in such rules.
> 5. This Conference therefore resolves that the rules as so amended be placed before the commercial and shipping interests for consideration, and, if approved by them, for ratification and use by voluntary agreement in the same manner as the York-Antwerp Rules 1890.
> 6. This Conference further resolves that, if the draft be not ratified by the commercial and shipping interests generally, the International Law Association be requested to arrange for further consideration of the draft by the interests directly concerned at a Conference to be specially convened for that purpose."

00.92 The new rules were immediately published in the press and were also circulated shortly after to the leading mercantile bodies throughout the world, and it was soon evident that they met with a very general measure of approval. No serious criticism of their provisions was raised, except in the United States, and the business community as a whole accepted the rules as a satisfactory solution of their demand for a revision which would provide a greater degree of uniformity in all cases of general average, whether under modern or future conditions of commerce. In the United States, however, the new rules were not received with the same approval, and special clauses providing for the partial application of the 1924 Rules became common.

6. York-Antwerp Rules 1950

The *Makis* Case

00.93 It was clearly the intention of the framers of the 1924 Rules,[8] and of the Stockholm Conference which adopted them, that all cases provided for by the numbered rules should be considered as general average, and that the lettered rules laid down general principles to be applied in those cases not specifically covered by the numbered rules. However, in 1928 the decision in *Vlassopoulos v British & Foreign Marine Insurance Co Ltd*[9] upset all preconceived ideas on this point.

It was held in that case that the lettered rules constituted a code of general average, and that the numbered rules were to be regarded as specific examples.

[7] For the text of the Rules, see Appendix 2B, below.
[8] For the text of the Rules, see Appendix 2B, below.
[9] *Vlassopoulos v British & Foreign Marine Insurance Co Ltd* [1929] 1 K.B. 187.

This meant that all the matters covered by the numbered rules were subject to the over-riding principles laid down in the lettered rules.

00.94 The situation following this decision caused embarrassment in commercial circles in this country and to overcome the difficulty an agreement was made in January 1929 between leading shipowners and underwriters in the United Kingdom. This agreement, known as the "Makis Agreement", was as follows:

> "The main object of the York-Antwerp Rules is to secure uniformity of practice in cases of General Average.
>
> In consequence of the decision in the case of Vlassopoulos v British & Foreign Marine Insurance Co. Ltd. (that of the 'Makis'), reported at 31 Lloyd's List Law Reports, p.315, questions have arisen as to the intention of the parties in framing the York-Antwerp Rules 1924, and it is desirable to set doubt at rest by agreeing that the rules shall be construed as if they contained the following provision:
>
> 'Except as provided in the numbered Rules 1 to 23 inclusive, the adjustment shall be drawn up in accordance with the lettered Rules A to G inclusive.'
>
> And it is hereby agreed that both outstanding and future cases shall be dealt with on this basis.
>
> This agreement shall be communicated to the Association of Average Adjusters of the United Kingdom with the request that all their Members and Associates shall act upon it."

The agreement was, of course, only binding upon the signatories, but it was generally respected by all concerned and ensured that the practice remained in line with that existing in other countries.

The general position regarding the 1924 Rules remained unsatisfactory, and after the Second World War had ended it soon became evident that these Rules should be revised. The development during that war of the American merchant marine rendered it more than ever important that a set of rules should be framed which would be acceptable without reservation by United States interests.

00.95 The question of revising the 1924 Rules was first raised at a Conference of the Comité Maritime International (a body devoted wholly to matters of maritime concern) at Antwerp in September 1947, with particular reference to r.XXII; and the International Law Association was invited to consider the desirability of amending this rule so as to substitute for the legal rate of interest prevailing at the final port of destination a fixed rate of interest for all countries.

The Conference of the International Law Association in Brussels in 1948 acceded to this request and also agreed to an arrangement whereby the Comité Maritime International was to undertake the task of examining the 1924 Rules with the object of facilitating their general adoption, and the Permanent Bureau of the Comité Maritime International invited its British branch, the British Maritime Law Association, to take the lead in investigating the position and in co-ordinating the work of the other national branches.

00.96 The British Maritime Law Association met in London in July 1948 under the Chairmanship of Sir Leslie Scott, and a sub-committee was appointed to examine and report on any amendments desirable with a view to facilitating the general adoption of the York-Antwerp Rules.

Committees were also set up by the national branches of the Comité Maritime International in Belgium, Denmark, France, Holland, Norway, Sweden, and in the

United States, and all the reports, memoranda and minutes of the British sub-committee were circulated to these national committees.

00.97 The views of these committees were ascertained and co-ordinated by the British Maritime Law Association Sub-Committee, for consideration by an International Commission appointed by the Permanent Bureau of the Comité Maritime International.

The Commission met in London on July 4 and 5, 1949. Each rule was considered in detail and decisions were reached on all points of difference. A drafting committee was appointed and instructed to prepare a draft of the amended Rules in accordance with decisions reached, to be submitted to the Permanent Bureau for circulation to the various national associations.

00.98 New draft Rules and various reports were placed before the Conference of the Comité Maritime International held at Amsterdam in September 1949, and after being considered and discussed fully were, with a few amendments, adopted and designated "The York-Antwerp Rules".

Delegates of all the nations represented, including the United States, agreed to recommend the adoption of the new Rules by their respective countries, and in a very short time the York-Antwerp Rules 1950 were adopted generally without reservation.

7. York-Antwerp Rules 1974

00.99 Although the 1950 Rules[10] were almost universally accepted, in the ensuing 20 years criticisms came to be made. These were in part the result of change in commercial procedures and shipping techniques, but in larger measure directed towards simplifying the task of average adjustment.

After valuable work by the Association Internationale de Dispacheurs Européens and the International Union of Marine Insurers, in November 1969 the Bureau Permanent of the Comité Maritime International resolved to set up an international sub-committee to study the subject. Mr William Birch Reynardson was appointed chairman, and Mr Henri Voet rapporteur.

00.100 A preliminary report and questionnaire were then circulated to national associations comprising the Comité Maritime International. Apart from questions directed to a number of specific Rules, these called for comment on matters not dealt with in the 1950 Rules, including the formalities of securing general average contribution, a franchise to eliminate small contributions, and a standard form of non-separation agreement. The replies were considered by a working group whose report was considered by the international sub-committee, which then appointed a drafting committee with Mr Lloyd Watkins as secretary. In February 1973 a draft text for the revised Rules was circulated to national associations. It was accompanied by the report of the President, which contained the following passage commenting on the revisions proposed at that time:

[10] For the text of the Rules, see Appendix 2B, below.

"The object of this detailed work was to clarify and simplify the Rules. After over twenty years it is not surprising the 1950 Rules were criticised in certain material respects.

The concept of General Average should not be allowed to be shrouded in academic mystique [. . .]. The principles upon which it is based must be clear and simple. If not, then unnecessary costs and delays will ensue. To be acceptable in the future the system must be seen to be both equitable and commercially viable [. . .]. It is hoped that the simplifications and clarifications which have been made will aid the practitioner and facilitate the drawing up of adjustments with the minimum of expense and delay."[11]

The XXXth Conference of the Comité Maritime International was held at Hamburg from April 1 to 5, 1974. Over 400 delegates representing 29 countries attended. The 1973 draft for revised York-Antwerp Rules was largely approved by the Conference, subject to important exceptions relating to rr.E, XIII and XVII,[12] and to other changes of lesser importance. At the plenary session on April 4, 1974, each of the revised Rules was approved by a vote showing a substantial majority, except in the case of r.XIII where the vote on the 1973 draft was a tie and the Swedish amendment re-introducing deductions "new for old" in a modified form was carried. The following resolution, proposed by Mr William Birch Reynardson, was then carried unanimously: **00.101**

"The delegates representing the National Associations of Maritime Law of those States as set out hereunder[13] :

1. Having noted with approval the amendments which have been made to the York-Antwerp Rules 1950 and which have been incorporated into a revised text of Rules to be known as the York-Antwerp Rules 1974.
2. Recommend that the York-Antwerp Rules 1974 should be applied in the adjustment of General Average claims as soon as is practical after July 1, 1974."

8. York-Antwerp Rules 1974, as Amended 1990

In April 1989, an International Convention on Salvage attended by representatives from 66 nations was held in London, the principal purpose of which was to amend the terms of the 1910 Brussels Convention for the Unification of Certain Rules of Law relating to Assistance and Salvage at Sea in view of the growing concerns for the protection of the environment, and the damage to the environment that would be caused by oil and chemical spillages resulting from marine casualties. **00.102**

By art.8 of the 1989 Convention, salvors owe a duty to carry out salvage operations with due care and, in performance of that duty, to exercise due care to prevent or minimise damage to the environment. However, to ensure that adequate

[11] CMI Documentation 1974, 1.58.

[12] These are noted in the commentary on the Rules in question, paras E.02, 13.04–13.05, 17.08, below.

[13] The resolution was carried by 29 States.

incentives are available to salvors, art.14 introduced a new special compensation which is payable when the ship or cargo to be salved threatens damage to the environment, and the values of the property salved were insufficient by themselves to provide an adequate reward. The special compensation is payable by the owner when the salvage operations had prevented or minimised damage to the environment, and is at least equivalent to the expenses incurred by the salvors, and in very special circumstances, even up to 200 per cent of the expenses.

00.103 Having completed their deliberations and adopted various recommendations and resolutions, the Conference added an Attachment 2 to their report:

> "CONSIDERING that payments made pursuant to article 14 are not intended to be allowed in general average REQUESTS the Secretary-General of the International Maritime Organisation to take the appropriate steps in order to ensure speedy amendment of the York-Antwerp Rules, 1974, to ensure that special compensation paid under article 14 is not subject to general average."

This request was implemented at a Conference of the Comité Maritime International held in Paris in June 1990 when an amendment was made to r.VI (alone) of the York-Antwerp Rules 1974, the full text of which is quoted in para.6.12 below. The Rules, in toto, were to be referred to as the "York-Antwerp Rules 1974, as amended 1990". It was recommended that they should be applied in the adjustment of claims in general average as soon as practicable after October 1, 1990, although as always this was dependent on contracts of affreightment being amended accordingly.

9. York-Antwerp Rules 1994

00.104 At the conclusion of the official meeting of the Comité Maritime International held in Paris in June 1990 at which r.VI was amended (see para.00.103, above), an informal meeting gave consideration to the important question of whether a full review of the York-Antwerp Rules was timely. Other rules also had an impact on pollution damage to the environment and the cost of avoiding or minimising same, and there was continuing concern that under English law it appeared that liabilities arising from a general average act could be admitted as general average. Thus, if a loaded tanker jettisoned 200 tonnes of oil to assist a refloating operation from an exposed shore, the resultant claims from local fishermen and hotel businesses would be a foreseeable consequence of that general average act, and therefore the liabilities arising would also be general average. Establishing the extent of such liabilities might take many years of litigation and the amount of the liabilities might well be wholly disproportionate to the values saved–both possibilities were considered to be unwelcome in the context of ensuring that any system of general average remained manageable and cost-effective.

Apart from pollution matters, changes in modern shipping techniques and the tendency for liner and container services to be more widely used made it relevant to examine the principles of general average to ensure that it was appropriate in the present commercial and legal world, and to reaffirm that in all respects the York-Antwerp Rules reflected modern commercial, technical, environmental and legal developments. If (as in fact transpired) UNCTAD intended to begin its own critical examination of the topic, it was highly desirable that, by reason of its own work, the CMI should be able to offer to UNCTAD the very best possible advice in their deliberations. Further, the European Association of Average Adjusters (AIDE) had already taken the first steps in a re-examination of the principles of general average and the York-Antwerp Rules and offered its full co-operation with the CMI.

Market soundings both in the United Kingdom and abroad indicated a general acceptance to review the York-Antwerp Rules, and at their meeting in December 1990 the Council of the CMI decided on this course and appointed Mr David Taylor to head an International Sub-Committee.

Their first task was to prepare a preliminary report and a questionnaire in **00.105**
two main parts. Part A sought general background information to provide a full awareness of legal, commercial and technical operating development which had occurred since the previous review in 1974, while Pt B sought opinions on the form and substance of the Rules together with proposals for specific amendments and additional subjects on which the then current Rules were silent.

This was circulated by the CMI Secretariat to national associations in July 1991 and some 20 replies had been received when the working group came to consider them in January 1992. Among those additional topics proposed for inclusion in the new Rules were:

- cost of measures to protect the environment imposed on the vessel in a port of refuge;
- currency of adjustment and rates of exchange;
- tug (or pushboat) and barges;
- contributing interests such as passenger vehicles, containers, etc. also contributory values on multimodal transport;
- differential salvage awards;
- non-separation agreements;
- time-limits for the production of documents to the adjuster.

The Working Group completed their analysis of the responses to the questionnaire in March 1992; in December a first meeting of the International Sub-committee was held in Brussels; and in July 1993 a situation Report was circulated to national associations preparatory to a final meeting of the International Sub-Committee in Paris in December 1993. By this time, those most closely concerned with the day-to-day practice of general average had largely mapped out the likely substance of the new York-Antwerp Rules to be discussed and promulgated at the full CMI Conference to be held at Sydney in October 1994.

During the same period UNCTAD had produced in November 1991 a paper **00.106**
entitled General Average–A Preliminary Review, to be followed in March 1994

with The Place of General Average in Marine Insurance Today. The second UNCTAD report reviewed current arrangements for insuring general average losses and liabilities available in insurance markets and through the P&I Clubs. The report noted difficulties experienced by developing countries in providing security and paying contributions, and the delays and costs that the process could involve. Drawing on recommendations made by AIDE and others, the report concluded with a number of recommendations to reduce the number of small and uneconomic general average cases and to simplify the procedures relating to general average and salvage security.

In turn, the International Union of Marine Insurers (IUMI), after their Conference at Berne in 1992, established a small working group to review marine insurers' experience of general average. This included the compiling and in-depth analysis of data of over 1000 general average incidents during recent years and the issuing of an impressive Report–General Average and its Impact on Marine Insurance–in June 1994. The Report suggested that the general average system appeared to operate heavily in favour of shipowners and detrimentally to shippers, and that the shipowners who most benefited from general average were the owners of old and sub-standard shipping. Further, the costs of the system were disproportionate to any benefits that could be recognised. Subsequently, the President of IUMI wrote to the President of CMI on September 27, 1994 expressing a concern that several proposals for changes in the Rules implied an expansion of general average and stating that under no circumstances could IUMI accept expansion of the existing Rules.

00.107 Thirty-nine national maritime law associations attended the CMI Conference at Sydney, held from October 2 to 8, 1994, together with numerous observers. With regard to the issue of pollution liabilities a compromise proposal was put forward by the British delegation (led by Lord Donaldson) that would exclude all such liabilities from general average but would allow costs of preventing or minimising damage to the environment in relation to certain general average acts, such as entry into a port of refuge. The exclusion of liabilities was achieved by an addition to r.C and the permissible allowances were set out in a new r.XI(d), which largely reflected the existing practice of adjusters under the 1974 Rules. Thus property insurances were content to see liabilities removed without any corresponding increase in allowances under the numbered rules, while the P&I Clubs saw that environmental costs closely related to the safety of property would continue to be met by property interests.

Other significant new rules included a Rule Paramount (which made more explicit the requirement for a test of reasonableness to be applied to all allowances), a new r.B (aimed at greater uniformity in the adjustment of tug and tow general averages), and the wording of a non-separation agreement, with Bigham clause, was brought in to the existing r.G. On procedural matters, r.E was extended to require parties claiming in general average to notify the adjuster within 12 months of the termination of the voyage and to give the adjuster liberty to use estimates to complete a case if information was not forthcoming. Both these last measures were aimed at reducing delays in the production of adjustments; the problem of delays in settlements was also recognised by an amendment to r.XXI which provided that interest should be calculated to run for three months after the issue of the adjustment.

A number of other proposals were considered and rejected by varying margins. These included proposals to allow jettison of cargo however stowed (r.I) and the abolition of deductions "new for old" (r.XIII), together with a change in the basis of valuation of cargo to meet the circumstances of through transport shipments. The exclusion of any allowances for temporary repairs of accidental damage, unless for the common safety, was also debated and rejected.

At a plenary session on October 7, 1994 the text of the new York-Antwerp Rules was unanimously adopted by the 36 Member Associations voting, together with the following resolution: **00.108**

> "The Marine Association of Australia and New Zealand as the host Association proposes with pleasure that the delegates representing the National Associations of Maritime Law of the States listed hereunder:
>
> 1. Having noted with approval the amendments which have been made to the York-Antwerp Rules, 1974, as amended 1990.
> 2. Propose that the new text be referred to as the York-Antwerp Rules, 1994.
> 3. Recommend that the York-Antwerp Rules, 1994 should be applied to the adjustment of claims in General Average as soon as practicable after 31st December 1994."

In his concluding Report, Mr David Taylor, Chairman of the International Sub-Committee, stated that:

> "The theme, which has been the theme of all recent periodical reviews of the York-Antwerp Rules, has been . . . to seek to simplify general average procedures, to clarify doubtful issues with a common goal of trying to ensure that the general average regime continues realistically to respond to the shipping, insurance, financial, trading and environmental techniques of the 1990s."

10. York-Antwerp Rules 2004

The International Union of Marine Insurers (IUMI) continued to express dissatisfaction with the revision of the Rules in 1994. During its 1998 conference in Berlin, a Working Group submitted a paper entitled General average–how should it be changed? This resulted in a formal request to CMI the following year for further reform of the York-Antwerp Rules to be given consideration. The International Union of Marine Insurers felt that the concept of general average reflected in the current York-Antwerp Rules was outdated. Recognising the difficulties of completely abolishing a concept embedded in the law of most maritime nations, its proposed solution was to restrict the categories of loss or expense that would be made good by general average contributions between the parties; more losses would be allowed to lie where they fell. **00.109**

The International Union of Marine Insurers' solution to the problems it perceived was to reduce the number of general averages by restricting general average to "common safety" situations, making it a prerequisite for all allowances that they should relate strictly to sacrifices and expenditure in time of actual peril. This would effectively eliminate the majority of the costs that would be allowed once in a port of refuge, e.g.:

(i) port charges during repairs necessary for the safe prosecution of the voyage;
(ii) cargo discharge, storage and reloading required for repairs;
(iii) wages, fuel etc. during repairs necessary for the safe prosecution of the voyage;
(iv) substituted expenses (such as towage to destination, transhipment of cargo and temporary repairs of accidental damage,) allowed up to general average expenses (i-iii above), saved by taking the alternative course of action.

00.110 Arguments for and against this radical proposal–and other incremental changes proposed by IUMI–were aired at subsequent CMI meetings in Toledo (2000) and Singapore (2001), and a Working Group was set up to give the matter more detailed consideration. Its report, dated March 7, 2003, was progressed further by an International Sub-Committee meeting at Bordeaux in June 2003, and a final version was made ready for the 2004 conference in Vancouver, setting out both sides of the debate as even-handedly as possible.

There was little support in the preliminary meetings or at Vancouver for the radical restriction to the "common safety" concept, with delegates taking the view that the existing system for dividing costs at a port of refuge was widely understood and generally worked well. The advantage that was recognised was that action can be taken promptly within a known framework, leaving legal issues to be sorted out later; any change would be likely to increase the number of costly disputes, particularly relating to the abandonment of voyages.

However, there was considerable support from the delegations (made up from the Maritime Law Associations of over 40 countries) for many of the incremental changes proposed by IUMI. A number of these were agreed and formed the basis of the new 2004 Rules. These consisted of:

(i) the exclusion of salvage from general average, thus amending r.VI, although credit would be given for any salvage paid by one party (usually ship) on behalf of others;
(ii) an amendment to r.XI so that crew wages would no longer be allowed while at a Port of Refuge;
(iii) an amendment to r.XIV so that savings to ship interests achieved by effecting temporary repairs to accidental damage at a port of refuge were accounted for first, before any allowance in general average is considered;
(iv) the removal of any allowance for commission;
(v) the adoption of a procedure whereby the rate of interest would be reviewed and set annually by CMI;

(vi) the introduction of a time-bar provision, where national jurisdictions permit.

Finally, minor amendments to the Rules were made to "tidy up" the drafting and provide a more coherent numbering system.

In their opening remarks, the IUMI delegation stressed the importance placed by their organisation on the reform process and the need for the insurance and commercial communities to have an alternative available to the 1994 Rules. **00.111**

It was agreed at the Vancouver conference, in both the international sub-committee and plenary sessions, that the new Rules should be given the title of "York-Antwerp Rules 2004" to make it clear that they were not simply an amendment to or modification of the 1994 Rules (as happened with the 1990 amendment of the 1974 Rules in respect of r.VI).

The Plenary Session of the Vancouver Conference adopted the following resolution:

"The delegates representing the National Associations of Maritime Law of the States listed hereunder

1. having noted with approval the amendments which have been made to the York Antwerp Rules 1994;
2. propose that the new text be referred to as the York-Antwerp Rules 2004;
3. recommend that the York-Antwerp Rules 2004 should be applied in the adjustment of claims in General Average as soon as practicable after 31 December 2004."

The 2004 Rules represented the first occasion when a new set of Rules had been approved without a consensus between shipowning and other interests. The changes were not supported by the representatives of shipowning interests at the conference. Speaking also on behalf of BIMCO, Intertanko and Intercargo, the International Chamber of Shipping (ICS) delegate told the conference that they considered it premature to produce a new set of rules after only 10 years and before the 1994 version had become the norm. With general average absorption clauses in hull policies (whereby the hull insurers pay all general average expenses up to a specified limit) removing some 50 per cent of general average cases and improvements in shipping standards, many of the problems highlighted by IUMI had fallen away. The ICS therefore felt that the 2004 Rules would be a source of unhelpful confusion.

Following the Vancouver conference, this position was reaffirmed by the various bodies representing shipowners' interests. The differences between the 1994 and 2004 Rules are largely neutral so far as the Protection and Indemnity clubs are concerned, since the "pollution compromise" achieved at the 1994 Sydney conference and reflected in rr.C and XI(d) was not disturbed. (The significant difference between the 1974 Rules and the 1994/2004 Rules remains, in that pollution liabilities directly attributable to a general average act, such as a release of cargo to lighten a vessel, are not excluded by the former.) In 2005, BIMCO issued a bulletin confirming its position that it remained unconvinced about the need for change. It was stated that all new and revised BIMCO charterparties **00.112** would refer only to "York-Antwerp Rules 1994" and the additional text to the effect of "or any subsequent modification thereto" would no longer be used to avoid any possible misinterpretation.

Although hull insurers were urged at subsequent IUMI Conferences to insert clauses into hull policies restricting liability for ship's proportion of general average to the extent permitted by the 2004 Rules, there seemed little appetite for doing so. The 2004 Rules were adopted by some oil majors but were rarely seen else-where and the exceptions to the 1994 Rules appearing in contracts of affreightment were rare, and were then as likely to specify the 1974 Rules as the 2004 Rules.

CMI were quite rightly concerned that this situation was contrary to the objective of uniformity and, during the latter part of 2011, began preliminary discussions with interested parties to see if a compromise set of rules could be sanctioned at the then forthcoming 2012 CMI meeting in Beijing. In the event, compromise proposals put forward by a CMI working group and the British Marine Law Association, which modified or put to one side the more contentious aspects of the 2004 Rules relating to salvage and crew wages, were not supported at the meeting. Many Maritime Law Associations and industry bodies felt there had been insufficient time for consultation. However many present felt that the compromises suggested would provide a framework for a new set of rules that could meet with general acceptance.

The CMI working group therefore recommended to the CMI Executive Council "that it should appoint a new International Working Group on General Average, with a mandate to carry out a general review of the York-Antwerp Rules on General Average, and, noting that the York-Antwerp Rules 2004 had not found acceptance in the ship-owning community, to draft a new set of York-Antwerp rules which met the requirements of the ship and cargo owners and their respective insurers, with a view to their adoption at the 2016 CMI Conference".

The new working group was formed during early 2013 and included representatives from the International Chamber of Shipping and IUMI, and others attending in an individual capacity, including senior insurance claims handlers, lawyers and average adjusters. A detailed questionnaire that was sent out to CMI's member Maritime Law Associations and other interested parties in May 2013, and 26 responses were received and discussed at the October 2013 CMI Conference in Dublin. There was no apparent wish to re-open the abolitionist debate but many constructive ideas were put forward both on matters of general principle and points of detail. The International Working Group will be continuing to scrutinise and develop these ideas for presentation to the CMI Conference at Hamburg in 2014.

SECTION 4

THE YORK-ANTWERP RULES 1994 AND 2004

INTRODUCTION

The York-Antwerp Rules 1994 and 2004, like all their predecessors,[1] apply only when the parties to the contract, whether it be of affreightment, of marine insurance[2] or of some other nature,[3] so agree; and they fall to be construed in the same manner as any other contractual terms which have been reduced into writing. Thus it is submitted that, in an English court, the actual intentions of the draftsmen of the Rules are not admissible aids to their construction, although they are interesting and important as a guide to the international commercial interpretation of the Rules.[4] On the other hand, reference may be made to decisions on the construction of the earlier rules in so far as the wording remains unaltered and their construction is not affected by the Rule of Interpretation which precedes the lettered rules. In the following pages each of the Rules is considered under three main headings, namely: **PRE.01**

(1) English law and practice on the subject-matter of the rule, and independently of the contractual provisions of the rule itself.
(2) Historical development and practice under the rule since its introduction in 1860 or subsequently.
(3) Construction of the individual words and phrases in the 1994 and 2004 Rules.

[1] See Appendix 2, below.
[2] For the relevant provisions of the Institute Clauses, see paras 50.63 et seq., below.
[3] See *Thomson v Micks Lambert & Co* (1933) 47 L.I.L.R. 5 (average bond).
[4] In *Vlassopoulos v British and Foreign Marine Insurance Co* [1929] 1 K.B. 187, Roche J. refers at 196 and 198 to the intentions of the draftsmen, but it is suggested that he was not considering their actual intentions but the intentions which must be imputed to them and to the parties who by contract had adopted the Rules.

Under the third heading an attempt has been made to forecast the construction which could be put upon each rule by an English court in the light of such decisions as there have been and the English legal rules of construction.

If general average is adjusted otherwise than in accordance with English law, the Rules may be interpreted differently,[5] although the wording was the work of international committees.[6] It is outside the scope of this work to consider such differences.

In setting out the text of the Rules the following scheme has been adopted. Where the differences between the 1994 and 2004 Rules are minor:

(1) Those passages which appear in both the 1994 and 2004 Rules are set out in bold non-italic script.
(2) Those passages which appear only in the 2004 Rules are set out in bold italic script.
(3) Those passages which occur only in the 1994 Rules are set out in non-bold italic script.

Where the differences between the 1994 and 2004 Rules are extensive, as for example in r.VI(a), both versions are set out in full.

[5] For the system of law which should govern the adjustment, see paras 30.06 et seq., below; and r.G.

[6] See Section 3, paras 00.70 et seq., above.

Rule of Interpretation

1. Historical Development and Practice

The 1890 Rules were numbered only and dealt with specific situations, and whether or not they should be treated as general average; they laid down no general principles. However, in *Anglo-Grecian Steam Trading Co Ltd v T. Beynon & Co*[1] Roche J. held that under those Rules it was not sufficient for a person claiming contribution in general average to prove the state of facts required by any individual numbered rule unless he could also prove that there had been a general average act in accordance with the general law, which he held to be expressed in s.66(2) of the Marine Insurance Act 1906.[2] **PRE.02**

In 1924 lettered rules dealing with general principles were introduced in an effort to obtain international uniformity. The inter-relationship of the general law, the lettered and the numbered rules was considered by Roche J. in *Vlassopoulos v British and Foreign Marine Insurance Co (The Makis)*.[3] In that case the ship's foremast collapsed at the loading port, causing a derrick to fall into the hold, and allowances were claimed in respect of the expenses incurred while the repairs were being carried out. The repairs were necessary for the safe prosecution of the voyage, and most of the expenses claimed therefore fell within the relevant provisions of rr.X and XI. However, neither ship nor cargo were at any time in peril, and on that ground allowance was refused. The judge described the relationship between the lettered and the numbered rules as follows:

> "In my judgment the true construction is this: that certain general Rules are laid down in order that if the parties choose to adopt the Rules by way of contract, as these parties have done, they may not be troubled thereafter by questions which arise under the old Rule XVIII as to what, if any, general law is to apply. They may have if they choose a self-contained code. . . . But when this has been done and a general set of Rules provided laying down the general principles which are to operate, then the Rules go on to deal with certain specific cases, and I am satisfied on the true construction of the Rules that those cases are dealt with not by way of mere illustration, but in

[1] *Anglo-Grecian Steam Trading Co Ltd v T. Beynon & Co* (1926) 24 Ll.L.Rep. 122. The report incorrectly refers to the 1924 Rules.

[2] See para.A.05, below.

[3] *Vlassopoulos v British and Foreign Marine Insurance Co (The Makis)* [1929] 1 K.B. 187.

> order to make definite and certain what the Rules decide about certain cases which are on the border line and which might be held to be on one side or the other of the line which is to be drawn under the general Rules. . . . It is, I think, as if the Rules had provided that Rules A, B, C, and so forth constitute the general rules for general average and then followed the words: 'And in particular 1, 2, 3, 4' and so on 'are cases of general average'."[4]

PRE.03 Whatever may have been the intention of the parties in the case referred to above, the construction propounded by Roche J. did not accord with international practice or meet with the approval of the leading British shipowners and underwriters, who subsequently concluded an Agreement, commonly known as the "Makis Agreement",[5] which provided: "Except as provided in the numbered Rules 1 to 23 inclusive, the adjustment shall be drawn up in accordance with the lettered Rules A to G inclusive." It is in this Agreement that the Rule of Interpretation has its origin.

York-Antwerp Rules 1950 and 1974

RULE OF INTERPRETATION

PRE.04 In the adjustment of general average the following lettered and numbered Rules shall apply to the exclusion of any Law and Practice inconsistent therewith.

Except as provided by the numbered Rules, general average shall be adjusted according to the lettered Rules.

York-Antwerp Rules 1994

PRE.05 Two changes were made in the rule, both merely consequences of the adoption of the Rule Paramount in the 1994 Rules,[6] and having no wider significance. First, the reference to the lettered and numbered Rules was omitted, in order to ensure that the Rule Paramount (which is neither lettered nor numbered) fell within the provisions of the first paragraph of the rule. Secondly, an express reference to the Rule Paramount was inserted in the last paragraph of the rule.

York-Antwerp Rules 2004

PRE.06 No change.

[4] This construction was accepted by Tucker J. in *Athel Line v Liverpool and London War Risks Insurance Association Ltd* [1944] 1 K.B. 87.

[5] Text of this Agreement is set out at para.00.94, above.

[6] See paras PRE.21 et seq., below.

RULE OF INTERPRETATION

In the adjustment of general average the following Rules shall apply to the exclusion of any Law and Practice inconsistent therewith.

Except as provided by the Rule Paramount and the numbered Rules, general average shall be adjusted according to the lettered Rules.

2. Construction

First Paragraph

The first paragraph of the rule ensures that the rules shall not be construed as a mere codification of any national law or any practice, national or international. They thus take effect as a contract between the parties and fall to be construed in the same manner as any other contract. They do not, however, constitute a complete or self-contained code and need to be supplemented by bringing into the gaps provisions of the general law which are applicable to the adjustment.[7] The practice of adjusters at the place of adjustment may also supplement the Rules, but law or practice on a matter which is fully dealt with by the Rules, for example a practice as to the interpretation of the Rules, is excluded by the Rule of Interpretation. In *The Bijela*[8] evidence as to the practice of adjusters in interpreting r.XIV was held on this ground to be inadmissible. Having stated the general rule that evidence of usage is admissible to explain or supplement the terms of a contract, but not to contradict or nullify them, the judge continued[9] : **PRE.07**

"But the matter does not rest there. There is an express provision in the Rule of Interpretation in the York-Antwerp Rules. That provides that in the adjustment of general average the lettered and numbered rules shall apply to 'the exclusion of any Law and Practice inconsistent therewith'. Therefore any attempt by the defendants to prove a practice that is inconsistent with the true construction of the rules is legally irrelevant and must be refused."

Second Paragraph

The second paragraph in effect reverses the decision in the *Makis* case.[10] Thus if the facts support a claim in general average under the numbered rules, it matters not that there has been no general average act within the meaning of r.A. Equally **PRE.08**

[7] *Goulandris Bros Ltd v B. Goldman & Sons Ltd* [1958] 1 Q.B. 74 at 91, per Pearson J.

[8] *Marida Ltd v Oswal Steel (The Bijela)* [1992] 1 Lloyd's Rep. 636, reversed on another point [1994] 2 Lloyd's Rep. 1.

[9] *Marida Ltd v Oswal Steel (The Bijela)* [1992] 1 Lloyd's Rep. 636 at 642.

[10] See para.PRE.02, above.

if a numbered rule, for example r.I, negatives any claim in general average arising out of the loss in question, no claim can be made under the lettered rules although the facts fall within the scope of such rules. There may be cases where any claim in general average is negatived, not expressly, but by implication from the wording of the numbered rules, with the same result. However, it must be a clear implication from the wording of the rule that any claim in general average is negatived. It is not sufficient that the claim should merely be excluded from the scope of the numbered rule in question.

PRE.09 If a claim in general average can be established under one of the numbered rules, it does not follow that all the lettered rules must be disregarded in relation to that claim. In the first place, if a claim is advanced under one of the numbered rules "it is the wording of the numbered rule which has to be construed but it should be construed taking into account the general principles of the York-Antwerp Rules as stated in the lettered Rules".[11] Secondly, the Rule of Interpretation requires that the numbered rules shall override the lettered rules only to the extent that there is inconsistency between them in any particular case. It should not be assumed that inconsistency exists, and an attempt should be made to reconcile all the provisions of the Rules so far as possible.[12]

PRE.10 Determining whether inconsistency exists is in some instances most difficult, but in cases of doubt the sensible approach would seem to be to keep in mind that many of the numbered Rules were introduced with the specific intention of resolving vexed questions, and differences in local law or practice, which regularly arose in applying the principles of general average in certain particular situations, and to seek to identify those particular issues which the numbered rule in question was intended to resolve.

For example, it is reasonably clear from its origins, content and wording that r.VII is intended to resolve the question whether the running of the ship's machinery, when afloat or when ashore, is an extraordinary measure, and whether the resulting damage is intentionally incurred and therefore a sacrifice. Thus if a claim is made under r.VII for damage to machinery or boilers it is irrelevant to inquire whether the requirements of r.A relating to these three matters have been fulfilled; r.VII is intended to provide a complete answer of its own on these questions. It is equally clear that r.VII is not intended to impinge on the matters covered by rr.B, D, E and G,[13] which will therefore remain applicable to any claim under that rule. Rule F is also unlikely to give rise to problems in this context, since by its nature it has no relevance to the case where the claim falls within the scope of

[11] Per Hobhouse J. in *Marida v Oswal Steel (The Bijela)* [1992] 1 Lloyd's Rep. 636 at 644.

[12] The numbered rules have been described as exceptions to the principles embodied in the lettered rules: *Macdonald* [1995] L.M.C.L.Q. 480; Rose para.1.30. However, many of the numbered rules, which pre-date the lettered rules, were originally adopted to clarify debatable issues, and that remains one of their principal functions, rather than a desire to vary the lettered rules (see paras PRE.10 et seq., below).

[13] Rule G will, of course, give way to such numbered rules as may be inconsistent with it, in particular rr.XVI and XVII. In its 1993 "Review of the law of General Average and Revision of the York-Antwerp Rules", AIDE raised the question whether the Rule of Interpretation should be re-worded to reflect "the distinction in practice, that whereas Rules A, C and G are subordinated to the numbered rules, the matters treated in Rules D, E and F are in effect paramount".

a numbered rule, its purpose being to allow recovery of expenses, not falling within the lettered rules, which are substituted for another expense which would have been recoverable under the numbered rules. Where matters become much more problematic is in considering whether r.C, or the remaining requirements of r.A, apply to a claim under r.VII.

In *The Alpha*[14] it was held that the provisions of rr.C and E remained applicable to a claim under r.VII, but that the requirement of reasonableness under r.A did not.[15] So far as concerns r.E this is clearly correct, but as regards r.C it seems an oversimplification. Rule VII contains provisions of its own on causation, and seems to be designed to provide a complete code on causation so far as concerns the chain of events between the endeavours to refloat and the damage to the machinery or boilers. However, the rule does not purport to provide its own code beyond that point, and the question whether losses and expenses consequential on the damage to the machinery or boilers (such as loss of charter hire, costs of repairs or expenses of an adjustment) are recoverable in general average is therefore governed by r.C. Many of the numbered rules require a similar distinction to be drawn. So far as concerns the requirement of reasonableness under r.A, it is this aspect of the decision in The Alpha which gave rise to the most concern and was the reason for the introduction of the Rule Paramount in 1994.[16] It seems unlikely that r.VII was consciously intended to dispense altogether with the requirement of reasonableness, or to substitute some different requirement.[17] On the other hand several of the numbered rules expressly incorporate a requirement of reasonableness (or of necessity, which is if anything a more stringent lest), and this militates against the view that such a requirement is automatically imported into every numbered rule. As a matter of construction of the 1974 Rules it must therefore be accepted that the decision in *The Alpha* is probably correct. **PRE.11**

Other numbered rules which have given rise to similar problems are rr.X(b) and XI(b). On the face of it, these rules confer allowances in general average for inter alia expenses incurred at a port of loading or of call during delay caused by repairs to accidental damage, where the repairs are necessary for the safe prosecution of the voyage. As we have already seen, it was held in *The Makis*[18] that a requirement of peril was to be incorporated into the numbered rules, and this decision led to the Rule of Interpretation, in the light of which it has been held in the USA that rr.X(b) and XI(b) are not subject to any overriding requirement of peril.[19] This conclusion seems inescapable on the wording of those rules. **PRE.12**

[14] *Corfu Navigation Co v Mobil Shipping (The Alpha)* [1991] 2 Lloyd's Rep. 515 at 519 (York-Antwerp Rules 1974).

[15] In the 10th and 11th editions of this work the view was expressed that neither r.C nor r.A would apply to a claim under r.VII.

[16] See paras PRE.21 et seq., below.

[17] In *Anglo-Grecian Steam Trading Co Ltd v Beynon & Co* (1926) 24 Ll.L.Rep. 122, which concerned voluntary stranding under the 1890 Rules, Roche J. said: "it is necessary for the plaintiffs to satisfy me and for me to be satisfied that the vessel was reasonably and intentionally run on shore".

[18] *Vlassopoulos v British & Foreign Marine Insurance Co (The Makis)* [1929] 1 K.B. 187.

[19] *Eagle Terminal Tankers v Insurance Co of USSR (The Eagle Courier)* (1981) A.M.C. 137, US Ct of Appeals 5th; *Ellerman Lines v Gibbs Nathaniel (The City of Colombo)* (1986) 26 D.L.R. (4th) 161; (1986) A.M.C. 2217, not following the decision to the contrary in *Orient Mid-East Lines v A Shipment of Rice (The Orient Transporter)* (1974) A.M.C. 2593, US Ct of Appeals 5th (YAR 1950).

PRE.13 Under the 1994 and 2004 Rules, in which the r.A requirement of reasonableness has by virtue of the Rule Paramount been made an essential of any claim, whether under the lettered or the numbered rules, the very fact that this one requirement has been singled out for special treatment in this manner is an indication that the remaining requirements of r.A are not paramount, and are not to be imported into the numbered rules.

RULE PARAMOUNT

1. HISTORICAL BACKGROUND

In the preceding paragraphs we have observed that the Rule of Interpretation has the effect that the numbered rules override the lettered rules in the case of inconsistency, but that it provides little or no guidance on the question whether inconsistency arises in any given case. The problem, which is also touched upon in the commentary under r.A,[1] usually arises in determining which, if any, of the provisions of the lettered Rules are applicable to a claim under the numbered Rules. The extent of the problem was brought into sharp focus in 1991 by the decision of the English court in *Corfu Navigation v Mobil Shipping (The Alpha)*.[2] It was held in that case that a claim under r.VII for damage to machinery sustained during attempts to refloat a grounded ship was not subject to the requirement of reasonableness in r.A. and was therefore entitled to succeed even though the attempts to refloat by using the ship's engines had been unreasonable. It was the view of many that the decision, although unfortunate, was correct as a matter of construction of the Rules. PRE.21

York-Antwerp Rules 1994

As a result of the decision in *The Alpha* there was a widespread view among delegates at the Sydney Conference in 1994 that the Rules should be changed so as to make it clear that the requirement of reasonableness embodied in r.A should apply to all claims whether under the lettered or numbered rules. The US delegation had proposed a Rule Paramount which would contain, as overriding provisions, both the requirement of reasonableness and the exclusion of pollution liabilities and clean-up costs. The latter provision was eventually transferred to r.C, but the Conference accepted the US proposal to the extent of adopting a Rule Paramount which made reasonableness an overriding requirement. PRE.22

[1] See para.A.107, below.
[2] *Corfu Navigation v Mobil Shipping (The Alpha)* [1991] 2 Lloyd's Rep. 515; see also para. PRE.11, above.

This course did not meet with universal approval. Some delegates, including the British MLA, took the view that the numbered rules already contained their own requirement of reasonableness (or necessity) wherever this was appropriate,[3] and that to require the adjuster to determine the reasonableness of the measures adopted would require him to resolve questions of navigation and ship management which could frequently only be done with the assistance of consultants, thereby increasing the costs of the adjustment; it would also encourage protracted analysis, with the aid of hindsight, of decisions often taken in the heat of the moment.[4] However, the majority of the delegates regarded these considerations as being of lesser importance than the need to exclude from allowances losses resulting from measures which it was unreasonable to adopt. A suggestion by the British delegation that the objections to the rule could be reduced if it were so expressed as to exclude from allowance sacrifices or expenditure "if unreasonably made or incurred" was defeated in plenary session.

York-Antwerp Rules 2004

PRE.23 No change.

RULE PARAMOUNT

In no case shall there be any allowance for sacrifice or expenditure unless reasonably made or incurred.

2. CONSTRUCTION

PRE.24 The rule must be read in the context of the Rule of Interpretation, which expressly provides that the Rule Paramount overrides the lettered Rules in the event of inconsistency. The title of the rule probably owes its origin to the phrase "Clause Paramount" which is frequently found in charterparties and bills of lading in order to describe a clause which incorporates the Hague Rules into the contract of carriage "and which overrides any express exemption or condition which is inconsistent with it".[5] It follows that, although the York-Antwerp Rules contain no explicit provision that the Rule Paramount overrides all of the numbered rules, it is inherent in its title that it should have this effect. The result is that it is a requirement of any claim whether under the lettered or numbered rules, just as it is under

[3] This view is not easy to accept. There are no grounds for suggesting that any of the numbered rules were adopted for the purpose of excluding or modifying the requirement of reasonableness. It is true that some of the provisions of the numbered rules are expressly made subject to a requirement of reasonableness, whereas others are not, but it is difficult to discern any rationale behind these differences in treatment, which seem to owe as much to chance as to design. See para.A.107, below.

[4] See also Hudson, p.32; *Macdonald* [1995] L.M.C.L.Q. 480, 490 et seq.; *Rose*, para.2.67. The fears seem exaggerated; the requirement is no more stringent than that of r.A, under which it is interpreted in a realistic manner (see para.PRE.25, below).

[5] *Nea Agrex v Baltic Shipping* [1976] Q.B. 933 at 943, per Lord Denning M.R.

English law, that the sacrifice or expenditure should be reasonably made or incurred.

"reasonably made or incurred" The wording is identical to that of the corresponding provisions of r.A and of English law,[6] the effect of which is discussed at paras A.94 et seq., below. Thus any claim, whether under the lettered or numbered rules, will be subject to the identical test of reasonableness. In spite of the rejection of the wording proposed by the British delegation, referred to above,[7] it appears that the approach to the interpretation of the Rule Paramount has followed that adopted in practice under r.A[8] ; the sacrifice or expenditure will be deemed to have been reasonably made or incurred unless the contrary is established, and the master will be given the benefit of the doubt. **PRE.25**

In determining whether a sacrifice was reasonably made, what must be considered is the reasonableness of the decision to adopt the measure which involves or causes the sacrifice. If the measure in question is then carried out in a negligent manner, that does not deprive it of its character as a general average act; however, any additional loss or damage resulting from that negligence may be excluded from general average by r.C (if the claim is under the lettered rules), and those parties whose property has been lost or damaged thereby may pursue any remedies available to them in respect of the negligence.[9]

The Rule Paramount provides a defence to a claim in general average if the sacrifice or expenditure was unreasonable, even though the claimant was not himself responsible for the unreasonable conduct. Thus a cargo-owner, whose cargo is unreasonably jettisoned by the master or damaged by unreasonable attempt by the master to extinguish a fire on board, will have no claim for contribution, at any rate against those interests who were not guilty of unreasonable conduct. It may be that in such a case the shipowner would be estopped from invoking the unreasonable conduct of his own servants or agents in order to resist a claim for contribution, and in any event, unless he is protected from liability by an exceptions clause, he will be liable in damages for the loss caused thereby. **PRE.26**

[6] i.e. the Marine Insurance Act 1906 s.66(2): see para.A.05, below.
[7] See para.PRE.22, above.
[8] See para.A.94, below.
[9] cf. *Federal Commerce and Navigation Co v Eisenerz* [1970] 2 Lloyd's Rep. 332; [1975] 1 Lloyd's Rep. 105. See also paras 00.67 et seq., above, para.12.14, below.

RULE A

DEFINITION OF GENERAL AVERAGE

There is a general average act when, and only when, any extra-ordinary sacrifice or expenditure is intentionally and reasonably made or incurred for the common safety for the purpose of preserving from peril the property involved in a common maritime adventure . . .[1] **A.01**

The words of this definition have remained unchanged since first formulated for the 1924 Rules. The essential features follow earlier legal definitions.

Earlier Legal Definitions

The first modern case in which the sanction of an English court of common law was given to the principle of general average was that of *Birkley v Presgrave*[2] in 1801. The principle does not appear to have been contested at the trial of this case, but was treated in argument as a thing long established and well known, and the dispute was only as to some particular point of its application. One of the judges, however, Lawrence J. began his judgment with the following sentence: **A.02**

> "All loss which arises in consequence of extraordinary sacrifices made or expenses incurred for the preservation of the ship and cargo comes within general average, and must be borne proportionably by all who are interested."[3]

This was no new departure, but a direct continuation of the historical antecedents discussed in Section 1 of this book in paras 00.01 et seq., above. Nevertheless the words of Lawrence J. have always been treated as of the highest authority.

[1] A second paragraph was added to r.A in 1994, but this is not concerned with the definition of general average.
[2] *Birkley v Presgrave* 1 East 220.
[3] *Birkley v Presgrave* 1 East 220 at 228. The words "all loss" in this definition, said Gorell Barnes J. in *The Leitrim* [1902] P. 256–266, must read with some limitation; they ought not to cover losses which "are the result of 'accidental circumstances' affecting the loser, and are not losses which the other persons interested ought in ordinary course to be treated as concerned with". For the test as to remoteness, see paras C.04–C.12, below.

They were adopted and used as a test in *Covington v Roberts*,[4] *Job v Langton*,[5] and in *Svendsen v Wallace*.[6]

A.03 Variations, substantially however amounting to much the same thing, have been offered by other judges, for example:

> "In order to give rise to a charge as general average, it is essential that there should be a voluntary sacrifice to preserve more subjects than one exposed to a common jeopardy. An extraordinary expenditure incurred for that purpose is as much a sacrifice as if, instead of money being expended for the purpose, money's worth were thrown away. It is immaterial whether a shipowner sacrifices a cable or an anchor to get the ship off a shoal, or pays the worth of it to hire those extra services which get her off": *Kemp v Halliday*,[7] per Blackburn J.

Similar terms have been used by the American Courts:

> "General average contribution is defined to be a contribution by all the parties in a sea adventure to make good the loss sustained by one of their number on account of sacrifices voluntarily made of part of the ship or cargo to save the residue and lives of those on board from an impending peril, or for extraordinary expenses necessarily incurred by one or more of the parties for the general benefit of all the interests embarked in the enterprise": The Star of Hope,[8] per Clifford J.

A.04 In cases of doubt or difficulty, however, the English courts still recognise the importance of the original maxim of the Rhodian law.[9]

Statutory Definition

A.05 General average is not a doctrine forming part of the law of insurance; it belongs to the law of carriage by sea. Nevertheless it has important consequences in the field of marine insurance, and the Marine Insurance Act 1906 s.66 contains a definition of a general average loss and of a general average act. There is judicial authority[10] for the proposition that this will now prevail for all purposes. Although

[4] *Covington v Roberts* (1806) 2 B. & P.N.R. 378.
[5] *Job v Langton* (1856) 6 E. & B. 779 at 790.
[6] *Svendsen v Wallace* (1884) 13 Q.B.D. 69 at 73.
[7] *Kemp v Halliday* (1865) 6 B. & S. 723 at 746; 34 L.J.Q.B. 233 at 242, see further *Hallet v Wigram* (1850) 9 C.B. 580 at 601; 19 L.J.C.P. 281 at 288, *Cargo ex Galam* (1863) 33 L.J.Ad. 97 at 102, *Johnson v Chapman* (1865) 19 C.B. (n.s) 563 at 583: *Fletcher v Alexander* (1868) L.R. 3 C.P. 375 at 381; *Walthew v Mavrojani* (1870) L.R. 5 Exch. 116 at 119; *Stewart v West India and Pacific S.S. Co* (1873) L.R. 8 Q.B. 88 at 93; *Whitecross Wire Co v Savill* (1882) 8 Q.B.D. 653 at 661, 662; *Ocean S.S. Co v Anderson* (1883) 13 Q.B.D. 651 at 662.
[8] *The Star of Hope* (1869) 9 Wall. 203 (US Sup. Ct.). This and many other American decisions tend to show that, in the US, measures to ensure the completion of the adventure may give rise to general average, although the property was not in physical danger.
[9] See the judgment of Watkin Williams J. in *Pirie v Middle Dock Co* (1881) 4 Asp. M.C. 388 at 390. Parsons, referring to this maxim, says: "This law was in force in the commerce of the Mediterranean and Adriatic seas more than a thousand years before the Christian era; nor can there be a better definition of the law of general average as it is in force today." (Boston, *Law of Shipping* (1869), p.339). See also *Austin Friars S.S. Co v Spillers and Bakers Ltd* [1915] 1 K.B. 833 at 835, per Bailhache J.; *Australian Coastal Shipping Commission v Green* [1971] 1 Q.B. 456 at 478.
[10] *Austin Friars S.S. Co v Spillers and Bakers Ltd* [1915] 1 K.B. 833 at 835, per Bailhache J.

the application of the Act is clearly confined to marine insurance, it was intended to codify the law and thus may be regarded as of a wider application.[11] The relevant provisions are as follows:

> **66.**—(1) A general average loss is a loss caused by or directly consequential on a general average act. It includes a general average expenditure as well as a general average sacrifice.
> (2) There is a general average act where any extraordinary sacrifice or expenditure is voluntarily and reasonably made or incurred in time of peril for the purpose of preserving the property imperilled in the common adventure.

It is clear that r.A of the York-Antwerp Rules is modelled very closely on the English statutory definition, and it may be useful to print the two definitions together for ease of comparison: **A.06**

(MIA) *There is a general average act where any* . . .

(YAR) There is a general average act when, and only when, any . . .

(MIA) *EXTRAORDINARY* . . .
(YAR) **EXTRAORDINARY . . .**

(MIA) *SACRIFICE* or *EXPENDITURE* is . . .

(YAR) **SACRIFICE** or **EXPENDITURE** is . . .

(MIA) *VOLUNTARILY* and . . .
(YAR) **INTENTIONALLY** and . . .

(MIA) *REASONABLY made or incurred in* . . .

(YAR) **REASONABLY** made or incurred for the . . .

(MIA) *TIME OF PERIL for the purpose of preserving the property* . . .
(YAR) **COMMON SAFETY** for the purpose of preserving from . . .

(MIA) *IMPERILLED in the* . . .

(YAR) **PERIL** the property involved in a . . .

(MIA) *COMMON ADVENTURE*.
(YAR) **COMMON MARITIME ADVENTURE**.

We now look more closely at the five essential features, all of which must be present to constitute a general average act: **A.07**

[11] *Australian Coastal Shipping Commission v Green* [1971] 1 Q.B. 456 at 478.

(1) intentional;
(2) peril (common safety);
(3) common maritime adventure;
(4) extraordinary;
(5) reasonable.

1. Necessity for Intentional Act

A.08 In order that a sacrifice or expenditure may constitute a general average act, under the terms of r.A it must be intentional, while English legal decisions and the statutory definition use the word "voluntary". When r.A was being discussed in 1924 at the Stockholm Conference it was urged by some of the delegates that the word "voluntarily" was capable of several interpretations, none of which implied quite the same decisiveness as "intentionally". Many acts might be done voluntarily without implying any precise intention. After careful consideration the Conference elected to adopt the word "intentionally" as emphasising more clearly the idea of deliberate choice. This was also designed to avoid the argument that an act was not voluntary when it resulted from overwhelming pressure of circumstances.

From a practical point of view, the use of the word intentional (or voluntary) is to distinguish the resultant loss from one that is entirely accidental in origin. Thus, if a vessel strands and rips open her bottom, the damage to the ship and to the cargo in any affected hold is the direct and immediate result of an accident, and the respective owners of the ship and the damaged cargo will each bear their own losses without contribution. But if, in order to refloat the stranded vessel and her cargo,

- cargo is jettisoned; and/or
- lighters are hired to offload the cargo; and/or
- salvage tugs are employed; and/or
- the ship's engines are damaged by working them when aground,

each or any of these losses, although having its origin in the initial accidental stranding, is really the result of an intentional act and will generally be admissible as general average.

A.09 Losses incurred by accident or through superior force are not made good in general average. The act must be the result of the exercise of reasoning power and discretion, directed to the particular problem of saving the vessel and cargo concerned. In *Athel Line Ltd v Liverpool and London War Risks Association Ltd*,[12] two vessels of the plaintiff line, sailing in convoy from Bermuda to the United Kingdom, put back to Bermuda under order of the convoy commodore. These orders were pursuant to Admiralty instructions, owing to the convoy ahead having

[12] *Athel Line Ltd v Liverpool and London War Risks Association Ltd* [1944] K.B. 87.

been attacked by an enemy raider with considerable losses. The plaintiffs' vessels lost six days on their voyage and extra fuel and stores were consumed. Accordingly the plaintiffs claimed from their War Risk underwriters the ships contribution towards these expenses in general average under rr.A and X(a) of the York-Antwerp Rules 1924. Tucker J. held that the language of r.A was inappropriate to cover mere obedience to lawful orders of a superior authority, and that the plaintiffs could not rely upon the acts of the masters of the vessels as general average acts. He also decided that the plaintiffs could not rely upon the acts of: (1) the commodore; or (2) the Admiralty, as the orders were given as part of the general naval and strategic dispositions in the North Atlantic, and not for the sole purpose of preserving from peril the property involved in the adventures in the plaintiffs' two vessels.

Must General Average Act be that of the Master?

A further important question is whether an intentional sacrifice or expenditure, in order to constitute a general average act, must be ordered or at any rate authorised by the master, or whether it may be the act of the crew or of a stranger to the adventure. The master is no doubt in most cases the proper person to decide whether a sacrifice or expenditure must be made or incurred, the conduct of the adventure and the care of the ship and cargo having been entrusted to him. If, however, an emergency arises at a time when the master is absent or for any other reason incapable of acting, a sacrifice or expenditure made or incurred under the direction of the mate or other officer discharging the master's duties would without doubt be treated as a general average act if it could have been so treated if performed by the master. Yet there may be exceptional cases in which a sacrifice has reasonably been made without any order from him (or his substitute), or even against his wish; and the question may arise in such cases whether the owner of the property sacrificed is entitled to contribution. There is little English authority on the point. **A.10**

In *Price v Noble*,[13] a claim for contribution was made in respect of the jettison of the ship's guns and part of her stores and tackle, after she had been captured by a French privateer and while she was in the possession of a prize master and crew. The mate of the ship and two of the crew had, however, been left on board; and in the emergency of the storm the prize crew called the mate to their aid in navigating the ship, and it was with his assistance and on his advice that the jettison was made. Afterwards the ship was recaptured, and her owner brought an action for a contribution in general average, and obtained a verdict which the defendants moved to set aside on the ground that the jettison was not ordered by the master, but by strangers to whom the respective owners of the ship and cargo had not entrusted their safety. The court, however, held that, as the goods had been jettisoned for the benefit of the residue of the property, the shipowners were entitled to contribution. It is true that Mansfield C.J. said in his judgment that the prize crew had consulted the mate and entrusted him with the navigation, and that the **A.11**

[13] *Price v Noble* (1811) 4 Taunt. 123.

stores seem to have been thrown overboard by his direction: but it seems clear that the mate's evidence to this effect was only used by his Lordship for the purpose of showing that the jettison was necessary. As the ship and cargo were in the possession of the prize crew, the mate's position was that of an adviser to the prize master, and the power to decide whether the sacrifice should be made or not was in the hands of the latter.[14]

A.12 In *Papayanni v Grampian S.S. Co*[15] the facts were that the defendant's ship, the Birkhall, being on fire, was taken by her master into the port of Philippeville, where the crew were unable by their own exertions to extinguish the fire. The captain of the port, to whom intimation of the state of affairs had been given, came on board, and ordered the ship to be scuttled. The master afterwards stated that in his opinion:

> "it was the best thing for the ship and cargo to scuttle the ship, though he was only obeying the orders of the captain of the port, and had nothing to do with it".

The action was for a general average contribution, and, as reported, the judgment of Mathew J. is contained in the following words:

> "This evidence shows that what was done was in the interest of ship and cargo. There is no evidence that there was any other motive for scuttling the ship. The captain, who had not parted with the possession of his ship, did not object. There seems to be clear evidence that he sanctioned what was done. The loss must be adjusted as a general average sacrifice."

The statement that the master "sanctioned" what was done suggests that Mathew J. based his judgment on a finding that the master was a party to the sacrifice. From the report, however, it seems clear that the master did not propose the scuttling of the ship; that he was not consulted about it; and was powerless to prevent it. Under these circumstances his approval of the sacrifice seems only material as being evidence that the scuttling was a proper measure: and it is improbable that the learned judge intended to found his decision on the master's assent, except in so far as it was evidence of the necessity of the sacrifice.

A.13 In both these cases, therefore, the only view consistent with the facts seems to be that the sacrifice was made by a stranger to the adventure; and they support the conclusion that it is not essential that the sacrifice should have been made under the authority of the master, but that the real question is whether it was necessary for the common safety. Such a rule is consistent with the principle of natural justice on which the law of general average is said to be founded: and if this be the correct view, it follows that a sacrifice made by the crew without the master's assent, and even against his wish, may be general average, though the fact that the

[14] There seems to have been no suggestion in any of the judgments that as the ship and cargo had not yet been condemned by a Prize Court, the prize master might be regarded as the person who had succeeded to the master's duty to the owners of the property to take the necessary steps for its preservation, and not as a stranger to the adventure.

[15] *Papayanni v Grampian S.S. Co* (1896) 1 Com. Cas. 448.

master was opposed to the sacrifice would be strong evidence that it was not imperative, and the clearest proof of its necessity would therefore be required.

A different rule has, however, been laid down by a majority in the Supreme Court of the United States. In *Ralli v Troop*,[16] a case of a ship on fire, which was scuttled by the harbour authorities, it was held that: **A.14**

> "The power and duty of determining what part of the common adventure shall be sacrificed for the safety of the rest, and how and when the sacrifice shall be made, appertain to the master of the vessel, magister navis, as the person entrusted with the command and the safety of the common adventure, and of all the interests comprised therein, for the benefit of all concerned, or to some one who, by the maritime law, acts under him or succeeds to his authority."

Applying this rule, the court held that a sacrifice of vessel or cargo by the act of a stranger to the adventure gives no right of contribution, and that the port authorities were strangers to the maritime adventure and to all interests included therein.[17]

In 1944 this question was again argued at length before Tucker J. in *Athel Line Ltd v Liverpool and London War Risks Association Ltd.*[18] Upon the view taken of the facts by the learned judge, it was not necessary to decide the point, and he observed that it was undesirable that he should express any opinion with regard to it. He did, however, say that "there was no clear authority". All the cases above referred to were cited and it was suggested that there might be a difference between English and American law in this respect.

If the master and crew abandoned a vessel completely and with no expectation of returning to her, measures taken by a stranger in order to bring her to safety would not be of a general average nature, under English law. Nor would measures be taken to destroy a vessel, for example because of a risk of pollution.

A different aspect of the same problem is now far more common, where the master does not exercise his own judgment but acts on the orders of his owners, or the owners themselves carry out the general average act. For example, in *Australian Coastal Shipping Commission v Green*[19] tugs were summoned not by the masters of the two vessels concerned but by the plaintiffs' shore officers. It was not argued that on this ground the hiring of the tugs could not be general average acts. No doubt the masters there assented to the steps that their employers had taken. However, it is submitted that the decision was right on a wider ground: the shipowner, as employer of the master, is entitled if he wishes and the opportu- **A.15**

[16] *Ralli v Troop* (1894) 157 U.S. 386.

[17] See also *Minneapolis S.S. Co v Manistee Transit Co* (1907) 156 Fed. Rep. 424; *Wamsutta Mills v Old Colony Steamboat Co* (1883) 137 Mass. 471; *Andree-Moran (No.16)* (1930) A.M.C. 631. This line of authority has been much criticised. cf. *The Roanoke* (1893) 46 Fed. Rep. 297; 53 Fed. Rep. 270; 59 Fed. Rep. 161; and *The Beatrice* (1924) A.M.C. 914, where the work of extinguishing the fire was done by the fire department, but by request of the owners with the approval of the officers and crew and for the safely of the particular ship and cargo, and it was held that the fire department was acting as the agent of the shipowner and that the damage done in putting out the fire was recoverable as general average (*Ralli v Troop* distinguished).

[18] *Athel Line Ltd v Liverpool and London War Risks Association Ltd* [1944] K.B. 87.

[19] *Australian Coastal Shipping Commission v Green* [1971] 1 Q.B. 456.

nity occurs, to call in the discretion which he has entrusted to the master, and to make the decision himself or by others of his servants or agents.

At the Stockholm Conference in 1924 an amendment was in fact moved to add the words "by the master or his representative" after the word "incurred", but was withdrawn. It may be assumed, therefore, that the intention of the Conference was that, provided the act otherwise possesses the necessary qualification required by r.A, the fact that it was not specifically ordered by the master will not bar a claim to allowance in general average. Nor is it required by r.A that the sacrifice must be preceded by a consultation between the master and the crew, as provided by many foreign codes. These must be regarded as wise omissions, for provisions to this effect would certainly narrow the scope of general average unduly. Provided that the act possesses the true elements of general average, the fact that the master was absent or in the emergency of the moment, acted on his sole initiative, should not on grounds of policy deny the compensation in general average to the interest concerned.

Since the early 1960s, when the incidents dealt with in *Australian Coastal Commission v Green* occurred, a revolution has taken place in global communications that has transformed the shipping industry as much as any other. The Master and Chief Engineer of most vessels are likely to be in daily contact with their Head Office as a matter of routine, and there will be a constant exchange of communications if the vessel is in any difficulty. Many decisions will therefore be made by those on shore and in practice the origin of such decisions is never investigated; only the nature of a course of action is considered.

Intervention by Outside Authorities

A.16 The majority of serious casualties that occur within coastal waters will quickly attract the attention of national, regional and port authorities, seeking to protect their national and local interests from pollution or other dangers arising from the incident. In the United Kingdom, following the "Braer" and "Sea Empress" casualties, Lord Donaldson carried out reviews recommending measures to protect the coastal environment which led initially to the engagement of the first emergency towing vessels (ETVs) to be employed by the Government. After the "Sea Empress" his emphasis shifted to the need to establish a clear chain of command and responsibility to deal with the complex and conflicting issues that arise following a major casualty. This resulted in the introduction of the position of the Secretary of State's Representative for Maritime Salvage and Intervention (SOSREP). Under Sch.3A of the 1995 Merchant Shipping Act (as amended) the SOSREP was given unprecedented powers to give directions to vessels, salvors and others within 12 miles of the UK coast in respect of safety matters, and within 200 miles in respect of possible pollution. These powers would include, for example, the choice of a port of refuge or, as occurred with a much publicised casualty in 2006 involving a container vessel, the decision to beach a badly damaged vessel.

The government of many maritime countries have official bodies that have a responsibility to intervene in casualties, for example, the Coast Guard organisations of the United States and Japan. In other countries a variety of organisations may become involved, often with overlapping or conflicting objectives.

The widespread interventions of such authorities give rise to problems of principle and practical difficulties in relation to general average, for which there is currently no case law to offer guidance.

Decisions Imposed by Third Parties

In the majority of cases, responsible governmental agencies will make or endorse decisions that are in the best interests of the property at risk. It is suggested that a Court would follow the line taken in *Papayanni v Grampian S.S. Co*[20] and, if the action or intention fell within the broad terms of r.A, allow the resulting expense or sacrifice as general average. **A.17**

Conflicting Interests of Third Parties

In some circumstances the authorities may impose a course of action that is partly directed to the safety of ship and cargo but is also dictated by other considerations relating to possible pollution, or other damage to national or local interests. A vessel may therefore be directed to a port or place of refuge that might not have been the owner's or master's first choice and, on entering port, additional costs are incurred regarding anti-pollution measures that go beyond what the owners or master might consider to be strictly necessary. **A.18**

As is recognised in the 1989 Salvage Convention and in rr.C, VI and XI(d) of the York-Antwerp Rules 1994 and 2004, the environmental impact of a casualty can rarely be ignored. The common thread that lies behind the Salvage Convention and the subsequent amendments to the York-Antwerp Rules is the compromise reached between property and liability insurers, whereby an enhancement of a cost due to environmental considerations will not be treated differently from what might be termed the "ordinary" cost of the measure taken. The practical difficulties of separating such enhanced costs would often be considerable–as noted below in para.6.09 Lloyd's arbitrators have never attempted to make such distinctions in their salvage awards. Further, the changes made in successive versions of the Rules have been guided by a desire to meet the changing facts of the commercial world as they exist; it would be artificial to attempt to calculate an "ordinary" cost which, because of contemporary concerns regarding the environment, can only exist as a hypothetical figure.

Environmental issues began to emerge as a significant factor in response to casualties during the currency of the 1974 York-Antwerp Rules which had no specific provisions concerning environmental liabilities or related expenses. Practitioners generally adopted the view that, where additional costs were incurred at the insistence of the relevant authorities in carrying out a general average act, they could be allowed properly as general average, as being an unavoidable part

[20] *Papayanni v Grampian S.S. Co* (1896) 1 Com. Cas. 448.

of achieving something of benefit of the common adventure. It is suggested that this approach remains correct in principle.

The foregoing comments are made in the context of the role of the authorities in connection with a general average act, but their intervention will often include a response to the casualty itself, i.e. the accident that precedes the general average act. Distinctions between these two areas of intervention may need to be made, and this is discussed further at paras 11.46–11.59 dealing with r.XI(d).

Punitive Actions by Authorities

A.19 In a small number of cases, the demands of a relevant authority may appear to be out of all proportion to the possible dangers to the environment that are presented by a particular casualty. The authorities may intervene to prevent a general average act (i.e. entering a port of refuge or lightening cargo) or impose terms to allow the act to proceed, that are manifestly unreasonable or disproportionate. Such actions may occur for political reasons or as an opportunity to earn revenue from, or be seen to "punish", a large corporate owner and his insurers.

As noted above, some enhancement of costs is seen as unavoidable in a modern context and therefore reasonable in terms of the Rule Paramount and r.A. However, where the conduct of the authorities appears to have a punitive aim it is suggested that the matter has to be looked at carefully, since fines are the concern of the liability insurers rather then general average.

Similarly, the authorities may impose additional measures or restrictions because an owner is seen to have been dilatory in complying with his statutory obligations following a casualty. Even if the additional expenses that followed were then unavoidable and were related to a general average act, the Rule Paramount would require a careful examination of any costs that the owner might have brought upon himself.

2. Necessity for Peril

A.20 Of the five essential features necessary to constitute a general average act, perhaps the most important is that there must be present a situation of real and substantial peril whereby the common safety of the adventure is threatened.

Unfortunately, this subject of peril is also one of the most difficult to deal with comprehensively. The infinite variety of circumstances surrounding maritime casualties make it impossible to formulate any general proposition with sufficient precision to enable those concerned to ascertain at a glance whether any particular situation has the necessary degree of peril to be treated as general average. However, by examining some of the decisions of the courts and other situations encountered in everyday practice, some working guidelines may be deduced.

There are, of course, certain situations of such extreme danger and gravity that there would and could be no dispute that ship and cargo were in peril, for example:

(1) a loaded vessel heavily aground on rocks for half her length and with one or more holds flooded;
(2) a loaded container vessel with cargo on fire;
(3) a vessel with her deck cargo of steel pipes shifted, and listing to 45$AG in heavy seas;
(4) a loaded vessel after a serious collision, with the engine room and the adjacent cargo hold flooded.

At the other end of the spectrum, it would hardly be suggested that the ship and cargo were in peril if, for instance, a vessel struck a quay wall on leaving port and merely indented the shell plating above the waterline, in no way reducing her strength or impairing her ability to continue the voyage in the normal manner.

It is between these two extremes, however, that the situation is less clear.

Is a Danger to Life Sufficient?

In practice it is unlikely that the ship and cargo will not be imperilled by a danger which threatens the lives of the persons on board the vessel. If the effect of sacrificing part of the property in fear of death has been to save that which remains, it may well be that a court would not inquire whether the saving of the property was actually in the mind of the master when he directed the sacrifice, but would impute such a motive to him. Yet if there could be a case in which a portion of the ship or cargo has been sacrificed in fear of death, without any expectation or possibility of advantage to the owners of the property which remains, there are no authorities except the dictum set out below which supports the view that there would be a liability to contribute to general average.[21] **A.21**

In *Montgomery v Indemnity Mutual Marine Insurance Co*,[22] Vaughan Williams L.J., delivering the judgment of the Court of Appeal, said: **A.22**

> "It is not, we think, true to say that it is only the danger to the ship, freight or cargo which necessitates and justifies sacrifice by the master of either a portion of the cargo or a portion of the ship. This may be done in fear of death, and if it is done upon a proper occasion all must contribute to the loss."

The contrary view was expressed in the American case of *Shoe v Low Moor Iron Co*,[23] as one of two grounds on which the right to contribution was denied.

[21] The definition of a general average act in the Marine Insurance Act 1906 (para.A.05, above) seems opposed to the dictum. In *The Gratitudine* (1801) 3 C.Rob. 240, Lord Stowell says that in the cases of extreme necessity when the lives of the crew cannot otherwise be saved, the whole cargo may be thrown overboard, and the ship must contribute its average proportion; but the case which he puts is evidently one in which the object is to save the lives of those on board by preserving the vessel. It may also be pointed out that general average is in many respects analogous to salvage, and that there was no power, until it was given by statute, to remunerate the salvor of life only at the expense of the property. The statement in *Mouses's Case* (1609) 12 Co. Rep. 63 that "everyone ought to bear his loss for the safeguard and life of a man" may also be cited; but it cannot safely be assumed that the court in making it had the question of general average in mind.

[22] *Montgomery v Indemnity Mutual Marine Insurance Co* [1902] 1 K.B. 734 at 740.

[23] *Shoe v Low Moor Iron Co* (1891) 46 Fed. Rep. 125; 49 Fed. Rep. 252.

It is to be noted that a jettison of cargo to enable the ship to receive the passengers and crew of another vessel in distress would not constitute a general average sacrifice. In *Dabney v New England Co*[24] the Supreme Court of Massachusetts held that the sacrifice had not been made to avoid a danger to the original adventure.

Must a Total Loss of Ship and Cargo be likely?

A.23 As a general principle, it is probably true to state that for an act to be considered a general average act, it must have been undertaken to preserve the ship and cargo from a situation which might or could develop into an actual or commercial total loss of the ship and cargo—other than by mere decay—before arrival at her final destination. Thus, it is to be assumed, for instance, that:

(1) if a fire is not extinguished, it is likely to consume the ship and cargo;
(2) if a stranded vessel is not refloated, she and her cargo will be broken up and lost in subsequent storms which are bound to occur at some time; or
(3) if a vessel with a complete machinery breakdown is not salved into a port of refuge, she will drift ashore and become a stranded vessel as in (2).

If a total loss of ship and cargo cannot be envisaged, it is doubtful whether the peril is sufficient to constitute a general average. In making this judgement it is suggested that the possibility of total loss has only to be a reasonable apprehension rather than a matter of certainty. For example, factors such as bad weather may be statistically unlikely in a given location at a certain time of year but, if they cannot be ruled out, they may reasonably be taken into account. The modern parlance would be to take the "worst case scenario" that a person with the necessary knowledge and experience might reasonably contemplate.

In *Orient Mid-East Lines Inc v S.S. Orient Transporter*[25] the United States Court of Appeals held that general average does not apply to expenses incurred to remove a ship intentionally grounded in an abandoned ship channel to permit repairs, and that the York-Antwerp Rules 1950 did not do away with the fundamental requirement that a ship be in a position of peril before the law of general average applies.

The facts in that case were that the vessel had completed loading a cargo at Beaumont and because voyage repairs to the boilers had not then been completed, she was taken under the guidance of a pilot to an abandoned ship channel in the Neches River and intentionally grounded on a soft silt bottom to permit repairs to be continued. The anchorage proved unsuitable and it was only with difficulty that the vessel was removed from the silt and mud.

[24] *Dabney v New England Co* (1867) 14 Allen 300.
[25] *Orient Mid-East Lines Inc v S.S. Orient Transporter* (1974) A.M.C. 2593.

> "The District Court found that the (vessel) was not in a position of peril when resting on the bottom of the Neches River. The facts support this finding. The vessel was far removed from any danger of collision with another ship and did not interfere in any way with navigation. The pilot . . . testified that the ship would not have been disturbed by heavy weather."

In earlier times it used to be suggested that if the quantum of danger was such that, in the absence of a sacrifice, the total loss of all property involved in the adventure was certain, there could be no " 'sacrifice" of part since this part was ex hypothesi already lost. This view has not been accepted by the English courts.[26] If a cargo is on fire, and the fire can only be put out by pouring in water, it has been decided that the damage done by pouring water in is to be allowed as general average.[27]

Continuation of Peril

When a ship is immobilised but in no immediate danger, it is a question of fact whether there is a peril sufficient to support a claim for general average contribution. In *McCall v Houlder Bros*[28] a vessel carrying perishable cargo had been towed into Las Palmas harbour with a damaged propeller. No greater peril could be suggested than that "if she had remained where she was, she would have rotted away". In the Law Journal report of the case, Mathew J. said: **A.24**

> "It is idle to say that she was not in peril, for she could do nothing but lay where she was . . . In my opinion, there existed under the circumstances described a common danger . . ."

Similar, but not identical, words are to be found in the *Law Times Reports* and *Aspinall. The Times Law Reports* have ". . . it was idle to think of discharging the cargo . . ." Commercial Cases omit these remarks altogether, although the point as to peril was one of the principal issues argued and was essential to the decision. It is submitted that mere inability to proceed further, even with a perishable cargo, is not by itself sufficient peril to support a general average claim where peril, or action for the common safety, is an essential requirement. However, in considering the above case, and the Troilus discussed in para.A.25, below, it should be remembered that under the York-Antwerp Rules allowances relating to expenses while at the port of refuge would have been made in any event because both vessels were plainly in need of repairs necessary for the safe prosecution of the voyage.

[26] *Pirie & Co v Middle Dock Co* (1881) 44 L.T. 426 at 430. It has also been rejected in the US: *Barnard v Adams* (1850) 10 How. 270. However, the question may still arise, namely, whether there can be a sacrifice of some particular item of property involved in the common adventure which is so far damaged or doomed to destruction as to be effectively lost, even if the rest of the adventure is saved: see the commentary of rr.III and IV of the York-Antwerp Rules.

[27] *Stewart v West India and Pacific S.S. Co* (1873) L.R. 8 Q.B. 88.

[28] *McCall v Houlder Bros* (1897) 66 L.J.Q.B. 408; 13 T.L.R. 280; 2 Com. Cas. 129; 8 Asp.M.C. 252; 76 L.T. 469. The last two are by the same reporter.

A.25 *The Troilus*[29] was a case concerned with salvage reward, for services rendered in towing a vessel with a fractured tail-shaft first to the quarantine anchorage off Aden, and subsequently to the United Kingdom. The principles of law to be applied were different from those of general average, but the facts afford a good illustration of the test as to when a vessel is in peril. The Admiralty assessors in the Court of Appeal advised that the vessel while off Aden was in "no immediate danger, but in the event of an unusual gale springing up she would certainly be in greater danger than a ship with all her main power available". The assessors in the House of Lords advised that she was in no greater danger than a vessel with motive power available, since she had proper tackle to keep her at anchor. It is submitted that, for general average purposes, the vessel was in peril on the basis of the advice given to the Court of Appeal, but not on the basis of the advice given to the House of Lords.

How Immediate Must the Peril be?

A.26 Some accidents are so serious that they undeniably place ship and cargo in immediate peril (of being totally lost), for example:

(1) a loaded container vessel with cargo on fire;
(2) a loaded vessel grounded on rocks in a severe storm.

Other accidents may create a situation potentially just as dangerous, but more in the future, rather than the immediate present. The simplest example may be a loaded vessel which suddenly loses her propeller, but in fine weather in the open sea. Clearly there is no immediate danger to ship and cargo, though it will be appreciated that if nothing be done, sooner or later a storm must break and/or the vessel will drift ashore.

A.27 In *Vlassopoulos v The British & Foreign Marine Insurance Co Ltd*[30] the propeller of the Makis fouled some wreckage while on passage from Bordeaux to Cardiff and the vessel was obliged to put into Cherbourg for repairs. Roche J. held that the ship and cargo were in danger and said:

> "It is not necessary that the ship should be actually in the grip or even nearly in the grip of the disaster that may arise from a danger. It would be a very bad thing if ship-masters had to wait until that state of things arose in order to justify them doing an act which would be a general average act.
>
> That is all, I think, which need be said with regard to that matter, unless I add this: that 'peril,' which means the same thing as 'danger' is the word used in the general rule (A), just as it is the word used in the Marine Insurance Act, Sec. 66. The word is not 'Immediate peril or danger.' It is sufficient to say that the ship must be in danger, or that the act must be done in order to preserve her from peril. It means, of course, that the peril must be real and not imaginary. It means that it must be substantial and not merely slight or nugatory. It must be a danger."

[29] *The Troilus* [1951] A.C. 820.
[30] *Vlassopoulos v The British & Foreign Marine Insurance Co Ltd* [1929] 1 K.B. 187.

In other words, it is the potential rather than the present peril or danger which is important, although it must be stressed in the words of Roche J. that the peril "must be real and not imaginary . . . it must be substantial and not merely slight or nugatory" ("nugatory" is defined in the Concise Oxford Dictionary as "trifling, worthless, futile".)

The wording of the York-Antwerp Rules "for the common safety for the purpose of preserving of peril" might appear to be looking further forward in time than the Marine Insurance Acts' "in time of peril". However, the Makis case (and other cases) makes it clear that the "time of peril" embraces the period when the peril is imminent but has not begun to act, so that in practice the two definitions do not conflict.

The facts in the *Makis* case, above, concerned an accident to the propeller, a vital part of the propulsion of any vessel, and on a voyage which—though short—is through relatively hazardous waters. What of situations such as the following: **A.28**

(1) A vessel loaded to the maximum draft to enter a certain port or waterway strikes some object causing a small leak into the forepeak tank, which fills. There is no danger to the ship and cargo at any time while at sea except . . . that her draft is increased and she cannot enter her port of discharge or the waterway en route without grounding?
(2) A vessel suffers some machinery breakdown such that her speed is reduced to seven knots. This is perfectly adequate for safety on her lengthy sea voyage, but inadequate to combat the strong currents in the Bosphorous (or wherever en route to her destination)?
(3) A vessel loses one or both anchors on a voyage to Bhavnagar. She can proceed in perfect safety to this port, but there is no prospect of her being able to lie there in safety to discharge her cargo, for in this particular port two anchors and several shackles of cable must always be used if the vessel is not to be driven ashore?

If the "peril" is so far distant, and preceded by a passage of complete safety, can the shipowner be entitled to call upon the general average system to make cargo interests contribute to the port of refuge expenses or the cost of extra tugs hired to avoid or combat that future peril?

It is submitted that such extra expenses are properly admissible as general average, provided only that the accident creating the future peril occurred on the current voyage, and while the cargo was on board. A distinction may be drawn, perhaps, between sacrifices and expenditure. A sacrifice of the cargo, or of any part of the ship, will generally be made only in times of extreme emergency and imminent danger, and when there is really no other alternative if the common adventure is to be saved. On the other hand, an expenditure (for example the putting into a port of refuge) can often be delayed for some short time while the facilities for repairs or cargo handling at various ports in the area are considered, and the cheapest or most efficient course of action decided upon.[31] **A.29**

[31] See, e.g. *Phelps v Hill* [1891] 1 Q.B. 605, CA.

Imagined Peril

A.30 A sacrifice made in the mistaken—though reasonable—belief that a peril in fact exists is not general average under English or American law, nor under the York-Antwerp Rules.

In *Joseph Watson & Son Ltd v Firemen's Fund Insurance Co of San Francisco*,[32] the captain saw what he (wrongly) assumed to be smoke issuing from the hold, which indicated to him that there was a fire. Acting on that mistaken assumption, he caused high-pressure steam to be directed into the hold for the purpose of extinguishing the supposed fire, and damaged the cargo therein.

Rowlatt J. held that the damage to the cargo was not a general average loss because the evidence failed to establish that there had been an actual fire in the hold and that, therefore, there had been no peril; he was not prepared to accept that there was a peril in every case where the captain believed it existed.

The facts in the American case of *The West Imboden*[33] were very similar to those prevailing in *Watson v Firemen's Fund* (above) in that steam and water were injected into the hold when the master mistakenly assumed that there was a fire therein because the deck above the hold was found to be hot, and when rain and heavy seas fell on the deck, it caused vapour and steam to arise. On arrival at destination, no fire was found to have existed, but a steam pipe in the hold was found to be broken near the deck and escaping steam had heated the deck.

In identical fashion, it was held that the damage to the cargo was not be a general average loss.

Wrongly Identified Peril

A.31 Where a peril does exist, a mistake on the part of the master as to the precise nature or degree of the danger, or of the action necessary, will not prejudice that sacrifice or expenditure being treated as general average. In *The Wordsworth*,[34] the vessel encountered heavy weather and the master erroneously came to the conclusion that a flooded forepeak was due to a hole in the ship forward and below the water-line. Fearing that the collision bulkhead might give way, and considering that it was the only way to save the ship, he opened the sluices of the collision bulkhead, thereby damaging cargo. When the water by this means had been reduced in the forepeak sufficiently to allow persons to go down and examine the inside, it was found that the leak arose from a break in the port hawse pipe and this break was soon repaired. Had the master known that the damage was to the port hawse pipe, he could have repaired the same without opening the sluices.

The damage to the cargo was allowed in general average upon the grounds that (as referred to in later cases):

[32] *Joseph Watson & Son Ltd v Firemen's Fund Insurance Co of San Francisco* [1922] 2 K.B. 355; 38 T.L.R. 752; 12 Lloyd's Rep. 133.

[33] *The West Imboden* (1936) A.M.C. 696.

[34] *The Wordsworth* (1898) 88 Fed. Rep. 313.

> "There was an actual peril to cargo, the Master being merely mistaken as to its degree." (*West Imboden*)
>
> "There was peril, for water was coming into the ship, although not in the manner supposed by the Captain, and no one knew what would be the result." (*Watson v Firemen's Fund*)

In *Corry v Coulthard*[35] the vessel met with gales and very heavy seas, rolling and straining very heavily, and the mainmast settled down in the ship about four inches, very suddenly slacking up the rigging and allowing the mast to roll about heavily. Being afraid of the heel of the mast working down to the plating and going through the bottom of the ship, the main mast was cut away and this loss was allowed as general average. **A.32**

It appears that the master was mistaken as to the danger of the mast going through the ship's bottom, but in the Court of Appeal, Cockburn C.J. held:

> "It is not necessary that the judgment of the master should be borne out by the facts when they come to be examined into.[36] The question in all this case is, not whether the event shows the wisdom of what was done, but whether, under all the circumstances, it was the exercise of a reasonable, prudent, sound judgment.[37] He sacrificed the mast because, if it had been allowed to remain where it was, it would in his judgment, have led to the common destruction of mast, ship and cargo."[38]

Although the master was mistaken as to the danger of the mast going through the ship's bottom, there was still a real danger, that is, of the mast lurching out of the ship and causing critical damage: ". . . whatever be the condition of the mast it was a source of danger to the ship . . .": also, "The jury found that (the master) was right in supposing there was a danger".

Thus the *Corry* case is on all fours with the decision in *The Wordsworth*[39] (also *Montgomery v Indemnity Mutual Marine Insurance Co*[40]): a real peril existed, unlike the situation in the *Watson* case.[41]

An interesting case encountered in practice relating to peril concerned a chemical tanker which carried a part cargo of phenol in two of her four stainless steel tanks. Phenol is a relatively weak acid, though it is classified as hazardous whether in liquid or solid form, and is rapidly absorbed through the skin and causes severe burns. Within three days of sailing, it was found that the phenol had inexplicably eaten through certain gasket seals in the tanks and had flooded the adjacent pump-rooms. The cargo was transferred into the other tanks but soon destroyed their gasket seals, with the result that the ship might now be considered to have one continuous and common tank. **A.33**

[35] *Corry v Coulthard*, Unreported December 31, 1876, Exch. D.C.; Court of Appeal, January 17, 1877. See 3 Asp. M.L.C. 546(n).

[36] *Ex Shepherd v Kottgen* (1877) 2 C.P.D. 578 at 583.

[37] Ex 3 Asp.M.L.C. 546(n) at 547.

[38] Ex 3 Asp.M.L.C. 546(n) at 547.

[39] *The Wordsworth* (1898) 88 Fed.Rep. 313.

[40] *Montgomery v Indemnity Mutual Marine Insurance Co* [1902] 1 K.B. 734.

[41] *Watson v Firemen's Fund* [1922] 2 K.B. 355; 38 T.L.R. 752; 12 Lloyd's Rep. 133.

The phenol having finally flooded the after pump-room next to the engine-room and accommodation, and considering that it would only be a short time before the phenol had eaten its way through the seals in the engine-room bulkhead, and fearing for the safety of his crew and the ship, the master ordered the whole cargo to be jettisoned.

Subsequent investigation showed that the seals in this particular bulkhead were made of a different material and would have been impervious to the ravages of the phenol, and it can be suggested, therefore, on the grounds of the cases of *Watson v Firemen's Fund*[42] and *The West lmboden*[43] that no real peril existed and that the jettison could not be treated as general average. However, it is submitted that those two cases are easily distinguished in that in neither was there the supposed fire which would have created the peril. In the chemical tanker case, a real accident had occurred and the hazardous acid had already broken bounds and escaped from its proper location, and it was only with hindsight that the master was to learn that the phenol would not gain access to the engine room and accommodation and endanger the crew and the ship. The additional requirement that the sacrifice must be reasonable was clearly satisfied. The master would have been foolhardy to adopt a "wait and see" attitude.

Fear of Peril

A.34 In the vast majority of cases, peril can exist only after some accident or other extraordinary circumstance has operated and caused damage which impairs the seaworthiness, manoeuvrability, or general ability of the ship to withstand the normal maritime perils.

It is not impossible that the ship and her cargo can be in peril, even though presently undamaged, but the impending disaster from which relief is sought by the supposed sacrifice or expenditure must then be immediately imminent and all but inevitable. Anchors can be lost by being dropped in an emergency to avoid a collision[44] and vessels may be intentionally run aground to avoid a collision, but the evidence in such cases should always be examined with even greater care as it is to be questioned whether the supposed sacrifice or expenditure was truly extraordinary,[45] or just a measure taken in the ordinary course of navigation, and one which was part of the shipowner's ordinary obligations under the contract of affreightment. Thus, the expense of moving a vessel out of port or to a typhoon anchorage when extremely bad weather is forecast is an ordinary voyage expense and not general average, though the position may be different if her moorings have already broken and/or other damage has been sustained.

A.35 In *Societe Nouvelle d'Armement v Spillers and Bakers Ltd*,[46] the expenditure in respect of which a claim was made in general average was the engagement of a

[42] *Watson v Firemen's Fund* [1922] 2 K.B. 355; 38 T.L.R. 752; 12 Lloyd's Rep. 133.

[43] *The West lmboden* (1936) A.M.C. 696.

[44] See para.A.73, below.

[45] See paras A.59–A.61, below. See also *Hamel v P&O S.N. Co* [1908] 2 K.B. 298, quoted in para.A.75, below.

[46] *Societe Nouvelle d'Armement v Spillers and Bakers Ltd* [1917] 1 K.B. 865.

tug to tow a French sailing ship in June 1915, from Queenstown to Sharpness, so as to minimise the risk of attack by enemy submarines. The evidence did not satisfy the learned judge that on this particular voyage the vessel would be exposed to any exceptional risk of attack, and no submarine was in fact sighted during the towage. On the facts he held that the risk of attack was not, for time of war, an extraordinary and abnormal one, and that, although the towage might have minimised the risk, it was impossible to say that it preserved the property in time of peril.

The Peril Must Affect All Interests

A sacrifice or expenditure incurred for the safety of one interest alone can never **A.36**
be general average; the peril sought to be avoided must affect all interests. Thus, if the refrigerating machinery of a reefer ship broke down, a deviation into a port of refuge for repairs could not be treated as general average as it would be solely for the safety of the refrigerated cargo.

Provided that the impending peril does affect all interests, no distinction will be made between any varying degrees of peril to which it might be suggested that the different interests were subject. Thus, if a vessel carrying both refrigerated cargo and, say, pig iron, were to suffer a total machinery breakdown, it is clear that delay and natural deterioration will cause the refrigerated cargo to become a total loss long before the pig iron. However, any general average or salvage services will remove them both from essentially the same risk of total loss by stranding or shipwreck, etc. and on these grounds the salvage or general average expenditure will be apportioned strictly pro rata over the values saved.[47]

Fire

Fire continues to be possibly the most alarming of any peril on board ship. **A.37**
Once started, it can quickly spread if unchecked, and on these grounds it can safely be asserted that any fire on board, however small, constitutes a real peril and that damage caused in extinguishing it can be treated as a general average sacrifice.

Groundings

Prima facie, any ship aground in a place where she is not intended to be is likely **A.38**
to be in peril, but it is a question of fact, to be decided on the circumstances existing in each particular case, whether or not the vessel is in any real and substantial peril.

When a vessel grounds in the open sea or on an exposed coastline there is seldom any doubt that the vessel is in peril, for even if safe enough at the time,

[47] American courts have declined to evaluate different degrees of peril to the various interests: *Willcox v American Smelting Co; The Trojan* (1913) 210 Fed.Rep. 9; and see *The St Paul* (1898) 82 Fed.Rep. 104; 86 Fed.Rep. 340. See also *The M Vatan* [1990] 1 Lloyd's Rep. 336, and also the further remarks, in para.6.25, below.

danger must be apprehended should bad weather come on. Difficulties are more likely to arise when the vessel grounds in more protected waters, such as inland seas and lakes, rivers and estuaries, or in ports and harbours. For such guidance as they may offer, the facts and fairly extensive extracts from the judgments in three English legal decisions now follow.

A.39 In *Trafalgar S.S. Co v British and Foreign Marine Insurance Co*[48] the Rodney grounded some distance below Point Indio Lightship after leaving Buenos Aires. Here she remained fast for nearly two hours, her engines being worked ahead and astern to enable the vessel to get off, and ultimately, owing to the rising water, she floated and proceeded on her voyage. The expense of opening up and repairing the damage to the machinery was claimed in general average, but Channell J. ruled that the vessel was not in peril and that the damage was not admissible in general average.

> "It seems to be an extremely common thing to go through this soft mud and occasionally to stick, and the evidence is very clear that you will not have any wind that will cause any damage to you from being aground, which will not, some 12 hours, it is said, before that wind comes to you, have raised the water so as to get you off. It seems, therefore, that, although, I suppose, people would generally say that in anything that can be called an open road-stead to be aground is to a certain extent to be in peril, yet in this particular place it rather seems that that is not so; it is a place where the water is shallow, where vessels habitually disregard it; they do not appear to wait until there is a southerly wind to raise the water, and it is not in practice considered to be a danger."

A.40 In *Charter Shipping Co Ltd v Bowring Jones & Tidy Ltd*[49] the case for the shipowners was that shortly after leaving the quay at Jacksonville the ship ran aground and was for a time, it was alleged, in danger of breaking her back. The engines were run full speed ahead and astern alternately, but that failed to refloat the vessel. She was refloated, however, with the assistance of a tug after being aground for nearly three hours.

In his judgment, Roche J. stated:

> "It is said, in the first place, that the vessel was not in a position of peril, that she was in no real danger, that she was in inland waters 20 miles from the sea, and that it was merely a matter of rising water and if necessary, the assistance of a tug to get her off. The danger was not very great, but still I am satisfied that there was a position of peril within the meaning of the rule (VII of the York-Antwerp Rules 1890); the danger was real and substantial enough to necessitate the use of the engines; and the risk of damage which was undergone, and the damage, if any, which resulted from their use and other circumstances, was damage within that rule of the York-Antwerp Rules."

A.41 In *Daniolos v Bunge & Co*[50] the case for the shipowners was that while the vessel was sailing up the narrow navigable channel in the Randers Fjord on

[48] *Shipping Gazette*, November 18, 1904.
[49] *Charter Shipping Co Ltd v Bowring Jones & Tidy Ltd* (1930)36 Lloyd's Rep. 272.
[50] *Daniolos v Bunge & Co* (1938) 62 Lloyd's Rep 65; affirming (1937) 59 Lloyd's Rep 175.

January 7, 1936, the strong ebb current caught her starboard bow and she grounded on her port side near Raaby Odde.

Efforts to refloat her by her own engines proved unsuccessful, and a tug was made fast. She was refloated momentarily, but was immediately caught again by the current and the wind and taken ashore on her starboard side on the north bank of the channel. Another attempt was made to refloat her, but, after moving about 150 yards ahead, she again went firmly aground and remained on the edge of the steep bank on the north side of the channel, being supported by only half her width on the starboard side, which was resting on a hard and uneven bottom of mud and stones.

Though continual efforts to refloat the ship were made, she remained aground until January 11, and was in constant danger of being taken further up the bank and of receiving damage to her bottom and internal structure, and of collision with passing vessels, with consequent loss or damage to her cargo. She was refloated at about 08.00 on January 11, the water having risen owing to the wind veering, and she proceeded to Randers, where the cargo was discharged.

Goddard J. decided that the vessel had not been in any real danger and stated:

> ". . . I cannot find here that there was any real danger to this ship. In determining whether there was real danger I think the first thing one has to look at, and what is more valuable to consider, is the views and conduct of the people who were on the spot at the time.
>
> That she would suffer some damage to her bottom in getting where she was, and that she would suffer some damage to her bottom in getting out from where she was, was only to be expected; but the damage that was in fact done, the damage that was found when she had gone into dry dock–assuming, as I do assume, that every bit of it that was found was done on this occasion–was not of a character which in my judgment exposed the cargo to any danger. The damage to the bilge keel, which is the point that is most insisted on, I think it equally follows that that was done when they were getting the ship out; but I am quite certain nobody ever thought for a moment that that ship was ever in a position of danger when she lay in the Randers Fjord."

This decision was affirmed in the Court of Appeal.

The vessel in *Daniolos v Bunge & Co* appears to have been of some 7500 dwt capacity and there are no recent cases dealing with modern vessels, some of which may carry that amount of cargo in a single hold. While the same principles are applicable, it may be necessary to take specialist advice regarding the risks of hogging and sagging (the centre of the hull being distorted upwards or downwards, respectively) that large vessels are particularly exposed to when aground and the structure of the vessel is unevenly supported.

Situations in which there may be insufficient peril to ship and cargo to constitute general average often occur in loading or discharging ports due to bad weather or similar factors. For example, when a vessel starts ranging alongside a discharging berth, the master may call for a tug to help hold the vessel off and reduce any further damage. Unless the conditions are exceptional there is unlikely to be any common peril, but there is a risk of the vessel sustaining further shell plating damage which would be expensive to repair. In such circumstances the tug costs may be properly recoverable under the Sue and Labour clause (e.g. cl.13 of Institute Time Clauses Hulls 1.10.83) of the vessel's policies.

A similar array of cases from the courts of the United States includes *Wilcox, Peck and Hughes v American Smelting and Refining Co*,[51] *The Mincio*,[52] *The Edward Rutledge*,[53] and *The National Defender*.[54]

Machinery Breakdowns

Main engines

A.42 If a vessel is totally immobilised at sea by, for instance, a complete breakdown of the main engine or its crankshaft, or by a breakage of the tailshaft and/or loss of the propeller, and has no other means of propulsion,[55] the common adventure must almost invariably be in peril, even if the accident occur in fine weather.[56] The cost of towage and/or salvage into a port of refuge will then unquestionably be treated as general average.

Twin-engined vessels

A.43 Some vessels are fitted with two (or more) engines for greater speed, manoeuvrability, and reliability. If one of these engines is completely immobilised, the vessel will sometimes put into port for repairs, but can it be said that the common adventure is in peril?

As a general rule the answer is "no", and it will usually be found that the decision to deviate for repairs was taken for economic reasons only, and that the safety of the vessel and her cargo was not in question. If for example both engines can propel the vessel at 15 knots, a single engine may produce 10 knots, and the deviation is simply to get the benefit of cheaper and/or better repair facilities, and/or to save time on the voyage.

Turbo-chargers

A.44 Turbo chargers make use of the exhaust gases from the main engine to provide additional power and/or efficiency. If a turbo charger sustains damage, it does not automatically mean that the ship and cargo are necessarily in peril; very often, the turbo charger can be blanked off at sea by the crew and the vessel can proceed at reduced speed. The ability to operate without a turbo-charger will vary with

[51] *Wilcox, Peck and Hughes v American Smelting and Refining Co* (1913) 210 Fed.Rep. 89.

[52] *The Mincio* (1936) A.M.C. 1765.

[53] *The Edward Rutledge* (1954) A.M.C. 2070.

[54] *The National Defender* (1969) A.M.C. 1219.

[55] In *Ballantyne v Mackhmon* (1896) 65 L.J.Q.B. 616, a schooner-rigged steamer ran out of fuel and burned all her spare wood and some part of her fittings and was towed into her destination. In his official deposition, the master stated there was "no damage to our vessel, and we could have proceeded under sail, and we were not in distress".

[56] See para.A.26, above.

different types of engines and the effects on the combustion process may lead in time to damage to other components. The matter may therefore need to be considered in the context of the length of the anticipated voyage and the expected weather and sea conditions.

Broken cylinder heads or liners

If a vessel's main engine suffers damage to a piston, cylinder head or liner that renders one unit unserviceable, it will often be possible to isolate that unit and for the main engine to continue to produce an acceptable level of power. The vessel is unlikely to be in peril unless the origin of the damage is likely to impinge on other units or there is a reduction in power sufficient to cause concern with regard to (for example) anticipated bad weather or ice conditions. **A.45**

Generators

A vessel may be fitted with three generators, of which only one is required to supply the normal electrical load at sea, with two being necessary when in port working cargo. When navigating in restricted or crowded waterways it is sometimes considered prudent to have two generators running in parallel in order to prevent a blackout occurring at an inopportune moment should one machine suffer damage, but in theory one generator should be capable of taking the load. It is seldom that a vessel will put into port for a single generator breakdown but not infrequent if two generators have failed. Prima facie, the third generator should be sufficient for all the vessel's needs on the sea voyage, and if she put into port it could be for fear of a future peril rather than the existence of a present peril. If the accidents which have befallen the two other generators are quite separate and unrelated, it is suggested that the entry into port for repairs does not constitute a general average act. However, the position might be otherwise if, for instance, the two generators broke down as the result of contaminated fuel oil which has also been used in the third generator. In such a case, a further breakdown might reasonably be anticipated within a short time. It will often be necessary to take technical advice to decide the point and this may involve seeking guidance from the vessel's Classification Society. **A.46**

Cranes, cargo pumps, auxiliary boilers, etc.

If a vessel is proceeding to a port where there are no discharging or repair facilities and sustains damage to her cranes, cargo pumps, auxiliary boilers for heating oil cargo, or other gear which makes it impossible for her to discharge her cargo at destination, she will probably put into some earlier port for necessary repairs. If the damage did not render the vessel unfit to encounter the ordinary perils of the seas and there are no dangers relating to the instability of cargo, then the common safety has not been endangered and the port charges cannot be treated as general average. **A.47**

Navigation aids, etc.

A.48 Modern ocean-going ships are fitted with radar, communications systems, and all manner of aids to navigation. The deck officers and pilots have come to rely on such equipment and if, for instance, the radar mast and all the various antennae sustain damage, repairs will be carried out at the very earliest opportunity–indeed, the vessel may put into an unscheduled port especially for such repairs. Without such equipment in working order, can the common adventure be said to be in peril? The question illustrates the frequent impossibility of dealing with such points in the abstract, since the answer will depend entirely on the size and type of vessel, the voyage contemplated, and the extent to which back-up systems are available. Working radio and radar equipment are required under flag state and international regulations, but a deviation into port to satisfy a legislative requirement will not of itself be sufficient to indicate the vessel was in peril.

Shortage of bunkers

A.49 A vessel proceeding west-bound across the North Atlantic in winter may meet with continuous adverse weather and make such little headway that it is thought likely that her bunkers will be exhausted before she reaches destination. Accordingly, she may turn about and run with the wind to a port, say, in Ireland to replenish bunkers. The expenses at that port will be allowed as general average, subject to any question of fault under r.D.

This is a good example of a situation where the peril is both real and substantial but the ship is not in the immediate grip of that peril: she would still have on board a fair supply of bunkers at the time the decision was taken to turn about and make for Ireland. Clearly, it would be ridiculous to deny a general average situation until all the bunkers had been consumed.

To survey the damage

A.50 After stranding, a vessel may put into port to obtain a diver's survey or other inspection to ensure that it is safe to proceed on the voyage. If the vessel is found to have little or no damage, it follows that the common adventure was not in peril and the entry into port was not a general average act. It has been the practice of some adjusters to allow the expenses of putting into port for a precautionary survey, even if minimal damage is found, on the grounds that this is a prudent measure that cargo interests would recognise and not wish to discourage. No doubt cases have been settled on this equitable basis, but there is no support for this practice in the York-Antwerp Rules, or under English law. If the grounding were more serious and significant damage was found which did not however disable the vessel, it could then be argued with more certainty that the circumstances are closer to those encountered in the cases described in para.A.31 than those shown in para.A.30.

Following a collision in coastal waters, it is common for the relevant authorities to instruct a vessel to proceed to the nearest port to enable enquiries to take place under their jurisdiction. Frequently, resort to a port of refuge is also necessitated by the damage sustained and the entry to and detention at the port is properly allowable as general average. However, if legal proceedings prolong the vessel's stay after she is otherwise ready to proceed, the extra detention will not be allowable and the same would apply if legal considerations were the sole reason for the call.

3. Necessity for a Common Maritime Adventure

One of the essential features of a general average act is that it must be for the purpose of preserving from peril the property involved in a common maritime adventure. The doctrine of general average is derived from the maritime law, and there is no authority at common law for extending it to property not engaged in a common maritime adventure in the nature of a voyage.[57] In *Morrison S.S. Co v Greystoke Castle*[58] Lord Uthwatt said: A.51

> "The principle involved in general average contribution is peculiar to the law of the sea and extends only to sea risks."

General average does not extend to the transport of goods by land, or by air,[59] nor does it apply to the intentional sacrifice of property on land, for example, to extinguish or contain a conflagration in a town or forest, or even in a dockside warehouse.

Storage and Specialist Vessels

Where a ship is used in port as a hulk or warehouse to store oil or other goods, the case may be thought more doubtful, but it is submitted that while the vessel is used only as a store and not for transport, there is no maritime adventure common to her and the goods which she contains, and no right of contribution between their respective owners.[60] It is conceivable that, on occasion, salvage services may be rendered to the storeship and her cargo, but this should be treated as pure A.52

[57] "With regard to salvage, general average, and contribution," said Bowen L.J. in *Falcke v Scottish Imperial Insurance Co* (1886) 34 Ch.D. 234 at 248, "the maritime law differs from the common law. This has been so from the time of the Roman law downwards. The maritime law, for the purposes of public policy and for the advantage of trade, imposes in these cases a liability upon the thing saved, a liability which is a special consequence arising out of the character of mercantile enterprises, the nature of sea perils, and the fact that the thing saved was saved under great stress and exceptional circumstances. No similar doctrine applies to things lost upon land, nor to anything except ships or goods in peril at sea." And dealing with a contract for the conveyance of goods by ship and railway, Lush J. said: "Goods may be damaged in their transit in ship or on the railway, but general average contribution can only arise in respect of damage on ship": *Crooks v Allan* (1879) 5 Q.B.D. 38 at 40.

[58] *Morrison S.S. Co v Greystoke Castle* [1947] A.C. 265 at 310.

[59] See McNair, *Law of the Air*, 3rd edn, Ch.10. For a case of jettison from a passenger airline on a normal scheduled flight, see *The Times*, March 28, 1960, and cf. *Re California Eastern Airways* (1951) U.S. Av.Rep. 327.

[60] cf. *European and Australian Co v P&O* (1866) 14 L.T. 704.

salvage and the ancillary allowances and principles of the general average system should not be introduced. There are some types of property or circumstances in which there is some exposure to maritime perils but which may not sit comfortably within the normal idea of a common maritime adventure. There is no direct case law to assist with these grey areas, the only indirect guidance coming from cases regarding whether particular property could be described as a ship for purposes of limitation of liability or other statutory or insurance purposes.

The following examples illustrate some of the problem areas.

Tankers may sometimes be chartered with the intention of loading cargo that will be held indefinitely as the purchaser speculates on the long-term movements in the price of oil. The voyage may be greatly extended beyond the normal passage between producing and consuming countries, but this remains an obvious maritime adventure.

More difficult questions arise when tankers are assigned for storage purposes to a particular oilfield for an indefinite period. Clearly, a fire would expose both ship and cargo to a common peril, but the common adventure is limited to the brief period that the cargo stays on board until transhipped into another vessel. General average allowances could be made in respect of extinguishing damage or fire-fighting expenses but allowances relating to the safe prosecution of any voyage would be very limited–it is suggested that these repairs necessary for the safe prosecution of the "voyage" could go no further than making the vessel able to offload its current cargo.

Where matters are taken a stage further and a tanker is converted into a Floating Production Storage and Offloading vessel (FPSO) or a vessel is specially built for the purpose, similar considerations would apply—as they would also to the specialised transhipment vessels, used for lightening or loading vessels in the bulk ore trades.

Off-shore construction and support vessels such as crane-barges, pipe-layers and diving support vessels often have property on board that is in different ownership so that general average liabilities may arise. Again "common safety" losses present no great problem but in place of an identifiable voyage from one place to another there will often be a contract to carry out a specified task or set of tasks in a given location. In this case it is suggested that allowances under r.XI can reasonably be made with a view to repairs necessary for the safe prosecution of the contractual works.

Another example of an undefined voyage can arise with vessels used in support of fishing fleets where their original cargo will decrease as stores are provided to the fishing boats at the same time as valuable catch is taken on board for processing and storage. Here, it is suggested that the "voyage" is the period for which the vessel was contracted to act as a support vessel.

While a drilling rig on passage to a new operational location with third party equipment on board is identifiably the same as a cargo vessel on passage, once stationary at a long-term drilling location its character may well have changed. It has been suggested that the well being drilled (which can have very significant value in terms of money invested in it to date) should contribute to measures to save the rig in the event of a serious fire, but this is in the nature of a financial loss that is remote from the property actually in physical danger.

In any of the circumstances outlined above, in which the principles of general average and the York-Antwerp Rules appear to be inappropriate or their application difficult, the solution is to deal with the matter by express terms in the relevant contracts and/or insurance policies. However it is suggested that, if the option chosen is to dispense with general average principles, the parties should be aware that many of the losses and expenses dealt with by these principles will not disappear in the event of a casualty; clear alternative provisions need to be made to avoid possible delays when in the grip of a casualty, or disputes in its aftermath.

Must more than One Interest be Imperilled?

A further question is whether general average can exist if the ship is the sole property imperilled, that is when no cargo is on board and the vessel is not under charter. **A.53**

The definitions of a general average act provided by the English courts all seem to contemplate that more than one interest must be in peril. Indeed, in *Kemp v Halliday*,[61] Blackburn J. expressly said: "It is essential that there should be a voluntary sacrifice to preserve more subjects than one." And the statutory definition in s.66(1) of the Marine Insurance Act 1906 speaks of "the property imperilled in the common adventure"; again implying that more than one interest must be concerned.

In the case of *The Brigella*,[62] the vessel being outward bound in ballast to her loading port, so that the only interest at stake was that of the shipowner, Gorell Barnes J. held that port of refuge expenses on this voyage could not be general average, as there could be no contribution. But this decision was expressly disapproved in *Montgomery v Indemnity Mutual Assurance Co*,[63] where the mast of *The Airlie* had been cut away in time of peril, the shipowner being also the owner of the cargo on board. The Court of Appeal affirmed the judgment of Mathew J., holding that " 'a general average act is not affected by the consideration whether there will be a contribution or not". Vaughan Williams L.J., in delivering the judgment of the Court of Appeal, said: **A.54**

> "The object of the maritime law seems to be to give the master of the ship absolute freedom to make whatever sacrifice he thinks best to avert the perils of the sea, without any regard whatsoever to the ownership of the property sacrificed; and, in our judgment, such a sacrifice is a general average act quite independently of unity or diversity of ownership."[64]

61 *Kemp v Halliday* (1866) L.R. 1 Q.B. 520.
62 *The Brigella* [1893] P. 189.
63 *Montgomery v Indemnity Mutual Assurance* Co [1902] 1 K.B. 734.
64 *Montgomery v Indemnity Mutual Assurance Co* [1902] 1 K.B. 734 at 740.

A.55 It must accordingly be regarded as settled that contribution is not an essential element in general average: but is it essential that there shall be more than one interest?

So far as the liability of underwriters to indemnify the assured against general average losses is concerned, it is clear from the Marine Insurance Act 1906 that the interests may be in common ownership. Section 66(7) provides that:

> "Where ship, freight, and cargo, or any two of those interests, are owned by the same assured, the liability of the insurer in respect of general average losses or contributions is to be determined as if those subjects were owned by different persons."

The Court of Appeal in *Montgomery v Indemnity Mutual Marine Assurance Co*,[65] quoted with approval a portion of the judgment of Story J. in the case of *Potter v Ocean Assurance Co*,[66] which definitely suggests that general average is payable where there is only a single interest at stake, and that inasmuch as the expenses may be said to have been incurred as much for the benefit of underwriters as for the shipowner, they are "in the nature of general average". It is to be noted, however, that this was an American decision, and that in the United States it has been held that in the case of a ship in ballast, or even in the case of a yacht, general average is payable. The American view seems to be founded upon the consideration of the liability of underwriters being deemed an interest at stake.[67]

A.56 Whatever may be the law in the United States, it is submitted that in the United Kingdom and under the York-Antwerp Rules, more than one interest must be imperilled if there is to be a general average act. The many definitions of a general average act found in the judgments of the courts, the statutory definition contained in the Marine Insurance Act, as well as the York-Antwerp r.A definition, all indicate that an essential element of general average is that the act shall be done for the preservation of more than one interest, and it is hard to see how the interest of underwriters can be included for this purpose.[68]

Vessels in Ballast

A.57 It should be noted that a general average situation can exist when a vessel is in ballast if she is under time-charter, in which case the time charterer's bunkers constitute the second interest. Additionally, under English Law a vessel sailing in ballast to load cargo under an existing voyage charter has the freight at risk under that charter as a separate interest, which is treated as if it were physical property

[65] *Montgomery v Indemnity Mutual Marine Assurance Co* [1902] 1 K.B. 734.

[66] *Potter v Ocean Assurance Co* (1837) 3 Sumner 27.

[67] *Dollar v La Fonciere* (1908) 162 Fed. Rep. 563, following *Potter v Ocean*, etc.

[68] cf. *Foscolo Mango v Stag Line Ltd* [1931] 2 K.B. at 60 per Scrutton L.J., where in considering the question of a reasonable deviation he said: "I think the interests to be considered must be those of the parties to the adventure in the contract adventure, which may include consideration of the position of underwriters." It is also worthy of note in this connection that in *Oppenheim v Fry* (1863) 3 B. & S. 873, where hull and machinery of *The Baroness Tecco* were insured, separately valued, with a clause "average payable on the whole or on each as if separately insured", the court clearly indicated that it thought that the expenses of extinguishing a fire might be general average as two interests, separately valued, were preserved. See per Blackburn J. at 884 (obiter).

and brought in to contribute on a general average basis. Both these situations are dealt with in the Association of Average Adjusters Rule of Practice B26 which is to be found in Appendix 3 and see also paras 17.59–17.61 and 50.81.

When the loss consists of the incurring of expenses, in the case of the ship alone being at risk, the expenses, or some of them, may be recoverable under the "suing and labouring" clause, contained in the hull policy. Many hull policies also contain a clause providing that in the event of the ship being in ballast, and not under charter, general average shall nevertheless be payable generally in accordance with the provisions of the York-Antwerp Rules. See Section 7, para.50.81, below.

Tug and Tow

The circumstances in which a tug and tow, or a linked flotilla of tug and barges, etc. may constitute a common maritime adventure are discussed under r.B. **A.58**

4. Necessity for an Extraordinary Sacrifice or Expenditure

General Principles

In order to constitute a general average act, the sacrifice or expenditure must be extraordinary in its nature. **A.59**

Ipso facto, any sacrifice of cargo by the master of the ship at a time of peril must be extraordinary. The cargo ought never, under those ordinary circumstances which alone are provided for by the contract of affreightment, to be exposed to a risk beyond that which is common to the entire adventure. Therefore, in case of exposure to any risk greater than ordinary, as by opening hatches during a gale to jettison cargo, such exposure, if followed by loss or damage, is treated as a sacrifice. However, some degree of exposure to risk on the part of the ship's gear and machinery may naturally be regarded as no more than the ship's ordinary duty, and not amounting to a sacrifice for which compensation should be made.

The question must then be asked:

> "In consideration of the payment of the agreed freight for the voyage, has the cargo-owner the right under the contract of affreightment to expect the shipowner to make such 'sacrifice' or incur such expenditure without requiring a supplementary contribution from the cargo-owner? Was the sacrifice or expenditure truly extraordinary and out of the usual course, or was it encompassed within the shipowner's obligations under, and performance of, the contract of affreightment?"

This point is further illustrated by r.VII.

The position is best illustrated by a few[69] of the many legal cases from sailing ship days.

[69] But see also *Birkley v Presgrave* (1801) 1 East 220; *Taylor v Curtis* (1815) 4 Camp. 337; *Soc. Nouvelle d'Armement v Spillers & Bakers* [1917] 1 K.B. 865.

Meaning of "Extraordinary"

A.60 If a vessel carried a press of sail in order to beat off a lee-shore or to escape from an enemy, and the sails were thereby blown away, the masts sprung, or the hull extraordinarily strained, such loss was in this country considered not to be the subject of general average contribution.

In *Covington v Roberts*[70] the Nancy had been captured by a French privateer, but as it blew a gale and the sea ran high the Frenchman could not board her; whereupon the master of the Nancy, in order to make her escape, carried an unusual spread of canvas, in consequence of which she was much strained, opened most of her seams, and carried away the head of her mainmast: but succeeded in getting clear away. The owner of the Nancy sued his underwriter on ship for this damage, as particular average. The underwriter contended that he was only liable for his share, treating it as a general average, as a loss occasioned by an exertion to save the whole concern; and *Birkley v Presgrove*[71] was cited in support of this view. But Sir J. Mansfield C.J. said:

> "In the case referred to, there was an article given up for the benefit of the whole concern. A cable was sacrificed. The language of Lawrence J. is, that all loss which arises in consequence of extraordinary sacrifices or expenses incurred for the preservation of the ship and cargo come within the description of general average. This is only a common sea risk. If the weather had been rather better, or the ship stronger, nothing might have happened."[72]

In *Power v Whitmore*[73] a ship was in imminent danger of being driven ashore during a gale, and in order to avoid this danger was stood out to sea with a press of sail greater than she was able to bear in such weather, with the result that serious damage was sustained to the masts, sails and the hull itself. It was held, as counsel for the shipowners had admitted in argument[74] that no part of this damage was the subject of general average.

A.61 In some countries the position was otherwise, and damage caused by carrying a press of sail was treated as general average. Those countries which rejected the allowance usually did so on the grounds that the shipowner was bound under his contract of affreightment to furnish the cargo with all the ordinary means of reaching its destination which are supplied by the ship and her tackle, each part used in its appropriate way, whether it be with greater or less strain put upon it; and this includes, upon occasion, the carrying a press of sail.[75]

[70] *Covington v Roberts* (1806) 2 Bos. & P.N.R. 378.
[71] *Birkley v Presgrave* (1801) 1 East 220.
[72] In *The Bona* (1895) P. 125 at 134, Lord Esher said that the court would not be disposed to extend *Covington v Roberts*.
[73] *Power v Whitmore* (1815) 4 M. & S. 141.
[74] *Power v Whitmore* (1815) 4 M. & S. 141 at 146.
[75] e.g. Ulrich, *Grosse Haverei*, p.41.

Damage and Expense in Using Auxiliary Engine

In *Wilson v Bank of Victoria*,[76] an auxiliary sailing vessel (that is one that normally proceeded under sail and used her engine only when the wind was light, or adverse) struck an iceberg and was dismasted while on voyage from Melbourne to Great Britain and was obliged to put into Rio de Janeiro as a port of refuge under her auxiliary steam power. The cost of repairs being prohibitive, the master effected only temporary repairs at Rio and proceeded to destination under steam, purchasing additional coals at both Rio and Fayal for this purpose. A claim was made for a general average contribution towards the cost of these coals, but disallowed on the grounds that the expenditure was merely the performance of a service owed by the shipowner to the cargo-owners under the contract of affreightment. As Blackburn J. said: **A.62**

> "(The measure taken) caused the disbursements for coals to be extraordinarily heavy, but it did not render it an extraordinary disbursement . . ."

Somewhat similar considerations applied in the case of *Harrison v Bank of Australasia*,[77] decided five years later. It concerned a sailing ship, also on voyage from Melbourne to Great Britain, which sprang a leak in a cyclone. The vessel was fitted with a donkey-engine for loading and unloading cargo, hoisting sails, and for pumping the ship. To save the vessel from foundering, the donkey-engine was used continuously throughout the voyage and, when the existing supply of bunkers was exhausted, the master was obliged to burn spare spars and ships stores, and to purchase additional bunkers from a passing steamer. Further, the donkey-engine needed repairs by reason of its excessive use. A claim for a general average contribution from cargo was allowed in respect of the ship's spars and stores, which truly constituted an extraordinary sacrifice of those items, but not for the cost of the coals consumed or of repairing the donkey-engine. **A.63**

An identical situation was decided in identical fashion in the case of *Robinson v Price*.[78]

The above cases are some of antiquity but give good practical examples of how the word "extraordinary" in the general definition given in r.A must be given effect to. Nonetheless the point can be a difficult one and part of the role of the numbered rules is to ensure uniformity as to where the line may be drawn in different circumstances, for example r.VII dealing with damage to a vessel's engines while trying to refloat. Reflecting on Blackburn's words in *Wilson v Bank of Victoria*, when considering temporary repairs in *The Bijela*,[79] Hoffman L.J. said: **A.64**

> "The cargo-owners certainly benefit from the temporary repairs which enable the voyage to be completed, but if the owner was under a duty under the contract of affreightment to make such repairs, the benefit may be said to be one for which the cargo-owners have already paid. On the other hand, there seems to be no rigid

[76] *Wilson v Bank of Victoria* (1867) L.R. 2 Q.B. 203.
[77] *Harrison v Bank of Australasia* (1872) L.R. 7 Ex. 39.
[78] *Robinson v Price* (1876) 2 Q.B.D. 91: (1877) 2 Q.B.D. 295.
[79] *Marida Ltd v Oswal Steel (The Bijela)* [1993] 1 Lloyd's Rep. 411 at 420.

> principle that sacrifice or expenditure cannot qualify for general average because the owner was under a duty under the contract of affreightment to make it. A policy of giving the owner or master a financial incentive in an emergency to give priority to the safety of the vessel or delivery of its cargo seems also the play a part."

There is no modern case law that offers guidance with regard to extra-ordinary expenditure but it is suggested that the following contemporary examples would not, in the absence of special circumstances, give rise to a claim for general average under r.A:

- The cost of using of diesel rather than heavy fuel oil after an auxiliary boiler failure make heating the heavy oil impossible.
- The cost of tugs engaged to assist in berthing a vessel that has damaged her bow thrusters.

Piracy

A.65 In the 12th edn, the problem of piracy merited only a footnote that noted that in *Hicks v Palington* (1590) Moore's (Q.B.) R 297, cargo given to pirates by way of ransom was a sacrifice that was a subject for general average contribution. At the time of the last edition, piracy in various forms had returned to many parts of the world, particularly off Somalia, and a more detailed commentary was provided.

The actions of pirates in each set of circumstances and subsequent events need to be looked at carefully in order to see whether the principles of General Average are properly applicable. In some cases the intention of the pirates is immediate theft, whether of ship's cash and crew valuables or the removal of part of the cargo. While hazardous and traumatic for all concerned, such situations are unlikely to give rise to circumstances that come within the terms of r.A. However, if the same pirates take the vessel to a remote location to remove valuable deck cargo, before abandoning the ship and the rest of the cargo the expenses of searching and recovering the property would almost certainly fall within r.A. The position regarding payment of ransom is dealt with in more detail below.

Consumption of fuel, etc.

A.66 Pirates may often steam a vessel for some distance to escape detection or off-load cargo. Any such fuel costs fall outside general average, as would any damage to the vessel done by pirates deliberately or through neglect while in their control.

Payment of ransom

A.67 Where the pirates' intention is to detain the vessel to obtain a ransom, rather than carrying out only a brief seizure for the purpose of theft, it will be necessary for them to hold the vessel while negotiations are carried out. In the case of Somalia, few attempts were made by the authorities to recover vessels from the pirates' coastal bases, due to the threat of violence against the crew. Such locations cannot generally be described as ports or places of refuge, and, even if so described, detention there is not for the common safety or to effect repairs necessary for the safe prosecution of the voyage, which are the only two grounds that permit the allowance of fuel and stores and wages and maintenance under r.XI.

Once the vessel has been released it is likely, if the detention period has been lengthy, that it will need to be taken to a safe port for replenishment and repairs required to complete the voyage safely; this port is likely to fall within the terms of rr.X and XI so that fuel, wages and port charges can be considered and allowed in the usual way.

That the payment of ransom to pirates may be the subject of contribution by all **A.68** parties to the common adventure has appeared to be acceptable to commercial interests since the time of Justinian.[80] The principle has found its way into legislation in many countries[81] although some have made payment of ransoms illegal, generally in order to meet shore-based concerns about organised crime. Under English law payment of ransom per se has not been illegal since the repeal of the 1782 Ransom Act.

However this remains a delicate area involving issues of public policy and legality. Detailed discussion of these issues in the context of a sue and labour claim can be found in *Arnould's Law of Marine Insurance*[82] and in *Royal Boskalis Westminster v Mountain*. These matters were also more recently considered in connection with a claim for an Actual Total Loss under a policy on cargo aboard the "Bunga Melati Dua"[82A] when she was captured by pirates off Somalia in August 2008. The cargo interests tendered notice of abandonment to their insurers but, following payment of a ransom, the vessel was released shortly afterwards, reaching destination in late October 2008. The cargo was sound but had missed the seasonal market and the assured claimed an actual total loss on the basis of having been irretrievably deprived of the goods at the moment of seizure. Unsurprisingly, given the well established pattern in Somali cases of seizure and subsequent release, this argument failed in the High Court and on Appeal. However, part of the claimants' subsidiary argument is relevant to the present topic. It was contended that although payment of ransom was not illegal it was a submission to extortion and was therefore against the public interest such that it should be no part of the Assured's duty under s.78(4) of the Marine Insurance Act 1906 to preserve his property from loss by paying a ransom. If payment of ransom could not be required it followed that the cargo was an Actual Total Loss when seized. In the Court of Appeal, Lord Justice Rix acknowledged that these were "morally muddied waters" but considered there was nothing at present to prompt the Courts to state that the payment of ransom should be regarded as a matter that was wholly unacceptable and undeserving of legal recognition. With reference to the Bribery Act of 2010 (at that time yet to come into force) he also distinguished between payment of ransom and payment of a bribe to obtain an improper

[80] See para.60.05.
[81] See s.706.6 of the German Commercial Code.
[82] Arnould, *Law of Marine Insurance*, 17th edn, para.913A.
[82A] *Masefield AG v Amlin Corporate Member Ltd* [2011] EWCA Civ 24.

advantage, stating it is common ground here that payment of a ransom is not illegal, whereas bribery or constructive bribery may well be.

A distinction may also exist between the initial payment of a ransom and the subsequent contribution to the resulting general average. The question of legality may be more difficult if the captors are an overtly political or terrorist organisation, given the extensive modern legislation prohibiting financial support for such entities. Where the payment of a ransom is illegal in the jurisdiction(s) of the parties to the adventure it is difficult to see how any right of contribution could be enforced.[83]

Kidnap of crews

A.69 In addition to stealing a vessel and its cargo, pirates may often detain the crew as an additional bargaining counter when making ransom demands or to deter close pursuit. It might therefore be argued that the expense of the search and recovery operations should be divided pro-rata on some basis to reflect the saving of life and property. Phillips L.J. in Royal Boskalis rejected a similar argument, citing the example of *The Bosworth (No.3)*[84] in which it was held that salvors who save lives as well as property may have their award enhanced to reflect that fact, but nonetheless property insurers bear the whole cost. There may be circumstances in which the crew are held to ransom separately, in which case this principle would not apply.

Sacrifices of Ship

A.70 The variety of ship's sacrifices which can occur is of necessity so considerable that many instances are not directly covered by previous decisions of the courts or by any of the specific provisions of the numbered rules of the York-Antwerp Rules. In such cases average adjusters rely upon the principles underlying the law and practice of general average and upon "custom" (using the word in its popular rather than in its legal sense). The "custom" of average adjusters carries no weight in litigation if the court considers that it conflicts with principle. Nevertheless where no such conflict arises or in case of doubt, there is, as Lowndes pointed out: "a natural tendency–difficult indeed to be reckoned on, since it is naturally stronger in some judges than others–to pay a sort of prima facie respect to such customs, as presumably falling in with the wishes and perhaps requirements of mercantile men."[85]

A.71 Lowndes stated the principle to be applied in the following terms:

[83] See for example *Regazzoni v KC Selthia* (1958) A.C. 301.

[84] *The Bosworth (No.3)* (1962) I.L.R. 483.

[85] 4th edn, p.112. "A general practice", says Lord Blackburn, "long continued amongst English adjusters, affords strong ground for thinking that the practice is one which is not in general inconvenient, and it throws a considerable onus on those who impugn it to show that the particular circumstances are such as to render an adherence to the practice in that case against principle": *Svendsen v Wallace* (1885) 10 A.C. 404 at 416. See also the judgments in *Balmoral S.S. Co v Marten* [1902] A.C. 511, as to the desirability of upholding a long-established practice of average adjusters.

> "The principle which underlies most if not all these matters of ordinary practice may be expressed as follows: while it is the duty of the master under his contract to apply each part of his ship and tackling to its proper uses in carrying on his voyage, without regard to the more or less of exposure to danger which the doing so may involve,[86] he is not bound to destroy any of them, nor to abuse any–understanding by this term 'abuse' the using it for purposes for which it was not intended nor constructed, and which, therefore, expose it to an extraordinary risk.[87] If he does so, he does it as general average, i.e. under an implied contract with all those whose property he shall bring into safety by so doing, that any loss he thereby incurs shall be made good by the contribution of all."

Cutting away to clear collision

A schooner, drifting in a strong tideway, was carried under the hawse of a ship at anchor and, the ship's bowsprit catching the stay between the two masts of the schooner, the latter was pressed over so as to be in danger of capsizing, to prevent which the schooner's masts were cut away. This was treated as general average. **A.72**

Two vessels, both at anchor, were in collision, and in attempting to get clear the anchor of one of them was hove up, but found to have hooked the chain of the other; whereupon, to get clear and avoid a second collision, the anchor was slipped. This was treated as general average.

Anchors and cables suddenly let go

An anchor is normally dropped only when the vessel has lost nearly all way, and its sole intended purpose is to hold the vessel in a certain position; it is not designed to serve as a brake.[88] If, therefore, an anchor is let go without the usual preparations in order to check the vessel and avoid some sudden danger, such as an impending collision or running aground, and in consequence the cable breaks, the loss is in practice treated as general average. However, the full facts relating to any such claim must be carefully ascertained, as it is not unknown for anchor cables to part from accidental or other causes. **A.73**

Anchors and cables slipped in efforts to refloat

When a vessel runs aground, her anchors will sometimes be carried out and dropped in deep water astern to serve as ground tackle to prevent the vessel riding further up the reef or beach and. at the appropriate time, to heave upon and haul the vessel clear of the strand. At the moment of refloating, it is occasionally necessary to slip the anchors. If they are not recovered, the loss is allowed as general average provided that the vessel was in a position of peril when aground. **A.74**

[86] See *Covington v Roberts* (1806) 2 Bos. & P.N.R. 378 (para.A.60, above).

[87] See *Birkley v Presgrave* (1801) 1 East 220 (para.A.77, below); *The Bona* [1895] P. 125 (para.7.03, below).

[88] But an anchor may be so used to enable a vessel to manoeuvre at slow speed with full engine-power.

Anchors and cables slipped in an emergency

A.75 It is possible for a vessel at anchor to slip the anchor and cable to avoid some impending danger such as collision or a typhoon. When this action is taken in the appropriate circumstances of real danger to the common adventure, the loss should, on principle, be allowed as general average.

On the particular facts ruling in *Hamel v P&O Steam Navigation Co*,[89] Lord Alverstone C.J. decided that the slipping of an anchor (afterwards recovered) was not a general average act but it is submitted that this decision does not necessarily conflict with the principle enunciated in the paragraph above. The following extract is taken from Commercial Cases, but the facts and judgment are variously reported in the different reports:

> "... the vessel, within a few minutes after leaving her berth to proceed on her voyage, got into difficulties, and for an hour or thereabouts she was engaged in endeavouring to avoid perils of the river. The vessel swung up in consequence of the tide catching her stern; she was in danger of colliding with a vessel higher up; and she had to slip her anchor to avoid collision with some other craft ... The slipping of the anchor, which was to some extent relied upon, was not a general average act; it was an ordinary measure taken in the ordinary course of navigation–a measure taken to avoid danger, and not a sacrifice of the anchor in the sense in which that word is used in general average cases. Moreover, the anchor was recovered afterwards."

Anchors and cables slipped because foul

A.76 Anchors slipped when a vessel is in peril because they become "foul"–that is, held fast by some obstruction under water, such as a rock or some other anchors or chains, are allowable as general average only when it was likely that the obstruction was of a temporary nature, so that the anchor might have been cleared if it had not been dangerous to wait. If the anchor was incapable of ever been freed, the slipping of the cable did not involve any sacrifice.

Jury-rig and analogous cases

A.77 A very ancient custom related to jury-rig. When a ship's mast or rudder was carried away, and a "jury" or "temporary" mast or rudder was fitted up at sea as a substitute, the value of the materials cut up or destroyed for the purpose such as spare spars or ropes, together with any damage done to the hull of the ship by cutting or adapting it to the purpose, was in practice treated as general average.

This practice is in accordance with the decision in *Birkley v Presgrave*,[90] so far as the articles thus used are applied to different uses from those for which they were originally intended.

[89] *Hamel v P&O Steam Navigation Co* [1908] 2 K.B. 298; 77 L.J.K.B. 637; 98 L.T. 861; 24 T.L.R. 535; 13 Com. Cas. 270; 11 Asp.M.C. 71.

[90] *Birkley v Presgrave* (1801) 1 East 220; see also *The Bona* [1895] P. 125.

Damage done in getting ship clear

On the same principle, damage done to a ship by the means taken to get her off a shore, or clear of a collision, or otherwise out of a situation of imminent danger, may frequently give rise to a claim for general average. For example if, after a ship has run aground, one of her boats is launched to carry out a hawser in order to heave her off, or otherwise to assist in floating her, and the boat is swamped or injured in the attempt, this damage is treated as general average; not so if the boat were got out merely to save the lives of the passengers or crew.[91] **A.78**

Damage done to ship by efforts to refloat

Damage done to the ship in heaving her afloat, such as hawsers broken, damage to anchors and chains,[92] a windlass or winch strained, or other damage directly caused to the ship's upperworks or bottom by the strain used, is general average. It may sometimes be difficult to distinguish between damage caused by having been on the ground, and by pulling off, but where this distinction can properly be drawn, the damage to the bottom caused by the efforts to refloat is clearly allowable as general average.[93] **A.79**

Damage to ship by discharging cargo

If a ship is damaged in the act of discharging cargo whilst aground or at a port of refuge, for example, where barges range against the ship's side, or if the hatches are damaged from the necessity of unusual haste, it seems clear that, provided the cost of discharging belongs to general average, this damage should be treated in the same way. In *The Felix*[94] damage to a vessel's propeller by timber jettisoned from on deck for the common safety was allowed in general average, although loss of the timber was disallowed under the York-Antwerp Rules 1890. **A.80**

Damage to ship by collision with salving vessel

If a tug, coming alongside a ship to render a salvage service, does damage to her upper works as may fairly be regarded as the natural consequence of approaching the vessel at such a time, the damage is, in practice, treated as general average.[95] **A.81**

Use of flares, etc.; damage to fenders and pumps

Flares used as signals of distress, or fenders put out to prevent collision, and smashed, or damage to the pumps caused by the stress of pumping a leaky ship, **A.82**

[91] See, however, the dictum as to sacrifices made in fear of death, para.A.21, above.
[92] *Roberts v The Ocean Star* (1860) Fed. Cas. 11908.
[93] See also York-Antwerp r.VII.
[94] *The Felix* (1927) A.M.C. 844.
[95] cf. *Australian Coastal Shipping Commission v Green* [1971] 1 Q.B. 456.

have not been treated as general average[96] : for that is the very purpose for which such things are carried in the ship. Fire extinguishers are considered in para.3.16, below.

Cutting away a cable

A.83 If a cable is cut in order that it may be used for a purpose for which it was not intended and such cutting and use are to meet an emergency which threatens the whole adventure, this is a general average sacrifice.

In *Birkley v Presgrave*[97] the Argo, bound for Sunderland, was, whilst entering that port, caught by a sudden squall, which rendered it necessary to let go the anchor. She was fastened with a warp to the South Pier, in order to secure her from the storm; but the warp soon parted. More cable was then paid away, and the ship was permitted to drive alongside the North Pier, to which she was made fast with hawser ends and towing lines, which were proper ropes, and such as were usually provided and employed for that purpose. Fearing that another ship would be adrift and come down upon the Argo, the master cut the cable, and therewith moored the Argo to the pier; and this he did for the preservation of the ship and cargo. Whilst they were so fastening her with the cable, the other ropes, through the violence of the storm and by another ship driving down upon the Argo, broke.

On these facts, however, the owner of the ship claimed as general average the value of the cable thus cut, and also that of the hawsers and towing lines. At the trial, the counsel for the plaintiff withdrew the demand in respect of the damage to the hawser-ends and towing lines, admitting that these were not claimable, as having only been applied to the ordinary purposes for which such things are provided: but claimed the cable, which had been "appropriated to a different use from what it was originally intended for, and which contributed to the preservation of the ship and cargo". This claim was admitted by the court. Lord Kenyon C.J. said:

> "All ordinary loss and damage sustained by the ship, happening immediately from the storm or perils of the seas, must be borne by the shipowners; but all those articles which were made use of by the master and crew upon the particular emergency, and out of the ordinary course, for the benefit of the whole concern, and the other expenses incurred, must be paid proportionably by the defendant as general average."

Damage caused by fighting

A.84 Damage so caused is probably not a general average loss, at all events if a ship is specially equipped to fight.

In *Taylor v Curtis*[98] the ship Hibernia on her voyage to St Thomas, was attacked by a privateer. She resisted, and a severe engagement ensued. The privateer was

[96] Where pumps were put to an abnormal use, as to pump out water impregnated with acid from the cargo, the damage was allowed in the US: see the 8th edn of this work, p.298.

[97] *Birkley v Presgrave* (1801) 1 East 220.

[98] *Taylor v Curtis* (1815) 4 Camp. 337 and on appeal (1816) 6 Taunt. 608.

beaten off, and the Hibernia delivered her cargo safe to the consignees. A claim as general average was made for damage sustained in her hull and rigging by the enemy's shot, for the cost of curing the seamen's wounds, and for gunpowder and shot expended. Gibbs C.J. decided against the claim.

> "The measure of resisting the privateer was for the general benefit, but it was part of the adventure. No particular part of the property was voluntarily sacrificed for the protection of the rest. The losses fell where the fortune of war cast them, and there it seems to me they ought to rest."[99]

This decision has been much questioned. Damage, says Benecke, which is the consequence of a determination to resist, may be looked upon as damage voluntarily sustained; the defence is intended for the preservation of the whole.[100] The argument that it was the duty of the crew to fight, says Phillips, proves too much; it is their duty to cut away a mast in case of need, or to make any sacrifice that may be requisite for the safety of ship and cargo.[101] It is however, not so easy to resist the argument from analogy with carrying a press of sail. If a ship sails on her voyage provided with guns and ammunition sufficient to resist an enemy, these are provided for that purpose and no other: and the use or expenditure of them, more or less, for their appropriate purpose, is not regarded as the subject of general average. The ship being so equipped, again, is surely a notice to the crew that they are hired to fight in case of need, and not merely to navigate the ship. **A.85**

Although armed guards may be carried in some areas where piracy is a particular threat, the days of the armed merchant vessel referred to in the above paragraphs have long since past.

As a matter of first principles, if a Master deliberately runs his vessel aground when under attack so that it is no longer of value as a target for ransom or theft, causing the pirates to withdraw, it is suggested that any grounding damage would fall within the terms of r.A and r.V (voluntary stranding). More difficult questions arise where a Master attempts to escape from pirates by steaming away at full speed or making evasive manoeuvers; during this time the vessel's superstructure may be damaged by the pirates' weapons as they try and force it to stop.

Unless the circumstances are exceptional it may be difficult in practice to distinguish between a level of damage that is an intrinsic part of such an incident and a more severe level that was intentionally sustained for the common safety. Further, although not armed as in the sailing ship days, those involved with a vessel passing through a known piracy area would expect some evasive measures to be taken by the vessel and might not consider this to be an extra-ordinary abuse of the vessel in this context.

[99] This passage from the judgment of Gibbs C.J. was cited and applied by Sankey J. in *Société Nouvelle D'Armement v Spillers & Bakers* [1917] 1 K.B. 865.

[100] *Benecke*, p.231.

[101] *Phillips*, para.1310.

Sacrifices of Cargo

A.86 In *McCall v Houlder*,[102] a ship having sustained damage to her propeller, was towed into a port of refuge where the cargo, which was perishable, could not be stored. In order to repair the propeller with the cargo on board she was tipped and, in consequence of the tipping, part of the cargo was damaged by seawater. Mathew J. held that the tipping was resorted to for the preservation of the ship and cargo and was a general average act and that the damage to the cargo being incidental thereto, although not contemplated, was a general average loss. There may, however, be cases where such damage is too remote, being caused by some extraneous and unforeseen event.

Cargo damaged by flooding of hold

A.87 Damage caused to cargo when the master flooded the hold following an accidental stranding, to steady the vessel upon the rocks to prevent pounding and the consequent break up of the ship, would be treated as general average.[103]

Cargo given as salvage

A.88 Should cargo be sacrificed by being given in kind as salvage for the entire property, such a sacrifice would be treated as general average.[104]

Cargo sold or pledged to raise funds

A.89 Cargo may also be sacrificed by being sold or pledged in order to raise funds in a port of refuge, when the owners of the ship and cargo are unable or unwilling to supply the sum needed for the purpose of releasing the ship from her obligations at such port and thereby enabling her to proceed on her voyage.

This case, however, is involved in complications which properly belong to a larger subject, namely the treatment of loss and expense incurred in order to raise funds required for general average purposes. This is dealt with under r.XX.

Partial loss of cargo by putting into port of refuge

A.90 The case of *Anglo-Argentine Live Stock Agency v Temperley S.S. Co*[105] provides an unusual example of a sacrifice of cargo. The facts were that the Edenbridge took on board in the River Plate a deck cargo of cattle and sheep for Britain, under a contract which provided that the vessel should on no account touch at any

[102] *McCall v Houlder* (1897) 2 Com. Cas. 129. cf. *Gage v Libby* (1867) 14 Allen (Mass.) 261, where wastage of a cargo of ice caused by opening the hold in order to renew a mast at a port of refuge was allowed in general average.

[103] *Pacific Mail S.S. Co v Dupre* (1896) 74 Fed. Rep. 250.

[104] On the same principle, where cargo is voluntarily given up to pirates by way of composition, the sacrifice is a subject for contribution: *Hicks v Palington* (1590) Moore 297. See also paras A.65–A.69, above.

[105] *Anglo-Argentine Live Stock Agency v Temperley S.S. Co* [1899] 2 Q.B. 403.

Brazilian or European Continental ports before landing her livestock. Soon after sailing she sprang a leak, and as the water could not be kept down, the master put into Bahia, a Brazilian port, for repairs. The consequence was that, by reason of an Order in Council then in force, the cattle could not be landed in Britain and they were taken instead to Antwerp where they realised much lower prices than they would have fetched in Britain. Bigham J. held that the owners of the livestock were entitled to recover in general average the difference in prices as a loss which was the direct and immediate consequence of the general average act. "The moment the vessel touched the Brazilian port", he said, "the plaintiffs' property was ipso facto rendered of less value than it was before, because by that act the plaintiffs were deprived of one of their means, and that the best, of realising their property."

Sacrifice of Goods not included in Bills of Lading or Cargo Manifests

The question, whether goods which are not shipped as cargo must be contributed for if they are sacrificed, does not appear to be covered by express authority. **A.91** On the other hand, the rule seems established in practice that any kind of property which is preserved from destruction must contribute unless there be some special reason for exempting it.[106] Arnould stated that the jettison of goods for which there is no bill of lading gives no claim to contribution.[107] He only cited foreign authorities, and probably had in his mind the case of a clandestine shipment in fraud of the shipowner, in which case the disallowance of contribution may well be justified.[108] With this exception, however, there is no valid reason for refusing contribution on the ground that no bill of lading has been given for the goods, if it be proved that they were sacrificed or damaged by a general average act.

Miscellaneous Property

Passengers' baggage and effects

The question whether passengers are entitled to contribution for the sacrifice of their effects has not been litigated in this country, and instances of such sacrifice **A.92** seem to have been too rare to give rise to any settled practice. It may be argued that as passengers' baggage is not made to contribute when saved, it ought not to be contributed for when sacrificed. The argument founded on the want of reciprocity does not appear to be convincing.

The contrary view was admirably expressed by Brown D.J. in an American case,[109] in which he held that there is a right of contribution for passengers'

[106] See para.17.19, below.

[107] Arnould, 2nd edn, p.904; but see *British Shipping Laws*, Vol.10; Arnould, *Marine Insurance*, 15th edn, para.929.

[108] Most of the foreign codes do not allow contribution for the sacrifice of goods, unless the captain has given a bill of lading for them or declared them in the manifest, and one of the authorities cited by Arnould is para.420 of the French Code de Commerce, which contains a provision to this effect. See also York-Antwerp r.XIX.

[109] *Heye v North German Lloyd* (1887) 33 Fed. Rep. 60.

baggage. His decision on this question, the only one raised on appeal, was affirmed by the Circuit Court of Appeals.[110]

He also came to the conclusion that passengers' baggage in the baggage compartment is liable to contribute, but it is clear that, even if he had formed a different opinion on that part of the case, his decision that passengers' baggage must be contributed for would not have been affected and it is submitted that on this point his judgment is correct.

Crew's effects

A.93 It can hardly be doubted that the master and crew are entitled to contribution for the sacrifice of their effects, and their right is generally recognised by the foreign codes. The "reciprocity" argument has little or no weight in their case; and their exemption from contribution may be explained on the ground that they have done their share towards the preservation of the ship by their personal efforts,[111] and also as regards their wearing apparel on the ground that it may be considered as attached to the person, which is not a contributory interest.[112]

5. Necessity for Reasonableness

A.94 According to the statutory definition and r.A, the sacrifice or expenditure must have been reasonably made.

In the case of sacrifice, one hopes, for instance, that it will be the low-valued cargo in the lower hold, which will be selected for jettison, rather than the valuable general cargo in the tweendeck, though by its very stowage and the greater ease with which it can be lifted out of the hold, the valuable general cargo is likely to be the first to be jettisoned. The master, as the person on the spot and in the agony of the moment, should be—and generally is—credited with the benefit of any doubt as to the wisdom of his actions, provided that a real peril exists; hindsight and the superior wisdom of the desk-bound operative should be ignored. Reference may be made to the remarks of Cockburn C.J. in *Corry v Coulthard*[113] quoted in para.A.32, above and of Hobhouse J. in *Corfu Navigation Co v Mobil Shipping Co Ltd*[114] with regard to the reasonableness of the courses of action taken by the respective masters.

A.95 The same principle holds good in the case of expenditure, except that here one may encounter the additional problem that some suppliers of labour and services choose to exploit a casualty and their charges rise accordingly. Thus, a party called upon to contribute to general average expenditure may seek to challenge the claim

[110] (1887) 36 Fed. Rep. 705. A lengthy extract from the judgment was quoted in para.A.94 of the 11th edn.
[111] Per Brown D.J. in *Heye v North German Lloyd*, fn.102, above.
[112] See para.17.79, below.
[113] *Corry v Coulthard*, Unreported December 21, 1876, Exch. Div.; January 17, 1877, CA.
[114] *Corfu Navigation Co v Mobil Shipping Co Ltd* [1991] 2 Lloyd's Rep. 515.

not only on the grounds that it was unreasonable for the master to adopt the measures which resulted in the expenditure but also on the grounds that the amount of the expenditure is itself unreasonable. With regard to the latter point it is clear that contribution can only be recovered in respect of such amount as was reasonably incurred, and that if the master or shipowner agree to pay an excessive sum, contribution can only be recovered in respect of the amount which it would have been reasonable to pay, and not towards the excess.

Thus, in *Anderson v Ocean S.S. Co*[115] the owners of cargo carried on board the Achilles refused to pay the full amount of general average claimed from them in respect of towage expenses, on the grounds that the amount paid by the shipowner to the towage contractor was exorbitant and the shipowner was only bound to pay a reasonable sum (or if he had agreed to pay an exorbitant sum he could not charge the cargo with the excess). In delivering the judgment of the House of Lords, Lord Blackburn said[116] : **A.96**

> "But I think there is neither reason nor authority for saying that the whole amount which the owners of the ship choose to pay is. as a matter of law to be charged to general average. And though I quite agree that there is some evidence here that the Achilles and her cargo were both in danger, and were both saved by the services of the Shanghai, and though I also agree that it is not a question of law whether the amount of the sum charged as a disbursement was exorbitant or not, still I cannot find that any question as to the amount was submitted to the jury."

A new trial was therefore ordered, since no question as the reasonableness of the amount paid had been put to the jury. The shipowner, who had paid £2,691.19.6d. to the towage contractor, contended that this was fixed under the terms of his agreement with the contractor. Upon the first trial, the case proceeded to the House of Lords apparently upon the footing that the jury had determined this question in favour of the shipowner, and all that was lacking was any finding as to the reasonableness of the shipowner's conduct. One the retrial, however, the jury found that there was no binding agreement between the shipowner and contractor which fixed the remuneration, and that the shipowners obligation was to pay a reasonable sum, which they determined to be £1,500. It was therefore to this reduced sum of £1,500, rather than the £2,691 paid by the shipowner, that cargo was finally held liable to contribute. For the full history of the retrial of this unusually hard-fought case see: (1885) 1 T.L.R. 324 at 413 and 615, and (1886) 2 T.L.R. 537 and 859.

In *Australian Coastal Shipping Commission v Green*[117] Lord Denning M.R. summarised the effect of the case as follows:

> "If the master of the Achilles agreed to pay an exorbitant charge, such that he ought never, in justice to the cargo-owners, to have agreed to, then the excess of the charge

[115] *Anderson v Ocean S.S. Co* (1884) 10 A.C. 107, HL, reversing sub nom. *Ocean S.S. Co v Anderson* (1883) 13 Q.B.D. 651.

[116] *Anderson v Ocean S.S. Co* (1884) 10 A.C. 107 at 117.

[117] *Australian Coastal Shipping Commission v Green* [1971] 1 Q.B. 456 at 483. See also *The Gratitudine* 3 Ch. Rob. 240 at 277.

(over and above a reasonable charge) would not flow from the general average act, but from the onerous clause which the master had agreed to. The only amount allowable as a 'general average loss' would be a reasonable charge."

It is submitted that, in determining what is a reasonable charge, it is the conduct of the shipowner or master, in all the circumstances and pressures of the casualty, which must be considered, rather than the conduct of the contractor who demanded the charge, and it is irrelevant that in other circumstances the same services might have been acquired at a much lower price. Thus, in *The Gratitudine*[118] the master hypothecated ship and cargo to a moneylender on most onerous terms, but since he had no practical alternative but to accept the contract, the loss under it was held to be general average.

Historical Development and Practice of Rule A

York-Antwerp Rules 1924

A.97 As originally drafted in 1924, r.A comprised two paragraphs (as it does in 1994), but upon discussion at Stockholm it was considered advisable that the two paragraphs should be separated and constitute individual rules (A and B). This was reportedly to avoid any misapprehension concerning the treatment of general average losses and expenditure specifically provided for by the numbered rules but not falling within the definition of general average contained in the first paragraph. (In fact, just such a misapprehension occurred in the *Makis* case.[119])

York-Antwerp Rules 1950 and 1974

A.98 No change, the two original paragraphs continuing their separate existence as rr.A and B.

York-Antwerp Rules 1994

A.99 To provide room for a new r.B on tug and tow without upsetting the existing order of the Rules, the previous rr.A and B were combined as two separate paragraphs in the latest r.A.

The first paragraph remains with its tried and tested wording, and the second paragraph also survives with only the most minor change to preserve an uniformity of wording within the same rule. To conform to the use of the word "expenditure" in the first paragraph, the word expenses in the second paragraph was similarly expressed as expenditures.

[118] *The Gratitudine* 3 Ch. Rob. 240 at 272-276.
[119] *Vlassopoulos v British & Foreign Marine Insurance Co Ltd* [1929] 1 K.B. 187.

First paragraph

The wording of this paragraph of r.A is clearly based upon and follows very closely the English statutory definition of a general average act[120] but the definitions which prevailed under the laws of leading maritime nations are given in generally similar terms. **A.100**

The reasons why the Stockholm Conference in 1924 selected the word "intentionally", rather than "voluntarily" to define the general average act have already been described earlier in para.A.08, above. **A.101**

Much discussion also ensued on the selection of the proper words to imply that the common safety of the adventure was the only justification for an act being treated as general average. The view has sometimes been expressed that the principle of common safety is peculiarly a British one and that other nations are inclined to widen the scope of general average so as to justify the inclusion as general average of acts performed merely for the benefit of the adventure, without the element of a common peril being present. No one at the conference, however, expressed any desire to widen the definition of general average so as to include in its scope losses or expenses other than those arising from an intention to save the common adventure from a common peril. In the end not only were the words "for the common safety" inserted in the definition, but the principle implied by these words was further emphasised by continuing with the phrase "for the purpose of preserving from peril the property involved in a common maritime adventure". The numbered rules dealing with "common benefit" could be seen as being consistent with this definition in that they are incurred as part of measures taken to ensure that the vessel will not be placed in peril if she puts to sea again to complete the voyage, so that they are part of a process of "preserving from peril". Alternatively, the usual and probably better view is to consider these numbered Rules as drawing their effect not from the r.A definition but as exceptions to this and other lettered Rules, that have been expressly agreed in the interests of international uniformity.

As regards the degree of imminence of the peril to avert which the sacrifice is made, the feeling of the Stockholm Conference was clearly in favour of not restricting the operations of general average only to cases in which the danger was immediate or imminent. This was emphasised by several of the representatives present and it is quite clear that the definition finally agreed upon was intended to imply that although the danger must be such as to threaten the common safety, it is not necessary that it be immediately pending. In so deciding, the Conference took the view which is generally held in all countries. **A.102**

York-Antwerp Rules 2004

No change, apart from the numbering of the paragraphs. **A.103**

[120] See para.A.06, above.

A.104 **RULE A**

(*1*) There is a general average act when, and only when, any extraordinary sacrifice or expenditure is intentionally and reasonably made or incurred for the common safety for the purpose of preserving from peril the property involved in a common maritime adventure.

(*2*) General average sacrifices and expenditures shall be borne by the different contributing interests on the basis hereinafter provided.

CONSTRUCTION

First Paragraph

A.105 **"general average act":** The five essential features necessary to constitute a general average act (intentional; peril (common safety); common maritime adventure; extraordinary (sacrifice or expenditure); reasonable) have each been discussed earlier, and antecedent references will be quoted again in this short section on the construction of each of these terms.

"when, and only when": In point of law these words seem to add little to the corresponding "where" of the Marine Insurance Act 1906, s.66(2), so far as English law is concerned; they are no doubt used for the sake of clarity and emphasis, and an attempt to have them removed as mere surplusage in 1994 was defeated.

"extraordinary": See paras A.59 to A.60, above.

A.106 **"sacrifice or expenditure": A general average act may take the form of either or both:**

(1) a *sacrifice* of physical property (for example the jettison of cargo and the freight attaching thereto, or the damage to a ship's engines sustained in efforts to refloat after stranding);

(2) an *expenditure* of money for the purchase of services to extricate the vessel and her cargo, etc. from the peril (for example for the hire of tugs to refloat a stranded vessel, or of lighters and labour to off-load cargo in similar circumstances, or of port or refuge expenses, etc.).

"intentionally": See paras A.08 to A.19, above.

A.107 **"reasonably":** See paras A.94 to A.96, above, also the commentary on the Rule Paramount in paras PRE.21 to PRE.26. However, for general average adjustments still subject to the York-Antwerp Rules 1974 (or even 1950 or 1924). it should be noted that the requirement that sacrifices and expenditures should be reasonably made or incurred applies solely to those claimable only under the lettered Rules (for example, a jettison of cargo[121] or damage to the bottom of a ship sustained in

[121] See also para.1.01, below.

efforts to refloat when aground and in a position of peril[122] under r.A, or substituted expenses under r.F). Claims under the numbered rules, in the absence of express wording[123] therein requiring it, are not subject to this requirement of reasonableness.

This was decided in the case of the Alpha.[124] The judgment was probably technically correct, but it was unwelcome, and accounted for the introduction of the Rule Paramount in 1994.

"intentionally and reasonably made or incurred": Both the adverbs apply to each of the verbs and thus the sacrifice "must be made or expenditure incurred intentionally and made or incurred reasonably".[125] A.108

The intention must be to preserve from peril, not merely to perform the act of sacrifice.[126] The rule does not specify by whom the sacrifice must be made or expenditure incurred and there is no decision on the point.[127] In the absence of any indication from the wording of the rule the common law will apply and it is suggested that the actor need not be the master. See paras A.10 to A.19.

"for the common safety": See paras A.20 to A.35, above, and note also that the meaning of these words is really defined by the remainder of the rule, but they are important because they occur in a number of the other rules as a shorter and more convenient phrase than "for the purpose of preserving from peril the property involved in a common maritime adventure". It should be noted that the phrase refers to the physical safety of the property and not to the successful conclusion of the voyage,[128] although in *McCall v Houlder*[129] the distinction seems not to have been very closely observed. A.109

"for the purpose of preserving from peril the property involved in a common maritime adventure": The peril need not be immediate, but it must be real and not imaginary. It is probably not enough that the act should be done in order to secure the general safety of all shipping in a given area, even though this includes the common adventure. The act must be specifically designed to secure the particular safety of the particular adventure.[130] A.110

"common maritime adventure": See paras A.51–A.58, above, also r.B.

[122] See also para.7.01, below.

[123] Rule XVIII mentions "reasonable cost of repairing" and "reasonable depreciation"; r.X(c) has "including insurance if reasonably incurred", while rr.XI(a) and (b) mentions "wages and maintenance of . . . crew reasonably incurred".

[124] *Corfu Navigation Co v Mobil Shipping Co Ltd* [1991] 2 Lloyd's Rep. 515.

[125] *Athel Line Ltd v Liverpool and London War Risks Insurance Association Ltd* [1944] K.B. 87 at 93, per Tucker J. In *The Seapool* [1934] P. 53 at 64, Langton J. seemed to incline to the view that "intentionally" only applied to "sacrifice . . . made".

[126] *Daniolos v Bunge & Co Ltd* (1937) 59 Ll.L. Rep. 175 at 180; affirmed (1938) 62 Ll.L. Rep. 65, CA.

[127] It was argued but not decided in *Athel Line Ltd v Liverpool and London War Risks Insurance Association Ltd* [1944] K.B. 87; cf. *Australian Coastal Shipping Commission v Green*, above.

[128] Contrast the phrase "For the safe prosecution of the voyage" in r.X(b).

[129] *McCall v Houlder* (1897) 66 L.J.Q.B. 408; 2 Com. Cas. 127. See para.A.24, above.

[130] *Athel Line Ltd v Liverpool and London War Risks Insurance Association Ltd* [1944] K.B. 87 at 95.

Second Paragraph

A.111 The second paragraph seems to give rise to no problems of construction. In both 1974 and 1994 it was suggested that it was superfluous and in 1994 it was proposed that it should therefore be deleted. However, this received no real support.

"different contributing interests": These are considered when dealing with r.XVII.

RULE B

TUG AND TOW

ENGLISH BACKGROUND AND FOREIGN LAW

The commentary on the preceding r.A dealt at length with the essential features necessary to constitute a general average act, and these included the requirement that there be a common maritime adventure involving more interests than one[1] whose safety was threatened by a situation of peril. **B.01**

A ship and the cargo she carries are necessarily involved in a common adventure, but what of the situation where a tug is towing or pushing one or more barges, an oil rig or other craft, on any of which there may or may not be cargo? Are they all engaged in a common adventure, and does a peril affecting one unit of the flotilla involve them all in a common general average?

Clearly the towage contract and/or the conditions of carriage must be closely examined for special provision regarding general average and unusual situations on the voyage[2] , but it is submitted that, unless there be independent commanders on board the various units of a linked flotilla, each capable of making independent decisions and giving effect thereto, all units and the cargoes they carry are engaged in a common maritime adventure which could be subject to a collective general average. However, the more important question of which units should contribute to a general average will depend upon which units, when linked together,[3] are imperilled by the same common danger. Furthermore, in the majority of tug and tow cases the alleged general average act is a disconnection of one or more units of the flotilla, and in such cases it is necessary to consider whether the disconnection is a sacrifice. It should not be so regarded unless the chances of survival of the disconnected unit are lessened, for example by lack of motive power or personnel on board.

[1] See para.A.54, above.

[2] All towage contracts have provisions affecting liability. See for example *The A Turtle* [2008] EWCH 3034; [2009] 1 Lloyd's Rep. 177. BIMCO towage terms. See also *The Key Singapore* [2004] EWCH 2227; [2005] 1 Lloyd's Rep. 91.

[3] Contrast the different approach which applies under the York-Antwerp Rules; para.B.14, below.

B.02 There is no reported English decision on the subject, and those in other jurisdictions are few in number and of rather doubtful authority. Before considering them, therefore, we shall examine some practical examples which, it is hoped, will illustrate some of the problems which arise and the principles which should be applied in resolving them.

1. A single barge under tow is holed and leaking badly after striking a rock or a passing vessel, but the tug is not herself in danger as a result of the incident. Measures taken to save the barge and her cargo will be general average as between those interests, but the tug will not contribute, since she is not imperilled. Even if the tug was imperilled by the accident (for example the barge was sinking in deep water and the tug was in danger of being dragged under) disconnection of the towing line would not be a sacrifice because it would not further reduce the small or non-existent chances of saving the barge.
2. One of a flotilla of barges runs aground in sheltered waters and cannot be freed by the tug, but the tug and the remaining barges are not in danger. Measures taken to save the grounded barge and her cargo will not be contributed to by the tug and the remaining barges. If the grounding occurs in exposed or dangerous waters with the result that the other units are imperilled, and the grounded barge is cast off, it must be considered, before concluding that the disconnection is a sacrifice, whether the grounded barge is in a worse situation as a result.
3. If an oil rig or other large structure is being towed by two or more tugs, an accident to one of those tugs is unlikely to place the other tug(s) or the tow in any peril, and they would not contribute to the general average–if any–on the damaged tug.
4. A complete main engine breakdown on the high seas of the (single) tug is the most likely situation where a common peril affecting the entire flotilla might exist. If the barge or tow can be detached and lie or anchor in safety until the tug has repaired at a port of refuge and returned to resume the voyage, the barge or tow should not be called on to contribute to any general average on the tug. However, if the barge or tow cannot be left in safety unattended and must be taken together with the tug to a port of refuge, it would appear correct that the whole flotilla and their cargoes should contribute to the general average expenses incurred.
5. On occasion, a severe storm and heavy seas could threaten the safety of both the tug and her tow, and the tug may cast the tow adrift, hoping perhaps to pick it up again when the weather abates, but with the prospect that she may not be able then to find the tow and that it may either sink or drift ashore.

From the point of principle, this perhaps is the most difficult situation. If by casting the tow adrift, both units stand an equally better chance of surviving the storm, it is submitted that there is no "sacrifice" and that anything which subsequently causes loss to either of them during the temporary suspension of the common adventure is a loss particular to the unit sustaining it, and not to be contributed to as general average by the surviving units or property. However, in the more likely situation where, by reason of its generally greater seagoing qualities, the tug casts the tow adrift with the object of giving itself alone a better chance of survival, leaving the tow to its fate and the likelihood of being swept ashore or lost in the storm, the casting adrift may be likened to a jettison of cargo, and any loss or damage to, or salvage of, the tow should be similarly considered and treated as general average to which the tug should contribute, unless the storm is so severe that whether the barge had remained in tow or been cast adrift she would inevitably have foundered even though the tug survived the storm.

In *The J.P. Donaldson*,[4] a tug which had been towing some sailing barges cast them off in a storm, to save herself from going ashore. The barges went ashore, and were lost with their cargoes. The tug arrived safely. She had been towing on the terms of receiving part of the freight which would have been earned by the barges. A claim for contribution in general average was made against the tug by the owners of the barges. **B.03**

It was held by the Supreme Court of the United States that no contribution was payable. The master of the tug was not in control of the barges in the sense necessary to empower him to make a sacrifice binding tug and barges as a single maritime adventure. In all respects, except that of performing the contract of towage, the barges were under the control of their own masters.

> "The master of the tug having no authority to decide, as between a barge and her cargo, what part shall be sacrificed for the safety of the rest, and thereby to subject what is saved to contribution in general average for what is lost, can surely have no greater authority by abandoning all the barges with their cargoes to subject the tug to a general average contribution."[5]

This case was distinguished by the United States District Court in *S.C. Loveland Co v USA*[6] where the libellant owned both the tug and two barges carrying government cargo. One of the barges was deliberately run on shore after a casualty to prevent it sinking. This measure was in no way directed towards the safety of the tug, the other barge or the cargo in it, but it was held that all should contribute in general average. **B.04**

It is submitted that neither decision is altogether satisfactory; of the two, *S.C. Loveland Co v USA*[7] is the more surprising, since by the time of the sacrifice there was, on the facts, no common danger threatening the whole adventure. But if there is such a danger, it is hard to see why the master of a tug should not be treated, at any rate, for some purposes and for the time being, as in control of tug, barges and cargo.

[4] *The J.P. Donaldson* (1897) 167 U.S. 399.

[5] *The J.P. Donaldson* (1897) 167 U.S. 605. See also *The John Perkins* (1822) Ware (U.S.) 87; 3 Kent Comm. 243n, where the cutting of a cable to prevent a collision with another vessel was not a ground for contribution from that vessel. cf. Phill., s.1311.

[6] *S.C. Loveland Co v USA* (1963) A.M.C. 260.

[7] *S.C. Loveland Co v USA* (1963) A.M.C. 260.

B.05 In *Northland Navigation Co Ltd v Patterson Boiler Works Ltd*[8] a tug towing a loaded barge from Vancouver to Prince Rupert encountered heavy seas which broke over the stern of the tug, flooding the bilge and entering the engine-room. The engine began to shudder and the tug let go the tow line and headed for shelter. Collier J. accepted that "It may well be that the tug and tow were in danger of going down, if the barge had not been let free" and stated, further, that:

> "The casting adrift of the barge, in the knowledge it would inevitably strand or go under, can be characterized as a general average sacrifice."

The barge with her cargo drifted ashore onto rocks, attempts to refloat her proved unsuccessful and the barge was abandoned, but the entire cargo was saved. Until that time when it was decided that the barge herself could not be refloated, the judge held that the expenses of attempting to save both barge and cargo were properly allowable as general average, but expenses subsequent to that time were particular charges on the barge's cargo. He further held that the tug should not contribute to such general average, basing this view on *Walthew v Mavrojani*[9] in that the common peril had expired and the tug was in safety when the general average expenses were incurred.

With respect, it is submitted that this decision also is highly suspect. This was not a separate general average affecting only the barge and her cargo, and commencing when the barge ran ashore; the real general average act was–as already accepted by the judge–the intentional casting adrift of the barge and her cargo at a time when the tug, plus the barge and her cargo, were in joint danger. The sacrifice made by the master of the tug was the full value of the barge and her cargo, less whatever could be salved from either or both the barge and her cargo. Thus, the general average in this case consisted essentially of the value of the lost barge plus all the expenses incurred in attempting to save the barge and her cargo.[10] The important point to note, however, is that the tug should contribute to the sacrifice of the barge and its cargo, which was made for the joint benefit of the tug and—as it happens—the cargo which was saved.

B.06 The most recent—and again unsatisfactory—legal decision comes from the Norwegian Court of Appeal and concerns the ship *Alppi*,[11] which, pursuant to a contract of towage, was in the course of being towed unmanned and in ballast from Norway to Spain. Very heavy weather was encountered in the English Channel and tug and tow were both in danger of being driven ashore. All attempts to tow the Alppi away from the shore proved unavailing and the master of the tug

[8] *Northland Navigation Co Ltd v Patterson Boiler Works Ltd* (1983) 2 C.F. 59.

[9] *Walthew v Mavrojani* (1870) L.R. 5 Ex. 116: see para.8.11, below for the facts of the case. There is, however, a crucial difference between the two cases, since in *Walthew v Mavrojani* the discharging of the cargo, which brought about the physical separation of the ship and cargo, was not the direct (or even indirect) cause of the expense subsequently incurred in refloating the ship; this expense, therefore, was neither incurred for the common safety, nor was it the direct result of an antecedent act which was itself a general average act.

[10] One sometimes encounters cases where cargo is jettisoned for the common safely but some is found floating and recovered. The allowance in general average is for the full value of that cargo, less its damaged value after recovery and the costs of salvage, etc. on those goods.

[11] *The Alppi v The Bjorn Eskil* (ND 1989, 397 Eidsiating Appeal Court).

decided to cast off the towing line in order to save the tug. The Alppi did drive ashore and became a total loss.

A general average adjustment was prepared in Oslo in which the loss of the Alppi was treated as general average to which the tug should contribute, and this claim was upheld in the court of first instance. The decision was reversed in the Court of Appeal, however, it being unanimously held that grounds in theory and/or legal usage for such a claim in general average had not been proved, and some stress appearing to be made of the fact that the Alppi carried no cargo:

> "Existing literature is primarily aimed at the situation where a ship pushes or tows a barge carrying a cargo. Even then opinions seem to differ whether there is any basis for applying the provisions [of general average]. Case law in this area is limited . . . Among international judgments, it is . . . only the Loveland[12] judgment which imposes the payment of a contribution, but then in connection with a barge carrying a cargo."

However, the fact that the Alppi was not carrying cargo provides no convincing reason why her loss should not be general average as between those interests (namely her and the tug) which were imperilled. The facts of the case correspond very closely with those outlined in the fifth example given in para.B.02, above, and it is submitted that under English law a loss occurring in these circumstances ought to be made good in general average, so long as it can genuinely be said that the tug as well as the tow was imperilled, while linked together.

Historical Development and Practice of Rule B

York-Antwerp Rules 1994

The subject of general average involving a tug and tow was considered of sufficient importance in 1994 to warrant a new lettered rule. This was achieved by incorporating the somewhat superfluous provisions of the existing r.B into r.A, thereby making room for the new r.B. The new rule, which largely reflects existing English practice, is based mainly on the provisions in r.XXV of the Rhine Rules (IVR 1979), and before dealing with r.B itself, it may be useful to consider the Rhine Rule. It is entitled Convoys and the relevant first two sections read as follows: **B.07**

1. For the purpose of this rule, a convoy is considered to be a group of vessels coupled with each other in such a way that none of the vessels has any freedom of independent movement.
2. When measures are taken to preserve a vessel and/or some or all vessels of such convoy and their cargo from a common peril, rr.I to XXIV shall be applied accordingly. A vessel forming part of a convoy is not in

[12] *S.C. Loveland Co v USA* (1963) A.M.C. 260.

common peril with another vessel of that convoy, if by a mere uncoupling of the connection with such other vessel she can be placed in safety.

In brief: s.1 defines a convoy as consisting of a group of vessels coupled together such that they must travel together, while s.2 states that if one or more of the vessels in the convoy should be in peril and (general average) measures be taken to preserve them, all the preceding Rhine Rules I to XXIV shall apply to such general average. Probably by way of confirmation that not every unit in the convoy need be involved in the general average, s.2 then continues with the statement that a vessel forming part of the convoy is not in common peril with the others if by a mere uncoupling of the connection she can be placed in safety.

The Rhine Rule may itself not be perfect, but in its translation into the new r.B of the York-Antwerp Rules, below, potential areas for argument have been introduced, particularly in the third paragraph.

York-Antwerp Rules 2004

B.08 No change other than the addition of paragraph numbers as part of the process of standardising the drafting of the Rules. For reasons unknown the second paragraph was not given a number of its own.

B.09 **RULE B**

(1) **There is a common maritime adventure when one or more vessels are towing or pushing another vessel or vessels, provided that they are all involved in commercial activities and not in a salvage operation.**

When measures are taken to preserve the vessels and their cargoes, if any, from a common peril, these Rules shall apply.

(2) **A vessel is not in common peril with another vessel or vessels if by simply disconnecting from the other vessel or vessels she is in safety; but if the disconnection is itself a general average act the common maritime adventure continues.**

CONSTRUCTION

First Paragraph–Paragraph (1) in the York-Antwerp Rules 2004

B.10 **"common maritime adventure"**: See paras A.51 et seq., above, for general remarks on this expression. Its use here is to secure an internationally uniform approach to the problem of whether and when a tug and tow constitutes a common maritime adventure and to resolve the doubt created by the differing decisions referred to above.[13] This first paragraph spells out that a linked flotilla of tug(s) and other vessels will constitute a common maritime adventure . . .

". . . provided that they are all involved in commercial activities and not in a salvage operation": All operations of towage or carriage of goods at sea or in rivers will surely be considered as a commercial activity, as indeed will any salvage operation, and the purpose of this proviso must simply be to ensure that if a vessel with her cargo—if any—is in peril and engages salvage assistance or towage, that particular operation shall not constitute yet another common maritime adventure and invite the possibility of a separate general average involving also the salvage vessel within the existing general average.

Second Paragraph–part of Paragraph (1) in the York-Antwerp Rules 2004

The first paragraph of the rule having declared that a tug and tow (or linked flotilla of tugs and barges etc.) will generally constitute a common maritime adventure, this second paragraph states that when the constituent parts of that adventure are threatened by a common peril, the York-Antwerp Rules shall apply to any extraordinary sacrifice or expenditure necessarily incurred for their joint preservation. **B.11**

"the vessels and their cargoes, if any": The words if any were included to reverse the reasoning in The Alppi[14] and to ensure that a general average situation could still arise in appropriate circumstances even though the tow might carry no cargo.

"a common peril": The wording, when compared with the more precise wording of the Rhine Rule[15] may create the impression that all units of the flotilla must be threatened to an equal degree if r.B is to apply. However, it is submitted that the rule can and should be construed as covering the situation where only part of the flotilla, for example one vessel and its cargo, is in peril.

In such a case, the intention of the rule appears to be that the units affected by the common peril will be parties to the general average, but the units not so affected will not contribute.

"these Rules shall apply": These words having something of an ex cathedra ring about them, it needs to be stressed that the York-Antwerp Rules will not apply unless they are expressly incorporated in the relevant contracts of carriage between any ship or barge in the flotilla and her cargo, and, perhaps even more importantly, the contracts of towage between the tug(s) and the individual units of the flotilla. **B.12**

The precise wording of the individual towage contract will need close examination, but it will be appreciated that towage contracts frequently contain very wide exemption clauses and indemnities in favour of the tug owner, and it is necessary to consider the effect of these clauses on rights and liabilities in general average. Thus under the United Kingdom Standard Conditions for Towage, except where **B.13**

[13] Paras B.03–B.06, above.

[14] See para.B.06, fn.10, above.

[15] Rule XXV(2), see para.B.07, above.

there has been a personal failure by the tugowner to make the tug seaworthy: (1) the tugowner is exonerated from any liability for damage to the tow; and (2) the hirer must indemnify the tugowner against damage to the tug and all "claims". As observed in the commentary on r.D,[16] the first of these provisions would not of itself exclude claims in general average for a sacrifice of the tow, but the second provision has the result that any sacrifice or expenditure for the common safety is effectively being made entirely for the benefit of the hirer, who would otherwise bear the full cost of the damage to both tug and tow, and of any claims; and this, it is suggested, is sufficient to exclude any liability of the tugowner in general average. Other towage contracts in widespread use, the International Ocean Towage Agreement, Lump Sum ("Towcon") and Daily Hire ("Towhire") are more even-handed in their provisions, but they stipulate that loss of or damage to the tow or tug respectively are "for the sole account of" the hirer or tugowner respectively "without any recourse", and again this is probably wide enough to exclude recourse in general average. In the circumstances it is hardly surprising that there has been no rush by tugowners to incorporate the York-Antwerp Rules within their contracts of towage.

Third Paragraph–Paragraph (2) in the York-Antwerp Rules 2004

B.14 This third paragraph is somewhat badly expressed, and could possibly give rise to different interpretations in everyday practice. It is in two parts, separated by a semi-colon, and the first part corresponds fairly closely with the second sentence of s.2 of the Rhine Rule, while the second part is new.

"A vessel is not in common peril with another vessel . . . if by simply disconnecting . . . she is in safety": This phrase endeavours to deal with an aspect of the problem of common peril which is peculiar to the situation of tug and tow, and it does so by excluding from the concept of common peril the case where a unit is in safety by mere disconnection. In such a case it therefore matters not that, in the connected state, all the units are affected by the same a common peril; indeed this is precisely the situation which the provision contemplates. Contrary to the view expressed in the 12th edition, there appears to be no adequate reason to restrict its operation to the case where the peril, while it may affect all units in the connected state, is intrinsic to one unit of the flotilla, such as the case where one of a flotilla of barges is damaged in a collision and leaking, or is on fire[17] ; certainly the language lends no support to such a restrictive construction. The effect of the provision is therefore that, because of its engine power and manoeuvrability, a tug which disconnects from the barge which she is towing, for example in order to save herself from damage or foundering in heavy weather, will frequently (but not always[18]) be relieved by this provision of any obligation to contribute to damage to the barge consequent on the disconnection.

[16] See, for instance, para.D.15, below, and the general rule under English law that a contractual or statutory provision exempting a party from liability will not be construed as referring to a liability to contribute in general average unless it expressly so provides.

[17] See also Rainey, *The Law of Tug and Tow*, 2nd edn (2002), pp.319–320.

[18] See para.B.15, below.

"she is in safety": The rule only negatives the existence of a common peril if by simply disconnecting the vessel is in safety. The equivalent words of the Rhine Rule require that by a mere uncoupling of the connection she can be placed in safety. The wording of r.B has been compared unfavourably with the equivalent Rhine Rule, and as causing potential problems in the case where, for example, a tug disconnects from a barge which has caught fire; the tug, in order to be in safety must be removed to a safe distance from the barge, with the result that she can be placed in safety as required by the Rhine Rule, although she is not immediately in safety as arguably required by r.B. However, the difference between the two rules is probably more apparent than real. The word disconnecting, which is less precise than the equivalent phrase in the Rhine Rule, must be given a common-sense meaning, and is capable of including a simple manoeuvre, under own power, to place the vessel outside the area of danger created by the other vessel(s) in the flotilla.[19] **B.15**

Nevertheless, the provision may give rise to some difficult questions of degree. In a typical case where a tug disconnects from the tow in bad weather in order to improve her chances of riding out a storm, what is to determine whether she is in safety? It is submitted that if the tug, having disconnected, can safely ride out the storm at the place where she disconnects she is in safety, whereas if she needs to make for a port of refuge or seek other shelter to ride out the storm, as occurred in *Northland Navigation Co v Patterson Boiler Works*[20] she is not in safety simply by disconnecting, with the result that the tug and tow will be regarded as having been in common peril at the time of the disconnection. Equal or greater difficulty could arise where a barge is disconnected from a sinking tug. However, that situation is unlikely to give rise to problems in practice, since it is difficult to envisage circumstances in which such a disconnection would fulfill the other requirements of a general average sacrifice.

"but if the disconnection is itself a general average act": The opening word but is misleading, since it suggests that the situation described, namely where the disconnection is a general average act, is an exception to, or qualification of, the provisions of the first part of the paragraph. In reality, however, the two provisions are wholly distinct. Thus if the vessel is in safety merely by disconnecting herself, with the result that the requirements of common peril are excluded by the first part of the third paragraph, the disconnection cannot be a general average act as regards that vessel, since it is not an act undertaken for the common safety, and it follows that the requirements of the second part must necessarily also be unsatisfied as regards that vessel. The purpose of the second part of the third paragraph is to deal with an entirely different problem, discussed in the next paragraph. **B.16**

[19] In any event, in the example given, even if the tug were held to be in common peril with the barge, no general average contribution would be payable by the tug to the loss incurred by the barge in consequence of the fire, unless the disconnection from the barge amounted to a sacrifice of the barge. This would only be the case if the danger affecting the barge was materially increased by the disconnection of the tug.

[20] *Northland Navigation Co v Patterson Boiler Works* (1983) 2 C.F. 59; para.B.05, above.

The requirement that the disconnection be a general average act will be met if it satisfies the requirements of a sacrifice of the disconnected vessel(s) in order to save the other or others. This will be the case if:

(1) the disconnecting vessel (usually the tug) is in common peril with the other vessel(s), a question considered in para.B.14, above; and
(2) the chances of the disconnected vessel(s) (usually the barge(s)) attaining safety are materially diminished by the disconnection, while the disconnecting vessel's chances are improved.

B.17 **"the common maritime adventure continues"**: Although anything but ideal, these words were designed to and should reverse the effect *Northland Navigation Co v Patterson Boiler Works*,[21] in which, on the erroneous grounds that the common adventure was then over, the court refused to award any contribution in general average from the tug in respect of losses and expenses sustained by the tow and its cargo, nominally subsequent to their being cast off by the tug, but effectively as the direct result of the casting off.

No indication is given as to when the adventure terminates, but assuming that the original adventure is not resumed and completed, it is submitted that for each of the units the adventure ends when they respectively reach a place of safety, but see also the more detailed commentary in r.G and r.XVII.

B.18 The rule is primarily concerned with the question of common peril, and provides scant guidance on how port of refuge and similar expenses are to be treated if the voyage is not abandoned as soon as the place of safety is reached. However it is clear that the rule does have the effect that port of refuge expenses falling within rr.X and XI are allowed in general average between the relevant interests. It is suggested that the following is the correct approach.

(1) Where the tug sustains damage which imperils all the interests and requires her to put into a port of refuge for repairs in order to complete the voyage, the port of refuge expenses allowed under rr.X and XI are general average as between all the interests, namely tug, barge(s) and cargo(es).
(2) Where the damage is sustained by the barge it will not normally imperil the tug or the other barges. In such a case, the port of refuge expenses will be general average as between the damaged barge and its cargo, but the tug and the other barges and their cargoes will not contribute for the reasons explained in para.B.11, above.
(3) The contracts between the parties will need close examination to see whether they contain specific provisions which override the Rules. For example it is common for towage contracts to provide that the barge is responsible for the expenses of the tug during detention at a port of refuge. In such a case it seems unlikely that the barge could recover general average contribution from its cargo in respect of these expenses, since they are a loss incurred by delay, and therefore excluded by r.C.

[21] *Northland Navigation Co v Patterson Boiler Works* (1983) 2 C.F. 59; para.B.05, above.

RULE C

CAUSATION, CONSEQUENCES AND DAMAGE TO THE ENVIRONMENT

General Introduction

Since 1924, when the lettered rules were first introduced, r.C has been the provision in the York-Antwerp Rules dealing generally with problems of causation and consequences. As a result of new provisions adopted in 1994, the rule now also deals with the largely distinct topic of damage to the environment. **C.01**

Causation and Consequences

To what extent must a general average act, whether involving sacrifice or expenditure, be followed to its more or less remote consequences? This question underlies a great many general average questions. Rules II, V, VIII, X, XI, XII and XIV of the York-Antwerp Rules are all concerned in whole or in part with settling disputed problems as to remoteness; so was the great dispute at common law as to port of refuge expenses.[1] **C.02**

It can never have been intended that every loss which would not have taken place, had the sacrifice been not made, must be replaced by contribution. The cutting away of a mast, for example, while saving the ship and cargo from some imminent danger, may, by retarding the ship's sailing, bring them within the action of some new danger, from which they would otherwise have been free through having reached their destination. Suppose that from this cause she were to fall into an enemy's hands, it could hardly be contended that the loss by capture should be replaced by contribution as a consequence of cutting away the mast.

On the other hand, if all losses and expenses were excluded from consideration unless consciously intended by the master at the time of the act, many consequences which flow naturally and foreseeably from the act would have to be disregarded, thus giving rise to an artificial result.

[1] See paras 10.01 et seq., below.

Damage to the Environment

C.03 The growing significance in general average of liabilities and expenses consequent upon actual or threatened environmental damage, in particular oil pollution, led to the introduction of special provisions on the subject in the 1994 Rules. The most important of these provisions, which is contained in the second paragraph of r.C, is an exclusion from general average of liabilities in respect of damage to the environment. This exclusion, which is best regarded as something distinct from the remainder of r.C, and potentially inconsistent with it, owes less to principle than to policy, and to the reluctance of insurers of hull and cargo (that is, property) to become insurers of liabilities through the mechanism of the general average system. Until the change effected to the rule in 1994 there was no reason in English law why liability for damage to the environment should not have been allowed in general average, whether the adjustment was governed by the York-Antwerp Rules or not.[2]

English Law and Background

Causation Generally

C.04 The Marine Insurance Act 1906, which has been held to codify the English law, and therefore to apply between the parties to the adventure as well as to claims under policies of marine insurance,[3] provides that the loss to be made good in general average must be "caused by or directly consequential on" the general average act.[4] When a rule of general application, r.C,[5] was introduced for the first time into the York-Antwerp Rules in 1924, its wording was modelled closely on the Act and it applied the test of "direct consequences". However, the English decisions on questions of causation, including those decided after the introduction of the Marine Insurance Act and of r.C, have continued to pay great regard to the rather more elaborate tests proposed by Lowndes and by Ulrich.[6]

The tests adopted by Lowndes and Ulrich

C.05 Lowndes prefaced his views by referring to the general rule of English law as to remoteness of damage, citing *Mayne on Damages* (3rd edn, p.39). He continued:

[2] See paras C.16 and C.28, below. However, a questionnaire circulated by AIDE, the results of which were published in their Report of September 1993, revealed that the law of different countries on the point was far from uniform, and the practice of adjusters varied.

[3] See para.C.11, below, and para.50.02, below.

[4] See para.C.11, below, and para.50.02, below.

[5] See para.C.18, below.

[6] See paras C.05–C.06, below. The position may be different where one of the numbered rules applies; see para.C.17, below.

"The first, and in fact the only inquiry in all these cases is, whether the damage complained of is the natural and reasonable result of the defendant's act; it will assume this character if it can be shewn to be such a consequence as in the ordinary course of things would flow from the act, or, in cases of contract, if it appears to have been contemplated by both parties. . . .[7] Applying this rule more closely to general average, it may be thought that, since we have to determine quod pro omnibus datum est, and since giving must always imply an intention to give, what we have here to ascertain must be, what loss at once has in fact occurred, and likewise must be regarded as the natural and reasonable result of the act of sacrifice? Or, in other words, what the shipmaster would naturally, or might reasonably have intended to give for all when he resolved upon the act? If then, upon the act of sacrifice any loss ensues, which the master did not in fact bring before his mind at the time of making the sacrifice, it would have to be considered whether it were a loss of which he naturally might or reasonably ought to have taken account."

The second test is that of the German writer Ulrich[8] : **C.06**

"General average comprises not only the damage purposely done to ship and cargo, but also: (1) all damage or expense which was to be foreseen as the natural (immediate) consequence of the first sacrifice, since this unmistakably forms part of that which was given for the common safely; (2) all damage or expense which, though not to be foreseen, stands to the sacrifice in relation of effect to cause, or, in other words, was its necessary consequence. Not so, however, those losses or expenses which, though they would not have occurred but for the sacrifice, yet, likewise, would not have occurred but for some subsequent accident."

The authorities on English law

In *McCall v Houlder Bros*[9] (decided under the York-Antwerp Rules 1890), the vessel's propeller was damaged when she struck a bar on leaving the loading port, and she was detained at her next bunkering port, as a port of refuge. As there were no facilities for the storage of the cargo, which was perishable, the vessel was tipped so that repairs to the propeller could be carried out. The tipping of the vessel was held to be a general average act. It was later discovered that as a result of the operation, cargo had been damaged by seawater entering the hold through a broken air pipe. The fracture had occurred during the striking of the bar, but was unknown to the master when he decided to tip the vessel. The cargo damage was allowed in general average. Mathew J. said: **C.07**

"it was not known what the result of the vessel striking when crossing the bar had been, but it was clear that if any damage had been done to the structure of the ship, the process of setting the ship down by the head might be attended by considerable risk to the cargo. The Master, it seems to me, acted prudently in determining to run that risk . . . It was said that the loss was particular average only, because it was not

[7] For the modem law on this topic, see *McGregor on Damages* (17th edn), Ch.6. It is at least possible that, the test for general average purposes having crystallised at this stage in the development of the common law, there is now a divergence between remoteness in general average cases and remoteness at common law. Cf. *Australian Coastal Shipping Commission v Green* [1971] 1 Q.B. 456.

[8] Ulrich, *Grosse-Haverei*, p.5.

[9] *McCall v Houlder Bros* (1897) 2 Com. Cas. 129 at 132. For a comparison of the various reports of this case see para.A.24, above.

> foreseen, and was not, therefore, a voluntary sacrifice. But it is not necessary that a particular loss should have been contemplated, if it be incidental to the general average act."

While Mathew J. did not expressly refer to the test of either Lowndes or Ulrich, his reasoning reflects that of Lowndes, since the risk of damage to the cargo, although not the precise manner in which it occurred, was or ought to have been something the master would take into account in deciding to tip the vessel.

A modern example of the same problem occurs on old ships with wasted and leaky bulkheads; water poured into one hold to extinguish a fire in that hold will frequently find its way into other holds and damage the cargo therein. It is the practice to allow the damage so caused, leaving it to the injured parties to enforce their remedies for unseaworthiness, if appropriate.

C.08 In *Anglo-Argentine Live Stock Agency v Temperley S.S. Co*[10] the vessel had loaded cattle and sheep in the River Plate for conveyance to Britain, under a contract which provided that on no account should the vessel call at any Brazilian or European Continental ports. After springing a leak the vessel was forced to put into Bahia in Brazil for repairs. In consequence, by reason of emergency legislation then in force, the cattle could not be landed in Britain and were taken instead to Antwerp, where they were sold for much less than they would have realised in Britain. The loss on sale was held to be allowable in general average as a direct and immediate consequence of the general average act of putting into Bahia. In the course of his judgment, Bigham J. cited the test of Lowndes and Ulrich, and said:

> "These two passages seem to me to express accurately the principles upon which the damages to be made good in general average are to be ascertained . . . and applying those principles to the present case, I think that as, when the master of the Edenbridge resolved upon the average act, he knew, or ought to have known, that he was sacrificing the advantages which the plaintiffs then possessed by reason of the ship not having touched a Brazilian port, he must be taken to have intended that the value of those advantages should be made good in general average; and the master's intention is the intention of the parties interested, whose agent he is. I am further of opinion that the damage in question is the necessary consequence of the general average act."

The loss in value was therefore allowed in general average.

C.09 In *Austin Friars S.S. Co v Spillers and Bakers*[11] the plaintiffs ship, bound for Sharpness dock with a cargo of maize, stranded just above the dock and was seriously damaged. Refloated with the aid of tugs, she was making water so fast that the master and pilot decided to take her into Sharpness, rather than beaching her further downstream as first intended. Because of the strong ebb tide both master and pilot contemplated (and the pilot actually intended) that the ship would strike the lower pier of the dock, and do some damage. She struck harder than intended and damaged herself to the extent of £1,600 and the pier to the extent of £5,000.

10 *Anglo-Argentine Live Stock Agency v Temperley S.S. Co* [1899] 2 Q.B. 403 at 410.

11 *Austin Friars S.S. Co v Spillers and Bakers* [1915] 1 K.B. 833 at 836; affirmed [1915] 3 K.B. 586, CA.

Bailhache J. held that "to put into Sharpness with the knowledge that in doing so the ship would strike the pier was a reasonable and prudent thing to do". On the question of causation he cited the tests of Lowndes and Ulrich, and said they were "admirable guides" to the decision in the case. The shipowner therefore recovered contribution in respect of the damage to the ship and in respect of the liability incurred for the damage to the dock.

The main ground on which the right to contribution was disputed was that there could be no contribution in general average where the act consisted of inflicting damage on the property of a third person, particularly when the damage amounted to a tort. However Bailhache J. held that,

> "the master has implied authority when occasion arises for a general average act to do whatever is necessary and prudent for the preservation of ship and cargo, even if this involves committing a trespass . . ."

In *Anglo-Grecian Steam Trading Co v Beynon (T) & Co*[12] the ship fouled the cable of a buoy while leaving port, as a result of which she lost power and fractured her aft peak. She was therefore in "distinct and considerable" danger. Since she was unable to clear the cable, it was decided to beach her, using tugs, in the centre of a nearby bay. The operation was carried out, but she took the ground rather sooner and rather further to the east than the pilot wished or expected. When the tide rose the tugs were unable to hold her, the tow ropes parted and she was carried onto rocks on the east side of the bay and damaged. **C.10**

Roche J. held that the initial stranding of the ship was voluntary, and that the decision to beach her was reasonable. He then turned to the question whether the damage was a sufficiently direct or immediate result of the stranding. He held that the chain of causation would have been broken if the vessels being carried onto the rocks was the result either of a supervening act of negligence or of some accident "not connected with the original beaching". Having held that there was no negligence, he referred to the statement of the law in *Anglo-Argentine Live Stock Agency v Temperley S.S. Co*,[13] and the test of Ulrich there cited, and concluded that the loss should be allowed because:

> "although the grounding on the rocks was not at any rate foreseen as either a necessary or even a probable consequence by the pilot, yet it was not a subsequent accident unconnected with the grounding."[14]

In the two cases referred to above, both Bailhache and Roche JJ. regarded the question of remoteness as governed by the provisions of s.66(1) of the Marine Insurance Act.[15]

[12] *Anglo-Grecian Steam Trading Co v Beynon (T) & Co* (1926) 24 Lloyd's Rep. 122.

[13] See para.C.08, above.

[14] *Anglo-Argentine Live Stock Agency v Temperley S.S. Co* (1926) 24 Lloyd's Rep. 122 at 127. The references to the York-Antwerp Rules 1924 are mistaken, as Roche J. explained in *Vlassopoulos v British & Foreign Marine Insurance Co* [1929] 1 K.B. 187 at 193.

[15] The second of those cases was decided under the York-Antwerp Rules 1890 but these contained no general provision on causation.

C.11 In the light of these decisions, it cannot be said that a precise rule has been laid down on remoteness in English law. The decisions have relied on the tests of both Lowndes and Ulrich but without providing any real indication of which is to be preferred. Yet the difference in approach between the two tests is considerable, since Lowndes approaches the problem by seeking to determine what loss the master did or ought to have taken into account, as a guide to presumed intention, whereas Ulrich lays emphasis on the lack of any intervening accidental cause. The tests will not always produce the same result. The Marine Insurance Act, which defines a general average loss as a loss "caused by or directly consequently on a general act", introduces a further complication. At first sight it seems to follow the approach of Ulrich rather than that of Lowndes, yet Bailhache J. in *Austin Friars S.S. Co v Spillers and Bakers*,[16] while holding that he was bound to apply the provisions of the Act as a codification of the common law, derived assistance from the test of Lowndes as well as that of Ulrich. And in *Anglo-Grecian Steam Trading Co v Beynon (T) & Co*,[17] Roche J., also holding that he was bound to apply the provisions of the Act, adopted the statement of the law in *Anglo-Argentine Live Stock Agency v Temperley S.S. Co*,[18] which follows Lowndes' approach, as a correct statement of the law.

C.12 As a matter of principle, it is submitted that the test of Lowndes is to be preferred, and particularly its last sentence, which interprets what has gone before. At the risk of introducing yet a third test, it is suggested that no consequence is too remote if:

(1) the master did in fact expect it to happen; or
(2) he "naturally might or reasonably ought" to have so expected; or
(3) he did appreciate, or naturally might have or reasonably ought to have appreciated, that there was a substantial risk of its happening.[19]

Loss by Delay

C.13 English law has been slow to allow loss by delay, mainly on the practical grounds that the loss depends frequently upon the private contractual arrangements of one of the parties to the adventure in some degree, and that it gives rise to considerable difficulties of quantification. Thus in *Anglo-Argentine Live Stock Agency v Temperley S.S. Co*, Bigham J. rejected that part of the claim that related to the wages of cattlemen employed by the charterers, and the cost of fodder for the cattle during the period of delay at the port of refuge. After holding that these expenses did not fall within r.X or XI of the York-Antwerp Rules 1890, he continued:

[16] *Austin Friars S.S. Co* [1915] 1 K.B. 833; see para.C.09, above.
[17] *Anglo-Grecian Steam Trading Co* (1926) 24 Ll.L.Rep. 122; see para.C.10, above.
[18] *Anglo-Argentine Live Stock Agency* [1899] 2 Q.B. 403; see para.C.08, above.
[19] "Necessary", "immediate" and "direct" are adjectives which have been used in US decisions: *Columbian Insurance Co v Ashby* 13 Pet. 331 (1839); Parsons, *Maritime Law*, p.304; *The Wordsworth* 88 Fed. Rep. 313 (1898). But a wider rule is sometimes applied: *Norwich & NY Transport Co v Insurance Co of NA* (1903) 118 Fed. Rep. 307; 129 Fed. Rep. 1006; 194 U.S. 637.

> "But it was said that though these two claims may not be recoverable under the York-Antwerp Rules, they are nevertheless recoverable at common law. I am, however, of opinion that they are not. Everyone concerned in the adventure suffers damage by the delay at the port of refuge. Each cargo-owner is delayed in the use or the sale of his goods. The freight-owner is delayed in getting payment of his freight, and the ship-owner is deprived of the use of his ship. Yet none of these cases afford the foundation of any claim in general average according to our common law."

In *The Leitrim*[20] the ship was delayed at a port of refuge while undergoing general average repairs. She was running under a time charter, which contained a clause providing that in the event of damage occurring which prevented the working of the vessel for more than 24 hours, the hire should cease. The ship-owner claimed in general average the loss of time freight through the delay, but the court decided against the claim. The grounds of the decision appear to be: **C.14**

(1) that the loss of hire was an "accidental circumstance peculiar to the shipowner";
(2) that "the loss of time is common to all the parties interested and all suffer damage by the delay, so that the damages by loss of time may be considered proportionate to the interests and may be left out of consideration"; and
(3) that great inconvenience could result if losses due to delay had to be assessed, and the practice of adjusters had been to exclude them.

Both of these cases on loss by delay were decided before the passing of the Marine Insurance Act 1906, but it was held in *Wetherall v The London Assurance*[21] that the provisions of s.66(1) of the Act did not affect the rules of the common law excluding loss by delay. The Leitrim was decided under the York-Antwerp Rules 1890, but since those Rules contained no general provisions equivalent to r.C the recoverability of the loss caused by delay was governed by English law. **C.15**

Damage to the Environment

There is no decision in English law on the question whether liabilities in respect of pollution or other damage to the environment are allowable in general average. However, *Austin Friars S.S. Co v Spillers and Bakers*[22] establishes that there is no objection to such a claim on the grounds of public policy, and liabilities of this nature may therefore be allowed, so long as they fall within the to the usual requirements of a general average loss, of which the most relevant are likely to be that the liability should be caused by or directly consequential on a general average act, and that it should be reasonably incurred. **C.16**

[20] *The Leitrim* [1902] P. 256.
[21] *Wetherall v The London Assurance* [1931] 2 K.B. 448: see para.C.19, below.
[22] *Austin Friars S.S. Co* [1915] 1 K.B. 833; [1915] 3 K.B. 586, CA: see para.C.09, above. See also para.C.28, below.

HISTORICAL DEVELOPMENT AND PRACTICE OF RULE C

C.17 Before 1924 there was no general provision in the Rules dealing with problems of remoteness and causation, although certain of the numbered rules contained provisions relevant to these questions in the particular circumstances to which they applied. The 1994 and 2004 numbered rules do likewise,[23] and in those particular circumstances the numbered rules override r.C to the extent of any inconsistency.[24]

York-Antwerp Rules 1924

C.18 Whilst English law excluded loss by delay and other indirect losses, in same countries the consequences of a general average act were not so limited.[25] In order to achieve uniformity on the point a general rule, reflecting the English law approach, was adopted at the Stockholm conference.

> Only such damages, losses or expenses which are the direct consequence of the general average act shall be allowed as general average.
>
> Damage or loss sustained by the ship or cargo through delay on the voyage, and indirect loss from the same cause, such as demurrage and loss of market, shall not be admitted as general average.

York-Antwerp Rules 1950

C.19 Under the 1924 Rule the express exclusion of loss by delay was limited to delay on the voyage. In *Wetherall v The London Assurance*[26] where the shipowner claimed loss by detention of the vessel during repairs of general average damage effected after the end of the voyage, it was held that the rule did not exclude such a claim. In other countries, however, it had been held that the rule did, by clear implication, exclude a claim for loss by delay after the end of the voyage.[27] In order to resolve these doubts, the words on the voyage in the second paragraph of the rule were changed to on the voyage or subsequently.

[23] e.g. rr.II, V, VIII, X, XI and XIV.

[24] See the Rule of Interpretation.

[25] In *The Champlain* (1923) it was decided in the Cour de Cassation, France, that damage to cargo through delay at a port of refuge into which the vessel had put in consequence of sea perils was properly allowable in general average. The same court decided in *The Willesden* (1926) and *The Madali* (1934) that demurrage during repairs was allowable in general average under French law.

[26] *Wetherall v The London Assurance* [1931] 2 K.B. 448. The claim failed anyway, because it was held that since r.C neither excluded nor permitted the claim, the matter was governed by English law, under which the claim was excluded by the decision in The Leitrim; see para.C.14, above.

[27] In *The Elini* (1938), the Rennes Court of Appeal held that the loss suffered by the shipowner through delay during repairs of general average damage after the completion of the voyage was not allowable in general average under r.C, even though under French law such a claim would have been allowed.

York-Antwerp Rules 1974

No change. C.20

York-Antwerp Rules 1994

The main single issue at the Sydney Conference was the way in which the increasingly important question of pollution liabilities[28] should be dealt with. A number of different views were advanced. The US delegation was in favour of a complete exclusion, by means of a Rule Paramount, of all pollution liabilities and of the costs of clean-up of pollutants. Other countries, and the P. and I. Clubs, took the view that pollution liabilities should be dealt with on the same footing as any other liabilities.[29] A third solution, proposed by the Association of Average Adjusters and AIDE, and supported by the British delegation, favoured a general exclusion of pollution liabilities but express allowance of certain of the costs of avoiding pollution; it was felt that this held a fair balance between ship and cargo interests, and that it would promote good practice by encouraging the prevention of pollution while excluding from general average liabilities in respect of pollution which had actually occurred. C.21

It was this third solution which was adopted at the Sydney Conference. The general exclusion of pollution liabilities is found in the lettered r.C; and the express allowances of costs of preventing or minimising pollution are found mainly in r.XI(d), but also in those provisions of r.VI of the 1994 Rules which deal with salvage awards enhanced by reason of the salvor's efforts in that regard. By virtue of the Rule of Interpretation these allowances in the numbered rules override the general exclusion in r.C. In addition, in order to prevent claims in respect of pollution costs from arising under any of the other numbered rules, amendments were made to rr.II, V and VIII.

Apart from the new paragraph dealing with pollution liabilities, certain improvements of a drafting nature were made in the rule. In particular the discrepancy between the apparent scope of the first paragraph (which refers to losses, damages or expenses) and the last paragraph (which referred only to loss or damage) has been eliminated[30]; and the somewhat misleading reference to loss of market as an example of indirect loss[31] has been altered. C.22

York-Antwerp Rules 2004

No change other than the numbering of the paragraphs and the substitution of "allowed" for "admitted" in the third paragraph. C.23

[28] For the sake of simplicity we refer in this introductory paragraph to "pollution liabilities". However r.C itself is in wider terms, and includes within its scope any "damage to the environment". See para.C.38, below.

[29] For English law on the subject see para.C.16, above. However there appears to be no uniformity of approach between different countries; see para.C.03, fn.2, above.

[30] See para.42, below.

[31] See para.41, below.

RULE C

(1) Only such losses, damages or expenses which are the direct consequence of the general average act shall be allowed as general average.

(2) In no case shall there be any allowance in general average for losses, damages or expenses incurred in respect of damage to the environment or in consequence of the escape or release of pollutant substances from the property involved in the common maritime adventure.

(3) Demurrage, loss of market, and any loss or damage sustained or expense incurred by reason of delay, whether on the voyage or subsequently, and any indirect loss whatsoever shall not be admitted/allowed as general average.

CONSTRUCTION

First Paragraph–Paragraph (1) in the York-Antwerp Rules 2004

C.24 **"losses, damages or expenses"**: This is a comprehensive expression which is clearly intended to include every kind of adverse consequence of a general average act. The effect of the first paragraph of r.C is therefore that all such consequences will initially be subjected to the same test, namely whether they are a direct consequence of the general average act. If they are, they can be allowed in general average, unless they fall within the specific exclusions of the second or third paragraphs of r.C. or of any of the numbered rules. If they are not a direct consequence, they are excluded from any allowance in general average unless they fall within a specific provision of a numbered rule.

C.25 **"the direct consequence of the general average act"**: These words are in essence the same as the wording of s.66(1) of the Marine Insurance Act 1906.[32]

The only case in the English Courts in which their interpretation has been considered is *Australian Coastal Shipping Commission v Green*.[33] In that case the plaintiff shipowners had engaged towage assistance for two of their vessels in distress, Bulwarra and Wangarra. Each towage contract was on the United Kingdom Standard Towage Conditions, which provided for an indemnity in wide terms in favour of the tug owner. In each case the towing line broke during the towage. Bulwarra's tug became a total loss; Wangarra's tug was salved and incurred salvage charges, and the tug owners claimed against the plaintiffs under the indemnity provisions. The claim in respect of Bulwarra failed, but the plaintiffs incurred expense in defending it. The claim in respect of Wangarra succeeded for an indemnity plus legal costs. The plaintiffs now sought to recover the ships

[32] "Caused by or directly consequential on a general average act".

[33] *Australian Coastal Shipping Commission v Green* [1971] 1 Q.B. 456.

proportion of all of the above sums from their hull insurers, under policies which provided for the adjustment of general average in accordance with the York-Antwerp Rules 1950.

Mocatta J. held that the liability incurred to the owners of the tug by reason of the breaking of the towing line was the direct result of the general average act within the meaning of r.C. on the grounds that, applying Lowndes' test, it was a liability which the plaintiffs "naturally might, or reasonably ought to have contemplated", and applying Ulrich's test as explained by Roche J. in *Anglo-Grecian Steam Trading Co v Beynon (T) & Co*,[34] that the liability to the tug owners consequent upon the breaking of the tow ropes was a possibility which was so connected with the act of engaging the tugs as not to break the chain of causation.[35]

This decision was upheld in the Court of Appeal, where Lord Denning M.R. said[36]: **C.26**

> "At the time when the Rules were made in 1924, all lawyers thought that they could tell the difference between direct and indirect consequences . . . Naturally enough, therefore, the framers of the York-Antwerp Rules used it too. But 40 years later the Privy Council poured scorn upon it[37] . . . To add to the confusion, Rule C of the York-Antwerp Rules gives loss of market as a typical instance of indirect loss, following, no doubt, *The Parana* (1877) 2 P.D. 118 whereas in *Czarnikow (C) Ltd v Koufos* [1969] 1 A.C. 350, 385, Lord Reid says that the loss of market there was directly caused by the defendant's breach of contract.
>
> In these circumstances I propose to go back to the concept, as I understood it in 1924, when the York-Antwerp Rules were made. Direct consequences denote those consequences which flow in an unbroken sequence from the act; whereas indirect consequences are those in which the sequence is broken by an intervening or extraneous cause. I realise that this is not very helpful; because the metaphor of breaking the chain of causation means one thing to one man and another thing to another. But still we have to do the best we can with it."

However, Lord Denning then rejected Ulrich's test and turned to foreseeability[38]:

"If the master, when he does 'the general average act', ought reasonably to have foreseen that a subsequent accident of the kind might occur—or even that there was a distinct possibility of it—then the subsequent accident does not break the chain of causation . . . If, however, there is a subsequent incident which was only a remote possibility, it would be different."

Neither Phillimore L.J. nor Cairns L.J. considered that any problem of causation arose where the expenditure was incurred under a contract which was itself a general average act; but they were prepared to accept the test of Ulrich for cases of sacrifice. All of the judges held that the legal costs incurred by the owners were recoverable, without giving separate consideration to them.

[34] *Anglo-Grecian Steam Trading Co v Beynon (T) & Co* (1926) 24 Lloyd's Rep. 122; see para.C.10, above.

[35] [1971] 1 Q.B. 456 at 471.

[36] [1971] 1 Q.B. 481.

[37] In *The Wagon Mound* [1961] A.C. 388, per Lord Simonds at 423.

[38] *The Wagon Mound* at 482.

C.27 In the light of this decision it appears that the approach of the English courts to general questions of causation under the York-Antwerp Rules will not differ from that adopted in the cases decided before the introduction of r.C. The effect of the first paragraph of r.C may be summarised by saying that a consequence is direct if it flows from the general average act without any intervening or extraneous cause; and that if the master ought reasonably to have foreseen such intervening or extraneous cause as a distinct possibility, the result is still a direct consequence of the general average act.

Other decisions on causation

C.28 In an English arbitration shipowners claimed contribution towards their liability for pollution, resulting from jettison of oil to refloat the vessel, as general average expenditure. The arbitrator found that the shipowners' liability was both a direct and a foreseeable consequence of the jettison, and the claim (which was governed by the York-Antwerp Rules 1950) succeeded. Under the 1994 or 2004 Rules, however, such a claim would be excluded by the second paragraph of r.C.

In *Federal Commerce and Navigation Ltd v Eisenerz GmbH*,[39] r.C was relied on by the party who had suffered loss, in order to show that it was not a general average loss. Damage to cargo occurred during discharge and reloading at a port of refuge.[40] Prima facie such damage is allowable in general average, however, it was found that the damage was caused by negligence of the master (amongst others) in failing to supervise the cargo operations. The shipowners could not be heard to say that the master's own negligence should be foreseen as a distinct possibility. So the chain of causation was broken, the loss was not a direct consequence of the general average act, and the cargo owners recovered in full for breach of the contract of carriage.[41]

C.29 In *Sea-Land Service Inc v Aetna Insurance*,[42] the Beauregard stranded accidentally and the master engaged a tug to tow her off. During the towage operation, the towing line broke, and the vessel, which was beginning to come free, was driven by wind and waves sideways to port as a result of which she sustained bottom damage. The shipowners' claim to have this damage made good in general average failed, because they were unable to prove that the vessel would not have drifted to port and sustained the same damage if no towage had been attempted. However, had they been able to do so the claim would have succeeded. The master did anticipate, or should have anticipated, that the towing line might part, and the damage would therefore have been the direct result of the engagement of the tug.

[39] *Federal Commerce and Navigation Ltd v Eisenerz GmbH* [1970] 2 Lloyd's Rep. 332; [1975] 1 Lloyd's Rep. 105 (S.C. Can.).

[40] See paras 00.68 et seq., above.

[41] Whilst this reasoning may be correct in relation to r.C, and the overall result of the case is correct, other aspects of the reasoning are questionable: see para.12.14, below.

[42] *Sea-Land Service* [1977] 2 Lloyd's Rep. 84; [1976] A.M.C. 2164 (U.S. Court of Appeals).

In *Corfu Navigation v Mobil Shipping*[43] (York-Antwerp Rules 1974) the claim was for damage to machinery in endeavouring to refloat, but questions of causation were regarded as being governed by r.C.[44] The claim was resisted on the ground that the master had not prepared adequately for the attempt and had not used proper means to refloat the vessel, and that his unreasonable conduct broke the chain of causation. Rejecting this argument, Hobhouse J. said:

> "The general average act is the refloating attempt involving the running of the engines in such a way as to risk the damage. The damage to the engines was the actual and immediate consequence of that act without the intervention of any other cause; like in the Australian Coastal Shipping case, the general average act itself contemplates the loss and there is really no room for the argument that the loss is anything other than the direct consequence of the act."

Intervening negligence

If the alleged general average act is unreasonable in its conception, its consequences are excluded from general average by the Rule Paramount.[45] However, the same result does not necessarily follow where the negligence occurs during the execution of the act. Where the negligence is that of a third party, such as a stevedore employed to discharge the cargo, there is certainly no general rule that it precludes a claim for any loss or damage which could have been avoided if the negligence had not occurred.[46] It will only do so, it is submitted, if the negligence was "something unexpected and unconnected with" the measure adopted for the common safety.[47] Thus the ordinary rules of remoteness already discussed will apply. **C.30**

Where the negligence is that of the party who decided upon the course of action which constitutes the general average act special problems may arise. In *Federal Commerce and Navigation Ltd v Eisenerz*[48] damage was caused to a cargo in discharging at a port of refuge, as a result of the negligence of the master, among others, in failing to supervise the operation properly. The question of causation was treated as being governed by r.C, and it was held that since the owners could not be heard to say that the master's own negligence should be foreseen as a distinct possibility, the chain of causation was broken.

Agency Fees to Shipowners or their Managers

When the ship has gone ashore, or some other maritime disaster has happened which imperils the whole adventure, the shipowner is bound to use his best **C.31**

[43] *Corfu Navigation* [1991] 2 Lloyd's Rep. 515 at 522, the decision which led to the introduction of the Rule Paramount, which would provide a defence to the claim under the 1994 Rules.

[44] See para.PRE.11, below, where the correctness of this view is discussed.

[45] See paras PRE.01 et seq., below.

[46] For English law on this question see *McGregor on Damages*, 17th edn, paras 6.046 et seq. and *Rahman v Arearose* [2001] Q.B. 351.

[47] See *Anglo-Grecian Steam Trading Co v Benyon* (1926) 24 Ll. L. Rep. 122, 127.

[48] *Federal Commerce and Navigation Ltd v Eisenerz* [1970] 2 Lloyd's Rep. 332; [1975] 1 Lloyd's Rep. 105 (S.C. Canada).

endeavours in the interest of all parties concerned. There is, however, no rigid rule of law that he is bound to do everything himself; and in a proper case he may employ experienced persons to act for the benefit of all parties, and charge their remuneration as a general average expenditure.[49]

In addition to the financial expenditure involved in any general average situation, the shipowner will probably expend a considerable amount of extra time and trouble organising salvage assistance, arranging repairs and the discharge and reloading of cargo at a port of refuge, etc. and the question arises: is he entitled to any remuneration for this extra time and trouble? In general terms, the answer is that he is entitled to his actual out-of-pocket expenses such as travel and communication expenses, but not to any remuneration. Rule of Practice No.A3 of the Association of Average Adjusters provides as follows:

> "*Agency Commission and Agency*
>
> That, in practice, neither commission (excepting bank commission) nor any charge by way of agency or remuneration for trouble is allowed to the shipowner in average, except in respect of services rendered on behalf of cargo when such services are not involved in the contract of affreightment."

C.32 It frequently occurs that the registered owner of a vessel will leave the day-to-day operation of his vessel to a firm of ship managers who may be recompensed on a fee or commission basis. If the ship managers are entitled under the terms of their agreement to make a special charge for extra services rendered in a general average situation, is that charge properly admissible in general average?

The position is by no means clear, but some guidance may be obtained from *Rose v Bank of Australasia*.[50] In that case, the Sir Walter Raleigh stranded on the coast of France near Cap Gris Nez when on a voyage to the United Kingdom with a general cargo. The owner of the ship operated from Aberdeen and, therefore, he instructed a firm in London with experience in salvage operations and disasters of this kind to take all necessary steps in his interest and the interest of others concerned in the adventure. This firm proceeded at once to do what they could to save the ship and cargo and sent one of their men to the scene of the disaster and arranged for a local firm to do the best possible to save the cargo. For these services the London firm was to get £750 and the French firm was to receive a percentage of the value of the cargo salved; this proved to amount to £1,500. The ship ultimately proved to be a total loss but the cargo was discharged, carried to the top of the cliff and later carted to Boulogne. A quantity of seawater-damaged cargo was attended to and spread out to prevent deterioration, and ultimately it was forwarded to London. These two payments of £750 and £1,500 were charged–in part, at least–to general average, and the cargo interests disputed liability.

[49] *Rose v Bank of Australasia* [1894] A.C. 687 (see para.C.32, below), disapproving *Schuster v Fletcher* (1878) 3 Q.B.D. 418.

[50] *Rose v Bank of Australasia* [1894] A.C. 687. In *The Westport (No.3)* [1966] 1 Lloyd's Rep. 342, an agent's remuneration was held to be recoverable by him as a "disbursement" within the Administration of Justice Act 1956 s.1(1).

Certainly with regard to the £750 it was alleged that these services were a matter for the shipowner himself and that it merely represented the discharge of a duty incumbent upon him. If he chose to employ others to do this job it must be treated as if he had done it himself.

The House of Lords decided that both amounts were properly allowable and Herschell L.C. said (p.697): **C.33**

> "There is no doubt that when a disaster of this kind happens the ship-owner is bound to use his best endeavours in the interest of all concerned; but whether he is to do anything himself, and what he ought to do himself without making a charge for it, must, it seems to me, depend upon the circumstances of the case; there can be no rigid rule of law laid down with regard to it. It would in some cases, as it strikes me, be most unreasonable not to allow the shipowner to employ others to do the work, whilst in other cases it would be most unreasonable that he should, or that if he did he should make any charge in respect of it . . . I quite concede that a ship-owner owes a duty to all interested; that he cannot throw the expense of doing what he ought to do himself upon some other interests because he chooses to employ somebody else. Whilst conceding that, it appears to me clear that there are many cases where the employment of others is a reasonable and right course to take; and where by such employment extraordinary expenditure is incurred for the general benefit, I am at a loss to see why it may not be distributed over those who receive the benefit."

The expense to the owner of sending a special agent to a port of distress has been allowed in American cases, when such procedure was reasonable and the agent's services were for the general benefit.[51]

Costs of adjustment

It might be argued that this rule excludes any allowance in general average of the fees and expenses of an adjuster, since the shipowner is probably not bound to employ an adjuster and may prepare his own average statement.[52] However, he is bound to produce an average statement of some kind (since the York-Antwerp Rules have so provided, by implication, since 1924)[53] and it is the invariable practice for such costs to be treated as part of the general average under the Rules. It is submitted that the practice is correct; a consequence may be direct, if in the circumstances it will invariably happen, although one of the parties can avoid it if he choose to do so. In the United States a commission of 2.5 per cent for settlement and collection is charged to general average and received by the adjuster.[54] **C.34**

[51] *Hobson v Lord* 92 U.S. 397 (1875); *Besse v Hecht* 85 Fed. Rep. 677 (1898); *The Eliza Lines* 102 Fed. Rep. 184 (1900); also *Rose v Bank of Australasia* [1894] A.C. 687.

[52] *Wavertree Sailing Ship Co v Love* [1897] A.C. 373. See para.30.04, below.

[53] *Chandris v Argo Insurance Co Ltd* [1963] 2 Lloyd's Rep. 65.

[54] *Moore-McCormack Lines v Esso Camden* (1957) A.M.C. 971.

Legal costs

C.35 It is clear from *Australian Coastal Shipping Commission v Green*[55] that where a general average act gives rise to legal proceedings which are reasonably prosecuted or defended, the costs so incurred by a party to the adventure are general average.

Second Paragraph–Paragraph (2) in the York-Antwerp Rules 2004

General observations

C.36 This paragraph, introduced in 1994, essentially denies any allowance in general average in respect of any of the consequences of either:

(1) actual or threatened damage to the environment, if caused by the property involved in the common adventure[56] ; or
(2) the escape or release of pollutant substances from the property involved in the common adventure, even though these consequences may be the direct result of a general average act. Subject to the exceptions described below, all the consequences of these events are excluded, whether they take the form of damage to property, the costs of cleaning up pollution or making good damage, or liabilities to third parties.

It does not debar the allowance in general average of:

(1) the value of property sacrificed, including oil, chemicals or other pollutant substances, even if the sacrifice causes damage to the environment or involves an escape or release of pollutants, for example a jettison of a cargo of chemicals, or a discharge of bunker oil in order to lighten a ship;
(2) those losses damages and expenses recovery of which is specifically sanctioned by the numbered rules, namely:
    (a) damage to the property involved in the common maritime adventure consequent upon a sacrifice or other general average act, which may still be allowed under r.II, III or V; and
    (b) certain costs of preventing or minimising damage to the environment, which may be recoverable under r.VI of the 1994 Rules, or r.XI(d).

C.37 **"In no case"**: As explained in the commentary on the Rule of Interpretation, claims under any of the numbered rules are not affected by any of the provisions of r.C which are inconsistent with them. These apparently all-embracing words

[55] *Australian Coastal Shipping Commission* [1971] 1 Q.B. 456: see paras C.25–C.26, above.

[56] See para.C.39, below, as to threatened damage, and the case where the damage to the environment arises from another source.

therefore exclude from general average only those claims which are sustainable solely under the provisions of r.A, such as the example mentioned in para.C.28, above, or under any of the other lettered rules. Their purpose is simply to emphasise that the losses, etc. referred to in this paragraph are excluded even if they are the direct consequence of the general average act.

"losses, damages or expenses": These words are identical to the corresponding wording in the first paragraph of the rule,[57] and are also intended to be of the same comprehensive nature. The exclusion contained in this paragraph therefore extends not only to physical loss or damage to the environment and to clean-up costs, but also to liabilities[58] incurred to third parties in respect of environmental damage. The original draft considered by the CMI Conference at Sydney contained an express reference to liabilities, but this was deleted at the instigation of hull and cargo insurers.[59]

"in respect of damage to the environment": The expression damage to the environment is the same as that used in the International Convention on Salvage 1989,[60] where it is defined as meaning: **C.38**

> "substantial physical damage to human health or to marine life or resources in coastal or inland waters or areas adjacent thereto, caused by pollution, contamination, fire, explosion or similar major incidents."

The Convention, and its definition of damage to the environment, are expressly referred to in r.VI(a) of the 1994 Rules, and it seems clear that the identical phrase damage to the environment used in r.C is intended to have exactly the same meaning, with the result that it effectively incorporates the definition of the phrase contained in the Salvage Convention. The 1984 CMI Report to I.M.C.O. on the draft Convention has the following comments on the definition:

> "By using the words 'substantial' and 'major' as well as the reference to 'pollution, explosion, contamination, fire' it is intended to make it clear that the definition does not include damage to any particular person or installation. There must be a risk of damage of a more general nature in the area concerned, and it must be a risk of substantial damage.
>
> During the Montreal Conference the words 'to human health or to marine life or resources' were added to exclude further from the concept cases where there may only be a risk of substantial physical damage to other property, e.g. warehouses or other buildings ashore.

[57] See para.C.24, above.

[58] At the Sydney conference in 1994 the US delegation was concerned that this wording did not, with complete certainty, exclude liabilities. Accordingly they made a formal statement in the plenary session of the Conference as follows: "The Delegation of the United States of America understands that the proposed York-Antwerp Rules 1994 exclude allowances in general average in respect of liability in consequence of the escape or release of pollutant substances from the property involved in the common maritime adventure." The British delegation entertained no such doubts.

[59] Some hull and cargo insurers, while not disputing that in certain circumstances liabilities would be allowable in general average under the York-Antwerp Rules, were anxious to avoid any express references to liabilities in the Rules, even in a provision excluding them from allowances.

[60] The Convention has the force of law in England: see the Merchant Shipping Act 1995 s.224 and Sch.11.

> The use of the words 'coastal or inland waters' serves to make it clear that cases where there is only a risk of damage to the environment on the high seas are excluded. This is felt to be important since there would often be a possibility of speculative and inflated claims based on loose assertions that general environment damage to fishing or other ecology was involved. It must be stressed, however, that damage in coastal waters emanating from a ship in danger on the high seas is not excluded.
>
> As can easily be seen, the definition includes much more than pollution. It is not limited to risk of damage caused by oil or other specific cargoes. The use of the words 'explosion' and 'fire' in particular shows that it is the intention to cover all major incidents comprehensively."

It follows that the provisions of r.C relating to damage to the environment are not confined to pollution, and comprise damage resulting from any major incident. However, they do not include the following kinds of damage:

(1) damage which affects only one person or installation. It follows from this that damage to a single pier, such as occurred in *Austin Friars S.S. Co v Spillers and Bakers*[61] would not be excluded by r.C even if caused by an event which falls within the definition such as explosion or fire;
(2) damage which affects only buildings or installations ashore;
(3) damage which affects only deep-sea waters, without threatening coastal areas.

However where the damage results from the escape or release of a pollutant these situations will fall within the subsequent words of the paragraph, discussed in para.C.40, below.

C.39 The words "in respect of" have a wide meaning and include any losses, damages or expenses which are the result of or attributable to damage to the environment arising from the general average act. They may be contrasted with narrower expressions used elsewhere in the Rules, such as "in consequence of" (the expression used later in the paragraph, and commented on in para.C.40, below). It seems probable that the intention was also to include losses, etc. which are the result of alleged or threatened damage to the environment, such as might arise if a national authority were to impose a fine on the shipowner in the erroneous belief that damage to the environment had occurred for which he was responsible, or were to insist on the taking of expensive measures in order to avoid damage (or further damage) to the environment. All such cases are therefore prima facie excluded from general average by r.C. although the great majority of losses and expenses incurred in order to prevent or minimise threatened damage to the environment will fall within the specific provisions of r.XI(d), and will therefore be allowable.

Although the wording of this part of the rule does not make it as clear as it might, the rule was not intended to exclude allowances in cases where the actual or threatened damage to the environment is not attributable to the property involved in the common maritime adventure or from any efforts made to safeguard the same, but to an external source. For example, the expense of measures

[61] *Austin Friars S.S. Co* [1915] 1 K.B. 833; [1915] 3 K.B. 586.

taken to protect the ship and cargo from the consequences of a conflagration on another vessel or at a shore installation should not be excluded by the rule, and should therefore be allowable so long as the measures comply with the requirements of r.A, or of one of the numbered rules.

"in consequence of the escape or release of pollutant substances": As explained in para.C.38, above, the expression "damage to the environment" does not cover every situation where loss, damage or expense is caused by an escape or release of a pollutant from the ship or cargo, and r.C therefore contains this further specific provision, the effect of which is to exclude all such losses, etc. from allowance in general average (unless they fall within the terms of one of the numbered rules). "Escape" covers the case where the pollutant substance is emitted accidentally, and "release" where it is emitted by design. The effect of the words "in consequence of" is that there must have been an actual (that is, not merely an alleged or threatened) escape or release of the pollutant substance if this part of the second paragraph of the rule is to apply. However, if the threatened pollution damage is such as would amount to "damage to the environment" the case would fall within the antecedent provision of the rule. **C.40**

"from the property involved in the common maritime adventure": These words serve a dual purpose. In the first place they exclude from the operation of this paragraph of r.C the case where general average expenses are incurred in consequence of the escape or release of a pollutant substance from another ship, or from a shore installation. Secondly, they make it clear that there must be an escape or release of the pollutant substance beyond the confines of ship and cargo; thus an escape or release of a pollutant from the ship into the cargo or vice versa falls outside the scope of the provision, with the result that the consequent loss or damage may be chargeable to general average. Damage to the outer hull of the ship, caused by an escape or release of her cargo or bunkers is only consistent with an escape or release beyond the confines of the ship and cargo, and is therefore prima facie barred by the rule. However, such damage will be allowable under r.II if it is the consequence of a sacrifice and is reasonably incurred.

Third Paragraph–Paragraph (3) in York-Antwerp Rules 2004

"loss of market": Earlier versions of r.C referred to loss of market as an example of indirect loss, whereas in English law it is usually regarded as a direct loss,[62] and a loss caused by a fall in the market at the destination is not too remote to be recoverable from a carrier by sea as damages for breach of contract.[63] The wording of the earlier versions could therefore have been interpreted as an indication that the expression "direct consequence" in r.C had a particularly narrow meaning, although it seems unlikely that this was actually the intention.[64] The **C.41**

[62] See *Australian Coastal Shipping v Green* [1971] 1 Q.B. 456 at 481, per Lord Denning M.R., para.C.26, above.

[63] See *Koufus v C. Czarnikow* [1969] 1 A.C. 350. See also para.C.05 fn.7, above.

[64] See *Australian Coastal Shipping v Green* [1971] 1 Q.B. 456 at 481, and at 487. The point is discussed at para.C.30 of the 11th edn, where this interpretation is rejected.

1994 and 2004 Rules eliminate this potential source of misunderstanding; loss of market is excluded in its own right, and cannot be treated as having any influence on the meaning of "direct consequence".

There is no authority on the meaning of "loss of market". It clearly bars recovery of any loss resulting from market fluctuation during a period of delay. Thus if goods shipped specially for the Christmas market are delayed in consequence of a general average act on the voyage, and arrive in January physically sound but of considerably reduced value, the cargo owner has no claim in general average. However, it is submitted that r.C does not exclude from general average a loss resulting from the goods becoming unsaleable, or less valuable, in the market at their destination, whether as a result of physical damage or as a result of legal or other obstacles. Thus the cargo's loss in value, in *Anglo-Argentine Live Stock Agency v Temperley S.S. Co*[65] should be allowed under r.C as it was under English law. That loss in value was not caused by delay, or by any other intervening cause but by the goods becoming subject to the prohibition on import at the intended destination, as a direct result of the general average act.

The exclusion of claims for loss of market does not, of course, mean that the value of the cargo at destination is ignored in calculating the amount to be made good for loss or damage caused by a general average sacrifice. r.XVI of the York-Antwerp Rules contains detailed provisions for calculating the amount made good, which is based on invoice value at destination.

C.42 **"any loss or damage sustained or expense incurred by reason of delay"**: The exclusion of loss, etc. by delay reflects English law on the subject.[66] Earlier versions of r.C referred only to loss or damage through delay, leaving open the argument that expense incurred through delay was not caught by the exclusion.[67] The 1994 and 2004 Rules remove any basis for this argument, since the words loss or damage sustained or expense incurred mirror the language of the first two paragraphs of the rule (discussed at paras C.24–C.37, above) and there can thus be no doubt that they are intended to be of equal width.

"whether on the voyage or subsequently": The reason for the introduction of this phrase in 1950 has already been discussed.[68]

C.43 **"delay"**: There are cases where it may be difficult to determine whether a loss is caused by a delay or by some other factor, for example:

(1) Water used to extinguish a fire puts the refrigerating machinery out of action and the contents are ruined because their temperature rises above that at which they can be stored. Such loss has been allowed.

[65] *Anglo-Argentine Live Stock Agency* [1899] 2 Q.B. 403. See para.C.08, above.

[66] See paras C.13 et seq., above.

[67] On the ground that expenses were specifically referred to in the first paragraph of r.C, but were omitted from the paragraph dealing with loss, etc. by delay. The merits of this argument are discussed at para.C.28 of the 11th edn, where the view is expressed that, despite the deficiencies in the drafting of the rule, expenses caused by delay did fall within the scope of this paragraph of the rule, and were therefore excluded from general average.

[68] See para.C.19, above.

(2) A vessel puts into a port of refuge loaded down to summer load line. By the time she leaves, winter load lines have come into force and she is obliged to leave part of her cargo. This is seldom allowed.

"any indirect loss whatsoever": This is simply the corollary of the provisions of the first paragraph of the rule, which allows in general average only those losses, damages and expenses which are the direct consequence of the general average act. The meaning of that expression is discussed above at para.C.25. **C.44**

RULE D

THE EFFECT OF FAULT

In the majority of cases in which a claim for contribution in general average is disputed, the defence raised is that the peril which gave rise to the general average act was caused by the fault of the person claiming contribution, for example the shipowner has failed to exercise due diligence to provide a seaworthy ship. The circumstances in which such a defence will succeed, both at common law and under the York-Antwerp Rules,[1] are here examined. With one possible exception,[2] there is no difference between English law and York-Antwerp Rules in their treatment of the effect of fault. Both have adopted the policy of keeping separate the adjustment of general average and the consequences of fault, thereby enabling the necessary action to be taken in response to a common peril, and the adjustment prepared, while leaving the parties free to dispute any issues of fault and its effect at a later stage. D.01

ENGLISH LAW AND BACKGROUND

General Rule in English Law

If the necessity for a general average act arose as a result[3] of the fault of one of the parties to the adventure,[4] the act retains its general average character and contribution is due between the parties to the adventure, subject to the important D.02

[1] Rule D: see paras D.22 et seq., below.

[2] Where the liability of the person claiming contribution is limited by statute or by contract: see paras D.08, D.10, D.32, below.

[3] The issue is whether the claimant "has by his own [actionable] fault occasioned the peril which immediately gave rise to the claim": *Strang Steel & Co v A. Scott & Co* (1889) 14 A.C. 601 at 608, per Lord Watson; and *Pirie & Co v Middle Dock Co* (1881) 44 L.T. 426 at 429. But fault after the peril has arisen may also be relevant: *Eisenerz GmbH v Federal Commerce & Navigation Co* [1975] 1 Lloyd's Rep. 105.

[4] *Strang Steel & Co v A. Scott & Co* (1889) 14 A.C. 601 at 609, PC; *Louis Dreyfus & Co v Tempus Shipping Co* [1931] A.C. 726 at 747, HL.

exception that the party at fault is not entitled to recover contribution from any other at whose suit the fault was actionable[5] at the time at which the sacrifice or expenditure was made or incurred.[6]

The justification for this exception has been attributed to the policy of the courts of avoiding circuity of action[7] and to the principle that a person shall not recover from any other person in respect of the consequences of his own wrong.[8] It has also been suggested that contribution is irrecoverable because the sacrifice or expenditure by the party at fault is made or incurred for the benefit of that party alone and not for the benefit of the adventure as a whole, since the party at fault would have been liable to the proposed contributor in respect of the loss averted by the general average act.[9] In the 9th edn of the present work this was considered the better view. But: (1) it encounters the same objection as the argument based on circuity of action in cases where the wrongdoer would be only partially liable[10] ; (2) it is inconsistent with the right of a party not at fault to recover contribution from another party not at fault; and (3) it seems artificial to suppose, on the facts, that the motive was not the preservation of all the property involved.

Actionable Fault

D.03 Although the exception is usually expressed in terms of actionable fault,[11] the fault will frequently be actionable only in an artificial sense, if at all, since the general average act may avert the damage in respect of which an action would have lain. Thus if a ship is unseaworthy at the commencement of a voyage, as a result of want of due diligence on the part of her owner, and in consequence the master engages towage assistance to save the vessel and cargo from danger, the engagement of towage assistance will usually prevent any loss or damage to the cargo in respect of which an action could be maintained; the cargo owner may have a claim in contract for nominal damages, but no tort has been committed. If, on the other hand, instead of the master engaging a tug under a towage contract, the ship and cargo had been salved and the cargo interests had incurred liability to the salvors, the shipowner would be liable for substantial damages.

However in such a case, if the contract of carriage imposed upon the shipowner the obligation to exercise due diligence to make the ship seaworthy, the cargo owner would have a defence to a claim for contribution. The true test of actionable fault is therefore whether, if the general average act had not been performed with the result that the peril had operated, the person claiming contribution would have been legally liable to the person against whom contribution is claimed for

[5] *Schloss v Heriot* (1863) 14 C.B. (N.S.) 59; *Strang Steel & Co v A. Scott & Co* (above) at 608; *Louis Dreyfus & Co v Tempus Shipping Co* (above) at 738, 747.

[6] *Goulandris Bros Ltd v B. Goldman & Sons Ltd* [1958] 1 Q.B. 74 at 104.

[7] *Schloss v Heriot* (above) at 64.

[8] *Goulandris Bros Ltd v B. Goldman & Sons Ltd* (above) at 95.

[9] *Tempus Shipping Co v Louis Dreyfus & Co* [1931] 1 K.B. 195 at 211, per Greer L.J. [1931] A.C. 726 at 742, per Lord Warrington (but see Viscount Dunedin at 734).

[10] *The Ettrick* (1881) 6 P. D. 127. See paras D.08 and D.10, below.

[11] See the cases cited in fns 5, 6, above.

the damage to the property of the latter.[12] A similar approach is adopted in determining whether an exceptions clause prevents the fault from being actionable.[13]

Effect of Contractual or Statutory Exemptions from Liability

The obligations normally undertaken by the carrier and the shipper under the contract of affreightment are described in outline elsewhere,[14] and it is these obligations which must in the first instance be determined in order to ascertain whether the peril which occasioned the general average act was caused by the failure of the party claiming contribution properly to perform his contractual obligations to the party from whom contribution is claimed. Where there is no contract between the parties it must likewise be determined whether the peril arose as a result of a failure by the person claiming contribution to comply with a duty owed to the other party in tort, or as a bailee. **D.04**

The next step is to ascertain whether the failure is actionable, or whether on the other hand it is excused by a statutory provision or (where the relationship between the parties is governed by contract) by the provisions of a contractual exceptions clause. The exempting provisions which may be relevant in determining this question take a number of different forms; they may, for example:

(1) prevent any legal responsibility at all from arising in circumstances when it would otherwise arise;
(2) exclude any liability for "loss or damage" arising from a specified cause;
(3) limit liability to a particular sum; or
(4) exonerate the shipowner from liability unless suit is brought within a specified period of time.

The effect of these provisions on the existence of actionable fault is examined below, and for this purpose no distinction in principle need be drawn between contractual and statutory exemptions.[15]

(1) Provisions which prevent any legal responsibility from arising

It has always been accepted that exceptions clauses of the first category nullify the existence of any actionable fault, for all purposes including general average. In *The Carron Park*[16] a clause stating "neglect or default whatsoever of. . . the **D.05**

[12] See *Louis Dreyfus & Co v Tempus Shipping Co* (above); *The Makedonia* [1962] 1 Lloyd's Rep. 316 at 339, 341. Such liability might arise out of the failure to perform the general average act (see paras 00.61 et seq., above), but liability which would have arisen solely out of such a failure must be ignored for the purpose of applying the test propounded here.

[13] See paras D.04 et seq., below.

[14] See paras 00.34 et seq., above.

[15] *Louis Dreyfus v Tempus Shipping* [1931] A.C. 726.

[16] *The Carron Park* (1890) 15 P.D. 203. The decision was approved and followed by the Court of Appeal in *Milburn & Co v Jamaica Fruit Importing & Trading Co* [1900] 2 Q.B. 540, where the relevant clause was in similar terms.

servants of the shipowner always excepted" was held to prevent the shipowner from being under any responsibility for the entry of water into the holds, as a result of negligence by the ship's engineers in the operation of her valves, and therefore to preserve unaffected by that negligence the shipowner's right to contribution in general average. In the light of *Louis Dreyfus v Tempus Shipping*[17] it is clear that statutory provisions in similar terms should receive exactly the same effect.

(2) Provisions which exclude liability for loss or damage

D.06 Until the decision of the House of Lords in *Louis Dreyfus and Co v Tempus Shipping Co*[18] it was not clear whether provisions of this second type had the same effect. In that case, fire broke out on the voyage as a result of the failure to exercise due diligence to make the ship seaworthy, in breach of the contract of carriage. Expenses were incurred at a port of refuge, and the shipowner claimed contribution. Under s.502 of the Merchant Shipping Act 1894, the shipowner was exempt from liability for "loss or damage" caused by fire arising without his actual fault or privity. It was argued by the cargo owners that the shipowner's breach was actionable; the section merely relieved him of certain consequences of his default—namely liability for "loss or damage", and that it had no relevance to a claim for general average. This argument was accepted by Wright J.[19] and Scrutton L.J.,[20] but rejected by the majority of the Court of Appeal and by the House of Lords. Slesser L.J. considered that the correct test was whether any actionable liability would have lain on the party claiming contribution if the sacrifice or expenditure had not been made, and if the property had been lost, and he concluded: "it must be admitted that whatever the shipowner did to save the cargo, if he had not done it no action would have arisen."[21] In the House of Lords, Lord Dunedin considered that "an actionable wrong for which you can recover nothing is a contradiction in terms".[22]

D.07 The same approach was adopted in *The Makedonia*,[23] where the exceptions clause provided that the deck cargo was "carried. . . at the sole risk of the owner of such cargo" and excused the carrier from liability for " 'loss, damage or delay". The ship, which was unseaworthy, broke down and salvage services were engaged by the owner, who sought to recover in general average the cargo's share of the salvage award. This claim failed with regard to the under-deck cargo, but succeeded with regard to the deck cargo. Dealing with the argument that the exception clause dealt only with physical loss or damage, and not with pecuniary loss, Hewson J. said: "the shipowners were, as I see it, averting a physical loss for which they would not have been liable."[24] A similar decision had already been

[17] *Louis Dreyfus v Tempus Shipping* [1931] A.C. 726.
[18] *Louis Dreyfus* [1931] A.C. 726.
[19] [1930] 1 K.B. 699.
[20] [1931] 1 K.B. 195 at 207–208.
[21] As above, at 218.
[22] [1931] A.C. 726 at 739.
[23] *The Makedonia* [1962] P. 190: [1962] 1 Lloyd's Rep. 316 at 339–341.
[24] [1962] 1 Lloyd's Rep. 316 at 341.

reached in Australia in *Westfal-Larsen v Colonial Sugar Refining Co*,[25] where the clause exempted the shipowner from responsibility for loss of or damage to goods on board, or for delay, unless caused by the personal want of due diligence of the owners or their manager to make the ship seaworthy, or by the personal act or omission or default of the owners or their manager. The ship was unseaworthy as a result of the negligence of the ship's engineers in taking on board the wrong type of fuel oil, she broke down on the voyage, and general average expenses were incurred. Neither the owners or their manager were personally at fault, and accordingly it was held by Walsh J. that the effect of the clause was that the cargo owners had no defence to a claim for contribution since "the threatened loss or damage to the goods, or delay in their transport, arose from a cause outside the area of the responsibility of the owners, as defined by the contract".[26]

(3) Provisions which limit liability

Where the terms of the contract or statute merely limit the amount of the party's liability, as opposed to excluding it, they do not nullify the existence of actionable fault. The result is that nothing can be recovered.[27] **D.08**

(4) Provisions which exclude liability unless suit is brought within a defined period

In general, provisions of this nature will have no effect on the question of actionable fault, for the reasons described in para.D.12, below.

The Effect of Certain Specific Provisions

Section 186 of the Merchant Shipping Act 1995 (fire)

In cases to which this section applies, the shipowner cannot be made liable at the suit of the other interests for loss or damage and accordingly his "fault" is not **D.09**

[25] *Westfal-Larsen v Colonial Sugar Refining Co* [1960] 2 Lloyd's Rep. 206.

[26] As above, at 211. The case concerned the Baltime exceptions clause, which has subsequently been held by the House of Lords to be confined to responsibility for physical loss or damage to the goods, or delay, and to provide no protection against claims for financial loss: see *Tor Line v Alltrans* [1984] 1 Lloyd's Rep. 123. In that case Lord Roskill expressed the view that Westfal-Larsen was wrongly decided, apparently on the ground that Walsh J. had erroneously interpreted the clause as providing protection against claims for financial loss as well as physical loss and damage. It is true that the construction of the clause adopted by Walsh J. leads inevitably to the conclusion that the clause covers financial loss, and therefore can no longer be regarded as wholly sound. However, the reasons for his decision that contribution was recoverable, contained in the passage quoted in the text, remain perfectly valid even on the narrower interpretation of the clause adopted by the House of Lords. The Tor Line case was not concerned with general average, and none of the relevant authorities on actionable fault are referred to.

[27] There is no direct authority for this proposition in relation to contractual limitations, but it is submitted that it follows from *The Ettrick* (1881) 6 P.D. 127, and the equation of statutory with contractual exemptions from liability in *Louis Dreyfus & Co v Tempus Shipping Co* [1931] A.C. 726, HL.

actionable and he can recover contribution in general average.[28] No distinction is to be made between this section which prevents the recovery of losses from a shipowner and an exceptions clause which negatives a duty which would otherwise rest upon the shipowner.[29]

Section 185 of the Merchant Shipping Act 1995 (limitation of liability)

D.10 This section gives legal effect to the Convention on Limitation of Liability for Maritime Claims 1976. The Convention by limiting, as opposed to negativing, liability leaves the fault of the shipowner actionable and he is accordingly unable to recover contribution in general average, as demonstrated by the decision in *The Ettrick*,[30] under an earlier statute to similar effect, where the Court of Appeal rejected the argument that, by paying the statutory limit into court the shipowner had purged his actionable fault.

Article IV, Rules 1 and 2 of the Hague and the Hague-Visby Rules

D.11 Article IV, rr.1 and 2 of both the Hague and the Hague-Visby Rules confer on the carrier exemption from liability for loss or damage to or in connection with[31] goods arising from a variety of causes. It follows that when the peril which occasions the general average act arises from one of these causes the defence of actionable fault cannot be raised in answer to a claim for contribution. Most of these Hague and Hague-Visby Rule exceptions have no application if the underlying cause of the loss or damage is the negligence of the carrier or of his servants or agents, but some protect the carrier even in the event of negligence by his servants or agents, namely the exception of act, neglect or default in the navigation or the management of the ship,[32] and the exception of fire.

Article III, Rule 6 of the Hague and the Hague-Visby Rules

D.12 Both the Hague and the Hague-Visby Rules contain examples of the fourth type of exemption clause referred to in para.D.04, above, which exonerate the carrier from liability unless suit is brought within a specified time. Thus art.III, r.6 of the Hague Rules provides that the carrier shall be "discharged from all liability in respect of loss or damage"[33] unless suit is brought within one year of the delivery of the goods or the date when the goods ought to have been delivered. In *Goulandris Bros v B. Goldman & Sons*[34] it was held that this provision did not

[28] See *Louis Dreyfus & Co v Tempus Shipping Co* [1931] A.C. 726, HL, decided under the equivalent provisions or the Merchant Shipping Act 1894 s.502.

[29] *Louis Dreyfus*, at 739, 750.

[30] *The Ettrick* 6 P.D. 127; *Louis Dreyfus & Co v Tempus Shipping Co* [1931] A.C. 726 at 747, HL.

[31] The Rules simply refer to "loss or damage", but this has been held to mean loss or damage to, or in connection with the carriage of, the goods: see *G.H. Renton & Co Ltd v Palmyra Trading Corp* [1957] A.C. 149; *Adamastos Shipping Co Ltd v Anglo-Saxon Petroleum Co Ltd* [1959] A.C. 133.

[32] See para.00.50, above.

[33] See fn.31, above.

[34] *Goulandris Bros v B. Goldman & Sons* [1958] 1 Q.B. 74.

prevent a cargo owner from raising actionable fault as a defence to the carrier's claim for contribution, even though he had not brought suit within one year for the purpose of establishing the actionable fault on the part of the carrier. The cargo owner was entitled to wait until an action for contribution was brought against him, whenever that might be, and to raise the defence of actionable fault at that time, because art.III, r.6 only brings about a discharge of liabilities and not a barring of defences.[35] The case was decided under the York-Antwerp Rules,[36] but the same conclusion will hold good where the claim is governed by English law. It also holds good, it is submitted, where the contract of carriage incorporates the Hague-Visby Rules rather than the Hague Rules[37] ; and it will apply a fortiori where the contract incorporates the two year time-bar contained in art.20 of the Hamburg Rules, which is merely procedural, barring the remedy rather than extinguishing the liability.

Fault on the Part of the Person from Whom Contribution is Claimed

We have so far been considering the effect of fault on the part of the person claiming contribution. What is the result in the converse case, where the accident which gave rise to the general average was caused by the fault of the party to the adventure from whom contribution is claimed? Clearly such a party cannot rely on his own fault as a defence to the claim for contribution, but if the fault was actionable at the suit of the person claiming contribution,[38] it will usually be more advantageous to the claimant to seek to recover his entire loss, as damages for breach of contract or in tort, and not merely a contribution towards it in general average. As a result, the claim in general average, although remaining perfectly valid, will often be subsumed in a larger claim for damages. **D.13**

Thus in *Dixon v Royal Exchange Shipping Co*[39] the cargo owners claimed from the shipowner the entire value of cargo jettisoned, as damages on the grounds that the jettison resulted from the shipowner's breach of contract in taking a deck cargo; the shipowner accepted liability for a contribution in general average, but it was held that he was liable for the entire loss. Equally, if a shipowner incurs general average expense as a result of the loading by a shipper of dangerous cargo, without the master's knowledge or consent,[40] the shipowner may recover the **D.14**

[35] An additional ground for the decision was that "loss or damage" in art.III, r.6 did not include a liability to contribute in general average. Sed quaere: see para.00.54, fn.57, and para.D.11, fn.31, above.

[36] Rule D of the York-Antwerp Rules 1950. Subsequent amendments to r.D have no effect on this conclusion.

[37] The equivalent wording in art.III r.6, of the Hague-Visby Rules is "the carrier shall be discharged from all liability whatsoever in respect of the goods", and whilst this is in some respects rather wider than the provision in the Hague Rules it still only brings about a discharge of liabilities, and not a barring of defence.

[38] See para.D.03. above, as to the meaning of actionable fault.

[39] *Dixon v Royal Exchange Shipping Co* [1886] 12 App.Cas. 11. See para.1.12, below. In *Gould v Oliver* (1840) 2 Man. & Gr. 208 the cargo owner, who had succeeded in a previous action in recovering a general average contribution to the loss of his deckload by jettison, brought a second action to recover his full loss and claimed damages on the grounds that the jettison was caused by bad stowage.

[40] See paras 00.63 et seq., above.

entire expense from that shipper and not merely a contribution; and since the fault of the shipper does not deprive the act of its general average character the shipowner may also claim contribution from the owners of any cargo on board at the time of the general average act, the only qualification being that he is not entitled to recover more than once for the same loss.

Exceptions Clauses as a Defence to a Claim for Contribution

D.15 As explained above, an exemption clause in a contract of affreightment which exempts one party (usually the shipowner) from liability for loss or damage from a specified cause will, by negativing the existence of actionable fault:

(1) protect that party from liability in damages for the entire loss; and
(2) preserve his right to claim contribution from the other parties to the adventure.

Occasionally attempts have been made rely on such exemption clauses as also providing a defence to a claim for contribution, and whilst this topic may more properly belong elsewhere, it can conveniently be dealt with here.

D.16 With the exception of clauses imposing a time bar for claims, the courts have consistently adopted the approach that contractual or statutory provisions exempting a party from liability for loss or damage to cargo, or to similar effect, will not be construed as referring to a liability to contribute in general average, unless they very clearly so provide.

Thus in *Schmidt v Royal Mail S.S. Co*,[41] where the bill of lading contained an exception of "fire on board", it was held that this did not prevent the charterer from claiming a general average contribution from the owner in respect of cargo sacrificed in extinguishing the fire. Blackburn J. expressed the view that:

> "the office of the bill of lading is to provide for the rights and liabilities of the parties in reference to the contract to carry, and is not concerned with liabilities to contribution in general average."

The same conclusion was reached in *Crooks v Allen*[42] where the provisions of the contract exempted the shipowner from liability "for any damage to any goods which is capable of being covered by insurance", and in *Burton v English*[43] where the contract provided that a deck load was to be carried "at merchants risk", it was held that the clause provided no defence to a claim for contribution to a loss by jettison.[44] In all of these cases the clause in question, whilst it prevented the shipowner from being held liable in damages, was held to have no bearing on his liability in general average.

[41] *Schmidt v Royal Mail S.S. Co* (1876) 45 L.J.Q.B. 646.
[42] *Crooks v Allen* (1879)5 Q.B.D. 38.
[43] *Burton v English* (1883) 12 Q.B.D. 218, CA.
[44] The same conclusion has been reached by the US courts in *Nicaraguan Lumber Co v Moody* (1954) A.M.C. 658.

In *Greenshields, Cowie v Stephen & Sons Ltd*[45] the same approach was adopted towards a statutory provision. A cargo of coal ignited spontaneously as a result of inherent vice. The cargo was sacrificed and the shipowner, in defence to a claim for general average contribution, relied on the implied exception of inherent vice in the contract of carriage, and the statutory exception of fire under s.502 of the Merchant Shipping Act 1894. These arguments were rejected, since the implied exception, while providing a defence to a claim for damage or non-delivery, had no relevance to a claim for contribution, and "the statute is not dealing with general average at all".[46] The result would have been different if there had been a breach of contract in the shipping of the coal, since the loss would then have arisen as a result of the actionable fault of the cargo owner who was claiming contribution. However, the shipowner had agreed to carry the coal with full knowledge of its nature. Claims for contribution in general average are, by art. III(a), expressly excluded from the scope of the Convention on the Limitation of Liability for Maritime Claims 1976, thus ruling out any argument of the kind raised by the defendant in the Greenshields case. **D.17**

It follows that if a party wishes to be relieved from the obligation to contribute, he must use words which expressly or by necessary implication refer to contribution in general average. This is sometimes done with regard to deck cargo and dangerous cargo.[47] **D.18**

Special considerations apply when the exception clause relied on is a contractual time limit for bringing actions. Here a different approach has been adopted by the courts, and the time limit will normally be construed as applying to a claim for general average contribution, at any rate where the obligation to contribute in general average is contractual.[48] The effect of such time limits is considered in more detail below.[49] **D.19**

General Average Resulting from Fault of Cargo

When a claim in general average is resisted on the ground of fault it is usually the fault of the shipowner which is in issue; but this is not always so. For example, cargo which has ignited spontaneously may be jettisoned, or damaged by **D.20**

[45] *Greenshields, Cowie v Stephen & Sons Ltd* [1908] A.C. 431.

[46] *Greenshields*, at 436, per Lord Halsbury. This phrase was relied upon by the cargo owners in their unsuccessful argument in *Louis Dreyfus & Co v Tempus Shipping Ltd* (para.D.06, above) as demonstrating that the statutory exception in s.502 of the Merchant Shipping Act was irrelevant for all purposes of general average. The House of Lords held that the views expressed by Lord Halsbury were confined to the context where the provision was relied upon as a defence to a claim for contribution. The decisions on actionable fault on the part of the claimant, and those on the effect of exceptions in favour of the person from whom contribution is claimed are fully consistent in their approach. In each case the question is where the loss would have fallen if the sacrifice or expenditure had not been made. In the *Greenshields* case, if the general average act had not been carried out, some of the resulting damage (namely that to the ship) would have been borne by the shipowner, and neither the statute nor the contractual exception of inherent vice would have entitled him to claim that loss from the cargo owner. It would therefore be illogical if those provisions were to protect him against a claim for contribution by the cargo owner.

[47] Art.IV r.6 of the Hague Rules (dangerous cargo); see para.00.65, above.

[48] See paras 00.26 et seq., above.

[49] Paras 23.01 et seq., below.

firefighting operations and the shipowner and other cargo-owners may seek to defend a claim for contribution by the owner of the sacrificed cargo on the ground that the sacrifice arose as a result of the fault of the cargo itself.

D.21 Until the decision in *Greenshields, Cowie & Co v Stephen & Sons Ltd*[50] the view was sometimes advanced that in such a case contribution could not be recovered in respect of sacrifice of cargo if it was the inherent vice of the cargo itself which had caused the danger. However, this view has been said to involve "a complete fallacy",[51] and it is now settled beyond argument that exactly the same principle applies in this case as in any other. Contribution can be recovered unless the danger arose as a result of actionable fault on the part of the owner[52] of the cargo sacrificed; it is no defence to the claim merely to show that the damage arose from the inherent vice of the cargo.[53]

Historical Development and Practice of Rule D

D.22 The 1924 rule reproduced the Antwerp Rule 1903,[54] with the substitution of the word "event" for "danger" and "fault" for "default".

The intention of those who drafted the rule seems to have been to try to separate rights under the contract of affreightment from rights in general average.[55] Logically such a separation must result in rights in general average being unimpaired by any breach of the contract of affreightment, whether or not the claimant be the party in default. In practice the rule has been interpreted as affirming that the rights in general average of innocent parties are unaffected by any breach of the contract of affreightment, but not as improving the position of the party in fault. This construction seems to accord with the intentions of the Antwerp Conference of 1903[56] and the Stockholm Conference of 1924.

York-Antwerp Rules 1924 and 1950

D.23 The rule was in the same terms as that set out below, except that it ended "but this shall not prejudice any remedies which may be open against that party for such fault".

[50] *Greenshields* [1908] A.C. 431, see para.D.17, above.

[51] *Pirie v Middle Dock Co* (1881) 4 Asp. M.L.C. 388 at 391, per Watkin Williams J.

[52] See paras 00.63 et seq., above, as to the obligation of the shipper with regard to the nature of the goods shipped, and the question whether those obligations are transferred to a bill of lading holder.

[53] See *Johnson v Chapman* (1865) 19 C.B. (N.S.) 563; *Pirie v Middle Dock Co* (1981) 4 Asp. M.L.C. 388; *Greenshields, Cowie v Stephen* [1908] A.C. 431. Consideration may need to be given in such a case to the separate question whether the cargo was effectively lost anyway. See paras 3.01 et seq., below.

[54] See para.00.80, above.

[55] See papers by Kennedy L.J. and T.G. Carver in *The Journal of Comparative Legislation*, Vol.V, pp.221, 224.

[56] Para.00.80, above.

York-Antwerp Rules 1974

In 1974 the final words of the rule were enlarged so as to provide "but this shall not prejudice any remedies or defences which may be open against or to that party in respect of such fault". The effect of this alteration is considered below.[57] **D.24**

York-Antwerp Rules 1994 and 2004

There was no change. A proposal was made[58] in 1994 to amend the rule to provide that a party from whom contribution was claimed should be obliged in the first instance to pay the contribution properly assessed on his interest, and only then be entitled to raise the issue of actionable fault, in separate proceedings to recover the amount already paid–"pay first sue later". However, the proposal was strongly criticised by cargo interests as being a serious inroad into the principle, adopted by many national laws, that actionable fault is a defence to a claim for contribution, rather than being merely a matter of counterclaim, and no national delegation could be found to support it. **D.25**

RULE D

Rights to contribution in general average shall not be affected, though the event which gave rise to the sacrifice or expenditure may have been due to the fault of one of the parties to the adventure, but this shall not prejudice any remedies or defences which may be open against or to that party in respect of such fault.

CONSTRUCTION

The object of the rule is to keep all questions of alleged fault outside the average adjustment and to preserve the legal position at the stage of enforcement. The first part of the rule permits an adjustment to be prepared on the assumption that the casualty occurred without the fault of any party to the adventure. The second part of the rule then operates as a proviso to the first, enabling the prima facie rights of the parties derived under the first part to be defeated by the remedies which are preserved by the second part.[59] **D.26**

To illustrate the operation of these principles, two examples are given below:

[57] See para.D.32, below.
[58] By the Association Internationale de Dispacheurs Europeens.
[59] *Goulandris Bros Ltd v B. Goldman & Sons Ltd* [1958] Q.B. 74 at 92–93.

Example (1)

D.27 The shipowner fails to exercise due diligence to provide a seaworthy ship, as the result of which the vessel sustains a machinery breakdown, and for the common safety, is obliged to put into a port of refuge to effect repairs.

A general average situation exists, the shipowner has incurred general average expenditure, and it is therefore perfectly in order for an adjustment to be prepared. However, the cargo are entitled to refuse payment of any general average contribution demanded of them.

If the preparation of the adjustment in such circumstances appears to be a somewhat futile operation, it should be noted that the adjustment will generally be required in any event in order that the shipowner may claim:

(1) the ship's proportion of general average from the hull insurers, whose policies customarily preclude the denial of liability on the grounds of unseaworthiness of the vessel;
(2) the cargo's proportion of general average from his Protecting and Indemnity Association, if unrecovered from the cargo interests themselves.

By determining the proportion of general average which attaches to ship and cargo respectively, the adjustment will thus establish a division of responsibility between the shipowner's hull and liability insurers. Further, the adjuster is concerned only with whether a general average situation exists, and it is not within his province to determine whether the ship was seaworthy or not, or whether the shipowner has failed to exercise due diligence.

Example (2)

D.28 The shipowner fails to exercise due diligence to provide a seaworthy ship, as the result of which a fire breaks out on board, cargo is damaged by measures taken to extinguish it and the shipowner incurs expenses admissible as general average within the terms of the York-Antwerp Rules. A general average adjustment is prepared showing these figures:

Shipowner's general average expenditure	100,000
Damage to cargo by extinguishing measures	900,000
	1,000,000

An owner of cargo delivered in sound condition is shown liable in the adjustment to pay a general average contribution of 10,000, effectively comprising:

1,000	due to the shipowner in respect of expenditure incurred by him, and
9,000	due to the owners of the damaged cargo.
10,000	

The cargo interest may legitimately decline to pay the 1,000 nominally due to the shipowner whose fault has brought about the stranding, but he must contribute his share of the loss suffered by the innocent owners of the damaged cargo. The adjustment is required in order to quantify the amount of this share, and it is necessary to collect security from the owners of the undamaged cargo for the claims of the owners of the damaged cargo, the shipowner being both bound and entitled to collect such security notwithstanding any allegation of fault which may be made against him.[60] A collective claim of 900,000 can then be made against the shipowner by all those parties who have suffered or made good the loss.

This procedure may again appear ponderous, but the cargo interests suffering the loss by the measures taken to extinguish the fire will at least recoup their loss with some degree of certainty and within a reasonable period of time, whereas it could take several years to prosecute and recover their direct claim against the shipowner—or he may be without funds or uninsured.

Problems in identifying the party at fault, proving the necessary facts, and enforcing remedies, may be even more intractable where the party at fault is not the shipowner, but, for example, the shipper of a container of dangerous goods, which, because they are misdescribed or inadequately described on shipment, cause an explosion which damages the ship and other goods, thereby necessitating sacrifices and expenses of a general average nature. In such a case the only matter which is reasonably clear at the outset is that any claim against the person at fault, even if he can be identified, is unlikely to be satisfied, and the only sensible course in such a case is that the owners of the surviving property should initially give security and contribute to the sacrifices and expenses on the basis of rights and obligations in general average, leaving it until later to assess whether there is any real prospect of effecting a recovery.

"event": In line with English law, this word refers to the original accident or occurrence which occasioned the sacrifice or expenditure.[61] Fault at subsequent stages may also be relevant, but will not necessarily have the same effect. Thus if the measures adopted to avert the peril are wholly unreasonable there will be no general average act within the definition of r.A, or within the requirement of the Rule Paramount,[62] and r.D will not become relevant at all. If the measures adopted are reasonable but are negligently carried out, r.C or the rule of English law as to remoteness will normally prevent recovery of any loss resulting from the negligence of the person claiming contribution.[63] Where that loss has fallen upon another party, a remedy will generally be afforded by the contract of carriage; the law of general average does not affect that remedy, and r.D is not needed to preserve it.[64] **D.29**

[60] See *Strang Steel & Co v A. Scott & Co* (1889) 14. A.C. 601.

[61] *Federal Commerce & Navigation Ltd v Eisenerz GmbH* [1975] 1 Lloyd's Rep. 105 at 110.

[62] See paras PRE.21-PRE.26 and A.94 et seq., above. The position is the same under English law: see the Marine Insurance Act 1906 s.66(1), para.A.05, above.

[63] See paras C.01 et seq., above.

[64] See paras 00.67 et seq., above.

D.30 **"fault"**: Fault is not defined and its meaning falls to be determined in accordance with the proper law of the contact,[65] or, it is submitted, more correctly in accordance with the law governing the adjustment. As a matter of English law it means a legal wrong which is actionable as between the parties at the time at which the sacrifice or expenditure is made or incurred.[66]

D.31 **"remedies or defences"**: This is similarly undefined and resort must be had to the appropriate system of law.[67] As a matter of English law the word "remedies" included defences as well as cross claims and the 1950 rule thus preserved for an innocent party to the adventure the equitable defence that a party at fault cannot recover contribution in respect of the consequences of his own wrong.[68]

D.32 **"open against or to that party"**: The party in question is the party to the adventure whose fault occasioned the event which gave rise to the general average act. The purpose of the reference to the remedies and defences open against that party is obvious, and has been considered above.[69] The reason for expressly preserving the remedies and defences open to the party at fault is less apparent. If it is merely to preserve his right to contribution where his fault is not actionable at all it is superfluous, at any rate in English law, since the 1950 rule clearly had this effect anyway. It is arguable that the addition of the words "or to" in 1974 produces the result that a party claiming contribution, even where his fault is actionable, can rely on any limit of liability which would have been open to him if the sacrifice or expenditure had not been made and the property imperilled had been lost, and can claim contribution to any loss in excess of that limit. The expression "remedies or defences" is probably wide enough to extend to a right to limit liability.[70] However in considering whether the remedy or defence is "open in respect of such fault" it is likely that the English court would adopt the same approach as in *The Ettrick*[71] and hold that a party's payment of the statutory or contractual limit did not deprive the their conduct of its character as an actionable fault, and therefore did not affect the result that such fault provided a defence to a claim to contribution. As held in *Goulandris Bros Ltd v B. Goldman & Sons Ltd*[72] such fault provides a pure defence and does not operate merely by way of cross-claim or circuity of action, with the result that the fact that the party at fault would have incurred only a limited liability in the event of loss of or damage to the goods is immaterial.

"in respect of such fault": This refers back to the earlier part of the rule, and to fault which has caused an event giving rise to the sacrifice or expenditure.[73]

[65] *Goulandris Bros Ltd v B. Goldman & Sons Ltd* [1958] 1 Q.B. 74 at 91. Cf. paras 30.31 et seq., below.

[66] *Goulandris*, at 104.

[67] *Goulandris*, at 93.

[68] *Goulandris*, at 98, 100.

[69] See para.D.26, above.

[70] See *Goulandris Brothers Ltd v B. Goldman & Sons Ltd* [1958] 1 Q.B. 74 at 100 as to the scope of the word "remedies".

[71] *The Ettrick* (1881) 6 P.D. 127; above, para.D.10.

[72] *The Ettrick* (1881) 6 P.D. 127.

[73] See para.D.29, above.

Deviation: An unjustifiable deviation is within the meaning of "fault" as a matter of English law. However, it merits separate mention as it gives rise to special rights or remedies, the other party to the contract being entitled to treat the deviation as going to the root of the contract and to declare himself no longer bound by the contract terms.[74] The effect of deviation upon rights to contribution in general average is discussed in the sections on Principles of Carriage by Sea and Enforcing Rights of Contribution.[75] **D.33**

United States Law

Rule D does not obviate the necessity for the inclusion of a Jason or similar clause in the contract of carriage. In the absence of such a clause, it is a defence to a claim for general average contribution that the necessity for the general average act arose from the fault of the carrier notwithstanding that he is protected from liability by an exceptions clause.[76] **D.34**

[74] *Hain S.S. Co Ltd v Tate & Lyle* (1936) 41 Com. Cas. 350 at 354, per Lord Atkin.
[75] See paras 00.39 et seq., above, and paras 30.59 et seq., below.
[76] See paras 00.55 et seq., above.

RULE E

ONUS OF PROOF

HISTORICAL DEVELOPMENT AND PRACTICE

York-Antwerp Rules 1924

Rule E appeared for the first time in the 1924 Rules and remained unaltered until 1994. In its original form it did no more than to provide that the burden of proof lay on the party claiming contribution, as follows: **E.01**

> The onus of proof is upon the party claiming in general average to show that the loss or expense claimed is properly allowable as general average.

York-Antwerp Rules 1950 and 1974

No change, though in 1974 the International Subcommittee of the C.M.I, had proposed a further paragraph reading: **E.02**

> Thereafter the onus of proof is upon the party refusing to contribute in general average to show that he is not liable to contribute.

This was rejected at the Hamburg Conference, not because it was thought to be incorrect but on the ground that it was unnecessary and might cause confusion.

York-Antwerp Rules 1994

Before the Sydney Conference, concern had been expressed at the length of time sometimes required in order to obtain the relevant information relating to losses and contributory values from the parties to the adventure. In an attempt to speed up this process two paragraphs were added to the rule, the first of which imposes a time limit of one year for notifying claims to the adjuster, and the second of which imposes a time limit for producing evidence to the adjuster of **E.03** losses and of contributory values. If these time limits are not complied with, the adjuster is entitled to make his own assessment on the material before him, which can only be challenged on limited grounds.[1] A further proposal[2] with the same object, namely to impose a time limit for commencing proceedings to recover contribution, had received little support and was not put forward at the Conference.

York-Antwerp Rules 2004

E.04 No change other than the numbering of the three paragraphs, as part of the process of standardising the drafting and layout of the Rules

RULE E

(1) **The onus of proof is upon the party claiming in general average to show that the loss or expense claimed is properly allowable as general average.**

(2) **All parties claiming in general average shall give notice in writing to the average adjuster of the loss or expense in respect of which they claim contribution within 12 months of the date of the termination of the common maritime adventure.**

(3) **Failing such notification, or if within 12 months of a request for the same any of the parties shall fail to supply evidence in support of a notified claim, or particulars of value in respect of a contributory interest, the average adjuster shall be at liberty to estimate the extent of the allowance or the contributory value on the basis of the information available to him, which estimate may be challenged only on the ground that it is manifestly incorrect.**

CONSTRUCTION

First Paragraph–Paragraph (1) in the York-Antwerp Rules 2004

E.05 This paragraph seems to present no real problems of construction and its effect has not been discussed in any reported English case.[3] It applies to claims under the numbered as well as the lettered rules,[4] and appears to state a very obvious truth, almost a truism it might seem. However, since national laws may differ on the point, it is no doubt considered desirable that the onus of proof that the loss is properly claimable as general average should be clearly and definitely thrown upon the claimant. So far as concerns English law it does no more than reflect the

[1] The British MLA and AIDE had both prepared drafts, not differing greatly in substance, of recommended additions to the rule. The International Standing Committee on General Average of CMI, then produced its own draft. The rule in its final form adopted the AIDE draft for the second paragraph, and the ISC draft, with one significant amendment, for the third paragraph.

[2] As with the proposals actually adopted at Sydney, this proposal also was advanced by the British MLA.

[3] In *The Seapool* [1934] P. 53 its effect was common ground between the parties; see p.61.

[4] *Corfu Navigation v Mobil Shipping* [1991] 2 Lloyd's Rep. 515, 519 (r.VII).

ordinary rule, that the onus lies upon a claimant to prove the facts necessary to support his claim. Once the claimant has established that an allowance is due, if the other parties wish to defeat the claim on the grounds of, for example, fault, the onus shifts to them to do so.

Standard of proof

The paragraph does not mention the standard of proof, which may vary from country to country.[5] English law requires that the necessary facts must be proved on the balance of probability. Equally r.E is not concerned with methods of proof, which are governed by the rules of evidence of the lex fori.[6] The mere production of a general average adjustment is not, in English law, proof of anything,[7] except where the York-Antwerp Rules 1994 or 2004 apply, and the adjuster has made an estimate of losses or contributory values under the third paragraph of r.E. But in practice it is almost unknown for the figures in an adjustment to be challenged in court, even if the principles applied are in dispute. **E.06**

To require that the claimant must prove his claim does not mean that he must have direct and precise evidence of every fact upon which it is based. Such evidence is often unobtainable in establishing what occurred during an emergency at sea; a recording angel does not stand by during an emergency jettison making a precise and accurate tally of each separate package or quantity of bulk cargo jettisoned. It is often necessary to reach a solution by drawing inferences from the facts that are definitely established, making use of common sense and experience. **E.07**

The greatest problems with regard to the onus of proof are likely to arise in cases of underwater damage to the bottom of a ship[8] alleged to have been sustained in efforts to refloat after stranding, and the problem can occasionally be exacerbated in these modern times, when ships are regularly drydocked only at intervals of two years or more. Where the balance of probabilities that the bottom damage might have been caused either by stranding or by efforts to refloat is equal, clearly the onus of proof has not been satisfied and there can be no allowance in general average. This contrasts with the case where it is known (or can be assumed) that a loss or damage is the result of two causes. Thus, if a cargo which has been force-discharged at a port of refuge arrives at final destination with shortage of 2 per cent and the normal shortage is only 1 per cent, it is reasonable to allow as general average the extra loss of 1 per cent as being caused by the forced discharge. **E.08**

[5] Selmer, *Survival of General Average*, p.62, instances the marked difference between the laws of Norway and Denmark in the degree of proof required to establish whether damage to the bottom of the ship was sustained in efforts to refloat.

[6] *Selmer*, 14th edn; paras 14–015 et seq.

[7] *Chandris v Argo Insurance Co* [1963] 2 Lloyd's Rep. 65 at 76. In the US an adjustment is prima facie proof of quantum, if a general average act has been proved and the contract contains a general average agreement: *The Clydewater* [1967] A.M.C. 1474.

[8] See the further remarks relating to r.VII in para.7.12, below, and the case of *Sea-Land Service Inc v Aetna Insurance Co* (1976) A.M.C. 2164, [1977] 2 Lloyd's Rep. 84, there referred to; also para.E.06, fn.5, above.

Effect on the preparation of an adjustment

E.09 The language of the first paragraph of r.E might suggest that if a party wishes to claim any loss or expenditure as general average the responsibility is on him to submit his claim to the average adjuster, supported by the necessary evidence, failing which the adjuster should ignore it. The practice is different, and when the shipowner has appointed an average adjuster to adjust what appears prima facie to be a case of general average, the adjuster will take upon himself the responsibility of acting as agent for all the parties to the adventure, seek and collect all the relevant evidence as to the nature of the casualty and the ensuing losses and expenses, and then act as both prosecuting and defence counsel in arguing the merits of each claim, and finally as arbitrator. Thus, if either the shipowner or cargo interests overlook a claim for an expenditure incurred or, say, some loss or damage to cargo caused by a forced discharge, the average adjuster will put in hand the inquiries necessary to elicit the production of the necessary documents to support the claim.

E.10 This practice is implicitly recognised in the second and third paragraphs of r.E, and it in no way offends against the first paragraph of the rule, which is concerned with the resolution of disputed claims once the evidence has been presented. But this does not mean that the average adjuster is free to ignore the burden of proof. Once he has collected what evidence he can, he must decide whether the facts necessary to support an allowance are established on the balance of probability. If they are not, or if the probabilities are equal, no allowance should be given.

E.11 **"the party claiming in general average"**: It is submitted that these words include not only those parties who are net creditors in the general average, but also those who have incurred any loss or expense which ought to be the subject of an allowance.

Second Paragraph–Paragraph (2) in the York-Antwerp Rules 2004

E.12 **"All parties claiming in general average"**: See para.E.11, above.

"the average adjuster": See the commentary under the third paragraph of the rule at para.E.15, below.

"the date of the termination of the common maritime adventure": The problems which may arise in identifying the date when the adventure terminates are discussed in the commentary under r.G.[9] Although the words of r.E differ from the corresponding expression in r.G—"the time . . . when . . . the adventure ends"—there does not appear to be any ground for distinguishing between them.

Third Paragraph

E.13 This part of the rule reflects the practice described in para.E.09, above, that the average adjuster will pursue the question whether a party is entitled to an allowance and seek to obtain evidence of allowable losses, even where a party has himself advanced no claim, or has failed to put forward any evidence in support

[9] See paras G.21 et seq., below.

of it. Although the obligations imposed by r.E are directed to the parties to the adventure, it is implicit that the average adjuster has to act properly and promptly in the performance of his duties. In particular, he should:

(1) formally request any claimants in general average (and in particular the shipowner) to furnish the necessary documentary evidence in support of their claims;
(2) send a prompt reminder for a copy of the commercial invoice from any cargo interests who have not furnished the same with their valuation form;
(3) whenever there is an indication that a cargo interest has suffered loss or damage make a prompt request that particulars of the same be provided;
(4) in any case where after the lapse of 12 months the evidence supplied is inadequate or inconclusive, promptly proceed to make a fair estimation of the claim or contributory value, as the case may be, and attempt to agree the same on this basis with the party concerned.

The concluding provisions of the paragraph are a significant departure from the English law rule that an adjustment has no legal effect, and certain questions to which this gives rise are discussed in paras E.15 and E.16, below.

"Failing such notification": That is the notification required under the provisions of the second paragraph of the rule, within the 12-month period there laid down. **E.14**

"evidence in support of a notified claim, or particulars of value in respect of a contributory interest": On the face of it, the evidence and particulars which must be supplied are those requested by the adjuster, however detailed, but there is probably an implied requirement that the adjuster shall act reasonably and in accordance with usual practice in deciding how much information to request.

"the average adjuster": In English law there is no legal requirement that a professional adjuster will be employed; the shipowner is at liberty to produce his own adjustment, as indeed is a cargo-owner. Consistently with this liberal approach, there is nothing to prevent the cargo-owner from employing his own professional adjuster, even if the shipowner also employs one. None of this matters in English law, because nothing in the adjustment binds any of the parties to the adventure.[10] In contrast, where the third paragraph of r.E applies, it renders the adjustment prima facie binding as regards allowances and contributory values, subject to challenge only on limited grounds, and thus confers a distinct legal status on the adjustment, thus raising the question, which is discussed in Section 5,[11] whether a professional adjuster must be employed. A further question, also discussed in Section 5 is, who is "the average adjuster" in the case where more than one is employed? **E.15**

[10] See *Wavertree Sailing Ship Co v Love* [1897] A.C. 373, and the other cases referred to in paras 30.35 et seq., below.
[11] Paras 30.38 et seq., below.

E.16 Once an adjustment has been produced by an adjuster who qualifies as "the average adjuster" which contains estimates of allowances and contributory values pursuant to the liberty conferred on the adjuster by r.E, any other adjuster who is subsequently employed will likewise be bound by the estimates of allowances and contributory values adopted in the original adjustment, unless they are manifestly incorrect.[12]

It is the practice in some countries for cargo interests to appoint their own co-adjuster, whose function is to assist in obtaining details of losses and contributory values from cargo, and to check, before publication, the adjustment prepared by the shipowner's adjuster.

E.17 **"shall be at liberty"**: The adjuster's liberty to make an estimate of allowances or contributory values arises as soon as the relevant 12-month period has expired (that is, 12 months from the termination of the adventure for notifying general average loss or expense, and 12 months from the date of the adjuster's request for furnishing evidence of the loss or expense or particulars of the contributory value). However, the adjuster is not obliged to exercise this liberty immediately. He may allow the parties further time, and take into account information which becomes available to him later, and there are some situations when he should take this course: see para.E.19 below.

E.18 **"to estimate the extent of the allowance or the contributory value"**: The purpose of this phrase is to give the adjuster power to make factual assumptions and estimates of value in order to fill in gaps in the information available to him. As this power will only have become exercisable because a party to the adventure has failed to notify a claim, or to supply the information required of him, in accordance with the provisions of the rule there may be a temptation to make assumptions and draw inferences which are adverse to the interests of that party. However, at any rate so far as concerns estimating contributory values, the rule contains no justification for adopting this course, and the adjuster must make his estimate even-handedly on the material available. The position is slightly different when it comes to estimating allowable loss and expense. Here the first paragraph of the rule places the onus of proof upon the party claiming the allowance, and the adjuster should give effect to this when making his estimate under the third paragraph. If, as a result of a party's failure to provide the required information, the adjuster is unable to conclude on the balance of probability that the party has suffered any allowable loss, or a particular item of loss, he should exclude it altogether.

E.19 **"on the basis of the information available to him"**: On the face of it, this means the information available at the time when the adjuster makes his estimate, and the adjuster is entitled to ignore any information subsequently received. However, there is probably an implicit requirement that the adjuster shall keep any estimate which he makes under review, and revise it if appropriate in the light

[12] The rule does not preclude the engagement of more than one adjuster, as occurred in *The Bijela*, where successive professional adjustments were drawn up (see the report of the proceedings at first instance at [1992] 1 Lloyd's Rep. 6236 at 638). However, if the York-Antwerp Rules 1994 or 2004 had applied, the second adjusters would have been bound by any such estimates properly made by the original adjusters under r.E.

of any relevant new information. Clearly there must come a point of time at which the adjuster becomes entitled to make a final estimate, which he is not obliged to change in the light of subsequent information, and, if the rule is not to be unworkable, this point must at the latest be the date when the adjustment is published. However, there are good practical reasons for saying that it is reached at an earlier date, namely when the preparation of the adjustment is so far advanced that to alter the amount in question would involve unreasonable delay and expense.

"which estimate may be challenged only on the ground that it is manifestly incorrect": The restriction on the right of challenge affects all parties equally, and it makes no difference whether the challenge is mounted by the party who failed to supply the information or another party. It was recognised at Sydney that this could sometimes operate rather harshly against parties not in default,[13] but it was decided to make the restriction all-embracing in the interests of simplicity and finality. **E.20**

Unfortunately the rule does not make clear at which date, and on the basis of what material, the correctness of the estimate falls to be determined, and this is by no means an easy question. To allow the party in default to challenge the estimate on the basis of new material, which he failed to produce to the adjuster at the proper time, seems to deprive the rule of some of its intended effect. On the other hand, it could in some cases produce even more objectionable results to refuse to allow innocent parties to produce new evidence, not before available to the adjuster, in support of a challenge mounted by them. Moreover, the choice of the present tense ("is manifestly incorrect") tends to support the view that the correctness of the estimate must be judged by reference to matters as they stand at the time of the challenge.[14] **E.21**

Nevertheless, the rule poses a substantial obstacle to any party who wishes to challenge the adjuster's estimate. It places the burden of proof on him, and he cannot discharge the burden of proof merely by showing that the estimate is wrong on the balance of probability. He must show that it is manifestly wrong, and the effect of this is that if, in the light of all the available information, there remains a reasonable possibility that the estimated amount is correct the challenge will fail, even though it has become apparent that a different amount is more likely to be correct.

Since the purpose of empowering the adjuster to make an estimate is to prevent the completion of the adjustment being held up by lack of factual information, the rule should not affect the right of a party to challenge the estimate on the ground that the adjuster has taken a wrong view of the law or of the effect of the York-Antwerp Rules.[15] However, the effect of the third paragraph of r.E is that the onus would lie upon that party to identify the error of law or of interpretation upon which the estimate was based. **E.22**

[13] In both the British MLA and the AIDE draft proposals the restriction on the right of challenge only applied to the party who had failed to supply the information.

[14] The ISC draft of the rule restricted the right of challenge to those cases where the adjuster had acted unreasonably, the effect of which would have been that information not available to him when he made his estimate could not be relied on.

[15] The rule would not, e.g. affect the right of a shipowner to challenge an amount allowed in respect of temporary repairs on the ground that it was based on an erroneous interpretation of r.XIV. It would not be necessary to show that the interpretation was "manifestly incorrect".

RULE F

SUBSTITUTED EXPENSES

As the name implies, substituted expenses are the expenses incurred in respect of a course of action undertaken as an alternative to—or in substitution for—the expense of an action that would be allowable as general average. F.01

For example, a vessel grounds and sustains damage to her bottom which obliges her to put into a port of refuge for the common safety and to effect repairs necessary for the safe prosecution of the voyage. Such repairs will involve discharging of the cargo and storing it ashore, drydocking and effecting permanent repairs, thereafter reloading the cargo and continuing the voyage all of which would be allowed as general average under the York-Antwerp Rules. However, some or all of these costly operations can often be avoided, or the time and expense necessary for them be reduced to the benefit of all the parties to the adventure, by the adoption of alternative courses of action such as the following:

(1) temporary[1] repairs may be effected afloat, with the cargo remaining on board;
(2) the vessel may be towed to destination with the cargo on board, after only minimal repairs;
(3) the cargo may be forwarded to destination by other vessels;
(4) extra blocks and cradles may be installed in the drydock sufficient to support the additional weight of all or part of the cargo while repairs are effected;
(5) overtime may be worked on repairs or the cargo operations;
(6) spare parts necessary for the repairs may be transported to the port of refuge by air, rather than by sea;
(7) the cargo (particularly if low valued) may be sold, and a replacement cargo purchased on completion of repairs.

[1] See r.XIV, which deals specifically with temporary repairs, a particular form of substituted expenses.

How should the expenses of these alternative courses of action be dealt with, and to what extent can they be charged to general average, either under English law or the York-Antwerp Rules?

English Law

F.02 It will be noted that in all the practical examples given above in para.F.01 the vessel is assumed to be in a port of refuge and that the expenses under consideration would be incurred with the object of the successful completion of the adventure, rather than the achievement of safety itself, with which alone general average under English law is concerned. Thus, none of the expenses of these operations could be charged directly to general average, but was there another approach?

F.03 Rightly or wrongly, English practice in the days of wooden sailing vessels always regarded the adventure as remaining in peril until the vessel had arrived in the port of refuge and completed any necessary discharge of cargo.[2] Consequently, the cost of discharge was allowable in general average, whether the necessity for the discharge arose from the damage which the ship had sustained, or from the cargo itself. Thereafter, the cost of storage for the cargo was treated as a special charge on the cargo, and the cost of reloading was a special charge on the freight. To the extent, therefore, that the undertaking of courses of action in examples (1) to (4) above resulted in the avoidance of any necessary discharge of cargo at the port of refuge, the question arose: could the cost of the operation be considered a substituted expense for those saved costs of discharge, storage, and reloading, plus possible savings in the repair costs to the ship, and could it then be charged to ship, freight and cargo in the same proportions that those interests would have borne the cost of the cargo operations and repairs?

F.04 The question was considered by Blackburn J. in the case of *Wilson v Bank of Victoria*[3] and, in the absence of a custom of the trade, he decided that the principle was not tenable at law. The case concerned an auxiliary sailing vessel which struck an iceberg while on voyage from Melbourne to Britain and was dismasted and otherwise damaged such that she could no longer sail. She put into Rio de Janeiro as a port of refuge under her auxiliary steam power and, the cost of repairs there being prohibitive, the master effected only temporary repairs at Rio and proceeded to destination under steam, purchasing coals at both Rio and Fayal for this purpose. The shipowner claimed a general average contribution towards the cost of these coals on the grounds—inter alia—that they were a substituted expense for the expenses that would have been incurred at Rio if permanent repairs had been effected there, some of which might have been expected to be charged to general average. The claim was denied and Blackburn J. said:

[2] See para.10.06, fn.4, below.
[3] *Wilson v Bank of Victoria* (1867) L.R. 2 Q.B. 203.

"... we think that the expenses actually incurred must be apportioned according to the facts that actually happened, and that there is no legal principle on which they can be apportioned according to what might have been the facts if a different course had been pursued.

No case or authority was cited to support the principle contended for, nor are we aware of any. If in any particular trade it has been found convenient to act on this principle, and that has been done to such an extent as to create a custom. . . the case would be different; but as it is, the principle proposed is not, we think, tenable at law."

As to reinforce his general refusal to accept the principle of substituted expenses, Blackburn J. had stated earlier in his judgment on the facts of this particular case:

"Inasmuch as the master could, by the expenditure of a comparatively small sum on temporary repairs and coals, bring the ship and cargo safely home, it was his duty to do so; and, though we do not decide a point which does not arise, we are not to be taken as deciding that his owners would not have been liable to the owners of the cargo if he had not taken this course."

Thus, the question raised earlier of whether the expense of an alternative course of action should be treated in the same manner as would have been applied to the expenses they replaced was answered firmly in the negative. **F.05**

As Lowndes himself wrote in 1873 with regard to temporary repairs as a possible candidate for the substituted expense treatment:

"The master's right, not only to enter a port of refuge, but to remain and incur expense there, is strictly limited to the necessity of the case. He must not subject the cargo to delay or expense which it is in his power, with safety to all, to prevent. He has not an absolute right to make a complete repair of the ship at the port of refuge, if a partial or temporary repair will suffice to render her seaworthy to carry the cargo to its destination. Hence, if there be two courses open to him at the port of refuge, by the first of which the ship will be completely repaired, but there will be a long delay or a considerable expense of general average, while by the second this delay or expense will be diminished, and the ship, though incompletely repaired, will be fit to sail on her voyage with her whole cargo, the second course is that which the master if legally bound to adopt. Having done so, he has no right to make a merit of his conduct, and claim compensation from the cargo, on the ground of his having rendered it a service by not having chosen the more expensive course.[4] In such a case, therefore, an adjustment on the basis of 'substituted expenses' would be incorrect."

However, from his support for other types of substituted expense, such as towage to destination (see para.F.06), it would appear that his objection was to this particular category of expense rather than the principle in general.

[4] Confirmation of this view was received from, e.g. Earl of Halsbury, L.C. in *Ruabon S.S. Co v London Assurance* [1900] A.C. 6, or Bowen L.J. in *Svendsen v Wallace Bros* (1885) 10 A.C. 404. There is no rule of (English) law that a person can be called upon for a payment towards the expense of another merely because he may have obtained some benefit from that other person's actions.

English Practice

F.06 Although in the case of *Wilson v Bank of Victoria* Blackburn J. had held that the principle of substituted expenses was not tenable at law, he did state that the case would be different if there had been a custom in the trade to apply the principle. No evidence of such a custom was presumably produced during the court hearing, nor did a custom necessarily exist, but one can see the principle of substituted expenses being explored even as early as 1851 by the highly respected L.R. Baily on p.78 of his work on general average:

> "When such extra expense has been incurred to avoid discharging the cargo, the excess of the expense actually incurred in temporary and permanent repairs, beyond what would have been incurred if the vessel had been permanently repaired at the intermediate port, should be divided as follows:–
>
> Ship, freight and cargo should bear the extra expense in the same proportion that they would have borne the expense for discharging, warehouse rent, and re-shipping, that would have been incurred if the cargo had been discharged; and the residue of the expenses should be paid by the shipowners."

Although there may have been no accepted custom to apply the principle of substituted expenses in 1867 it does appear that commercial men favoured the principle, certainly in so far as it applied to towage of a vessel to destination, or the forwarding of her cargo, and they set about creating or evidencing the custom. Lowndes endeavoured to introduce a Rule of Practice on the subject of towage at the semi-annual meeting of the Association of Average Adjusters in November 1870, and although unsuccessful on that occasion, he received the unanimous support of members when in 1876 he persuaded the representative of the Liverpool Underwriters' Association to propose a similar rule, also one on the forwarding of cargo.

With regard to some of the examples set out in para.F.01 above, English practice developed as follows:

Example (1): Temporary Repairs

F.07 This particular example is dealt with more fully in the chapter dealing with r.XIV, and it is sufficient here to state that following the remarks of Blackburn J. in *Wilson v Bank of Victoria* that, "Inasmuch as the master could, by the expenditure of a comparatively small sum on temporary repairs and coals, bring the ship and cargo safely home, it was his duty to do so", English practice (absent the York-Antwerp Rules) has been not to allow the cost of temporary repairs to accidental damage as general average.

Example (2): Towage to Destination

F.08 Towage to destination would but rarely be considered an obligation under the contract of affreightment, and the subsidiary reasoning in *Wilson v The Bank of*

Victoria which would deny temporary repairs to accidental damage being allowed in general average would not be applicable here, where a shipowner incurs the expense of having his vessel towed to destination with her cargo to avoid the (generally larger) expenses that would have been incurred to discharge, store and reload the cargo, and effect repairs at the port of refuge. In 1876 a Rule of Practice on the subject was passed unanimously by the Association of Average Adjusters.

F14 Towage from a Port of Refuge

> "That if a ship be in a port of refuge at which it is practicable to repair her, and if, in order to save expense, she be towed thence to some other port, then the extra cost of such towage shall be divided in proportion to the saving of expense thereby occasioned to the several parties to the adventure."

Example (3): Forwarding Cargo from a Port of Refuge

Not only did commercial men in 1876 consider that the cost of towage from a port of refuge should be treated on a substituted expense basis, but also where cargo was forwarded from a port of refuge to avoid the cost of storing it there. At the same meeting of the Association of Average Adjusters in 1876, the members passed unanimously another Rule of Practice proposed by the Representative of the Liverpool Underwriters' Association. **F.09**

F15 Cargo Forwarded from a Port of Refuge

> "That if a ship be in a port of refuge at which it is practicable to repair her so as to enable her to carry on the whole cargo, but, in order to save expense, the cargo or a portion of it, be transhipped by another vessel, or otherwise forwarded, then the cost of such transhipment (up to the amount of expense saved) shall be divided in proportion to the saving of expense thereby occasioned to the several parties to the adventure."

The substituted expense would sometimes be greater than the expenses avoided at the port of refuge, the shipowner undertaking the forwarding of the cargo largely to preserve the goodwill of cargo interests. Up to the expenses avoided at the port of refuge, the substituted expenses will be allowed and apportioned over the savings that accrued to the parties and the general average, and any excess would be borne by the carrier.

Example (4): Drydocking with Cargo on Board

If a loaded vessel requires to drydock for underwater repairs, it will usually be necessary to discharge all or part of the cargo in order to achieve a weight that both the ship and the drydock can safely bear. However, to avoid the heavy cost of discharging, storing and reloading the cargo, it is sometimes possible to install extra blocks and cradles in the drydock to support the additional weight and to leave the cargo on board. **F.10**

The cost of installing the extra blocks and cradles is treated as a substituted expense for, and allocated in the same manner as would have applied to the cost of discharging, storing and reloading the cargo. The practice appears well founded. It has also been accepted (obiter) in the US case of Browning v Thebaud.[5]

Example (7): Loss by Sale of Cargo at a Port of Refuge

F.11 In case of a vessel carrying a low-valued cargo such as coal which it was necessary to discharge at a port of refuge, in order to avoid the storage expenses, etc. thereon, the cargo was sometimes sold and a fresh cargo purchased on completion of repairs. The loss on the sale and repurchase was treated as a substitution for the expenditure saved, and divided in the proportions in which that expenditure would have fallen.

In 1902 the Association of Average Adjusters introduced a Rule of Practice on the subject:

F16 Cargo Sold at a Port of Refuge

> "That if a ship be in a port of refuge at which it is practicable to repair her so as to enable her to carry on the whole cargo, or such portion of it as is fit to be carried on, but, in order to save expense, the cargo, or a portion of it, be, with the consent of the owners of such cargo, sold at the port of refuge, then the loss by sale including loss of freight on cargo so sold (up to the amount of expense saved) shall be divided in proportion to the saving of expense thereby occasioned to the several parties to the adventure; provided always that the amount so divided shall in no case exceed the cost of transhipment and/or forwarding referred to in the preceding rule of the Association."

(Examples 5, 6 and 7 are discussed fully in paras F.25–F.28, below)

Historical Development and Practice of Rule F

York-Antwerp Rules 1890–The old Rule X(d)

F.12 A month prior to the International Conference held at Liverpool in August 1890 to produce the York-Antwerp Rules of 1890, the British Association of Average Adjusters had held an Extraordinary General Meeting to consider what proposals they would put forward. One possibility was a new rule on substituted expenses which would effectively combine the provisions of their own two Rules of Practice rr.F14[6] and F15[7] passed in 1876 and dealing with the specific examples of towage to destination and forwarding cargo to destination; however, this was rejected.

At the Liverpool Conference itself, a proposal was made to allow as a substituted expense the cost of forwarding cargo, alone. This proposal was seconded and extended to include towage as follows:

[5] *Browning v Thebaud* 42 Fed. Rep. 796 (1890).
[6] See para.F.08, above.
[7] See para.F.09, above.

"If a ship under average be in a port or place at which it is practicable to repair her, so as to enable her to carry on the whole cargo, and if, in order to save expense, either she is towed thence to some other port or place of repair or to her destination, or the cargo or a portion of it is transhipped by another ship, or otherwise forwarded, then the extra cost of such towage, transhipment and forwarding or any of them (up to the amount of the extra expense saved) shall be payable by the several parties to the adventure in proportion to the extraordinary expense saved."

York-Antwerp Rules 1924—The new Rule F

Rule X(d) dealing with just two specific examples of substituted expenses remained unchanged in 1924, but it was supplemented on this occasion with a new lettered r.F which served as a general statement of the principle of substituted expenses, with wording as follows: **F.13**

"Any extra expense incurred in place of another expense which would have been allowable as general average shall be deemed to be general average and so allowed but only up to the amount of the general average expense avoided."

As originally proposed by the Drafting Committee, the rule opened as follows: "Any extra expense or loss incurred in place of another expense or loss. . .". But after discussion, the delegates at the 1924 Conference unanimously agreed to omit the words "or loss", indicating their intention[8] that only expenses were to be taken into account, in accordance with the Rule of Practice[9] of average adjusters in this country.

York-Antwerp Rules 1950

Between 1924 and 1950, it is believed that in practice substituted expenses falling to be dealt with under r.F were charged, entirely to general average up to the amount of the general average expenses avoided, and without regard to any possible savings to other interests. To the present editors, this appears to be the correct construction to be placed upon the 1924 wording of r.F. However, an alternative view– that all parties who had benefited by a substituted expense should **F.14**

[8] Although it was most certainly the intention that there should be no allowance in general average for substituted losses incurred in place of another expense or loss which would have been allowable as general average, it is submitted that unless the wording of r.F expressly prohibits such a substitution there may be grounds (subject to r.C and the law of the port of destination) for the allowance of certain substituted losses akin to general average sacrifices. For instance, an adjustment has been seen where a motor-vessel proceeding in ballast under charter to load cargo was obliged to put into a port of refuge with accidental damage to her main engine. Temporary repairs necessary for the safe prosecution of the voyage were effected but these necessitated the use at all times of diesel oil instead of the usual fuel oil. As the vessel already had on board a complete supply of fuel oil, the extra diesel oil required could only be shipped by shutting out an equivalent weight of cargo. The loss of freight thereon, together with the cost of the temporary repairs, was allowed as general average on a substituted expense basis. Given that the Rules do not envisage substituted losses, any intention to make such an allowance on equitable grounds should generally be supported by a specific agreement between the parties in advance of the proposed course of action.

[9] Rule F17. See para.70.44, below.

contribute thereto[10] —may have had its adherents, and this alternative view was expressed as late even as 1948 in the 7th edition[11] of this Work.

To avoid any possible doubt upon the construction to be given to r.F, in 1950 the words "without regard to the saving, if any, to other interests" were added. It was then quite plain that, up to the amount of the general expenses avoided, substituted expenses were to be charged entirely to general average and that the savings to other interests were to be ignored.

A proposal that the words "or loss" should be added after the third word of the rule, "expense", was not accepted as it might have led to abuse. It was appreciated that extra losses were incurred occasionally in order to avoid general average expenditure, but it was felt that, in practice, it was better to deal with these substituted losses by a special agreement.

York-Antwerp Rules 1974

F.15 There was no change to r.F, but the suggestion was again made by one country that the words or loss should be added after the word expense. Rule X(d), introduced in 1890, was rescinded on this occasion in favour of the principle established by the later rr.F and XIV whereby, if the savings to general average were sufficient, the whole of the substituted expenses were chargeable to general average, and all other savings were ignored.

York-Antwerp Rules 1994

F.16 Perhaps because of the difference in approach between the English law view of substituted expense and that of many other countries, the interpretation of r.F continued to give rise to considerable debate in text books and elsewhere. The topic was discussed in a number of Chairman's Addresses to the Association of Average Adjusters including those by J.R. Danson (1946), J.P. Duke (1981), D.J. Wilson (1988), C. S. Hebditch (1990), and extensively in the 11th and 12th editions of this Work. Whilst points of difficulty do exist, it should be noted that the principle is taken at face value and generally accepted willingly by commercial interests. In particular, r.F was recognised as facilitating arrangements to forward cargo or tow a vessel to destination with minimal additional formalities, avoiding the need for special agreements to allocate liability for such expenditure in each case.

There were a number of proposals before and at the Sydney conference to limit the scope of interpretation and practical application of the rule. The United States Maritime Law Association stated that it was not content with the current status of the treatment of substituted expenses in the lettered and numbered rules and was giving consideration to a proposal to lead to the restoration of (old) r.X(d) and the application of its principles to all substituted expenses. Subsequently, they put forward the

[10] For example, see the commentary on the English Rules of Practice F14-F15 in paras F.08-F.09, and F.11, above.

[11] See pp.363–364.

proposal that the alternative course against which the substituted expenses actually incurred would be compared, would need to be reasonably incurred. Although both proposals were withdrawn, the United States Maritime Law Association achieved their ends by securing the passage of their Rule Paramount.[12]

York Antwerp Rules 2004

No change. **F.17**

RULE F

Any additional expense incurred in place of another expense which would have been allowable as general average shall be deemed to be general average and so allowed without regard to the saving, if any, to other interests, but only up to the amount of the general average expense avoided.

CONSTRUCTION

"Any additional expense": The only change to r.F in 1994 was the substitution of the word "additional" in the phrase under discussion for the previous extra, and it was reported that no change in meaning or practice was intended, merely a clarification "to express what has always been the intention and also is expressed in the French text, which uses the word 'supplémentaire' ". It had been contended by many (including the editors of the several editions of Lowndes) that the word "extra" should be read as a shortened form of "extraordinary" or that the rule should be changed to include the latter word. However, whatever word might be chosen or implied, a clear meaning is prevented by the absence of any indication of what exactly the expense was "extra" or "additional" to, or in what respect it had to be "extraordinary". **F.18**

The obligation placed on the shipowner to complete the voyage by all reasonable means at his disposal was seen under English law as an impassable barrier that shut out the allowance of substituted expenses. However, this approach has to be modified in the context of the York-Antwerp Rules, which accept that some aspects of this obligation may give rise to legitimate general average allowances. **F.19**

In the Commercial court in *The Bijela* Hobhouse J.[13] rejected a claim for temporary repairs based on his construction of r.XIV (see paras 14.30–14.33) but he recognised the particular relationship between the shipowner's obligations and the York-Antwerp Rules as they have developed over time:

> "Accordingly the 'prima facie' position is that the expenses of repair were particular average expenses incurred by the Shipowners in the course of fulfilling

[12] See para.PRE.22, above.
[13] *Marida Ltd v Oswal Steel* [1992] 1 Lloyd's Rep. 636.

> their contractual obligations under the contracts of carriage. The existence of the obligation is not decisive of the question before me. Many types of general average expenditure are incurred by the master in the fulfillment of his duties to the interests involved in common adventure, including to the cargo-owners, and the function of general average is to provide a superimposed scheme for the sharing of the burden of that expenditure in an equitable fashion. It is simply the starting point."

F.20 In the Court of Appeal in the same case, Hoffman L.J. delivered a masterful review of the topic as part of his dissenting judgment. He noted that the courses of action contemplated by the old r.XI(d), i.e. forwarding of cargo and towage to destination, both fell outside the range of a Shipowner's contractual obligations. Referring to the more generalised terms of r.F he noted:

> "As the most recent edition of the standard work, Lowndes & Rudolph on General Average and the York-Antwerp Rules (11th edn, (1990), p.144) puts it, the substituted expense must be an alternative to, or in substitution for–what prima facie might be thought of as being in the normal or standard means of dealing with a given situation.
>
> What is less clear is whether all cases falling within r.F must exhibit all the features which I have identified in connection with two cases in the old r.X(d). In particular, is it necessary that the course of conduct giving rise to the substituted expense should have fallen outside the obligations contained in the contract of affreightment? Or is it sufficient that the expenditure was a less usual and more expensive way by which the owner complied with his contractual obligation, e.g. to repair the ship? Lowndes & Rudolph suggest that the expenditure of the latter kind could fall within the rule."

The present editors continue in the view that it is not necessary for the course of action to fall completely outside the contractual obligations; if the intention were otherwise the more generalised terms of r.F would be largely unnecessary. However, in the context of the rule an "additional" expense must at least be something that goes beyond the ordinary voyage expenses that might have been contemplated when the common adventure began. Those anticipated voyage expenses would normally include some element for contingencies, such as additional fuel consumed during bad weather or expenses arising out of problems such as port congestion. Such costs of earning freight may be enhanced by factors outside the shipowner's control but this is a commercial risk that is taken as part of earning freight. The requirement to repair accidental damage to the ship and complete the voyage in a timely manner also remains part of the obligations under the contract of affreightment so that to qualify under r.F as "additional" any expenses incurred in this regard must involve something that is beyond the normal or standard means of conducting that repair. In practice, one is therefore left in some instances to decide questions on the basis of degree and impression.

F.21 This point has been discussed at length by a number of authors and it is difficult to reach an entirely satisfactory conclusion when discussing the point in the abstract. Happily, the two most common and financially significant allowances under r.F, (forwarding cargo and towage to destination) do not give rise to any concerns in this regard since both actions will fall (in the absence of special contract terms) outside the shipowner's normal obligations. These and other less clear-cut examples are now discussed below–temporary repairs are dealt with in the chapter regarding r.XIV.

Towage to Destination

A shipowner is rarely under any obligation to have his vessel towed to destination, even if this is the only alternative to accepting that a voyage is frustrated because of the time or cost required for repairs. Equally, he is rarely under any obligation to arrange such towage merely to reduce the cost or time required for a vessel to carry out repairs necessary for the safe prosecution of a voyage. F.22

The cost of towage is therefore "additional" but credit must be given for any voyage expenses saved (principally the cost of fuel) because of the voyage being completed under tow—the net figure is the true "additional" expense (see also paras F.23 and 6.17).

Where a vessel is under time-charter and the towage is funded by the shipowner, the primary saving in voyage expenses will be realised by the charterer who would otherwise have paid for the fuel. The shipowner will only receive as a general average allowance the net cost of the towage, leaving him with a shortfall unless he has made an agreement with the time-charterer to resolve this anomaly.

Forwarding Cargo to Destination

In the absence of special terms in the contract of affreightment a shipowner is also under no obligation to forward cargo in order to reduce the effects of a delay in the voyage. The costs of doing so are clearly "additional" and forwarding cargo is one of the most common examples of a substituted expense that generally finds favour with all parties. To arrive at the actual additional cost of such forwarding (before any comparison is made with the general average expenses saved), credit must be given for the ordinary voyage expenses saved by reason of the original vessel not having to complete the voyage, such as wages, fuel and stores, port charges, etc. F.23

The cost of forwarding must also be reviewed to ensure that the amount claimed is reasonable, as required by the Rule Paramount. The party claiming the forwarding expenses, (usually the shipowner, sometimes the charterer) must be able to demonstrate that the forwarding vessel was engaged at appropriate market rates, although such rates may be increased by the circumstances of vessel being in difficulty or a remote location. Where a container vessel enters a port of refuge that is on an established route, perhaps used by the same owner or members of the same consortium, it may be possible to forward some or all of the cargo using empty "slots". It may therefore be necessary to investigate whether the forwarding has resulted in any actual extra cost in addition to handling expenses.

Drydocking with Cargo on Board

The normal practice is for Shipowners to drydock their vessel in ballast condition, although container vessels may sometimes drydock for short periods with a F.24

modest amount of cargo on board if this can be fitted onto their normal voyage rotation.

Drydocking with part cargo on board creates extra stresses on the vessel, and possibly the drydock, requiring additional blocks and other measures. Some degree of greater caution will also be required, particularly if the vessel has sustained hull damage. Nonetheless, the attendant costs will generally be significantly less than the cost of discharging, storing and reloading cargo that would otherwise be allowable as general average. The general practice is therefore to recognise this as an unusual or "additional" cost and to allow the extra cost of the drydocking with the cargo on board up to the savings in discharging cargo, etc. and the detention expenses during cargo operations.

Overtime Working

F.25 With the three examples discussed in paras F.22 to F.24 there can be little debate that the costs are "additional". By contrast, overtime working, whether in cargo handling, port movements or damage repairs is a familiar part of shipping operations and overtime costs are incurred as a matter of normal commercial expediency. In such circumstances can the cost of working overtime on repairs to accidental damage be described as "additional" and therefore the excess cost be allowed under r.F in lieu of savings in detention expenses (wages, fuel, port charges) that would otherwise have been allowed in general average? In contrast to the use of airfreight (see para.F.26) to carry spares which is now acknowledged as universal, the position regarding overtime does not lend itself to a simple answer. In the absence of a casualty, owners will sometimes pay for the excess cost of overtime work but sometimes they will choose not to–the same applies to a casualty situation where there is no cargo onboard. When looking at a general average situation it is therefore difficult to say whether the overtime worked can be described as "extra" or "additional". The presence or absence of likely savings in particular average repair costs could be used as an indicator, but in reality this is only one of a number of financial and commercial decisions that may be behind the shipowners' decision. In general, practitioners appear to take the view that it is better to avoid such speculation and to allow the excess cost of overtime working, subject to there being appropriate savings and the following criteria:

- The overtime is not a fixed part of the trading terms of the party engaged. For example, engine manufacture's travelling service engineers are much in demand and will expect to work overtime to complete a job as soon as possible, in order to move on to the next assignment.
- The overtime is not a necessary part of a particular repair process, for example post weld heat treatment of a rudder stock, that has to continue on a 24-hour basis for technical reasons.
- The overtime is worked at the shipowner's option and is not enforced by the repairers, for example because of limited drydock availability.

It has been suggested that a strong indication that the cost of overtime is not "extra" (1974 Rules) or "additional" (1994, 2004 Rules) is the fact that, on British insurance policies, it is usual for hull insurers to allow overtime costs as particular average where the vessel is sailing on a "liner" service to a fixed and advertised schedule. In 1995 the Advisory Committee of the Association of Average Adjusters dealt with the similar point that can be made regarding temporary repairs.

> "The Committee observes that in the absence of a general average situation, or a contract of affreightment incorporating the York-Antwerp Rules, the proper home for temporary repairs is particular average. However, it should be borne in mind that the definition of Particular Average, in the Marine Insurance Act 1906, is a negative one, i.e. it is something that is not general average, viz:
>
> > Section 64(1) 'A particular average loss is a partial loss of the subject matter insures, caused by a peril insured against, and which is not a general average loss.'
>
> If a contract of affreightment provides for York-Antwerp Rules and a temporary repair cost comes within the criteria set by Rule XIV, that the cost cannot be particular average because it has become general average; to ignore this would be to state incorrectly the claim on the hull policy."

While the point is unlikely to be taken by insurers or other parties where insignificant amounts are involved, (and where it is academic if the general average is being claimed under an absorption clause, which will often be the case) hull and loss of earnings insurers will generally expect the customary treatment of overtime costs to be followed. Thus the excess cost of overtime will be a first charge on general average, up to savings in general average expenditure; if these savings are insufficient the balance is a charge on particular average up to savings in repair costs; any excess overtime costs remaining will finally be applied to the loss of hire policy, if there is one, or must be borne by the shipowner.

Air Freight

The use of air freight to move spare parts is now so universal that the debate surrounding its status as a possible substituted expense is largely of historic interest. However, the point still arises occasionally with particularly large spare parts and it is a good illustration of the way in which technical innovations can change practice. **F.26**

In *Western Canada S.S. Co Ltd v Canadian Commercial Corp*,[14] shipowners recovered contribution towards the expense of flying by a specially charted Halifax bomber a new tailshift from Wales to Singapore, in so far as it exceeded the freight for such a voyage by sea, on the grounds that port of refuge expenses in a larger amount were thereby saved, and would otherwise have been allowed in general average. The defendants' contention that such an expense was usual and not "additional" was rejected. Judgment in this above case was given in 1960 and related to events which took place in 1947.

[14] *Western Canada S.S. Co Ltd v Canadian Commercial Corp* (1960) 2 Lloyd's Rep. 313.

A sub-committee of the Association Internationale de Dispacheurs Europeens, reporting in 1969 on the simplification of the York-Antwerp Rules, suggested that air freight on engine parts by scheduled flights was now quite a normal means of transport and should be treated as part of the cost of repairs and not as a substituted expense, but that this stage had not then been reached with chartered aircraft. F.27

In 1991 the United States Association changed their existing Rule of Practice, and added a useful exposition on the proper treatment of air freight on chartered aircraft:

> *"Rule XXI–Air Freight*
>
> The cost of ordinary air freight on repair parts shall be allowed as part of the reasonable cost of repairs.
>
> The cost of any extraordinary shipments by air, such as chartered aircraft or similar means, shall be dealt with by the Adjuster considering (1) the reasons for such shipment and/or (2) the savings resulting therefrom. The Adjuster shall insert a note in the average statement in explanation of the allowances or charges made."

and in explanation of the second paragraph:

> "The word 'extraordinary' primarily refers to shipment by chartered airplane. The circumstances envisaged are:
>
> 1) The size of the part is such that it will not fit on regular scheduled airplanes at tariff rates. If the cost of the chartered airplane is reasonably incurred, then the cost of the shipment follows the cost of repairs, e.g. Particular Average, General Average or Owners. One example of what might be regarded as not reasonable is when it is known for some time that an oversized part is required at a scheduled repair port, and that the part could have been shipped by sea well in advance of that time.
> 2) The part could have been shipped by ordinary airfreight, but some saving results from the use of a chartered airplane. For example, if the repair port is remote and the shipment would require three changes of airplane, resulting in seven days of transit, while a chartered airplane would deliver the part in two days, there has been a saving of five days. The Adjuster would determine the saving involved in G.A., and/or P.A. and explain the saving in the note following the invoice."

Sale of Cargo

F.28 As noted above suggestions that r.F should extend to losses as well as additional expenses have been consistently resisted, so that the Association of Average Adjusters Rule of Practice F16 (dealing with cargo sold at a port of refuge to save storage expenses) is the only one on the topic of substituted expenses not to have found its way into the ambit of the York-Antwerp Rules. In practice, the sale of cargo would not usually be contemplated without receiving the written agreement of cargo interests and it is a relatively straightforward matter to ensure that such an agreement includes provision for an equitable distribution of any losses that may be incurred.

F.29 **"incurred in place of another expense which would have been allowable as general average"**: For this rule to have any application there must have been an alternative course of action which, if adopted, would have involved expenditure which could properly be charged to general average. As recorded earlier in para.F.16, above, in the preparatory stages preceding the Sydney Conference in 1994 the United States Maritime Law Association had proposed an amendment whereby a substituted expense would qualify for consideration as general average only when the expense of the alternative course of action "would have been reasonably incurred and allowable as general average". This proposal was not maintained when the all-embracing Rule Paramount put forward by the same USMLA was accepted at Sydney, for this latter proposal clearly comprises the former.

This requirement of reasonableness has probably always existed in respect of claims under any of the lettered rules by reason of the provisions of r.A, as noted in A.B. Dann's address to the Association of Average Adjusters in 1976:

> "When one is considering substituted expense for allowance in general average one cannot allow expenses substituted for something which, being unreasonable, could not have been allowed in general average at all."

The alternative course of action should be one that is physically possible in the circumstances that the ship and cargo find themselves and not lead to the frustration of the voyage on grounds of delay or cost. Nor should it be a course of action that would be in breach of the contract of affreightment or threaten the legality of the adventure.[15] **F.30**

It should be a natural and logical alternative, and not a matter of artificial invention. As an extreme example, the continuing hire payable on containers at a port of refuge is a loss by delay and excluded by r.C, but the suggestion has been made that the hire can be charged to general average as a "substituted" expense for the cost of unstuffing the containers and storing the contents in a warehouse. Such a course of action would be clearly unreasonable, and outside normal shipping practice. A further example of an excessively contrived alternative that is often quoted is the possibility of bringing a floating drydock to a vessel at a port of refuge, and again such an alternative would clearly be outside normal practice. The use of semi-submersible barges to remove vessels for repair has been encountered with regard to damaged naval vessels, however, the special considerations of security and lack of financial constraints would not be found with merchant vessels and, although less obviously artificial, is also unlikely to qualify as a realistic alternative for the purposes of r.F. **F.31**

In practice some alternative courses of action are never likely to be taken because of the actual "substituted" action being commercially the most attractive solution by a considerable margin. Thus, there are few ports of refuge in which a large tanker would be able to discharge its cargo and the only alternative if repairs are to be effected is to charter a vessel to conduct a ship to ship transfer and to store the cargo. It is very rare that this course of action, which would be allowable under r.X(c), will be followed through with in its entirety and the chartered vessel, once it has the cargo aboard, will normally proceed to destination. The net cost

[15] See *Marida Ltd v Oswal Steel: The Bijela* [1993] 1 Lloyd's Rep. 411 at 421, per Hoffmann L.J.

(i.e. after deducting voyage savings, see para.F.23) of carrying the cargo to destination will be allowed under r.F in substitution for the charter hire that would have been incurred during storage duties and while returning the cargo to the original vessel after repairs, which would have been allowed in general average.

F.32 **"and so allowed without regard to the saving, if any, to other interests"**: One area of particular criticism of substituted expenses has arisen from the change in approach in 1974 from the old r.X(d), (under which amounts allowed as substituted expenses were apportioned between the various parties in proportion to the savings in expense they enjoyed, see para.F.12), to the approach of allowing the substituted expense wholly to the general average "without regard to savings to other interests".

It would seem likely that this change was made in the interests of simplicity. By referring only to savings in expense even the old r.X(d) failed to guarantee a completely equitable result because it did not take account of less easily quantifiable, but potentially just as significant, commercial benefits. However, the disadvantage of this simple approach is that, although the whole general average community should by definition benefit from a reduction in general average expenses and/or a speedier completion of the voyage, one party may also receive other benefits that are significant. The most common example cited is that of towage to destination, allowed under r.F, which may also result in the vessel moving from an area with very high repair costs to one where steel prices are dramatically lower. At the time of writing, the cost for basic steelwork ranges very widely according to location and differences in time required for repairs can also be significant; these issues are therefore of considerable interest to hull and loss of earnings insurers in the case of a major casualty.

The York-Antwerp Rules 2004 will prevent such windfalls for shipowners and their insurers in the case of temporary repairs, since the amended r.XIV requires savings in repair costs to be accounted for first, before any general average savings are considered. In all other cases, the imperfect result that may sometimes follow the simple approach adopted in the York-Antwerp Rules has to be accepted.

F.33 **"but only up to the amount of the general average expenses avoided"**: The allowance in general average for substituted expenses must clearly not exceed the cost of the alternative expenses which would have been incurred and allowed as general average. Thus, if cargo is forwarded to destination at a cost (after crediting normal voyage expenses saved) of 150,000 but the alternative expenses of storing the cargo, etc. at the port of refuge amount only to 120,000, only 120,000 of the forwarding expenses can be charged to general average and the excess of 30,000 will, in the absence of special agreement, be for the account of the party incurring the expenditure—usually the shipowner.

Rule G

Valuation of Losses and Contributory Values; Non-Separation Agreement

Rule G is concerned only with the valuation of the property involved in the common adventure: the rule specifically leaves open the question of the place at which the adjustment is to be prepared and the law of the adjustment. These latter topics are dealt with separately in Section 5. G.01

Since the 1994 Rules, r.G has also incorporated provisions that are equivalent to the standard form of Non-Separation Agreement which permits certain general average allowances to continue after cargo has left the vessel in order to be forwarded to destination.

English Law and Background

The Time and Place of Valuation

In any adjustment there are two sets of values to be considered. Firstly there is that of the general average loss which is to be allowed and secondly there is the contributory value of each contributing interest, and it is worth stressing here that only by assessing the allowance in general average for property sacrificed on precisely the same basis as contributory values are calculated—at the termination of the adventure—can the equitable aims of the general average system be achieved whereby it should be financially immaterial to any party to the adventure whether his goods or property were sacrificed, or those of another. G.02

Sacrifices

Where the general average loss consists of a sacrifice it is generally agreed that the state of facts, real in the case of contributing interests and assumed in the case of the thing sacrificed, which forms the basis of the adjustment is that existing at the termination of the adventure. This will be the date of discharge at the port of G.03

destination unless the voyage is wholly broken up earlier, in which case it will be the date when the voyage was broken up. This is decided by Fletcher v Alexander,[1] in which a ship bound from Liverpool to Calcutta with a cargo consisting entirely of salt stranded on a sandbank. In order to refloat, a very large portion of the salt was thrown overboard and she was then towed off the bank and brought back to Liverpool in a leaky state. Of the salt not jettisoned, the greater part was either washed out by sea-water or so damaged as not to be fit for reshipment.

Bovill C.J. referred to the valuation of the contributing interests in the following terms:

> "If after jettison or the matter which is the subject of general average has arisen, the remainder of the goods are totally lost, and so no benefit accrues to the owners of the other goods from the jettison, no contribution can be claimed. The whole law on the subject is founded on the principle that the loss to the individual whose goods are sacrificed for the benefit of the rest is to be compensated according to the loss sustained on the one hand and the benefit derived on the other."[2]

Of the valuation of the thing sacrificed, he said:

> "It is clear that the value of the goods at the time of the jettison is not to be taken as the test, because, if the whole adventure is afterwards brought to an end by the loss of ship and cargo, there will be no contribution at all. The rules as to contribution and adjustment seem to me to depend upon the probable state of things at, and to have reference to, the time and place of adjustment,[3] that is to say, when and where the adjustment ought to take place . . . In the present case, it is almost a matter of certainty that, if the salt which was jettisoned had remained on board, it could not have reached the port of adjustment, Liverpool, in a sound state. What, then, is the loss which the owner has sustained by the jettison? The only loss I can suggest is the value of the salt if it had arrived in an unsound state."[4]

Thus, although property may have been in sound condition when it was jettisoned or otherwise sacrificed, the allowance in general average will not be for the full sound value if it can confidently be asserted that such property would have suffered loss or damage during the remainder of the voyage subsequent to the sacrifice. The allowance for property sacrificed must be subjected to the same vicissitudes of the continuing voyage as were suffered by the properties which arrived at destination, and reduced accordingly.

Expenditure

G.04 For many years there was a dispute between the writers of textbooks as to whether the same rule applied to expenditure. However, it is thought that this controversy may now be allowed to subside, and the answer taken to be laid down

[1] *Fletcher v Alexander* (1868) L.R. 3 C.P. 375.

[2] *Fletcher* (1868) L.R. 3 C.P. 375, 382.

[3] In this and other early reported cases, the phrase place of adjustment equates with termination of the adventure. The matter is discussed further at para.30.05, below.

[4] *Fletcher* (1868) L.R. 3 C.P. 375, 383.

by Sankey J. in 1921, which has not since been overturned.[5] In the case of expenditure, as with sacrifices, contributory values are assessed at the termination of the adventure; if none of the interests survive, there is no contribution.[6] Where the York-Antwerp Rules apply, there can be no doubt that this is the result.[7]

Historical Development and Practice of Rule G

York-Antwerp Rules 1924

Detailed provisions relating to the assessment of contributory values and amounts made good for general average losses had appeared in the numbered rules of the first York-Antwerp Rules from 1860. Those same provisions were expressed in briefer and even more general terms in r.G, introduced in 1924 as part of the new set of lettered rules setting out the fundamental principles of general average, r.G then read: **G.05**

> "General average shall be adjusted as regards both loss and contribution upon the basis of values at the time and place when and where the adventure ends.
>
> This rule shall not affect the determination of the place at which the average statement is to be made up."

The *first paragraph* merely expressed what was generally accepted worldwide. However, it was purposely silent on the vexed question of when and where the adventure ended on those increasingly common occasions when the vessel had on board cargo for a number of ports of discharge.

A Draft Code of General Average prepared in 1914 by Mr. H.C. Dowdall K.C. had proposed that: **G.06**

> "Section 5(1) General average shall be adjusted as regards both loss and contribution upon the basis of values at the first port of discharge after the general average act occurs, or at any earlier place at which the voyage may be broken up. Such port or place is hereinafter called the place of adjustment.
>
> (2) . . .
>
> (3) The provisions of this section shall not affect the determination of the place at which the average statement is to be made up."

However, the more generally accepted practice in this country and the Continent was to adjust general average as regards both loss and contribution upon the basis

[5] *Chellew v Royal Commission on the Sugar Supply* [1921] 2 K.B. 627; [1922] 1 K.B. 12.

[6] The contrary view, championed by Lowndes, is discussed at length in the 10th edn, paras 345 et seq. The point was left open by the Court of Appeal in the Chellew case: see [19221 1 K.B. 12 at 20, per Scrutton L.J. See also *The Mary Thomas* [1894] P. 108; *Green Star Shipping v The London Assurance* [1933] 1 K.B. 378 at 390; *Morrison S.S. Co Ltd v Greystoke Castle* [1947] A.C. 265 at 285, 312.

[7] See para.G.21, below. See also the *Chellew* case in the Court of Appeal, and *Green Star Shipping v The London Assurance* (see fn.6, above).

of values at the port of destination of the part of the cargo concerned, and in respect of the ship at the last port to which any of the cargo on board at the time of the general average act was consigned. The central proposal in the Draft Code to adopt the first port of discharge as the termination of the adventure was not generally acceptable. In fact, it will be noted that r.G leaves the matter quite open, while the rule follows exactly the opening and concluding words of the Draft Code of 1914.

The second paragraph of r.G was in accordance with and gave contractual effect to the decision of the Privy Council in the case of *Wavertree Sailing Ship Co v Love.*[8]

The applicable law and practice

G.07 The lack of any reference in r.G to the law and practice which should apply to the adjustment of any general average was an important omission; the subject had previously even merited a rule of its own–r.XVIII of the York-Antwerp Rules 1890.[9] Although the practice was well settled that adjustments should be prepared in accordance with the law and practice obtaining at the termination of the adventure, the difficulty was to determine or agree on every occasion precisely where the adventure did end. This, together with the (unfulfilled) anticipation that because the York-Antwerp Rules were by 1924 a fairly comprehensive and self-contained set of rules "it should be a matter of indifference at which port the adventure was deemed to be terminated",[10] probably accounts for the omission in the 1924 Rules.

York-Antwerp Rules 1950 and 1974

G.08 No change.

York-Antwerp Rules 1994

G.09 The existing wording of r.G was again retained unaltered, but a further two paragraphs were added which constituted what previously had been popularly known as a "Non-Separation Agreement" and the "Bigham Clause". These had customarily been used on an ad hoc basis and attached to the individual general average security documents on those occasions when cargo was forwarded to destination by other vessels from a port of refuge. However this need to make special arrangements with each of the cargo interests is now obviated by their incorporation within the York-Antwerp Rules themselves.

[8] *Wavertree Sailing Ship Co v Love* [1897] A.C. 373. See para.30.04, below.

[9] See Appendix 2B, below.

[10] See G.R. Rudolf *The York-Antwerp Rules* (1926), p.61.

Non-Separation Agreements

Background

If the cargo is forwarded to destination—even in continuation of the voyage—the common adventure ceases when the original carrying vessel and her cargo part company,[11] and all allowances in general average to the shipowner under r.XI(b) for crew wages, bunkers, and daily port charges during repairs will cease at that time. The cargo cannot be called upon to contribute to general average expenses incurred after leaving the ship.[12] **G.10**

Except in those cases where the voyage by the original vessel has been frustrated, it would seem unfair that the shipowner should suffer these disallowances and possibly bear also part of the cost of the forwarding when, by that forwarding, the cargo interests receive the distinct advantage of a much earlier delivery of their cargo than would otherwise have been the case, plus the additional benefit of being required to contribute only to a reduced general average, that has been saved the above mentioned allowances under r.XI, and also the cost of storing the cargo allowable under r.X(c).

Standard Non-Separation Agreement

Accordingly, it has been the custom for over a century[13] to ask cargo interests, in return for the forwarding of their cargo and an earlier delivery, to agree to contribute to a general average adjusted as though their cargo had remained at the port of refuge during the repairs to the ship, and been carried to destination in the original carrying vessel. **G.11**

This is achieved by incorporating what is termed a "Non-Separation Agreement" into the average bond and average guarantee signed by the consignees and the cargo insurers, respectively. The wording of the Agreement can be tailor-made, to suit any particular circumstances, but a Standard Form of Non-Separation Agreement has been in use in the British market since 1967:

> "It is agreed that in the event of the vessel's cargo or part thereof being forwarded to original destination by other vessel, vessels or conveyances, rights and liabilities in general average shall not be affected by such forwarding, it being the intention to place the parties concerned as nearly as possible in the same position in this respect as they would have been in the absence of such forwarding and with the adventure continuing by the original vessel for so long as justifiable under the law applicable or under the Contract of Affreightment."

The basis of contribution to general average of the property involved shall be the values on delivery at original destination unless sold or otherwise disposed of short of that destination, but where none of her cargo is carried forward in the

[11] See para.G.41, below.
[12] *Royal Mail S.P. Co v English Bank of Rio* (1887) 19 Q.B.D. 362.
[13] See also Rule of Practice F15 (para.70.42, below) adopted in 1876.

vessel she shall contribute on the basis of her actual value on the date she completes discharge of her cargo.

Interpretation of the Agreement

G.12 The object of the Agreement is to place the parties to the adventure in the same position with regard to their rights and liabilities in general average as if the cargo had been justifiably retained at the port of refuge and carried to destination in the original carrying vessel after repairs. Thus, and assuming that the delay for repairs was not sufficient to frustrate the adventure and the contract of carriage, the effect of the Agreement would be:

(1) The wages and maintenance of the crew, bunkers consumed and daily port charges throughout the detention undergoing repairs at the port of refuge would be allowable as general average under r.XI(b).
(2) The contributory values of the property will be:
   (i) For the cargo: calculated in the normal way as per r.XVII on delivery at the original destination, unless sold or otherwise disposed of short of that destination.
   (ii) For the ship (and bunkers, etc.): calculated in the normal way as per r.XVII but on the date on which the ship completes discharge of her cargo (at the port of refuge, assuming the whole cargo to be forwarded).

The *extra cost* of forwarding the cargo (that is after deduction of voyage savings) would be charged to general average under r.F as a substituted expense for any necessary cost of storing the cargo at the port of refuge allowable under r.X(c). It is important to note that items such as crew wages cannot be used to rank as savings for allowances under r.F or r.XIV (temporary repairs) if they are allowed under a non-separation agreement, since this would result in a double allowance in general average.

Bigham Clause

G.13 For the greater protection of cargo interests fearful of what they may be undertaking when signing a non-separation agreement, it was a common practice to include what is commonly known as the "Bigham Clause", which originated in the United States:

> "It is understood that the amount charged to cargo under this agreement shall not exceed what it would have cost the cargo owners if cargo was delivered to them at. . . (port of refuge) and forwarded by them to destination."[14]

In other words, cargo interests cannot be called upon to contribute towards "general average" expenditure incurred during an extended period of repairs more

[14] See paras G.17, G.50, below regarding the equivalent wording incorporated in 1994 into Rule G.

than it would have cost them to forward the cargo themselves from the port of refuge to destination. The clause is a sensible addition to the non-separation agreement from the point of view of the cargo interests and in the ABT Rasha[15] Clarke L. in the Court of Appeal referred to a non-separation agreement incorporating a Bigham clause as a reasonable agreement that held "obvious attractions . . . from point of view of both shipowners and cargo owners." In any negotiations regarding either or both provisions the question may arise as to whether the cargo interests have the right to refuse to sign a non-separation agreement in any form, and to insist upon taking delivery at the port of refuge and to pay there the freight and any other charges due upon the goods. Under the laws of Canada and of the United States it is clear that the cargo-owner has this right.

Thus in *Ellerman Lines v Gibbs Nathaniel (Canada); The City of Colombo*[16] the vessel, while on a voyage from Cochin to Toronto, was detained for 69 days for repairs at Montreal, only 350 miles from Toronto.[17] It was held that the owners of the Toronto cargo were under no obligation to allow the shipowner to retain and carry their cargo to Toronto in the original ship, after repairs, but were entitled to delivery at any port where the vessel put in, on payment of full freight and of any other charges due upon the cargo. The Court referred with approval to the American case of the *Domingo De Larrinaga*[18] in which it was held that consignees of damaged cargo (which had been discharged to allow an inspection of the hull) were entitled, on payment of full freight, to refuse to have their goods re-loaded and take delivery, even where the shipowners had arranged to tow ship and cargo to destination. **G.14**

Whilst there is no English authority on the point, these decisions have much to recommend them. Undoubtedly the shipowner is entitled to keep possession of the goods for a reasonable time for the purpose of earning his freight, for as Sir James Hannen said in The Blenheim[19] : **G.15**

> "The shipowner has a lien on the cargo for the purpose of enabling him to earn his freight, and the cargo owner is not entitled to insist on delivery of the cargo without payment of freight before the completion of the voyage on which the freight is to be earned."

But, having paid the freight, and any extra expenses incurred by the shipowner in making a special discharge of the cargo, and furnishing security in respect of general average sacrifices and expenditures incurred up to the time of taking delivery, any cargo owner should be entitled to demand delivery of his cargo at an intermediate port of call and a termination of his liability to contribute to continuing general average expenses.

[15] *ABT Rasha* [2000] 2 Lloyd's Rep. 575, see also paras 50.14.

[16] *Ellerman Lines v Gibbs Nathaniel (Canada); The City of Colombo* (1986) 26 D.L.R. (4th) 161; (1986) A.M.C. 2217. See also *The Julia Blake* (1882) 107 U.S. 418; *The Domingo De Larrinaga* (1928) A.M.C. 64.

[17] The delay was such that it might have given rise to the frustration of the adventure, but the issue of frustration was not raised.

[18] *Domingo De Larrinaga* (1928) A.M.C. 64.

[19] *The Blenheim* (1885) 10 P.D. 167; 54 L.J.P. 81; 5 Asp. M.C. 522.

York Antwerp Rules 2004

G.16 No change other than the introduction of paragraph numbers.

G.17 **RULE G**

(1) **General average shall be adjusted as regards both loss and contribution upon the basis of values at the time and place when and where the adventure ends.**

(2) **This rule shall not affect the determination of the place at which the average statement is to be made up.**

(3) **When a ship is at any port or place in circumstances which would give rise to an allowance in general average under the provisions of Rules X and XI, and the cargo or part thereof is forwarded to destination by other means, rights and liabilities in general average shall, subject to cargo interests being notified if practicable, remain as nearly as possible the same as they would have been in the absence of such forwarding, as if the adventure had continued in the original ship for so long as justifiable under the contract of affreightment and the applicable law.**

(4) **The proportion attaching to cargo of the allowances made in general average by reason of applying the third paragraph of this Rule shall not exceed the cost which would have been borne by the owners of cargo if the cargo had been forwarded at their expense.**

CONSTRUCTION

G.18 The first two paragraphs of r.G are concerned only with general principles and by reason of the Rule of Interpretation,[20] must yield to the specific provisions of the *numbered* rr.XVI (Amount to be made good for cargo lost or damaged by Sacrifice) and XVII (Contributory Values) in the event of any conflict. The purpose of these two paragraphs is to define in general terms at what time and place the values of the property at risk at the time of a general average act should be assessed, for the purpose of calculating both the allowance to be made in general average for any property sacrificed, and also the values on which the property saved should be called upon to contribute to such sacrifice or to any general average expenditure.

First Paragraph

G.19 **"as regards both loss and contribution"**: The effect of the first sentence of the rule is that the amount to be made good in respect of any general average loss,

[20] See para.PRE.04, above.

whether consisting of sacrifice or of expenditure, and the amount of contribution due from the other interests are assessed on the basis of the actual value of those interests, and the notional value[21] of any property sacrificed, at the end of the adventure.

This rule, together with r.XVII therefore resolves the doubt which existed at common law[22] as to whether in the case of general average expenditure contributory values fall to be assessed as at the time and place of the expenditure or whether, as in the case of sacrifices, these values must be assessed as at the termination of the adventure. Thus, a person who has incurred general average expenditure runs the risk of a subsequent change in the values of the contributing interests as a result of a subsequent casualty[23] : and the contributing interests themselves run the risk of the contribution of some being increased by a casualty reducing the value of the remainder.[24]

"loss": In this rule the word is used in contradistinction to "contribution", and includes "loss", "damage" and "expense", although in other rules it is to be contrasted with damage (for example rr.II, III, and IV). The word is apt to cover expenditure as well as sacrifice,[25] but the "values" referred to in the rule are those of the property at risk in the common adventure,[26] and these values have no relevance to the valuation of expenditure, which therefore falls to be valued at the time when it was made, as it does under English law.[27] In practice, since expenditure is not at risk in the adventure, the correct time and place for its valuation will only be of practical importance in connection with rates of exchange. So far as concerns these, expenditure is to be exchanged at the rate prevailing on the date when the expenditure was made.[28] **G.20**

"upon the basis of values at the time and place when and where the adventure ends": As previously mentioned, the rule does not define when and where the adventure ends.[29] A similar difficulty exists at common law.[30] A solution to the problem is not assisted by the fact that the rule expresses the noun "adventure" in the singular, thereby possibly creating the impression that, however complex the voyage, there is only one single adventure, and which editors since the 8th edition have submitted must be the "common maritime adventure" referred to in r.A. **G.21**

This may well be the case where a single shipment of cargo is carried to a single port of discharge, but less obviously so where the vessel loads a number of shipments at various ports of loading for two or more ports of discharge, possibly even with some transhipment cargo under "through" bills of lading. In any such

[21] See paras G.03, G.04, above.

[22] See para.G.05, above.

[23] See *Chellew v Royal Commission on the Sugar Supply* [1921] 2 K.B. 627; [1922] 1 K.B. 12, CA.

[24] See *Green Star Shipping v The London Assurance* [1933] 1 K.B. 378. See para.G.29, below.

[25] "A general average loss includes a general average expenditure as well as a general average sacrifice" (Marine Insurance Act 1906 s.66(1)).

[26] Namely the notional value of property sacrificed and the actual values of other property: see paras G.03, G.04, above.

[27] See para.G.03, above.

[28] See para.40.23, below.

[29] For the Rule of Practice governing the ascertainment of the end of the adventure for purposes of insurance claims where the vessel is in ballast, see para.70.12 (r.B26), below.

[30] See paras G.06, G.07, above.

situation it might more accurately reflect the situation to state that there are several commercial adventures at risk, with different termini and of different lengths, but that for part of those lengths they and the ship all coincide and are common. This section of the overall voyage can undoubtedly be considered as a common maritime adventure.

G.22 Rule A is concerned only with defining a general average act, something which occurs at a particular moment during the overall voyage and is relevant to all those separate adventurers who happen to be bound up with the ship at the particular time of the general average act. Rule G addresses the separate issue of the evaluation of the general average losses and of the properties which shall contribute. The present editors submit that for this purpose of evaluating the losses and contributory values, there may be several adventures which, in the absence of an earlier abandonment of the voyage, will each terminate at their several destinations. As a basic concept, the relevant maritime adventures for cargo and freight will generally end when their community of interest with the ship separates on discharge[31] from the ship at the different ports of discharge, and that for the ship ends on completion of discharge at the final port of discharge. Container vessels often operate on continuous service loops that do not have any obvious terminus. In such cases the final port is generally considered to be the one at which the last of the cargo on board at the time of the general average act is discharged.

Potential difficulties in defining the precise termination of the adventure in individual circumstances will be discussed in greater detail as indicated in paras G.23–G.43.

Voyage to a Single Destination

G.23 No problems are anticipated in the straightforward situation where the vessel is bound for a single port of discharge and, together with such cargo as has not been lost or destroyed by a general average sacrifice, she arrives there successfully. In the absence of alternative provisions in the contract of affreightment, the law and practice applicable at that destination governs the adjustment, and general average losses and contributory values are both to be assessed on the basis of the values ruling at that place and at the time of discharge (in practice, on the last day of discharge for all the cargo).

Voyage to Two or More Ports

G.24 If a vessel incurs general average expenditure or makes a general average sacrifice when carrying cargo for two or more ports of discharge, does the adventure end at the first port, or at the second (or final) port of discharge? This problem has been touched upon earlier in para.G.22, but the principle involved is of sufficient

[31] The practice is to take the last day of discharge at each of the ports of discharge, this being the relevant date under r.XVI (see para.16.20, below) until 1974.

importance and financial consequence that a more detailed study is warranted here.

To illustrate the problem in simple form, let it be assumed that on a voyage to ports A and B the ship and cargoes A and B are each worth 1,000,000, and that during the early part of the voyage as part of fire-extinguishing operations cargo is water damaged and the sacrifice valued at 300,000 or 10 per cent of the total contributory values (including amounts made good). The voyage to port A is successfully completed thereafter without further incident, but the ship and cargo B are totally lost before arrival at port B.

Let the sacrifice of 300,000 be exclusively of cargo for port A

The interests of cargo A will be best served by suggesting that port A is the termination of that adventure which is common to all the contributors, and that the subsequent portion of the voyage is a matter with which cargo A has no concern. Thus, the general average would be apportioned on values as at A and, effectively, ship and cargo B should contribute their due proportion of say 200,000 towards cargo A's loss of 300,000. **G.25**

Cargo B would object, that the voyage is not yet over and that it may perish on the second stage to port B. To assess their value for contribution at A is to fly in the face of the rule that there can be no contribution unless there is benefit, and the extent of that benefit can only be assessed on arrival at B. Further, how can cargo A exercise any lien on or enforce contribution from the ship and cargo B at port A?

Let the sacrifice of 300,000 be exclusively of cargo for port B

On this occasion, cargo A will protest if it be similarly suggested that the common adventure ends on the completion of discharge of their cargo at A, and that they should thereupon become liable immediately to pay their due portion of 100,000 towards cargo B's loss of 300,000. They will rightly maintain that if (as in fact happened), the ship and remaining cargo B were lost before arrival at B, cargo B would have lost nothing by the earlier sacrifice, for that water damaged cargo would similarly have been totally lost, and, accordingly, that nothing is to be made good in general average. **G.26**

In the absence of any contrary law ruling at port A, it is submitted that for the purpose of r.G there are two adventures involved here with different terminii, but united and common at the time of the sacrifice. The adventure for cargo A, ended on completion of discharge at port A. The adventure for the ship and cargo B. would have terminated for both on completion of discharge at port B but did in fact terminate on their prior loss at sea. Rights of contribution to general average can be enforced only at the place where any adventure ends,[32] and while port A was the appropriate place to exercise these for cargo A, not until their safe arrival at port B could the ship and cargo B be required to contribute towards any general average sacrifice sustained by them. Their rights to any general average **G.27**

[32] See paras 30.41 et seq., below.

expenditure incurred by them, however, survive the total loss and would be payable wholly by surviving cargo A.

G.28 If we return now to cargo A, its adventure terminates on completion of discharge at port A and it cannot be called upon to contribute to any subsequent salvage or general average suffered by the ship and cargo B after leaving port A. It will be obliged to provide proper general average security before delivery at port A, but its obligation to contribute to any losses sustained by the ship and cargo B and its rights to receive anything from them are obviously deferred until they have successfully completed the adventure—or been lost. Thus, the final stage of the adventure to port B remains of considerable interest to cargo A, and in accordance with the view expressed elsewhere in this series,[33] the adventure does not terminate at the first port of discharge, but continues in part until the last port of discharge of the cargo on board at the time of the general average act.

G.29 It is appropriate here to record the facts of a case which supports the view that the common adventure does not cease at the first port at which any of the cargo is discharged (except as regards the cargo discharged there), but continues in part until the last port of discharge. In *Green Star Shipping Co Ltd v The London Assurance*,[34] the vessel was loading at New York when fire broke out in the holds, in consequence of which general average expenditure was incurred by the shipowners. Cargo valued at $18,000 was discharged and not reloaded. The vessel duly sailed from New York with the remainder of the cargo but was involved in a collision and sank. The salved value of ship and cargo, excluding the cargo discharged at New York, was about $142,000 but general average expenditure resulting from the collision amounted to $180,000.

Roche J. held that[35] :

> "This 18,000 dollars worth of cargo was the only property in the adventure which was available for the purpose of contribution in the first general average, because the expenditure occasioned by the second general average, the collision, fell to be deducted from the values of ship and cargo (see York-Antwerp Rule XVII)[36] for the purposes of the adjustment of the first general average. After this deduction was made the values of the rest of the cargo and of the ship were nil."

Later in his judgment he reverted to the matter thus[37] :

> "The cargo which went on from New York was reduced in value by the collision and second general average from about 19,000 dollars to nothing. Had there been no

[33] Carver, *British Shipping Laws*, Vol.3; *Carriage by Sea*, 13th edn, paras 1451–1452. For a fuller discussion see the 12th edn, paras 945–947. See also *British Shipping Laws*, Vol.10: Arnould, *Marine Insurance*, 16th edn, para.992.

[34] *Green Star Shipping Co Ltd v The London Assurance* [1933] 1 K.B. 378. The case was decided under the York-Antwerp Rules 1890 but there is no difference between the Rules and English law on the point.

[35] *Green Star* [1933] 1 K.B. 378 at 382.

[36] Of the 1890 Rules which provided that: "The contribution to a general average shall be made upon the actual values of the property at the end of the adventure . . . deduction also being made from the value of the property of all charges incurred in respect thereof subsequently to the general average." The 1890 Rules, however, contained no equivalent of r.G or of the Rule of Interpretation.

[37] *Green Star* [1933] 1 K.B. 378 at 385.

> collision the full contribution recoverable from cargo in respect of the first general average (fire) would have been recovered. But if the cargo which went on to meet with the collision had not met with that collision and been thereby reduced in value, the cargo which remained at New York would not have been liable to make contribution up to 100 per cent., as it in fact did in the circumstances as altered by the collision."

It is possible that Roche J. considered that the appropriate sound values for ship and all the cargo were New York values, on the basis that the common adventure ended there, r.XVII providing for the deduction of charges incurred even after the end of the adventure. However, this seems unlikely in view of the way in which he expresses himself in the second passage quoted above, and it can hardly be correct to take the physical condition of the goods at one port but to deduct charges incurred up to a subsequent port. It seems more probable that the ship and the cargo reloaded were valued at their actual destination. The case may therefore be regarded as authority for the view that, at any rate where the York-Antwerp Rules apply, the adventure continues in part until the last port of discharge. **G.30**

Voyage with Cargo for Onward Transit from Discharge Port

In the absence of any specific provisions in the bill of lading, the common adventure as regards the cargo transhipped ends at the transhipment port and the cargo becomes legally liable there and then to contribute to any earlier general average. It contributes on the value in which it is at that time and place, regardless of what may happen to it on any subsequent stage of its scheduled transport. **G.31**

However, on practical and commercial grounds, it may be difficult for the shipowner to hold up the cargo at the transhipment port and exercise his lien there and collect general average security at what, for the cargo, is but an intermediate port. In the circumstances, the shipowner may permit the cargo to go forward to final destination in the normal way, but taking steps to ensure that the cargo is not released at final destination until the proper general average formalities have been fulfilled.

For practical convenience, as stated in para.17.27, below, the contributory value will be assessed on the value of the cargo at its final destination, except that damage known to have occurred subsequent to leaving the original vessel will not be deducted.

Voyage Abandoned Short of Destination(s)

In *Fletcher v Alexander*[38] the facts of which are set out in para.G.03, the vessel returned to the loading port after stranding and the voyage was there abandoned. The owners of the jettisoned salt refused to furnish a substitute cargo, and when the ship was repaired, her owner took in a fresh cargo of salt on his own account, and sent it to Calcutta, where it arrived, and was sold at a profit. **G.32**

[38] *Fletcher v Alexander* (1868) L.R. 3 C.P. 375.

On behalf of the owner of the salt it was contended that he was entitled to the sum which the jettisoned salt would have produced had it been carried in the ship to Calcutta. Since the event proved that in that case it would have been sold at a profit, as the second cargo was, he was entitled to such profit. As a consequence of this contention, it was argued that Calcutta was the proper place, and the date of the ship's arrival there the proper time, for adjusting the general average.

Bovill C.J. held that, although in general the port of destination was the proper place for adjusting a general average, when the voyage was broken up, and the adventure brought to an end at some other place, the average should be adjusted there. Thus, if at some intermediate port the entire voyage is wholly abandoned owing to an excepted peril, general average losses and contributory values are both to be assessed on the basis of the values of the property at that place. For example, in respect of:

Cargo Sold at the Port of Refuge

G.33 If cargo is damaged solely by an accidental cause, the contributory value will be the net sale proceeds of the cargo after deducting any charges incurred to achieve such proceeds (for example reconditioning charges). If the cargo is damaged solely by a general average sacrifice, the contributory value will be the net sale proceeds, as before, plus any amount made good in general average. The amount made good will be assessed by deducting the net sale proceeds from the sound value at the port of refuge, which in the normal case is likely to be the sound value at the scheduled destination, less the estimated cost of getting the cargo there.

Cargo Forwarded to Original Destination

G.34 Cargo interests may well decide to forward sound or moderately damaged cargo to the scheduled destination in the anticipation that its value there is likely to be greater than any sale proceeds at the port of refuge, but as stated earlier, general average losses and contributory values ought both to be assessed on the values at the place where the voyage was abandoned and general average security presumably obtained.

In practice, this will be achieved by adopting the actual sound or damaged values as at the scheduled destination, but deducting there from such charges as were incurred to achieve those destination values (for example the forwarding freight). Loss or damage from any new cause known to have occurred during the forwarding passage must clearly be added back to the actual values at destination, but any natural extension of existing damage may reasonably be ignored or treated as a quid pro quo for the likely higher values at intended destination as compared with sale proceeds at the port of refuge.

G.35 The preceding remarks are predicated on the assumption that an accident caused the voyage to be justifiably abandoned: in the unusual event that a general average sacrifice dictated the abandonment of the voyage (for example a voluntary stranding from which the vessel could not be refloated), general average allowances and contributory values should be based on values at the intended destination(s), on the grounds that the loss of the value at destination was a direct result of the general average act.

Part Cargo is left behind at a Port of Refuge

Such a situation occurred in the case of *Hill v Wilson*,[39] see also para.30.16, below, The *Virago* stranded during the course of a voyage from Riga to Hull with a general cargo, and, after jettisoning a small part of the cargo, was got off and towed into Copenhagen. There the cargo was discharged, much of it sold, some of it forwarded to destination, and. after repairs, the vessel completed the voyage with the remainder of the cargo. **G.36**

The matter at issue was simply whether English or Danish law should govern the adjustment of the general average, and Lindley J. decided that English law was applicable, both for the ship and the cargo, including that left behind and sold at Copenhagen. He was not concerned with the amounts to be made good in general average or with contributory values, but on the particular facts of case, where it may reasonably be assumed that the damage to the cargo necessarily sold at Copenhagen was of accidental origin, there seems little doubt that such cargo should contribute on its net sale proceeds at Copenhagen, while the cargo forwarded in other vessels or carried to destination by the Virago would contribute on its value at final destination, Hull.

With regard to the cargo jettisoned, the amount to be made good in general average should be based on the likely condition in which the cargo would, but for the jettison, have arrived at Copenhagen: (1) if badly damaged and requiring to be sold at Copenhagen, on its value at that port; or (2) if sound, or in fit condition to be carried to Hull, on its value there.

Where the Cargo is sold at the Port of Refuge, the Costs will be dealt with as follows:

(1) Damaged solely by an accidental cause

Provided that the discharge was not for the common safety, or the cargo be left behind as some form of general average sacrifice (dealt with at para.G.38 below): **G.37**

(a) As regards the cargo discharged and sold, both the common adventure and the voyage itself obviously terminate at the port of refuge.
(b) The cargo is not liable for any general average expenses or losses sustained subsequent to its discharge.
(c) The shipowner's general average lien must be exercised at the port of refuge, but will be at least partly subject to the safe arrival of the other property at the scheduled destinations.

[39] *Hill v Wilson* (1879) 4 C.P.D. 329.

(d) The contributory value will be the net sale proceeds of the cargo after deducting any charges incurred to achieve such proceeds (for example reconditioning expenses).

(2) Damaged solely by a general average sacrifice

G.38 (a) For the net *sale proceeds*, the common adventure and the voyage itself terminate at the port of refuge, and the proceeds do not contribute to any general average expenses or losses sustained subsequent to the discharge of cargo. If a general average lien needs to be exercised, it is at the port of refuge.

(b) The amount made good effectively travels with the ship and other cargo to the intended destination. Thus, the common adventure continues and the amount made good is subject to the same vicissitudes as are suffered by the other properties.[40] However, assuming that no further casualties are encountered:

(i) The amount made good in general average will be the sound CIF invoice value at the scheduled destination, less the net sale proceeds at the port of refuge.

(ii) The contributory value, to include the amount made good, will be the sound CIF invoice value.

(3) Sound or damaged from any cause, but the sale necessitated by some form of general average sacrifice

G.39 The guiding principle to be borne in mind whenever cargo is left behind at a port of refuge as the direct result of a general average act or sacrifice is that the owner should be placed in the same position as he would have been in if his cargo had remained on board or been reloaded on the original vessel and carried on to the intended destination.

Cargo Forwarded from a Port of Refuge by Other Vessels

G.40 A vessel may enter a port of refuge and on survey, be found to be a constructive total loss, or requiring repairs which will take so long as to destroy the commercial purpose of the voyage. In either situation the adventure is potentially frustrated[41] and, if the cargo be sound or in such condition as to warrant forwarding to destination the shipowner must elect within a reasonable time:

(1) to exercise his implied right of transhipment[42] and to complete the contract voyage in another bottom at his own expense in order to earn freight still at risk; or

[40] See para.17.32, below; also Report No.34 of the Advisory Committee of the Association of Average Adjusters.

[41] See paras 00.42 et seq., above, as to the circumstances in which the adventure is frustrated.

[42] See para.00.45, above.

(2) to abandon the voyage and leave it to the cargo interests to make their own arrangements for forwarding goods to destination, or himself make the forwarding arrangements as agent for the cargo interests and at their expense.

In all of these circumstances the adventure terminates, as regards the ship, when the cargo has been discharged at the port of refuge.[43] But so far as concerns the transhipped cargo, does the adventure terminate at the port of refuge or does it continue until arrival at the scheduled destination?

In principle the answer to this question is clear enough. It involves drawing a distinction between; (1) the case where the shipowner, in the exercise of a liberty conferred upon him and in order to earn his freight, tranships and forwards the cargo in continuation of the voyage and at his own expense; and (2) the case where the cargo is forwarded by the cargo interests, or by the shipowner acting as their agent and looking to them for reimbursement of the costs of forwarding: **G.41**

(1) *In continuation of the voyage*: In this case it can hardly be said that the voyage is broken up. There is simply the substitution by the shipowner of one vessel for another under circumstances entitling him to make such substitution. The contract, and therefore the adventure which is constituted by it, still exists. All rights under it, including the right to exercise a lien and recover general average on delivery of the cargo to the consignee, still remain in force. In this case, therefore, it is submitted that the proper place for adjustment is the port of destination.[44]

(2) *Forwarding by or on behalf of cargo owners*: In this case, the voyage has been broken up at the place of transhipment and this is the proper place for adjustment. The shipowner will usually hold the cargo at the port of refuge until proper general average security has been furnished, but if he does defer his rights until arrival he may instead forward the goods under a bill of lading taken out in his own name, in which case he will be able to exercise a lien on them at the destination. However, even in that case, it is submitted that the voyage still terminates at the port of refuge.

Which of these two courses the shipowner will adopt is likely to depend upon whether the costs of completing the voyage at his expense exceed any freight still at risk, and whether in the shipowners view the adventure has been frustrated, thereby entitling him to abandon the voyage at the port of refuge. But the crucial distinction between the two cases is that in the first case, where the transhipment is in continuation of the voyage, the shipowner will bear the costs of forwarding, being remunerated for carriage to the scheduled destination by the contract freight **G.42**

[43] See para.G.10, above.

[44] cf. *Barnard v Adams* (1850) 10 How. 270 at 307; *McLoon v Cummings* (1873) 73 Penn. St.Rep. 98; *Bradley v Cargo of Lumber* (1886) 29 Fed. Rep. 648.

originally agreed,[45] whereas in the second case the cargo bears the expenses, and if the shipowner pays them in the first instance, he does so merely as a financing exercise, and is entitled to be reimbursed.

G.43 In practice, however, the distinction is not always easy to draw because one party to the adventure (normally the shipowner) may pay the costs in the first instance but claim to recover them from the other party; and at the time of the adjustment it may still be in dispute who is liable to pay the costs. In such cases it is generally true to say that forwarding should be regarded as being in continuation of the voyage unless:

(1) there has been some express notice of abandonment of the voyage by the shipowner, or some conduct which shows clearly that he regards the voyage as terminated at the port of refuge; and
(2) the abandonment is either agreed to by the cargo interests or is justified by the frustration of the adventure[46] or by the express terms of the contract of carriage.

On occasion the cargo is forwarded (or carried forward) under the terms of a special agreement which may, for example, require the shipowner to fund the forwarding expenses but oblige the cargo owners to reimburse him if the contract was justifiably terminated at the port of refuge, for example on the grounds of frustration.

Second Paragraph

G.44 **"This rule shall not affect the determination of the place at which the average statement is to be made up"**: This second paragraph reproduces what was held to be the common law in *Wavertree Sailing Ship Co v Love*[47] and its purpose is presumably to make it clear that the rule does not affect the determination of either the law governing the adjustment[48] or the place where the adjustment is actually prepared.[49]

Third Paragraph

G.45 This paragraph essentially reproduces the first paragraph of the Standard Form of Non-Separation Agreement in use in the British market since 1967, the background and interpretation of which is dealt with at length, in paras G.10 to G.15, above.

"When a ship is at any port or place": See commentary in para.10.31, below.

[45] In certain limited circumstances the cost of forwarding cargo is allowed in general average as a substituted expense: see paras F.09 and F.23, above.
[46] See paras 00.41 et seq., above.
[47] *Wavertree Sailing Ship Co v Love* [1897] A.C. 373: see paras 30.03 et seq., below.
[48] See paras 30.06 et seq., below.
[49] See paras 30.04 et seq., below.

"in circumstances which would give rise to an allowance in general average under the provisions of Rules X and XI": The circumstances which would give rise to an allowance in general average under the provisions of rr.X and XI are best recorded with an extract from r.XI(b):

> "When a ship shall have entered or been detained in any port or place in consequence of accident, sacrifice or other extraordinary circumstances which render that necessary for the common safety, or to enable damage to the ship caused by sacrifice or accident to be repaired, if the repairs were necessary for the safe prosecution of the voyage . . ."

A construction of these various phrases is given in paras 11.27–11.29, with further references to paras 10.30 to 10.32 and 10.46, below. The general average allowances referred to include the cost of cargo operations in rr.X(a) and (b), and crew wages and maintenance, fuel and stores consumed, and port charges under r.XI(b) and expenses incurred minimising pollution under r.XI(d).

Where the transhipment takes place from a port of refuge at which repairs cannot be effected, allowances under the second paragraph of r.X(a) (i.e. the cost of removal, including towage to a second port of refuge) will also be made under a Non-Separation Agreement (1974 Rules) or r.G (1994 and 2004 Rules). However, the move to a second port has to be consistent with what would have been done if the voyage had continued. If the shipowner chooses to go further than the nearest suitable repair port in search of cheaper repair costs or to re-position the vessel for a new voyage, such a removal is outside the scope of r.X(a). **G.46**

"and the cargo or part thereof is forwarded to destination by other means": **G.47**
Although forwarding will customarily be carried out by another ship, if the port of refuge is close to the scheduled destination the cargo may be forwarded by lighters, or by rail, etc. Although unstated, it would appear reasonable to assume that the forwarding must have been undertaken by the shipowner or the charterer at his expense for the general provisions of this Non-Separation Agreement to apply.

"subject to cargo interests being notified if practicable"[50] : Non-Separation Agreements were customarily agreed and signed in the appropriate circumstances only after a casualty, and it is understandable that some slight reservations might be felt in certain quarters about the wisdom of contractually giving away that agreement, or right to object, in advance. This particular phrase was insisted upon by the US delegation at Sydney in 1994. They feared—probably unnecessarily—that the incorporation of the Non-Separation Agreement within the York-Antwerp Rules might override the decision in the *City of Colombo*[51] case and that by including this phrase cargo interests would be given the opportunity to object to the forwarding, or the continuing general average allowances, if considered appropriate.[52] It was appreciated, however, that such notification may not always

[50] This phrase is dealt with out of order and appears in the space. . . in the next following phrase for construction.

[51] *Ellerman Lines v Gibbs Nathaniel (Canada)* (1986) A.M.C. 2217.

[52] It is interesting to record that in *Shoe v Craig* (1912) 194 Fed. Rep. 678, where a vessel was towed to destination without consulting the cargo, in spite of the fact that their office was only a few

be practicable, particularly with multi-bill of lading shipments by container vessels.

G.48 **"rights and liabilities in general average shall. . . remain as nearly as possible the same as they would have been in the absence of such forwarding"**: As stated in para.G.12, above, the object of a Non-Separation Agreement is to place the parties to the adventure in the same position with regard to their rights and liabilities in general average as if the cargo had been justifiably retained at the port of refuge and carried to destination in the original carrying vessel after repairs. The rights in general average will be the continuing daily allowances to the shipowner under rr.X and XI, and the liabilities for all parties will be to contribute to the general average on the basis of their values as set out in the third paragraph of r.XVII.

"as if the adventure had continued in the original ship": This phrase forms an integral part of and reinforces the idea expressed in the immediately preceding wording that, contrary to the fact that ship and cargo have actually parted company, the adventure should be deemed to continue.

G.49 **"for so long as justifiable under the contract of affreightment and the applicable law"**: If a vessel is badly damaged, circumstances may be such that the cost or time required for repairs or the perishable nature of a cargo would render the voyage frustrated, according to the terms of the contract of affreightment or applicable law. Absent forwarding, allowances in general average would then be limited to:

(a) Cargo discharge or other measures if for the common safety.
(b) Storage of cargo if discharged for the common safety.
(c) Wages and maintenance, fuel and stores and port charges, etc.

Of the above, (b) and (c) continue only up to the ship's condemnation or the abandonment of the voyage or the completion of the discharge of cargo. The scope for any allowances under a Non-Separation Agreement or r.G (or under r.F for any forwarding cost) is therefore minimal. Where the frustration of the voyage is readily apparent, if the shipowner nonetheless wishes to exercise his option to forward cargo to destination, a special agreement is necessary to establish what compensation he wishes to receive.

For commercial reasons and for the added convenience of not having to deal with cargo during the repair process, transhipment of cargo is often arranged very promptly after arriving at a port of refuge—this is particularly the case with container vessels if the port is on an established container route. It sometimes occurs that the full extent of the damage only becomes apparent when, some weeks later, the vessel is able to enter an available drydock. Having taken advantage of the forwarding operation, is it then open to cargo interests to refuse to

blocks away from that of the shipowner, the judge noted this position and stated that: "I do not believe that a substituted expense is ever allowable in general average unless all parties in interest have first agreed to it."

contribute to the detention expenses during the repairs because their duration might be such as might have frustrated the voyage?

Assuming the vessel is repaired, this is generally a strong indication that frustration on the basis of repair costs would not be justified. The cargo interests would need to establish a frustrating delay which may often prove difficult in view of the lack of legal authority setting out the period required—as exemplified by the difficult task that a shipowner would face if trying to advance a case for frustration by delay in his own interest. However, it is not considered that the fact that cargo had been notified of the intention to forward would of itself prevent cargo raising the point that continuation of the original voyage might not have been justified under the contract of affreightment or applicable law, unless the notice was given in terms that acceptance involved express or implied agreement as to the general average allowances that were envisaged when the "bargain" inherent in the situation was struck. With a bulk cargo, or similar voyages involving a limited number of interests, the general average security may in fact be claused accordingly and will be requested at the same time as the notification of forwarding is given.

Forwarding of cargo is often seen with container vessel casualties where the number of interests involved and the speed with which forwarding arrangements are usually made will make notification of cargo interests impracticable—and also very probably unpopular with cargo interests that would see it as involving an unnecessary delay. The prompt forwarding of cargo in such cases is of clear general benefit to all parties and it would be regrettable if a greater degree of formality became necessary to forestall objections to allowances under r.F or r.G that were made with the advantage of hindsight.

If a clear case can in fact be made that full examination of the damage indicates a delay for repairs that would frustrate the voyage, it was suggested in the previous edition that the rule or the agreement it came from is so worded that it probably modifies the common law rule that frustration may occur as a result of prospective delay; thus, if a delay of two months is required to frustrate the contract, allowances could continue for that period. The present editors consider that it is difficult to find support for this view in the wording and that once the circumstances give rise to frustration the effects of this situation are immediate.

Fourth Paragraph

"The proportion attaching to cargo of the allowances made in general G.50
average by reason of applying the third paragraph of this Rule shall not exceed the cost which would have been borne by the owners of cargo if the cargo had been forwarded at their expense": This paragraph is essentially the old Bigham Clause commented on in paras G.13 to G.15, above, and constitutes the second limitation on the continuing daily general average allowances which can be made under the Non-Separation Agreement. Cargo interests cannot be called upon to contribute towards "general average" expenditure incurred during an extended period of repairs more than it would cost to forward the cargo themselves from the port of refuge to destination.

G.51 A typical situation in which r.G would apply might be as follows:

A loaded vessel limps into a port of refuge with severe grounding damage that requires repairs necessary for the safe prosecution of the voyage.

An inspection at the anchorage takes place to see whether temporary repairs could be effected afloat but it is decided the vessel must be dry-docked for permanent repairs, which will require discharge of all cargo. Although storage facilities are available ashore they are likely to be very expensive and a vessel is found to take the cargo to destination. Following a ship to ship transfer of cargo at the anchorage, the vessel drydocks and repairs are carried out. The costs will be dealt with as follows:

(a) STS Operation: The cost of discharging cargo is allowable under r.X and is allowed directly to General Average. If the STS operation is more expensive than discharge ashore the excess costs would form part of (b).

(b) Transhipment to destination (less voyage expenses saved by the original vessel not completing the voyage) is allowed under r.F in substitution for the greater costs of storing and reloading cargo (r.X(c)). It is important to emphasise that this allowance is not in any way dependent on the signing of a Non-Separation Agreement where the 1974 Rules are applicable or the effect of r.G's third paragraph under the 1994/2004 Rules.

(c) Detention expenses during repairs–i.e. wages and maintenance of crew, (not under 2004 Rules) fuel and stores consumed, and port charges including allowances under r.XI(d) regarding expenses incurred to minimise damage to the environment are all expenses that are incurred after the common adventure has ended when ship and cargo parted company. These expenses can only be allowed under a Non-separation Agreement (1974 Rules) or by relying upon r.G (1994 and 2004 Rules).

G.52 In most cases cargo's proportion of the expenses under (c) will be relatively modest and it will be evident that the Bigham Clause cap in the fourth paragraph of r.G will not apply.

In rarer cases (see the ABT Rasha discussed in para.50.14 of Section 7 relating to General Average and Insurance) the expenses may be much more significant. If in the above example there had been no repair facilities at the initial port of refuge (A), the cost of towing the vessel to a second port of refuge (B) would be allowed under the second paragraph of r.X(a). If, as before, the cargo was transhipped from port A, the towage to port B can only be allowable by virtue of r.G or a Non-Separation Agreement.

Once the cost of towage to B and the r.XI allowances at B have been added together, cargo's proportion of the total can be calculated. This figure is then compared with the cost that would have been borne by the owners of cargo, if the cargo had been forwarded at their expense. In calculating the cost of forwarding if arranged by cargo, it is suggested that:

(i) The "what if" calculation is on the basis of the voyage being terminated at port A by agreement, and it must therefore be assumed that no costs of discharge (unless for the common safety), storage, etc. are allowed in general average and are entirely for cargo's account.
(ii) Similarly, even if the contract of affreightment had provided for shipowners to pay the costs of discharge at destination, they would probably have no obligation to pay for such costs if cargo elect to end the voyage short of destination.

In the rare cases where cargo's proportion of allowances under r.G, para.3 exceed the cost calculated under the fourth paragraph, the excess is disallowed and may, in appropriate circumstances, be recoverable from hull insurers as part of the "proportion of the (general average) loss that falls on the Shipowner"—see MIA 66 (4) and para.50.14 below.

RULE I

JETTISON OF CARGO

Jettison is the classic example of a general average sacrifice; it forms the subject of the earliest known reference to general average[1] and was by far the earliest example of general average to come before the English courts. At no time in any of the maritime nations of the world has there ever been any doubt that underdeck cargo thrown overboard at a time of peril for the common safety should be made good in general average. So widely held and applied has been this basic concept that, either by oversight or because it was thought to be stating the obvious, the York-Antwerp Rules have never made any specific provision for such an allowance. **1.01**

Thus, losses by jettison must be claimed under the general principles of r.A and it is there, perhaps, that the subject should be treated. However, during the litigious nineteenth century there was very considerable dispute concerning the jettison of cargo carried on deck, and as r.I was originally framed to deal with this vexed topic, this is a convenient place to deal with the whole subject of jettison.

ENGLISH LAW AND BACKGROUND

The first reference to contribution towards jettison recorded in our law books occurred in 1285 in the reign of Edward I.[2] The second is given in Coke's Reports, as occurring in the sixth year of King James I's reign, under the title of Mouse's Case.[3] The modern law concerning the master's right to jettison cargo in case of imminent danger begins with the case of The Gratitudine[4] in 1801, where Lord Stowell gave judgment as follows: **1.02**

[1] See para.00.01, above.
[2] See para.00.10, above.
[3] *Mouse's Case* (1609) 12 Co. Rep. 63.
[4] *The Gratitudine* (1801) 3 C.Rob. 240.

"It must unavoidably be admitted that in some cases he [the master] must exercise the discretion of an authorized agent over the cargo, as well in the prosecution of the voyage at sea, as in intermediate ports, into which he may be compelled to enter. The case of throwing overboard parts of the cargo at sea is of that kind. Nothing can be better settled than that the master has a right to exercise this power in case of imminent danger. He may select what article he pleases; he may determine what quantity; no proportion is limited; a fourth, a moiety, three-fourths, nay, in cases of extreme necessity, when the lives of the crew cannot otherwise be saved,[5] it never can be maintained that he might not throw the whole cargo overboard. The only obligation will be that the ship should contribute its average proportion."

1.03 As the passage cited above shows, jettison has two important aspects. First, it entitles the owner of cargo thrown overboard to contribution in general average from the property saved. Secondly, it provides a defence to the shipowner against any claim by the owner of the cargo lost for failure to carry it safely to its destination.[6] In each case the jettison must be such as to qualify as a general average act, that is, the goods must be thrown overboard, not accidentally carried away by heavy weather, and this must be reasonably done in order to preserve the vessel and the remainder of the cargo from a loss threatening the whole adventure. Thus, where the master of a vessel which was about to be attacked threw a quantity of dollars into the sea merely to prevent it falling into enemy hands, and not for the preservation of the property involved in the common adventure, no right to contribution in general average could arise.[7] Likewise, in each case the consequences of jettison may differ if the need for it was caused by fault of one of the parties to the adventure.[8] But the principle remains that the master of a ship is entitled to jettison cargo in circumstances of necessity and if he does so, his owners have a defence to a claim for the loss of the cargo but are subject to a liability to contribute in general average.

Jettison of Deckload

1.04 To the rule that jettison is general average there is one ancient and well-established exception: goods carried on a ship's deck if thrown overboard are, generally speaking, not made good by contribution, although if saved they must contribute like anything else. The reason is that a ship's deck is generally an improper place for cargo.[9] Where

[5] As to sacrifices made "in fear of death", see paras A.21–A.22, above.
[6] This is further considered at paras 00.67 et seq., above.
[7] *Butler v Wildman* (1820) 3 B. & Ald. 398.
[8] See para.D.02, above.
[9] "According to the rules of maritime law, the placing of goods upon the deck of a sea going ship is improper stowage, because they are hindrances to the safe navigation of the vessel; and their jettison is therefore regarded, in a question with the other shippers of cargo, as a justifiable riddance of incumbrances which ought never to have been there, and not as a sacrifice for the common safety": per Lord Watson, *Strang v Scott* [1889] 14 A.C. 601 at 609.

The carrying of cargo on deck is absolutely forbidden by many old sea laws: e.g. by the decrees of the Hanseatic League (AD 1477) 2 Pard. 483; by the old law of Genoa (AD 1441) 4 Pard. 463: by the Ordonnance of Louis XIV, para.13. The Hague Rules except from the definition of "goods", cargo which by the contract of carriage is stated as being carried on deck, and is so carried (Art.I(2)).

this is not so, as in some coasting[10] and other trades, or on container vessels where the carrying of deck loads is justified by custom, or if all parties have agreed that cargo shall be carried on deck, the exception is not applicable.

Former practice in England

The practice in this country, followed by adjusters for years, was to exclude from the benefit of general average all cargo carried on deck; if carried without the shipper's consent, the loss by jettison or accident was made to fall on the shipowner; if with his consent, the loss from either of these causes fell on the shipper. **1.05**

Even where there was a well-known usage of trade to carry deckloads, as in the case of the North American and Baltic timber trades, the same rule was followed.

This practice was disturbed in the year 1837 by the decision of the Court of Common Pleas in *Gould v Oliver*,[11] but a succession of important legal decisions, given over the next half-century and summarised below, gradually clarified and resolved the position to that set out in para.1.04, above, and followed today. **1.06**

In *Gould v Oliver* a deckload of timber was jettisoned for the common safety on a voyage from Quebec to London, and it was admitted on both sides that it was the custom of the trade between those ports to carry a portion of the timber on deck. After a full review of the authorities, Tindall C.J. decided that the jettison of the deckload was properly admissible in general average.[12]

In *Milward v Hibbert*[13] it was decided that the underwriters on ship were liable to contribute, as general average, for a jettison of pigs from Ireland to London, carried on deck in accordance with the custom of the trade.

In *Johnson v Chapman*[14] part of the deck cargo of timber was necessarily jettisoned during the voyage from Quebec and the shipowner resisted the cargo-owner's claim for a general average contribution to the loss on the grounds that the timber was already in a state of wreck when jettisoned, but not on the grounds that the cargo was carried on deck. Willes J. decided in favour of the cargo-owner's claim, but the important part of his judgment—in the present context—was that here was a charterparty contract with a single shipper which expressly provided for a full cargo, including a deckload: **1.07**

> ". . . it is not necessary to refer to any custom affecting the voyage, because, according to the contract between the parties, there was to be a deck cargo. Then, immediately you find that the deck cargo is within the contemplation of the parties, you must deal with it as if shipping a deck cargo was lawful. When you have established that it is a deck cargo, lawfully there by the contract of the parties, it becomes subject to the rule of general average."

[10] cf. the passage in the judgment of the Court of Appeal in *Wright v Marwood* (1881) 7 Q.B.D. 62, which suggests a more general right to contribution in the case of coasting voyages. See also per Walton J. in *Appollinaris Co v Nord Deutsche Insurance Co* [1904] 1 K.B. 252 at 259.

[11] *Gould v Oliver* (1837) 4 Bing. N.C. 134.

[12] This decision was not accepted at Lloyd's and amongst the British adjusters as final, and there ensued some further unsatisfactory litigation and a change of practice ("general contribution"), which may be pronounced even more unsatisfactory. See 10th edn, para.109.

[13] *Milward v Hibbert* (1842) 3 Q.B. 120.

[14] *Johnson v Chapman* (1865) 19 C.B. (N.S.) 563; 35 L.J.C.P. 23.

1.08 In *Wright v Marwood*[15] there was again a contract with the shipper specifying that his cargo of 100 head of cattle from New York to Portsmouth in England were to be carried on deck, but on this occasion the vessel was a general ship carrying the goods of various parties. The cattle were jettisoned for the common safety and, on the authority of *Johnson v Chapman*,[16] the loss was held at the original trial to be general average. In the Court of Appeal, however, it was held that there was no right of contribution, even from the shipowner, by whom the goods were carried on deck, and the earlier case was distinguished on the grounds that the present vessel was a general ship carrying the goods of various parties:

> "... whatever may be the agreement between deck cargo and shipowner, the other cargo owners are no parties to it. nor bound to inquire into it, or notice it, as they are bound to take notice of a custom."

It should be noted that in that case no custom allowing cattle to be carried as deck cargo was alleged or proved.

1.09 In *Burton v English*[17] the sole question for determination was whether the words in the charterparty "at merchant's risk" excluded the liability to contribute for the jettison of deck cargo.[18] It was not disputed that but for this clause the liability would have arisen, as there was a custom of the trade to carry timber on deck from the Baltic to London, and the ship was chartered to carry a full cargo.

1.10 In what might be considered to be the final clarification of English law on the subject of deck-load jettison. Lord Watson, in delivering the advice of the Privy Council in *Strang v Scott*[19] said that the exception in the case of deck cargo does not apply either:

> "(1) In those cases where, according to the established custom of navigation, such cargoes are permitted, or
> (2) In any case where the other owners of cargo have consented that the goods jettisoned should be carried on the deck of the ship."

He thus accepts the principle that there is a right to contribution when all the parties to the adventure have agreed to the carriage of a deck cargo, for example, by a provision in the bill of lading that: "The carrier shall have liberty to carry livestock and/or cargo on deck." If this be the correct principle, the case where there are only two parties who have expressly contracted for a deck cargo is an a fortiori one.[20]

[15] *Wright v Marwood* (1881) 7 Q.B.D. 62.
[16] *Johnson v Chapman* (1865) 19 C.B. (N.S.) 563; 35 L.J.C.P. 23.
[17] *Burton v English* (1883) 10 Q.B.D. 426; 12 Q.B.D. 218.
[18] It did not. For an account of this aspect of the case see also para.D.15 et seq.
[19] *Strang v Scott* (1889) 14 A.C. 601 at 609. Lord Watson's judgment was referred to by Lord Dunedin in the House of Lords in 1931 as an "authoritative statement" of the law, though it is true that this was on another point, namely, on the right of a person to claim contribution where the necessity had arisen through his own default: see *Louis Dreyfus & Co v Tempus Shipping Co* [1931] A.C. 726 at 735.
[20] See *The Freda* (1920) 226 Fed. Rep. 551.

What is a custom of the trade?

To constitute a custom of the trade to carry cargo on deck, much more is required than the occasional or even frequent carrying of deckloads. There must be a practice so general and universal in the trade that everyone in that trade must be taken to know that his goods will or may probably be put on deck. It must also be consistent with the express terms of the contract of affreightment. **1.11**

Cotton, for example, in earlier times, used often to be carried on the decks of steamers between ports in the United States and Great Britain. This was done, sometimes by express agreement with the shippers, sometimes without the shippers consent or even knowledge, the shipowner in the latter case, according to the general understanding for many years, taking the risk upon himself.

In *Dixon v Royal Exchange Shipping Co*[21] an attempt was made to establish that the practice set out above amounted to a custom of the trade such as would enable the jettison of a deckload to be treated as a general average act. Action was brought by the owner of the deckload against the shipowner for the full value of the deckload on the grounds that the shipowner was in breach of his contract by stowing the cotton on deck; the shipowner contended that he was not liable for more than his share of the loss, treated as general average. The case went to the Court of Appeal, and was there decided against the shipowner. Brett M.R. (afterwards Lord Esher) said: **1.12**

> "It is suggested that there is a practice which it must be taken that they knew. Now the only practice which it can be taken in law that they impliedly knew (that is, taken that they knew, although they did not) is a general practice; so general and universal in the trade and at the port from which these goods were taken, that everybody who ships cotton on board a ship at New Orleans for England must be taken to know that his goods probably will, or may probably be put on deck . . . To say that there is a practice, or to say that there is a frequent practice, is only to say that it is sometimes done, leaving it open that as often, or oftener, it is not done. Such evidence as that is not evidence to go to a jury, upon which they would be justified in finding a general usage."

Effect of special clauses

Where there is a recognised custom of the trade that cargo is carried on deck, with the result that such cargo does prima facie qualify for contribution in general average, general exemption clauses in favour of the carrier, such as a provision that the deck cargo is carried "at merchant's risk", will not exclude the right of contribution.[22] **1.13**

[21] Court of Appeal, May 18, 1885; affirmed in House of Lords (1886) 12 A.C. 11. A similar decision was given by the Court of Appeal in *Newell v Royal Exchange Shipping Co* (1885) 33 W.R. 868.

[22] See in particular *Burton v English* (1883) 10 Q.B.D. 218. The question is discussed generally at para.D.15 et seq.

Jettison as a result of inherent vice of cargo

1.14 The fact that the cargo jettisoned was suffering from inherent vice, such as spontaneous heating, which rendered it a danger to the ship and other cargo, does not of itself preclude the right of contribution in general average. However, if the shipment of the cargo constituted a breach of contract,[23] any claim for contribution may be defeated by the existence of actionable fault. The question is discussed generally in the commentary on r.D.[24]

Practice of adjusters

1.15 As a matter of practice, jettison of deck cargo is not treated by adjusters as general average in this country, unless the carriage of a deck cargo on the particular voyage is sanctioned by custom. The rule (No.F1) of the Association of Average Adjusters dealing with this point is as follows:

> "The jettison of a deckload carried according to the usage of trade and not in violation of the contracts of affreightment is general average.
>
> There is an exception to this rule in the case of cargoes of cotton, tallow, acids and some other goods."[25]

The practice, therefore, is in accordance with the view expressed by Lowndes on this subject.[26] It is, however, important to remember that should an adjustment be challenged in the courts, the law as determined by the authorities will prevail over the practice of adjusters, unless, of course, the parties have contracted to contribute in general average in accordance with the practice of adjusters.[27]

1.16 The reason for the rule which disallows contribution for the jettison of deck cargo can hardly apply to an inland voyage by river or canal; for on such a voyage it is difficult to suppose that the deck is an improper place for cargo.[28] Therefore, even without evidence of custom, it is apprehended that in the unlikely event of a jettison of deck cargo on such a voyage for the general safety there will be a right to contribution.

[23] See paras 00.63 et seq. as to the duties of the shipper with regard to the shipment of dangerous goods.

[24] Paras D.20-D.21, above.

[25] The rule of the Average Adjusters' Association of the United States in dealing with this subject is as follows: "Where cargo consisting of one kind of goods is, in accordance with a custom of trade, carried on and under deck, that portion of the cargo loaded on deck shall be subject to the same rules of adjustment in case of jettison, or expenses incurred, as if the same were laden under deck." See also *Gourlie*, pp.86–87. Specific provision is made in the codes of some European countries relating to jettison of deckload.

[26] See 9th edn of this work, para.116.

[27] See e.g. *Stewart v West India and Pacific S.S. Co* (1873) L.R. 8 Q.B. 88.

[28] See judgment of Walton J. in *Apollinaris Co v Nord Deutsche Insurance Co* [1904] 1 K.B. 252.

Bulk cargo pumped or baled out

Where part of a cargo of wheat had been pumped into the sea by the ships pumps, working in the ordinary way to keep down a leak, it was held that that was not a general average loss.[29] **1.17**

But where water is baled out of a ship, in an extraordinary manner, for the general safety and under such conditions that some of the cargo is necessarily thrown out with it, this is in practice treated as a jettison. The same rule is applied in the United States when, as happens on the Great Lakes, cargo such as grain is deliberately pumped overboard by salvage pumps to lighten the vessel.

Jettison of ship's stores

A jettison of ship's stores is treated as on the same footing with a jettison of cargo.[30] **1.18**

The practice of adjusters here introduces a distinction analogous to that of deck and under-deck cargo. Many ships are lumbered with all kinds of useless articles on deck, which increase the risk and are sure to be thrown overboard on the first approach of danger. To guard against the abuse of this practice, the rule in this country, as in Germany and many other states, is that no jettison of ship's materials off the upper deck is treated as general average unless it be of such articles as are necessary for the navigation of the ship and, therefore, are carried on deck in conformity with the custom of the trade.

Historical Development and Practice of Rule I

York Rules 1864

By 1864 the situation with regard to the jettison of a deckload, which in earlier times had been universally disallowed, was changing and becoming less settled. Certainly in the timber trades, at least, ships were being constructed expressly to carry large deckloads and their greater safety had been tacitly recognised in Britain by the repeal of earlier Acts of Parliament[31] prohibiting the carriage of deckloads of timber on certain voyages. In certain other trades, for example cotton, livestock, tallow, tar and rosin, it was becoming increasingly frequent for part of such cargoes to be shipped on deck, though not so invariably as to constitute what would be termed a recognised custom of the trade. **1.19**

In the United States, where there was a considerable timber trade with up to one-third of the cargo being shipped on deck, there was no case law on the subject,

[29] *Hills v London Assurance Co* (1839) 9 L.J. Ex. 25: 5 M. & W. 569.

[30] *Price v Noble* (1811) 4 Taunt. 123 (guns, two anchors, two chains and other stores from the middle deck). Such sacrifices demand close scrutiny: *The Santa Ana Maria* 49 Fed. Rep. 878 (1892).

[31] 8 & 9 Vict., c.93, ss.24-26; 16 & 17 Vict., c.107.

but a uniform practice was applied excluding from general average the jettison of any deckload. In the European countries it is believed that the same practice was followed except, possibly, on short coastal voyages where the law permitted the carriage of deckloads.

1.20 In an attempt to secure world-wide uniformity, the following rule was passed at the 1864 Conference at York:

> "*Rule I. Jettison of Deck Cargo*
>
> A jettison of timber or deals, or any other description of wood cargo, carried on the deck of a ship in pursuance of a general custom of the trade in which the ship is then engaged, shall be made good as general average, in like manner as if such cargo had been jettisoned from below deck.
>
> No jettison of deck cargo, other than timber or deals, or other wood cargo, so carried as aforesaid, shall be made good as general average.
>
> Every structure not built in with the frame of the vessel shall be considered to be a part of the deck of the vessel."

Proposals were made at the 1864 Conference to make tar, cotton, tallow, cattle and coastal voyages subject to the same provisions, but these proposals were defeated.

The wording of the rule itself calls for no explanation other than, possibly, the last paragraph, which was an endeavour to define what constituted the "deck". The wording would exclude cargo in most types of deckhouses, but was sufficient to cover cargo carried in the poop. In practice, a great deal of silk and other light valuable cargo was stowed there.

York-Antwerp Rules 1877

1.21 The 1877 Conference was held at Antwerp and European delegates attended in much greater force than at York. Their opinions held sway, and by 26 votes to 10 the 1864 rule was completely reversed and the following substituted:

> "*Rule I. Jettison of Deck Cargo*
>
> No jettison of deck cargo shall be made good as general average. Every structure not built in with the frame of the vessel shall be considered to be a part of the deck of the vessel."

York-Antwerp Rules 1890

1.22 The 1890 Conference was at Liverpool and the British Association of Average Adjusters was primarily responsible for drawing up proposed amendments for the new Rules. In the intervening years English law on deckload jettison had been clarified considerably by the cases discussed in paras 1.06–1.10 above, which had decided that the jettison of a deckload carried in accordance with a recognised custom of the trade, and not in violation of the contract of affreightment, was general average as between all the parties to the adventure.

English law and commercial practice having overtaken the York-Antwerp Rules, r.I needed to be reconsidered if it was to be kept in line with current requirements. The British Association proposed, inter alia, that:

> "A jettison of wood, tar, and resin, or any of them, carried on deck in accordance with a general custom of the trade, when not in violation of the contract of affreightment, shall be made good as general average if the jettison be made for the common safety."

This proposal was withdrawn, however, in deference to the wishes of the European delegates, who were unanimously opposed to the new rule. The previous 1877 rule was reaffirmed, and contracts of affreightment in the timber trade continued, increasingly, to be drawn up with provisions for the York-Antwerp Rules, but excluding the word "No" in r.I.[32]

York-Antwerp Rules 1924

This increasing practice influenced the drafting Committee for the 1924 Rules to add to the old rule the words: "unless such cargo is carried in accordance with the recognised custom of the trade" and to delete the word "deck" from both the title and the text. This amendment was accepted by the Stockholm Conference, if with a certain continuing reluctance on the part of some of the European delegates. **1.23**

A considerable discussion took place at the Stockholm Conference with regard to the definition of a deck contained in the old rule. In the end it was decided to omit any reference to the deck. Many technical objections were raised as to the wording and the view eventually prevailed that any definition was unnecessary and that it should be left to be decided as a matter of fact in each case as it arose whether the place of stowage, be it technically on deck or under deck, was a place sanctioned by the custom of the particular trade as a proper place for the carriage of the cargo jettisoned.

In the form finally agreed, the rule read as follows:

> *"Rule I.–Jettison of Cargo*
>
> No jettison of cargo shall be made good as general average, unless such cargo is carried in accordance with the recognised custom of the trade."

York-Antwerp Rules 1950 and 1974

No change, but it may be recorded that the President's Report and Draft Text for the 1974 Rules published by the Comité Maritime International in February 1973 stated: **1.24**

[32] See e.g. *De Hart v Compania Anomina "Aurora"* [1903] 1 K.B. 109; [1903] 2 K.B. 503; 8 Com. Cas. 42, 314.

> "No provision was made for containers because it was felt that generally a custom to carry containers on deck was already held to exist,[33] and that in any event a provision covering containers as such would probably not be sufficient to cover technological developments in the future."

By now the custom must be firmly established, although there is still no English decision on the question.

York-Antwerp Rules 1994

1.25 No change. A proposal was made, but received little support, that, "Jettison of cargo, wherever stowed, shall be made good as general average when made for the common safety".

York-Antwerp Rules 2004

1.26 As part of the process of tidying up the drafting of the Rules the words "made good as general average" were changed to "allowed as general average". Their effect is not altered.

1.27

RULE I

JETTISON OF CARGO

No jettison of cargo shall be *made good/allowed* as general average, unless such cargo is carried in accordance with the recognised custom of the trade.

CONSTRUCTION

1.28 **"cargo"**: It is submitted that "cargo" in this and throughout the Rules means property in the possession of the shipowner under a contract of affreightment, including containers and commercial vehicles, whether loaded or not. It also includes mails and motorcars carried in the vessel on which the owners are passengers, and passengers' luggage provided that it is not retained in the possession of the passenger, for example for use on the voyage.[34]

1.29 **"unless such cargo is carried in accordance with the recognised custom of the trade"**: Previous editions of the work have recorded that the construction of this rule has not been debated in the courts and that the exact scope of this

[33] But see *Du Pont de Nemours International v Mormacvega* [1972] A.M.C. 2366; [1973] 1 Lloyd's Rep. 267, affirmed [1974] 1 Lloyd's Rep. 296, in which the shipowners' assertion that in 1967 there was a custom in the shipping industry of carrying containers on deck and that a bill of lading not claused for deck shipment would be presumed to have been issued subject to the custom was not upheld; the custom was not sufficiently ancient.

[34] By the express terms of r.XVII mails, passengers' luggage, personal effects, and accompanied private motor vehicles do not contribute in general average: see para.17.74 et seq., below.

particular exception is difficult to determine and may well be surprisingly narrow. In practice, it is believed that the words are interpreted in the light of the remarks of Brett M.R. in *Dixon v Royal Exchange Shipping Co*[35]:

> "... a general practice; so general and universal in the trade and at the port from which these goods were taken, that everybody who ships (cotton) on board a ship at (New Orleans) for (England) must be taken to know that his goods probably will, or may probably be put on deck . . ."

In principle, however, it is not the knowledge of the individual shipper whose goods are, in the event, carried on deck which is relevant, but the knowledge of shippers in general. Thus it should suffice if a shipper is aware that his or some other shipper's goods will probably be carried on deck. Conversely the shipper of cargo which is unsuitable for underdeck stowage, and who knows that it will be carried on deck, should not be entitled to contribution in the event of its jettison unless shippers in general were aware that such cargo would probably be carried on the voyage as deck cargo.

"carried": It is submitted that this refers more to the manner rather than the fact of carriage–in fact, that it is equivalent to "stowed", with particular reference to the place of stowage.[36] Goods carried by sea are of such infinite variety that it would otherwise be possible to argue in very many cases that so few goods of the particular description have ever been carried on the particular route that there is no recognised custom to carry them at all. If, however, "carried" means "stowed", it is possible to contend that all goods of certain broad categories are or may be carried on deck, and that other goods, again described in very broad categories, will or should always be carried in the hold.

"recognised custom": These words prompt the inquiries "Recognised by whom?" and "What is a custom?" It is submitted that no formal recognition by the courts or by trade bodies is necessary, and that the word "custom" does not bear the restricted meaning attaching to custom in the strict legal sense. Each case will have to be judged on its own facts, but it is suggested that the right approach is to consider whether a person familiar with the trade would, upon being apprised of the method of stowage adopted, comment "That is a usual stowage in this trade". See also paras 1.11, 1.12, above. **1.30**

"trade": This word has to be construed in relation both to the type of goods being carried in the vessel and to the route upon which she is trading.

The idea which lies behind the rule and which must form the basis of its construction is that no party to the adventure should be asked to contribute towards a loss by jettison of goods which are peculiarly liable to be jettisoned, for example deck cargo, unless the cargo was carried in accordance with the custom of the trade and the party had reason to expect the presence of such goods by reason of the construction or trade of the vessel.[37] However, the words must be given their

[35] Court of Appeal, May 18, 1885; affirmed in House of Lords (1886) 12 A.C. 11.

[36] See para.1.23 above for the reason why express reference to deck cargo has been omitted from the rule since 1924.

[37] *Strang v Scott* (1889) 14 A.C. 601 at 609.

natural meaning, and the exception contained in the rule cannot be extended to allow contribution towards a jettison of cargo carried in an unusual manner but in a manner sanctioned by the contract of affreightment, and this remains so even where the whole cargo is in one ownership. Furthermore, the operation of the first part of the rule cannot be confined to deck load, however defined, although jettison of underdeck cargo is universally admitted to be the classic example of a general average sacrifice. On the other hand, it will be much easier to prove that underdeck cargo is "carried in accordance with the recognised custom of the trade". It should be added that as a result of the inclusion of the Rule of Interpretation, contribution is not recoverable under r.A if it is barred by this rule.

The burden of proving that the exception applies and contribution is recoverable lies, by the terms of r.E, on the claimant.

RULE II

LOSS OR DAMAGE BY SACRIFICES FOR THE COMMON SAFETY

ENGLISH LAW AND BACKGROUND

Damage Incidental to Jettison of Cargo

Damage which is incidental to a jettison, so that the jettison cannot reasonably be made without incurring it, must be regarded as part of the loss by jettison and included in the general average; for example holes cut in the deck, or bulkheads or bulwarks stove in, in order to get at the cargo or throw it over. So if goods are damaged by reason of the opening of the hatches to throw cargo overboard, from seas which break over the deck, all such damage is properly and in practice made the subject of general average, being the necessary consequence of the measure for the common safety. This rule is as old as the Roman law, and may be regarded as universally accepted,[1] even though the practice was at one time otherwise.[2] The same principle applies to damage done by chafing or breakage of packages, or otherwise from the derangement of stowage consequent on a jettison: for example if the cargo consisted of barrels, well secured in their places while the hold was full, but which could not be prevented from shifting after a portion of the cargo had been thrown out; or if goods were lost or damaged in consequence of having been brought on deck in order to get access to less valuable goods for the purpose of jettison.[3] 2.01

[1] *The Brig Mary* (1842) 1 Sprague 17. See also Abbott on *Merchant Shipping*, 5th edn, p.136, which was adopted by Cresswell J. in *Hallett v Wigram* (1850) 9 C.B. at 608: "From the rule thus established by the Rhodians, various corollaries have been deduced. Thus, if in the act of jettison, or in order to accomplish it, other goods in the ship are broken, damaged or destroyed, the value of these also must be included in the general contribution."

[2] See para.2.03, below.

[3] *Benecke*, p.213.

Damage from Sacrifice of Ship

2.02 In a similar manner, loss of or damage done to cargo, in consequence of a sacrifice of some part of a ship is allowable as general average, being perfectly analogous to damage occasioned by seas shipped while the hatches are open for jettison. Modern examples of loss of or damage to cargo caused in this manner are infrequent, but might occur where, for example, sound plating is cut away in order to separate collided vessels when one is sinking, leading to water ingress into a hold and damage to cargo contained therein.

Historical Development and Practice of Rule II

Glasgow Resolutions 1860

2.03 There being differences of opinion on the treatment of losses to cargo by chafage and breakage consequent upon the stowage being deranged after a jettison, a Resolution was passed at the Glasgow Conference as follows:

> "(3) That the damage done to cargo by chafing and breakage, resulting from a jettison of part of the remainder of the cargo, ought not to be allowed in general average."

At this particular time the belief was widely—if mistakenly—held that, in principle, an allowance could not be made in general average unless the property in respect of which the claim arose had been selected to be damaged for the general benefit. Further, it was considered that such loss was only a remote and uncertain consequence of the jettison. On practical grounds, it was thought wise to exclude such losses to prevent all damage sustained during the voyage from being claimed as resulting from the jettison.

York Rules 1864 and York-Antwerp Rules 1877

2.04 At the York Conference in 1864 the whole subject of damage consequent upon a jettison was considered afresh, the previous Glasgow Resolution was reversed and a new first paragraph added affirming the allowance of damage by water going down the hatches during a jettison. The rule was as follows:

> *Rule II. Damage by Jettison*
>
> Damage done to goods or merchandise by water which unavoidably goes down a ship's hatches opened, or other opening made, for the purpose of making a jettison shall be made good as general average, in case the loss by jettison is so made good.
>
> Damage done by breakage or chafing, or otherwise from derangement of stowage consequent upon a jettison, shall be made good as general average.
>
> In 1877 the two paragraphs of the rule were brought into accord by the addition at the end of the second paragraph of the concluding words of the first paragraph: "in case the loss by jettison is so made good".

York-Antwerp Rules 1890

The 1877 and earlier editions of r.II made no mention of damage to ship, and other cases of damage to cargo which arose in practice (for example a mast might be cut away for the common safety and, in falling, tear a hole in the deck through which water might gain access to the cargo[4]). These losses, also, were customarily allowed as general average, but to avoid any possible doubt there might be on the matter, the rule was completely recast in 1890 to make it more general in its provisions: **2.05**

Rule II. Damage by Jettison and Sacrifice for the Common Safety

> Damage done to a ship and cargo, or either of them, by or in consequence of a sacrifice made for the common safety, and by water which goes down a ship's hatches opened or other opening made for the purpose of making a jettison for the common safety, shall be made good as general average.

York-Antwerp Rules 1924, 1950 and 1974

No change. **2.06**

With the introduction of the lettered rules, in particular rr.A and C, in 1924, there was no longer any real need for this r.II. However, it was thought preferable by those drafting the 1924 Rules to leave the old Rules undisturbed as much as possible, well known as they were to the business community, and only to effect such amendments or deletions as appeared to be absolutely necessary to bring them into harmony with modern conditions. This being so, the 1890 rule was left unaltered.

York-Antwerp Rules 1994

Purely as a minor "tidying-up" operation, and to ensure that properties involved in the adventure other than ship and cargo should also be covered by the rule, the wording was made more general. Even in its revised form, however, and for the reasons set out in para.2.11, the scope of the rule was confined to loss or damage to the property involved in the common maritime adventure. **2.07**

The title of the rule was also amended on this occasion.

York-Antwerp Rules 2004

No change other than the substitution of "allowed" for "made good" as part of the general tidying-up of the drafting of the Rules. **2.08**

[4] See paras 2.01 and 2.02, above.

2.09
RULE II

LOSS OR DAMAGE BY SACRIFICES FOR THE COMMON SAFETY

Loss of or damage to the property involved in the common maritime adventure by or in consequence of a sacrifice made for the common safety, and by water which goes down a ship's hatches opened or other opening made for the purpose of making a jettison for the common safety, shall be *made good/allowed* as general average.

Construction

2.10 The rule deals with three different cases of loss or damage to any of the property involved in the common maritime adventure, namely: (1) by a sacrifice (for example, damage to the ship's propeller by a log jettisoned for the common safety); (2) in consequence of a sacrifice (for example by chafage or breakage of packages consequent on the derangement of stowage resulting from a jettison); and (3) the special case of water going down an opening made for the purpose of a jettison, that is, a specific example of heading (2).

2.11 **"the property involved in the common maritime adventure"**: This expression was added to the wording of the rule in 1994 in substitution for the previous and more limited "ship and cargo". . To the extent that loss of or damage to any of the property involved in the common maritime adventure (for example, containers, freight and time-charterers' bunkers) may now be made good under the rule, the new wording is wider in its coverage. However, it does not extend to loss or damage to property not involved in the common maritime adventure, or to liability to the owners of such property, for example liability to the owners of a fishery damaged by oil pollution consequent upon a general average sacrifice. The reason for this is to prevent any allowance being made, via the "back-door" of r.II for pollution and similar liabilities, of the kind which are intended to be universally excluded by the provisions of the lettered r.C which were introduced in 1994.[5] The effect of the wording is that any claim for an allowance in respect of damage to property which is not involved in the common maritime adventure can be brought only under the lettered rules, and it will therefore be excluded by r.C if the loss or damage falls within the category of "damage to the environment or in consequence of the escape or release of pollutant substances from the property involved in the common maritime adventure".[6] Where the damage falls outside this category, any loss incurred in respect of damage to property outside the common maritime adventure may be recoverable under r.A, and r.II does not prevent such a recovery.

[5] For an explanation concerning the overriding effect of the numbered rules upon the lettered rules, see the Rule of Interpretation, para.PRE.04, above.

[6] For the meaning of this expression see paras C.38 et seq., above.

"by or in consequence of": It seems unlikely that this phrase is intended to affect the ordinary rule as to causation discussed under r.C.[7]

"sacrifice": See commentary in para.A.106, above.

"for the common safety": See commentary in para.A.109, above. 2.12

It should be noted that loss of or damage to the property involved in the common maritime adventure in consequence of a sacrifice for the common safety is recoverable even if the original sacrifice itself is irrecoverable because of the provisions of r.I. This is illustrated by a decision given in the United States District Court (Southern District of New York).[8]

The S.S. Felix shipped a cargo of mahogany and cedar logs, partly on deck, at Belize for carriage to New York, under a bill of lading which contained a clause providing that general average should be adjusted according to the York-Antwerp Rules 1890. During the voyage the vessel stranded and it became necessary to jettison part of the deck cargo in order to lighten her. In doing so, damage was caused to the hull and equipment of the steamer and a log which had been jettisoned became jammed between the propeller and the stern frame, stopped the engines and damaged one of the propeller blades, damage being also caused to the engines in endeavouring to clear the log from the propeller. It was held that all this damage, both to hull and machinery, was allowable in general average in accordance with the terms of r.II, notwithstanding the fact that the jettison of the deck cargo was not allowable in general average under r.I.[9]

[7] See paras C.25 et seq., above, and the commentary on the similar expression in r.V at para.5.18, below.

[8] *Ove Lange, Trustee v George D. Emery & Co and Insurance Co of North America* Unreported, January 1926.

[9] Rule I of the 1877 and 1890 Rules excluded any contribution in respect of jettison of deck cargo. For text of that rule see para.1.21, above.

RULE III

EXTINGUISHING FIRE ON SHIPBOARD

ENGLISH LAW AND BACKGROUND

If a ship is on fire and the fire is quenched by pouring water into the hold, or by scuttling the ship in shallow water, or by filling the hold with steam, the damage done by this means to the ship, cargo, or freight is properly the subject of general average contribution. In broad terms, this is the law and practice of all countries and it was only with regard to damage caused to such portions of the ship and bulk cargo, or to such separate packages of cargo, as were or had been on fire, that there was until 1974 a possible divergence of opinion.[1] 3.01

FORMER PRACTICE OF ADJUSTERS

Damage to cargo done by the means used to extinguish a fire was probably treated as general average in this country until at least the 1820s, but a contrary practice was then established, possibly initiated by Stevens. In the 4th edition of his Essay on Average published in 1822 he gave it as his opinion that such damage should be treated as general average.[2] He suggested a doubt, however, in saying: 3.02

> "When claimed as a general average, it is objected to on the ground that the damage done to the goods is secondary and accidental, and not primary and intentional (as in cutting away a mast, etc.), which it ought to be to establish such a claim."[3]

This perhaps meant that the water was poured in for the purpose of quenching the fire and not of wetting the goods, and was not aimed at any particular package. On whatever ground it may have rested, however, we find that the practice of

[1] See para.3.07, below.
[2] And see, to the same effect, Benecke, p.243.
[3] Stevens, *Average*, 4th edn, p.243.

excluding such claims from contribution was completely established before the year 1851, Baily spoke of it as a settled rule.[4]

Manley Hopkins[5] considered the practice to be wrong, though he was prepared to accept that it might be advisable to pursue it solely on the grounds of expediency, and with the proviso that the practice was not justified by a defence which was shown to be fallacious.

3.03 Until the year 1873 then, the practice of adjusters in case of fire was this: if a hole was cut in a ship,s deck, in order to pour water down it to flood the cargo and quench the fire, the cost of repairing the deck was replaced in general average, but the damage done to the goods by the water poured down was not replaced. If a hole was cut in a ship's side in order to scuttle the ship for the same purpose, the damage done to the ship by cutting the hole was allowed as general average, but the damage done to the ship and goods by the water that flowed in through the hole was not allowed. This practice held good only until it was challenged in *Stewart v West India and Pacific S.S. Co.*[6]

In that case a parcel of 180 serons of bark had been shipped at Santa Martha on board the steamer Venezuelan, bound for London, under a bill of lading containing the clause, "average, if any, to be adjusted according to British custom". While the Venezuelan was at Santa Martha, loaded and about to sail, a fire broke out in her forehold, which was only extinguished by pouring in water down the hatchways, and through holes cut in the deck, and by cutting a hole in the side of the ship and filling her fore-compartment with water. By the water thus poured or let into the ship, 152 of the 180 serons of bark were destroyed. The owner of it claimed contribution from the shipowner, as general average. The question was tried on an agreed case, in which it was admitted that if these measures had not been taken, the remaining cargo would in all probability have been destroyed, and the ship most seriously damaged, if not rendered a total wreck. It was admitted also that "it has been the practice of British average adjusters, in adjusting losses, to treat a loss occasioned by water in the manner above described as not a general loss".

3.04 The judgment of the Court of Queen's Bench was delivered by Quain J. who said:

> "The first question argued before us was, whether the loss in question was a loss which properly formed the subject of a general average contribution, according to the law of England . . . On these facts we are clearly of opinion that the loss was, according to the general law, properly the subject of a general average contribution. It was a voluntary and intentional sacrifice of the bark, made under pressure of imminent danger, and for the benefit, and with a view to secure the safety, of the whole adventure then at risk."

[4] Baily, *General Average*, p.60. However, as pointed out by Lord Coleridge C.J. in *Whitecross Iron v Saville* (1882) L.R. 8 Q.B.D. 653, Baily's own view was that "in defence of this practice no valid reason can be urged". In *Achard v Ring* (1874) 31 L.T. (N.S.) 647; 2 Asp M.C. 423 (para.3.05, below), where the views of textbook writers were held not to be admissible as evidence of a similar custom, the jury found that no such custom was proved.

[5] Manley Hopkins, *Handbook on Average* (1857), p.38.

[6] *Stewart v West India and Pacific S.S. Co* (1873) L.R. 8 Q.B. 88.

Accordingly, he held that, if the case depended wholly on the common law applicable to general average losses, the plaintiffs would be entitled to recover. However, as the parties had agreed to make the custom of British average adjusters a part of their contract, the case had to be decided in accordance with the custom as the parties had agreed it to be, and judgment was given for the defendants.

Practice Altered

The effect of this decision was that the practice was rescinded. The Association of Average Adjusters, at their 1873 annual meeting, passed a resolution: "That damage done by water poured down a ship's hold to extinguish a fire be treated as general average."[7] **3.05**

However, the principle established by the decision does not appear to have been accepted unreservedly by average adjusters, for the Rule of Practice was passed only by 11 votes to six and a modifying rule[8] was introduced the following year. Nor was the decision unreservedly accepted by shipowners, merchants, underwriters or maritime lawyers, for *Stewart v West India and Pacific S.S. Co* was carried to the Exchequer Chamber,[9] who upheld the decision in favour of the defendants solely on the basis of the special clause, and pointedly refrained from expressing any view on English law on the subject. However, notwithstanding the reluctance of the Court of Exchequer Chamber to reach a decision on the point, in 1874 in the case of *Achard v Ring*,[10] where the only issue was whether there was a custom of Lloyd's to exclude from general average damage caused by water when a ship was scuttled extinguish a fire, Cockburn C.J. entertained no doubts on the correct answer under English law:

> "It is quite clear that this [alleged] custom is in opposition to, and in derogation of, the law of the land relating to insurance, and to the matter of average as between the shipowner and the owner of the goods."

The jury found that no such custom existed.

Against this background of uncertainty it took two further decisions, *Pirie v Middle Dock Co*[11] and *Whitecross Wire Co v Saville*[12] before the English law on the point was established beyond argument. In the latter case the whole matter was argued afresh in the Court of Appeal unhampered by precedent. The iron ship, Himalaya, bound for Wellington, New Zealand, had arrived at that port, and had landed the greater portion of her cargo, when a fire broke out on board, which was extinguished by pouring water into her hold. Among other portions of the cargo damaged by the water poured in was a quantity of iron wire belonging to the plaintiffs. The owners of the wire made a claim on the shipowners for contribution **3.06**

[7] Rule F2. See Appendix 3, para.70.29, below.

[8] The modifying rule is quoted in para.3.07, below; it was rescinded in 1974 and wording identical with r.III of the York-Antwerp Rules 1974, substituted in its place.

[9] *Stewart v West India and Pacific S.S. Co* (1873) L.R. 8 Q.B. 362.

[10] *Achard v Ring* (1874) 31 LT (N.S.) 647; 2 Asp. M.L.C. 423.

[11] *Pirie v Middle Dock Co* (1881) 44 L.T. (N.S.) 427

[12] *Whitecross Wire Co v Saville* (1882) 8 Q.B.D. 653: cf. *Garrets v Behr & Mathew* (1933) 47 Lloyd's Rep. 219.

towards their damage, as general average, which was resisted on the ground firstly that there was no real sacrifice of the cargo, which was doomed to loss by fire anyway, and secondly that, since the ship was iron, there was no risk of her being rendered a total loss by the fire. Pollock B. gave judgment in the claimant's favour, which was upheld unanimously on appeal:

> "It must be shown", said Lord Coleridge,[13] "that an imminent peril existed, and that the master deliberately and for the sake of preserving the adventure sacrificed that in respect of which contribution is claimed . . . I am unable to come to the conclusion that this is not a case of general average; the facts seem to me to fall within the definition of a general average act . . . No authority is against our decision."

Brett L.J. said[14]:

> "If there is an imminent danger, and if the captain sacrifices part in order to save the rest of the adventure, a claim for a general average contribution arises . . . if the fire had not been extinguished [the ship] would have been brought almost to the state of a wreck . . . here the captain intentionally inundated the cargo and thereby necessarily damaged it by water . . . All the circumstances seem to me to exist which constitute a general average loss."

If any doubt could possibly have remained after these decisions as to the right to recover in general average for the damage done by pouring water into the hold to extinguish a fire, it was set at rest by the judgment of the House of Lords in *Greenshields v Stephens*[15] : and the same principle obviously applies in the case of other reasonable steps, such as scuttling,[16] taken for the same purpose.

Damage to Packages Already on Fire

3.07 In 1874, the year after the Association of Average Adjusters had adopted the Rule of Practice to allow as general average damage caused by water poured into a hold to extinguish fire, the rule was modified by another, namely:

> "That goods in a ship which is on fire, or the cargo of which is on fire, affected by water voluntarily used to extinguish such fire, shall not be the subject of general average if the packages so affected be themselves on fire at the time the water was thrown upon them."[17]

This latter rule was passed without discussion and it is not now possible to deduce with certainty the reasons which prompted the rule. Lowndes wrote in the 1888 edition of this work:

13 *Whitecross* (1882) 8 Q.B.D. 653 at 659.

14 *Whitecross* (1882) 8 Q.B.D. 653 at 662.

15 *Greenshields v Stephens* [1908] A.C. 431: cf. *Pacific Mail S.S. Co* (1896) 74 Fed. Rep. 564.

16 So held in *Papayanni v Grampian S.S. Co* (1896) 1 Com. Cas. 448; and *Achard v Ring*, para.3.05, above.

17 The rule (F3) was rescinded in 1974 and wording identical with r.III of the York-Antwerp Rules 1974, substituted in its place (see Appendix 3, para.70.30, below). Packages which were on fire at the time the water was thrown upon them are no longer excluded from an allowance in general average.

> "It is based on the argument of common sense, that the water which in the same act damages and saves a package already kindled cannot be said to do that package, on the whole, any harm."[18]

This view was questioned in all subsequent editions.

The loss by fire of the rest of the cargo might have been inevitable if the water had not been poured over it; and the argument that the water had on the whole done no harm might equally well have been advanced in such a case with regard to that part of the cargo. If the package which had been on fire retained some value, and the damage done by the water could be separated from that done by the fire,[19] it seems more in accordance with principle to allow the former.[20]

The above remarks are now of historical interest only. At their annual meeting in 1974 the Association of Average Adjusters rescinded the Rules of Practice denying any allowance in general average for damages to packages which were already on fire at the time the water was thrown upon them, and substituted for it the wording[21] of r.III of the York-Antwerp Rules 1974.

Smoke Damage

In the years prior to the 1974 Rules an increasing number of claims were put forward in general average for damage to cargo caused by the extra smoke allegedly generated by modern methods of extinguishing fires. As smoke is a natural product of combustion (fire), damage caused thereby should be treated, prima facie, as accidental in origin and not the subject of any allowance in general average. However, there was a divergence of practice among adjusters. **3.08**

When Lowndes first wrote this work, the only effective means of fighting a fire was with water, but the damage so caused to a valuable general cargo could be extremely costly. Today, many ships carry supplies of carbon dioxide gas with which to suppress a fire, and water is used only as a last resort. Carbon dioxide is an inert gas which does not interact with other substances and it cannot, therefore, cause damage to even the most delicate and susceptible cargo (though cases have

[18] The rule observed in practice in the US is the same: Gourlie, General Average, p.157. And in *Slater v Hayward Rubber Co* (1857) 26 Conn. 128, it was held that where goods on fire are jettisoned, no contribution in general average is due. See also *Crockett v Dodge* (1835) 3 Fairf. 190, where a vessel was scuttled in order to extinguish a fire in her cargo of lime. The lime was destroyed in consequence of the scuttling, but the ship was saved. It was held that no contribution was due in respect of the lime because the lime was already doomed. If the lime had not been doomed, contribution would have been payable (*The Rapid Transit* 52 (1893) Fed. Rep. 320; see also *Columbian Insurance Co v Ashby* (1839) 13 Pet. 331 at 340).

[19] In an American case, where it was impossible to distinguish between the damage done by smoke and that done by steam turned into the hold to extinguish the fire, it was held that a claim for contribution had not been made out: *Reliance Marine Insurance Co v NY & Cuba Mail S.S. Co* (1896) 77 Fed. Rep. 317.

[20] In *Greenshields Cowie v Stephens & Sons, Shipping Gazette*, December 29, 1906 Channell J. said that in English law it would be a question of fact in each case whether a part of the cargo already on fire was effectively in a state of wreck, or whether it retained some value which was sacrificed by the extinguishing measures. The case was decided under the York- Antwerp Rules 1890, as to which see below.

[21] Rule F3. See Appendix 3, para.70.30, below.

been encountered in practice where its cooling effect has created a vacuum in containers whereby the containers themselves suffer buckling damage). For this reason, its use is vastly to be preferred to the indiscriminate application of water to flood an affected hold. Even if it cannot always extinguish a fire completely, carbon dioxide will often keep an outbreak under control for weeks on end until, say, the arrival at destination where professional fire-fighting services are available.

However, this manner of fighting or controlling fires almost certainly results in more smoke damage to cargo than used to be the case when water was applied more promptly. Of itself, the carbon dioxide does not produce smoke, but it can aggravate the formation of smoke, by reducing the degree and intensity of combustion, for example from a fiercely flaming conflagration to a smouldering affair.[22] Further, and assuming an effective sealing of the hold has been made, the air pressure will be greater and smoke may be forced further into the packages than it might otherwise be.

If, then, damage caused by water used to extinguish a fire is treated as general average, should not any increased damage by smoke be similarly allowed?

3.09 There is no case law on the subject in this country, but the problem has been considered by the courts of the US, with varying results. In *Reliance Marine Insurance Co v New York & Cuba Mail S.S. Co*[23] fire broke out in a cargo of hemp on board the Seneca. The hatches were closed, live steam from the boilers was let into the 'tween decks for about seven hours, and the ship put back to Cuba where part of the cargo was discharged into lighters and the ship then submerged. The insurers of 64 bales of tobacco claimed compensation in general average for damage to the tobacco by smoke driven into the compartment for the purpose of extinguishing the fire. The evidence was contrary and inconclusive whether the tobacco was damaged by smoke, and District Judge Brown held that a general average claim was not allowable for damage done through the undesigned and unavoidable spread of fire or smoke in the proper efforts to extinguish them. In the course of his judgment he said:

> "Here not only is there very great doubt whether the tobacco was tainted by smoke at all, but if it was, the smoke was an incident of the fire, and caused by the fire, and not by the act of man . . . If the smothering of the fire by closing the ship's hatches, or by forcing water or steam upon the fire, temporarily increased the smoke, the fire was none the less the true and original cause of all the smoke, and hence of all the damage it may have done; and this damage, if there was any such damage, must be classed with fire damage, as particular average and not as general average, because done by

[22] An excellent example drawn from practice was as follows: during the course of discharging a cargo of groundnuts at Rotterdam, a docker started a fire when he foolishly searched for his lost hook with a lighted match. The flames spread over the fatty bags at enormous speed and the dockers ran for their lives. The crew failed to extinguish the blaze with foam extinguishers and the fire assumed such proportions that the master ordered the hatches to be closed and sealed. Carbon dioxide gas was then injected for several days and eventually succeeded in extinguishing the fire. However, the whole of the cargo in the hold was very seriously damaged by smoke; if the hold had been flooded (and there was no nautical reason why it should not have been) there would have been considerable damage to cargo by water, but very little smoke.

[23] *Reliance Marine* (1896) 70 Fed. Rep. 262; 77 Fed. Rep. 317; 165 U.S. 720.

> smoke alone, as an incident of the fire, and not by the steam voluntarily employed to extinguish it . . . Only when the damage is done by the agency employed to extinguish the fire, as in the case of water damage, can the damage be deemed a voluntary' sacrifice . . ."

This judgment was affirmed on appeal, but, seemingly, on grounds of lack of evidence rather than principle. Shipman J. said:

> "We are of opinion that more damage was caused to the tobacco by the pressure of steam, which carried smoke or its contents, than would have been caused if no steam had been introduced into the lower 'tween decks . . . We have, therefore, in this case, an ordinary and extraordinary smoke damage; and no one can tell how much is ordinary, and how much is extraordinary. Under such circumstances, it is unnecessary to consider what might or might not be a proper rule of adjustment in a case where such ordinary and extraordinary damages were susceptible of a separation, and, severally, of exact ascertainment."

However, in *Starlight Trading Inc v S.S. San Francisco Maru*[24] a fire broke out in No.5 hold of the vessel while the hatch cover was open for discharging a cargo of textiles in cartons. The hatch was thereupon closed and sealed, carbon dioxide was introduced into the hold, and the fire extinguished, after about 42 hours. When the hold was re-opened, the cargo was found to be extensively damaged by smoke. The court found that if the hatch had not been sealed the cargo would probably escaped damage by smoke, and accordingly allowed the damage as general average. In reaching this conclusion the court purported to apply the law as laid down in *Reliance Marine*,[25] but it appears to have assumed, without discussion, the point left open in the earlier case, namely whether the smoke damage, although the product of the fire itself, could properly be treated as a sacrifice. **3.10**

Although there is no English case law on the point, in 1974 the Association of Average Adjusters adopted a Rule of Practice,[26] based on r.III of the York-Antwerp Rules 1974,[27] which excludes any compensation for damage by smoke or heat. **3.11**

Complex Fire Extinguishing Operations

Apart from the problem of smoke damage, the use of carbon dioxide to suppress or control a fire, often without extinguishing it completely or immediately, creates other general average problems which can best be likened to those dealt with under "Complex Salvage Operations".[28] An imaginary example, based on a number of cases seen in practice, may illustrate the problem. **3.12**

A vessel loaded a full cargo of copra and tapioca products in Indonesian ports for the lengthy voyage via the Cape to Rotterdam and Hamburg. The cargo for Hamburg was stowed at the bottom of each of the vessel's five holds and the cargo for the first port of discharge, Rotterdam, was stowed above. Whilst

[24] (1974) A.M.C. 1523 (S.D.N.Y.).
[25] *Reliance Marine* (1896) 70 Fed. Rep. 262; 77 Fed. Rep. 317; 165 U.S. 720.
[26] Rule F3. See para.70.30, below.
[27] Para.3.21, below.
[28] See paras 8.04 et seq., below.

still in the southern hemisphere, the cargo in No.2 hold spontaneously ignited: the hold was sealed, large quantities of carbon dioxide gas were injected and the vessel put into Cape Town as a port of refuge. For a further 10 days carbon dioxide was injected into the hold and the temperature dropped sufficiently for the attending surveyors to consider it safe for the vessel to proceed on her voyage.

Some few days before arrival at Rotterdam, the cargo in No.2 hold again heated and the fire reasserted itself. A common peril threatened the whole adventure but the fire was again suppressed with carbon dioxide gas and the following course of action was decided upon and carried out. At Rotterdam No.2 hold was left unopened (although it contained cargo for that port) and only the Rotterdam cargo in the other four holds was discharged. The vessel then proceeded to Hamburg and No.2 hold was again kept sealed whilst the cargo in Nos 1 and 3 holds was completely discharged (stability requirements dictated that the after holds, Nos 4 and 5 should not be discharged). Only then were the hatches on No.2 hold lifted. The influx of fresh air caused the fire to erupt and within minutes there was a great conflagration which was extinguished only by flooding the hold.

The expenses of putting into Cape Town and of the carbon dioxide used in the firefighting were clearly allowable in general average and to be contributed for by all interests, but which interests should contribute to the general average damage caused by the flooding of No.2 hold?

3.13 There may be those who, with a strong natural sense of equity, would contend that the whole of the cargo originally shipped should contribute towards the general average damage caused by flooding No.2 hold. In support of their view they might maintain that:

(1) The whole of the cargo was on board when the fire reasserted itself and imperilled the common adventure a few days before arrival at Rotterdam; further, that the whole of the cargo was on board when the first steps were taken to extinguish the fire, that is, the injection of carbon dioxide gas into the hold.
(2) The whole course of action, both fire fighting and discharge, was planned at the outset as one continuous operation and carried out as such.
(3) In *Reliance Marine Insurance Co v New York & Cuba Mail S.S. Co*[29] cargo removed from a ship before it was scuttled to extinguish a fire was nevertheless found liable to contribute towards the general average caused by the scuttling.
(4) The alternative view produces a ludicrous result in that the more cargo that is discharged before the final flooding of the hold is undertaken, the greater will be the burden and general average contribution falling on those interests that do contribute.

[29] *Reliance Marine* (1896) 70 Fed. Rep. 262; 77 Fed. Rep. 317; 165 U.S. 720.

However, and in spite of a seemingly inequitable result, it is submitted that the correct view is that the general average damage to the Hamburg cargo in No.2 hold should be borne only by the ship and such cargo as was on board at the time when the hold was flooded.

(1) There was nothing exceptional about the method adopted to fight the fire and shippers of cargo have the right to expect that a carrier will prosecute the voyage as cheaply and efficiently as possible.
(2) The fire fighting and discharge may have been planned as one continuous operation, but the discharging of Nos 1, 3, 4 and 5 holds was not undertaken with the object of, nor did it in any way assist in saving or benefiting the ship and cargo in No.2 hold.
(3) The cargo was discharged in the normal way at destination under the contract of affreightment, unlike the case of *Reliance Marine Insurance Co v New York & Cuba Mail S.S. Co*. Further, in that case, the discharge was for the common benefit in the sense that a valuable shipment of tobacco would have been destroyed by the scuttling, thereby increasing the total amount of the general average allowances. In the present case, the discharge was exclusively for the benefit of the particular cargo interests concerned and the case of *Royal Mail Steam Packet Co v English Bank of Rio*[30] is more in point.
(4) The alternative view would lead to strange results if consistently applied. For instance, a vessel may be involved in a serious collision just outside her port of discharge, which then becomes a port of refuge for all cargo other than that destined for that port. It would not be suggested that the cargo for that port should contribute to temporary repairs necessary to complete the voyage, or to detention expenses.

So far as concerns the Rotterdam cargo in No.2 hold, the decision to over-carry that cargo to Hamburg, rather than discharging it at Hamburg, may properly be regarded as a sacrifice of that cargo for the benefit of the ship and all the Hamburg cargo, and it follows that each of those interests should contribute to any additional damage caused by the over-carriage.

Increased Cost of Discharging Cargo at Destination after a Fire

It is customary for stevedores to claim "dirty money" or other enhanced rates of pay if called upon to discharge a cargo which has been damaged, say by fire and subsequent flooding of the hold. Or, a cargo of grain which has been similarly damaged may have to be discharged by grab, rather than elevator, again at extra cost. In practice, the extra cost of discharging is generally considered to be the direct and natural result of the fire and/or the flooding of the hold and, in so far as the extra cost relates to cargo damaged by a general average sacrifice, it is allowed as general average, for example: 3.14

[30] *Royal Mail Steam Packet Co v English Bank of Rio* (1887) 19 Q.B.D. 362: see below para.8.12.

Actual cost of discharge....................	10,000
Less: Normal cost	4,000
Extra cost	6,000
Whereof: Attributable to damage by	
Fire..........................	3,500
Water.........................	2,500
	6,000

The extra cost (2,500) of discharging the cargo damaged by water used to extinguish the fire would be allowed as general average.

Increased Cost of Discharging Cargo at Destination during a Fire

3.15 When a vessel arrives at destination with a fire in the cargo, the cost of discharging may be considerably increased. In order to get at the seat of the fire with the least possible delay, the discharge may take place in overtime hours or the men be paid danger money; or a smouldering cargo of fishmeal, instead of being discharged steadily tier by tier, may be attacked with grabs; or a cargo may be hastily discharged on to a dock wall and require additional handling and transport to the warehouse. Provided that the extra cost was incurred in order to extinguish the fire as quickly as possible and exclusively for the common safety of ship and cargo, it is allowed as general average.

Cost of Refilling Fire Extinguishers, etc. After Use

3.16 It is difficult to justify on established legal grounds the allowance in general average of the cost of refilling foam fire extinguishers and carbon dioxide gas cylinders.[31] They have been used for the very purpose for which they were intended. However, it is the invariable practice to allow the cost of refilling. The Association of Average Adjusters of the United States even have a rule of practice on the subject:

> "Rule XIX. Fire Extinguishers. The cost of replacing gas or any commodity used in efforts to extinguish a fire on board a vessel shall be allowed in general average even though the gas or commodity was on board the vessel at the time the fire was discovered."

In similar fashion, on purely practical grounds it is customary to allow as general average the cost of putting into port specially to replenish stocks of carbon dioxide gas, etc. previously used to extinguish a fire; also to allow wages and maintenance of crew during extra detention at a port of refuge while waiting for carbon dioxide gas cylinders to be refilled.

[31] e.g. *Harrison v Bank of Australasia* (1872) L.R. 7 Exch. 39; *Robinson v Price* (1876) 2 Q.B.D. 91.

Historical Development and Practice of Rule III

Glasgow Resolutions 1860

The second resolution put before the International Conference at Glasgow in 1860 was, "that the damage done to ship, cargo, and freight, in extinguishing fire, shall be allowed in General Average", and this was passed by a majority of 22:6 after very little discussion. **3.17**

In the printed version of the Rules published soon after the Conference, there is a note under r.2:

> "This, it will be observed, includes the damage done by water to property which was actually on fire at the time when the water extinguished that fire."

It is suggested that this note may not necessarily have been intended to be explanatory or directive, but, rather, to draw attention to what was thought by some of the delegates to be a fault in the wording of the rule.

York Rules 1864

Such discussion as took place on this occasion was concerned only with the form of wording of the rule, and the final version, passed unanimously, was as follows: **3.18**

> "Damage done to a ship and cargo, or either of them, by water or otherwise, in extinguishing a fire on board the ship, shall be general average."

It may be noted that the rule makes no mention of "freight", and it was the intention of the Conference to deal with freight in a more general way in the Bill that might be brought before Parliament.

York-Antwerp Rules 1877

The 1864 Rule was confirmed at Antwerp in 1877, but with additional wording proposed by Richard Lowndes: ". . . except that no compensation be made for damage done by water to packages which have been on fire." The Association of Average Adjusters had passed a British Rule of Practice of similar effect in 1874[32] and, no doubt, were pleased to see their views accepted by 36 votes to 4 at the International Conference. It is difficult to believe that Lowndes had any particular motive in his choice of the words "which have been on fire", rather than the words in the British Rule: "on fire at the time the water was thrown upon them", but their effect was, of course, quite different.[33] **3.19**

[32] The rule is quoted para.3.07, above.
[33] This distinction was relevant only up to and including the 1950 edition of the rule.

York-Antwerp Rules 1890

3.20 In the first, positive, part of the rule were added the words: "including damage by beaching or scuttling a burning ship" although they may not have been strictly necessary. In the second, negative, part of the rule were added: "such portions of the ship and bulk cargo."

> "Damage done to a ship and cargo, or either of them, by water or otherwise, including damage by beaching or scuttling a burning ship, in extinguishing a fire on board the ship, shall be made good as general average; except that no compensation shall be made for damage to such portions of the ship and bulk cargo, or to such separate packages of cargo, as have been on fire."

There existed, almost certainly, a school of thought which maintained that if any part of a bulk cargo was on fire, no allowance could be made in general average for damage caused by water or otherwise to any other part of the bulk cargo in that particular hold, and the additional wording in second part of the rule was intended to resolve this problem. However, in *Greenshields Cowie & Co v Stephens & Sons*[34] the Court of Appeal declined to place this construction on the rule, holding that it excluded from contribution only "so much as has been actually ignited".

York-Antwerp Rules 1924 and 1950

3.21 No change was made in the rule, either in 1924 or 1950, but on each occasion the point had been raised that the exception in the second half of the rule should be deleted. In its report[35] prior to the Amsterdam Conference in 1949, the Drafting Committee agreed that it was "illogical not to allow in general average damage sustained through extinguishing operations to such portions of the ship and cargo as have been on fire", but, for a reason which bears no close examination, recommended that the rule should be left in its then existing form.

York-Antwerp Rules 1974

3.22 Two important changes were made to the second, negative part of this rule at the Hamburg Conference in 1974.

First, the previous exclusion in the second half of the rule that no compensation should be made for damage "to such portions of the ship and bulk cargo, or to such separate packages of cargo, as have been on fire" was deleted, thus facilitating considerably the work of both the cargo surveyor and the average adjuster. As Mr N.G. Hudson said in his address to the Association of Average Adjusters in 1973:

> "The cargo surveyor will not need to make a separation of water damaged cargo into parcels suffering water damage only and those which have additionally been touched by fire. The other parties to the adventure will not now have to pay for the additional

[34] *Greenshields Cowie & Co v Stephens & Sons* [1908] 1 K.B. 51. There was an appeal to the House of Lords, but not on this point.
[35] *International Maritime Committee Bulletin*, No.104, p.111.

> labour cost involved in making this separation, nor if it has been overlooked, will the average adjuster have to rely on guesswork. Nor will it be necessary to explore the realm of semantics to decide what is a 'portion' of a bulk cargo, or whether there is a distinction between a package which is 'charred' and one which is 'scorched.' Everyone will benefit by this real and practical simplification."

Second, the vexed subject of smoke damage and the increasing number of claims being put forward for such damage as the result of modern methods of firefighting, discussed earlier[36] in this work, was addressed. It was resolved, and uniformity of practice achieved, by the addition to the rule of the words: "except that no compensation shall be made for damage by smoke or heat however caused."

York-Antwerp Rules 1994

At an early stage of the proceedings leading to the 1994 Rules, the Netherlands Maritime Law Association drew attention to the fact that the exclusion of any compensation in general average for damage by smoke or heat however caused introduced in 1974 worked unfairly if the heat or smoke damage was attributable to general average measures. However, as the 1974 exclusion was purposely introduced on the grounds of practical expediency alone, the Netherlands did not press further with any proposals they might have had for change. **3.23**

At a later stage of the proceedings, a somewhat similar point was made by the US delegation and this achieved greater success. It concerned refrigerated cargoes, which were likely to suffer deterioration if it proved necessary to turn off the refrigerating equipment in order to extinguish a fire, or the refrigerating equipment was put out of action by water used to extinguish a fire–a general average act. The damage to the cargo from this cause would be the direct consequence of the general average act, but, rightly or wrongly, it had been argued that no allowance in general average could be made on the grounds that the deterioration was the consequence of heat however caused, as excluded by the rule.

The United States Maritime Law Association proposed, therefore, that the exclusion of damage by heat however caused should be modified to exclude only damage by heat of the fire, and this was accepted at Sydney.

York-Antwerp Rules 2004

No change other than the substitution of allowed for made good and allowance for compensation. **3.24**

RULE III **3.25**

EXTINGUISHING FIRE ON SHIPBOARD

> **Damage done to a ship and cargo, or either of them, by water or otherwise, including damage by beaching or scuttling a burning ship, in extinguishing a fire**

[36] See para.3.08, above.

on board the ship, shall be made good/allowed as general average; except that no compensation/allowance shall be made for damage by smoke however caused or by heat of the fire.

CONSTRUCTION

3.26 **"Damage"**: The word is used in contradistinction to "loss", and cargo which is lost by water used to extinguish a fire (for example sugar) may, more properly, be recoverable under the lettered rules rather than under r.III. Similarly, if cargo is jettisoned because part of it is on fire, the loss, if it is recoverable at all (see *Slater v Hayward Rubber Co*[37]), should be claimed under the lettered rules.

"ship and cargo": For a commentary on "cargo" see r.I.[38] Damage caused by the means used to extinguish a fire to property not carried under a contract of affreightment will be made good under the lettered rules, as will damage to crews clothing while fighting a fire. Loss of freight will be claimed under r.XV.

"by water or otherwise": The word "otherwise" is understood to comprise those other means of extinguishing fires such as steam, carbon dioxide gas, and foam, etc.

"extinguishing": Contribution under this rule is confined to damage done in extinguishing an existing fire, as opposed to damage done in preventing a fire, for example by pouring water on a bulk cargo which is heating dangerously and will otherwise ignite. Damage done as a result of preventive measures might, however, be recoverable under the lettered rules.

3.27 **"fire"**: To constitute fire there must be actual ignition, that is visible flames, a ruddy glow, or incandescence. "Mere heating which has not arrived at the stage of incandescence or ignition is not within the specific word fire".[39] However, measures taken to deal with, for example, a dangerous level of spontaneous heating of cargo may qualify as general average under the lettered rules.

"no compensation/allowance shall be made for damage by smoke however caused or by heat of the fire": Damage caused by smoke, whether naturally resulting from the fire itself or whether enhanced by the use of CO_2 gas or other modern methods of extinguishing a fire, is hereby excluded from compensation in general average absolutely on the grounds of practical expediency, as recounted in paras 3.08 to 3.10 and 3.23, above.

To the extent that damage caused by heat resulting from the fire itself can be separated from that resulting directly from the means used to extinguish the fire, the former is excluded from general average and the latter allowed.

[37] *Slater v Hayward Rubber Co* (1857) 26 Conn. 128.

[38] See para.1.28, above.

[39] *Tempus Shipping v Louis Dreyfus & Co* [1930] 1 K.B. 699 at 708; *Harris v Poland* [1941] 1 K.B. 462.

RULE IV

CUTTING AWAY WRECK

ENGLISH LAW AND BACKGROUND

A class of case which at one time gave rise to much difference of opinion consists in the cutting away of ship's materials when they are in what is called a state of wreck. **4.01**

When a ship's mast had been carried away, and was held fast alongside, with the yards, sails, and rigging, and this wreck, beating against the ship's side, threatened to stave it in, and thus endangered ship and cargo, supposing that in such a case the master, instead of waiting to try how much he could save of this "wreck", for the common safety cut it all away, was any part of this loss properly the subject of general average? With modern ships the problem arises less frequently, but is still occasionally encountered. For example, an anchor may accidentally[1] run out to the bitter end in deep water, with the result that it is impossible to get it back on board, and it may therefore be cut away for the common safety. See also the example given in para.4.19, below.

Emerigon,[2] and other foreign writers, held that an allowance should in such cases be made, as general average, for so much as the articles thus sacrificed, in their actual condition, may reasonably be taken to be worth. And this was always the rule in many foreign countries. In this country and the United States, however, a contrary practice prevailed until it was disapproved in the latter part of the nineteenth century by a series of legal decisions in both[3] countries. At this present time, therefore, the law and practice in most countries is the same and, but for the York-Antwerp Rules, favours an allowance in general average of the damaged **4.02**

[1] If an anchor is deliberately run out to the bitter end in an emergency, in the hope that it may ground and prevent the ship drifting, and it subsequently becomes necessary to detach it, the consequent loss would be treated as a direct consequence of the original sacrifice: see para.4.19, below.

[2] *Assurances*, Ch.12, para.41; p.422 of Boulay-Paty's ed.

[3] In the US, *The Margarethe Blanca* (1882) 12 Fed. Rep. 728; 14 Fed. 59; *The Mary Gibbs* (1884) 22 Fed. Rep. 463. A working scale for such allowances was prepared by Captain F. A. Martin on behalf of the New York Board of Underwriters.

value of any wreck cut away for the common safety if that wreck would have survived the storm (or other emergency). However, the contrary practice of British and American average adjusters was, to some extent, incorporated into the York-Antwerp Rules from their inception in 1860 and remains to this day, for the soundest of practical reasons.[4] To the extent that the York-Antwerp Rules are now of almost universal application, the law on this subject is of less practical importance than when Lowndes himself prepared the first four editions of this work.

Principle Established by Decided Cases

4.03 The principle may be expressed thus: whatever, when cut away or parted from for the common safety, is already "in a state of wreck", is not admissible as general average. That is "in a state of wreck" which is in such a state that, even if it had not been thus cut away or parted from, and though the ship and cargo had nevertheless escaped the danger, that thing would certainly have perished or become of no value. It is not enough that it would perhaps or very likely have perished: on the other hand, it is not necessary that its perishing should be demonstrably certain; but if, according to the ordinary course of human events, no expectation could be entertained that it could be saved (a matter on which the judgment of experts may be called in), then it must be treated as "in a state of wreck" or of no value.

Cases on State of Wreck

4.04 In *Johnson v Chapman*,[5] the facts of which have already been considered in para.1.07, Willes J. said:

> "The cargo appears to have broken away, appears to have got loose on deck: it was not washed overboard; it had not become valueless; it was not spoiled with water; and if the weather had been fine it would have been restowed, and it might have come on and been just as valuable except getting a little wetting with salt water. It was in fact once restowed, or part of it, during the voyage, so that it clearly was not in a state of wreck, in the sense of having become lost property, which they could not recover, or make use of if they recovered it."

4.05 In arriving at this conclusion Willes J. gave an example of what truly constituted a state of wreck:

> "If a mast were sprung and a part of it were to go overboard with a quantity of spars and sails attached to it hanging on by a stay which must give way in a minute or two, whilst in the meantime, by battering against the side of the vessel, it adds to the danger, and if the stay were cut to let it go at once, it would be very difficult to say that that was anything more than wreck. A lawyer could not lay it down as a matter of pure law that all cumber cut loose is wreck. But what I say is, if it was virtually lost, if not recoverable, if the act of cutting the rope was only hastening the moment at which it would be lost, you would properly call that wreck, and you would not say it

[4] See York-Antwerp r.IV, para.4.16, below.

[5] *Johnson v Chapman* (1865) 19 C.B. (N.S.) 563 at 582; 35 L.J.C.P. 23 at 28.

was general average. The reason given is, because you cannot keep it. There is no intentional sacrifice in cutting it away. You must lose it, and the losing it a minute or two sooner can make all the difference of its doing great injury or not; but you cannot help losing it."

Three cases have been tried in the English courts in which the attempt was made to exclude from general average the value of a mast cut away while still in situ, on the ground that by reason of previous damage to it or its supports the mast had been rendered of no value and virtually a wreck. **4.06**

The first of these, *Corry v Coulthard*[6] is unfortunately not reported, but from the references to it in the case next cited we may gather that the mast, an iron one, having become loose, the master, fearing that if it broke it would go through the bottom of the ship, cut it away. The question having been raised whether this was general average, the judge, Cleasby B, directed the jury that the question turned on whether "if the weather had moderated, the mast could possibly have been saved". The jury found for the plaintiff, that is, in favour of general average. The case was carried up to the Court of Appeal, on the question of misdirection: but the court unanimously pronounced that the question had been rightly put to the jury. Brett L.J. said:

"You do not mean to say that it was so valueless that a man, in a calm, would have thrown it overboard: it was worth money. . . Wreck means rubbish, I suppose."

In *Shepherd v Kottgen*,[7] the barque Rollo met with a heavy gale, and portions of the rigging gave way, owing to which the mainmast began to lurch violently, so that the crew feared it would rip up the decks and endanger the ship's safety. To prevent this, the master, after vainly attempting to secure the mast, cut it away. At the trial, Manisty J. put the question to the jury in the following form: "Are you of opinion that that mast was virtually a wreck and valueless and gone at the time it went over?" The jury found that the mast was a wreck: and, to a further question from the learned judge, "Do you find whether it was hopelessly lost?" they answered "Yes". On this the judgment was given against general average. **4.07**

In the Divisional Court[8] the judgment was set aside upon the ground that the question should have been put to the jury in the same form as in *Corry v Coulthard*.[9] The Court of Appeal,[10] whilst it adopted and concurred with the law as laid down in the Divisional Court, differed from it in thinking that the law as laid down to the jury by Manisty J. amounted to the same thing and restored the original judgment.

Bramwell L.J. said: **4.08**

[6] Heard in Exch. Div., December 21, 1876, and in the Court of Appeal, January 17, 1877; mentioned in *Shepherd v Kottgen* (1877) 2 C.P.D. 578 at 583.

[7] *Shepherd v Kottgen* (1877) 2 C.P.D. 578 at 583.

[8] Shepherd (1877) 2 C.P.D. 578.

[9] *Corry v Coulthard* Unreported December 31, 1876.

[10] *Shepherd* (1877) 2 C.P.D. 585.

"Where the thing destroyed has some peculiar condition attached to it, so that it will be lost whether the whole adventure is saved or not, then its destruction cannot be deemed a sacrifice. I think that this proposition applies to the present facts. The mast was in such a state that it must have been lost, whether the vessel got safely to port or not. Consequently there was no sacrifice of it when it was cut away, and the plaintiffs have no claim for contribution."

Brett L.J. said:

"Now, consistently with the decision of this court in Corry v Coulthard,[11] and in accordance, as it seems to me. with what was intimated by the court in that case, the following proposition may be stated: If anything on board a ship, which is cut or cast away because it is endangering the whole adventure, is in such a state or condition that it must itself certainly be lost, although the rest of the adventure should be saved without the cutting or casting away, then the destruction of the thing gives no claim for general average. Or the proposition may be stated in the following terms: where, whether the act relied upon as the act of sacrifice had been done or not, the thing in respect of which contribution is claimed would, by reason of its own state or condition, have been of no value whatever, or would have been certainly or absolutely lost to the owner, although the rest of the adventure had been saved, there is nothing lost to the owner by the act, and therefore there is nothing sacrificed, that is to say, there is no sacrifice."[12]

Cotton L.J. said:

"'Hopelessly lost' must mean 'impossible to be saved.' In the language of everyday life a thing is impossible when, according to the ordinary course of human events, no expectation can be entertained that it will happen . . . Where the thing said to have been voluntarily abandoned or destroyed is in such a state, by reason of a peril peculiar to itself, that if the act of supposed sacrifice had not been done, it would have very shortly been destroyed, without the rest of the common adventure being lost, the act of slightly hastening the moment of loss, is not an act of sacrifice which enables the owner of the thing to claim contribution."

4.09 In *Montgomery v Indemnity Mutual Marine Insurance Co*[13] the facts were that the Airlie encountered bad weather, in which she rolled and lurched violently. The mainmast, which was made of iron, and hollow, settled down, and the master, fearing that it would break and fall on the deck and cause the loss of the vessel, cut away the windward rigging, after which the mast fell on the side and was cut adrift. It was afterwards found that the mast had been in no greater peril than the rest of the adventure. It had broken across about 12 inches from the keelson. The upper portion had crushed into the lower in telescope fashion and rested securely on the keelson. Mathew J. said:

[11] See para.4.06, above.

[12] cf. the judgment of Bigham J. in *Iredale v China Traders' Insurance Co* [1899] 2 Q.B. 356 at 360, where he suggests obiter that whether the thing sacrificed is in a state of wreck has to be ascertained subjectively in the light of the facts known at the time of the sacrifice. It is submitted that this is not correct and that the true test is whether the thing sacrificed was in fact in a state of wreck, to be ascertained in the light of all the facts known at the time of making the adjustment.

[13] *Montgomery v Indemnity Mutual Marine Insurance Co* [1901] 1 Q.B. 147.

> "The mast was not in such a condition that it must have been lost whether the rest of the adventure had been saved or not. It could not be said that the mast had no value, or that it was impossible to be saved. There was a chance of saving it, and that chance was thrown away for the safety of the whole adventure. The master would seem to have exercised his judgment reasonably, and it was not necessary that his views should be borne out by the facts when they came to be afterwards examined. For the defendants reliance was placed on the case of Shepherd v Kottgen[14] where the mast was cut away, but was held to have been already lost. There it appeared that the rigging had been loosened in the storm, and that all that was done was to anticipate by a few minutes an inevitable loss. The mast of the Airlie before the rigging was cut was firmly upheld, and could have stood and been saved if the master had not ordered it to be cut away. Upon the question of fact I am of opinion that there was a general average sacrifice."[15]

Proposed Rules of Practice

The principle to be extracted from these decisions has been set out above.[16] Lowndes proposed that this principle should be applied to particular cases in the form of a set of working rules for which reference may be made to the fourth to ninth editions of this work. **4.10**

Historical Development and Practice of Rule IV

Glasgow Resolutions 1860

If a ship's mast carried away in a gale, but was held fast alongside by the rigging and that rigging was cut away in order to get rid of the mast because it threatened to stave in the ships side and endanger the ship and cargo, it was the custom in most foreign countries in 1860 to allow as general average the value, in their then damaged condition, of the lost mast, spars, sails and rigging. Nevertheless, all but two of the delegates at the 1860 Conference at Glasgow voted in favour of the Resolution (No.5): **4.11**

> "That the loss sustained by cutting away the wreck of masts accidentally broken ought not to be allowed in general average."

This resolution was based on the inveterate practice[17] of British and American adjusters. Even if the theoretical grounds for the practice would be considered

[14] *Shepherd* (1877) 2 C.P.D. 578.

[15] cf. *May v Keystone Yellow Pine Co* (1902) 117 Fed. Rep. 287, where the rudder of a ship, partly torn loose in a gale, was cut away to prevent it from beating a hole in the ship. But for the storm it could have been replaced in position; and its value in its damaged condition was allowed in general average.

[16] See para.4.03, above.

[17] *Stevens* (1816), p.18, considered that the situation in which these articles were placed by the breaking of the mast rendered them of no value whatever. *Benecke* (1824), p.185, denied that the articles were valueless, but, having recourse to his favourite doctrine that where there was no choice

unsound today, they carried some weight in 1860, and the practical difficulties of placing a value in their then damaged condition on the sacrificed mast, spars, sails and rigging were probably sufficient to sway the voting in favour of the Resolution.

York Rules 1864

4.12 The wording of the 1860 Resolution was amended slightly in 1864 and carried by a large majority, three votes only being given against it:

> "Loss or damage caused by cutting away the wreck or remains of spars, or of other things which have previously been carried away by sea-peril, shall not be made good as general average."

York-Antwerp Rules 1877, 1890, 1924 and 1950

4.13 No change.

York-Antwerp Rules 1974

4.14 The wording of the 1864 Rule survived unchanged for 110 years; but as it related essentially to sailing ships, the question was raised when considering any necessary revision for the 1974 Rules whether the rule was obsolete and should be deleted. No strong opinions were expressed one way or another and the view prevailed, as expressed by the President of the International Sub-Committee:

> ". . . that the Rule does serve some function in a limited number of cases and, perhaps more important, it serves to express a principle which is nowhere else expressed in the Rules."

Accordingly, a modernised text omitting any reference to spars was passed at the Hamburg Conference in 1974:

> "Loss or damage sustained by cutting away wreck or parts of the ship which have been previously carried away or are effectively lost by accident shall not be made good as general average."

York-Antwerp Rules 1994

4.15 No change, although the suggestion was again made that the rule was obsolete.

there could be no sacrifice, considered that, generally speaking, it would be impossible to work the vessel without cutting away the broken mast and the rigging in which it was entangled, so that this act was not optional but dictated by necessity, and consequently was not a sacrifice. Baily (1851), pp.33–34, considered that no allowance could be made in general average for the sacrifice of an article which was itself the immediate cause of the danger necessitating the sacrifice.

York-Antwerp Rules 2004

No change other than the substitution of allowed for made good as part of the process of tidying up the drafting of the Rules. **4.16**

RULE IV

CUTTING AWAY WRECK

Loss or damage sustained by cutting away wreck or parts of the ship which have been previously carried away or are effectively lost by accident shall not be *made good/allowed* as general average.

CONSTRUCTION

In the case of cargo, and parts of the ship which have not previously been carried away, the rule simply embodies the principle that there can be no sacrifice of that which is valueless, or doomed anyway.[18] However, in the case of parts of the ship which have been previously carried away the rule, for reasons of practical convenience, extends this principle. **4.17**

There may be great practical difficulties in determining:

(1) whether, for instance, a mast or spars (or other part of the ship) previously carried away in a storm but still lying alongside the ship attached by the rigging were "hopelessly lost" or might have survived the storm had they not been cut away; and
(2) if they had so survived, what their likely value would have been in damaged condition.

These are solved by assuming that any part of the ship which has previously been carried away by accident shall be considered to be valueless when cut away for the common safety, and not the subject of any general average allowance.

"Loss or damage": The wording of the rule as a whole is less than perfect, and a difficulty arises from the introduction of the word "damage". It is possible to visualise, for instance, that a broken mast on an auxiliary sailing vessel might be cut away for the common safety, and, before clearing the vessel, cause damage to the propeller. The loss of the mast is plainly excluded by the wording of the rule. The propeller was not itself previously harmed, by accident or otherwise. Is the damage to it to be excluded, because it was sustained through cutting away the mast? It is submitted that the loss or damage referred to are the financial consequences to the shipowner solely through cutting away the wreck or parts of the **4.18**

[18] See paras 4.01–4.10, above.

ship, and that the damage to the propeller is not excluded. This accords with principle.[19]

"wreck": See paras 4.03 to 4.09, above.

4.19 **"parts of the ship which have been previously carried away . . ."**: This is the part of the rule which involves the departure from principle referred to above. If a part of the ship has been carried away, is then secured to the ship in the hope that it can be saved, and is subsequently cut away for the common safety, the rule excludes contribution, whether or not the part in question was valueless, or effectively doomed anyway. The words carried away denote that the part in question must have become detached accidentally; if it was detached deliberately this part of the rule will not be applicable. In an example drawn from practice the pipe-laying ramp of an offshore construction barge was damaged in a collision, as a result of which it was subsequently detached from the barge by the crew, and secured alongside to prevent it sinking. A storm approached, causing the ramp to range heavily against the side of the barge, causing significant damage to both, and the master decided to cut away the ramp, after which it was lost. In these circumstances it was necessary to decide whether the ramp was in a state of wreck, or already effectively lost by accident. If the ramp had been carried away (i.e. detached from the barge) by the original collision itself, these considerations would have been immaterial, since the rule would have excluded contribution anyway.

"by accident": See the commentary above. If the original damage, rather than being accidental, was the result of a general average sacrifice, any further loss caused by the cutting away would in most circumstances be recoverable as a direct result of that sacrifice.

[19] e.g. see Ove Lange, *Trustee v George D. Emery & Co and Insurance Co of North America* Unreported January 1926, the facts of which are recorded at para.2.12, above.

RULE V

VOLUNTARY STRANDING

LAW AND BACKGROUND

When a ship is voluntarily run upon a sandbank, or purposely sunk in shallow water, in order to escape the pursuit of an enemy or the imminent danger of being dashed to pieces on rocks, or sinking in deep water, or to extinguish a fire on board, and if the ship or the cargo suffers damage by reason of that measure, the rule in almost every country is to treat the damage thereby caused as general average. It is the result of an extraordinary measure taken for the common safety, and involving almost certain injury to the bottom of the ship, and considerable risk to the cargo in the lower hold, from leakage caused by the shock below. It is the substitution of a danger affecting mainly, if not exclusively, the lower portion of the ship and cargo for a danger of total loss, that is, a danger affecting all parts equally. In this sense it is the sacrifice of a part for the benefit of the remainder. **5.01**

English Law

It is surprising that no case has ever come before the courts of this country involving the voluntary stranding of a vessel and depending for a decision on English law, unencumbered by the York-Antwerp Rules. The chance of such a case being brought for trial must now be considered extremely remote for the following reasons: **5.02**

(1) the almost universal use of the York-Antwerp Rules, with their specific provision[1] on the subject;
(2) driving ashore (whether voluntarily, or by accident) is no longer the common occurrence that it was in sailing ship days, despite a very recent example of such an event when MSC Napoli was beached in Lyme Bay in 2007.

[1] Rule V, para.5.14, below.

Of the textbook writers, Abbott, Shipping (in the last edition published (1827) in Lord Tenderden's lifetime), laid down that:

> "damage voluntarily done to a ship by . . . "running it on a rock, shallow, or strand to avoid the danger of a storm or of an enemy, and the expense of recovering the ship from this latter situation . . . are to be sustained by a general contribution."[2]

There is no doubt that the great current of academic opinion sets that way. The Consolado del Mare, Roccus, Targa, Emerigon, Abbott, are cited by Arnould, who concludes: "there is no rule more clearly established than this by the uniform course of maritime law and usage."[3]

5.03 Nevertheless, the lack of binding authority led to there being, at least throughout the nineteenth century, a considerable difference of opinion amongst adjusters and amongst the writers of textbooks, including the authors of earlier editions of this work[4]; in fact, it is probable that more discussion took place and more was written on the subject of voluntary stranding than on any other single example of a general average sacrifice. In addition there used to be a Custom of Lloyd's excluding from general average all damage to ship and cargo resulting from a voluntary stranding except such damage as was done by beaching or scuttling a burning ship to extinguish a fire. Whilst this Custom remained in being, any British adjuster was bound to attach considerable weight to the Custom, even if he was not obliged to follow it blindly, and it was partly to refute this old and possibly invalid Custom that previous editions of this work were designed. This reason no longer applies, for in 1968 the Association of Average Adjusters rescinded the old Custom and substituted wording identical with the then current (1950) r.V of the York-Antwerp Rules, to be followed in 1996 with the 1974 wording of r.V of the York-Antwerp Rules[5]:

> "When a ship is intentionally run on shore for the common safety, whether or not she might have been driven on shore, the consequent loss or damage shall be allowed in general average."

Law in the United States

5.04 The law in the United States is better defined, and from the many cases which have come before the courts of that country it is possible to deduce the governing principles.

1. Even if the ship must inevitably ground somewhere, and the only act of volition consists of selecting a place for grounding where she will suffer least, this is enough: the damage done is general average.[6]

[2] Abbott, *Shipping*, 5th edn, (1827) p.349.
[3] Arnould, *Insurance*, 2nd edn, p.915. See also 16th edn, para.943.
[4] See the 1st to 9th editions.
[5] Rule F4, para.70.31, below.
[6] *Sims v Gurney 4 Binney's Penns Rep. 513 (Supreme Court of Pennsylvania); Barnard v Adams* 10 Howards S.C.Rep. 270 (Supreme Court).

2. The consequences need not be those which were intended by the master provided that the subsequent stranding is the result of the action of those in command; if while the master is running the ship for one point on the strand, she takes the ground on another, that loss is general average.

This principle is well illustrated by a number of American cases,[7] also the English case of *Anglo-Grecian Steam Trading Co Ltd v T. Beynon & Co*[8] in which Roche J. said:

> "It is said . . . that the ship was not intentionally run on shore. Now that depends on this. On the facts as I have found them it was intended to beach her and she did take the beach during the operation of beaching her: but she took the beach before the person in control of the operation expected she would . . . I hold that there was an intentional beaching, none the less because the actual taking of the ground . . . occurred sooner than anticipated and not precisely in that place of the beach area which was expected and desired. Of course the pilot did not intend to put her on the rocks, neither do I find that he put her on the rocks. She got on the rocks because, after getting on the beach, by the operation of natural causes, she was moved from the place she took on the beach towards the rocks and on to the rocks."

3. A voluntary stranding is equally the subject of general average, whether the stranded ship is afterwards saved and repaired, or is totally lost by the stranding.[9]
4. The stranding must be the consequence of an intentional act.
If the master does not intend to strand the vessel there can, of course, be no claim in general average on the basis of a voluntary stranding.[10]
Similarly if there was an intention to strand, but, because of the force of the elements or for some other reason, the master is unable to influence the course of the vessel any subsequent stranding will not be a voluntary stranding.[11]

Conclusions

To sum up, in the United States, the law now seems to be that although some stranding was inevitable, the loss is allowable in general average, but that if the same stranding was inevitable, it is not. Or, as was stated in Phillips on Insurance: **5.05**

> "On the whole, then, if the intentional stranding is, under the particular circumstances, the direct result of voluntary agency, rather than of the action of the elements,

[7] *Rea v Culler* (1846) 1 Sprague 135; *Sturgess v Cary* (1854) 2 Curtis, Cir. Ct. 59; *The Star of Hope* (1869) 9 Wall 203; *Norwich & NY Transport Co v Insurance Co of North America* (1902) 118 Fed. Rep. 307.

[8] *Anglo-Grecian* (1926) 24 Lloyd's Rep. 122 at 125.

[9] *Columbian Insurance Co v Ashby* (1839) 13 Pet. 343. In *Iredale v China Traders' Insurance Co* [1899] 2 Q.B. 356 at 363, Bigham J. said that he believed English law on the point to be the same as that laid down in this case.

[10] *Walker v US Insurance Co* (1824) 11 Sarg. & Rawle's Penns. Rep. 61.

[11] *Shoe v Low Moor Iron Co* 49 Fed. Rep. 252 (1891).

> and the actual stranding is another than the one impending, and not merely an incidental and inconsiderable modification of it, the case is one for general average."[12]

Historical Development and Practice of Rule V

Glasgow Resolutions 1860

5.06 At the International Conference held at Glasgow in 1860 the principle appears to have been generally accepted by those delegates who spoke that damage done to a ship and her cargo by a voluntary stranding was properly allowable as general average. However, it was the opinion of L.R. Baily, undoubtedly the most respected and persuasive delegate present (and at this time the senior partner of Richard Lowndes), that in this particular instance it was better to depart from sound principle and adopt a practical rule which excluded from general average any loss caused by voluntary stranding:

> "The practical difficulties are so great that however correct in theory it may be to allow such damages, I would in practice reject them from general average: for when a ship is run ashore, much water is already in her, and she and her cargo have both sustained much damage previously. By running her on shore these injuries may be increased; but who in the world is to say what that increase is? Is it not better to waive your principle, and make a practical rule to prevent litigation?"

Accordingly, Baily put forward the resolution:

> "That the damage done to ship, cargo, and freight, by running a ship on shore . . . shall not be allowed in General Average."

In this form, the resolution was perfectly clear and unambiguous, and generally acceptable as a working rule to those present, but it flew in the teeth of the principles upon which general average was founded and, as Judge Marvin (United States) said, they should not give up a good principle when they might avoid the inconvenience. Further discussion ensued and a number of amendments were proposed which on practical grounds would exclude from general average any damage caused by voluntary stranding without denying the basic principle that such damage might properly be admissible as general average.

Finally, the following Resolution proposed by Lord Neaves was passed:

> "That, as a general rule in the case of the stranding of a vessel in the course of her voyage, the loss or damage to ship, cargo, or freight shall not be the subject of general average, but without prejudice to such a claim in exceptional cases, upon clear proof of special facts."

[12] Phillips, *Insurance*, p.1313.

York Rules 1864

After the 1860 Glasgow Conference, a number of reports and questionnaires were circulated amongst the delegates and a more specific and tighter wording was put forward for discussion at the International Conference held at York in 1864. It was proposed that damage caused by a voluntary stranding should be allowed as general average only if the stranding was to avoid capture or foundering. **5.07**

In the discussion which followed, the same points raised at the 1860 Conference were again stressed, namely that by the specific laws of some countries, also on the grounds of general principle, damage caused by voluntary stranding was allowable as general average: however, the practical difficulties of carrying out the principle, and the abuses and frauds to which it was open, made it preferable to limit allowances in general average to the minimum.

It was finally agreed to accept the wording of L.R. Baily, as follows:

> "When a ship is intentionally run on shore because she is sinking or driving on shore or rocks, no damage caused to the ship, the cargo and the freight, or any or either of them, by such intentional running on shore, shall be made good as general average."

This rule, as was the intention, removed from general average those cases of voluntary stranding most likely to offer opportunities for fraud and abuse, but it suffered from the defect that, to those not aware of the background, it might appear that these two instances of voluntary stranding were not allowable in general average on principle. This was not necessarily so, even in Britain, where for the previous 40 years or more such allowances were not generally made.[13] As the Chairman, Sir Fitzroy Kelly (afterwards Lord Chief Baron of the Exchequer) said at the 1864 Conference:

> "The law of England, as it then stood, that where an injury had been bona fide done, whether to ship, freight or cargo, by the voluntary act of the master, in order to prevent some greater calamity, then the consequences whatever they might be, would belong to general average. On this principle, the law, as regards voluntary strandings, would be the same in England as in the United States."

York-Antwerp Rules 1877

The existing 1864 York Rule was unanimously confirmed at the Conference at Antwerp in 1877. **5.08**

York-Antwerp Rules 1890

At the Conference at Liverpool in 1890 Charles McArthur proposed that the rule might be clarified by additional wording on two subjects: **5.09**

[13] See para.5.03, above.

(1) The rule in 1877 form mentioned only those situations where damage caused by voluntary stranding was excluded from general average; it failed to provide for those positive situations where the damage could be made good. It may have been that silence gave consent, and that it was the intention of those who framed the earlier rule that all those cases not expressly excepted should be treated as general average; if so, it was better to express it. For those countries (and he instanced France, Germany, Italy, Holland, Sweden, Norway, Denmark, Russia, Spain, Portugal, the United States, and the Argentine Republic) which had codes providing for voluntary stranding, there was no problem but in Britain, at least, there was a custom of Lloyd's[14] to disallow such claims.

(2) The words "driving on shore or on rocks" required greater definition. In the 4th edition of this work, Richard Lowndes stated at p.137 concerning the 1877 rule:

> "It was understood, I believe, that this rule was only applicable to a stranding in extremis, when a loss was inevitable, and it may be read in this sense; but the vagueness of the terms used is to be regretted."

MacArthur, therefore, proposed the following amendment, which was carried nem con:

> "When a ship is intentionally run on shore, and the circumstances are such that if that course were not adopted, she would inevitably sink or drive on shore or on rocks, no loss or damage caused to the ship, cargo, and freight, or any of them by such intentional running on shore shall be made good as general average. But in all other cases where a ship is intentionally run on shore for the common safety, the consequent loss or damage shall be allowed as general average."

York-Antwerp Rules 1924

5.10 At the Stockholm Conference in 1924, at the suggestion of the Association of Average Adjusters, it was unanimously agreed that the words "sink or" should be deleted from the 1890 rule. There now remained but a single exception to the allowance in general average of loss or damage caused by voluntary stranding: where the ship would inevitably drive on shore or on rocks if that course was not adopted.

York-Antwerp Rules 1950

5.11 The words "but loss or damage incurred in refloating such a ship shall be allowed as general average" were added to the first paragraph of the rule in 1950 to clarify a point on which there was no dispute in practice, but on which the wording of the 1924 rule was open to the opposite construction:

> "When a ship is intentionally run on shore, and the circumstances are such that if that course were not adopted she would inevitably drive on shore or on rocks, no loss or

14 See para.5.03, above.

damage caused to the ship, cargo and freight or any of them by such intentional running on shore shall be made good as general average, but loss or damage incurred in refloating such a ship shall be allowed as general average.

In all other cases where a ship is intentionally run on shore for the common safety, the consequent loss or damage shall be allowed as general average."

York-Antwerp Rules 1974

In their replies to the questionnaire circulated by the Comité Maritime International in 1970, National Associations were practically unanimous in suggesting that r.V should not be changed. However, the West German Association considered that difficulties[15] would be removed and some simplification achieved if it were no longer necessary to differentiate between those cases of voluntary stranding, where the vessel would inevitably drive on shore or on rocks, and other cases of voluntary stranding. This view found favour and the new 1974 rule allowing loss or damage caused by running a ship on shore for the common safety in all circumstances was passed at the Hamburg Conference without comment. 5.12

It probably reflects the law of most countries on the subject and also sound principle.

York-Antwerp Rules 1994

As previously recorded in paras C.36 and 2.11, above, important new provisions were introduced in 1994 to r.C to exclude any allowance in general average for damage to the environment, or consequent on the escape or release of pollutant substances from the property involved in the common maritime adventure. By reason of the Rule of Interpretation, the provisions of the lettered r.C would be subservient to any contrary provisions in any of the numbered rules, and if the exclusionary provisions of r.C were always to retain their force, it was essential that potentially contrary provisions such as existed in rr.II, V and VIII should be neutralised. 5.13

The 1974 r.V permitted the allowance in general average of any loss or damage consequent upon a voluntary stranding for the common safety, but limiting wording added in 1994 ensures that the only loss or damage allowable in general average from a voluntary stranding under r.V is that caused to the property involved in the common maritime adventure, that is, the ship and cargo, etc. and not to local beaches and fishing grounds, etc.

York-Antwerp Rules 2004

No change. 5.14

[15] The difficulty would be in determining under the 1950 rule whether a ship would "inevitably" drive on shore or on rocks. It is believed that one of the reasons why "sinking" was removed from the 1924 rule was this same difficulty in determining whether a vessel would "inevitably" have sunk; the matter could have been only one of conjecture.

RULE V

VOLUNTARY STRANDING

When a ship is intentionally run on shore for the common safety, whether or not she might have been driven on shore, the consequent loss or damage to the property involved in the common maritime adventure shall be allowed in general average.

CONSTRUCTION

5.15 **"intentionally"**: For comments on the general meaning of the word, see under r.A.[16] The relevant intention is an intention to run on shore, not to run on shore at a precisely defined spot, though it must be stressed that conditions must exist which make it possible for the master or those on board to carry out that intention and exercise some control over the manoeuvre and to run the vessel ashore at some spot other than that on which the elements would have driven her.[17]

In Anglo-Grecian Steam Trading Co Ltd v Beynon & Co[18] it was intended to put the vessel ashore at a defined point in the centre of Whitmore Bay, but the vessel touched the ground sooner and more to the eastward than had been intended or expected. Roche J. held[19] that under the 1890 rule:

> "there was an intentional beaching none the less because the actual taking of the ground, which after all must be a matter of some uncertainty, occurred sooner than was anticipated and not precisely in that place of the beach area which was expected and desired."

"run on shore": These words are equivalent to "stranded"[20] and mean going with the bottom on the shore. They do not cover running the vessel against the side of structures or objects attached to the shore, the vessel being still afloat, although damage so caused may be a sacrifice or extraordinary expenditure within the meaning of r.A.

Contact with Harbour Installations

5.16 In *The Seapool*[21] the vessel was intentionally run broadside against a pier with the object of using the pier as a lever to get the head of the ship into such a

[16] See particularly paras A.08 et seq., above.

[17] See para.5.05, above.

[18] *Anglo-Grecian* (1926) 24 Lloyd's Rep. 122. See also the American cases quoted in para.5.04, fn.7, above.

[19] *Anglo-Grecian* (1926) 24 Lloyd's Rep. 122 at 125.

[20] For the meaning of "stranded", see *Dobson v Bolton* (1799) 1 Park. Ins. 239: *C'Dougle v Royal Exch. Ass. Co* (1816) 4 Camp. 283; 4 M. & S. 503: *Wells v Hopwood* (1832) 3 B. & Ad. 20.

[21] *The Seapool* [1934] P. 53. So far as the damage to the pier is concerned, it should have been regarded rather as an extraordinary expenditure.

position that she could steam out to sea in a gale when her anchor had dragged, her port cable had parted and she was in great peril. As a result, the vessel was severely damaged and her owners became liable to pay and paid for the damage to the pier. Langton J. held that this was not a loss which fell within the terms of r.V but that it was covered by r.A as an extraordinary sacrifice. So far as r.V is concerned he said[22]:

> "On the other side, however, it was contended that 'stranding' is a well-known term. It is a term which occurs both in Continental law and in English law and it has a well ascertained meaning. 'Stranding' means going with the bottom on the shore and for my part I have always so understood it. I find it difficult to imagine that anybody could consciously have used language such as this if they had intended to include running a ship against the end of a pier, while the bottom of the ship was clear of the ground. It is true that some colour may be lent to the argument by the fact that in this particular case the ship appears to have bumped upon the ground whilst she was lying against the end of the pier, but, apart from that-which seems to me an extraneous circumstance–I see very little colour in this argument at all."

In similar fashion, when a ship, having lost her anchors, or being very leaky, so that it is dangerous to remain in the river or roadstead, is run into a dock when it would under ordinary circumstances have been improper to do so and is damaged by striking against the pier in entering it, the damage both to ship and pier should be treated as general average under r.A. Similarly it might be an extraordinary sacrifice of the ship to enter a narrow channel, and risk damage by grounding, in order to avoid a peril at sea. **5.17**

In *Austin Friars S.S. Co Ltd v Spillers & Bakers Ltd*,[23] the steamship Winchester, bound for Sharpness dock, stranded in the Severn near to the dock, and when she was got off was so seriously damaged and making so much water, that her master and the pilot decided (reasonably and prudently it was found) to take her at once into the dock, although in consequence of the strong ebb tide they expected that she would strike the pier and suffer some damage. She did collide with the pier and was not only damaged, but also did damage to the pier. Bailhache J. and the Court of Appeal held that the owners of the ship were entitled to a contribution in general average from the cargo owners in respect both of the damage to the ship and of their liability to compensate the dock authorities for the damage to the pier, the loss being in each case the direct consequence of the act of putting into the dock, which in the circumstances was a general average act.

It will be noticed that Sharpness dock was the ship's place of discharge, but she would not have been taken into the dock in that state of the tide but for the purpose of averting greater damage to the whole adventure. For that purpose, said the Court of Appeal, there was in the circumstances no difference between a port of refuge and a port of discharge.

"for the common safety": See under r.A.[24] **5.18**

[22] *The Seapool* [1934] P. 53 at 62.
[23] *Austin Friars* [1915] 1 K.B. 833; [1915] 3 K.B. 586, CA.
[24] See particularly paras A.20 et seq., above.

"consequent loss or damage": Rule C limits that which may be made good in general average to the direct consequences of a general average act, but, in the light of the Rule of Interpretation, this limitation does not affect the numbered rules. Indirect loss and damage may, therefore, be recoverable under this part of the rule, a fear expressed by the Drafting Committee for the 1950 Rules,[25] although it is thought that in practice the word "consequent" is construed restrictively and comprising only the "direct" loss or damage caused by a voluntary stranding, as that word has been interpreted in r.C.[26]

Whether wages and maintenance of crew can be allowed whilst the vessel is intentionally stranded is dealt with in para.11.11, below.

"to the property involved in the common maritime adventure": As recorded in para.5.13, above, this expression was added in 1994 to ensure that if, for instance, the cargo tanks of an oil tanker became ruptured as the result of a voluntary stranding for the common safety, the only allowance in general average is for the resulting loss of oil and damage to the ship or cargo, that is, the property involved in the common maritime adventure. Any claim for damage to the environment caused by the leaking oil or for any expense incurred by a party to the adventure consequent on such damage, although a direct result of the voluntary stranding, is outside the scope of r.V, and cannot be recovered under r.A, because it is excluded by the provisions of r.C.[27] However, where the damage to the property of third parties consequent on a voluntary stranding does not fall within the exclusion in r.C, any expense incurred by a party to the adventure by reason of that damage may be recoverable under the lettered rules. Examples might be damage to a pier or a structure on shore caused by contact with the vessel in the course of her stranding.

[25] International Maritime Committee, Bulletin No.104, p.111.

[26] The French Association of Average Adjusters has resolved that wages and provisions of the crew, after the termination of the voyage but during repairs the cost of which is allowed in general average under this rule, are also to be allowed in general average.

[27] See particularly paras C.36-C.40, above for the scope of this exclusion.

Rule VI

Salvage Remuneration

English Law and Practice

The concept of rewarding those that save life and property at sea goes back to ancient history and was described in more modern times as the "clearest general right" **6.01**

In the days of sailing ships, salvage was usually on a small scale. For example, people in small boats might put out from the shore to a wreck to rescue the sailors and the cargo that floated out of the wreck. The scope for refloating a grounded ship or extinguishing a fire was very limited, because the equipment and techniques available to salvors were not very sophisticated. With the development of steamships and motor ships and more especially of tugs, salvage became a specialist business in its own right. One result of this is that modern salvage services, especially in serious and difficult situations, are usually given by highly qualified professional salvors who have at their disposal purpose-built salvage tugs and other special salvage equipment, and the operations are managed by salvage masters of great experience and technical skill.

In 1898 the English Admiralty Court, in the classic case of the "Glengyle",[1] summarised the principle of public policy that the salvor and in particular the professional salvor ought to be encouraged by generous awards to maintain tugs and other salvage equipment in constant readiness. The judge in that case put it this way:

> "The maintenance of salvage steamers . . . is for the general benefit of owners and underwriters and others interested in seagoing vessels and their cargoes and the crews and passengers of those vessels and . . . the Admiralty Court will be liberal in its awards in respect of services rendered by salvage steamers even though the awards may fall somewhat heavily on individual owners. The owners of salvage steamers invest a large amount of capital in them and maintain them and their crews divers and

[1] *Glengyle* [1898] A.C. 519; 67 L.J.P. 87, P. 97, 102. This approach was endorsed by the Court of Appeal.

> appliances and have no remuneration to look forward to except that which may be earned by occasional salvage services."

To give rise to an entitlement to a salvage award the following factors must all be present:

- There must be a recognised subject of salvage, i.e. a ship and or its cargo.
- There must be a degree of danger that the property is exposed to.
- The services must be rendered by "volunteers", e.g. parties not already bound to offer the services by contract.
- There must be at least some degree of success by which the salved property has benefited.

Prior to the International Convention on Salvage 1989 the Master's authority to bind cargo interests to a salvage contract rested under English law on the doctrine of the Master being an "agent of necessity" rather than on any implied term. To create an agency of necessity there had to be circumstances in which the Master was obliged to act without first communicating with cargo interests.[2]

The 1989 Convention, (enacted as a schedule to the Merchant Shipping Act 1995) provided under art.6.2 that:

> "The master shall have the authority to conclude contracts for salvage operations on behalf of the owner of the vessel. The master or the owner of the vessel shall have the authority to conclude such contracts on behalf of the owner of the property on board the vessel."

The law of salvage is complex and reference to books such as *Kennedy & Rose: Law of Salvage* is recommended for a more detailed analysis.

6.02 The word "salvage" is used in many different ways including:

(i) the act performed when rescuing a vessel in distress;
(ii) the payment due for performing (i);
(iii) the residual value of badly damaged goods.

In addition, efforts to rescue maritime property from peril are categorised under separate headings which need to be distinguished, although they share the same broad objective.

English law, as codified by the Marine Insurance Act 1906, will classify the cost of the rescue operations under one of the following three headings:

- Sue and labour (or particular) charges—s.78;
- General average—s.66;
- Salvage charges—s.65,

[2] *The Choko Star* [1990] 1 Lloyd's Rep. 516 (CA).

depending on the circumstances in which the services were performed, by whom, the nature of their employment, and the rights of the various parties against each other, etc.

"Sue and labour" charges is a term peculiar to marine insurance, and means expenses incurred by the assured or his "factors, servants or assigns", exclusively for the purpose of saving his own property from loss by a peril insured against; where several interests are imperilled and the expense is incurred for the common benefit, such expenses cannot be sue and labour charges.

"General average", as will be appreciated already from the commentary on r.A, relates to the saving conjointly of the property involved in a common maritime adventure by the parties to the adventure, and for the purposes of English law a general average act is deemed by s.66(2) of the Marine Insurance Act 1906, to include:

> "... any extraordinary ... expenditure ... voluntarily and reasonably ... incurred in time of peril for the purpose of preserving the property imperilled in the common adventure."

"Salvage charges" are defined by s.65(2) of the same Act as meaning:

> "... the charges recoverable under maritime law by a salvor independently of contract. They do not include the expenses of services in the nature of salvage rendered by the assured or his agents, or any person employed for hire by them..."

Under the terms of the 1989 Salvage Convention an award for salvage (made **6.03**
under Art.13) is payable by "all of the vessel and other property interests in proportion to their respective salved values". The Convention applies (Art.6) to "any salvage operations save to the extent that a contract otherwise provides expressly or by implication".

Some contracts, such as Lloyd's Open Form 2011, preserve the position whereby the master or owner signs on behalf of all the property at risk which remains separately liable to the salvor to pay their proportion of the award, which is in keeping with the English law position reflected in The Raisby discussed in para.6.05 below.

Other contracts, which may still be referred to loosely as salvage contracts, will provide that the shipowner is solely responsible to pay the contractor, whether the contract is on a "no cure-no pay" basis or provides for a daily rate or lump sum payment.

The salvor's right to an award is established by bringing the property to a place **6.04**
of safety. Once there:

- the salvor is entitled (under the 1989 Salvage Convention and in most jurisdictions where the Convention does not apply) to exercise a maritime lien on the property;
- the values to be used in any salvage arbitration are crystallised and the entitlement to or amount of a salvage award will not be affected by any partial or total loss suffered by the property later in the voyage.

This is in contrast to the general average position in which the possessory lien for contribution can only be exercised at destination and the contributory values are those existing on completion of discharge. Where a serious casualty involves both a claim by salvors and other general average loss or expenditure it may thus be necessary to delay ship and cargo at the port of refuge while salvage security is provided and to delay cargo at the port of destination until general average security is forthcoming. In practice the main inconvenience is felt in any delay at the port of refuge, which is particularly likely to arise when a large number of cargo interests are involved. If the amounts involved are relatively modest the shipowner may provide salvage security on behalf of cargo and recover the subsequent payment made as general average, on the basis of general average security collected at destination. In larger cases the shipowner may provide only interim security to the salvor (generally using the International Salvage Union's standard form ISU2) which undertakes to hold cargo at destination until satisfactory security is provided to salvors.

Earlier Practice of Adjusters

6.05 The law and practice prevailing generally in maritime nations was to treat salvage as general average but this approach was questioned and later strongly resisted by British adjusters and legal commentators during the nineteenth century. Lowndes wrote in 1873 that:

> "As jettison is regarded as the type or simplest form of general average sacrifice, so salvage, it has been said, may be regarded as the type of a general average expenditure. This, however, is only from one point of view. Salvage is always an extraordinary expense, and is always incurred in order to rescue the thing salved from danger: in these respects it is the perfect form of general average expenditure; but it is not always incurred for the common safety of ship and cargo. Whenever it is so, it is general average."

However, it is likely that by this time some British adjusters were beginning to follow a different practice and were drawing a firm distinction between salvage and general average. The basis of this divergence is given more fully in previous editions but it rested on the fact that salvage created an independent and separate liability upon all the parties, such that it could not be regarded as something undertaken by one party for the common interest. An eminent authority in London, Manley Hopkins, wrote in his *Handbook of Average* (1868), p.63:

> "When salvage services to a ship and cargo are paid for in one sum, in accordance with a previous agreement or a subsequent compromise, by an award of referees . . . or by the decision of the Admiralty Court, that amount is frequently allowed to form an item of the general average contribution, and is divided on the same values as the other common expenses. But if special valuations of ship, goods, and freight were made by or for the arbitrators . . . it is the better plan to adhere to those valuations in dividing the salvage."

The strands of the law on salvage became yet more clearly defined following the decision in 1885 in *The Raisby*[3] in which it was held that a salvor was not entitled to sue the shipowner for cargo's proportion of a salvage award given by an arbitrator, to which cargo had failed to respond. From that date until about 1927 it is reasonably certain that British adjusters, in contrast with those in most other countries, drew a clear distinction between salvage and general average and treated them separately. Salvage was apportioned over the values at the place where the salvage services terminated, as adopted at the salvage proceedings, and the proportion of salvage attributable to each interest simply formed a deduction to be applied in arriving at the contributory value of that interest for apportioning the general average proper.

This distinction became a little costly, however, following the introduction in the York-Antwerp Rules 1924 of an allowance of two per cent commission and five per cent interest on disbursements which were allowed as general average. Adjustments prepared in the United States or on the European Continent would show an allowance for commission and interest on salvage awards, but not so in Britain. To remedy this apparent anomaly, in 1926 a Special Committee of the Association of Average Adjusters was formed, including representatives of underwriters and shipowners. They recommended a rule of practice stating: **6.06**

> "That in the application of Rules XXI and XXII of York-Antwerp Rules, 1924, no distinction shall be drawn in practice between General Average Expenses and Expenses for Salvage Services rendered by Agreement . . ."

and this was passed unanimously in 1927 and confirmed in 1928 without discussion.

The purpose of the rule was clearly to ensure that commission and interest should be allowable on salvage awards in general, but it did not direct that salvage should be charged to general average and re-apportioned over the general average contributory values.

Thus, for the next 15 years there was a "multiformity" of practice among British adjusters; some treated salvage as general average, while others continued to keep it quite separate, but nevertheless allowed commission and interest thereon.

This situation was remedied in 1942 and 1943 by rescinding the old Rule of Practice and adopting a new one stating that: "Expenses for salvage services rendered by or accepted under Agreement shall in practice be treated as General Average".

With the introduction of the new Rule of Practice clause in 1942–1943, uniformity of practice among British adjusters was achieved, and, moreover, they were in line with the rest of the world. At the same time, it must be pointed out that the British Rules of Practice are not mandatory or binding on members, and it was always open for any adjuster to depart from the provisions of the rule in appropriate circumstances, and some invariably did so in those cases where ship and cargo negotiated separate and differential salvage awards.

[3] *Cardiff S.S. Co v Barwick* (1885) 54 L.J. 65; 53 L.T. 56; 5 Asp. M.C. 473.

Historical Development and Practice of Rule VI

6.07 As noted above, in all maritime countries other than the United Kingdom, salvage (at any rate under contract) was invariably treated as general average and, apportioned over the values which arrived at destination. In this country, however, it was possible to draw a number of legal distinctions[4] between general average and salvage and the practice of British adjusters was not uniform.[5]

The first attempt to introduce a rule dealing with salvage into the York-Antwerp Rules was at the Conference in Liverpool for the 1890 Rules, when the British Association of Average Adjusters proposed a rule:

> "Payment for salvage services rendered to a stranded or otherwise disabled ship shall be dealt with as general average; except that payment for salvage services assessed by legal process on specific values shall be charged directly to the interests specified."

The proposal was withdrawn, however, following strong criticism from T.G. Carver and Charles McArthur.

York-Antwerp Rules 1974

6.08 To overcome these difficulties, and to ensure greater international uniformity, the following provision was introduced in 1974 as r.VI[6]:

> "Expenditure incurred by the parties to the adventure on account of salvage, whether under contract or otherwise, shall be allowed in general average to the extent that the salvage operations were undertaken for the purpose of preserving from peril the property involved in the common maritime adventure."

This provision made it clear that under the York-Antwerp Rules there was to be no distinction in principle between salvage, whether performed under a contract or not, and general average. However, salvage expenditure was only allowable to the extent that the salvage operations were undertaken for the purpose of preserving from peril the property involved in the common maritime adventure. This limitation soon gave rise to problems when salvage awards began to reflect measures taken by the salvors to minimise pollution, in response to widespread international concern following a number of major casualties involving the spillage of oil from tankers.

[4] This subject is discussed in paras 6.04–6.06, above. See also the address of the Chairman of the Association of Average Adjusters, 1973, pp.28–29, and 1988, pp.10–17.

[5] See paras 6.04–6.06, above.

[6] Rule VI in previous editions of the York-Antwerp Rules had dealt with an entirely different subject—Carrying Press of Sail—but this was considered obsolete in 1974 and abolished. The various texts of the old r.VI from 1864 to 1950 are set out in Appendix 2A, below.

Salvage awards enhanced by the avoidance of pollution

Lloyd's Standard Form of Salvage Agreement 1980 (LOF 1980). Lloyd's Standard Form of Salvage Agreement 1980 stated that the salvor agreed to use his best endeavours to prevent the escape of oil from the vessel while performing a salvage operation and, in their assessment of any salvage award, Lloyd's Arbitrators would take into account this additional obligation on the part of salvors and their skill and efforts in complying with it. 6.09

This element of enhancement was quite clearly outside the scope of the words in r.VI and should in theory have been excluded from general average and have fallen on the shipowner alone and his liability insurers. However, it was not anticipated that arbitrators would specify in their awards the extent of any enhancement so that, as with life salvage (see para.6.27), the enhanced award would be payable by property interests. Before the issue of LOF 1980, London market insurers and the International Group of P&I Associations had issued a joint statement (or "Funding Agreement") in the following terms:

> "In order that the revision of Lloyd's Open Form can proceed as quickly as possible, the International Group of P&I Clubs for their part and The Institute of London Underwriters and Lloyd's Underwriters Association for their part confirm the following:
>
> . . . (2) The Underwriters will continue to accept that Salvage Awards are recoverable by ship, cargo and freight under the existing forms of policies for those interests, notwithstanding that such Awards may have been enhanced to take account of measures taken to prevent the escape of oil from the ship."

The decisions of these leading sections of the international insurance market are widely followed in other parts of the world and it was sensible that average adjusters should give effect to them in their general average adjustments. It was always open to any uninsured cargo interest to dispute his liability for the element of enhancement in any salvage award, although Lloyd's arbitrators do not specify in their awards the extent of any enhancement, and would be extremely reluctant to do so.

A second innovation introduced by LOF 1980[7] was that when the vessel to which salvage services were rendered was a tanker wholly or partly laden with oil, and the salvage was wholly or partly unsuccessful, or could not be completed, for reasons occurring without the fault of the salvor, the salvor was entitled to be awarded his expenses, plus a discretionary increment of up to 15 per cent, to the extent that the sum in question exceeded the amount recoverable under the ordinary salvage award. The shipowner alone or, in practice, his P&I Club, was liable to the salvor for any sums awarded under this special provision.

Salvage cases involving containers and their contents which may involve numerous interests of low value have caused considerable problems in LOF cases for a number of years. The expense of collecting security and establishing contributory values has often proved prohibitive. Salvors and their solicitors have 6.10

[7] Cl.1(c).

frequently relied on adjusters to assist in these tasks. The not dissimilar problems, in the context of general average, of assessing contributory values and collecting security are discussed elsewhere in this Work.[8] As a matter of practice an adjuster would leave out of account such low value cargo in the interests of economy. However, if such interests were found to have a contributory value in the salvage arbitration, this was not possible and made it less easy to make savings.

However, there developed a practice in LOF arbitrations, to save expense in a case where the salvors' claim had been settled with represented interests but remained on foot against unrepresented interests, of permitting the salvors to adduce evidence of the settlement figure and put that before the arbitrator.[9] This practice was usually restricted to cases where the unrepresented interests were 10% or less of the salved fund and would not apply to any unrepresented interest which objected to the settlement figure upon being given notice of the intention to proceed to arbitration. This practice did not deal in any way with the issue of low contributory values.

In LOF 2011 there are two provisions designed to save time and expense. The first represents an extension of the existing practice and the second tackles the question of low contributory values. These clauses provide:

> Clause 14, "Subject to the express approval of the Arbitrator, where an agreement is reached between the Contractors and the owners of salved cargo comprising at least 75% by value of salved cargo represented in accordance with Clause 7 of these Rules, the same agreement shall be binding on the owners of all salved cargo who were not represented at the time of the said approval."
>
> Clause 15, "Subject to the express approval of the Arbitrator, any salved cargo with a value below an agreed figure may be omitted from the salved fund and excused from liability for salvage where the cost of including such cargo in the process is likely to be disproportionate to its liability for salvage."

The clauses are self-explanatory. Both are subject to the express approval of the arbitrator for their operation in particular cases. Objection to the settlement figure by an unrepresented interest in what would otherwise be a case for the application of cl.14 would be likely to cause an arbitrator to decline to approve the settlement. In such a case an application should be made under cl.15 to have the objecting interest left out of account if the value is sufficiently low. The application of cl.15 is likely to make the adjuster's task easier and bring about savings there.

6.11 The International Salvage Convention 1989. This Convention adopts and in many respects extends both of the above anti-pollution elements of the 1980 Lloyd's Open Form. First, under art.13, para.l(b) of the Convention it is expressly provided that the skill and efforts of the salvors in preventing or minimising damage to the environment[10] shall be taken into account in fixing the amount of the award. Secondly, art.14 of the Convention provides for special compensation to be payable by the shipowner to the salvor if the vessel or its cargo threatened

[8] See paras 17.01 et seq., and 30.01 et seq.

[9] See Brice on *Martie Law of Salvage*, 5th edn, para.8–142

[10] "Damage to the environment" is defined in Annex 1(d) of the Convention: see para.C.38, above.

damage to the environment and the amount of the salvor's remuneration under art.13 is not at least equal to the amount of special compensation. The basic amount of special compensation is equal to the expenses incurred by the salvor but, if the salvage operations have actually prevented or minimised damage to the environment, a discretionary increment of up to 30 per cent, or in exceptional cases up to 100 per cent, may be awarded to the salvor.

The Salvage Convention did not acquire the force of law in England until 1995, but many of its important features were incorporated into Lloyd's Open Form 1990 and thus applied by contract to many salvages.

York-Antwerp Rules 1974 as amended 1990

In order to deal with the problems caused by the 1989 Salvage Convention the rule was expanded, following a special conference of the Comité Maritime International held in Paris in June 1990, by the addition of two new paragraphs, the first of which allowed in general average the element of enhancement of the award for the salvor's efforts in avoiding or minimising damage to the environment, and the second of which excluded from general average any special compensation payable under Art.14 of the 1989 Convention, or under any similar provision. In addition, some changes in wording were made to the first paragraph of the 1974 rule, as follows: **6.12**

(1) on account of salvage was replaced by in the nature of salvage:
(2) to the extent that was replaced by provided that;
(3) undertaken was replaced by carried out.

The main purpose of these changes was to reflect the fact that the allowance of the element of enhancement of the award under art.13, para.l(b) of the Convention was inconsistent with the 1974 version of r.VI.[11] The effect of the new phraseology is considered in more detail below.

York-Antwerp Rules 1994

No changes were made on this occasion to the wording adopted in 1990, but a number were suggested. Of these the subject of differential settlements and costs, and whether they should be brought into the general apportionment,[12] was the most important. There was a gulf which remains difficult to bridge between those who feel that material inequity is worked by r.VI when it obliges otherwise advantageous individual settlements to be "cast into the general average pot", and those who regard it as an imperfect but nevertheless practical tool to give effect to the community of interest that underlies the notion of general average. **6.13**

[11] See para.6.08, above.
[12] This subject is discussed at para.6.19, below.

RULE VI

SALVAGE REMUNERATION

(a) Expenditure incurred by the parties to the adventure in the nature of salvage, whether under contract or otherwise, shall be allowed in general average provided that the salvage operations were carried out for the purpose of preserving from peril the property involved in the common maritime adventure.

Expenditure allowed in general average shall include any salvage remuneration in which the skill and efforts of the salvors in preventing or minimising damage to the environment such as is referred to in Article 13 paragraph l(b) of the International Convention on Salvage, 1989 have been taken into account.

(b) Special compensation payable to a salvor by the shipowner under Article 14 of the said Convention to the extent specified in paragraph 4 of that Article or under any other provision similar in substance shall not be allowed in general average.

CONSTRUCTION

Rule VI(a), First Paragraph

6.14 **"Expenditure . . . in the nature of salvage"**: The change in wording from the 1974 rule (expenditure on account of salvage) is probably superfluous since the words which follow[13] make it clear that the rule is not confined to salvage charges in the strict sense.[14] However the new wording is more accurate, certainly so far as English law is concerned.

Since the new wording lacks the rather expansive phrase of the 1974 Rule, on account of salvage, it can be said that it applies only to expenditure on services which are themselves in the nature of salvage, or strictly incidental thereto, and does not apply to all consequential expenses, such as legal costs in attempting to resist or reduce a salvage claim.[15]

"by the parties to the adventure": When, as sometimes occurs, the insurers of ship or cargo organise and make all arrangements for salvage and pay all or part of a salvage award direct to the salvors, the amount of that payment is

[13] i.e. the phrase "whether under contract or otherwise": see paras 6.14–6.15, below.

[14] For the English definition of "salvage charges", see para.6.03, above. The Marine Insurance Act 1906 draws a clear distinction between "salvage charges" and "charges in the nature of salvage", incurred by the assured under contract (s.65(2)). Rule VI is clearly intended to apply to all such charges.

[15] However, such expenses are recoverable under r.C as a direct consequence of the general average act of engaging salvors, see para.C.35 above and *Australian Coastal Shipping Commission v Green* [1971] 1 Lloyd's Rep. 16.

nevertheless treated as general average, even though insurers can hardly be termed "parties to the adventure".

"salvage, whether under contract": The original text put forward for discussion at the Hamburg Conference in 1974 was "salvage, whether under maritime law or under contract". At the last moment difficulty arose over the French text since there is no equivalent in French jurisprudence for the expression "maritime law", whilst the word "loi" on its own offended those who favour accurate translation. This apart, there is no problem in comprehending the English words "salvage under contract", which comprise all contracts of any classification, whether they be strictly for salvage charges, or merely for services in the nature of salvage, both as detailed in s.65(2) of the Marine Insurance Act 1906, and discussed earlier in paras 6.02 to 6.03, above.

"... or otherwise": These words comprise all those awards of salvage made under maritime law where no contract has been entered into with the salvors, for example because the ship has already been abandoned by her entire crew. Prior to the introduction of r.VI in 1974, the award for salvage services in such circumstances would not have been treated as general average in the United Kingdom or the United States, at least, on the grounds that the services would have been rendered on a pure volunteer basis and with the representatives of the ship and cargo not being in any position to make an "intentional" sacrifice or expenditure within the terms of r.A. **6.15**

The position is now changed and, by the express terms of r.VI, the absence of an actual contract for salvage services does not affect the issue and any award is to be treated as general average and apportioned over the values at final destination rather than those at the time and place where the salvage services terminated. Commission and interest under rr.XX and XXI are also allowable when the salvage is treated as general average.

An exception to this provision might occur in those rare cases where the ship and her cargo are a true "derelict", that is, abandoned by the crew and by the owners of the property, without hope on their part of recovering it and without intention of returning to it. The "common maritime adventure" might then be said to be at an end, in which case any salvage award would probably be treated as a particular charge on the property salved.

"shall be allowed in general average": In addition to the proviso (dealt with below in para.6.21) any expenditure in the nature of salvage must also satisfy the overriding requirements of Rule Paramount and be reasonably incurred if it is to be allowable as General Average. Although a case dealing with cargo's liability to pay under a Lloyd's Open Form award, the *Pa Mar*[16] illustrates the approach that a court might adopt. A vessel on a loaded voyage from the Black Sea to China became immobilised in the Red Sea due to multiple generator failures. An LOF was agreed and the vessel was towed first to Aden, thence to Colombo and Singapore. Salvors claimed that the whole towage was rendered pursuant to the LOF and an award was given; on appeal the appeal arbitrator treated the services under LOF as terminating at Colombo. Mr Justice Clarke agreed that it was **6.16**

[16] *The Pa Mar* [1999] 1 Lloyd's Rep. 338.

reasonable to have taken salvage services on LOF terms, applying the tests for agency of necessity as given by Lord Justice Slade in the Choko Star. The reasonable owner would have a full assessment of the damage at Aden, and he ruled that the cargo-owners were not bound by the amendment of the LOF to take the vessel to Colombo and beyond. Nonetheless, as with all situations under the Rule Paramount (or r.A) when the test of reasonableness is applied, the benefit of the doubt should be given to the party in the difficult position of making the decision at a time of emergency.

The values over which salvage expenses allowable as general average under the terms of this rule will be apportioned are the net arrived values of the property at destination in accordance with r.XVII and, to the extent that these values differ from the values at the termination of the salvage services, the salved values assessed by the court or by an arbitrator will be ignored.

Expenses saved to be credited

6.17 The salvage expenses allowable as general average under the terms of this rule are, in practice, the net expenses after crediting any voyage expenses saved under the contract of carriage by reason of the salvage services.

Thus, where a vessel is towed to (or towards) her destination, it will usually be found that the shipowner (or time-charterer) has been saved the cost of bunkers that would normally have been consumed on the main engine, and credit for this must clearly be given against the cost of the towage itself.

Although there is no express provision in the rule to this effect, it is one of the fundamental principles of the equitable system of general average that none of the parties to the adventure ought to make a "profit" from the general average act, and it is to be noted that the United States Association of Average Adjusters has a Rule of Practice (No.V) on this subject adopted in 1902:

> "Where salvage services are rendered to a vessel, or she becomes disabled and is necessarily towed to her port of destination, and the expenses of such towage are allowable in general average, there shall be credited against the allowance such ordinary expenses as would have been incurred, but have been saved by the salvage or towage services."

Commenting on this Rule of Practice in his admirable textbook Marine Insurance & General Average in the United States, the late Leslie J. Buglass states:

> "However, in applying this rule it is the practice of average adjusters to offset the saving in voyage expenses (usually fuel and stores etc . . .) by the extra wages, etc., of the crew incurred as a result of the enhanced duration of the voyage due to the vessel being under tow."

This same practice was repeated here in para.6.16 of the 11th edition with tacit approval; but, it was suggested in the last edition that the practice is incorrect in principle when the additional delay results from accidental damage, because it makes an allowance for wages that would not be permitted by the terms of r.XI.

However, the practice would now appear to be universal and is based on the view of adjusters that it is part of a legitimate accounting exercise to find the net benefit to the shipowner. In 2002 the United States Association of Average Adjusters added an additional sentence to their Rule of Practice to reflect this, stating that in calculating the savings there shall be taken into consideration such factors as additional fuel, if any, and crew's wages for the longer time under tow, or similar expenses, to arrive at the net savings.

A similar need to credit savings can arise, for instance, where cargo is discharged during salvage operations and, for convenience or other reasons, it is on-carried by that other vessel to destination as part of the salvage services. On the authority of cases such as *Guthrie v Northern China Insurance Co Ltd*[17] and *The Winson*,[18] the cargo interests will receive their cargo free of any freight which might have been payable on delivery at destination by the original carrying vessel. The freight thus saved ought to be credited to the general average and debited to those cargo interests who escaped payment of the normal freight. **6.18**

Differential salvage awards, settlements and costs

It sometimes happens that ship and cargo interests will be separately represented at any salvage proceedings and that they will make separate settlements with the salvors whereby, for instance, the ship interests may pay a 5 per cent award and the cargo interests pay 6 per cent. The benefit or prejudice of these separate settlements will be lost to the individual parties as the aggregate of these payments for salvage must be charged to general average and re-apportioned on a pro-rata basis.[19] This view was adopted in the 10th edition of this work as the proper construction of the 1974 Rules, and was indorsed in 1983 by the Advisory Committee of the Association of Average Adjusters in its Report No.40. The Committee was: **6.19**

> "... unanimously of the opinion that Rule VI is mandatory as between the parties to a Contract of Affreightment providing for adjustment of General Average according to York-Antwerp Rules 1974. The Committee accordingly takes the view that subject to the overall requirement of reasonableness in the amounts claimed by parties to the adventure, differential expenditure, including costs, on account of the salvage should be allowed in General Average and apportioned as such."

It will be noted that the Committee's views include a reference to an overall requirement of reasonableness. Under the 1994 Rules, the Rule Paramount makes reasonableness an overriding requirement in any event, and the requirement therefore extends even to those expenditures which do fall within the express terms of r.VI, such as a settlement figure agreed with and paid to the salvors, or even to the salvage award itself, and to all the associated legal and other expenses that may be allowed under r.C. **6.20**

[17] Guthrie (1902) 7 Com. Cas. 130.

[18] *The Winson* [1982] 1 Lloyd's Rep. 117 at 123.

[19] American case law already provided for this method of adjustment: *The Jason* (1908) 162 Fed. Rep. 56; (1910) 175 Fed. Rep. 414.

Determining the reasonableness of conduct which has resulted in differential awards, settlements and costs may present the adjuster with considerable difficulty. The mere fact that one interest has settled at a slightly lower figure than another does not of itself lead to the conclusion that the latter has acted unreasonably, but where the discrepancies in the amounts paid or the costs incurred are very substantial the party putting forward the larger claim should be asked to justify the reasonableness of his conduct. Moreover, just as a settlement figure may be unreasonable, so in some circumstances may a refusal to settle. Thus a party who has had a large salvage award made against him when he ought reasonably to have settled the earlier claim, should not necessarily recover in full.

6.21 **"Provided that the salvage operations were carried out for the purpose of preserving from peril the property involved in the common maritime adventure"**: In broad terms r.VI provides that salvage awards and expenditure shall be treated as and allowed in general. This proviso makes it clear that the purpose of the operations should not merely be judged when they were first embarked upon, but kept under review as they proceed. If there comes a point at which it can properly be said that a separate stage of the operations, not falling within the subsequent words of the rule, is being carried out, the operations may no longer fall within r.VI. The following examples illustrate areas in which this proviso may be applicable:

6.22 **(a) The property involved in the common adventure must have been in peril.** This is an obvious requirement and in accordance with the general provisions of r.A. Examples of where a salvage contract was entered into where the property was not in any real peril, and perhaps merely to save delay, include:

- *Ballantyne v Mackinnon*,[20] where a schooner-rigged steamer ran out of fuel and was "salved" into her destination but, as the master stated in his official deposition: "There was no damage to our vessel, and we could have proceeded under sail. . .";
- *Trafalgar S.S. Co v British & Foreign Marine Insurance Co*[21] where a ship grounded in the River Plate and was in no danger, as any wind which might cause damage would previously have raised the water sufficiently to get her off the ground.

6.23 **(b) Salvage awards enhanced by the avoidance of pollution.** These problems are now dealt with specifically in the succeeding paragraphs of the 1994 rule.[22]

6.24 **(c) Services go beyond the extrication from peril of the salved property.** With the object of preserving the highest possible salved values and increasing the services and expense they can put before the arbitrator, it sometimes appears in practice that salvors are performing services which go beyond the mere extrication from peril of the salved property, after the property has been brought to safety in port and could be returned to its respective owners.

[20] *Ballantyne v Mackinnon* (1896) 65 L.J.Q.B. 616.
[21] *Trafalgar S.S. Shipping Gazette*, November 18, 1904.
[22] See paras 6.29 et seq., below.

Examples of these additional services include the following:

(1) The engine room of a loaded vessel is flooded by accident and she is immobilised and in some peril. Salvors may stop the leak, pump out the engine room, and tow the vessel to a safe berth-all proper salvage, to which ship and cargo should contribute. Salvors may now continue to perform the valuable service of de-watering and preserving all the flooded machinery.

(2) Cargo may similarly be reconditioned by salvors after damage by accident.

It is submitted that the words of r.VI(a) require it to be demonstrated, at each separate stage of such operations, that the operations were being carried out for the purpose of preserving from peril the property involved in the common adventure. Once this purpose has been achieved, it would seem that any further operations cannot fall within r.VI,[23] nor under the similar wording of r.A. However, difficult situations arise where different interests reach the point of safety at different times. For example, cargo may be removed and taken to safety before a grounded ship is refloated. Whether or not the cost of refloating the ship should be charged to general average will depend upon whether the removal of the cargo and the refloating can be regarded as a continuous salvage operation, a topic discussed in more detail under r.VIII.[24]

(d) Rescue from different risks. Occasionally ship and cargo are rescued from different risks, as distinct from different degrees of risk. Thus, a vessel which has sustained a machinery breakdown may need to engage the services of a single tug to tow her to a port of refuge for the common safety. If, however, she has on board a perishable cargo of fruit, the services of a second and even third tug may be engaged to expedite the voyage in order that the cargo does not perish before arrival. In these circumstances, should the cost of all the tugs be allowed in general average, or should the cost of the second and third tugs be charged to cargo and freight alone? **6.25**

There is a decision of the Admiralty Court[25] to the effect that in such circumstances a salvage award may depart from the normal principle of rateable contribution in proportion to salved values, although the decision has been widely criticised and is seldom followed.[26] The wording of r.VI seems to require that, in

[23] See para.6.12, above.

[24] See paras 8.04–8.16, below.

[25] *The Velox* [1906] P. 263, where a disabled ship with a cargo of fresh fish was towed to her destination, by a single salving vessel, and non-proportionate awards were made against ship and cargo.

[26] On the grounds that the approach which it adopts is contrary to established practice, and impossible to apply fairly or consistently: see The M. Vatan [1990] 1 Lloyd's Rep. 336; Kennedy, *Law of Salvage*, paras 1192–1195; Brice, *Maritime Law of Salvage*, paras 4.28–4.30. The criticisms appear soundly based. The distinction sometimes drawn between the situation where the salved interests are exposed to different degrees of risk (where it is never suggested that the ordinary rule of rateable contribution should be departed from) and the situation where they are exposed to different kinds of risk is artificial. The expense attributable to the predicament of one particular interest will frequently be very difficult to identify, and even in a case as apparently clear-cut as the example given above it cannot be said that the shipowner derives no benefit from the second and third tugs. The

the example given, the cost of all three tugs must be allowed in general average. So long as all of the interests remain imperilled, and the operations are carried out for the purpose of preserving them from peril, the cost of the operation falls within the rule, which provides no justification for adjustment based on differing kinds of degrees of risk, or expenditure. One possible way of avoiding this conclusion, on the facts of our example, would be to say that the second and third tugs were engaged on a separate operation, to which r.VI did not apply at all, but apart from its artificiality[27] this approach still faces the difficulty that the second and third tugs are in fact salving the ship as well as the cargo, whether or not they would have been engaged if the cargo were not perishable.

6.26 The situation is rather different when ship and cargo have become separated when the salvage operations in question are performed. Here, the operations carried out on each interest will usually be truly separate, rather than a single operation performed for the general benefit. Thus, a vessel carrying a timber cargo partly on deck may develop a severe list whereby the deck lashings are broken and part of the deck cargo lost overboard. Salvage services rendered to the ship and her remaining cargo will obviously be treated as general average, but payments made for recovering timber washed ashore or collected by local fishing vessels or other craft should be borne exclusively by the particular cargo rescued.

This situation must be distinguished from:

(1) the case where the cargo, instead of being washed overboard accidentally, is jettisoned for the common safety: here one would allow as general average the full value of the cargo jettisoned, less its recovered value after deducting any salvage expenditure thereon;

(2) those cases, discussed in the commentary on r.VIII where the cargo is intentionally discharged from the ship, as part of a complex salvage operation, to enable the ship to be salved and the voyage to be prosecuted.

6.27 **(e) Life salvage.** Apart from statute, the saving of life at sea attracts no right to salvage unless associated with the saving of property. However, where salvors succeed in saving both life and property, the amount awarded to them for the salving of the property is traditionally increased to take into account their skills and efforts in saving life.[28] It is not the practice of salvage arbitrators in this country to quantify the increase in the amount of the award attributable to the saving of life, and the full amount of the award is payable rateably by the salved property interests, in the usual way. Similarly, where the salvage expenditure falls to be treated as general average (as under r.VI) the practice is that the entire amount of the salvage award is included in the general average, without reduction to reflect

duration and risk of the towage is reduced, as will be the cost of the first tug; the ship will be repaired sooner and able to earn freight; and the cargo will doubtless arrive with a greater value on which to contribute.

[27] If, instead of three tugs, one very powerful (and more expensive) tug were engaged, the argument that part of the expense of towage was the expense of a separate operation could not even be contemplated.

[28] This practice is confirmed in numerous decisions, see, e.g. *The Fusilier* (1865) 3 Moo. P.C. (N.S.) 51. It is also embodied in the International Convention on Salvage 1989 art.13, para.1(e).

the fact that the award in part remunerates the salvors for operations other than the preservation from peril of the property involved in the common adventure.

The Merchant Shipping Act 1894 imposed a statutory liability to pay salvage remuneration for the saving of life alone.[29] This liability, which was imposed on the owners of the ship, her cargo and apparel was, like other salvage remuneration, payable rateably by these interests in proportion to the value of the property which survived.[30] However, whilst liability for salvage under the Act could not exceed the value of the property which survived,[31] the purpose of the award was solely to remunerate the salvors for their efforts in saving life; it was unnecessary that the property should have survived by the efforts of the life salvors, or even that the life salvors should have made any efforts to salve the property.[32] For this reason salvage payable under the Act is not admissible in general average.[33]

Rule VI(a), Second Paragraph

"damage to the environment": This phrase is probably intended to bear the same meaning as under the 1989 Salvage Convention, where it is so defined as to exclude any case where the only risk is of deep-sea pollution which does not affect coastal or inland waters.[34] The same definition was imported into the 1990 and 1995 Lloyd's Open Forms. For this reason, when the vessel to be salvaged is a tanker laden with oil which is not in coastal waters, salvors occasionally insisted on being engaged under LOF 1980[35] rather than LOF 1990 or 1995, with the effect considered in the next paragraph. **6.28**

"such as is referred to in Article 13 paragraph l(b) of the International Convention on Salvage, 1989": The provisions of that Article relating to enhanced awards for preventing or minimising damage to the environment have already been explained in outline. The Convention was incorporated into the 1990 and 1995 versions of Lloyd's Open Form, with the result that Art.13, para.l(b) applied to any salvage performed on those terms. Moreover, by virtue of s.224 of the Merchant Shipping Act 1995, the Convention had the force of law in the United Kingdom and governed salvage operations commenced after January 1, 1995 and is therefore applicable to the 2011 Lloyd's Open Form. A Funding Agreement made in January 1991 between the International Group of P&I Clubs and London Market Insurers provided that the insurers would pay any award under LOF 1990, even though the award might be enhanced by the salvor's efforts in avoiding or minimising damage to the environment.[36] **6.29**

[29] Merchant Shipping Act 1894 s.544, repealed by the Merchant Shipping (Salvage and Pollution) Act 1994. See also art.16 of the 1989 Salvage Convention.

[30] *The Fusilier* (1865) 3 Moo. P.C. (N.S.) 51 at 55.

[31] Where the value of the property is insufficient there was a discretion to award payment out of the Merchant Marine Fund.

[32] *The Cairo* (1874) L.R. 4 A. & E. 184.

[33] Salvage payable by virtue of a similar statute in the US is treated as general average.

[34] See para.C.38, above.

[35] See para.6.09, above.

[36] The Agreement extends to the case where the contract of affreightment incorporates the York-Antwerp Rules 1974. For the purposes of the Agreement, references in the contract or the policy to the 1974 Rules take effect as if the reference were to the 1974 Rules as amended in 1990.

The only further point which need be made is that the phrase "such as is referred to in Article 13, paragraph l(b) of the International Convention on Salvage" indicates that an award may fall within r.VI(a) even if it is not actually made under the Convention itself, so long as the element of enhancement is made in respect of preventing or minimising damage to the environment falling within the scope of that phrase as defined in the Convention.[37]

Rule VI(b)

6.30 **"Special compensation ... under Article 14 of the said Convention"**: See para.6.10, above. The Funding Agreement referred to in the previous paragraph provides that the P&I. Clubs will take responsibility for Special Compensation awarded under Art.14.

"to the extent specified in paragraph 4 of that Article": The shipowner alone is liable for this special compensation, but art.14, para.4 stipulates that the special compensation is only payable to the extent that the amount so assessed exceeds the amount awarded under para.13. The purpose of the words under review is to make it clear that it is only this excess amount which is excluded from general average. All amounts payable under art.13 are included even though they may be enhanced by measures taken to avoid pollution.

"or under any provision similar in substance": In practice special compensation is often likely to be dealt with under the Special Compensation P&I Club Clause (SCOPIC). Article 14 provides compensation for the salvor at a "fair rate" and the meaning of this phrase became a matter of controversy in cases such as the "Nagasaki Spirit",[38] with decisions going to the Appeal Arbitrator and as far as the House of Lords. While the concept of special compensation was still welcomed by all parties, these disputes were proving to be very costly.

Discussions between the International Salvage Union and the International Group of P&I Clubs began in 1997. They were later joined by London property underwriters and, after 18 months' discussion, the SCOPIC Clause, together with its associated appendices, codes of practice and security form, was agreed.

The essential features of SCOPIC[39] have remained unchanged and the practical operation of the clause is as follows:

1. The SCOPIC clause incorporates the provisions of Art.14.
2. The salvor is contracted to assist on terms expressly incorporating the SCOPIC clause (such as LOF 2011).
3. The salvor has the option to "invoke" (i.e. to formally bring into effect) the SCOPIC clause. He will normally do this whenever he considers that

[37] See para.C.38, above.
[38] *Semco Salvage & Marine v Lancer Navigation* [1997] 1 Lloyd's Rep. 323.
[39] See Appendix 4, below, para.80.11.

the cost of the Salvage might exceed the likely Art.13 award. He may invoke SCOPIC from day one, or at any time after, but his SCOPIC remuneration will be calculated only from the time he invokes the clause.
4. The method, cost and progress of the salvage operation are monitored and reported to all the parties on a daily basis by the salvage master and by representatives of the salved property. The most important is the Shipowners' Casualty Representative (SCR). His duties and powers and the reporting procedures are all clearly set out in the clause.
5. The daily cost of the salvage operation is calculated according to a special tariff incorporated in the SCOPIC clause, and an uplift of 20 per cent is added. This total sum is called the SCOPIC remuneration.
6. The P&I Club puts up an immediate guarantee of US$3 million as security for SCOPIC remuneration. The amount may be increased or reduced as appropriate by agreement.
7. When the salvage is complete, the Art.13 salvage award is assessed in the usual way, by negotiation or arbitration, and is paid by the owners of salved property or their underwriters. If SCOPIC remuneration exceeds the Art.13 remuneration, then the amount of the excess is paid by the shipowners, who will normally be covered by their P&I insurance.
8. If the SCOPIC remuneration is less than the Art.13 award, then the award is reduced by 25 per cent of the difference.

Example 1

A vessel is aground and badly damaged so that the salvor considers the chances of success to be marginal and therefore invokes the SCOPIC clause. In the event the ship and cargo are salved but are badly damaged, reducing the salved fund. **6.31**

SCOPIC expenses are calculated, using the tariffs at:	US$1,000,000
Article 13 Award is given by the Arbitrator as:	750,000
SCOPIC remuneration equals:	US$1,250,00

The art.13 award is paid by the property insurers and the SCOPIC remuneration is paid by the P&I Club. If the ship and cargo had been a total loss the full SCOPIC remuneration would be payable by the Club.

Example 2

A similar situation to the above, but the salvage operation goes much better than expected after SCOPIC has been invoked, resulted in a larger salved fund and award. **6.32**

Article 13 Award	US$1,000,000
SCOPIC expenses	750,000
Difference	US$1,250,00

No SCOPIC remuneration is payable and the Art.13 amount payable by property insurers is reduced by the "penalty".

Article 13 Award	US$1,000,000
Less 25 per cent of difference (US$250,000)	62,500
Amount payable by property insurers	US$1,937,500

The penalty is intended to discourage salvors from invoking SCOPIC in cases were it is not warranted.

In both examples only the art.13 payments would be allowable as general average under the 1994 Rules.

York-Antwerp Rules 2004

6.33 Once the restriction of the "common benefit" allowances in the York-Antwerp Rules was no longer pursued, the main focus of the IUMI representations at CMI meetings prior to and at Vancouver was to restrict the circumstances in which salvage could be allowed as general average, reflecting the English law position as it had developed in the late ninteenth century.

6.34 The IUMI proposal was based on the view that the re-distribution of salvage was, in many circumstances, not necessary and gave rise to additional expense. The arguments for and against were set out as follows in the CMI Working Party Report that was distributed prior to the Vancouver conference:

"6.2.1 *Arguments* ***for exclusion*** *of salvage from General Average:*

- *Inclusion of salvage involves unnecessary duplication of the apportionment of the salvage remuneration between contributing interests.*
- *In most cases the proportions are not changed significantly but the cost of read-justment may be relatively high.*
- *It requires collection of two sets of security to cover basically the same moneys.*
- *It prolongs the whole operation, sometimes for years.*
- *It involves additional hassle for cargo underwriters.*

6.2.2 Arguments ***for inclusion*** *of salvage in General Average:*

- *It produces a fairer result at the end of the case.*
- *In some cases to leave salvage where it falls after salvage settlement or arbitra-tion can cause serious injustice; e.g. sacrifices made good in General Average are added back in computing the values under Rule G.*
- *A second casualty can also materially affect the values at the end of the adven-ture and thus the apportionment.*
- *In some cases the salvage remuneration can be assessed on the basis of rough figures, leaving the fine tuning of the apportionment to be done later in General Average. This can expedite salvage settlements and save costs.*
- *Some jurisdictions e.g. Netherlands contain laws, which require the shipowner to pay salvage in full and collect from cargo in General Average–this is recog-nised by the IUMI proposals.*
- *In many serious casualties General Average security will still be collected because the shipowner's likely financial exposure may not be fully known and the possible extent of cargo sacrifices cannot be determined without delaying the release of cargo.*

- *It redresses the balance if one party to the adventure is able to use commercial or other pressures to reach a particularly favourable negotiated settlement with salvors leaving other parties to pay the full cost at arbitration.*
- *Even if salvage is not allowed in General Average, it will still be treated as a special charge (which will be deducted in calculating contributory values) therefore the adjustment cannot be completed until the final amount of the salvage charges paid by each interest is available."*

The representatives of shipowning interests spoke against any change and it was narrowly rejected during the international sub-committee session at Vancouver. However, during the final plenary session the majority of delegates favoured the exclusion and the existing rule was replaced with the following: 6.35

RULE VI

SALVAGE REMUNERATION

"(a) Salvage payments, including interest thereon and legal fees associated with such payments, shall lie where they fall and shall not be allowed in General Average, save only that if one party to the salvage shall have paid all or any of the proportion of salvage (including interest and legal fees) due from another party (calculated on the basis of salved values and not General Average contributory values), the unpaid contribution to salvage due from that other party shall be credited in the adjustment to the party that has paid it, and debited to the party on whose behalf the payment was made.

(b) Salvage payments referred to in paragraph (a) above shall include any salvage remuneration in which the skill and efforts of the salvors in preventing or minimising damage to the environment such as is referred to in Article 13 paragraph 1(b) of the International Convention on Salvage 1989 have been taken into account.

(c) Special compensation payable to a salvor by the shipowner under Article 14 of the said Convention to the extent specified in paragraph 4 of that Article or under any other provision similar in substance (such as SCOPIC) shall not be allowed in General Average and shall not be considered a salvage payment as referred to in paragraph (a) of this Rule."

CONSTRUCTION

"Salvage payments": Following the publication of the 2004 Rules considerable concern was expressed regarding the lack of any definition of this term within the amended rule. In particular it was questioned whether the rule related only to salvage payments made in respect of "salvage charges" as defined by the Marine Insurance Act 1906 and under contracts such as Lloyd's Open Form (which impose a separate liability on each party) or whether it extended to contract salvage or similar services which were contracted for and funded initially by the shipowners. It was noted that historically r.VI had embraced both categories, referring (in 1994) to expenditure "in the nature of salvage". 6.36

Because of these concerns a small sub-committee was set up by the Association of Average Adjusters in November 2004 which reported in January of the following year. The sub-Committee concluded that the clause as drafted was indeed ambiguous, but noted that it had been in use in an IUMI G.A. Working Group Report in September 1999. From this and other IUMI and CMI preparatory papers it was clear that the intention was for the rule to relate only to situations where the salvage contract (or relevant law applicable in the absence of any contract) already provided for a basis of distribution between the salved interests.

Subsequent discussions with insurers confirmed this understanding and the following probationary Rule of Practice was put forward at the Association's Annual General Meeting in May 2005:

> "For the purpose of applying Rule VI of the York Antwerp Rules 2004 the term 'salvage payments' shall be interpreted to mean payments made in respect of salvage services and for which there is contractual and/or legal provision for apportionment and payment between the salved interests upon termination of the salvage services independent of the York Antwerp Rules 2004."

The proposal was seconded by the claims director of a leading insurance company.

"the unpaid contribution to salvage due from that other party shall be credited in the adjustment to the party that has paid it." Even if a salvage contract on LOF or similar terms provides for separate liability on the part of ship and cargo it sometimes happens that the shipowner will pay the salvor in full for reasons of commercial expediency or perhaps to avoid the delay that might occur in the voyage while cargo interests provide salvage security at a port of refuge. The shipowner then relies on general average security obtained at destination to recover the proportion attaching to cargo.

6.37 The extent to which salvage is re-admitted when paid by one party on behalf of others is on very limited terms. It is purely an accounting transaction, so that credit is given without the amount being considered as general average. No allowance for interest can therefore be made for the period that the paying party is out of pocket and, also taking into account the abolition of the 2 per cent allowance for commission, there is less incentive for shipowners to take the commercially practical route of settling cargo's proportion for modest salvage services in the first instance.

The Association of Average Adjusters of the United States approved a new Rule of Practice in October 2005 that deals with this last point.

> "XXII. Salvage Settlements under York Antwerp Rules 2004–Allowance for Interest
>
> (Adopted–October 5, 2005)
>
> When the adjustment is subject to the York Antwerp Rules 2004 and includes, applying the provisions of Rule VI (a) of those Rules, contributions to salvage paid by one party to the adventure on behalf of another party to the adventure as well as

> on its own behalf, the provisions of Rule XXI of the Rules will apply to the paying party's salvage payments, including interest thereon and legal fees associated with such payments, as if they were General Average expenditure."

The likely savings envisaged by IUMI may not in fact always be significant. **6.38**
With Lloyd's Open Form and similar cases, the amount of salvage paid will still have to be ascertained and deducted from contributory values as a special charge. It may also be necessary to calculate separate salved values in addition to the contributory values at destination, in order to make the accounting credit in the manner called for by the rule.

However, the exclusion of salvage from general average will in many cases extend the effectiveness of general average absorption clauses (under which the hull insurers pay general average in full up to a specified limit). Previously, in cases involving salvage, the absorption clause limit has often been exhausted by an actual payment for contract salvage or by the anticipated award under Lloyd's Open Form, necessitating the collection of general average security to recover other items of expenditure.

Paragraphs (b) and (c) of the rule serve the equivalent purpose of the second **6.39**
paragraph of r.VI(a) and r.VI(b) of the 1994 Rules, in excluding any form of special compensation from general average.

Rule VII

Damage to Machinery and Boilers

English Law and Background

When dealing with the conditions which needed to be present in order to constitute a general average act, whether under r.A or under English law, it was stated that the sacrifice or expenditure must be extraordinary in its nature. As a result of this requirement, damage to a ship caused by carrying press of sail while the ship was afloat was not allowed in general average.[1] A similar rule applies where a ship's engines are damaged by straining them in order to escape from a situation of danger; while the vessel remains afloat, cargo interests have a right to expect the full use of the vessel's engine to extricate herself from that danger without being called upon to contribute to any damage caused by straining the engine. **7.01**

Damage by Setting Sail to Force Ship off Ground

Although no allowance in general average was made in this country for damage caused by carrying a press of sail when the ship was afloat, the situation was different when the ship is aground and in a position of peril. The Customs of Lloyd's, as collected in 1874,[2] provided that: **7.02**

> "Sails damaged by being set, or kept set to force a ship off the ground, or to drive her higher up the ground for the common safety, are general average."

And Lowndes was of the view that this was correct in principle:

[1] See particularly para.A.60, above; also *Covington v Roberts* (1806) 2 Bos. & P.N.R. 378; *Power v Whitmore* (1815) 4 M. & S. 141. From 1860 to 1974, when it was deleted on the grounds of obsolescence, the York-Antwerp Rules had always included a rule denying any allowance in general average for damage to ship or cargo by carrying a press of sail when the vessel was afloat; see the various forms of the old r.VI, in Appendix 2, below.

[2] Now Rule of Practice F6, para.70.33, below.

> "When a ship is aground, for example, and at tide times sails are set on her in the hope of forcing her off the bank, by which means she is got afloat, but the sails are blown to pieces, this loss in practice is treated as general average. On account of the greater resistance offered by a ship that is aground, this may be considered as an abusing of the sails, or applying them to a purpose for which they were not intended."

Damage to Engines used to Refloat

7.03 When a vessel is aground in a position of peril and the engines are kept going in order to back her off or over the ground, the machinery may be strained, bearings overheat, or the propeller strike the ground and sustain damage, etc. Damage done in this manner is analogous to the loss of sails blown away when set in order to force a ship off the ground and is likewise treated as general average.

In *The Bona*,[3] the question arose whether the act of working a vessel's engines for the purpose of getting her off a strand, on which she was hard and fast, was a general average act. The consequent damage to the engines had been allowed in general average, under r.VII of the York-Antwerp Rules 1890, which formed part of the contract; and the actual question in the case was whether the coal consumed in working the engines should also be allowed. This was considered to depend upon whether the use of the engines was, at law, a general average sacrifice; if so, the coal formed part of the sacrifice. The Court of Appeal affirming Sir Francis Jeune P. held that it was. Lord Esher M.R. said the question depended on:

> "Whether the engines were used not only under unusual circumstances, but in an unusual and abnormal manner . . . The manoeuvre which this captain determined to follow, knowing that it was a dangerous manoeuvre to the property of his owners, was to use the engines so as to force the ship off the ground . . . That is not using the ship and her equipment in the ordinary way. It is putting them to an abnormal use intentionally, knowing the risk, for the purpose of saving the ship and cargo from the imminent danger in which they were."[4]

Historical Development and Practice of Rule VII

York-Antwerp Rules 1890

7.04 The British Association of Average Adjusters were largely responsible for drafting the proposed Rules put forward for discussion at the International

[3] *The Bona* [1895] P. 125; cf. *Trafalgar S.S. Co v British and Foreign Marine Insurance Co* (para.6.22, above): *The Mincio* (1936) A.M.C. 1765; *Willcox v American Smelting Co; The Trojan* (1913) 210 Fed. Rep. 89. In *Walford de Baerdemaecker v Galindez* (1897) 2 Com. Cas. 127, damage done to the boilers of a steamship through using cannel coal, which was part of the cargo, in an emergency, when the supply of bunker coal had been exhausted, was allowed in general average. Cf. also *Charter S.S. Co Ltd v Bowring Jones & Tidy Ltd* (1930) 36 Lloyd's Rep. 272. In this case trouble experienced with engines and boilers subsequent to a stranding, was claimed as general average arising through working engines to refloat and it was held that a small part of the damage to engines was so caused and therefore claimable, but that no part of the boiler trouble so arose.

[4] *The Bona* [1895] P. 125 at 138.

Conference at Liverpool in 1890, and, they having passed a domestic Rule of Practice on this very subject, and to similar effect, only a few months previously, it is not surprising that the following rule was introduced and agreed in 1890:

> *"Damage to Engines in Refloating A Ship*
>
> Damage caused to machinery and boilers of a ship which is ashore and in a position of peril, in endeavouring to refloat, shall be allowed in general average when shown to have arisen from an actual intention to float the ship for the common safety at the risk of such damage."

York-Antwerp Rules 1924

At the Stockholm Conference the Drafting Committee for the 1924 Rules suggested amending the 1890 rule to read: **7.05**

> *"Damage by Use of Machinery*
>
> Damage done to a ship or cargo and caused by the use for the common safely of the machinery and boilers of a ship which is ashore and in a position of peril shall be allowed in general average . . ."

The important difference between the suggested new wording and the wording of the 1890 rule was, of course, that the new wording would not have limited the damage to be made good in general average to that sustained only by the machinery and boilers, but would extend to any damage done to the ship and her cargo. It would have covered, for example, injury to the hull by excessive vibration of the engines,[5] or to the cargo by leakage of water through plates started by the same vibration. There is nothing objectionable in principle to such allowances, but in practice it can be difficult to distinguish between such damage caused by the stranding itself and that caused by the subsequent working of engines. For these practical reasons, and also the possibility that the proposed new rule would be construed to admit in general average the damage done to the bottom of a ship when being forced off the ground by the use of her engines, it was decided to retain the wording of the 1890 rule as the first part of the 1924 rule.

Some difference of opinion was revealed in the discussion on the last clause of the draft rule put forward:

> "but where a ship is afloat no loss or damage caused by working the machinery and boilers shall be made good as general average."

It was evidently the view of some of the delegates present that when damage was caused to a vessel's engines by being strained when in imminent danger of running

[5] cf. *Compania de Nav. Olazarri v Merchants Marine Insurance Co Ltd* Unreported, 1905, where damage to a ship through straining of the hull caused by the working of the engines in the endeavour to refloat her when stranded was held to be general average. Such damage is very rarely allowed in the US.

ashore, this should be treated as general average. In the end, however, the limitation imposed by the final clause in the draft rule was passed unanimously.

York-Antwerp Rules 1950

7.06 Although a second section, dealing with damage caused by working the machinery and boilers when afloat, was added to r.VII at the 1924 Conference at Stockholm, the original 1890 title ("Damage to Engines in Refloating a Ship") was retained unaltered, although it was not entirely apt to cover the new wording. The titles form part of the Rules, to which the parties have by contract agreed, and may therefore be used as an aid to interpreting what is stated in the Rules where the latter is ambiguous or unclear: but where the meaning of the Rules is clear, it cannot be altered by the title. Nevertheless, it was found in practice that in certain countries the title was being used to override the wording of the rule itself. It was contended, from the title, that the rule applied only to damage to engines in refloating, and that an allowance for damage to machinery and boilers while the vessel was afloat was not prohibited if the vessel had not been ashore. To avoid this form of interpretation, the title of r.VII was amended in 1950 to "Damage to Machinery and Boilers".

A further amendment in 1950 consisted of the addition of the following italicised words in the second part of the rule:

> "but where a ship is afloat no loss or damage caused by working the machinery and boilers, including loss or damage due to compounding of engines or such measures, shall in any circumstances be made good as general average."

These additional words were necessary because in the courts of Italy, at least, it had been held that "compounding of engines" (effectively, the cutting out of one of the cylinders, or altering a triple or quadruple expansion steam engine in such a way as to admit steam directly to some or all of the intermediate or low pressure cylinders instead of feeding it successively from one cylinder to another) was not working the engines:

> "Damage caused to machinery and boilers of a ship which is ashore and in a position of peril, in endeavouring to refloat, shall be allowed in general average when shown to have arisen from an actual intention to float the ship for the common safety at the risk of such damage; but where a ship is afloat no loss or damage caused by working the machinery and boilers, including loss or damage due to compounding of engines or such measures, shall in any circumstances be made good as general average."

York-Antwerp Rules 1974

7.07 Two alterations of some note were made in this rule in 1974:

(1) The words "including loss or damage due to compounding of engines or such measures" were deleted for the reasons that:

(a) Compounding can be done only on steam-engines, and they becoming obsolete, compounding of engines was of very infrequent occurrence.

(b) The French text of the 1950 rule ("y comprise la perte ou avarie due . . . un forcement de machines ou une mesure de ce genre") did not exactly correspond with the English text and needed harmonising if the provision were retained.

(2) Two changes were made affecting the machinery and boilers to which the rule applied:

(a) The word "any" was added in the positive part of the rule ("Damage caused to . . . machinery and boilers") to ensure that, for instance, damage to auxiliary machinery, boilers and pumps, etc. could be allowed under the rule.

(b) The word "propelling" was added in the second, negative, section of the rule ("no loss or damage caused by working the . . . machinery and boilers"), thereby confirming the expressed opinion of the Drafting Committee of the 1950 Rules[6] and enabling an allowance to be made in general average for loss or damage to auxiliary machinery, boilers and pumps etc. caused by a general average act when the vessel was afloat.

York-Antwerp Rules 1994

No change, but the correct, if unwelcome, decision on r.VII in The Alpha[7] prompted the United States Maritime Law Association to propose the highly important new Rule Paramount requiring sacrifices and expenditure to be reasonably made or incurred before any allowance in general average could be made under any of the York-Antwerp Rules. **7.08**

York-Antwerp Rules 2004

No change other than tidying up the drafting by the substitution of allowed as general average for made good as general average in the second part of the rule. **7.09**

[6] The Drafting Committee for the 1950 Rules reported: "In the discussions both in the International Commission and in the Drafting Committee consideration has been given to defining what is meant by 'machinery' and it has been found impossible to find any clear definition. The Drafting Committee therefore feels that it should state in its report that what is meant is the main engines and the propelling machinery of a vessel and not machinery such as pumps even though these form part of the main engines."

[7] *Corfu Navigation Co v Mobil Shipping Co Ltd* [1991] 2 Lloyd's Rep. 515. See para.PRE-21, above, for an account of this case.

RULE VII

DAMAGE TO MACHINERY AND BOILERS

Damage caused to any machinery and boilers of a ship which is ashore and in a position of peril, in endeavouring to refloat, shall be allowed in general average when shown to have arisen from an actual intention to float the ship for the common safety at the risk of such damage; but where a ship is afloat no loss or damage caused by working the propelling machinery and boilers shall in any circumstances be *made good/allowed* as general average.

CONSTRUCTION

7.10 **"Damage caused to any machinery and boilers"**: Although the wording of the first part of this rule is expressed in positive terms, the rule as a whole is effectively negative in character. Allowances which can be made in general average under this rule are strictly limited to the damage caused:

- *to* machinery and boilers;
- *by* working the propelling machinery and boilers,

in efforts to refloat a ship which is ashore and in a position of peril.

Other Loss or Damage during Efforts to Refloat

7.11 Any loss or damage other than to machinery or boilers caused by the efforts to refloat is recoverable, if at all, under the lettered r.A. Examples include:

(1) The extra bunkers and stores consumed whilst working the machinery in actual efforts to refloat (but not the normal consumption by auxiliary engines, etc. for supplying domestic light, heat and power whilst aground).[8]
(2) Damage to hull by excessive vibration of the engines.
(3) Damage to the bottom plating or rudder of the ship caused by forcing or hauling her off or over the ground or to the cargo by leakage of water resulting from the damage to the bottom.
(4) Damage caused in endeavouring to drive a ship higher up the ground, or to keep her on a rock.

The principles involved are admirably stated by a book published in the United States[9] :

[8] See *The Bona* [1895] P. 125); at para.7.03, above.
[9] E.W. Congdon, *General Average* (1913), pp.74–75.

"In respect of damages to the hull below the water line the legal presumption is, except in cases of voluntary stranding, that they were accidentally caused, and it is only upon evidence removing this presumption that consideration can be had as to whether they were sustained as a natural consequence of the measures taken to float the vessel.

The damage may not have been designed or foreseen by the master, but if it was a natural result of these measures it is regarded as an incident to them and, as such, partakes of their voluntary character, but a mere surmise or supposition that it was sustained in 'getting off' rather than in 'getting on' or by the accidental pounding of the vessel on the bottom while stranded, is insufficient to warrant allowance in general average.

A careful investigation of all the circumstances is necessary, the nature of the damage being usually determined from the evidence given by the master and by the opinion of disinterested experts."

Burden of Proof

Thus, there is no doubt in principle that damage caused to the bottom by efforts to refloat a vessel which is ashore and in a position of peril is properly allowable as general average. The real difficulty in practice is for the shipowner to demonstrate with some degree of certainty that not only did the damage occur during the refloating operations, but that it was actually caused by or the result of the particular method or means used to refloat, rather than just a natural consequence of the grounding itself; also that it would not have occurred even if no attempt to refloat had been made. Rule E[10] provides that the onus of proof is upon the party claiming in general average, and this onus is not necessarily discharged merely because some attending surveyor expresses the opinion in his report that such and such damage was attributable to efforts to refloat. In practice disputes can usually be avoided by the instruction of a surveyor to represent the general interest when the vessel is examined in drydock and, where practicable, inviting hull and cargo interests to survey the damage at the same time. 7.12

A US case where the shipowner was unable to discharge this burden of proof is *Sea-Land Services Inc v Aetna Insurance Co*[11] where the vessel grounded with her forefoot in the rubble of the breakwater when entering Rio Haina in very rough weather. A tug pulled for 10 minutes and the vessel was beginning to move when the towline broke, whereafter the wind and waves pushed the vessel to a slightly new position where she sustained considerable additional damage to the bottom. The shipowner maintained that the vessel's bow was so firmly embedded when she first ran aground that, but for the movement started by the tug when the towline broke, the vessel could not have swung into the new position.

As a matter of pure fact, the District Court Judge found (and the Court of Appeals confirmed by a majority) that it was more likely than not that the ship would have shifted by wind and current to roughly the new position regardless of whether the tow had been attempted, and the claim in general average for refloating damage was accordingly denied. As a matter of principle, the standard was "whether the towing materially increased the possibility of the shift from A to B".

[10] On the subject of bottom damage see para.E.08, above.

[11] *Sea-Land Services Inc v Aetna Insurance Co* (1976) A.M.C. 2164; [1977] 2 Lloyd's Rep. 84.

7.13 **"ashore"**: The word "stranded" appeared in the original draft for this rule prepared in 1890 by the Association of Average Adjusters, but because it had a well-defined and narrow meaning in this country, it was purposely discarded in favour of the word "ashore". Strictly, even the word "ashore" must mean that the vessel has grounded on the shore, but it is suggested that it would be construed as if it read "'aground" and would thus include grounding upon a permanently submerged bar or reef or, possibly, submerged rocks.

"in a position of peril": It is a condition precedent that the vessel should be in a position of peril before any allowance can be made under this rule and further reference is requested to the specific examples on groundings given in r.A.[12]

7.14 **"when shown"**: These words reinforce the provisions of r.E to the effect that the burden of proof lies upon the claimant.

"actual intention to float the ship . . . at the risk of such damage": These words were almost certainly intended in 1890 to be extremely restrictive and to limit the scope of the rule to a case in which the master actually contemplated damage to machinery and boilers as a possible result of his actions in endeavouring to refloat the ship, and to exclude a claim if he did not actually foresee such damage even if he ought to have done so. However, as stated in all editions of this work since 1955, an actual contemplation of all reasonably foreseeable damage will no doubt be held to have been shown on very little evidence, unless and until evidence is given to rebut the presumption.

Under r.C, actual contemplation of the damage is not necessary.[13] Thus in *Australian Coastal Shipping Commission v Green*[14] Lord Denning, M.R. stated:

> "If the master, when he does a 'general average act' ought reasonably to have foreseen that a subsequent accident of the kind [the tow-rope parted and fouled the tug's propeller] might occur, or even that there was a distinct possibility of it, then the subsequent accident does not break the chain of causation. The loss or damage is the direct consequence of the original general average act."

The wording of r.VII may in theory be stricter, but in practice any difference is more apparent than real. Moreover, it is difficult to see any reason in principle why a more stringent test should apply under r.VII than in other cases. It would be strange result if, for example, damage to the hull caused by excessive vibration of the engine in refloating should be allowed under rr.A and C, although the master did not actually contemplate the damage, while damage to machinery incurred at the same time should be disallowed because of a stricter test laid down by r.VII.[15] In *The Alpha*,[16] where there was evidence that the chief engineer warned the

[12] See paras A.38 et seq., above.

[13] See paras C.25-C.27, above.

[14] *Australian Coastal Shipping Commission v Green* [1971] 1 Q.B. 456; 1 Lloyd's Rep. 16, CA. See also *Sea-Land Services Inc v Aetna Insurance Co* (1976) A.M.C. 2164: [1977] 2 Lloyd's Rep. 84, where the United States Court of Appeals similarly accepted that the master did or should have anticipated that the towline might part.

[15] The shipowner might seek to get round this anomaly by founding his claim for damage to the machinery on rr.A and C. This would raise the question whether r.VII, by imposing a more stringent test, by implication prohibited such a claim from being advanced under the lettered rules.

[16] *The Alpha* [1991] 2 Lloyd's Rep. 515.

master that the engine was over-heating as a result of the attempts to re-float, but the master decided to continue with the attempt, it was held that the requirement of the rule was satisfied, but its precise effect, and the extent (if at all) to which it differs from the ordinary requirements of r.C, was not discussed.

"for the common safety": See commentary under r.A:[17] and the discussion of complex salvage operations in paras 8.04 et seq., below. **7.15**

"but where a ship is afloat": As a result of the inclusion of the Rule of Interpretation, the second part of this rule will be decisive against any claim to contribution in respect of loss or damage to machinery or boilers falling within its terms, even if such contribution would otherwise have been recoverable under the lettered rules.

"no loss or damage caused by working the propelling machinery and boilers": This exclusion is not limited to loss or damage to the propelling machinery and boilers (as the title to the rule would suggest) but applies to any kind of loss or damage caused by working the propelling machinery and boilers whilst the ship is afloat. However, the exclusion, unlike the opening part of the rule, applies only to propelling machinery and boilers, with the result that it does not exclude allowance for damage caused by working other ship's machinery, such as pumps or windlasses, while the vessel is afloat.

The word working is intended in practice to cover any and every use of the propelling machinery or boilers, even if that use might better be considered an abuse of their normal functioning.

[17] See paras A.20 et seq., above.

RULE VIII

EXPENSES LIGHTENING A SHIP WHEN ASHORE AND CONSEQUENT DAMAGE

English Practice and Background

The expense of a forced discharge and the attendant loss or damage to cargo, etc. requires consideration under two separate classifications: **8.01**

(1) where the discharge takes place at a time of peril when a ship is ashore;
(2) where the discharge takes place in the comparative safety of a port of refuge.

We are here concerned only with the first mentioned situation, and reference should be made to rr.X(b) and (c) and XII for the treatment of the expenses and attendant losses and damages at a port of refuge.

If, in order to refloat a vessel which is aground and in a position of peril, cargo is discharged onto the beach or into lighters, the cost of discharge has been universally allowed as general average since time immemorial.[1] In similar fashion, loss or damage sustained by the cargo whilst being discharged, or whilst on the beach or in the lighters, has also been always treated as general average.[2]

However in cases of wreck, where the cargo is discharged not for the common safety but for its own preservation, there is no ground for claiming as general average the costs of discharge, nor any damage which the cargo may sustain in the process.

On the subject of loss or damage to the cargo, there are circumstances in which the discharging of cargo for the common safety can scarcely be distinguished from a jettison. For example, if a ship is stranded she may be in extreme danger **8.02**

[1] See for example *Job v Langton* (1856) 6 E. & B. 779, per Lord Campbell.

[2] There is a sentence in the Roman law (Dig. lib. XIV. tit. 2, f.4) (see para.60.06, below) to the effect that if, to lighten a ship, a part of the cargo is put into a boat or lighter, and if the boat and goods on board are lost before reaching the shore, the loss of the goods is allowable as general average, as in the case of jettison—"proinde tanquam si jactura facta esset". This is simply one example of the more general rule stated in the text.

unless she can be lightened sufficiently to float her off by the next rise of tide; for which purpose a portion of the cargo may be thrown out not intending its destruction but with the hope that it may be fetched into safety by barges, or transport from the shore or it may have to be landed through heavy rains, with no means of protection. In cases of this kind, where exposure of the cargo to great risk or even certainty of damage is deliberately adopted to avert the greater evil of extreme danger to the entire property, all damage or loss of cargo which occurs in consequence of such exposure, and in spite of reasonable care to prevent it is clearly the subject of general average. It is perfectly analogous to damage by water going down when the hatches are open for jettison; that is to say, the particular damage was not intended, but, for the common safety, a measure was resorted to which naturally produced that damage.[3]

8.03 In the context of r.VIII, we are concerned only with the expenses of lightening the ship as a necessary preliminary to refloating her (together with any cargo remaining on board). However, although the expense of refloating should more properly be dealt with under r.A, it is probably convenient to deal with it here. Prima facie, it would be logical to assume that the succeeding expense of refloating the vessel which is stranded and in a position of peril should be as readily admissible in general average as is the cost of discharging the cargo to facilitate that operation and which preceded it. In fact, the situation under English law (though not necessarily under English practice) is less straightforward, and is discussed in the following paragraphs.

Complex Salvage Operations

8.04 The operations by which a ship and cargo are rescued from a situation of peril may be divided into three classes:

(1) Those which throughout deal with the property as a whole, and, in saving any part, save all at once; as, for example, when a loaded ship is towed off a sandbank. These expenses are always treated as general average.

(2) Those which consist in the rescuing of portions of the property, disconnectedly, so that the saving of one portion has no reference to, and does not assist in, the saving of another portion; such as the recovery of goods or ships materials strewn along a beach, or floating about at sea, after the ship has broken up. These expenses are never treated as general average, but charged individually to the separate interests salved.

(3) Those which have for their object the saving of the whole property, or so much of it as can be saved, not all at once, but by a series of distinct operations, each of which has or may have the twofold effect of immediately rescuing from danger one portion of the property, and of facilitating the eventual recovery of the remainder; as when, a ship being ashore, and her floating uncertain, some of the cargo is first taken out, and it then becomes possible to tow her off when she has been lightened. These last

[3] See *McCall v Houlder* (1897) 2 Com. Cas. 129.

may be called "complex salvage operations", although it is not the salvage operations themselves which are necessarily so complex, but rather the legal problems at issue.

The leading cases on complex salvage operations are discussed below. When studying them, it should be borne in mind that these decisions were properly governed by the very strict views on general average which have always been maintained by the English courts, including the following: **8.05**

(1) That general average is at an end when physical safety has been attained (as contrasted with some other countries, where the more liberal theories of common benefit and completion of the adventure hold sway).
(2) That when ship and cargo part company (as when cargo is discharged in order to lighten a vessel for refloating), the previous community of interest is likely to be severed and that expenses incurred thereafter are more for the individual benefit of a particular interest, than for the common adventure.

On the basis of these two principles, the preponderant view of English legal decisions is that, where cargo is removed from a stranded vessel and placed in a position of safety ashore, in the absence of exceptional circumstances such cargo cannot be called upon to contribute towards the expenses of refloating the vessel (and any cargo remaining on board) incurred subsequent to its removal.

However, this strict assessment by the English courts of the legal rights and responsibilities of the various parties in complex salvage situations has never been wholly acceptable to commercial interests, particularly those whose business is of an international character. It seemed inequitable to them, where a salvage operation was planned and carried out as one continuous operation and with no dramatic changes in the condition of the stranded property, that cargo landed safely ashore should escape contribution towards the subsequent expenses incurred in refloating the ship and any cargo still remaining on board. In many cases the cargo discharged would owe its good fortune and immunity merely to the fact that it was stowed near the hatches, or in holds where its removal would be most efficacious in refloating the ship. Other anomalies present themselves. **8.06**

In practice, therefore, there was a tendency to ignore certain aspects of the decisions which follow and, except in sauve qui peut cases and situations such as occurred in *Royal Mail Steam Packet Co v English Bank of Rio*,[4] to treat the whole cost of complex salvage operations as general average, at any rate up to the point of time when the safety of all the property at risk has been attained. These divergencies from the strict legal position are noted below in connection with each of the cases considered. Where the York-Antwerp Rules apply, these divergencies are more easily justified by the terms of r.VIII.

[4] *Royal Mail* (1887) 19 Q.B.D. 362. See para.8.12, below.

The Authorities

8.07 In *Job v Langton*,[5] the barque Snowdon, on a voyage from Liverpool to St Johns, Newfoundland, ran ashore in Malahide Bay, on the coast of Ireland. The vessel at low water was high and dry; and it became necessary to discharge the whole of the cargo and the ballast before she was got off. After the cargo was discharged and placed in store in Dublin, the vessel was got off at considerable cost, with the aid of a steam-tug, and by cutting a channel for her. She was then towed to Liverpool and repaired. The cargo was, in order to save its market, sent on by another vessel; but, by agreement, the question before the court was to be determined as if the Snowdon, after being repaired, had carried on her cargo. The question was, whether the expenses incurred in getting off the ship and taking her to Liverpool to repair, after the entire cargo was discharged, were chargeable to general average, or to particular average on the ship alone. Lord Campbell, delivering the judgment of the Court of Queens Bench, pronounced that the expenses were not chargeable to general average, but to the ship alone:

> "The expenses, to constitute general average, must therefore be brought within the second category, 'extraordinary expenses incurred for the joint benefit of ship and cargo . . .' Although the stranding was fortuitous, all expenses incurred from the misadventure till all the cargo had been discharged confessedly constituted general average. But how can it be said that the subsequent expenses in getting off the ship and taking her to Liverpool for repair were of the same character? The employment of the steam-tug, and the cutting of the channel by which the ship was rescued cannot, as was contended for, be part of the same operation as the unloading of the cargo; for the case expressly finds that 'the steam-tug did no work at the ship until after the cargo was landed, and the coals and ballast taken out of her.' We therefore, do not see how these expenses are to be distinguished from the expenses of repairing the ship when she had been brought to Liverpool, which, it is admitted, must fall exclusively on the owner of the ship or the underwriter on the ship, as particular average. If the owner of the ship was to earn the stipulated freight by carrying the cargo to Newfoundland, it was his duty to repair her and to carry her to a place where she might be repaired . . ."[6]

The decision in *Job v Langton*[7] is unquestionably correct as a matter of English law, but it is suggested that, in modern practice, all the expenses incurred in refloating the ship and towing her to Liverpool would be allowed as general average.

8.08 In *Moran v Jones*[8] tried in the same court in the following year, *Job v Langton* was distinguished. The ship Tribune, shortly after sailing from Liverpool to Callao, ran aground on East Hoyle Bank. She was in ballast, under charter to fetch a cargo from the Chinchas on which the freight was at risk: but she had on board, by the charterer's permission, a small quantity of goods belonging to other parties. Two days after she ran ashore, the weather being more moderate, assistance was

[5] *Job v Langton* (1856) 6 E. & B. 779.
[6] *Job v Langton* (1856) 6 E. & B. 779 at 790.
[7] *Job v Langton* (1856) 6 E. & B. 779.
[8] *Moran v Jones* (1857) 7 E. & B. 523.

procured from Liverpool, and men were employed saving from alongside the wreck of the ship's foremast which had been cut away, the materials of the ship, and the goods, all of which were sent in lighters to Liverpool. Afterwards, a stream anchor was carried out, the ship was scuttled [sic], about 300 tons of ballast were thrown overboard, and then the ship, being kept free by pumping, floated. She was then towed by two steamers back to Liverpool, and there repaired. The question raised was, whether the sum of £643, which had been expended after the cargo was taken out, for the purpose of floating the ship and bringing her to Liverpool for repair, should be treated as general average.

Lord Campbell said[9] : **8.09**

> "In this case we never doubted that the defendant, as underwriter on the freight was liable for a contribution to general average in respect of the sum of £643, the expenses incurred in order to get the ship off from the bank on which she was stranded, whether the goods were or were not liable to contribute to this portion of the loss. It is admitted that the ship could not have been got off and completed her voyage unless these various expenses had been incurred. Therefore, without these expenses, there would have been a total loss of the freight, amounting to the sum of £6,750 . . .
>
> But the sum for which this defendant is liable will depend, to a certain degree, upon the question whether, under the circumstances stated, these goods are to contribute in respect of the £643. And upon this question likewise we are bound to give our opinion. The goods had been taken from the ship and put on board a lighter before these expenses were incurred; and if this had been a separate operation by which they were intended to be saved for the benefit of the owners of the goods, we should have thought (as in Job v Langton[10]) that the goods were not liable to contribute to the expenses subsequently incurred. Looking, however, to the facts stated in this special case, it seems to us that the act of putting the goods in the lighter was only part of one continuous operation, viz, getting the ship off the bank on which she was stranded, and sending her to Liverpool, where she might be repaired with a view to prosecute the original adventure. When she got to Liverpool, the operation of saving her from shipwreck was completed, and the whole expense of the repairs fell upon the owner as owner, and must be borne by him in that capacity, or by the underwriters on the ship; but the expenses of the continuous operation, for the common benefit of ship, goods and freight, are the subject of a general average. In Job v Langton,[11] we considered that the goods had been saved by a distinct and completed operation, and that afterwards a new operation began which could not be properly distinguished from the repairs done to the ship to enable her to pursue the voyage . . . But in the case on which we have now to adjudicate, the goods were put into a lighter by the master of the ship, along with materials of the ship saved from the wreck and they remained in the custody and under the control of the master till the ship was repaired, when they were reloaded in the ship and carried forward, without any interference by the owner of the goods, to their destined port. Unless it had been intended that an operation should be undertaken and completed by which both ship and goods should be rescued from the peril to which they were exposed nothing might have been done and the goods might have perished. Because the goods happened to be saved in the earliest part of the operation, this can be no sufficient reason for saying that they ought not to contribute to all the expenses of the operation which contemplated the benefit of all the interests imperilled by the stranding . . ."

[9] *Moran v Jones* (1857) 7 E. & B. 523 at 532.
[10] *Job* (1856) 6 E. & B. 779.
[11] *Job* (1856) 6 E. & B. 779.

8.10 In holding that the landing of the goods and the salving of the ship were parts of a continuous operation, the court in *Moran v Jones*[12] was, to some extent at least, influenced by the fact that the whole series of operations was necessary to enable the adventure to be successfully prosecuted; a circumstance which, as has been pointed out, does not according to English law make the operation as a whole general average. It is very questionable whether, on the particular facts of the case, the judgment in Moran v Jones can be supported.[13] Nevertheless, the general sentiments expressed by Lord Campbell (and particularly the phrase "one continuous operation") are more attractive to commercial interests and most adjusters, and the case is preferred in practice to *Job v Langton*.[14]

8.11 In *Walthew v Mavrojani*,[15] the ship Southern Belle, while lying at Calcutta laden with a cargo of linseed for London, was driven from her moorings by a cyclone and left fast aground on a mud-bank. A survey was held on her, and it was recommended that the cargo and ballast should be discharged, and the ship dismantled, it being in the surveyor's opinion otherwise impossible to remove the ship from the strand. By October 19, the whole of the cargo was safely warehoused in Calcutta. On that day a surveyor examined the ship and advised that she would not float without extraordinary means being employed to get her off the strand. Tenders having been invited, a firm at Calcutta contracted with the plaintiffs agents to float the ship; but on November 24, their efforts having proved unavailing, they declared their inability to perform the contract and abandoned the attempt. The plaintiff's agents then made a fresh contract with Messrs Burns & Co for £2,300 to float the ship, and they, by constructing an embankment round the vessel, so as to form a dock which they afterwards filled with water, succeeded on December 31, in floating her. Thereafter, the ship was repaired and reloaded with the cargo, which was delivered at destination.

Here the question was raised, whether this £2,300 was the subject of general average. In the Court of Exchequer it was held not to be so, but this was appealed against.

[12] *Moran v Jones* (1857) 7 E. & B. 523.

[13] See the remarks of Bovill C.J., in *Walthew v Mavrojani* (1870) L.R. 5 Exch. 116 at 122, on *Moran v Jones*. "I take it to be settled now", said Wills J. in *Royal Mail Steam Packet Co v English Bank of Rio* (1887) 19 Q.B.D. 370, "that the circumstances which impose a liability in the nature of general average must be such as to imperil the safety of ship and cargo and not merely such as to impede the successful prosecution of the particular voyage. I take it also to be settled that if the cargo as a whole be landed and in safety, the expenses of getting the ship afloat incurred thereafter are not general average: Job v Langton, a case with which Moran v Jones has been supposed to conflict, but which does not seem to me, so far as principles are concerned, to be open to that observation. It is the decisions, if anything, which are at variance, not the principles upon which they are based." And Grantham J. said, Royal Mail at 377: "As that case (i.e. *Moran v Jones*) has not been since followed, even if it has not been overruled, we could not act upon that decision unless the facts were absolutely identical."

In *Svendsen v Wallace* (1884) 13 Q.B.D. 80, Brett M.R. said that, in his opinion, Moran v Jones could not be supported; Bowen L.J. said (at [93]): "The inferences of fact drawn by the Court of Queen's Bench may or may not have been correct, but the decision has reference only to the special facts of the case."

[14] *Job* (1856) 6 E. & B. 779.

[15] *Walthew v Mavrojani* (1870) L.R. 5 Exch. 116.

The decision of the court was unanimous that the expense should not be general average. Bovill C.J. said[16]:

"Whereas to ground a claim for general average there must be a danger, actual or impending, common to both ship and cargo, here the cargo was safe and the ship only in peril; it was indifferent to the owners of the cargo whether the ship floated or not, and there was therefore no sacrifice made, or extraordinary expense incurred, to save both ship and cargo, or for the common benefit of both."

The judgment in this case is faultless from the perspective of English law. However, on the basis that the doctrine of "completion of the adventure" is preferred by commercial interests, it is submitted that, in practice, the costs of refloating the vessel would now be allowed as general average.

In *Royal Mail Steam Packet Co v English Bank of Rio*,[17] the Tagus, on a voyage from Rio de Janeiro to Southampton, having on board specie (coin) of the value of £125,000, partly belonging to the defendants, and a general cargo, ran aground on an island near Bahia and lay in a dangerous position. The weather being bad, the master landed the specie on the next day on the island, afterwards jettisoned some of the cargo, and with the assistance of several tugs got the ship off the ground. After the specie was landed, it was taken to Bahia and forwarded in another vessel: but the parties agreed that for the purpose of ascertaining whether any general average contribution was due from the defendants it should be treated as having been carried by the plaintiffs in the Tagus to Southampton. **8.12**

The plaintiffs claimed a contribution from the defendants in respect both of the jettison, the expense of floating the ship, and the cost of landing the specie and conveying it to Bahia; and a special case having been stated, their counsel argued before a Divisional Court that the specie was landed on the island, and sent on to Bahia, as part of a continuous salvage operation, undertaken for the common preservation of ship, cargo and freight, of which the jettison and the employment of the tugs formed another part. The court held, however, that the landing of the specie was not part of the general average act, and that the specie was not bound to contribute to the expense of getting the ship off the shore.

Wills J. after reviewing the authorities, said[18]: **8.13**

"Cases, no doubt, may occur in which it may be difficult to say whether the purpose for which the goods are removed is that of lightening the ship or of saving the goods, and there will no doubt from time to time be instances in which it is impossible to separate the one purpose from the other. 'The mere fact that the cargo is unladen, although it is done in part for the purpose of saving the goods, yet if it is also done for the purpose of lightening the vessel and as a means of causing her to float, and of saving her from the common peril will not necessarily divest the transaction of its character as an act performed for the joint benefit of ship and cargo': McAndrews v Thatcher[19] in the Supreme Court of the United States. It is impossible with reference

[16] *Walthew* (1870) L.R. 5 Exch. 116 at 124.
[17] *Royal Mail* [1887] 19 Q.B.D. 362.
[18] *Royal Mail* [1887] 19 Q.B.D. 362 at 374.
[19] *McAndrews v Thatcher* (1865) 3 Wallace 347 at 370. But English law may differ from that of the

> to such a matter to lay down any right or inflexible rule. The question will be one of circumstance and degree, and each case must depend upon its own facts . . . The whole of the specie in this case weighed, we are told, about a ton and a half. The Tagus is a vessel of some 3,000 tons burthen. The ease to the vessel could be nothing at all. The combined value and smallness of total weight would be certain in any case to save the specie from jettison. Its value and the facility with which it could be got ashore would be certain, in any case where it was possible to land it, to save it from being left on board, and I cannot doubt that its removal was carried out, not in any sense or degree as a means of securing the common safety of ship and cargo, but simply for the purpose of saving the specie itself. I think, therefore, that when the general average loss was incurred, in whatever sense, restricted or enlarged, that phrase can be properly used, it had ceased to be at risk, that upon no reasonable view of the facts can its removal be considered as a part of the means taken for saving any common adventure. I am consequently of opinion that it is not liable, using the words of the special case, 'to contribute to the jettison or to any of the expenses of getting the ship off the ground incurred after it was landed.'"[20]

Practice and the law are here the same, and the result would be the same under the York-Antwerp Rules.

8.14 In *Kemp v Halliday*,[21] the Chebucto encountered heavy gales when on voyage from Liverpool to Rio de Janeiro with a general cargo and it became necessary for the common safety to put into Falmouth as a port of refuge. Part of the cargo was discharged ashore and repairs were commenced, but before these had been completed, a hurricane caused the ship with that part of the cargo still on board to sink at her moorings. The ship and cargo were raised together as a single operation and, in order to determine the main point at issue (that is. whether the ship was a constructive total loss) the court had first to decide whether the expense of raising the ship and cargo was general average.

8.15 Blackburn J. decided that the expense of this operation was general average chargeable to the ship and that portion of the cargo on board, but "not as against the part that was safe". So far the decision presents no difficulties and practice and the law are as one. No average adjuster would contemplate charging to the cargo safely ashore any proportion of the expense of raising the ship and other cargo, for the simple reason that the expense resulted from a new and separate accident

US on this point. In the 8th edn, of this work the following propositions were submitted as the result of three American cases: when a vessel strands near her destination and her cargo is discharged and delivered at destination by lighters, or other similar means, the salvage and other extraordinary expenses up to the time of delivery of the cargo are general average, and the subsequent expenses of floating the ship are chargeable to the ship unless she is floated without much expense or delay after the cargo has been delivered. In the latter event all the extraordinary expenses are to be treated as general average. See *McAndrews v Thatcher* 3 Wall 347 (1865); *The Julie Blake* 107 U.S. 418 (1882); *L'Amerique* 35 Fed. Rep. 835 (1888). If the casualty occurs short of destination, and the cargo is reloaded, or intended to be reloaded, all the expenses are treated as general average: *NY & Cuba Mail S.S. Co v Reliance Marine Insurance Co* 70 Fed. Rep. 262 (1895); (1896) 77 Fed. Rep. 317; 165 U.S. 720; The Joseph Farwell 31 Fed. Rep. 844 (1887). When the services have not been continuous, expenses incurred after a separation of interests are not general average: *Pacific Mail S.S. Co v N.Y.H. and R. Mining Co* 69 Fed. Rep. 414 (1895); 74 Fed. Rep. 564 (1896).

[20] For cases where specie has been held liable to contribute, see *The St Paul* 82 Fed. Rep. 340 (1898); *The Mullhouse* Fed. Cas. 9910 (1859).

[21] *Kemp v Halliday* (1865) 6 B. & S. 723; 34 L.J.Q.B. 233.

which did not imperil the cargo ashore and was in no way connected with the original accident.

However, Blackburn J. then continued with the remarks for which the case is generally remembered:

> "I do not mean to say that in every case where a ship with a cargo is submerged, and the two are in fact raised together by one operation, the expenditure incurred must necessarily be for the common preservation of both. I think it is in every case a question of fact whether it was so; and if the cargo could easily and cheaply be taken out of the ship, and saved by itself, it would not be proper to charge it with any portion of the joint operation; which in that case would not be incurred for the preservation of the cargo."[22]

The view expressed here is, it is submitted, questionable in law, and it is not followed in practice. If it is reasonable to raise the ship and cargo as a joint operation (and this will usually be preferable to a situation where each cargo interest is competing to have his cargo removed separately), the fact that the cargo, or some of it, might have been saved by a different, perhaps cheaper, method should not deprive the joint operation of its character as a general average act.

Further Removal of Cargo

It is to be remembered that we have been speaking only, thus far, of the expenses of removing the ship and cargo, from the strand or bottom, to the nearest place of actual safety. This very often is only the first portion of the extraordinary expenditure which the accident has necessitated. The cargo may be in safety, but on rocks, or on a beach above high-water mark, or in barges; it is at all events safe from perils of the seas.[23] It may be of little or no value, however, in that position; it must be removed either to a market or to a port of shipment for its own or some other market. Here we come upon a fresh set of complications. Who is to bear the expense of this removal from a place of bare actual or physical safety to one of mercantile safety? Shall this be treated as general average, as a charge on the specific cargo saved, or on the freight, or on the cargo and freight conjointly? **8.16**

It is submitted that the expense of the further removal of the cargo to a place of mercantile safety falls to be dealt with in accordance with whether or not the expense of the preliminary stage in the saving of the cargo was or was not a general average expenditure.

Freight Earned by Substituted Ship

If the ship is not floated or raised, or is found not capable of repair so as to carry the cargo, and the shipowner avails himself of his privilege of substituting another ship and sends it to the nearest port to fetch the goods, it seems obvious that the **8.17**

[22] Kemp (1865) 6 B. & S. 723; 34 L.J.Q.B. 233 at 243.

[23] It may, however, be necessary to remove the cargo to another place for shelter, or to be conditioned. In this case the place mentioned in the text would not be considered a place of safely: *Rose v Bank of Australasia* [1894] A.C. 687.

same principle should apply: the cost of bringing the goods to the port should be general average if the expense of the preliminary stage was general average, if not, a charge on the cargo and freight; and the cost of loading the goods should be a charge on the freight alone.[24]

Historical Development and Practice of Rule VIII

York-Antwerp Rides 1890

8.18 The cost of discharging cargo, etc. from a vessel which was aground and in a position of peril, and any attendant loss or damage to the cargo, has always and universally been allowed as general average. The following rule was therefore accepted without discussion when first introduced in 1890:

> "When a ship is ashore and, in order to float her, cargo, bunker coals and ship's stores, or any of them are discharged, the extra cost of lightening, lighter hire and re-shipping (if incurred), and the loss or damage sustained thereby, shall be admitted as general average."

Although this wording contained no explicit provision that the ship and cargo should be in a position of peril before the cost of discharging cargo, etc. could be allowed as general average, it can confidently be asserted that this omission was but an oversight on the part of those who framed the Rules and that this condition precedent would never have been far from their minds. Nevertheless, the omission did not go unnoticed, and the courts of Holland, at least, in applying this rule held[25] that it was not necessary that the ship should be in peril: it was sufficient merely that she be ashore in order to charge the cost of discharging, etc. to general average.

York-Antwerp Rules 1924

8.19 This defect in the 1890 rule was remedied at Stockholm in 1924 by introducing the necessity for the discharge to be done "as a general average act". The definition of a general average act contained in r.A preserves to the full the necessity of the common safety being involved and the element of peril being present.

York-Antwerp Rules 1950 and 1974

8.20 No change.

York-Antwerp Rules 1994

[24] This question was raised in *Rose v Bank of Australasia* [1894] A.C. 687; but under the circumstances of the case it was unnecessary in the House of Lords to decide it.

[25] The cases are reported in the 5th edn of this Work, p.596 and in the 6th edn, p.608.

Following the introduction in 1994 of the major new provisions in r.C[26] to prevent the allowance in general average of any liabilities to third parties resulting from damage to the environment or the escape or release of pollutant substances from the property involved in the common maritime adventure, it became essential to make changes here and in rr.II and V to ensure that the then existing provisions in those numbered rules could not override[27] the fundamental new principle set forth in the lettered r.C. **8.21**

The 1974 wording of r.VIII covered "... the loss or damage sustained" (by discharging, etc.) and this wording would generally have been considered sufficiently wide to permit the allowance in general average of third-party claims arising from damage to the environment caused by, for instance, a loss of oil from a broken pipeline during discharging operations from a stranded tanker in efforts to refloat.

New and precise wording was introduced in 1994 to make it clear that loss or damage only "to the property involved in the common maritime adventure" was allowable.

York Antwerp Rules 2004

No change other than the substitution of allowed for admitted. **8.22**

RULE VIII

EXPENSES LIGHTENING A SHIP WHEN ASHORE, AND CONSEQUENT DAMAGE

When a ship is ashore and cargo and ship's fuel and stores or any of them are discharged as a general average act, the extra cost of lightening, lighter hire and re-shipping (if incurred), and any loss or damage to the property involved in the common maritime adventure in consequence thereof, shall be admitted/allowed as general average.

Construction

"ashore": See commentary on r.VII.[28] **8.23**

"cargo": See commentary on r.I.[29]

"discharged": The first draft of this rule, submitted to an Extraordinary General Meeting of the Association of Average Adjusters prior to the Liverpool Conference in 1890, used the words "discharged into lighters". The words "into lighters" were struck out in order to ensure that the provisions of the rule should

[26] See paras C.36 et seq., above.
[27] See the *Rule of Interpretation*, para.PRE.04, above.
[28] See para.7.13, above.
[29] See para.1.28, above.

apply also to a discharge direct on to the beach. The rule only applies to discharging. The cost of refloating the vessel therefore falls to be dealt with under r.A, and any damage to the vessel in refloating is governed by r.A or r.VII.

8.24 **"as a general average act"**: This phrase is defined in general terms by r.A. However, the effect of the numbered rules must also be considered when determining what is a general average act. For example where the 2004 Rules apply, and where the cargo is discharged by salvors who are remunerated by "salvage payments" of the kind referred to in r.VI, the cost of the operation will be borne by the parties in accordance with the apportionment of the salvage remuneration, and will not be re-apportioned in general average under r.VIII. However, any extra costs of lightening, lighter hire or re-shipping in respect of which there is no provision for apportionment between the parties other than the general average system are allowed under this rule. Moreover, any loss or damage caused to cargo in the course of discharge, etc. will be allowed under this rule, even when the operation is carried out by salvors, since r.VI does not exclude such loss or damage from allowances.

"extra cost": If the cargo, etc. is reshipped, the whole cost of the operation will constitute "extra" cost. The word "extra" assumes importance more particularly when the discharge takes place at or near the intended port of destination. If, for any reason, the cargo is not reshipped into the original carrying vessel (for example because the cargo would customarily have been discharged into lighters, craft or other vessels) it would be manifestly unjust that the carrier or other parties should be relieved of the normal expenses of discharging and lighter hire, etc. merely because the ship was ashore. In such a case, it is only the increase in cost which is admissible in general average.

"re-shipping": The word is wide enough to cover the costs of bringing the cargo and ship to the place of re-shipment, and the loading and re-stowage operation, whether the cargo is re-shipped on the same or a substitute. It does not cover the costs subsequently incurred in completing the voyage, such as charter hire on a substitute vessel.

8.25 **"to the property involved in the common maritime adventure"**: The reason for the introduction of this phrase in 1994 is explained in para.8.21, above. Its effect is that any liability incurred to third parties for damage to their property falls outside the scope of the rule. It follows that all such liabilities must now be claimed under rr.A and C, and are thus subject to the exclusionary provisions of r.C. Examples of loss or damage which might be successfully claimed under rr.A and C are damage to lighters or mobile cranes, hired for the lightening operation, for which the shipowner was responsible under the contract of hire.

8.26 **"in consequence thereof"**: This phrase refers to the consequences of:

(1) the discharge as a general average act;
(2) the act of lightening from the ship ashore, plus the period in the lighter, in so far as these are extra to any normal lightening;
(3) the period while on the beach or on shore; and
(4) the act of re-shipping, if incurred.

Thus, any loss or damage to cargo, fuel and/or stores from an external cause sustained during the operations or intervening period just mentioned may be allowed in general average. This is perfectly in accordance with the fundamental principles of general average; if by reason of a general average act (the forced discharge), cargo, etc. is exposed to increased risks over and above those it would expect to encounter if it had remained undisturbed on board ship, the resulting loss or damage should be borne by all the properties involved in the common maritime adventure.

RULE IX

CARGO, SHIP'S MATERIALS AND STORES USED FOR FUEL

ENGLISH LAW AND BACKGROUND

When sail gave way to steam there were bound to be occasions at sea when the ship's bunkers were exhausted–or about to become so—and, for the common safety, it was necessary to burn cargo or ship's materials in the furnaces. 9.01

The use of cargo for nominally ship's purposes at a time of peril very clearly constitutes an extraordinary sacrifice which is properly allowable as general average (see para.A.59, above), but the position with regard to a supposed sacrifice of the ship's materials was rather less certain. Was such "sacrifice" truly extraordinary and out of the usual course, or was it comprised within the shipowner's obligations under and performance of the contract of affreightment? The question was resolved in 1872 by the decision in *Harrison v Bank of Australasia*[1] in which it was held that spare spars, planks, and other ship's materials used upon emergency for fuel for the ship's engines to avert some danger and when there has been no original insufficiency in the supply of bunkers, are the subject of general average. The facts of the case are recorded in para.A.63, above.

In the subsequent case of *Robinson v Price*,[2] a question substantially the same was decided in the Court of Appeal. The ship John Baring, bound with timber from Quebec for London, was supplied with a donkey-engine adapted for the loading and discharge of cargo and ballast and also for pumping the ship, to aid the ships hand pumps, when required. At the time of sailing the ship had five tons of coal on board, which was found to be a sufficient supply of fuel for all purposes of the ship while at sea, other than pumping, for a much longer voyage than that from Quebec to London. While at sea the ship fell in with bad weather, and sprang so bad a leak that she could hardly be kept free by constant pumping. For this purpose it presently became necessary to have the pumps worked by the donkey-engine, and as the supply of coal threatened to run short, the captain ordered some

[1] *Harrison v Bank of Australasia* (1872) L.R. 7 Ex. 39.
[2] *Robinson v Price* (1876) 2 Q.B.D. 91.

of the ship's spare spars, and a portion of the cargo, to be used with the coal to keep up the fire of the donkey-engine: by which means the ship was eventually brought safe into port. The questions for the court were whether the burning of the spare spars and whether the burning of the cargo, were to be made good as general average.

9.02 The judgment of the court was delivered by Lush J. who said:

> "The circumstances under which the ship's spars and the cargo were used as fuel for the donkey-engine satisfy all the conditions of a general average claim. The peril was imminent; the sacrifice voluntary, in the sense of being an act of will on the part of the master; it was, in the emergency, necessary in order to save the ship from sinking, and was, of course, made with a view to the safety of the whole adventure–ship, freight, and cargo. Prima facie, therefore, the case of the plaintiff is made out. But it was objected that, as the ship was furnished with a donkey-engine, adapted and intended, in the case of need, for pumping as well as for loading and discharging the cargo, the owner was bound to provide sufficient fuel for its use; that if this had been done the resort to the spars and cargo would not have been required; that it was not done and, therefore, the use of the spars and cargo was not a necessity brought about by the perils of the sea, but a necessity occasioned by his own default.
>
> Although we cannot accede to the proposition in its terms, we entirely accede to the principle which underlies it. We think that a shipper of cargo is entitled, in time of peril, to the benefit not only of the best services of the crew, in order to save his goods, but of the use of all the appliances for that purpose with which the ship is provided. It follows that, where a ship is fitted up with auxiliary steam pumping power, it is the duty of the owner to make some provision for supplying the engine with fuel. Not that he is bound to have on board enough for every possible emergency, but he is bound to have a reasonable supply, having regard to the nature of the voyage, the season of the year, the quality of the cargo, the condition of the ship, and what experience has shewn to be prudent to provide against under those conditions. If he fails to do so, he cannot call upon the owners of cargo to contribute towards that reasonable supply. That would be to make them pay for that which he ought to have provided at his own expense. If, under such circumstances, the opportunity occurs during a time of peril of buying coals from a passing steamer, we think it clear that he could not charge their cost as an extraordinary expenditure entitling him to general average.
>
> That statement of the case not being so explicit as it might have been upon this point, we thought it right to send it back to the learned counsel who settled it between the parties, to find from the evidence he had taken one way or the other upon this question. He has returned it to us, with a statement as follows: 'I find that the John Baring, when she left Quebec, had on board a reasonable supply of coal for the donkey-engine for pumping purposes.' This finding concludes the defendants. The prima facie claim to general average contributions is not displaced by any default on the part of the owner, and our judgment must be for the plaintiff."

9.03 This decision was affirmed upon appeal.[3] Lord Coleridge said:

> "In my opinion the judgment of the Queen's Bench Division was perfectly right. The facts are now stated so distinctly as to preclude all argument. It is impossible to say that under the circumstances this sacrifice of the spars and cargo was not general average." Bramwell and Brett L.JJ. concurred.

[3] *Robinson* (1877) 2 Q.B.D. 295.

There seems to be no distinction in point of principle between burning cargo to feed a ship's donkey-engine, and burning it to feed the ordinary working engines of a steamer.

What is Sufficient Supply of Fuel?

There is "no obligation cast upon the shipowner to have more than a reasonable and ordinary supply of fuel on board, having regard to the character of the voyage and the character of the weather that was to be expected".[4] Account must be taken inter alia of the distance to be covered to destination or the next intended bunkering port, the distance expected to be covered each day, having regard to the weather likely to be encountered at that particular season of the year, the state of cleanliness of the vessel's bottom, and the condition of the engines and/or boilers; the anticipated daily consumption of fuel at the expected speed of the vessel. With these factors in mind, the required quantity of bunkers can be calculated but, to the sum so produced, must be added a reasonable margin[5] to cover emergencies according to what prudent owners usually do in the particular trade. **9.04**

Thus in *E.B. Aaby's Rederi v Union of India (No.2)*[6] Donaldson J. said that the supply of fuel should be "sufficient to get the vessel to the next bunkering port in all reasonably foreseeable circumstances". In that case the voyage was from Portland to Bombay via Yokohama as an intended bunkering port. It was common ground between the parties that a reserve of 25 per cent over the anticipated consumption was sufficient, and Donaldson J. expressed the view that in calculating the margin a further allowance should be made for adverse winds and currents expected on the voyage, as well as unpumpable fuel and possible error in calculating the quantity of fuel on board. The appropriate reserve will vary from voyage to voyage, and on a westward crossing of the North Atlantic in winter would probably be at least 33 per cent. Equally on a short voyage the reserve expressed as a percentage of the anticipated consumption will be considerably greater.

If it is necessary for purposes of bunkering to divide a voyage into stages, the **9.05**
vessel must load a reasonably sufficient quantity of fuel at the commencement of

[4] Per Keating J., *Shand v Ash* (1872) Mitchell's Mar. Reg. 242.

[5] The US cases' of *Hurlburt v Turnure* 81 Fed. Rep. 208 (1897) and *The Abbazia* 127 Fed. Rep. 495 (1904), may offer some guidance as to what constitutes a "reasonable margin". The first of these cases is also worth recording for its decision on a point which may not have come before the British courts. A steamship bound from a Cuban port to New York had but 91/2 days' supply of coal, whereas the customary supply was for 10 days. Ordinarily, the voyage would have taken eight days, but she encountered a hurricane which delayed her so that she was obliged, from lack of coal, to put into Newport News, which she reached in 12 days, having consumed considerable quantities of ship's materials and cargo. It was held that the ship must bear the expense of putting into Newport News, and also the loss of ship's materials and cargo during the time the coal she ought to have taken would have lasted, but that the remainder of the loss was general average.

[6] *E.B. Aaby's Rederi v Union of India (No.2)* [1976] 2 Lloyd's Rep. 714, 718; affirmed [1978] 1 Lloyd's Rep. 351. The shipowners' claim was for the costs of towage into Yokohama. Since r.IX does not apply to such a case it fell to be determined under the lettered rules, and the claim was defeated because the shipowners failed to establish that they had exercised due diligence to provide an adequate supply of the correct type of fuel.

each stage in order to comply with the warranty of seaworthiness.[7] The vessel must load sufficient fuel to enable her to reach the intended bunkering port where the next stage is to begin; the fact that in the course of the voyage there may be an opportunity to rebunker at a port en route will not justify the owners in embarking on the voyage with a smaller margin than would be prudent if no such ports existed.[8]

Problems occasionally arise when a grade of fuel is supplied which is unsuitable for the vessel, and which causes increased consumption.[9] In such circumstances it seems clear enough that the shipowner must demonstrate that the quality as well as the quantity of fuel was satisfactory.

In order that the interested parties may make an assessment of the adequacy or otherwise of the supply of fuel, the Association of Average Adjusters have the following Rule of Practice:

"B9 *Claims arising out of Deficiency of Fuel*

That in adjusting general average arising out of deficiency of fuel, the facts on which the general average is based shall be set forth in the adjustment, including the material dates and distances, and particulars of fuel supplies and consumption."

Historical Development and Practice of Rule IX

York-Antwerp Rules 1890

9.06 The following rule, proposed by the Association of Average Adjusters, was unanimously accepted at the Conference at Liverpool in 1890:

"Cargo, Ship's Materials and Stores Burnt for Fuel

Cargo, ship's materials and stores, or any of them, necessarily burnt for fuel for the common safety at a time of peril, shall be admitted as general average, when and only when an ample supply of fuel had been provided; but the estimated quantity of coals that would have been consumed, calculated at the price current at the ship's last port of departure at the date of her leaving shall be charged to the shipowner and credited to the general average."

It will be noted that an allowance in general average was conditional upon an ample supply of fuel having been provided for the voyage and, further, that the value of the "coals" that would normally have been consumed should be credited to the general average and charged to the shipowner.

[7] *The Vortigern* [1899] P. 140. CA: *Greenock S.S. Co v Maritime Insurance Co* [1903] 2 K.B. 657, CA.

[8] *Timm & Son v Northumbrian Shipping Co* [1939] A.C. 397.

[9] e.g. *E.B. Aaby's Rederi v Union of India* (see para.9.04, above).

York-Antwerp Rules 1924

At the Stockholm Conference in 1924, three changes were made in the rule: **9.07**

(1) The word "cargo", which was the first word on the 1890 rule (and of the title) was deleted in order that the cargo-owner's right to contribution should not depend upon the adequacy of the original supply of fuel, a matter with which he would not normally be concerned. Thenceforth, if cargo was burnt as fuel for the common safety at a time of peril, the value of that cargo would be allowable as general average under the lettered r.A. and regardless of whether or not an ample supply of fuel had been provided.

(2) The more comprehensive word "fuel"' was substituted for "coals" in order that the rule should be kept up-to-date and apply to the more advanced oil-fired ships.

(3) Lastly, words were omitted which indicated that the sum to be credited to the general average in respect of the value of the fuel that would have been consumed should automatically be debited to the shipowner. This latter amendment was prompted by the consideration that it is sometimes the charterer who is responsible for the cost of supplying the fuel for the voyage.

York-Antwerp Rules 1950 and 1974

No change. **9.08**

York-Antwerp Rules 1994

In that the 1974 r.IX dealt only with ship's materials and stores burnt for fuel, **9.09**
and that it would generally be impossible to burn such solid items in the diesel marine engines in fairly universal use today, there were suggestions from a few countries that r.IX might be deleted. Having regard to the fact that only in the case of tankers loaded with an oil cargo was there now likely to be an alternative source of fuel available on board and that the sacrifice of cargo would be covered by r.A, it would have been sensible to have adopted the suggestion to delete the rule.

However, there were two proposals retain the rule in an amended form, applicable to both ship's materials and cargo. One, from the United States Maritime Law Association was to the effect that:

(1) general average should in all cases continue to be credited with the value of the fuel that would normally have been consumed; and

(2) allowances for ship's materials and stores could only be made when an ample supply of fuel had been provided.

The other, from the British Maritime Law Association, was to the effect that:

(1) the general average received no credit for the value of the fuel saved;
(2) the requirement of an ample supply of fuel was omitted altogether.

As a somewhat illogical compromise, the conference decided to adopt the British proposal with the modification that, in the case of the use of ship's materials and stores, but not cargo, the general average was to be credited with the value of the fuel saved.

York-Antwerp Rules 2004

9.10 No change, other than the substitution of "allowed" for "admitted".

RULE IX

CARGO, SHIP'S MATERIALS AND STORES USED FOR FUEL

Cargo, ship's materials and stores, or any of them, necessarily used for fuel for the common safety at a time of peril, shall be *admitted/allowed* **as general average, but when such an allowance is made for the cost of ship's materials and stores the general average shall be credited with the estimated cost of the fuel which would otherwise have been consumed in prosecuting the intended voyage.**

CONSTRUCTION

9.11 **"cargo"**: As submitted in para.1.28, above, this means property in the possession of the shipowner and/or charterer under a contract of affreightment.

"ship's materials and stores": These words are nowhere defined, but they clearly do not include cargo even if owned by the shipowner. Nor, it is submitted, do they include any material placed on board for the purpose of being used as fuel for the vessel. For instance, a motor vessel which customarily uses fuel oil whilst at sea and the more expensive diesel oil only whilst manoeuvring, may exhaust or be unable to use her supply of fuel oil and be compelled to use diesel oil to continue the voyage. The extra cost involved would not be admissible in general average. In any case, it could hardly be contended that the adventure was "in peril" whilst an alternative supply of bunkers remained.

9.12 Under all versions of this rule until 1994, allowances in general average in respect of ship's materials and stores could be made "when and only when an ample supply of fuel had been provided". The effect of these words was to override r.D and to make it a condition precedent to a claim under the rule that the ship was seaworthy, so far as the provision of fuel was concerned, at the beginning of the relevant stage of the voyage, irrespective of whether under the contract of carriage the shipowner was under any liability for unseaworthiness or failure to use due diligence to make the ship seaworthy. Furthermore, the words "only when" prevented any such claim being made under the lettered rules.

The omission of these words in the 1994 and 2004 versions of r.IX renders it irrelevant, so far as the adjustment itself is concerned, whether or not a sufficient quantity of fuel was originally supplied (as to which see para.9.04, above). Where the material used as fuel is cargo, as will usually be the case, this is reasonable enough. However, where it is ship's materials or stores, the question of the claimant's actionable fault will almost inevitably be raised, and, in this context, the Rule of Practice quoted in para.9.05, which is applicable to claims both under English law and under the Rules, requires the adjuster to set out in the adjustment the facts upon which the adjustment is based, including the material dates and distances, and particulars of fuel supplies and consumption. Although, under r.D, the proof of such fault lies on the claimant, in the case of a general average arising out of a deficiency of fuel, where actionable unseaworthiness is obviously a strong possibility, cargo interests should not be obliged to do their own detective work; far better that, where the original supply of fuel was deficient, and the owner's contractual responsibility for the deficiency is apparent, the adjustment should never be prepared with its attendant costs.

If the omission was on the ground that, if it is the duty of the charterer to provide and pay for the fuel, it is unreasonable that the shipowner should be deprived of his right to claim contribution simply because the supply of fuel was inadequate, this seems to ignore the fact that even if it be the charterer's duty to provide and pay for fuel, it remains the master's duty to ensure that he has such a supply before he sails,[10] or at least to give the charterer accurate information as to the quantity and type of fuel required, to enable him to provide the requisite quantity of fuel.[11] Moreover, where the owner of the cargo from whom the shipowner is claiming contribution is not the charterer, the failure of the latter to comply with his obligation to provide fuel would, under most bill of lading terms, provide no excuse to the shipowner, whose claim could therefore be resisted on the grounds of actionable fault.

"for the common safety": See commentary under r.A.[12] 9.13

"at a time of peril": For the purposes of r.A and the other rules which refer to "the common safety', the peril must be real but it need not be immediate. It may have been intended in 1890, by the emphatic use of the twin expressions "for the common safety" and "at a time of peril", to make it necessary for the ship to be in the grip of the peril before this rule could apply, but it is submitted that in modern times the words do not have so drastic an effect. In practice, the words "at a time of peril" are considered not to modify the ordinary meaning of "for the common safety".

This particular problem was raised at the Stockholm Conference in 1924 when one delegate questioned at what time a state of peril began and the master became entitled to burn the cargo or ship's stores. Was it only when the very last drop of fuel had been exhausted? It was his opinion–and it appears the sensible approach–that a "time of peril" would commence at a much earlier stage if the cargo and/or

[10] *Park v Duncan* (1898) 25 R. 528. Ct. of Sess.; *McIver v Tate* [1903] 1 K.B. 382.

[11] *The Captain Diamantis* [1977] 1 Lloyd's Rep. 362.

[12] See paras A.20 et seq., above.

ship's stores, etc. were such that they would not burn alone, but only in conjunction[13] with the ship's bunkers.

For the sake of completeness, it may be mentioned that a state of peril would be deemed to exist when the ship's own supply of fuel had been consumed, even though the cargo was itself "fuel".

9.14 **"the general average shall be credited with the estimated cost of the fuel which would otherwise have been consumed . . ."**: It is entirely appropriate and in accordance with equitable principles that a credit should be given to general average when general average has been charged with something which should properly be provided by the ship interests, whether shipowner or charterer. The rule, however, provides that this credit shall be given only in those infrequent cases where ship's materials and stores may be used, and not in the more likely situation where cargo is consumed. The distinction which the rule draws between ship's materials and cargo, which resulted from the compromise referred to in para.9.09 above, appears to lack any rational justification. If it gives an immediate impression of being a concession to the cargo, in that the whole of its value will be made good, the reality is that the "no credit" provision is an unwarranted gift to the party responsible for paying for normal bunker consumption.

[13] *Park v Duncan* (1898) 25 R. 528. Ct. of Sess.

RULE X

EXPENSES AT PORT OF REFUGE, ETC.

ENGLISH LAW AND PRACTICE

In contrast to the situation relating to most other of the York-Antwerp Rules, English law and practice on the subject of Port of Refuge Expenses played little or no part in the development of r.X; in fact, it might be truer to state that English mercantile interests may have been only too willing to escape from the somewhat complex and not entirely logical provisions of English law and practice. Except for those few cases where a general average may still have to be adjusted in accordance with English law and practice, the following paras 10.02 to 10.20 are not required reading. **10.01**

At first sight, it would seem that the act of putting into a port of refuge, if justifiable, must fall within the definition of an act of general average. On the other hand, it might be argued, and certainly used to be, that when the ship has been damaged by an accident so as to have been rendered unseaworthy, it immediately becomes the duty of the shipowner to take measures at his own expense, to restore her to a seaworthy condition in which the voyage can be continued. If so, can it be said that the master's act in bearing up for the nearest place where the ship can be repaired is any more than the performance of the shipowner's duty? **10.02**

This question gave rise to very considerable controversy throughout most of the nineteenth century, culminating in the bringing of two important test actions before the courts.[1] The decisions given in those two cases were not received with wholehearted satisfaction (Lowndes referred to them as "bundle of contradictions"), but they did enable the Association of Average Adjusters to revise and frame a number of Rules of Practice which ensured uniformity of practice amongst British adjusters. The most important of these rules are quoted immediately below, followed by a review of the situation leading up to the legal cases and the cases themselves. **10.03**

[1] *Atwood v Sellar* (1880) 5 Q.B.D. 286; *Svendsen v Wallace* (1885) 10 A.C. 404.

Rules of Practice

10.04 *"F8 Resort to Port of Refuge for General Average Repairs: Treatment of the Charges Incurred*

That when a ship puts into a port in consequence of damage which is itself the subject of general average, and sails thence with her original cargo, or a part of it, the outward as well as the inward port charges shall be treated as general average: and when cargo is discharged for the purpose of repairing such damage, the warehouse rent and reloading of the same shall, as well as the discharge, be treated as general average (See Atwood v Sellar)."

"F9 Resort to Port of Refuge on Account of Particular Average Repairs: Treatment of the Charges Incurred

That when a ship puts into a port of refuge in consequences of damage which is itself the subject of particular average (or not of general average) and when the cargo has been discharged in consequence of such damage, the inward port charges and the cost of discharging the cargo shall be general average, the warehouse rent of cargo shall be a particular charge on cargo, and the cost of reloading and outward port charges shall be a particular charge on freight. (See Svendsen v Wallace.)"

The other Rules of Practice relating to the treatment of expenses at a port of refuge (F10, F13, F18) can be found in Appendix 3.

Practice of average adjusters prior to 1879

10.05 In most countries except Great Britain the entire expense incurred by putting into a port to repair was (as it still is) treated as general average: that is to say, the pilotage and port-charges going into the port and coming out; the cost of discharging the cargo, whether for its own safety or that of the ship, or both, for example if the ship were leaky and the cargo damaged; or to repair the ship, for example to lighten her and enable her to enter a dry dock; the warehouse rent of the cargo so discharged, and the cost of reloading it.[2] On the other hand, the cost of repairing the ship at the port of refuge was dealt with as general average only if the damage were occasioned by a sacrifice for the common safety, but not otherwise.[3]

10.06 In Britain, for a long period, the same rule prevailed in practice. But about the beginning of the nineteenth century a practice grew up amongst British adjusters, that only so much of the expense of putting into port to repair should be treated as general average as was incurred up to the time when the ship and cargo were placed out of danger. The pilotage and port charges incurred in going into the port

[2] As to fuel, see *Gourlie*, p.243.

[3] Temporary repairs at an intermediate port (where permanent repairs cannot be made), if necessary to enable the ship to proceed on her voyage, are treated as general average in the US: *Hobson v Lord* (1875) 92 U.S. 397; *Bowring v Thebaud* (1890) 42 Fed. Rep. 796; *The Star of Hope* (1873) 17 Wall. 651; *Phillips on Insurance*, 5th edn, para.1500.

of refuge and the expense of discharging the cargo, whether for safety or to repair[4] the ship, were treated as general average but all subsequent expenses were allotted to the particular interests immediately concerned. The warehouse rent of the cargo was made a specific charge on the cargo, and the expenses of setting forth again on the voyage (for example the cost of re-loading the cargo, and the outward pilotage and port charges) were treated as a specific charge on freight.[5]

This treatment was applied irrespective of whether the damage to the ship which occasioned the putting in had been the result of an accident or of a sacrifice for the common safety.

Eventually, after holding its ground for almost a century, the practice was assailed, and it is interesting to record that Richard Lowndes was the protagonist. In his early career he was the staunchest advocate of the British practice (at the conference leading to the York Rules of 1864 he was the only delegate to urge its retention) and he continued to support the practice strongly in the first two editions of this work. By 1874, however, he was beginning to entertain doubts as to the correctness of his earlier views and, by the time the 3rd edn was published, the volte-face was complete. 10.07

His new views were based, not on the theory of "completion of the adventure", but rather on the principle that when a master decides to put into a port of refuge, he effectively decides at the same time to leave that port after repairs. In similar fashion, a decision to discharge the cargo necessarily entailed its subsequent reloading, etc. From 1876 onwards, Lowndes gave effect to these new views in his business practice, but, in the first instance, limited their application to those cases where the necessity to put into a port of refuge arose from a general average sacrifice as opposed to an accidental cause. His adjustments were "after more or less of discussion, passed by underwriters",[6] but eventually one such case came before the courts.

The Authorities

Atwood v Sellar[7]

The ship Sullivan Sawin, on a voyage in the year 1877 from Savannah to Liverpool, met with a gale in which, for the common safety, the master was compelled to cut away her fore-topmast and this in its fall did such damage to her hull that the master was obliged to put into Charleston to repair it, for which 10.08

[4] The expense of discharging the cargo at a port of refuge in order to effect repairs was invariably charged to general average, even when the ship and cargo were in perfect safety in the port. To a modern eye, this practice hardly appears to accord with the theory that the general average terminated as soon as physical safety had been attained, but it should be remembered that in the times when the practice originated ships were built of wood and that, as a general rule when the cargo had to be discharged, it was usually because the ship was leaking and matters of this kind were best regulated by simple rules of thumb.

[5] The beginning of this practice may be seen in some of the earlier editions of *Stevens on Average*, and in *Benecke*.

[6] 3rd edn, p.107.

[7] *Atwood v Sellar* (1879) 4 Q.B.D. 342.

purpose he had to discharge a portion of the cargo and to place it in a warehouse. After repairing, this cargo was reloaded and the vessel then completed her voyage to Liverpool. The agreed case stated by an arbitrator set out the practice of adjusters. It was stated, that the practice for the last 70 or 80 years in all such cases, whether the putting in were the result of a sacrifice or of an accident, was to allow in general average the expense of going into port and discharging the cargo, but to treat the warehouse rent as a special charge on the cargo and the reloading, together with the outward port charges, as a special charge on the freight. The plaintiffs in this case claimed that all of the expenses should be treated as general average. The defendants contended that they were only liable to pay in conformity with the practice.

10.09 In the Queen's Bench Division,[8] judgment was given by a majority of the court, in favour of the plaintiffs. Cockburn C.J. began by considering what, independently of the practice of average adjusters, was the principle or rule of law applicable to this case. That the expenses in question (those of leaving the port, and of warehousing and reshipping the cargo) should, according to legal principles, be made the subject of general average, appeared to him to flow necessarily from the fundamental principle on which the whole doctrine of general average rests; namely, that all loss which arises from extraordinary sacrifices made, or expenses incurred, for the preservation of the ship and cargo, must be borne proportionately by all who are interested.

10.10 The Court of Appeal[9] unanimously confirmed the judgment of the Queen's Bench Division. Their judgment was delivered by Thesiger L.J. who stated:

> "The going into port, the unloading, warehousing, and reloading of the cargo and the coming out of port, are at all events part of one act or operation contemplated, resolved upon, and carried through for the common safety and benefit and properly to be regarded as continuous. The shipowner is at least entitled to reship the goods and prosecute his voyage with them; and the expenses necessary for that purpose, being ex hypothesi consequent upon a damage voluntarily incurred for the general advantage, should legitimately be the subject of general average contribution . . ."

After carefully reviewing the previous decisions and dicta, Thesiger L.J. concluded:

> "The result of this review of the authorities is to confirm the opinion which, apart from authority, we entertain and have already expressed upon the question submitted to us. The practice, then, of the average adjusters, as stated in the special case, appears to us to be neither founded upon true principles, nor to be in accordance with the views of the textwriters, and, so far as there is case authority upon the matter, it appears to us to be opposed to legal decisions."

10.11 This decision was regarded as conclusive on the question immediately before the courts, where the ship had put into port on account of a sacrifice, and no attempt was made to carry the case up to the House of Lords. It was not so clear, however, whether the change in practice was to stop here, or whether it should be

[8] *Atwood* (1879) 4 Q.B.D. 342.
[9] *Atwood* (1880) 5 Q.B.D. 286.

extended to the case of putting into a port of refuge on account of accidental damage, as contended by Lowndes in the 3rd edn of this work.[10] With the usual courage of his convictions, and with the tacit approval of the marine insurance market in Liverpool (but not London), Lowndes changed his practice and allowed as general average the costs of entering and leaving port, and of discharging, warehousing and reloading cargo, even in those cases where the necessity to seek a port of refuge arose from accidental damage. As anticipated, this changed practice was challenged in the courts.

Svendsen v Wallace

Having got a straightforward case where the facts were simple, the advocates of the Custom of Lloyd's, as defendants representing the cargo, resisted the allowance in general average, of the cost of warehousing and reloading the cargo and of the expenses of leaving the port to resume the voyage. Their first plea was that this was a contrary to ancient and well-known custom amongst shipowners, shippers and consignees of cargo, assured, underwriters and average adjusters, applicable to voyages from Rangoon to Liverpool. Secondly, they pleaded that, independently of the custom, this mode of treating the expenses in question was right in principle. **10.12**

The facts were these: *The Olaf Trygvason*, on a voyage with a cargo of rice from Rangoon for Liverpool, sprang a dangerous leak in bad weather, which obliged the captain, for the safety of ship and cargo, to put into Rangoon for repair. When in port the cargo was necessarily landed in order to repair the ship and also, as was pointed out in the House of Lords, but not till then, for the common safety as the vessel continued to take on water. The cargo was warehoused, and after the ship had been repaired it was re-shipped. **10.13**

At Guildhall and in the Queens Bench Division, the first plea relating to custom was dismissed, both courts holding that there was no reasonable evidence of a usage controlling the contract. The next step, therefore, was to obtain the judgment of Lopes J. on the question of whether the practice referred to was right in principle. He decided against the defendants saying he was bound, by the decision in *Atwood v Sellar*, for he could see no practical distinction between the two cases.[11]

A majority decision in the Court of Appeal reversed Lopes J.; Brett M.R. regarded the expenses subsequent to entry and unloading as disconnected from the going in; the proximate motive in warehousing cargo being quite detached from any question of preservation or safety of the ship, and the proximate motive in coming out being the intention to proceed with the voyage, not that of escaping from danger. He continued: **10.14**

> "When the cargo is landed, it may or may not, according to its own nature, or the circumstances of the locality, require to be warehoused or otherwise protected. It may in consequence of partial damage already suffered, or from its own nature, require for its own safety to be manipulated, as, for instance, to be unpacked or dried; but such acts cannot possibly be necessary for the safety or preservation of the ship. She is at

[10] At pp.109, 110.
[11] *Svendsen v Wallace* (1883) 11 Q.B.D. 616 at 617.

that moment safe or unsafe; but these acts cannot contribute in any way to her safety if she is unsafe. They cannot be said to be a part of the act of going into port to repair; they have no reference to the act of repairing, or of putting the ship into a position in which she can be repaired. They are, therefore, not within the principle. The repairing of the ship has nothing to do with the safety of the cargo. It is done in respect of the ship alone. The reloading of the cargo and the outward expenses are expenses of acts done when both ship and cargo are safe from existing danger, and are, therefore, not within the rule. They cannot be said to be a part of the act of placing the ship in a position to be repaired. Unless, therefore, we are bound by authority to hold otherwise, I am of opinion that, according to the law of England, when a ship is obliged, for the safety of ship and cargo, to go into and goes into a port of distress in order to repair damage done by sea peril, the expenses of going into the port are general average expenses: that if it is necessary for the safety of both ship and cargo to unload the cargo, or if it is necessary to unload the cargo in order to repair the ship, though it is not necessary for the safety of the cargo, the expense of unloading the cargo is a general average expense; but if the unloading of the cargo is not for either of these causes the expense of unloading is not a general average expense. I am of opinion, in the same way and in the same case, that the expenses of warehousing, guarding, or manipulating the cargo, of repairing the ship, of reloading the cargo, of taking the ship out of port, of the charges of going out of port, are not general average expenses."[12]

10.15 Distinguishing *Atwood v Sellar*, Brett M.R. said:

"The real ground of the decision was, I think, that where the putting into port for repairs is the necessary consequence of a previous general average sacrifice, the law of England is as elastic in respect of the subsequent acts done and expenses incurred in the port as the American and other laws are stated to be in all cases of a ship necessarily putting into a port of distress to repair. And for that proposition there were, before the decision in Atwood v Sellar,[13] many weighty dicta by English writers of authority and English judges, but all which dicta threw a distinction between the going into a port of distress in consequence of a voluntary sacrifice, and of putting into port in consequence of a particular average damage. I adopt that distinction because do not think that we are bound in the present case by the decision in Atwood v Sellar,[14] and the propriety of that decision, with reference to the facts on which it was decided, we are not at liberty to question."[15]

Baggallay L.J. dissented exclusively on the ground that the decision in *Atwood v Sellar*, which he considered to be right, obliged them in consistency to decide the present case in the same way.

10.16 This decision was affirmed in the House of Lords,[16] Lord Blackburn finding that: the cargo owners were not chargeable with a general average contribution in respect of reshipping the cargo; the further question of the expenses coming out he expressly left undecided. These expenses were small and enough had already been paid to cover them. Lord Blackburn also discussed and criticised *Atwood v Sellar*[17] and in view of his observations it is probably doubtful if the decision of

12 *Svendsen* (1884) 13 Q.B.D. 69 at 77.
13 *Atwood* (1880) 5 Q.B.D. 286.
14 *Atwood* (1880) 5 Q.B.D. 286.
15 *Svendsen* (1884) 13 Q.B.D. 69 at 79.
16 *Svendsen* (1885) 10 A.C. 404.
17 *Atwood* (1879) 4 Q.B.D. 342.

the Court of Appeal in that case can be regarded as an entirely satisfactory authority. Lords Watson and Fitzgerald concurred, but gave no reasons.

Principles to be deduced

It is submitted that the Rules of Practice of the Association of Average Adjusters accurately state the law subject to the following reservations: 10.17

(1) *Atwood v Sellar* is only to be relied upon as authority for the proposition that the cost of discharging, warehousing and reloading is to be treated as general average if such cost, on the facts of the particular case, can be said to have been incurred for the preservation of both ship and cargo and that therefore such cost is of its own right an extraordinary expenditure of a general average nature or is necessarily incident to a general average act.

(2) *Svendsen v Wallace* is not to be relied upon as authority for the proposition that where the cost of reloading and outward port charges are a particular charge on freight, such charge falls on the cargo owner if, and to the extent that, freight is prepaid and non-returnable.[18] None of the judgments expressly deals with this point and as the freight was partly prepaid in this case, such a proposition seems inconsistent with the speech of Lord Blackburn, who said that if: "the cost of reshipping is properly charged to freight the defendants [cargo-owners] are not liable to pay any part of it."[19] Rule F9, read literally, accurately summarises the decision in the case so far as the incidence of the cost of reloading cargo is concerned and it is suggested that the charges fall on the shipowner whether or not the freight is at risk. 10.18

This case is also no authority for the proposition that the inward port charges and the cost of discharging cargo are, in every case, general average expenditures, irrespective of whether or not the vessel put into a port of refuge for the preservation of both ship and cargo. This is made clear by the decision in *Hamel v P&O S.N. Co*,[20] although it related to damage during discharge and not to the cost of such discharge.

In that case a ship, having through perils of navigation sustained damage which prevented her from proceeding upon her voyage, put back into port for repairs. To enable her to be repaired it was necessary to unload the cargo, during which process the cargo was damaged. The cargo was at no time in any danger and Alverstone C.J. held that the cargo owners were not entitled to contribution in general average from the owners of the ship on the grounds that: 10.19

> "if the consequence of a peril of the sea is merely to render one part of the venture abortive, merely to render the ship unfit to proceed or the cargo unfit to be carried

[18] cf. Rules of Practice, Nos F9 and F12, Appendix 3, paras 70.36 and 70.39, below.
[19] *Svendsen* (1885) 10 A.C. 404 at 416.
[20] *Hamel v P&O S.N. Co* [1908] 2 K.B. 298.

further on the voyage, acts done merely to make the ship lit to proceed or done merely to make the cargo fit to be carried further on the voyage are not general average acts and do not afford ground for a general average contribution."

10.20 For more detailed discussion of the application of these principles reference is invited to the 12th and earlier editions.

Historical Development and Practice of Rule X(A)

Glasgow Resolutions 1860

10.21 At the International Conference at Glasgow in 1860, the complex treatment of port of refuge expenses by British average adjusters[21] was set aside in favour of the "completion of the adventure" theory practised elsewhere in the world, and the following Resolution was passed by 24 votes to 5:

> "(6) That the expense of warehouse rent at a port of refuge on cargo necessarily discharged there, the expense of re-shipping it, and the outward port charges at that port, ought to be allowed in general average."

It was deemed unnecessary to make provision for dealing with inward port charges and the expense of discharging cargo as these were universally allowed as general average.

York Rules 1864

10.22 On this occasion, the wording of the rule was much improved and made more precise, but its provisions were still directed exclusively to the cost of storing and reloading cargo and the outward port charges, it being taken for granted that the inward port charges and cost of discharging would be universally allowed as general average in the appropriate circumstances.

The first sentence of the rule was passed unanimously, the only discussion taking place on the last sentence, which was added as an amendment by L.R. Baily.

> *"Rule VII. Port of Refuge Expenses*
>
> When a ship shall have entered a port of refuge under such circumstances that the expenses of entering the port are admissible as general average, and when she shall have sailed thence with her original cargo or a part of it, the corresponding expenses of leaving such port shall likewise be so admitted as general average: and whenever the cost of discharging cargo at such port is admissible as general average, the cost of reloading and stowing such cargo on board the said ship, together with all storage charges on such cargo, shall likewise be so admitted. Except that any portion of the cargo left at such port of refuge, on account of its being unfit to be carried forward,

[21] See para.10.06, above.

> or on account of the unfitness or inability of the ship to carry it, shall not be called on to contribute to such general average."

York-Antwerp Rules 1877

At the Conference at Antwerp in 1877, the 1864 rule was re-affirmed in its main provisions, but the final sentence was expunged after considerable discussion. This discussion is not reported but from one of the reports issued prior to the Conference it may be conjectured that it proceeded on the basis that as any portions of cargo which had been left behind in a port of refuge had equally benefited with the rest by putting into a port of refuge they should not be exempted from contribution to general average. **10.23**

York-Antwerp Rules 1890

The 1877 rule made no attempt to define what was a port of refuge, nor did it make provision for expenses incurred as the result of an accident which occurred in a port of refuge, for example during the course of loading cargo, or when sailing but before having left the confines of the port. Only if a vessel entered a port as a port of refuge could the old rule apply **10.24**

These two main deficiencies were remedied at the International Conference at Liverpool in 1890 and specific mention was at last made that inward port charges should be admissible as general average. The wording of the rule was changed to the form we know it today and the rule was sub-divided into three sections (a, b and c) to deal individually with the various charges incurred at a port of refuge. Rule X(a) deals only with inward and outward port charges:

> "When a ship shall have entered a port or place of refuge, or shall have returned to her port or place of loading, in consequence of accident, sacrifice, or other extraordinary circumstances which render that necessary for the common safety, the expenses of entering such port or place shall be admitted as general average; and when she shall have sailed thence with her original cargo, or a part of it, the corresponding expenses of leaving such port or place, consequent upon such entry or return, shall likewise be admitted as general average."

York-Antwerp Rules 1924

No change. **10.25**

York-Antwerp Rules 1950

The rule of 1890 and 1924 was continued unchanged, but on this occasion a second paragraph was added to give recognition and authority to a practice which was already followed to a very large extent throughout the world, but on which at one time there had been some diversity of opinion, particularly in England.[22] **10.26**

[22] See Rule of Practice No.C3, para.70.26, below.

If, for the common safety, a vessel was obliged to put into a port of refuge at which there were no repair facilities, it would usually be necessary—after the immediate emergency was over—to move the vessel to another port where repairs could be carried out. In practical terms, both ports might be considered to be "ports of refuge", but it was argued, and with some reason, that if the vessel and her cargo were already in safety at the first port of refuge, it could hardly be suggested that the move to the second port was for the common safety, the only grounds for allowing the inward and outward port changes under the York-Antwerp Rules.

The practical view prevailed and the second paragraph was added in 1950:

> "When a ship is at any port or place of refuge and is necessarily removed to another port or place because repairs cannot be carried out in the first port or place, the provisions of this Rule shall be applied to the second port or place as if it were a port or place of refuge. The provisions of Rule XI shall be applied to the prolongation of the voyage occasioned by such removal."

The intention of the Conference was that the expenses incurred in proceeding to and entering "the second port or place", of detention there and of sailing thence to the point of deviation from the intended voyage or an equivalent point should be treated in the same manner as those incurred in relation to the first port. The Conference did not intend any distinction to be drawn between ports of refuge, loading and call. The practice of average adjusters gives effect to these intentions.[23]

York-Antwerp Rules 1974

10.27 In making the addition to this rule at the 1950 Conference, it appears to have been overlooked that when a vessel required to move from one port of refuge to another because repairs could not be carried out at the first port, she would often be disabled and in need of towage assistance to the second port. As the numbered rules of the York-Antwerp Rules have to be construed strictly, this omission concerning the cost of towage gave rise to numerous arguments in practice, it being contended (as with the 1924 rule) that if the vessel and cargo were already in safety at the first port of refuge, the cost of towage was not for the common safety and should be treated as part of the cost of repairs.

This strict construction of the rule was not in keeping with the true intention, and the situation was made clear in 1974 by the addition of the words: "and the cost of such removal including temporary repairs and towage shall be admitted as general average."

[23] See also Rule of Practice No.C3, para.70.26, below. Another Rule of Practice (No.C4, para.70.27, below) provides that a ship shall be deemed to be at a port or place of refuge, within the second paragraph, when the wages and maintenance of her master, officers and crew during any extra period of detention there would be admissible in general average under r.XI.

York-Antwerp Rules 1994

No change of any substance in practical effect, but two commas previously appearing after place of refuge and extraordinary circumstances in lines 1 and 3 of the first paragraph were deleted on this occasion. The purpose of this was to make it clear that the requirements imposed by the subsequent words of the rule ("in consequence of accident . . . for the common safety") applied equally to both a port or place of refuge and a port or place of loading. **10.28**

The second paragraph of the rule remains unchanged, but a number of delegates had proposed that temporary repairs and towage costs incurred in moving a vessel from one port of refuge at which repairs could not be effected to another should follow the cost of the repairs carried out at the second port, rather than be charged automatically to general average. On this matter, see also para.14.11, below.

York-Antwerp Rules 2004

No change other than "allowed" in place of "admitted", the addition of the words "of refuge" in the second paragraph and the numbering of the paragraphs. **10.29**

RULE X(a)

EXPENSES AT PORT OF REFUGE, ETC

***(i)* When a ship shall have entered a port or place of refuge or shall have returned to her port or place of loading in consequence of accident, sacrifice or other extraordinary circumstances which render that necessary for the common safety, the expenses of entering such port or place shall be admitted/allowed as general average; and when she shall have sailed thence with her original cargo, or a part of it, the corresponding expenses of leaving such port or place consequent upon such entry or return shall likewise be admitted/allowed as general average.**

***(ii)* When a ship is at any port or place, of refuge and is necessarily removed to another port or place of refuge because repairs cannot be carried out in the first port or place, the provisions of this Rule shall be applied to the second port or place of refuge as if it were a port or place of refuge and the cost of such removal including temporary repairs and towage shall be admitted/allowed as general average. The provisions of Rule XI shall be applied to the prolongation of the voyage occasioned by such removal.**

Construction

First Paragraph

The broad intention of the first paragraph of this sub-rule is clear, namely: that where, solely for the common safety, a ship puts into any port or place, or, having **10.30** left the confines of a loading port, puts back to the loading port, the expenses of entering or returning to that port or place shall be allowed in general average. Further, that if she sails thence in continuation of the common adventure, the expenses of leaving that port or place shall similarly be allowable.

"shall have entered": These words apply when a vessel puts into a port of refuge from the sea or other waters outside the confines of the port, as opposed to putting back to a port of loading before having left its confines.

10.31 **"port or place"**: The 8th and 10th editions of this work construed only the word "place", submitting that, in the words of Scrutton L.J.[24] :"place" should be interpreted as ejusdem generis with "port", "as a locality having some or many of the characteristics of a port."

Subsequent editions have taken the view that the words "port or place" are better construed, not in isolation, but as part of the complete phrase from which they are taken: "port or place of refuge". The word "refuge" governs "port or place" and signifies the purpose[25] of the resort to the port or place and is one of the essential characteristics of a port. This view was approved by Moore-Bick J. in the Trade Green.[26] Rejecting an argument, based on the dicta of Scrutton L.J. and others that a "place" must be in the nature of a port, he referred to the earlier authorities and said:

> "The precise subject matter differs from case to case, but given the particular context in which the question arose in each case it is not difficult to see why reference to a "place" should have been construed in that way. The subject matter of the York-Antwerp Rules is very different, however. The phrase as found in r.X(a) is "port or place of refuge" and it is followed by the words . . . in consequence of accident, sacrifice or other extraordinary circumstances which render that necessary for the common safety. I would agree with the comment in para.10.34 of Lowndes & Rudolf that any place which provides the shelter needed for the common safety would fall within these words."

Where an undamaged vessel seeks shelter in a protected bay merely to avoid a threatened storm or gale, this can never constitute a general average act. But, if some accident has already occurred which places the ship and her cargo in peril, it is immaterial whether the vessel puts into a proper port or a mere place of refuge to secure the common safety. It is often impossible for large tankers and bulk carriers to enter many of the ports of the world when they are in trouble, and they are then obliged to put into sheltered bays and anchorages in order to carry out repairs or other measures necessary to prosecute their voyages in safety. It may be remarked that American adjusters have long interpreted "port or place"' to include a sheltered bay or anchorage.

This distinction between "port" and "place" is usually of little consequence in the context of this r.X(a) as it is unlikely that any charges will be incurred for the

[24] *Humber Conservancy Board v Federated Coal & Shipping Co* (1927) 29 Lloyd's Rep. 177 at 179, a case concerning a claim for pilotage dues under the Pilotage Act 1913, which were chargeable if the vessel made use of "any port". However, the Act incorporated the Merchant Shipping Act, which defined a port as including a place.

[25] *Maritime Insurance Co v Alianza Co* [1907] 2 K.B. 660.

[26] *Trade Green* [2000] 2 Lloyd's Rep. 451, 456.

use of a "place" of refuge, but the point becomes material when considering allowances for crew wages, etc. under r.XI(a).[27] On occasion it may be decided that part or all of the cargo of a large tanker needs to be removed to carry out temporary or permanent repairs. With only a limited number of terminals able to take such vessels it will be necessary to conduct a ship to ship (STS) transfer of the cargo. The authorities may allow such an operation to be carried out in the location where the vessel has taken refuge or at a location nearby specially designated for such purposes; alternatively they may insist the STS discharge takes place outside coastal waters. Although "place of refuge" is construed widely it cannot readily be applied to an unspecified location possibly out of sight of land, and wages and maintenance of crew during the operation would not then be allowable.

In many cases there may only be one port in the vicinity that the vessel can proceed to in order to achieve safety, but in others there may be several ports that can be considered. In making a selection the master must be given a wide discretion, but he remains bound by the general obligations to complete the voyage with reasonable despatch. In addition, the Rule Paramount requires that his choice is made reasonably, with the interests of all parties to the adventure in mind. Thus the selection of a port of refuge that offered the opportunity to load additional cargo, in preference to one in which superior repair facilities would have reduced the period of detention, would not be a reasonable choice.

"of refuge": These words import the qualification that the presence of the ship **10.32**
in the port or place is "for the purpose of preserving from peril the property involved in a common maritime adventure".[28]

If a ship is obliged to enter a port for the common safety, but it so happens that she would in any event have entered that port as a port of call, can she be said to have entered a port of refuge? It is suggested that the port of call becomes a port of refuge but that "the expenses of entering such a port or place" are only so much of the total expenses as exceed the cost of entering the port as a port of call.

"or shall have returned to her port or place of loading": Reference is requested to the remarks in para.10.24, above.

"in consequence of . . .": See para.10.28, above.

"accident": It is suggested that the word involves some element of suddenness, the unforeseen and the fortuitous, but an accident is easier to recognise than to define. Thus, abnormal wear of machinery would not of itself be an accident but sudden breakage of machinery, even if due to normal wear and tear, might well be. In such a case the consequence may be an accident, though the cause was not.[29]

"sacrifice": See commentary in paras A.59 et seq. above and para.50.04, below.

"other extraordinary circumstances": If there be a genus which includes **10.33**
"accident" and "sacrifice" these words will be construed ejusdem generis, but in any event it is suggested that they should be construed strictly and full weight

[27] See para.11.07, below.
[28] cf. r.A.
[29] See also the *Makis* decision on this word in r.X(b) (para.10.50, below), *Mills v Smith* [1964] 1 Q.B. 30: and *R. v Morris* [1972] 1 W.L.R. 728.

given to the adjective. Examples of such circumstances are serious depletion of the crew by an epidemic on board, a shortage of bunkers, drunken football supporters running amok on a ferry, or (an unusual case encountered in practice) where the master is murdered and the assailant is unknown and still at large. Further, the term might be construed to cover such situations as, for instance, where bearings slowly overheat and a serious breakdown can be expected within a short time unless precautionary repairs are carried out.

"for the common safety": For a full commentary on these important words, see paras A.20 et seq., above, in r.A.

10.34 **"expenses of entering such port"**: If port dues for the whole or a part of the time during which the vessel remains in port are payable on entry, these are part of the expenses of entering the port, but any other port dues fall to be considered under r.XI(b).[30] It is submitted that damage suffered in entering port would not be an expense within this rule, though it might give rise to a claim for contribution under the lettered rules.

The "expenses of entering such port" are usually construed in practice to include the cost of reaching a berth within the port. For example, a ship may put into a port of refuge with machinery trouble, but only as far as the anchorage, it being thought that repairs can be accomplished there. On opening up, however, the damage is found to be more extensive than was expected, or shore cranes or other facilities are required, and the vessel will then shift to a berth within the port. It can be argued with good reason that the cost of this move should be dealt with in the same manner as the cost of the repairs, but in practice the cost of the move will often be treated as the "expense of entering such port" and allowed as general average.

10.35 **"and when she shall have sailed thence with her original cargo, or a part of it . . ."** Introduced in 1864, these words are perfectly adequate for those countries which admit a general average situation only when a vessel has cargo on board. However, for the benefit of those countries following the English legal system, which contemplates a general average situation even when the vessel is in ballast but under charter,[31] the words might with convenience be translated as "when she shall have sailed thence in continuance of her original voyage". This probably reflects the precise intention of the framers of the rule and would also be appropriate to those hull insurance conditions which accept a general average even when the vessel is in ballast and not under charter.

"corresponding expenses": Where a ship put back to her port of loading and, whilst she was there detained, ice formed in the river through which she had to proceed to sea. Bigham J. held, obiter,[32] that the shipowner could not recover contribution in respect of the expense of cutting a passage through the ice, as the expenses contemplated by the rule were "the ordinary expenses of leaving the place of loading 'corresponding' to the expenses of entering such place". This seems a somewhat narrow construction to put upon the words. It is suggested that what is meant is that if the expense of getting to point A in a harbour is, allowed

[30] See para.11.25, below.
[31] See paras 17.59–17.61, below.
[32] *Westall v Carter* (1898) 3 Com. Cas. 112 at 114 (1890 Rules).

as the expense of entering the port, then, in the reverse direction, the expense of sailing outward from point A will be so allowed even if it greatly exceeds the corresponding expense of entry.

Second Paragraph

The broad intention[33] of this paragraph is clear, namely: if a ship is necessarily removed from a port or place of refuge at which repairs are impossible to another port or place in order that repairs may be effected, the second port or place shall also be treated as a port of refuge to which all the provisions of rr.X and XI will apply. Further, the cost of moving to the other port, including any necessary temporary repairs and towage, plus crew wages, etc. and bunkers, shall also be allowed as general average. **10.36**

"necessarily removed . . . because repairs cannot be carried out": It is suggested that the repairs contemplated are those necessary to complete the voyage, which may or may not be permanent repairs. If it is possible, in a commercial sense, to effect such repairs, the paragraph will not apply. In *The Bijela*[34] Hobhouse J. held that the paragraph did not apply if either temporary or permanent repairs were possible at the first port of refuge, and on the wording of the paragraph this conclusion seems inevitable.

"necessarily removed to another port": The other port to which the vessel is removed for repairs should be a necessary choice and, if only by reason of the new Rule Paramount, that choice should be reasonable to all the parties to the adventure. Cases are occasionally encountered in practice where the repairs necessary to complete the voyage might have been effected at a "neighbouring" port but, perhaps because the cargo has been forwarded under a Non-Separation Agreement.[35] the vessel then proceeds even on a trans-Atlantic or trans-Pacific voyage simply to secure the most advantageous repair charges. The costs of proceeding to such a repair port, or during any resulting over-extended delay, will only rarely be admitted as general average.

"the provisions of this Rule shall be applied to the second port . . .": This r.X deals, effectively, only with the cost of:

(1) entering and leaving a port of refuge:
(2) discharging cargo; or
(3) storing and reloading cargo,

and, whilst it might have made the matter clearer if r.XI had also been expressly mentioned, there can be no doubt that the port charges and crew wages, etc.

[33] See also paras 10.26–10.27, above.

[34] *Marida v Oswal Steel* [1992] 1 Lloyd's Rep. 636 at 644. The decision was upheld in the Court of Appeal [1993] 1 Lloyd's Rep. 411, Hoffmann L.J. dissenting but reversed in the House of Lord ([1994] 1 Lloyd's Rep. 1), but in neither of those tribunals did the point under the second paragraph of r.X(a) arise directly for decision. In the House of Lords the views of Hobhouse J. on the point are referred to without criticism, and it is submitted that his decision on the second paragraph of r.X(a) remains valid. The case is discussed in more detail in connection with r.XIV, para.14.31 et seq., below.

[35] See r.G, above.

incurred during the detention at the second port of refuge are independently recoverable under the provisions of r.XI(b), which applies to any port or place, whether it be a first or second port of refuge.

10.37 **"The provisions of Rule XI shall be applied to the prolongation of the voyage occasioned by such removal"**: Rule XI provides, inter alia, for the allowance in general average of crew wages, etc. and fuel and stores consumed during the periods:

(1) deviating into and out of a port of refuge; or
(2) detained in a port of refuge.

Both periods might naturally be construed as a "prolongation of the voyage", but in the particular context and development of the York-Antwerp Rules, the term "prolongation of the voyage" applies particularly to period (1) above.[36]

The important point to note is that the wages and maintenance of the crew and any fuel and stores consumed during any deviation to and from the second port of refuge are allowable as general average.

Historical Development and Practice of Rule X(B)

Glasgow Resolutions 1860, York Rules 1864 and York-Antwerp Rules 1877

10.38 These are considered under r.X(a)[37] as the rule was not then divided.

York-Antwerp Rules 1890

10.39 The 1877 r.VII had stated that:

> "Whenever the cost of discharging cargo . . . is admissible as general average, the cost of reloading and stowing such cargo . . . shall likewise be so admitted."

But it failed to provide under what circumstances the discharge of the cargo should be admitted as general average. This was remedied at the International Conference at Liverpool in 1890 as follows:

> *"Rule X(b)*
>
> The cost of discharging cargo from a ship, whether at a port or place of loading, call or refuge, shall be admitted as general average, when the discharge was necessary for the common safety or to enable damage to the ship, caused by sacrifice or accident during the voyage, to be repaired, if the repairs were necessary for the safe prosecution of the voyage."

[36] See also para.11.10, below.
[37] See paras 10.21-10.23, above.

York-Antwerp Rules 1924

The amendments made on this occasion consisted of allowing the cost of "handling on board" as well as of actual discharging, and of extending the allowance to the cost of handling and discharging, not only cargo, but fuel and stores as well. Before 1924 a certain difference in practice, at any rate in this country, had existed regarding the treatment of the cost of moving cargo from one hold to another or on to deck, without an actual discharge overside, in order to effect repairs: also of the cost of handling or discharging fuel or stores, neither of which were mentioned in the old rule. These difficulties were removed by the amendments made at that time. **10.40**

A further amendment to the 1890 rule was the deletion of the words "during the voyage" appearing in that rule after the words "sacrifice or accident". These words were left out both by the Committee of the Association of Average Adjusters in their proposals for revision of the 1890 Rules and also by the Drafting Committee appointed by the International Law Association. The intention of the omission of these words was to include within the scope of the rule cases in which a vessel has sustained damage which is entirely unsuspected at the time of her arrival at a port of loading, and it is not until her draught is increased by reasons of loading cargo that the damage becomes apparent (for example by water entering a hold; this incursion of water would constitute an "accident" within the meaning of the York-Antwerp Rules). In such circumstances, if cargo has to be discharged in order to effect repairs necessary for the safe prosecution of the voyage, and a claim is made by the shipowner for general average contribution, it would, of course, be open to the owner of the cargo called upon to contribute to exercise any rights of defence or counterclaim which he may have under the contract of affreightment.

"*Rule X(b)*

The cost of handling on board or discharging cargo, fuel or stores, whether at a port or place of loading, call or refuge, shall be admitted as general average when the handling or discharge was necessary for the common safety or to enable damage to the ship caused by sacrifice or accident to be repaired, if the repairs were necessary for the safe prosecution of the voyage."

York-Antwerp Rules 1950

No change. **10.41**

York-Antwerp Rules 1974

The existing 1950 rule was retained unaltered on this occasion but certain new wording was added at the end of the rule to deny general average allowances in two specific instances. Firstly: **10.42**

> ". . . except in cases where the damage is discovered at a port or place of loading or call without any accident or other extraordinary circumstance connected with such damage having taken place during the voyage."

An example of the situation envisaged by this wording might be as follows: while a vessel is in a port loading cargo, or at a port of call, the opportunity is taken to open up the main engine for routine survey and inspection and a crack is discovered in the crankshaft for which repairs necessary for the safe prosecution of the voyage are essential. As there has been no sudden breakage or breakdown (which in itself would constitute an "accident"[38] within the meaning of the York-Antwerp Rules), there will now be no allowance in general average for any discharge, etc. of cargo unless it can reasonably be shown that the fracture owed its origin to some "accident"[39] or other extraordinary circumstance"[40] having taken place during the current voyage. Secondly:

10.43 "The cost of handling on board or discharging cargo, fuel or stores shall not be admissible as general average when incurred solely for the purpose of re-stowage due to shifting daring the voyage unless such re-stowage is necessary for the common safety."

It is not uncommon for cargoes (particularly deck cargoes of timber or containers) to shift in heavy weather, and for the carrying vessel to put into a port of refuge for the common safety and to re-stow the cargo. Whilst the cost of entering and leaving the port of refuge in such circumstances is admissible as general average, the cost of re-stowing is so allowed only if the common safety is at risk even in the port, that is, if the vessel may still capsize in the port unless the list is righted. In the majority of cases the vessel and her shifted cargo are in no danger once within the port and the re-stowage is carried out essentially for the "safe prosecution of the voyage".[41]

Although there were no words in the York-Antwerp Rules 1950 to permit the allowance in general average of the cost of discharging or handling cargo except when necessary for the common safety, or to enable damage to the ship caused by sacrifice or accident to be repaired, if the repairs were necessary for the safe prosecution of the voyage, it is believed that in certain parts of the world, and notably on the West Coast of the United States, the Rules were construed on a less than strict basis and that the cost of re-stowing shifted cargoes was treated as general average.

To make the matter clear beyond doubt, express wording, as above, was introduced in 1974.

It may here be remarked that wages and maintenance of crew. etc. during detention of a vessel to re-stow cargo which has shifted were customarily allowed as general average under the 1950 Rules and the framers of the 1974 Rules accordingly felt that no special provision on this subject was needed in r.XI(b) of the

[38] See para.10.32, above.
[39] See para.10.32, above.
[40] See para.10.33, above.
[41] See para.10.48, below.

1974 Rules. The matter was again raised in 1994 and reference may be made to para.10.66, below.

York-Antwerp Rules 1994

No change, but there were proposals to reverse the provisions of 1974 that the cost of restowing a shifted cargo should be chargeable to general average only when necessary for the common safety. It was suggested that at the end of the second paragraph should be added "or for the safe prosecution of the voyage", an expression which would have permitted the allowance in general average of the cost of restowing almost every shifted cargo. This proposal was not accepted by the International Sub-Committee. **10.44**

York Antwerp Rules 2004

No change other than "allowed" for "admitted", "allowable" for "admissible", and the numbering of the paragraphs. **10.45**

RULE X(b)

***(i)* The cost of handling on board or discharging cargo, fuel or stores whether at a port or place of loading, call or refuge, shall be admitted/allowed as general average, when the handling or discharging was necessary for the common safety or to enable damage to the ship caused by sacrifice or accident to be repaired, if the repairs were necessary for the safe prosecution of the voyage, except in cases where the damage to the ship is discovered at a port or place of loading or call without any accident or other extraordinary circumstance connected with such damage having taken place during the voyage.**

(ii) The cost of handling on board or discharging cargo, fuel or stores shall not be admissible/allowable as general average when incurred solely for the purpose of restowage due to shifting during the voyage, unless such restowage is necessary for the common safety.

CONSTRUCTION

In its positive provisions, this sub-rule deals with the cost of handling or discharging cargo, fuel and stores in two distinct sets of circumstances, namely: (1) where necessary for the common safety; and (2) to enable damage caused by sacrifice or accident to be repaired, if the repairs were necessary for the safe prosecution of the voyage. **10.46**

"The cost of handling on board": As already mentioned, this expression relates to the situation where cargo, fuel or stores need to be shifted for the common safety or to effect repairs necessary for the safe prosecution of the voyage, but where it is not necessary that they be discharged ashore from the vessel.

"or discharging": The word "discharge" means simply to relieve a vessel of her cargo, fuel or stores, that is, to get them out of the vessel. This definition is important when dealing, for instance, with the cost of discharging worthless cargo, to which further reference will be made in paras 10.72 et seq., below. The word cannot be construed and extended to include also transporting to a dumping site.

"cargo": See under r.I.[42]

10.47 **"for the common safety"**: See commentary under r.A.

In the context of the present rule relating to expenses incurred when the vessel is within the comparative safety of a port of refuge, it is clear that the same words "common safety" must relate to a serious situation when ship and cargo are truly in the "grip of a disaster". Examples of situations where the discharge or shifting of cargo, etc. might be necessary for the common safety would include where the ship is holed and making water or where the ship or cargo is on fire.

10.48 **"repairs necessary for the safe prosecution of the voyage"**: This expression looks to a time in the future when the common safety will be endangered if the voyage continues. The degree of damage to the ship necessary to meet the requirements of the expression is the same as–and no less than–would be necessary to endanger the "common safety" of the adventure if the vessel were at sea.

For example, a vessel may lose her propeller at sea and thereby be rendered unfit to encounter the ordinary perils of the sea. A resort to a port of refuge will be justified for the "common safety", but once within a port where repairs can be effected, safety will have been attained, and some alternative expression is required if (as was intended by the early framers of the Rules) general average allowances are to continue. The alternative expression chosen was "necessary for the safe prosecution of the voyage", and it merely provides for a situation in port which, if the ship were at sea, would endanger the "common safety". It does not introduce another lower standard of damage which will permit general average allowances to be made under this or other of the York-Antwerp Rules.

10.49 Difficult problems with regard to the cost of discharging cargo can arise when the voyage either is, or might be, lawfully abandoned[43] at a port of refuge. If the discharge is necessary for the common safety, the cost is always allowable as general average, but where the discharge is only for the purpose of repairs that would have been necessary for the safe prosecution of the voyage, and that voyage is not prosecuted, it is submitted that the cost should fall on the cargo interests alone,[44] subject to any express provision in the contract of affreightment. This applies even in those cases where no formal declaration of the abandonment of the voyage is made, and also to those cases where no decision to abandon could be taken until the discharge had been wholly or partly carried out.

It has been argued that, because rr.X(c) and XI(b) provide for the allowance in general average of certain storage charges and wages, etc. of crew until the completion of discharge even though the voyage has been abandoned previously, the cost of discharge itself must be allowable. This argument is untenable, however equitable it may appear. It is well recognised that the numbered rules fall to be construed strictly, and there are special reasons why wages and maintenance of

[42] See para.1.28, above.

[43] For the circumstances in which the shipowner is entitled to abandon the voyage, see para.10.67, below, and paras 00.43 et seq., above.

[44] *Medina Princess* [1965] 1 Lloyd's Rep. 361 at 522; *Myrto* [1984] 2 Lloyd's Rep. 341.

crew, etc. are allowed after the abandonment of the voyage which have no application to the cost of discharge.

"sacrifice or accident": These words presumably have the same meanings as in sub-rule (a).[45] It will be noticed that the words "extraordinary circumstances"[46] are omitted so that if such circumstances (as opposed to sacrifice or accident) necessitate putting into a port of refuge for repairs, the expenses of entering the port, and the corresponding expenses of leaving will be allowed in general average, but the cost of handling and discharging the cargo will not be allowed unless such handing or discharging were necessary for the common safety. An example of a case which would be within sub-rule (a) but not (b) is that of a ship whose main shaft is out of alignment on sailing with the result that the bearings slowly overheat and the ship is obliged to put into a port of refuge for the common safety, but is safe as soon as she is within the port. **10.50**

In *Vlassopoulos v British and Foreign Marine Insurance Co*[47] (the *Makis* case), Roche J. construed "accident" in the sub-rule as being confined to accidents which involved a threat to the common safety, but this decision was influenced by the fact that (as Roche J. held) under the 1924 Rules the lettered rules governed the interpretation of the numbered rules. With the inclusion of the Rule of Interpretation, this decision is no longer applicable.

"except in cases where the damage to the ship is discovered at a port or place of loading or call without any accident or other extraordinary circumstances connected with such damage having taken place during the voyage": These words were added to the sub-rule in 1974, on which occasion some effort **10.51** was made to reduce the incidence of general average cases by increasing the stringency of the criteria by which it should be determined whether a general average situation exists. It was felt that the outstanding candidate for exclusion was the "port of call" type general average where damage was merely discovered at a port of loading or of call without any accident or other extraordinary circumstance having taken place during the voyage.

Two examples already mentioned may serve as a guide to the practice probably intended to be established.

(1) Concurrently with the loading of cargo, the opportunity is taken to open up the main engine for routine survey and inspection, and a crack is discovered in the crankshaft for which repairs necessary for the safe prosecution of the voyage are essential. The crack has progressed gradually over a lengthy period and its origin antedates the commencement of the current voyage.[48]
No allowances can be made in general average for discharging cargo, etc. or for detention expenses at the port.

(2) At some date prior to the commencement of the current voyage a crack is caused in the ship's side plating which passes completely unnoticed. On

[45] See para.10.32, above.
[46] cf. r.X(a), para.10.33, above.
[47] *Vlassopoulos* [1929] 1 K.B. 187 at 201.
[48] See para.10.42.

loading cargo, however, the ship's draught increases and water pours through the crack into the hold, necessitating the discharge of cargo in order to carry out repairs necessary for the safe prosecution of the voyage.

Although the crack itself was sustained before the commencement of the voyage, what might be termed a new accident has intervened with the cargo on board (the incursion of sea water), and the cost of discharging cargo, etc. and other detention expenses at the port can be treated as general average. The shipowner's right to claim contribution from the cargo would be subject to any defence or counterclaim of the cargo owner for breach of the contract of affreightment, for example breach of any absolute warranty of seaworthiness or of the Hague Rules duty to use due diligence to make the ship seaworthy. However, provided a general average situation can be established under the York-Antwerp Rules, the shipowner should be able to recover cargo's proportion of general average from his Protecting and Indemnity Association, subject to the conditions of entry.

10.52 When drafted in 1974 it was considered unnecessary to define the extent of "voyage" for the purpose of this rule as the functions mentioned were sufficiently general to make such a definition unnecessary; that is to say, that if provision had been made for allowance of costs of "handling on board", there was no further need to provide that "voyage"' begins at the commencement of loading. On the grounds that the Drafting Committee intended that the voyage begins only at the commencement of loading, and that there should be a community of interests at the time of the accident, it is submitted that:

(1) Where a vessel sails in ballast from A under charter to load at B and sustains damage during the passage which is discovered only during or after loading the cargo at B, but before leaving B, there is no general average unless some "new accident" has occurred such as suggested in example (2) above.

(2) Where the vessel loads at A and B and damage sustained during the passage from A to B is discovered during or after loading cargo at B, but before leaving B, there is an acceptable general average for the ship and cargo A (other than for the cost of discharging, etc. cargo loaded at B). On the basis outlined in (1) above, no general average exists vis-à-vis cargo B, and it would be appropriate, therefore, to exclude the value of cargo B from contribution.

(3) Where the vessel loads at A and B and damage sustained during the passage from A to B is discovered after leaving B, all property on board at the time of any deviation to a port of refuge must be brought in to contribute, but cargo B may plead a breach of the contract of affreightment.

10.53 **"The cost of handling on board or discharging cargo, fuel or stores shall not be admissible as general average when incurred solely for the purpose of restowage due to shifting during the voyage":** As stated above,[49] this second

[49] See para.10.43, above.

paragraph of the sub-rule was added in 1974 to emphasise that where cargo, fuel or stores had shifted during the voyage and the sole object of the handling on board or discharge was to restow properly and to correct the vessel's trim and stability for the safe prosecution of the voyage, the cost would not be admissible as general average. Where, however, the handling or discharge was also necessary: (1) because the common safety was at risk even within the comparative shelter of the port of refuge; or (2) to enable damage to the ship caused by sacrifice or accident to be repaired, if the repairs were necessary for the safe prosecution of the voyage, the cost of handling on board or discharging only as much cargo as was necessary for either of these purposes would be recoverable under the positive provisions of the first paragraph of the sub-rule.

"unless such restowage is necessary for the common safety": In the light of the commentary in the previous paragraph these words are possibly superfluous, but they may serve to emphasise that the cost of restowing a shifted cargo, etc. is allowable as general average when necessary for the common safety. (It must be reiterated that the cost is also allowable when the handling or discharge is necessary for repairs for the safe prosecution of the voyage.) **10.54**

Historical Development and Practice of Rule X(C)

This sub-rule deals essentially with the costs of: (1) storage; and (2) reloading of cargo discharged at a port of refuge. Under the laws of almost all countries, the cost of both operations were charged in appropriate circumstances to general average, but in this country the practice[50] was to charge the costs of storage and reloading as special charges on cargo and freight, respectively. **10.55**

To secure international uniformity, the costs of both operations were made the subject of general average from the very first international conference at Glasgow in 1860. The wording of the Glasgow Resolution 1860, the York Rule 1864, and the York-Antwerp Rule 1877 has already been discussed.[51]

York-Antwerp Rules 1890

It was on this occasion that the single rule entitled "Expenses at Port of Refuge etc.," was sub-divided into three sections, of which r.X(c) read as follows: **10.56**

> "Whenever the cost of discharging cargo from a ship is admissible as general average, the cost of re-loading and storing such cargo on board the said ship, together with all storage charges on such cargo, shall likewise be so admitted. But when the ship is condemned or does not proceed on her original voyage, no storage expenses incurred after the date of the ship's condemnation or of the abandonment of the voyage shall be admitted as general average."

[50] See para.10.06, above.
[51] See paras 10.21–10.24, above.

The first sentence was almost identical with the wording in the 1877 rule, and although the second sentence was new, it was probably nothing more than a re-statement of the existing practice.

York-Antwerp Rules 1924

10.57 *"Rule X(c)"*

> Whenever the cost of handling or discharging cargo, fuel or stores is admissible as general average, the cost of reloading and stowing such cargo, fuel or stores on board the ship, together with all storage charges (including fire insurance, if incurred) on such cargo, fuel or stores, shall likewise be so admitted. But when the ship is condemned or does not proceed on her original voyage, no storage expenses incurred after the date of the ship's condemnation or of the abandonment of the voyage shall be admitted as general average. In the event of the condemnation of the ship or the abandonment of the voyage before completion of discharge of cargo, storage expenses, as above, shall be admitted as general average up to date of completion of discharge."

Under the 1890 Rules this sub-rule related only to the cost of storage and reloading cargo. In the 1924 Rules an amendment was introduced (as was done in the case of sub-rule (b)) extending this sub-rule to cover such costs in relation to fuel and stores. Two other amendments were made in the first sentence of the sub-rule. First, the word "stowing" was substituted for the misleading expression "storing" ("storing such cargo on board the said ship") and the second amendment consisted of including the cost of fire insurance (if incurred) as one of the charges of storage ashore.

10.58 The last of the 1924 amendments consisted of adding the third sentence of the sub-rule, extending the allowance of storage expenses ashore until all the cargo was discharged, even though at that date the ship had been condemned or the voyage abandoned. A similar amendment was made to r.XI(b) allowing the continuation of allowances for wages and maintenance on the same basis, with the intention of encouraging shipowners not to pay off their crew prematurely. It is assumed that the continuation of allowances for storage was also intended to encourage the safeguarding of cargo until its owners could make arrangements to deal with it appropriately. It must be stressed that once the voyage has been abandoned or the ship condemned, the cost of discharging cargo can be treated as general average only if necessary for the common safety.

York-Antwerp Rules 1950

10.59 The 1950 version of the sub-rule was the same as that of 1924 save that for the words "(including fire insurance, if incurred)" were substituted "(including insurance, if reasonably incurred)", thus permitting the allowance of premiums for reasonable but wider insurances where, for instance, cargo was discharged into lighters rather than into a warehouse.

One objection to the deletion of the word "fire" was that it might foster the idea that the shipowner was under some duty to effect insurances against all manner of extraneous risks. To counter this suggestion it was proposed at the Amsterdam Conference that it be minuted that the intention was not to impose any duty of effecting insurance upon the shipowner and that no such obligation should rest upon him.

It is clear that the carrier, as bailee of the cargo, must take all necessary steps to ensure that cargo discharged ashore at a port of refuge is properly kept and cared for, but, as was stated at the Amsterdam Conference, the carrier is under no duty or obligation to effect wide insurances on the cargo discharged ashore.

York-Antwerp Rules 1974

On this occasion, the wording of the sub-rule was rearranged for greater clarity, but no changes in previous practice were intended or made. **10.60**

York-Antwerp Rules 1994

The 1974 wording was left unchanged on this occasion but a probably unnecessary and therefore confusing addition was made at the end of the first paragraph: "The provisions of Rule XI shall be applied to the extra period of detention occasioned by such reloading or restowing." The effect of this addition will be discussed below in para.10.66. **10.61**

York-Antwerp Rules 2004

No change except "allowable" for "admissible" and "allowed" for "admitted" **10.62**

RULE X(c) **10.63**

> **Whenever the cost of handling or discharging cargo, fuel or stores is admissible/allowable as general average, the costs of storage, including insurance if reasonably incurred, reloading and stowing of such cargo, fuel or stores shall likewise be admitted/allowed as general average. The provisions of Rule XI shall be applied to the extra period of detention occasioned by such reloading or restowing.**
>
> **But when the ship is condemned or does not proceed on her original voyage, storage expenses shall be admitted/allowed as general average only up to the date of the ship's condemnation or of the abandonment of the voyage or up to the date of completion of discharge of cargo if the condemnation or abandonment takes place before that date.**

CONSTRUCTION

This sub-rule is complementary to the sub-rule (b) above. Between them they provide a complete code for the treatment of the cost of handling on board, discharging, reloading and stowing cargo, fuel and stores on board the ship, and **10.64** of storage ashore, whether the adventure be terminated at the port or placed concerned or continued therefrom.

"Whenever the cost of handling or discharging cargo, fuel or stores is admissible as general average": If a claim is to be admissible under this sub-rule the facts must be such that a claim for the costs of handling or discharging cargo, etc. can be substantiated under sub-rule (b).[52]

"the costs of storage": The word "storage" comprises both:

(1) the action of transporting cargo fuel or stores to a warehouse or other place of storage; and
(2) the period during which the property remains in store and for which rent or hire will be charged.

On occasion, cargo which has been discharged for the common safety or to enable repairs to be effected to the ship which are necessary for the safe prosecution of the voyage, is not reloaded for various reasons. The cost of storage on such cargo is invariably allowed as general average up to the time when the vessel resumes her voyage, but thereafter its treatment will depend upon individual circumstances. If the cargo is left behind merely because it has been damaged by accidental causes, the cost of storage after the vessel has sailed will be treated as a special charge on cargo. If, however, the cargo is not reloaded for reasons directly caused by a general average act. for example: (a) the cargo was damaged by a general average sacrifice; (b) the ship cannot reload the cargo because she is already down to her marks owing to flooding of the holds to extinguish a fire; (c) water used to extinguish a fire renders part of the cargo dangerous and liable to combust spontaneously, the cost of storage for a reasonable time will still be allowed as general average.

10.65 **"including insurance, if reasonably incurred"**: Insurances under this part of the sub-rule are not limited to the risks of fire alone: other appropriate and reasonable risks may be insured against.

In The Mormacmar cargo discharged ashore into a warehouse at a port of refuge was destroyed by fire, and no insurances on the cargo whilst ashore were placed by the carrier. It was held by Medina D.J. that:

> "The respondents . . . were trustees of the goods thus placed ashore and their duty to keep and care for[53] the goods necessarily included, under the circumstances, the duty to place insurance against the risk of fire, collapse of structures and rising of navigable water."

In *Marine Insurance & General Average* in the United States, Leslie J. Buglass states:

> "It is highly desirable that any cargo discharged from the vessel should be insured against shore perils (including fire) and, if it is stored on lighters, also have effective

[52] See para.10.45, above.
[53] Carriage of Goods by Sea Act, 46 U.S. Code, s.1303(2).

> marine insurance. The amount to be insured is the estimated value of the cargo in its sound or damaged condition, as the case may be. Such insurance should also contain a clause to the effect that, it take precedence over any other insurance effected on the goods because such insurance is for the benefit of the owners of the goods or the original insurers. Sometimes, such insurances also incorporate a clause stipulating that in the event of damage to goods, the general average has first lien (on the proceeds of any claim under the insurance) for any unpaid salvage and/or general average or special charges."

As discussed by John Wilson (joint editor of the 11th and 12th editions) in another book,[54] the decision in the Mormacmar is a little surprising if the shipowner had done all he reasonably can to care for the cargo. If a bulk cargo is involved enquiries can be made with the cargo insurer to see whether any additional insurance is in fact required. If the number of interests involved with a containerised or other general cargo make such enquiries impracticable any insurance should be effected on limited conditions appropriate for the risks of storage at that particular location, with the additional clauses suggested by Buglass. Any damage that occurs during the acts of discharging and loading will be allowable under r.XII so that any insurance should relate only to the period of storage.

"The provisions of Rule XI shall be applied to the extra period of detention occasioned by such reloading or restowing": This sentence was added in 1994 at the suggestion of the United States Maritime Law Association and received the support of the International Sub-Committee, they reporting that it was felt to be a clarification of the then present practice and not an extension of general average. The ship's readiness to proceed had always been construed as referring to her readiness as a laden ship–that is, with previously discharged cargo reloaded and stowed. 10.66

"when the ship is condemned": This may arise when the ship has suffered such damage by excepted perils that repairs would be commercially impossible, and the shipowner is in consequence discharged from his obligation to repair her and continue the voyage.[55] 10.67

"or does not proceed on her original voyage": Even where the ship is not condemned, it may be impracticable for her to proceed upon her original voyage. For example, the delay during the necessary repairs may be so great as to frustrate the contract of carriage; or the extent of the damage and the repair facilities at the port of refuge may be such that the only practicable course is to abandon the voyage or tranship the cargo, and take the original ship in ballast to another port for repairs. The circumstances in which matters of this nature will entitle the shipowner to abandon the voyage are dealt with in Section 2 of this work,[56] where it is also noted that the shipowner has the right to tranship the cargo, if he so wishes.

However, in the application of the second paragraph of r.X(c) it appears to matter not whether the shipowner is justified in abandoning the voyage. On the

[54] See Wilson, *The Insurance of Average Disbursements & Other Subsidiary Interests Following a Marine Casualty* (Association of Average Adjusters, 1988).

[55] See *Assicurazioni Generali v Bessie Morris S.S. Co* [1892] 1 Q.B. 571: [1892] 2 Q.B. 652; *Kulukundis v Norwich Union* [1937] 1 K.B. 1; see para.00.43, above.

[56] See paras 00.43 et seq., above.

wording of the rule, the only relevant consideration is whether or not the vessel proceeds on the original voyage. Thus if, for good reason or bad, the shipowner decides not to continue the voyage from the port of refuge, storage charges will cease to qualify as general average expenditure from the date of abandonment or, if later, of the completion of discharge. If the shipowner wrongfully abandons the voyage he will be liable in damages and the provisions of r.D will apply.

So long as the shipowner is justified in abandoning the voyage at the port of refuge, he will be entitled to recover in full from the cargo owner any storage charges which he incurs thereafter on the cargo.[57] However, it seems unlikely that this right would extend to entitle the shipowner to recover the expense of destroying or disposing of worthless cargo; such remedies as the shipowner has to recover these expenses are discussed below.[58]

10.68 **"storage expenses"**: The second paragraph of r.X(c) makes no mention of the other expenses, apart from storage, referred to in the first paragraph of the rule–that is, insurance, reloading and stowage. However the intention appears to be that insurance charges should be dealt with in the same way as storage charges and, if reasonably incurred, allowed up to the same date and that once storage charges have ceased to qualify for contribution in general average, any subsequent reloading and stowage expenses involved in forwarding the cargo from the port of refuge will also be disallowed. Where cargo has to be left at the port of refuge because it has been damaged as a result of a general average sacrifice, any storage expenses reasonably incurred will be allowed under r.XVI or under the lettered rules.

10.69 **"the date of the ship's condemnation or of the abandonment of the voyage"**: It is suggested that the date is not that of the casualty or frustrating event but:

(1) in the case of the ship's condemnation, the date upon which it is ascertained that the ship is commercially irreparable[59];
(2) in the case of abandonment of the voyage, the date upon which:
 (a) it is ascertained that the voyage is frustrated.[60] or
 (b) the parties agree to abandon the voyage; or
 (c) the shipowner gives notice that he is abandoning the voyage; or
 (d) the decision is taken to tranship the cargo[61] whichever is earlier.

10.70 It is submitted that "the abandonment of the voyage" in r.X(c) includes the case where the decision is taken to tranship, even when the transhipment is in continuation of the voyage.[62] This interpretation reflects the earlier phrase–"when the ship . . . does not proceed on her original voyage", which clearly includes the case where the original ship does not proceed on the voyage. It would also reflect the

[57] See *China Pacific v Food Corp of India* [1982] A.C. 939 at 960; *Notara v Henderson* (1872) L.R. 7 Q.B. 225.
[58] See paras 10.72 et seq., below.
[59] See para.10.66, above.
[60] See paras 00.37 et seq., below.
[61] See para.10.70, below.
[62] See paras G.41 et seq., below.

usual practice in cases of transhipment, which is to treat cargo handling expenses at the port of refuge as a particular charge on freight, except in so far as they fall to be made good in general average as a substituted expense.

"Up to the date of completion of discharge": It is suggested that these words should be read as including that date. **10.71**

"cargo": See commentary on r.1.[63]

The rule does not provide for the case where part of the cargo is sold or disposed of at the port of refuge. For the method of adjustment in such a case reference should be made to rr.XVI and XVII.

Discharging and Disposal of Worthless Cargo

Cargo may be damaged and rendered worthless by accident (fire, stranding, collision, etc.) or by general average sacrifice (for example water used to extinguish a fire), and require to be disposed of. Dumping cargo at sea is now illegal under many jurisdictions and the requirements of the environmental authorities at a port of refuge may be exacting and often very expensive. **10.72**

Where cargo has been damaged by sacrifice it is generally accepted practice to regard the resultant disposal costs as a foreseeable consequence of that sacrifice.

Where the cargo has been damaged by accident, more complex problems can arise, as illustrated in the following examples. All the following examples assume a loaded vessel that has been involved in a serious collision which has resulted in the flooding of one or more holds. The vessel has entered a port of refuge to effect repairs necessary for the safe prosecution of the voyage.

Case A

A mixed general cargo of bags, bales, boxes, crates, and drums, etc. is largely submerged in the affected hold. It is discharged ashore, transported to a warehouse, and there sorted and separated into categories such as: **10.73**

(1) fit to be reloaded after repairs to the ship;
(2) fit to be reloaded into the original or a following vessel after reconditioning;
(3) severely damaged, and to be sold locally; and
(4) worthless, and to be dumped.

It is submitted that the various expenses should be dealt with as follows:

[63] See para.1.28, above.

Discharging

10.74 As general average in accordance with r.X(b),[64] the discharge being necessary in order to carry out repairs to the ship necessary for the safe prosecution of the voyage. The fact that some of the cargo may be worthless does not affect the issue.

Transporting to warehouse

10.75 As general average in accordance with r.X(c)[65] as part of the cost of "storage" (putting into store).

Sorting and separating

10.76 As special charges on the cargo involved, this being exclusively for the benefit of that cargo, and of no concern to the general average, the damage being the result of an accident.

Reconditioning

10.77 As special charges on the particular cargo involved.

Dumping

10.78 The costs of disposal of accidentally damaged cargo is not allowable as general average. The port or local health authorities will generally look to the shipowner (as the person in possession of the cargo and with a valuable asset within their jurisdiction that can be detained), to pay for the costs of disposing of cargo that cannot be re-loaded or otherwise on-carried. The cover provided by most P&I clubs includes the cost of removing and disposing of damaged or worthless cargo, in so far as there is no other recourse to recover such expenses and after deduction of any proceeds of sale. If the voyage is justifiably abandoned there are (subject always to the law applicable to the contract of affreightment) generally good legal grounds for saying that the shipowner is entitled to call upon the cargo owner to take delivery at the port of refuge. If the cargo interests fail to take delivery or accept responsibility for their cargo they are liable in damages for the costs incurred by the shipowners.

Warehouse rent (storage)

10.79 As general average in accordance with r.X(c)[66] up to the time when the ship leaves port after repairs: thereafter, the rent will be a special charge on the cargo

[64] See para.10.45, above.
[65] See para.10.63, above.
[66] See para.10.63, above.

still being reconditioned. (It is assumed that the worthless cargo will already have been dumped.)

Reloading

(a) **Into the original vessel**. As general average in accordance with r.X(c).[67] 10.80

(b) **Into a following vessel**. As special charges on the cargo concerned. It is probable that the cost of reloading into another vessel will be no more than the charge that would have been incurred in reloading into the original vessel and which would have been allowed as general average, but one must take facts as one finds them, and the fact is that the common adventure is over for the cargo left behind when the original vessel leaves the port of refuge, and it contributes on its value at that port. 10.81

Case B

The submerged cargo in the affected hold is recognised at a very early stage to be worthless and requiring dumping. However, and with ecological problems in mind, the local authorities take about a month to approve a suitable site for the dumping. Accordingly, the worthless cargo is discharged into barges and stored there until final arrangements can be made concerning the dumping. The worthless cargo is then transferred to trucks and transported to the dumping site. 10.82

The ship completes repairs and sails from the port of refuge before the dumping takes place.

It is submitted that the various expenses should be dealt with as follows:

Discharging into barges

As general average in accordance with r.X(b)[68] the discharge being necessary in order to carry out repairs to the ship necessary for the safe prosecution of the voyage, and even though it is known at the time that the cargo is worthless. 10.83

Barge hire

From a commonsense point of view, this charge is part of the cost of disposing of the worthless cargo, but as the numbered rules of the York-Antwerp Rules must be construed strictly, the barge hire counts as "storage" and, up to the time the original vessel leaves the port of refuge on completion of repairs, it can be allowed as general average in accordance with r.X(c).[69] 10.84

[67] See para.10.63, above.
[68] See para.10.45, above.
[69] See para.10.63, above.

Dumping

10.85 The barge hire subsequent to the original vessel leaving the port of refuge, the cost of discharging from the barges and loading into the trucks, and the transport to and discharge at the dumping site, are subject to the same considerations as in case A, see para.10.78.

Case C

10.86 The vessel is carrying a bulk cargo of phosphate and in order to carry out repairs necessary for the safe prosecution of the voyage, it is necessary to discharge the entire cargo and it is recognised that the cargo in the affected hold is worthless and requires dumping.

The cargo is discharged into lorries, the sound being transported to a storage area and the worthless to a dumping site. The transport costs, whether to the storage area or to the dumping site, are identical.

It is submitted that the various expenses should be dealt with as follows:

Discharging

10.87 As general average in accordance with r.X(b).[70]

Transporting to dumping site

10.88 As with other costs of disposing of worthless cargo, payable by the shipowner and/or his P&I club.

The fact that it costs no more to transport the worthless cargo to a dumping site than to a storage area is no reason to expect general average to bear that cost. It is not a substituted expense, for there is never any reason to do anything other than dump the cargo, and while the word "storage" in r.X(c)[71] comprises the cost of transporting to a "store", a dumping site can in no way be construed as being a "store".

Case D

10.89 The vessel carries a bulk cargo of grain products which needs to be discharged in order to effect repairs. It is recognised that the cargo remaining in the affected hold is worthless. Authority is given for this damaged cargo to be discharged into barges and taken to an approved disposal area. Attempts are first made to pump out this cargo afloat, but it has tended to cake and solidify, with the result that the operation proves so difficult that, eventually, the vessel drydocks, the damaged shell plating is removed, and the worthless cargo is bulldozed from the hold into

[70] See para.10.45, above.
[71] See para.10.63, above.

the drydock, loaded onto a conveyor belt and discharged to the dumping barge alongside.

It is submitted that the various expenses should be dealt with as follows:

Afloat

Hire of pumps, etc. for discharging. As general average in accordance with r.X(b),[72] the discharge being necessary in order to carry out repairs necessary for the safe prosecution of the voyage. 10.90

Hire of barges. As costs of disposing of worthless cargo, and payable by the shipowner and/or his P&I club. 10.91

The purpose of the barge is to transport the worthless cargo to the dumping ground, and not to "store" the cargo as in case B.

In drydock

Drydocking, dues, and removal of damaged plating. As particular average on ship, except that any extra drydock dues incurred over and above the normal period of repairs can sometimes be considered as costs of discharge and allowed as general average in accordance with r.X(b).[73] The drydock has been stemmed solely for repairs, and the damaged shell plating has to be removed for permanent repairs to the collision damage. 10.92

Hire of bulldozers, etc. As part of the costs of discharge and allowed as general average. 10.93

Hire of conveyor belt (payloader). It has already been suggested in para.10.45, above, that the word "discharge" means simply to relieve the vessel of her cargo, that is, to get it out of the vessel. The present cost of transferring the worthless cargo from the drydock bottom to the dumping barge might, therefore, be considered as something other than "discharge". However, on this occasion it appears legitimate to consider it as a substituted expense for the more difficult and expensive operation of pumping out the cargo afloat, already attempted and partly effected. Accordingly, it is submitted that this charge should be treated as "discharging" and allowed as general average. 10.94

Hire of barges. As costs of disposal of worthless cargo, as above. 10.95

American Practice

In his *Marine Insurance and General Average in the United States*, 3rd edn, p.253, Buglass states that: 10.96

[72] See para.10.45, above.
[73] See para.10.45, above.

> "Sometimes cargo which has been discharged in order to effect repairs is damaged to such an extent as to be worthless and has to be dumped at the port of refuge. Under American practice, any expenses incurred in dumping such cargo at the port of refuge is allowed in general average. The entire operation of discharging the cargo, storing it and either reloading it into the vessel or dumping it if worthless, is considered to be one continuous general average act, and the entire cost is treated accordingly."

CREDIT: EXPENSES SAVED AT DESTINATION

10.97 In each of the above cases A/D it has been suggested that the cost of discharging the cargo from the ship at the port of refuge should be allowed as general average. There can be no dispute with regard to that portion of the cargo which is reloaded into the original carrying vessel after repairs, but what of the worthless cargo which is dumped, or the damaged cargo which is sold at the port of refuge or forwarded by other vessels after reconditioning? Can it be suggested that this cargo is at "destination" and that the charges fall, therefore, on the carrier if he is responsible for discharging the cargo at destination, or on the cargo interests themselves under, for example a "free in and out" contract? It is submitted that the correct answer is that the discharge takes place at an unintended port–a port of refuge–and that the cost is properly allowable as general average in accordance with a strict construction of r.X(b). The question then arises whether the expenses of discharge saved at destination should be credited to the general average.

There are two of the numbered rules that contain an express reference to giving credit against a general average allowance:

- Rule IX–where ships materials and stores (but not cargo) are used as fuel, credit must be given for the fuel saved.
- Rule XV–where loss of freight is allowed as general average, the contingent expenses saved by not incurring costs to earn the freight must be credited against the amount made good.

Other rules may involve the crediting or deduction of certain costs to arrive at the extra expense that is allowable, for example:

- Rule F—when a vessel is towed to destination, voyage expenses saved are deducted in order to arrive at the "additional" (or "extra" in the 1974 Rules) cost of that operation which can then be considered as a substituted expense.
- Rule VIII—when establishing the "extra cost of lightening" a vessel that is grounded near enough to destination for it to be unnecessary to reload the cargo.
- Rule XI(b)—when calculating the allowances for wages, fuel and port charges during the extra period of detention at a port of call that becomes a port of refuge.

Other rules do not contain any express reference to credits or the words "extra" or "additional", but the usual practice of adjusters is to give credit for ordinary voyage expenses saved:

- Rule VI—when a salvage operation involves towing the vessel to a port of call.
- Rule X—when a vessel enters a port of call which has become a port of refuge.

Two opposing schools of thought exist regarding the crediting of savings of the type now under discussion. One view considers that the credits and calculations outlined above indicate a general requirement to make proper credit where some saving or advantage has arisen to any of the parties to the adventure, in accordance with the principles of equity that lie at the ancient foundations of general average.

The opposing view is that, as part of the process of pragmatic compromise, the framers of the York-Antwerp Rules have made express provision for allowing only extra expenses or giving credit where it was deemed necessary; where no express provision was made on grounds of simplicity and economy in adjusting cases, none need be invented. One can make a case for either view although the latter argument is perhaps weakened by the examples of rr.VI and X, assuming the practices indicated are accepted. Perhaps all one can ask is that practitioners should be consistent in the view that they adopt—for example a "strict constructionist" should not deny credit for discharge expenses saved while allowing under r.X the costs of putting in to a port for survey following an incident when no damage is found.

However, it is suggested that on the rare occasions that courts consider the York-Antwerp Rules they will tend to favour strongly the strict construction of the Rules, particularly the numbered ones.

Replacement Cargo

A rare situation which could present itself in case D above, concerns the likely need to obtain a new cargo or solid ballast to stow in the empty hold from which the cargo has been washed out after the collision, or is dumped in the port of refuge. **10.98**

It will be appreciated that a ship may not be sufficiently strong to withstand a storm and heavy seas if one hold—particularly in the centre of the ship—is completely empty: she might break in two unless the cargo is evenly spread throughout her length. But the grain cargo remaining in the ship cannot simply be part transferred to an empty hold, for international regulations require that a bulk cargo of "liquid" grain must fill any hold in which it is carried to avoid it shifting in heavy weather and possibly causing the ship to list and capsize.

It is possible, therefore, that the shipowner may find it necessary to incur considerable extra expense to:

(1) bag 25 per cent of the cargo to stow on top of the bulk grain; or
(2) purchase a suitable amount of solid ballast to put in the empty hold, and dispose of it after the voyage or
(3) seek an additional part cargo for the empty hold.

Such additional expenses will be for the sole purpose of prosecuting the original voyage in safety, but there is no York-Antwerp rule—lettered or numbered—which will admit those expenses as general average. There is no peril affecting the ship and cargo while they remain in the port of refuge, and the expenses must therefore constitute simply an additional voyage expense to the shipowner caused by an accident. Although not relevant to the subject of general average, these expenses might be recoverable from the insurers on freight, but only if the freight is at risk.

Rule XI

Wages and Maintenance of Crew and other Expenses Putting in to and at a Port of Refuge

While r.X deals with the cost of entering a port of refuge and the cargo handling operations, etc. that may take place there, r.XI deals firstly with the costs of wages and fuel etc involved in getting to such a port. It then sets out the allowances for wages, fuel and port charges whilst there—the latter often being referred to collectively as "detention expenses" and, since 1994, also deals with various anti-pollution expenses. 11.01

English Law and Practice

Wages and maintenance of crew during the detention at a port of refuge were allowable as general average under the law of many countries, some of whom also admitted the wages and maintenance of crew whilst at sea, bearing up for a port of refuge and regaining position after leaving the port. In neither set of circumstances, however, has it ever been the practice in the United Kingdom[1] to allow such crew wages, etc. 11.02

Two reasons are offered for the English rule. The first is that the general average is terminated as soon as the port of refuge is reached, so that the expenses in question do not really form part of the cost of the general average operation, but of the delay in port in order to repair, which, in the case at least of accidental damage, falls within the shipowner's duty under his contract. The second reason is based on the principle, that, to constitute general average, an expenditure must be extraordinary in its kind, not the mere augmentation of an ordinary expenditure. The services of the crew during the whole voyage are due to the cargo, being, like

[1] US case law on the subject includes *Campbell v Alknomac* (1798) Bee 124; Fed. Cas. 2350; *Star of Hope* 9 Wall. 203 (1869); *Hobson v Lord* 92 U.S. 397 (1875). The allowance ceases when the voyage is abandoned, or the vessel is ready to resume her voyage: The Joseph Farwell 31 Fed. Rep. 844 (1887).

the use of the ship itself, purchased by the engagement to pay freight. The shipowner must take the chance of a longer or shorter voyage.

Lowndes continued with:

> "The English rule has been sanctioned by a series of decisions in our courts, which, though unsatisfactory enough as regards the reasons on which they are based, having for the most part been given at a time when the subject of general average was little understood, must now, it is presumed, be regarded as of binding authority."

Some of these decisions were set out in a footnote.[2] Nevertheless, it is clear that the point is still open for argument.[3]

To return to Lowndes' own text:

> "It would certainly have been more satisfactory if we could say that the arguments in favour of the allowance of wages and provisions had been laid before, and at least listened to by, the judges of the English courts. There is really something to be said in support of a practice which is of great antiquity, and very general amongst seafaring communities.
>
> Let us confine ourselves to the case of a ship which has put into port to repair damage which is itself the subject of general average.
>
> The shipowner contends that he is entitled to an indemnity for his loss of the ship's employment during the detention caused by the sacrifice made for the common safety. If he is entitled to a complete compensation for such loss, this ingredient in it is too important to be let out of sight. His right to compensation for loss of time is recognised by the courts when it is a question of damages under a collision suit. In such a case he received compensation for it, under the name of demurrage.
>
> But, it may objected, if the claim is for demurrage, why limit this to the cost of keeping the crew? Why not also bring in the loss of time? The answer is: The shipowner's loss of time is balanced by a corresponding loss on the part of the owners of the cargo. The delay is or may be prejudicial to the latter in two ways: they may lose their market—but against this may be set the chance of a rise in the market during the delay; they also lose the interest, during the delay, on the cost of their merchandise. This loss of interest bears the same proportion to the value of the goods which the shipowner's loss, by being deprived of the use of the ship, bears to the value of the ship. At any rate, if not always precisely the same, these two losses may not unfairly be set off against one another.[4] If insurance be left out of sight, it makes little or no difference, as between the owners of cargo and the owner of the ship, whether both these losses are brought in, or both left out. But, over and above this loss of time, the shipowner has to bear an additional burden by having to pay and maintain his crew, who would be paid off at the end of the voyage. He is not really compensated for the sacrifice which necessitated the delay, unless this outlay is made good to him.
>
> If, then, at any future time the courts should lay down the principle that, when there is a delay caused by a sacrifice, the loss thereby occasioned is to be completely compensated in general average, it may become necessary to reconsider the present

[2] 4th edn, p.240. The case most directly in point is *Power v Whitmore* (1815) 4 M. & S. 141, in which Lord Ellenborough thus briefly dismissed the claim: "General average must lay its foundation in a sacrifice of a part for the sake of the rest; but here was no sacrifice of any part by the master, but only of his time and patience."

[3] See *Atwood v Sellar* [1880] 5 Q.B.D. 286 at 291, CA; and *The Leitrim* [1902] P. 256 at 268.

[4] This argument is supported by the decision of Barnes J. in *The Leitrim* [1902] P. 256, which was followed and applied by Rowlatt J. in *Wetherall (J.H.) & Co v The London Assurance* [1931] 2 K.B. 448. See also *Anglo-Argentine Live Stock Agency v Temperley S.S. Co* [1899] 2 Q.B. 403 at 412.

rule as to the crew's wages and provisions. It is by no means improbable that in this respect a distinction may be drawn between the case of putting into port to repair accidental damage, and that in which the putting in has been necessitated by a sacrifice for the common safety.

At present, however, we do not seem to be ripe for such a change; the exclusion from general average of the crew's wages, during the delay[5] in the course of a voyage not terminated by wreck, must be taken to be a settled rule."

Historical Development and Practice of Rule XI(a)

York-Antwerp Rules 1924

Wages and maintenance of crew during the detention at a port of refuge were allowable as general average under the laws of many countries (though not Britain), and it is not surprising that the York-Antwerp Rules have made similar provision[6] since 1860. There was less international uniformity, however, with regard to the treatment of wages and maintenance of crew whilst at sea, bearing up for a port of refuge and regaining position after leaving the port, and it was not until 1924 that a rule on this subject was introduced. **11.03**

> *"Rule XX. Expenses Bearing up for Port, etc.*
>
> Fuel and stores consumed, and wages and maintenance of master, officers and crew incurred, during the prolongation of the voyage occasioned by a ship entering a port or place of refuge or returning to her port or place of loading shall be admitted as general average when the expenses of entering such port or place are allowable in general average in accordance with Rule X(a)."

If the expenses of entering a port of refuge were to be allowed as general average in accordance with r.X(a).[7] it was only logical that the expenses of bearing up for that port of refuge and subsequently regaining position should also be allowed.

York-Antwerp Rules 1950

The new rule on wages, etc. introduced in 1924 was numbered XX, and was inconveniently separated from the original but continuing r.XI on the same subject. In 1950, the opportunity was taken to combine the two rules in one r.XI. The only other changes were that: (1) the words "wages and maintenance", etc. were placed before the words "fuel and stores"; and (2) an over-cautious draftsman introduced the word "reasonably" in the second line. **11.04**

[5] See *Anglo-Argentine Live Stock Agency v Temperley S.S. Co* [1899] 2 Q.B. 403.
[6] See r.XI(b), para.11.25, below.
[7] See para.10.29, above.

York-Antwerp Rules 1974

11.05 No change.

York-Antwerp Rules 1994

11.06 No change.

York-Antwerp Rules 2004

11.07 The title was changed to a more contemporary, "Putting in to and at a port of refuge", and "allowed" was substituted for "admitted".

RULE XI(a)

WAGES AND MAINTENANCE OF CREW AND OTHER EXPENSES BEARING UP FOR AND IN/PUTTING IN TO AND AT A PORT OF REFUGE.

Wages and maintenance of master, officers and crew reasonably incurred and fuel and stores consumed during the prolongation of the voyage occasioned by a ship entering a port or place of refuge or returning to her port or place of loading shall be *admitted/allowed* as general average when the expenses of entering such port or place are allowable in general average in accordance with Rule X(a).

CONSTRUCTION

11.08 **"wages"**: These are defined by sub-rule (c).[8]

"maintenance": This word is construed to include not only the cost of food and drink supplied for the crew, but also the cost of laundering, bedding, etc. If it is necessary for the crew or part of them to be housed ashore at a port of refuge, either because of some immediate danger to the ship or because their own accommodation has been damaged and rendered uninhabitable, it would include the cost of lodging.[9]

"crew": This does not include "cattlemen",[10] or other supernumaries who are not employed by the shipowner under the command of the master. In the case of passenger vessels and cruise liners it includes all those stewards and other

[8] See para.11.41, below.

[9] See *Board of Trade v Anglo-American Oil Co* (1911) 16 Com. Cas. 151, where maintenance of a distressed seaman under the Merchant Shipping Act 1906, s.41(1) was held to mean his board and lodging. See also the Opinion No.22 of the Advisory Committee of the Association of Average Adjusters.

[10] See *Anglo-Argentine Live Stock Agency v Temperley S.S. Co* [1899] 2 Q.B. 403.

personnel employed solely to serve and attend upon the passengers, provided that they are engaged under articles or entered in the vessel's crew list.

Vessels on short sea ferry services may have two regular crews, only one of which will be on board ship at any time. The wages of the "working" crew alone can be considered for allowance under the rule, but it is clear that the "leave pay" considered as "wages" under r.XI(c) will be substantial.

"fuel": This includes all fuel consumed in the main engine, generators and other auxiliary machinery, including fuel that is consumed to heat, cool or otherwise maintain the condition of cargo. **11.09**

"stores": In earlier times this word may have been construed to cover only lubricating oils, grease, and waste, etc. consumed in the necessary running and maintenance of engines in the engine room, but this limited construction no longer applies. The Advisory Committee of the Association of Average Adjusters gave it as their opinion (No.21) that:

> ". . . there is no difference of practice between the adjusters of the United States and the adjusters in this country which is to allow under the York-Antwerp Rules for such deck, engine room or steward's stores as may be consumed during the vessel's detention, and which are not covered by allowances elsewhere provided for in the York-Antwerp Rules."

"the prolongation of the voyage": This phrase relates to the extra period spent at sea during a vessel's resort to and from a port of refuge. The period commences from the moment of deviation from the intended route, ceases temporarily on the ship's arrival at the port of refuge, resumes when she leaves that port, and ends finally when the original point of deviation has been regained. **11.10**

In the common case where the ship sails from the port of refuge on a direct course for her destination and does not pass the original point of deviation, account must obviously be taken and credit given for the unperformed leg of the voyage. Where the vessel is disabled and proceeds at slow speed into the port of refuge, but after repairs is able to resume the voyage at normal full speed, a variety of methods for calculating the precise extent of this "prolongation of the voyage" present themselves, and there is no international uniformity of practice amongst adjusters.

This was accepted by an AIDE Working Group in a Report prior to the meetings at Sydney at which the York-Antwerp Rules 1994 were promulgated. A majority of members of the Working Group favoured a re-drafting of r.XI(a) to clarify exactly what was intended, but, unfortunately, no text was offered to meet this perceived need for clarification, with the result that no change in the wording was made in 1994 and average adjusters are seemingly left free to pursue their own individual interpretations of the meaning of the phrase. This divergence in possible methods was reflected in the 12th edition in which seven different methods were described and analysed. It would appear that practice has now become more uniform in favour of the simplest method, referred to in the 12th edition as the "Time Only" basis. This takes the total time under way into the port of refuge, adds the time spent regaining position on the original track and then credits the time that would have been spent on passage (at normal speed) between the points of deviation and regaining position. This method was singled out for criticism in the last edition, particularly in cases where the vessel steams to the port of refuge at reduced speed, in which case a general average allowance made on the "Time Only" basis not only reflects the additional distance involved in the deviation but also the extra time involved arising from the damaged condition of the ship. As a matter of construction this criticism is soundly based, however it is evident that practitioners prefer the simplicity of the "Time Only" method (which is akin to similar calculations used under charter parties), and the application of the same method in all cases.

It is convenient to state here that the combined allowances for wages and maintenance of crew made under r.XI(a) and (b) are calculated in the United Kingdom to the nearest half-day,[11] but in the United States to the nearest whole day.[12] Thus, a total allowance of 80 hours would count as three and a half days, but only three days in the United States.

Allowances Commence only from Moment of Deviation

11.11 In practice the rule is interpreted as meaning a prolongation in both time and distance. No allowance is therefore made in general average for wages and maintenance of crew, etc. until a vessel makes a positive move and deviation towards a port of refuge. Thus:

(1) A vessel involved in a collision may anchor immediately pending a diver's inspection or the arrival of tugs, but not until she commences to weigh anchor and head towards a port of refuge can the allowance of wages and maintenance of crew, etc. commence.

(2) Not until a vessel refloats from an accidental stranding can the allowance of wages and maintenance of crew, etc. commence (though payments to crew for overtime worked in jettisoning or discharging cargo, or other efforts to refloat, can be allowed as general average, also the fuel and stores consumed in working the winches and in actual efforts to refloat—assuming the vessel to be in peril).

If a collision or other accident renders it necessary to put the vessel ashore to prevent her sinking, or because the authorities refuse entry into the port of refuge until temporary repairs have been effected, crew wages, etc. will generally be allowable while the vessel is "voluntarily stranded". It will be necessary to demonstrate only that the vessel and her cargo were in peril, that she has deviated from her intended voyage, and that the stranding place is a "place of refuge" within the meaning outlined in para.10.31, above.

11.12 **"port or place of refuge"**: If a ship can be said to have entered a port or place of refuge when, for the common safety, she enters a port which she would in any

[11] Opinion No.5 of the Advisory Committee of the Association of Average Adjusters.
[12] Rule of Practice XVIII of the Association of Average Adjusters of the United States.

event have entered as a port of call,[13] there is no prolongation of the voyage within the meaning of this sub-rule.

It occasionally happens that a vessel aground and in peril will discharge part of her cargo into lighters, which may then be towed to some nearby safe anchorage or port. After refloating, the vessel deviates to that anchorage or port solely to reload the cargo. Although not expressly dealt with within this rule, the wages and maintenance of the crew, etc. during any deviation and whilst reloading cargo are allowed in general average, under the wording added to Rule X(c) in 1994. .

"when the expenses of entering such port or place are allowable in general average in accordance with Rule X(a)": This sub-rule can operate only when the expenses of entering the port or place are allowable under r.X(a), that is, "in consequence of accident, sacrifice or other extraordinary circumstances, which render that necessary for the common safety".

Historical Development and Practice of Rule XI(b) (Rule XI(c) in York-Antwerp Rules 2004)

Glasgow Resolutions 1860

In most countries other than England, wages and maintenance of crew during the detention at a port of refuge were allowable as general average. This majority view prevailed at the International Conference at Glasgow in 1860 and the following Resolution was passed: **11.13**

> "(8) That the wages and provisions for the ship's crew ought to be allowed to the shipowner in general average, from the date the ship reaches a port of refuge in distress until the date on which she leaves it."

York Rules 1864

The general principle that wages and maintenance of crew at a port of refuge should be made good as general average, as stated in the first sentence of the rule quoted below, was accepted unanimously by the delegates to the York Conference in 1864. A proposal that there should be no allowance for wages and maintenance if the ship was condemned at the port of refuge was, however, strongly contested. The general view was that wages and maintenance should be allowed up to the date of the ship's condemnation, but in deference to the British viewpoint, the proposal was deleted and the problem left as an open question. **11.14**

[13] See commentary under r.X(a), para.10.32, above. See also para.10.31, above, for meaning of "port or place".

The second sentence of the rule was added after the reported discussion, no doubt to conform with an identical provision in r.VII (now r.X(a)).[14]

"When a ship shall have entered a port of refuge under the circumstances defined in Rule VII, the wages and cost of maintenance of the master and mariners, from the time of entering such port until the ship shall have been made ready to proceed upon her voyage shall be made good as general average. Except that any portion of the cargo left at such port of refuge on account of its being unfit to be carried forward, or on account of the unfitness or inability of the ship to carry it, shall not be called on to contribute to such general average."

York-Antwerp Rules 1877

11.15 On this occasion, the first sentence of the 1864 rule was affirmed unchanged, but the second sentence was deleted to correspond with an identical deletion from r.VII (now r.X(a))[15] :

"When a ship shall have entered a port of refuge under the circumstances defined in Rule VII, the wages and cost of maintenance of the master and mariners, from time of entering such port until the ship shall have been made ready to proceed upon her voyage, shall be made good as general average."

York-Antwerp Rules 1890

11.16 Apart from renumbering the rule and greater precision in the wording used, no material changes were made on this occasion, but an extra sentence was added to provide for the situation where the ship was condemned or the voyage abandoned, stating that the wages and maintenance of the master, officers and crew, incurred after the date of the ship's condemnation or of the abandonment of the voyage, shall not be admitted as general average.

York-Antwerp Rules 1924

11.17 The 1890 rule was affirmed unchanged, but a new sentence was added at the Stockholm Conference providing (consistently with r.X(c)) that the allowance of wages and maintenance should continue, in the event of condemnation of the ship or abandonment of the voyage, until completion of discharge of cargo. It was supposed that, without this provision, the owner of a ship which had been condemned might be tempted to discharge the crew in order to save expense, and that this course would not be to the advantage of the cargo, having regard to the possibility among other things of a sudden outbreak of fire on board.

11.18 Another innovation in 1924 was r.XX, providing for the allowance in general average of fuel and stores consumed during the extra detention in a port or place of refuge, thus belatedly recognising that steam (and motorships) had ousted sail.

[14] See para.10.22, above.
[15] See para.10.29, above.

Wages and maintenance of crew during the same period had been allowable under the Rules since 1860.

> *"Rule XX (second paragraph)*
>
> Fuel and stores consumed during extra detention in a port or place of loading, call or refuge shall also be allowed in general average for the period during which wages and maintenance of master, officers and crew are allowed in terms of Rule XI, except such fuel and stores as are consumed in effecting repairs not allowable in general average."

York-Antwerp Rules 1950

The whole of the 1924 r.XI became the first paragraph of the 1950 r.XI(b) and, whilst there was no change in the substance of the rule, there were improvements in the drafting. The 1924 rule referred to the vessel entering or being detained in any port or place under the circumstances or for the purpose of the repairs mentioned in r.X, but these words did not make it clear to which sub-sections of r.X reference was intended. Clarification was achieved by spelling out in the 1950 rule that wages, etc. were allowable when the vessel had entered or been detained in any port or place in consequence of accident, sacrifice or other extraordinary circumstances which rendered that necessary for the common safety, or to enable damage to the ship caused by sacrifice or accident to be repaired, if the repairs were necessary for the safe prosecution of the voyage. **11.19**

> "(b) When a ship shall have entered or been detained in any port or place in consequence of accident, sacrifice or other extraordinary circumstances which render that necessary for the common safety, or to enable damage to the ship caused by sacrifice or accident to be repaired, if the repairs were necessary for the safe prosecution of the voyage, the wages and maintenance of the master, officers and crew reasonably incurred during the extra period of detention in such port or place until the ship shall or should have been made ready to proceed upon her voyage, shall be admitted in general average. When the ship is condemned or does not proceed on her original voyage, the extra period of detention shall be deemed not to extend beyond the date of the ship's condemnation or of the abandonment of the voyage or, if discharge of charge is not then completed, beyond the date of completion of discharge."

The opportunity was also taken in 1950 to incorporate within r.XI(b) part of the old and inconveniently situated r.XX dealing with the allied subject of fuel and stores consumed at a port of refuge. **11.20**

> "Fuel and stores consumed during the extra period of detention shall be admitted as general average, except such fuel and stores as are consumed in effecting repairs not allowable in general average."

Another new paragraph was added to this sub-rule in 1950. In accordance with an Opinion of the Advisory Committee of the Association of Average Adjusters issued in 1944, the practice in the United Kingdom was to treat port charges incurred during the extra period of detention of a ship (that is, beyond the period permitted by the initial charge payable on entering the port), in the same manner **11.21** as the cost of the operations being undertaken during the period for which such dues were charged.

This did not accord with the practice in other countries, in most, if not in all, of which such dues were invariably allowed in general average in full. But it became apparent during the discussions of the British Maritime Law Association's Sub-Committee that British underwriters were not prepared to agree to the allowance of port charges on a basis other than that of the British practice, and they proposed the wording in the current rule:

> "Port charges incurred during the extra period of detention shall likewise be admitted as general average except such charges as are incurred solely by reason of repairs not allowable in general average."

11.22 A different wording was put forward for discussion at the Amsterdam Conference, but British underwriters again offered as an amendment their own wording and this was accepted by the Conference without discussion.[16]

The wording of the final form of this paragraph left much to be desired and it is a fact that average adjusters abroad interpreted the new rule as being a confirmation of their old practice, while British adjusters again began to differ in their treatment of "daily" port charges until 1955. It was then agreed, on a strict interpretation of the wording, and in the interests of international uniformity, to follow the practice adopted in other countries.

York-Antwerp Rules 1974

11.23 In conformity with the changes made concurrently in r.X(b), an important new paragraph was added to this sub-rule in 1974 to deny general average allowances in those cases where damages were merely discovered at a port of loading or of call without any accident or other extraordinary circumstances connected with such damage having taken place during the voyage. (An example of the situation envisaged by the new wording is given in para.10.51, above.) Some minor changes were also made in the wording of the sub-rule relating to condemnation of the ship and abandonment of the voyage, but in all other respects the 1950 sub-rule remained unaltered.

York-Antwerp Rules 1994

11.24 No changes of any real consequence were made on this occasion, but the minor changes made in 1974 had made mention of crew wages, etc. and fuel and stores consumed, but overlooked the concomitant port charges that would be incurred. This oversight has now been remedied and, for ease of reference, the additional wordings are printed in italics in the full text of the sub-rule copied in the next paragraph. Additionally, the five paragraphs of the rule were re-arranged in what was thought to be a more logical order.

[16] See para.11.29, below, also the annual report for 1955 of the Association of Average Adjusters.

RULE XI(b) 11.25

When a ship shall have entered or been detained in any port or place in consequence of accident, sacrifice or other extraordinary circumstances which render that necessary for the common safety, or to enable damage to the ship caused by sacrifice or accident to be repaired, if the repairs were necessary for the safe prosecution of the voyage, the wages and maintenance of the master, officers and crew reasonably incurred during the extra period of detention in such port or place until the ship shall or should have been made ready to proceed upon her voyage, shall be admitted in general average.

Fuel and stores consumed during the extra period of detention shall be admitted as general average, except such fuel and stores as are consumed in effecting repairs not allowable in general average.

Port charges incurred during the extra period of detention shall likewise be admitted as general average except such charges as are incurred solely by reason of repairs not allowable in general average.

Provided that when damage to the ship is discovered at a port or place of loading or call without any accident or other extraordinary circumstance connected with such damage having taken place during the voyage, then the wages and maintenance of master, officers and crew and fuel and stores consumed and port charges incurred during the extra detention for repairs to damages so discovered shall not be admissible as general average, even if the repairs are necessary for the safe prosecution of the voyage.

When the ship is condemned or does not proceed on her original voyage, the wages and maintenance of the master, officers and crew and fuel and stores consumed and port charges shall be admitted as general average only up to the ship's condemnation or of the abandonment of the voyage or up to the date of completion of discharge of cargo if the condemnation or abandonment takes place before that date.

York-Antwerp Rules 2004

At the Vancouver Conference various proposals were put forward to remove existing allowances for wages and maintenance under rr.XI(a) and XI(b), and/or fuel and stores and/or port charges while at a port of refuge. A number of delegates felt particularly strongly that wages were a loss by delay and should not be singled out for a special allowance when r.C excluded all other such losses. On the other hand, it was noted that the allowance of wages had been an accepted part of general average in many jurisdictions prior to the first York-Antwerp Rules. A compromise was suggested by the Canadian delegation to exclude wages only while at the port of refuge, retaining the status quo for the deviation to the port and subsequent regaining of position. 11.26

Rule XI(a) is therefore unchanged, but all reference to wages is now removed from the new r.XI(c) which was formerly r.XI(b), a change having been made in the ordering of the paragraphs. The rule reads as follows:

> *"(c)(i) When a ship shall have entered or been detained in any port or place in consequence of accident, sacrifice or other extraordinary circumstances which render that necessary for the common safety, or to enable damage to the ship caused by sacrifice or accident to be repaired, if the repairs were necessary for the safe prosecution of the voyage, fuel and stores consumed during the extra*

period of detention in such port or place until the ship shall or should have been made ready to proceed upon her voyage, shall be allowed in general average, except such fuel and stores as are consumed in effecting repairs not allowable in general average.

(ii) Port charges incurred during the extra period of detention shall likewise be allowed as general average except such charges as are incurred solely by reason of repairs not allowable in general average.

(iii) Provided that when damage to the ship is discovered at a port or place of loading or call without any accident or other extraordinary circumstance connected with such damage having taken place during the voyage, then fuel and stores consumed and port charges incurred during the extra detention for repairs to damages so discovered shall not be admissible as general average, even if the repairs are necessary for the safe prosecution of the voyage.

(iv) When the ship is condemned or does not proceed on her original voyage, fuel and stores consumed and port charges shall be admitted as general average only up to the date of the ship's condemnation or of the abandonment of the voyage or up to the date of completion of discharge of cargo if the condemnation or abandonment takes place before that date."

CONSTRUCTION

11.27 Whereas the previous sub-rule XI(a) provides for the period while at sea proceeding to or from a port of refuge, the present sub-rule XI(b) (or XI(c) in the 2004 Rules) deals with the period spent within any port or place (of refuge) and permits the allowance in general average of:

(1) wages and maintenance of crew (not under 2004 Rules);
(2) fuel and stores consumed; and
(3) port charges incurred,

during the extra period of detention in the port when the ship shall have:

(a) "**entered**" in consequence of accident, sacrifice or other extraordinary circumstances which render that necessary for the common safety;
(b) been "**detained**" in consequence of accident, sacrifice or other extraordinary circumstances which render that necessary for the common safety. For example a serious collision in the port causes severe leakage, or a fire in the cargo threatens the common safety even within the port;
(c) been "**detained**" to enable damage to the ship caused by sacrifice or accident to be repaired, if the repairs were necessary for the safe prosecution of the voyage. For example, some accident to the ship occurs in the port which in no way threatens the common safety while within the port, but which requires repair before the voyage can be safely prosecuted.

Thus, the scope of this sub-rule is undoubtedly very wide, but there are a few situations where wages and maintenance of crew, etc. during any extra detention would not be allowed as general average, for example:

(1) to recondition damaged cargo, whether the damage be from accidental cause or by general average sacrifice;
(2) to rectify some defect in the ship which constitutes neither accident[17] nor sacrifice,[18] but merely an extraordinary circumstance[19] (for example overheated bearings, or a slowly extending fracture in a crankshaft), if the work is done at a port of loading or of call at which the vessel has called in the normal course of her voyage. See also the commentary on r.X(b);
(3) where a vessel has been ordered out of port for the safety of the port (for example in fear of an explosion on board ship);
(4) during the extra time it may take to discharge damaged cargo at its intended destination, even though the damage may be caused by, for example, flooding the hold for the common safety.

A number of aspects of r.XI(b) (r.XI(c) of York-Antwerp Rules 2004) were considered in the *Trade Green*[20] which can most conveniently be dealt with together. **11.28**

The vessel had carried a cargo of rice in bags from Bangkok to Aquaba under bills of lading providing for York-Antwerp Rules 1974, and while discharging alongside a fire broke out in the engine room. On the instructions of the port authority the vessel was taken by tugs to an anchorage outside the port where the fire was brought under control by the vessel's crew. The vessel was towed "dead-ship" back to the berth the following day to complete discharge. The tug charges were the largest part of the general average and were allowed by the adjusters on the basis that the services of the tugs were the consequence of an order to leave the berth and were therefore port charges recoverable under r.XI(b). Cargo interests challenged the adjustment and four preliminary issues came before Moore-Bick J.

"Detained": The primary contention put forward by cargo was that the voyage within the meaning of the Rules had ended when the vessel berthed at Aquaba and that the vessel had therefore not been "detained" in a way contemplated by r.XI(b), which looked to a situation in which the vessel was prevented from continuing her progress to her final destination. The contrary argument that the words "voyage" and "common maritime adventure" have essentially the same meaning was rejected by the judge, who considered that rr.X and XI were both concerned with the interruption of the vessel's progress to destination and that the choice of the word "voyage" in these Rules (as opposed to "adventure" found in other Rules) had to be given its effect as a progression from the loading port to arrival at the port of discharge. He therefore found that, in the absence of any detention of the vessel, there could be no allowance under r.XI(b).

The grounds for this decision were viewed by many practitioners with some surprise. It had never been previously suggested that a distinction (relevant to

[17] See para.10.32, above.
[18] See para.10.32, above.
[19] See para.10.33, above.
[20] *Trade Green* [2000] 2 Lloyd's Rep. 451.

these circumstances) should be made between "voyage" and "adventure" in the manner suggested in this case. A valid distinction exists between the contract voyage under the bill of lading and the common adventure, since the latter continues when there has been a prior abandonment of the contract voyage. However, the use of "voyage" in rr.X and XI is a reminder that the repairs under consideration are those required to bring ship and cargo to the end of the contract voyage and not merely to the nearest place at which the common adventure can be safely ended by discharging cargo.

The meaning given to the term "voyage" by practitioners in the context of the York-Antwerp Rules is supported by a questionnaire sent to the participating national committees prior to the Stockholm Conference that produced the 1924 Rules. The first question was, "what is the duration of a sea voyage for the purpose of performing a General Average act?"

The answer supplied by the English Committee (which was full of contemporary luminaries and headed by Lord Justice Kennedy) was:

> "A voyage begins when a ship either enters upon a chartered voyage or when she takes on board any cargo for carriage, and terminates when delivery of the whole cargo is completed or abandoned or partly completed and for the rest abandoned (*Williams v London Assurance; Whitecross Wire Co v Savill*)."

The other national committees took a similar view in responding to the questionnaire and it is likely that adjusters will continue to treat the voyage as something that concludes only on completion of discharge of cargo.

It is suggested that since it is common ground that the tug charges imposed on the *Trade Green* made no contribution to the common safety and that the time this occupied was not necessary for effecting repairs necessary for the safe prosecution of the voyage—these being the two triggers of an allowance under r.XI(b)—the claim for these expenses could have been rejected on these simple grounds.

The general average claim having failed because of the decision that there was no detention during the voyage, the judge expressed the following obiter views on the remaining issues.

"Port or place": The judge rejected the proposition that a "place" must be in the nature of a "port" (see also para.10.31, above).

11.29 "Port charges": As noted above, the tug charges were allowed by the adjusters on the basis that they were port charges incurred within an extra period of detention. The judge noted the absence of direct authorities and therefore considered the language of r.XI(b) and the context provided by rr.X and XI as a whole.

> "In this context I think that the natural meaning of the expression 'port charges' in r.XI(b) is apt to include any charges which the vessel would ordinarily incur as a necessary consequence of entering or staying at the port in question. That would obviously include standard charges and levies of all kinds and may also extend to charges for standard service such as garbage removal which may or may not be optional but would be regarded as ordinary expenses of being in port. It is unnecessary to decide that point in the present case, but I note that this is the view put forward by the editors of Lowndes & Rudolf at para.11.32. Ordinary tug charges for assisting

> the vessel into and out of the port might well fall within r.XI(b), therefore, but it is much more difficult to bring the towage charges in the present case within it. They were not ordinary charges which any vessel using the port could expect to incur and apart from the fact they were levied by the port authority bore little similarity to port charges in the accepted sense. I do not think that r.XI(b) can be construed so as to cover all sums charged by the port authority regardless of the circumstances; in my view it is much more limited in its scope. It is true that in the present case the services of the tugs and the charges for those services were imposed on the vessel by the port authority, but they were imposed in response to an unusual situation and were not imposed in the common interests of the ship and cargo. In these circumstances I do not think that they can properly be regarded as port charges within the meaning of r.XI(b)."

If, by this passage, Moore-Bick J. meant that any charges beyond the standard ones, which any vessel using the port would incur, cannot qualify as "port charges" it is contrary to established practice and it is submitted that it goes too far.

The usual situation to which the rule applies is where a vessel puts into a port of refuge for the common safety, either because she has sustained hull or machinery damage, or because of an emergency affecting her cargo. In such circumstances it is very likely, and often a certainty, that the ship will incur charges by reason of her use of the port which exceed those which a ship in full operating condition would incur, and those charges are therefore treated as general average because they are a direct consequence of the decision to use the port. The most common example would be the requirement of a tug to stand by a vessel at the anchorage while her main engine is repaired. Sometimes bad weather or poor holding ground will mean that the master calls for a standby tug which is therefore evidently required for the safety of ship and cargo. On other occasions the port authority instigates the requirement out of concern to avoid disruption to the port operations or damage to its facilities, so that it becomes a condition of entering and staying at the port. Frequently a combination of these motives may be found.

The practice of viewing "port charges" as something that could go beyond standard harbour dues etc also extended under the 1974 Rules to costs of anti-pollution measures required by a Port Authority prior to allowing entry to a port or granting permission to remain there. Such allowances were expressly sanctioned by r.XI(d) of the 1994 Rules (and unchanged in the 2004 Rules) when it was emphasised that no extension of allowances under the 1974 Rules (or adjusters' practice under them) was being made.

However, it was never considered sound adjusting practice to simply allow all charges within a port of refuge without questioning their purpose. Expenses not relating to the objective of ensuring the common safety or keeping the vessel in port to effect repairs necessary for the safe prosecution of the voyage–for example the crew going ashore for medical treatment, or a shift to a bunker berth, would be excluded. Additionally, as noted in para.11.27, above, the clearly defined circumstances that permit the allowances of wages also apply to port charges. It will also be noted that the examples in para.11.27 of situations in which wages would not be allowed (which also appeared in the 12th edition) included example 3, that of a vessel that had been ordered out of a port for the safety of the port.

11.30 **"Extra period of detention"**: Had they lost on the other issues, counsel for the defendants argued that the towage charges had not been incurred during the extra period of detention which he defined as the time after which the vessel would otherwise have been able to leave the port; since the vessel would have remained at Aquaba for some time to discharge cargo the towage charges were not incurred during any extra period of detention in terms of r.XI(b). The judge agreed that (at a port of call) the extra period of detention is the period after which she would have been ready to leave port having completed scheduled operations there.

If detention can only be allowed at ports of call after all the scheduled activities at that port have been completed, this gives rise to some curious anomalies. If a vessel enters a port of refuge following a cargo fire which has been fought using Co2 and remains there for several days while the cargo cools, the detention would in practice be allowed from the time of her arrival. However, on the Trade Green approach, if the vessel had entered a port of call no allowance could be made during the same period because the vessel had yet to carry out her cargo handling operations at that port of call–likewise in the event of a fire at a loading port when only part cargo had been loaded.

It is suggested that the existing and universal practice is to be preferred, namely to allow the period during which the ordinary scheduled activities at the port are interrupted or postponed because of the taking of measures for the common safety, or the carrying out of repairs necessary for the safe prosecution of the voyage.

First Paragraph–Paragraph c(i) in the York-Antwerp Rules 2004

11.31 **"shall have entered"**: See commentary on r.X(a).[21]

"any port or place": These words are clearly wide enough to cover the port of loading whether or not the ship had sailed and returned thereto, a port of call, a port of refuge and a port to which the ship has removed from a port of loading, call or refuge for repairs.[22]

"accident, sacrifice or other extraordinary circumstances": See commentary on r.X(a).[23]

"the common safety": See commentary on r.A.[24]

"necessary for the safe prosecution of the voyage": See commentary on r.X(b).[25] "The voyage" is the voyage which is the common maritime adventure, and detention during repairs postponed until after the voyage (including repairs at the discharging part) is outside the scope of this sub-rule.[26] It is submitted that permanent repairs may not be necessary for the safe prosecution of the voyage if

[21] See para.10.29, above.
[22] See also commentary under r.X(a), para.10.29, above.
[23] See paras 10.32-10.33, above.
[24] See para.A.109, above.
[25] See para.10.45, above.
[26] *Wetherall (J.H.) & Co v The London Assurance* [1931] 2 K.B. 448. The adventure continues until discharge is completed, even if the voyage ends earlier: *Whitecross Wire Co v Savill* (1882) 8 Q.B.D. 653.

temporary repairs can be effected more speedily: but this is really a question of fact to be determined in each case.

"wages": These are defined by sub-rule (c)[27] or (b) in 2004 Rules. 11.32

"maintenance": See commentary on r.XI(a).[28]

"crew": See commentary on r.XI(a).[29]

"reasonably": This word was first introduced in the 1950 edition of this sub-rule, probably to give effect to the suggestion by the Scandinavian Committees that the duty to discharge part of the crew, if practicable, should not be entirely overlooked. When an extended stay in a port of refuge is to be expected, it is sometimes found that part of the crew will be signed off and repatriated, and a new crew engaged when the vessel is ready to resume her voyage. In such circumstances, the wages, etc. of the crew whilst on board ship are allowed in general average, also the cost of signing off, repatriation and re-engagement, up to the wages, etc. saved thereby.

"extra period of detention": Where a ship puts into a port of refuge and is 11.33 there detained for the reasons specified in the sub-rule, the cost of wages, etc. during the whole period of detention will usually be admissible in general average. The word "extra" will take effect in such cases as detention at a port of call, in which case crew wages, etc. will be admissible only during the extra period of detention in addition to what is required to fulfil the purpose of her scheduled call at the port.

When fire breaks out in the cargo of a ship at one of her ports of discharge an "extra period of detention" thereby results to the ship, and much discussion has taken place concerning the period during which the fire continues to burn. As the Chairman of the United States Association of Average Adjusters said in his annual address in 1962:

> "It is considered by some that the detention period should commence at the time the fire is extinguished while others are of the view that the full period of time during which efforts are being made to extinguish the fire should be included in General Average."

It is submitted that the latter view is correct and that the vessel has been "detained . . . in consequence of accident . . . which render(s) that necessary for the common safety" within the meaning of the sub-rule while fire-fighting operations are being carried out. The practice in the United States is also to commence allowances under the sub-rule from the time of the first act to extinguish the fire.

"until the ship shall or should have been made ready to proceed upon her voyage": Since the 11th edn of this work it has been asserted that it is the condition of the ship alone which governs how long the "extra periods of detention" can be said to run. This view was difficult to reconcile with some of the propositions also made in the same editions with regard to certain types of delay not directly connected with the condition of the ship itself, namely: 11.34

[27] See para.11.41, below.
[28] See para.11.07, above.
[29] See para.11.07, above.

11.35 (1) Fog or gales, will not be admissible in general average on the grounds that weather conditions are generally variable and irregular, and a similar delay might just as easily occur at sea on the voyage itself.

(2) Ice conditions may be allowable provided that it can be shown that such ice conditions were to be expected and were, or ought to have been, within the contemplation of the master when he decided to put into the port of refuge.

(3) A strike of pilots or tugs might also be allowable, depending upon circumstances. Strikes being less accurately predictable than ice conditions, but not so uncommon in modern times and in certain countries with troubled labour relations as to be beyond the bounds of foreseeability.

(4) Waiting for convoy (in war-time), was not admissible in general average, but the practice might be questioned if convoys sailed on known dates or at regular intervals.

The governing factor in making the above distinctions appears to be a test of foreseeability.

The words "until the ship shall have been made ready to proceed upon her voyage" first appeared in the York-Antwerp Rules of 1864 and the additional words "or should have been" appeared in 1890. The longevity of this wording and the lack of any pressure for amendments can perhaps be explained by a broader meaning being assigned to the idea of the ship being ready than was admitted in the 11th and 12th editions. When r.X(b) was amended in 1974 to expressly exclude the cost of re-stowing shifted cargo (unless for the common safety) it appears to have been generally accepted that allowances for detention expenses during the period of such operations had been correctly made in the past and would continue to be made in the future, even when the cost of the operation itself was excluded. It would appear that the concept of the ship being ready to resume the voyage extended to the readiness of a ship with regard to:

- the context of its cargo carrying voyage, i.e. with cargo on board and in all respects ready to continue the maritime adventure;
- not being impeded by any circumstance that could have been foreseen as likely to flow from the original general average act that brought the vessel to the port of refuge.

Similarly, where a grounded vessel had its cargo discharged into lighters and then refloated, after which the vessel and lighters both moved to a nearby port to re-load the cargo it would appear that the usual practice was to allow the detention expenses during the re-loading even in the absence of a continuing peril or repairs being necessary for the safe prosecution of the voyage. This practice was confirmed by the additional sentence added to r.X(c) in 1994 (see para.10.63) and such allowances were evidently viewed as a natural and foreseeable consequence of the initial general average act.

However, the position is somewhat unsatisfactory because the wording of r.XI(b), which as a numbered rule falls to be construed strictly and on its own merits, makes no reference to foreseeability. The rule admits two specific triggers for an allowance for detention expenses, that is: being detained for the common safety or to effect repairs necessary for the safe prosecution of the voyage. However, the approach is not entirely at odds with the general principles set out in the lettered rules. When Lowndes pressed for the allowance under English law for the cost of storing and reloading cargo as general average, he did so on the basis that such costs were a foreseeable consequence of a general average act, rather than out of any recognition of the principle of common benefit.

A further example of this dilemma relates to the delays on port that may sometimes occur when the vessel is ready to proceed but is arrested by salvors pending provision of security by ship or, more usually, cargo.

The American adjuster and author Buglas, follows the same line as this work with regard to delays caused by weather and ice conditions and then continues:

> "Occasionally a vessel is subjected to extra delay at port of refuge while arrangements are made to obtain the release of the vessel from arrest by salvors. In such cases it is customary to allow detention in general average. This may not be strictly in accord with Rule XI but American average adjusters have usually taken a broad view of such delays. The rationale behind such allowances is that, with the best will in the world, it takes time to provide salvors with security at a foreign port. Therefore, if the time taken is reasonable it is customary to allow wages, etc. of crew during such reasonable delay. (It would be unusual to allow a delay of more than two or three days solely for this purpose.) The reasoning is that when the master signs a salvage contract (the general average act) it is apparent that some delay may be unavoidable in providing security and that, therefore, such reasonable and unavoidable delay flows directly from the general average act. It should be stressed that any unreasonable or avoidable delay would not qualify for a general average allowance. Thus, if the delay is due solely to lack of funds or credit, the delay becomes unreasonable and such extension of the detention at a port of refuge would not qualify as general average."

It is understood that a similar approach is also followed by some European adjusters, who report that it is generally accepted.

As Buglas admits, it is difficult to find support for this practice in the wording of r.XI(b) and the addition of the word "expenses" in the third paragraph of r.C since 1994 might be put forward as an additional obstacle to it.

While noting the areas in which universal practice, or the practice in certain locations, goes beyond a strict construction of r.XI(c) it should be emphasised that all adjusters should give proper weight to the words "should have been made ready". Thus, if repairs are prolonged because of owners' work undertaken in addition to repairs necessary for the safe prosecution of the voyage, or other avoidable delays occur, allowances should be curtailed accordingly. Detention arising from arrests by governmental bodies seeking security in respect of pollution liabilities or in relation to civil or criminal actions would also clearly fall outside the scope of this rule.

Second Paragraph

"fuel and stores": See commentary on r.Xl(a). **11.36**

"except such fuel and stores as are consumed in effecting repairs not allowable in general average": A ship in port consumes power to provide lighting and heating for crew, refrigeration and ventilation of cargo holds, etc.; the cost of all fuel and stores consumed for these routine ship's purposes during the extra detention is chargeable direct to general average. However, if additional fuel and stores are consumed in shifting a vessel to a dry dock or other repair berth, or to provide extra lighting for repairs not allowable in general average, the cost of the additional fuel and stores is not allowable as general average.

Third Paragraph–Paragraph c(iii) in the York-Antwerp Rules

11.37 **"Port charges"**: It is difficult to give an exhaustive list of what are comprised in "port charges" but the words certainly include port and dock dues payable on a day to day basis and may also include the cost of gangway watchmen, launch hire and garbage removal, etc. and perhaps also charges for water and electricity supplied from ashore for use on ordinary ship's purposes during the extra period of detention. As noted in para.11.29 above, this paragraph which appeared in the 11th and 12th editions was referred to in the Trade Green in support of the judge's view that only standard or ordinary port charges were contemplated. It has however always been the practice of adjusters to regard this list as being illustrative rather than exhaustive.

"Except such charges as are incurred solely by reason of repairs not allowable in general average": Examples of such charges would include the cost of putting the vessel in drydock to repair grounding damage, or a shift to a berth with craneage facilities to enable spares required for repairs to accidental damage to machinery to be loaded.

Fourth Paragraph–Paragraph c(iii) in the York-Antwerp Rules 2004

11.38 **"Provided that when damage to the ship is discovered at a port or place of loading or call without any accident or other extraordinary circumstances connected with such damage having taken place during the voyage"**: See commentary on r.X(b).[30]

Fifth Paragraph–Paragraph (c(iv) in the York-Antrewp Rules 2004)

11.39 **"When the ship is condemned or does not proceed on her original voyage"**: See commentary on r.X(c).[31]

"the date of the ship's condemnation or of the abandonment of the voyage": See commentary on r.X(c).[32]

[30] See paras 10.45 and 10.55, above.
[31] See para.10.67, above.
[32] See para.10.69, above.

HISTORICAL DEVELOPMENT AND PRACTICE OF RULE XI(C) (RULE XI(B) IN YORK-ANTWERP RULES 2004)

York-Antwerp Rules 1950

With the ending of the Second World War a great change in labour relations and working conditions was set in motion, many countries including legislation to create a "welfare" state with social security, etc. while notionally shorter working hours on board a ship in fact meant the payment of considerably more overtime to the crew. This resulted in some doubt as to really what was comprised within the term wages in r.XI and practice varied with regard to payments for compulsory social insurance, pension funds and crew overtime, etc. This was resolved in 1950 with the introduction of sub-rule (c), a definition of the term wages. Henceforth, all such payments would be treated as wages whether imposed by law upon the shipowners or made under the articles of employment, and the sub-rule has remained unchanged ever since.[33] **11.40**

York-Antwerp Rules 1994

RULE XI(c) **11.41**

For the purpose of this and the other Rules wages shall include all payments made to or for the benefit of the master, officers and crew, whether such payments be imposed by law upon the shipowners or be made under the terms or articles of employment.

York-Antwerp Rules 2004

The order of the sub-paragraphs was changed with XI(c) becoming XI(b) with no alteration to the wording. **11.42**

CONSTRUCTION

Although given in a different context, the following definition of wages by the Advisory Committee of the Association of Average Adjusters is apt for general average purposes: **11.43**

> "The term 'wages' comprises the gross amount of all those payments made by the Shipowners to the members of the crew on a monthly, weekly or other periodic basis including leave pay, overseas allowance, etc. and the employer's contribution to State and other Insurance and/or Pension Schemes which relate to those payments, and also

[33] Parallel sub-rule (d) relating to crew overtime was also introduced in 1950, but this was subsequently regarded as superfluous and deleted in 1994. The wording of this sub-rule (d), and a commentary thereon, appears in paras 11.36, 11.37 of the 11th edn.

payments of overtime to the crew in pursuance of their normal watch keeping and/or other duties which may loosely be termed regular overtime."

Examples of "regular overtime" include crew acting as night-watchmen, engineers on generator watches, and catering staff preparing early, late, and weekend meals, all resulting from the 24-hours-a-day nature of life on board ship.

As distinct from "regular" overtime, extra overtime may be paid or special payments made for specific tasks that arise following a casualty, for example working double watches while fighting a fire or tank-cleaning to enable an inspection or repair to be carried out. Such payments will depend upon the employment contracts and flag state regulations under which the crew are employed. Provided the payments are made in accordance therewith, and proper evidence is given to show payments have been received by the crew, such expenses can be allowed under r.A (if they relate to general average acts) or as particular average if the terms of the relevant policies permit.

In the majority of cases crews are employed by crewing agencies, which may be a subsidiary company of the shipowner or a third party specialist company. Such an agency will pass on to the owner a number of costs that are in addition to the payments made to the crew, for example air fares and other expenses relating to crew changes, and the Agency's own charges for the service provided. Many of these changes are not part of the "payments made to or for the benefit of the master officers and crew" and therefore fall outside the definition given by this r.XI(c). In practice, allowances are often made on the basis of the all inclusive monthly rate provided by the crewing agency since the time required to break down the charges into the different elements would be disproportionate to the sums involved. However, where a lengthy detention involves, for example, the change-over of a crew the distinction should be born in mind.

It should also be noted that in practice the costs of medical expenses etc relating to the crew while at a port of refuge are not allowed under r.XI.

Historical Development and Practice of Rule XI(d)

English Law and Practice

11.44 Just as liability for actual pollution or environmental damage may in certain circumstances be allowed in general average in English law,[34] so may the costs of taking measures to avoid or minimise such damage. Nevertheless, the avoidance of pollution or environmental damage, is not in itself an objective which gives rise to a claim in general average; it follows that the costs of avoidance measures are not as such allowable in English law, even if they are carried out as part of an operation performed for the common safety: they are only allowable if they are a necessary part, or a direct consequence, of such an operation. The position is the

[34] See para.C.15, above.

same under the pre-1994 versions of the York-Antwerp Rules. The cost of such measures was often allowed in general average, particularly when the operation of which they formed part was undertaken by salvors acting on a "no cure no pay" basis and the salvage award was increased as a result of the salvors' skill and efforts in preventing or minimising pollution.[35] In 1990 this practice with regard to salvage was sanctioned under the York-Antwerp Rules by the amendment effected to r.VI.[36]

With regard to preventative measures in other circumstances, the practice of British adjusters was generally as follows:

- Measures taken immediately following (say) a grounding form part of the initial accident and are for the account of owners and their liability insurers, as would be the cost of any actual clean up operations during this and any subsequent stage.
- Additional measures taken as part of a refloating operation, whether instigated by the shipowner or as a condition set by the authorities prior to permitting the operation, would be allowed as a part of, or direct consequence of, the general average act of refloating the vessel. While conditions set by the authorities might be driven by wider concerns than the safety of ship and cargo, compliance was generally unavoidable if the general average act was to proceed.
- Preventive measures taken as a condition of entering a port of refuge–as general average under r.X(a).
- Preventive measures taken as a condition of remaining in a port of refuge–as port charges in terms of r.XI(b).[37]

Making the distinction between measures that flowed from the original casualty, and those that flowed from a particular action being taken could often be difficult in practice. It is understood that such problems were encountered by the administrators of the International Oil Pollution Compensation Funds (IOPC) under which compensation for the cost of "preventive measures" would depend partly on the purpose for which they were taken.[38] After initially applying a "primary purpose" test it was accepted that operations would often have a dual purpose and that it was sometimes appropriate to apportion the expenses between the purposes that were identified in each particular case.

As noted above, the practice of adjusters prior to the 1994 Rules was generally to focus less on the intention behind the measures in question and more on the directness of any link with a general average act, and the 1994 changes have confirmed this approach.

[35] See para.6.09, above.

[36] See para.6.11, above.

[37] Reference is requested to para.11.29 regarding the more restricted view of the term "port charges" given by the judge in the Trade Green.

[38] See Ch.19 of Shipping and the Environment by Colin de la Rue which gives a detailed and interesting analysis of pollution matters in relation to general average.

York-Antwerp Rules 1994

11.45 Rule XI(d) forms part of the "pollution compromise" adopted at the 1994 CMI Conference at Sydney, the basic feature of which was to exclude from general average liabilities and clean-up costs in connection with pollution which had actually occurred, but to admit certain of the costs of avoidance measures. Rule XI(d) was selected as the vehicle for the provisions which allow the costs of these avoidance measures. Rule XI(d) of the 1974 Rules (which dealt with crew overtime during repairs at a port of refuge) having been deleted on the grounds that it was superfluous. However, in contrast with the other sections of r.XI, the new r.XI(d) is by no means confined to expenses incurred at or in entering a port of refuge, and its provisions would no doubt have been considered worthy of a separate rule of their own but for a natural reluctance to add to or alter the numbering of the rules.

The general exclusion of losses and expenses relating to pollution or damage to the environment is contained in the second paragraph of r.C, and the overall intention is that unless such costs are recoverable under r.XI(d) or the second paragraph of r.VI(a) they are excluded altogether from general average. The formulation of r.XI(d) as part of the pollution compromise also had the added benefit of providing a uniform framework for the existing practice of many adjusters as outlined in para.11.44.

York Antwerp Rules 2004

11.46 The rule differs only in that para.(iii) refers to XI(c) rather than XI(b), reflecting the change in order of the preceding sections of the rule.

11.47 **RULE XI(d)**

The cost of measures undertaken to prevent or minimise damage to the environment shall be allowed in general average when incurred in any or all of the following circumstances:

(i) as part of an operation performed for the common safety which, had it been undertaken by a party outside the common maritime adventure, would have entitled such party to a salvage reward;

(ii) as a condition of entry into or departure from any port or place in the circumstances prescribed in Rule X(a);

(iii) as a condition of remaining at any port or place in the circumstances prescribed in *Rule X(b)/Rule XI(c)*, provided that when there is an actual escape or release of pollutant substances the cost of any additional measures required on that account to prevent or minimise pollution or environmental damage shall not be allowed as general average;

(iv) necessarily in connection with the discharging, storing or reloading of cargo whenever the cost of those operations is admissible as general average.

CONSTRUCTION

"to prevent or minimise": The wording is the same as that used in the International Convention on Salvage 1989.[39] The inclusion of a reference to minimising damage to the environment makes it clear that the allowances granted by the rule do not cease to apply as soon as some environmental damage has occurred. However, the rule does require a clear distinction to be drawn between the costs of avoiding further damage, and expenses in respect of damage already incurred. It is no fault of the draughtsman of the rule that the distinction will sometimes be difficult to draw. For example, the costs of minimising the amount of a pollutant substance which escapes is clearly within the rule even though some has already escaped and caused damage to the environment, as are the costs of limiting the area over which the escaped pollutant is able to disperse.[40] But assume that the pollutant has already contaminated a coastline. Can the costs of a clean-up operation be allowed? If the operation is undertaken by or on behalf of the shipowner, if it will reduce "damage to the environment",[41] and if it is undertaken in the circumstances described in one of the sub-paragraphs of the rule, the costs could be argued to fall within the words of the rule. However, it was definitely not the intention of the framers of the rule that such clean-up costs should ever be allowed, even when the shipowner was required to give a guarantee in respect of clean-up costs as a condition of entering or remaining in a port of refuge (see sub-paras (ii) and (iii) below). 11.48

"damage to the environment": Again the words are the same as those of the 1989 Salvage Convention, and their effect has been discussed in the context of r.C.[42] It will be noted that the opening provisions of r.XI(d), unlike r.C, contain no additional reference to "the escape or release of pollutant substances". It follows that the actual or threatened escape or release of a pollutant does not of itself bring r.XI(d) into play, and it must in each case be determined whether the result of the escape or release would be "damage to the environment". In the specific cases referred to in sub-paras (ii) to (iv) of the rule, this requirement will be fulfilled when the actual or threatened pollution is sufficiently major to cause substantial damage to human health or to marine life or resources. However, in the case of a deep-sea salvage operation, which would otherwise fall within r.XI(d)(i), even a major escape or release of pollutant substances may give rise to no actual or threatened damage to the environment,[43] with the consequence that the costs of preventing or minimising the escape would not fall within r.XI(d). 11.49

[39] Art.8, para.l(b), which imposes on salvors a duty "to exercise due care to prevent or minimise damage to the environment". Art.13, para.l(b) requires that their skill and efforts in that regard must be taken into account in fixing their remuneration.

[40] However, where the claim is made under sub-para.(iii) costs of this nature are not allowable; see paras 11.55–11.58, below.

[41] See the definition of "damage to the environment" in the 1989 Salvage Convention: see para.C.38, above.

[42] See para.C.38, above.

[43] i.e. because there is no threat of damage which affects "coastal or inland waters or areas adjacent thereto": see the definition of "damage to the environment" set out in para.C.38, above.

Sub-paragraph (i)

11.50 The purpose of sub-para.(i) is to ensure that a party to the adventure who carries out salvage operations for the common safety, or who hires a contractor to perform the operations at a fixed price or rate, can recover in general average the costs of those measures for preventing or avoiding damage to the environment which, had they been performed by a salvor working on a "no cure no pay" basis, would have entitled him to an award under the 1989 Salvage Convention. Under the Convention the salvor owes a duty to the owners of ship and cargo to exercise due care to prevent or minimise such damage, and his skill and efforts in so doing are taken into account in fixing the reward; r.VI then provides that the full amount of the award shall be allowed in general average. Against this background it would clearly be inequitable that a shipowner who performed the operations himself, or hired a contractor to do so, should not be able to recover the costs of those measures for preventing or minimising environmental damage which formed part of the operations. If he were unable to do so, a shipowner would be encouraged to engage salvors on a "no cure no pay" basis, which would usually mean that cargo's liability would in the end be greater.

The sub-paragraph does not impose any requirement such as probably exists under English law[44] to the effect that the preventive measures should be a necessary part of, or directly caused by, the operation performed for the common safety. It simply requires that they should be part of that operation. This clearly covers the case where the measures in question are taken to prevent the salvage operations themselves from causing environmental damage, and it probably includes every other case where the measures can properly be regarded as ancillary to the operation being performed for the common safety. The latter must always be the predominant purpose of the operation as a whole. The expression for the common safety is the same as that used in r.A, and its meaning is discussed in the context of that rule.[45]

11.51 **"as part of an operation performed for the common safety"**: The operation being performed for the common safety is one that would entitle a party to a salvage award (see para.11.53) that is to say a salvage operation which is defined in Art.12 of the Salvage Convention 1989 as:

> "Any act or activity undertaken to assist a vessel or any other property in danger in navigable waters or in any other waters whatsoever.".

Under Art.8 of the Convention the salvor's duty under Art.8.1(b) to "exercise due care to prevent or minimise damage to the environment" is related to the performance of Art.8.1(a), which is the duty to carry out the salvage operations with due care. Thus, there is no general duty in relation to the environment outside the salvor's main task, for example to clean up pollution of beaches already caused by an initial grounding prior to the salvor's attendance.

44 See para.11.44, above.
45 See paras A.20, et seq., above.

The words "an operation performed" also serve as a reminder that any costs to be considered under this sub-paragraph need to be part of a positive measure to extricate the property from danger, rather then merely an aspect of the accident itself; in short, a consequence not just of "being there" but rather of "doing something about it". To this extent the compromise reached in r.XI(d) is consistent with the broader principles of general average.

Situations in which an owner responds to a casualty without engaging salvors on "no cure, no pay" terms often occur in the vicinity of loading and discharging ports where tugs and pollution response equipment are available as part of the terminal facilities. Following a grounding, anti-pollution vessels may be deployed immediately in case of any pollution and begin to clean up or contain any pollution that is already occurring. It is submitted that such operations fall outside the rule. After this initial response, attention will turn to the condition of the vessel and the steps necessary to refloat it. The actual operations may often begin with the removal of bunkers from double bottom tanks, in case of damage during the grounding or planned refloating operations, and the cost of doing this, together with the anti-pollution vessels standing by, would form the first part of the active salvage phase that does come within the rule.

In many cases the response to the casualty may be overseen by a port authority or other governmental agency; such authorities may go further and dictate what is to be done or set specific pre-conditions for any refloating attempts, all of which may result in additional costs being incurred by owners. In some cases the authorities will deploy their own vessels and personnel, the cost of which will be debited to owners. In reviewing such costs, the question of the motivation behind the authorities' actions can be ignored, since the determining factor is whether the activities actually carried out are within the broad spectrum of the steps that might have been taken by a salvor acting in accordance with Art.13 of the Salvage Convention.

Response Plans

Shipowners trading in some jurisdictions are required to lodge with the appropriate authorities a contingency plan that provides contact details and a response plan that can be activated in the event of a serious casualty. Frequently, a shipowner will pay a retainer to a specialist company or individual in that jurisdiction, with additional payments being made if the plan is activated. 11.52

The primary function of such response companies is to enable the shipowner to comply with legislation so that he can continue to trade. In the event of a casualty they will also seek to reassure the authorities that the shipowner is responding properly and to avoid or minimise any fines or other sanctions that might be imposed. In the absence of special circumstances, none of these activities justify any allowance in general average.

When a professional salvor is engaged on terms such as Lloyd's Open Form 2000, the salvage master will liaise closely with the authorities regarding the salvage plan and any environmental issues arising from it. In such circumstances the role of the response company may be peripheral and will be unlikely to justify any allowances for their costs in general average. However, where the shipowner is engaging tugs on contract terms and is controlling operations himself, it may be that the active intervention required of the response company would be sufficient to allow the additional costs of liaising with the authorities as general average.

11.53 **"which . . . would have entitled such party to a salvage reward"**: Under the Salvage Convention 1989, which has been incorporated into English law,[46] the right to a salvage award arises when "salvage operations which have had a useful result" have been rendered.[47] The requirement that the operations should have had a useful result may sometimes be of practical significance. Rule XI(d)(i) contemplates that the outcome of the salvage operation must be such that, if the operation had been performed by a salvor outside the common maritime adventure, it would have entitled him to a reward under Art.13 of the Convention. Thus if the property is not saved, or if the operations referred to in the opening words of r.XI(d) did not contribute to its preservation, there can be no claim under r.XI(d)(i).[48] It is not sufficient that the operations should have given rise to a right to special compensation under art.14 of the Convention, since this does not it is submitted, amount to a "salvage reward". Just as special compensation under art.14 is excluded from r.VI,[49] so it falls outside the scope of r.XI(d)(i).

Once it is established that the operation in question would, if undertaken by a party outside the common maritime adventure, have entitled him to an award under art.13 of the Salvage Convention, the actual costs of the measures undertaken as part of the operation to prevent or minimise environmental damage are allowable in general average. The rule does not require the adjuster to consider the amount by which, if the salvage operation had been undertaken by a stranger to the adventure, the award would have been enhanced under the provisions of art.13, para.1(b) of the Convention, or even to consider whether it would have been enhanced at all.

"had it been undertaken by a party outside the common maritime adventure": The reason for the insertion of these words is to overcome the rule that a person who is under a pre-existing duty to render services for the purpose of safeguarding the property cannot claim a salvage reward.[50]

Sub-paragraph (ii)

11.54 **"as a condition of entry into or departure from any port or place"**: The purpose of sub-para.(ii) is to allow in general average the cost of those measures

[46] See the Merchant Shipping Act 1995 s.224.

[47] Salvage Convention 1989 art.12 para.1.

[48] The principle which normally prevails in general average, outside the context of r.XI(d)(i), is rather different. So long as the sacrifice or expenditure was reasonably made or incurred for the purpose of preserving the property from a common peril, and so long as some property is preserved (in the absence of which there would be no contributing interests), contribution is due. It is unnecessary to inquire whether the particular sacrifice or expenditure in question was instrumental in preserving the property.

[49] See r.VI(b), para.6.30.

[50] The 1989 Salvage Convention gives effect to this rule by art.17, which provides: "No payment is due under the provisions of this Convention unless the services rendered exceed what can reasonably be considered as due performance of a contract entered into before the danger arose."

which must be undertaken, by reason of the requirements of local law, or of the legally constituted port or other authorities, if the ship is to be allowed to enter or leave the port or place. The distinction between these costs and the costs of measures undertaken as a condition of remaining at the port is discussed at para.11.58, below.

Even if the authorities or the local laws require a particular measure to be adopted in relation to environmental damage, the cost of that measure will only be allowable if it falls within the opening words of the rule–that is, if it is undertaken to prevent or minimise damage to the environment, the scope of which expression is discussed above at para.11.40. For example, if the authorities require the shipowner to give a guarantee covering: (1) liability to third parties in respect of pollution damage; or (2) clean-up costs,[51] the costs of so doing will not be recoverable.

"in the circumstances prescribed in Rule X(a)": Rule X(a), the commentary on which will be found at paras 10.30 to 10.35, above, essentially provides that the costs of entering and leaving a port of refuge shall be allowed in general average only when it was necessary to enter the port for the common safety.

Sub-paragraph (iii)

"as a condition of remaining at any port or place": Whereas sub-para.(ii) deals with costs when incurred as a condition of entry or departure, sub-para.(iii) deals with costs incurred as a condition of remaining at a port or place. This sub-paragraph contains a proviso regarding an actual release or escape of pollutant substances which is not found in the other three–the effect of this proviso is discussed in para.11.57. **11.55**

"in the circumstances prescribed in Rule XI(b)"[52] : Rule XI(b), the commentary on which is at paras 11.25 to 11.39, above, provides that crew wages and certain other expenses shall be allowed in general average during detention at any port or place where the detention is necessary either for the common safety or to enable repairs necessary for the safe prosecution of the voyage to be effected. It follows that, unlike sub-para.(ii), this sub-paragraph is not confined to those cases where the anti-environmental damage measures were imposed as a condition of an operation performed for the common safety, and extends to cases where the vessel is detained to effect repairs necessary for the safe prosecution of the voyage. **11.56**

"provided that when there is an actual escape or release of pollutant substances the cost of any additional measures required on that account to **11.57**

[51] Clean-up costs are intended to be excluded from the scope of r.XI(d): see para.11.48, above.

[52] Some confusion arose, at the Sydney Conference and subsequently, concerning the identity of the rule which was intended to be referred to in sub-para.(iii) of r.Xl(d). In its original draft form (r.XI(d) is based on a draft submitted by the British MLA, which received the recommendation of the International Standing Committee of CMI), this sub-paragraph referred to r.XI(b); the draft which was before the Plenary Session of the Conference, when it voted to adopt the York-Antwerp Rules 1994, referred to r.X(a), as did the *CMI Newsletter* No.3 of 1994; the first official CMI, publication of the Rules referred to r.X(b), but CMI, later published an amendment which changed the reference from r.X(b) to XI(b). In the version of the Rules published in the 1994 CMI Yearbook the reference is to r.XI(b).

prevent or minimise pollution or environmental damage shall not be allowed as general average": Whenever there is an actual escape or release of pollutant substances the rule excludes from any claim under sub-para.(iii) the cost of any measures over and above those which would be required anyway, as a precaution, even if there had been no actual escape. Thus it will exclude the costs of additional measures taken to minimise the amount of pollutant which escapes, or the area over which it spreads, even though these costs fall within the scope of the opening words of r.XI(d).[53] The cost of those precautionary measures which would have been required anyway, even if there were no escape or release, will continue to be allowed, so long as these measures did actually continue to be required and the costs in question were actually incurred. The phrase "escape or release" is the same as that used in r.C, and it probably also contemplates that there should be an escape or release beyond the confines of the property involved in the common maritime adventure.

It may sometimes be difficult, when an actual escape or release occurs, to identify which additional measures are to be regarded as having been required on that account within the meaning of the proviso. Clearly this phrase includes any extra measures required to be undertaken in order to deal with the actual escape or release, such as stopping the spread of a pollutant which has already escaped. The cost of measures of a precautionary nature, required by the authorities merely in case the escape or release should recur, and which go beyond those which the authorities would have required if no escape or release had previously occurred, are not expressly dealt with in the rule. However, it is suggested that such expenses are incurred "on that account" (i.e. because of the spill) in that they would not have been called for otherwise, and therefore should not be allowed.

11.58 Because the proviso relating to an actual spill or escape appears in (iii) but not in (ii) it is necessary to identify whether particular measures are being allowed under (ii)–as a condition of entry or (iii)—as a condition of remaining. In many cases the requirements of a port authority may not be set out particularly clearly and they may set conditions that relate to occupation of a berth or anchorage as a pre-condition of entry. It was suggested in the 12th edition that allowances under (iii) should commence when the common safety had been attained in a port of refuge, however this does not always provide a complete answer since r.XI(b), which is referred to in (iii), deals with detention in a port for the common safety as well as for necessary repairs. The rule is designed as a compromise and such compromises often require cut-off points that are clear, whether or not they are entirely consistent with principle. From an entirely practical point of view it is easy to see that the proviso in (iii) might be particularly difficult to apply while a vessel is struggling into a port of refuge and a broader approach is therefore justified in (ii).

Any allowance under r.XI (d) is in respect of "measures undertaken" and it is submitted that the intention of the rule is that the question of whether (ii) or (iii) is applicable should be determined on the basis of when the respective measures

[53] See para.11.47, above.

were actually taken, and the costs incurred, rather than when the conditions were set by the authorities.

Sub-paragraph (iv)

"necessarily in connection with the discharging, storing or reloading of cargo": The requirement that the costs to which this sub-paragraph relates must be necessarily incurred is fairly stringent, but would probably be satisfied whenever the costs are reasonably incurred in taking those measures to prevent or minimise damage to the environment which are insisted on by the legally constituted authorities at the port or place in question, or commercial enterprises such as stevedores and warehousemen without whose co-operation the discharge, storing and re-loading of the cargo cannot be achieved, or which any reasonably prudent person would take in the circumstances of the case. 11.59

It will be noted that only cargo is referred to, unlike r.X(c) which also refers to "fuel or stores". Operations to shift or remove bunkers would therefore fall outside this sub-paragraph but, in practice, will often fall within sub-para.(i).

"whenever the cost of those operations is admissible as general average": The cost of discharging cargo at a port or place of refuge is admissible in general average under the provisions of r.X(b)[54] when necessary for the common safety, alternatively to enable damage to the ship to be repaired, if the repairs were necessary for the safe prosecution of the voyage. And whenever the cost of discharging is so allowable, the cost of storing and reloading such cargo is admissible under r.X(c).[55] Similar charges to lighten a vessel when ashore are admissible as general average in the terms of r.VIII.

[54] See para.10.45, above.
[55] See para.10.63, above.

RULE XII

DAMAGE TO CARGO IN DISCHARGING, ETC.

ENGLISH PRACTICE AND BACKGROUND

When cargo is discharged from a ship under such circumstances that the operation is a general average act, that is to say an extraordinary act performed for the common preservation of ship and cargo, and when such discharging[1] entails damage or partial loss to the cargo, such damage or loss falls within the definition of general average, and in practice is so treated.[2] 12.01

Thus, when a ship, being in a leaky state or needing repairs, is for the common safety taken into a port of refuge and it is necessary to discharge the cargo there, then, if the discharging is for the common safety of all, and is on this, or indeed any other, ground properly treated as a general average act, any damage or loss of cargo which follows from so discharging it is properly to be treated as general average loss.[3] It is otherwise where the cargo is not in danger but has to be discharged to enable the ship to be repaired after sustaining a particular average loss.[4]

Until 1996 the British practice was to allow such damage only when the damage was necessarily caused in the discharging. A Rule of Practice on the subject in force from 1886 until 1996, read as follows:

[1] As to when the cargo is negligently damaged in the course of discharge, see *Federal Commerce and Navigation Co Ltd v Eisenerz GmbH* [1970] 2 Lloyd's Rep. 332; [1975] 1 Lloyd's Rep. 105; para.12.14, fn.16, below.

[2] Thus, a loss of cargo in barges, into which it had been discharged to enable the vessel to make a port of refuge, should be allowed as general average. See *Abbott* (5th edn), p.346, cited with approval by Cresswell J. in *Hallett v Wigram* (1850) 9 C.B. 580 at 608, and by Mathew J. in *McCall v Houlder* (1897) 2 Com. Cas. 129 at 132. See also per Wills J. in *Royal Mail Steam Packet Co v English Bank of Rio* (1887) 19 Q.B.D. 362 at 372, and the American cases *Hennew v Monroe* (1826) 8 Martin, La., 227 (IV. 449; O.S.); *Lewis v Williams* (1820) 1 Hall, N.Y. 430; *Gourlie* (1820) 213; *Heyliger v N.Y.F. Insurance Co* (1814) 11 Johns. R. 85.

[3] But not damage or deterioration which would have occurred if the cargo had remained on board: *Spafford v Dodge* (1817) 14 Mass. 65: *Gourlie*, p.214.

[4] *Hamel v P&O Steam Nav. Co* [1908] 2 K.B. 298. Lord Alverstone C.J.

> *"F18 Treatment of Damage to Cargo caused by Discharge, Storing and Reloading*
> That damage necessarily done to cargo by discharging, storing, and reloading it, be treated as general average when, and only when the cost of those measures respectively is so treated."

However, in 1996 a new Rule of Practice was adopted in terms identical to r.XII, and containing no reference to necessarily. The discussion later in this section of the effect of r.XII is therefore equally applicable to the Rule of Practice. Broadly speaking it enables allowance to be made for any damage in discharging and associated operations which should reasonably have been anticipated as a serious possibility. This approach is entirely consistent with the English law rules on causation.

Why Damage should Follow Discharging

12.02 There are three principal reasons why discharging cargo at a port of refuge may lead to its being damaged: (1) the cargo may have to be discharged with unusual haste, as when the ship is leaking; or (2) in a place where it is not usual to unload so large ships or cargoes of that kind, so that there are not the proper appliances: or, (3) the cargo may be of such a nature, for example coal, that it cannot be landed without suffering loss by breakage or the like, so that to discharge it at a port of refuge, in addition to the port of destination, is simply doubling the ordinary wastage. In any of these cases, what the discharging actually costs is the money outlay plus the damage to cargo consequent upon the decisions to discharge it. Allowance is also made in practice for cargo pilfered during a forced discharge, so far as such loss might reasonably be anticipated. Damage to cargo merely through delay at a port of refuge is not, however, allowed, whether it be left on the vessel or stored on shore, nor is a loss by fire or other accident while the cargo is stored, made good.[5]

HISTORICAL DEVELOPMENT AND PRACTICE OF RULE XII

Glasgow Resolutions 1860

12.03 The practice in this country in 1860 was to allow in general average any loss or damage to cargo caused by a forced discharge for the common safety whilst the vessel was at sea or ashore, but until 1883 to exclude such loss or damage if the discharge took place at a port of refuge in the manner customary at that port.[6] This

[5] The dictum to the contrary in *The Brig Mary* (1842) 1 Sprague 17 is not followed by American adjusters.

[6] See the textbooks of the period, or the Custom of Lloyd's: V. Damage to Cargo in Discharging. Damage done to cargo by discharging it at a port of refuge, in the manner and under the circumstances customary at that port, is not allowed as general average.

British practice applicable to a port of refuge was accepted by 19 votes to 6 at the International Conference at Glasgow in 1860:

> "(4) That the damage done to cargo, and the loss of it and the freight on it, resulting from discharging it at a port of refuge in the way usual in that port with ships not in distress, ought not to be allowed in general average."

York Rules 1864

No change was made in the effect of the earlier Glasgow Resolution but its wording was rearranged: **12.04**

> "(IX) Damage done to cargo by discharging it at a port of refuge shall not be admissible as general average in case such cargo shall have been discharged at the place and in the manner customary at that port with ships not in distress."

York-Antwerp Rules 1877

No change, but it is believed that opposition to the rule was mounting. **12.05**

York-Antwerp Rules 1890

Probably as the result of the decisions in *Atwood v Sellar*[7] and *Svendsen v Wallace*[8] the practice of British average adjusters changed between 1877 and 1890. In 1883 the Association of Average Adjusters introduced a rule of practice to the effect that whenever the cost of discharging cargo was general average, all loss or damage necessarily arising to cargo therefrom should also be allowed in general average, and in 1886 this was extended to cover damage done by "discharging, storing and reloading".[9] **12.06**

It is not surprising, therefore, that at the International Conference held at Liverpool in 1890 the York-Antwerp Rule was amended to reflect this progress.

The first draft put forward in 1890 had opened with: "Damage done to, or loss of cargo by discharging, storage, reloading and stowing . . ." but this was considered too wide and warning was given that the word "storage" would cause difficulty, almost certainly on the grounds that it was likely to be construed as covering losses sustained during the period of storage. It is clear from the discussion that the only losses to be made good were those necessarily sustained in the act of handling the cargo, that is, when putting it out of the ship, into the warehouse, or back into the ship: loss or damage, even if almost inevitable, sustained during the period of storage was not to be covered. Accordingly "storage" was changed to "storing", and "necessarily caused in the act of" was inserted before the various cargo operations.

[7] *Atwood v Sellar* (1880) 5 Q.B.D. 286.

[8] *Svendsen v Wallace* (1885) 10 A.C. 404.

[9] Rule of Practice F18. See para.70.45, below.

"(XII) Damage done to or loss of cargo necessarily caused in the act of discharging, storing, reloading and stowing, shall be made good as general average when and only when the cost of those measures respectively is admitted as general average."

York-Antwerp Rules 1924

12.07 Minor changes to the wording were introduced on this occasion:

(1) The insertion of the words "fuel or stores" after the word "'cargo" and of the word "handling" before the words "discharging, storing", so that the rule should correspond with the alterations then being made in r.X(b) under which "the cost of handling on board or discharging cargo, fuel or stores" at a port of refuge was to be allowed as general average.
(2) The omission of the word "necessarily" before the word "caused". The phrase "necessarily caused"' had been found difficult of construction and it was thought that the wording adopted in 1924 indicated with sufficient precision what damage or loss was allowable as general average.

York-Antwerp Rules 1950

12.08 Prior to the International Conference at Amsterdam, the Belgian Committee pointed out that they considered r.XII too restrictive in that it covered loss or damage to cargo caused only in the act of handling, etc. They instanced the case of refrigerated cargo being discharged at a port of refuge at which no refrigerated storage facilities existed; the master knew perfectly well that such cargo must suffer damage as the result of the forced discharge, and they considered that this damage should be allowed as general average. They proposed, therefore, that the words, "caused in the act of handling, etc." should be replaced by: "in consequence of handling, etc."

The International Committee were sympathetic to this view, and the Drafting Committee proposed an alternative form of wording "caused by[10] handling, etc." but, as it was open to abuse, felt some doubt as to the advisability of making any amendment and recommended that the question should be discussed at the Amsterdam Conference.

Considerable discussion ensued and the question raised: What was the cause of damage sustained in such circumstances by perishable cargo? Was it the act of handling, etc. or was it decay or deterioration? If damage by delay were to be allowed under r.XII, it would conflict with the general principle laid down in r.C.[11]

[10] At the Conference itself, the Belgian delegation proposed that the wording should be "directly caused by" in the hope that it would avoid some of the abuses which the wording might otherwise allow. It would restrict the allowance to those cases in which goods would not have suffered from the delay of the vessel but for being discharged into an inefficient store.

[11] The example of a perishable cargo inevitably calls into question the relationship between r.XII and r.C. However, there are other cases where the lack of suitable storage facilities ashore will necessarily cause loss by causes other than delay, for example a steel cargo wetted by rainwater as a result of storage in a leaky warehouse. According to Hudson, the practice was to allow inevitable loss or

Having regard to the difficulty of amending the rule in any agreed form and the difficulty of choosing the right words to express any possible amendment, the Conference eventually decided to retain the existing wording of the 1924 rule.

York-Antwerp Rules 1974

No change. **12.09**

York-Antwerp Rules 1994

Where those in 1950 feared to tread, their successors in 1994 plunged boldly and introduced the previously desired change. The words of the rule, "*caused in the act of* handling, discharging, storing, reloading and stowing . . ." were amended to, ". . . *sustained in consequence of* their handling, discharging, storing, reloading and stowing . . ." The new wording adopted a British proposal, the original purpose of which was to bring consequential loss and damage within the rule, so long as it was the natural consequence of the handling, discharging, storing etc. rather than the result of a supervening event, such as a fire in the warehouse, thus bringing the rule into line with the general principles set out in r.C (but without the specific exclusion of loss by delay). This was clearly an extension of the previous rule which, for instance, might have included (as desired in 1950) deterioration of refrigerated cargo discharged at a port of refuge at which no refrigerated storage facilities existed. By mid-1994, however, when insurers were reluctant that there should be any expansion of general average, it was pointed out that the amendment was also of a limiting nature, required because the existing caused in the act of was too wide, and included loss or damage not necessarily the natural consequence of the discharging, etc. but the result of some extraneous cause such as negligence of stevedores.[12] **12.10**

York-Antwerp Rules 2004

No change, other than the substitution of "allowed as general average" for "made good/admitted as general average". **12.11**

RULE XII

DAMAGE TO CARGO IN DISCHARGING, ETC.

Damage to or loss of cargo, fuel or stores sustained in consequence of their handling, discharging, storing, reloading and stowing shall be made good/ allowed as general average, when and only when the cost of those measures respectively is admitted/allowed as general average.

damage of this kind caused by deficient storage facilities, despite the apparent conflict between this practice and the wording of the rule.

[12] e.g. as in *Federal Commerce and Navigation Co v Eisenerz GmbH* [1970] 2 Lloyd's Rep. 332; [1975] 1 Lloyd's Rep. 105.

Construction

12.12 Since r.VII deals with damage to cargo when discharged from a ship ashore, the prime intention of r.XII is to deal with the situation when the discharge takes place in a port of refuge.

"cargo": See commentary under r.I.[13]

"in consequence of": This phrase requiring a more extensive commentary than normal, it will be dealt with after the various cargo operations to which it refers. See para.12.14, below.

12.13 **"handling"**: Although this word might be construed to comprise the complete range of cargo movements mentioned in the rule, there is no doubt that when introduced in 1924, (see paras 12.07, also 10.46, above), this single word was clearly intended as an abbreviation for the phrase "handling on board" in r.X(b), that is, it related to the situation where cargo, etc. was moved from one compartment of the ship to another, or on to deck, without an actual discharge overside.

"discharging": By custom, the operation of discharging includes also the transit to the warehouse or other place where the cargo, etc. is stored.[14]

"storing": When first introduced in 1890, this word was intended to cover only the operation of placing and stacking the cargo, etc. in the warehouse or other place of storage. In everyday use it is, of course, perfectly capable of bearing the construction that it covers the keeping of the goods in storage. Thus loss sustained during that period is allowable under the rule provided that it is sustained in consequence of the storing of the goods ashore, or of one of the other operations referred to in the rule. (See also paras 12.17 to 12.19, below.)

"reloading": By tradition[15] and analogy with discharging, above, this term will include the unstacking and return conveyance of the cargo, etc. from the warehouse to the ship, its transfer on board, and also its . . .

". . . stowing": on board the ship.

12.14 **"in consequence of"**: Introduced in 1994, these words replaced the previous "*caused in the act of*", an expression almost incapable of being misconstrued and which imposed no requirement that the loss or damage sustained during the mentioned cargo operations should be such as would have been contemplated or foreseen as likely to occur.[16]

[13] See para.1.28, above.

[14] See Rule of Practice F12(b) in para.70.39, below.

[15] Under earlier English practice, the cost of discharging and conveyance to the warehouse was general average, the warehouse rent was a special charge on the cargo itself, and the relocating expenses, etc. were a special charge on the freight.

[16] In spite of the Canadian decision to opposite effect in *Federal Commerce and Navigation Co v Eisenerz GmbH* [1970] 2 Lloyd's Rep. 332; [1975] 1 Lloyd's Rep. 105. In that case the Oak Hill discharged and reloaded cargo at Levis as a port of refuge. During these operations two grades of pig-iron became intermingled and damaged. It was found that this was due to negligence of the stevedores and of the master, who had failed to supervise their work. The charterers claimed damages, and the owners pleaded that they were liable for no more than a contribution in general average under r.XII of the York-Antwerp Rules 1950.

The Supreme Court of Canada held that the damage could only be general average if it was a direct consequence of the general average act, and that as the master could not be allowed to foresee his own

The 1994 wording does introduce the concept of consequences and is accordingly less easy to construe in practice, nor does it state in terms whether the consequences be limited to direct, or include also indirect.[17] Simple examples of both direct and indirect losses have already been given in para.12.02, above. It appears probable that the framers of the rule intended that, to be treated as general average, any loss or damage should be the direct consequence of the cargo handling operations mentioned in the rule. How this requirement is to be applied in various situations is considered in more detail below, but first it is useful to consider what general approach common sense and sound principle would suggest is appropriate.

On those occasions when, as provided by rr.X(b) and X(c), the operations of handling on board, discharging, storing, reloading and stowing cargo, fuel or stores are treated as general average acts and their cost charged to general average, the owners of such shifted cargo, etc. have an equal right to expect that if their property is thereby exposed to greater risks than would be expected if it remained undisturbed on board the ship, and those greater risks operate, either during the handling operations themselves or whilst stored ashore, the loss or damage sustained thereby should similarly be allowed as general average, either under r.XII itself, or rr.A and C. **12.15**

Losses during Cargo Handling Operations

The risks attendant upon the active processes of cargo handling, etc. are wholly avoided if the goods remain undisturbed in the ship, and it follows that even if the goods should be unnecessarily lost or damaged during discharging operations, etc. as the result of negligence of stevedores, that loss should be allowed as general average.[18] For what they may be worth, all rights of recourse against any party responsible for a loss admitted in general average must accrue to the general average itself, but there should never be any doubt that the merchant or other party initially suffering the loss should have a prime right to compensation in general average from his fellow adventurers for that loss. **12.16**

The following examples of loss or damage covered by the rule may be mentioned:

(1) total loss of or damage to packages dropped into the sea, onto the quay, or into the hold during discharge or reloading operations;

negligence this test was not satisfied. Hence the charterers' claim for the whole loss succeeded. It is submitted that the court's reasoning is not wholly satisfactory, although it led to the correct conclusion. The damage was general average within the 1950 r.XII, whether or not it was within r.C, for the Rule of Interpretation so provides. But since there was fault on the part of the owners, in the negligence of their master, they could not rely on the general average act as a defence to the charterers' claim for the whole loss.

[17] "Direct consequences denote those consequences which flow in an unbroken sequence from the act: whereas indirect consequences are those in which the sequence is broken by an intervening or extraneous cause," per Lord Denning in *Australian Coastal Commission v Green* [1971] 1 Q.B. 456 at 481.

[18] There is no rule in English law that subsequent negligence by a third party breaks the chain of causation between the defendant's actionable conduct and the damage sustained by the claimant: see e.g. *Rahman v Arearose Ltd* [2001] Q.B. 351, CA.

(2) loss of contents from bags burst, or containers damaged, by the rough handling of stevedores at the port of refuge;
(3) rain or weather damage to baled goods or steel pipes whilst being transported to the warehouse.

Losses during the Period of Storage

12.17 The risks attendant upon the passive condition of storage are always present to some degree, whether the goods are aboard or ashore—indeed, they may even be reduced while ashore–and different considerations apply. If cargo, etc. is discharged at a port of refuge into what is thought to be suitable and adequate storage and some unexpected accident occurs, for example:

(1) a fire in the warehouse;
(2) the roof of the warehouse is torn off by a hurricane;
(3) a lighter is cast from its moorings in a gale and sunk,

the consequent loss or damage to the cargo would not normally be made good in general average for the reason that, whilst it is always possible to envisage that such events may happen, the chances of their actual occurrence are somewhat remote and it is unlikely that they would be seriously taken into account by the master when considering the discharge.[19]

However, if the facilities for storage at the port of refuge are known to be insufficient or inadequate, the possibility of damage would be fairly within the contemplation of the master and it is, and should, accordingly, be allowed as general average, either under r.XII or C, for example:

(1) weather and dirt damage to cargo stored in the open;
(2) damage by rain through the defective roof of an ancient warehouse;
(3) similar damage to goods in a lighter through worn and inadequate tarpaulins.

Moreover a certain amount of pilferage of food, drink, and other valuable small goods is almost inevitable in any warehouse, whatever its condition.

12.18 A topic on which some difference of opinion may exist concerns the deterioration which a perishable or frozen cargo may sustain as the result of a forced discharge, for example:

(1) A cargo of apples may be bruised by rough handling and in consequence the fruit go rotten.

[19] An insurance against this class of accident is frequently arranged at the time of the discharge and the premium charged to general average. Any claims on the policy, however, would be paid to the owners of the cargo.

Provided that this damage may fairly be attributable to the actual handling, it should be allowed in full.

(2) A cargo of new potatoes may sustain little or no damage by the forced discharge, but the detention may cause the potatoes to become a little soft and lose their "scraping" qualities.

It is probable that the same loss would have occurred even if the potatoes had remained in the vessel and had not been discharged, accordingly the loss was not sustained as a consequence of any of the operations described in the rule, and should not be allowed.

Refrigerated cargoes give rise to special problems, for example: **12.19**

(1) Refrigerated cargo is left on board during repairs, while the vessel has no power. The consequent deterioration is not a consequence of any of the operations to which the rule applies, and is not allowable.
(2) Refrigerated cargo is put ashore during drydock repairs. There is no power ashore or on board.
The position is as in (1) above. Again the deterioration is not a consequence of any of the operations to which the rule applies.
(3) Some refrigerated cargo is discharged in order to enable the vessel to drydock. Power is available on board but not ashore. The deterioration is allowable, being the consequence of the discharge and storage ashore of the cargo.
(4) Power is available on board and ashore, but refrigerated containers stored ashore are not connected up, as a result of negligence Here the negligence is probably sufficiently grave and unpredictable to break the chain of causation between the storage ashore and the damage. It would be otherwise if the failure of the shore power was due to a more predictable event such as a power cut at a port where such events were not infrequent.

"only when the cost of those measures respectively is admitted as general average": Claims for loss of or damage to cargo, etc. sustained in consequence of handling on board or discharging, etc. are allowable under this rule only when the cost of those various measures is admissible in general average. The circumstances in which such cost is allowable are as follows: **12.20**

- *Handling on board and discharging*, under r.X(b), when necessary for the common safety or to enable damage to the ship caused by sacrifice or accident to be repaired, if the repairs were necessary for the safe prosecution of the voyage.
- *Storing, reloading and stowing*, under r.X(c), when the handling or discharging (as above) was admissible in general average.

Rule XIII

Deductions from Cost of Repairs

English Law and Background

When any part of a ship's hull, gear, or machinery, etc. is sacrificed for the common safety, and when the ship is afterwards repaired, the sum allowable in general average as compensation for this damage is the reasonable[1] cost of repairs, with an appropriate deduction for the advantage—if any—which the owner derives from having new work in place of old.[2] 13.01

Deductions "New for Old"

By an ancient and widespread custom prevailing amongst almost all maritime countries, the deduction from the cost of repairs was fixed at one-third of the cost of repairs, with certain equally well-defined exceptions. No deduction was made during a vessel's first voyage,[3] which in the days of sail could often take a year; anchors were allowed in full, while chain cables were subject to a deduction of one-sixth only; and unbroached stores, such as coils of rope taken from a store-room, or spare sails which had never been bent, were allowed without deduction. 13.02

[1] For an indication of the considerations which apply when construing the term "reasonable cost of repairs", see the commentary, para.18.12, below, on r.XVIII of the York- Antwerp Rules 1974.

[2] The notion of betterment causes difficulty in other branches of the law. In the case of claims in tort for damage to a ship caused by collision it has long been the law that no "new for old" deduction is made, since the benefit thus obtained by the claimant "arises only from the impossibility of effecting . . . indemnification without exposing him to some loss or burden, which the law will not place on him": see *The Gazelle* (1844) 2 W. Rob. (Adm.) 279, 281. The same approach has been applied in the case of other chattels, and of buildings; see *Harbutt's Plasticine Ltd v Wayne Tank and Pump Co Ltd* [1970] 1 Q.B. 447; *Bacon v Cooper Metals* [1982] 3 All E.R. 397. However, where the damage is so extensive that complete replacement of a chattel is necessary, and no market exists for a second hand replacement in similar condition, it has been held that the proper measure of damage is the cost of a new product less an appropriate allowance for betterment: see *Voaden v Champion* ("The Baltic Surveyor") [2001] 1 Lloyd's Rep. 739; [2002] 1 Lloyd's Rep. 623 (CA).

[3] *Pirie v Steel* (1837) 2 M. & Rob. 49; 8 C. & P. 200.

These customary deductions, "new for old", may have been appropriate in the days of wooden sailing ships, but with the introduction of the more durable iron and steel ships, and machinery in place of sails, it was considered that a deduction of one-third from the cost of repairs was unnecessarily severe on shipowners. In 1884, therefore, the Association of Average Adjusters appointed a special committee to make inquiry into the subject. In accordance with their recommendations, a detailed Rule of Practice[4] was introduced, and this has been amended from time to time to accord with the latest developments in shipbuilding, and in 1974 in the interests of simplification.

Historical Development and Practice of Rule XIII

York-Antwerp Rules 1890, 1924 and 1950

13.03 A rule on the subject of deductions from the cost of repairs, "new for old", was first introduced into the York-Antwerp Rules at the Conference held in Liverpool in 1890, and the wording followed very closely that of the British Rule of Practice passed by the Association of Average Adjusters in 1887.

The technical advances and developments made over the years in the shipbuilding industry were matched by appropriate amendments in the rule in 1924 and 1950, but, as in all its editions the rule was essentially technical in its provisions, none of the lengthy wordings is quoted here, but they may be referred to in the Appendices of the 7th and 11th editions of this work.

York-Antwerp Rules 1974

13.04 With a view to simplifying the process of general average adjustment, a complete and radical change was suggested for r.XIII in 1974: that no deductions "new for old" should be made from the cost of any repairs allowable in general average.

Although the principle that some deduction should be made from the cost of repairs to represent the betterment of the ship by reason of new material replacing old is in many cases eminently sound, it was doubted whether, in modern practice, the extra work of assessing the deductions was entirely justified or worthwhile, more particularly as the 1950 and earlier rules on this subject suffered from the defects common to rule-of-thumb methods of applying principles, and were somewhat arbitrary in their provisions. Moreover, while the deductions might be justified where expendable items such as sails, rigging and ropes, etc. were concerned, it was generally illusory to assume that even the oldest vessel was in any way improved, or that any benefit which could be realised in cash was conferred upon the shipowner, by, say, the fitting of a new strake of plating; the vessel would still end her useful trading life and be sent to the breakers' yard at

[4] F19, see para.70.46, below.

much the same time as she would normally have done. Accordingly, the following wording was put forward for discussion at the Hamburg Conference in 1974:

> "No deductions 'new for old' shall be made from the cost of permanent or temporary repairs to the ship in any circumstances.
>
> There shall be no allowance in general average in any circumstance for cleaning and painting of bottom."

Contrary to what might have been expected from the replies by the National Associations to the questionnaire circulated by the Comité Maritime International in 1970, the proposal to abolish deductions "new for old" was most strenuously resisted by a number of countries. A counter-proposal, based upon a recommendation made at the 1967 Assembly of AIDE, was put forward by a number of delegations. The voting at the working session of the Hamburg Conference showed a majority of 11 to 8 in favour of the abolition of deductions "new for old". However, the proposal was raised again at a plenary session of the Conference in the form of an amendment proposed by Sweden. The result of a vote, taken on the "abolition" text first, as being the most radical, was a 12 to 12 tie, so that it failed. The amendment was then put to the vote and passed in preference to the retention of the 1950 text. **13.05**

York-Antwerp Rules 1994

No change, but it is worthy of record that the abolition of deductions "new for old" was again briefly considered, but the principle being in many cases sound,[5] and the simplified deductions of the 1974 rule causing no difficulties in practical application, it was decided to retain the first section of the rule unchanged. **13.06**

York-Antwerp Rules 2004

No change. **13.07**

RULE XIII

DEDUCTIONS FROM COST OF REPAIRS

> **Repairs to be allowed in general average shall not be subject to deductions in respect of "new for old" where old material or parts are replaced by new unless the ship is over fifteen years old in which case there shall be a deduction of one third. The deductions shall be regulated by the age of the ship from the 31st December of the year of completion of construction to the date of the general average act, except for insulation, life and similar boats, communications and navigational apparatus and equipment, machinery and boilers for which deductions shall be regulated by the age of the particular parts to which they apply.**

[5] Even if the renewal of a strake of plating may not extend the life and increase the value of an old vessel, the renewal of a main engine or similar most certainly does, and the case of the 22-year old Alpha is a reminder that such examples can occur: *Corfu Navigation Co v Mobil Shipping Co Ltd* [1991] 2 Lloyd's Rep. 52.

The deductions shall be made only from the cost of the new material or parts when finished and ready to be installed in the ship.

No deductions shall be made in respect of provisions, stores, anchors and chain cables.

Drydock and slipway dues and costs of shifting the ship shall be allowed in full.

The costs of cleaning, painting or coating of bottom shall not be allowed in general average unless the bottom has been painted or coated within the twelve months preceding the date of the general average act in which case one half of such costs shall be allowed.

CONSTRUCTION

13.08 Whether the cost of repairing damage to the ship is in principle allowable in general average falls to be decided under the lettered rules or under rr.II, III, IV, V, VII, IX, or XIV, If the cost is so allowable under any of these rules, other than r.XIV, r.XVIII(a), read with this rule regulates the amount to be allowed in general average. In cases falling within r.XIV, no deductions "new for old" are made.

"life and similar boats": It is suggested that by "similar boats" is meant boats similarly carried on board during passage, for example launch, cutter, gig, etc. and not merely boats carried for a purpose analogous to that of a life-boat.

"cost of the new material or parts when finished and ready to be installed in the ship": Deductions are confined to the cost of the new material, the cost of manufacturing the new article from the new material, the cost of such final preparation of the new material or the new article as may be necessary for fitting, and such local transportation costs as occur upon the repairers' or manufacturers' premises or in the drydock or yard. Although possibly not in accordance with a strict construction of the rule, in practice no deduction is made from the cost of transporting, for instance, a new propeller, tailshaft, or other machinery part from specialist manufacturers to the repair yard.[6]

Credit for Scrap Materials

13.09 In Britain, at least, the practice has existed for a century or more to make deductions "new for old" from the gross cost of new materials or parts, that is, before dealing with any credit received for the old materials sold or taken over as scrap. This practice was criticised as being inequitable by the Chairman in his address to the Association of Average Adjusters in 1963[7] and he instanced the case of a new bronze propeller costing £6,000 with a credit of £2,000 for the scrap propeller, and where a difference of £667 can result in the net amount allowed in general average. However, having regard to the many other arbitrary results that inevitably flow from a rule-of-thumb such as r.XIII, it is to be doubted whether any

[6] See para.13.07, fn.6 (12th edn).
[7] A.A.A. 1963 Report, p.5.

great weight should be attached to this criticism; it is more important that the practice should be uniform rather than that it should be unassailably correct.

"stores": It is difficult if not impossible to devise an accurate definition of this word in its context, but it was formally recorded at the Stockholm Conference in 1924 that the word was intended to include hawsers, ropes, and sheets. In practice it is probably construed also to include such expendable items as paints, oils, and tools.

"Drydock and slipway dues and costs of shifting the ship shall be allowed in full": This sentence means only that any allowance in general average under r.XVIII for the cost of drydocking and dues, etc. incurred to repair damage caused by sacrifice shall not be subject to deductions "new for old": it does not mean that the whole cost of drydocking and dues is necessarily chargeable to general average irrespective of what other work or repairs may be carried out in the drydock concurrently.[8] 13.10

"The costs of cleaning, painting or coating of bottom shall not be allowed in general average unless the bottom has been painted or coated within the 12 months preceding the date of the general average act in which case one half of such costs shall be allowed": As this r.XIII deals only with "Deductions from Cost of Repairs" and is in any case subservient to r.XVIII, there can be no doubt that this particular section of r.XIII is badly worded and might have been better expressed on lines such as the following: 13.11

> "The costs of cleaning, painting or coating of those parts of the bottom damaged by a general average act shall be subject to a deduction of one-half, except that when the bottom has not been painted or coated within the 12 months preceding the date of the general average act, no allowance shall be made."

In its present form, this 1974 wording is open to a construction quite opposed to the equitable principles of general average, and with the highly expensive "grit-blasting"' taking the place of the old-fashioned "scraping", cargo interests could find themselves severely prejudiced.

For example, a vessel may strand for her full length and, quite apart from any damaged plating, the whole of the bottom paint may be removed, scored or scuffed by the stranding alone—an accident. In principle, none of the costs of grit-blasting or repainting should be charged to general average, but it is conceivable that 50 per cent of such costs might be charged to general average under the existing wording if, for instance, the propeller or other underwater part was damaged by refloating operations.

Another area for doubt which could be resolved by precise wording concerns the cost of supplying and applying new anti-fouling paint to replace that destroyed only by exposure to the atmosphere during the period in drydock necessary for the repair of damage caused by a general average act. For example, a vessel may strand without damage, but the efforts to refloat cause damage to the propeller, and exposure to the atmosphere during the period of drydocking necessary for the 13.12

[8] For a fuller commentary on this subject, see paras 18.14–18.15, below.

propeller repairs may destroy the qualities of the anti-fouling paint. It is probably correct to say that the paint has not been destroyed by a general average act (the refloating operations) but by delay, to be excluded by the terms of r.C. However, if there are specific provisions in a numbered rule (as there may be here), those provisions override the general provisions of a lettered rule in accordance with the Rule of Interpretation. The introduction in the last few years of silicon based paints, which can withstand exposure to the atmosphere during drydocking, should mean that these problems are less frequently encountered than in the past. Since the silicon based paints remain soft, they are more likely to be damaged as a direct result of the grounding itself, or by the efforts to refloat.

13.13 A further criticism of this part of the rule is that while the ability of modern bottom coatings to withstand exposure to the atmosphere has reduced the cases where the coating will need to be replaced on drydocking, the exclusion of any allowance for replacing the bottom coating unless renewed within the last 12 months is potentially very unfair, since modern coatings may have a life of five to ten years. The following technical information may be of interest:

> Until, say, the 1970s, most ships drydocked about once every year for routine maintenance and "scraping and painting" of bottom. As the water was gradually let out of the drydock, men on rafts scraped off the weeds and barnacles, also any loose paint, rust and scale. Bare patches of steel were touched up with primer, followed by a full coat of anti-corrosive to protect against the natural corrosive action of salt water, and then a full coat of anti-fouling to arrest the attachment of seaweed and other marine growths. The whole process was relatively unsophisticated, cheap, and took place generally during the first and last day in drydock.
>
> Reasonably appropriate to this unsophisticated process were the rule of thumb provisions of Rule XIII in the 1890, 1924 and 1950 York-Antwerp Rules, which basically provided that: "No painting bottom to be allowed if the bottom has not been painted within six months previous to the date of the accident." (How much of the cost was to be allowed if the bottom had been painted within the previous six months was unspecified, and was no doubt discretionary, but hull insurance conditions almost invariably excluded any claim whatever for bottom painting.)
>
> Today, a classification society will typically require a ship to be drydocked every five years, with an intermediate in-water survey in between, although some types of vessels more than 15 years old must be inspected in drydock twice every five years; and the modern approach to painting the bottom is far more sophisticated—and highly expensive.

New provisions are very necessary for this section of r.XIII and it is to be regretted that no change whatever was made in 1994 or 2004.

Rule XIV

Temporary Repairs

English Law and Background

Repairs carried out to a ship may be either complete and of a permanent character, or they may be of a temporary nature only, sufficient to enable the remaining voyage to be prosecuted in safety, but of no lasting benefit to the ship and requiring to be removed at destination or elsewhere and replaced with full permanent repairs. **14.01**

Temporary repairs reasonably effected to damage caused by a general average sacrifice (for example by a voluntary stranding[1]) cause no problem; the cost of such repairs follows the nature of the damage itself and is charged to general average.

For temporary repairs to damage caused by accident, the position under English law is, with one exception, precisely the same: the cost of the temporary repairs similarly follows the nature of the damage itself and is borne wholly by the shipowner or his insurers as particular average. The exception is when those temporary repairs are made at a time of peril, for the common safety, and involve the sacrifice of property on board ship intended for some other purpose, thereby constituting a general average act and justifying in its own right the allowance in general average of the value of the property sacrificed, Lowndes gives as an example[2]:

> "A very ancient, general, and undisputed custom . . . relates to jury-rig. When a ship's mast or rudder is carried away and a 'jury' or temporary mast or rudder is fitted up at sea as a substitute, the value of the materials cut up or destroyed for the purpose . . . (is) in practice treated as general average."

[1] See paras 5.01 et seq., above.
[2] See para.A.77, above.

With regard to temporary repairs of accidental damage effected, not at a time of peril, but in the safety of a port of refuge, various reasons may be put forward for the decision to effect only temporary repairs, for example:

(1) Repair facilities in the port of refuge may not exist–or be inadequate–for full permanent repairs.
(2) Repair costs at the port of refuge may be much higher than at destination or elsewhere.
(3) Temporary repairs may be effected with the cargo remaining on board, whereas permanent repairs would require a costly discharge of the cargo.
(4) Temporary repairs may be effected in much less time than permanent, thereby saving delay and expense.

For all or any of these reasons, can the cost of the temporary repairs be charged to general average, either wholly or in part?

14.02 As already stated English law is unequivocal in its refusal to recognise any allowance in general average for temporary repairs of accidental damage to enable the adventure to be completed, based on authority dating from Roman times. As recorded in the Digest, a vessel bound for Ostia suffered considerably by storm; her mast, yard and some other furniture were burnt by lightning. She put into Hippo, and after having speedily provided what was requisite, she completed her voyage and delivered her cargo in good condition. A question arose whether the proprietors of the cargo ought to contribute to the repairs of the vessel, and this was decided in the negative because the expenses had been incurred "rather to fit out the ship than to preserve the cargo".[3]

14.03 Nevertheless, Lowndes recorded in 1873 that before the decision in *Wilson v Bank of Victoria*[4] six years earlier there had been a tendency in practice to look with favour on such claims. Thus in the 2nd edn of his General Average published in 1856, Lowndes' senior partner, Lawrence R. Baily, wrote:

> "To avoid the expense that would result from discharging cargo at a port of refuge, a vessel is sometimes repaired there in a temporary manner.
>
> When the sum of the cost of such temporary repairs, and the cost of the repairs effected subsequently in a proper manner, is greater than the cost would have been for repairing the vessel in a proper manner at the port of refuge, the excess of the expense actually incurred in temporary and proper repairs over the expense which would have been incurred for repairing the vessel in a proper manner at the port of refuge, should . . . be charged to general average."

It is interesting to note that Baily's method prescribed for calculating the allowance was used as the basis for the amendment to r.XIV of the 2004 Rules, which avoids the often unduly generous allowances under earlier versions of the rule.

[3] L. 6 de leg. Rhod.—see para.60.07, below, with the particular translation above by Hoffmann L.J. in *Marida Ltd v Oswal Steel (The Bijela)* [1993] 1 Lloyd's Rep. 411 at 420.

[4] *Wilson v Bank of Victoria* (1867) L.R. 2 Q.B. 203

However, the practice could no longer be justified after the decision in *Wilson v Bank of Victoria*, the facts of which are set out in para.F.04, above. The claim in that case, which was not for the cost of the temporary repairs themselves (which seem to have been very minor),[5] but for the expense of extra fuel consumed in the auxiliary engine on the remainder of the voyage (which expense would have been avoided if the permanent repairs had been carried out, and could thus be regarded as part of the overall cost to the shipowner of effecting temporary repairs rather than permanent), was advanced on two grounds: **14.04**

(1) the extra fuel costs were a substituted expense for the cargo handling and storage costs which would have been incurred at the port of refuge, Rio, if permanent repairs had been effected there;
(2) the extra fuel costs were an extraordinary expense incurred for the common benefit.

The court rejected the first argument on the simple ground that English law did not recognise the principle of substituted expenses:

> "... we think that the expenses actually incurred must be apportioned according to the facts that actually happened, and that there is no legal principle on which they can be apportioned according to what might have been the facts if a different course had been pursued."

The second argument was rejected on the ground that the expense of the extra fuel, although extraordinarily heavy compared with that which would have been incurred if the vessel had been able to proceed under sail, was not extraordinary in kind. It might have been rejected on the additional ground that in English law general average does not extend to the concept of the common benefit, and, inasmuch as the vessel had been equipped with an adequate supply of fuel before departing from Rio, there was no threat to the common safety at the time when the expense was incurred.

The decision is sometimes explained on the additional ground, hinted at by Blackburn J.,[6] that:

> "Inasmuch as the master could, by the expenditure of a comparatively small sum on temporary repairs and coals, bring the ship and cargo safely home, it was his duty to do so."

However, this did not form the actual ground of the decision nor, it is submitted, would it have been a sufficient ground in itself.[7] It must be read in the context of

[5] One reason why the shipowner may have refrained from claiming the temporary repair costs themselves is that he could not establish that the cost of temporary repairs plus the cost of permanent repairs effected later exceeded the cost of permanent repairs if effected at Rio, the port of refuge, (see p.210 of the Report). Thus even under the practice described in para.14.03 no allowance would have been due.

[6] *Wilson* (1867) L.R. 2 Q.B. 203, p.211.

[7] See para.00.61, above. There is no rule that excludes expense from general average on the grounds that the master was under a duty to incur it.

the facts of the case, where a decision to effect permanent repairs would have been so unreasonable and have caused so much delay that it would almost certainly have amounted to a breach of the contract of affreightment. That will not always be the case, since there appears to be no rule that the shipowner is obliged to effect temporary rather than permanent repairs whenever that is the quicker or cheaper course.[8] Thus whether or not permanent repairs would have been a legitimate alternative must be a question of fact and degree.

14.05 In only one case decided under English law has the court given any encouragement to an allowance for the cost of temporary repairs of accidental damage in order to complete the voyage. That case is *Plummer v Wildman*[9] where the facts were as follows: the ship Cambridge sailed from Kingston with a cargo of sugars and rum for London, and a day or two later was in collision with a brig whereby her false stern and knees were broken and the master was in consequence obliged to cut away part of the rigging of her bowsprit, and to return to Kingston to repair the damage sustained by the accident and the cutting away. Upon her return the cargo was necessarily re-landed and warehoused in order that such temporary repairs might be done as would enable her to prosecute her voyage. Permanent repairs were effected on the vessel's arrival in London and this cost was not included in the claim for contribution.

The combined judgments of Lord Ellenborough C.J., Le Blanc and Bayley JJ., as reported, occupy no more than a page, but it is possible to deduce from the language used that an allowance might be made in general average in respect of the cost of temporary repairs to accidental damage sufficient only "to enable the ship to prosecute her voyage home, and were afterwards of no benefit to the ship". Nevertheless, such a deduction was not drawn by the contemporary writers Stevens (1816)[10] or Benecke (1824).[11] nor by any writer since, and *Plummer v Wildman*[12] must today be considered either to be overruled, or not to be an authority for the rule deduced from it.[13] Indeed in *Power v Whitmore*[14] Lord Ellenborough himself, perhaps regretting the width of the views expressed in *Plummer v Wildman*, sought to explain the decision on the grounds that the temporary repairs had been of damage caused by sacrifice.

[8] In *Marida v Oswal Steel (The Bijela)* [1992] 1 Lloyd's Rep. 636; [1993] 1 Lloyd's Rep. 411; [1994] 2 Lloyd's Rep. 1 permanent repairs would have taken about the same time as temporary repairs, but would have resulted in far greater expenses which would have been claimed in general average. Hobhouse J. expressed the view that the shipowners could not have been held to be in breach of contract if they had decided to effect permanent repairs.

[9] *Plummer v Wildman* (1815) 3 M. & S. 486.

[10] *Essay on Average* (1816): "It is surprising that any discussion should have taken place on this subject, or that there could ever have been any doubt that the owner of the ship was bound to keep his ship in repair."

[11] *Marine Insurance* (1824): "But the repairs done to a vessel are always a benefit to her, and I doubt whether, according to the above distinction, any part of those repairs which in themselves are of the nature of a particular average, can ever be construed into a general average."

[12] *Plummer* (1815) 3 M. & S. 486.

[13] Fuller views on this case are expressed in para.952 of Arnould, *Law of Marine Insurance and Average*.

[14] *Power v Whitmore* (1815) 4 M. & S. 141, 149.

Historical Development and Practice of Rule XIV

York-Antwerp Rules 1890

Deductions "new for old" are made from the cost of permanent repairs to damage caused by general average sacrifice to represent the supposed betterment or improvement in the value of the ship by reason of having new parts in place of old. By their very nature, however, temporary repairs make no improvement to the ship and will be removed on some later occasion when the damage is properly repaired. In consequence, no deductions "new for old" should be made from the cost of temporary repairs and a rule to this effect was introduced in 1890 as follows: "No deductions 'new for old' shall be made from the cost of temporary repairs of damage allowable as general average." **14.06**

It should be noted, however, that in the 1890 Rules there was no provision to show in what circumstances temporary repairs could be allowed as general average, and this question would continue to be determined by the law and practice governing the adjustment.[15]

York-Antwerp Rules 1924

The question of the proper treatment of temporary repairs at a port of refuge was one upon which much difference of opinion existed among the jurists of various nations. In England the question had been settled by the decision in *Wilson v Bank of Victoria*,[16] and at any rate so far as temporary repairs of particular average damage were concerned, no allowance in general average was possible except where a sacrifice was made. **14.07**

The practice in foreign countries, whether or not based on sound legal authority,[17] relating to the treatment of the cost of temporary repairs to accidental damage at a port of refuge has been reported in the various editions of Rudolf or Lowndes & Rudolf since 1926 essentially as follows: in the United States, reasonable temporary repairs of damage arising from excepted perils, made at some intermediate port, where permanent repairs could not be made, if necessary to remove the disability of the ship to proceed on her voyage, were regarded as general average. Such repairs had to be purely temporary in their nature and must serve no permanent purpose. Temporary repairs made solely to save the excessive cost of permanent repairs were not general average. When permanent repairs could be made at a port of refuge, but at a large expense, and it would necessitate the discharge of cargo and the incurring of heavy general average expenses, and, perhaps, serious damage to cargo in handling, it was the practice to treat the temporary repairs as general average. In Italy also the practice was to allow purely temporary repairs of particular average damage as general average provided

15 See para.14.07, below.

16 *Wilson* (1867) L.R. 2 Q.B. 203.

17 In the 11th and 12th edns of this work it is questioned whether the practice reported as prevailing in the US, Germany and other countries was in accordance with the law of those countries.

permanent repairs were not possible or practicable. In other countries (Germany, Holland and Scandinavia, for example) the cost of temporary repairs of particular average damage was allowed as general average if by effecting such repairs greater general average expenses were saved.

14.08 With a diversity in the practice of the different countries, a rule on the subject was desirable, and at the Stockholm Conference in 1924 a provision was introduced dealing with this vexed question based almost word for word on the draft rule suggested by the Association of Average Adjusters:

> "Where temporary repairs are effected to a ship at a port of loading, call or refuge, for the common safety, or of damage caused by general average sacrifice, the cost of such repairs shall be admitted as general average; but where temporary repairs of accidental damage are effected merely to enable the adventure to be completed, the cost of such repairs shall be admitted as general average . . . only up to the saving in expense which would have been incurred and allowed in general average had such repairs not been effected there.
>
> No deductions 'new for old' shall be made from the cost of temporary repairs allowable as general average."

York-Antwerp Rules 1950

14.09 In the United Kingdom, at least, the 1924 rule attracted two schools of thought in respect of the cost of "temporary repairs of accidental damage effected merely to enable the adventure to be completed":

(1) That the cost should be a first charge on the savings to general average alone.

(2) That the cost should be apportioned over all savings. If temporary repairs were undertaken at a port of refuge with the ancillary benefit in mind of a saving, for instance, in the cost of permanent repairs, it could hardly be said that the temporary repairs were effected merely to enable the adventure to be completed, and it was only equitable to apportion the cost over all savings.

Having confirmed that foreign adjusters adopted the first view above, the Association of Average Adjusters passed a Uniformity Resolution[18] in 1928 giving effect to this view. Thereafter, a uniform interpretation of r.XIV was applied throughout the world, but it was thought wise in the 1950 Rules to remove all possible doubt on this matter by adding the words "without regard to the saving, if any, to other interests, but" in the space . . . left in the 1924 rule quoted above. In addition the part of the rule dealing with repairs to accidental damage was placed in a separate paragraph.

[18] See Appendix 3, para.70.50, below.

York-Antwerp Rules 1974

As stated above, extra wording was added to the rule in 1950 to make it clear that the cost of temporary repairs to accidental damage should be a first charge on savings to general average alone, even if, in effecting those temporary repairs, the shipowner might be actuated by some motive in addition to the mere completion of the adventure (for example a saving in the cost of permanent repairs). However, the draftsmen of the 1950 rule had left the word "merely" in the phrase: "Where temporary repairs of accidental damage are effected merely to enable the adventure to be completed . . .". There is little doubt that the word "merely" was intended solely to contrast the provisions of the second paragraph with the first limb of the first paragraph (where the repairs must be necessary for the common safety), but the word may have created some difficulty in construction. **14.10**

For the sake of clarity in general application, in 1974 the words "in order" were substituted for the word "merely". Even if this substitution did not overcome every problem, there was no doubt in practice that, if one of the reasons for effecting temporary repairs was to enable the adventure to be completed, the second paragraph would apply. The repairs must, of course, have been necessary for this purpose, and no more than was necessary to complete the voyage.

York-Antwerp Rules 1994

No change, but the second paragraph of the rule, dealing with the allowance in general average of the cost of temporary repairs to accidental damage, probably excited more attention and criticism in the years leading up to 1994 than any other section of the York-Antwerp Rules. This attention was no doubt fuelled by the passage through the British courts of the celebrated case of *The Bijela*.[19] **14.11**

Suggestions for reform in 1994 included:

(1) the deletion of this second paragraph altogether (coupled with the proposal for r.X(a) that temporary repairs should not be charged direct to general average, but follow the treatment of the permanent repairs);
(2) that in no circumstances should the cost of temporary repairs be admitted as general average except where such repairs involved an extraordinary sacrifice of any of the property engaged in the common maritime adventure;
(3) that temporary repairs of accidental damage should be allowable in general average only if permanent repairs would have been practicable at the port at which the temporary repairs were effected.

None of these suggestions was accepted and r.XIV thus remained precisely as before, but in its practical application it is subject to two potential changes.

[19] *Marida Ltd v Oswal Steel (The Bijela)* [1992] 1 Lloyd's Rep. 636; [1993] 1 Lloyd's Rep. 411; [1994] 2 Lloyd's Rep. 1.

(a) the view previously and widely held that temporary repairs to accidental damage could be charged to general average only when facilities for permanent repairs existed at the same port of refuge, was disapproved in *The Bijela*[20];

(b) Rule XIV is now subject to the new Rule Paramount[21] and the requirement of reasonableness imposed thereby.

These two potential changes will be discussed below in paras 14.34 and 14.31 respectively.

York-Antwerp Rules 2004

14.12 In the period before the Vancouver Conference, criticism of r.XIV became focused on two matters:

(1) The rule contained no definition of temporary repairs, which enabled allowances to be made in respect of repairs which enhanced the value of the vessel, by enabling her to trade without the necessity of effecting permanent repairs, for long after the termination of the voyage.

(2) The net cost to the shipowner and his hull insurers of deferring permanent repairs and effecting temporary repairs was frequently far less than the amount actually expended on the temporary repairs, since it enabled the permanent repairs to be effected more cheaply than if they had been effected at the port of refuge.

Both of these criticisms were addressed, the first obliquely and the second directly, by adding a proviso, considered in detail below, to the second paragraph of the rule the purpose of which is to limit the amount allowable under that paragraph to the net overall cost to the shipowner of effecting temporary repairs and deferring (or dispensing altogether with) permanent repairs. As pointed out at a late stage in the debate at Vancouver, the same proviso should logically apply to all repairs of accidental damage, whether effected for the common safety, or to enable the adventure to be completed, but under the wording adopted it does not apply to repairs of accidental damage effected for the common safety.

In addition:

(1) for ease of reference, the three paragraphs of the rule were designated by the letters (a), (b) and (c);

(2) "allowed" was substituted for "admitted" as part of the process of standardising the drafting of the Rules.

[20] *Marida* [1992] 1 Lloyd's Rep. 636; [1993] 1 Lloyd's Rep. 411, [1994] 2 Lloyd's Rep. 1.

[21] See para.PRE.23 above.

RULE XIV 14.13

TEMPORARY REPAIRS

(*a*) Where temporary repairs are effected to a ship at a port of loading, call or refuge, for the common safety, or of damage caused by general average sacrifice, the cost of such repairs shall be admitted/allowed as general average.

(*b*) Where temporary repairs of accidental damage are effected in order to enable the adventure to be completed, the cost of such repairs shall be admitted/ allowed as general average without regard to the saving, if any, to other interests, but only up to the saving in expense which would have been incurred and allowed in general average if such repairs had not been effected there. Provided that, for the purposes of this paragraph only, the cost of the temporary repairs falling for consideration shall be limited to the extent that the cost of temporary repairs effected at the port of loading, call or refuge, together with either the cost of permanent repairs eventually effected or, if unrepaired at the time of the adjustment, the reasonable depreciation in the value of the vessel at the completion at the voyage, exceeds the cost of permanent repairs had they been effected at the port of loading, call or refuge.

(*c*) No deductions "new for old" shall be made from the cost of temporary repairs allowable as general average.

Construction

General Observations

The first two paragraphs of the rule provide for the allowance in general average of the cost of temporary repairs carried out in a port of loading, call or refuge, and falling within two main categories: 14.14

First paragraph—Temporary repairs:

(a) for the common safety (for example the plugging of a hole in the ship's shell plating to prevent her sinking within the port);

(b) to damage caused by a general average sacrifice (for example by a voluntary stranding,[22] or efforts to refloat.[23] etc.).

The cost of such temporary repairs is charged direct to general average and this will be in accordance with the law and practice of probably all countries.

Second paragraph—This deals with the cost of temporary repairs to accidental damage which are not necessary for the common safety within the port (as in First paragraph above), but are necessary in order to enable the continuing voyage to be prosecuted and completed[24] in safety. The intention of the rule seems clear: that 14.15

[22] See r.V.

[23] See r.VII.

[24] The provisions of the second paragraph of the rule apply only to those cases where the temporary

the cost of such temporary repairs to accidental damage should be treated as general average on a substituted expense basis. Thus, if, instead of temporary repairs, permanent repairs had been carried out in the port and these would have taken longer to effect than temporary, and/or would involve the discharge of cargo, the cost of the temporary repairs should be compared with the alternative cost of the daily port charges and crew wages, etc. which would have been incurred during the extra detention for permanent repairs, and/or the cost of discharging, storing and reloading the cargo necessary for permanent repairs. Such alternative expenses might generally be expected to be charged to general average under rr.X and XI and, up to these general average expenses avoided, the cost of the temporary repairs to accidental damage should be charged to general average.

First Paragraph—Paragraph (a) in the York-Antwerp Rules 2004

14.16 **"temporary repairs"**: The finer points of construction on the term "temporary repairs" are associated with the second paragraph of this rule and are discussed in that context.

"port of loading, call or refuge": The first paragraph of this rule deals only with temporary repairs effected at a port of loading, call or refuge for the common safety, or of damage caused by general average sacrifice. Temporary repairs, of course, are frequently carried out at sea, and the cost may similarly be allowed as general average under the lettered rules. When temporary repairs to damage caused by general average sacrifice are carried out at destination the cost may also be allowed as general average, but the adjuster will then need to satisfy himself that it was reasonable to carry out only temporary repairs. If facilities for permanent repairs do not exist at the port of destination, or if permanent repairs can be effected more cheaply at some other port, it would clearly be reasonable to allow the cost, but it might be otherwise if such repairs are done solely for the convenience of the shipowner. The meaning of the phrase is considered further in the context of the second paragraph of the rule.[25]

14.17 **"for the common safety"**: See the general commentary on r.A[26] but, for greater relevance to situations where the vessel is already within the comparative safety of a port of refuge, see the commentary in para.10.47, above. For temporary repairs to be necessary for the common safety when the vessel is in port, they must have been required to combat some truly dire emergency such as a danger of sinking at the berth.

"damage caused by general average sacrifice": If damage is caused to the ship by a general average act or sacrifice, for example in extinguishing a fire on

repairs enable the vessel to proceed direct to her destination. When a ship is at any port or place of refuge at which permanent repairs cannot be carried out, and she is necessarily removed to another port or place of refuge, the cost of any temporary repairs necessary for that removal can be allowed direct to general average under the terms of the second paragraph of r.X(a) and without regard to savings.

[25] See para.14.26, below.

[26] See paras A.20, et seq., above.

board,[27] by a voluntary stranding,[28] or in efforts to refloat,[29] etc. the cost of any necessary temporary repairs to such damage at a port of refuge is charged direct to general average without conditions such as are expressed in the second paragraph of the rule for repairs to accidental damage.

Second Paragraph–Paragraph (b) in the York-Antwerp Rules 2004

"temporary repairs" **14.18**

How long is " temporary"?

One of the original theories behind the allowance in general average of the cost of temporary repairs was that they were of no lasting benefit[30]; they were undertaken merely to enable the vessel to proceed on her voyage; at the end they would be taken out and the damage fully and permanently repaired. Today, however, those temporary repairs, even though no stronger than necessary to complete the immediate voyage, may enable the vessel to continue trading for a prolonged period, say until her next annual or special survey. In the discussions preceding the York-Antwerp Rules 1950 the French delegation proposed that if permanent repairs were not effected within six months of the completion of the adventure, only 50 per cent of the cost of temporary repairs should be made good in general average. This proposal did not find favour with the other delegates, it being argued that the period was too short and that it was sometimes not possible to obtain a licence to do permanent repairs or, alternatively, to find a suitable shipyard willing to undertake the work. And if the suggested period of six months were extended, say, to two or three years, general average adjustments would be held up.

In similar discussions preceding the 1994 Rules, an Italian proposal that no allowance in general average should be made unless permanent repairs were carried out within a "reasonable time" was indorsed by the United States Maritime Law Association, but with a specific limit of six months[31] after the completion of the voyage. These proposals were rejected.

[27] See r.III.

[28] See r.V.

[29] See r.VIII.

[30] *Plummer v Wildman* (1815) 3 M. & S. 486. Among the early proposals for the new 1994 York-Antwerp Rules was a set of definitions by AIDE, one of which stated that: ". . . the expression 'temporary repairs' shall mean such repairs as confer no lasting material benefit to the ship." It was not proceeded with.

[31] It may be of interest to record that this period of six months' use for temporary repairs was considered to be "of some benefit to the ship" in the early American case of *Brooks v Oriental Insurance Co* 7 Pick 259 (1828), when Putnam J. endeavoured to follow what he thought to be English law as declared in *Plummer v Wildman* (1815) 3 M. & S. 486. In his case a schooner sustained damages on two occasions about six months apart which were temporarily repaired at the time and permanent repairs to both effected on the vessel's return home to Salem immediately following the second temporary repairs. The cost of the second temporary repairs was allowed as general average, but not of those for the earlier accident, which "were of some benefit to the ship".

14.19 Provided that sufficient general average expenses are saved by not effecting permanent repairs at the port of refuge, the whole cost of the temporary repairs will be allowed as general average, subject to any limit imposed by the new provisions of the 2004 rule, where it applies, irrespective of whether the vessel continues trading after the voyage with the temporary repairs in place. However, certain important considerations must be borne in mind:

(1) The temporary repairs which can be considered for an allowance in general average are only those which are necessary to complete the current cargo voyage. If the temporary repairs are designedly stronger, and with the object of enabling the vessel to continue trading beyond the termination of the current voyage, clearly the shipowner must bear the cost of the extra stiffeners or strengthening.

(2) The original theory of "no lasting benefit" cannot be totally ignored, with its implication that the temporary repairs will be removed and full permanent repairs undertaken on some future occasion. Thus, if temporary repairs are carried out in the expectation that full permanent repairs are unlikely ever to be effected, the "temporary" repairs must themselves be considered as permanent. If in the particular economic climate prevailing at the time of the accident the shipowner would not give consideration to permanent repairs because temporary repairs would suffice for the expected life of the ship, there is no real "substitution" of expense.

An extreme example of this situation occurs where a vessel is proceeding on her last voyage to the breakers' yard and sustains accidental damage which obliges her to put into a port of refuge for repairs. The repairs undertaken will obviously be limited to the very minimum necessary for the vessel to arrive at the breakers' yard and should all be considered as permanent.

(3) Where permanent repairs have not been effected by the date of the adjustment, the provisions of the 2004 Rules, where they apply, are likely in practice to reduce the amount allowable in respect of the temporary repairs: see para.14.38 below.

14.20 Occasional difficulties may arise in practice in deciding whether certain repairs undertaken on grounds of simple economy but of uncertain durability should be treated as temporary or permanent. For instance, a fractured bedplate may be repaired by the Metalock process, or new tips may be brazed into the damaged blades of a bronze alloy propeller. A new bedplate or propeller might be the ideal permanent repair, but possibly an unnecessarily expensive one. It is usually considered that if these alternative repairs survive for six months or so, it is probable that they will last as long as the original bedplate or propeller–the position can often be ascertained from the recommendations or conditions imposed by the vessel's Classification Society. It is submitted, therefore, that such repairs should be considered as permanent unless they fail in service.

Fitting of spare propellers

In a report by the Advisory Committee of the Association of Average Adjusters dated December 13, 1937, the Committee expressed their view that: **14.21**

> "Where a vessel has lost her propeller, the cost of replacing this at a port of refuge with a spare propeller is, in the absence of exceptional circumstances, a temporary repair within the meaning of Rule XIV."

It may be remarked that the Committee were considering a case where the working manganese propeller had been replaced with a spare cast-iron propeller; for technical reasons, cast iron propellers are not encountered in modern times.

Temporary repairs are a general average expense and not a sacrifice

In another report of the same Committee dated February 10, 1942, the view was expressed that temporary repairs of accidental damage allowed as general average under r.XIV should be regarded as a general average expense, and not a sacrifice. Hence the cost should not be treated as an amount made good to be included in the value of the ship for contribution. **14.22**

Removal of temporary repairs

If the cost of effecting temporary repairs is allowable in general average under any of the provisions of r.XIV, it follows that the cost of removing those same repairs (if any) falls to be dealt with under the same provision. **14.23**

Abortive temporary repairs

A number of cases have been encountered in practice where temporary repairs to accidental damage have been attempted at a port of refuge in order to save general average detention, but have failed, necessitating the effecting of permanent repairs. On the theory that the cost of temporary repairs should be chargeable to general average because they are of no value to the ship, it might be equitable to allow the cost in general average in such cases. However, the rule is quite explicit on this point, and as, in fact, the temporary repairs effected no savings to general average, their cost cannot be allowed. **14.24**

"accidental damage": In this second paragraph of r.XIV, the temporary repairs under consideration are those to accidental damage, necessary in order to enable the voyage to be completed, but not for the common safety. The meaning of the term "accident" has been considered in paras 10.32 and 10.50, above, but a further example may be appropriate here. **14.25**

An elderly vessel springs a leak in her plating during heavy weather and puts into a port of refuge for temporary repairs. On a close inspection of the damage, the classification surveyor discovers that the surrounding plating is thoroughly wasted and insists on far more extensive repairs than are strictly necessary to restore the vessel to her pre-accident condition. The split plating itself would probably be regarded as accidental damage (even though resulting from general debility) and the temporary repairs thereto considered for an allowance in general average. The additional repairs required by the surveyor, however, would be in respect of pure wear and tear and would not be considered for any allowance. Nor would the crew wages, etc. during any extra detention for such wear and tear repairs, or the cost of discharging, etc. any additional cargo to gain access for the wear and tear repairs.

14.26 **"port of loading, call or refuge"**: These words appear in the first paragraph of r.XIV, but not in the second paragraph of the 1994 rule. It is suggested that this omission was unintended and that the wording of the second paragraph should apply only to temporary repairs of accidental damage carried out at a port of loading, call or refugee.[32] In the 2004 rule, in which a proviso has been added which places a further limit on the allowable cost of temporary repairs claimed under the second paragraph, the words do appear in the proviso, thereby reinforcing the conclusion that they apply to the provisions of the second paragraph as a whole.

It appears, however, that the words "loading call or refuge", which are the same as those used in r.X(b), will be given a wide meaning. Thus in *The Bijela*,[33] the facts of which are summarised at para.14.31 below, the view was expressed by the Court of Appeal that a port did not lose its character as a port of loading when the vessel had completed loading and sailed from it, and that any port at which the vessel might legitimately call in the course of her voyage, whether scheduled or in order to deal with an emergency, was a port of call.[34] In the House of Lords the argument that the relevant port, Providence, was not a port of loading, call or refuge was abandoned.

Temporary repairs in a roadstead, etc.

14.27 Nevertheless, the phrase clearly requires that the repairs be carried out at a port, rather than at sea, although the effecting of temporary repairs at sea is an increasingly common occurrence with the mammoth vessels in service today. For example, a very large bulk carrier may load a precisely calculated maximum quantity of cargo which enables her to leave the loading port only when the tide is at peak height, and then with just a few inches of water beneath her bottom.

If any miscalculation is made in navigation or timing, the vessel may strand and rupture her bottom and the pumps be unable to cope with the inflow of water. With her increased draft, there will be no possibility of returning to the loading port, and temporary repairs necessary before the vessel can proceed elsewhere

[32] In *Marida Ltd v Oswal Steel (The Bijela)* [1993] 1 Lloyd's Rep. 411 at 416 Neill L.J. accepted that: "the temporary repairs covered by the second paragraph are those effected at a port of loading, call or refuge".

[33] *Marida Ltd v Oswal Steel (The Bijela)* [1992] 1 Lloyd's Rep. 636; [1993] 1 Lloyd's Rep. 411, [1994] 2 Lloyd's Rep. 1.

[34] See [1993] 1 Lloyd's Rep. 411 per Neil L.J. at 417, Mann L.J. at 419 and Hoffman L.J. at 424.

may need to be carried out at an anchorage, open roadstead, or in some nearby bay.

Carried out within the shelter and safety of a port, those same repairs might be considered as being only "necessary for the safe prosecution of the voyage"[35] (or "to enable the adventure to be completed"). However, and depending on the precise location and its exposure to wind, tides, and passing ships, those repairs may now be necessary for the "common safety",[36] and, if capable of being considered as an "extraordinary sacrifice or expenditure" within the meaning of r.A.[37] be treated as general average.

Temporary repairs at destination

On occasion, it may be necessary to carry out temporary repairs at destination to accidental damage before it is possible to discharge the cargo, and whether this cost can be charged to general average raises a problem, often of considerable monetary interest. It most frequently arises with tankers carrying cargoes of crude oil, which can only be discharged at a temperature of at least 135F. Steam for heating and discharging the cargo is often provided by auxiliary boilers, and if they suffer damage it is generally impossible to discharge the cargo by any means other than repairing one or more of the boilers. Circumstances may differ and there is as yet no authoritative answer to this problem; but in no case yet encountered in practice has any allowance in general average been justified. **14.28**

"in order to enable the adventure to be completed": See the commentary in para.14.10, above. The repairs need not be necessary for the common safety; it suffices if they are necessary in order to enable the vessel to reach the port of destination and discharge her cargo there. The expression may be considered as an alternative to "necessary for the safe prosecution of the voyage" appearing elsewhere in the Rules and construed in para.10.48, above.[38]

"without regard to the saving, if any, to other interests": Although construed in the order in which it appears in the rule, this particular phrase might more sensibly be reserved until after "but only up to the saving in expense . . ." dealt with in the next paragraph. **14.29**

If, instead of effecting permanent repairs at a port of refuge, temporary repairs alone are carried out, assumed savings to general average may result, while the shipowner may be able to save on the cost of permanent repairs effected at a cheaper port of repair,[39] or a shorter period off-hire for his vessel, and the cargo interests may benefit by an earlier delivery of their cargo at destination.

[35] See para.10.48, above.

[36] See paras A.20 et seq., above.

[37] See paras A.59 et seq., above.

[38] See *Trade Green Shipping v Securitas Bremer (The Trade Green)* [2000] 2 Lloyd's Rep. 45 where it was held in the context of r.XI that a distinction was to be drawn between the two expressions; the safe prosecution of the voyage was complete when the vessel arrived at her destination, although the cargo remained on board and the adventure was therefore not completed. For a discussion of the decision see the commentary on rr.X and XI.

[39] Under the 2004 Rules this saving will be taken into account in determining the allowable cost of the temporary repairs. See para.14.37, below.

If savings to general average can be shown, the cost of temporary repairs to accidental damage will be a first charge against the savings to general average alone, and not apportioned over all savings effected. (See also paras 14.09 and F.32, above.)

14.30 **"but only up to the saving in expense which would have been incurred and allowed in general average if such repairs had not been effected there"**: As stated in para.14.15, above, the intention of this section of the rule seems clear: that the cost of temporary repairs to accidental damage should not be looked upon as a simple repair charge, but be treated on a "substituted expense" basis, that is, as a substitution for those alternative and probably larger expenses which would have been charged to general average if permanent repairs had instead been effected in the port of refuge. Permanent repairs would generally have taken longer than the temporary repairs and, if the damage was to the bottom of the ship, they might also have necessitated the discharging, storing and reloading of the cargo. The port charges and crew wages, etc. during the additional detention, and the costs of any discharging, storing and reloading of cargo, are normally allowable as general average under rr.X(b), X(c) and XI(b) and, up to the amount of these additional and alternative expenses avoided by effecting only temporary repairs, the cost of the temporary repairs should in practice be charged to general average.

14.31 Whether the precise wording used in r.XIV adequately and clearly expressed this intention was queried here from the 8th edition onwards. Allowances under rr.X(b), X(c) and XI(b), for port charges, crew wages and cargo operations are all subject to the requirement that the repairs were "necessary for the safe prosecution of the voyage", and although the temporary repairs will generally fulfil this criterion, it is self-evident that if those temporary repairs were sufficient to prosecute the voyage in safety, permanent repairs could not possibly be necessary for that purpose (or were greater than was necessary for that purpose). On this basis, the additional port charges, crew wages, and cargo operations would not have justified any allowance in general average, and there could be no "saving in expense which would have been . . . allowed in general average" against which to set the cost of the temporary repairs.

This particular quandary was resolved, and the construction placed upon the wording of r.XIV by adjusters worldwide for the previous 70 years confirmed, in the case of *Marida Ltd v Oswal Steel (The Bijela)*.[40] In that case, the vessel grounded very shortly after leaving her loading port of Providence, Rhode Island, thereby sustaining considerable damage to her bottom and leakage into the double bottom tanks. She put into Jamestown as a port of refuge (a port at which permanent repairs were impossible), effected temporary repairs afloat, thereafter resuming her voyage and delivering the cargo of shredded scrap at Kandla in India and then proceeding to Singapore for permanent repairs. If she had not effected temporary repairs, she would have had to return to Providence, discharge her cargo, and then proceed to drydock at New York for permanent repairs, before returning to Providence to reload the cargo.

[40] *Marida* [1992] 1 Lloyd's Rep. 636; [1993] 1 Lloyd's Rep. 411; [1994] 2 Lloyd's Rep. 1.

Final judgment was given in the House of Lords, overruling the decisions of the courts below, and Lord Lloyd of Berwick pointed to the concluding words of the second paragraph of r.XIV and said:

> "The second paragraph of Rule XIV obliges us to suppose that the temporary repairs had not been effected at Jamestown. What then would have happened? The answer is simple. She would have gone into dry-dock in New York. Was the discharge of the cargo necessary to enable the damage to the ship to be repaired in dry-dock? The answer is clearly yes. Were those repairs necessary to enable the vessel to proceed safely to (destination), always assuming that she had not already been repaired in Jamestown? The answer, again, is clearly yes."

The rationale of this judgment presumably means that when one is obliged to ignore the course actually adopted of temporary repairs, the next most reasonable alternative course then becomes and must be deemed necessary, as required for the hypothetical allowances under rr.X(b) and XI(b) against which the cost of the temporary repairs will be set. Further, when the alternative course takes on this mantle of necessity, a fortiori it must also be assumed to be reasonable, as required by the Rule Paramount,[41] and not such as could amount to a breach of the contract of carriage.

The only limitations to this general premise might occur in those situations where the adoption of the standard alternative course of permanent repairs would not be practical at all,[42] would entitle the parties to the adventure to abandon the voyage, because it would be so costly , or the vessel was a commercial total loss, or it would take so long that the adventure would be frustrated. **14.32**

In the latter circumstances one must endeavour to answer the question posed by Lord Lloyd in his judgment, quoted above: "What then would have happened?" It must surely be accepted that the reasonable course then to adopt would be to abandon the voyage, whereupon it is to be noted that all general average allowances cease effectively on the date of that abandonment and that there would thus be no–or insufficient–allowances against which to set the cost of the temporary repairs effected. It is submitted that the shipowner, not actually having exercised his option to forward the cargo in another vessel, is not entitled to rely upon the general average allowances which might have been available if that option had been exercised.[43]

It may also be added that although a real-life abandonment of the voyage might result in the cargo interests being obliged to pay a second freight or other comparable charges to get their cargo to destination, these additional charges cannot be invoked to increase any allowance for the cost of temporary repairs, since r.XIV permits only the "saving in expenses which would have been . . . allowed in general average" to be taken into account.

It should be noted that in *The Bijela* Hoffmann L.J., who delivered a dissenting judgment in the Court of Appeal, took the view that for the purpose of determining **14.33**

[41] See para.PRE.23, above.

[42] For the views expressed by Hoffman L.J. in *The Bijela* on this situation see para.14.34, below and para.F.30, above.

[43] See r.G, para.G.41, above.

what general average expenses had been saved by the temporary repairs it was necessary to assume that the temporary repairs could not have been carried out.[44] However, the House of Lords, although agreeing with Hoffmann L.J. in the result, expressly declined to adopt this part of his reasoning. Thus immediately after the passage quoted in para.14.31, above, Lord Lloyd continued:

> "It is not necessary to assume that the vessel could not have been repaired at Jamestown in order to give effect to the two rules [rules X and XIV]. It is only necessary to assume that she was not so repaired, as r. XIV requires."

The more limited assumption made by the House of Lords will not, it is submitted, satisfy the requirements of the second paragraph of r.X(a), which extends the port of refuge allowances of r.X to a second port of refuge to which the ship is necessarily removed because repairs cannot be carried out in the first port or place.[45] It seems to follow that, in determining what expenses have been saved by the temporary repairs:

(1) expenses of the kind provided for under r.X(a) which would have been incurred in proceeding to, entering or leaving the second port or place of refuge cannot be taken into account;
(2) expenses which would have been incurred in discharging, handling, storing and re-loading cargo at the second port would be taken into account, since these are allowable, under r.X(b) and (c) at any port of loading call or refuge, and the second port, if not the port of loading (as was the case in The Bijela), would be a port of call within the meaning of that expression.[46]

In *The Bijela* the expenses falling into the second category presumably exceeded the cost of the temporary repairs, with the result that it was immaterial whether or not the expenses falling into the first category could be taken into account, although this does not emerge clearly from the report.[47]

[44] *The Bijela* [1993] 1 Lloyd's Rep. 411 at 423.
[45] One of the grounds on which Hobhouse J. rejected the claim ([1992] 1 Lloyd's Rep. 637 at 644) was that, since repairs could be carried out at Jamestown, the requirements of the second paragraph of r.X(a) were not satisfied. Hoffmann L.J. ([1993] 1 Lloyd's Rep. 411 at 424) held that they were satisfied because it was necessary to assume that the temporary repairs at Jamestown were not an available option. The House of Lords, for the reasons set out in fn.47 below, found it unnecessary to express any view on the point.
[46] See para.14.26, above.
[47] The cost of the temporary repairs was US$282,606. The r.X(b) and (c) expenses which would have been incurred in discharging, storing and re-loading the cargo at Providence plus the r.X(a) expenses which would have been incurred in proceeding to Providence and thereafter to and from New York amounted to US$ 535,000, but no breakdown of this figure between the two categories of expenses is given in the reports. Lord Lloyd appeared to regard the question as being determined by a concession on the part of the cargo owners that Providence, if the vessel had returned there and discharged her cargo before proceeding to New York, would have been a port of loading, call or refuge, concluding: "by this I understand it to be accepted that the expenditure at Providence would have been allowable in general average subject only to [the] point that repairs at New York were not 'necessary for the safe prosecution of the voyage'". But this hardly meets the problem which arises in relation to the costs of proceeding to, entering and leaving Providence and New York under the more specific terms of r.X(a).

Where permanent repairs impossible at the port of refuge

Vessels which sustain severe damage may, on occasion, be obliged for the common safety to put into ports of refuge at which facilities do not exist for the carrying out of permanent repairs (for example a drydock for repairs to the bottom). Temporary repairs may then be the only option, sometimes sufficient to enable the vessel to prosecute the whole voyage in safety, at other times adequate only to enable the vessel to reach another and better-equipped port of refuge. **14.34**

In the latter case, the cost of any temporary repairs for a necessary removal to the second port of refuge can be charged direct to general average in accordance with the second paragraph of r.X(a).[48] With regard to the case where temporary repairs to accidental damage enable the vessel to proceed to destination, it was the practice of some average adjusters prior to the decision in The Bijela[49] to consider that if the temporary repairs were effected at a port of refuge at which there were no facilities for carrying out permanent repairs, there was no alternative but to do this class of repairs and there was no substitution of expense. Accordingly, there could be no allowance in general average for the cost of the temporary repairs.[50]

This practice was followed by the adjusters first employed to adjust the case of *The Bijela*,[51] where substantial temporary repairs sufficient to enable the adventure to be safely completed were effected at a port of refuge at which permanent repairs were impossible. However, in *The Bijela* both Neill L.J. and Hoffmann L.J. in the Court of Appeal regarded this as being immaterial, and Hoffman L.J. drew attention to the fact that a British proposal to introduce a specific provision to that effect into the 1950 Rules was withdrawn after opposition from the Americans. In the House of Lords, the argument that the owners were obliged to show that permanent repairs could have been carried out at the port of refuge was not even pursued. However, Hoffman L.J. considered that, since r.XIV was based, however loosely, on the substitution principle, the second paragraph could only take effect if permanent repairs were possible somewhere—i.e. either at the port of refuge or some port which could have been substituted for it under the provisions of r.X. The requirement for there to have been a practical alternative in order for there to be a valid substitution has long been recognised by adjusters when dealing with both r.F and r.XIV. In the House of Lords, Lord Lloyd noted that the point had been conceded and that it was therefore unnecessary to consider what would have been the position if the nearest place for effecting permanent repairs had been "on the other side of the world".

It is submitted that the alternative has to be "practical" in the physical sense of technically feasible and also "reasonable" in the sense that such measures would

[48] See para.10.36, above.

[49] *Marida Ltd v Oswal Steel (The Bijela)* [1992] 1 Lloyd's Rep. 637; [1993] 1 Lloyd's Rep. 411; [1994] 2 Lloyd's Rep. 1.

[50] The practice would have originated as an inherited "carry-over" from the earliest r.X(d) on substituted expenses, which opened with the words "If a ship under average be in a port or place at which it is practicable to her . . .". See also under para.14.31 and its lengthy fn.32 in the 11th edn.

[51] See para.30.35, below.

not be disproportionate to the circumstances of the case, which removing a vessel for an inordinate distance to effect repairs might well be.

Where there is more than one alternative that could be envisaged in the circumstances of a particular case, the substituted temporary repair costs can only be compared against the alternative that would have resulted in the lowest allowable general average expenditure.

14.35 **"there"**: The second paragraph of the rule omits to state where the temporary repairs under discussion must have been effected: but it would be reasonable to assume that it must be at a port of loading, call or refuge where alternative general average expenses can be incurred, and not at sea. (The draft rule submitted by the Danish Committee for the York-Antwerp Rules 1950 made special mention of this point.)

The Proviso Added in 2004

(The commentary in paras 14.36 to 14.39 below does not apply to the 1994 Rules)

14.36 **"for the purpose of this paragraph only"**: As this phrase makes clear, the limit on the allowable cost of temporary repairs which is imposed by the proviso in the second paragraph of the rule, will not apply to the cost of temporary repairs of damage caused by sacrifice, or effected for the common safety, which are allowed under the first paragraph. However, as a matter of principle there seems to be no reason the proviso should not have been made applicable to all temporary repairs of accidental damage, whether effected for the common safety or to enable the adventure to be completed. It is only in the case of temporary repairs of damage caused by sacrifice, where the cost of permanent repairs is allowable in its own right, that the provisions of the proviso are inappropriate.

14.37 **"the cost of temporary repairs falling for consideration shall be limited"**: The effect of the proviso is to limit the amount allowable in respect of the cost of temporary repairs to the net additional cost (or in the case of unrepaired damage the net financial detriment) incurred by the shipowner resulting from his decision to carry out temporary repairs and to defer or dispense with permanent repairs. The limit operates separately from, and is additional to the limit imposed by the first sentence of this paragraph, which limits the allowance to the amount of the general average expense thereby avoided. Examples of the way in which it operates are given below.

Where the ship has been repaired by the date of the adjustment

Cost of temporary repairs at port of loading, call or refuge	£500,000
Cost of permanent repairs	£1,250,000
	£1,750,000
Cost of permanent repairs if effected at port of loading, call or refuge	£1,500,000
Cost of temporary repairs for the purpose of second paragraph of r.XIV	£1,250,000

Where the ship is unrepaired at the date of the adjustment

Cost of temporary repairs at port of loading, call or refuge	£500,000
Depreciation[52]	£1,150,000
	£1,650,000
Cost of permanent repairs if effected at port of loading, call or refuge	£1,500,000
Cost of temporary repairs for the purpose of second paragraph of r.XIV	£1,150,000

In ascertaining the "cost" of the relevant permanent and temporary repairs for purpose of applying the proviso, it is only out-of-pocket expenses that are relevant. Thus no account is taken of any benefit which the shipowner obtains by reason of the permanent repairs eventually effected being completed in a shorter time than would have been possible if they had been effected at the port of loading call or refuge is.

"the cost of temporary repairs effected at the port of loading, call or refuge": Self-evidently this refers to the cost of the temporary repairs actually effected in the course of the voyage. The meaning of "temporary repairs" and "port of loading, call or refuge" has been discussed earlier: see paras 14.18 et seq. and paras 14.16 and 14.26. 14.38

"the cost of permanent repairs eventually effected": This refers to the actual cost of the repairs effected after the termination of the adventure.

"if unrepaired at the time of the adjustment": The effect of this phrase is that the time of the adjustment may be of considerable importance, since the reasonable depreciation at the date of the adjustment may differ from the cost of permanent repairs effected later. Moreover it calls into question what is the relevant "time of the adjustment" where, as in *The Bijela*[53] more than one adjustment is prepared. A similar issue arises under r.XVIII and under the time bar provisions of the new r.XXIII, introduced in 2004. It is submitted that the time of the first adjustment should be taken as the relevant time.

"the reasonable depreciation in the value of the vessel": The purpose of r.XIV(b), in its 2004 form, is to compensate the shipowner for the net overall cost, or financial detriment, to him of carrying out temporary, as opposed to permanent, repairs at the port of loading, call or refuge. It follows that the reasonable depreciation should be arrived at by comparing the value of the vessel at the end of the voyage in her actual (i.e. temporarily repaired) state with the value which she would have had if she had been permanently repaired at the port of loading, call or refuge.

"at the completion of the voyage": Although the decision in The Trade Green[54] might suggest that the "completion of the voyage" occurs as soon as the

[52] The meaning of this expression is discussed below.

[53] See the judgment of Hobhouse J. at first instance [1992] 1 Lloyd's Rep. 636 at 638–639. See also para.30.37, below.

[54] *Trade Green Shipping v Securitas Bremer* [2000] 2 Lloyd's Rep. 45. See paras 11.28 and 14.28, above.

vessel reaches her final port of destination, the phrase is almost certainly intended to refer to the termination of the adventure, namely the completion of discharge at that port.

14.39 **"the cost of permanent repairs had they been effected at the port of loading, call or refuge"**: The repetition of the phrase "the port of loading, call or refuge" might suggest that the proviso envisages that permanent repairs must be possible at the port where the temporary repairs were carried out–precisely the conclusion which was rejected in The Bijela in relation to the first sentence of r.XIV(b). This was certainly not the intention, and to interpret the proviso in this manner would be likely to deprive it of its intended effect in precisely those cases which it was primarily intended to deal with—i.e. where the savings in the cost of permanent repairs by deferring them until after the completion of the adventure are substantial. The purpose of the phrase is no doubt to contrast the permanent repairs eventually effected–i.e. after the completion of the voyage, with the hypothetical permanent repairs which would have been effected during the voyage, and it is submitted that the phrase means no more than the port at which the permanent repairs would have been carried out had they been effected, instead of the temporary repairs, in the course of the voyage.

Since the purpose of the proviso is to identify the net overall cost to the shipowner of carrying out the temporary repairs, any costs which would have been incurred in moving the vessel to the port where the permanent repairs would have been carried out, to the extent that they would have fallen on the shipowner, should be included in the cost of repairs.

Third Paragraph–Paragraph (c) in the York-Antwerp Rules 2004

14.40 **"deductions 'new for old'"**: See r.XIII.

RULE XV

LOSS OF FREIGHT

ENGLISH LAW AND BACKGROUND

When is Loss of Freight Made Good?

Freight is one of the properties involved in the common maritime adventure. **15.01**
Thus a loss of freight at the risk of the carrier[1] falls to be made good in general average in the same circumstances as loss or damage to ship or cargo, namely when the carrier's right to receive freight is intentionally sacrificed by a general average act.

Examples of a sacrifice of freight are given in the succeeding paragraphs, but the ultimate question is always whether, as a direct result of a general average act, the carrier has been deprived of the right to receive the freight or a part of it. For this purpose it is necessary to have regard to the effect of the contract of affreightment, and some of the more important points may be summarised here.[2]

(1) If freight is not at the risk of the carrier at the time of the general average act,[3] there can be no sacrifice of freight as such, since the freight will be payable whether or not the cargo reaches the destination. The risk has passed to the cargo owner and the freight is treated as an additional element in the value of the cargo,[4] for the purposes of computing both the contributory value of the cargo (see paras 17.24 and 17.29, below) and the amount made good on a sacrifice of the cargo (see para.16.31, below).

[1] See above as to freight at the risk of the cargo owner. For the meaning of "carrier" in this context see para.15.02, below.
[2] See also para.17.53, below.
[3] See para.17.53, below, as to whether freight is at the risk of the carrier or of the cargo owner.
[4] cf. *Maldonado v British and Foreign Marine Insurance Co* 182 Fed. Rep. 744 (1910), and see para.17.51, below.

(2) Since freight is payable without deduction on damaged cargo, provided it retains its commercial identity,[5] there can be no sacrifice of freight where cargo is merely damaged as a result of a general average act.

(3) If freight is payable on a lump sum basis, or on the intake quantity, there can be no sacrifice of freight by, for example, a jettison of part of the cargo.[6]

(4) In the absence of contrary agreement, freight is payable only on delivery at the scheduled destination, and the carrier is not entitled to a proportion of the freight if he delivers the cargo short of destination.[7]

15.02 In the commentary on r.XVII will be found a description of the various types of freight contract, and a discussion of the circumstances in which freight is at the risk of the carrier.[8] It is also important to bear in mind that, in determining whether freight is at the risk of the carrier, and in computing the value of the freight, it is the immediate contract with the cargo owner alone which is relevant.[9] If freight is not at carrier's risk under that contract it neither contributes nor is it made good, regardless of whether it is at a charterer's risk or at the shipowner's risk under an antecedent contract. On the other hand, if freight is at carrier's risk under the immediate contract with the cargo owner, the carrier under an antecedent contract may be entitled to share in any amount made good, in the same way as he would have been liable to participate in making contribution upon that freight.[10] For example:

Shipowner A charters his ship to B	@ $40 per ton, at risk
B puts it on the berth	@ $48 per ton, at risk
The amount made good will be:	@ $48[11] per ton
Of which: B's share is	$8[12] per ton
Shipowner's share	$40[13] per ton
If the shipowner had chartered to B	@ $56 per ton
(so that B was making a loss of $8 per ton)	
The amount made good will still be	$48[14] per ton
Of which: B's share	nil
Shipowner's share	$48[15] per ton

[5] See para.17.53, below.

[6] See fn.17, below. See para.16.36, below, for the effect of a lump sum freight term on the amount made good for sacrifice of cargo.

[7] But see *British Shipping Laws*, Vol.III: Carver, *Carriage by Sea*, 13th edn, paras 1685–1690. The courts will sometimes imply an agreement to pay pro rata freight.

[8] See paras 17.49 et seq., below.

[9] See paras 17.49 et seq., below, for the application of the same rule to contribution in respect of freight.

[10] See para.17.94, below.

[11] See para.15.26, below.

[12] See para.15.26, below.

[13] See para.15.26, below.

[14] See para.15.26, below.

[15] See para.15.26, below.

Time-charter hire, since it accrues continuously while the ship is on hire, is never at risk in the same way as voyage freight, and is therefore not treated as a separate interest for the purpose of general average.[16]

Examples of Sacrifices of Freight

(1) By loss of or damage to cargo resulting from a general average act

If cargo is jettisoned or otherwise destroyed by a general average, such that the value of the cargo is itself made good in general average, the loss to the carrier[17] of the freight due and at risk on that cargo must similarly be made good provided that the original voyage is successfully completed. The same is the case if, as a result of a general average act the cargo is so damaged as to lose its commercial identity[18] by reason, for instance, of water used to extinguish a fire: the loss to the carrier of the freight at risk thereon is made good as general average. **15.03**

(2) By the necessity to discharge and leave behind some of the cargo at a port of refuge

(A) An outbreak of fire in the cargo of a vessel already loaded down to her marks may be extinguished at a port of refuge by the use of water. If her cargo absorbs the water and it cannot all be pumped out, an equivalent weight of cargo will require to be discharged and left behind at the port of refuge. The loss of freight thereon will be made good as general average. **15.04**

(B) A vessel loaded down to her summer loadline may put into a port of refuge and, when ready to resume her voyage, find that winter loadlines are applicable. Accordingly, she will be obliged to reduce her draft by discharging and leaving behind some of the cargo. The loss of freight thereon will not be made good as general average, arising as it does from delay.

(C) The cargo may be so damaged that it is unfit to be carried to the destination:

[16] See para.17.64, below. The situation will rarely arise in which the owner of time-charter hire will be entitled to share in the amount made good on voyage freight, since a sacrifice of cargo will normally cause no loss of hire.

[17] Freight is occasionally payable at destination on a lump sum basis, or on the "intake" quantity. Provided that a worthwhile quantity of cargo is delivered at destination, the whole freight is payable and the carrier suffers no loss by a jettison or other sacrifice. For a fuller account and example, see para.16.36, below.

[18] See *Duthie v Hilton* (1868) L.R. 4 C.P. 138, where it was held that a cargo of cement in a flooded hold had been "destroyed" or had "ceased to exist as cement"; *Asfar v Blundell* [1896] 1 Q.B. 123: *Montedison v Icroma* [1980] 1 Lloyd's Rep. 91. Damage falling short of a loss of commercial identity is insufficient to prevent the liability for freight from arising.

15.05 (a) *By accident alone.* There can be no claim in general average for the freight lost. In *Iredale & Porter v China Traders Insurance Co Ltd*[19] a vessel on voyage from Cardiff to Esquimalt was obliged to put into a port of refuge in the River Plate owing to the dangerous overheating of her cargo of coals. It was found that none of the cargo could with safety be forwarded to destination and it was accordingly sold at the port of refuge. A claim in general average by the shipowner for his loss of freight was disallowed, it being held that owing to the condition of the cargo, the freight was already lost when the vessel put into the port of refuge.

15.06 (b) *By sacrifice alone.* Sound cargo may be rendered unfit for carriage to destination by a general average sacrifice, for example the use of water to extinguish a fire in other cargo in the ship. The loss of freight to the carrier caused by such a sacrifice is made good in general average.

In *Pirie v Middle Dock Co*[20] fire broke out in a cargo of coals and this was extinguished by pouring a large quantity of water into the hold. The vessel put into a port of refuge and the whole cargo was discharged there and sold, it being found that a considerable portion of the cargo was completely charred and burnt, and the remainder so damaged by saturation with water that it was practically impossible to forward it to its destination. The shipowner thereby lost his freight, and it was held that on that portion of the cargo which was not within the immediate reach of the fire and which was too much damaged by water to be forwarded to its destination, the freight should be made good in general average.

15.07 (c) *By combination of both accident and sacrifice.* It is possible for two separate causes to operate on the same portion of cargo and for the combined effect to produce a total loss or loss of specie of that cargo whereby the carrier will lose his freight. For example, let us again take a cargo of coals, the whole of which has heated dangerously and on part of which water has been poured as a general average sacrifice.

The damage to that part of the cargo damaged by both heating and water may well be allocated 50:50 (or other proportion) to each cause, but by reason of the fact that freight is payable either in full or not at all (see para.15.02, above) the loss of freight must be attributed wholly either to the heating or to the water damage. If, but for the use of the water, the cargo could have been economically made fit for further carriage to the intended destination, the loss of freight can be allowed as general average. However, if as in the *Iredale*[21] case the coals would be sold even with only the damage by heating, no allowance for freight can be made good in general average. The water will have caused no loss of freight.

(3) By damage to the ship

15.08 (i) The ship may be so damaged that the cost of repairing her sufficiently to enable her to complete the voyage is greater than her value when repaired plus the freight at risk;[22] (ii) though worth repairing, the time required for those repairs

[19] *Iredale & Porter v China Traders Insurance Co Ltd* [1900] 2 Q.B. 515.
[20] *Pirie v Middle Dock Co* (1881) 44 L.T. 426; 4 Asp. M.C. 3788.
[21] See para.15.05, above
[22] See para.00.43, above.

necessary to enable the ship to continue the voyage may be so long that the voyage is frustrated; or (iii) in either case, the shipowner has an option either to abandon the voyage or to tranship the cargo and forward it to destination. If he elects to abandon the voyage, the question whether the loss of freight is made good depends upon whether the damage resulted from an accident or general average sacrifice. However, in the case where the ship is worth repairing but the time required for repairs would frustrate the contract, it must also be considered whether the loss is in any event excluded by r.C as a loss by reason of delay: see para.15.12 below.

(a) By accident alone. Clearly there can be no allowance in general average for any loss of freight from such a cause. **15.09**

(b) By sacrifice alone. It is difficult to visualise a situation in practice where a sacrifice does not follow some previous accident to the ship, but if such a situation did arise, the resulting loss of freight would be allowable in general average. **15.10**

(c) By combination of both accident and sacrifice. A typical example might occur where the estimated cost of repairing damage caused by stranding and by efforts to refloat would together amount to more than was worth spending on the vessel. It is suggested that the ratio of the damages one to another—whether it be 1:3 or 3:1—has no direct bearing on whether the loss of freight at risk can be allowed as general average. **15.11**

The crucial factor is whether, but for the refloating (or sacrifice) damage, the vessel would have been worth repairing, and could have been repaired without frustrating delay. If the answer is yes, the proximate cause of the loss of freight would appear to be the damage caused by sacrifice, and the freight should be made good in general average.[23]

Where the ship is so damaged as to be not worth repairing, the loss of freight is on no view attributable to delay, but to the effective loss of the ship, and it is unnecessary to enquire how long the repairs would have taken if the vessel had been repaired. However, where the ship is worth repairing but voyage is abandoned because the length of time required would frustrate the adventure, it may be a difficult question whether the consequent loss of freight is incurred by reason of delay. The decisions under freight policies on the effect of the exclusion of claims "consequent on loss of time"[24] may suggest that the claim for loss of freight would be excluded by r.C. However, those decisions turned ultimately on the construction of the particular exceptions clause, and the reasoning is not necessarily applicable to r.C.[25] Moreover it has been questioned whether the same clause would invariably exclude claims for loss of voyage freight resulting from delay while **15.12**

[23] Compare paras 18.02 et seq., below, on the question whether the damage to the ship is made good in similar circumstances.

[24] *Bensaude v Thames and Mersey Marine Insurance Co* [1987] A.C. 609; *Naviera de Canarias SA. v Nacional Hispanica Aseguadora* [1978] A.C. 853.

[25] See in particular per Lord Diplock in *Naviera de Canarias* at [1978] A.C. 881 to 882.

repairs were carried out.[26] In the case where the ship is so damaged by a general average sacrifice that she cannot be repaired in time to enable the adventure to be completed there would appear to be strong argument to the effect that the effective cause of the loss of freight is the damage to the ship rather than delay.

Amount to Be Made Good for Freight Lost

Normal voyage expenses saved to be credited

15.13 Where the carrier sustains a loss of freight as the result of a general average sacrifice, the amount to be made good is the gross freight lost, less those expenses which the carrier would have incurred to earn such freight, but which in consequence of the sacrifice, he escapes.[27]

In the case of the whole voyage being abandoned short of destination, those expenses will include the wages and maintenance of the crew and the bunkers that would have been consumed in prosecuting the remainder of the voyage until final completion of discharge of cargo, plus the port charges and discharging expenses, etc. to be incurred at the port(s) of destination, and canal dues en route, if any. Where only part of the freight is lost (for example by jettison) and the vessel herself continues to destination, the only expenses likely to be saved are the cost of discharging the (jettisoned) cargo, as it is seldom that other voyage expenses will in any way be reduced by reason of the sacrifice.

Freight on cargo taken to fill up

15.14 If, after a jettison, the ship puts into a port of refuge, and there takes in fresh cargo in the space left vacant through the jettison, editions of this work prior to the tenth have stated that the new freight thus earned must go in diminution of the shipowner's claim for loss of freight unless that new cargo might equally have been received on board even if there had been no jettison.[28]

It would probably be more correct to state that the new freight thus earned (less the extra expenses incurred to earn it) should go in diminution of the total general average, and that regardless of whether the shipowner's original freight was at risk or not.

15.15 In the US case of *The Rosamond*,[29] a deck cargo of timber was jettisoned for the common safety and the vessel put into a port of refuge for repairs. Thereafter, she secured a new deck cargo and an additional freight. The freight on the original deck cargo had been prepaid absolutely, and the shipowner could have been in the happy position of earning two freights on the same voyage. Further, the value of

[26] See per Lord Diplock in *Naviera de Canarias* [1978] A.C. at 883; *Robertson v Petros M. Nomikos* [1939] A.C. 371 per Lord Atkin at 377.

[27] See also Rule of Practice, No.F20, para.70.47, below. See also *Nathl Hooper* (1839) 3 Sumner 543; *Mutual Insurance Co v Cargo Brig George* (1845) Olcott 89. Rule of Practice, No.14, of the Average Adjusters Association of the US provides for deduction of the expenses saved through not earning the freight.

[28] Baily, *General Average*, p.134.

[29] *The Rosamond* (1940) A.M.C. 195.

the original deck cargo jettisoned did not fall to be made good in general average.[30] The Circuit Court of Appeals held, in effect, that the new freight, less the additional expense incurred in earning it, should be credited to the general average, as follows:

> "We think fairness requires a holding in such a case at this with its peculiar facts that: If the net new freight exceeds the general average expense, then there has in fact been no loss and no contribution is due from anyone; if the general average expense exceeds the amount of the net new freight, then only the amount of the excess should be apportioned among the contributing interests. We arrive at this result because the event causing the loss also enabled the ship to carry new cargo. Were it not for the event, such new cargo would not have been obtained. It is only right, we think, that the ship's profit be restricted to the amount of the excess of the net new freight over the general average expense."

Historical Development and Practice of Rule XV

York Rules 1864

A jettison or similar sacrifice of cargo carries with it the loss to the carrier of any freight payable at destination on the cargo sacrificed. This simple truth was given formal expression in r.XI at the International Conference at York in 1864 and passed unanimously: **15.16**

> "In every case in which a sacrifice of cargo is made good as general average, the loss of freight, if any, which is caused by such loss of cargo, shall likewise be so made good."

York-Antwerp Rules 1877

No change. **15.17**

York-Antwerp Rules 1890

A possible lacuna in the 1864 rule was revealed in 1881 by the decision in *Pirie v Middle Dock Co.*[31] A cargo of coals was necessarily sold at a port of refuge in consequence of damage by water used to extinguish a fire; the shipowner thereby lost the freight that would have been payable on delivery at destination and it was held that this loss should be made good in general average. As the cargo owner received his coals freight-free and suffered no loss as the result of the general average act (in fact he made an unexpected profit) nothing was made good in general average for the damage to the cargo. **15.18**

[30] The bill of lading incorporated the York-Antwerp Rules 1890 r.1 of which stated: "No jettison of deck cargo shall be made good as general average."

[31] *Pirie v Middle Dock Co* (1881) 44 L.T. 426.

Under the existing York-Antwerp Rule it might have been possible to argue that an allowance in general average for loss of freight was conditional upon an allowance being made for the cargo itself, and to avoid this situation, the rule was amended as follows and unanimously agreed at the International Conference at Liverpool in 1890:

> "Loss of freight arising from damage to or loss of cargo shall be made good as general average, either when caused by a general average act, or when the damage to or loss of cargo is so made good."

York-Antwerp Rules 1924

15.19 On this occasion the existing 1890 rule was retained unchanged but at the suggestion of the Association of Average Adjusters, a second paragraph was added[32] of identical effect to one of their own Rules of Practice[33] passed in 1894.

York-Antwerp Rules 1950 and 1974

15.20 No change.

York-Antwerp Rules 1994

15.21 No change.

York-Antwerp Rules 2004

15.22 No change, other than the substitution of "allowed" for "made good", as part of the process of standardising the drafting of the rules.

15.23

RULE XV

LOSS OF FREIGHT

Loss of freight arising from damage to or loss of cargo shall be made good/allowed as general average, either when caused by a general average act, or when the damage to or loss of cargo is so made good/allowed.

Deduction shall be made from the amount of gross freight lost, of the charges which the owner thereof would have incurred to earn such freight, but has, in consequence of the sacrifice, not incurred.

[32] It may also be remarked that a third paragraph relating to new freight earned on goods carried in lieu of goods sacrificed was suggested, but not approved. This subject is dealt with paras 15.14–15.15, above.

[33] No.F20. See para.70.47, below.

Construction

The provisions of r.XV follow and are in total accord with English law and practice, and reference to paras 15.01–15.15, above, is requested for a more detailed analysis and examples. **15.24**

"freight": See para.15.01, above, and paras 17.49 et seq., below, for the meaning of freight in this context. **15.25**

"arising from damage to or loss of cargo": Rule XV deals only with loss of freight arising from damage to or loss of cargo. Loss of freight arising out of damage to or loss of the ship is not made good under this rule, although it may be made good under the lettered rules.

"Deduction shall be made . . . not incurred": It is manifestly right that the allowance in general average to the owner of freight sacrificed should be limited to the actual loss he has sustained and this can only be arrived at by allowing him the net freight, after deduction of the charges he would have had to pay to earn it. Such charges are limited, of course, to those which have been avoided in consequence of the sacrifice, for example the estimated cost of discharging at destination. They do not extend to the wages and maintenance of the crew or port charges paid during the remainder of the voyage, unless these charges have been saved in whole or in part by reason of the sacrifice (see also para.15.13, above). **15.26**

Where freight is not at risk to the carrier, similar savings in the costs that would have been incurred to discharge the cargo jettisoned may be made by him, but in practice these savings are ignored. General average aims to provide a partial indemnity against losses, not to enforce the sharing of profits; and a general average adjustment must not place a person in a worse position than he would have been in if the adventure, instead of being saved, had been totally lost at the time of the general average act.

As to the deduction of freight or hire payable by the carrier under an antecedent charter, see para.15.02, above.

RULE XVI

AMOUNT TO BE ALLOWED FOR CARGO LOST OR DAMAGED BY SACRIFICE

ENGLISH LAW AND PRACTICE

The basic principle which regulates the amount to be made good for loss of or damage to cargo caused by a general average sacrifice is that the owner of the goods is to be so compensated that: **16.01**

(1) he shall be in the same position as if, not his goods, but those of some other person had been thus sacrificed, or (what amounts to the same thing);
(2) it will be financially immaterial to him whether his cargo was sacrificed or delivered in similar condition to the cargo of the other interested parties.

To give full effect to this principle, interest ought to be allowed to the owner of cargo sacrificed from the time of the termination of the adventure until he actually receives the amount made good to him. Otherwise he is not put on an equality with those other owners of cargo who receive their cargo when the vessel arrives. In practice, however, such interest is never allowed in this country.[1]

Amounts Allowable when Voyage Completed

In case of total loss of part cargo

Whenever there has been a general average sacrifice of cargo and the ship reaches her intended port of destination with at least part of her cargo, the amount of the loss to be made good in general average for a total loss of part of the cargo **16.02**

[1] See Rule of Practice No.A2, para.70.02, below; cf. r.XXI, York-Antwerp Rules. In the US such interest is allowed: The Brig Mary 1 Sprague 17 (1842). See also paras 21.01–21.05, below.

is always[2] based upon the net market value of the goods; that is to say, the sum which the goods would have been worth, or would have fetched if, immediately upon delivery[3] to the consignee, he had sold them in the market, deducting therefrom all those expenses which he would have incurred subsequent to the general average act to realise that sum, and which he escapes if the goods are totally lost. Hence, the freight must be deducted if it is payable only on right delivery at destination; so must the expenses of landing the cargo and, in appropriate circumstances, any duty or sale charges. Expenses incurred before the general average act (such as the cost of marine insurance), or payable whether or not the ship and/or cargo arrive at destination, are not deducted.

In the case of non-delivery, either of a number of packages or of a whole consignment, the amount to be allowed as general average is the net market value of the cargo short-delivered, calculated as above. In the case of goods arriving at destination in a totally worthless condition, the amount to be allowed is also the net market value, calculated as above, plus the charges—if any—incurred by the consignee in dumping the cargo.

Net market value

16.03 The net market value at the last day of discharge is in all cases the basis of compensation. The expression "net market value" assumes that there is a market at the destination for the particular goods sacrificed. This will usually be the case with basic commodities for which there is a wide need and demand, but in the case of goods or manufactured products imported for a particular need, there may be no general market. It is then generally found appropriate to adopt both for the purpose of compensation and for contribution the invoice price with an addition of say 10 per cent to represent the net market value.

Basic commodities (for example grain) are often bought and sold many times during the course of a voyage at varying prices which reflect the general market value on the particular date of sale, and the fact that the particular receiver of the goods at destination may have paid a higher or lower price than the eventual

[2] It is, however, said, that if jewels or other valuables are described in the bill of lading as articles of inferior value, they are to be contributed for as of such inferior value. See *Benecke*, p.294; Arnould, 2nd edn, p.947; *British Shipping Laws*, Vol.10; *Arnould's Law of Marine Insurance*, 16th edn, para.979: Code de Com, Art.418; cf. *Lebeau v Gen Steam Nav Co* (1872) L.R. 8 C.P. 88. So also, according to the Laws of Wisby and some of the older writers, if valuables are packed in a box without any intimation to the master of their value, they shall be contributed for only upon the value of the box, or of the goods the master might reasonably suppose it to contain. See Arnould, above. Phillips, however, considers that if the omission to give notice of the contents of the box was not due to the fault or negligence of the shipper, the contribution should be for their value: *Phillips*, para.1372. See also r.XIX of the York-Antwerp Rules.

[3] In practice, the last day of discharge is the date customarily adopted. In the case of certain commodities (such as wool) which are only sold at stated intervals, the practice is to adopt the values as determined at the next following sale.

market value on the last day of discharge is disregarded; it is the latter which is made the basis of both compensation and contribution.[4]

Until 1974, the above remarks would have been equally applicable to a claim under the York-Antwerp Rules. However since 1974 the Rules have provided that the value of the goods shall be ascertained from the commercial invoice rendered to the receiver.

When goods delivered damaged

Where cargo is delivered at destination in damaged condition, the amount to be allowed as general average is as follows: **16.04**

(1) When the cargo is sold, the general practice among adjusters (according to the 8th and 9th editions of this work) was to allow the difference between the sound market value of the goods on the date of their sale and the amount they actually realised. Prima facie, this was an exception to the general rule that the relevant date for comparison purposes is the last day of discharge, and it is submitted that (particularly having regard to the change in practice brought about by the York-Antwerp Rules 1950[5]) modern practice would be to allow the difference between the sound market value of the goods on the last day of discharge and the amount they actually realise.

(2) When the cargo is accepted by the consignee in its damaged condition:

(a) if it requires repair or reconditioning, the amount to be allowed is the actual cost of repair or reconditioning, plus, if the cargo is even then in less than sound condition, a further sum to represent the depreciation in value;

(b) it frequently occurs that a surveyor acting on behalf of the general average interests, or on behalf of cargo underwriters, will agree with the consignees a measure of depreciation to represent the damage. If that depreciation is expressed as a flat sum per package, or on the whole consignment, that sum is the amount to be allowed as general average. If, however, the agreed depreciation is expressed as a percentage (and this is usually the case), the amount to be allowed as general average is the sum that results from the application of that percentage to–almost invariably–the gross sound market value of the goods on the last day of discharge. The reason why the percentage is applied to the gross sound market value rather than the net, is that, in agreeing on that percentage depreciation, the consignee and the surveyor will both be thinking in terms of the saleable value at destination, and this will include freight and landing charges paid at

[4] This, which had for many years been the practice amongst adjusters, was confirmed by the Court of Appeal in *Rodocanachi v Milburn* (1886) Q.B.D. 67 at 76. This was an action against the shipowner for non-delivery, but the principles laid down by Lord Esher M.R. are equally applicable to the case of general average. See per Gorell Barnes J. in *The Leitrim* [1902] P. 256 at 267.

[5] See para.16.19, below.

destination. As an example, a cargo of grain might have the following value:

Gross Sound Market Value	£20,000
Less: freight and landing charges	8,000
Net Sound Market Value	£12,000

If the surveyor agrees a depreciation of 10 per cent it is almost certain that he will have based this figure on the expectation that the grain could only be sold in its damaged condition for £18,000, that is a loss of £2,000. To allow in general average only 10 per cent of the net sound market value, that is £1,200, would not give a proper indemnity to the consignee.

Were the surveyor to agree a depreciation of, say, 80 per cent on the above consignment of grain, or were it to be sold for £4,000, the loss to the merchant in either case would be £16,000, and this is the sum which is allowable as general average, even though it exceeds the contributory value of £12,000. This particular problem will again be mentioned in para.16.33, below, when dealing with r.XVI.

Exception where goods replaced at port of loading

16.05 Where the vessel returns to her port of loading as a port of refuge, or puts into some other nearby port and sacrificed goods are replaced there, the amount allowed in practice is the actual cost of replacing them.[6]

Amounts Allowable when Voyage Terminated Short of Destination

16.06 When the voyage is terminated short of destination for both ship and cargo, either by the wreck of the ship or some other justifiable cause, the allowance in general average for cargo sacrifices must be regulated by the value of the cargo at the time and place where the voyage was abandoned, though it must be recognised that if the damaged goods either were, or would have been, forwarded to their original destination, the value at the place where the voyage was abandoned is the value at the original destination, less the cost of getting them there, and that amounts made good should be based on original destination value.

Subsequent total loss of ship and cargo

16.07 On the authority of *Chellew v Royal Commission on the Sugar Supply*,[7] when a sacrifice is followed by a total loss of ship and cargo, there is of course no allowance in general average. When a jettison is followed by a wreck with partial salvage, the sum allowable is so much as presumably would have been saved had the jettisoned goods been left on board and shared the fortunes of the remainder.

[6] *Gourlie*, p.480.
[7] *Chellew v Royal Commission on the Sugar Supply* [1922] 1 K.B. 12.

Reduction in value for actual or notional damage

If the goods jettisoned had previously been damaged, or if, though not damaged at the time, it can confidently be asserted that, had they remained on shipboard with the rest of the cargo, they must inevitably have suffered damage before reaching their destination, the amount to be made good is to be reduced to their value in the damaged state.[8] **16.08**

In carrying out this principle, it is to be borne in mind that the owner of goods jettisoned has a prima facie claim to their value in a sound state; consequently, the burden of proof rests with those who wish to admit a lower value; and the allowance should not be reduced except upon reasonably clear evidence that the damage either actually existed, or, if in the future, that it was almost inevitable. In practice when the goods were sound at the time of jettison, and when other cargo arrives partly sound and partly damaged, so that it is uncertain whether the goods jettisoned would have been damaged or not, they are treated as if sound.[9]

Reduction in amount made good to achieve equality

To give effect to the cardinal principle that the owner of cargo sacrificed shall be placed in the same position as if, not his goods, but those of some other person had been sacrificed, it is necessary in the adjustment to contrive certain reductions in the amounts effectively allowable in general average such that they should be subject to and reflect the same vicissitudes of the continuing voyage as were suffered by those goods which were saved by the general average act. Thus: **16.09**

(1) Reduction for actual or notional damage. As outlined in para.16.08, if all the cargo in the same compartment of the ship arrives at destination in a damaged condition, it is reasonable to assume that the sacrificed goods would have arrived similarly damaged and the general average allowance must be based accordingly. **16.10**

(2) Amount made good must contribute: also hypothetical salvage. Any amount made good in general average in respect of property sacrificed must be brought in as a contributing interest rateably with the property preserved, and this will again be referred to with a figured example in para.17.15, below, when dealing with r.XVII. However, this is a convenient opportunity to offer an identical and parallel example where—under English law or the York-Antwerp Rules 2004—salvage is or might be treated separately and apart from general average ("hypothetical" salvage). **16.11**

Assume that a vessel and her cargo are stranded in a position of peril and that, in order to refloat, salvage services are engaged and that cargo B with a value of

[8] e.g. *Fletcher v Alexander* (1868) L.R. 3 C.P. 375. On the same principle, if the goods jettisoned were subject to leakage or breakage, allowance ought to be made for the ordinary leakage or breakage in estimating their value: 2 Phillips, para.1366; *British Shipping Laws*, Vol.10: Arnould, *Marine Insurance*, 16th edn, para.979. No deduction should be made solely on account of the peril existing at the time of the sacrifice: *Rogers v Mechanics Insurance Co* (1842) 2 Story 173.

[9] Baily, *General Average*, p.137n.

1,000 is jettisoned. An award of salvage of 25 per cent—750 is made on the values of the properties saved, that is:

Ship on	1,000	pays	250
Cargo A on	1,000	"	250
Cargo B on	—	"	—
Cargo C on	1,000	"	250
	3,000	pays	750

To make good in general average the whole of the value of 1,000 to the owners of jettisoned cargo B would be totally inequitable and place them in a particularly favoured position, especially as they also escape any liability for salvage. Accordingly, this position is remedied in any general average adjustment prepared in accordance with English law in the following manner:

16.12

The amount to be allowed in general average in respect of the jettison of Cargo B	1,000		
would be reduced by the amount of salvage to which the other salved property was subject, i.e. 25 per cent =	250		
Amount to be allowed in general average	750		
This sum would be apportioned as follows (Cargo B also being required to contribute):			
Ship on arrived value	1,000		
Less: ppn. Salvage	250		
	750	pays	187.50
Cargo A (as for Ship)	750	"	187.50
Cargo B (on amount made good)	750	"	187.50
Cargo C (as for Ship)	750	"	187.50
	3,000	pays	750.00

The overall financial result to each of the parties to the adventure is that the shipowner and merchants A and C each have salved property worth		1,000.00
Less: ppns.salvage	250.00	
general average	187.50	
	437.50	437.50
		562.50
whereas merchant B receives the general average contributions payable by the shipowner and merchants A and C, i.e.:	187.50 × 3 =	562.50

Equality of sacrifice has thus been preserved.

(3) Second general averages. In similar fashion, if a second general average sacrifice or expenditure is made or incurred during the remaining part of the voyage, 16.13

the amount made good in respect of property sacrificed in the first general average must contribute also to the second general average. A figured example showing the general principle is given in para.17.88, below. Expenditure incurred in consequence of the sacrifice, and made good in the first general average, such as the expense of dumping sacrificed cargo, will not contribute to the second general average.

Historical Development and Practice of Rule XVI

York-Antwerp Rules 1877

The only new rule introduced at the Antwerp Conference in 1877 was the relatively simple and straightforward statement that: **16.14**

> "The value to be allowed for goods sacrificed shall be that value which the owner would have received if such goods had not been sacrificed."

As such, it was accepted unanimously.

York-Antwerp Rules 1890

Having regard to the provisions of the then current rule on contributory values,[10] it appears reasonably clear that allowances under the 1877 rule for cargo sacrifices were intended to be based on market values at the termination of the adventure. However, the wording of the rule was not altogether certain on this point and was capable of being construed to give the owner of sacrificed cargo the price for which he had sold it under a forward contract. For greater precision on this matter, and to ensure that any allowance was based on market values, the wording was altered in 1890 as follows: **16.15**

> "The amount to be made good as general average for damage or loss of goods sacrificed shall be the loss which the owner of the goods has sustained thereby, based on the market values at the date of the arrival of the vessel or at the termination of the adventure."

York-Antwerp Rules 1924

In the 1924 revision the words "where this ends at a place other than the original destination" were added at the suggestion of the Association of Average Adjusters, the intention being to indicate that a premature termination of the adventure was referred to. A more important amendment consisted of the addition of a second paragraph which read: **16.16**

[10] See para.17.03, below.

"Where goods so damaged are sold after arrival, the loss to be made good in general average shall be calculated by applying to the sound value on the date of arrival of the vessel the percentage of loss resulting from a comparison of the proceeds with the sound value on date of sale."

Prior to the 1924 amendment of the rule there were three main methods of ascertaining the allowance to be made in general average in respect of the goods sold, although it cannot be said that any of these were, or could be, consistently applied, as so much depended on the particular circumstances of the case.

16.17 Provided that there was no change in the market value of the goods between the last day of discharge[11] and the date on which they were sold, it was immaterial which of the three methods was employed—they would all give an identical result for the amount to be allowed in general average. However, when a change in market values did take place, wide differences in the amounts to be made good in general average could arise, as demonstrated below[12]:

	On a *rising* market	On a *falling* market
Sound value on last day of discharge	100	100
Sound value on date of sale	120	80
Proceeds realised	90	60
Method 1		
Sound value on last day of discharge	100	100
Less: Proceeds realised	90	60
Less: Allow as general average	10	40
Method 2		
Sound value on date of sale	120	80
Less: Proceeds realised	90	60
Less: Allow as general average	30	20
Method 3		
Sound value on date of sale	120	80
Less: Proceeds realised	90	60
	30	20
	= 25%	25%
Less: Allow 25 per cent of sound value on last day of discharge	25	25

[11] Although the rule specified the "date of arrival of the vessel" the practice was to adopt the sound value on last day of discharge in preference to that on date of arrival of the vessel, this being justified on the grounds that, even if the goods had arrived sound, some time would have been occupied in discharging the goods and preparing them for sale and that therefore the values on the last date of discharge had a greater relevance in assessing the loss. A similar practice existed with regard to the first paragraph of the rule.

[12] For a more complete discussion on the three methods and their respective merits and demerits, reference is requested to the 7th to 9th edns of this work.

International uniformity was desirable on such an important matter and Method 3 above was adopted at the Stockholm Conference in 1924 by 24 votes to 8 of those present and voting. This method was very familiar to anyone conversant with the calculation of cargo claims under a contract of marine insurance, and it was claimed by the advocates of this method that it provided a perfect solution of the many difficulties inherent in the other methods.[13] **16.18**

York-Antwerp Rules 1950

As revised in 1950, the rule read as follows: **16.19**

> "The amount to be made good as general average for damage to or loss of goods sacrificed shall be the loss which the owner of the goods has sustained thereby, based on the market values at the last day of discharge of the vessel or at the termination of the adventure where this ends at a place other than the original destination.
>
> Where the goods so damaged are sold and the amount of the damage has not been otherwise agreed, the loss to be made good in general average shall be the difference between the net proceeds of sale and the net sound value at the last day of discharge of the vessel or at the termination of the adventure where this ends at a place other than the original destination."

So far as the first paragraph of the rule was concerned, the only amendment was the substitution of "the last day of discharge of the vessel" for "the date of the arrival of the vessel", thus giving validity to what had always been the practice. The justification for the adoption of the later date was that it approximated more closely to the date upon which the owner could have sold his goods had they arrived in a sound condition.

The second paragraph was completely redrafted and Method 3 discussed above was abandoned in favour of Method 1 (value on last day of discharge less proceeds of sale). This was done at the request of the United States, which had never accepted the 1924 r.XVI and customarily excluded it when providing for York-Antwerp Rules in contracts of affreightment. Under Method 1, market fluctuations between the last day of discharge and the date of sale would influence the amount to be allowed in general average for damage to cargo, but it was the only method which would provide the owner of cargo sold damaged with an allowance in general average which, together with the actual sale proceeds, would amount to the sum he would have received for the goods but for the sacrifice, namely, the sound value on the last day of discharge. Although general average would bear the whole burden of these market fluctuations, it was felt that the owner of the

[13] It is also of interest to note that the proper interpretation of r.XVI in the 1890 Rules came before the French courts in the case of *Sprunt & Sons v Cap. Mal and French Government* ("Seine"), where in respect of bales of cotton sold in damaged condition at destination, general average allowances had been made on the basis of Method 1. However, the market had risen considerably in the interval between the last day of landing and the date of sale, and the consignees objected, claiming that they were entitled to a greater allowance under either of Methods 2 or 3. The adjustment was upheld in the courts below, but the Cour de Cassation held in favour of Method 3 (réglement par quotité).

damaged goods could claim with some justification that an additional loss by a market fluctuation due to a delayed sale was just as much a consequence of the sacrifice as the loss directly attributable to the damage itself.

In redrafting the second paragraph, the last day of discharge of the vessel was again adopted rather than the date of arrival.

York-Antwerp Rules 1974

16.20 The principles of the previous rule remained unchanged in 1974, but important amendments to the wording were necessary to correspond with the radical new provisions introduced at this time in r.XVII[14] relating to contributory values. The value shown in the commercial invoice rendered to the receiver of the cargo at the time of discharge was henceforth to be adopted as (or in place of) the "market value at the last day of discharge".

York-Antwerp Rules 1994

16.21 No change, but to give contractual recognition and authority to a commonly adopted working practice it had been proposed here, and also in r.XVII, to amend the expression "at the time of discharge" (from the vessel suffering the general average) to "at the time of delivery under the contract of carriage" (at the ultimate destination of the goods). The reasons for the proposed change, and the effects–if any–of its defeat, will be discussed below in paras 16.26 to 16.30, below.

York-Antwerp Rules 2004

16.22 Two changes were made as part of the process of rationalising the drafting of the rules:

(1) the expression "made good" was changed to "allowed";
(2) the two paragraphs were numbered (a) and (b).

RULE XVI

AMOUNT TO BE MADE GOOD/ALLOWED FOR CARGO LOST OR DAMAGED BY SACRIFICE

(a) **The amount to be made good/allowed as general average for damage to or loss of cargo sacrificed shall be the loss which has been sustained thereby based on the value at the time of discharge, ascertained from the commercial invoice rendered to the receiver or if there is no such invoice from the shipped value. The value at the time of discharge shall include the cost of insurance and freight except insofar as such freight is at the risk of interests other than the cargo.**

[14] See para.17.08, below.

(b) **When cargo so damaged is sold and the amount of the damage has not been otherwise agreed, the loss to be made good/allowed in general average shall be the difference between the net proceeds of sale and the net sound value as computed in the first paragraph of this Rule.**

CONSTRUCTION

The first paragraph enunciates the general principle to be applied in ascertaining the amount to be made good in general average for damage to or loss of goods sacrificed and the second paragraph lays down the method to be adopted in a particular case, namely when damaged goods are sold and the amount of damage has not been otherwise agreed. Whether or not the owner of the goods is entitled to have his loss made good in general average at all is a question which falls to be decided under other rules, that is, rr.A, C, D, E, I, II, III, V, VIII, IX, XII, and XIX. 16.23

First Paragraph

"The amount to be made good as general average for damage to or loss of cargo sacrificed shall be the loss which has been sustained thereby": The basic principle set forth in para.16.01 above, that the owner of goods sacrificed should be so compensated that he shall be in the same position as if, not his goods, but those of some other person had been thus sacrificed is here preserved in the opening wording of the rule, also the principle set out in r.IV that there can be no sacrifice of what is already irrevocably lost. However, as will be recorded shortly, an indemnity based on fluctuating market values was changed in 1974 on the grounds of practical simplicity to an indemnity on an "agreed value" basis related to invoice values. 16.24

"based on the value at the time of discharge": Although unstated, it is well understood that the discharge referred to is from the vessel suffering the general average, also that this discharge is the termination of the common adventure[15] for the cargo concerned. 16.25

Transhipment Cargo

In practice, and more particularly since the advent of containerisation, this discharge may be merely one staging post in the particular adventure on which the cargo is engaged, and it may not yet have reached its final scheduled destination. The cargo could be due for transhipment by another ocean-going vessel to a more distant seaport, and thence even by road, rail or barge for delivery to the consignee at some inland destination. Upon its discharge from the vessel suffering the 16.26

[15] The termination of the adventure is not precisely defined either in r.G, or here in r.XVI or r.XVII, but see, for instance, the more extended wording of this r.XVI prior to 1974: ". . . based on the market values at the last day of discharge of the vessel or at the termination of the adventure where this ends at a place other than the original destination." See also the discussion in paras G.23 et seq., above.

general average, such cargo may justifiably regard itself to be still in transit and its own particular adventure to be continuing, but, in conformity with fundamental principles, the rule specifies that any claim in general average for loss or damage to such cargo shall be "based on the value at the time of discharge" from the vessel suffering the general average. Thus:

(1) If cargo damaged by the general average act continues its journey to ultimate destination, any subsequent accident causing additional loss or damage will not reduce the value on which it contributes, nor extinguish to any degree the allowance to be made in the general average per the original carrying vessel.
(2) As the calculation of any claims in general average for loss of or damage to cargo almost invariably requires a consideration of both sound and damaged values of the cargo concerned, it would appear evident that these values must similarly both be assessed as at this time of discharge from the vessel suffering the general average.

Calculation of Claims with Transhipment Cargoes

16.27 The sound value (at least) of the damaged cargo at the time of discharge is, by the express provision of the rule since 1974 to be "ascertained from the commercial invoice rendered to the receiver" (see also para.16.31 below). If, as is likely, the complete transit to ultimate destination be covered by a single "through" bill of lading or contract of carriage, and the commercial invoice shows a single CIF or C&F price which includes all the prepaid freight(s), handling charges and—where appropriate—insurance costs for the complete journey, it is that single invoice price which represents and is to be adopted as the sound value of the cargo concerned, most certainly if the freights and other ancillary charges are prepaid and non-returnable ship and/or cargo "lost or not lost". Deduction from the ultimate destination invoice price of either the known or the notional costs of forwarding the cargo to that ultimate destination from the port at which it was originally discharged is justified only in those cases where such charges have not been prepaid on a non-returnable basis and would be saved to the consignee if the ship or cargo were to be lost or abandoned prior to delivery at the ultimate destination. As is stated later in the rule (see also para.17.29, below): "The value at the time of discharge shall include the cost of insurance and freight except insofar as such freight is at the risk of interests other than the cargo."

16.28 The damaged value at the time of discharge (or to be more precise, the value of the lost or damaged cargo), may or may not be ascertained from the commercial invoice. If, for instance, it has been jettisoned, it will have no value: if it be sold in damaged condition, the actual net proceeds of sale will generally be adopted as the damaged value under the second paragraph of the rule. (See also the commentary in para.16.32, below). The important point, as stated earlier, is that the value of the loss or damage is crystallised at the time of discharge from the vessel suffering the general average, and damage sustained thereafter from a subsequent accident cannot be taken into account.

The fact that the loss or damage should effectively be valued on discharge from the vessel suffering the general average does not mean that a detailed survey of all the cargo discharged must be carried out at that port. In practice, seriously damaged cargo may well be detained and either sold or reconditioned there, but where it is thought sensible to forward the cargo to its intended destination in the normal way, it will be equally sensible in calculating the general average allowances to adopt the degrees of damage assessed by the surveyors at that destination, even if it might be suggested that there has been some natural progression of the original damage during the final stages of the voyage.

Ever since multimodal transport became common, simplicity and practical considerations have usually dictated that average adjusters should adopt practices such as are outlined above,[16] but to give them greater authority and recognition, and to avoid any doubts which might be attributed to what might be termed a "pre-1974 approach", it had been proposed at Sydney in 1994 that the expression "at the time of discharge" (from the vessel suffering the general average), here and also in the parallel r.XVII, be amended to "at the time of delivery under the contract of carriage" (at the ultimate destination of the goods). **16.29**

A number of the delegates at Sydney, however, were critical of the proposal, possibly sensing that under r.XVII an increased proportion of the general average might thereby be cast upon the cargo interests, or that general average was being "dragged ashore" and extended to land transit, and three attempts to secure its passage in varying formats were all defeated.

In the event, the doubts entertained by those at Sydney who advocated a change in the rule have proved unfounded, and in practice the ultimate destination invoice values are adopted as the sound value in the calculation of allowances for loss or damage to cargo. For the purpose of demonstrating that this practice is in accordance with sound principle, two examples will be given in which it will be assumed that the CIF invoice price at final destination is 10,500, and that if that price could be projected back to the port of discharge, it would be 10,000. These examples demonstrate that only when ultimate destination values are adopted can a full and proper indemnity be provided to the suffering cargo interest. **16.30**

(1) A consignment of paper is delivered at ultimate destination with 50 per cent depreciation for damage caused by water used to extinguish a fire, and the consignee obviously suffers a loss of 50% x 10,500 = 5,250, and not the notional 5,000 assessable on supposed values at the earlier port of discharge.

(2) The same consignment is jettisoned for the common safety. Again, the loss suffered by the consignee will clearly be the full 10,500 ultimate destination price he has paid unless he is able to obtain any recovery from the carriers or cargo handlers for their unperformed services.

[16] See, for instance, the 1981 Resolution of AIDE.

16.31 **"ascertained from the commercial invoice"**: See commentary under r.XVII in para.17.26, below.

"rendered to the receiver": See commentary under r.XVII in para.17.28, below.

"if there is no such invoice from the shipped value": See commentary under r.XVII, in para.17.28, below, and note that when dealing with the allowances in general average permitted by this r.XVI, in the case of:

(1) *goods shipped "on consignment"*, a "shipped" value is not necessarily the equivalent of an FOB invoice value, which latter would include an element of profit to the shipper/exporter;
(2) *personal and household goods*, the value of those goods is but rarely increased by the amount of the freight payable for transporting them.

"The value . . . shall include the cost of insurance and freight except insofar as such freight is at the risk of interests other than the cargo": See commentary under r.XVII in para.17.29, below.

Second Paragraph

16.32 **"When cargo so damaged is sold"**: The provisions of the second paragraph apply only to those cases where damaged cargo is sold and . . .

"the amount of the damage has not been otherwise agreed": If the damage has been otherwise agreed (i.e. agreed in a manner at variance with the second paragraph of the rule), the claim will be dealt with under the provisions of the first paragraph of the rule. In practice the damage is very often agreed as a percentage of the sound value of the goods, or at so much per unit of weight or measurement, the percentage or amount having been recommended by cargo surveyors who have inspected the damaged cargo.

"the loss to be made good/allowed . . . shall be the difference between the net proceeds of sale and the net sound value as computed in the first paragraph of this Rule": In calculating the amount to be allowed as general average in terms of the second paragraph of the rule, the basic idea of Method 1[17] (sound value less proceeds) has been preserved and the term "net proceeds of sale" still means the actual gross proceeds of sale less the expenses of making the cargo ready for sale and of the sale (for example the cost of sorting, repacking, transportation, selling commission, etc.). However, in the interests of simplicity and economy the term "net sound value" is no longer based on market values, but is ascertained or computed from the invoice to the receiver in accordance with the provisions of the first paragraph of the rule. Thus, and as mentioned earlier, one is comparing unlike terms, that is, a "market" value with an "invoice" value, but this particular anomaly was knowingly and purposely intended by the framers of the current rule.

[17] Described in para.16.17, above.

However, a further and unintended comparison of unlike terms which would appear to be required on occasion by the specific wording of the rule is not applied in practice. This particular anomaly, which was carried over from the 1950 rule, is that when the goods are sold at destination the term "net proceeds of sale" will almost invariably include freight (whether prepaid or payable at destination), whereas the term "net sound value" will exclude freight on those occasions when it is "at the risk of interests other than the cargo".[18] **16.33**

Thus, if goods with an FOB invoice value of 7,500 and on which freight of 2,500 was payable only on right delivery at destination arrived in damaged condition and were sold for net proceeds of 6,000, the loss to be allowed in general average in accordance with a strict construction of the wording would be only:

Net Sound Value (i.e. FOB)	7,500
Deduct: Net Proceeds of Sale	6,000
	1,500

However, this would be manifestly unfair to the receiver who has had to pay freight of 2,500 to achieve his net sale proceeds of 6,000, and in practice the loss is (and was under the 1950 wording) calculated by a comparison of like values, that is:

Net Sound Value (as before)		7,500
Deduct: Net Proceeds of Sale	6,000	
Less: Freight	2,500	
	3,500	3,500
	Loss:	4,000

In similar fashion, if goods arriving at destination in damaged condition are sold in a "duty paid" condition, the allowance in general average should be assessed by a comparison of like values, that is:

Sound CIF invoice value		10,000
Add: Normal duty at 25%	2,500	
Less: Refund by customs	1,000	
+Duty Paid	1,500	1,500
		11,500
Deduct: Net Proceeds of Sale		5,000
	Loss:	6,500

[18] See para.17.29, below.

Calculation of Claims

16.34 There should be no difficulty in dealing with claims for cargo jettisoned or destroyed by a general average act; the value which the cargo lost would have had upon discharge[19] is to be ascertained from the commercial invoice– although it will not in all cases be the same as the invoice price. However, there can be problems when cargo is delivered in a damaged condition and particularly if it is sold. The following examples are given relating to a shipment of 100 bales with an invoice price of 10,000 on CIF terms or 7,500 on FOB terms.

On CIF terms (10,000)

(1) The 100 bales and delivered at destination damaged to the extent of 20 per cent.

(a) If the market is rising (for example sound value 12,500) it will profit the receiver to agree a 20 per cent depreciation with a surveyor to ensure that an allowance is made in general average of 20 per cent of 10,000 = 2,000.
Were he to sell the cargo for say, 80 per cent of 12,500 = 10,000, there would be nothing to make good in general average.

(b) If the market is falling (for example sound value 8,000) it will profit the receiver to sell the cargo and ensure that no percentage depreciation is agreed with a surveyor. If the cargo were sold to produce a 20 per cent depreciation (that is 6,400) the allowance in general average would be:

Invoice value	10,000
Less proceeds	6,400
	3,600

On FOB terms (7,500)

16.35 *(2) The 100 bales are delivered damaged at destination and a depreciation of 20 per cent is agreed with the surveyor.*

It is suggested that the 20 per cent depreciation is likely to have been assessed on a landed value basis (that is inclusive of freight), and that, therefore, the 20 per cent depreciation should be applied, not to the FOB price of 7,500 but to the notional CIF value of 10,000 to produce an allowance in general average of 2,000.

(This problem already existed under the 1950 Rules and was dealt with in the manner outlined. It was discussed further in para.16.04, above.)

[19] See paras 16.24 et seq., above, for a discussion on the expression "value at the time of discharge."

(3) The 100 bales are delivered at destination damaged to the extent of 20 per cent, and are sold for:

(a) 10,000 when the sound value if 12,500.

As stated in Example (1)(a), it will profit the receiver to agree a 20 per cent depreciation with a surveyor, failing which no allowance in general average can be made. Further, and as stated in Example (2), it is suggested that the 20 per cent depreciation should be applied, not to the FOB price of 7,500, but to the notional CIF value to produce an allowance in general average of 2,000.

(b) 6,400 when the sound value is 8,000.

As stated in Example (1)(b), it will profit the receiver to sell the goods for 6,400 and, as the price paid will effectively include a freight constituent of 2,500, the allowance in general average should again be assessed on a CIF basis, that is:

Notional CIF price....................	10,000
Less: proceeds	6,400
	3,600

One further small problem received judicial consideration in the United States courts in the case of *Christie v Davis Coal & Coke Co.*[20] Particularly in the bulk oil trade one occasionally finds that freight is at risk to the carrier but, provided any worthwhile quantity of cargo is delivered at destination, payable in full on the "intake" quantity. Thus, and for example 1000 tons of cargo might be shipped with: 16.36

an FOB invoice value of	80 per ton =	80,000
and freight at risk of	20 per ton =	20,000
	100	100,000

If 300 tons of the cargo were to be jettisoned, the cargo interests would be obliged to pay the full freight of 20,000, and in valuing the cargo jettisoned for allowance in general average, it is necessary to take into account not only the FOB

[20] *Christie v Davis Coal & Coke Co* 95 Fed Rep 837 (1899).

value of 80 per ton but also the proportion of the freight paid of 20 per ton, that is a total allowance of 30,000.[21]

[21] It could be suggested that the contributory values to be calculated in accordance with r.XVII of the York-Antwerp Rules 1974 would be as follows:

CARGO–700 tons delivered at FOB invoice value80		= 56,000
	Add: Made Good	30,000
		86,000
FREIGHT–At Risk and Earned (less costs of earning same)		20,000
		106,000

However, this is clearly wrong as the combined contributory values of cargo and freight cannot exceed 100,000.

In fact, the cargo will contribute only on the FOB element of 300 × 80 = 24,000 of the total amount made good of 30,000, the shipowner (or carrier) continuing to bear the contribution attaching to the full freight at his risk of 20,000. This problem, is very similar to that of the time-charterers' bunkers mentioned in para.17.44, below, but an easier way of confirming the correctness of the contributory values would be to calculate them in accordance with English law or the 1950 Rules, i.e.

CARGO–700 tons delivered at landed value 100		= 70,000
	Add: Make Good	30,000
		100,000
	Deduct: Freight	20,000
		80,000
FREIGHT–At Risk and Earned (less costs of earning same)		20,000
	Combined Contributory Values	100,000

Rule XVII

Contributory Values

Once it has been established that a general average loss has occurred and the amount to be made good has been determined, the following questions arise: **17.01**

(1) Which of the properties associated with the ship, her passengers and crew, her freight or earnings, also the cargo, should contribute to the general average?
(2) On what basis should the contributory values be calculated for those interests called upon to contribute?

A slightly different presentation has been adopted when dealing with r.XVII. to ensure that all the material on any individual property or contributing interest appears in one continuous section. For ready reference, the subject-matter of this section which also deals with contributory interests is as follows:

Historical Development and Practice of Rule XVII

Glasgow Resolutions 1860

17.02 Contributory values were assessed in the mid-nineteenth century by a variety of methods in which sound reason does not always appear to have played a great part. For instance, in France and Holland ship and freight contributed on only 50 per cent of their respective values, while in Hamburg, Sweden and Denmark cargo was made to contribute on its invoice value regardless of loss or damage sustained during the voyage. The situation was not much better in England.

An attempt to secure international uniformity was made at the Glasgow Conference in 1860 with the passing of the following Resolutions:

> "(9) That when the amount of expenses is less than the value of the property finally saved, the contributing values of ship, freight, and cargo, ought to be their values to the owners of them respectively, at the termination of the adventure.
> (10) That, when the amount of expenses is greater than the value of the property saved, the proceeds of the property so saved ought to be applied towards those expenses, and the excess of the expenses over the proceeds ought to be apportioned as if the whole property had finally reached its destination.
> (11) That, in fixing the value of the freight, the wages and port charges up to the date of the general average act ought not to be deducted, and the wages and port charges after that date ought to be deducted from the gross freight at the risk of the shipowner."

Although Resolutions Nos 9 and 11 were sound in principle, the same cannot be said of No.10, having regard to the decision in 1922 of *Chellew v Royal Commission on the Sugar Supply*.[1]

York Rules 1864

17.03 The following changes in the Glasgow Resolutions were made at York in 1864.

Resolution No.10 relating to general average expenses in excess of the contributory values was withdrawn in the face of strenuous opposition from Continental delegates. The sound principle established by Resolution No.11 was changed in favour of an arbitrary provision that the contributory value of freight should be three-fifths of the amount at risk. This measure was adopted in order to avoid certain practical difficulties arising from the varying liability of the shipowner to pay crew wages under different national laws. The substance was then combined into a single rule and couched in clear language which was to serve as the framework of the rule on contributory values for the next 110 years.

> "The contribution to general average shall be made upon the actual values of the property at the termination of the adventure, to which shall be added the amount made good as general average for property sacrificed: deduction being made from the

[1] *Chellew v Royal Commission on the Sugar Supply* [1922] 1 K.B. 12.

shipowner's freight and passage-money at risk of two-fifths of such freight, in lieu of crew's wages, port charges, and all other deductions; deduction being also made from the value of the property of all charges incurred in respect thereof subsequently to the arising of the claim to general average."

York-Antwerp Rules 1877

The decision taken in 1864 to adopt an arbitrary contributory value for freight of three-fifths of the amount at risk was unanimously reversed in 1877 and a return made to principle with the following words: **17.04**

"... deduction being made from the shipowner's freight and passage-money at risk, of such port charges and crew's wages as would not have been incurred had the ship and cargo been totally lost at the date of the general average act or sacrifice."

No alteration was made to the remainder of the rule.

York-Antwerp Rules 1890

An oversight in previous editions of the rule was remedied at the International Conference held at Liverpool in 1890. From the shipowner's freight and passage money at risk were deducted such port charges and crew's wages as would not have been incurred had the ship and cargo been totally lost at the date of the general average act or sacrifice, and from the value of property in general were deducted all charges incurred in respect thereof subsequently to the general average act. In so far as those port charges, crew's wages, and other charges were made good in general average, it was essential for sound principle that the amounts so made good should also contribute to the general average, and to rectify this earlier omission, suitable wording was added in the appropriate places in 1890. **17.05**

A further paragraph relating to passengers' luggage was also added at the end of the rule in 1890. This was prompted by the decision in the United States courts of *Heye v North German Lloyd*[2] in which it was held that, except for apparel and other articles taken for use on the voyage, passengers' baggage stored in the baggage compartment was liable to contribute in general average. The delegates to the Conference recognised that considerable inconvenience and ill-will would arise if general average security were demanded from the large number of passengers travelling by sea in 1890 and it was unanimously agreed that passengers' luggage and personal effects not shipped under bill of lading should be exempted from contribution. The 1890 rule now read as follows:

"The contribution to a general average shall be made upon the actual values of the property at the termination of the adventure to which shall be added the amount made good as general average for property sacrificed; deduction being made from the shipowner's freight and passage-money at risk, of such port charges and crew's wages as would not have been incurred had the ship and cargo been totally lost at the date of

[2] *Heye v North German Lloyd* 33 Fed. Rep. 60 (1887); 36 Fed. Rep. 705 (1888).

> the general average act or sacrifice, and have not been allowed as general average; deduction being also made from the value of the property of all charges incurred in respect thereof subsequently to the general average act, except such charges as are allowed in general average.
>
> Passengers' luggage and personal effects, not shipped under bill of lading, shall not contribute to general average."

Considerable discussion also took place on a proposal of similar effect to the Glasgow Resolution No.10 of 1860, but this was eventually withdrawn.

York-Antwerp Rules 1924

17.06 The following amendments to the rule were made in 1924:

(1) The word "net" inserted before the word "values", so as to read, "the contribution to a general average shall be made upon the actual net values of the property, etc."
(2) The words "'if not already included" inserted after the provision that amounts made good in general average shall be added to the actual net values, in order to correct an anomaly in the 1890 rule revealed by the case of The Strathdon,[3] in which the cost of general average repairs had been brought in twice to contribute to the general average.
(3) The omission of the word "port" before the words "charges and crew's wages", in the provision dealing with the deductions to be made from freight and passage money at risk, in order to permit the deduction of the cost of bunkers and stores bought (and consumed) after the general average act.
(4) The words "in earning the freight" added to qualify the description of the charges to be deducted from the amount of freight at risk.
(5) The omission of the superfluous words "or sacrifice" in the old rule, after the words "at the date of the general average act".

In order to bring about uniformity in the treatment of ulterior freight the Drafting Committee for the 1924 Rules put forward the following paragraph for inclusion in r.XVII:

> "When a ship is in ballast, but under charter, the ship and the freight (computed as above) earned under the charter, shall contribute to general average."

Exception was taken to this proposal by several of the Continental delegates present at the Stockholm Conference, as perhaps might have been expected, as only the United Kingdom recognises such freight as a contributory interest, and this proposal was rejected by a considerable majority.

Two other additions to the rule were proposed, of similar effect to the original Glasgow Resolution No.10, but neither of these suggestions was put forward by

[3] *The Strathdon* 94 Fed. Rep. 206 (1899); 101 Fed. Rep. 600 (1900).

the Drafting Committee for the consideration of the Stockholm Conference as there was little reason to suppose that either of them would find favour with the majority of the delegates present.

York-Antwerp Rules 1950

No change, but at the time of the drafting of the 1950 Rules, the Netherlands proposed that mails and time-charter hire should be included in the second paragraph of the rule and so excluded from any liability to contribute. This proposal was subsequently withdrawn. **17.07**

York-Antwerp Rules 1974

Simplification in the processes of preparing an adjustment was the objective governing most of the changes made in the rules in 1974, and a major contribution to that objective was the changes in r.XVII relating to contributory values. **17.08**

(1) In respect of cargo, instead of being based on fluctuating free-market values, the contributory value of cargo was now to be based on the invoice price to the receiver (essentially on CIF or FOB terms, depending on whether or not the freight was at risk to the carrier) at the time of discharge, with no percentage addition for anticipated profit.

The intended simplification was undoubtedly achieved in those (say 95 per cent of) cases where cargo was delivered at destination in sound condition, and it is also probably true to state that cargo interests in general benefited in that they often contributed on a lesser value than formerly, in that no addition for profit was made to the invoice value of the cargo. However, in the case of cargo delivered damaged, whether by accidental cause or by general average sacrifice, the calculations became more complicated, and certain anomalies crept into the actual allowances in general average for damage by sacrifice by reason of the occasional comparisons required by rr.XVI and XVII of unlike and dissimilar values–that is, invoice values and real market values as evidenced by sale proceeds. The equitable nature of the general average system would normally require a comparison of like with like.

(2) In respect of ship, the contributory value was now to be based on her "free" market value, ignoring the beneficial or detrimental effect of any demise or time charterparty to which the ship might be committed. This change was in the interest of international uniformity.

A further suggestion that freight should contribute on a "forfeit" basis was not proceeded with as it would often have led to unreasonable results not justified by the insignificant simplification achieved.

York-Antwerp Rules 1994

17.09 The rule passed in 1974 remained essentially unchanged, but certain additions were made on this occasion:

(1) At the end of the second paragraph was added wording which will prevent awards which fall upon the shipowner for special compensation under Art.14 of the International Convention on Salvage 1989 being treated as an "extra charge" in terms of r.XVII and thereby reducing the contributory value of the ship. York-Antwerp r.VI(b)[4] specifically states that such compensation shall not be allowed in general average, and that provision would have been partly frustrated if, by reducing the contributory value of the ship, the ship thereby paid a lesser proportion of the admissible general average.

(2) Consequent on the introduction in 1994 of a Non-Separation Agreement in r.G,[5] a new third paragraph was necessary here in r.XVII to provide for the basis of assessing contributory values when cargo was forwarded to destination.

(3) The final paragraph of the 1974 rule excepted from contribution to general average passengers' luggage and personal effects not shipped under bill of lading. On practical grounds, these exceptions have been extended in 1994 to comprise "mails, passengers' luggage, personal effects and accompanied private motor vehicles".

A fourth set of changes had been proposed, identical for both rr.XVI and XVII, to amend the expression "at the time of discharge" (from the vessel suffering the general average) to "at the time of delivery under the contract of carriage" (at the ultimate destination of the goods). This suggestion was to give contractual recognition and authority to a working practice already commonly adopted, but it was strenuously opposed and defeated at Sydney in October 1974, and in this respect r.XVII remains in its 1974 format. The reasons for the proposed change, and the effects–if any—of its defeat, are discussed earlier in paras 16.26 to 16.30, above.

17.10 **RULE XVII**

CONTRIBUTORY VALUES

The contribution to a general average shall be made upon the actual net values of the property at the termination of the adventure except that the value of cargo shall be the value at the time of discharge, ascertained from the commercial invoice rendered to the receiver or if there is no such invoice from the shipped value. The value of the cargo shall include the cost of insurance and freight unless and insofar as such freight is at the risk of interests other than the

[4] See para.6.30, above.
[5] See para.G.17, above.

cargo, deducting therefrom any loss or damage suffered by the cargo prior to or at the time of discharge. The value of the ship shall be assessed without taking into account the beneficial or detrimental effect of any demise or time charter-party to which the ship may be committed.

To these values shall be added the amount made good as general average for property sacrificed, if not already included, deduction being made from the freight and passage money at risk of such charges and crew's wages as would not have been incurred in earning the freight had the ship and cargo been totally lost at the date of the general average act and have not been allowed as general average: deduction being also made from the value of the property of all extra charges incurred in respect thereof subsequently to the general average act, except such charges as are allowed in general average or fall upon the ship by virtue of an award for special compensation under Art.14 of the International Convention on Salvage, 1989 or under any other provision similar in substance.

In the circumstances envisaged in the third paragraph of Rule G, the cargo and other property shall contribute on the basis of its value upon delivery at original destination unless sold or otherwise disposed of short of that destination, and the ship shall contribute upon its actual net value at the time of completion of discharge of cargo.

Where cargo is sold short of destination, however, it shall contribute upon the actual net proceeds of sale, with the addition of any amount made good as general average.

Mails, passengers' luggage, personal effects and accompanied private motor vehicles shall not contribute in general average.

York Antwerp Rules 2004

The substance of the rule was unchanged but a new arrangement of the paragraphs was a considerable aid to the clarity of this rule and the 2004 version is therefore shown in full. 17.11

RULE XVII

CONTRIBUTORY VALUES

a.

(i) The contribution to a general average shall be made upon the actual net values of the property at the termination of the adventure except that the value of cargo shall be the value at the time of discharge, ascertained from the commercial invoice rendered to the receiver or if there is no such invoice from the shipped value.

(ii) the value of the cargo shall include the cost of insurance and freight unless and insofar as such freight is at the risk of interests other than the cargo, deducting therefrom any loss or damage suffered by the cargo prior to or at the time of discharge.

(iii) The value of the ship shall be assessed without taking into account the beneficial or detrimental effect of any demise or time charterparty to which the ship may be committed.

b. To these values shall be added the amount allowed as general average for property sacrificed, if not already included, deduction being made from the

freight and passage money at risk of such charges and crew's wages as would not have been incurred in earning the freight had the ship and cargo been totally lost at the date of the general average act and have not been allowed as general average; deduction being also made from the value of the property of all extra charges incurred in respect thereof subsequently to the general average act, except such charges as are allowed in general average or fall upon the ship by virtue of an award for special compensation under Art. 14 of the International Convention on Salvage, 1989 or under any other provision similar in substance.

c. In the circumstances envisaged in the third paragraph of Rule G, the cargo and other property shall contribute on the basis of its value upon delivery at original destination unless sold or otherwise disposed of short of that destination, and the ship shall contribute upon its actual net value at the time of completion of discharge of cargo.

d. Where cargo is sold short of destination, however, it shall contribute upon the actual net proceeds of sale, with the addition of any amount allowed as general average.

e. Mails, passengers' luggage, personal effects and accompanied private motor vehicles shall not contribute to general average.

17.12 Before proceeding to construe the precise text of the rule, it will be worthwhile setting out what are the general principles which govern the assessment of contributory values. The first principle is that it should be financially immaterial to a party to the adventure whether his own property is sacrificed, or that belonging to someone else; it follows that the basis of calculating the contributory value of property which is saved is exactly the same as that adopted for calculating the amount to be made good in general average for property sacrificed. Thus, just as in computing the amount to be made good it must be determined what has been the true loss to the owner of property sacrificed, so in ascertaining the contributory values upon which contribution shall be based it is necessary to determine which owners of property have benefited, and to what extent, by a safe arrival.

17.13 The next and self-evident principle to state is that only those interests which were on board the ship or at risk at the time of the general average act can be called upon to contribute, and then only provided that success attends the continuing adventure and that some property with value arrives at its intended destination or some other place where the adventure is terminated. A general average becomes "crystallised" and enforceable only on safe arrival at destination, and a prior total loss of the adventure before such arrival extinguishes any earlier general average.[6]

This is evidenced in broad terms by r.G:

> "General average shall be adjusted as regards both loss and contribution upon the basis of values at the time and place when and where the adventure ends."

Thus, and to the extent that any property suffers further loss or damage during the remainder of the voyage subsequent to the general average act, its contribu-

[6] *Chellew v Royal Commission on the Sugar Supply* [1922] 1 K.B. 12.

tory value will be reduced to the value it has in the actual condition in which it arrives at destination.

A further principle must now be applied: the arrived value of properties at 17.14
destination must be reduced by all those charges incurred subsequent to the general average act in order to realise that destination value and which would have been avoided if, instead of being saved by the general average act, the property had at that time been totally lost. Thus, and for example:

(1) If cargo has a destination value of.	100,000
but this includes a freight payable only on right delivery at destination of.	20,000
The contributory value of the cargo will be	80,000
	80,000
(2) If the shipowner has freight at risk to him payable only on right delivery of the cargo at destination (as above) of.	20,000
but in order to earn that freight he must incur voyage expenses subsequent to the general average act of.	8,000
The contributory value of the freight will be	1,12,000
(3) If the ship has an arrived destination value of.	1,000,000
but the shipowner has already carried out full permanent repairs to the damage giving rise to the general average of	1,100,000
The contributory value of the ship will be	1,900,000

In other words, destination values must be converted (reduced) to the equivalent values of the property immediately following the accident which gave rise to the general average. In practice, charges incurred subsequent to the general average act which are themselves allowable as general average are not deducted from the destination values to arrive at the contributory values, for the reasons expressed in the following paragraph; if general average charges were first deducted, they would then have to be added back as amounts "made good".

The final principle to apply in arriving at the contributory values of the property 17.15
is that to the sums produced thus far must be added any amount made good in general average for loss of or damage to the property. As a simple proof of this requirement, assume that if a voyage had been successfully concluded without accident, the values at destination would have been:

Ship	1,000
Cargo A	1,000
Cargo B	1,000
Cargo C	1,000
	4,000

Let it also be assumed that Cargo B is jettisoned for the common safety. A general average of 1,000 falls to be apportioned, and if this were between only those parties whose property arrived, the figures would be:

Ship on	1,000	pays	334
Cargo A on	1,000	"	333
Cargo B on	–	"	–
Cargo C on	1,000	"	333
	3,000	pays	1,000

The financial result of such an apportionment would be that the shipowner and merchants A and C would have property with an effective value of 667, whereas merchant B would have cash amounting to 1,000. This is so clearly inequitable that merchant B is also made to contribute to the general average on the amount of the loss nominally made good to him in general average, that is:

Ship on	1,000	pays	250
Cargo A on	1,000	"	250
Cargo B on	1,000	is liable for	250
Cargo C on	1,000	pays	250
	4,000	pays	1,000

The equitable result now is that each of the parties to the adventure reaches destination with property or cash in the sum of 750.

17.16 The fundamental principles[7] set forth above in paras 17.12 to 17.15 might be summarised and paraphrased into "rule" form as follows:

> "general average sacrifices and expenses shall be borne by . . .
> . . . the ship and other properties on board at the time of the general average act . . .
> . . . in proportion to their actual values at the termination of the adventure
> . . . after deducting therefrom all charges incurred subsequent to the general average act (other than those allowed as general average) which would not have been incurred if the adventure had been totally lost at the date of the general average act . . .

[7] In the 11th and 12th edns further refinements were suggested with regard to contributory values. If the charges incurred subsequent to a general average act by any individual property exceed its net value at the termination of the adventure, it is clear that the property cannot be called upon to contribute to the general average. However, as that property would have been financially better off if, instead of being saved, the adventure had been totally lost, it was questioned whether that property should be assessed at a negative contributory value and be paid a general average contribution as part compensation for the expenses it has incurred. Likewise it was suggested that where freight was not at risk the contingent expenses of carrying the freight after the general average act should be deducted from the value of the ship, in order to preserve the principle that the overall values should be unchanged by the circumstances of whether freight was at risk or not. Both suggestions are based on a sophisticated appreciation of the principles involved, but it would appear that practitioners and commercial interests are reluctant to pursue such refinements when the recent trend has been to simplify as much as possible both the processes and the principles involved in general average.

". . . to which values shall be added the amount made good for property sacrificed, if not already included."

We now construe the current r.XVII, but dealing first with the general principles enunciated at intervals throughout the rule, and concluding with provisions which relate specifically to particular contributing interests.

Remarks of a general nature concerning English and/or foreign law and practice will precede the specific provisions of r.XVII for each of these particular properties.

CONSTRUCTION

General Principles

"The contribution to a general average shall be made upon the actual net values of the property at the termination of the adventure": This provision is in accordance with the fundamental principles outlined in paras 17.12, 17.13, above, and the only words to which particular attention need be drawn are: 17.17

"contribution": Technically, a general average contribution is the sum paid by or to any individual party to the adventure after taking into account any loss or expense borne by him and allowed in the general average. However, practitioners are well aware that what is intended is that the total general average shall be apportioned (over the actual net values).

"actual net values": It is submitted that the word "actual" excludes any consideration of potential claims which the owner may have against persons who are not parties to the adventure for damage to the property, for example collision damage.[8] 17.18

In certain cases, parties to the adventure other than the owner of the damaged property may have their own right of action against the wrongdoer, as in *Morrison S.S. Co v Greystoke Castle (Cargo Owners)*.[9] In the United States it has been held that, since the owner of sacrificed cargo has a maritime lien over the carrying vessel for the contribution due to him, he is entitled to share pro-rata in any sums recovered by the owners of the carrying vessel against a colliding vessel as damages for loss of or damage to the carrying vessel.[10]

"the property": Lowndes wrote that: 17.19

> "The ship, the cargo, and the freight, constitute, generally speaking, the whole of the property on shipboard liable to contribute to general average. Should there be any kind of property, not coming under any of these heads, which is preserved from destruction by a general average act, this likewise must contribute, unless there be some special reason for exempting it . . . If there be anything else on shipboard, not

[8] See also paras 50.92 et seq., below.

[9] *Morrison S.S.* [1947] A.C. 265: see para.50.92, below.

[10] *Armour v Green Star Shipping Co* (1930) 37 Lloyd's Reg. 178 (District Ct): (1931) 39 Lloyd's Reg. 199 (Circuit Ct of Appeals). See para.G.29, above, for the circumstances out of which the claim arose. English law does not recognise a maritime lien for general average contribution.

> constituting merchandise in the proper sense of the word, yet possessing a substantial value, it ought to contribute. For example, the unconsumed stores of a troop ship,[11] or those laid in by a passenger charterer[12]; planks or other materials used as dunnage, or covering boards, or for the construction of temporary bulkheads for cargo, or the like, should properly be brought in as contributing. It is only the small value of such articles which occasions their being, in practice, frequently disregarded."

This rule laid down by Lowndes, that any kind of property saved by a general average act must contribute in the absence of special reasons for exemption, is based on the fundamental principle of general average.[13]

17.20 **"at the termination of the adventure"**: This important phrase, relevant to rr.G, XVI and XVII, receives no precise definition in the York-Antwerp Rules, but some of the problem areas associated with the phrase are discussed at length in paras G.21 et seq., and also in paras 16.25 to 16.30, above. In practice, however: (1) if a complete cargo is being carried to a single port of destination, the adventure terminates upon completion of discharge at the destination or upon the earlier abandonment of the voyage; (2) if parts of the cargo are consigned to several different ports of destination, in the absence of an earlier termination of the whole voyage, the ship is valued at the last port of discharge of any part of the cargo on board at the time of the general average act, and each part of the cargo (and any freight at risk thereon) at its own respective port of discharge from the ship. This includes cargo shipped under a "through" bill of lading for further on-carriage whether by sea and/or land.

If the ship is in ballast and under charter, and the adjustment is being prepared for purposes of a claim on an English policy of marine insurance, Rule of Practice B.26[14] will apply and the adventure will be deemed to terminate:

(a) upon completion of discharge at the final port of discharge of the cargo carried under the charter, if the vessel is under a voyage charter entered into by the shipowner before the general average act;
(b) at the first loading port upon the commencement of loading cargo, if the vessel is under a time charter.

Adjustment to values of ship and cargo

17.21 **"To these values shall be added the amount made good as general average for property sacrificed, if not already included . . ."**: The provision that

[11] Government stores in a transport are liable to general average. See British Shipping Laws, Vol. 10: Arnould, *Marine Insurance*, 16th edn, para.973. So determined in the US: *United States v Wilder* (1838) 3 Sumner, U.S. 308.

[12] Arnould, 4th edn, p.793.

[13] Magens (Vol.1, p.62), and Stevens (p.44) maintained that "what pays no freight pays no average"; but the latter author inconsistently allowed (p.45) that this rule should not be construed literally: "or it would be very unjust that the master, or owner, or any other person who had goods on board, should not contribute, merely because he pays no freight for the carriage of them." By goods he meant "the wares or cargo for sale, laden on board the ship".

[14] See para.70.12, below.

any amount made good in general average must also contribute to the general average is one of the fundamental principles of general average, the reasons for which have already been explained with a figured example in para.17.15, above.

The final words—if not already included—were added in 1924 for the reason mentioned in para.17.06, above, and relate to those cases where the general average sacrifice has already been repaired before the termination of the adventure: for example the ship may have suffered a general average sacrifice which has been repaired at a port of refuge. In such cases the amount made good is already included in the actual net value of the property at the termination of the adventure and does not have to be added to that value.

"... deduction being also made from the value of the property of all extra charges incurred in respect thereof subsequently to the general average act, except such charges as are allowed in general average": This wording encompasses another of the fundamental principles to be observed in assessing the contributory value of any property, and a number of simple figured examples were given in para.17.14, above. From the actual net values at the termination of the adventure must be deducted all those charges incurred subsequent to the general average act in order to realise that destination value and which would not have been incurred if, instead of being saved by the general average act, the property had at that time been totally lost. **17.22**

The concluding words except such charges as are allowed in general average dispense with the need to deduct such of those charges incurred subsequent to the general average act as are themselves allowed as general average. If they were deducted, sound principle would require them to be treated as "made good" and added back again as per the rule wording analysed in the previous para.17.21 that is:

Freight at risk to shipowner	20,000
Less: Voyage expenses subsequent to the general average act	8,000
Contributory value of freight	12,000

The "voyage" expenses" in the example are expenses which have not been allowed as general average, but if crew wages incurred during a detention at a port of refuge of 1,000 were also to be deducted as "charges subsequent to the general average act", the calculation of the contributory value would have to proceed as follows:

Freight at risk to shipowner	20,000
Less: Voyage expenses subsequent to the general	9,000
average act (8,000 + 1,000)	11,000
Add: Made good (in general average)	1,000
Contributory value (as before)	12,000

The word extra was added in 1974 particularly to cope with a potential problem anticipated with the valuation of cargo. Prior to 1974 the assessment of cargo **17.23** values often started with their landed market values, from which needed to be deducted freight (unless prepaid and non-returnable), landing and warehousing charges, duty, and brokerage, etc. With the change in 1974 to bare invoice values, these particular deductions could no longer be made, but extra charges (for example by reason of damage) might so fall to be deducted.

SPECIFIC PROVISIONS

Cargo–English Law and Practice

17.24 Cargo contributes on its actual or assumed landed market values on the last day of discharge at destination or other place where the adventure ends. In practice, market values are adopted for all those basic commodities regularly traded on the exchanges of the world, such as grain, coffee, cotton, rubber, oil, etc. but in the case of manufactured products (where a similar "market" might not exist) it is the general custom in respect of goods delivered at their intended destination to base the contributory value on the CIF invoice value to the receiver of the goods, plus say 10 per cent[15] for assumed profit. If the goods are damaged as at the last day of discharge, the damaged value forms the basis of contribution, but damage sustained from a new cause subsequent to the discharge from the vessel (the subject of the general average) should properly be ignored.

17.25 From the above values are deducted such expenses as the cargo owner has incurred to realise that value and which he would escape if the adventure had been totally lost at the time of the general average act. These expenses might include freight (unless prepaid and/or payable "lost or not lost"), landing and warehousing charges, duty and brokerage. Particular charges attaching to the cargo which would not be incurred if the adventure had been totally lost at the time of the general average act are also deducted.[16] (Additional information can be found in paras 416 to 418 of the 10th edn.)

CARGO AND YORK-ANTWERP RULE XVII

Construction

First Paragraph (paragraph (a) in 2004 Rules)

17.26 **"except that the value of cargo . . .":** The opening word indicates that the contributory value of cargo is to be assessed in a manner which may differ from the general provisions of the rule dealt with earlier.

". . . shall be the value at the time of discharge . . .": However, the basic principle that contributory values shall be based on the condition and arrived

[15] In *Mormacsaga v Crelinston Fruit Co* (1969) A.M.C. 1621, the court added 15 per cent when assessing the value of cargo not replaceable locally.

[16] *The Eliza Lines* (1900–1902) 102 Fed. Rep. 184; 114 Fed. Rep. 307.

values at the time and place when and where the adventure ends, in accordance with r.G and the opening words of r.XVII is preserved thus far.

"... ascertained from the commercial invoice ...": Following the alteration in the Rules in 1974,[17] contributory values are now based on the invoice price to the receiver, without the addition of any profit margin. It should be noticed that the invoice must be a commercial one; it must state a price payable on a genuine sale. If it does not, it should be disregarded.

Transhipment cargo. For transhipment cargo carried under a "through" bill of lading or contract of carriage for further transport after its discharge from the vessel suffering the general average, although its own particular adventure may yet be continuing, the common maritime adventure terminates on the present discharge and such cargo must contribute on its value and in its condition at that time. This value, however, will still be "ascertained from the commercial invoice rendered to the receiver", and if that invoice be on a CIF ultimate destination basis, with all the freights, transport, handling charges and insurance, etc. for the complete journey prepaid and non-returnable ship and/or cargo "lost or not lost", the value at the intermediate port of discharge will–if sound–be precisely the same as at the ultimate destination. No deduction from the ultimate destination CIF invoice price should be made for the notional expense of getting the cargo from the (first) port of discharge to the ultimate destination. **17.27**

Account must clearly be taken of loss or damage already present on discharge from the vessel suffering the general average, but additional loss or damage sustained thereafter from a new cause will not reduce the value on which such cargo contributes. (A more extensive commentary on the problems with transhipment cargo appears in paras 16.26 to 16.30, above.)

"... rendered to the receiver": Some goods, particularly basic commodities, are often bought and sold many times during the course of a voyage, and invoices will obviously be prepared to substantiate each individual sale. The particular invoice which is most likely to record the value at the termination of the adventure is the invoice rendered to the actual receiver of the goods and the rule provides accordingly. **17.28**

The adoption of invoice values undoubtedly simplifies adjustments, but invoices themselves are not without their problems. Various deductions from the basic price are frequently made and it is not necessarily the final price quoted on the invoice which should always be taken for contribution purposes. Some of the more common deductions are as follows:

"Less 5 per cent to Commission Agent"	—	Do not deduct
"Less 2 per cent Cash Discount"	—	Deduct
"Less 4 per cent for Ordinary Loss"	—	Deduct
"Less 2 per cent Advertising Allowance"	—	Do not deduct
"Less 2½ per cent for Letter of Credit"	—	Deduct
"Less 5 per cent Quantity Rebate"	—	Deduct

[17] See para.17.08, above.

"if there is no such invoice from the shipped value": Some goods are shipped without an invoice being rendered to the receiver (for example personal and household effects, goods sold "on consignment", and possibly government and foreign aid cargoes). In such cases, the adjuster must assess the contributory value as best he can from the shipped value.

17.29 **"The value of the cargo shall include . . .":**

(a) **". . . the cost of insurance . . ."**: The use of the expression "cost of insurance"' suggests that where the cargo is not insured, the contributory value should be assessed (subject to the following remarks on freight) on C&F or FOB terms.

(b) **". . . and freight unless and insofar as such freight is at the risk[18] of interests other than the cargo"**: Freight will form part of the contributory value of the cargo to the extent that it is at risk to the cargo at the time of the general average act, either by reason of it having been prepaid on non-returnable conditions, or being payable subsequently on "lost or not lost" conditions. The words "insofar as" cover those cases where the freight is partly prepaid and partly at carrier's risk, the partly prepaid portion only being included in the contributory value of the cargo.

17.30 **"deducting therefrom any loss or damage suffered by the cargo prior to or at the time of discharge"**: The value of any loss or damage suffered by the cargo prior to or at the time of discharge must clearly be deducted in accordance with general principle, and, having regard to the basis of valuation set out in the earlier part of the rule, it is submitted that the loss or damage must similarly be valued on the "invoice" basis. Thus cargo sold at destination in damaged condition by the receiver will not contribute on the actual sale proceeds; it will be necessary to ascertain what would have been the value in sound condition, calculate the percentage depreciation, and deduct this percentage from the invoice value.

This last sentence is best illustrated by example, and using the same facts and figures as is para.16.34, above, that a shipment of 100 bales with a CIF invoice price of 10,000 delivered at destination damaged to the extent of 20 per cent. If the market is rising (for example, sound value 12,500) and the cargo is damaged by accidental causes and sold for 10,000, it would appear quite illogical to adopt that damaged value of 10,000 as the contributory value when similar cargo in sound condition will contribute on the same CIF value of 10,000. The wording of the rule requires that the contributory value shall be based upon and "ascertained from the commercial invoice"

i.e	10,000
but "deducting therefrom any loss or damage", i.e.	
20 per cent	2,000
Contributory Value.	8,000

[18] The party to whom the freight is at risk is discussed in paras 17.53–17.56, below.

Although perhaps more relevant to the construction of r.XVI, it is interesting and convenient here to calculate the allowance in general average and the contributory value for the same consignment with an arrived sound value of 12,500 where the damage has been caused by general average sacrifice. As stated in para.16.34, above, if the receiver agrees a depreciation of 20 per cent with the surveyor, the allowance in general average would be calculated by applying this 20 per cent depreciation to the invoice value of 10,000, that is 2,000.
The contributory value would be assessed as:

Invoice value.	10,000
Less: damage	2,000
	8,000
Add: made good	2,000
Contributory value	10,000

On the other hand, if as per r.XVI, the "cargo so damaged is sold and the amount of the damage has not been otherwise agreed", nothing will be made good in general average as there is NO "difference between the net proceeds of sale (10,000) and the net sound value (10,000)". The contributory value, accordingly, will be assessed as:

Invoice value.	10,000
Less: damage.	2,000
	8,000
Add: made good	
Contributory value	8,000

Third Paragraph (paragraph (c) in 2004 Rules)

"In the circumstances envisaged in the third paragraph of Rule G, the cargo . . . shall contribute on the basis of its value upon delivery at original destination unless sold or otherwise disposed of short of that destination": The "third paragraph of Rule G", introduced in 1994, constitutes the first half of what was popularly known as a Non-Separation Agreement,[19] and the second half of the Agreement, relating to the valuation of the various properties, was clearly more appropriately sited here in r.XVII than in r.G.[20] The wording under discussion provides that cargo forwarded from a port of refuge by other vessels in circumstances entitling the shipowner to retain the cargo there during repairs shall contribute to the continuing general average on the basis of its value, not when it left the ship at the port of refuge, but "upon delivery at original destination unless sold or otherwise disposed of short of destination". 17.31

[19] For a description, see paras G.10–G.12, above.
[20] See para.17.26, above.

Fourth Paragraph (paragraph (d) in 2004 Rules)

17.32 **"Where cargo is sold short of destination, however, it shall contribute upon the actual net proceeds of sale . . .":** This particular paragraph was added in 1974 at the request of the British delegation to legislate for a problem encountered in practice, as detailed in Report No.34 of the Advisory Committee of the Association of Average Adjusters dated May 7, 1968. The wording makes an exception to the general provision that cargo shall contribute on the basis of the value shown in the commercial invoice rendered to the receiver in the case of cargo sold short of destination. The actual net proceeds of sale, plus any amount made good as general average will be the contributory value.

Where the voyage is justifiably and wholly abandoned at a place short of the scheduled destination, cargo which is undamaged or not requiring to be sold at that place will often be forwarded to its intended destination. The contributory value should then be assessed in the normal way from its destination invoice price, deducting therefrom all charges incurred by the cargo interests themselves subsequent to the abandonment to get their cargo to the intended destination.

SHIP–ENGLISH LAW AND PRACTICE

17.33 The ship contributes upon her value at the completion of discharge at the final port of destination, or other place where the adventure ends, and in that condition—whether sound or damaged—in which she then finds herself. From this value should be deducted the cost of any repairs already carried out subsequent to the general average act, and to this value should be added any sum made good in general average for damage to the ship.

Unless the ship has actually been sold at the time and place when and where the adventure ends, thereby placing a fairly precise and unarguable value upon her,[21] it will be necessary to seek the assistance of a recognised ship valuer. In practice it is seldom that a ship valuer will actually inspect the ship, and it is customary to seek an opinion of the sound[22] market value of the vessel at the relevant time and place, and to deduct from this value the cost of repairing all damage carried by the vessel, to arrive at a damaged value.

17.34 It is also necessary to define those constituent parts of the ship which will be included in the global value assessed by the ship valuer (in the same way that, when buying a house, it is well understood that this does not include the furniture, curtains and carpets, etc. unless expressly mentioned). Using the definition contained in Rule of Construction No.15 of the Marine Insurance Act 1906, as a starting point, the term "ship" includes the hull, materials and outfit, stores and provisions for the officers and crew, the ordinary fittings requisite for the trade in

[21] *Bell v Smith* (1806) 2 Johnson R. 98.

[22] The term "sound" is a relative one, and will take account of the routine maintenance and upkeep work likely to be necessary, having regard to the time elapsed since the last drydocking and special survey. For this reason, the cost of normal wear and tear repairs is not deducted from the sound value.

which she is engaged, the main engine, the generators and other auxiliary machinery. It does not include, for instance, the bunkers, unbroached stores and spare gear, etc. which are usually paid for separately by the purchaser of any vessel, nor does it include property on board the ship belonging to other parties, for example leased equipment or containers.

The market value of a ship in sound condition represents the current opinions of shipowners and can be adopted when there is a sufficiently extensive market for ships of that kind. In the case of ships of a peculiar build, or having qualities which specially adapt them to a limited trade, the value in the market may not come near to the real value.[23] In such a case it may be necessary to take account of the initial building cost, to make a deduction for age and wear and tear, and to allow, likewise, for changes which have taken place in the cost of materials or the price of labour since the ship was built, and for later improvements in construction which may diminish her value. **17.35**

Many vessels are operated under long-term charters which can affect their market values. The majority of these chartering arrangements are straightforward business transactions between parties at arm's length, whilst others have as part of their objective the securing of tax or other advantages offered by different countries. The assessment of market values in such cases presented considerable problems under adjustments prepared only in accordance with English law. **17.36**

The effect of a long-term time charter on the value of a ship for salvage purposes was the subject of two cases fought in the Admiralty Court. In *The San Onofre*,[24] the vessel was committed to a time charter which had several years to run at a relatively disadvantageous rate of hire. The President, Sir Samuel Evans, held that the contractual arrangements between the owners and the charterers were immaterial and must be disregarded, and he adopted the (higher) free-market value of the vessel.

In a later case, *The Castor*[25] the vessel was similarly subject to a time charter which had several years to run, but this particular charter was more profitable than could have been secured at the time. In following *The Harmonides*[26] and similar collision cases, the President, Lord Merrivale, said: **17.37**

> "It seems to me inconsistent with authority, and wrong in principle to exclude from consideration the earning power of the Castor under the charterparty, under which, so long as it subsists, she could alone earn money for her owners."

[23] An interesting case where the vessel was actually sold illustrates the occasional extremes in values which can be encountered. A Panamanian flag vessel on a voyage from the US to Europe was obliged to put into an east coast US port with severe damage, estimated to cost $4,000,000 to repair. Her sound value on an "international" basis was $6,000,000, resulting in a contributory value of $2,000,000. However as she had been damaged in US waters, she became eligible under the US Wreck Act for the import to the US flag and operation in US coastwide trading and, as such, she was sold in her damaged condition for $10,000,000. This was adopted as the contributory value.

[24] *The San Onofre* [1917] P. 96.

[25] *The Castor* [1932] P. 142.

[26] *The Harmonides* [1903] P. 5.

Accordingly, he valued the vessel at a higher figure than her free-market value. Lord Merrivale was able to find grounds to distinguish the case of *The Castor* from *The San Onofre*, but they do appear to conflict and it may be that one of the cases would now be decided differently.[27]

17.38 In the United States, a case was heard in the Circuit Court of Appeals where the facts were similar to *The San Onofre*.[28] In *The Kia Ora*[29] circuit Judge Woods said:

> "Free on the market at the time she was stranded, her market value would have been \$3,000,000; but the fact that she was under requisition of the British government reduced her market value to \$1,772,600. It seems clear that her real value, as properly found by the District Court, was her value under the actual conditions of requisition, not what would have been her value with that condition removed."

Many other countries take no account of the beneficial or detrimental effect of a vessel's long term charter engagements, and this matter was resolved by the provisions introduced into r.XVII in 1974 that, "the value of the ship shall be assessed without taking into account the beneficial or detrimental effect of any demise or time charterparty to which the ship may be committed."

17.39 No inflexible rule can be laid down regarding the valuation of the ship. The principle is that the ship is to be valued at that sum for which the owner as a reasonable man would be willing to sell her, and this sum must be ascertained by the adjuster as well as he can.[30] Rule B24 of the Association of Average Adjusters provides:

> "*Contributory Value of Ship*
>
> That in any adjustment of general average there shall be set forth the certificate on which the contributory value of the ship is based, or if there be no such certificate, the information adopted in lieu thereof, and any amount made good shall be specified."

The adjuster should also consider any special circumstances in a case that may mean that the figure given by an expert valuer will need to be reviewed carefully in order to reach a contributory value that is fair to all parties. Examples of such circumstances now follow in paras 17.40–17.42.

Sound Value higher than the Valuer's Estimate

17.40 Problems of some financial consequence can arise with the contributory value of a ship when the shipowner elects to carry out repairs even though the vessel would appear to be a commercial total loss on the basis of her estimated values in sound condition and as scrap. An example presented for the consideration of the Advisory Committee of the Association of Average Adjusters in 1981/1982 will demonstrate the position:

[27] e.g. see the discussions in *Kennedy's Law of Salvage*, 5th edn, paras 1050–1059 in the British Shipping Laws Series.

[28] *The San Onofre* [1917] P. 96.

[29] *The Kia Ora* (1918) 252 Fed. Rep. 507.

[30] See *African S.S. Co v Swanzy* (1856) 2 K. & J. 660; *Grainger v Martin* (1862) 4 B. & S. 9. See also *The Harmonides* [1903] P. 1.

Estimated sound value of vessel, on completion of the adventure		1,000,000
Estimated net proceeds of sale as scrap on completion of the adventure		250,000
		750,000
Actual cost of repairs effected to damage caused by:		
Accident (Stranding)	375,000	
Sacrifice (Refloating)	900,000	
	1,275,000	> 750,000

Prima facie, the ship was not worth repairing, and unless it can be shown that some unusual or exceptional circumstances prevailed (for example part repairs already effected and unexpected damage revealed only on drydocking or opening up: or violent fluctuation in exchange rates affecting the expected cost of repairs), it must be assumed that the estimated sound value of the ship of 1,000,000 is suspect, and that the true value to the shipowner was much greater. On the basis that it was reasonable for the shipowner to effect repairs, the ship must have been worth to him in sound condition a minimum of:

Estimated scrap value	250,000
Repairs effected	1,275,000
Sound Value	1,525,000

Thus, the Advisory Committee were able to reach an unanimous opinion that the correct contributory value was:

Estimated scrap value	1,250,000
Add: made good	1,900,000
	1,150,000

Or, put in another way, to correspond with the normal method adopted on more routine cases:

Sound value (as above)	1,525,000
Deduct: repairs	1,275,000
	250,000
Add: made good	1,900,000
	1,150,000

Contributory Value less than Scrap Value

If the previous example may give the impression that the contributory value of the ship should never drop below her net scrap value, it must be stated that this can happen on occasion without the sound value assessed by an experienced ship valuer being in the least suspect. Assume, for example, a vessel with unchallengeable values as follows: **17.41**

Sound	1,000,000
Scrap	500,000

The vessel sustains severe accidental damage during the early part of a voyage and this is fully repaired at a port of refuge for 400,000. Having left the port of refuge, she has the misfortune to suffer another severe accident, repairs to which are effected at destination, again for 400,000.

Applying the fundamental principles set out in paras 17.12 to 17.13, above, and in the precise wording of r.XVII, below, the contributory value of the ship should be assessed at 200,000 (that is less than her scrap value of 500,000) and calculated as follows:

"Actual net value . . . at the termination of the adventure"	600,000
(i.e. sound value 1,000,000 less second repairs 400,000)	
"Deduction being also made from the value of the property of all extra charges incurred in respect thereof subsequently to the general average act"	400,000
(i.e. The first repairs at the port of refuge)	
Contributory value	200,000

This is the only benefit conferred on the owner of the ship by the first general average act; had the ship been totally lost at that time (of the first accident), the shipowner would have lost his ship worth, sound 1,000,000 but would have saved the cost of repairing the

First damage.	400,000	
Second damage	400,000	
	800,000	800,000
		200.000

If neither of the two damages had been repaired before arrival at destination, the contributory value could not be less than her arrived and scrap value of 500,000, for it would not then be reasonable to effect any repairs, but in the particular circumstances of the example above, the repairs on both occasions would be reasonably effected as their individual costs of 400,000 were less than the difference between the sound and scrap values.

Adjustment for Duration of Repairs

17.42 If a vessel will be under repair and out of commission for six months, this will clearly affect the price that any-prospective purchaser would be willing to pay for her. If two vessels were for sale, identical in every respect except that one can be traded immediately and the other only in six months' time, it is reasonably obvious that a lesser price will be paid for the latter. It is submitted, therefore, that where a lengthy period of repairs is involved, this is a factor which should be taken into consideration when assessing her value in damaged condition.

The point might also be raised that ship values can change dramatically in six months, but it must be reiterated that for general average purposes the value of the vessel must be assessed as at the time of the termination of the adventure, and not on the basis of reported sales of similar vessels six months later when the repairs were completed.

Even assuming a static ship sale market during a six months period under repair, any prospective purchaser of such a damaged vessel would surely take into account interest at current rates on the purchase price and his subsequent outlay on repairs in assessing the price he was willing to pay for that damaged vessel.

If, for example, a similar vessel in sound condition might change hands at 10,000,000, the sort of calculations which would be likely to run through the mind of a prospective purchaser might include the following:

Notional present sound value of vessel		10,000,000
Deduct: repair costs (3 equal instalments payable in 2, 4 and 6 months)		6,000,000
		4,000,000
Deduct: Interest at 12 per cent p.a. on repair cost instalments:		
2,000,000 for 4 months	80,000	
2,000,000 for 2 months	40,000	
	120,000	
		120,000
		3,120,000
		3,880,000
Present purchase price 100/106 per cent		3,660,377

Set out in an alternative manner to build up to that anticipated sound value of 10,000,000 in six months' time:

Present purchase price, as above	3,660,377
Interest thereon for six months @ 12 per cent p.a.	219,623
Repair costs	6,000,000
Interest on progress payments for repair	120.000
	10,000,000

Containers

The containers themselves generally do not form part of the ship's permanent equipment and, whether owned by the shipping line, leasing company or slot charterers they contribute as a separate interest. The York-Antwerp Rules will apply if the containers are carried subject to a contract providing for the Rules. Having regard to the large number of containers carried on board, their different types, ages, and condition of depreciation, the assessment of contributory values is a matter of some difficulty. **17.43**

In a Report dated August 29, 1975, the Advisory Committee of the Association of Average Adjusters considered that the method most correct in principle was to adopt the current replacement cost, less depreciation for age etc. However, on grounds of simplicity, they suggested that insured values could well be adopted. In the majority of container ship cases the usual practice is to adopt the values used by leading insurers for standard types of containers, and such values will usually also be adopted for the purposes of a salvage arbitration. Some specialist containers, particularly those designed for the bulk carriage of liquids and chemicals, can have comparatively high values which may merit closer attention by the adjuster.

Bunkers

17.44 Whether owned by the shipowner or by a time-charterer, bunkers remaining on board the vessel at the completion of the adventure and which were on board at the time of the general average act should contribute as a separate interest to any general average. They contribute on their value at the time and place where the adventure ends, plus any amount made good in general average for bunkers previously consumed (or sacrificed) during any resort to a port of refuge, etc.

Where the vessel is engaged under time charter and, as is customary under such charters, the time charterer provides the bunkers, it has always been the practice to treat these bunkers as a separate contributing interest. The practice with regard to bunkers that are the property of the shipowner has been less uniform. The reported values for ship sales on which the ship valuer will primarily base his opinion, are customarily exclusive of bunkers and unbroached stores for which a separate price may be agreed. There is therefore a danger that a significant part of the total contributory values may be missed if the valuer's figure alone is used, without enquiry into the quantity and value of bunkers on board at the material time. It is accepted that the valuer's figure implies an accuracy that cannot actually be achieved short of selling the vessel, and some adjusters have felt that calculating a separate figure for bunkers simply compounds this misleading impression. However, except in cases involving relatively low percentage levels of contribution, the difference can be material and other interests would be entitled to object if the value of bunkers is not properly accounted for.

It should also be noted that when a vessel is engaged under time charter, she is generally placed "off-hire" during any time lost as the result of, for instance, a general average deviation and detention, and the bunkers consumed during that period are debited by the time-charterer to the shipowner. Any amount "made good" in general average for bunkers consumed during this period is accordingly credited to the party out-of-pocket for the expense–that is the shipowner. However, the bunkers still remain the property of the time-charterer and it is he who will be called upon to pay the general average contribution attaching to the amount made good. This practice was confirmed by the Advisory Committee of the Association of Average Adjusters in their Report No.37, dated April 15, 1977.

The Ship and York-Antwerp Rule XVII

17.45 In any general average subject to the York-Antwerp Rules the contributory value of the ship is assessed in accordance with the fundamental principles outlined in paras 17.11 to 17.15, above, and the general remarks in para.17.33, above, that is, it contributes on its net sale proceeds or free market value at the time and place when and where the adventure ends. From this value is deducted the cost of any repairs already carried out subsequent to the general average act, and any sum made good in general average for damage to the ship is added.

The only special provisions in r.XVII relating particularly to the ship are to be found in the following three places:

End of first paragraph, paragraph a(iii) in 2004 Rules

"The value of the ship shall be assessed without taking into account the beneficial or detrimental effect of any demise or time charterparty to which the ship may be committed": This proposal to assess the contributory value of a ship free of charter commitments was made by the Norwegian delegation in the interests of international uniformity and was carried by a large majority at the Hamburg Conference in 1974. A discussion on the reason for this provision has already been given in paras 17.35 to 17.37, above. 17.46

It is also to be noted that:

(1) The beneficial or detrimental effect on the value of a ship secured by existing fixtures on a voyage basis for voyages subsequent to that on which the general average occurred would also be ignored in practice.
(2) In salvage cases, the courts and arbitrators of any country may still take account of the effect of these time charterparties in valuing the salved property and assess their awards accordingly. Any distribution they decide on must be reviewed in the general average adjustment, and the total award for salvage be apportioned in accordance with r.VI over the contributory values determined in the manner provided by this r.XVII.

End of second paragraph, paragraph (b) in 2004 Rules

"(except such charges as . . .) fall upon the ship by virtue of an award for special compensation under Art. 14 of the International Convention on Salvage, 1989 or under any other provision similar in substance": Article 14 of the International Convention on Salvage provides that where the value of the property salved is insufficient to provide an adequate reward to salvors for their services, but those services have prevented or minimised damage to the environment, special compensation shall be paid by the shipowner to the salvors. It is specifically provided in r.VI(b) of the York-Antwerp Rules that such special compensation shall not be allowed in general average, and the wording under discussion was added to r.XVII in 1994 to prevent any award for special compensation under the International Convention on Salvage (or similar provisions) ranking as a deduction from the contributory value of the ship. 17.47

Third paragraph, paragraph (c) in 2004 Rules

"In the circumstances envisaged in the third paragraph of Rule G, . . . the ship shall contribute upon its actual net value at the time of completion of 17.48

discharge of cargo": (at the port of refuge) See the commentary in para.17.31 above, relating to cargo; this is the comparable addition relating to the ship, and is self-explanatory.

FREIGHT

General Remarks

17.49 The term "freight" is a wide one capable of many meanings but in its simplest form it is the remuneration payable for the carriage of goods by sea in a ship. It is sufficiently wide to comprise the payment made under a bill of lading or a voyage charterparty, or the hire paid under a time charterparty[31]; it can also include the profit derivable by a shipowner from the employment of his ship to carry his own goods or movables, but it does not include passage money.[32] Freight may be at risk to the carrier and payable only upon right delivery at destination, or it may be pre-paid absolutely, ship and/or cargo lost or not lost, or it may be partly pre-paid and partly at risk. On a voyage basis, it may be charged on the tonnage or volume of cargo loaded, or even on a lump-sum basis, and, in the case of time charters, on the vessel's deadweight cargo-carrying capacity at a rate per ton per month.

The variations are endless, and it is not uncommon to find that a ship is operating under several forms of freight contract at one and the same time. For instance, a shipowner may hire his vessel to a charterer on a time basis: the time charterer may sublet the vessel on a voyage charter-party basis: and the sub-charterer may operate the vessel "on the berth" and issue bills of lading under some of which the freight is pre-paid absolutely, whilst others may provide for freight to be payable only on right delivery.

17.50 Having regard to these many types of freight and the manner in which it is paid, it will be appreciated that the subject of when freight should contribute to general average and on what value can be complex. However, before dealing with the complexities it may be helpful to state the general principles.

Where freight at risk to the carrier

As a separate interest in its own right, freight contributes in general average when, and only when, it is at risk to the carrier at the time of the general average act, and is earned or made good.

Where freight pre-paid[33]

17.51 Where the freight has been earned by the time of the general average act it does not contribute as a separate interest, but is treated as part of the value of the goods,

[31] See paras 17.64 et seq., below.
[32] Marine Insurance Act 1906 s.90.
[33] The word "pre-paid" is used in the text as a shorthand expression to describe any freight which is not at the risk of the carrier at the time of the general average act. As to the circumstances in which freight is at the risk of the carrier, see para.17.53, below.

with the result that it is the cargo owner who will effectively bear the contribution.[34] This was decided in *Frayes v Worms*[35] where it was held that the charterer, who was also the owner of the goods at the time of the general average act. was liable to contribute in respect of pre-paid freight, because, in the words of Byles J. "in substance the goods are augmented in value by the pre-payment he has made".[36] The modern approach, exemplified by the York-Antwerp Rules, is simply to treat pre-paid freight as an element in the value of the cargo rather than as a contributing interest.

When vessel engaged under several freight contracts

Where the vessel is operating under more than one freight engagement, the question whether, and the amount on which, freight contributes (or is contributed for) is governed by the terms of that contract which is most immediate to the cargo owners themselves. **17.52**

If the immediate contract between the carrier and the cargo provides for the freight to be pre-paid, any antecedent charter arrangements will be ignored for general average contribution purposes and, for instance, the shipowner would not be required to contribute to a general average in respect of freight at risk to him and payable by a charterer only on right delivery. The only relevance of antecedent charters is that, where freight is at risk to the carrier under the immediate contract with the cargo owners, and is therefore a contributing interest, the shipowner would be obliged to participate in the contribution, in respect of charterparty freight at risk to him.

When is Freight at the Risk of the Carrier?

As will be clear from the above, it is essential to determine whether freight is at the risk of the carrier or of the cargo owner at the time of the general average act. For a full discussion of this subject reference should be made to the works on carriage by sea.[37] However, the principles may be summarised as follows: **17.53**

(1) The basic rule is that freight is earned and payable only on right and true delivery of the cargo. Thus it is effectively at the carrier's risk throughout the adventure.
(2) The rule is frequently modified by express terms of the bill of lading or charterparty which advance the date at which freight (or part of it) is earned, and/or the date at which it is payable (for example a term that freight shall be deemed earned on signing bills of lading, and payable 10 days after signature). Whilst the question is always one of the interpretation of the contract as a whole, it will generally be true to say that once

[34] Because he will contribute on the arrived value of the goods, without deduction of freight: see para.17.29, above.
[35] *Frayes v Worms* (1865) 19 C.B. (N.S.) 159.
[36] *Frayes* (1865) 19 C.B. (N.S.) 159 at 177.
[37] e.g. *British Shipping Laws*, 13th edn, Vol.2: Carver, *Carriage by Sea*, paras 1661–1702.

the date arrives at which freight is either earned or payable[38] it will cease to be at the risk of the carrier, and will thereafter be an element in the value of the goods for the purpose of general average. Thus in the example given immediately above, freight will cease to be at the risk of the carrier as soon as the bills of lading are issued, although not payable for a further 10 days.

(3) Freight is payable in full even if the cargo is damaged on delivery, provided that it retains its "specie" or commercial identity.[39] This rule is unaffected by a term providing for payment "on right and true delivery", which is taken to mean delivery to the right person and at the right place. Thus so long as the goods retain their commercial identity freight will contribute in full.

We may now proceed to consider in more detail the circumstances in which freight contributes in general average under various types of freight engagement, and the contributory value of such freights.

When Cargo on Board

If wholly pre-paid

17.54 If the freight has been wholly pre-paid.[40] then the risk in that freight rests not with the carrier but with the owner of the cargo. As such, the freight becomes merged in the value of the cargo and does not contribute as a separate entity.

[38] For the general principle see *Allison v Bristol Marine Insurance* (1879) 1 App. Cas. 209. Many of the older cases discuss the question whether a prepayment is a mere loan to the carrier, and thus repayable if the freight is not earned by delivery of the cargo, or is a true (or "absolute") payment of freight, in which case the risk is transferred to the cargo owner. A pre-payment will be regarded as falling into the former category only if the terms of the contract indicate that it remains at carrier's risk, or if there is nothing in the contract to indicate that the pre-payment is a payment of or on account of freight. The present editors have not encountered any modern form of bill of lading or charterparty where a provision for pre-payment could be construed as amounting merely to a loan.

For modern applications of the rule see: *Campania Naviera General SA v Kerametal* [1981] 2 Lloyd's Rep. 559; [1983] 1 Lloyd's Rep. 373, CA "Freight non-returnable cargo and/or vessel lost or not lost . . . to be paid . . . 75 per cent within five days after the master signed bills of lading and the balance on right and true delivery." Vessel and cargo lost in a storm within five days of signing bills of lading. Held: no freight payable.

Vagres Cia Maritima v Nissho Iwai [1988] 2 Lloyd's Rep. 330. "Freight deemed earned as cargo loaded," 95 per cent to be paid in advance and balance after completion of discharge. Vessel and cargo lost after cargo loaded and advance freight paid. Held: balance was payable although discharge never took place.

Bank of Boston v European Grain & Shipping [1989] 2 W.L.R. 440. "Freight deemed earned on signing bills of lading," payable five days after surrender of the bills. After signing the bills, but (probably) before freight became payable, the carrier wrongfully abandoned the voyage. Held: freight was earned and payable.

[39] See *Dakin v Oxley* (1864) 15 C.B. (N.S.) 646; *Asfar v Blundell* [1896] 1 Q.B. 123; *Montedison v Icroma* [1980] 1 Lloyd's Rep. 91.

[40] See para.17.51, above.

If wholly at carriers risk

If the payment of freight, whether under a bill of lading or voyage charterparty, is made conditional upon the arrival and delivery of cargo at destination, it is clear that the rescuing of the ship and cargo from total loss confers upon the carrier an advantage to the extent of the amount of freight that is at risk and earned, less those expenses incurred subsequent to the general average act to earn that freight and which he would have escaped if the adventure had been totally lost. This difference represents the contributory value of the freight in such a case.[41] **17.55**

If partly pre-paid and partly at risk

As already mentioned, freight for any voyage may be partly pre-paid and partly at risk. Thus, in the case of a general cargo, some of the bills of lading may evidence that the freight has been wholly pre-paid and/or is payable "ship and/or cargo lost or not lost", while other bills of lading may evidence that the freight is payable only on right delivery at destination. In the case of a voyage charterparty, part of the freight may be pre-paid, with the balance at risk to the carrier, and the situation may be the same even under individual bills of lading, for example 90 per cent may be payable within seven days of signing the bill of lading and the balance on right delivery at destination, etc. **17.56**

Whenever any part of the freight is at risk, only that part of the freight contributes to any general average, and its contributory value is calculated by deducting the full expenses of earning the whole freight, as detailed in para.17.69.

Deductions from freight earned

These may comprise the cost of: **17.57**

(1) crew's wages and other benefits from the time of the general average act until completion of discharge at the final port of destination or other port where the voyage is abandoned;
(2) provisions for the crew purchased subsequent to the general average act and consumed before the termination of the adventure as in (1) above;
(3) bunkers and stores purchased subsequent to the general average act and consumed before the termination of the adventure as in (1) above (the cost of bunkers may include, on occasion, a proportion of the port charges at the bunkering port);
(4) canal dues, light dues, pilots, tugs and other port charges at all ports of call necessary for the current cargo voyage and until the termination of the adventure as in (1) above (the cost of entering a last port of discharge forms a proper deduction from the contributory value of the freight, but not the cost of leaving that port);

[41] See per Gorell Barnes J. in *The Brigella* [1893] P. 189 at 196.

(5) discharging cargo at the various ports of discharge, unless payable by the cargo interests under an FIO contract,

except such of the above charges as have been allowed as general average.

17.58 The Rule of Practice of the Association of Average Adjusters dealing in general terms with the contributory value of freight is r.F22, as follows:

> "*Contributory Value of Freight*
> That freight at the risk of the shipowner shall contribute to general average upon its gross amount, deducting such charges and crew's wages as would not have been incurred in earning the freight had the ship and cargo been totally lost at the date of the general average act and have not been allowed as general average."

When the Vessel is in Ballast

Under voyage charterparty

17.59 It is universally accepted that freight which is at risk to the carrier shall contribute to a general average occurring when the cargo is on board, but there is no such unanimity with regard to the freight due to be earned and contracted for under the terms of a voyage charterparty whilst the vessel is proceeding in ballast to the loading port. In most countries, such freight is ignored[42] as a contributing interest to any general average (if a general average situation be admitted at all), or assumed to be comprised within the value of the ship. However, in those countries where English law applies, provided that the vessel has sailed and is proceeding on the voyage described in the charterparty, the freight earned under the terms of that contract will be brought in as a separate contributing interest to any general average occurring on a preliminary ballast passage to the loading port.

English law

17.60 In the case of *S.S. Carisbrook Co v London and Provincial Marine Insurance Co*,[43] the facts were that a vessel was chartered to proceed from England to Savannah, and there, having discharged her cargo (if any), to load a cargo of cotton and proceed therewith to Liverpool, Manchester or Bremen. She sailed in ballast from Fleetwood to Savannah, and in the course of the voyage a general average sacrifice was made. She subsequently arrived at Savannah, loaded her cargo, and earned her freight by completing the voyage. The shipowners having sued the underwriters on the ship for a particular average loss, the underwriters contended that the shipowners were liable to contribute as in general average[44] in

[42] Chartered freight docs not contribute in the United Slates if there was no cargo on board: see Rule of Practice, No.14 and cf. *The Brig Mary* (1842) 1 Sprague 17. There is a resolution of the French Association of Average Adjusters to the like effect.

[43] *S.S. Carisbrook Co v London and Provincial Marine Insurance Co* [1901] 2 K.B. 861; [1902] 2 K.B. 681, CA.

[44] Where the interests at risk are owned by the same person, so that there is no contribution, losses in the nature of general average must nevertheless be adjusted between him and his insurers as if the

respect of the chartered freight, and both Matthew J. and the Court of Appeal held on the authority of *Williams v London Assurance Co*,[45] that their contention was well founded. In the course of his judgment, Collins M.R. said[46]:

> "Looking at the matter in point of principle, and apart from authority, it would seem to me that the freight should be one of the contributories in such a case as this. The vessel in a round charter such as this is earning the only freight that is payable from the moment it breaks ground down to the time it delivers the cargo at the ultimate port; it is in process of earning that just as much before the goods are put on board as afterwards."

The earlier authorities on which the Carisbrook case was based were *Williams v London Assurance Co and The Progress*,[47] to which extended coverage was given in paras 427 to 428 of the 10th edn of this Work.

The effect of these legal decisions is summed up in Rule of Practice B26 of the Association of Average Adjusters, part of which reads as follows: **17.61**

> *"Vessel in Ballast and under Charier: Contributing Interests*
> For the purpose of ascertaining the liability of Underwriters on British[48] policies of insurance, the following provisions shall apply:
> When a vessel is proceeding in ballast to load under a voyage charter entered into by the shipowner before the general average act, the interests contributing to the general average shall be the vessel, such items of stores and equipment as belong to parties other than the owners of the vessel (e.g. bunkers, wireless installation and navigational instruments) and the freight earned under the voyage charter computed in the usual way after deduction of contingent expenses subsequent to the general average act. Failing a prior termination of the adventure, the place where the adventure shall be deemed to end and at which the values for contribution to general average shall be calculated is the final port of discharge of the cargo carried under the charter but in the event of the prior loss of the vessel and freight, or either of them, the general average shall attach to any surviving interest or interests including freight advanced at the loading port deducting therefrom contingent expenses subsequent to the general average act."

Deductions from freight earned

For the purpose of calculating the contributory value of freight to a general average occurring when the vessel is proceeding in ballast to a loading port under the terms of a voyage charterparty, all those expenses borne by the carrier detailed in para.17.57, above, may be deducted, and also: "(6) the cost of loading the cargo and all port charges entering, leaving, and at the port(s) of loading". **17.62**

interests were owned by different parties *Montgomery v Indemnity Mutual Marine Insurance Co* [1902] 1 K.B. 734, C.A.; Marine Insurance Act 1906 s.66(7).

45 *Williams* (1813) 1 M. & S. 318.

46 *S.S. Carisbrook* [1902] 2 K.B. 681 at 690.

47 *The Progress* (1810) 1 Edw. 210.

48 It must be stressed that the rule applies only to claims on British policies of insurance.

Future chartered freight

17.63 In his endeavours to secure profitable employment for his ship, it frequently occurs that an owner will fix his vessel to load cargoes for one or more voyages subsequent to that on which she is currently engaged. Although contracted for the freights earned on these subsequent voyages are not brought in as separate entities to contribute to any general average occurring on the current voyage. The Rule of Practice of the Association of Average Adjusters on this subject is B27, as follows:

> "*Chartered Freight (Ulterior): Contribution to General Average*
> That when at the time of a general average act the vessel has on board cargo shipped under charterparty or bills of lading, and is also under a separate charter to load another cargo after the cargo then in course of carriage has been discharged, the ulterior chartered freight shall not contribute to the general average."

It is submitted that this Rule of Practice reflects the law[49] and is correct in principle, although inconsistent with the judgment in *Norson v Jones*,[50] for ulterior freight is not a party to the common adventure in respect of which general average is to be adjusted. In this respect it can be distinguished from the homeward freight of a round voyage which does of course contribute.[51] The only occasion upon which it might be taken into account under adjustments prepared in accordance with English law, and that only indirectly, is if the value of the ship is increased by having future fixtures at a rate of freight above the market rate. Where the adjustment is governed by the York-Antwerp Rules, it is submitted that these future fixtures would be ignored.

Time Charters

17.64 By custom, freight has always been considered to be payable on a voyage basis, but many vessels are engaged on a long-term or time basis (for example six or 12 months: seven or 15 years) and payment is made on a daily or monthly hire basis, regardless of whether the vessel is in ballast or loaded, the quantity of cargo carried, or the nature or number of voyages undertaken during the period of the time charter. The essential feature of any time charter for this purpose is that payment—or hire—is earned on a daily or monthly basis; so that a charter for a round voyage at so much per month would be treated as a time charter. But a

[49] e.g. the remarks of: (1) Lord Stowell in *The Progress* (1810) 1 Edw. A.R. 210, "If there had been two distinct voyages, as is sometimes the case in charterparties, distinguishing the outward from the homeward voyage, the case would have assumed a different aspect"; (2) Collins M.R. in *S.S. Carisbrook Co v London and Provincial Marine Insurance Co* (1902) 2 K.B. 681, CA, "No doubt there are differences of convenience when there is a cargo carried to the intermediate port as distinguished from the case where no cargo is carried to the intermediate port, and if cargo is carried under a charter which entitles the ship to a freight at the intermediate port, one can easily understand why the average adjusters should make a difference and limit the contribution in respect of such an average sacrifice, on what I may call the first part of the voyage, to the freight which was to be earned at the first port where the cargo was to be discharged."

[50] *Norson v Jones* (1857) 7 E. & B. 523.

[51] See para.17.59, above.

charter for 12 months, to perform as many voyages as possible and with freight payable on a voyage basis, would be treated as a voyage charter, and freight for subsequent voyages thereunder as ulterior freight within the principle stated above.

Time-charter hire

If a vessel is time-chartered for a number of years, to be at the absolute disposal of the charterer, and the charterer employs her to make a series of voyages, carrying perhaps 20 different cargoes in the time, is the total hire under the charter to contribute to a general average that may occur on, say, the first of these voyages? **17.65**

This is a case in which it is difficult to separate the freight from the value of the ship. The value of this vessel to her owner is made up of two ingredients—the freight he is to receive for the period during which she has been hired, and the value now of a vessel which is not to come into his possession for any purpose of profit, until the end of the charter period.[52]

For this reason, time-charter hire due to a shipowner, or time-chartered owner, is not treated as a contributing interest in its own right, although shipowner and disponent owner may be obliged to participate in making any contribution in respect of voyage freights under a bill of lading or sub-charterparty.

Voyage freights when vessel under time charter

The practice with regard to voyage freights, when the ship is operating under a time charter, is as follows.

When cargo on board. In accordance with the principles already set out[53] the time charterer (or, where the vessel is sub-chartered, the sub-charterer who is the party to the immediate contract with cargo interests) will contribute on freight due to him from the cargo interests and at risk. Contribution will be calculated in the manner set out in para.17.45, above, and will be sub-divided between the parties in the manner illustrated in para.17.94, below. **17.66**

When in ballast. The rule[54] under English law that freight becomes a contributing interest from the moment that the vessel breaks ground on the approach voyage provided for in the charter does not apply in practice when the vessel is operating under a time charterparty. In such a case, therefore, neither the time-charter hire nor any voyage freight in the course of being earned by the time charterer is brought in to contribute to the general average as a separate entity. This is laid down as part of r.B26 of the Association of Average Adjusters: **17.67**

> "... When a vessel is proceeding in ballast under a time charter alone or a time charter and a voyage charter entered into by the time charterer, the general average shall attach to the vessel and such items of stores and equipment as are indicated above. Failing a prior termination of the adventure, the adventure shall be deemed to

[52] See para.17.36, above.
[53] See paras 17.50–17.58, above.
[54] See paras 17.59–17.61, above.

end and the values for contribution to general average calculated at the first loading port upon the commencement of loading cargo. . . . In practice neither time charter hire, as such, nor time charterer's voyage freight shall contribute to general average."

Passage Money

17.68 Passage money, being usually paid in advance and not liable to be refunded if the ship is lost, is not made to contribute: but in cases where passengers were carried at so much a head payable on arrival, the passage money was in English practice, said Lowndes, made to contribute.[55]

FREIGHT AND YORK-ANTWERP RULE XVII

17.69 Rule XVII (second paragraph) deals with freight in the following terms:

> "deduction being made from the freight and passage money at risk of such charges and crew's wages as would not have been incurred in earning the freight had the ship and cargo been totally lost at the date of the general average."

This provision is exclusively concerned with the contributing value of freight, rather than with defining the circumstances in which freight contributes at all. It follows that the latter question will depend upon the law governing the adjustment, and when English law applies the position will be as described in paras 17.53 to 17.63, above. Thus, for example:

(1) Freight will universally be called upon to contribute as a separate entity to general average when it is in respect of cargo already on board ship at the time of the general average act and is at risk to the carrier. Whether freight at risk to the carrier under a voyage charter party will be brought in to contribute to a general average occurring while the vessel is proceeding in ballast to a loading port will depend on the law and practice governing the adjustment.[56] In places where English law prevails or is followed, such freight will contribute: in others such as the United States and France, it will not.

(2) Where the vessel is operating under a time charter, the liability to contribute will be as described in paras 17.64, 17.67, above.

17.70 **". . . the freight and passage money at risk . . .":** The wording reflects the principle, already stated in para.17.50, above, that it is only freight at risk to the carrier at the time of the general average that is a contributing interest.

As mentioned in para.17.49, above, a ship may be operating under numerous forms of freight contract at one and the same time, but in any chain of contracts it

[55] Lowndes, 4th edn, Appendix O, p.636.
[56] See paras 30.02 *et seq.*, below.

is the freight payment terms in the contract which is most immediate to the cargo owners themselves which will govern whether that freight should contribute to a general average. If the freight under that "final" contract is pre-paid, it will not be called upon to contribute and any freights or time-charter hire at risk to earlier operators in the chain will be ignored. However, if that final freight is at risk to the carrier and brought in to contribute, there may be a sub-division of the contributory value between the various operators in the chain as detailed in the example in para.17.94, below.

It will be noted that passage money is also mentioned, but this is rarely at risk.

"deduction being made . . . of such charges and crew's wages as would not have been incurred in earning the freight had the ship and cargo been totally lost at the date of the general average act and have not been allowed as general average": This wording is a mere re-statement of a fundamental principle in assessing any contributory value, as discussed earlier in para.17.14. The types of charges likely to be deductible, and the English Rule of Practice F22, are set out in paras 17.57,17.58, above. **17.71**

Mails, Passengers' Luggage, Personal Effects and Accompanied Private Motor Vehicles

General Remarks

The concluding fifth para. of r.XVII[57] makes special provision exempting these particular properties from liability to contribute to any general average, but in the absence of such provision, the position under English law (if any) and the commercial practice would generally be as follows. **17.72**

Mails

On principle, there seems to be no reason why articles of pecuniary value carried by post should not contribute, and there is no English authority to prevent the collection of general average contributions from mails. However, it is believed that in practice articles carried under a mail contract have never been made to contribute. A sufficient reason for the exemption of ordinary correspondence is that letters cannot have a definite pecuniary value. On principle, indeed, there seems to be no reason why articles of pecuniary value carried by post should not contribute, though it is unlikely that the mail contract will include agreement to the application of the York-Antwerp Rules. There are also almost insuperable practical difficulties in the way of enforcing a lien on, and valuing, mails and tracing the owners. In practice, the appropriate allowance in general average is made for loss of or damage to mails by a general average act and the amount so made good is brought in as a contributory factor, but no contribution is customarily levied on mails, not so lost **17.73**

[57] See para.17.11, below.

or damaged. However, if the circumstances warrant it and the amount justifies the trouble involved, there is no English authority to prevent the collection of general average contributions from mails.

Passengers' Luggage and Personal Effects

17.74 If the doctrine that only goods put on board as merchandise are liable to contribute is accepted as the rule of English law,[58] it follows that all the effects of a passenger are exempt[59]: and the general practice in this country seems to have been to exempt them. If passengers' effects were to be held liable to contribution, the liability would be restricted to such effects as are stowed in the baggage had, thus exempting the property which the passenger retains in his own care for use on the voyage, and which, in this sense, is attached to his person.[60] Yet there are practical objections even to this limited responsibility. It must often be difficult, if not impossible, at the time of disembarkation to obtain a proper valuation of the effects of each passenger to fix the amount of his contribution, and to enforce payment or exact security for the claim; and after the passengers have left the ship and dispersed, a right of action only enforceable by a number of separate law-suits, most of them for trifling amounts, would be an illusory remedy. Thus the right to contribution from passengers would in most cases probably resolve itself into a claim for damages against the shipowner, for failing to enforce the right on behalf of the party whose property has been sacrificed.[61]

It is submitted that the best solution is to ascertain whether the articles are: (1) carried as "goods" under a contract of affreightment; or (2) carried as incidental to a contract for the carriage of a passenger.[62] In (1) the goods contribute and receive in the ordinary way; in (2) the articles do not contribute, but probably receive contribution if damaged by a general average act.

Passengers' Accompanied Private Motor Vehicles

17.75 The accompanying "luggage" of a passenger on a ferry will often include a car–and even a caravan—for his personal use and transportation after disembarking from the ship. These private motor vehicles can have considerable value, and this will clearly be taken into account in any award to salvors unless carried out under a contract such as Lloyd's Standard Form of Salvage Agreement (LOF

[58] *Brown v Stapyleton* (1827) 4 Bing. 119; 12 J. B. Moore 334, quoted in para.17.86, below.

[59] See Abbott, 5th edn, p.356; Stevens, p.44. Benecke, however, maintained (p.308) that passengers ought to contribute for their trunks and luggage, and Beawes (6th edn, p.243) limited the exemption to apparel in use.

[60] In *The Willem III* (1871) L.R. 3 A. & E. 487, Sir Robert Phillimore held that the wearing apparel of passengers and other effects carried by them for their daily personal use were not liable to pay salvage; and it was admitted that wares or merchandise belonging to them were liable to contribute.

Lord Justice Kennedy considered (*Civil Salvage*, 2nd edn, p.59) that there was no legal principle for the exemption, from payment of salvage, of such luggage and valuables as are not in daily use and are in the custody of the ship (cf. 4th edn, p.383).

[61] See para.30.42, below.

[62] cf. per Day J. in *R. v Judge of City of London Court* (1883) 12 Q.B.D. 115.

2011) which excludes private motor vehicles as well as personal effects. On principle, there is no reason why such vehicles should not be called upon to contribute to any general average, but as a matter of general commercial practice passengers are rarely, if ever, called upon to contribute to any general average in respect of their accompanied cars and caravans. The delay, inconvenience and ill-will which would result if passengers were obliged to complete general average formalities before being allowed to drive from the ship and/or port of destination would generally far outweigh the value of any contribution paid by them.

Many "tickets" for the carriage of passengers' cars and caravans make no provision regarding general average, and whilst this does not preclude the levying of a general average contribution, any adjustment would have to be prepared in accordance with the law of destination: the York-Antwerp Rules could have no application.

Under the 1994 and 2004 York-Antwerp Rules the owners of accompanied private motor vehicles are freed from the requirement to contribute to any general average, and the notional contribution which could be said to apply to such property will now be shared by the ship and any other commercial property on board.

Mails and Passengers' Luggage, etc. and York-Antwerp Rule XVII

"Mails, passengers' luggage, personal effects and accompanied private motor vehicles shall not contribute in general average": 17.76

"Mails": These comprise letters and packages, etc. consigned by the official postal services or by a private enterprise carrier as part of a general consignment entrusted to that carrier by the public at large.

"passengers' luggage, personal effects": The belongings of a passenger contained in suitcases and bags, etc. plus those of his smaller possessions of a personal nature frequently worn, used or carried around, are comprised within these two terms. The previous qualification in r.XVII that such property was "not shipped under bill of loading" having been removed in 1994; it is now immaterial whether the luggage, etc. was for use on the voyage or not. However, the terms are probably insufficient to comprise accompanied personal property such as a container-load of furniture and household goods being transported to a new home, which therefore remain liable to contribute to any general average, and should be insured appropriately.

"accompanied private motor vehicles": It is submitted that the freedom from liability to contribute to a general average is intended to apply also to a caravan without motive power, provided only that it is accompanied by its towing vehicle and passengers.

The fact that the owners of the various properties detailed in this section of the rule are freed from any requirement to contribute in general average carries no reciprocal denial of the right of those owners to claim a contribution towards any general average loss or damage suffered by their property, for example by water used to extinguish a fire.[63] Nevertheless, and although unresolved by the rule, it is submitted that whatever amount is made good in general average for loss or damage to mails and passengers' luggage, etc. should contribute to that general average.

MISCELLANEOUS OTHER PROPERTIES

Lives of the Passengers and Crew

17.77 The lives which are preserved by the general average act are not brought in to contribute; by reason, it has been said, of the impossibility of assessing them at a pecuniary value.[64]

Wages of Master, Officers and Crew

17.78 The wages of the crew are referred to in many commercial codes, but always to exclude them from contribution, and this has been the long established custom in England also. In point of fact, this is a right not depending on custom, for since the Merchant Shipping Act of 1854,[65] their wages are no longer at risk to the crew and dependent on the successful completion of the voyage of the earning of freight.

Personal Effects of the Master, Officers and Crew

17.79 By custom and inveterate practice, these are never brought in to contribute to any general average and, indeed, if passengers are expressly exempted from any such liability in respect of their luggage and personal effects,[66] the officers and crew must have an even better claim to such exemption.[67]

Commercial Vehicles and their Loads

17.80 Casualties involving commercial vehicles carried on ro-ro services can give rise to additional complications because of the frequently different ownership of the motive "tractor" unit, the trailer carrying the goods and the goods themselves; often only the latter will have insurance cover appropriate to deal with a serious general average or salvage situation, so that the provision of security can cause difficulty and delay. Operators of such vessels will invariably have Absorption Clauses (see Section 7) in their hull policies which will avoid the need

[63] Unless the passenger ticket or conditions of carriage provide otherwise. These sometimes provide that baggage and personal effects not shipped under bill of lading shall neither contribute nor be contributed for in general average.

[64] *Park on Insurance*, 8th edn, p.293.

[65] 17 & 18 Vict., c.104. para.183.

[66] See para.17.76, above.

[67] *Heye v North German Lloyd* (1887) Fed. Rep. 60.

to collect contributions up to a specified level, however a major salvage claim or extensive extinguishing damage may easily exceed that threshold. If the contract of carriage makes no reference to the York-Antwerp Rules, the matter would have to be dealt with according to the law of destination so far as general average is concerned.

Bullion and Specie

By reason of its small bulk and great value, bullion or specie can often be removed to safety with comparative ease in a number of general average situations. In addition, its virtual indestructibility and immunity to damage means that there will often be good prospects for its recovery after a disaster, even from a sunken vessel. **17.81**

It has been suggested,[68] therefore, that bullion and specie are not subject to quite the same degree of risk or peril in any general average situation as are the ship and other parts of the cargo on board. Nevertheless, if on board ship throughout any general average situation, bullion and specie contribute on their full value, and the balance of authority is firmly against any special treatment in their favour.[69]

Jewels and Other Valuables

Jewels, precious stones and other small articles of great value, if shipped as cargo, must contribute.[70] When such articles are brought on board by a passenger as part of his effects, the extent to which they are exempted from contribution is variously stated by the textwriters.[71] If the correct rule be that only goods shipped as merchandise are liable to contribute,[72] there is no necessity to consider specially the case of jewels and other valuables. If, however, this be not the rule of English law, it seems obvious that valuables which are stowed away as part of a passenger's luggage ought to be treated in the same way as his other effects in the baggage compartment. Jewellery and other valuables which he retains in his own care for use or ornament during the voyage ought, it is submitted, to be exempt on the analogy of wearing apparel in use. It may be urged with some show of reason that other valuables which the passenger keeps in his own care ought to contribute, especially if he carries them for purposes of trade. Yet the practice not to exact **17.82**

68 e.g. *The Emma* (1844) 2 W.Rob. 315.

69 *The Longford* (1881) 6 P.D. 60, an approach favoured in *The M. Vatan* [1990] 1 Lloyd's Rep. 336.

70 *1 Park*, 8th edn, p.293; *Peters v Miligan* (1787), p.296; per Park J. in *Brown v Stapylelon*, para.17.86, below.

71 Beawes, 6th edn, p.243 says that money and jewels must contribute, and only exempts apparel in use. On the principle that what pays no freight, pays no average, Magens (Vol.1, p.62), and Stevens (p.44) exempt the jewellery as well as the apparel of passengers. Abbott (5th edn, p.356), says that jewels or other things belonging to the persons of passengers or crew, and taken on board for their private use and not for traffic, do not contribute. Arnould (Vol.2, 2nd edn, p.936) states that all small articles of value contribute, unless carried about the person, or forming part of the wearing apparel, but see *British Shipping Laws*, Vol.10: Arnould, *Marine Insurance*, 16th edn, para.972. Marshall (4th edn, p.432), exempts jewels or ornaments when belonging to the persons of the people on board.

72 See para.17.86, below.

contribution in respect of valuables in the passenger's own care, partly due, perhaps, to the difficulty of ascertaining their existence without resort to inquisitorial methods of an extreme kind, may be supported on the ground that they do not run the same risks as merchandise or luggage in the hold. For they can usually be saved with the person, and therefore incur no greater danger than the passengers themselves.

Bank Notes and Securities

17.83 Phillips is of opinion that bank notes ought not to contribute, as they "are not so properly actual property, to the amount promised to be paid, as the evidence of demands, which evidence may be supplied by others in case of their being lost".[73] Arnould, on the other hand, following Weskett, considered that they ought to contribute, on the ground that they are convertible into money, and are saved by the sacrifice from becoming valueless.[74] In practice, bank notes, when shipped as cargo, contribute on their paper and printing costs; but if, for example, they are stolen by salvors and presented, they are contributed for, and contribute, on their face value. Circulated bank notes in the shops, casinos, and banks on board passenger liners should similarly contribute on their face value though if there be no contract of affreightment their liability may need be governed by the law of destination rather than the York-Antwerp Rules. It is submitted that no other instrument or security ought to be made to contribute, the loss of which does not necessarily put an end to the obligation which it creates. Although at common law, according to the weight of authority, an action could not have been maintained on a bill or note which had been lost or destroyed, relief could have been obtained in equity when there was no remedy at common law[75] and now by statute in an action on a bill of exchange or other negotiable instrument the defendant will be prevented from setting up the loss of the instrument if a satisfactory indemnity be given him against other claims.[76]

Shops and Banks on Board Ship

17.84 The stock and cash in the shops on board ship, and the circulated cash or other valuables in the bank, are also brought in to contribute to general average: however, the liability may need be governed by the law of destination rather than the York-Antwerp Rules.

[73] 2 Phillips, para.1397.

[74] Arnould, Vol.2, 2nd edn, p.936, but the editors of the *British Shipping Laws*, Vols 9 & 10: Arnould, *Marine Insurance*, 16th edn, take a different view: see para.973; Weskeit. lit. Contrib. No.1.

[75] See *Hansard v Robinson* (1827) 7 B & C. 90; *Ramuz v Crowe* (1847) 1 Exch. 167; *Crowe v Clay* (1854) 9 Exch. 604: *Chitty Bills*, 11th edn, p.191.

[76] Bills or Exchange Act 1882 ss.70, 89: *King v Zimmerman* (1871) L.R. 6 C.P. 466; see also s.69 of that Act. No case has yet come to the editors' notice of a consignment of trading stamps; but see *Building and Civil Engineering Holidays Scheme v Post Office* [1966] 1 Q.B. 247.

Leased Equipment

Vessels may carry leased equipment for which they are responsible, for example temporary deck cranes or generators. The terms of the lease agreement will usually determine which party is responsible for the payment of general average and salvage. 17.85

Provisions and Stores

As already recorded in para.17.19, above, Lowndes wrote that "the unconsumed stores of a troop ship, or those laid in by a passenger charterer . . . should properly be brought in as contributing", and it is submitted that this must be correct in principle, and also in practice if the value of the stores unconsumed at the end of the voyage is sufficient to warrant the contribution. Nevertheless, the matter was decided other wise in the case of *Brown v Stapyleton*.[77] 17.86

The question in that case was whether provisions, and victualling stores, shipped by the defendants on a vessel which they had chartered for the conveyance of convicts to Australia, intended for the use of the convicts, but unconsumed at the time of the general average act, were liable to contribute. The Court of Common Pleas held that the claim could not be supported.

Best C.J.:

> "It is not every object of value which has been held liable to a contribution for average, but only such stores as are termed merces. Merces has never been held to extend to provisions, but includes only the cargo put on board for the purposes of commerce; and the practice shows that this has been the understanding of all times. Magens, Molloy, Stevens, and other writers, all expound the word 'merces' in this way; ail in terms exclude provisions. They concur in saying that things of light weight, but of considerable value, must contribute, if they belong to the cargo, but not if they belong to the passengers. Provisions are laid in for the passengers, and must be esteemed to belong to them."

Bingham's report of the judgment of Park J. leaves it doubtful whether the learned judge agreed unreservedly with the rule laid down by the Chief Justice; but Moore's report makes it clear that he assented to the proposition that only goods which are shipped as merchandise are liable to contribute. 17.87

Moore:

> "Provisions have always been held to be excepted from the rule of contribution, which only applies to merchandise put on board for the purpose of traffic. In the term merchandise is included jewels and articles of like nature, not being the wearing apparel or ornaments of the passengers, but the subject of traffic."[78]

[77] *Brown v Stapyleton* (1827) 4 Bing. 119; 12 J.B. Moore, 334.

[78] (1827) 12 J. B. Moore, p.338. Phillips (Vol.2, para.1399) said that the assumption in this case that only goods which are merces contribute, is erroneous, or at least very questionable.

If the claim to contribution had been allowed, it would have been based only on the value of the stores unconsumed at the end of the voyage.

Double General Averages

17.88 On occasion, the properties involved in a common maritime adventure may have the misfortune to be involved in two (or more) general averages on the same voyage. The contributory values for each general average will be calculated separately, and in accordance with the general principles outlined in paras 17.12 to 17.13, above, or the precise wording of r.XVII (paras 17.10, 17.11, above). In practical terms, this means that the contributory values for the second general average must be calculated first, and the proportion of that second general average deducted in arriving at the contributory values for the first general average. This on the principle that if the adventure had been totally lost at the time of the first general average, the expenses of the second general average would have been avoided.

As a simple example, let it be assumed that a

SHIP with a sound value of	6,000,000
loads CARGO for a Port A worth	7,000,000
and for Port B worth	5,000,000
Total Sound Values.	18,000,000

General Average No.1. Whilst proceeding to Port A, the vessel sustains a complete main engine breakdown and is salved into a port of refuge where repairs to the ship costing 400,000 are effected. The total of the salvage and other general average expenses amounts to 780,000

General Average No.2. Having discharged her cargo at A and resumed the voyage to B. the vessel is involved in a collision whereby the ship sustains damage costing 600,000 to repair, and the cargo in one of the holds damage to the extent of 400,000. The total of the salvage and other general average expenses amounts to 1,000,000

GENERAL AVERAGE NO.2 APPORTIONED

SHIP on sound value		6,000,000		
Less: Damage No.2		600,000		
. . . .		5,400,000	pays	540,000
CARGO b on sound value	5,000,000			
Less: Damage, ...	400,000			
	4,600,000	4,600,000	pays	460,000
		10,000,000	pays	1,000,000
				= 10 per cent

GENERAL AVERAGE NO.1 APPORTIONED

SHIP on "Net" destination value (as above)	5,400,000

Less: Damage No.1	400,000			
Ppn. 2nd G.A.				
(as above)......................	540,000			
	940,000	940,000		
		4,460,000	pays	223,000
CARGO A on sound value................		7,000,000	pays	350,000
CARGO B on destination value				
(as above).......................	4,460,000			
Less: Ppn. 2nd G.A. (as above),	460,000			
	4,140,000	4,140,000	pays	207,000
		15,600,000	pays	780,000
				= 5 per cent

Solely for the purpose of demonstrating the principle, the whole of the proportions of the second general average have been deducted from the damaged values of the ship and cargo B in order to arrive at their contributory values for the first general average. In practice, however, correct principle requires that only the proportions of the second general average, excluding commission and interest, should be deducted. These particular items are really book-keeping devices to achieve a greater equality of sacrifice between the parties to the adventure, and do not affect the values of the properties. It would be wrong for cargo A to pay a varying proportion of the first general average, dependent simply on whether it took a short or long time to prepare the adjustment. **17.89**

On occasion, a general average situation may arise from a single accident, but where the port of refuge happens to be the intended destination for part of the cargo. For example, a vessel loaded with cargo for ports A and B is involved in a serious collision shortly before arrival at port A and she is salved into that port. Cargo for port A is discharged in the normal way, whereafter the vessel is detained undergoing repairs necessary for the safe prosecution of the voyage to port B. **17.90**

The award for salvage and costs, etc. amounts to	1,200,000
The port of refuge general average expenses to...............	400,000
Total general average................................	1,600,000

Cargo A must clearly contribute to the salvage award, etc. but it does not contribute to general average expenses incurred after it has been discharged, and with the object of completing a voyage in which it has no interest. These port of refuge expenses fall solely upon the ship and cargo B.

In practice the general average would be shown as follows: **17.91**

	GENERAL AVERAGE Payable by:	
	ALL INTERESTS	SHIP AND CARGO B
Salvage award and costs etc.	1,200,00	
Port of refuse expenses		400.000
	1200,000	400,000

					APPORTIONED		TOTAL
SHIP ON	600,000	pays …	360,000	+	240.000	=	600,000
CARGO B ON	400,000	pays …	240,000	+	160,00	=	400,000
	1,000,000	pays …	600.000	+	400.000	=	1,000.000
CARGO A ON	1,000,000	pays …	600,000		—	=	600,000
	2,000,000		1,200,000	+	400,000	=	1,600,000

17.92 It was suggested in the 11th and 12th editions that general averages of this type should be apportioned in the same manner as "double" general averages, however this view has never been widely followed and the method used in the above example was preferred by the Advisory Committee of the Association of Average Adjusters in 1992.

The exclusion of small contributory values

17.93 It is a fundamental principle of general average that all properties saved should contribute to the general average sacrifices and expenses incurred, in proportion to their values at the termination of the adventure. However, commercial good sense dictates that properties with small values should be exempted from the requirement to contribute if the contribution they would pay is less than the costs which would be incurred to obtain general average security from them, assess the value, and finally collect the contribution when the adjustment is issued. The problem arises most often in the container trades, notwithstanding the use of General Average Absorption Clauses and other special insurances (see Section 7) which have greatly reduced the number of uneconomic security collections. In particular, low value consignments are likely to be found in consolidated shipments where a forwarding agent assembles a number of smaller separate packages into a container load.

In practice, in the days immediately following the casualty giving rise to a general average act, the adjusters will seek to make a very provisional assessment of the total general average and the likely total contributory values, and calculate the likely rate of contribution. If, for instance, this works out to say two per cent of the total contributory values and they also consider (purely for example) that it costs 100 to collect general average security and the eventual contribution from any individual consignment, it would be uneconomic to collect security from those small consignments with values of less than 5,000. The necessary instructions can therefore be sent to the ship's agents at the various ports of destination to release such cargo without general average formality. Even after security has been collected, the adjuster may wish to keep the position under review in order to save time and cost in the eventual settlement process.

Freight contributory value—subdivision between shipowner and time-charterer

17.94 If voyage freight at risk to the time charterer contributes to a general average, the contributory value of that freight will be calculated to arrive at the identical result that would have been achieved if the freight had been at risk to the shipowner, but that contributory value will then be apportioned[79] between the time charterer and the shipowner in proportion to their respective interests in the freight. For example:

Gross voyage freight at risk and earned			100,000
Deduct: Wages of crew		5,000	
Bunkers purchased	25,000		
Less: unconsumed	20,000		
		5,000	
Port charges and cost of discharging Cargo		10,000	
Contributory value of freight			20,000
			80,000

Sub-divided[80]

The Time-Charterer contributes on gross voyage freight earned		100,000
Deduct: Bunkers used (as above)	5,000	
Port charges and cost of discharging cargo	10,000	
Time hire payable to shipowner after general average act	25,000	
		40,000
Time charterer contributes on		60,000
The Shipowner contributes on time hire	25,000	
Deduct: Wages of crew	5,000	
Shipowner contributes on		20,000
Contributory value of freight (as before)		80,000

Similar principles will apply where the freight is payable to a voyage charterer. They will also apply, in those cases where more than one charterparty is interposed between the cargo owners and the shipowner, in calculating the amount to be contributed by each charterer.

General average in excess of 100 per cent of the contributory values

On some rare occasions, total general average expenses and allowances can 17.95
exceed the contributory values, and the question then arises:

> "Can any party to the adventure be legally required to pay a general average contribution in excess of 100 per cent, of the contributory value of their property?"

[79] Unless the time charterparty provides (as does the Baltime Charter): "Hire not to contribute to general average", in which case the time charterer pays the contribution attaching to the whole of the freight.

[80] Under the usual terms of a time charterparty, the time-charterer is responsible for providing the bunkers and paying for all port charges and cargo expenses, etc. while the shipowner pays and feeds the crew.

In accordance with the provisions of r.G and the opening words of this r.XVII, it is clear that no contribution can be exacted from an interest which has no contributory value at the termination of the adventure. It is also clear that if, as in *Chellew v Royal Commission on the Sugar Supply*,[81] all the property is totally lost during the voyage, those who have financed any earlier general average expenditure must bear it alone and no contribution is due from other interests. What of the position, however, where some property is saved by a general average act and a general average adjustment needs to be prepared? If, for instance, general average expenditure of 10,000 has been incurred by the shipowner, but property to the value of only 1,000 has been saved, can the owner of that property be called upon to pay the whole of the 10,000?

17.96 Ordinary common sense and commercial logic dictate that the answer must be "No"', for the owner of that property would clearly prefer that his properly had been totally lost, rather than that he should be "taxed" with a liability in excess of its value. In Green Star Shipping Co v The London Assurance[82] Roche J. based his judgment on the assumption that contribution in general average could not exceed the contributory value and said:

> "The salved value of the cargo was rather over 26,000 dollars. The owners of that cargo are liable to make contribution up to its full value and the [shipowners] have received this contribution amounting to 26,249 dollars. Apart from this they have not received and are not entitled to receive any further contribution from owners of cargo."

Although the assumption of Roche J. may have been based on the law of Philadelphia, it can certainly be stated that the law of a number of countries specifically states that a general average contribution cannot exceed the contributory value; it is also to be doubted whether any country which has no specific law on the subject could logically arrive at any other conclusion.

17.97 However, and although this basic principle is widely accepted almost as a truism, it is submitted that it applies only to the capital items of any general average, whether sacrifice, expenditure, or adjustment charges, etc. The same common sense and commercial logic which dictate the basic principle must surely also sustain the view that interest is payable in addition on the debt or contribution, and broadly from the time of the expenditure or sacrifice by the creditor until at least the time when the general average adjustment is issued.

Interest is a legal and equitable right, admirably explained by Lord Wright in *Riches v Westminster Bank Ltd*[83]:

> "The essence of interest is that it is a payment which becomes due because the creditor has not had his money at the due date. II may be regarded as representing the profit he might have made if he had had the use of the money, or conversely the loss he suffered because he had not that use. The general idea is that he is entitled to compensation for the deprivation."

[81] *Chellew* [1921] 2 K.B. 627 [1922] 1 K.B. 12, C.A. The same view seems to have been taken by the House of Lords in *Morrison S.S. Co Ltd v Greystoke Castle* [1947] A.C. 265 at 285, 312.

[82] *Green Star* [1933] 1 K.B. 378 at 383.

[83] *Riches* [1947] A.C. 390 at 400. See also Dr Lushington's remarks in *The Aalia* (1864) 5 N.R. 164.

Brandon J. in "*The Mecca*"[84]:

> "In my view the purpose, and the sole purpose, of awarding interest, whether in an action for damages or a limitation action . . . is to compensate for the fact that the damages are paid late."

The period during which interest accrues must surely follow the provisions of r.XXI or the remarks of Megaw J. in *Chandris v Argo Insurance Co Ltd*[85]:

> "In my judgment (and I think this is borne out by the authority of the House of Lords in decisions which I shall mention later) . . . the right to receive, and the liability to pay, contribution arise on the occurrence of the loss. . . . That liability arises as soon as the general average loss has occurred, if it involves contribution. It is not postponed until the amount of the contribution is, or can be assessed."

With regard to the question of whether interest is comprised within, or allowable in addition to an imposed maximum liability (for example a limitation fund in a collision action), the remarks of Brandon J. quoted above are sufficient evidence that interest is payable in addition to the limitation fund itself.

The infrequency with which the problem is encountered does not warrant that **17.98** too much space or time be spent on the subject, but the following suggestions are offered as a practical and commercial approach in those cases where the total general average is likely to exceed the contributory values:

(1) The adjustment should be limited to general average expenditure alone (as was probably intended by Glasgow Resolution No.10 in 1860, and the proposals in 1890 and 1924), and general average sacrifices of property should be excluded and ignored. The extra work and costs involved of adjusting the sacrifices will generally be totally unwarranted and uneconomic because the amounts made good (exclusive of interest) will simply increase the contributory values by an identical amount and pay 100 per cent—or more.
(2) The capital items of the general average should be limited to 100 per cent of the total contributory values, with the necessary reductions being applied exclusively to the net creditors of the general average, they being the parties obliged to suffer at the hands of the debtors, who cannot be compelled to pay more than a basic 100 per cent of their contributory values.
(3) Interest[86] should be allowed on the reduced general average in the normal way, but no two per cent commission.[87]

In most such cases the expenditure in excess of contributory values will fall on the shipowner who may be able to seek recovery under special clauses in his Hull and Machinery policy such as cl.13.5 of Institute Time Clauses Hulls 1.10.83 or cl.9 of the International Hull Clauses 2003.

[84] *The Mecca* [1968] 2 Lloyd's Rep. 27.
[85] *Chandris* [1963] 2 Lloyd's Rep. 65.
[86] See r.XXI.
[87] See r.XX—not allowable in any event under the 2004 Rules.

RULE XVIII

DAMAGE TO SHIP

ENGLISH LAW AND BACKGROUND

When the Ship is Repaired

As stated when discussing r.XIII,[1] when any part of a ship's hull, gear, or machinery, etc. is sacrificed for the common safety, and when the ship is afterwards repaired, the sum allowable in general average as compensation for this damage is the reasonable[2] cost of repairs, with an appropriate deduction for the advantage, if any, which the owner derives from having new work in place of old.[3] 18.01

When the Ship is not Repaired

Since the 1st edn of this Work in 1873 it has been stated that when the injury to the ship, whether caused by the sacrifice alone or by that conjointly with accidental damage, is so extensive that she is not worth repairing and is therefore sold, the allowance in general average is not necessarily the estimated cost of replacing the articles sacrificed. We are in that case to inquire whether or not the sacrifice was that which caused the loss of the ship. If the accidental damage, apart from the sacrifice, would have sufficed to condemn the ship, all that can be allowed by way of compensation for the sacrifice is the difference between the sum which the ship would have fetched, other things remaining the same, had the sacrifice not been made and the sum which she actually fetched. This difference is all which 18.02

[1] Para.13.01, above.

[2] For an indication of the considerations which apply when construing the term "reasonable cost of repairs", see the commentary, para.18.12, below. By a Rule of Practice (No.A.4) it is the duty of the adjuster in adjusting particular average on a ship, or general average which includes repairs, to satisfy himself that such reasonable and usual precautions have been taken to keep down the cost of repairs as a prudent shipowner would have taken if uninsured. See also Rule of Practice No.A.5 (machinery), paras 70.05, below.

[3] See r.XIII, above.

the shipowner has really lost by the sacrifice. If, on the other hand, it is the damage done by the sacrifice which has turned the scale, that is to say, if the ship, in spite of all her previous accidental damage, would have been worth repairing and would have been repaired but for her masts having been cut away, or some similar sacrifice made for the general safety, then the amount allowable in general average for this sacrifice is the value of the ship before the damage—with her net freight, in case this be lost by the sale of the ship–minus the estimated cost of repairing the accidental damage and the net proceeds of the sale; this difference being, in the case supposed, the measure of the shipowner's actual loss through the sacrifice.

18.03 This approach was adopted by the Court of Appeal in *Henderson v Shankland*[4] where a vessel on voyage from Chittagong to Dundee encountered heavy weather and sustained considerable damage. The heavy weather continuing and the vessel being on her beam ends, the mainmast and foremast were cut away. She was subsequently towed into Calcutta, where it was ascertained that the cost of repairing her would exceed her repaired value and she was accordingly condemned as a constructive total loss and sold.

An adjustment was prepared on the instructions of the shipowners, in which the allowance for general average damage was calculated by estimating the cost of repairing the general and particular average damage separately, which came to 63 per cent and 37 per cent respectively. The loss shown by deducting the net proceeds from the sound value was then divided pro rata to these percentages and 63 per cent allowed in general average.[5]

The court decided, however, that the proper method of adjustment was first to ascertain the value of the ship immediately after the particular average damage and before the general average sacrifice, by deducting the estimated cost of particular average repairs from the sound value, and then deducting from the result so obtained the proceeds realised by the sale of the wreck.

18.04 As an example:

Sound (repaired) value of ship		1,000,000
Estimated cost of repairing:		
Accidental damage	800,000	
General average damage	250,000	
	1,050,000	> 1,000,000

The ship is clearly a constructive total loss and not worth repairing, and if she can be sold for scrap for say 120,000, only 80,000 of the estimated cost of repairing the general average damage (250,000) can be charged to general average, calculated as follows:

[4] *Henderson v Shankland* [1896] 1 Q.B. 525.

[5] According to L.J. Buglass Marine Insurance and General Average in the United States (p.212), some American adjusters use this method when there is an actual or commercial total loss of the ship and the York-Antwerp Rules do not apply.

Sound (repaired) value of ship		1,000,000
Deduct:		
Estimated cost of repairing accidental damage	800,000	
Sale proceeds of ship	120,000	
	920,000	920,000
Allow as general average		80,000

In *Henderson v Shankland* it was held that, in calculating the cost of repairing the particular average damage, no deductions "new for old" should be made. However this aspect of the decision has been criticised,[6] with some justification, on the ground that if the cost of repairs is to be used as the measure of depreciation caused by the particular average damage, any betterment which those repairs would have produced should be taken into account. An alternative method of producing an equally acceptable result is to take as the sound value of the ship not her value immediately before the damage, but her value in the repaired state–i.e. including any betterment which the repairs would have yielded. **18.05**

When the injury to the ship caused by sacrifice is less extensive, and the ship is worth repairing but the damage has not been repaired by the time the general average adjustment is ready to issue, the practice is to allow the reasonable depreciation in the value of the vessel by reason of the sacrifice, but not exceeding the estimated cost of repairs. **18.06**

HISTORICAL DEVELOPMENT AND PRACTICE OF RULE XVIII

York-Antwerp Rules 1924 and 1950

This rule appeared for the first time in the 1924 Rules,[7] the only amendment in the 1950 Rules being the substitution of "subject to deduction in accordance with Rule XIII" for "deductions being made as above (Rule XIII) when old material is replaced by new". **18.07**

> "The amount to be allowed as general average for damage or loss to the ship, her machinery and/or gear when repaired or replaced shall be the actual reasonable cost of repairing or replacing such damage or loss, subject to deduction in accordance with Rule XIII. When not repaired, the reasonable depreciation shall be allowed, not exceeding the estimated cost of repairs.
>
> Where there is an actual or constructive total loss of the ship the amount to be allowed as general average for damage or loss to the ship caused by a general average act shall be the estimated sound value of the ship after deducting therefrom the estimated cost of repairing damage which is not general average and the proceeds of sale, if any."

6 *British Shipping Laws*; Arnould, *Law of Marine Insurance and Average*, para.1120.
7 r.XVIII of the 1890 Rules dealt with a different subject-matter.

The rule appears to have been based on English law and practice, with which it was in complete accord; the first paragraph of the rule closely followed the provisions of s.69 of the Marine Insurance Act 1906,[8] for the ascertainment of the liability of underwriters under a marine policy in the event of a partial loss of a ship, and the second paragraph of the rule was in accordance with the decision in *Henderson v Shankland*.[9]

York-Antwerp Rules 1974

18.08 No change whatever was made in the general provisions and intention of the rule in 1974 but the layout and some of the wording was altered in order to define more clearly and to secure greater uniformity of practice on two particular points:

(1) The words "constructive total loss" in the second paragraph of the 1950 rule were not defined, and as this expression had varying legal meanings in different jurisdictions,[10] one meaning was selected and the words "constructive total loss" were changed in 1974 to: "When the cost of repairs of the damage would exceed the value of the ship when repaired."
(2) There were occasional differences in practice under the 1950 Rules where damage to the vessel was, in fact, repaired, but where the figures would demonstrate that the vessel was a commercial[11] total loss.

The following figures illustrate the problem:

[8] "69. Where a ship is damaged, but is not totally lost, the measure of indemnity, subject to any express provision in the policy, is as follows:
(1) Where the ship has been repaired, the assured is entitled to the reasonable cost of repairs, less the customary deductions, but not exceeding the sum insured in respect of any one casualty.
(2) Where the ship has only been partially repaired, the assured is entitled to the reasonable cost of such repairs, computed as above, and also to be indemnified for the reasonable depreciation, if any, arising from the unrepaired damage, provided that the aggregate amount shall not exceed the cost of repairing the whole damage, computed as above.
(3) Where the ship has not been repaired, and has not been sold in her damaged slate during the risk, the assured is entitled to be indemnified for the reasonable depreciation arising from the unrepaired damage, but not exceeding the reasonable cost of repairing such damage, computed as above."

[9] *Henderson* [1896] 1 Q.B. 525. See also para.18.03, above.

[10] In the UK the term is statutorily defined in the Marine Insurance Act 1906 s.60, part of which reads as follows: "In particular there is a constructive total loss ... In the case of damage to a ship, where she is so damaged by a peril insured against that the cost of repairing the damage would exceed the value of the ship when repaired." It is thought that in the USA there is a constructive total loss if the damage exceeds 50 per cent of the repaired value (*Wood v Lincoln and Kennebevk Insurance Co* 6 Mass. R. 479 (1810), and *Peek v Merchant Insurance Co* 3 Mason 27 (1822), and in France if the damage amounts to 75 per cent of the value.

[11] i.e. where the estimated cost of repairing the damage would not exceed the value of the ship when repaired, but where, on commercial grounds, a prudent shipowner would choose to scrap his vessel rather than repair. For an example see para.18.21, below.

Actual cost of repairing:		
Accidental damage	75,000	
General average damage	15,000	
Estimated scrap value of vessel	125,000	
Estimated value of vessel when repaired	______	100,000
	115,000>	100,000

18.09 Because the cost of repairing the accidental damage (75,000) plus the estimated scrap value of the wreck (25,000) were alone equal to the repaired value of the vessel, some adjusters used to make no allowance in general average for the cost of repairing the damage caused by sacrifice. On the other hand, the majority maintained that, provided the shipowner acted reasonably, and repairs were in fact carried out, the cost of those repairs fell to be dealt with under the first paragraph of the rule. Only in those cases where the vessel was an actual total loss, or where she was sold for scrap because the estimates demonstrated that she was a constructive total loss, did the second paragraph apply.

By separating the provisions of the 1974 rule into two sections: "(a) when repaired or replaced: (b) when not repaired or replaced", it was made clear that the previous majority view should now prevail.

It should also be noted that this earlier problem was resolved in that if the shipowner does elect to carry out repair to his vessel even though she is an apparent commercial total loss on the basis of her estimated values in sound condition and as scrap, the repaired value of the vessel to the shipowner would be assumed to be 115,000 in the example above, rather than the 100,000 estimated by the ship valuer.

York-Antwerp Rules 1994

18.10 Proposals for change of some importance to both paragraphs of the rule had been put forward, but, in the event, none was accepted at Sydney.

With regard to paragraph (a), the logical proposal that the last two paragraphs of r.XIII dealing with the charges for drydocking and for cleaning and painting of bottom should be transferred to and form part of the present r.XVIII had received fairly widespread support. However, no agreement could be obtained on the necessary revisions, because there was a fundamental conflict of views on the issue of apportionment of the charges where repairs of both general and particular average damage were effected concurrently.[12]

With regard to paragraph (b) of the rule, AIDE had earlier recommended that the Henderson v Shankland[13] formula be abandoned in favour of a proportional division between accidental and sacrificial damage. This would always have had the effect of increasing general average allowances to the shipowner and, because any increase in the general average system was to be avoided in 1994 if possible, no national delegation adopted this suggestion and the matter was not debated at Sydney.

[12] See paras 18.14 et seq., below.
[13] *Henderson v Shankland* [1896] 1 Q.B. 525.

York-Antwerp Rules 2004

18.11 No change.

RULE XVIII

DAMAGE TO SHIP

The amount to be allowed as general average for damage or loss to the ship, her machinery and/or gear caused by a general average act shall be as follows:

(a) When repaired or replaced, the actual reasonable cost of repairing or replacing such damage or loss, subject to deduction in accordance with Rule XIII;

(b) When not repaired or replaced, the reasonable depreciation arising from such damage or loss, but not exceeding the estimated cost of repairs. But where the ship is an actual total loss or when the cost of repairs of the damage would exceed the value of the ship when repaired, the amount to be allowed as general average shall be the difference between the estimated sound value of the ship after deducting therefrom the estimated cost of repairing damage which is not general average and the value of the ship in her damaged state which may be measured by the net proceeds of sale, if any.

CONSTRUCTION

Section (a)

18.12 **"the actual reasonable cost of repairing . . . such damage"**: When any part of the ship's hull, machinery or gear is sacrificed for the common safety, and when the ship is afterwards repaired the sum allowed as compensation for this damage is the actual reasonable cost of repairing it, with the appropriate deduction, if any, in accordance with r.XIII to represent the advantage which the owner derives from having new material in place of old.

The cost of repairing such damage must be taken to be the cost of repairing it at the time and place where it ought to be repaired. Should it be necessary for the ship, after the sacrifice, to go into some port of refuge, and there repair this damage, the reasonable cost of repairing at that place, however expensive it may be, is the sum allowable. Otherwise, the cost of repairing at the place of destination, and at the time of the ship's arrival, is to be taken, provided the repair either is or ought to be effected then and there. It may happen, however, that from motives of economy, the repairs are deferred until the vessel reaches some cheaper place, in which case, under ordinary circumstances, the sum allowable must be reduced to the actual cost at the place selected for the purpose. These rules are founded on the principle that the owner is entitled to no more than compensation for his actual loss, and that he is bound to do what is reasonable to make that loss as light as may be.

If the damage to the ship caused by general average sacrifice does not affect the 18.13
seaworthiness of the vessel, repairs may be deferred until some more convenient opportunity, even until the vessel undergoes her next quadrennial special survey. If, at that time, inflation has resulted in an increase in the cost of repairs, it may be necessary to reduce the allowance in general average to the cost that would have been incurred if the repairs had been effected at the first reasonable opportunity. In practice, this is often construed as the first routine drydocking or overhaul after the casualty.

Charges for drydocking, tank cleaning and gas freeing

As a preliminary to the effecting of repairs to any ship, it may often be neces- 18.14
sary to place the vessel in drydock. and/or to clean and render gas-free her bunker or cargo tanks. The charges for such measures will generally be regarded as forming part of the cost of those repairs, and the question then arises: How should the charges be treated when the measures are necessary not only for the purpose of effecting repairs to damage caused by a general average sacrifice, but also—as is usual—for repairs to accidental damage and other upkeep maintenance work effected concurrently?

As a typical example of this everyday and costly situation, an oil tanker may strand and her bottom thereby sustain damage by the stranding itself, also by the efforts to refloat. Repairs to both classes of damage necessitate tank-cleaning, gas-freeing and drydocking, and the work is effected concurrently with other repairs on shipowner's or charterer's account, and even with other accidental damage, all of which require the same services (but for differing periods as indicated in the column headings below).

The British practice for allocating these charges is likely to be on the following lines:

		Stranding Damage (12 days)	*General Average Damage* (4 days)	*Owners' Work* (4 days)
(1) *Where the vessel drydocks especially for repairs after the stranding*				
Entry and leaving charges	2,000	1,000	1,000	–
Dues for 4 days	2,400	1,200	1,200	–
Dues for 8 days	4,800	4,800	–	–
12 days	9,200	7,000	2,200	–
Tank-Cleaning and Gas-Freeing	15,800	7,900	7,900	–
	25,000	14,900	10,100	–

(2) *Where the repairs are deferred to a routine overall*				
Entry and leaving charges	2,000	500	500	1,000
Dues for 4 days	2,400	600	600	1,200
Dues for 8 days	4,800	4,800	–	–
12 days	9,200	5,900	1,100	2,200
Tank-Cleaning and Gas-Freeing	15,800	3,950	3,950	7,900
	25,000	9,850	5,050	10,100

The practice abroad varies from country to country and possibly from adjuster to adjuster, but it may confidently be asserted that some proportion of these common charges will always be allocated to any damage caused by a general average sacrifice.

18.15 Apportionment in the manner described above, or similar, is accepted in practice by all interests. It corresponds with the way in which particular average is dealt with,[14] and falls into the same pattern as that used for loss of hire claims. However, in the perhaps unlikely event of the question being brought to court for decision it may be doubted whether the practice would be upheld. Justification for it might be attributed to the decision of the House of Lords in The Vancouver,[15] but after the decision of the House of Lords in The Carslogie[16] it is questionable to what extent, if at all, that case remains a reliable authority. Moreover *The Vancouver* was concerned only with a claim under a marine insurance policy and the decision has not been extended to any other sphere. In the case of a claim against other parties to the adventure for a loss caused by sacrifice, where it is incumbent on the claimant to prove the amount of loss caused to him by the sacrifice, a court might well adopt an approach similar to that in collision cases, where damages are claimed in tort from the defendant owners of a colliding ship, and the claimant carries out other repairs concurrently with those attributable to the collision. Here the rules have been worked out in considerable detail, and do not involve apportionment of the expenses with which we are here concerned. If applied to general average, their effect would be broadly as follows.

(1) Where the general average damage is repaired and the owner takes the opportunity to repair other damage (or carry out other work) which is not immediately necessary to maintain or restore the seaworthiness of the ship and which could have been deferred, the expenses of the type described above will be attributed to the repairs of the general average

[14] Under Rule of Practice D5.
[15] *Marine Insurance Co Ltd v China Transpacific S.S. Co Ltd* (1886) 11 App. Cas. 573.
[16] *The Carslogie* [1952] A.C. 292; [1951] 2 Lloyd's Rep. 441.

damage, except to the extent that they have actually been increased by the carrying out of the other work.[17]

(2) Conversely, where the general average damage does not render the vessel unseaworthy, but the other damage does, all of the expenses in question are to be attributed to the non-general average damage, except to the extent that the carrying out of the general average repairs has actually increased those expenses.[18]

(3) Where each set of repairs was required immediately for the seaworthiness of the ship the expenses will be attributed to the repair of the damage which first occurred.[19] Thus if a ship damages her bottom in an accidental stranding, and then damages her propeller in refloating, and the damage from each cause is sufficient to require immediate drydocking, the drydock charges (except insofar as they are increased by the repair of the general average damage) are attributed to the accidental damage.

Costs of cleaning, painting or coating of bottom

If any part of the coatings on the bottom of a ship be damaged directly by a general average act, such as a voluntary stranding, or by efforts to refloat from a position of peril, the cost of repainting the damaged area ought properly to be dealt with on the principle enunciated above of establishing as nearly as possible the real amount of the loss, if any, sustained by the owner. Thus, if the paintwork was already damaged by an accidental grounding which would necessitate its renewal, or if the damaged paintwork was not renewed until a time at which it would normally have been renewed, the shipowner clearly sustains no loss by the apparent damage from the general average act, and no allowance in general average should be made. At the other end of the spectrum, if the bottom had been painted only a month before the general average act and was otherwise undamaged, the whole cost of repainting the area damaged by the general average act should be allowable if effected soon after the damage. **18.16**

To provide for these and intermediate situations we have only the generally inadequate provisions in the final paragraph of r.XIII.[20]

Cost of opening up for examination—no damage found

Another practical problem worthy of mention is whether, if no damage be found, the cost of opening up machinery or other parts to check whether damage **18.17**

[17] *The Chekiang* [1926] A.C. 637; *The Ferdinand Retzlaff* [1972] 2 Lloyd's Rep. 120. It apparently makes no difference that the repair of the general average damage might also have been deferred for a time: *The Oinoussian Friendship* [1987] 1 Lloyd's Rep. 258.

[18] *The Carslogie* [1952] A.C. 292. It makes no difference whether the general average damage occurred before or after the other damage.

[19] *The Haversham Grange* [1905] P. 307 (CA) as explained in *The Carslogie*. The justification for this is that the party responsible for the subsequent damage is entitled to rely on the fact that the damage for which he is responsible was suffered by a ship which was already in such a condition that she required immediate docking.

[20] See paras 13.11–13.13, above.

may have been caused by general average sacrifice (for example in efforts to refloat) can be charged to general average. There is an English law case relating to cargo insurance, *Lysaght v Coleman*[21] from which it might be possible to argue that there can be no allowance for the cost of opening up if no damage be found, but it is submitted that this particular decision has no application to general average.

Accordingly, if it is reasonable to open up any representative bearing or cylinder (but not necessarily all), or to draw the tailshaft, etc. to examine for possible damage by general average sacrifice, the reasonable cost may be charged to general average even if no damage be found.

Costs for cleaning dock after an escape of oil from the ship

18.18 A ship may be drydocked to repair damage caused by a voluntary stranding, or in refloating, in the course of which her bunker tanks have been breached. When the dock is pumped out bunker oil, previously retained by the pressure of water, may flow into the dock, and a cleaning up charge will be made by the dockyard. Provided that the escape of oil was not reasonably preventable, for example by pumping out the bunker tank, and that the charge for cleaning up is reasonable, the charge should be treated as part of "the actual reasonable cost of repairs" and therefore allowed under r.XVIII, even though, if the claim were brought under the lettered rules, it would be excluded by r.C on the grounds that it was incurred "in consequence of the escape or release of pollutant substances". No similar exclusion is to be found in r.XVIII.[22]

Section (b)

18.19 **"when not repaired . . ."**: The rule does not state at what date the ship has to be unrepaired, if this sentence is to apply. Three possibilities exist. The relevant date may be:

(1) That of the adjustment, though it is suggested that if the repairs had not been completed by the time the adjuster was ready to issue his adjustment, but were likely to be effected on some future occasion, he would almost certainly allow the estimated cost of repairing the damage (less the customary deductions), rather than, or in substitution for, the more nebulous "reasonable depreciation".
(2) That favourite of the courts, " 'a reasonable time".
(3) The termination of the adventure, on the ground that the right to contribution has then accrued and cannot be defeated.[23] In practice, however, it is submitted that this particular date would be adopted only in those rare cases where the vessel is totally lost after the termination of the

[21] *Lysaght v Coleman* [1895] 1 Q.B. 49. CA.
[22] The views expressed in this paragraph are in accordance with Opinion P8 dated October 5, 1998 of the Advisory Committee of the Association of Average Adjusters.
[23] See the commentary to r.G, above.

adventure and with the general average damage still unrepaired. It is, of course, possible to argue that the shipowner has sustained no loss at the time of the total loss from his earlier general average sacrifice, but, on the analogy of comparable marine insurance cases, the shipowner's claim in general average for the unrepaired damage would appear to be well founded.

"the reasonable depreciation": No guidance is given on how this shall be assessed. The failure to do so in this sentence is peculiar, but it is suggested that it is without significance, and that the reasonable depreciation is the reduction in the sale value of the vessel represented by the unrepaired general average damage, but not exceeding the estimated cost of repairs, less any appropriate deduction under r.XIII. **18.20**

In practice, it is suggested that reasonable depreciation is adopted as the basis for ascertaining the amount to be allowed as general average in the following circumstances:

(1) When, so far as can be foreseen, the vessel is unlikely to be repaired in full, or at all. For instance, an old vessel destined shortly for the breakers' yard may sustain general average damage to her shell plating. If that damage does not affect the seaworthiness of the vessel, it may well remain unrepaired. The price paid by the shipbreakers is unlikely to be affected by the existence of the damage and, in such circumstances, the reasonable depreciation would appear to be nil.

(2) When the vessel is totally lost after the termination of the adventure with the damage still unrepaired (as mentioned in para.18.19, above).

(3) When the vessel is sold for future trading in her damaged condition. In such a case, the loss by sale resulting from the unrepaired damage will usually reflect the "reasonable depreciation". An example, drawn from practice, may illustrate the point. The cost of repairing damage to the bottom of a ship by general average sacrifice was estimated by an expert surveyor at £1,000,000; the vessel was sold for future trading for £600,000 less than her true sound value and this £600,000 the adjuster allowed as the "reasonable depreciation". It may be remarked that where the vessel is sold, no deductions "new for old" need be taken into consideration. An actual sale provides positive evidence of the true loss caused by the sacrifice, whereas r.XIII provides but an arbitrary means of arriving at a similar, but less certain figure.

The above three examples relate to comparatively minor damage which does not affect the ability of the vessel to continue trading for some time. However, it may also be necessary to found a claim for "reasonable depreciation" when a major damage results in the decision to scrap the vessel. The estimated cost of repairs may be less than the value of the ship when repaired (see para.18.22, below) but greater than any prudent owner would spend, taking into account also the value of the vessel as scrap. Thus: **18.21**

Sound (repaired) value of ship		1,000,000
Estimated cost of repairing:		
Accidental damage	700,000	
General average damage,	250,000	
	950,000 <	1,000,000
Scrap value of ship,	120,000	
	1,070,000<	1,000,000

No commercial man would spend 950,000 to repair a ship with a sound value of 1,000,000 when for 880,000 plus his scrap proceeds of 120,000 he can purchase a similar vessel to the one damaged.

On figures as in the above example, the reasonable depreciation caused by the general average damage would be calculated as follows:

Sound (repaired) value of ship	1,000,000
Deduct: Estimated cost of repairing accidental damage,	700,000
Pre-general average value	300,000
Deduct: Sale proceeds of ship,	120,000
Reasonable depreciation to be allowed as general average,	180,000

18.22 **"when the cost of repairs of the damage would exceed the value of the ship when repaired"**: This wording was substituted in 1974 for the previous "constructive total loss", and is effectively the British statutory definition[24] of that term. When the cost of repairs would exceed the value of the ship when repaired, or when the ship is an actual total loss, the amount to be allowed as general average is:

> **"the difference between the estimated sound value of the ship after deducting therefrom the estimated cost of repairing damage which is not general average and the value of the ship in her damaged state which may be measured by the net proceeds of sale, if any."**

This provision is based on the decision in the English courts of *Henderson v Shankland*,[25] the effect of which is discussed in paras 18.03 to 18.05, above. In calculating the estimated cost of repairing the particular average damage the rule does not permit any deductions new for old to be made, and it follows that, for the reasons explained in para.18.05 above, the estimated sound value of the ship is to be taken as her notional value when repaired rather than her value immediately before the accident.

18.23 For the sake of completeness, this commentary on r.XVIII ends with the mention of an injustice which a shipowner will occasionally suffer owing to the strict construction which must be given to the numbered Rules. Fortunately, the number of cases in which the situation arises is fairly small,[26] and it was for

[24] Marine Insurance Act 1906 s.60(2)(ii).

[25] *Henderson v Shankland* [1896] 1 Q.B. 525.

[26] The number of cases may be small but the amount involved may be substantial. In one case the normal scrap value of a vessel would have been about $130,000 but, owing to potential hazards and liabilities created by a general average sacrifice, she could only be sold for a token payment of about 10c.

this reason that the matter was not taken further in the post–1924 revisions of the rules.

A vessel may become a commercial total loss and the sale proceeds of the wreck be reduced as a result of a general average sacrifice, for example owing to the lack of equipment such as anchors and cables which were sacrificed as a general average act. There is no good or sound reason why this loss should not be made good in general average except that r.XVIII does not permit it, for example:

Estimated sound value			50,000
Estimated cost of repairing accidental damage		40,000	
Normal proceeds of sale	20,000		
Less: sacrificed anchors, etc.	1,000		
Actual proceeds of sale	19,000	19,000	
		59,000	59,000
Allowance in General Average		Nil	

RULE XIX

UNDECLARED OR WRONGFULLY DECLARED CARGO

ENGLISH LAW AND BACKGROUND

None known, but see para.A.91, above. **19.01**

Historical Development and Practice of Rule XIX

This rule appeared for the first time in the 1924 Rules and has been reproduced verbatim in all subsequent versions of the rules. It embodies a principle which appears in the laws of many countries, especially in the great majority of those possessing a Commercial Code, which in itself is an argument in favour of its inclusion in rules intended for international use, though the occasions upon which it is invoked are infrequent. The provision that damage or loss to "goods loaded without the knowledge of the shipowner or his agent" shall not be allowed in general average agrees with the usual practice of excluding from the benefits of general average such goods as do not appear on the ship's manifest or for which no bill of lading has been issued. The addition of "goods wilfully misdescribed at time of shipment" is justifiable upon the practical ground that if valuable goods, such as platinum, are shipped as (say) tinware, they will not be accorded the careful stowage and treatment which their real value would deserve and may be sacrificed without much consideration. It would be highly inequitable in such a case if the owner, who has probably wilfully misdescribed them in order to obtain a low rate of freight, should be entitled to receive compensation in general average at their correct value. The penalty inflicted by r.XIX is severe in that it excludes such goods from receiving any compensation in general average at all. Where goods, however, are properly described on shipment but a value is declared which is lower than their real value, the second paragraph of the rule permits compensation but only at the declared value. Whether the goods have been concealed or misdescribed or their value has been wilfully misdeclared, they remain liable to contribute on their true value, which is perfectly just, for that value has been saved by the general average act. **19.02**

19.03 RULE XIX

UNDECLARED OR WRONGFULLY DECLARED CARGO

Damage or loss caused to goods loaded without the knowledge of the shipowner or his agent or to goods wilfully misdescribed at time of shipment shall not be allowed as general average, but such goods shall remain liable to contribute, if saved.

Damage or loss caused to goods which have been wrongfully declared on shipment at a value which is lower than their real value shall be contributed for at the declared value, but such goods shall contribute upon their actual value.

Construction

Second paragraph

19.04 **"contributed for at the declared value"**: If goods of a value of £100 are declared on shipment to have a value of £50 and are totally lost by sacrifice the amount allowed in general average will be £50. It is suggested that if such goods are damaged so that their value is reduced to £60, a proportionate part of the loss, that is, 50/100 × (100–60) = £20, will be allowed in general average.

Rule XX

Provision of Funds

English Law and Background

The business of raising funds for general average, like general average itself, belongs to that portion of the contract of affreightment for which no party to the adventure is alone responsible. It follows that the cost of supplying the funds is a mere appurtenance to the liability to pay the general average, and should fall conjointly on all. 20.01

Historical

When the merchants sailed with the ships, often having on board large sums of money, or goods by the sale of which money could be raised, those merchants were the ordinary financiers in any emergency, being bound in case of need to supply the master with either money or goods for sale. They were repaid and secured in the same method as in the case of jettison; that is to say, if the ship arrived, they were put on a par with their co-adventurers by a prompt and secure repayment, but if she perished on the voyage, they got nothing beyond the consolation that they were no worse off than if they had lent or sold nothing.[1] 20.02

When the merchants began to live ashore, the authority of the master was so far extended that he had power to do for the merchants that which they would presumably have done, or have been obliged to do, had they been there: that is, in the case of necessity, the master was empowered:

(1) in the first instance, to hypothecate, the ship and the freight by means of a bottomry bond;

[1] *Consolado*, Ch. 61 (106) (2 Pard. 109); Ch. 62 (107) (2 Pard. 110).

(2) if the security offered by the ship and the freight was insufficient, to hypothecate[2] also the cargo by means of a respondentia bond;
(3) in the last resort, and only when all other means of raising the necessary funds had failed, to sell as much of the cargo[3] as was required.

20.03 It would take too long here to enter into a full discussion of the law of bottomry[4] or of these forced sales but one or two points may be mentioned.

The expense of the bottomry or respondentia bond, or the loss on sale of the cargo, was charged eventually to those parties who were liable to pay for the expenses which necessitated the loan or sale. If the expenses at the port of refuge were wholly recoverable as general average, the loss would be recovered in the same way[5]; if, as commonly used to occur, the expenses were chargeable partly as general average, partly specifically on the cargo and freight, and partly to the shipowner, the bottomry premium or loss by sale was divided rateably between those interests in the proportion that they bore to the expenses themselves.

Bottomry and Respondentia Bonds

20.04 The master's right to raise money by a bottomry loan on the ship and freight comes into force only when he has exhausted all ordinary means of obtaining the necessary funds: that is, when no money is to be had by applying to the shipowner, or by pledging his personal credit or that of the shipowner. It has from very old times been requisite that the shipowner should first be communicated with whenever it was possible to do so without unduly delaying the voyage.

Only if the security offered by the ship and freight is insufficient to attract the funds necessary at the port of refuge is the master permitted to hypothecate the cargo in addition, and it is a legal requirement that the owners of the cargo be first communicated with; no bond on cargo is valid if this precaution has been neglected.

Should the loan not be repaid on the due date at destination, the lender has a maritime lien upon the property charged which can be enforced by proceedings in rem in the Admiralty Court.[6] If necessary, the property pledged can be sold, but only if the proceeds of the ship and freight are insufficient to repay the loan will any part of the cargo be used to satisfy the balance, and then only if the cargo was included in the bond.

[2] In *The Gaetano and Maria* (1882) 7 P.D. 137 at 145. Brett L.J. said: "This authority of the master of the ship to hypothecate the ship or cargo is peculiar. . . . It arises from the necessity of things; it arises from the obligation of the shipowner and the master to carry the goods from one country to another, and from its being inevitable from the nature of things that the ship and cargo may at some time or other be in a strange port where the captain may be without means, and where the shipowner may have no credit because he is not known there, that for the safety of all concerned and for the carrying out of the ultimate object of the whole adventure, there must be a power in the master not only to hypothecate the ship, but the cargo."

[3] *The Gratitudine* (1801) 3 C.Rob. 240; *Australasian S.N. Co v Morse* (1872) L.R. 4 P.C. 222, and other cases.

[4] For such a discussion, see Franck, De Bodmeria; *British Shipping Laws*, Vol. 3: Carver, *Carriage by Sea*, 12th edn, paras 775–785; and *The James W. Elwell* [1921] P. 351. In practice bottomry is believed to be obsolete.

[5] *The Constancia* (1846) 4 Not. of Cas. 677; *The Gratitudine* (1801) 3 C.Rob. 240.

[6] See *British Shipping Laws*; Thomas, Maritime Liens, Ch.8.

Forced Sale of Goods at Port of Refuge

As stated earlier,[7] where cargo was sold at an intermediate port in order to raise funds to pay for repairs or other expenses necessary to enable the voyage to be prosecuted, any loss by sale sustained by the owner of that cargo was added to the cost of those repairs or other necessary expenses and dealt with in the same manner as the principal sums themselves. **20.05**

The amount of that loss by sale would usually be quantified by deducting the net proceeds at the port of refuge from the sum the goods would have fetched at destination (after payment of any freight, etc. due there). If the ship was lost before arrival at destination, however, the cargo owner could nevertheless claim the net proceeds realised by his cargo at the port of refuge. This was decided in *Atkinson v Stephens*,[8] where, in the course of the argument. Alderson B. said:

> "The owner of the goods is entitled to the amount which they actually fetch, although the vessel does not arrive; but if she does, then he is entitled to [the sum] which such goods would fetch in the market."

On occasion, and largely because any freight due at destination would no longer be payable on cargo sold at a port of refuge,[9] it was possible for the cargo owner to make an unexpected profit from the sale because he was entitled to the whole of the net proceeds of sale, even though they exceeded what he would have obtained at destination.

In *Richardson v Nourse*[10] the question was, whether the owner of goods sold in Mauritius to pay for repairs to the ship and other port of refuge expenses was entitled to their net value at the port of destination, or to their actual proceeds, the latter being the larger sum of the two. Three arbitrators, to whom the matter had been referred, had pronounced that the owner was entitled to the larger sum; and the court, on being appealed to, refused to disturb their award. **20.06**

In the course of his judgment, Abbott C.J. said:

> "I cannot say that their decision was wrong; for by holding that the owner of a ship may lose but that he can never gain, by such a sale as this, we shall furnish the strongest possible inducement to him to take care that all the goods are conveyed to their place of destination."

Whenever cargo was sold at an intermediate port to raise funds and the shipowner thereby lost the freight that would have been payable at destination on the cargo sold, his loss of freight would similarly be added to the principal sums expended at the intermediate port and dealt with accordingly.[11]

[7] Para.20.03, above.
[8] *Atkinson v Stephens* (1852) 7 Exch. 567.
[9] Nor is freight pro rata itineris due on the cargo sold at the intermediate port: *Hopper v Burness* (1876) 1 C.P.D. 137.
[10] *Richardson v Nourse* (1819) 3 B. & Ald. 237.
[11] e.g. *Pirie v Middle Dock Co* (1881) 44 L.T. 426.

Cost of Raising Funds in Modern Times

20.07 The section thus far is but an edited version of what Lowndes himself wrote more than a century ago on the subject of raising funds, and what he wrote remains an accurate statement of the law on the subject. However, modern means of communication and the facility to remit funds from one country to another almost instantaneously make it unnecessary to raise funds at an intermediate port by such expensive and extremely short-term[12] forms of finance.[13] In modern times, therefore, it would appear that the cost of raising funds is, in practice, limited to the actual charges made by a bank for remitting funds, but excluding interest.[14]

Historical Development and Practice of Rule XX

20.08 Mercantile men have always recognised that the ability and willingness to advance funds on behalf of third parties merited the payment of an advancing commission, and general average disbursements—"for which no man is directly responsible"[15]—are no exception to this rule. In Germany, for example, a commission of one per cent was allowed on general average disbursements; in Belgium, two per cent and in the United States, 2.5 per cent. In this country, however, the practice was not to allow a commission for advancing funds, and this practice dated possibly from the time of *Schuster v Fletcher*.[16]

York-Antwerp Rules 1924

20.09 When the York-Antwerp Rules came to be revised in 1924 a demand was made that the practice of foreign countries should be introduced and embodied in the Rules.

> "*Rule XXI, Provision of Funds*
>
> A commission of 2 per cent, on general average disbursements (. . . [17]) shall be allowed in general average, but when the funds are not provided by any of the contributing interests, the necessary cost of obtaining the funds required by means of a bottomry bond or otherwise, or the loss sustained by owners of goods sold for the purpose, shall be allowed in general average. The cost of insuring money advanced to pay for general average disbursements shall also be allowed in general average."[18]

[12] Bottomry bonds were almost invariably repayable within three days of arrival at destination.

[13] Thus in *The Halcyon Isle* [1981] A.C. 221 (PC) Lord Diplock was able to declare (p.232) that "Bottomry is now obsolete".

[14] Interest is treated separately under r.XXI; see para.21.01 et seq, below.

[15] See also para.20.01, above.

[16] *Schuster v Fletcher* (1878) 3 Q.B.D. 418.

[17] Additional wording placed here in 1950.

[18] See also Rules of Practice of the Association of Average Adjusters: No.A2: "That, in practice, interest and commission for advancing funds are only allowable in average when, proper and necessary steps having been taken to make a collection on account, an out-of-pocket expense for

York-Antwerp Rules 1950

A period of cheap money prevailed at the time when the 1924 Rules were revised, and various suggestions were put forward to limit the amount charged to general average for advancing commission. One suggestion was to reduce the rate to one per cent while another was that commission should be allowed only on those disbursements incurred (which presumably meant paid) before the end of the voyage. In somewhat haphazard fashion it was agreed to adopt the proposal of the US sub-committee to retain the rate of commission and the existing wording of the rule, but in the space above (. . .) to add wording to exclude commission on wages and maintenance of master, officers and crew (regarded as the enhancement of ordinary voyage expenses, and not as extraordinary expenses for this purpose) and on fuel and stores not replaced during the voyage. **20.10**

York-Antwerp Rules 1974

No change. **20.11**

York-Antwerp Rules 1994

An early proposal that all general average disbursements should attract the two per cent commission was regarded by the insurance community as another example of the unwanted expansion of the general average system, and was accordingly withdrawn at the Sydney Conference. Other proposals which did succeed were essentially "modernising" drafting refinements: reference to the ancient system of raising funds by means of a bottomry bond was deleted, as also were the words "money advanced to pay for" in the final paragraph. **20.12**

York-Antwerp Rules 2004

Although the allowance of commission on general average disbursements has a long history in the laws of many countries, and may be justified on the grounds that it provides an incentive to the parties to provide the necessary funds, the feeling was growing, before the Vancouver conference, that the cost of providing funds is, in the great majority of cases, no more than the interest payable on the amounts expended, allowed separately under r.XXI, and that any further allowance is unnecessary, particularly since it is the practice to allow separately, under r.C, the communication and banking expenses (other than interest) and other incidental costs incurred in the raising and transmitting of funds. There was some discussion before Vancouver as to whether the commission should be retained, and a provision added to the effect that no further allowance should be permitted in respect of the expense of raising or providing funds, but in the end it was **20.13**

interest and/or commission for advancing funds is reasonably incurred." No.A3: "That, in practice, neither commission (excepting bank commission) nor any charge by way of agency or remuneration for trouble is allowed to the shipowner in average, except in respect of services rendered on behalf of cargo when such services are not involved in the contract of affreightment."

resolved at the conference to abolish the allowance of commission under r.XX, and the leave intact the existing practice with regard to out of pocket expenses.

The remaining two paragraphs of the rule were numbered (a) and (b).

RULE XX

PROVISION OF FUNDS

A commission of 2 per cent, on general average disbursements, other than the wages and maintenance of master, officers and crew and fuel and stores not replaced during the voyage, shall be allowed in general average.

(a) The capital loss sustained by the owners of goods sold for the purpose of raising funds to defray general average disbursements shall be allowed in general average.

(b) The cost of insuring general average disbursements shall also be admitted/allowed in general average.

CONSTRUCTION

First Paragraph (not applicable to the 2004 Rules)

20.14 **"commission"**: The two per cent commission allowed by the 1994 and earlier rules is a "flat" allowance credited to those (whether parties to the adventure, their insurers or the deposit funds) who advance funds to settle accounts which are allowable as general average. It is not in the nature of a rate of interest, that is, two per cent is earned on payment and regardless of the length of time between disbursement of the funds by the original payor and reimbursement to him by other parties to the adventure or by his own underwriters. So much is clear from the wording of the rule, particularly if it is compared with r.XXI.

The 2 per cent commission referred to in the previous paragraph is the modern equivalent of the variable premium payable on arrival at destination to the lender of money obtained abroad by means of a bottomry bond, all reference to which was deleted, on the grounds that it was obsolete, when r.XX was amended in 1994.

20.15 **"general average disbursements"**: The commission is allowed on all general average disbursements other than "'the wages and maintenance of master, officers and crew and fuel and stores not replaced during the voyage" and certain other exceptions discussed below.

The term "general average disbursements" is not synonymous with "general average expenditure", which is of much more limited application[19]: general average disbursements embrace any general average sacrifice or expenditure which, at the time of issuing the adjustment, is represented by an actual outlay of cash. Thus, if cargo damaged by a general average sacrifice is accepted by the consignee with a percentage allowance for depreciation, no commission is allowed; but if that same damage is repaired by the outlay of cash on reconditioning, the expense incurred would attract a two per cent commission. The position is the same with general average damage to ship; if repaired, two per cent commission is allowed on the cost of repairs charged to general average, but if unrepaired, no commission is payable.

It has been suggested that the fact that an account has not been paid, that is, disbursement has not yet been made by the date of the adjustment, is no reason for disallowing the commission if a liability has been incurred which will in due course have to be discharged, but that there was no settled practice in this respect.

If it be recognised that the commission is earned only by advancing funds, and not by a mere guarantee to pay, it will be readily understood that commission cannot be charged on items unpaid at the date of the adjustment. Those outstanding accounts may well be settled from general average contributions or other payments made by other parties.

Salvage awards payable under the terms of a contract such as Lloyd's Standard Form of Salvage Agreement were in practice treated as general average disbursements attracting two per cent commission provided that the services were engaged for the purpose of saving a common adventure. **20.16**

This is confirmed by r.VI which extends to salvage whether under contract or otherwise. Under the 2004 Rules the position is, of course, entirely different, since not only has commission been abolished, but remuneration for salvage on "no cure no pay" terms is no longer general average expenditure.

"other than the wages and maintenance[20] of master, officers and crew": Commission is not allowed on wages and maintenance of master, officers and crew for the reason explained in para.20.10, above, and this regardless of whether the crew are "replaced during the voyage". (These particular words govern only "fuel and stores".) **20.17**

Although it might be contended that as commission is not allowable on wages, etc. of crew, neither should it be allowed on other expenses charged to general average on a substituted expense basis and in lieu of wages, etc. this is not the practice. An exclusion such as this, may not be construed more widely than its actual wording, and commission is allowed on the substituted expenses.

"and fuel and stores not replaced during the voyage": Commission is allowed on fuel and stores only when they are replaced during the voyage. The position is the same with time-chartered vessels, but the commission is credited to

[19] See para.50.03, below.

[20] For definitions of the words "wages" and "maintenance" see paras 11.08 and 11.41, above.

the time-charterer only if he does not debit the shipowner with the cost of the bunkers consumed whilst off-hire (for example during a general average deviation and detention). If, as is customary, the shipowner is debited with the cost of bunkers consumed during an off-hire period, the commission (if any) is credited to the shipowner.

Second Paragraph–Paragraph (a) in the York-Antwerp Rules 2004

20.18 **"The capital loss sustained by the owner of goods sold for the purpose of raising funds to defray general average disbursements shall be allowed in general average"**: All reference to the archaic method of raising funds by means of a bottomry bond was deleted from the rule in 1994, yet mention of the even less likely sale of cargo for the same purpose was surprisingly retained. As recorded more fully in paras 20.02 to 20.06, above, it is only as an absolutely last resort, when all other means of raising funds have failed (including the prior requirement to hypothecate the ship and freight, and then the cargo itself), that the master is empowered to sell the cargo. Even then it is a legal requirement that he must first communicate with the owners of the cargo, unless it is impossible to do so.

In the absence of more specific conditions then imposed by the forced seller, the loss to be allowed in general average in terms of the rule is limited to the capital loss sustained by the owner of the goods (that is based essentially on bare CIF invoice values), and only in so far as the funds realised are used to settle general average disbursements. As the funds realised by sale are the absolute property of the owner of the goods, he is of course, under the 1994 and earlier rules, entitled to two per cent commission on those funds used to settle general average disbursements.

Third Paragraph (Paragraph (b) in the 2004 Rules)

20.19 **"The cost of insuring general average disbursements shall also be allowed in general average"**: It is an almost universal practice to effect insurance on money advanced for general average disbursements, for if a total loss of ship and cargo should occur after the making of general average disbursements, or should the ship or cargo be reduced in value by a subsequent accident so as to be worth less than the amount of general average expenses, it would be impossible in practice to recover the whole of the general average from the interests concerned. It has certainly been the practice in this country, and probably in all others, to allow the cost of such insurance in general average, and the rule in this respect, therefore, embodies a custom prevalent throughout the world.

The cost of insurance is only allowable when the general average disbursements have been financed by a contributing interest from their own funds or from money borrowed on terms that it is repayable regardless of the safe arrival at destination of ship and cargo. The proceeds of cargo sold for the purpose of raising funds falls into this category, and should therefore be insured.

THE INSURANCE OF GENERAL AVERAGE DISBURSEMENTS

General average expenses incurred at a port of refuge are customarily financed by the shipowner, and in order that he may recover the proportion of those expenses attaching to the cargo interests, the shipowner is granted a lien on and may hold the cargo until satisfactory security has been provided by them to meet their proper contribution. However, that lien can be exercised only on arrival at destination, and if the ship and cargo become a total loss between the port of refuge and the final destination, the shipowner will be unable to recover any part of his general average expenditure from the cargo interests. **20.20**

A graphic example occurred in the case of *Chellew v Royal Commission on the Sugar Supply*[21] where, during the course of a voyage from Cuba to Europe, the Penlee encountered a hurricane and sustained damage which obliged her to put into Horta as a general average act. Upon completion of the repairs, the vessel resumed her voyage from Horta, but a few days later she and her cargo of sugar were totally destroyed by fire. The shipowners sought to recover from the cargo interests their proportion of the general average expenses incurred at Horta, but this claim was denied. In the course of his judgment in the Court of Appeal, Scrutton L.J. said:

> "The person incurring the expenditure runs a risk of loss which he can cover by insurance of his interest in the arrival of the interests on which he has a lien for contribution to his expenditure."

Such an insurable interest in the general average expenses payable by cargo interests had previously been confirmed in 1849 by Lord Denman C.J. in *Briggs v The Merchant Traders' Ship Loan and Assurance Association*.[22]

Even if the subsequent accident does not render the ship and cargo a total loss it may reduce the contributing values of the surviving property below the amount of the general average expenditure, and against this eventuality it is also usual practice to insure. However it is not necessary to insure against the risk of damage to any of the common property for which the common maritime adventure ceases at the port of refuge, since the contribution due on that property crystallises upon discharge at the port of refuge. For example, if the ship abandons the voyage at the port of refuge and the cargo is transhipped and forwarded to destination under a non-separation agreement, the contribution due on the ship is unaffected by any subsequent loss or damage to her.

In point of fact, and assuming the ship to be already fully insured with conditions such as the Institute Time Clauses. Hulls, if the ship and cargo were totally lost between the port of refuge and the destination as the result of some new accident, the shipowner would be entitled on the principle of "successive losses"[23] **20.21**

[21] *Chellew* [1922] 1 K.B. 12; 91 L.J.K.B. 58; 126 L.T. 103; 27 Com. Cas. 1; 37 T.L.R. 903; 15 Asp. M.L.C. 393; 8 Lloyd's Rep. 305.

[22] *Briggs* (1849) 13 Q.B. 167; 18 L.J.Q.B. 178; 13 Jur. 787; 78 R.R. 341.

[23] Marine Insurance Act 1906 s.77. (The same principle attaches, of course, to insurances on cargo,

to recover from his hull insurers the whole of the general average expenses already incurred by him, plus the subsequent total loss. Likewise if, as a result of a subsequent accident, the contributory values are reduced to below the level of the disbursements the shortfall would be recoverable from hull insurers. However, as general average has a prior existence independent from insurance, it is probably reasonable that he who advances general average expenses on behalf of other parties should insure against the possibility of failing to recover the proportion of those expenses attaching to the other parties. (See also the only other recorded English legal decision concerning the insurance of average disbursements, *Green Star Shipping Co Ltd v London Assurance*,[24] where only the proportion of general average expenses attaching to the cargo had been insured.)

In current practice, it is generally found that the full general average expenses are insured, and not merely the proportion of those expenses attaching to the cargo. The justification for this, one must suppose, is that no-one likes to see an expenditure of money rendered worthless and abortive by a subsequent total loss of the property the expenditure was designed to save.

20.22 It is also generally found in current practice that the extent of the insurance cover is considerably increased in that the general average disbursements are covered not only against the risk of total loss, or loss which reduces contributory values to less than the general average disbursements, but also against the risks of any loss or damage to the ship, cargo or freight, etc. which reduces its value during the remainder of the voyage. The justification for such an extended insurance is that it helps to preserve the original anticipated percentage of general average contribution. Thus, if the anticipated contributory values were:

SHIP	500,000
CARGO	500,000
	1,000,000

and the general average expenses 100,000, the contribution would be 10 per cent. However, if for instance the ship were to strike a quaywall when arriving at destination and sustain damage costing 200,000 to repair, the contributory values would be reduced to:

SHIP	300,000
CARGO	500,000
	800,000

and the general average of 100,000 would now represent 12.5 per cent of the contributory values. Instead of paying 10 per cent [??]ts 500,000 = 50,000, cargo interests would be called upon to pay 12.5 per cent = 62,500.

and would protect the cargo interests if they had advanced general average expenditure or had provided separate security to salvors and paid their own proportion of any salvage award.)

[24] *Green Star* [1933] 1 K.B. 378; 145 L.T. 180; 36 Com. Cas. 258; 43 Lloyd's Rep. 523; 39 Lloyd's Rep. 213.

Such an increase would be avoided if the average disbursement of 100,000 were insured on "full" conditions.[25] The insurance policy would cover the proportion of general average attaching to the reduction in the value of the property (200,000) and, effectively, constitute another contributing interest. The general average might now be considered to be apportioned as follows: 20.23

SHIP	300,000	pays	30,000
POLICY	200,000	pays	20,000
CARGO	500,000	pays	50,000
	1,000,000	pays	100,000

and it will be noted that the general average contribution attaching to the cargo interests returns to the originally expected figure of 50,000.

In practice, the indemnity provided by the "full" conditions is usually rather less complete than as set out in the simple example above, for it is not the total general average that is insured, but only those expenses and losses which are represented by an outlay of money at the port of refuge and/or short of destination. Thus, claims allowable in general average for, for example jettison or other sacrifice of cargo, or for repairs to general average damage to the ship carried out at destination or subsequently, do not represent any outlay of money that needs protecting during the remainder of the voyage, and they are accordingly not declared on the insurance. (Such claims for jettison of cargo, or for general average repairs to ship at destination, are only contingent claims in general average, allowable only if some part of the property survives and there is a successful conclusion of the adventure.)[26] 20.24

[25] In May 1987 two new sets of Average Disbursement Causes agreed by the Association of Average Adjusters and the Institute of London Underwriters were issued. The (A) set is on "full" conditions and effectively covers that proportion of the general average expenses insured attaching to any reduction in the value of the contributing interests. The (B) set is on "limited" conditions and a claim can arise only when the values of the property at destination are less than the amount of the disbursements insured.

[26] For a fuller discussion on the subject of the insurance of average disbursements (also the insurance of other subsidiary interests following a casualty), see the booklet by D.J. Wilson published by the Association of Average Adjusters in 1988.

Rule XXI

Interest on Losses made good in General Average

English Law and Practice

With the almost universal adoption in contracts of affreightment of the York-Antwerp Rules, very few general average adjustments are prepared today which are subject only to English law.[1] In the few such adjustments seen by the present editors, commission for advancing funds and interest on outlays and losses have never been encountered, and this practice probably derives from the Rule of Practice A2 of the Association of Average Adjusters: 21.01

> "Interest and Commission for Advancing Funds
>
> That, in practice, interest and commission for advancing funds are only allowable in average when, proper and necessary steps have been taken to make a collection on account, an out-of-pocket expense for interest and/or commission for advancing funds is reasonably incurred."

Although this rule[2] does not deny that commission and interest may be allowable, it does appear to limit any allowance to an actual out-of-pocket expense paid to a bank or some other financier in respect of a specific advance related exclusively to the average expenses in question, and then only if steps have been taken to obtain collections on account from, presumably, hull underwriters and/or cargo interests.

The rule seems to be unduly narrow in its outlook and disregards the fact that money, whether provided by one of the parties to the adventure, or by others, is often a scarce and expensive commodity and its use should be paid for. The present editors prefer the views of *Lowndes* himself (1st to 3rd edns): 21.02

[1] In *E.B. Aaby's Rederi A/S v Union of India* [1974] 3 W.L.R. 269, HL, commission and interest were the only points of distinction between a claim for general average contribution which was, and one which was not, based on the York-Antwerp Rules.

[2] For a history of this rule, interested readers are referred to the annual reports of the Association of Average Adjusters (1878), pp.18 et seq.; (1879), pp.30 et seq.; (1880), pp.28 et seq.; (1905), pp.56 et seq.; (1906), pp.2 et seq.; (1907), pp.46 et seq.

"If the disbursements have been in the first instance paid by the shipowner, and cannot be refunded to him until after some lapse of time, is the owner entitled to charge interest on his outlay? Custom, founded probably on obsolete notions about usury, is against this: (a) but it may be doubted whether such a custom, which is plainly opposed to the true principle of general average, would be held binding in a Court of Law. The person who makes the advance for the sake of all ought certainly to be compensated for the use of his money. In the United States[3] more rational practice prevails.

(a) This custom is subject to one exception. If the shipowner advances money which he is not bound to advance, he may charge interest like any one else. He is not bound to pay salvage on cargo; the cargo being directly liable to the salvor. He is not bound to remit money to a foreign port, by sending out a letter of credit, or cash, in anticipation of the completion of the accounts; although he would be bound to accept the master's draft on him, when the accounts are closed. In many cases a bottomry premium is saved by such remittance, and it is then customary to allow interest or a commission to the owner. This whole subject, however, is at present in an unsatisfactory condition."

(4th to 7th edns):

"The expenses of doing this, including a rate of interest just sufficient to place all parties in a position of ultimate equality, so that no one should either wish, or shun, to advance more than his share, should be charged as a pendant to the capital expenditure itself."

21.03 Or the opinion of T. E. Scrutton, K.C. and J. A. Hamilton, K.C. given in about 1904:

"1. We are of opinion that, where a shipowner makes disbursements and finds funds for general average expenditure . . ., his outlay should . . . be treated as a sacrifice of the use of money, which he would otherwise have employed profitably elsewhere, and in principle, such sacrifice should be made good by an allowance of interest in general average. We know of no rule which requires a shipowner to possess and furnish gratuitously the funds required at a port of refuge, and the cases upon a master's authority to raise money on bottomry indicate the contrary.

2. We do not think that interest can be allowed to a consignee of goods sacrificed until after the arrival of the ship at the port of delivery, because in his case the goods, while on the voyage, are not interest bearing to him, and he makes no sacrifice of the employment of his money elsewhere during that time.

3. After the vessel's arrival at its port of destination, and pending the adjustment and collection of the contribution, we think that, in principle, interest may be allowed both to shipowner and cargo owner, though the point is more doubtful than the two previous ones. It may be said that there is no element of maritime sacrifice in waiting till a complicated adjustment can be completed, but there seems nothing unbusinesslike in interest up to the time when the amount of reimbursement is first determined in fact, and not merely determinable in theory, being allowed to a co-adventurer, who has laid out his money for the common good, and the contrary

[3] A commission of 2½ per cent is in practice allowed in the US, together with interest at the legal rate prevailing at the place of adjustment: *Simms v Hilling* 8 Serg. & R. 103 (1822). Commission is also allowed for collecting and settling the general average: *Barnard v Adams* (1850) 10 How. 270; *Sturgess v Cary* (1854) 2 Curl. 59. U.S. Interest is also allowed beyond the date of issuing any general average statement up to the estimated date when settlement will be effected (e.g. two or three months).

would work hardship. The shipowner, at any rate, should, it seems, have interest on his outlays till the date of the average statement, when contributions first become ascertained debts, if not till actual payment. Similarly, the cargo owner should have interest on the arrived value of goods sacrificed to the same date, though possibly it should not commence till such a time has elapsed alter arrival as would be requisite, in ordinary course, to sell and obtain payment for the goods. To the shipowner, in respect of materials sacrificed and damage done to the ship for general average purposes, interest should not begin to run till the corresponding replacements or repairs have been paid for."

The views quoted above were expressed in the context of the common law rule which in general excluded any award of interest by way of damages or compensation for late payment.[4] That rule was re-affirmed by the House of Lords in 1984,[5] but there are important exceptions to it: **21.04**

(1) Under a long-standing practice of the Admiralty Court, interest was awarded in damage actions, and it is now recognised[6] that this power extends to all claims within the Admiralty jurisdiction of the High Court, which include claims for general average contribution.
(2) Since 1934 there has existed a statutory power which, in its current form, entitles the court or arbitrator to award interest, at such rate as they think fit, on any sums claimed in the proceedings. In the case of a court, the power is to award simple interest from the date when the cause of action arose until the day of judgment, or of payment if earlier.[7] An arbitrator has wider powers–to award simple or compound interest from the date when the cause of action arose until payment.[8]

By virtue of these powers, which are almost invariably exercised in favour of the claimant,[9] a court is entitled to award interest from the date of the sacrifice or expenditure:

(a) in the case of a court, until judgment for, or earlier payment of, the amount stated in the adjustment;
(b) in the case of an arbitrator, until actual payment.

One important limitation on the powers described in the previous paragraph is that no interest can be awarded in any proceedings on principal sums paid before **21.05**

4 *London Chatham & Dover Ry Co v South Eastern Ry Co* [1893] A.C. 429.
5 *President of India v La Pintada Cia* [1985] A.C. 104.
6 *President of India* [1985] A.C. 104 at 121. See also *The Aldora* [1975] Q.B. 748.
7 Supreme Courts Act 1981 s.35A; County Courts Act 1984 s.69. The court cannot award interest for any period after the judgment until payment, but interest runs automatically on a judgment or award at a rate fixed by Statutory Instrument (since 1993 8 per cent). Equally there is no power to award interest for any period during which interest already runs.
8 Arbitration Act 1996 s.49.
9 The award of interest is made simply on the basis that the successful claimant has been out of pocket. Interest is normally refused only on some exceptional ground, such as culpable delay by the claimant which has caused prejudice to the defendant.

the proceedings were commenced.[10] This hiatus has been to some extent remedied by the Late Payment of Commercial Debts (Interest) Act 1998.

Historical Development and Practice of Rule XXI

York-Antwerp Rules 1924

21.06 It is one of the fundamental principles of general average that it should be financially immaterial to the parties to the adventure, upon adjustment, whose property or purse was selected to suffer for the general benefit. It is obvious, therefore, that unless interest be allowed, the full extent of the loss suffered by the owner of property sacrificed or by the disburser of general average expenditure is not made good to him. It had long been the practice in many countries to allow interest on general average sacrifices and expenditures, but the custom in this country was otherwise.[11] To remedy this obvious and unnecessary discrepancy a new York-Antwerp Rule, based on a draft[12] proposed by the Association of Average Adjusters, was introduced at the Stockholm Conference in 1924:

> *"Rule XXII. Interest on Losses made good in General Average*
>
> Interest shall be allowed on expenditure, sacrifices and allowances charged to general average at the legal rate per annum prevailing at the final port of destination at which the adventure ends, or where there is no recognised legal rate, at the rate of 5 per cent. per annum, until the date of the general average statement, due allowance being made for any interim reimbursement from the contributory interests or from the general average deposit fund."

The reported discussion shows that the delegates would have preferred a standard rate of interest to the "legal" rate proposed, but, the discussion turning on whether the standard rate should be 5 or 6 per cent, the matter was resolved by the simpler expedient of passing the rule in its proposed form.

York-Antwerp Rules 1950

21.07 The 1950 rule reproduced r.XXII of the 1924 Rules with the omission of the words "at the legal rate per annum prevailing at the final port of destination, or where there is no recognised legal rate . . ." thus providing for a uniform

[10] See *President of India v La Pimada Cia* [1985] A.C. 104 where the limitations of the statutory power were criticised by Lords Scarman and Roskill. For the limits on the Admiralty jurisdiction to award interest see at 119–121, per Lord Brandon; Arbitration Act 1996 s.40.

[11] See Rule of Practice A2 quoted in para.21.01, above.

[12] The "Draft International Code for General Average" intended for discussion by the International Law Association at a meeting which would have been held at The Hague in September 1914 also included a proposal that: "Interest at the current rate shall be paid on all loss, damage or expense from the time of accrual or date of payment to the date of adjustment."

rate of 5 per cent irrespective of whether or not there can be said to be some different legal rate of interest at the final port of destination. The amendment gave effect to a resolution adopted by the International Law Association at its Conference in Brussels in September, 1948. The reason for the resolution was that interested parties, in particular underwriters, took the view that "legal rates" of up to 8 per cent or even 10 per cent which prevailed in some parts of the world were exorbitant in view of the cheap money policies of that year.

It was further shown that there was no "recognised legal rate" in England, nor in the majority of the main importing countries, and that profits (or losses) not warranted by the reason behind the rule were being made. An example quoted was of a British ship bound for "Ruritania", where the legal rate of interest might be 10 per cent per annum. Although the owner might (at that time) be able to finance his general average disbursements for five per cent, he would nevertheless receive credit in accordance with the rule at 10 per cent.

The reporting Committee unhesitatingly expressed the view that no case could be made out for retaining in the rule the reference to legal rate of interest at the port of destination, and that the fixing of a definite rate of interest to be applied in all cases would more accurately give effect to the principles underlying the concept of general average.

York-Antwerp Rules 1974

The rate of interest was increased from 5 to 7 per cent. As had been pointed out by the British Maritime Law Association, any arbitrarily fixed rate of interest will sometimes be too high, and sometimes too low. At the time of the Hamburg Conference in 1974, world interest rates generally exceeded 7 per cent; they have since been very much higher, subsiding from their peaks in say 1982–1983, but except in countries such as Japan and Switzerland with very strong currencies, seldom below the regulation 7 per cent. **21.08**

York-Antwerp Rules 1994

The provisions of this rule aroused a fair measure of interest and discussion for the revisions which took place in 1994, but the eventual changes were small: (1) the rate of interest to be allowed on losses made good in general average would continue after 1994 at the same existing rate of seven per cent per annum; but (2) the period during which interest would be earned would be extended by three months, to run from the date of issue of the general average adjustment. The reason for this latter amendment is set out in the commentary in para.21.12, below. **21.09**

Other proposals for the rule were designed to resolve the complex problems associated with rates of exchange and the currency of the adjustment, but these failed to secure any agreement, and the rule therefore remains silent on the subject. The alternative proposals are discussed in the commentary in Section 6 at paras 40.42 et seq., below.

York-Antwerp Rules 2004

21.10 Before the Vancouver Conference it was widely recognised that to lay down a fixed rate of interest in the Rules could give rise to injustice, since commercial rates would fluctuate substantially during the periods between the revisions of the Rules. The Working Group set up by CMI to report on the matter initially favoured a fluctuating rate, linked by a formula to LIBOR. However, this was considered too complicated, and a proposal was made, which received general support, that the rate should be fixed annually by the Assembly of CMI. Another matter which was discussed was whether different rates should be fixed for different currencies, but again this was considered too complicated, and unnecessary in view of the fact that 80 per cent of adjustments are in US Dollars, and the great majority of the remainder in currencies which are closely linked to the dollar. This is reflected in the Guidelines adopted at Vancouver for fixing the rate:

Guidelines for the Assembly of the Comite Maritime International when deciding the annual interest rate provided for in YAR Rule XXI

The Assembly is empowered to decide the rate of interest based upon any information or consideration, which in the discretion of the Assembly are considered relevant, but may take the following matters into account:

The rate shall be based upon a reasonable estimate of what is the rate of interest charged by a first class commercial bank to a ship owner of good credit rating.

Due regard shall be had to the following:

- *That the majority of all G.A. adjustments are drawn up in USD.*
- *That therefore the level of interest for one-year USD loans shall be given particular consideration.*
- *That most adjustments which are not drawn up in USD are drawn up in GBP, EUR or JPY.*
- *That, if the level of interest for one-year loans in GBP, EUR or JPY differs substantially from the level of interest for one year loans in USD, this shall be taken into account.*
- *That readily available information about the level of interest such as USD–prime rate and LIBOR shall be collected and used.*
- *Any amendment of these guidelines shall be made by a decision of a conference of the CMI.*

RULE XXI

Interest on Losses made good in General Average

(a) Interest shall be allowed on expenditure, sacrifices and allowances in general average at the rate of 7 per cent per annum, until three months after the date of issue of the general average adjustment, due allowance being made for any payment on account by the contributory interests or from the general average deposit fund.

(b) Each year the Assembly of the Comite Maritime International shall decide the rate of interest which shall apply. This rate shall be used for calculating interest accruing during the following calendar year.

CONSTRUCTION

First Paragraph–Paragraph (a) in the York-Antwerp Rules 2004

Although this rule determines when the allowance of interest shall cease (three months after the date of issue of the general average adjustment), it does not state on what date interest begins to accrue. Resort can legitimately be had therefore to the object of the rule which is to ensure full and fair compensation to any interest which has suffered in the common cause, and to the practice of average adjusters. 21.11

It is impossible to provide for every individual circumstance, but it is believed that the general practice is to commence the allowance of interest on:

(1) *general average expenditure* (or any sacrifice or allowance represented by an actual outlay of cash)—from the date of payment;

(2) *cargo claims*—from the last day of discharge.

"expenditure, sacrifices and allowances": The word "allowances" occurs only in this rule, and is more apt to describe the shipowner's right to contribution in respect of fuel and stores consumed (r.XI(a) and (b)) and the cargo owner's right to contribution under r.XX in respect of goods sold to raise funds than "expenditure" or "sacrifice". The three words between them cover all forms of claim in general average. It seems unlikely, however, that they extend to the right conferred by r.VI of the 2004 Rules to recover the amount of a salvage payment paid in respect of another interest, since that right is, as the rule makes clear, a separate right of recourse, rather than a right in general average, and will only figure in the adjustment if the payment has not been previously reimbursed. In respect of payments of this kind, therefore, any right to interest will be governed by the law of the forum.

"until three months after the date of issue of the general average adjustment": Allowances for interest on losses made good in general average under the previous 1924, 1950, and 1974 Rules continued only until the date on which the average adjuster completed and issued his adjustment, and no interest accrued during the period thereafter and until settlement of the various contributions due. 21.12

Perhaps until about the early 1970s, when money was "cheap", when general average deposits were more frequently provided as security, and when debit balances under the adjustment were settled far more promptly, no real injustice was caused to any of the parties to the adventure by this loss of interest during the period between the date of issuing the adjustment and settlement thereunder.

However, possibly due to the very high rates of interest prevailing in later years, there had been a very marked tendency on the part of many debtors under any general average adjustment to decline or delay payment of their contributions for as long as possible and for any excuse. This resulted in the creditors under the adjustment being kept out of their money for lengthy periods and without compensating interest during the delay, and was the reason for adopting the new wording, the meaning of which is self-explanatory.

21.13 The English statute and case law on the award of interest after the expiry of the three month period is referred to in para.21.04, above.

It is the practice of English courts and arbitrators, in the exercise of their statutory powers, to award interest at a commercial rate, which might exceed the rate allowed under the rule. However, the creditor cannot take advantage of this possibly more favourable rate and claim statutory interest from the date of the sacrifice or expenditure, as the statutory power to award interest does not apply during a period in which the claimant has a contractual right to interest,[13] such as is conferred by r.XXI. It follows that statutory interest can only be awarded from the date on which the interest ceases to accrue under r.XXI. The fact that the right to interest under the rule ceases after three months from the publication of the adjustment should not provide any reason for the court or arbitrator to refuse to exercise its discretion to award interest thereafter.

The court's powers do not extend to the awarding of interest upon interest, with the result that any interest to which the claimant had become entitled under this rule would have to be left out of account in computing statutory interest. There is no such restriction on arbitrator's powers.

21.14 **"due allowance being made for any payment on account"**: In practice[14] effect is given to this part of the rule by crediting the contributory interests concerned with the full amount of interest allowable to them under the earlier words of the rule, and then debiting them with interest on the amount of the payment on account for the period between such payment and three months after the date of the general average statement, and crediting a like amount to the source of the funds from which the payment on account was made, for example deposit fund or contributory interests (or their underwriters) as the case may be. The alternative–a straightforward reduction in the amount of interest credited to a party–might work an injustice, since the saving in interest would benefit the parties to the adventure in proportion to their liability in general average, whereas the funds which made the interim payment possible may have been provided by the parties in quite different proportions, or even by only one of the parties. The rule makes no provision for interim reimbursement from other sources, for example as damages from a colliding vessel, and the treatment of interest in such a case is best explained by example.

[13] Supreme Courts Act 1981 s.35A(4); County Courts Act 1984 s.69(4).

[14] The same practice prevails in the US.

A shipowner incurs general average expenditure of 150,000 consequent upon a collision for which the other vessel is two-thirds to blame. One year after the expenditure was incurred, a recovery is effected from the colliding vessel of:

2/3 × 150,000	100,000
Interest for 1 year @ 12 per cent	12,000
	112,000

and the general average adjustment is issued six months thereafter showing the following figures:

General average expenditure		150,000
Interest @ 7 per cent for 1 year on	150,000	10,500
Credit: Recovery	100,000	
Interest for 9[15] months on	50,000	2,625
		163,125
Credit: Recovery	100,000	(100,000)
Interest 1 year @ 12 per cent	12,000	(7,000)[16]
	112,000	
Net General Average		56,125

Paragraph (b) (applicable to 2004 Rule only)

"the Assembly of the Comite Maritime International shall decide the rate of interest which shall apply . . . during the following calendar year": The reasons why this provision was adopted in 2004, and the matters to be taken into account by the Assembly in deciding the rate of interest are described in para.21.10 above. 21.15

The applicable yearly rates of interest are published on the CMI website.[17] At the date of publication the following rates have been fixed, applicable to the calendar years 2005 to 2008:

- 2005—4.5%;
- 2006—4.5%;
- 2007—5.5%;
- 2008—5.75%.

15 Six, plus three months after the adjustment.
16 General average cannot be credited with interest at a greater rate than is allowable under r.XXI.
17 *http://www.comitemaritime.org* [Accessed September 20, 2013].

Rule XXII

Treatment of Cash Deposits

Note: The Collection of cash deposits forms but one small part of the overall general average security and enforcement system; for a complete survey, reference is requested to the Chapter on Assessing and Enforcing Rights of Contribution at paras 30.01 et seq., below.

Historical Development and Practice of Rule XXII

York-Antwerp Rules 1924

Prior to 1924 there was considerable diversity of practice in the treatment of cash deposits collected from cargo interests, which was not always satisfactory to the depositors. In some countries the deposits were retained in the shipowners' own banking accounts, or in their businesses, and cases occurred of the deposits being lost if the shipowners became bankrupt before completion of the adjustment. For the greater protection of depositors and also in the interests of uniformity, the Association of Average Adjusters proposed a new rule in accordance with the practice in this country and based to a large extent on the wording of the then current Lloyd's Average Bond,[1] a document itself designed to be fair to all parties. **22.01**

"*Rule XXIII. Treatment of Cash Deposits*

Where cash deposits have been collected in respect of cargo's liability for general average, salvage or special charges, such deposits shall be paid into a special account, earning interest where possible, in the joint names of two trustees (one to be nominated on behalf of the shipowner and the other on behalf of the depositors) in a bank to be approved by such trustees. The sum so deposited, together with accrued interest, if any, shall be held as security for and upon trust for payment to the parties entitled thereto of the general average, salvage or special charges payable by the cargo in

[1] See Appendix 3, paras 1101–1104 in the 10th edn of this work. The present Lloyd's Average Bond (Appendix 4, para.80.03, below) makes no reference to deposits.

respect to which the deposits have been collected. The trustees shall have power to make payments on account or refunds of deposits which may be certified to in writing by the average adjuster. Such deposits and payments or refunds shall be without prejudice to the ultimate liability of the parties."

York-Antwerp Rules 1950

22.02 Because it conflicted with the anti-trust laws in certain States, r.XXIII of the York-Antwerp Rules 1924 was never acceptable in the United States, and contracts of affreightment were often worded: "General average to be adjusted in accordance with York-Antwerp Rules 1924, Rules 1/15 and 17/22 inclusive . . ." thereby excluding the application of this particular rule. To overcome this objection the rule was amended in 1950, all words being omitted from which it might be inferred that the deposit account was in the nature of a trust. The alteration did not affect the liability of the two representatives to deal with the deposits in accordance with their mandate, but, as noted below, it did alter the procedure to be adopted if they were in doubt concerning the rights of the parties to the deposit funds.

Another minor addition to the rule was that deposits were to be paid without any delay into the special bank account, and r.XXIII was renumbered XXII.

York-Antwerp Rules 1974

22.03 No change.

York-Antwerp Rules 1994

22.04 No change.

York-Antwerp Rules 2004

22.05 No change.

Rule XXII

TREATMENT OF CASH DEPOSITS

Where cash deposits have been collected in respect of cargo's liability for general average, salvage or special charges, such deposits shall be paid without any delay into a special account in the joint names of a representative nominated on behalf of the shipowner and a representative nominated on behalf of the depositors in a bank to be approved by both. The sum so deposited, together with accrued interest, if any, shall be held as security for payment to the parties entitled thereto of the general average, salvage or special charges payable by cargo in respect of which the deposits have been collected. Payments on account or refunds of deposits may be made if certified to in writing by the average adjuster. Such deposits and payments or refunds shall be without prejudice to the ultimate liability of the parties.

Construction

This rule is largely enabling in character. Thus, it does not direct that the cargo owner shall provide a deposit to secure the payment of cargo's liability in general average or for salvage or special charges. Whether the cargo owner can be compelled to pay such a deposit depends upon the law of the place where the cargo owner seeks to take delivery. In England, the shipowner can exercise his lien on the cargo until its owner either pays what is demanded as contribution or pays a deposit or otherwise provides reasonable security for payment of what may be due.[2] On the other hand, it does provide what shall be done with any deposits which are in fact paid, and ensures that the interests of the cargo owner are fully protected against the risk of misappropriation. 22.06

With the advent of complex legislation aimed at tackling money-laundering and funding of terrorism, setting up joint accounts can be time consuming and expensive. Particularly when multiple cargo interests are involved the parties generally accept that deposits can be held in a properly designated client account controlled by the adjuster.

"Where cash deposits have been collected . . . in a bank to be approved by both": The first sentence of the rule is of a procedural nature only and self-explanatory; no analysis is thought to be necessary. Once the deposit has been paid to the carrier or to his agent, the carrier falls under the obligation imposed by the rule to open the special account and to pay in the money, and is responsible if the money is lost before that time. 22.07

"The sum so deposited . . . shall be held as security . . .": It is perhaps worth stating that the principle security provided by the consignee in order to obtain delivery of his cargo and release from the shipowners' lien is, in fact, the undertaking he gives when signing an average bond and agreeing "to pay the proper proportion of any salvage and/or general average . . . ". When a general average deposit is paid, the deposit is nominally only a collateral security to the principal undertaking in the average bond, to be cashed only if the consignee fails to honour any proper demand for the general average contribution (or a payment on account thereof, as also provided in the average bond). It is not an advance payment, as such, of the contribution ultimately found to be due.

In practical terms, this distinction may appear over-fine, but it could be important, for instance, if the trustees of the deposit funds chose to exchange

[2] See paras 30.50 et seq., below.

the deposits[3] into some other currency without first seeking the consent of the depositors. (Compare Examples 1 and 2 in para.22.11, below.)

22.08 **"Payments on account or refunds of deposits may be made if certified to in writing by the average adjuster"**: The rule does not require that payments or refunds shall be made if certified by the adjuster, and it is submitted, contrary to the view expressed in the 11th and 12th edns of this Work, that no such requirement is to be implied. The effect, therefore, is that the deposit must be retained intact unless both the adjuster and the representatives of ship and cargo determine otherwise. In practical terms, from the point of view of the representatives, payments on account from the deposit funds to those cargo interests whose property has been sacrificed, or refunds of deposits where: (1) the original estimates on which the deposits were based subsequently prove to be excessive; or (2) a deposit was taken when general average damage to that cargo will make it a creditor of the general average,[4] can usually be safely left to the discretion of the adjuster. In other cases, particularly where there is a possibility that any liability will be resisted on the grounds of actionable fault, it would be sensible to consult first with the major interests which might be affected by the payment or refund. Unlike the pre 1977 Lloyd's Average Bond,[5] r.22 does not protect the representatives from claims for negligence in respect of payments or refunds authorised by them. Nor does it protect the adjuster.

This rule and r.E contain the only provisions in the York-Antwerp Rules which refer to the average adjuster and authorise him to make certain decisions which are binding on the parties. The question what is meant by "the average adjuster" in this context is considered in paras 30.35 et seq., below.

22.09 **"Such deposits and payments or refunds shall be without prejudice to the ultimate liability of the parties"**: The payment of a general average deposit by a cargo owner or insurer is made simply to obtain the release of the cargo from the shipowner's lien.[6] The above words clearly indicate that the payment of the deposit can in no way be construed as an admission by the depositor that a general average situation exists, or prevent him—at any later stage—from challenging any of the allowances made by the adjuster in the general average adjustment, or challenging liability (wholly or in part) if he can demonstrate that "the event which gave rise to the sacrifice or expenditure may have been due to the fault of one of the parties to the adventure" (r.D).

[3] In the *Worms and Co v Deutsche Levante Link* (1924) the German Supreme Court confirmed the decision of two lower courts that a deposit paid in Rumanian Lei should be returned to the depositors for its full amount, less the general average contribution due in German Marks (a depreciated currency).

[4] *The Norway* (1865) Br. & L. 404 at 411 PC.

[5] The Bond, on which r.XXII was based, used to provide: "AND IT IS HEREBY DECLARED AND AGREED than any payment . . . on account which shall be made by the Trustees . . . in pursuance of any Certificate . . . given by the said Adjusters . . . shall discharge such Trustees from all liability in respect of the amounts so paid and it shall not be necessary for them to inquire into the correctness of the Statement or Certificate."

[6] The pre–1977 form of Lloyd's Average Bond used to provide: "PROVIDED ALWAYS that the deposits . . . shall be treated as payments made without prejudice and without admitting liability in respect of the said alleged salvage and/or general average . . . and as though the same had been made by the Depositors respectively for the purpose only of obtaining delivery of their goods . . ."

A similar situation exists if part or the whole of a deposit is refunded to the depositor; this cannot be construed as an admission by the shipowner that a general average situation did not exist.[7]

Nor is the position altered if the depositor permits payments to be made ex the deposit, either to settle his alleged proportion of any salvage award, or to make a payment on account to other parties to the adventure who have financed large average expenditures or sustained large sacrifices. However, problems of some financial consequence might arise if, for instance, payments from the deposit funds were made without seeking the prior approval of some of the major depositors when the deposits are in one currency, but the liability is in another, and exchange rates have moved. The situation is best explained by example, and for this purpose the same currencies and rates of exchange are adopted as elsewhere[8] when dealing with problems of rates of exchange.

Examples

Common Facts

An American shipowner carrying a Japanese cargo incurs salvage services and port of refuge expenses in Yen, which he settles in his own operating currency of US Dollars @ $1.00 = Y 250. **22.10**

Provisional estimates of the total general average and contributory values suggest a contribution in the region of seven or eight per cent of the contributory values, and general average, deposits at the rate of 10 per cent are required.

Japanese Consignee "A", with cargo worth Y 25,000,000 (@ 250 = $100,000), is required to pay a 10 per cent deposit of .... Y 2,500,000

The general average adjustment is shown in the shipowners' operating currency of USD and the final contribution is eight per cent. Consignee "A" is therefore called upon to pay $8,000

The rate of exchange ruling at the time of the adjustment and settlement is .... $1.00 = Y 125

Example 1—Deposit Retained in **Yen**. **22.11**

	Debit	Credit
Consignee "A"– Wants his Deposit		Y 2,500,000
Pays General Average	$ 8,000	
	@ 125 =	1,000,000
Net: HE RECEIVES		Y 1,500,000

[7] The pre–1977 form of Lloyd's Average Bond used to provide: ". . . and in like manner all amounts returned by the Trustees to the Depositors shall be received by the latter respectively without prejudice to any claim which the Master or Owner of the said Ship may have against them respectively."

[8] See paras 40.01 and 40.32 et seq., below.

Example 2—Deposit Exchanged into **Dollars.**
(@ 250 = S 10.000)

	Debit	Credit
Consignee "A"– Wants his Deposit		$ 10,000
Pays General Average	$ 8,000	$ 8,000
Net: HE RECEIVES		$ 2,000
	@ 125 =	Y 250,000

Note: On the assumption that the deposit is merely security for payment of a future liability, it is submitted that the holders of the deposit funds have no right to transfer those deposits into any other currency—even the currency of the liability—except with the prior permission of the depositors, or if the bill of lading, contract of affreightment, or average bond expressly permits it.[9] The fact that the deposit may be in a "weak" currency does not alter the position, even if it should encourage the holders of the deposit funds to seek the necessary permission to make the exchange. Accordingly, it is submitted that unless Consignee "A" gave consent to the exchange of his deposit into US Dollars, under Example 2 he has the right to sue for the Y 1,250,000 lost to him by the exchange.

22.12 *Example 3*—Deposit Retained in **Yen.**
—Payment on Account taken of $ 5.000 @ 200 = Y 1,000,000

	Debit	Credit
Consignee "A"– Wants his Deposit		Y 2,500,000
Liable for General Average	$ 8,000	
Less: Payment on Account	5,000 =	1,000,000
		Y 1,500,000
Balance to Pay	$ 3,000	
	@ 125 =	375,000
Net: HE RECEIVES		Y 1,125,000

Note: Unless Consignee "A" gave consent to the payment on account taken from his deposit, it is presumably possible for him to base a case for a refund of Y 1,500,000 (as in *Example 1*) on the grounds that his ultimate liability for general average is $ 8,000 and, in terms of r.XXII, any "*payments* (on account) . . . *shall*

[9] The concluding part of a common American bill of lading clause reads as follows:
"Such cash deposit as the Carrier or his agents may deem sufficient as additional security for the contribution of the goods and for any salvage and special charges thereon, shall, if required, be made by the goods, shippers, consignees, or owners of the goods to the Carrier before delivery. Such deposit shall, at the option of the Carrier, be payable in United Slates money, and may be remitted to the adjuster. When so remitted the deposit shall be held in a special account at the place of adjustment in the name of the adjuster pending settlement of the General Average and refunds or credit balances, if any, shall be paid in United States money."

be without prejudice to the ultimate liability." It is submitted[10] that this is not correct in practice (particularly when the deposit is being used to finance the Consignee's own proportion of a salvage award), and that *ultimate liability* refers to an overall liability to contribute to general average, rather than for a precise sum, but the point is of sufficient importance to make the strong recommendation that a clause dealing with matters of rates of exchange in general average should be incorporated in every bill of lading, contract of affreightment, or the average agreement itself. Failing this, the prior consent of at least some of the major cargo interests will always need to be obtained before any exchange, or use, can be made of deposits funds.

[10] For the sake of completeness, reference might be made to the case of *Noreuro Traders Ltd v E. Hardy & Co* (1923) 16 Lloyd's Rep. 319, where the rates of exchange applicable to payments on account was a problem touched upon, but that case is today of doubtful authority and, in any case, was not concerned with general average deposits.

RULE XXIII

TIME BAR FOR CONTRIBUTIONS TO GENERAL AVERAGE

ENGLISH LAW AND BACKGROUND

Until the adoption of the York-Antwerp Rules 2004, when a time bar was, for the first time, incorporated into the Rules, all questions of limitation of action were governed by the law of the country where the claim for contribution was made, and any foreign law which those courts might apply under their conflict of laws rules. This remains the position for all claims for contribution except where the contract of affreightment incorporates the 2004 Rules.

Section 5 of the Limitation Act, 1980 provides for a limitation period of six years for actions "founded on simple[1] contract", after which the action will be time-barred. This immediately raises the question whether, as between the parties to the adventure,[2] rights and obligations in general average are so founded, or whether they arise independently of contract, simply as an incident of the carriage of goods by sea. This question is discussed generally in Section 1,[3] where it is concluded that, although this will not invariably be the case, in most cases the obligation to pay contribution will in practice be contractual. For example, it has been held that a clause in a bill of lading,[4] or charter party[5] which provides that general average shall be adjusted or settled according to the York-Antwerp Rules imposes a contractual obligation to contribute, and in such circumstances it is not open to the claimant to seek to avoid the limitation period by advancing his claim under the mercantile law independently of the contract.[6] The provisions of the Act **23.01**

[1] i.e. a contract not made under seal.

[2] The same problem does not arise between the parties to the adventure and their insurers, where the rights and obligations are founded on the contract of insurance.

[3] Paras 00.16 et seq., above.

[4] *Castle Insurance Co v Hong Kong Shipping Co* [1984] A.C. 226.

[5] *Union of India v E.B. Aabys Rederi* [1975] A.C. 797. See also *Alma Shipping Corp v Union of India* [1971] 2 Lloyd's Rep. 494; paras 00.26–00.27, above.

[6] See the cases cited above, fn.5.

will apply also in the case where the contract under which the claim arises contains an arbitration clause.[7]

Even where the obligation to contribute is not, strictly speaking, contractual, the courts might nevertheless apply the Limitation Act, since the words "founded on contract" are widely interpreted, and have been held applicable to analogous claims,[8] although there is no decision on whether the Act applies to a non-contractual general average claim. If the Limitation Act is inapplicable, the claim may nevertheless become barred, in the event of undue delay in prosecuting it, under the equitable doctrine of laches.

Accrual of the Cause of Action

23.02 Where the Limitation Act 1980 is applicable, the six year period within which the action must be commenced begins to run at the date when the cause of action accrues. This date may vary, depending upon precisely how the claim arises.

Claims under policies of insurance

23.03 The question of when the cause of action accrues under a policy of insurance for a general average loss, was considered in *Chandris v Argo Insurance Co Ltd*,[9] in which the defendant insurers relied upon the statute as a defence to a claim by their assured for indemnity against their proportion of general average sacrifices and expenditure made and incurred by them. The assured contended that the cause of action accrued upon the issue and publication of an adjustment, the defendants that it accrued when the sacrifices were made or the expenditure incurred, or alternatively on the termination of the adventure.

Megaw J. held: (1) that by reason of the terms of the policy and the York-Antwerp Rules incorporated therein, the parties had contemplated and provided that an average statement should be produced (but not that it should be binding on them); but (2) that the publication of an adjustment had not been made a condition precedent to the existence of a cause of action; and (3) that in the absence of an express term to that effect, liability to contribute arose when the sacrifice was made or expenditure incurred.[10]

23.04 Although the case was not directly concerned with a claim for indemnity against liability to contribute to the general average loss of another party to the

[7] Arbitration Act 1996 s.13. See also s.14 for the steps involved in commencing the arbitration for the purposes of the Act.

[8] *Re Diplock* [1948] Ch. 465, 514; *Kleinwort Benson Ltd v The Sandwell B.C.* [1994] 4 All E.R. 890, 942–943. As recorded in the latter case, the 1939 Limitation Act, on which the 1980 Act was based, was intended to give effect to the recommendations contained in the Fifth Interim Report of the Law Revision Committee, which included the recommendation that the limitation period should be six years for all actions founded on tort or simple contract (including quasi contract) (emphasis supplied). See also Goff & Jones, *Law of Restitution*, 6th edn, paras 43–001 to 43–002 and 43.010; *Halsbury's Law*, Vol.28, para.863.

[9] *Chandris* [1963] 2 Lloyd's Rep. 65.

[10] The decision on the third point was based in part on *Noreuro Traders v E. Hardy & Co* (1923) 16 Lloyd's Rep. 320 and dicta in *Tate & Lyle Ltd v Hain S.S. Co Ltd* (1934) 151 L.T. 249 (reversed on another point (1936) 41 Com. Cas. 350) and *Morrison S.S. Co Ltd v Greystoke Castle* [1947] A.C. 265 at 283, 312, and in part on s.66(3) of the Marine Insurance Act 1906.

adventure, there are several passages in the judgment which indicate that Megaw J. would have held, primarily on the basis of the wording of s.66(5) of the Marine Insurance Act 1906 that the cause of action against insurers in respect of such a claim also arose when the sacrifice was made or expenditure incurred. However, if the issue arose today, it is believed that the court would prefer to follow the approach adopted in other cases of liability insurance, where, unless the policy otherwise provides, the cause of action is not treated as arising until the assured's liability to the third party is established by judgment or agreement,[11] in which case even the publication of an adjustment, which is not of itself binding upon the parties,[12] would not suffice to create a cause of action. The wording of s.66(5) of the Marine Insurance Act hardly seems specific enough to require a different approach to be adopted in the case of insurance against liability to contribute in general average; but the existence of a lien to enforce the right to contribution, which is exercisable although the assured's liability may be in dispute, might be regarded as a sufficient practical reason for holding that the cause of action against insurers should arise at an earlier stage.

Claims between the parties to the adventure

In *Schothorst and Schuitema v Franz Dauter GmbH*[13] it was argued that in the **23.05**
case of a claim between parties to the adventure time started to run only on the publication of an adjustment. Kerr J. rejected this argument, holding that the reasoning of Megaw J. in *Chandris v Argo Insurance*[14] applied equally to a claim for contribution made by one party to the adventure against another party to the adventure, so that time began to run at the date of the general average sacrifice or expenditure.

The same conclusion was reached in *Castle Insurance Co v Hong Kong Shipping Co*[15] where the Privy Council held that the shipowner's claim under the bills of lading[16] for contribution from cargo arose when the sacrifice was made or the expenditure incurred. It made no difference that the bills of lading contemplated that an adjustment would be prepared in accordance with the York-Antwerp Rules.

It should be noted that the cause of action can only be said to accrue in a rather artificial sense before the adventure is terminated, since only then can it be known

[11] *Post Office v Norwich Union Fire Insurance Society* [1967] 2 Q.B. 363: *Bradley v Eagle Star Insurance Co* [1989] A.C. 957, in neither of which was *Chandris v Argo Insurance* cited to the court or referred to in the judgments. See also Sir Jonathan Mance in [1995] L.M.C.L.Q. at 37–40; *McGillivray on Insurance Law*, 10th edn, para.28–3. The decision in *Chandris v Argo Insurance* was approved by the Privy Council in *Castle Insurance Co v Hong Kong Shipping Ltd* [1984] A.C. 226, 236–238, but that was a case under an average bond and guarantee rather than a policy of insurance, and Post Office v Norwich Union was not cited to the Judicial Committee.

[12] See para.30.35 et seq., below.

[13] *Schothorst and Schuitema v Franz Dauter GmbH* [1973] 2 Lloyd's Rep. 91.

[14] Para.23.03, above.

[15] *Castle Insurance Co v Hong Kong Shipping Co* [1984] 1 A.C. 226.

[16] A different conclusion was reached on the shipowner's claim under the average bonds and guarantees: see para.23.06, below.

what property is to contribute and what its value is.[17] But the accrual of a cause of action is in any event an artificial concept, as a number of cases have shown in other branches of the law.[18]

Claims under average agreements

23.06 Where the defendant has entered into a bond, guarantee or other form of undertaking whereby he agrees to pay such general average as may legally be due, the undertaking creates a fresh cause of action, in respect of which time cannot begin to run until the undertaking is given.[19] However, it does not follow that time will necessarily begin to run even at that date, since the terms of the undertaking may, expressly or by implication, provide that the publication of an adjustment shall be a condition precedent to making any claim thereunder. Thus in *Castle Insurance Co v Hong Kong Shipping Co*[20] it was held that the Lloyd's bond executed by the consignees, and the average guarantees executed by the insurers of he cargo, made it clear by implication that the claim thereunder was not to arise until the adjustment had been completed. There can in practice be few forms of undertaking which would give rise to a different interpretation, since one of the forms of guarantee simply contained a promise to pay any contribution which may be legally chargeable.

Limitation Periods under Foreign Law

23.07 In the case of claims between the parties to the adventure, the rules described above will apply where the action or arbitral claim for contribution is brought in England and the adjustment is governed by English law.[21] Where the claim is brought in England but the adjustment is governed by foreign law, the effect of the Foreign Limitation Periods Act, 1984 is that the limitation provisions of the law governing the adjustment will apply, except insofar as they conflict with English public policy.[22] Where the claim is contractual, a similar result is achieved by the Contracts (Applicable Law) Act 1990. Where the law governing the adjustment is English, but the action is brought in another country, the question whether the English limitation period is applicable will depend upon the conflict of laws rules of the country in which the claim is brought.

[17] See the commentary on r.G, paras G.01 et seq, above. As pointed out by *Rose*, paras 2.77 et seq., these matters are relevant to the valuation of the claim, which in the event of a subsequent total loss may be reduced to nil, rather than the existence of the cause of action.

[18] e.g. *Central Electricity Generating Board v Halifax Corp* [1963] A.C. 785.

[19] *Union of India v E.B. Aaby's Rederi* [1975] A.C. 797.

[20] The Contrary view expressed by Kerr J. in *Schothorst and Schuitema v Franz Dauter* [1973] 2 Lloyd's Rep. 91, 97 was disapproved.

[21] See paras 30.06 et seq., below as to the law governing the adjustment.

[22] For example, if their application would cause undue hardship to either party: s.2(2), Sch.1 art.16; *The Logan* (1936) A.M.C. 993; *Transpacific S.S. Co v Marine Office of America* (1957) A.M.C. 1070; *Argyll Shipping Co v Hanover Insurance Co* [1968] A.M.C. 2195; *The Beatrice* [1957] 1 Lloyd's Rep. 220.

United States

The Courts of the United States have held that the cause of action accrues at the termination of the adventure, although the alternative which they had to consider was the publication of an adjustment, and not the date of the sacrifice or expenditure. **23.08**

The fact that a defendant, in order to obtain the release of his cargo, has entered into an undertaking to pay general average, does not extend the time limit. However, there is no statute of limitations directly applicable to a claim for general average, and the claim will be barred only by laches.

Contractual Limitation Periods

Charterparties and bills of lading frequently contain general provisions which limit the time within which claims must be brought, and which may curtail or (more unusually) extend the limits which would otherwise apply. In English law, such provisions are valid, and it is a question of interpretation of the contract terms as a whole whether the provision extends to claims for general average contribution. Where a charterparty imposed a 12-month time limit from arrival at the port of discharge for claims under the charter, and incorporated the York-Antwerp Rules 1950, it was held that a claim for contribution by the owner against the charterer involved a "dispute under this charter-party" and was therefore time-barred.[23] However, where the defendant has entered into a separate undertaking to contribute to general average, the expiry of the time limit contained in the contract of carriage does not provide a defence to a claim on the undertaking.[24] **23.09**

Where the relevant contract of affreightment incorporates the Hague or Hague-Visby Rules, it is possible that a claim by the cargo owner for contribution towards a sacrifice of his cargo would be held to fall within the provisions of art.III r.6 and become time-barred on expiry of one year of the date when the goods were, or should have been, delivered.[25]

The cases upon which the remarks in the previous paragraph are based were concerned with charter-parties or bills of lading which imposed no special time limit for claims in general average. Where the contract does impose a special time limit of that nature, for example by incorporation of the York-Antwerp Rules 2004, it would doubtless be held that the special time limit overrides any inconsistent general provisions, such as art.III r.6 of the Hague Rules, provided that the special limit is not shorter than that under art.III r.6. **23.10**

23 *Alma Shipping Corp v Union of India* [1971] 2 Lloyd's Rep. 494;

24 *Union of India v E.B. Aaby's Rederi* [1975] A.C. 797;

25 *Goulandris v Goldman* [1958] 1 Q.B. 74, 106 Pearson J. appears to have envisaged that art.III r.6 of the Hague Rules, which is rather narrower than the equivalent provision of the Hague Rules, would apply to such a claim, although they did not apply to the cargo owners cross-claim for damages equal to the shipowner's claim for contribution: see para.00.52 et seq., above.

HISTORICAL DEVELOPMENT OF RULE XXIII

York-Antwerp Rules 2004

23.11 Until 2004, the York-Antwerp Rules contained no provision which regulated the time within which proceedings for general average contribution had to be commenced. National laws impose widely different time bars, and also differ in their approach to time limits where an average bond or guarantee has been signed. In English law for example, as mentioned above,[26] such a bond or guarantee is likely to be held to create a fresh cause of action arising upon the publication of the adjustment, the effect of which will often be to postpone the beginning, let alone the end, of the limitation period until many years after the end of the adventure. For a substantial period before the Vancouver Conference pressure had been growing from hull and cargo underwriters for the incorporation of a time bar into the Rules, expressed in such terms that it would lead to the speedier completion of adjustments.

However, there had always existed substantial opposition to incorporating a time bar provision into the Rules, on the grounds that in many jurisdictions limitation rules are mandatory, and cannot be departed from by private contract; it follows, according to this view, that the Rules, since they have only contractual force, are not a suitable vehicle for imposing a time bar, and that it would be preferable, for example, to persuade UNCITRAL to incorporate a time bar for claims in general average into the draft International Convention on Issues of Transport Law, by which means it would eventually acquire the force of law.

23.12 Against this background, the matter was widely debated both before and at Vancouver, and the view that a time bar provision should be incorporated into the Rules prevailed, broadly speaking on the following grounds:

(1) the provision would be enforceable in many countries, and thus produce a much greater level of uniformity than previously existed;

(2) It would serve as a guideline, and might provide an incentive to legislators to incorporate a similar provision into their domestic law.

RULE XXIII

TIME BAR FOR CONTRIBUTIONS TO GENERAL AVERAGE

(a) Subject always to any mandatory rule on time limitation contained in any applicable law:

(i) Any rights to general average contribution, including any rights to claim under general average bonds and guarantees, shall be

[26] Para.23.06, above.

extinguished unless an action is brought by the party claiming such contribution within a period of one year after the date upon which the general average adjustment was issued. However, in no case shall such an action be brought after six years from the date of the termination of the common maritime adventure.

(ii) These periods may be extended if the parties so agree after the termination of the common maritime adventure.

(b) This Rule shall not apply as between the parties to the general average and their respective insurers

CONSTRUCTION

Part (a)

"Subject always to any mandatory rule on time limitation": These introductory words are a recognition of the fact that, as explained in para.23.11 above, the time bar provisions may not be effective in all jurisdictions. In English law there is no rule which prevents the provisions from taking effect according to their terms. 23.13

"Any rights to general average contribution . . . shall be extinguished": This provision is substantive rather than procedural, in that it extinguishes the right, not merely the remedy.

"including any rights to claim under average bonds or agreements": The rule abolishes the sharp distinction which exists in English law between the time bar applicable to a claim under the contract of carriage and that applicable to a claim under a bond or guarantee. All such claims are subject to the same time limits.

"unless an action is brought": The requirements for bringing an action will depend upon the jurisdiction in which the claim is brought. In England they are satisfied by issuing a claim form out of the court. The word "action" should be understood in a non-technical sense, and as including arbitration in the case where an arbitration agreement is in force between the claimant and the defendant.[27] 23.14

"within a period of one year after the date upon which the general average adjustment was issued": When more than one adjustment is issued, as in The Bijela,[28] it is submitted that the one year begins to run from the date of the first adjustment.

It is probable that an adjustment is "issued", for the purpose of the rule, when it is delivered to the claimant, or he is informed that it is ready for collection.

[27] Compare the non-technical approach adopted in *The Merak* [1965] P. 223, holding that "suit" in art.III r.6 of the Hague Rules included arbitration.

[28] *Marida v Oswal Steel (The Bijela)* [1994] 2 Lloyd's Rep. 1 (HL) reversing [1993] 1 Lloyd's Rep. 411, affirming [1992] 1 Lloyd's Rep. 637. See para.14.31, above.

The importance which the rule attaches to the date of the issue of the adjustment, and the comparatively short time thereafter within which an action must be commenced, seem to contemplate that the matters, if any, in issue between the parties after the adjustment has been issued will be limited and well defined, and raise the question whether a professional adjuster must be employed. This question is discussed in Section 5.[29]

"in no case shall such an action be brought more than six years after the termination of the common maritime adventure": The rule has adopted the English limitation period of six years, but whereas under English law[30] the period starts to run from the date of the sacrifice or expenditure, under the rule it does not start until the date of termination of the adventure, a question which is discussed in the context of r.G.[31] The important feature of the provision is that it contains a cut-off time limit, which will apply to all claims in general average, including those under bonds or guarantees, irrespective of the date of the issue of the adjustment, and even if no adjustment has been issued. This fulfils the desire of ship and cargo underwriters to ensure that adjustments are completed without undue delay.

The language may suggest that the time bar, insofar as it depends on the expiry of six years after the termination of the adventure, is procedural rather than substantive. It is submitted, however, that this is probably not the case, and that the effect is that if the claimant fails to bring the action within six years of the termination of the adventure his claim itself is extinguished, because he is irrevocably disabled from complying with the condition necessary to prevent its extinguishment under the provisions of the previous sentence.

23.15 **"These periods may be extended if the parties so agree after the termination of the common maritime adventure"**: By implication the rule purports to prevent the parties from agreeing to extend the time limits before the termination of the adventure, the reason being, no doubt, to discourage the parties from inserting provisions laying down longer periods in their charters or bills of lading. However, in English law at any rate, since the effect of the York-Antwerp Rules is purely contractual, there is nothing to prevent the parties from agreeing at any time to incorporate, exclude or vary any parts of the Rules as they see fit.

Part (b)

23.16 **"This rule shall not apply as between the parties to the general average and their respective insurers"**: The time limit for claims under insurance policies will therefore depend upon the general law, as to which see paras 23.03 to 23.04, above.

[29] Para.30.38 et seq., below.

[30] See para.23.05, above.

[31] Para.G.21 et seq., above.

SECTION 5

ASSESSING AND ENFORCING RIGHTS OF CONTRIBUTION

This Section deals with the means by which rights of contribution are assessed and enforced, and the subject is discussed in two parts: **30.01**

(1) The preparation of the adjustment.
(2) The recovery of contribution.

Whilst the second part deals mainly with procedural matters, many of the topics discussed in the first part are concerned more with substantive rights in general average than with the means of enforcing those rights, and could be said to merit a section of their own. The two topics are discussed in the same section partly for convenience, and partly because they are to some extent related. For example, the question of which courts or other tribunals have jurisdiction over disputes concerning general average may depend on the law governing the adjustment, and many general average clauses, the interpretation of which is discussed in this section, deal both with substantive rights and with the means of determining disputes and recovering payment.

1. THE PREPARATION OF THE ADJUSTMENT

Shipowner's Obligation

In former times the adjustment of general average often took place on the quay-side at the end of the voyage, with settlement being made in kind rather than in cash. In modern conditions however, the enforcement of rights of contribution is in practical terms impossible unless an adjustment is prepared, particularly where multiple interests are involved. It has been held that, where the York-Antwerp Rules apply, a written adjustment must be prepared,[1] and although there is no **30.02**

[1] *Chandris v Argo Insurance Co Ltd* [1963] 2 Lloyd's Rep. 65.

decision directly on the point in cases not governed by the rules, the remarks of Lush J. in *Crooks v Allen*[2] and of Lord Herschell in *Wavertree Sailing Ship Co v Love* suggest that they recognise that such an obligation to exist. The question whether a professional adjuster must be employed is dealt with below.[3]

30.03 The obligation of producing the adjustment lies upon the shipowner, who is usually willing to undertake the task anyway because he is a creditor in the general average, but even where the only general average loss is a sacrifice of cargo, the shipowner is obliged to prepare the adjustment.[4] The reason why this burden is imposed on him is that he alone of the parties to the adventure is in a position, by the exercise of his lien, to obtain security and, equally important, to obtain particulars of the value of the various consignments of cargo. However the shipowner is not required to bear all the costs of the adjustment himself, and the costs of preparing it are a general average expense.[5]

Where Should the Adjustment be Prepared?

30.04 The simple answer to this question is that there is no requirement imposed by law that the adjustment be prepared at any particular place. The York-Antwerp Rules are also silent on the question. Accordingly, so long as the correct governing law is selected in its preparation, it matters not where the adjustment is prepared nor where the adjuster carries on business, does his calculations or publishes the adjustment. As Blackburn J. is reported to have observed in *Mavro v Ocean Marine Insurance Co*[6]: "it does not matter who stated the average, whether a Turk or a Frenchman or the arbitrator in England."

In *Wavertree Sailing Ship v Love*[7] it was contended that the shipowner was bound to have an average statement drawn up by an average adjuster at the port of discharge. The voyage had ended at Sydney, New South Wales, and the cargo interests had entered into a bond by which they undertook to furnish particulars of the value of their goods for the purpose of enabling general average to be "ascertained and adjusted in the usual manner". The shipowners employed a Liverpool firm of adjusters, there being no difference between the law of England and the law of New South Wales relating to general average. The Privy Council rejected the argument of the cargo interests that the shipowner was obliged to employ an adjuster at Sydney. Lord Herschell said:

> "The shipowner was not bound to employ a member of any particular class of persons or indeed to employ any one at all. He might if he pleased make out his own average statement, and he may do the same at the present time if so minded. If he engages the services of an average stater, it is merely as a matter of business convenience on his

[2] *Crooks v Allen* (1879) 5 Q.B.D. 38, below, para.30.47.
[3] See para.30.38, below.
[4] *Crooks v Allen* (1879) 5 Q.B.D. 38, below, para.30.47.
[5] See para.C.34, above.
[6] *Mavro v Ocean Marine Insurance Co* (1875) 32 L.T. 743 at 745; 2 Asp. M.L.C. 590 at 592. The expression is omitted from the report in L.R. 10.C.P. 414.
[7] *Wavertree Sailing Ship v Love* [1897] A.C. 373.

part. The average stater is not engaged, nor does he act on behalf of any of the other parties concerned, nor does his statement bind them."[8]

The decision in the case was approved in *Castle Insurance Co v Hong Kong Shipping Co*[9] and is undoubtedly correct. Many firms of average adjusters have offices or correspondents in other countries, but there is no reason in law why an adjustment governed by the law of one country should not be prepared in another. However, some of Lord Herschell's remarks, in particular the statement that the employment of a professional adjuster is merely a matter of business convenience on the shipowner's part, need re-examination in the light of modern practice, particularly when the agreement between the parties requires that general average shall be adjusted "in the usual manner". The question is discussed at para.30.38, below.

The "place of adjustment"

In many of the reported cases, such as Simonds v White[10] such phrases as "the **30.05**
place of adjustment" are used to describe the place where the adventure ends, and it was upon this use of the phrase that the cargo interests in *Wavertree Sailing Ship Co v Love* based their argument that the adjustment should be prepared where the adventure ends. However, as Lord Herschell pointed out, the phrase "place of adjustment" is used to describe the place where the adventure ends because, in the absence of contrary agreement, that is the place:

(a) at which the interests involved in the common adventure are to be valued;
(b) whose law and practice is to be adopted in the adjustment;
(c) where rights of contribution are enforced; and
(d) whose courts would be resorted to in the event of a dispute.

The reasons why (c) and (d) occurred at the place where the adventure ended is that it is there that the property was situate when the lien was is exercised, and if there is was a dispute over the validity of the exercise of the lien it would naturally be at the place of discharge that the matter would be contested. However, in these respects their significance is mainly historical. In modern times, when the lien is almost invariably given up in exchange for security, the main significance of the place where the adventure ends is that it is the place at which sacrifices and contributing interests are valued, and, in the absence of contrary agreement, the place whose law governs the adjustment.

[8] Wavertree at 380. See also *The Santa Anna Maria* 49 Fed. Rep. 878 (1892): *The Alpine* 23 Fed. Rep. 815 (1884); *Chandris v Argo Insurance Co Ltd* [1963] 2 Lloyd's Rep. 65; *Union of India v E.B. Aaby's Rederi A/S* [1974] 3 W.L.R. 269. For a discussion of the circumstances where the parties agree to be bound by an adjustment see para.30.35, below.

[9] *Castle Insurance Co* [1984] A.C. 226.

[10] *Simonds v White* (1824) 2 B. & C. 805, see para.30.08, below.

The effect of a contractual provision that general average shall be adjusted at a stipulated place is considered below at paras 30.17 et seq.

The Law Governing the Adjustment

30.06 The traditional view, supported by all the English authorities, is that the adjustment of general average between the various parties to the adventure is, in the absence of agreement to the contrary, governed by the law of the place at which the voyage terminates.[11] This place, as already observed, is called "the place of adjustment". It seems unlikely, at any rate where the contract of carriage contains no express choice of governing law for the contract as a whole,[12] that the validity of this traditional view has been affected by the Contracts (Applicable Law) Act 1990, which enacts the 1980 Rome Convention on the Law Applicable to Contractual Obligations. Whenever the obligation to contribute is contractual,[13] the provisions of the Convention will apply in determining the governing law.

The basic rule laid down in the Convention, in the absence of a choice of the governing law by the parties themselves,[14] is that the contract is governed by the law of the country with which it is most closely connected.[15] However, the Convention qualifies this basic rule by providing that "a severable part of the contract which has a closer connection with another country may by way of exception be governed by the law of that other country". Applying this provision to general average:

(1) There are good reasons for regarding the obligation to contribute in general average as a severable part of the contract of affreightment, if only because it will usually involve interests other than the two parties to the contract of carriage, and in the absence of contractual provision regulating the adjustment it would fall outside the purview of the contract of carriage.[16]

(2) The reasons why general average is regarded as having its closest connection with the place where the adventure ends are effectively those summarised in para.30.05, above. It could be said that they are mainly historic, and have lost much of their force in the light of modern practice, whereby the lien is almost invariably given up in exchange for security,

[11] See the cases referred to in paras 30.08–30.11 and 30.14–30.16, below. See also Dicey and Morris, *The Conflict of Laws*, 10th edn, r.159 (the current (14th) edition does not deal specifically with general average); *British Shipping Laws*, Vol. 2: Carver, *Carriage by Sea*, 13th edn, para.1453; Arnould, *Law of Marine Insurance*, 16th edn, Vol.2, para.992. Previous editions of this work, as well as the majority of the decisions under English law, refer to the termination of the "voyage" whereas the York-Antwerp Rules, in the context of contributory values, refer to the "end" (r.G) or "termination" (r.XVII) of the "adventure". However, this difference in terminology does not appear to have any practical significance.

[12] As to the case where there is such a clause, see para.30.22, below.

[13] See art.1.1: and see paras 00.20–00.32, above, as to when the obligation is contractual.

[14] For the case where the parties themselves choose the governing law see art.3.1, para.30.22, below.

[15] Art.4.1.

[16] See paras 00.20 et seq., above.

and any disputes are determined long after the delivery of the cargo. However, if the parties are unable to reach agreement on the matter of security, the traditional view of the importance of the place where the adventure ends retains its validity in the last resort. Moreover, it is hallowed by tradition, and there is no sign that the mercantile community regards it as obsolete. For example, the general average provisions of the Institute Time Clauses and the International Hull Clauses are based on the assumption that, in the absence of agreement, the adjustment is governed by the law of the place where the adventure ends. The same assumption is made in recent case law,[17] although the point has not arisen directly for decision since the Convention came into force.

The presumptions laid down by the Convention as to the country with which the contract is most closely connected seem inapplicable to the obligation to contribute in general average.[18]

This rule causes no difficulty where all the cargo on board at the time of the general average act is destined for the same port, and where the voyage to that port is actually completed, but problems arise where the voyage is broken up short of the original destination, and where the cargo is destined for different ports. The various circumstances are considered below under the same headings as those employed in the discussion, under r.G, of the place of valuation of the properties involved in the common maritime adventure. The place of valuation, as we have seen, also depends on the place where the adventure ends, and the problems to which it gives rise are therefore very similar to those involved in determining the law governing the adjustment. However, they are not identical, and those relating to the place of valuation are essentially more complicated. The rules stated below are, of course, subject to variation by express agreement between the parties.[19] **30.07**

The York-Antwerp Rules contain no provisions which determine the law or place of adjustment, or which define the place at which the adventure ends.[20] Where the Rules apply, the role of the governing law and practice will clearly be of far less importance than in the rare cases where the Rules are not incorporated.

[17] i.e. *Sameon Co SA v Petrofina SA* (CA), Unreported April 30, 1997; *Galaxy Special Maritime Enterprise v Prima Ceylon Ltd* [2006] 2 Lloyd's Rep. 27 (CA).

[18] i.e. the general presumption contained in art.4.2 and the special presumption relating to contracts of carriage contained in art.4.4. It is uncertain whether these presumptions apply at all to a severable part of the contract, but, if they do, it would seem that they must be applied to the severed part (see Plender: The European Contracts Convention, para.6.08). In these circumstances, art.4.2 is inapplicable because there is no characteristic performance of the severable part of the contract, each party being merely obliged to pay his share of the general average loss (see art.4.5); and art.4.4 is inapplicable because the severable agreement to contribute in general average is not "a contract for the carriage of goods", or "a contract which has as its main purpose the carriage of goods".

[19] See paras 30.17 et seq., below.

[20] r.XVIII of the York-Antwerp Rules 1890 (see Appendix 2B, below) made provision to the effect that any matter not dealt with by the rules should be determined according to the law and practice which would have governed the adjustment if the contract of affreightment had not incorporated the rules. So far as it went this was unexceptionable, in fact almost a truism, but since the rule gave no positive guidance in identifying the relevant law and practice it was of little or no practical significance, and in 1924 it was abandoned.

However, as explained in para.PRE.07, above, the law and practice governing the adjustment may still have a part to play.

Where the voyage is to a single destination and is wholly performed

30.08 In this case the relevant place is the port of destination and the law to be applied is that of that port.

In *Simonds v White*,[21] an English shipper and owner of cargo, carried from Gibraltar to St Petersburg under a bill of lading governed by English law, as the law of the ship's flag had been compelled at St Petersburg, in order to obtain possession of his goods, to pay a sum of money as contribution towards general average, resulting from the ship having been obliged to put into a port of refuge on the voyage. This contribution, it was admitted, was assessed correctly according to the law of Russia, but amounted to a larger sum than the merchant would have been liable for had the average been adjusted according to English law. The merchant sued the shipowner for the amount which he had thus been compelled to pay in excess of his liability under English law.

Abbott C.J., in delivering the judgment of the court, said that there was one point upon which the laws of all maritime states were agreed, namely, that the place at which a general average should be adjusted was the place of the ship's destination or delivery of the cargo. He continued:

> "The shipper of goods tacitly, if not expressly, assents to general average as a known maritime usage, which may, according to the events of the voyage, be either beneficial or disadvantageous to him. And by assenting to general average he must be understood to assent also to its adjustment at the usual and proper place; and to all this it seems to us to be only an obvious consequence to add that he must be understood to consent also to its adjustment according to the usage and law of the place at which the adjustment is to be made."

For these reasons it was determined that, as between the shipowner and the owner of cargo, the adjustment, being admittedly correct according to the law of Russia, must be regarded as final.[22]

30.09 In *Lloyd v Guibert*,[23] the Court of Exchequer Chamber, while laying down that for many purposes the law of the flag must be resorted to, in order to determine the rights under a contract of affreightment, expressly stated that this was not the rule for general average:

> "The adjustment of a general average at the port of discharge, according to the law prevailing there, is binding upon the shipowner and the merchant, as they must be taken to have assented to adjustment being made at the usual and proper place, and, as a consequence, according to the law of that place."

[21] *Simonds* (1824) 2 B. & C. 805.

[22] See also *Dalglish v Davidson* (1824) 5 Dowl. & Ryl. 6: *Wavertree Sailing Ship Co v Love* [1897] A.C. 373 (see para.30.04, above).

[23] *Lloyd v Guibert* (1865) L.R. 1 Q.B. 115.

Where the voyage is to two or more ports of destination

The problems which arise where cargoes destined for different ports are on board at the time of a general average act concern mainly the ascertainment of contributory values and of the amount of loss to be made good, and are dealt with under r.G. In this section we are concerned with the effect which the delivery of cargo at different ports will have on the law governing the adjustment, but the problems are related, since they each involve an aspect of the place of adjustment.[24] **30.10**

There is no direct authority on the law which governs the adjustment in such a case. Effectively there are three possibilities:

(1) the law of the first port of discharge of any cargo on board at the time of the general average governs the entire adjustment;
(2) the law of the last port of discharge governs;
(3) the law of the place where each parcel of cargo is discharged governs the adjustment between that cargo (and any freight at risk thereon) and ship, but liabilities between cargoes for different destinations will be governed by the law of the place where the debtor cargo is discharged.

Neither of the first two possibilities is entirely practicable, and the favoured solution is the third. The reasoning adopted in *Simonds v White*[25] and *Wavertree Sailing Ship Co v Love*[26] is that the law of the place where the adventure ends governs the adjustment of general average, because it is at that place that the property is situated and the lien[27] will be exercised, and it is to the courts of that place that the parties must resort if there are disputes. This reasoning would suggest that the law of each country where cargo is discharged should apply to the adjustment of any general average contributions due from the owners of the cargo discharged there. **30.11**

This is in line with the practice adopted in determining the place or places at which contributory interests should be valued, and with *Green Star Shipping v The London Assurance*,[28] and it is submitted that it is probably correct, despite the inconvenience involved in preparing an adjustment in accordance with several systems of law.[29] The adjustment would need to be prepared in the manner adopted in the case cited by Lowndes:

> "The steamer Sarnia, having on board cargo, partly destined for Halifax in Nova Scotia and partly for Portland in the United States, met with an accident which obliged her to put back into Liverpool, where her cargo was discharged, for repairs; after which she proceeded and delivered her cargo at both ports without further

[24] See paras G.02 and 30.05, above.
[25] *Simonds* (1824) 2 B. & C. 805.
[26] *Wavertree* [1897] A.C. 373.
[27] See paras 30.41 et seq., below.
[28] *Green Star Shipping* [1933] 1 K.B. 378.
[29] Similar problems arise if the various contracts of affreightment make provision for the adjustment of general average, but subject to different codes: See paras 30.25 et seq., below.

mishap. The adjustment of general average, as between ship, freight and cargo, was prepared by adjusters from Halifax and the United States, associated together. They drew up a joint statement containing two columns for general average, one headed 'Halifax', and the other 'Portland'; and they certified that the amounts shown in the first column were the amounts payable according to British law and should be paid by the owners of the cargo delivered at Halifax, and the amounts shown in the second were according to American law and should be paid by the owners of the cargo delivered at Portland. And this was acted on."

30.12 Using hypothetical figures, and on the assumption that all expenses had been financed by the shipowner, the adjustment might have looked as follows:

	GENERAL Halifax	AVERAGE Portland
Cost of:		
Entering Port of Refuge	5,000	5,000
Discharging Cargo	10,000	10,000
Storing Cargo		5,000
Reloading Cargo	–	10,000
Outward Port Charges	–	2,500
Commission and Interest	–	1,500
	15,000	34,000

APPORTIONED

SHIP	30%			
HALIFAX CARGO	30%	Pays	4,500	
PORTLAND CARGO	40%	Pays		13,600
	100%			

The position would be far more complex[30] were sacrifices of cargo also to be involved, and it cannot be stressed too strongly that shipowners and charterers should endeavour to ensure that all time and voyage charter-parties and bills of lading in force at any one time on the same ship should make identical provisions for the adjustment of general average.

Where the scheduled voyage involves the forwarding of cargo from a transhipment port under a through bill of lading

30.13 This is another situation which is not covered by authority, but it is submitted that, in line with the views expressed in para.G.31, above, the common adventure ends at the port of transhipment, and the on-carriage in another vessel is disregarded. It follows that the adjustment is governed by the law of the port of transhipment.

[30] See the further example given in paras 30.28 et seq., below.

Where the intended voyage is justifiably and wholly abandoned at a port short of destination(s)

If at some intermediate port or place owing to an excepted peril the voyage is, by agreement or by necessity, wholly broken up and ship and cargo finally part company, the place of adjustment is that at which the voyage is broken up and the relevant law is the law of that place. **30.14**

In *Fletcher v Alexander*[31] the facts of which are set out in para.G.03, above, the vessel returned to the loading port after stranding, and the voyage was there abandoned. Bovill C.J. held that, although in general the port of destination was the proper place for adjusting a general average, yet, when the voyage was broken up, and the adventure brought to an end at some other place, the average should be adjusted there, and by the law which there prevailed.

The same view is adopted in *Mavro v Ocean Marine Insurance Co*[32] where Cockburn C.J. said:

> "The adjustment must be made at the port of destination, if it be reached, but if the voyage is interrupted by some supervening cause, which necessitates or justifies its termination at some intermediate place, that place is the proper place of adjustment."[33]

Where the voyage is successfully completed by the ship and some of the cargo, but other cargo is justifiably left behind at a port of refuge

In both *Fletcher v Alexander*[34] and *Mavro v Ocean Marine Insurance Co*[35] the entire voyage was abandoned at the port of refuge, which was therefore held to be the proper place of adjustment. What of the case where part of the cargo is left at the port of refuge, but the remainder is carried to the port of destination in the original vessel? This fell to be decided in *Hill v Wilson*[36] in which the Virago sailed from Riga with a general cargo, bound for Hull, and was stranded and injured, but after jettisoning a small part of the cargo was got off and towed into Copenhagen, where the cargo was discharged and the ship was repaired at large expense. A small quantity of cargo was forwarded to the destination by sister ships, but the whole of the goods belonging to the plaintiffs, being damaged, were sold, as was admittedly proper, at Copenhagen; the ship, with a portion of her original cargo belonging to other shippers, proceeded on her voyage and arrived at Hull. The plaintiffs claimed the proceeds of sale less such charges and general average expenses as the defendant shipowner might be entitled to deduct under English law. The shipowners claimed that, as between themselves and the plaintiffs, the voyage ended at Copenhagen, and that general average as between them must be adjusted at, and by the law of Copenhagen, which was more favourable to the shipowners than the law of England, as giving them a pro rata freight and in **30.15**

[31] *Fletcher v Alexander* (1868) L.R. 3 C.P. 375.
[32] *Mavro v Ocean Marine Insurance Co* (1874) L.R. 9 C.P. 595; L.R. 10 C.P. 414.
[33] *Mavro* (1874) L.R. 10 C.P. 414 at 416.
[34] See fn.31, above.
[35] See fn.32, above.
[36] *Hill v Wilson* (1879) 4 C.P.D. 329.

other respects. The portion of cargo sold at Copenhagen amounted to about seven-eighths of the whole.

It seems to have been common ground that liability for pro rata freight was to be determined by the law governing the adjustment.[37] Lindley J. stated that if the Danish adjustment was to be binding upon the plaintiffs, the shipowners would have to establish:

(1) that the voyage actually terminated at Copenhagen; and
(2) that it terminated there by agreement or by necessity.

Dealing with the first point, he continued[38]:

> "With respect to 90 tons of the original cargo, there was no termination whatever of the voyage at that port, but only a suspension of it whilst the ship was under repair. The plaintiffs' goods were no doubt sold at Copenhagen, and as to them the voyage obviously terminated there; but this of itself cannot make an average adjustment there binding on the plaintiffs, as will be seen at once by supposing all the rest of the cargo to have been brought home in the Virago after a short detention for repairs."

The case therefore seems to be authority for the view that where some of the cargo is carried on in the original vessel to the port of destination, the law applied at that port will govern the entire adjustment, both as regards the cargo left behind at the port of refuge, and the cargo forwarded by sister ships. For the reasons given in the next paragraph it is submitted that the result would be the same even if all the cargo carried on to Hull had been forwarded in other vessels rather than carried in the Virago, so long as the forwarding was in continuation of the voyage.

Where the cargo is forwarded from a port of refuge by other vessels

30.16 When the ship is at the port of refuge it may be found that she is a commercial total loss, or that she cannot be repaired without delay which would frustrate the adventure. In such a case the shipowner has a right to tranship the cargo at the port of refuge and to forward it to destination by another vessel or vessels. This right is discussed in detail in paras G.40 to G.43, above, where it is also explained that transhipment and forwarding may be effected in either of two ways:

(1) in continuation of the voyage, that is under arrangements made by the shipowner and at his risk and expense. In this case the adventure continues, and the law of the place of destination will therefore apply; or
(2) under arrangements made by or on behalf of cargo interests and at their risk and expense. In this case there is a breaking up of the common adventure at the port of refuge, whose law will therefore govern the adjustment.

[37] But see para.30.31, below.
[38] *Hill* (1879) 4 C.P.D. 329 at 334.

Hill v Wilson[39] makes it clear that it is only a total abandonment of the voyage at the port of refuge that will have the effect that the law of the port of refuge governs the adjustment, and consequently if any of the cargo is forwarded in continuation of the voyage the law of the scheduled destination will govern the whole adjustment, even though the remaining cargo is sold at the port of refuge or forwarded at the expense of cargo interests.

The non-separation provisions of r.G do not appear to affect the above conclusions.

Contractual Provisions Governing the Adjustment

It is usual for the bill of lading or charterparty to contain a clause which makes express provision for the place of or the law governing general average, often combined with the incorporation of the York-Antwerp Rules. Clauses which specify the law which is to govern the adjustment, or which provide for adjustment according to the York-Antwerp Rules do not appear to have given rise to problems in practice, but the interpretation of those clauses which purport to specify the place of general average has proved more difficult. The effect of the more common provisions is discussed here, and the impact of contractual time limits on claims in general average is dealt with in the commentary on r.23 of the York-Antwerp Rules. **30.17**

Clauses which specify the place of general average

Claases of this nature most commonly provide that general average shall be "adjusted" or "settled" at a particular place; sometimes a more comprehensive phrase is used, such as "adjusted, stated and settled", sometimes an even more elliptical one, such as "general average, if any, in London".[40] Whilst some of these clauses contain additional provisions which explain their meaning, many are not conspicuous for their clarity and provide no unambiguous answer to many potential questions. Is the effect of such a clause to specify: (1) the place where the appointed average adjuster is to carry on business, do his calculations, or produce his adjustment; (2) the place whose tribunals are to have jurisdiction over any disputes regarding general average; (3) the place whose law and practice is to govern the adjustment; and/or (4) the place where security must be provided and contribution must be paid? **30.18**

It is impossible to lay down any fixed rules for resolving these questions, since the result will depend on the terms of the clause as a whole, and may be affected by other terms of the contract of affreightment, such as the presence of an arbitration clause.[41] Nevertheless, there are a number of comments which may usefully be made: **30.19**

[39] *Hill* (1879) 4 C.P.D. 329.
[40] See cl.29 of the Sugar Charterparty 1969.
[41] See para.30.21, below.

(1) As a general rule, clauses which specify the place of general average have the effect that the adjustment of general average will be governed by the law and practice of the specified place.[42]

(2) The purpose of clauses specifying a place for adjustment or settlement of general average may be presumed to be the selection of a single law and practice to govern the adjustment. Not surprisingly, it does not appear that it has ever been suggested that such clauses, without more, also have the effect that losses and contributions are to be assessed by reference to the values at that place.

(3) "Adjusted": In *Sameon v Petrofina*,[43] where the clause stipulated that general average should be "adjusted" in London, Langley J. expressed the view that "the word adjusted is normally to be taken as referring to the process of assessment of rights of contribution in a non-binding manner", and the Court of Appeal agreed, Staughton L.J. saying:

> "to my mind the word 'adjusted' in the context of the charterparty in this case means simply calculated by someone who purports to know something about general average. Whether or not he need be a professional is something we need not decide today".

It was therefore held that the clause did not amount to an agreement that London should be the place of payment, or that the English courts should have jurisdiction over disputes relating to general average.

(4) "Settled": It was held in *Alma Shipping Corp v Union of India*[44] that a clause providing that general average was to be "settled" in London meant that the adjustment was to be prepared in London, but did not provide for a forum for settlement of disputes. The same decision was reached by the House of Lords in *Union of India v E.B. Aaby's Rederi*.[45] The question whether the specified place for settlement was also the place for payment of contributions did not arise in those cases, but Lord Dilhorne[46] was of the opinion that the clause did impose an obligation to make payment at the specified place, and Lord Salmon also inclined to this view.[47]

Incorporation of York-Antwerp Rules

30.20 As already indicated, clauses which provide that the adjustment shall be governed by the York-Antwerp Rules do not in practice appear to have given rise to disputes. This is perhaps surprising, since some forms of clause provide for the incorporation of a particular version of the York-Antwerp Rules as amended, or

[42] See *Wavertree Sailing Ship Co v Love* [1897] A.C. 373 at 381; *Union of India v E.B. Aaby's Rederi* [1975] A.C. 797 at 808–809, 811, 817; *Sameon v Petrofina* (Commercial Ct, March 13, 1996; Unreported April 30, 1997 CA).

[43] See fn.42, above.

[44] *Alma* [1971] 2 Lloyd's Rep. 494 at 501.

[45] *Union of India* [1975] A.C. 797.

[46] *Union of India* [1975] A.C. 797 at 815.

[47] *Union of India* [1975] A.C. 797 at 817.

with subsequent modifications or the like. Such provisions are ambiguous, because they may be intended to incorporate only such modifications as are, strictly speaking, amendments to the specified version of the Rules, or they may be intended to incorporate the current version of the Rules. The only example of an amendment of the Rules in the narrow sense is the 1990 amendment of the York-Antwerp Rules 1974, and it may be doubted whether the parties intended the provision to have such a narrow effect. On the other hand, as illustrated by the CMI resolutions quoted in Section 3,[48] successive versions of the Rules are, technically, new sets of Rules which replace rather than amend the preceding version, although in substance they may be regarded as amendments of the previous version. Problems of a similar nature have arisen under clauses which incorporate Hague Rule legislation "as amended". In The Marinor[49] it was held that such a clause incorporated legislation which replaced rather than amended the legislation specified in the clause, but the reasoning behind the decision may not apply to a non-statutory code such as the York-Antwerp Rules.

In view of the difficulties of construction of provisions of this nature it would be best to avoid them, and to use language which makes it clear whether the intention is to incorporate the current version of the Rules, or only "amendments" in the strict sense.

Arbitration clauses and general average

Where the contract of affreightment contains an arbitration clause in the usual **30.21**
form, disputed claims for contribution in general average will fall within the scope of the clause, even though the contract contains a clause dealing specifically with the settlement of general average.[50] The courts are reluctant to impute to the parties the intention that there should be one procedure for determining disputed claims in general average, and a different procedure for determining all other disputed claims,[51] and it follows that the presence of an arbitration clause in the contract weighs against interpreting a general average clause as providing an agreed machinery for determining disputed claims. Similar considerations would apply in the case of an exclusive jurisdiction clause.

However where, in order to procure the release of the shipowner's lien over the cargo or for some other sufficient consideration, a party to the contract has entered into a fresh agreement to pay general average, such as a Lloyd's Average Bond or a letter of undertaking, an arbitration clause in the original contract of affreightment will not apply to a claim under the fresh agreement.[52]

48 Paras 00.101, 00.108 and 00.111, above.

49 *Noranda Inc v Barton (Time Charter) Ltd (The Marinor)* [1966] 1 Lloyd's Rep. 301.

50 *Alma Shipping Corp v Union of India* [1971] 2 Lloyd's Rep. 491 ("any dispute arising under this charter"); *Union of India v E.B. Aaby's Rederi* [1975] A.C. 797 ("all disputes . . . arising out of this contract"). The result would be otherwise if the general average clause clearly provided its own separate machinery for determining disputed claims in general average.

51 See *Swiss Bank Corp v Novorossivsk Shipping* [1995] 1 Lloyd's Rep. 202 at 206; cf. *The loanna* 11978] 1 Lloyd's Rep. 238.

52 *Union of India v E.B. Aaby's Rederi* [1975] A.C. 797.

Choice of law governing the contract of carriage

30.22 The cases discussed earlier in this section[53] establish that the adjustment of general average is separated from the law governing the contract of carriage as a whole, and is ruled by the law of the port of destination. Does the same result follow where there is an express choice of law in the contract of carriage, not, by its terms, extending to general average? For example a bill of lading may provide: (1) that the contract shall be governed by the law of France; and (2) that general average shall be adjusted in London. In such a case it is submitted that English law and practice apply to the adjustment of general average,[54] and this will be so whether or not the obligation to contribute is contractual, since English law allows the parties to select different laws to govern different parts of their contract.[55] But what if stipulation (1) alone is included, and (2) omitted, but the port of discharge is in England? It could be said that this case is indistinguishable from Lloyd v Guibert,[56] so that again the adjustment of general average would be governed by English law and practice. However, Lloyd v Guibert was not dealing with the case of an express choice of law, and as a matter of construction there seem good reasons for holding that a choice of governing law will prima facie cover all aspects of the contract, including the obligation to contribute in general average, where that is contractual.[57]

Average bonds and the law governing the adjustment

30.23 The law governing an average bond, just as the law governing the contract of carriage as a whole, may differ from the law governing the adjustment. In *Schothorst and Schuitema v Franz Dauter GmbH*[58] the question arose whether a claim for contribution in general average made under a Lloyd's average bond, which contained no express choice of governing law, was a claim to enforce a contract governed by English law. Kerr J. rejected a submission that the bond was governed by Belgian law because the voyage ended at Antwerp, and took the

[53] See paras 30.08 et seq., above. See in particular *Simonds v White* (1824) 2 B. & C. 805 and *Lloyd v Guibert* (1865) L.R. 1 Q.B. 115.

[54] See para.30.06, above.

[55] See the Rome Convention on the law applicable to contractual obligations: art.3.1.

[56] Lloyd (1865) L.R. 1 Q.B. 115.

[57] This is the approach which has been adopted in the cases on the applicability of arbitration clauses to claims in general average; see para.30.21, above. The question is ultimately one of construction, but where the wording of the clause is wide enough to apply to all aspects of the contract, and there is nothing in the other provisions of the contract, construed in the context of the surrounding circumstances, to indicate that it was not intended to apply to general average, it should be allowed to take effect according to its terms. The matter must now be considered in the light of the Rome Convention (see para.30.06, above). Whilst the Convention does not make specific provision for interpreting the scope of choice of law clauses. Art.3.1 supports the view that if there is an express choice of law which is, on the face of it, wide enough to cover the adjustment of general average, and if the contract contains no other terms which cut down its scope, it will take effect according to its terms, unless it can be demonstrated with reasonable certainty from the circumstances of the case that the parties did not intend that it should apply to general average. In the ordinary case, it is difficult to see how this could be demonstrated with the required degree of certainty.

[58] *Schothorst* [1973] 2 Lloyd's Rep. 9l. Cf. *Armar Shipping v Caisse Algerienne* [1981] 1 W.L.R. 207, and see para.30.66, below.

view[59] that it incorporated English law by reference to the contract of carriage. The judge did not, however, say that the adjustment (which had been prepared in Rotterdam) should be completed in accordance with English law and practice as to questions of general average; and it is submitted that as to such matters Belgian law was appropriate, there being no express choice of law in the contract of carriage.[60] A similar approach was adopted by the court of Appeal in *Galaxy Maritime Enterprise v Prima Ceylon Ltd*[61] where there was no contract between the parties other than the average bond, and it was held that although the bond itself was probably governed by English law, the adjustment, and questions of actionable fault, were governed by the law of the place where the adventure ended.

Adjustment as Between Cargo-Owners

Where the cargo is carried under several bills of lading all incorporating the same version of the York-Antwerp Rules, it is the normal practice of British adjusters to treat that version of the Rules as governing all rights of contribution, not only between the shipowner and each cargo owner, but between cargo owners inter se. However, since it is not immediately obvious that there is any contract to that effect between the cargo owners, the question arises whether this practice can be justified, or whether rights of contribution between cargo owners should be adjusted by the law of the place where the adventure ends, as suggested by some writers,[62] however inconvenient that might be. 30.24

The proper starting point must be to construe the meaning of the words of the bill of lading in their context. Having regard to the nature of general average, it is submitted that a merchant holding a bill of which provides "general average to be adjusted according to the York-Antwerp Rules 2004" would be likely to understand that provision as meaning that it was to be adjusted according to those Rules not only between him and the shipowner, but also between him and the other cargo owners; thus if his cargo were to be sacrificed, he would rightly expect to receive contribution assessed under the 2004 Rules not only from the shipowner, but also from other cargo owners. If that is correct, it must follow that the holder of such a bill of lading assents to the shipowner contracting on the same terms with other cargo owners, and, since general average creates direct legal relations between cargo owners, gives the shipowner authority so to do so.[63]

Conflicting Provisions Regarding General Average

If the contracts of affreightment contain no specific provisions regarding the adjustment of general average, as might have been the case when Lowndes was 30.25

[59] The submission was withdrawn, and the view expressed obiter.

[60] Whilst not entirely clear from the report, it appears that the contract of carriage was governed by English law by implication rather than by express choice.

[61] *Galaxy Maritime Enterprise* [2006] 2 Lloyd's Rep. 27.

[62] *Carver*, para.1350, where, however, certain ways of avoiding this result are suggested.

[63] For other types of bills of lading clauses which create direct rights and obligations between the bill of lading holders inter se, see *Grange v Taylor* (1904) 9 Com. Cas. 223 and *Berry, Barclay v Louis Dreyfus* (1929) 35 Lloyd's Rep. 173. See also *The Satanita* [1897] A.C. 59.

active, any adjustment would be prepared in accordance with the law(s) of the port(s) of destination, and in para.30.11, above, an example was given of a Lowndes' adjustment relating to general average expenditure incurred by the shipowner alone, and with the cargo destined for Halifax, N.S. and Portland, United States. The total amount of the general average varied in accordance with the differing laws of the United Kingdom and the United States, with the result that the shipowner might have received from the Halifax cargo a general average contribution of say one per cent of its value, whereas the Portland cargo might have paid two and one-half per cent. In similar fashion, if the general average had consisted solely of a general average sacrifice of the cargo for one of those ports of destination, the owner of the cargo sacrificed might receive from the cargo destined to the other port either more or less than he would expect under the law of the country where his own cargo was discharged. In either case this profit or loss would be just the "luck of the draw" and would lie where it fell.

30.26 Is the position the same where specific provisions regarding the adjustment of general average are incorporated in the contracts of affreightment, but the shipowner fails to ensure that his contracts with each of the cargo owners contain identical provisions? For example, some of the bills of lading may incorporate the 1994 Rules and some the 2004 Rules, or other provisions; or the bills of lading may contain differing provisions relating to the place or law of adjustment. In such a situation problems similar to those mentioned in para.30.11, above, will arise and, if there are material differences between the provisions, it will be necessary to prepare an adjustment in accordance with more than one legal regime. However, there is a further question, namely whether the shipowner or carrier who incorporates into his contract of carriage with any particular cargo owner a provision that general average shall be adjusted in a particular manner, impliedly agrees with that cargo owner to contract in similar terms with all the other cargo interests.

30.27 There is no authority on this question,[64] but it is submitted that a clause in a bill of lading such as "general average to be adjusted in accordance with the York-Antwerp Rules 1994" imports that it should be so adjusted and settled as though all the interests had agreed thereto and not merely the shipowner and that bill of lading holder.[65] From this it follows that there is an implied (if not express) term of the nature already mentioned. While it is the shipowner or

[64] But see *US Shipping Board v R. Durrell & Co Ltd* [1923] 2 K.B. 739, where it was held that a shipowner does not undertake that all other bills of lading relating to cargo carried on the same voyage shall contain the same provisions as to demurrage. However, the grounds for the decision would seem inapplicable to provisions regarding general average.

[65] The shipowners undoubtedly acquires authority, under such a provision, to contract on similar terms with the remaining cargo owners. Otherwise the owner of cargo carried under a bill of lading incorporating the 1994 Rules could insist that general average should be adjusted under the common law as between him and the remaining cargo owners, even if the latter cargo was also carried under bills of lading incorporating the 1994 Rules. This is obviously absurd. For other types of bills of lading clauses which create direct rights and obligation between the bill of lading holders inter se, see *Grange v Taylor* (1904) 9 Com. Cas 112 and *Berry, Barclay v Louis Dreyfus* (1929) 35 Ll. L. Rep. 173. The question whether the shipowner was obliged to contract in similar terms with all the bill of lading holders did not arise in those cases. See also *The Satanita* [1987] A.C. 59.

carrier[66] who will usually be the sufferer if settlements come from cargo interests whose bills of lading contain different provisions regarding general average, cargo may also be affected if the general average mainly consists of cargo sacrifices.

The problem is best illustrated by a figured example. It should be noted that the **30.28** differences between the 1974 and 1994 Rules have been exaggerated for the purposes of the illustration.

A vessel loads cargo in India and Egypt for Ruritania. The cargo from India is shipped under bills of lading providing for general average to be adjusted in accordance with the York-Antwerp Rules 1994, whereas the Egyptian cargo is subject to the York-Antwerp Rules 1974. As a result of a casualty, damage to the Indian cargo is sustained that would warrant allowances in general average as follows:

General Average per:	
YAR 1974	YAR 1994
80,000	200,000

It was suggested in the last edition that, there being no agreement to the contrary binding all the parties to the adventure, the proper course is to prepare an adjustment under the law of the destination, since as between the cargo owners there has been no agreement which displaces the law of the place where the adventure ends. Examples of this approach are set out in paras 30.30 to 30.31 of the 12th edn.

In practice, it is likely that an adjustment will be drawn up showing separate columns for each code of general average, so that each cargo interest is called upon to contribute according to the version of the York Antwerp Rules applicable to them. The effect of this approach is shown in the following examples.

The Ship and the Indian cargo have agreed to an adjustment under York- **30.29** Antwerp Rules 1994, namely:

	1994 Rules	Credit Make Good	Balance To Pay	To Receive
Ship–pays 30%	60,000	—	60,000	
Indian cargo is liable for 30%	60,000	200,000	—	140,000
Egyptian cargo pays 40%	80,000	—	80,000	—
100% liable for	200,000	200,000	140,000	140,000

[66] The party liable under the implied term is the party liable to cargo under the bill of lading contract—i.e. normally the shipowner but occasionally the charterer. Where it is the shipowner who is liable to cargo, but the charterer was responsible for the form of the bills of lading, the shipowner may be entitled to an indemnity: see *British Shipping Laws*, Vol. II: Carver, *Carriage by Sea*, 13th edn, paras 704–719, 737–739.

The Egyptian cargo is not bound by this adjustment, not having agreed to York-Antwerp Rules 1994. The relevant features of the adjustment are the amount payable by the ship to Indian cargo and the total contribution of 140,000 to which the Indian cargo is entitled under York-Antwerp Rules 1994. However, when the York-Antwerp Rules 1974, as stipulated in the Egyptian bills of lading, are applied the adjustment would be as follows:

	1974 Rules	Credit Make Good	Balance To Pay	Balance To Receive
Ship–pays 30%	24,000	—	24,000	—
Indian Cargo is liable for 30%	24,000	80,000	—	56,000
Egyptian cargo pays 40%	32,000	—	32,000	—
100% liable for	80,000	80,000	56,000	56,000

It can readily be seen that whereas, under the 1994 Rules, the Indian cargo is entitled to receive 140,000 (from Ship 60,000 and 80,000 from the Egyptian cargo), the Egyptian cargo, according to 1974 Rules, will only contribute 32,000.

Is the carrier liable to the Indian cargo for the shortfall of 38,000 on the basis that the carrier has an obligation to ensure that all cargo is subject to the same provisions for adjustment of general average? There is no known authority to make such an assumption, but as noted above, this is likely to be the case. It should be noted that the problem is more pronounced in cases of cargo sacrifice when a cargo receiver/insurer may be affected. In cases of shipowners' expenditure they may suffer a shortfall by failing to ensure that all contracts of affreightment contained the same provisions for the adjustment of general average, but if they have issued the bills of lading they have no recourse against any other party. If the charterers (or several slot charterers on a container ship) have issued bills of lading in varying terms, the position may be different, particularly if the charter party or slot charter specified what version of the York-Antwerp Rules was to be used.

30.30 Where different terms are included in bills of lading, the adjuster may approach the parties concerned with a view to agreeing, in the interests of simplicity and economy, to adopt the most appropriate version of the York-Antwerp Rules, which will usually be the version shown in the majority of the bills of lading. However it should be emphasised that the cargo interests are under no obligation to agree.

Assume next that it is the Egyptian cargo which sustains the damage. Under Ruritanian law the adjustment would be:

	Ppn. GA	Credit Make Good	Balance To Pay	Balance To Receive
Ship— 30% liable for	45,000	—	45,000	—
Indian cargo— 30% liable for	45,000	—	45,000	—
Egyptian cargo— 40% liable for	60,000	150,000	—	90,000
100% liable for	150,000	150,000	90,000	90,000

However, ship and Egyptian cargo have agreed to adjustment under York-Antwerp Rules 1994, namely:

	Ppn. GA	Credit Make Good	Balance To Pay	Balance To Receive
Ship— pays 30% liable for	24,000	—	24,000	
Indian cargo— 30% liable for 30%	24,000	—	24,000	—
Egyptian cargo— 40% liable for	32,000	80,000	—	48,000
~~100%~~ liable for	80,000	80,000	48,000	48,000

As already noted in para.30.30, above, the Indian cargo is not affected by the latter adjustment, but the amount payable by the ship is governed by this adjustment rather than by the Ruritanian law adjustment.

Also to be noted is that in this case, unlike that where the Indian cargo sustained the damage, no loss has been suffered by either cargo interest as a result of the breach of the implied term. Indian cargo is better off than if the Egyptian bill of lading had incorporated York-Antwerp Rules 1994, and Egyptian cargo is better off than if the Indian bill of lading had incorporated York-Antwerp Rules 1974.

(a) In general average the Egyptian cargo is entitled to:

24,000 from ship
45,000 from Indian cargo
69,000

(b) The carriers' liability in damages for breach of the implied term is nil.

The Role of the Law Governing the Adjustment

30.31 We have already seen[67] that there may be a difference between the law governing the contract of carriage in general and the law governing general average. Normally this gives rise to little difficulty in practice; for example, few people would doubt that the question whether freight had become payable was governed by the proper law of the contract of carriage, whereas the method of valuing the contributing interests was governed by the law of the adjustment. However, it may be difficult in some instances to determine whether a particular problem should be characterised as one of contract or of general average: such as the interpretation of the words "at merchant's risk" ' in *Burton v English*.[68]

30.32 There is, strangely enough, no discussion of the problem in any of the decided cases. For example, in Hill v Wilson,[69] the facts of which are summarised at para.30.15 above, the owner was entitled to pro rata freight under Danish law, but not under English law. It was assumed that the entitlement to pro rata freight depended upon which law governed the adjustment, although if the same question arose today it would almost certainly be regarded as depending upon which law governed the contract of carriage as a whole. As a matter of principle, it is submitted that since the interpretation and effect of the contract is, in general, governed by its proper law,[70] that law should be applied to all such questions other than those concerned exclusively with general average. Thus the question whether fault is actionable, or whether freight has been earned or is still at risk, are questions which can and normally will arise quite independently of any claim for general average, and should therefore be governed by the law governing the contract of carriage, even when they arise in the context of a claim for contribution. In *Drew Brown v The Orient Trader*,[71] the question whether a statutory exception of fire protected the carrier against liability for a fire which broke out after a deviation was treated as a question to be answered by reference to the proper law of the contract. In *Galaxy Special Maritime Enterprise v Prima Ceylon Ltd*[72] where there was no contract between the parties other than the average bond, it was held that the question whether the peril arose as a result of actionable fault, and the question whether the shipowner had acted properly in entering into a salvage agreement were matters to be determined by the law of the place where the adventure ended, rather than the proper law of the bond.

30.33 Equally, it is submitted that questions such as that which arose in *Burton v English*[73] are to be determined under the proper law of the contract of carriage, since the effect of a clause such as "at merchant's risk" may have to be considered in a number of different situations, and it would be illogical that it should receive

67 See paras 30.06, et seq., above.
68 *Burton v English* (1883) 12 Q.B.D. 218.
69 *Hill* (1879) 4 C.P.D. 329.
70 See the Contracts (Applicable Law) Act 1990 Sch.1 art.10.1.
71 *Drew Brown v The Orient Trader* [1972] 1 Lloyd's Rep. 35; [1973] 2 Lloyd's Rep. 174.
72 *Galaxy Special Maritime Enterprise* [2006] 2 Lloyd's Rep. 27.
73 See fn.69, above.

one interpretation in the context of a general average claim and a different interpretation in any other context.

On the other hand, the question whether fault which is not actionable is a defence to a claim for general average, and the nature of the remedies or defences open to a party against whom contribution is claimed,[74] should be a matter for the law governing the adjustment. For example, if a contract of carriage governed by United States law provided for general average to be adjusted in London in accordance with English law, and contained an exception of negligent navigation, it would be irrelevant whether the contract contained a Jason Clause or a New Jason Clause[75] and contribution could be recovered even though the peril was brought about by negligent navigation of the ship. 30.34

The Legal Status of an Adjustment

Not binding in the absence of agreement

As noted at the beginning of this Chapter,[76] the shipowner is, in cases governed by the York-Antwerp Rules and probably in other cases as well, obliged to procure a written adjustment; however, the adjustment is not, in the absence of agreement, binding upon either the shipowner or any of the other parties. Thus in *The Bijela*[77] the shipowner engaged a firm of average adjusters to prepare a general average statement. Being dissatisfied with the statement which they produced, he then engaged another firm of adjusters, who produced a statement which was more favourable to him, and which was held by the House of Lords to be correct. It was never suggested that the shipowner was bound by the first statement. In the absence of special circumstances giving rise to an estoppel there is no reason why a party who, or whose agent, produces a statement should not withdraw it and contend that it was wrong. Equally, although there are obvious conveniences in having a second adjustment prepared in such a case, it would have been open the shipowners, or any other party dissatisfied with the first adjustment, to challenge it in court without having a second adjustment prepared. In the absence of clear words to that effect, clauses specifying a place or mode of adjustment will not affect the general rule in English law that the statement produced by the average adjuster is not binding on the parties.[78] In the case of particular average it has been held that even where the contract calls for an adjustment by a named adjuster his adjustment is not binding.[79] 30.35

The mere fact that the contract between the parties provides expressly for the preparation of an adjustment, so as to make the completion of the adjustment an

[74] cf. *Goulandris v B. Goldman & Sons* [1958] 1 Q.B. 74, and see paras D.29–D.32, above.
[75] As to the origin and effect of Jason and New Jason clauses, see paras 00.51 et seq., above.
[76] Paras 30.02 et seq., above.
[77] *Marida v Oswal Steel (The Bijela)* [1992] 1 Lloyd's Rep. 637, [1993] 1 Lloyd's Rep. 411 (CA), [1994] 2 Lloyd's Rep. 1.
[78] See the cases cited in fn.8, above, and *Castle Insurance Co v Hong Kong Islands Shipping Co* [1984] A.C. 226 at 238. The rule is by no means universal. In some countries (Sweden for example) an adjustment is binding in the absence of an appeal to the court within a specified period of time.
[79] See *Attaleia v Bimeh Iran* [1993] 2 Lloyd's Rep. 497.

essential ingredient of a cause of action for contribution, does not have the effect that the adjustment so prepared is binding.

Not essential to a cause of action in the absence of agreement

30.36 Equally, in the absence of express or implied agreement, such as is normally the case under an average bond or guarantee,[80] an average adjustment is not essential to the existence of a cause of action, and time will therefore start to run, for the purpose of the Limitation Act, from the date of the sacrifice or expenditure. The question is discussed in detail in the commentary on r.XXIII.

Effect of York-Antwerp Rules

30.37 Whilst the position is essentially the same under the York-Antwerp Rules, and the adjustment is not binding in the absence of agreement, the Rules contain provisions which confer a distinct legal status on the adjustment, or upon the adjuster, which may affect the parties' rights in various ways, as indicated below.

(1) Under r.E the adjuster is empowered in certain circumstances to make estimates of allowances or contributory values, which may only be challenged on limited grounds.
(2) Under r.XIV of the 2004 Rules the cap on the allowance for temporary repairs may depend upon whether or not permanent repairs have been affected "at the time of the adjustment". A similar situation may arise in practice, under r.XVIII,[81] in relation to the allowance for damage to the ship resulting from general average sacrifice, although the rule itself contains no reference to the date of adjustment.
(3) Under r.XXI interest runs at the stipulated rate until three months after the date of the issue of the adjustment.
(4) Under r.XXIII of the 2004 Rules one of the triggers of the two-pronged time-bar provision is date upon which the adjustment was issued.

These rules are clearly predicated upon the assumption that there is a single average statement which can be identified as "the adjustment", and are therefore not easy to reconcile with the liberty, mentioned in para.30.35 above, of any party who is dissatisfied with an adjustment to prepare his own. The position, it is submitted, is that, since it is the shipowner upon whom the burden of preparing the adjustment falls, the adjustment prepared on the instructions of the shipowner will be the relevant adjustment for the purpose of the Rules, as it is under the Lloyd's Average Bond,[82] any adjustment prepared on the instructions of the cargo owner only being relevant in the unusual case where the shipowner has refused, or perhaps delayed inordinately, to proceed with obtaining an adjustment. Where

[80] The agreement may be express or implied. The Lloyd's Average Bond and Guarantee has been held to amount to such an agreement: see para.23.06, above.
[81] See para.18.19, above.
[82] *Castle Insurance Co v Hong Kong Shipping Co* [1984] A.C. 226, 240–241.

the shipowner has procured more than one adjustment, as in *The Bijela*,[83] practical considerations seem to require that it is the first adjustment which is the relevant one for the purpose of the Rules. Thus a shipowner who is dissatisfied with an estimate made by the adjuster under r.E, or who has failed to comply with the time bar under r.XXIII of the 2004 Rules, cannot be permitted to improve his position by procuring another adjustment.

The Average Adjuster

Need a professional adjuster be employed?

Unless the parties agree to the contrary, expressly or by implication, there is no requirement that a professional adjuster be employed.[84] In *Chandris v Argo Insurance Co Ltd*[85] it was held that a contract of insurance, which provided for an adjustment according to the York-Antwerp Rules 1924, was not subject to any implied requirement that a professional adjuster be employed, although that was the usual practice.[86] However, in *Castle Insurance Co v Hong Kong Islands Shipping Co*[87] Lord Diplock, after referring to the passage in Lord Herschell's judgment in *Wavertree Sailing Ship Co v Love* quoted at para.30.04 above, to the effect that there was no implied requirement to employ a professional adjuster, expressed the view that in some future case it might be necessary: **30.38**

> "... to consider whether changes in mercantile practice which have taken place since 1897 have made such an implication necessary, at any rate in the case of contracts contained in bills of lading for carriage in a general ship."

Changes to the York-Antwerp Rules in 1994 and 2004 add force to the argument that, when the Rules apply, the implication of such a term may be necessary. In particular there appear to be strong grounds for contending that the provisions of r.E which entitle the adjuster to make binding estimates of allowances and contributory values[88] contemplate the employment of an independent professional, if the shipowner is not to be a judge in his own cause.

Later in his judgment in *Castle Insurance Co v Hong Kong Shipping Co*[89] Lord Diplock expressed the view that the Lloyd's form of Average Bond employed in that case, by referring to adjustment "in the usual manner", does require the employment of a professional adjuster, in the case of carriage in a general ship, that being the usual practice. The decision adopts a realistic view of the complexities of an adjustment involving numerous interests. The current Lloyd's Average Bond (LAB 77) and the Average Guarantees in common use (see Appendix 4) no longer include the words "in the usual manner", but it is suggested that the other

[83] See para.30.35, above.
[84] See the quotation from Lord Herschall in *Wavertree Sailing Ship Co v Love*, above, para.30.04.
[85] *Chandris* [1963] 2 Lloyd's Rep. 65.
[86] *Chandris* [1963] 2 Lloyd's Rep. 65 at 76.
[87] *Castle Insurance Co* [1984] A.C. 226 at 237.
[88] See paras E.13 et seq., above.
[89] [1984] A.C. 226 at 240.

references in these documents to the "average adjusters" would lead to a similar view.

In some countries the employment of a professional adjuster is mandatory. In Sweden, for example the adjuster is appointed by the government, and he is required to be "learned in the law".

The responsibilities of the adjuster

30.39 While the adjuster is normally engaged by the shipowner, his fees are, as noted in the commentary on r.C, part of the general average expenditure. In *Wavertree Sailing Ship Co v Love*[90] Lord Herschell asserted robustly that the adjuster does not act on behalf of any of the other parties to the adventure, but in the case of an adjuster whose fee will be debited to the general average this assertion may need to be reconsidered in the light of the decision of the House of Lords in *Morrison S.S. Co v Greystoke Castle*[91] which may produce the result that the adjuster is engaged on behalf of all the parties to the adventure, and is therefore under some responsibility for safeguarding their interests, although only the shipowner is directly liable to him for the fee. If Lord Herschell's remarks are correct, it may be doubted whether the adjuster owes any duty of care except to the party who engages him. However, since adjustments prepared by professional adjusters are in practice normally accepted and acted upon by the other interests, and since there is a sufficiently close proximity between the adjuster and those other interests, such that it can be said that the adjuster assumes a responsibility towards them, he would probably be held to owe to them a duty of care, at any rate in relation to statements of fact contained in the adjustment.[92]

30.40 It is possible for all interests jointly to instruct an average adjuster and also to agree to be bound by his adjustment. In such a case the adjuster is in the position of an arbitrator, does not owe a duty of care to the parties,[93] and is immune from liability unless he acts in bad faith.[94] However, if the adjuster is to have the status of an arbitrator or quasi-arbitrator, and thus enjoy the immunity, it is essential that,

> "there should be a formulated dispute between at least two parties which his decision is required to resolve. It is not enough that the parties who may be affected by the decision have opposed interests, still less that the decision is on a matter which is not agreed between them".[95]

In some European countries the adjuster's position is equivalent to that of a judge of first instance, and his decision binding on the parties unless appealed against.

[90] *Wavertree Sailing Ship Co* [1897] A.C. 373.
[91] *Morrison S.S.* [1947] A.C. 265. See para.00.19, above.
[92] See *Henderson v Merrett Syndicates Ltd* [1995] A.C. 145; *White v Jones* [1995] A.C. 207.
[93] *Tharsis Sulphur and Copper Co Ltd v Loftus* (1872) L.R. 8 C.P. 1.
[94] Arbitration Act 1996 s.29.
[95] *Arenson v Arenson* [1977] A.C. 405 at 424. See also *Sutcliffe v Thackrah* [1974] A.C. 727.

2. Enforcing Rights of Contribution

(A) The Lien for General Average Contribution

Shipowner's Common Law Lien

The shipowner has, at common law, a lien on the cargo while in his possession or in that of his servants as a carrier, not only for the freight, but also for the cargo's share of general average. The lien is a possessory lien, which entitles the shipowner to retain possession of the cargo until his claim is satisfied or properly secured, without regard to the question whether the consignee is under any personal liability to contribute.[96] It is thus immaterial to the shipowner, at the stage of exercising the lien, that a mere consignee of cargo, not being the owner at the time of the sacrifice or expenditure, is not liable for general average in the absence of agreement.[97] **30.41**

Procedure in exercising the lien

Under the ordinary rules of the common law relating to the exercise of possessory liens, the person who is entitled to exercise the lien has a right to demand immediate payment of the amount for which the lien subsists, and need not content himself with security; but conversely he is obliged, at the time when he exercises his lien, to quantify his demand correctly, or at any rate to give to the owner of the goods sufficient particulars from which the latter can ascertain and tender the correct amount. If the lienor fails to follow this procedure his continued detention of the goods becomes unlawful, and the lien is therefore lost.[98] **30.42**

In the case of general average, however, these ordinary rules are usually impossible to follow in practice, since the amount for which the lien is exercisable is almost always impossible to quantify at the time of discharge. The practice is therefore for the shipowner to make an estimate of the amount of contribution which is likely to be due on each consignment of cargo, and to obtain a secured undertaking from each consignee to pay the amount due on his consignment. The practice is recognised by legal authority, and was described as follows in *Castle Insurance Co v Hong Kong Islands Shipping Co*[99]: **30.43**

[96] "It is a possessory lien at common law, by virtue of which he (the master or owner of the ship) is entitled to hold the goods till his lien be satisfied": per Lord Kingsdown, in *Cargo ex Galam* (1863) Br. & L. 167 at 182. The same lien which the master has for general average, he has likewise for special or particular charges on cargo incurred during the transit: *Hingston v Wendt* (1876) 1 Q.B.D. 367.

[97] See paras 30.56 et seq., below.

[98] See *Albemarle Supply Co v Hind* [1928] 1 K.B. 307, applying *Scarfe v Morgan* (1838) 4 M & W 270, *Dirks v Richards* (1842) 4 M & G 574, *Huth v Lamport* (1886) 16 Q.B.D. 735 and *Ramsey v North Eastern Ry* (1863) 14 C.B.N.S. 641. Even if the person exercising the lien does give sufficient particulars, the goods owner will be excused from tendering the correct amount if the former makes it clear that he will not part with possession of the goods until his excessive demand is met in full. See the cases cited above and para.30.45, below.

[99] *Castle Insurance Co* [1984] A.C. 226. A similar practice is recognised by law in the US: *Wellman v Morse* (1896) 76 Fed. Rep. 563.

> "There attaches to all cargo that has been preserved in consequence of a general average sacrifice or expenditure a lien in favour of those concerned in ship or cargo who have sustained a general average loss. The lien attaches to the preserved cargo at the time when the sacrifice is made or the liability to the expenditure incurred. The lien is a possessory lien and it is the duty of the master of the vessel to exercise the lien at the time of discharge of the preserved cargo in such a way as will provide equivalent security for contributions towards general average sacrifices made or expenditure incurred not only by those concerned in the ship but also by those concerned in cargo in respect of which a net general average loss has been sustained. The lien, being a possessory one and not a maritime lien, is exercisable only against the consignee, but it is exercisable whether or not the consignee was owner of the consignment at the time of the general average sacrifice or expenditure that gave rise to the lien: a fact of which the shipowner may well be unaware. At the time of discharge the sum for which the lien is security (save in the simplest cases, which do not include that of a general ship) is unquantifiable until after there has been an average adjustment. Indeed in the case of some consignees of cargo that has been preserved in part only or damaged in consequence of a general average loss, so far from being liable to a net general average contribution they may eventually turn out to be entitled to a net payment in general average. The disadvantages and legal complications which would result from the master's actually withholding delivery to its consignee of cargo preserved by general average acts . . . need not be repeated here. In practice what happens is what happened in the instant case; the master, acting on behalf of the shipowner and of any persons interested in cargo who will be found on the adjustment to be entitled to a net general average payment, releases the preserved cargo to the consignees upon the execution by each consignee of an average bond in one or other of Lloyd's standard forms accompanied, in the comparatively rare cases of cargo that is uninsured or underinsured, by a deposit in a bank in joint names of money as security or, more usually, by a letter of guarantee from the insurer of the cargo."[100]

It is clear from this case that, where the shipowner seeks security for his claim rather than immediate payment, he will not be required to quantify his claim precisely, or to give particulars from which the cargo owner is able to do so.[101] The information which the shipowner who exercises his lien for the purpose of obtaining security is required to give is considered in more detail below.[102]

30.44 Since the lien is a possessory rather than a maritime lien, it ceases to exist when the shipowner parts with possession of the goods, but he may land the goods while maintaining his lien so long as he retains exclusive control against the person claiming possession.[103] Whilst a lienor has no power of sale at common law,[104] s.12 of the Torts (Interference with Goods) Act confers a right of sale on following the prescribed procedure. The Court also has power to order sale under s.13 of the Act, or, in the case of perishable goods, under rules of court.[105] A shipowner need not land cargo on which he has a lien in order to stop demurrage accruing, provided that the exercise of the lien by retaining the goods on board is reasonable.[106]

[100] *Castle Insurance Co* [1984] A.C. 226 at 234, per Lord Diplock delivering the judgment of the Privy Council.

[101] As he is required to do if he demands outright payment. See para.30.42, above.

[102] See para.30.45 and fn.115, below.

[103] *Mors-Le-Blanch v Wilson* [1873] LR. 8 C.P. 227.

[104] *Thames Ironworks Co v The Patent Derrick Co* (1860) 1 J. & H. 93.

[105] Civil Procedure Rules Pt 25.1(1)(c)(v).

[106] *Lyle & Co v Cardiff* (1899) 5 Com. Cas. 87; *Smailes v Hans Dessen & Co* (1906) 12 Com. Cas. 117. It would seem that in some cases, if the consignee refuses to take delivery of the goods or to

The position regarding the cost of exercising a lien was considered in a General Average context by Mr. Justice Popplewell in *Metall Market v Vitorio Shipping Co Ltd*,[107] in which a shipowner sought to recover the costs of exercising a lien in order to secure an average bond from the receiver. Contrasting this situation with the "Winson", where a salvor stored cargo as a bailee, he said:

> "I conclude that the principle to be derived from these authorities is that where a gratuitous bailee incurs expenses in carrying out his duties in preserving and caring for the goods, he has a correlative right to recover such expenses from the owner of the goods, provided that he is not denying possession of the goods to the owner solely on the grounds that he is exercising a lien. Where, however, he is exercising a lien adversely to the goods owner, who is seeking possession, and that is his sole ground for denying possession to the owner who would otherwise be entitled to possession but for the lien, he has no such right. In the latter circumstance the exercise of the lien and the retention of possession adversely to the goods owner are treated as being solely for the benefit of the lienee, for which he is not entitled to be reimbursed, even if his costs include those of preserving the goods."

Mr Justice Popplewell had based his decision largely on *Somes v British Empire Shipping Co*[108] regarding retention of a vessel by a shipyard for non-payment of repair bills, which was considered to govern all cases where a lien was exercised for the benefit of the lienor. In the Court of Appeal[109] Sir Bernard Rix disagreed that Somes provided any such overriding principle of law. After a detailed review of maritime and non-maritime cases he concluded that the Somes principle had "no application outside the case of the artificer's (ship repairers) lien", and that no case applying the Somes principle could be found relating to the shipping context of carriage of goods by sea. He concluded:

> "Above all in the context of general average, there is in my judgment no room for the strictness of the Somes principle. General average becomes part of English law through the general, internationally recognised, law of the sea deriving from the Lex Rhodia. The shipowner has an obligation, as well as a right, to collect general average contribution, or security for it, from all contributors and on behalf of all parties to the adventure. Mr Karia submits that there could have been no question in this case of the only other cargo interest involved, the steel pontoons carried on deck, being a net payee of general average contributions. In my judgment that does not undermine the shipowner's duty to collect general average contributions on behalf of all contributing interests (although it could of course mean that, if the duty were not complied with, then the shipowner would not be liable in damages as a result). However, quite apart from that obligation, there is no reason why the lien for general average should be subject to a strict but narrow principle deriving from the English

satisfy the lien on them, a master might be justified in carrying the goods back to the port of shipment, and there enforcing his lien against the shipper, on the principle that one who has a lien on goods may do what is reasonable to enforce it, and, if he cannot do so on the spot without incurring expense, may carry the goods to some place where he can: *Edwards v Southgate* (1862) 10 W.R. 528.

[107] [2012] EWHC 844 (Comm.).

[108] See *Somes v British Empire Shipping Co* (1858–60) E.B. & E. 353 at 367, Ex. Ch.; 8 H.L.Cas. 338.

[109] [2013] EWCA Civ 650.

common law's artificer's lien, as the citation from The Prins Knud makes abundantly clear."

It should be noted that many bills of lading include express terms which enable the shipowner to recover the costs of exercising a lien for general average or other purposes.

Limitations against abuse

30.45 In the event that the shipowner were to abuse the power of lien by demanding outright payment of a disputed amount, or by insisting upon unreasonable security, a number of safeguards are available to the consignee.

(1) The shipowner who insists on outright payment, rather than security, does so at his peril if he exaggerates his claim and fails to give the necessary particulars from which the consignee can ascertain the correct amount to tender, since his lien may then be lost. In addition the consignee can obtain a right to the delivery of his goods, and, consequently, a right of action for damages, if they are not delivered, by tendering to the shipowner or captain a sum sufficient to meet his rightful demand; the problem with this procedure, however, is that the duty of determining the amount to be tendered is thus cast upon the consignee, unless the shipowner or master shall have made his demand in such a manner as to imply a resolution on his part to take no smaller sum.[110] A more useful remedy, therefore, is to commence proceedings for delivery up of the goods, and apply to the court for an order for delivery of the goods upon paying the disputed sum into court.[111] In practice, for the reasons already described, outright payment is rarely, if ever, demanded or tendered.

(2) In the usual case, where the shipowner detains the goods for the purpose of obtaining security, rather than actual payment, he is obliged to accept security which is reasonable both in its form and in the amount of any deposit which is demanded[112] and if he refuses a reasonable offer of security, or makes it plain that he will accept nothing other than the unreasonable security which he demands, the lien is discharged.[113] Where the York-Antwerp Rules apply, the consignee is

[110] As to the law with regard to the making of tenders in cases of disputed liability, see the cases referred to in para.30.42, fn.99, above. See also *Allen v Smith* (1862) 12 C.B. (N.S.) 638; affirmed (1863) 9 Jur. (N.S.) 1248, Ex.Ch.; *Ashmole v Wainwright* (1842) 2 Q.B. 837; *Nicholson v Chapman* (1793) 2 H.Bl. 254; *Kerford v Mondel* (1859) 28 L.J. Exch. 303; *The Norway* (1865) Br. & L. 404 at 410–411, PC; per Lord Blackburn in *Anderson v Ocean S.S. Co* (1884) 10 App. Cas. 107 at 115; *Huth v Lamport* (1885–86) 16 Q.B.D. 442 at 735, para.30.51, below. According to Lord Esher in *Huth v Lamport* (p.736) the tender must be by way of outright payment. The point was left open by Lindley L.J. and Mathew J.

[111] Civil Procedure Rules Pt 25.1(1)(m).

[112] *Huth v Lamport* (1885-86) 16 Q.B.D. 442.

[113] See para.30.42, above. As to what is reasonable security see para.30.51, below.

entitled to insist that any deposit paid by him shall be held on the terms laid down in r.XXII. The consignee is entitled to such information as will enable him to ascertain whether the amount of any deposit claimed is reasonable, and any failure to provide such information is a breach of the contract of carriage.[114] As in the case of a demand for outright payment, the consignee may commence proceedings in court, and apply for an order for delivery of the goods, in which case the court will determine whether the security demanded is reasonable.

Remedy of Cargo Owner

Such are the remedies available to the owner of the ship. The owner of goods sacrificed for all is not in so advantageous a position simply because, not being in possession like the shipowner, he can have no direct right of lien.[115] However, as the shipowner can and must exercise a lien on the cargo for a sum sufficient to satisfy not only his own claim to contribution (for example for general average expenditure that he has incurred, or loss of freight) but also that of the unfortunate cargo owner, the latter can exercise a lien, albeit indirectly. If the shipowner fails to exercise his lien by requiring payment or the giving of reasonable security for payment before delivering the surviving cargo, he will be liable in damages to the owner of the sacrificed cargo. **30.46**

Cases which establish these propositions

In *Crooks v Allan*[116] the Sardinian took fire at sea, which made it necessary, in order to protect the whole from destruction, to flood the cargo with water, thus occasioning a general average loss to the plaintiff's goods. The ship returned to Liverpool, and there the shipowners, conceiving (wrongly, as it turned out[117]) that they were not liable to contribute to the damage to the cargo because of the terms of the bills of lading and not proposing themselves to make any claim upon the cargo, took no steps as to collecting a general average, but simply discharged the damaged cargo and handed it over to the Liverpool Salvage Association to be distributed and disposed of as might be most for the benefit of the parties concerned. The plaintiffs brought an action in which they asserted that it was a breach of duty by the shipowners first to fail to obtain security in the usual form from the owners of other cargo, and secondly not to inform the owners of the **30.47**

[114] *The Norway* (1864) Br. & L. 377 at 397–398. In that case Dr Lushington held that it was the duty of the master, when he demands a deposit for general average, to furnish the consignee "with some memorandum from an average adjuster as to the probable amount of contribution from the cargo for the general average".

[115] In the US the owner of goods sacrificed has a lien, enforceable in Admiralty, against the vessel and other interests for the amount due to him. In England he can in effect obtain security from the shipowner by commencing an Admiralty action in rem: see paras 30.67, 30.69, below.

[116] *Crooks v Allan* (1879) 5 Q.B.D. 38; 49 L.J.Q.B. 201.

[117] See para.D.16, above.

sacrificed cargo of the identity of the other contributing interests, and of their contributing values.

Lush J., after dealing with another point, said:

> "The next question is whether a shipowner is bound to exercise the power he is invested with, when a general average loss has arisen, and to afford the means in his power for adjusting the general average claims and liabilities, and secure their payment to the parties entitled. It seems strange that such a point has not been formally decided in this country. It has been decided in America in favour of the shipper. I am not aware that it has ever been judicially questioned here, and I can only account for the absence of direct authority by supposing that the universal practice has been accepted as proof of the obligation. It is clear that the shipowner has a lien for general average on the whole of the cargo liable to contribution, and can require, before he parts with it, security for its due payment. In early times the master, when he had jettisoned part of the cargo to save the whole adventure, took and rendered contribution in kind. The ordinary course now is, and has been for a very long time, for the shipowner to require before he delivers the cargo, an average bond or agreement for the payment of what shall be found due from each shipper for his proportion of the loss. He is the only person who has the power to require this security.
>
> The right to detain for average contribution is derived from the civil law, which also imposes on the master of the ship the duty of having the contribution settled, and of collecting the amount, and the usage has always been substantially in accordance with this law, and has become part of the common law of the land.
>
> I am therefore of opinion . . . that he [the shipowner] is liable to this action for not having taken the necessary steps for procuring an adjustment of the general average and securing its payment."[118]

As a result of this decision the shipowners collected and gave the requisite information, and caused an adjustment of general average to be drawn up, which was settled by all parties concerned, including the shipowners and their underwriters, without further question.

30.48 The decision in *Crooks v Allen*[119] that it was the master's duty to enforce the lien for general average contribution against each of the other cargo owners for the benefit of the owner of the goods sacrificed, was affirmed by the Privy Council in *Strang v Scott*,[120] where it was stated that the master was the agent of the owner of sacrificed cargo for the purposes of exercising the lien, and was applied in *Nobel's Explosives Co v Rea*,[121] where the shipowners were held liable in damages to the owners of goods jettisoned for delivering the other cargo without taking security from the consignees. The rule has also been recognised as settled law in *Hain S.S. Co Ltd v Tate & Lyle*,[122] *Morrison S.S. Co Ltd v Greystoke*

[118] *Crooks* (1879) 5 Q.B.D. 38 at 41.

[119] *Crooks* (1879) 5 Q.B.D. 38.

[120] *Strang v Scott* (1889) 14 App. Cas. 601.

[121] *Nobel's Explosives Co v Rea* (1897) 2 Com. Cas. 293. There was no evidence that the contribution was irrecoverable from the other cargo owners, and the decision effectively imposes on the shipowner who fails to obtain security for the other interests an obligation to pay the contribution due from those interests.

[122] *Hein S.S.* (1934) 39 Com. Cas. 259 at 281, per Greer L.J.; approved in the House of Lords (1936) 41 Com. Cas. 350 at 356, per Lord Atkin.

Castle[123] and in *Castle Insurance Co Ltd v Hong Kong Islands Shipping Co*,[124] where it was also pointed out that in releasing the cargo against reasonable security the master was acting not only on behalf of the shipowner but on behalf of all the creditors in the general average. In so far as *Hallet v Bousfield*[125] is a decision to the contrary, it must be regarded as having been wrongly decided.

The shipowner's exercise of his lien for the benefit of the owner of sacrificed cargo will only secure the contribution owed by other cargo owners, since the shipowner is under no obligation imposed by law to provide security for his own contribution. However, the cargo owner can in effect obtain security in respect of the shipowner's contribution by commencing an Admiralty action in rem and arresting the ship or a sister ship.[126]

The other aspect of the decision in *Crooks v Allen*,[127] that it was the shipowner's duty not only to obtain security from the consignees of other cargo, but also to procure an adjustment of general average, has not arisen for decision in any subsequent case. Normally the shipowner has incurred expense himself, and is therefore willing to undertake the task voluntarily. In any event the usual practice is for the shipowner to employ a professional adjuster, whose fees will form part of the general average expenditure. **30.49**

(B) SECURITY FOR GENERAL AVERAGE CONTRIBUTION

Average Bonds or Agreements

The usual procedure, as indicated in *Castle Insurance Co v Hong Kong Islands Shipping Co*,[128] is for the shipowner to give up his lien in exchange for security, and the security will consist firstly in the signing of an average bond[129] by the receiver of the goods whereby he undertakes to pay the proper proportion of any salvage and/or general average and/or other charges attaching to the goods, and also to provide the information necessary to value the cargo and any loss or damage thereto. The receiver will also be required to furnish either: **30.50**

[123] *Morrison S.S.* [1947] A.C. 265 at 283.

[124] *Castle* [1984] A.C. 226 at 234. See para.30.50, above. See also *The Santa Ana* (1907) 154 Fed. Rep. 800.

[125] *Hallet v Bousfield* (1811) 18 Ves. 187, a case in which Lord Eldon refused an injunction to restrain the shipowner from delivering the cargo without obtaining security for the plaintiff's claim. In commenting on this case in Strang v Scott (1889) 14 App. Cas. 601, Lord Watson observed (at 606): "Courts of equity are chary of granting injunctions which may lead to inconvenient results; and it does not follow from *Hallett v Bousfield* that a master might not be restrained from making delivery of the cargo, at the instance of all or most of those entitled to contribution, without taking security for their claims."

[126] See para.30.67, below. In the US the owner of goods sacrificed has a lien, enforceable in Admiralty, against the vessel and other interests for the amount due to him.

[127] See fn.117, above.

[128] *Castle* [1984] A.C. 226 at 234, see para.30.43, above. See also *Crooks v Allen*, para.30.47, above.

[129] For typical form of bond, see Appendix 4, para.80.03, below.

(1) A cash deposit,[130] more particularly in those cases where:

(a) The cargo is uninsured, or where a general average guarantee offered by insurers is considered unsuitable.

(b) The amount of the general average is substantial and the shipowner has given salvage security on behalf of the cargo and/or expects to need ready cash to make payments on account before the general average adjustment is completed to those parties to the adventure who have sustained large losses or expenditures.

A bank guarantee is sometimes accepted in lieu of a deposit but this can be expensive and the bank charges are not admissible in general average.

(2) An unlimited guarantee[131] from his insurers, whereby they guarantee the due payment of the proportion of the general average and other charges attaching to the cargo. Most forms of guarantee impose a primary liability on the insurer.[132]

Alternatively, cargo owners and insurers may enter into a tripartite agreement with the shipowner. The Lloyd's approved forms of such agreements are set out in Appendix 4.[133] However, it is open to the parties to make their own formal or informal agreement as they please,[134] provided that it is reasonable as to the form and the amount of security, and as to the terms upon which it is held.[135]

30.51 The wording of the average bond and guarantee is not fixed by the York-Antwerp Rules. Variations may be found where adjusters and insurers have amended the wordings, either as a matter of general practice or to suit the circumstances of a particular case, and jurisdiction clauses are now commonplace. It was held in the *Jute Express* [1991] 2 Lloyd's Rep. 55 that the words in the standard average bond referring to general average "which is payable" mean "and which is legally due", thus preserving the right to challenge any alleged liability for contribution. Nonetheless, to put the matter beyond doubt in other jurisdictions, the words "properly due" are used on the average guarantee and in some cases the phrase "legally and properly due" may also be used.

In cases involving a large number of interests (and/or a relatively low percentage rate of contribution from each interest) it may be decided not to request Average Bonds from receivers who are insured, in order to reduce the cost and paper work involved in the security collection. This decision can be made on a case by case basis, but BIMCO's Documentary Committee have drafted a recommended wording for insertion into the contract of carriage with the intention of making the collection of an Average Bond unnecessary in all cases. The wording was drawn

[130] For typical form of deposit receipt, see Appendix 4, para.80.06, below. Rule of Practice, No.B36, para.70.22, below, deals with interest on deposits. Rule XXII of the York-Antwerp Rules regulates the terms on which deposits are held.

[131] For typical form of guarantee, see Appendix 4, para.80.05, below.

[132] *Castle Insurance Co v Hong Kong Shipping Co* [1984] A.C. 226, 241–2. See also para.30.52 below.

[133] See paras 80.03, et seq., below.

[134] As in *Union of India v E.B. Aaby's Rederi* [1975] A.C. 797.

[135] See para.30.51, below.

up in consultation with the British Association of Average Adjusters, but has yet to come into wide use.

30.52 The customary procedure for collecting general average security was reviewed in the "Lehmann Timber" [2012] EWHC 844 (Comm.) which dealt with an appeal from an Arbitration award. Following release by Somali pirates after a 42-day detention, the vessel proceeded to the first discharge port in Germany where part cargo was discharged to receivers who had provided Average Bonds and an insurers' Average Guarantee. The receivers at St. Petersberg (MMO) provided only an insurers' guarantee for a small proportion of the cargo and declined to provide an Average Bond or a cash deposit for the remainder of the cargo. After waiting off St. Petersberg, the owners took the cargo to Hamina in Finland where it was discharged into a warehouse, incurring significant storage costs. The Tribunal found MMO liable for both their general average contribution and the storage costs. MMO appealed on two questions of law, the first of which was whether the owners were entitled to maintain a lien on the part of their cargo for which an insurers' Average Guarantee had been provided. MMO argued that by accepting the Average Guarantee the owners had lost their lien which could only be maintained until satisfactory security had been provided and because the terms of the Guarantee stated expressly that it was accepted "in consideration of the delivery in due course of the goods specified to the consignees thereof without collection of a deposit." Mr Justice Popplewell disagreed:

> "In my judgment this argument is unsound. The GA Guarantee was intended to operate in conjunction with a general average bond. The wording of the guarantee is expressed to be in consideration of delivery "without collection of a deposit" but it says nothing of delivery without a bond being in place from consignees. The factual matrix against which the GA Guarantee falls to be construed is that it was sought in conjunction with a bond in accordance with the almost invariable practice of the last 200 years or more. In those circumstances it is at the very lowest arguable that the Insurers could successfully contend that the GA Guarantee was not intended to respond in the absence of a bond with which it was expected to go hand in hand. The legal analysis might be that the guarantee is to be construed as a secondary liability guaranteeing only such liability as was undertaken under a GA bond by the consignees; or it might be that the circumstances indicated that the provision of a GA bond was a condition precedent to liability under the GA Guarantee. In either event the GA Guarantee would provide no sufficient security without a GA bond, which was never provided by MMO. In those circumstances the retention of the GA Guarantee could not be said to be inconsistent with the continued existence of the lien."

This conclusion appeared to be at odds with Lord Diplock's comments in the "Potoi Chau" in which the Judicial Committee Privy Council held that the signing of Average Bonds was a new contractual obligation and that by each of the forms of guarantee used in that case the insurers had assumed a primary liability.

In the Court of Appeal Sir Bernard Rix upheld the judgment on this issue while departing from the view that the guarantee was necessarily insufficient as security in its own right.

> "39. In my judgment, however, these submissions fail. On the facts the owner was clearly unwilling to give up its lien in the absence of a bond from the consignee in

addition to an insurer's guarantee or cash deposit. In the light of the authorities, long standing practice, and the arbitrators' findings, the owner was equally clearly fully entitled to take up that position, which was found to be reasonable in every respect. It may be perfectly true that, in the circumstances, by the time, whenever that was, that the bills came into the consignee's hands, and the consignee presented them to the owner, a bond might not have added in any practical way to the sources of its liability to the owner. However, the very refusal by the consignee to provide its bond would have given the owner pause for thought, and in my judgment rightly so. In any event, the bond would probably have clarified the consignee's liability very helpfully. Moreover, it would have postponed the running of the limitation period considerably, which in the context of the lengthy delays which can overtake the settlement of a general average adjustment can be of substantial importance (as the facts of The Potoi Chau illustrate). There were other advantages which the bond would have given, such as the right to a payment on account. In my judgment, the clarity and certainty of the obligations undertaken by the consignee under the bond are a sufficient justification, were any needed, for the owner's continuing request for one.

40. I say that on the assumption, which I am prepared to make in the light of The Potoi Chau, that the insurer's guarantee may well have been sufficient security on its own without the presence of any additional liability on the part of the consignee, whether derived from an average bond or from the bills of lading. I am willing to make that assumption despite the arbitrators' and the judge's views that the guarantee was conditional on the consignee's liability, and I am prepared to assume that those views were mistaken. Nevertheless, it is still impossible to my mind to say that the owner is not entitled to the clear, and clearly stated, undertaking of the consignee in addition. The consignee is the party most interested in the delivery of the goods and it is only fitting that it should be primarily responsible for any general average contribution. Although the insurer ought to be creditworthy, not all insurers turn out to be so, and the clearly accepted liability of the consignee is something to which history obviously accords proper regard: and I can see no reason why history should be discarded."

In view of the above comments, it is considered that, subject to the actual wording used, an average guarantee will impose a primary liability on the insurer.

Reasonable security

30.53 What is reasonable depends upon the circumstances of each case, but a demand for the deposit of a sum larger in amount than that of any anticipated contribution, or that the deposit shall be paid to the shipowner or his agent, or that the contribution shall be determined by some person appointed by the shipowner without recourse to a legal tribunal is unreasonable.

In *Huth v Lamport*[136] the then existing Liverpool form of Average Agreement was challenged and held by Mathew and Smith J.J., and by the Court of Appeal, to be unreasonable.

Lord Esher said[137]:

"If the shipowner requires the consignee to enter into a bond in particular terms, the question arises whether the bond is unreasonable, and if part of what is insisted upon

[136] *Huth v Lamport* (1885) 16 Q.B.D. 442; (1886) 16 Q.B.D. 735.
[137] *Huth* (1886) 16 Q.B.D. 735 at 737.

> is unreasonable, the whole instrument is unreasonable. That the bond is unreasonable, considered as one which the master may impose on the consignee, is. I think, clear. First, it makes the shipowner's average adjuster an arbitrator, and that is unreasonable. Then there is a peculiar kind of appeal from the decision of the average adjuster, which prevents the parties from taking the opinion of a legal tribunal. Further, the terms of the deposit are unreasonable, inasmuch as it requires a deposit in the joint names of the representative of the shipowner and the average adjuster. Then as to the mode in which payments are to be made out of the deposit. The average adjuster of the shipowner is to be the judge, and what purports to be a deposit is to be drawn upon for such disbursements as these two, without the consent of the depositor, think ought to be paid to the shipowner. For these different reasons the bond is one which, I think, the Liverpool shipowners have no right to impose upon the owner of any cargo which arrives there."

Earlier in his judgment he criticised the terms of the bond on the additional ground that it entitled the shipowner to draw from the deposit the whole amount of disbursements made by him, although it might turn out on the final settlement that a substantial part of those disbursements fell to be borne by him as his share of the general average.

If the shipowner demands security by way of a deposit, he is bound to set against the sum he demands, and place to the credit of the consignee, the amount of any claim which the latter may rightfully have upon the ship, in respect of a jettison or other sacrifice of goods.[138]

Where the shipowner is obliged to obtain security for the benefit of the owner **30.54** of sacrificed cargo, as well as obtaining it for his own benefit, the security must not only be reasonable as regards the consignees who are asked to provide it, but the shipowner is also obliged to ensure that it provides reasonable protection to the owner of the sacrificed cargo, a question considered in more detail below.[139]

Guarantees

As indicated in para.30.50, above, security for the payment of the cargo's **30.55** contribution to general average is today customarily provided by a guarantee given by the underwriters of the cargo rather than by a deposit. The question may arise, however, whether a shipowner who accepts a guarantee, instead of requiring a deposit, fulfils his duty to the cargo owner to whom a general average contribution is owing. In one respect a guarantee can never be as good a security as a deposit of money, for it may become inadequate or even valueless through the insolvency of the guarantor. It may therefore be argued that a shipowner fails in his duty to the cargo owner, if he agrees to substitute a guarantee for a deposit. It must, however, be remembered that in another respect a guarantee of the whole amount of the contribution may be a better security than a deposit; for the amount of the contribution is uncertain at the time when the security is given, and there is

[138] *The Norway* (1865) Br. & L. 404, 3 Moo. P.C. (N.S.) 245, P.C.
[139] See para.30.53, below.

a possibility that it will exceed the deposit, especially where the currency of the deposit differs from the currency of the adjustment.[140]

It is submitted that the shipowner fulfils his obligation if he obtains such security for the payment of the contribution as a prudent man would be content to take for his own benefit.[141] The guarantee of the Corporation of Lloyd's[142] or that of a bank[143] or insurance company of high standing would normally satisfy this test.

There can be no doubt that a guarantee for a part only of the contribution would be an insufficient security. There is, however, a practice in cases where the general average is of a minor nature and there are a great many cargo interests, to take security only from the larger of them. Alternatively in such a case it may be suggested to the ship's insurers that they should pay the whole loss, to avoid disproportionate expense in collecting contributions, but the increasing use of Absorption Clauses has meant that such calculations, which can be difficult to make in the early stages of a case, are less often required.

Cash Deposits

30.56 Cash deposits are normally required in the circumstances already described in para.30.38, above.

As has already been seen, it is a breach of contract by the shipowner to use his lien so as to demand a deposit which exceeds the maximum amount for which the consignee could realistically be liable to contribute, or so as to seek to impose unreasonable terms as to the manner in which the deposit is held.[144] The York-Antwerp Rules, where they apply, govern the terms upon which the deposit is held.[145]

30.57 It is the usual practice of the consignees of the cargo, when they have been obliged to make a cash deposit in order to obtain delivery of their goods, to claim the amount of the deposit from their insurers, who generally agree to reimburse them this amount in whole or in part, according as to whether the goods are fully or only partly insured. The assured then hand over to the insurers the receipt given for the deposit, sometimes accompanied by a formal assignment to the insurers of their interest in the deposit, up to the amount provided by the insurers.

140 For the currency in which deposits are to be held, see para.22.11, above.

141 The judgments of Mathew J. and Lindley L.J. in *Huth v Lamport* (para.30.51, above) suggest that the shipowner's duty is to take reasonable security. Even a trustee is not expected, save in the investment of the trust funds, to take greater precautions in managing trust affairs than an ordinary prudent man of business would take in managing similar affairs of his own: per Lord Blackburn, in *Speight v Gaunt* (1883) 9 App. Cas. 1 at 19; per Lord Watson, in *Learoyd v Whlteley* (1887) 12 App. Cas. 727 at 733.

142 Those forms which have been officially adopted by the Committee of Lloyd's are set out in Appendix 4, paras 80.03, et seq., below.

143 Provided that the guarantee is not of limited duration. Some banks will not give a guarantee lasting for more than one year, although they will usually renew it. Unless the bank is obliged to renew the guarantee from year to year, this would, it is suggested, be insufficient.

144 See paras 30.45, 30.47, above.

145 r.XXII, above.

The receipt customarily given to the depositor is a special Lloyd's form of General Average Deposit Receipt.[146] These receipts are transferable documents of title, which entitle any holder to present the same and claim the refund eventually found to be due. Unless special arrangements are made when the insurers reimburse their assured for the deposit paid, the whole of the bank interest earned on the deposit will be paid to the holder of the Deposit Receipt, regardless of the period for which each party has been out of pocket for the amount of the deposit.[147]

(C) ENFORCEMENT BY ACTION

Shipowner's Right to Sue

The shipowner is entitled to sue to recover contribution from the owners of surviving cargo. If the ownership of the cargo remains unchanged throughout the voyage there is no difficulty in identifying the proper defendant. If, however, there is a change in ownership, the person liable is the owner of the cargo at the time of the sacrifice or expenditure, although the liability may be retained by the shipper, or passed on to subsequent assignees of the goods, by appropriate contractual stipulations.[148] Thus in *Walford de Baerdemaecker v Galindez*[149] it was held that the special terms of the bills of lading imposed the obligation to contribute on the shippers alone, irrespective of the ownership of the goods at the time of the sacrifice. In *Castle Insurance Co v Hong Kong Shipping Co*[150] it was held that a clause in a bill of lading which provided "General Average shall be adjusted, stated and settled according to York-Antwerp Rules 1950" imposed upon the consignee or indorsee of the bill of lading a contractual obligation to pay any general average contribution on the cargo shipped under that bill of lading. **30.58**

An unauthorised deviation, unless waived by the bill of lading holder, would prevent the shipowner from enforcing the bill of lading holder's contractual liability to contribute as a party to the bill of lading contract.[151] Whether it will also prevent him from claiming contribution under the general law has been discussed in para.00.39, above. **30.59**

Enforcing an average agreement

Where the shipowner has obtained security in the form of an average agreement or bond, he will of course be entitled to enforce the liability to contribute against **30.60**

[146] See para.80.06, below.

[147] See Rule of Practice B36, para.70.22, below.

[148] *Hain S.S. Co v Tate & Lyle* (1936) 41 Com. Cas. 350 at 356, per Lord Atkin; *Morrison S.S. Co v Greystoke Castle* [1947] A.C. 265; *Castle Insurance Co v Hong Kong Islands Shipping Co* (1984) 1 A.C. 226 at 233–234, para.00.43, above.

[149] *Walford de Baerdemaecker v Galindez* (1897) 2 Com. Cas. 137.

[150] *Castle Insurance* [1984] 1 A.C. 226 at 235.

[151] *Scaife v Tobin* (1832) 3 B. & Ad. 523; *Hain S.S. Co v Tate & Lyle*. For the liability in these circumstances of a consignee who has signed an average bond, see paras 30.59 et seq., below.

the parties to the agreement in accordance with its terms.[152] The Lloyd's average bond imposes upon those consignees who sign it the obligation to pay:

> "the proper proportion of any salvage and/or general average and/or special charges which may hereafter be ascertained to be due from the goods or the shippers or owners thereof under an adjustment prepared in accordance with the provisions of the contract of affreightment governing the carriage of the goods or, failing any such provision, in accordance with the law and practice of the place where the common maritime adventure ended and which is payable in respect of the goods by the owners thereof."

Under an agreement in these terms general average will be payable provided that it was properly chargeable against the owner of the consignment at the time of the general average; and the amount due is to be calculated in accordance with the terms of the contract between the latter and the shipowner. The previous form of Lloyd's average bond[153] was to the same effect, although less clear in its terms.[154]

It seems probable that no liability arises under the bond until an adjustment has been published,[155] but the bond does not have the effect that the adjustment is binding on the parties.[156]

Effect of deviation or actionable fault on liability under the bond

30.61 The concluding words of the Lloyd's average bond, "and which is payable . . ." preserve the right of the signatory to rely on actionable fault as a defence to a claim under the bond.[157] but it remains to consider: (1) what is the effect of deviation on liability under the bond; and (2) at whose suit must the fault be actionable if it is to provide the signatory with a defence.

In *Hain S.S. Co v Tate & Lyle*[158] the ship deviated before the general average occurred but the deviation was waived by the charterer, who was the owner of the goods at the time of the general average act. The bills of lading were subsequently indorsed to the receivers, who obtained delivery upon entering into a Lloyd's average bond. In these circumstances the House of Lords held that although the consignees, who had not waived the deviation, had been discharged by the

[152] See para.30.50, above. For the effect of such agreements upon the limitation period, see para.23.06, above.

[153] See 10th edn, paras 1101 et seq. for the previous form.

[154] *Hain S.S. Co v Tate & Lyle*, para.30.59, below. See also *Castle Insurance Co v Hong Kong Islands Shipping Co* [1984] 1 A.C. 226, para.00.28, above, and para.30.43, above. In *Thompson v Micks, Lambert & Co* (1933) 39 Com. Cas. 40, the consignee was held liable under the previous form of Lloyd's average bond to pay general average in accordance with the York-Antwerp Rules, which were incorporated into the contract between the shipowner and the cargo owner, although the consignee had never become a party to that contract. His argument that the bond, by referring to adjustment "in the usual imanner", required an adjustment under the law of the destination rather than the Rules, was rejected.

[155] See para.23.06, above.

[156] *State Trading Corp of India v Doyle Carriers* [1991] 2 Lloyd's Rep. 55.

[157] *State Trading Corp* [1991] 2 Lloyd's Rep. 55 at 62.

[158] *Hain S.S.* (1936) 41 Com. Cas. 350.

deviation from any liability under the bills of lading, they were nevertheless liable under the bond since the deviation would have provided no defence to a claim against those who owned the cargo at the time of the general average.

It must be kept in mind that in *Hain S.S. Co v Tate & Lyle* the ship had returned to her proper route before the general average occurred and the court did not regard the accident as having been caused by the deviation.[159] The case therefore did not raise the same questions as arise where the consignee who enters into the average agreement contends that the event which gave rise to the general average was caused by the actionable fault of the shipowner.[160] In such a case it is submitted that the general approach described in para.30.59, above, holds good, and that if the consignee can establish that the event which gave rise to the general average was caused by fault which is actionable at the suit of the party who was the owner at the time of the cargo, contribution is not payable under the agreement.[161] **30.62**

What of the case where the shipowner's fault is not actionable by the owner of the cargo at the time of the general average, but is actionable by the consignee who enters into the average agreement? Such a situation could arise where the charterparty confers on the shipowner wider exemptions from liability than the bill of lading and the charterer, who owns the cargo at the time of the general average, subsequently indorses the bill of lading to the consignee who takes delivery upon entering into an average agreement. In such a case there seems to be no reason why the consignee, although prima facie liable in terms of the agreement, should not rely on the shipowner's breach of the bill of lading contract in order to defeat the claim by circuity of action.[162] **30.63**

Charterer's liability to contribute

If the charterer is the owner of a freight at risk, contribution on freight may be recovered from him in accordance with the terms of the charter, or of any average agreement entered into by him. However, in the absence of agreement to the contrary, a charterer as such is not liable to pay cargo's contribution upon cargo not owned by him. Although there is no direct authority on the point, it is submitted that a clause such as that under consideration in *Castle Insurance Co v Hong* **30.64**

[159] Despite the remarks of Lord Wright at 361, which probably refer to the situation which would have existed if the charterers had not affirmed the contract, and the responsibility of the shipowner as a common carrier were in issue: see *British Shipping Laws*, Vol. 3: Carver, *Carriage by Sea*, 13th edn, para.1202.

[160] See paras D.01 et seq., above, as to the effect of actionable fault.

[161] It could be argued that the terms of r.D lead to the opposite conclusion, and that the only relevant consideration is whether the fault is actionable at the suit of the person who entered into the average agreement. The latter, if not a bill of lading holder, may have no cause of action in contract or tort in respect of any fault by the shipowner: see *Leigh & Sillavan v Aliakmon Shipping* [1986] A.C. 785.

[162] In *Hain S.S. Co v Tate & Lyle* (1836) 41 Com. Cas. 350 the consignee did not contend that the general average was to avert a loss for which the shipowner, as common carrier, would have been liable to the consignee, thus providing the consignee with a defence on the grounds of actionable fault. This would have given rise to the question whether, the bill of lading contract having been abrogated, the shipowner owed the duties of a common carrier to anyone except the owner of the goods at the time.

Kong Islands Shipping Co[163] which simply provides for the method of adjustment and settlement, would not, when incorporated into a charterparty, amount to a contractual agreement on the part of the charterer to pay general average assessed on cargo owned by another. The purposes of such a clause is primarily to agree the terms upon which cargo owner should contribute, the charterer being obliged to procure that such terms are incorporated in the bills of lading. In some forms of charterparty, such as the Gencon, this is put beyond doubt, since the liability to contribute is expressly imposed upon the proprietors of the cargo.

A charterer who owns the cargo, and who has obtained delivery of his goods over which the shipowner was asserting a lien, is bound to pay general average in accordance with the terms of the charter, and is not entitled to rely upon a cesser clause in the charter.[164]

Cargo Owner's Right to Sue

30.65 The cargo-owner may sue the shipowner in respect of contributions in respect of ship and, sometimes, freight. He also has a direct right of action against other cargo-owners.[165] In the case of a collision as a result of which he has become liable to contribute in general average, the cargo owner may also recover from the owners of the other colliding ship a part of the contribution which he has been compelled to pay directly proportional to the extent of the responsibility of that ship for the collision.[166]

Charterer's Right to Sue

30.66 Where the charterer is the owner of freight at risk which has been sacrificed by a general average act, he will have rights of suit against the other parties to the adventure similar to those of the owner of sacrificed cargo. It seems unlikely, however, that a charterer who did not have a possessory interest in the cargo could successfully claim to recover, from the owners of a colliding ship, any general average contribution which he had become liable to pay on freight.[167]

[163] *Castle Insurance* [1984] 1 A.C. 226; para.30.56, above.

[164] *Marvigor Cia. Naviera SA v Romano Export State Company for Foreign Trade* [1977] 2 Lloyd's Rep. 280.

[165] *Strang v Scott* (1889) 14 App. Cas. 601, 606; *Dobson v Wilson* (1813) 3 Camp. 480, where the master had sold part of the cargo to procure his release from prison for debt, and it was held that the goods had not been sacrificed for the safety of the ship and the residue of the cargo.

[166] *Morrison v Greystoke Castle* [1947] A.C. 265. See also paras 50.92 et seq., below.

[167] Because of the rules governing the recoverability of financial loss in tort, the charterer has no cause of action in tort in respect of loss of freight (see *Elliott Steam Tug v Shipping Controller* [1922] 1 K.B. 127: *Candlewood Corp v Mitsui* [1986] A.C. 1) and it is difficult to see how he could have any greater rights in respect of contribution on freight saved. However, in *The Okehampton* [1913] P. 173, it was held that a charterer who had received the cargo from the shipper, placed it on board and issued a bill of lading in his own name was in possession of the cargo and therefore entitled to claim damages in tort for loss of freight thereon.

Jurisdiction

High Court

30.67 Where the defendant is domiciled in a state to which: (1) the EC Judgments Regulation 44/2001; or (2) the Brussels or Lugano Conventions apply, the jurisdiction of the court must be exercised only where permitted by the provisions of the Regulation or the relevant Convention. The basic provision of all of these is that a person should be sued in the courts of the country where he is domiciled, but jurisdiction also exists: (1) if the defendant has agreed that the English courts shall have jurisdiction; and, (2) in matters relating to contract, if England is the place for performance of the obligation in question. Where the defendant is not domiciled in a Regulation or Convention country, the court may assume jurisdiction: (1) when the defendant is present in England, so that proceedings can be served on him here; (2) when the defendant has agreed that the English courts shall have jurisdiction; and (3) in certain other cases also, most relevantly when the action is brought upon a contract which was made within the jurisdiction, is to be performed in England or which is governed by English law.[168]

30.68 The law governing the adjustment, the place where contributions are to be paid, and the question whether a clause specifying a place of adjustment amounts to an agreement that the courts of that place shall have jurisdiction has already been discussed in paras 30.06 et seq., above. So far as concerns average bonds, there is little clear authority on the law which governs them, or the place where payment under them is to be made, and the Lloyd's average bond contains no express provision on these matters. In *Schothorst and Schuitema v Franz Dauter*[169] Kerr J. expressed the view that the average bond should derive its proper law from the law governing the contract of carriage as a whole rather than the law governing the adjustment. It is submitted, however, that an average bond is rather more closely connected with the law governing the adjustment than that governing the contract of carriage, and in *Armar Shipping v Caisse Algerienne*[170] the views of Kerr J. were not adopted. However, on the facts of the latter case the Court of Appeal declined to hold that the proper law of the bond was the same as the law of the adjustment, since the bill of lading contract (to which the defendant was not a party) conferred upon the carrier a right to select the place of adjustment, and the selection had not been made when the bond was executed; the proper law of the bond could not "float" until the selection had been made, but must be ascertainable when the contract was formed.

[168] Civil Procedure Rules Pt 6.20. The jurisdiction probably extends to a claim to enforce a quasi-contractual claim (see *Rousou's Trustee v Rousou* [1955] 3 All E.R. 486) and therefore, it is suggested, to a claim in general average even where the obligation to contribute is not contractual. Where the obligation to contribute is contractual, it is submitted that the court can exercise jurisdiction under this sub-rule, whatever the proper law of the contract of carriage as a whole, so long as the law of adjustment is English. Sed quaere: see *Armar Shipping v Caisse Algerienne* [1981] 1 W.L.R. 207 at 212; [1980] 2 Lloyd's Rep. 450 at 456.

[169] *Schothorst* [1973] 2 Lloyd's Rep. 91.

[170] *Armar Shipping* [1981] 1 W.L.R. 207; [1980] 2 Lloyd's Rep. 450.

30.69 A claim arising out of a general average act falls within the Admiralty jurisdiction of the High Court, which is defined in s.20(2) of the Senior Courts Act 1981,[171] and includes:

(a) any claim for loss of or damage to goods carried in a ship;
(b) any claim arising out of any agreement relating to the carriage of goods in a ship or to the use or hire of a ship;
(c) any claim:
  (i) under the Salvage Convention 1989;
  (ii) under any contract for or in relation to salvage services; or
  (iii) in the nature of salvage . . .;
(d) any claim arising out of an act which is or is claimed to be a general average act.

This jurisdiction is exercisable in rem, as outlined in para.30.69, below.

County courts

30.70 The county court has jurisdiction over certain admiralty claims, as defined in s.27(1) of the County Courts Act 1984.[172] Unlike the equivalent statutory provision which defines the admiralty jurisdiction of the High Court,[173] s.27(1) makes no specific reference to claims in general average, but it does include all of the other types of claim referred to in para.30.64, above, and it follows that, except in most unusual circumstances,[174] a claim in general average will fall within the admiralty jurisdiction of the county court, as a "claim arising out of any agreement relating to the carriage of goods in a ship or to the use or hire of a ship". The financial limit of the court's jurisdiction is £5,000, or £15,000 in the case of salvage claims. The limit will not apply if the parties have made a written agreement to submit the dispute to a specified county court.

Proceedings in rem and arrest

30.71 So long as service of the writ upon the ship can be effected in England the admiralty jurisdiction of both the High Court and the county court is exercisable in rem in accordance with the relevant statutory provisions.[175] Whilst these are too

[171] Now the Senior Courts Act 1981.

[172] The abolition was effected by the High Court and County Courts Jurisdiction Order 1991, SI 1991/724 (made under the Courts and Legal Services Act 1990) art.2(8) and Sch.1 art.12(b) preserves the limit in relation to proceedings under the county courts' admiralty jurisdiction. The limit of £5,000 (modified in the case of salvage claims) is contained in the County Courts Act 1984 s.27(2).

[173] i.e. the Senior Courts Act 1981 s.20(2): para.30.67, above.

[174] See paras 00.20–00.29, above, as to the circumstances in which a claim in general average can be said to arise out of the contract of carriage.

[175] For the High Court see the Senior Courts Act 1981 s.21(4), and for the county court, see the County Courts Act 1984 s.28(4). However, where the defendant shipowner is domiciled in a Regulation or Convention country an action in rem must be brought in a country whose courts have jurisdiction under the relevant provisions.

complicated to discuss in detail here, their effect in relation to claims in general average is, broadly speaking, as follows:

(1) an action for contribution due from the shipowner may be pursued in rem against:
  (a) the ship in connection with which the claim arose, provided that it is still owned by him at the time when the action is commenced; or
  (b) any other ship owned by him at the time when the action is commenced;
(2) an action for contribution due from the charterer may be pursued in rem against any ship owned by him at the time when the action is commenced;
(3) an action for contribution due from a cargo-owner, not being the ship-owner or charterer, cannot be pursued by an action in rem.

The obvious advantage of an action in rem, where the claimant is unsecured or inadequately secured, is that he may arrest the vessel against which the action is brought and thus obtain security for his claim.

Jurisdiction in the United States

Cases involving questions of general average may come within the jurisdiction of either the District Courts of the United States (Federal Courts), or the State Courts. The District Courts, however, have exclusive jurisdiction in Admiralty, and proceedings in rem against vessels and in salvage cases are necessarily brought before them. The owner of goods sacrificed has, in the United States, a lien on the vessel and other interests for the amount due to him. Since the United States District Courts in Admiralty by their process in rem afford the most convenient means of enforcing this right, and of enforcing the shipowner's lien on the cargo, it is by the District Courts that almost all cases involving general average are now heard. **30.72**

Arbitration

Parties to a dispute may of course refer it to arbitration once it has arisen, and this gives rise to no specific problems in connection with general average. The question whether an arbitration clause in a contract of carriage extends to disputes concerning general average has been considered earlier.[176] **30.73**

Responsibility for Collecting Contributions

We have seen that the shipowner is responsible for obtaining security for the cargo owner's claims in general average and for procuring an adjustment.[177] The **30.74**

[176] Paras 00.26 et seq., above. See also para.30.21, above.
[177] See paras 30.47 et seq., above.

reason why it has been held that he is under these duties is that the cargo owner is usually in no position to take these steps himself. But does the shipowner's responsibility extend to the actual collection of general average contributions from the other interests? Whilst there is no authority on the point there would seem to be no valid reason for imposing on him this burden, which could be very onerous, provided that he has taken proper steps to obtain security.[178] If this is correct, it follows that any party who is a creditor in the general average is responsible for taking the necessary steps, at his own expense, to enforce payment.

The one limited exception to this is that where the shipowner has obtained security in a form which gives him alone the legal right to enforce it, he must be under an obligation to allow the cargo owner to bring proceedings in his name to enforce the security, against a suitable indemnity in respect of the costs. Since the coming into force of the Contracts (Rights of Third Parties) Act 1999 this situation is unlikely be common. Under the Lloyd's Average Bond, for example, although the promise of payment is, on the face of it, made solely to the shipowner it is not confined to the sums due to the shipowner in respect of his own losses, and having regard to the shipowner's well-established obligation to obtain security for the claims of cargo owners, it is submitted that it extends to these losses as well as his own. In these circumstances it is likely that it would be held that the contract contained in the bond purports to confer a benefit on all creditors in the general average, with the result that they would be entitled, under the Act, to enforce it in their own name.

30.75 In practice, because of his familiarity with the case, his possession of all the general average security and claims documents and his previous dealings with many of the parties involved, the average adjuster is usually entrusted in the first instance with the collection and settlement of all cargo debit and credit balances shown due in the adjustment. His fees for these services will be charged to general average in the adjustment itself. However, it was held in *Sameon Co SA v Petrofina SA*[179] that the right of suit in respect of unpaid contributions remains vested in the party to the adventure to whom contribution is due and there is no binding custom or practice whereby the legal obligation is to make payment to the adjuster. And in *Mora Shipping Inc v Axa Corporate Solutions Assurances Assurance SA*,[180] where the bond required payment to be made to either the shipowner or the adjuster, it was held that the choice of whether to pay the shipowner or the adjuster lay with the person liable on the bond.

30.76 It follows from the above that, provided that the shipowner has taken proper steps to obtain security, the risk that contribution may be irrecoverable from one or more of the parties to the adventure, for example by reason of insolvency or exchange controls or other legal or practical obstacles, falls on those parties to

[178] It was held in *Nobel's Explosives v Rea* (1897) 2 Com. Cas. 293 (para.30.48, above) that a shipowner who fails to take proper steps to obtain security for the benefit of the cargo owner is liable in damages to the cargo owner, but the case does not support the proposition that the shipowner is under any further obligations with regard to the collection of contributions due to the cargo owner.

[179] *Sameon Co SA v Petrofina SA* Unreported April 30, 1997 CA.

[180] *Mora Shipping Inc v Axa Corporate Solutions Assurances Assurance SA* Unreported July 28, 2005 CA.

whom the lost contribution is due, that is those parties whose property has been sacrificed or who have incurred general average expenditure, and pro rata to the general average allowances credited to each of them. No further contribution can be levied against those parties who have paid their full proportion of the general average.

SECTION 6

THE CURRENCY OF THE ADJUSTMENT

RATES OF EXCHANGE AND THE PROBLEM OF SET-OFF

When a general average occurs on any international voyage, problems of considerable financial consequence can arise if the rates of exchange alter between the time of the general average act and the date of settlement under the general average adjustment. To illustrate the problem, the following example concerns an American-owned ship which incurs a general average expenditure of $100,000 to which the Japanese-owned cargo should contribute 60 per cent. **40.01**

The rates of exchange current:

At the time of the general average expenditure	S 1.00 = Y 250
When the adjustment is issued	S 1.00 = Y 125
If the adjustment is drawn up in Yen (@ 250)	= Y 25,000,000
The shipowner would receive from cargo interests 60 per cent	= Y 15,000,000
Converted @ 125, this would produce	$ 120,000
As the shipowner requires to balance his books only	$ 60,000
He would make a PROFIT of	$ 60,000
If the adjustment is drawn up in Dollars i.e.	$ 100,000
The shipowner would receive from cargo interests 60 per cent	$ 60,000
which precisely balances his books, but . . .	
By reason of the great appreciation in the value of the Yen, at 125 this would cost only	Y 7,500,00
Instead of, as in the previous example	15,000,000
showing a SAVING to cargo interests of	Y 7.500,000

What then, are the legal principles and practice which now govern the situation?

English Law Before 1974

40.02 Until 1974 English law and practice on claims involving foreign currency was governed by a rule whose origins could be traced to decisions in the sixteenth century or earlier.[1] The first limb of the rule was that the English court could only give judgment in sterling, and the second limb was that the rate of exchange to be applied in converting any foreign currency into sterling was the rate prevailing at the date when the cause of action arose. Judgment would be given in sterling, months or years later, by which time rates of exchange might have moved, resulting in either a profit or loss in his own currency to the claimant. This rule, which came to be known as the "breach-date-sterling rule" was firmly settled by decisions of the House of Lords[2] and applied to claims for damages in tort[3] or for breach of contract[4] and to claims to recover debts, even when the debt was expressed in a foreign currency.[5]

40.03 In *Noreuro Traders Ltd v E. Hardy & Co*[6] the same rule was held to be applicable to a claim for general average contribution. In that case the voyage, which ended at Antwerp, was completed immediately before the outbreak of the First World War, but the adjustment, which was in Belgian francs, was not completed until 1921. One issue between the parties concerned the rates of exchange to be applied in convening the ultimate liability in francs into sterling for purposes of an English judgment.[7] On this point Rowlatt J. decided in favour of the pre-war rate of exchange.[8]

40.04 The practice of British adjusters prior to 1974 was to draw up the adjustment in the national currency at the port of destination, partly on the basis of authorities such as *Simmonds v White*[9] and *Fletcher v Alexander*[10] and partly on the assumption that foreign courts would follow the British line of only giving judgement in their national currency. This latter assumption seems to have been substantially mistaken at least so far as most European countries were concerned.[11]

[1] For the history of the rule see the judgments of Lord Wilberforce and Lord Cross in the House of Lords in *Miliangos v George Frank Textiles Ltd* [1976] A.C. 443 at 466–467, 491–95, [1976] 1 Lloyd's Rep. 201 at 209, 225–229.

[2] See fn.3, 5, below.

[3] *The Volturno* [1921] 2 A.C. 544. H.L.

[4] See, e.g. *De Fernando v Simon Smits* [1920] 3 K.B. 409.

[5] *Re United Railways of Havana and Regla Warehouses* [1961] A.C. 1007.

[6] *Noreuro Traders Ltd v E. Hardy & Co* (1923) 16 Lloyd's Rep. 319.

[7] The other issue was the rate of exchange to be applied in converting the payments on account, as to which, see para.22.11, above.

[8] It is not clear from the judgment whether Rowlatt J. regarded the correct date for conversion as being the date of the sacrifice or expenditure or the date when the voyage terminated. The former seems more likely—see also para.40.23, below.

[9] *Simmonds v White* (1824) 2 B & C, 805.

[10] *Fletcher v Alexander* (1868) LR 3 C.P. 375.

[11] See F.A. Mann, *The Legal Aspect of Money*, 3rd edn (1971) pp.351 to 376 which contains a comparison of the position in different countries in 1971, noting that most Continental countries either permitted judgment to be given in a foreign currency or else applied the rate of exchange prevailing on the date of payment whereas "there is room for the impression that the Anglo-American countries have failed to produce persuasive arguments in favour of a rule which, on cogent grounds, the rest of the Western world has rejected."

The effect of the breach-date-sterling rule was that the chance of profit or the risk of loss rested entirely with the foreign claimant or creditor, if sterling fluctuated against his own currency. At the time when major world currencies were based on the gold standard this would normally have been of little or no financial consequence: and in those cases where there were appreciable fluctuations the rule tended to work to the advantage of the claimant, since sterling was in general a strong currency. However, in the final years of this legal régime, not only had the gold standard disappeared, but sterling tended to be weak, with the result that foreign claimants showed a declining interest in availing themselves of the British justice system when it produced judgments (and settlements) in depreciated sterling. In these circumstances, the breach-date-sterling rule began to be called into question, and by a series of decisions between 1974 and 1979 it was effectively swept aside.[12] **40.05**

The Modern English Law

The modern law on currency and rates of exchange is embodied in three decisions of the House of Lords concerning debt, damages in tort and damages for breach of contract.

(1) Debt

In *Miliangos v George Frank (Textiles) Ltd*[13] the plaintiffs claimed payment for a quantity of polyester yarn sold to the defendants under a contract in which the price was expressed in Swiss francs. The proper law of the contract was Swiss law and the money of account and of payment was Swiss francs. It was held (Lord Simon of Glaisdale dissenting) that the rule adopted by the House of Lords in earlier cases that an English court could not give judgment for payment of a sum of foreign currency could not be justified and must be abandoned[14] and that the plaintiffs were entitled to judgment in Swiss francs. **40.06**

[12] i.e. the three decisions of the House of Lords referred to in the next following paragraphs, which were preceded by two important decisions of the Court of Appeal: in *Jugoslovenska Oceanska Plovidba v Castle Investment Co* [1974] Q.B. 292. it was held that English arbitrators had power to make an award in a foreign currency; in *Schorsch Meier v Hennin* [1975] Q.B. 416, a revolutionary case, it was held that where the claim was for a foreign currency debt judgment could be given in the currency of the debt.

[13] *Miliangos v George Frank (Textiles) Ltd* [1976] A.C. 443; [1976] 1 Lloyd's Rep. 201.

[14] In *Miliangos v Frank*, the House of Lords exercised its discretion under its 1966 Practice Direction to depart from the decision in *Re United Railways of Havana and Regla Warehouses*; and in *The Despina R* and *The Folias* (intra) the House of Lords took the view that *The Volturno*, and the decisions on damages for breach of contract (see para.40.03, above) turned entirely upon the old rule which required a judgment to be in sterling, and therefore as being of no application once that rule had been abolished.

(2) Damages in Tort

40.07 In *The Despina R*[15] the plaintiffs' ship was damaged in collision for which the other ship was 85 per cent to blame. The plaintiffs had incurred expenses for repairs, etc. in Chinese R.M.B., Japanese yen and United States dollars, but had settled these various expenses in their operating currency of United States dollars. It was unanimously held that, given the new ability of an English court to give judgments in a foreign currency, to give a judgment in the currency in which the loss was sustained (that is, United States dollars) produced a more just result than one which fixed the plaintiff with a sum in sterling taken at the rates of exchange ruling at the date of the breach or of the loss.

(3) Damages for Breach of Contract

40.08 *The Folias*[16] concerned a claim for damage to a cargo of onions owing to the failure of the vessel's refrigerating machinery and for which the shipowner was responsible. The Brazilian receivers of the cargo had rendered their claim to the charterers of the vessel in Brazilian cruzeiros and this had been settled by them by purchase of the necessary Brazilian cruzeiros with French francs. In turn, they presented their claim against the shipowners in French francs. It was unanimously held that, in contractual as in other cases, a judgment could be given in a currency other than sterling, and that according to the normal principle of restitutio in integrum, the charterers recoverable loss was the sum of French francs which they had expended, rather than Brazilian cruzeiros.

40.09 The purpose underlying these decisions was described as follows by Lord Wilberforce in Miliangos v Frank,[17] in the context of a claim in debt:

> "I do not for myself think it doubtful that, in a case such as the present, justice demands that the creditor should not suffer from fluctuations in the value of sterling. His contract has nothing to do with sterling: he has bargained for his own currency and only his own currency,"

and in *The Despina R*,[18] in the context of a damages claim:

> ". . . to give a judgment in the currency in which the loss was sustained produces a juster result than one which fixes the plaintiff with a sum in sterling taken at the date of the breach or of the loss. . . . To fix such a plaintiff with sterling commits him to the risk of changes in the value of a currency with which he has no connection: to award him a sum in the currency of the expenditure or loss, or that in which he bears the expenditure or loss, gives him exactly what he has lost and commits him only to the risk of changes in the value of that currency, or those currencies, which are either his currency or those which he has chosen to use."

[15] *The Despina R* [1979] A.C. 685; [1979] 1 Lloyd's Rep. 1.
[16] *The Folias* [1979] A.C. 685; [1979] 1 Lloyd's Rep. 1.
[17] *Miliangos v Frank* [1976] A.C. 443 at 465; [1976] 1 Lloyd's Rep. 201 at 208.
[18] *The Despina R* [1979] A.C. 685 at 696–697; [1979] 1 Lloyd's Rep. 1 at 5.

From a practical point of view the major effect has been to remove from the creditor the risk of profit or loss on exchange fluctuation (unless he has bargained for a currency of account other than his own currency). The profits and losses themselves are totally unavoidable, but they now fall upon the debtor, unless his own currency happens to be that in which the claim is calculated. A subsequent decision of the House of Lords[19] provided a vivid illustration of how great these profits or losses may be.

The modern law may be summarised as embodying two principles. The first is that where the parties have agreed, expressly or by implication, on a currency which shall be used as a measure of the obligation–"the currency of the contract"– the courts will give judgment in that currency; the second is that where there is no currency of the contract the damage should be calculated, and judgment given, in the currency in which the loss was felt by the claimant, or "which most truly expresses his loss".[20] The determination of that currency, and the rates of exchange for converting other currencies are considered in more detail below. **40.10**

Application of the modern law to general average

None of the three cases upon which the modern law is founded was concerned with general average, and it may be objected that general average differs from debt in that there is normally no specified currency of account, and from damages in that the right of recovery does not arise out of any breach of duty. However, in the case where the parties have agreed upon a currency of account for general average, the situation cannot be distinguished from Miliangos[21] and there can be no doubt that the court would apply the same rule. Even in those cases where there is no agreement, it is illogical to have a special rule for general average which differs from the rules applicable to any other monetary claims. The principle of restitutio in integrum, upon which the decision of the House of Lords in *The Despina R* and *The Folias*[22] is based, is no less applicable to general average than to damages, and it should therefore prevail in the absence of any binding practice to the contrary.[23] It follows that the ordinary rules of law summarised in the previous paragraph should apply equally to general average. **40.11**

One additional effect of the abolition of the rule that the English court must give judgment in sterling is that, where the adjustment is governed by English law, there will now be no difference between the currency in which the adjustment should be prepared and the currency in which the judgment will be recovered if the claim is enforced by proceedings in England. The adjuster ought to give effect to the principles set out in para.40.10, above and, if he does so correctly, the court will give judgment in the currency of the adjustment. **40.12**

[19] *The Texaco Melbourne* [1994] 1 Lloyd's Rep. 473; see para.40.27, below. In that case the debtor profited from the fluctuation.

[20] Per Lord Wilberforce in *The Folias* [1979] A.C. 701; [1979] 1 Lloyd's Rep. 1 at 8. See para.40.21, below.

[21] *Miliangos* [1976] A.C. 443; [1976] 1 Lloyd's Rep. 201.

[22] *The Despina R* [1979] A.C. 685; [1979] 1 Lloyd's Rep. 1.

[23] No uniform practice of average adjusters has yet emerged, see para.40.20, below.

Even where the adjustment is governed by foreign law[24] there is no reason why the English court should not give judgment in the currency of the adjustment, provided that the adjuster has correctly applied the foreign law in selecting that currency. The situation which arose in *Noreuro Traders v E. Hardy & Co*[25] where it was accepted that the adjustment fell to be made in Belgian francs but all the losses had to be re-converted from francs into sterling at the rate prevailing on the date when they were incurred, or on the date when the adventure terminated,[26] could no longer apply.

Determining the Currency of Adjustment

40.13 We shall now consider in more detail the currency or currencies in which the adjustment should be prepared, and the exchange rates which should be used when conversion from one currency to another is necessary. As Lord Wilberforce stated in The Folias[27]:

> "The first step must be to see whether, expressly or by implication, the contract provides an answer to the currency question. This may lead to selection of the 'currency of the contract.'"

Express provision for currency of adjustment

40.14 It cannot be recommended too strongly that every bill of lading and charter-party should include special provisions specifying a single currency in which any general average adjustment is to be prepared and settled, for example: "General Average shall be adjusted, stated and settled at [ ] according to York-Antwerp Rules [ ] in [currency]."

There is no legal objection to such a contractual provision in English law, and, provided that the specified currency is an accepted international trading currency, or bears some relationship to the particular trade on which the vessel is engaged, such a provision should be commercially acceptable, and this would resolve the many problems which can occur where no such currency provision is made.

40.15 Some clauses confer upon the shipowner the option to select the currency of the adjustment. There is no reason in English law why such a clause should not be enforceable, but the courts might be reluctant to allow the option to be used so as to enable the shipowner to engage in a free currency speculation at the expense of the other parties to the adventure, on the basis that the selection by the shipowner of a currency which had no connection with the loss was an invalid exercise of the option.

[24] The selection of the currency in which the adjustment should be made is determined by the substantive law governing the obligation—see *The Folias* [1979] A.C. 685 at 700. In general average this is the law governing the adjustment.

[25] *Noreuro Traders* (1923) 16 Lloyd's Rep. 319, para.40.03, above.

[26] It is not clear in the report of the case which date was adopted. See also para.40.03, above.

[27] *The Folias* [1979] A.C. 685 at 700; [1979] 1 Lloyd's Rep. 1 at 7.

Where the contract makes provision for a specific currency, all expenditure and sacrifices should be converted into that currency for the purposes of the adjustment, with the result that the adjustment will be in a single currency. The dates on which, subject to any special terms of the contract, other currencies are to be converted into the currency of the contract are considered below.[28] **40.16**

Implied currency of the adjustment

In the absence of a clause expressly specifying the currency of the contract for general average purposes, can any particular currency of the contract be implied? There are a number of possibilities, namely: **40.17**

(1) the currency in which other payments under the contract, such as freight, are expressed;
(2) where there is an express choice of the law governing the adjustment, the currency of the country whose law governs the adjustment; and
(3) the currency of the country or countries where the adventure ends.

The first possibility may be dismissed, for as Lord Wilberforce said in *The Folias*[29]:

> "In the present case the fact that U.S. dollars have been named as the currency in which payments in respect of hire and other contractual payments are to be made, provides no necessary or indeed plausible reason why damages for breach of the contract should be paid in that currency. The terms of other contracts may lead to a similar conclusion."

Equally, the second possibility has little to recommend it. The losses suffered in the general average may have little or no connection with the country whose law is chosen and there is no reason why a choice of law, or a choice of place, for the adjustment should be treated as an indication that the parties intended that the currency of that country should be used. In *The Folias*[30] the parties had expressly chosen English law and arbitration; but that was not considered to indicate an intention to choose English currency for payment of damages.

The third possibility deserves more serious consideration. Before 1974 it was generally considered that, because general average was historically settled at destination, and it was there that the shipowner could exercise his lien, the currency or currencies of the ports of destination, or where the adventure ended, should be adopted. This viewpoint derived some support from r.G of the **40.18**

[28] See para.40.23, below.

[29] *The Folias* [1979] A.C. 685 at 701; [1979] 1 Lloyd's Rep. 1 at 8. The observations to the contrary in *Jugoslavenska Oceanska Plovidba v Casile Investment Co* [1974] Q.B. 292 at 298 can no longer be regarded as sound. For a case in which it was held, applying *The Folias*, that a provision in a charterparty that the cost of overtime should be shared between owners and charterers imported no choice of the currency in which overtime expenses were incurred: see *Food Corp of India v Carras* [1980] 2 Lloyd's Rep. 577.

[30] *The Folias* [1979] A.C. 685; [1979] 1 Lloyd's Rep. 1.

York-Antwerp Rules, and from the finding in *Noreuro Traders Ltd v E. Hardy & Co*[31] that on a voyage to Antwerp, the general average adjustment fell to be made in Belgian francs, and from a similar American case, *The Arkansas*.[32]

40.19 Against this argument ranks the fact that the place where the adventure ends may be fortuitous, and even where it ends at the contractual destination, the currency of that country may have little connection with the losses suffered, particularly those suffered by the shipowner. Nor is the currency of the destination likely to lead to greater simplicity in adjustment, since the great majority of general averages consists simply of expenditure by the shipowner alone, whereas there may be ports of discharge in several different countries. The practice of preparing the adjustment in the currency of the place of destination, although widespread before 1974, was not universal, nor of particularly long standing.

40.20 On the whole, it seems preferable to recognise that a historical viewpoint will provide no solution to the problem. Therefore, while one cannot rule out the possibility that the currency of the place where the adventure ends might be held to be an implied choice of currency, the present editors adhere to the view first expressed in the tenth edition[33] that there will normally be no currency of the contract for general average purposes except where a currency of adjustment has been expressly agreed upon.

The currency in which the loss was felt by the claimant

40.21 In the absence of any express or implied currency of the contract for general average, we return to the views expressed by Lord Wilberforce in *The Folias*[34]:

> "If then the contract fails to provide a decisive interpretation, the damage should be calculated in the currency in which the loss was felt by the Plaintiff or 'which most truly expresses his loss.' "

Further clarification is afforded by Lord Wilberforce in *The Despina R*,[35] starting with the passage in which he describes the two main alternatives:

> "The first is to take the currency in which the expense or loss was immediately sustained. This I shall call 'the expenditure currency.' The second is to take the currency in which the loss was effectively felt or borne by the plaintiff, having regard to the currency in which he generally operates or with which he has the closest connection–this I shall call 'the plaintiff's currency.' "[36]

Lord Wilberforce then rejects "the expenditure currency" in favour of "the plaintiff's currency":

[31] *Noreuro Traders* (1923) 16 Lloyd's Rep. 319 at 320.
[32] *The Arkansas* (1929) A.M.C. 581.
[33] 10th edn (1975), para.471, anticipating the approach in *The Folias*.
[34] *The Folias* [1979] A.C. 685 at 701; [1979] 1 Lloyd's Rep. 1 at 8.
[35] *The Folias* [1979] A.C. 685 at 701.
[36] *The Folias* [1979] A.C. 685 at 696; [1979] 1 Lloyd's Rep. 1 at 4–5.

> "My Lords, in my opinion, this question can be solved by applying the normal principles . . . of restitutio in integrum and that of the reasonable foreseeability[37] of the damage sustained. It appears to me that a plaintiff, who normally conducts his business through a particular currency, and who, when other currencies are immediately involved, uses his own currency to obtain those currencies, can reasonably say that the loss he sustains is to be measured not by the immediate currencies in which the loss first emerges but by the amount of his own currency, which in the normal course of operation, he uses to obtain those currencies. This is the currency in which his loss is felt, and is the currency which it is reasonably foreseeable he will have to spend."[38]

Returning to "the plaintiff's currency", he observes:

> "I should refer to the definition I have used of this expression and emphasise that it does not suggest the use of a personal currency attached, like nationality, to a plaintiff, but a currency which he is able to show is that in which he normally conducts trading operations."[39]

Thus, we arrive at the conclusion that: **40.22**

(1) Where a currency for general average purposes has been expressed in the bill of lading or contract of affreightment, the general average sacrifices and expenditures of the various parties to the adventure should be exchanged into that single currency of the contract, and settlement between the parties effected in that currency.
(2) In the absence of an expressed currency of the contract, no particular currency can generally be implied, but the general average sacrifices and expenditures of the various parties to the adventure should be shown in the operating currencies of those who have sustained the sacrifices and financed the expenditures, that is the currency in which they each feel their loss.

How settlement should take place between the parties will be discussed later.

Rates of Exchange

In each case, the court and the adjuster should seek to give effect to the principle of restitutio in integrum, and this will normally involve adopting the rate prevailing on the date(s) when the loss was felt by the claimant. As a general rule these dates will be as follows: **40.23**

- **In the case of expenditures**–on the various dates when the accounts were paid or, when the payment is made through an agent, when the agent was placed in funds.[40]

[37] See para.40.24, fn.44, below, as to the reference to reasonable foreseeability.
[38] *The Folias* [1979] A.C. 685 at 697; [1979] 1 Lloyd's Rep. 1 at 5.
[39] *The Folias* [1979] A.C. 685 at 698; [1979] 1 Lloyd's Rep. 1 at 6.
[40] See *Food Corp of India v Carra* [1980] 2 Lloyd's Rep. 577. Where the adjustment is made in the operating currency of the claimant there will frequently be no need to undertake any exchange

- In the case of cargo sacrifices–on the date of the last day of discharge at each of the ports of discharge.[41]
- Adjustment charges and agency fees, etc.—payable only when the adjustment has been issued, should be exchanged at the rates of exchange ruling at the date of completion of the adjustment.
- Commission and interest—where allowable, are calculated on the principal sum in the currencies of the adjustment and cause no exchange problems.

Ascertaining the Claimants' Currency of Loss

40.24 The certainty which existed under the breach-date-sterling rule was replaced by a degree of uncertainty as to what constitutes the appropriate currency, and this uncertainty was recognised by Lord Wilberforce himself[42]:

> "Finally it is said (and this argument would apply equally if the expenditure currency were taken) that uncertainty will take the place of certainty under the present rule. Undoubtedly the present (sterling-breach-date) rule produces certainty–but it is often simpler to produce an unjust rule than a just one. The question is whether, in order to produce a just or juster rule, too high a price has to be paid in terms of certainty."

Undoubtedly, as Lord Wilberforce had stated earlier in his judgment[43]:

> "The plaintiff has to prove his loss: if he wishes to present his claim in his own currency, the burden is on him to show to the satisfaction of the tribunal that his operations are conducted in that currency and that in fact it was his currency that was used, in a normal manner, to meet the expenditure for which he claims or that his loss can only be appropriately measured in that currency (this would apply in the case of a total loss of a vessel which cannot be dealt with by the "expenditure" method). The same answer can be given to the objection that some companies, particularly large multi-national companies, maintain accounts and operate in several currencies. Here again it is for the plaintiff to satisfy the court or arbitrators that the use of the particular currency was in the course of normal operations of that company and was reasonably foreseeable."[44]

40.25 Two collision cases demonstrate the difficulty of determining what, in fact, was the relevant currency in which the plaintiff truly felt his loss. In *The Lash Atlantico*[45] the managers of the vessel operated in United States dollars (as did the

exercise; it will merely be necessary to ascertain how much of his own operating currency the claimant has expended. This was the case *in The Despina R and The Folias.*

[41] On the grounds of practical expediency, and because the precise date on which a consignee may have paid for his cargo is rarely known—whether, e.g. on shipment, or 90 days after landing, etc.—the last day of discharge is recommended for a common approach in exchanging the currency of the commercial invoice rendered to the receivers into his operating currency.

[42] *The Folias* [1979] A.C. 698; [1979] 1 Lloyd's Rep. 6.

[43] *The Folias* [1979] A.C. 698; [1979] 1 Lloyd's Rep. 6.

[44] Lord Wilberforce is here referring to the test of remoteness in the tort of negligence. In general average the question will be whether the loss was the direct consequence of the general average act (see paras C.01 et seq., above). It is submitted that, as a general rule, a claimant's right to recover general average contribution calculated in his operating currency will not be affected by r.C of the York-Antwerp Rules (or by the common law relating to remoteness).

[45] *The Lash Atlantico* [1985] 2 Lloyd's Rep. 464; [1987] 2 Lloyd's Rep. 114, CA.

managers of *The Despina R*), but the owners produced their annual balance sheet in Greek drachmas and the accounts rendered by the managers to the owners were expressed in drachmas. The Registrar awarded damages in US dollars, the Admiralty Court in Greek drachmas, and the Court of Appeal in US dollars.

In *The Transoceanica Francesca*,[46] the Italian owners first presented their claim in Italian lire but amended this subsequently to United States dollars. In support of this latter, more favourable, currency the owners were able to point out that the vessel was operating under a long-term charterparty under which the hire was paid in US dollars, and that they maintained a US dollar bank account into which all the earnings of the vessel were paid, and from which all trading expenses were disbursed–including the cost of repairs in the subject collision claim. However, the decision of the Registrar and of the Admiralty Court was that the US dollar account was a mere "buffer", or convenient dollar float, and that the real profits or losses on the trading of the vessel were converted into, and felt in, Italian lire. **40.26**

The approach in *The Transoceanica Francesca*[47] is entirely in accordance with the principles of restitutio in integrum upon which *The Despina R*[48] and *The Folias*[49] are based, and a similar approach was adopted by the House of Lords in *The Texaco Melbourne*.[50] In that case the claim was for non-delivery of a cargo of oil at the Ghanaian port of Takoradi. The plaintiff oil company carried on business in Ghana and maintained its bank accounts in Ghanaian cedis; if the cargo had been duly delivered the plaintiffs would have sold it and received payment in cedis. Although the plaintiffs conducted all their international oil trading operations in US dollars, exchange control regulations prevented them from maintaining funds in dollars, and the necessary dollar funds were provided by their bank for each operation. In these circumstances the House of Lords had little difficulty in holding that the plaintiffs had felt their loss in cedis. The decision supports the view that in identifying the currency in which the loss is felt the most important factor is the currency in which the plaintiff maintains his funds rather than that in which operations are conducted or in which the loss is immediately suffered. The House of Lords rejected the argument that because the international oil trade is conducted in dollars, and if the plaintiffs had bought a substitute cargo they would have paid for it in dollars, the loss was to be measured in dollars. If the plaintiffs had bought a replacement cargo they would have sold it for cedis or converted the proceeds of sale into cedis. **40.27**

The case also makes it clear that the approach laid down in The Despina R and The Folias will be applied however great is the fluctuation in currency values. At the date when the cargo should have been delivered there were 2.75 cedis to the dollar: at the date of judgment there were 375. Thus the damages recovered by the plaintiff represented, at the date of judgment, less than one per cent of the value of the original cargo, and the liability of the defendants, who presumably kept

[46] *The Transoceanica Francesca* [1987] 2 Lloyd's Rep. 155.
[47] *The Transoceanica Francesca* [1987] 2 Lloyd's Rep. 155.
[48] *The Despina R* [1979] A.C. 685; [1979] 1 Lloyd's Rep. 1.
[49] *The Folias* [1979] A.C. 695; [1979] 1 Lloyd's Rep. 7.
[50] *The Texaco Melbourne* [1992] 1 Lloyd's Rep. 303; [1993] 1 Lloyd's Rep. 471. CA; [1994] 1 Lloyd's Rep. 473, HL.

their funds in dollars, was virtually extinguished. Thus the adoption of the immediate operating currency is not appropriate where it is shown that the loss was really felt in another currency. *The Lash Atlantico*[51] is to be explained on the basis that although the accounts and the balance sheet were expressed in drachmas, there was no evidence that any payments were made in that currency, or that funds were held in that currency by the owners.

40.28 As a simple generalisation, it will generally be true that, for example a British shipowner feels his loss in sterling, a German shipowner in deutschmarks, and cargo interests in the national currency of the country of the port of destination. In the case of cargo, however, this is always subject to the usual inquiry whether the local national currency in fact represents the true loss sustained by the party concerned. In some countries where the value of the local currency is unreliable, trading operations even between locals may customarily be conducted, and funds held, in an international currency such as the US dollar. In such a case, the place of business of the claimant may provide little guidance in ascertaining the currency in which his loss is truly felt. If there is no adequate evidence as to the currency in which the loss was felt the correct conclusion may be that it was felt in the currency in which it immediately arose—"the expenditure currency".[52]

40.29 Certain passages in the judgments of the House of Lords in *The Despina R*[53] might be taken to support the view that the claimant may advance his claim either in the currency in which he felt the loss or in sterling at his option. However, this approach would be inconsistent with the general principles upon which *The Despina R*[54] and *The Folias*[55] are based, and difficult to reconcile with subsequent decisions in which those principles have been applied.[56] The court and the adjuster should always seek to give recovery of the claim in the currency which, on the evidence before it, best reflects the claimant's loss.

Contributory values

40.30 In any general average adjustment, and regardless of the number of currencies in which the general average allowances may need to be shown, contributory values must necessarily be shown in a single currency for the purpose of apportioning the total general average. It matters not which currency is chosen: it may

[51] See fn.45, above. See also *Kinetics Technology v Cross Sea Shipping* (2001) 2 Lloyd's Rep. 313 a case involving damage to cargo. Although manufactured in Italy, the goods were in transit between two US companies and the transaction was denominated in US Dollars, which was held to be the currency of loss rather than Italian Lire.

[52] See *The Despina R* [1979] A.C. 685 at 698; [1979] 1 Lloyd's Rep. 1 at 6, per Lord Wilberforce. Such an approach should not be adopted too readily where the currency in which the loss was immediately felt is much stronger than the national currency of the claimant and there is incomplete evidence about his operating currency. Lord Wilberforce appears to envisage that it will always be in the interests of the claimant to provide full information about his operating currency (see the passage cited at para.40.24, above) but there are cases where this may not be so.

[53] In particular the opening section of the passage quoted, para.40.25, above: "If he wishes to present his claim in his own currency . . .".

[54] *The Despina R* (1979) A.C. 685; [1979] 1 Lloyd's Rep. 1.

[55] *The Folias* [1979] A.C. 685; [1979] 1 Lloyd's Rep. 1.

[56] See in particular *The Texaco Melbourne* [1979] 1 Lloyd's Rep. 303.

be that of any one of the destinations, or even, for convenience, the currency of a port of shipment, or an international trading currency such as the US dollar. However, any necessary exchange into that currency should be made at the rate prevailing—for cargo on the last day of discharge at each individual port of discharge, and for the ship at the rate ruling on the last day of discharge at the final port of discharge.

The Question of "Set-Off"

When general average sacrifices and/or expenditures are incurred by both ship and cargo interests, and those losses are felt in different currencies, it is clearly necessary to strike a balance between the respective claims in some common currency—in practice, the currency of the creditor. The question then arises whether those claims should be exchanged into the common currency at the rates of exchange ruling: **40.31**

(1) when the losses were sustained:
(2) when the adjustment is issued;
(3) at the date of judgment or agreement on liability and quantum; or
(4) when payment is made.

Lord Russell of Killowen mentioned this problem in his judgment in the House of Lords in the collision action of *The Despina R*.[57]

> "I have not overlooked the arguments advanced based upon complications involved in departure from The Volturno in fields such as set-off, counterclaim, limitation of liability, insolvency. They do not arise in this case, and should not be incapable of just solutions when they do arise. I do not propose to advance hypothetical solutions."

Two simple examples will illustrate the problem, and for this purpose it will be convenient to adopt the same currencies and rates of exchange used throughout this section. **40.32**

£0.75 = $1.00 = Y250 at the time of loss or expenditure
$1.00 = Y125 at the time when claims agreed.

Example 1

An American and a Japanese vessel collide in the English Channel and both sustain serious damage which obliges them to put into Falmouth for repairs. Both vessels are equally at fault and repairs and other expenses to each vessel cost £300,000 and this is settled by the:

American owner @ £0.75 = $ 1.00 = $ 400,000
Japanese owner @ £0.75 = Y 250 = Y 100,000,000

[57] *The Despina R* [1979] A.C. 685 at 704; [1979] 1 Lloyd's Rep. 1 at 10.

Example 2

A Japanese vessel carrying an American cargo with a value identical to that of the ship strands in a position of peril and engages the services of salvage tugs to refloat. An award of £600,000 is made and. both ship and cargo having provided separate salvage security, they each pay £300,000 settled as follows:

American cargo	@ £0.75	= $ 1.00	=	$ 400,000
Japanese ship	@ £0.75	= Y 250	=	Y 100,000,000

40.33 If the respective claims of the parties in both Examples 1 and 2 are set-off against each other and exchanged *at the time of loss or when the expenditure was incurred*, it will be readily appreciated that no money changes hands as each party has already borne his precise and proper share of 50 per cent of the total damage, or salvage award. This would be the situation under the old breach-date-sterling rule. However, if the respective claims were to be maintained in their settlement currencies and set-off against each other only when the claims were agreed and/or a general average adjustment was issued, the financial position of the parties would be totally different. The value of the claims would then be:

American claim—	$ 400,000 @125 =	Y 50,000,000
Japanese claim—	Y 100,000,000 @ 125 =	$ 800,000

The claim of the Japanese ship is now double the value of that of the American cargo and the American would pay to the Japanese 50 per cent of the difference between their respective claims, whether for collision damages or as a general average contribution, that is Y25,000,000 @ 125 = $200,000.

40.34 Support for maintaining the respective claims in their settlement currencies and setting them off against each other only when the claims have been agreed and/or a general average adjustment has been issued, can be found in current English case law in collision actions and the continental système des masses for general average.

Set-off in collision actions

When giving judgment in 1977 in the court of first instance in *The Despina R*,[58] Brandon J. addressed himself to this problem of set-off of the respective claims and gave it as his provisional view, and without the benefit of argument, that this set-off should effectively take place at the date of judgment ("date on which the amount of the two liabilities are established by agreement or decision") rather than at the time of loss. The Court of Appeal in that case also suggested that a solution to these special problems could be found such as Brandon J. provisionally offered.[59]

58 *The Despina R* [1978] Q.B. 396 at 415.
59 *The Despina R* [1978] Q.B. 396 at 437.

In *The Transoceanica Francesca*[60] Brandon J.'s view was adopted and the respective claims of the two vessels were exchanged at rates ruling on the date on which the amount of both liabilities was finally agreed. Thus the Italian plaintiff, whose lire claim exceeded the defendant's (US dollar) claim if exchanged at the time of the collision, but fell short of the defendants claim if exchanged at the date when both claims had been agreed[61] found himself transformed from a creditor into a debtor.[62]

Set-off in general average in English law

While there is no direct authority on the point, there are strong arguments that in principle in the adjustment of general average under English law the competing claims should be set off against each other at the date when the losses were sustained, (or, more probably, the date of the end of the voyage in question), and that the practice in collision actions should not be followed. **40.35**

(1) Both-to-blame collision cases do not fall within the ordinary categories of cross-claims in respect of which a set-off arises.[63] By contrast, where general average losses are suffered by several contributing interests on a single common adventure, the claims to have those losses made good in general average give rise to set-off in the true sense; no party is entitled to advance a claim in respect of his losses without giving credit for the losses suffered by the other parties to the adventure, and the only claim which can be recovered by proceedings is for the balance of the general average account.[64]

(2) Since there is no recoverable claim except for the balance of account, currency fluctuations should not be allowed to operate upon the full amount of each party's loss, when he has no right in law to bring proceedings to recover his full loss, and has in fact already recouped himself in whole or in part, by means of the extinction or reduction of his own liability to contribute. That liability arises at the time of the loss or, at any rate, at the termination of the adventure[65] and it can make no difference that it has not been quantified or agreed upon at that date.

(3) The effect of the old breach-date-sterling rule was that set-offs took place at the date when the losses were sustained, or the cause of action arose. Any currency fluctuations would only operate on the net balance

[60] *The Transoceanica Francesca* [1987] 2 Lloyd's Rep. 155.

[61] There appears to have been no complete agreement on quantum, since the appropriate currency in which the claim was to be calculated remained in dispute until determined by the Court (para.40.26, above). The agreement, referred to in the report, which determined the date of set-off, was presumably an agreement on all the individual items, subject to the currency argument.

[62] For conflicting views on the merits of this approach see J. A. Knott, "The Wealth-time Continuum Revisited: Set-off in Marine Collison Claims", *Lloyd's Maritime & Commercial Law Quarterly*, May 1981, and D. J. Wilson, "Rates of Exchange Revisited", Hull Claims Analysis 4, 12, 174.

[63] As to the latter, see *Hanak v Green* [1958] 2 Q.B. 9.

[64] See the judgment of the Privy Council in *Grant v Norway* 3 Moo.(N.S.) 245 at 267–269, per Knight-Bruce L.J.

[65] See *Chandris v Argo Insurance Co* [1963] 2 Lloyd's Rep. 65 and para.40.23, above.

payable by the debtor.[66] None of the reasons for changing that rule demands any change in the previous law relating to the date when set-off takes effect: in fact the principle of restitution in integrum requires that on this point the law should remain unchanged.

40.36 The examples which follow show the effects of the set-off when the necessary currency conversion is effected at the rates of exchange ruling at the time of the loss.

Examples

Note: The common features throughout are those:

(1) The ship is Japanese, and the owners feel their loss in Japanese Yen. (Y 25,000,000–worth at the time of loss $100,000).
(2) The CARGO is generally destined for the United States and the owners feel any loss in US Dollars (usually US$ 100,000–worth at the time of loss Y 25,000,000).
(3) The RATES OF EXCHANGE will be:

$1.00 @ Y 250 at the time of the expenditure or loss
$1.00 @ Y 125 at the time of settlement under the Adjustment

(4) The contributory values will be:

SHIP—	$ 4,000,000
CARGO—	6,000,000
	$10,000,000

40.37 *Example 1*

Port of Refuge Expenses by Shipowner	Y 25,000,000
Jettison of Cargo	$100,000

Note: The Shipowner has spent Y 25,000.000 @ 250 = $100,000
Equivalent to 2½ per cent of Contributory Value of Ship ($4,000,000)
The Cargo has lost $100,000
Equivalent to 1.66 per cent of Contributory Value of Cargo ($6,000,000)

It follows that the Cargo will be a Debtor to the Ship and the Adjustment should be prepared in Yen, i.e.

Port of Refuge Expenses by Shipowner	Y 25,000.000
Jettison of Cargo $100,000 @ 250[67]	Y 25,000,000
	Y 50.000,000

[66] The same will be the case where the contract of affreightment contains a currency clause for general average claims (see para.40.14, above).

[67] The cargo owners' loss of $100,000 is converted into Yen at the rate of exchange prevailing at the date when the loss was incurred, i.e. $1.00-Y 250.

Apportionment and Settlement

				Credit Own Loss	*To Receive*	*Balance To Pay*
SHIPS	4,000,000	pays	Y 20,000,000	Y 25,000,000	Y 5,000,000	–
CARGO	6,000,000	pays	30,000,000	25,000,000	___	Y 5,000,000
	10,000,000	pays	Y 50,000,000	Y 50,000,000[68]	Y 5,000,000	Y 5,000,000
						@ 125 =$40,000

Example 2 **40.38**

The losses are the same as for Example 1, i.e.:

Port of Refuge Expenses by Shipowner.. Y 25.000,000
Jettison of Cargo $100,000

but the cargo is consigned to two separate receivers, of whom:

"A" with Cargo worth $1,000,000 sustains the whole of the jettison
"B" with Cargo worth 5,000,000 sustains no loss
$6,000,000

A preliminary calculation will disclose that the respective degrees of loss suffered by the parties are as follows:

SHIP ($100,000)	—2½ per cent of Contributory Value	($4,000,000)
CARGO "A" ($100,000)	—16 per cent of Contributory Value	($1,000,000)
CARGO "B"	—NIL per cent of Contributory Value	

It follows, therefore that:

The SHIP	–is a Debtor to "A", but a Creditor of "B"
CARGO "A"	–is a Creditor of both Ship and "B"
CARGO "B"	–is a Debtor to both Ship and "A"

There being Creditors in two currencies, the Adjustment is prepared in both those currencies, i.e.: **40.39**

		Yen	*US $*
Port of Refuge Expenses...	Y 25,000,000 @ 250	Y 25,000.000	$100,000
Jettison of Cargo	$100,000 @ 250	Y 25.000.000	100.000
		Y 50.000.000	$200,000

APPORTIONED

SHIP—	$4,000,000 Pays	Y 20,000,000	$ 80,000
CARGO 'A'	1,000,000 Pays	5,000,000	20,000
CARGO 'B'	5,000,000 Pays	Y 25,000,000	$ 100,000
	10,000,000 Pays	Y 50,000,000	$200,000

40.40 FINANCIAL SETTLEMENT

	SHIP (*40 per cent*)	*CARGO "A"* (*10 per cent*)	*CARGO "B"* (*50 per cent*)
Shipowner v Cargo "A" (In $ as "A" the Net Creditor)			
S/O liable "A"–$AM 40 per cent × $100,000 = $40,000			
"A" liable S/O–10 per cent × $100.000 = 10,000	$30,000 @ 125= Y3,750,000	$30,000	
A Shipowner Pays "A" ($30,000)			
Shipowner v Cargo "B" (In Yen as Shipowner the Creditor)	(12,500,000)		Y12,500,000 @ 125= $100,000
"B" liable S/O–50 per cent × Y 25M = Y 12,500,000			
Cargo "A" v Cargo "B" (In $ as "A" the Creditor)			
"B" liable "A"–50 per cent × $100,000 = $50,000		($50,000)	50,000
	Receives (Y 8,750,000)	Receives ($80,000)	Pays $150,000

40.41 The following example uses the approach adopted in collision cases (and by continental adjusters for many years prior to the change in English Law and usually refered to as the Systeme des Masses) of effecting the set off at the date of the final adjustment, which is closest to the date of settlement that can in practice be achieved. The ship and cargo have equal contributory values.

	General Average	
Japanese Shipowners' Disbursements		Y 100,000,000
American Cargo Sacrifices	$400,000	

APPORTIONED

Japanese Shipowner	(50 per cent)	pays	$200,000	Y 50,000,000
American Cargo	(50 per cent)	pays	200,000	50,000,000
	100 per cent)	pays	$400,000	Y 100,000,000

FINANCIAL SETTLEMENT BETWEEN PARTIES

Japanese Shipowners pays to American Cargo	$200,000 @ 125 = Y 25,000,000
receives from Cargo	50,000,000
NET: Shipowner RECEIVES	Y 25,000,000
American Cargo pays to Japanese Shipowner	Y 50,000,000 @ 125 = $400,000
receives from Shipowner	200,000
NET: Cargo PAYS	$200,000

Proposals for the York-Antwerp Rules

The problems of currencies and rates of exchange were the subject of discussion during the development of the 1994 Rules. The International Sub-Committee was in principle, in favour of introducing additional wording into r.XXI to regulate these matters and the British Maritime Law Association submitted a draft wording which provided that, except where the parties had already agreed that the adjustment should be prepared in a specific currency, it should be prepared in SDRs. **40.42**

The SDR is a unit of account created by the International Monetary Fund purely as an official reserve asset and comprising a "basket" of the currencies of the five member countries of the IMF with the largest exports of goods and services during the five-year period preceding any revision, weighted to reflect broadly their relative importance in international trade and finance. The overall effect of adopting SDRs as a unit of account is that it smoothes out some of the extremes of fluctuation between any two of the five individual currencies and the benefits of this system was demonstrated in the 12th edition by several detailed examples.

Members of AIDE, however, were unenthusiastic about the use of SDRs and put forward an alternative text with the adjustment being: **40.43**

> "prepared in such currency or currencies as may be equitable in the interests of the parties, having regard to the currencies in which the major claimants in general average have sustained financial loss."

This gave the impression of being based on English legal precedents, but it was objected that rates of exchange should not be left to be determined by any individual on grounds of supposed equity. In the event, no agreement could be reached at Sydney in October 1994 on how best this topic could be incorporated within the York-Antwerp Rules, with the result that those Rules remained silent on the matter of rates of exchange, as do the 2004 Rules.

40.44 In the years following the change in English Law away from the breach-date sterling rule the US dollar dominated world trade and adjusters rarely encountered any objections if they drew up adjustments in this currency, rather than trying to identify one or more currencies of loss that applied to the particular case. Disbursements would be exchanged into US dollars at the date of settlement and cargo sacrifices would be exchanged at rates prevailing on the final date of discharge at the port where the cargo in question was landed. With a single currency, no set-off would be required.

If the circumstances of the case were such that actual currencies of loss had to be identified and used in order to produce an equitable result, it would appear that the majority of British adjusters have preferred the set-off to be done at the closest possible date to the issuing of the adjustment, rather than adopting the methods shown in paras 40.38–40.40. As noted above, this approach has always been more in line with the way in which Continental law has approached such matters. In the absence of any clear guidance from the English Courts (except with regard to collision cases where different principles may apply), or from the York-Antwerp Rules, the current editors can only repeat the recommendation that a clear provision regarding currency of adjustment is included in every contract of affreightment.

SECTION 7

GENERAL AVERAGE, INSURANCE AND RECOVERIES

Introduction

This section covers a wide range of topics and for ease of reference these are set out below: **50.01**

1. Claims on Policies for General Average Losses

Definitions and Background

50.02 A general average loss, as defined by s.66(1) of the Marine Insurance Act 1906 "is a loss caused by or directly consequential on a general average act.[1] It includes a general average expenditure as well as a general average sacrifice."

A general average expenditure is simply the expenditure or outlay of money in order to purchase services or facilities which will relieve the property in the common adventure from the peril in which it finds itself, for example the hire of labour and lighters to discharge cargo from a vessel ashore, the hire of tugs to tow the vessel to a port of refuge, or the expenses of entering a port of refuge.

A general average sacrifice, even though it must be subsequently quantified in money terms in any general average adjustment, in the first instance comprises or is constituted by the intentional causing of loss or damage to one or more of the physical properties at risk in the common adventure—ship, cargo or freight, etc. for example the jettison of cargo and the freight attaching thereto, or the damage to machinery of a stranded vessel caused in efforts to refloat.

Commission, interest, and adjustment charges, where applicable, will follow the treatment of the capital sums on which they are based and will constitute sacrifice or expenditure, as appropriate.

A general average contribution, as defined by s.66(3) of the Marine Insurance Act 1906,[2] is the sum payable:

(1) *By* any party to the adventure after setting off against his rateable proportion of the total general average any credit due for sacrifices or expenditures incurred by him.
(2) *To* any party to the adventure in respect of general average sacrifices or expenditures incurred by him, after setting off his own liability to contribute to the total general average.

Example

50.03 A figured example may assist in appreciating the distinctions between these various terms, essential if one is to understand the differing legal rights of an assured when making a claim for any particular form of general average loss on a policy of marine insurance.

[1] A general average act is defined by the Marine Insurance Act 1906 s.66(2) and given extensive coverage (above) when dealing with r.A of the York-Antwerp Rules.

[2] "Where there is a general average loss, the party on whom it falls is entitled, subject to the conditions imposed by maritime law, to a rateable contribution from the other parties interested, and such contribution is called a general average contribution."

1. Claims on Policies for General Average Losses

A vessel strands in a position of peril and. in order to refloat, is obliged to engage salvage services, (each party paying their own proportion of the award), to jettison cargo, to work the ship's engines, and subsequently to put into a port of refuge for the common safety.

The general average is made up of the following:

			General average
SHIPOWNER'S	Sacrifice—Refloating damage to machinery		30,000
	Expenditure—In the port of refuge		25.000
	Salvage payment		100,000
			155,000
CARGO A'S	Expenditure—Salvage payment		100,000
CARGO B'S	Sacrifice—Jettison	250.000	
	Expenditure—Salvage payment	75,000	325,000
CARGO C's	Expenditure—Salvage payment		100,000
			680,000

APPORTIONMENT AND SETTLEMENT

	Contributory Value		Ppn. G.A.	Credit Allowance in G.A.	CONTRIBUTION To Pay	CONTRIBUTION To Receive
SHIP—Sound Value	1,200,000					
Less: Damage	230,000					
	970.000					
Add Made Good	30,000					
	1,000,000	liable for	170,000	155,000	15,000	–
CARGO A–Value	1,000,000	liable for	170,000	100,000	70,000	–
CARGO B–Value (incl. Jettison)	1,000,000	liable for	170,000	325,000	–	155,000
CARGO D–Value	1,000,000	liable for	170,000	100,000	70.000	–
	4,000,000	liable for	680,000	680,000	155,000	155,000

The proportion of general average attaching to each of the contributing interests is a uniform 170,000, but the contributions payable by ship, and cargos A and C are 15,000, 70,000 and 70,000 respectively (totalling 155,000), while the contribution receivable by cargo B is 155,000.

Under s.66(2) of the Marine Insurance Act 1906, a general average act will be constituted whenever: **50.04**

> "... any extraordinary sacrifice or expenditure is voluntarily made or incurred in time of peril ...".

and the peril may arise from any cause whatever, whereas a policy of marine insurance generally covers the property insured against the risk of loss or damage only from certain specified perils.

The initial accident or occurrence creating the peril may in terms of the policy, be specifically covered or excluded, or unmentioned, and the peril which the general average act seeks to avoid may similarly be covered, excluded, or unmentioned in the policy. In determining whether a claim for general average arises on any particular policy, the governing factor is the peril sought to be avoided, as provided by s.66(6) of the Marine Insurance Act 1906:

> "In the absence of express stipulation, the insurer is not liable for any general average loss or contribution where the loss was not incurred for the purpose of avoiding, or in connection with the avoidance of, a peril insured against."

50.05 In the majority of cases, the accident which gives rise to the peril (for example fire) is the same peril which the general average act seeks to avoid (destruction by fire). Where, as is usual, fire is one of the perils insured against by the policy, both the damage caused by the fire, and the sacrifices made and the expenditures incurred to extinguish that fire, will be recoverable on the same policy. However, less straightforward cases can occur, and the following examples may assist in understanding the doctrine set forth in the above s.66(6) of the Act:

(1) A vessel and her cargo may be in peril arising from a complete main engine breakdown at sea, the result of pure wear and tear. The expense of repairing that damage to the main engine is most unlikely to be recoverable on the hull policy, but if the engine breakdown was likely to result in the risk of loss by the vessel drifting ashore, or by heavy weather or collision (all insured perils), the general average losses or expenses would be recoverable.

(2) In Pyman S.S. Co Ltd v Admiralty[3] the propeller shaft of a vessel broke in the North Sea during the First World War. A heavy gale was blowing at the time and there was an added danger that the vessel might drift on to an enemy minefield. Salvage services were rendered, and the arbitrator apportioned his award as to 75 per cent marine and 25 per cent war, and this was upheld in the Court of King's Bench and the Court of Appeal. The cause of the breakage of the propeller shaft is irrelevant to the question of liability for the ensuing general average.

(3) A vessel struck a mine, sustaining very severe damage and incurring substantial general average expenditure. The whole claim was settled by the war risk insurers. About a year after the extensive repairs, the main engine crankshaft broke in mid-ocean and the damage was reasonably attributed to the earlier striking of the mine and the cost of repairs was again settled by the war risk insurers. The general average expenses, however, being incurred to avoid the perils of drifting ashore, or of loss

[3] *Pyman S.S. Co Ltd v Admiralty* [1918] 1 K.B. 480; [1919] 1 K.B. 49; 14 Asp. M.L.C. 171 at 364: 34 T.L.R. 174: 35 T.L.R. 79.

by heavy weather, were chargeable to the marine insurers on risk at the time of the breakage of the crankshaft.

(A) General Average Sacrifice

Section 66(4) of the Marine Insurance Act 1906 provides: **50.06**

> "Subject to any express provision in the policy, . . . in the case of a general average sacrifice he, [the assured] may recover . . . from the insurer in respect of the whole loss without having enforced his right of contribution from the other parties liable to contribute."

Thus, the assured may proceed directly and immediately against the insurers for the whole of his loss, and on payment, insurers are thereby subrogated[4] to the general average contributions eventually recovered from the other parties to the adventure when the general average adjustment has been prepared and settled. Rights of subrogation are dealt with above, in paras 50.41–50.53. It is also worthy of record that:

(1) Although an assured shipowner may generally proceed directly and immediately against his insurers for the whole of his loss, if he prejudices their rights of subrogation by omitting to collect general average security from cargo interests, the insurers may be entitled to deny liability for such proportion of the sacrifice damage to the ship as would have been, having regard to the circumstances of the case, recoverable from the cargo.[5]

(2) Where an assured shipowner proceeds first against cargo interests for their due contribution to damage to the ship caused by general average sacrifice, but fails to recover that contribution on grounds such as a breach of the contract of carriage, he may still proceed against his insurers for the whole of the ship sacrifice.

This basic right had been re-established in 1868 by the case of *Dickenson v Jardine*[6] where goods were jettisoned under circumstances which entitled the plaintiff to a general average contribution from the owners of the ship and other cargo. The goods were insured by a policy which included jettison among the perils insured against and the plaintiff sued the insurers for the whole amount insured, without having first collected the contributions to which he was entitled from the other parties to the adventure. It was held that he was so entitled to recover, and that the liability of insurers could not be varied by an alleged custom in London between merchants and insurers to hold the latter liable only for the **50.07**

[4] Marine Insurance Act 1906 s.79.

[5] See also the Association of Average Adjusters Rule of Practice B32, which requires the adjuster to report on whether the shipowner has taken necessary steps to enforce their lien on cargo, and *The Vasso* [1993] 2 Lloyd's Rep. 309 with regard to an insurers entitlement in respect of a failure by the assured to sue and labour.

[6] *Dickenson v Jardine* (1868) L.R. 3 C.P. 639.

share of the loss cast upon the owner of jettisoned goods in the general average adjustment. Having settled the loss, the insurers were entitled to stand in the place of the assured and were subrogated to the general average contributions recovered from the other parties to the adventure.

Thus, the initial claim on any policy of marine insurance for loss of or damage to the property insured by a general average sacrifice is calculated in precisely the same manner and on the same established principles as though the loss were from an accidental cause, that is on a particular average or total loss basis, and whether the loss is to ship, cargo or freight, etc.

50.08 These insurance principles for calculating claims may produce either a greater or lesser sum than the allowance which will be made in general average in accordance with the provisions of the contract of affreightment, particularly in the case of the insurance of cargo, and some simple examples now follow to illustrate the direct claims[7] upon the policies compared with the allowances in general average. The rights of subrogation attaching thereto will be dealt with subsequently in paras 50.42 to 50.51, below.

Cargo

(In the two examples below, the cargo is assumed to have an invoice value of 10,000 and to be insured subject to the Institute Cargo Clauses for: Case A–12,000, so valued and Case B–8,000, so valued.)

50.09 **(1) In the event of a total loss,** for example by jettison.

The allowance in general average per r.XVI of the York-Antwerp Rules 1994 will be based upon the invoice value, that is 10,000.

The measure of indemnity, in accordance with s.68(1) of the Marine Insurance Act 1906 "is the sum fixed by the policy"', that is in Case A—12,000 and Case B—8,000.

(2) In the event of a partial loss, for example by the jettison of 50 per cent of the cargo insured, or of damage to the complete consignment by water used to extinguish a fire, assessed at 50 per cent of the value.

The allowance in general average per r.XVI of the York-Antwerp Rules will be based upon the invoice value, that is, 50 per cent of 10,000 = 5,000.

The measure of indemnity, in accordance with s.71(1) or (3) of the Marine Insurance Act 1906 is 50 per cent of the insured value of the goods, that is:

Case A—50% × 12,000 = 6,000
Case B—50% × 8,000 = 4,000

[7] It is possible for a policy of marine insurance to be valued or unvalued, and for the sum insured to be less than the insured or insurable value. These variables can affect the amount of a claim upon the policy, but for the sake of simplicity and brevity it will be assumed in the text and examples throughout this section that, ship and cargo are insured by valued policies and that the sum insured is the full insured value, and that freight is insured by an unvalued policy, with varying sums insured.

The insurers' rights of subrogation when the general average adjustment is completed and issued say two years later, will be considered in paras 50.47, 50.48, below.

Ship

(In the example below, the ship is assumed to have a sound market value of 5,000,000 and to be insured subject to the Institute Time Clauses, Hulls for Case A–6,000.000 so valued and Case B–4,000,000, so valued.)

The claim upon a policy of marine insurance for damage to a ship caused by a general average sacrifice is governed by the provisions of s.69 of the Marine Insurance Act 1906.[8] as refined by any special conditions in the policy. In practice, and ignoring any "deductible" stipulated in the policy, the assured generally recovers from his insurers the actual and reasonable cost of repairing the damage, in full, without deductions "new for old", and regardless of the insured value of the ship, other than as a limiting factor on the maximum claim payable. **50.10**

In the event of damage, for example, to the propeller and main engine by efforts to refloat after stranding.

The allowance in general average per r.XVIII of the York-Antwerp Rules 1994 will be the "actual reasonable cost of repairing . . . such damage. . . ."		100,000
subject to deductions "new for old" in accordance with r.XIII	(say)	5,000
		95,000

The measure of indemnity, in accordance with s.69(1) of the Marine Insurance Act 1906 will be "the reasonable cost of the repairs, less the customary deductions" (that is also 95,000), but by reason of cl.14 of the Institute Time Clauses, Hulls, which states that "claims payable without deduction new for old", the claim will be for 100,000 in both cases A and B.

Freight

(In the example below, the vessel is assumed to be carrying 10,000 tons of cargo on which the freight is at risk to the shipowner and payable only on right delivery of the cargo at destination at the rate of 100 per ton, that is 1,000,000. This is insured by an unvalued policy subject to the Institute Time Clauses, Freight for Case A—1,200,000 and Case B—800,000. In both cases 1000 tons of cargo are jettisoned at a time of peril.)

The allowance in general average in accordance with r.XV of the York-Antwerp Rules 1994 will be for the "gross freight lost" 100,000 **50.11**

[8] See para.50.06, above.

Deduct: "charges which the owner thereof would have incurred to earn such freight, but has, in consequence of the sacrifice, not incurred." (e.g. discharging expenses) say 5,000

95,000

The measure of indemnity, in accordance with s.70 of the Marine Insurance Act 1906 will be: "such proportion . . . of the insurable value . . . as the proportion of the freight lost by the assured bears to the whole freight at the risk of the assured under the policy."

The insurable value of the freight may be assumed to be:

Gross freight at risk—10,000 tons @ 100 =		1,000,000
Add: charges of insurance	say	3,000
		1,003,000

The claims on the respective policies would be, therefore:

Case A–1,000/10,000 × 1,003,000 =	100,300
except that cl.13(1) of the Institute Time Clauses Freight limits any claim to "the gross freight actually lost", i.e.	100,000
Case B–If total insurable value 1,003,000 pays 100,300	
Then sum insured 800,000 pays in proportion	80,000

(B) General Average Expenditure

50.12 Section 66(4) of the Marine Insurance Act 1906 provides:

> "Subject to any express provision in the policy, where the assured has incurred a general average expenditure, he may recover from the insurer in respect of the proportion of the loss which falls upon him . . ."

Unlike a policy claim for general average sacrifice, where the assured can recover the whole of his loss immediately and directly from insurers, in the case of general average expenditure he can recover only the proportion which falls upon him. As an example if the shipowner has financed the whole of any general average expenditure (100,000), and the value of his ship represents 25 per cent of the total contributory values, he can usually proceed directly against his insurers for only 25 per cent of his general average expenditure, that is, 25,000 (unless his policy includes an absorption clause and the total general average falls within its limit—see paras 50.33–50.35). He must either wait until the general average adjustment has been completed and settled before recovering the balance of 75 per cent from cargo and other contributing interests, or seek payments on account from those other contributing interests in accordance with the terms of their general average guarantee, or from any general average deposit funds.

50.13 However, where the cargo or other contributing interests have sustained general average sacrifices of their property, or have financed part of the general average (for example by settling their own proportion of any salvage award), it follows that the "proportion of the loss (general average

expenditure) which falls upon him"[9] will not be the above-mentioned 25,000 but a higher amount. For instance, if the shipowner has incurred general average expenditure amounting, as before, to 100,000 but the cargo sacrifices or expenditures amount to. 200,000
Total general average . . 300,000
The proportion attaching to ship—25 per cent is . . . . 75,000.

There are some circumstances in which the "proportion of the loss" which falls on the shipowner may be greater that the proportion of the loss calculated to attach to the ship in the usual manner. **50.14**

The "*ABT Rasha*"[9A] was a large tanker carrying crude oil from Saudi Arabia to Rotterdam when she suffered damage to her rudder and put into Port Elizabeth, South Africa, as port of refuge. Cargo was transhipped to Rotterdam on another vessel and cargo interests signed a non-separation agreement which included a Bigham clause (see paras G.13). The Bigham clause in question stated that the amount payable by cargo "shall not exceed what it would have cost the cargo-owners if cargo had been delivered to them at Algoa Bay and forwarded by them to destination". After transhipping the cargo the "ABT Rasha" was towed to Dubai for dry-docking and repairs.

An adjustment was produced which showed that cargo's proportion of general average amounted to US$3,601,776.22. After taking into account the effect of the Bigham clause the adjusters then calculated that the cost to cargo had they taken delivery at the port of refuge and forwarded to destination at their own expense, would have amounted to US$2,814,349.94 which was therefore the limit to cargo's payment in respect of general average. The balance of US$787,426.28 was claimed from hull and machinery underwriters under s.66(4) of the Marine Insurance Act 1906 as part of the proportion of the loss falling on the assured.

The Court of Appeal reversed the decision of the lower court. They found that a non-separation agreement with a Bigham clause was in principle a reasonable agreement for shipowners and cargo-owners to make in a case of this kind; whether it would be reasonable on the facts of a particular case depended on the facts. If the non-separation agreement had the effect both between shipowners and cargo-owners, and as between shipowners and their hull underwriters, of treating certain expenses as general average expenses, it made no sense to treat the other paragraphs of the non-separation agreement differently. The Bigham clause in the non-separation agreement was an indivisible part of the whole agreement. The shipowners' proportion of the general average expenses assessed in accordance with the agreement had to be arrived at by taking the whole of the expenses defined as general average expenses and assessing what proportion of those expenses were attributable pro rata to ship and cargo to determine whether the cargo's proportion was more than the Bigham cap, i.e. the amount it would have cost cargo interests to take delivery and pay for the forwarding themselves. If this was the case, cargo's proportion would be the amount of the cap and the ship's share the remainder.

9 Marine Insurance Act 1906 s.66(4).
9A [2002] 2 Lloyd's Rep 575.

The Court of Appeal concluded that s.66(4) cannot be held to limit "proportion" to rateable proportion when it does not expressly do so. The proportion of the loss which falls on the shipowner was, under s.66(4), that calculated in accordance with the whole non-separation agreement including the Bigham clause and recoverable under cl.11.1 of the Institute Time Clauses as "ship's proportion of general average". Clause 11.1 of the Institute Time Clauses covers ship's proportion of those general average expenses including that proportion of those expenses which, apart from the agreement, would not have been general average. The shipowners claim under the hull policy for the "excess" Bigham expenses therefore succeeded.

Under-insurance

50.15 The party who has financed a general average expenditure is limited in his recovery from insurers to the "proportion of the loss which falls upon him"[10] and that sum may be further reduced if the property is insured for less than its real worth–or that on which the contributory value is based in accordance with the York-Antwerp Rules or other applicable law.

Section 73 of the Marine Insurance Act 1906 provides:

"(1) Subject to any express provision in the policy, where the assured has paid, or is liable for, any general average contribution, the measure of indemnity is the full amount of such contribution, if the subject-matter liable to contribution is insured for its full contributory value; but, if such subject-matter be not insured for its full contributory value, or if only part of it be insured, the indemnity payable by the insurer must be reduced in proportion to the under insurance, and where there has been a particular average loss which constitutes a deduction from the contributory value, and for which the insurer is liable, that amount must be deducted from the insured value in order to ascertain what the insurer is liable to contribute.

(2) Where the insurer is liable for salvage charges the extent of his liability must be determined on the like principle."

We are here discussing general average expenditure, and it may be noted that the above s.73 of the Act mentions only general average contribution. However, it is well understood that s.73 applies to general average expenditure in accordance with the provisions of s.75(1) of the Marine Insurance Act 1906:

"Where there has been a loss in respect of any subject-matter not expressly provided for in the foregoing provisions of this Act, the measure of indemnity shall be ascertained, as nearly as may be, in accordance with those provisions, in so far as applicable to the particular case."

50.16 A simple example will illustrate the basic principle set forth in s.73 of the Act. In *S.S. Balmoral Co v Marten*[11] decided in 1902, the Balmoral incurred general

[10] Marine Insurance Act 1906 s.66(4).

[11] *S.S. Balmoral Co v Marten* [1902] A.C. 511.

average expenditure and salvage services and her salved and contributory value was established at £40,000. She was insured by a valued policy for £33,000 and the House of Lords, affirming previous decisions of the Court of Appeal and of Bigham J. held that the insurers were liable for 33/40ths of the general average and salvage expenditure.

The terms of s.73 of the Marine Insurance Act undoubtedly give effect to the Balmoral decision: furthermore, by incorporating a great deal of the wording of the Custom of Lloyd's on the subject (adopted by the Association of Average Adjusters as a British Rule of Practice in 1876),[12] they appear also to indorse the more refined English practice of that time: **50.17**

> "If the ship or cargo be insured for more than its contributory value, the underwriter pays what is assessed on the contributory value. But where insured for less than the contributory value, the underwriter pays on the insured value; and when there has been a particular average for damage which forms a deduction from the contributory value of the ship that must be deducted from the insured value to find upon what the underwriter contributes. This rule does not apply to foreign adjustments, when the basis of contribution is something other than the net value of the thing insured."

It may be noted that the adjusters' Rule of Practice refers on a number of occasions to the simple expression "contributory value", whereas s.73 of the Marine Insurance Act quoted in para.50.15, above, on two occasions uses the expression "full contributory value". It is submitted that "full contributory value' means the value upon which the interest contributes even if that be less than the sound value at the termination of the adventure.

Example: Assume a general average has been adjusted with the following contributory values: **50.18**

SHIP		*FREIGHT*	
Sound Value	1,000,000	Gross Freight at risk and earned	1,000,000
Deduct:Damage,	200,000	*Deduct*: Contingent Expenses,	200,000
Contributory Value	800,000	Contributory Value	800,000

Taking first the freight, with a gross sum at risk and earned of 1,000,000 the deductions of 200,000 will almost invariably comprise simply the routine voyage expenses incurred by the shipowner to earn that freight subsequent to the general average act. The insurers of the freight will not be liable for these expenses, and it is perfectly equitable, therefore, that an insured value of 800,000 should pay the full general average contribution attaching to the net contributory value of 800,000.

In the case of the ship, however, with a sound value of 1,000,000, the deductions (for damage) of 200,000 probably comprise items for which the insurers may be liable, for example as particular average. In such a case, it would be manifestly inequitable that an insured value of 800,000 should respond for the whole **50.19**

[12] Now forming the first section of r.B33; see para.70.19, below.

of any general average expenditure attributable to a net contributory value of 800,000. This was recognised in the old Custom of Lloyd's and indorsed by the Marine Insurance Act by providing that, to the extent that the insurers were liable for any particular average deductions made in arriving at the contributory value, those same deductions should also be made from the insured value when assessing any degree of under-insurance. Thus, and assuming for the sake of example a proportion of general average expenditure of 80,000, where the insurers are liable to pay:

(1) The whole of the deductions of 200,000

If contributory value 800,000 pays 80,000

Then insured value	800,000
Less Damage Claim	200,000
	600,000 pays in proportion 60,000

(2) None of the deductions of 200,000 (for example on a policy the excludes partial losses)

If contributory value 800,000 pays 80,000

Then insured value	800,000
Less Damage Claim	Nil
	800,000 pays in full 80,000

(3) 120,000 ex the deductions of 200,000 (for example by reason of a large policy deductible, or because some of the damage was not caused by insured perils)

If contributory value 800,000 pays 80,000

Then insured value	800,000
Less Damage Claim	120,000
	680,000 pays in proportion 68,000

50.20 The old Custom of Lloyd's and the Marine Insurance Act both make reference only to the deduction of particular average from the insured value, but the insurers could be liable for other expenses which have constituted deductions in arriving at the net contributory value of any property, for example general average thirds "new for old", or salvage when treated separately and not directly as general average as may now occur under the York-Antwerp Rules 2004. Accordingly, and to achieve a greater equity in the assessment of any degree of under-insurance, the Association of Average Adjusters added in 1922 a second section to their Rule of Practice B33:

> "That in practice, in applying the above rule for the purpose of ascertaining the liability of underwriters for contribution to general average and salvage charges, deduction shall be made from the insured value of all losses and charges for which underwriters are liable and which have been deducted in arriving at the contributory value,"

which substitutes all losses and charges for the more narrow particular average in the Act and the first section of their rule.

The position regarding under-insurance as set out in the Marine Insurance Act may of course be modified by an express term in the policies and this is frequently seen with Hull insurances. The International Hull Clauses 2003 provide: **50.21**

> "8.1 This insurance covers the vessel's proportion of salvage, salvage charges and/or general average, without reduction in respect of any under-insurance, but in case of general average sacrifice of the vessel the Assured may recover in respect of the whole loss without first enforcing their right of contribution from other parties."

Where other clauses are used, cover notes should be checked for wordings with similar effect for example "vessel deemed to be fully insured for general average".

Unlike an insurance on ship, freight is almost invariably insured by means of an unvalued policy. **50.22**

In order to calculate the liability of the insurers of a freight insured by an unvalued policy for 800,000 where the gross amount at risk and earned was 1,000,000, but the contributory value 800,000, and assuming a proportion of general average expenditure of 80,000 attaching thereto, it is necessary to have regard to a number of the provisions of the Marine Insurance Act:

Section 81 relating to the effect of under-insurance states that:

> "Where the assured is insured for an amount less than the insurable value . . . he is deemed to be his own insurer in respect of the uninsured balance."

The insurable value of the freight, as provided by s.16(2): ". . . is the gross amount of the freight at risk of the assured, plus the charges of insurance."

By s.67(2) of the Act:

> ". . . the insurer . . . is liable for such proportion of the measure of indemnity as the amount of his subscription bears to the . . . insurable value in the case of an unvalued policy."

Thus, the claim for the proportion of general average expenditure of 80,000 attaching to freight should be dealt with as follows:

If insurable value 1,003,000 pays 80,000

Then sum insured 800,000 pays in proportion 63,809

This last example would accord with the practice of all British adjusters as their interpretation of the final section of their Rule of Practice B33, added in 1926: **50.23**

> "In adjusting the liability of underwriters on freight for general average contribution and salvage charges, effect shall be given to Section 73 of the Marine Insurance Act, 1906, by comparing the gross and not the net amount of freight at risk with the insured value in the case of a valued policy or the insurable value in the case of an unvalued policy."

To complete this section on the rights of an assured to recover for general average expenditure, one final example is given for cargo: **50.24**

(The cargo is assumed to have an invoice or market value of 100,000 and to be insured subject to the Institute Cargo Clauses for Case A–120,000, so valued and Case B–80,000, so valued.

Salvage services are rendered to the vessel and her cargo and the owners of the above cargo are obliged to settle direct with salvors for their proportion of the total award, that is 10,000.)

This sum of 10,000 is the "proportion of the loss which falls upon him" in accordance with s.66(4) of the Marine Insurance Act 1906 and the claim upon insurers will therefore be based on the full sum of 10,000.

In Case A—where the value of the property is fully insured, the measure of indemnity will be the actual amount of (and no more than) the sum paid of 10,000.

In Case B—where the value of the property is under-insured, the measure of indemnity "must be reduced in proportion to the underinsurance",[13] that is to 80,000/100,000 (i.e. "times") 10,000 = 8,000.

Had the insured property also suffered damage by accidental cause and the insurers paid a particular average claim, some further calculations would be necessary to comply with the last lines of s.73(1) of the Marine Insurance Act 1906 such as are explained in paras 50.30, 50.31, above, but by reason of the principles applied in calculating claims on cargo insurance policies, the proportion of the salvage award or general average expenditure recoverable from insurers will almost invariably be 80 per cent in Case B.

(C) General Average Contributions

50.25 The rights of an assured to recover from his insurers in respect of general average contributions payable to other parties to the adventure are governed by the following provisions of the Marine Insurance Act 1906, s.66(5):

> "Subject to any express provision in the policy, where the assured has paid, or is liable to pay, a general average contribution in respect of the subject insured, he may recover therefor from the insurer,"

together with s.73, the full text of which was quoted in para.50.15, above.

50.26 The term general average contribution has been defined earlier in para.50.02 and attention drawn with words and a figured example in paras 50.06 to 50.08, above, to the fact that although the amount of a general average contribution may often be the same as the proportion of general average shown in a general average adjustment as attaching to a particular property, the terms are not synonymous.

However, in those simple cases where the amount of the contribution is identical with the proportion of general average (that is because the particular property has not suffered loss or damage by a general average sacrifice, or because the owner of the property has not incurred a general average expenditure), the rights of the assured to recover from the insurers of his ship, cargo or freight, etc. are

[13] Marine Insurance Act 1906 s.73(1).

precisely the same as for general average expenditure, and reference may therefore be directed to what has been written in paras 50.12 to 50.24, above. However, a contribution paid towards the sacrifice of another party to the adventure is treated vis-à-vis the paying contributor in the same manner as general average expenditure, and not in the preferential manner associated with an insurance claim in respect of a general average sacrifice.

The situation can be mathematically more complex where an insured party is called upon to pay a general average contribution which is for a different sum than the proportion of general average shown in the general average adjustment as attaching to his property, and two examples now follow to illustrate the problem. **50.27**

Cargo

A general average adjustment shows figures such as the following in respect of an individual cargo interest with an invoice or market value of 10,000:

Arrived value	9,000	
Add: Made Good	1,000	
	10,000 liable for **proportion general average** 5,000	

Credit: Amount made good in general average for:		
Sacrifice damage to property	1,000	
Credit: Salvage payment	1,800	2,800
Balance to Pay (= **Contribution**)		2,200

Adopting the same insured values as used in earlier examples of:

Case A–12,000
Case B–8,000

the positions are as follows:

In Case A–where the cargo is fully insured, the measure of indemnity will be for the full general average contribution of 2,200 (in addition to the earlier claims presumed paid by insurers in respect of the: **50.28**

Sacrifice–10 percent × 12,000 =	1,200
Salvage payment	1,800
	3,000)

In Case B—where the cargo is under-insured, in simple practical terms the measure of indemnity for the general average contribution of 2,200 may well be calculable by a straight comparison of the insured and contributory values, that is: **50.29**

If contributory value 10,000 pays contribution	2,200
Then insured value 8,000 pays in proportion	1,760

However, the proper approach (and this applies even in Case A) must be to examine and re-assess the rights of the assured against his insurers to recover for each constituent part of his claim for damage, salvage, and the eventual general average contribution, and from the combined total to deduct such sums—if any—which have already been paid by the insurers.

Thus, the final claim on a policy subject to the Institute Cargo Clauses might well be calculated as follows:

Sacrifice—10 per cent × 8,000 800
Salvage—If salved value 9,000 pays 1,800
Then insured value 8,000
Less: claim paid, 800
7,200 pays in proportion 1,440
Contribution—If contributory value 10,000 pays 2,200
Contribution—Then insured value 8,000 pays in proportion 1,760
Total Liability 4,000

Credit: Previous payments for Sacrifice	800	
Credit: Previous payments for Salvage	1,440	cr.
	2,240	2,240
Balance to Pay		1,760

It will be noted that the total liability of 4,000 happens to be 8,000/10,000ths of the proportion of general average attaching to the cargo of 5,000, but this would not apply in Case A. It will also be noted that the insurers in this example have previously paid the precisely correct claims for sacrifice and salvage, but these payments might have been for different amounts—or not at all. The matter might also be rendered more complex by the addition of interest on general average allowances.

Ship

50.30 A general average adjustment might show figures such as the following in respect of the ship:

Sound Value	5,000,000		
Less: Damage–P.A. 1,000.000			
Less: Damage–G.A., 200.000	1,200,000		
	3,800,000		
Add: Made Good	200,000		
	4,000,000 liable for		
	ppn. G.A.		1,000,000
Credit: Amounts Made Good in General Average			
Credit: Sacrifice damage	200,000	cr.	
Credit: Expenditure by Shipowner	500,000	700,000	
Balance to Pay (= **Contribution**)		300,000	

Adopting the same insured values for the ship as used in earlier examples of: 50.31

Case A–6,000,000
Case B–4,000,000

and assuming the ship to be insured subject to the Institute Time Clauses, Hulls, but ignoring any deductible:

In Case A—where the ship is fully insured, it can safely be said that the measure of indemnity for the general average contribution of 300,000 will be the full sum of 300,000, but that calculations such as are shown below in Case B will nevertheless need to be made.

In Case B—where the ship is under-insured, the final general average contribu- 50.32
tion payable to other parties to the adventure of 300,000 will never be looked at in isolation; as with cargo Case B above, an overall adjustment must be prepared dealing with each constituent part of the shipowners claim against his insurers and account taken of any earlier payments on account made by them. For the above example, and assuming that the contributory value of the ship represents 50 per cent of the total contributory values, the overall measure of indemnity would be assessed as follows:

Particular Average.			1,000,000
General Average, proportion attaching to Ship 1,000,000			
Whereof: Sacrifice 50% ×	200,000 =	100,000	100,000
Whereof: Expenditure 50% ×	1,800,000 =	900,000	
	2,000,000 =	1,000,000	
Proportion G.A. Expenditure/Contribution, as above, 900,000			
If Contributory' Value 4,000,000 pays 900,000			
Then Insured Value	4,000,000		
Less: P.A.	1,000,000		
	3,000,000	pays in proportion	675,000
		Measure of Indemnity	1,775,000
Credit: Payments on Account in respect of:			
Particular Average	say	850,000	
General Average Sacrifice		170,000	
General Average Expenditure		400,000	
	say	1,420,000	1,420,000
		Balance to Pay,	355,000

In practice, the figures will be rendered more complex by the addition of interest on general average allowances, but the balance to pay of 355,000 has no real or direct connection with the final general average contribution of 300,000 payable to the other parties to the adventure, and is dependant entirely on what sums have previously been advanced by insurers on account of their eventual liability.

(D) Absorption Clauses and other Special Insurances

Absorption clauses

50.33 As noted above, where a shipowner has incurred general average expenditure he is entitled to recover only the ship's proportion of that expenditure under a standard hull and machinery policy. The balance can only be recovered from cargo interests, which will involve the collection of general average security and the preparation of a full general average adjustment.

Historically with general cargo vessels and now with container vessels, the cost of collecting security from hundreds of cargo interests can be costly and time consuming for all concerned. If the general average expenses are relatively modest, the process of contribution becomes uneconomic and highly undesirable for commercial interests. The solution to this problem has been the inclusion of absorption clauses, so called because the hull insurer agrees to absorb or pay general average expenditure in full, rather than just ship's proportion. In this way the shipowner can recover certain types of expenditure according to the well understood frame-work of the York-Antwerp Rules, without the commercial and insurance community being involved in the collection of security and settlements required for the "contribution" part of the general average process.

It is now the exception to see a hull policy for an ocean going vessel without an absorption clause of some kind. This applies to all classes of vessel; while collecting security from a single cargo interest aboard a bulk carrier usually involves no great cost, the process is still quite rightly considered commercially inappropriate when relatively modest expenditure is involved. The amounts specified as to the limit do need to be tailored to the type of vessel insured and for large container vessels additional arrangements may need to be made beyond a hull policy absorption clause (see para.50.36).

Until recently, no standard wording for an absorption clause has existed and a variety of forms are seen in circulation. Some wordings have particular deficiencies, for example:

> "In cases where General Average is estimated not to exceed US$50,000 (or equivalent in any other currency) the Assured shall have the option of deciding whether or not they will claim the whole General Average amount under this insurance or claim from the cargo as they think fit. In such cases of charging the whole to this insurance no commission or interests to be charged."

This wording begs the questions of "estimated by whom?" and "estimated at what stage?". Other wordings refer to paying cargo's proportion up to a specified figure. Although clear in its objective, this approach makes it necessary to estimate the value of cargo in order to assess the proportion of general average attaching to it. This may present no real difficulty with a bulk commodity but may give problems with a containerised cargo where the number of items may run into thousands, and manifest details frequently provide very limited details on which to base a valuation.

In September 2002 BIMCO circulated their recommended wording for a standard general average absorption clause. This coincided with the redrafting of the Institute Time Clauses Hulls under the new title of International Hull Clauses 2002 and many features of the BIMCO wording were incorporated in IHC 2002, the first time such a clause had appeared in Institute form. IHC 2002 was intended as a model for a new type of hull form and was published partly with a view to encouraging comment as to how a modern policy document should be structured. Following the minimal adoption of the Institute Time Clauses 1.11.95, a period of consultation was considered essential. The inclusion of an Absorption Clause was welcomed but many improvements were suggested and the IHC 2003 Clauses when published had clearly moved much closer to the BIMCO wording—most notably in that claims made under the clause would not be subject to a deductible. **50.34**

This important clause is shown in full with brief comments given in brackets.

40.1 If the Underwriters have expressly agreed in writing and subject to the provisions of Clause 8, the following shall apply in the event of an accident or occurrence giving rise to a general average act under the York-Antwerp Rules 1994 or under the provisions of the general average clause in the contract of affreightment. **50.35**

(Although included in the wording, express agreement by underwriters and the agreement of a specified amount are needed to activate the clause.)

40.2 The Assured shall have the option of claiming the total general average, salvage and special charges up to the amount expressly agreed by underwriters, without claiming general average, salvage or special charges from cargo, freight, bunkers, containers or any property not owned by the Assured on board the vessel (hereinafter the "Property Interests").

40.3 The Underwriters shall also pay the reasonable fee and expenses of the average adjuster for calculating claims under this Clause 40, in addition to any payment made under Clause 40.2.

40.4 If the Assured claims under this Clause 40, the Assured shall not claim general average, salvage or special charges against the Property Interests.

40.5 Claims under this Clause 40 shall be adjusted in accordance with the York-Antwerp Rules 1994, excluding the first paragraph pf Rule XX and relating to commission and interest.

(Although the provisions of general average clause in the contract of affreightment may be used to affirm the existence of a general average act, whatever those terms may be, the actual adjustment under this clause must be in terms of York-Antwerp Rules 1994. The exclusion of Commission (r.XX) and Interest (r.XXI) has been a normal feature of the bespoke clauses used in the past.)

40.6 Claims under this Clause 40 shall be payable without the application of the deductible(s) in Clause 15.

(Although a long standing feature in some insurance markets such as Scandinavia, the removal of the deductible was a departure for a London market wording. However, the purpose of the absorption clause was seen as being not only to offer a benefit to the assured owner but also to remove the administrative burden and costs of smaller general average cases, where the costs of distribution between property interests were clearly uneconomic. The high levels of deductible now carried by many major owners would prevent access to the absorption clause in many cases, giving rise to the temptation to at least seek cargo's contribution. This would clearly defeat the object of the exercise and the removal of the deductible was a far-sighted solution to this problem.)

> 40.7 *Without prejudice to any other defences that the Underwriters may have under this insurance or at law, the Underwriters waive any defences to payment under this Clause 40 which would have been available to the Property Interests, if the Assured had claimed general average, salvage or special charges from the Property Interests.*

(Generally, cargo interests under a Contract of Affreightment have a broader range of defences open to them to decline making a contribution than Hull Underwriters have to enable them to decline liability under a hull policy. Where security has been collected from cargo, the P&I Club will generally pay any contributions that are refused on the grounds of a breach of a contract of affreightment, but they would not respond if the same defenses were to be used by a hull underwriters, leaving the shipowner in limbo. This provision removes that potential difficulty.)

> 40.8 *In respect of payments made under this Clause 40, the Underwriters waive their rights of subrogation against the Property Interests, save where the accident or occurrence giving rise to such payment is attributable to fault on the part of Property interests or any of them.*
>
> 40.9 *Claims under this Clause 40 shall be payable without reduction in respect of any under-insurance. (This over-rides Section 73 of the Marine Insurance Act 1906).*
>
> 40.10 *For the purposes of this Clause 40, special charges shall mean charges incurred by the Assured on behalf of or for the benefit of a particular interest to the adventure, for which charges the Assured is not responsible under the contract off affrieghtment.*

(The clause also refers to "Special Charges", which are defined in cl.40.10. When general average guarantees and bonds are obtained from cargo interests following a casualty, the wording will almost invariably refer to special charges as well as general average and salvage.

If cargo is discharged ashore following a fire in order to be inspected and/or reconditioned, the reconditioning costs relating to extinguishing damage will be general average (payable by all parties) and the costs relating to fire damage will be a special charge falling on the individual cargo interests. For practical reasons it is often difficult to distinguish between likely general average expenses and special charges at the time decisions are being made whether or not to collect security from cargo. By bringing both within the terms of the absorption clause this uncertainty is removed and a further incentive to avoid uneconomic security collections is provided.)

Special insurances

As noted above, the inclusion of an absorption clause in the hull policies of blue-water cargo vessels is now common-place, and hull insurers may therefore find that they are expected to take on this additional exposure for little or no extra premium. A container vessel operator may therefore find that his hull insurer may be unwilling to provide a level of absorption clause that meets his needs fully, if he is to avoid the commercial disruption and cost of collecting security from a large number of interests to cover a moderate general average case. One option is then to take out a special insurance that provides a second "layer" by covering cargos' contributions up to a more satisfactory level. In this way collection of security and contributions from cargo only has to be made in the case of a very serious casualty. **50.36**

Frequently, a container vessel owner will pool his vessels as part of a consortium which may also charter in tonnage to supplement the vessels of its members. The owner will also therefore be issuing his bills of lading as a slot-charterer on vessels he does not own and will be expected to ensure that "his" cargo provides general average and salvage security if the need arises, unless he is prepared to meet those contributions himself for commercial reasons. The "top up" cover that is taken out to form a layer above the absorption clause may also be extended to cover contributions due from cargo carried under his bills of lading when acting as a slot charterer. Again the intention is that cargo interests are not troubled for security or contributions except in serious cases when the limits of the special insurances are exceeded. **50.37**

With absorption clauses or special "top up" policies the limits of cover will be a matter of balancing premium costs against potential exposure to delays in transit and customer dissatisfaction.

(E) General Average Deposits

The circumstances in which a general average deposit may be required, as security for the general average contribution which will eventually be ascertained to be due, have been set forth earlier in para.30.54. Whether the insurers under a typical marine insurance policy are under any legal obligation to reimburse to their assured the deposit paid by them is a question which has not been satisfactorily resolved.[14] **50.38**

In practice, whatever be the strict rights of the assured under the policy, it is the practice of cargo insurers to reimburse the amount of the deposit to their assured provided that: **50.39**

(1) the sum insured and the insured value of the goods are at least equal to the invoice value[15] (failing which a proportional reduction will be made); and

[14] See *Brandeis v Economic Insurance Co* (1922) 11 Lloyd's Rep. 42.
[15] When the York-Antwerp Rules 1974 or subsequent rules are applicable.

(2) the deposit is not excessive, and is properly held[16] (for example in accordance with r.XXII of the York-Antwerp Rules).

(F) Rights of Recovery Where Common Ownership

50.40 Section 66(7) of the Marine Insurance Act provides:

> "Where ship, freight and cargo, or any two of those interests, are owned by the same assured, the liability of the insurer in respect of general average losses and contributions is to be determined as if those subjects were owned by different persons."

This subsection appears to be intended to codify the decision in *Montgomery v Indemnity Mutual Marine Insurance Co*,[17] in which it was held by Matthew J. and the Court of Appeal that the fact that all the contributory interests were in the same ownership did not prevent a sacrifice of part of the ship from being a general average act. Section 66(7) now places this beyond argument, at any rate so far as concerns the relationship between insurer and insured.

The section gives rise to no difficulty with regard to expenditure or contribution, since in these cases, quite apart from any question of common ownership, the insured can claim only his own proportion of expenditure, or the contribution for which he is liable. Thus in the case of expenditure by a common owner of ship and cargo, the common owner can claim the ship's proportion from the hull insurers (the Act requiring one to assume that he could recover cargo's contribution from himself in his capacity as cargo owner) and may recover cargo's contribution from the insurers of the cargo. However, in the case of sacrifices there is a difficulty, for here, as has already been noted,[18] where no question of common ownership is involved the insured is entitled to claim in full from the insurer, and need not reduce his claim by the amount of contributions which he is entitled to receive. Does the same rule apply where there is common ownership of the contributory interests? At first sight s.66(7) might suggest that it does. However in *Montgomery v Indemnity Mutual Marine Insurance Co*[19] the Court of Appeal held, reversing Matthew J. on this point, that the common owner, in claiming from hull underwriters the loss caused by the sacrifice, had to give credit for cargo's contribution "because the shipowner already has in his own pocket his contribution as cargo owner". It seems open to doubt whether this aspect of the decision is codified by s.66(7). Nevertheless, in practice the insurer of property sacrificed is treated as entitled to credit for contributions due from other interests in the same ownership, and it is submitted that this practice would be reconciled with s.66(7) on the

[16] See *Salvage Association v Suzuki* (1929) 35 Lloyd's Rep. 45. In *Brandeis v Economic Insurance Co* (above) the insurers declined to follow the practice of reimbursing the deposit because they regarded the terms upon which the deposit was paid (i.e. not into joint names, and with no security for its return) as unreasonable and imprudent.

[17] *Montgomery* [1901] 1 K.B. 147; [1902] 1 K.B. 734. In *Chalmer's Marine Insurance Act 1906*, 10th edn, p.110, this is said to have been the intention of the subsection, which was twice altered during the passage of the Bill through Parliament.

[18] See para.50.06, above.

[19] *Montgomery* [1902] 1 K.B. 734.

grounds that the Court of Appeal rightly treated a contribution due in respect of an interest in common ownership on the same footing as a contribution actually paid, and that the insured would therefore have to give credit for it, just as he would if the contribution had been paid to him by a third party.

2. Rights of Insurers on Payment

Subrogation

Having settled any claim for general average, whether sacrifice, expenditure, contribution or deposit, the insurer is entitled to "stand in the shoes" of the assured and, in the words of s.79(2) of the Marine Insurance Act 1906: **50.41**

> ". . . is thereupon subrogated to all rights and remedies of the assured in and in respect of the subject-matter insured as from the time of the casualty causing the loss, in so far as the assured has been indemnified . . ."[20]

Those rights and remedies may be against the other parties to the common adventure in so far as they are liable to contribute to any general average loss or expenditure sustained by the owner of the insured property greater than his own rateable proportion of the total general average, and for which the insurer has already made settlement with the assured. Alternatively they may arise out of the actionable fault of a party to the adventure or a third party—these latter categories are dealt with under s.11 on recoveries below at paras 50.92 to 50.100.

As stated in para.50.06, above, an assured may proceed directly and immediately against his insurers for the whole of any loss caused by general average sacrifice, and the insurers are thereby subrogated to the general average contributions eventually received from the other parties to the adventure when the general average adjustment has been prepared and settled. **50.42**

Thus, and to take the first example given in para.50.09, above, where cargo with an invoice value of 10,000 was totally lost by jettison, the insurers by a policy subject to the Institute Cargo Clauses and with a sum insured and insured value:

In Case A—of 12,000, were immediately liable to pay the assured	12,000
In Case B—of 8,000, were immediately liable to pay the assured	8,000

[20] With regard to s.79(1) of the Act dealing with cases "Where the insurer pays for a total loss" and giving him additional rights entitling him ". . . to take over the interest of the assured in whatever may remain of the subject-matter so paid for", it is to be noted that the right to recover from third parties (i.e. the other contributing interests) passes to the insurer, not under the principle of abandonment outlined above, but only under the more limited principle of subrogation applying to claims for both total and partial loss, and under which the insurer can make no windfall profit, his subrogation rights being limited to the amount he has paid (*Att-Gen v Glen Line Ltd* [1930] 37 Lloyd's Rep. 55; 36 Com. Cas. 1; 46 T.L.R. 451).

In the general average adjustment, the allowance in general average (in accordance with the York-Antwerp Rules, 1994) would be for the invoice value of 10,000
and, assuming that the total general average represented 20 per cent of the overall contributory values, this particular cargo interest would be debited with a proportion of general average amounting to 2,000
Net general average contributions receivable from other parties to the adventure 8,000

50.43 To how much of this contribution received of 8,000 are the insurers entitled? In Case A—where insurers have settled a loss of 12,000, there is no problem; the assured has already been fully indemnified for his loss and the insurers are entitled to the whole of the recovery of 8,000.

In Case B—where insurers have settled a loss of 8,000, the matter will be resolved on the following equitable basis:

		CREDIT	
		INSURERS	ASSURED
Credit: Amount Made Good	10,000		
To Insurers: Up to the amount settled		8,000	
To Assured: The Balance			2,000
Debit: Proportion General Average	2,000		
To Insurers:			
If C.V. 10,000 liable for 2,000			
Insd. V. 8,000 pays in ppn		(1,600)	
To Assured: The balance			(400)
General Average Contribution Received	8,000	6,400	1,600

50.44 Viewed from a strictly legal standpoint, such a solution is probably wrong, and, up to the amount settled by insurers (8,000), they are entitled to the whole of the recovery (8,000) received here from third parties. Section 27(3) of the Marine Insurance Act 1906 provides that:

> "Subject to the provisions of this Act, and in the absence of fraud, the value fixed by the policy is, as between the insurer and assured, conclusive of the insurable value of the subject intended to be insured, whether the loss be total or partial."

In Case B, the assured has insured his goods for an agreed value of only 8,000, he has received that full sum in settlement of his claim, and, consequently, has no sound legal argument to participate in any recovery from third parties of 8,000 or less.

This is borne out by the case of *Boag v Standard Marine Insurance Co Ltd*[21] where (and to use the figures in our example above) the assured had first insured his goods for 8,000 **50.45**
but, with market values rising, had later effected a policy with different insurers, and without the knowledge of the original insurers, covering "increased value" for 2,000

his goods for	8,000
for	2,000
	10,000

The goods were jettisoned, and the allowance in the general average adjustment was for the full market value of 10,000
Less: Proportion of general average attaching thereto 2,000
Net Recovery 8,000

It was held that the original insurers for 8,000 were entitled to the whole of the net recovery of 8,000, and the "increased value" insurers[22] to nothing. The insured merchant was in no way concerned in the action, or in the recovery, he having collected the full value of his cargo (10,000) from the two sets of insurers.

The *Boag* case follows established legal precedent and must be considered sound in principle, but strong support for the equitable approach adopted in practice (and accepted by insurers with murmurs only at 10-year intervals) is to be found from the alleged market custom in the mid-nineteenth century, as evidenced by the case of *Dickenson v Jardine*,[23] the facts of which are recounted in para.50.07, above. **50.46**

It is clear that the insurers of those days endeavored not to settle immediately their direct liability on the policy for the whole of a general average sacrifice, but required the assured first to "send round the hat" to the other parties to the adventure, and thereafter to claim from insurers only in respect of the proportion of general average attaching to the insured cargo. Again using the figures from our example above, it may thus be surmised that the assured would first collect the 8,000 contributions due from his co-adventurers and then proceed to his insurers for their liability in respect of the proportion of the loss falling upon him of 2,000.

Such liability would no doubt have been settled on the following basis:

If contributory value 10,000 pays proportion general average	2,000
Then insured value 8,000 pays in proportion	1,600

thus producing the identical result to that adopted in modern everyday practice. One may also refer to the judgment of Willes J. In *Dickenson v Jardine*[24]:

> "The result is that the owner has two remedies: one for the whole value of the goods against the underwriter; the other for a contribution in case the vessel arrives safely in port: and he may avail himself of which he pleases, though he cannot retain the proceeds of both so as to be repaid the value of his loss twice over."

[21] *Boag* (1937) 57 Lloyd's Rep. 83; 42 Com. Cas. 214.

[22] In many of the "trade" insurance clauses, provision is now made whereby the original insured value is deemed to be increased to the total amount insured at the time of loss, thereby enabling increased value insurers to participate in any recovery.

[23] *Dickenson* (1868) L.R. 3 C.P. 639.

[24] *Dickenson* (1868) L.R. 3 C.P. 639.

50.47 Identical legal principles and customary practice apply to a case of partial loss or damage to insured property by a general average sacrifice, such as our earlier second example in para.50.09, where cargo with an invoice value of 10,000 was partly jettisoned to the extent of 50 per cent, or was damaged by water used to extinguish a fire to the extent of 50 per cent, and was insured by a policy subject to the Institute cargo Clauses for 12,000 or 8,000.
Insurers were immediately liable to pay:

In *Case A* 50 per cent of 12,000 = 6,000
In *Case* B 50 per cent of 8,000 = 4,000

50.48 In the general average adjustment the allowance in general average (in accordance with the York-Antwerp Rules 1974) would be for 50 per cent of the invoice value of 10,000, i.e. 5,000
and, again assuming a 20 per cent rateable proportion of general average, this particular cargo would be debited with a proportion of general average of 20 per cent of 10,000 (including amount made good) 2,000
Net general average contributions receivable from other parties to the adventure 3,000

In Case A—where insurers have settled a loss of 6,000, they would be entitled to the whole recovery of 3,000.

In Case B—where insurers have settled a loss of 4,000, sound legal principles might suggest that they were also entitled to the whole recovery of 3,000, but customary practice will apportion this sum on the following equitable basis:

		CREDIT	
		INSURERS	*ASSURED*
Credit: Amount Made Good	5,000		
To Insurers: Up to the amount settled		4,000	
To Assured: The Balance			1,000
Debit: Proportion General Average			
(As in Example in para.50.43)	2,000	(1,600)	(400)
General Average Contribution Received	8,000	6,400	1,600

Interest on amounts made good

50.49 It is necessary also to consider insurers rights to the interest which will be allowed on the principal sums in accordance with r.XXI of the York-Antwerp Rules 1994.

Such interest is apportioned in practice in accordance with Rule of Practice B37 of the Association of Average Adjusters:

2. Rights of Insurers on Payment

"Apportionment of Interest on Amounts Made Good

That in practice (in the absence of express agreement between the parties concerned) interest allowed on amounts made good shall be apportioned between assured and underwriters, taking into account the sums paid by underwriters and the dates when such payments were made, notwithstanding that by the addition of interest, the underwriter may receive a larger sum than he has paid."

This equitable basis for the apportionment of the interest has also been questioned at times by insurers, but has been pronounced legally correct in an opinion given in 1955 by the then Eustace Roskill QC.[25]

To illustrate the principle of the apportionment we revert to Case B in our **50.50**
first example of the total loss by jettison and the allowance in general average of 10,000

There would also be allowed interest at 7 per cent per annum from the date on which the goods would have been discharged at destination (say January 1, 2011) until three months after the date on which the adjustment was issued
(say January 1, 2013), or 1,400

Total allowance in general average 11,400

Deduct: Proportion general average (20 per cent) attaching to 10,000 2,000

General Average Contributions received from other parties to the adventure 9,400

The goods were insured only for 8,000, which sum was settled in full by insurers on say April 1, 2011.

The apportionment would be as follows: **50.51**

		CREDIT	
		INSURERS	ASSURED
Credit: Amount Made Good	10,000	8,000	2,000 (as before)
Interest thereon from 1.1.11 to 1.1.13	1,400		
To Insurers: On 8,000 from 1.4.11 to 1.1.13		980	
To Assured: On 8,000 from 1.1.11 to 1.4.11			140
And On 2,000 from 1.1.11 to 1.1.13			250
	11,400	9,980	2,420
Debit: Proportion general average (as before)	2,000	1,600	400
General average contribution received	9,400	7,380	2,020

[25] See Opinion No.23 of the Advisory Committee of the Association of Average Adjusters. A similar approach was adopted in *H. Cousins & Co v D. & C. Carriers* [1971] 2 Q.B. 230 at 242–243, where the question arose as to the apportionment between insured and insurers of interest on a subrogated claim awarded by the court under its statutory powers.

General average deposits

50.52 As previously stated, there is no clear and certain liability on the part of insurers to reimburse their assureds for general average deposits paid to secure the release of their goods from the shipowner's lien, but it is the common practice to do so.

General average deposits will usually be for an amount estimated to be slightly in excess of the eventual general average contribution required, and as by the terms of r.XXII of the York-Antwerp Rules 1994 such deposits will be banked in a special account and customarily earn interest, there should generally be some refund due to the holders of the general average deposit receipt when the adjustment has been issued, and after satisfying the liability to contribute to the general average or other charges.

Lloyd's Form of General Average Deposit Receipt[26] contains wording at the foot:

> "N.B.—The refund, if any, will be made only to the bearer of, and in exchange for, this Receipt, and will be the whole balance of the deposit after satisfying the General Average and/or Salvage and/or Charges, without deduction or set oft" of any other claims of the Shipowner against the Shipper or Consignee,"

and unless the average adjusters have been notified by the insurers that only part of the deposit has been refunded to the assured, they will be obliged to return the whole balance of the deposit to the holder of the receipt.

50.53 Further, and in accordance with Rule of Practice No. B36 of the Association of Average Adjusters:

> *"Interest on Deposits"*
>
> That, unless otherwise expressly provided, the interest accrued on deposits on account of salvage and/or general average and/or particular and/or other charges, or on the balance of such deposits after payments on account, if any, have been made, shall be credited to the depositor or those to whom his rights in respect of the deposits have been transferred."

the whole of the bank interest earned on the deposit will be credited to the holder of the deposit receipt (the insurer) regardless of the date on which he refunded the deposit to the assured. Thus, the transfer of the deposit receipt to the insurers may be likened to the purchase today by a bank of a bill of exchange payable in 90 days or other period of time.

3. Rates of Exchange

50.54 The currency (or currencies) in which a general average adjustment should be prepared and in which settlement of the general average contributions takes place

[26] See para.80.06, below.

between the various parties to the common adventure is discussed at length in Section 6, earlier, and we arrive at the conclusion that:

(1) Where a currency for general average purposes has been expressed in the bill of lading or contract of affreightment, the general average sacrifices and expenditures of the various parties to the adventure should be exchanged into that single currency of the contract, and settlement between the parties effected in that currency.
(2) In the absence of an expressed currency of the contract, no particular currency can generally be implied, but the general average sacrifices and expenditures of the various parties to the adventure should be shown in the operating currencies of those who have sustained the sacrifices and financed the expenditures, that is, the currency/ies in which they feel their loss.

Where, as is often the case, the general average consists solely of expenditure incurred by the shipowner, the adjustment will be prepared, and settlement take place, in the currency in which he feels his loss. **50.55**

Where the owners of both ship and cargo have sustained general average losses, and in different currencies, their respective claims in general average must be set off against their general average liabilities to each other, and the adjustment will be prepared, and settlement made:

(1) In the currency of the net creditor, if there be only one creditor (or more than one creditor, but all in the same currency).
(2) In the several currencies of the various net creditors where there are a number of creditors who feel their loss in different currencies.

Regardless of the currency/ies in which a general average adjustment is prepared and settled, or in which a general average sacrifice or expenditure is incurred, any claim upon a policy of marine insurance must be expressed in the currency of the policy, that is, that in which the property was insured: this is the currency of the contract. It follows that conversions from one or more "foreign" currencies into the currency of the policy will often need to be made, and, as for the preparation of the general average adjustment itself,[27] certain rules must be laid down for the appropriate dates on which (and the consequent rates of exchange at which) these conversions are to be made. **50.56**

Cargo

Policy claims for general average sacrifice, that is, physical loss of or damage to the cargo, are generally calculated by direct reference to the currency of the policy itself (that is, the currency in which the goods are insured) and conversion problems with rates of exchange should seldom arise. However, in the case of **50.57**

[27] See para.40.01, above.

general average expenditure, or general average sacrifices represented by an expenditure of cash (for example repair or reconditioning charges), contributions and deposits, the expenditure may often be in a currency other than that of the policy, and a conversion will need to be made.

A policy of marine insurance being one of indemnity, any necessary exchanges are made at the rate(s) ruling on the date(s) when payment was made by the assured, and. assuming the goods to be insured for their full value, the policy claim reimburses him precisely[28] for the amount(s) he has expended, or produces an equivalent value if the goods were insured in a currency other than that in which he directly feels his loss.

Subrogation

50.58 Where cargo has been sacrificed, the owner will often receive a net general average contribution from the other parties to the adventure, and, for the purpose of subrogating the insurers in respect of any direct claim previously paid by them, the general average contribution if in another currency will need exchanging into the currency of the policy at the rate ruling on the date when the contribution was received.

Adopting—and adapting—figures previously used in paras 50.09 and 50.47 to 50.52, above, let it be assumed that goods with an invoice value of $10,000 are shipped from the United States to Japan and insured for $8,000. As a general average act, the goods are jettisoned during the voyage and the insurers pay promptly a total loss of the sum insured of $8,000. In the general average adjustment, and on the principles outlined in Section 6, above, the allowance for this jettison is likely to be the invoice value of $10,000, but expressed in Yen and at the rate of exchange ruling on the last day of discharge at the intended destination of $1.00 = Y250, that is:

	Y2,500,000
Less: Proportion General Average	500,000
Net General Average Contribution Received	Y2,000,000
Worth, at time of receipt @ Y125 = $1.00	$16,000

50.59 Although the insurers settled a total loss and are entitled in terms of s.79(1) of the Marine Insurance Act 1906: ". . . to take over the interest of the insured in whatever may remain of the subject-matter so paid for . . .", and thereby make a profit on a few isolated occasions, in this particular instance nothing remains of the subject-matter insured, and the rights of the insurers against the other parties to the adventure are those of subrogation and extend only, per s.79(2) of the Marine Insurance Act 1906, "in so far as the assured has been indemnified", that is $8,000.

[28] Unlike the shipowner, who often finances general average expenditure on behalf of all the contributing interests, a cargo owner is rarely called upon to advance more than "the proportion of the loss (expenditure) falling upon him" as per the Marine Insurance Act 1906 s.66(4).

In fact, and in accordance with the practice stated in para.50.43, above, the net general average contribution received of Y2,000,000 = $16,000 would be apportioned as follows (ignoring interest):

		CREDIT	
		INSURERS	ASSURED
Credit: Amount Made Good	Y2,500,000 = $20,000	$8,000[29]	$12,000
Debit: Proportion General Average	500,000 = $4,0000	(3,200)	(800)
	Y2,000,000 = $16,000	$4,800	$11,200

Ship

As stated earlier, the majority of general average cases consist solely of expenditure by the shipowner, and in such cases the adjustment will generally be prepared in the operating currency of the shipowner. If as is frequently the case, he also insures his vessel in that same operating currency, the claim on the policy for the ship's proportion of the total general average should be a straightforward affair and present no problems with regard to rates of exchange. 50.60

On those occasions when, perhaps on the insistence of the mortgagees or for other reasons, the ship has been insured in a currency other than the shipowner's operating currency, it will be necessary to exchange each item of the shipowner's claim in the general average adjustment into the currency of the policy at the published rates of exchange ruling on the various dates when the shipowner settled each item. The proportion attaching to the ship of this total general average in the currency of the policy now forms the basis of the insurance claim.

Where the general average also includes sacrifices of cargo and those sacrifices are at a greater rate than the general average losses incurred by the shipowner, the general average is likely to be prepared and settled in the currency/ies of the cargo creditors, and the shipowner will be shown as a net debtor to (some of) the other contributing interests and be called upon to pay a general average contribution. The claim on his policy will then be based on: 50.61

(1) The *whole* of his own general average losses, exchanged into the currency of the policy where necessary at the rates ruling on the various dates when he settled the expenses.
(2) The amount of his net contribution to the cargo interests exchanged into the currency of the policy at the rate ruling on the date of settlement of the contribution.

An illustration may be helpful: the ship is insured in US $ and the adjustment is prepared in Yen. with rates of exchange of $1.00 = Y250 at the time of the general average, and $1.00 = Y125 when the adjustment is issued and the contribution paid. 50.62

[29] Limited to the original claim paid of $8,000—*Yorkshire Insurance Co Ltd v Nisbel Shipping Co Ltd* [1961] 2 All E.R. 487.

The General Average Adjustment

Shipowner's	Expenses at port of refuge	$80,000	@ 250 =	Y20,000,000
	Adjustment charges	20,000	@ 125 =	2,500,000
		100,000		Y22,500,000
Cargo	Sacrifices	200,000	@ 250 =	50,000,000
		300,000		Y72,500,000

Apportionment and Settlement

		GENERAL AVERAGE	CREDIT ALLOWANCE IN G.A.	BALANCE TO PAY	BALANCE TO RECEIVE
SHIP—	50% pays	Y36,250,000	22,500,000	13,750,000	13,750,000
CARGO—	50% pays	Y36,250,000	50,000,000	–	13,750,000
	100% pays	Y72,500,000	72,500,000	13,750,000	13,750,000
				@ 125 =	
				$110,000	

Claim on Ship Policy (If fully insured)

Ship's proportion General Average. Y36.250.000
Whereof: Own expenses . . . . Y22.500,000 = $100,000
Contributions to Cargo . . . . Y13,750,00 = $110,000
. . . . Y36,250.000 = $210.000

4. General Average Clauses

50.63 We have already observed that English marine insurance law, as codified in the Marine Insurance Act, contains its own definitions of a general average act, and of general average losses and contributions,[30] and that these definitions will apply between the parties to the adventure, where the general average is to be adjusted in accordance with English law.[31]

50.64 However, modern policies almost invariably contain specific provisions designed (subject to certain limits[32]) to equate the liability of the insurer under the policy in respect of general average with that of the assured vis-à-vis the other

[30] See s.66(1), (2) and (3).
[31] See para.A.05, above.
[32] See para.50.65, below.

parties to the adventure. The relevant provisions of the Institute Clauses are here analysed, and for reasons which will become apparent it is necessary to draw a distinction between insurances on ship or freight, and insurances on cargo.

Insurances on ship or freight

The standard Institute Clauses on Hulls and on Freight, whether for voyage or time, include the following clause: **50.65**

> "Adjustment to be according to the law and practice obtaining at the place where the adventure ends, as if the contract of affreightment contained no special terms upon the subject[33]; but where the contract of affreightment so provides the adjustment shall be according to the York-Antwerp Rules."

As the wording makes clear, the insurers are not prepared to allow their liability to be governed by any provisions in the contract of affreightment other than provisions for the application of unmodified York-Antwerp Rules or the law and practice of the place where the adventure ends. The effect of the clause is that if the contract of affreightment provides for the adjustment of general average in accordance with the York-Antwerp Rules (of any vintage), insurers will accept liability for the proportion of general average attaching to the ship or freight in accordance with those York-Antwerp Rules, in plain unmodified form; in all other circumstances, their liability shall be governed by a general average adjustment drawn up in accordance with the law and practice (on general average alone) of the place where the adventure ends. For ease of understanding, this is now set out in tabular form:

General Average Provisions in contract of affreightment:	Insurers' Liability to be Governed by:
(1) None	Law and practice of place where the adventure ends.
(2) Law and practice of the place where the adventure ends	Law and practice of the place where the adventure ends.
(3) Law and practice of the place where the adventure ends, in any modified or extended form,	Law and practice of place where the adventure ends, alone, and ignoring any modification.
(4) York-Antwerp Rules	York-Antwerp Rules
(5) York-Antwerp Rules in any modified or extended form.	York-Antwerp Rules in plain form, and ignoring any modification.
(6) Any other code of general Average	Law and practice of place where the adventure ends.

[33] This phrase was introduced in order to avoid the result in *De Hart v Campania Aurora* [1903] 1 K.B. 109; [1903] 2 K.B. 503.

Provided that, in each case, the liability of insurers shall not exceed the proportion of general average actually due from the insured.

Cargo insurances

50.66 Cargo insurers are well aware that the shippers of general cargo seldom have the opportunity to exercise any influence on the terms of any provision regarding general average in the contract of affreightment, and the standard Institute Cargo Clauses accordingly place no restrictions on the liability of insurers for any general average loss properly adjusted in accordance with the general average provisions in the contract of affreightment, whatever they may be. The wording of the relevant clause (No.2) is as follows:

> "This insurance covers general average and salvage charges adjusted or determined according to the contract of affreightment and/or the governing law and practice . . ."

Thus, cargo insurers accept liability for general average as adjusted in accordance with any provisions regarding general average in the contract of affreightment, subject only to the exception that the general average should not have been:

> ". . . incurred to avoid or in connection with the avoidance of loss . . . excluded . . . in this insurance."

Effect of the Institute Clauses

50.67 There are no decided cases in which the current provisions of the Institute Clauses relating to general average have been construed by the courts, but the following observations on their interpretation may be made:

(1) They do not affect the ordinary principle that the insurer is not liable for general average when the sacrifice or expenditure was made or incurred in connection with the avoidance of a peril expressly excluded by the policy.[34]

(2) Subject to any express provisions in the policy (such as are contained in the Institute Cargo Clauses[35]) they do not override the general rule that the insurer is only liable for a general average loss where the loss was incurred for the purpose of avoiding, or in connection with the avoidance of a peril insured against. However, whether a loss falls within this category may fall to be determined by the law of the place where the adventure ends, or by the relevant provisions of the contract of affreightment.[36]

[34] The Institute Cargo Clauses expressly affirm this principle (see para.50.66, above).

[35] See para.50.66, above.

[36] See para.50.65, above.

5. Excess Liabilities

For a variety of reasons, the insured value of a vessel in a policy covering her hull and machinery, etc. may on occasion be less than her real sound market value. In spite of such under-insurance, however, the measure of indemnity in respect of claims for damage to the ship caused by accident (particular average) or by general average sacrifice will be the full cost of repairs,[37] up to a limit of the insured value. The only headings of general average claim which will suffer and be reduced by reason of any under-insurance are general average expenditure and contributions, and to the extent as explained earlier in paras 50.15 to 50.32, and, in so far as concerns the ship, more particularly paras 50.16, 50.19 and 50.30 to 50.32, above. **50.68**

Additional insurance cover to meet all or part of any claim for general average expenditure unrecoverable on the hull and machinery policy can be provided by a separate policy covering excess liabilities on conditions such as the Institute Time Clauses, Hulls—Excess Liabilities, or the Institute Time Clauses, Hulls—Disbursements and Increased Value (total loss only, including excess liabilities), and include the following wording:

> "General Average, Salvage and Salvage Charges recoverable under the insurances on hull and machinery but not recoverable in full by reason of the difference between the insured value of the Vessel as staled therein (or any reduced value arising from the deduction therefrom in process of adjustment of any claim which law or practice or the terms of the insurances covering hull and machinery may have required) and the value of the Vessel adopted for the purpose of contribution to general average, salvage or salvage charges, the liability under this insurance being for such proportion of the amount not recoverable as the amount insured hereunder bears to the said difference or to the total sum insured against excess liabilities if it exceed such difference."

An example to illustrate the operation of this clause may best be provided with some of the figures used in the example given earlier in paras 50.42 and 50.44, where: **50.69**

The sound market value of the vessel at the termination of the adventure was	5,000,000
the insured value	4,000,000
and where Hull insurers were liable for a claim for particular average damage to the ship of	1,000,000
The proportion of general average expenditure and/or contribution attaching to the ship was	900,000

and the claim therefore on the Hull and Machinery policy was shown as follows:

[37] Marine Insurance Act 1906 ss.66(4), 69.

If Contributory Value	4,000,000	pays 900,000	
Then Insured Value	4,000,000		
Less: Particular Average	1,000,000		
	3,000,000	pays in proportion	675,000
		SHORTFALL	225,000

If a policy has been effected to cover Excess Liabilities for:

(a) 500,000 or
(b) 1,000,000

the respective claims will be calculated as follows:[38]

If Contributory Value 4,000,000			pays G.A. expenditure	900,000
and Hull policy on net				
insured value of		3,000,000	" "	675,000
Difference		1,000,000	pays "	225,000
Insured for:	(a)	500,000	pays in proportion	112,500
Insured for:	(b)	1,000,000	pays in full	225,000

Order in which Headings of Claim to be Marshalled

50.70 A problem of only rare occurrence which can affect the claim on a policy covering excess liabilities concerns the order in which the various headings of claim on a policy covering the hull and machinery of a vessel must be marshalled when they collectively exceed the insured value of that policy.

For example, a vessel may be insured for 4,000,000 so valued, and sustain very severe damage which the owner nevertheless elects to repair. Ignoring any "excess" customarily applied to any claim on a Hull policy, the various headings of claim against the policy (calculations are shown later) might be:

General Average	sacrifice—	360,000
	thirds—	100,000
	expenditure—	90,000
Particular Average—		3,500,000
		4,050,000

50.71 This sum being in excess of the insured value of 4,000,000, some part of the claim must be reduced by 50,000 and the question arises: which is it to be? In accordance with an opinion given by F. D. Mackinnon (later Mackinnon L.J.).

[38] Effectively: Sound Value 5,000,000
Less: Particular average 1,000,000
4,000,000

the claim on the hull and machinery policy must be marshalled in the following order:

Particular Average
General Average — sacrifice
— thirds
— expenditure

Thus, it is the claim for general average expenditure which must be reduced, with a resulting increase in the claim on any policy covering excess liabilities.

Example

A vessel is insured as follows: **50.72**

4,000,000 on Hull and Machinery, so valued, subject to the Institute Time Clauses, Hulls (No excess)
1,000,000 on Increased Value, so valued, subject to the Institute Time Clauses. Hulls—Disbursements and Increased Value (Total Loss only, including Excess Liabilities)

5,000,000

Her sound value at the time of the accident is 6,000,000. and an adjustment is prepared showing the following figures:

			General Average		
		P.A.	1/3rd off	Thirds Deducted	In full
Repairs to SHIP	4,200,000	3,500,000	300,000		400,000
Less: Thirds "new			100,000	100,000	
for old"			200,000	……..	200,000
G.A. Expenditure	900,000				900,000
	5,100,000	3,500,000	—	100,000	1,500,000

GENERAL AVERAGE APPORTIONED **50.73**

SHIP	Sound Value	6,000,000		
SHIP	*Less*: Damage	4,200,000		
		1,800,000		
SHIP	*Add*: Made Good	600,000		
		2,400,000	pays	900,000
CARGO—Net Value		1,600,000	pays	600,000
		4,000,000	pays	1,500,000

50.74 CLAIM ON HULL AND MACHINERY POLICY

1) Particular Average				3,500,000
2) General Average Sacrifice—60% × 600,000				360,000
3) General Average Thirds Deducted				100,000
4) General Average Expenditure—60% × 900,000			= 540,000	
If Contributory Value	2,400,000	pays	540,000	
Then Insured Value	4,000,000			
Deduct: All losses and charges for which insurers are liable and which have been deducted in arriving at the contributory value (i.e. Particular Average and Thirds)	3,600,000	pays		
	400,000	in ppn.	90,000	
	Limited by Insured Value to			40,000
				4,000,000

50.75 CLAIM ON EXCESS LIABILITIES POLICY

If Contributory Value	2,400,000	pays G.A. Expenditure	540,000
And Hull Policy on net insured value	400,000	"	40,000
Difference	2,000,000	pays G.A. Expenditure	500,000
Policy for	1,000,000	pays in proportion	250,000

6. Losses in Excess of the Insured Value

50.76 Where the subject-matter insured is totally lost by an insured peril, s.68 of the Marine Insurance Act 1906[39] provides that the measure of indemnity is the sum for which the property was insured, and. in the absence of any express provisions in the policy, this is the maximum liability of the insurers[40] in respect of any one accident. However, even in respect of a single accident it is possible for the total damage sustained and expenses incurred to exceed the sum insured, and it is always possible that during the course of any one voyage the ship and her cargo may meet with two or more accidents, producing a similar financial result. Consideration will now be given to some representative situations and the liability of ship and cargo insurers under standard insurance conditions to respond for these substantial losses.

[39] "Subject to the provisions of this Act, and to any express provision in the policy. where there is a total loss of the subject-matter insured,—(1) If the policy be a valued policy, the measure of indemnity is the sum fixed by the policy."

[40] e.g. *Aitchison v Lohre* (1879) 4 A.C. 755; 4 Asp. M.L.C. 168.

General Average Followed by Total Loss from New Cause

In *Chellew v Royal Commission on the Sugar Supply*[41] the Penlee sustained damage in a hurricane and put into Horta as a port of refuge. Upon completion of repairs she resumed her voyage but a few days later she and her cargo were totally destroyed by fire. As explained previously in para.20.20, the cargo were held not to be liable for any part of the general average expenses incurred at Horta, the whole of these consequently falling upon the shipowner. 50.77

On the grounds that the total loss arose from a new and separate accident, and that general average expenditure incurred and settled constitutes a partial loss which has "been repaired or otherwise made good", in accordance with s.77 of the Marine Insurance Act 1906[42] making provision for successive losses, the shipowner would be entitled to recover from his hull insurers:

(1) The whole of the general average expenses, being the "proportion of the loss which falls upon him" as stated in s.66(4) of the Marine Insurance Act and as explained by *Green Star Shipping Co Ltd v London Assurance.*[43]
(2) The sum insured in respect of the subsequent total loss.

Although in the above example the cargo interests sustained no more than the total loss, had they been obliged, for instance, to provide separate security to salvors at the port of refuge, they similarly would be entitled to recover from their insurers both the salvage payment and the subsequent total loss.

General Average Followed by Total Loss from Same Cause

To illustrate this particular situation, let it be assumed that a loaded vessel strands in a position of peril and sustains damage to her bottom which is temporarily repaired at a port of refuge after refloating. During the ensuing continuation of the voyage, and without the intervention of any new cause, the temporary repairs fail and the ship and her cargo sink and are lost. 50.78

As in the first example, the shipowner would be unable to recover from the cargo interests any contribution to the general average expenses incurred by him at the port of refuge, and his claim upon his insurers in respect of this double loss from a single accident might normally be expected to be limited to the sum insured. However, and in the absence of any insurance on average disbursements,[44] the shipowner should be able to recover what might reasonably have been

[41] *Chellew* [1922] 1 K.B. 12.
[42] "(1) Unless the policy otherwise provides, and subject to the provisions of this Act. the insurer is liable for successive losses, even though the total amount of such losses may exceed the sum insured. (2) Where, under the same policy, a partial loss, which has not been repaired or otherwise made good, is followed by a total loss, the assured can only recover in respect of the total loss: Provided that nothing in this section shall affect the liability of the insurer under the suing and labouring clause."
[43] *Green Star* [1933] 1 K.B. 378; 39 Lloyd's Rep. 213: 36 Com. Cas. 258: 8 Asp. M.L.C. 225.
[44] See paras 20.19–20.24, above.

expected to be the ship's proportion of those general average expenses under cl.13.5/6 of the Institute Time Clauses, Hulls:

> "13.5 When a claim for total loss of the Vessel is admitted under this insurance and expenses have been reasonably incurred in saving or attempting to save the Vessel and other property and there are no proceeds, or the expenses exceed the proceeds, then this insurance shall bear its pro rata share of such proportion of the expenses, or of the expenses in excess of the proceeds, as the case may be. as may reasonably be regarded as having been incurred in respect of the Vessel . . .; but if the Vessel be insured for less than its sound value at the time of the occurrence giving rise to the expenditure, the amount recoverable under this clause shall be reduced in proportion to the under-insurance.
>
> 13.6 The sum recoverable under this Clause 13 shall be in addition to the loss otherwise recoverable under this insurance but shall in no circumstances exceed the amount insured under this insurance in respect of the Vessel."

50.79 These clauses also have particular application in situations such as the following:

(1) Where a salvage tug is willing to proceed to the assistance of a distressed vessel and her cargo only on the basis of a guaranteed daily hire, and the ship and her cargo sink and are totally lost before the arrival of the tug.
(2) Where expenses are incurred in attempts to refloat and save a ship and her cargo ashore on rocks, but bad weather causes the vessel to break up and be lost together with her cargo.

From the expenses incurred must be deducted the proceeds or value of any property saved, whether ship or cargo, and of the balance the ship insurers will pay:

> ". . . its pro rata share . . . as may reasonably be regarded as having been incurred in respect of the vessel . . . reduced in proportion to the underinsurance."

Although the clause gives no precise guide, it is submitted that the abortive salvage expenses—or the excess over any proceeds—should be apportioned over the approximate values of the property sought to be saved, and in the condition in which it was likely to be saved.

This approach was adopted in the Canadian case *Ultramar Canada Inc v Mutual Marine Office Inc*,[45] under the very similar provisions of the equivalent clause in the American Institute Clauses. It was also held in that case that the clause applied even though one of the purposes for which the expense was incurred was the avoidance of pollution, rather than solely the saving of insured property.[46]

[45] *Ultramar Canada Inc* [1995] 1 F.C. 341 (Fed. Ct Can., Trial Division).

[46] This in itself is no doubt correct, but it leads on to the question whether, for the purpose of giving effect to the clause, any of the expenses should be apportioned to the avoidance of pollution rather than to the salving of property. In the Ultramar case all of the expenses were apportioned between hull and cargo and none to the avoidance of pollution, and this seems questionable. It was also held that in assessing the values of the different properties any amount made good in general average in respect of a sacrifice should be added to the value of the interest which had suffered the sacrifice. It is submitted, however, that there is no good reason for adopting this course.

6. *Losses in Excess of the Insured Value*

Where no Total Loss, but Loss and Expenses Exceed the Insured Value

In *Aitchison v Lohre*[47] the "Crimea" encountered heavy weather and sustained severe damage and was in danger of sinking. She was rescued by a steamer which was awarded £800 salvage, and afterwards repaired. Even after deducting thirds "new for old", the cost of repairs exceeded the insured value, and the shipowner endeavoured to recover the salvage award in addition under the sue and labour clause. The insurers were held liable for the cost of repairs up to the sum insured, but not for any part of the salvage expenses. As Lord Blackburn said in the House of Lords: **50.80**

> "I think that general average and salvage do not come within either the words or the object of the suing and labouring clause. . . . the object (of the clause) is to encourage exertion on the part of the assured; not to provide an additional remedy for the recovery by the assured, of indemnity for a loss which was by the maritime law a consequence of the peril."

The principle established is now codified in s.78(2) of the Marine Insurance Act 1906:

> "General average losses and contributions and salvage charges, as defined by this Act, are not recoverable under the suing and labouring clause."

7. Vessels in Ballast

Under English law in order to constitute a general average act, it is essential that there should be a common adventure and this normally consist of a ship and its cargo. However, a general average may exist when a ship is in ballast in the following circumstances. **50.81**

1. When on a ballast passage to load under a voyage charter under which freight is at risk.
   See para.17.59. English law treats the freight at risk as if it were a physical entity that forms the other element of the common adventure.
2. Where the vessel is on a ballast passage under time charter.
   See paras 17.44 to 17.67. In this instance the time charterer's bunkers provide the necessary other elements of the common adventure. The time charter hire and time charterers voyage freight at risk in such circumstances are ignored under English practice.
3. Where the vessel is proceeding in ballast and not under charter, in terms of an express provision in the hull policy.

[47] *Aitchison* (1879) 4 A.C. 755; 4 Asp. M.L.C. 168.

In the absence of any Charter, English law would not recognize a general average because only a single interest was at risk—the vessel. While expenses such as towage would be recoverable as sue and labour (see for example cl.13 of ITC Hulls 1.10.83), the owner would not be able to recover detention expenses at a port of refuge that would otherwise be recoverable as general average. In order to put the Assured in the same position irrespective of the lack of any charter arrangements, English insurance conditions have for many years included a "ballast general average" clause. This example appears in IHC 2003:

> 8.3 When the vessel sails in ballast, not under charter, the provisions of the York-Antwerp Rules, 1994 (excluding Rules XX and XXI) shall be applicable, and the voyage for this purpose shall be deemed to continue from the port or place of departure until the arrival of the vessel at the first port or place thereafter other than a port or place of refuge or a port or place of call for bunkering only. If at any such intermediate port or place there is an abandonment of the adventure originally contemplated, the voyage shall thereupon be deemed to be terminated.

Because such clauses offer additional benefits beyond the strict legal position it is usual for allowances for Commission and Interest (r.XX and XXI) to be excluded.

It will be noted that the allowances are not open ended and will cease when there is "an abandonment of the adventure originally contemplated".

Such a clause is unnecessary in the United States as the result of the decision in the case of *Potter v Ocean Insurance Co*[48] to the effect that the liability of the insurers was an additional interest at risk on any voyage.

8. Differing Codes of General Average

50.82 On occasion, bills of lading will be issued to shippers of cargo on the same voyage with differing provisions regarding the adjustment of general average. If the allowances in general average under the differing codes would be materially different, it will be necessary to prepare the general average adjustment with two (or more) separate columns showing the differing general average allowances, and with separate apportionments.

This subject has already been touched upon in para.30.12, above, and a hypothetical example given where a shipowner had financed the whole of the general average in respect of a vessel bound for Halifax, N.S., and Portland in the United States.

[48] *Potter* (1837) 216 Fed. Rep. 303; 3 Sumner 27.

		GENERAL AVERAGE	
		HALIFAX	PORTLAND
Cost of:	Entering port of refuge	5,000	5,000
	Discharging cargo	10,000	10,000
	Storing cargo	–	5,000
	Reloading cargo	–	10,000
	Outward port charges	–	2,500
	Commission and Interest	–	1,500
		15,000	34,000
HALIFAX CARGO	—30% pays	4,500	–
PORTLAND CARGO	—40% pays	–	13,600
SHIP	—30% bears	4,500	10,200
		15,000	3,000

50.83 Assuming standard cargo insurance conditions and the value fully covered by insurance, the insurers of the cargo will be liable to indemnify their assureds for the general average contributions properly charged to them respectively of 4,500 to the Halifax cargo, and 13,600 to the Portland cargo.

What is the position, however, of the insurers of the ship? They cannot be called upon to pay both proportions of general average attaching to the ship of 4,500 and 10,200, for the same expenses are essentially duplicated in both general average columns. The correct solution is to claim a part of each "contribution" corresponding to the proportion of the total value of the cargo represented by the cargo subject to that same particular code of general average, that is:

30/70ths	of the ship's ppn. G.A.—4,500—per Halifax adjustment =	1,929
40/70ths	of the ship's ppn. G.A.—10.200—per Portland adjustment =	5,828
70/70ths	Claim on Hull Insurers	7,757

For the purpose of claiming general average "contributions" from the insurers of any freight that may be at risk, similar (but not necessarily identical) principles can be applied.

9. Unrepaired General Average Damage

50.84 A ship insured for a period of 12 months from January 1, may sustain damage by a general average sacrifice on February 1, but repairs be deferred. During the course of a subsequent voyage, but within the currency of the same policy, the vessel is totally lost on November 1.

In accordance with the comments in para.18.20, above, it is conceivable that the reasonable depreciation in the value of the vessel arising from such unrepaired damage may be treated as general average in any average adjustment. The shipowner might then reasonably expect to recover from the cargo and other contributing interests the proportions of such depreciation attaching to their property, but in accordance with the provisions of s.77(2) of the Marine Insurance Act 1906,[49] he cannot recover from his own hull insurers the proportion of the depreciation attaching to the ship.

10. Constructive Total Loss

50.85 The subject of constructive total loss is one of great complexity, and for a thorough review, interested readers are referred to the almost 90 pages of text in the *British Shipping Law* Series, *Arnould on Marine Insurance*. In this present volume, however, it is necessary to refer only to the relatively limited extent to which general average may be taken into account for the purpose of demonstrating a constructive total loss on a policy of marine insurance covering a ship. Section 60(2) of the Marine Insurance Act 1906 provides that:

> "In particular, there is a constructive total loss—
> (ii) In the case of damage to a ship, where she is so damaged by a peril insured against, that the cost of repairing the damage would exceed the value of the ship when repaired.
> In estimating the cost of repairs, no deduction is to be made in respect of general average contributions to those repairs payable by other interests, but account is to be taken of the expense of future salvage operations and of any future general average contributions to which the ship would be liable if repaired."

50.86 In essence, the Marine Insurance Act requires that in order to demonstrate a constructive total loss, the estimated cost of repairs should exceed the repaired (or sound) value of the ship. However, the value of the ship may be difficult to determine or become a matter of dispute so that in practice all standard forms of hull insurance prefer to use the known insured value as a point of reference. Thus under ITC Hulls 1.10.83 the benchmark is the insured value itself, while under IHC 2003 it is 80 per cent of the insured value, which is in line with policies in Scandinavia and elsewhere. The rationale for adopting 80 per cent of the insured value is that it more clearly reflects the commercial realities when a vessel is seriously damaged. If an uninsured owner is faced with a repair bill amounting to 80 per cent of the insured value he would be likely to regard the vessel as not worth repairing because of the loss of earnings during a lengthy repair period and the cost of financing the repairs themselves. According to Phillips the "general rule in the United States was that if ship or goods were damaged to more than half of the value the assured may abandon and recover for a total loss". However, the American Institute Hull Clauses have long required that the cost of recovery and repairing the vessel must exceed the insured value.

49 "Where, under the same policy, a partial loss, which has not been repaired or otherwise made good, is followed by a total loss, the assured can only recover in respect of the total loss: provided that nothing in this section shall affect the liability of the insurer under the suing and labouring clause."

10. Constructive Total Loss

In the examples which follow, it will be assumed that the vessel is insured for an agreed value of 1,000,000 under ITC Hulls 1.10.83 (which make the insured value the required figure) and that the cargo on board would contribute 50 per cent towards any general average sacrifice or expenditure.

(1) Estimated cost of repairs to ship— 50.87

Particular Average	800,000
General Average sacrifice	300,000
	1,100,000

Although the vessel might be repaired at a net cost to the shipowner of 950,000 after crediting the 150,000 contribution payable towards the general average repairs by the cargo interests, s.60 of the Act makes it clear that:

> "In estimating the cost of repairs, no deduction is to be made in respect of general average contributions payable by other interests."

Thus, the vessel is a constructive total loss, and the Act recognises that, regardless of who may be paying for the repairs, it is uncommercial to spend 1,100,000 on repairs to a vessel worth only 1,000,000. Identical considerations would apply to a vessel damaged in a collision for which the "other" vessel was responsible; the potential recovery would be ignored since the issue is deciding the state of facts as to whether the vessel is a constructive total loss, and not who may be eventually be liable to contribute to that loss.

(2) Estimated cost of: 50.88

Repairs to ship—Particular Average	800,000
General Average expenses or cargo sacrifice	300,000
	1,100,000

In this instance, the vessel is not a constructive total loss, for the Act provides:

> ". . . but account is to be taken of the expense of future salvage operations and of any future general average contributions to which the ship would be liable if repaired,"

that is, it is only the ship's proportion (50 per cent or 150,000) of the shipowners general average expenditure, or the shipowners contribution to the general average sacrifice or expenditure of the cargo which may be taken into account.

(3) Estimated cost of: 50.89

Repairs to ship—	Particular Average		800,000
	General Average	150,000	
	General Average (Refloating) Expenses	150,000	300,000
			1,100,000

Following the principles set out in the first two examples, a constructive total loss can be demonstrated, with the ranking items:

Estimated cost of:			
Repairs to ship—	Particular Average		800,000
	General Average sacrifice		150,000
Refloating vessel—	50% of 150,000		75,000
			1,025,000

In the 11th and 12th editions it was suggested that the vessel was not a constructive total loss because the contribution by cargo to ship sacrifice (75,000) should be set off against ships proportion of expenditure (also 75,000) leaving only the costs of repairs totalling 950,000 as ranking items. It is submitted that this view was incorrect because it confused the process of financial settlement between parties with the prevailing state of facts that showed the vessel to beyond commercial repair.

Future Salvage Operations

50.90 In defining what constitutes one particular class of constructive total loss for a ship, s.60(2)(ii) of the Marine Insurance Act 1906 states that: "In estimating the cost of repairs . . . account is to be taken of the expense of future salvage operations." The question arises as to the particular time-base from which the salvage operations are to be regarded as "future"; is it that of the casualty, or of the tendering of a notice of abandonment? Or, expressed more directly: "Can the cost of salvage operations incurred after a casualty, but before the tendering of notice of abandonment to the insurers, be used in the assessment of whether a vessel is a constructive total loss?"

The correct answer to this question continues to be a matter of debate and there is no clear authority to be found in cases decided before or after the passing of the Marine Insurance Act. Whilst the use of the word "future" in connection with general average contributions (para.50.88) has a clear meaning (in the sense of contributions that will be payable in due course after an adjustment has been drawn up) the same cannot be said in qualifying the word "salvage".

Reference is often made to *Hall v Hayman*, a re-insurance case that followed the settlement of a total loss due to grounding by the original insurers. The re-insurance policy contained a clause providing that the insured value of $34,000 was to be taken as the repaired value. An initial attempt to refloat the vessel at a cost of $1,830 was made shortly after the casualty in November, before ice conditions made further attempts impossible, and notice of abandonment was given in early December. The following spring, an unsuccessful salvage operation took place at a cost of $2,000 followed by a successful refloating which cost $9,800. The cost of the spring salvage operations, ancillary costs and estimated repair costs came to only $30,500 and the main issue dealt with by Bray J. was therefore whether the value of the wreck could be taken into consideration. On this he found that the Marine Insurance Act had changed the common law as reflected in

Macbeth v Maritime Insurance Co because the value of the wreck could not come within the term "expenditure" now used by s.60(1) of the Act, something he considered likely to be an unfortunate and unintended consequence of the new statute.

The possibility of including the cost of the first salvage attempt ($1,830) had been initially conceded by counsel for the plaintiffs on the basis that it predated the notice of abandonment, but the costs were re-presented in argument on the basis that the operations had been instigated by insurers. Bray J. dealt with this point as follows:

> "I now take the figures that I have before me and deal with them. The first salvage is 1830 dollars. That was the attempt that was made to salve her between the date of stranding, the 16th Nov., and the date the 9th Dec.; in fact, it was made very soon after the ship stranded, and it was a failure. It is said that I ought to allow that nevertheless. Mr. Bailhache conceded that if that had been done by the shipowners, he could not have claimed that as part of the repairs, because they were not future salvage operations, but he said it had in fact been done by the underwriters, and t herefore I ought to include it. I do not see that. In estimating the cost of repairs, I do not think I have anything to do with the underwriters. It is all upon the assumptions as to what a prudent uninsured owner would do, and I have got to see whether on the 9th Dec. the cost of the repairs, as stated in the Act, including those items which are mentioned in the Act, would or would not exceed the value when repaired. I cannot take into consideration anything that was done before, which, as a matter of fact, neither improved the position nor worsened it. Therefore I cannot allow 1830 dollars."

The 18th edn of Arnould para.29–33 considers that *Hall v Hayman* cannot be regarded as a decision on the point, preferring the view that the relevant date is that of the casualty:

> "In *Hall v Hayman*, in which a series of attempts was made to refloat a stranded vessel, it was assumed by the plaintiff's counsel that the relevant date was that of giving notice of abandonment and it was therefore conceded that the cost of the first attempt, made before notice was given, could not be included in the cost of repairs. This was accepted as correct by Bray J., but the case cannot be regarded as a decision on the point. The same point was argued on behalf of underwriters, and considered but not decided by Porter J. in Carras v London & Scottish Assurance Co. On principle it seems that the relevant date is the date of the casualty. Section 60 of the Marine Insurance Act 1906, is concerned with the question of what constitutes a constructive total loss, and this, as we have seen, is quite independent of notice of abandonment. If notice of abandonment is rightly given the loss dates back to the casualty, and the test for ascertaining whether or not there is a constructive total loss ought presumably to be applied, actually or notionally, at the same date."

Lord Justice Donaldson took a similar view in his Chairman's Address to the Association of Average Adjuster's annual general meeting in 1982. He considered that taking the notice of abandonment as the operative date could not be right because it ignored the distinction between the factual situation of a vessel being a constructive total loss and an election to treat her as a total loss for the purposes of a claim on underwriters.

This view has frequently been objected to (including in the 12th edn of this Work) on the basis that the word "future" becomes surplusage, and it is regrettable that the opportunity was not taken in the International Hull Clauses 2003 to put the matter beyond doubt, one way or the other.

50.91 The courts of the United States adopt the view that expenses incurred prior to the tendering of notice of abandonment may be included in the computation for the purpose of demonstrating a constructive total loss and also form an additional claim under the sue and labour clause. The effect of these decisions is modified[50] by wording in lines 138/139 of the American Institute Hull Clauses (June 2, 1977):

> ". . . but expenses incurred prior to notice of abandonment shall not be considered if such are to be claimed separately under the sue and labor clause."

The assured is thus presented with the choice of how the claim is presented. For example, assuming an insured value of 1,000,000:

(a) Refloating Expenses	350,000
Repairs (or unrepaired damage)	750,000
	1,100,000

or (b) The sum insured of 1,000,000, but losing his refloating expenses and giving credit to the insurers for the value of the vessel.

11. Recoveries from Third Parties

50.92 The following paragraphs relate to recoveries in the context of collision claims, but many of the principles involved would apply to other kinds of recovery, for example, mis-declared dangerous goods that started a fire on board a loaded container vessel.

A collision between two vessels will frequently result in the need for one or both vessels to incur general average sacrifices and expenditures and these will be apportioned between ship and cargo, etc. in the customary manner. Assuming that the "other" vessel is wholly or partly to blame for the collision, what are the respective rights of the ship and cargo interests in a common maritime adventure to claim against that other vessel for such general average sacrifices and expenditure, or the general average contributions that may have been paid by the various parties to the adventure? In particular, do the cargo interests have the right to sue the wrongdoing vessel direct for general average contributions paid to the owner of the carrying vessel?

[50] See *Bradie v Maryland Insurance Co* 37 U.S. 378 (1838); *Young v Union Insurance Co* 24 Fed. Rep. 279 (1885); *Cia. Mar Astra v Archdale* (1954) A.M.C. 1674; [1954] 2 Lloyd's Rep. 469; *Northern Barge Line v Royal Insurance Co* (1974) A.M.C. 136.

In 1891 it was held in the case of *The Marpessa*[51] that cargo interests had no such right to claim direct against the other vessel for general average contributions paid to the carrying vessel, it being considered that the immediate cause of such contributions was not the collision, but the contract of carriage between the ship and cargo. This decision applied only to general average contributions, and cargo interests were not precluded from proceeding directly against the other vessel for physical loss or damage to their property directly sustained in the collision, or by a general average sacrifice of their cargo immediately thereafter. Equally, the cargo interests were not necessarily placed in the position that they had been obliged to pay a general average contribution with no means whatever to recover the same; in his own claim for damages against the other vessel, the owner of the carrying vessel would include the whole of the general average expenses, etc. and any recovery would be apportioned subsequently between the ship and cargo interests. Nevertheless, and as the example below will demonstrate, the financial results to the cargo interests could be materially different where they to have the right to claim directly against the colliding vessel. **50.93**

In 1947 this right was recognised when *The Marpessa* was partly overruled by the House of Lords (Viscount Simon and Lord Simonds dissenting) in the case of *Morrison S.S. Co v Greystoke Castle; The Cheldale.*[52] Henceforth it was established that cargo interests had the right to recover in their own name, as damages from the owners of a colliding vessel, in respect of any general average contribution paid to the owners of the carrying vessel. However the House of Lords reaffirmed the right of the owner of the carrying ship to claim the whole of the general average expenditure, including cargo's proportion, from the colliding ship,[53] with the result that there are now two possible routes by which cargo's proportion can be claimed. **50.94**

Where both vessels are at fault for the collision, under what might be termed *The Marpessa*[54] régime, if the carrying vessel included in its claim against the other vessel the whole of the general average expenditure, the cargo interests could find on occasion that they failed to recover any part of the general average contribution they paid to the owner of the carrying vessel. Their own claim simply served as a set-off for the owner of the carrying vessel against his own collision liability to the other vessel, benefiting both shipowners, but not the cargo. This would occur particularly where the claims against the earning vessel were so large that the owner limited liability (as happened in the *Greystoke Castle*[55] case). **50.95**

An example may assist:

Vessels A and B collide and are held to be equally at fault.

[51] *The Marpessa* [1891] P. 403.

[52] *The Cheldale* [1947] A.C. 265; 80 Lloyd's Rep. 55.

[53] [1949] A.C. 265, at p 279. See also *Macieo Shipping Ltd v Hipper Shipping Lines* [2000] 1 Lloyd's Rep. 645. Although the owners claim failed on other grounds Steel J. noted that owners would not have been obliged to give credit against their claim for any monies recovered under the general average adjustment.

[54] *The Marpessa* [1891] P. 403.

[55] *Greystoke Castle* [1947] A.C. 265; 80 Lloyd's Rep. 55.

Vessel A incurs general average expenditure of	200,000
of which Cargo A pays 60% =	120,000
Cargo A might expect, therefore, to recover from the owner of Vessel B 50% of 120,000 =	60,000

50.96 Under *The Marpessa*[56] régime, the respective claims of the two vessels would be, say:

Claim of Vessel A

Particular Average and Demurrage—	600,000
General Average (100%)—	200,000
	800,000

Claim of Vessel B, which sank as the result of the collision, in ballast, and without loss of life:

Sound Value	8,000,000

A single liability settlement between the two vessels might proceed as follows:

A liable to B for 50% of 8,000,000 =	4,000,000
B liable to A for 50% of 800,000 =	400,000
Net, A liable to B for	3,600,000
Limited to	2,000,000

There is no recovery from vessel B, and vessel A having limited liability, there can be no application of the "cross liabilities" principle under standard insurance conditions such as the Institute Time Clauses, Hulls.

50.97 Under the post-*Greystoke Castle*[57] principle, the claim of shipowner A against B would be reduced to:

Particular Average and Demurrage—	600,000
General Average (200.000 – 120.000)—	80,000
	680,000

but he would still end up by limiting liability and paying B 2,000,000.

Cargo A, however, would recover from B 50 per cent of the general average contribution of 120,000 they had paid to shipowner A, that is, 60,000.

50.98 Other side effects or corollaries arising from the *Greystoke Castle*[58] decision included the following:

[56] See fn.51, above.
[57] *Greystoke Castle* [1947] A.C. 265; 80 Lloyd's Rep. 55.
[58] *Greystoke Castle* [1947] A.C. 265; 80 Lloyd's Rep. 55.

(1) The general average contribution claimable from the wrongdoing vessel would include sundry charges and allowances, previously unclaimable, such as commission and interest allowable under rr.XX and XXI of the York-Antwerp Rules, the fees and charges of the ships agents collecting general average security, and of the average adjusters preparing the adjustment, etc.

(2) If cargo interests were entitled to claim general average contributions from the other vessel, it followed—if with rather less certainty—that the shipowner also could include in his claim against the other vessel expenses such as the average adjusters' fees and expenses.

As mentioned above, many claims against colliding vessels are still presented on a *Marpessa* basis, with the owner of the carrying vessel claiming for himself and on behalf of the cargo interests the whole of any general average expenditure, including adjustment charges, etc. but with interest at commercial rates, rather than as under the York-Antwerp Rules. Provided that neither vessel has limited liability, this method will generally result in the cargo interests recovering their full entitlement from the other vessel. **50.99**

The only point to which they should pay attention and protect themselves if possible concerns the matter of legal and adjustment costs. Under the *Greystoke Castle* principle, the costs of recovering a simple general average contribution should be minimal, for the degree of liability attaching to the other vessel has already been determined, as has the amount of the general average contribution paid to the owner of the carrying vessel. Under the Marpessa method, however, it is not impossible that cargo interests could find themselves contributing unnecessarily on a pro rata basis to many of the heavy costs incurred by the shipowner for determining liability for the collision, and for apportioning the recovery.

If cargo interests are assuming that shipowners are putting forward their claim on a Marpessa basis, i.e. including 100 per cent of the general average, it is important that they verify that this is in fact the case. If it is not, they need to consider how their claim for cargo's proportion of general average is going to be recovered, having particular regard to matters such as the provision of separate security and any relevant time bar. Whilst the shipowner has the right to make such a recovery, he cannot be obliged to do so, since his actual duties extend only to the carriage, preservation and delivery of the cargo: they do not extend to benefitting cargo by litigation. Accordingly, cargo owners must keep a very careful eye on any time bar which might affect the claim. **50.100**

APPENDICES

APPENDIX 1

THE ROMAN CIVIL LAW

THOSE portions of the Digest and Institutes of Justinian which bear on the subject of general average are brought together in a convenient form, and illustrated by copious notes, in the first volume of M. Pardessus's "Collection de Lois Maritimes", from which the following extracts are taken.)

SECTION 1

WHAT LOSSES ARE THE SUBJECT OF GENERAL AVERAGE

1. Lege Rhodiâ cavetur, "ut, si levandae navis gratiâ jactus mercium factus est, omnium contributione sarciatur quod pro omnibus datum est."

1. The Rhodian law decrees that, if goods are thrown overboard to lighten a ship, all shall make good by contribution that which has been given for all (*a*). **60.01**

2. Si conservatis mercibus deterior facta sit navis, aut si quid exarmaverit, nulla facienda est collatio, quia dissimilis earum rerum causa sit, quae navis gratiâ parentur, et earum pro quibus mercedem aliquis acceperit: nam et si faber incudem vel malleum fregerit, non imputaretur ei qui locaverit opus: sed, si voluntate vectorum, vel propter aliquem metum, id detrimentum factum sit, hoc ipsum sarciri oportet.

2. If, the goods being preserved, the ship suffers damage or loses any of her tackling, there shall be no contribution, there being no distinction between things provided for the use of the ship and other things for which a man receives hire or payment: for, if a smith breaks his anvil or hammer, he cannot charge it against the person who employed him on the work. But if it is by the will of the passengers (*b*), or on account of some danger, that this damage was done, this must be made good (*c*). **60.02**

3. Cùm arbor, aut aliud navis instrumentum, removendi communis periculicausâ, dejectum est, contributio debetur.

3. When a mast or other appurtenance of the ship is cut down for the sake of removing a common danger, contribution is due (*d*). **60.03**

4. Arbore caesâ, ut navis cum mercibus liberari possit, aequitas contributionis habebit locum.

4. When a mast is cut, that the ship with the goods may escape, the equity of contribution shall come in (*e*). **60.04**

(a) Dig. Lib. 14, Tit. 2, Fr. 1; 1 Pard. 104. M. Pardessus is of opinion that this sentence contains all that the Romans really borrowed from the Rhodians (Vol. 1. p. 23), and that the Rhodians in turn borrowed it from the Phoenicians (Vol. 1, Intra. xxix.).

(b) "Vectores" may be translated passengers or merchants on board. The context shows that there were sometimes "vectores sine sarcinâ", passengers who had no wares: but this was probably exceptional. (See 1 Pard. 105, n. 3.)

(c) Dig. Lib. 14, Tit. 2, Fr. 2, para. 1; 1 Pard. 105.

(d) 1 Pard. 107.

(e) Fr. 5, para. 1: Pard. 108.

60.05 5. Si navis à piratis redempta sit, Servius, Ofilius, Labeo, omnes conferre debere aiunt. Quod verò praedones abstulerint, eum perdere cujus fuerit: nec conferendum ei qui suas merces redemerit.

5. If a ship has been ransomed from pirates, Servius, Ofilius, Labeo, all agree that there should be a contribution. But what the robbers have taken away, he must lose whose property it was; nor shall there be a contribution for him who has ransomed goods of his own (*f*).

60.06 6. Navis onustae levandae causâ, quia intrare flumen vel portum non potuerat cum onere, si quaedam merces in scapham trajectae sunt, ne aut extra flumen periclitetur, aut in ipso ostio vel portu, eaque scapha submersa est, ratio haberi debet inter eos qui in nave merces salvas habent, cum his qui in scaphâ perdiderunt, proinde tanquam si jactura facta esset. . . . Contrà, si scapha cum parte mercium salva est, navis periit, ratio haberi non debet eorum qui in navi perdiderunt, quia jactus in tributum nave salvâ venit.

6. If, for the purpose of lightening a laden ship, because she cannot enter a river or haven with her cargo on board, some of the goods are transhipped in a lighter, to avert danger either from remaining outside or in the harbour or port itself, and if the lighter is sunk, a contribution shall be made between those who have their goods safe in the ship, and those who have lost theirs in the lighter, just as if there had been a jettison.

If, on the other hand, the lighter with a part of the goods is saved, and the ship perishes, there shall not be a contribution towards the loss of those in the ship, on the plea that a jettison would have been contributed for if the ship had been saved (*g*).

. . . Quid enim interest, jactatas res meas amiserim, an nudatas deteriores habere coeperim? Nam sicut ei qui perdiderit sub-venitur, ita et ei subveniri oportet qui deteriores propter jactum res habere coeperit.

. . . What difference does it make, whether by a jettison I lose my goods, or by an exposure of them for the purpose I receive them damaged? As he who loses them is compensated, so compensation should be made to him who receives his goods damaged by reason of the jettison (*h*).

60.07 7. Navis adversâ tempestate depressa, ictu fulminis deustis armamentis et arbore et antennâ, Hipponem delata est, ibique tumultuariis armamentis ad praesens comparatis, Ostiam navigavit et onus integrum pertulit. Quaesitum est an hi quorum onus fuit, nautae pro damno conferre debeant. Respondit non debere: hic enim sumptus instruendae magis navis quam conservandarum mercium gratiâ factus est.

7. A ship damaged in a storm, her mast and yards having been struck by lightning, was taken into Hippo, and having there been equipped for the occasion with temporary spars and gear, performed her voyage to Ostia and delivered her cargo undamaged. The question was raised whether the owners of the cargo should contribute towards the shipowner's loss: and it was determined that they should not: for these expenses were incurred rather for the purpose of refitting the ship than of preserving the cargo (*i*).

60.08 8. Cum depressa navis aut dejecta esset, quod quisque ex ea suum servasset, sibi servare respondit, tanquam ex incendio.

8. When a ship is sunk or wrecked, whatever of his own property each owner may have saved, he shall keep for himself, as if rescued from a fire (*k*).

(f) Fr. 2, para. 3: 1 Pard. 106.
(g) Fr. 4; 1 Pard. 107.
(h) Fr. 4, para. 2; 1 Pard. 108.
(i) Fr. 6; 1 Pard. 108.
(k) Fr. 7; 1 Pard. 108.

Section 2

Computation of Losses and Contributing Interests

9. Portio autem pro aestimatione rerum quae salvae sum, et earum quae amissae sunt, praestari debet: nec ad rem pertinet, si hae quae amissat sunt pluris venire poterunt, quoniam detrimenti, non lucri, fit praestatio. Sed in his rebus quarum nomine conferendum est, aestimatto debet haberi, non quanti emptae sint, sed quanti venire possunt.

9. An apportionment is to be made according to the valuation of the property saved and of that sacrificed: nor does it affect the case if that which was sacrificed might have been sold at a profit, since the compensation is made for loss sustained, not for expected gain. But for the contributing values the estimate is to be taken, not on what they cost, but on what they might have been sold for (*l*). **60.09**

10. Amissae navis damnum collationis consortio non sarcitur per eos qui merces suas naufragio liberaverunt: nam hujus aequitatem tunc admitti placuit, cùm jactus remedio caeteris in communi periculo, salvâ nave, consultum est.

10. If a ship is cast away, the loss shall not be borne by a contribution on the part of those who have rescued their goods from the shipwreck; for this equitable right is only admissible when a jettison has been purposely made for rescuing the remainder in a common danger, and when the ship is saved (*m*). **60.10**

11. Cùm jactus de nave factus est, et alicujus res quae in navi remanserunt deteriores factae sunt, videndum an conferre cogendus sit, quia non debet duplici damno onerari, et collationis, et quòd res deteriores factae sunt. Sed defendendum est, hunc conferre debere pretio praesente rerum: itaque, verbi gratiâ, si vicenûm merces duorum fuerunt, et alterius aspargine decem esse coeperunt, ille cujus res integrae sunt, pro viginti conferat, hic pro decem.

Potest tamen dici etiam illa sententia, distinguentibus nobis deteriores ex qua causa factae sunt; id est, utrùm propter jacta nudatis rebus damnum secutum est, an verò alia ex causa, veluti quod alicubi jacebant merces in angulo aliquo, et unda penetravit; tunc enim conferre debebit: an ex priore causa collationis onus pati non debet, quia jactus etiam hunc laesit. Adhuc numquid et si aspargine propter jactum res deteriores factae sunt? Sed distinctio subtilior adhi-benda est, quid plus sit in damno, an in collatione: si, verbi gratiâ, hae res viginti fuerunt, et collatio quidem facit decem, damnum autem duo: deducto hoc quod damnum passus est, reliquum conferre debeat? Quid ergò, si plus in damno erit quàm in collatione, utputa decem aureis res deteriores factae sunt, duo autem collationis sunt? Indubitatè utrumque onus pati non debet. Sed hic videamus num et ipsi conferre oporteat: quid enim interest, &c.

11. When a jettison has been made from a ship, and some of the goods remaining in the ship are damaged, it is to be considered whether the owner of those goods shall be compelled to contribute, seeing that he should not be burdened with a double loss, both of the contribution and of the damage done to his goods. The right view is, that he should contribute upon the present value of his goods: thus, for example, if two men had goods each worth twenty, and one by wetting was brought to the value of ten, he whose goods are sound should contribute on twenty, the other on ten. **60.11**

In giving this judgment, however, a distinction should be made according to the cause of the deterioration; that is, whether the damage to the goods arose from their having been exposed on account of the jettison, or from some other cause, such as, that the goods were stowed in some corner where the water penetrated: in the latter case, they should contribute; in the former case they should be relieved from this burden, since their owner is himself a sufferer by the jettison. Again, how if it is by wetting on account of the jettison that the goods were damaged? Here a more subtle distinction is to be drawn, as to which is most, the damage or the contribution. If, for instance, these goods were worth twenty, and the contribution would make ten, but the damage two; deducting from this value the amount of the damage, should the remainder contribute? How, again, if the damage is more than the contribution: suppose the goods to be deteriorated by ten pounds, while the contribution is two? Undoubtedly the owner ought not to bear both burdens. But here we have to see whether contribution should not be made to him: for what difference does it make. &c. (No. 6, ante) (*n*).

(l) Fr. 2, para. 4; 1 Pard. 106.
(m) Fr, 5; 1 Pard. 108.
(n) Fr. 4, para. 2; 1 Pard. 108. The distinctions here suggested seem to indicate that the simple remedy for all these difficulties now universal, namely the bringing in the amount made good as a contributor, had not at this time suggested itself.

60.12 12. Si navis quae in tempestate jactu mercium unius mercatoris levata est, in alio loco submersa est, et aliquorum mercatorum merces per urinatores extractae sunt datâ mercede, rationem haberi debere ejus cujus merces in navigatione levandae navis causâ jactae sunt, ab his qui postea sua per urinatores servaverunt, Sabinus aeque respondit: eorum verò qui ita servaverunt, invicem rationem haberi non debere ab eo qui in navigatione jactum fecit, si quaedam ex his mercibus per urinatores extractae sunt: eorum enim merces non possunt videri servandae navis causâ jactae esse, quae periit.

12. If a ship, which in a tempest has been relieved by the jettison of one man's goods, shall afterwards in another place be sunk, and the goods of some merchants are brought up by divers for a stated reward, it is rightly held by Sabinus that he whose goods were jettisoned to save the ship is entitled to contribution from those who afterwards recovered theirs by means of divers: but, on the other hand, that there shall be no contribution from him whose goods had been jettisoned towards those whose goods were rescued by the divers: for these last goods cannot be said to have been cast out for the sake of preserving the ship which perished (*o*).

60.13 13. Cum in eadem nave varia mercium genera complures mercatores coëgissent, praetereaque multi vectores servi liberique in ea navigarent, tempestate gravi ortâ, necessariò jactura facta erat. Quaesita deinde sunt haec: an omnes jacturam praestare oporteat; et si qui tales merces imposuissent quibus navis non oneraretur, velut gemmas, margaritas, et quae portio praestanda est; et an etiam pro liberis capitibus dari oporteat, et qua actione ea res expediri possit. Placuit, omnes quorum interfuisset jacturam fieri conferre oportere, quia id tributum ob servatam rem deberent itaque dominum etiam navis pro portione obligatum esse; jacturae summam pro rerum pretio distribui oportet; corporum liberorum aestimationem nullam fieri posse; ex conducto dominos rerum amissarum cum nautâ, id est, cum magistro, acturos. Itidem agitatum est an etiam vestimentorum cujusque et annulorum aestimationem fieri oporteat; et omnium visum est, nisi si qua consumendi causâ imposita forent, quo in numero essent cibaria, eò magis, quòd, si quando ea defecerint in navigationem, quod quisque haberet in commune conferret.

13. Where in the same ship a number of merchants had shipped various kinds of goods, and also many passengers, slaves and free, were on board, a violent storm having arisen, it was necessary to make a jettison. Hereupon the following questions arose: whether all should take part in the contribution? whether those who had on board such goods as were no burden to the ship, as gems or pearls, should contribute, and if so, in what proportions; whether the lives even of freemen should be taken account of; and in what form of action the matter should be settled? It was determined, that all to whose interest it was that the jettison should be made should contribute, because they owed this ransom on account of their property preserved; therefore that the master of the ship was likewise bound for his proportion; that the amount of the jettison should be distributed rateably on the value of the property; that freemen's lives could have no value set upon them; that the owners of the goods cast over must proceed against the master of the ship ex conducto (p). At the same time it was discussed whether the wearing apparel and rings of those on board were to be valued; and it was determined that everything should, except such things as were put on board in order to be consumed, under which head came provisions; and this so much the more because, in case of deficiency while at sea, whatever each one had was brought into the common stock (*q*).

60.14 14. Servorum quoque qui in mare perierunt, non magis aestimatio facienda est, quam si qui aegri in nave decesserint, aut aliqui sese praecipitaverint.

14. As for slaves who perished in the sea, no greater valuation is to be set on them than if they had died of disease on shipboard, or had thrown themselves into the sea (*r*).

60.15 15. Si res quae jactae sunt apparuerint, exonerator collatio: quòd si jam contributio facta sit, tunc hi qui solverint agent ex locato cum magistro, ut is ex conducto experiatur, et quod exegerit reddat.

15. If goods which have been jettisoned are recovered, the contribution is discharged: but if the contribution has already been made, then those who have paid it may proceed ex locato against the master, that he may take his course ex conducto, and refund what he had demanded (*s*).

Res autem jacta domini manet, nec fit apprehendentis, quia pro derelicto non habetur.

The goods jettisoned however remain the property of their first owners, for they are not to be treated as derelict (*t*).

(o) Fr. 4. para. 1: 1 Pard. 107.
(p) See note (u). post.
(q) Fr. 2. para. 1: 1 Pard. 105–106.
(r) Fr. 2. para. 5: 1 Pard. 106.
(s) Fr. 2, para. 7: 1 Pard. 107.
(t) Fr. 2, para. 8; 1 Pard. 107; see also Fr. 8: 1 Pard. 109.

SECTION 3

REMEDIES AND MODE OF PROCEDURE

16. Si, laborante nave, jactus factus est, amissarum mercium domini, si mercedes vehendas locaverant, ex locato cum magistro navis agere debent; is deinde, cum reliquis, quorum merces salvae sunt, ex conducto, ut detrimentum pro portione communicetur, agere potest. Servius quidem respondit, ex locato agere cum magistro navis debere, ut caeterorum vectorum merces retineat, donec portionem damni praestent. Imò, etsi retineat merces magister, ultrò ex locato habiturus est actionem cum vectoribus: quid enim si vectores sint qui nullas sarcinas habeant? Planè commodius est, si sint, retinere eas. At si non, [et] totam navem conduxerit, ex conducto aget, sicut vectores qui loca in nave conduxerunt: aequissimum enim est commune detrimentum fieri eorum qui, propter amissas res aliorum, consecuti sunt ut merces suas salvas haberent.

16. If. when the ship is labouring, a jettison has been made, the owners of the goods sacrificed, if they have been shipped for carriage, should proceed ex locato against the master: who can then proceed against the others, whose goods are safe, ex conducto (*u*), that the loss may be distributed proportionally. Servius, however, is of opinion that they should proceed ex locato against the master of the ship, that he may retain the goods of the other merchants, until they have paid their share of the loss. Yes, but though the master may retain the goods, there must likewise be a right of action against the merchants (vectores: see note (b), p.419). ex locato (*x*): for how if there are merchants who have no goods on board? Clearly it is more convenient, if there are any, to retain them. But if not, and if he has freighted the whole ship, let him proceed ex conducto, as on passengers who have hired places in a ship: for it is most equitable that the loss should fall in common amongst those who, by means of the sacrifice of other persons' property, have succeeded in obtaining their own in safety. **60.16**

17. Si quis ex vectoribus solvendo non est, hoc detrimentum magistri navis non erit: nee enim fortunas cujusque nauta excutere debet.

17. If any of the merchants is insolvent, this loss must not fall on the captain; for a sailor cannot be expected to hunt out each man's stability. **60.17**

(u) Locator is he who lets his ship, or room in it, on hire; conductor, he who engages to pay for the use; hence the actio ex lacato, is a suit against the master or owner of the ship, to enforce the obligations undertaken by him in letting his ship; the actio ex conducto is by the master against the merchants, to enforce the duties which this contract imposes upon them. (Sandars, Inst. Just. 457.)

(x) This apparently should be ex conducto. Instances of this confusion, says Pardessus, are not uncommon in the Roman law. (1, 105, n. 2.)

APPENDIX 2A

GLASGOW RESOLUTIONS (1860), YORK RULES (1864) AND YORK-ANTWERP RULES (1877)

Glasgow Resolutions (1860)	York Rules (1864)	York-Antwerp Rules (1877)
	Rule I. Jettison of Deck Cargo	**Rule I. Jettison of Deck Cargo**
	A jettison of timber or deals, or any other description of wood cargo, carried on the deck of a ship in pursuance of a general custom of the trade in which the ship is then engaged, shall be made good as general average, in like manner as if such cargo had been jettisoned from below deck.	No jettison of deck cargo shall be made good as general average.
	No jettison of desk cargo, other than timber or deals, or other wood cargo, so carried as aforesaid, shall be made good as general average.	
	Every structure not built in with the frame of the vessel shall be considered to be a part of the deck of the vessel.	Every structure not built in with the frame of the vessel shall be considered to be a part of the deck of the vessel.
	Rule II. Damage by Jettison	**Rule II. Damage by Jettison**
	Damage done to goods or merchandise by water which unavoidably goes down a ship's hatches opened, or other opening made, for the purpose of making a jettison shall be made good as general average, in case the loss by jettison is so made good.	Damage done to goods or merchandise by water which unavoidably goes down a ship's hatches opened, or other opening made, for the purpose of making a jettison shall be made good as general average, in case the loss by jettison is so made good.
(3) That the damage done to cargo by chafing and breakage, resulting from a jettison of part of the remainder of the cargo, ought not to be allowed in general average.	Damage done by breakage or chafing, or otherwise from derangement of stowage consequent upon jettison, shall be made good as general average.	Damage done by breakage and chafing, or otherwise from derangement of stowage consequent upon a jettison, shall be made good as general average, in case the loss by jettison is so made good.

Glasgow Resolutions (1860)	York Rules (1864)	York-Antwerp Rules (1877)
	Rule III. Extinguishing Fire on Shipboard	**Rule III. Extinguishing Fire on Shipboard**
(2) That the damage done to ship, cargo and freight in extinguishing a fire, ought to be allowed in general average.	Damage done to a ship and cargo, or either of them, by water or otherwise, in extinguishing a fire on board the ship, shall be general average.	Damage done to a ship, and cargo, or either of them by water or otherwise, in extinguishing a fire on board the ship, shall be general average; except that no compensation be made for damage done by water to packages which have been on fire.
	Rule IV. Cutting away Wreck	**Rule IV. Cutting away Wreck**
(5) That the loss sustained by cutting away the wreck of masts accidentally broken ought not to be allowed in general average.	Loss or damage caused by cutting away the wreck or remains of spars, or of other things which have previously been carried away by sea-peril, shall not be made good as general average.	Loss or damage caused by cutting away the wreck or remains of spars, or of other things which have previously been carried away by sea-peril, shall not be made good as general average.
	Rule V. Voluntary Stranding	**Rule V. Voluntary Stranding**
(1) That, as a general rule in the case of the voluntary stranding of a vessel in the course of her voyage, the loss or damage to ship, cargo, or freight, ought not to be the subject of general average, but without prejudice to such a claim in exceptional cases upon clear proof of special facts.	When a ship is intentionally run on shore because she is sinking or driving on shore or rocks, no damage caused to the ship, the cargo and the freight, or any or either of them, by such intentional running on shore, shall be made good as general average.	When a ship is intentionally run on shore because she is sinking or driving on shore or rocks, no damage caused to the ship, the cargo and the freight, or any or either of them, by such intentional running on shore, shall be made good as general average.
	Rule VI. Carrying a Press of Sail	**Rule VI. Carrying a Press of Sail**
(7) That the damage done to ship, cargo and freight, by carrying a press of sail, ought not to be allowed in general average.	Damage occasioned to a ship or cargo by carrying a press of sail shall not be made good as general average.	Damage occasioned to a ship or cargo by carrying a press of sail shall not be made good as general average.
	Rule VII. Port of Refuge Expenses	**Rule VII. Port of Refuge Expenses**
(6) That the expense of warehouse rent at a port of refuge on cargo necessarily discharged there, the expense of re-shipping it, and the outward port charges at that port, ought to be allowed in general average.	When a ship shall have entered a port of refuge under such circumstances that the expenses of entering the port are admissible as general average, and when she shall have sailed thence with her original cargo or a part of it, the corresponding expenses of leaving such port shall likewise be so admitted as general average; and whenever the cost of discharging cargo at such port is admissible as general average, the cost of reloading and stowing such cargo on board the said ship, together with all storage charges on such cargo, shall likewise be so admitted. Except that any portion	When a ship shall have entered a port of refuge under such circumstances that the expenses of entering the port are admissible as general average, and when she shall have sailed thence with her original cargo or a part of it, the corresponding expenses of leaving such port shall likewise be admitted as general average: and, whenever the cost of discharging cargo at such port is admissible as general average, the cost of reloading and stowing such cargo on board the said ship, together with all storage charges on such cargo, shall likewise be so admitted.

Glasgow Resolutions (1860)	York Rules (1864)	York-Antwerp Rules (1877)
	of the cargo left at such port of refuge, on account of its being unfit to be carried forward, or on account of the unfitness or inability of the ship to carry it, shall not be called on to contribute to such general average.	
	Rule VIII. Wages and Maintenance of Crew in Port of Refuge	**Rule VIII. Wages and Maintenance of Crew in Port of Refuge**
(8) That the wages and provisions for the ship's crew ought to be allowed to the shipowner in general average, from the date the ship reaches a port of refuge in distress until the date on which she leaves it.	When a ship shall have entered a port of refuge under the circumstances defined in Rule VII, the wages and cost of maintenance of the master and mariners, from the time of entering such port until the ship shall have been made ready to proceed upon her voyage, shall be made good as general average. Except that any portion of the cargo left at such port of refuge on account of its being unfit to be carried forward, or on account of the unfitness or inability of the ship to carry it, shall not be called on to contribute to such general average.	When a ship shall have entered a port of refuge under the circumstances defined in Rule VII, the wages and cost of maintenance of the master and mariners, from the time of entering such port until the ship shall have been made ready to proceed upon her voyage, shall be made good as general average.
	Rule IX. Damage to Cargo in Discharging	**Rule IX. Damage to Cargo in Discharging**
(4) That the damage done to cargo, and the loss of it, and of the freight on it, resulting from discharging it at a port of refuge in the way usual in that port with ships not in distress, ought not to be allowed in general average.	Damage done to cargo by discharging it at a port of refuge shall not be admissible as general average in case such cargo shall have been discharged at the place and in the manner customary at that port with ships not in distress.	Damage done to cargo by discharging it at a port of refuge shall not be admissible as general average in case such cargo shall have been discharged at the place and in the manner customary at that port with ships not in distress.
	Rule X. Contributory Values	**Rule X. Contributory Values**
(9) That when the amount of expenses is less than the value of the property finally saved, the contributing values of ship, freight, and cargo, ought to be their values to the owners of them respectively, at the termination of the adventure.	The contributions to a general average shall be made upon the actual values of the property at the termination of the adventure, to which shall be added the amount made good as general average for property sacrificed; deduction being made from the shipowner's freight and passage-money at risk of two-fifths of such freight, in lieu of crew's wages, port charges, and all other deductions; deduction being also made from the value of the property of all charges incurred in respect thereof subsequently to the arising of the claim to general average.	The contribution to a general average shall be made upon the actual values of the property at the termination of the adventure, to which shall be added the amount made good as general average for property sacrificed; deduction being made from the shipowner's freight and passage-money at risk, of such port charges and crew's wages as would not have been incurred had the ship and cargo been totally lost at the date of the general average act or sacrifice; deduction being also made from the value of the property of all charges incurred in respect thereof subsequently to the arising of the claim to general average.

Glasgow Resolutions (1860)	York Rules (1864)	York-Antwerp Rules (1877)
(10) That, when the amount of expenses is greater than the value of the property saved, the proceeds of the property so saved ought to be applied towards those expenses, and the excess of the expenses over the proceeds ought to be apportioned as if the whole property had finally reached its destination.		
(11) That, in fixing the value of the freight, the wages and port charges up to the date of the general average act ought not to be deducted, and the wages and port charges after that date ought to be deducted from the gross freight at the risk of the shipowner.		
	Rule XI. Loss of Freight In every case in which a sacrifice of cargo is made good as general average, the loss of freight, if any, which is caused by such loss of cargo, shall likewise be so made good.	**Rule XI. Loss of Freight** In every case in which a sacrifice of cargo is made good as general average, the loss of freight, if any, which is caused by such loss of cargo shall likewise be so made good.
		Rule XII. Amount to be made good for Cargo The value to be allowed for goods sacrificed shall be that value which the owner would have received if such goods had not been sacrificed.

APPENDIX 2B

YORK-ANTWERP RULES OF 1890, 1924, 1950, 1974 (AND AS AMENDED 1990), 1994 AND 2004

The Comité Maritime International publishes the York-Antwerp Rules in an English and a French text. Only the English texts are reproduced in this Appendix. The French text of the York-Antwerp Rules 1994 and 2004 can be found on the CMI website *http://www.comitemaritime.org*.

York-Antwerp Rules (1890)	York-Antwerp Rules (1924)	York-Antwerp Rules (1950)
		Rule of Interpretation In the adjustment of general average the following lettered and numbered Rules shall apply to the exclusion of any Law and Practice inconsistent therewith. Except as provided by the numbered Rules, general average shall be adjusted according to the lettered Rules.
	Rule A There is a general average act when, and only when, any extraordinary sacrifice or expenditure is intentionally and reasonably made or incurred for the common safety for the purpose of preserving from peril the property involved in a common maritime adventure.	**Rule A** There is a general average act when, and only when, any extraordinary sacrifice or expenditure is intentionally and reasonably made or incurred for the common safety for the purpose of preserving from peril the property involved in a common maritime adventure.
	Rule B General average sacrifices and expenses shall be borne by the different contributing interests on the basis hereinafter provided.	**Rule B** General average sacrifices and expenses shall be borne by the different contributing interests on the basis hereinafter provided.
	Rule C Only such losses, damages or expenses which are the direct consequence of the general average act shall be allowed as general average.	**Rule C** Only such losses, damages or expenses which are the direct consequence of the general average act shall be allowed as general average.

York-Antwerp Rules (1890)	York-Antwerp Rules (1924)	York-Antwerp Rules (1950)
Rule of Interpretation In the adjustment of general average the following lettered and numbered Rules shall apply to the exclusion of any Law and Practice inconsistent therewith. Except as provided by the numbered Rules, general average shall be adjusted according to the lettered Rules.	**Rule of Interpretation** In the adjustment of general average the following lettered and numbered Rules shall apply to the exclusion of any Law and Practice inconsistent therewith. Except as provided by the numbered Rules, general average shall be adjusted according to the lettered Rules.	**Rule of Interpretation** In the adjustment of general average the following lettered and numbered Rules shall apply to the exclusion of any Law and Practice inconsistent therewith. Except as provided by *the Rule Paramount and* the numbered Rules, general average shall be adjusted according to the lettered Rules.
	Rule Paramount In no case shall there be any allowance for sacrifice or expenditure unless reasonably made or incurred.	**Rule Paramount** In no case shall there be any allowance for sacrifice or expenditure unless reasonably made or incurred.
Rule A There is a general average act when, and only when, any extraordinary sacrifice or expenditure is intentionally and reasonably made or incurred for the common safety for the purpose of preserving from peril the property involved in a common maritime adventure.	**Rule A** There is a general average act when, and only when, any extraordinary sacrifice or expenditure is intentionally and reasonably made or incurred for the common safety for the purpose of preserving from peril the property involved in a common maritime adventure. General average sacrifices and expenditures shall be borne by the different contributing interests on the basis hereinafter provided.	**Rule A** There is a general average act when, and only when, any extraordinary sacrifice or expenditure is intentionally and reasonably made or incurred for the common safety for the purpose of preserving from peril the property involved in a common maritime adventure. General average sacrifices and expenditures shall be borne by the different contributing interests on the basis hereinafter provided.
Rule B General average sacrifices and expenses shall be borne by the different contributing interests on the basis herinafter provided.	**Rule B** There is a common maritime adventure when one or more vessels are towing or pushing another vessel or vessels, provided that they are all involved in commercial activities and not in a salvage operation. When measures are taken to preserve the vessels and their cargoes, if any, from a common peril, these Rules shall apply. A vessel is not in common peril with another vessel or vessels if by simply disconnecting from the other vessel or vessels she is in safety; but if the disconnection is itself a general average act the common maritime adventure continues.	**Rule B** There is a common maritime adventure when one or more vessels are towing or pushing another vessel or vessels, provided that they are all involved in commercial activities and not in a salvage operation. When measures are taken to preserve the vessels and their cargoes, if any, from a common peril, these Rules shall apply. A vessel is not in common peril with another vessel or vessels if by simply disconnecting from the other vessel or vessels she is in safety; but if the disconnection is itself a general average act the common maritime adventure continues.
Rule C Only such losses, damages or expenses which are the direct consequence of the general average act shall be allowed as general average.	**Rule C** Only such losses, damages or expenses which are the direct consequence of the general average act shall be allowed as general average.	**Rule C** Only such losses, damages or expenses which are the direct consequence of the general average act shall be allowed as general average.

† Where the 2004 Rules differ from the 1994 Rules, the 2004 Rules are printed in italics.

York-Antwerp Rules (1890)	York-Antwerp Rules (1924)	York-Antwerp Rules (1950)
	Damage or loss sustained by the ship or cargo through delay on the voyage, and indirect loss from the same cause, such as demurrage and loss of market, shall not be admitted as general average.	Loss or damage sustained by the ship or cargo through delay, whether on the voyage or subsequently, such as demurrage, and any indirect loss whatsoever, such as loss of market, shall not be admitted as general average.
	Rule D Rights to contribution in general average shall not be affected, though the event which gave rise to the sacrifice or expenditure may have been due to the fault of one of the parties to the adventure; but this shall not prejudice any remedies which may be open against that party for such fault.	**Rule D** Rights to contribution in general average shall not be affected, though the event which gave rise to the sacrifice or expenditure may have been due to the fault of one of the parties to the adventure; but this shall not prejudice any remedies which may be open against that party for such fault.
	Rule E The onus of proof is upon the party claiming in general average to show that the loss or expense claimed is properly allowable as general average.	**Rule E** The onus of proof is upon the party claiming in general average to show that the loss or expense claimed is properly allowable as general average.
	Rule F Any extra expense incurred in place of another expense which	**Rule F** Any extra expense incurred in place of another expense which

York-Antwerp Rules (1974)	York-Antwerp Rules (1994)	York-Antwerp Rules (2004)
Loss or damage sustained by the ship or cargo through delay, whether on the voyage or subsequently, such as demurrage, and any indirect loss whatsoever, such as loss of market, shall not be admitted as general average.	In no case shall there be any allowance in general average for losses, damages or expenses incurred in respect of damage to the environment or in consequence of the escape or release of pollutant substances from tinl property involved in the common maritime adventure. Demurrage, loss of market, and any loss or damage sustained or expense incurred by reason of delay, whether on the voyage or subsequently, and any indirect loss whatsoever, shall not be admitted as general average.	In no case shall there be any allowance in general average for losses, damages or expenses incurred in respect of damage to the environment or in consequence of the escape or release of pollutant substances from tinl property involved in the common maritime adventure. Demurrage, loss of market, and any loss or damage sustained or expense incurred by reason of delay, whether on the voyage or subsequently, and any indirect loss whatsoever, shall not be *allowed* as general average.
Rule D	**Rule D**	**Rule D**
Rights to contribution in general average shall not be affected, though the event which gave rise to the sacrifice or expenditure may have been due to the fault of one of the parties to the adventure, but this shall not prejudice any remedies which may be open against or to that party for such fault.	Rights to contribution in general average shall not be affected, though the event which gave rise to the sacrifice or expenditure may have been due to the fault of one of the parties to the adventure, but this shall not prejudice any remedies or defences which may be open against or to that party in respect of such fault.	Rights to contribution in general average shall not be affected, though the event which gave rise to the sacrifice or expenditure may have been due to the fault of one of the parties to the adventure, but this shall not prejudice any remedies or defences which may be open against or to that party in respect of such fault.
Rule E	**Rule E**	**Rule E**
The onus of proof is upon the party claiming in general average to show that the loss or expense claimed is properly allowable as general average.	The onus of proof is upon the party claiming in general average to show that the loss or expense claimed is properly allowable as general average. All parties claiming in general average shall give notice in writing to the average adjuster of the loss or expense in respect of which they claim contribution within 12 months of the date of the termination of the common maritime adventure. Failing such notification, or if within 12 months of a request for the same any of the parties shall fail to supply evidence in support of a notified claim, or particulars of value in respect of a contributory interest, the average adjuster shall be at liberty to estimate the extent of the allowance or the contributory value on the basis of the information available to him, which estimate may be challenged only on the ground that it is manifestly incorrect.	The onus of proof is upon the party claiming in general average to show that the loss or expense claimed is properly allowable as general average. All parties claiming in general average shall give notice in writing to the average adjuster of the loss or expense in respect of which they claim contribution within 12 months of the date of the termination of the common maritime adventure. Failing such notification, or if within 12 months of a request for the same any of the parties shall fail to supply evidence in support of a notified claim, or particulars of value in respect of a contributory interest, the average adjuster shall be at liberty to estimate the extent of the allowance or the contributory value on the basis of the information available to him, which estimate may be challenged only on the ground that it is manifestly incorrect.
Rule F	**Rule F**	**Rule F**
Any extra expense incurred in place of another expense which	Any additional expense incurred in place of another expense	Any additional expense incurred in place of another expense which

York-Antwerp Rules (1890)	York-Antwerp Rules (1924)	York-Antwerp Rules (1950)
	would have been allowable as general average shall be deemed to be general average and so allowed without regard to the saving, if any, to other interests, but only up to the amount of the general average expense avoided.	would have been allowable as general average shall be deemed to be general average and so allowed without regard to the saving, if any, to other interests, but only up to the amount of the general average expense avoided.
	Rule G General average shall be adjusted as regards both loss and contribution upon the basis of values at the time and place when and where the adventure ends. This rule shall not affect the determination of the place at which the average statement is to be made up.	**Rule G** General average shall be adjusted as regards both loss and contribution upon the basis of values at the time and place when and where the adventure ends. This rule shall not affect the determination of the place at which the average statement is to be made up.
Rule I. Jettison of Deck Cargo No jettison of deck cargo shall be made good as general average.	**Rule I. Jettison of Cargo** No jettison of cargo shall be made good as general average, unless such cargo is carried in accordance with the recognised custom of the trade.	**Rule I. Jettison of Cargo** No jettison of cargo shall be made good as general average, unless such cargo is carried in accordance with the recognised custom of the trade.
Rule II. Damage by Jettison and Sacrifice for the Common Safety Damage done to a ship and cargo, or either of them, by or in consequence of a sacrifice made for the common safety, and by	**Rule II. Damage by Jettison and Sacrifice for the Common Safety** Damage done to a ship and cargo, or either of them, by or in consequence of a sacrifice made for the common safety, and by	**Rule II. Damage by Jettison and Sacrifice for the Common Safety** Damage done to a ship and cargo, or either of them, by or in consequence of a sacrifice made for the common safety, and by water which

York-Antwerp Rules (1974)	York-Antwerp Rules (1994)	York-Antwerp Rules (2004)
would have been allowable as general average shall be deemed to be general average and so allowed without regard to the saving, if any, to other interests, but only up to the amount of the general average expense avoided.	which would have been allowable as general average shall be deemed to be general average and so allowed, but only up to the amount of the general average expense avoided.	would have been allowable as general average shall be deemed to be general average and so allowed without regard to the saving, if any, to other interests, but only up to the amount of the general average expense avoided.
Rule G	**Rule G**	**Rule G**
General average shall be adjusted as regards both loss and contribution upon the basis of values at the time and place when and where the adventure ends. This rule shall not affect the determination of the place at which the average statement is to be made up.	General average shall be adjusted as regards both loss and contribution upon the basis of values at the time and place when and where the adventure ends. This rule shall not affect the determination of the place at which the average statement is to be made up. When a ship is at any port or place in circumstances which would give rise to an allowance in general average under the provisions of Rules X and XI, and the cargo or part thereof is forwarded to destination by other means, rights and liabilities in general average shall, subject to cargo interest, being notified if practicable, remain as nearly as possible the same as they would have been in the absence of such forwarding, as if the adventure had continued in the original ship for so long as justifiable under the contract of affreightment and the applicable law. The proportion attaching to cargo of the allowances made in general average by reason of applying the third paragraph of this Rule shall not exceed the cost which would have been borne by the owners of the cargo if the cargo had been forwarded at their expense.	General average shall be adjusted as regards both loss and contribution upon the basis of values at the time and place when and where the adventure ends. This rule shall not affect the determination of the place at which the average statement is to be made up. When a ship is at any port or place in circumstances which would give rise to an allowance in general average under the provisions of Rules X and XI, and the cargo or part thereof is forwarded to destination by other means, rights and liabilities in general average shall, subject to cargo interest, being notified if practicable, remain as nearly as possible the same as they would have been in the absence of such forwarding, as if the adventure had continued in the original ship for so long as justifiable under the contract of affreightment and the applicable law. The proportion attaching to cargo of the allowances made in general average by reason of applying the third paragraph of this Rule shall not exceed the cost which would have been borne by the owners of the cargo if the cargo had been forwarded at their expense.
Rule I. Jettison of Deck Cargo No jettison of cargo shall be made good as general average, unless such cargo is carried in accordance with the recognised custom of the trade.	**Rule I. Jettison of Cargo** No jettison of cargo shall be made good as general average, unless such cargo is carried in accordance with the recognised custom of the trade.	**Rule I. Jettison of Cargo** No jettison of cargo shall be *allowed* as general average, unless such cargo is carried in accordance with the recognised custom of the trade.
Rule II. Damage by Jettison and Sacrifice for the Common Safety Damage done to a ship and cargo, or either of them, by or in consequence of a sacrifice made for the common safety, and by water which	**Rule II. Loss or Damage by Sacrifices for the Common Safety** Loss of or damage to the property involved in the common maritime adventure by or in consequence of a sacrifice made	**Rule II. Loss or Damage by Sacrifices for the Common Safety** Loss of or damage to the property involved in the common maritime adventure by or in consequence of a sacrifice made for

York-Antwerp Rules (1890)	York-Antwerp Rules (1924)	York-Antwerp Rules (1950)
water which goes down a ship's hatches opened or other opening made for the purpose of making a jettison for the common safety, shall be made good as general average.	water which goes down a ship's hatches opened or other opening made for the purpose of making a jettison for the common safety, shall be made good as general average.	goes down a ship's hatches opened or other opening made for the purpose of making a jettison for the common safety, shall be made good as general average.
Rule III. Extinguishing Fire on Shipboard Damage done to a ship and cargo, or either of them, by water or otherwise, including damage by beaching or scuttling a burning ship, in extinguishing a fire on board the ship, shall be made good as general average; except that no compensation shall be made for damage to such portions of the ship and bulk cargo, or to such separate packages of cargo, as have been on fire.	**Rule III. Extinguishing Fire on Shipboard** Damage done to a ship and cargo, or either of them, by water or otherwise, including damage by beaching or scuttling a burning ship, in extinguishing a fire on board the ship, shall be made good as general average; except that no compensation shall be made for damage to such portions of the ship and bulk cargo, or to such separate packages of cargo, as have been on fire.	**Rule III. Extinguishing Fire on Shipboard** Damage done to a ship and cargo, or either of them, by water or otherwise, including damage by beaching or scuttling a burning ship, in extinguishing a fire on board the ship, shall be made good as general average; except that no compensation shall be made for damage to such portions of the ship and bulk cargo, or to such separate packages of cargo, as have been on fire.
Rule IV. Cutting away Wreck Loss or damage caused by cutting away the wreck or remains of spars, or of other things which have previously been carried away by sea-peril, shall not be made good as general average.	**Rule IV. Cutting away Wreck** Loss or damage caused by cutting away the wreck or remains of spars, or of other things which have previously been carried away by sea-peril, shall not be made good as general average.	**Rule IV. Cutting away Wreck** Loss or damage caused by cutting away the wreck or remains of spars, or of other things which have previously been carried away by sea-peril, shall not be made good as general average.
Rule V. Voluntary Stranding When a ship is intentionally run on shore, and the circumstances are such that if that course were not adopted, she would inevitably sink or drive on shore or on rocks, no loss or damage caused to the ship, cargo and freight, or any of them by such intentional running on shore shall be made good as general average. But in all other cases where a ship is intentionally run on shore for the common safety, the consequent loss or damage shall be allowed as general average.	**Rule V. Voluntary Stranding** When a ship is intentionally run on shore, and the circumstances are such that if that course were not adopted, she would inevitably drive on shore or on rocks, no loss or damage caused to the ship, cargo and freight, or any of them by such intentional running on shore shall be made good as general average. But in all other cases where a ship is intentionally run on shore for the common safety, the consequent loss or damage shall be allowed as general average.	**Rule V. Voluntary Stranding** When a ship is intentionally run on shore, and the circumstances are such that if that course were not adopted, she would inevitably drive on shore or on rocks, no loss or damage caused to the ship, cargo and freight, or any of them by such intentional running on shore shall be made good as general average, but loss or damage incurred in refloating such a ship shall be allowed as general average. In all other cases where a ship is intentionally run on shore for the common safety, the consequent loss or damage shall be allowed as general average.
Rule VI. Carrying Press of Sail. Damage to or Loss of Sails Damage to or loss of sails and spars, or either of them, caused by forcing a ship off the ground or by driving her higher up the ground, for the common safety, shall be made good as general average; but where a ship is afloat, no loss or damage caused	**Rule VI. Carrying Press of Sail. Damage to or Loss of Sails** Damage to or loss of sails and spars, or either of them, caused by forcing a ship off the ground or by driving her higher up the ground, for the common safety, shall be made good as general average; but where a ship is afloat, no loss or damage caused	**Rule VI. Carrying Press of Sail. Damage to or Loss of Sails** Damage to or loss of sails and spars, or either of them, caused by forcing a ship off the ground or by driving her higher up the ground, for the common safety, shall be made good as general average; but where a ship is afloat, no loss or damage caused

York-Antwerp Rules (1974)	York-Antwerp Rules (1994)	York-Antwerp Rules (2004)
goes down a ship's hatches opened or other opening made for the purpose of making a jettison for the common safety, shall be made good as general average.	for the common safety, and by water which goes down a ship's hatches opened or other opening made for the purpose of making a jettison for the common safety, shall be made good as general average.	the common safety, and by water which goes down a ship's hatches opened or other opening made for the purpose of making a jettison for the common safety, shall be *allowed* as general average.
Rule III. Extinguishing Fire on Shipboard Damage done to a ship and cargo, or either of them, by water or otherwise, including damage by beaching or scuttling a burning ship, in extinguishing a fire on board the ship, shall be made good as general average; except that no compensation shall be made for damage by smoke or heat however caused.	**Rule III. Extinguishing Fire on Shipboard** Damage done to a ship and cargo, or either of them, by water or otherwise, including damage by beaching or scuttling a burning ship, in extinguishing a fire on board the ship, shall be made good as general average; except that no compensation shall be made for damage by smoke or heat however caused or by heat of the fire.	**Rule III. Extinguishing Fire on Shipboard** Damage done to a ship and cargo, or either of them, by water or otherwise, including damage by beaching or scuttling a burning ship, in extinguishing a fire on board the ship, shall be *allowed* as general average; except that no *allowance* shall be made for damage by smoke however caused or by heat of the fire.
Rule IV. Cutting away Wreck Loss or damage sustained by cutting away the wreck or parts of the ship which have previously been carried away by accident shall not be made good as general average.	**Rule IV. Cutting away Wreck** Loss or damage sustained by cutting away the wreck or parts of the ship which have previously been carried away by accident shall not be made good as general average.	**Rule IV. Cutting away Wreck** Loss or damage sustained by cutting away wreck or parts of the ship which have *been* previously carried away *or are effectively lost* by accident shall not be *allowed* as general average.
Rule V. Voluntary Stranding When a ship is intentionally run on shore for the common safety, whether or not she might have been driven on shore, the consequent loss or damage shall be allowed in general average.	**Rule V. Voluntary Stranding** When a ship is intentionally run on shore for the common safety, whether or not she might have been driven on shore, the consequent loss or damage to the property involved in the common maritime adventure shall be allowed in general average.	**Rule V. Voluntary Stranding** When a ship is intentionally run on shore for the common safety, whether or not she might have been driven on shore, the consequent loss or damage to the property involved in the common maritime adventure shall be allowed in general average.
Rule VI. Salvage Remuneration Expenditure incurred by the parties to the adventure on account of salvage, whether under contract or otherwise, shall be allowed in general average to the extent that the salvage operations were undertaken for the purpose of preserving from peril the property	**Rule VI. Salvage Remuneration** (a) Expenditure incurred by the parties to the adventure in the nature of salvage, whether under contract or otherwise, shall be allowed in general average provided that the salvage operations were carried out for the purpose of preserving from peril	**Rule VI. Salvage Remuneration** *a. Salvage payments, including interest thereon and legal fees associated with such payments, shall lie where they fall and shall not be allowed in general average, save only that if one party to the salvage shall have paid all or any of the proportion of salvage (including*

York-Antwerp Rules (1890)	York-Antwerp Rules (1924)	York-Antwerp Rules (1950)
to the ship, cargo and freight, or any of them, by carrying a press of sail, shall be made good as general average.	to the ship, cargo and freight, or any of them, by carrying a press of sail, shall be made good as general average.	to the ship, cargo and freight, or any of them, by carrying a press of sail, shall be made good as general average

York-Antwerp Rules (1974)	York-Antwerp Rules (1994)	York-Antwerp Rules (2004)
involved in the common maritime adventure. **York-Antwerp Rules (1974) as Amended 1990** (a) Expenditure incurred by the parties to the adventure in the nature of salvage, whether under contract or otherwise, shall be allowed in general average provided that the salvage operations were carried out for the purpose of preserving from peril the property involved in the common maritime adventure. Expenditure allowed in general average shall include any salvage remuneration in which the skill and efforts of the salvors in preventing or minimising damage to the environment such as is referred to in Art.13 paragraph 1 (b) of the International Convention on Salvage, 1989 have been taken into account. (b) Special compensation payable to a salvor by the shipowner under Art. 14 of the said Convention to the extent specified in paragraph 4 of that Article or under any other provisions similar in substance shall not be allowed in general average.	the property involved in the common maritime adventure. Expenditure allowed in general average shall include any salvage remuneration in which the skill and efforts of the salvors in preventing or minimising damage to the environment such as is referred to in Art. 13 paragraph 1(b) of the International Convention on Salvage, 1989 have been taken into account. (b) Special compensation payable to a salvor by the shipowner under Art. 14 of the said Convention to the extent specified in paragraph 4 of that Article or under any other provisions similar in substance shall not be allowed in general average.	*interest and legal fees) due from another party (calculated on the basis of salved values and not general average contributory values), the unpaid contribution to salvage due from that other party shall be credited in the adjustment to the party that has paid it, and debited to the party on whose behalf the payment was made.* *b. Salvage payments referred to in paragraph (a) above shall include any salvage remuneration in which the skill and efforts of the salvors in preventing or minimising damage to the environment such as is referred to in Article 13 paragraph 1(b) of the International Convention on Salvage 1989 have been taken into account.* *c. Special compensation payable to a salvor by the shipowner under Article 14 of the said Convention to the extent specified in paragraph 4 of that Article or under any other provision similar in substance (such as SCOPIC) shall not be allowed in general average and shall not be considered a salvage payment as referred to in paragraph (a) of this Rule.*

York-Antwerp Rules (1890)	York-Antwerp Rules (1924)	York-Antwerp Rules (1950)
Rule VII. Damage to Engines in Refloating a Ship Damage caused to machinery and boilers of a ship, which is ashore and in a position of peril, in endeavouring to refloat, shall be allowed in general average, when shown to have arisen from an actual intention to float the ship for the common safety at the risk of such damage.	**Rule VII. Damage to Engines in Refloating a Ship** Damage caused to machinery and boilers of a ship, which is ashore and in a position of peril, in endeavouring to refloat, shall be allowed in general average, when shown to have arisen from an actual intention to float the ship for the common safety at the risk of such damage; but where a ship is afloat no loss or damage caused by working the machinery and boilers shall be made good as general average.	**Rule VII. Damage to Machinery and Boilers** Damage caused to machinery and boilers of a ship, which is ashore and in a position of peril, in endeavouring to refloat, shall be allowed in general average when shown to have arisen from an actual intention to float the ship for the common safety at the risk of such damage; but where a ship is afloat no loss or damage caused by working the machinery and boilers, including loss or damage due to compounding of engines or such measures, shall in any circumstances be made good as general average.
Rule VIII. Expenses Lightening a Ship when Ashore, and Consequent Damage When a ship is ashore and, in order to float her, cargo, bunker coals and ship's stores, or any of them are discharged, the extra cost of lightening, lighter hire and re-shipping (if incurred), and the loss or damage sustained thereby, shall be admitted as general average.	**Rule VIII. Expenses Lightening a Ship when Ashore, and Consequent Damage** When a ship is ashore and cargo and ship's fuel and stores or any of them are discharged as a general average act, the extra cost of lightening, lighter hire and re-shipping (if incurred), and the loss or damage sustained thereby, shall be admitted as general average.	**Rule VIII. Expenses Lightening a Ship when Ashore, and Consequent Damage** When a ship is ashore and cargo and ship's fuel and stores or any of them are discharged as a general average act, the extra cost of lightening, lighter hire and re-shipping (if incurred), and the loss or damage sustained thereby, shall be admitted as general average.
Rule IX. Cargo, Ship's Materials and Stores Burnt for Fuel Cargo, ship's materials and stores, or any of them, necessarily burnt for fuel for the common safety at a time of peril, shall be admitted as general average, when and only when an ample supply of fuel had been provided; but the estimated quantity of coals that would have been consumed, calculated at the price current at the ship's last port of departure at the date of her leaving, shall be charged to the shipowner and credited to the general average.	**Rule IX. Ship's Materials and Stores Burnt for Fuel** Ship's materials and stores, or any of them, necessarily burnt for fuel for the common safety at a time of peril, shall be admitted as general average, when and only when an ample supply of fuel had been provided; but the estimated quantity of fuel that would have been consumed, calculated at the price current at the ship's last port of departure at the date of her leaving, shall be credited to the general average.	**Rule IX. Ship's Materials and Stores Burnt for Fuel** Ship's materials and stores, or any of them, necessarily burnt for fuel for the common safety at a time of peril, shall be admitted as general average, when and only when an ample supply of fuel had been provided; but the estimated quantity of fuel that would have been consumed, calculated at the price current at the ship's last port of departure at the date of her leaving, shall be credited to the general average.

York-Antwerp Rules (1974)	York-Antwerp Rules (1994)	York-Antwerp Rules (2004)
Rule VII. Damage to Machinery and Boilers Damage caused to any machinery and boilers of a ship which is ashore and in a position of peril, in endeavouring to refloat, shall be allowed in general average when shown to have arisen from an actual intention to float the ship for the common safety at the risk of such damage; but where a ship is afloat no loss or damage caused by working the propelling machinery and boilers shall in any circumstances be made good as general average.	**Rule VII. Damage to Machinery and Boilers** Damage caused to any machinery and boilers of a ship which is ashore and in a position of peril, in endeavouring to refloat, shall be allowed in general average when shown to have arisen from an actual intention to float the ship for the common safety at the risk of such damage; but where a ship is afloat no loss or damage caused by working the propelling machinery and boilers shall in any circumstances be made good as general average.	**Rule VII. Damage to Machinery and Boilers** Damage caused to any machinery and boilers of a ship which is ashore and in a position of peril, in endeavouring to refloat, shall be allowed in general average when shown to have arisen from an actual intention to float the ship for the common safety at the risk of such damage; but where a ship is afloat no loss or damage caused by working the propelling machinery and boilers shall in any circumstances be *allowed* as general average.
Rule VIII. Expenses Lightening a Ship when Ashore, and Consequent Damage When a ship is ashore and cargo and ship's fuel and stores or any of them are discharged as a general average act, the extra cost of lightening, lighter hire and re-shipping (if incurred), and the loss or damage sustained thereby, shall be admitted as general average.	**Rule VIII. Expenses Lightening a Ship when Ashore, and Consequent Damage** When a ship is ashore and cargo and ship's fuel and stores or any of them are discharged as a general average act, the extra cost of lightening, lighter hire and re-shipping (if incurred), and any loss or damage to the property invoked in the common maritime adventure in consequence thereof, shall be admitted as general average.	**Rule VIII. Expenses Lightening a Ship when Ashore and Consequent Damage** When a ship is ashore and cargo and ship's fuel and stores or any of them are discharged as a general average act, the extra cost of lightening, lighter hire and reshipping (if incurred), and any loss or damage to the property involved in the common maritime adventure in consequence thereof, shall be *allowed* as general average.
Rule IX. Ship's Materials and Stores Burnt for Fuel Ship's materials and stores, or any of them, necessarily burnt for fuel for the common safety at a time of peril, shall be admitted as general average, when and only when an ample supply of fuel had been provided; but the estimated quantity of fuel that would have been consumed, calculated at the price current at the ship's last port of departure at the date of her leaving, shall be credited to the general average.	**Rule IX. Cargo, Ship's Materials and Stores Burnt for Fuel** Cargo, ship's materials and stores, or any of them, necessarily used for fuel for the common safety at a time of peril, shall be admitted as general average, but when such an allowance is made for the cost of ship's materials and stores the general average shall be credited with the estimated cost of the fuel which would otherwise have been consumed in prosecuting the intended voyage.	**Rule IX. Cargo, Ship's Materials and Stores used for Fuel** Cargo, ship's materials and stores, or any of them, necessarily used for fuel for the common safety at a time of peril shall be *allowed* as general average, but when such an allowance is made for the cost of ship's materials and stores the general average shall be credited with the estimated cost of the fuel which would otherwise have been consumed in prosecuting the intended voyage.

York-Antwerp Rules (1890)	York-Antwerp Rules (1924)	York-Antwerp Rules (1950)
Rule X. Expenses at Port of Refuge, etc.	**Rule X. Expenses at Port of Refuge, etc.**	**Rule X. Expenses at Port of Refuge, etc.**
(a) When a ship shall have entered a port or place of refuge, or shall have returned to her port or place of loading, in consequence of accident, sacrifice, or other extraordinary circumstances, which render that necessary for the common safety, the expenses of entering such port or place shall be admitted as general average; and when she shall have sailed thence with her original cargo, or a part of it, the corresponding expenses of leaving such port or place consequent upon such entry or return, shall likewise be admitted as general average.	(a) When a ship shall have entered a port or place of refuge, or shall have returned to her port or place of loading, in consequence of accident, sacrifice or other extraordinary circumstances, which render that necessary for the common safety, the expenses of entering such port or place shall be admitted as general average; and when she shall have sailed thence with her original cargo, or a part of it, the corresponding expenses of leaving such port or place consequent upon such entry or return, shall likewise be admitted as general average.	(a) When a ship shall have entered a port or place of refuge, or shall have returned to her port or place of loading, in consequence of accident, sacrifice or other extraordinary circumstances, which render that necessary for the common safety, the expenses of entering such port or place shall be admitted as general average; and when she shall have sailed thence with her original cargo, or a part of it, the corresponding expenses of leaving such port or place consequent upon such entry or return shall likewise be admitted as general average. When a ship is at any port or place of refuge and is necessarily removed to another port or place because repairs cannot be carried out in the first port or place, the provisions of this Rule shall be applied to the second port or place as if it were a port or place of refuge. The provisions of Rule XI shall be applied to the prolongation of the voyage occasioned by such removal.
(b) The cost of discharging cargo from a ship, whether at a port or place of loading, call or refuge, shall be admitted as general average, when the discharge was necessary for the common safety or to enable damage to the ship, caused by sacrifice or accident during the voyage, to be repaired, if the repairs were necessary for the safe prosecution of the voyage.	(b) The cost of handling on board or discharging cargo, fuel or stores, whether at a port or place of loading, call or refuge, shall be admitted as general average when the handling or discharge was necessary for the common safety or to enable damage to the ship caused by sacrifice or accident to be repaired, if the repairs were necessary for the safe prosecution of the voyage.	(b) The cost of handling on board or discharging cargo, fuel or stores whether at a port or place of loading, call or refuge, shall be admitted as general average when the handling or discharge was necessary for the common safety or to enable damage to the ship caused by sacrifice or accident to be repaired, if the repairs were necessary' for the safe prosecution of the voyage.

York-Antwerp Rules (1974)	York-Antwerp Rules (1994)	York-Antwerp Rules (2004)
Rule X. Expenses at Port of Refuge, etc.	**Rule X. Expenses at Port of Refuge, etc.**	**Rule X. Expenses at Port Of Refuge, etc.**
(a) When a ship shall have entered a port or place of refuge, or shall have returned to her port or place of loading, in consequence of accident, sacrifice or other extraordinary circumstances, which render that necessary for the common safety, the expenses of entering such port or place shall be admitted as general average; and when she shall have sailed thence with her original cargo, or a part of it, the corresponding expenses of leaving such port or place consequent upon such entry or return shall likewise be admitted as general average.	(a) When a ship shall have entered a port or place of refuge, or shall have returned to her port or place of loading, in consequence of accident, sacrifice or other extraordinary circumstances, which render that necessary for the common safety, the expenses of entering such port or place shall be admitted as general average; and when she shall have sailed thence with her original cargo, or a part of it, the corresponding expenses of leaving such port or place consequent upon such entry or return shall likewise be admitted as general average.	a. (i) When a ship shall have entered a port or place of refuge or shall have returned to her port or place of loading in consequence of accident, sacrifice or other extraordinary circumstances which render that necessary for the common safety, the expenses of entering such port or place shall be *allowed* as general average; and when she shall have sailed thence with her original cargo, or a part of it, the corresponding expenses of leaving such port or place consequent upon such entry or return shall likewise be *allowed* as general average.
When a ship is at any port or place of refuge and is necessarily removed to another port or place because repairs cannot be carried out in the first port or place, the provisions of this Rule shall be applied to the second port or place as if it were a port or place of refuge and the cost of such removal including temporary repairs and towage shall be admitted as general average. The provisions of Rule XI shall be applied to the prolongation of the voyage occasioned by such removal.	When a ship is at any port or place of refuge and is necessarily removed to another port or place because repairs cannot be carried out in the first port or place, the provisions of this Rule shall be applied to the second port or place as if it were a port or place of refuge and the cost of such removal including temporary repairs and towage shall be admitted as general average. The provisions of Rule XI shall be applied to the prolongation of the voyage occasioned by such removal.	(ii) When a ship is at any port or place of refuge and is necessarily removed to another port or place *of refuge* because repairs cannot be carried out in the first port or place, the provisions of this Rule shall be applied to the second port or place *of refuge* as if it were a port or place of refuge and the cost of such removal including temporary repairs and towage shall be *allowed* as general average. The provisions of Rule XI shall be applied to the prolongation of the voyage occasioned by such removal.
(b) The cost of handling on board or discharging cargo, fuel or stores whether at a port or place of loading, call or refuge, shall be admitted as general average, when the handling or discharge was necessary for the common safety or to enable damage to the ship caused by sacrifice or accident to be repaired, if the repairs were necessary for the safe prosecution of the voyage, except in cases where the damage to the ship is discovered at a port or place of loading or call without any accident or other extraordinary circumstances connected with such damage having taken place during the voyage.	(b) The cost of handling on board or discharging cargo, fuel or stores whether at a port or place of loading, call or refuge, shall be admitted as general average, when the handling or discharge was necessary for the common safety or to enable damage to the ship caused by sacrifice or accident to be repaired, if the repairs were necessary for the safe prosecution of the voyage, except in cases where the damage to the ship is discovered at a port or place of loading or call without any accident or other extraordinary circumstances connected with such damage having taken place during the voyage.	b. (i) The cost of handling on board or discharging cargo, fuel or stores whether at a port or place of loading, call or refuge, shall be allowed as general average, when the handling or discharge was necessary for the common safety or to enable damage to the ship caused by sacrifice or accident to be repaired, if the repairs were necessary for the safe prosecution of the voyage, except in cases where the damage to the ship is discovered at a port or place of loading or call without any accident or other extraordinary circumstances connected with such damage having taken place during the voyage.
The cost of handling on board or discharging cargo, fuel or stores shall not be admissible as general average when incurred solely for the	The cost of handling on board or discharging cargo, fuel or stores shall not be admissible as general average when incurred solely for	(*ii*) The cost of handling on board or discharging cargo, fuel or stores shall not be *allowable* as general average when incurred solely for the

York-Antwerp Rules (1890)	York-Antwerp Rules (1924)	York-Antwerp Rules (1950)
(c) Whenever the cost of discharging cargo from a ship is admissible as general average, the cost of reloading and storing such cargo on board the said ship, together with all storage charges on such cargo, shall likewise be so admitted. But when the ship is condemned or does not proceed on her original voyage, no storage expenses incurred after the date of the ship's condemnation or of the abandonment of the voyage shall be admitted as general average.	(c) Whenever the cost of handling or discharging cargo, fuel or stores is admissible as general average, the cost of reloading and stowing such cargo, fuel or stores on board the ship, together with all storage charges (including fire insurance, if incurred) on such cargo, fuel or stores, shall likewise be so admitted. But when the ship is condemned or does not proceed on her original voyage, no storage expenses incurred after the date of the ship's condemnation or of the abandonment of the voyage shall be admitted as general average. In the event of the condemnation of the ship or the abandonment of the voyage before completion of discharge of cargo, storage expenses, as above, shall be admitted as general average up to date of completion of discharge.	(c) Whenever the cost of handling or discharging cargo, fuel or stores is admissible as general average, the cost of reloading and stowing such cargo, fuel or stores on board the ship, together with all storage charges (including insurance, if reasonably incurred) on such cargo, fuel or stores, shall likewise be so admitted. But when the ship is condemned or does not proceed on her original voyage, no storage expenses incurred after the date of the ship's condemnation or of the abandonment of the voyage shall be admitted as general average. In the event of the condemnation of the ship or the abandonment of the voyage before completion of discharge of cargo, storage expenses, as above, shall be admitted as general average up to the date of completion of discharge.
(d) If a ship under average be in a port or place at which it is practicable to repair her, so as to enable her to carry on the whole cargo, and if, in order to save expenses, either she is towed thence to some other port or place of repair or to her destination, or the cargo or a portion of it is transhipped by another ship, or otherwise forwarded, then the extra cost of such towage, transhipment, and forwarding, or any of them (up to the amount of the extra expense saved) shall be payable by the several parties to the adventure in proportion to the extraordinary expense saved.	(d) If a ship under average be in a port or place at which it is practicable to repair her, so as to enable her to carry on the whole cargo, and if, in order to save expenses, either she is towed thence to some other port or place of repair or to her destination, or the cargo or a portion of it is transhipped by another ship, or otherwise forwarded, then the extra cost of such towage, transhipment and forwarding, or any of them (up to the amount of the extra expense saved) shall be payable by the several parties to the adventure in proportion to the extraordinary expense saved.	(d) If a ship under average be in a port or place at which it is practicable to repair her, so as to enable her to carry on the whole cargo, and if, in order to save expense, either she is towed thence to some other port or place of repair or to her destination, or the cargo or a portion of it is transhipped by another ship, or otherwise forwarded, then the extra cost of such towage, transhipment and forwarding, or any of them (up to the amount of the extra expense saved) shall be payable by the several parties to the adventure in proportion to the extraordinary expense saved.
Rule XI. Wages and Maintenance of Crew in Port of Refuge, etc.	**Rule XI. Wages and Maintenance of Crew in Port of Refuge, etc.** (For corresponding provision, see Rule XX, *infra.*)	**Rule XI. Wages and Maintenance of Crew and other Expenses bearing up for and in a Port of Refuge, etc.** (a) Wages and maintenance of master, officers and crew reasonably incurred and fuel and stores consumed during the prolongation of the voyage occasioned by a ship entering a port or place of refuge or returning to her port or place of

York-Antwerp Rules (1974)	York-Antwerp Rules (1994)	York-Antwerp Rules (2004)
purpose of restowage due to shifting during the voyage, unless such restowage is necessary for the common safety. (c) Whenever the cost of handling or discharging cargo, fuel or stores is admissible as general average, the costs of storage, including insurance if reasonably incurred, reloading and stowing of such cargo, fuel or stores shall likewise be admitted as general average. But when the ship is condemned or does not proceed on her original voyage, storage expenses shall be admitted as general average only up to the date of the ship's condemnation or of the abandonment of the voyage or up to the date of completion of discharge of cargo if the condemnation or abandonment takes place before that date.	the purpose of restowage due to shifting during the voyage, unless such restowage is necessary for the common safety. (c) Whenever the cost of handling or discharging cargo, fuel or stores is admissible as general average, the costs of storage, including insurance if reasonably incurred, reloading and stowing of such cargo, fuel or stores shall likewise be admitted as general average. The provisions of Rule XI shall be applied to the extra period of detention occasioned by such reloading or restowing. But when the ship is condemned or does not proceed on her original voyage, storage expenses shall be admitted as general average only up to the date of the ship's condemnation or of the abandonment of the voyage or up to the date of completion of discharge of cargo if the condemnation or abandonment takes place before that date.	purpose of restowage due to shifting during the voyage, unless such restowage is necessary for the common safety. c. Whenever the cost of handling or discharging cargo, fuel or stores is *allowable* as general average, the costs of storage, including insurance if reasonably incurred, reloading and stowing of such cargo, fuel or stores shall likewise be *allowed* as general average. The provisions of Rule XI shall be applied to the extra period of detention occasioned by such reloading or restowing. But when the ship is condemned or does not proceed on her original voyage, storage expenses shall be *allowed* as general average only up to the date of the ship's condemnation or of the abandonment of the voyage or up to the date of completion of discharge of cargo if the condemnation or abandonment takes place before that date.
Rule XI. Wages and Maintenance of Crew and other Expenses bearing up for and in a Port of Refuge, etc. (a) Wages and maintenance of master, officers and crew reasonably incurred and fuel and stores consumed during the prolongation of the voyage occasioned by a ship entering a port or place of refuge or returning to her port or place of	**Rule XI. Wages and Maintenance of Crew and other Expenses bearing up for and in a Port of Refuge, etc.** (a) Wages and maintenance of master, officers and crew reasonably incurred and fuel and stores consumed during the prolongation of the voyage occasioned by a ship entering a port or place of refuge or returning to her port or place of	**Rule XI. Wages and Maintenance of Crew and other Expenses *putting in to and at a* Port of Refuge, etc.** a. Wages and maintenance of master, officers and crew reasonably incurred and fuel and stores consumed during the prolongation of the voyage occasioned by a ship entering a port or place of refuge or returning to her port or place of

York-Antwerp Rules (1890)	York-Antwerp Rules (1924)	York-Antwerp Rules (1950)
		loading shall be admitted as general average when the expenses of entering such port or place are allowable in general average in accordance with Rule X (a).
When a ship shall have entered or been detained in any port or place under the circumstances, or for the purposes of the repairs, mentioned in Rule X, the wages, payable to the master, officers and crew together with the cost of maintenance of the same, during the extra period of detention in such port or place until the ship shall or should have been made ready to proceed upon her voyage, shall be admitted as general average. But when the ship is condemned or does not proceed on her original voyage, the wages and maintenance of the master, officers and crew, incurred after the date of the ship's condemnation or of the abandonment of the voyage, shall not be admitted as general average.	When a ship shall have entered or been detained in any port or place under the circumstances, or for the purposes of repairs mentioned in Rule X, the wages payable to the master, officers and crew, together with the cost of maintenance of the same, during the extra period of detention in such port or place until the ship shall or should have been made ready to proceed upon her voyage, shall be admitted as general average. But when the ship is condemned or does not proceed on her original voyage, the wages and maintenance of the master, officers and crew, incurred after the date of the ship's condemnation or of the abandonment of the voyage, shall not be admitted as general average. In the event of the condemnation of the ship or the abandonment of the voyage before completion of discharge of cargo, wages and maintenance of crew, as above, shall be admitted as general average up to the date of completion of discharge.	(b) When a ship shall have entered or been detained in any port or place in consequence of accident, sacrifice or other extraordinary circumstances which render that necessary for the common safety, or to enable damage to the ship caused by sacrifice or accident to be repaired, if the repairs were necessary for the safe prosecution of the voyage, the wages and maintenance of the master, officers and crew reasonably incurred during the extra period of detention in such port or place until the ship shall or should have been made ready to proceed upon her voyage, shall be admitted in general average. When the ship is condemned or does not proceed on her original voyage, the extra period of detention shall be deemed not to extend beyond the date of the ship's condemnation or of the abandonment of the voyage or, if discharge of cargo is not then completed, beyond the date of completion of discharge. Fuel and stores consumed during the extra period of detention shall be admitted as general average, except such fuel and stores as are consumed in effecting repairs not allowable in general average. Port charges incurred during the extra period of detention shall likewise be admitted as general average except such charges as are incurred solely by reason of repairs not allowable in general average.

York-Antwerp Rules (1974)	York-Antwerp Rules (1994)	York-Antwerp Rules (2004)
loading shall be admitted as general average when the expenses of entering such port or place are allowable in general average in accordance with Rule X (a).	loading shall be admitted as general average when the expenses of entering such port or place are allowable in general average in accordance with Rule X (a).	loading shall be *allowed* as general average when the expenses of entering such port or place are allowable as general average in accordance with Rule X (a).
(b) When a ship shall have entered or been detained in any port or place in consequence of accident, sacrifice or other extraordinary circumstances which render that necessary for the common safety, or to enable damage to the ship caused by sacrifice or accident to be repaired, if the repairs were necessary for the safe prosecution of the voyage, the wages and maintenance of the master, officers and crew reasonably incurred during the extra period of detention in such port or place until the ship shall or should have been made ready to proceed upon her voyage, shall be admitted in general average.	(b) When a ship shall have entered or been detained in any port or place in consequence of accident, sacrifice or other extraordinary circumstances which render that necessary for the common safety, or to enable damage to the ship caused by sacrifice or accident to be repaired, if the repairs were necessary for the safe prosecution of the voyage, the wages and maintenance of the master, officers and crew reasonably incurred during the extra period of detention in such port or place until the ship shall or should have been made ready to proceed upon her voyage, shall be admitted in general average.	b. *For the purpose of this and the other Rules wages shall include all payments made to or for the benefit of the master, officers and crew, whether such payments be imposed by law upon the shipowners or be made under the terms of articles of employment.*
Provided that when damage to the ship is discovered at a port or place of loading or call without any accident or other extraordinary circumstance connected with such damage having taken place during the voyage, then the wages and maintenance of master, officers and crew and fuel and stores consumed during the extra detention for repairs to damages so discovered shall not be admissible as general average, even if the repairs are necessary for the safe prosecution of the voyage.	Fuel and stores consumed during the extra period of detention shall be admitted as general average, except such fuel and stores as are consumed in effecting repairs not allowable in general average.	
When the ship is condemned or does not proceed on her original voyage, wages and maintenance of the master, officers and crew and fuel and stores consumed shall be admitted as general average only up to the date of the ships condemnation or of the abandonment of the voyage or up to the date of completion of discharge of cargo if the condemnation or abandonment takes place before that date.	Port charges incurred during the extra period of detention shall likewise be admitted as general average except such charges as are incurred solely by reason of repairs not allowable in general average.	
Fuel and stores consumed during the extra period of detention shall be admitted as general average, except such fuel and stores as are consumed in effecting repairs not allowable in general average.	Provided that when damage to the ship is discovered at a port or place of loading or call without any accident or other extraordinary circumstance connected with such damage having taken place during the voyage, then the wages and maintenance of master, officers and crew and fuel and stores consumed and port charges incurred during the extra detention for repairs to damages so discovered shall not be admissible as general average, even if the repairs are necessary for the safe prosecution of the voyage.	

York-Antwerp Rules (1890)	York-Antwerp Rules (1924)	York-Antwerp Rules (1950)
		(c) For the purpose of this and the other Rules wages shall include all payments made to or for the benefit of the master, officers and crew, whether such payments be imposed by law upon the shipowners or be made under the terms or articles of employment.

York-Antwerp Rules (1974)	York-Antwerp Rules (1994)	York-Antwerp Rules (2004)
Port charges incurred during the extra period of detention shall likewise be admitted as general average except such charges as are incurred solely by reason of repairs not allowable in general average.	When the ship is condemned or does not proceed on her original voyage, the wages and maintenance of the master, officers and crew and fuel and stores consumed and port charges shall be admitted as general average only up to the date of the ship's condemnation or of the abandonment of the voyage or up to the date of completion of discharge of cargo if the condemnation or abandonment takes place before that date.	
(c) For the purpose of this and the other Rules wages shall include all payments made to or for the benefit of the master, officers and crew, whether such payments be imposed by law upon the shipowners or be made under the terms or articles of employment.	(c) For the purpose of this and the other Rules wages shall include all payments made to or for the benefit of the master, officers and crew, whether such payments be imposed by law upon the shipowners or be made under the terms or articles of employment.	c. (i) When a ship shall have entered or been detained in any port or place in consequence of accident, sacrifice or other extraordinary circumstances which render that necessary for the common safety, or to enable damage to the ship caused by sacrifice or accident to be repaired, if the repairs were necessary for the safe prosecution of the voyage, *fuel and stores consumed* during the extra period of detention in such port or place until the ship shall or should have been made ready to proceed upon her voyage, shall be *allowed* as general average, except such fuel and stores as are consumed in effecting repairs not allowable in general average. (ii) Port charges incurred during the extra period of detention shall likewise be *allowed* as general average except such charges as are incurred solely by reason of repairs not allowable in general average. (iii) Provided that when damage to the ship is discovered at a port or place of loading or call without any accident or other extraordinary circumstance connected with such damage having taken place during the voyage, then fuel and stores consumed and port charges incurred during the extra detention for repairs to damages so discovered shall not be *allowable* as general average, even if the repairs are necessary for the safe prosecution of the voyage. (iv) When the ship is condemned or does not proceed on her original voyage, fuel and stores consumed and port charges shall be *allowed* as general average only up to the date of the ship's condemnation or of the abandonment of the voyage or up to

York-Antwerp Rules (1890)	York-Antwerp Rules (1924)	York-Antwerp Rules (1950)
		(d) When overtime is paid to the master, officers or crew for maintenance of the ship or repairs, the cost of which is not allowable in general average, such over time shall be allowed in general average only up to the saving in expense which would have been incurred and admitted as general average, had such overtime not been incurred.
Rule XII. Damage to Cargo in Discharging, etc. Damage done to or loss of cargo necessarily caused in the act of discharging, storing, reloading and stowing, shall be made good as general average when and only when the cost of those measures respectively is admitted as general average.	**Rule XII. Damage to Cargo in Discharging, etc.** Damage to or loss of cargo, fuel or stores caused in the act of handling, discharging, storing, reloading and stowing shall be made good as general average, when and only when the cost of those measures respectively is admitted as general average.	**Rule XII. Damage to Cargo in Discharging, etc.** Damage to or loss of cargo, fuel or stores caused in the act of handling, discharging, storing, reloading and stowing shall be made good as general average, when and only when the cost of those measures respectively is admitted as general average.
Rule XIII. Deductions from Cost of Repairs In adjusting claims for general average, repairs to be allowed in general average shall be subject to the following deductions in respect of "new for old", viz.:	**Rule XIII. Deductions from Cost of Repairs** In adjusting claims for general average, repairs to be allowed in general average shall be subject to the following deductions in respect of "new for old", viz.:	**Rule XIII. Deductions from Cost of Repairs** In adjusting claims for general average, repairs to be allowed in general average shall be subject to deductions in respect of "new for old" according to the following rules, where old material or parts are replaced by new.

York-Antwerp Rules (1974)	York-Antwerp Rules (1994)	York-Antwerp Rules (2004)
		the date of completion of discharge of cargo if the condemnation or abandonment takes place before that date.
(d) When overtime is paid to the master, officers or crew for maintenance of the ship or repairs, the cost of which is not allowable in general average, such over time shall be allowed in general average only up to the saving in expense which would have been incurred and admitted as general average, had such overtime not been incurred.	(d) The cost of measures undertaken to prevent or minimise damage to the environment shall he allowed in general average when incurred in any or all of the following circumstances: (i) as part of an operation performed for the common safety which, had it been undertaken by a party outside the common maritime adventure, would have entitled such party to a salvage reward; (ii) as a condition of entry into or departure from any port or place in the circumstances prescribed in Rule X (a); (iii) as a condition of remaining at any port or place in the circumstances prescribed in Rule X (a), provided that when there is an actual escape or release of pollutant substances the cost of any additional measures required on that account to prevent or minimise pollution or environmental damage shall not be allowed as general average: (iv) necessarily in connection with the discharging, storing or reloading of cargo whenever the cost of those operations is admissible as general average.	(d) The cost of measures undertaken to prevent or minimise damage to the environment shall he allowed in general average when incurred in any or all of the following circumstances: (i) as part of an operation performed for the common safety which, had it been undertaken by a party outside the common maritime adventure, would have entitled such party to a salvage reward; (ii) as a condition of entry into or departure from any port or place in the circumstances prescribed in Rule X (a); (iii) as a condition of remaining at any port or place in the circumstances prescribed in Rule XI (c), provided that when there is an actual escape or release of pollutant substances the cost of any additional measures required on that account to prevent or minimise pollution or environmental damage shall not be allowed as general average: (iv) necessarily in connection with the discharging, storing or reloading of cargo whenever the cost of those operations is allowable as general average.
Rule XII. Damage to Cargo in Discharging, etc Damage to or loss of cargo, fuel or stores caused in the act of handling, discharging, storing, reloading and stowing shall be made good as general average, when and only when the cost of those measures respectively is admitted as general average.	**Rule XII. Damage to Cargo in Discharging, etc.** Damage to or loss of cargo, fuel or stores sustained in consequence of their handling, discharging, storing, reloading and stowing shall be made good as general average, when and only when the cost of those measures respectively is admitted as general average.	**Rule XII. Damage to Cargo in Discharging, etc.** Damage to or loss of cargo, fuel or stores sustained in consequence of their handling, discharging, storing, reloading and stowing shall be allowed as general average, when and only when the cost of those measures respectively is allowed as general average.
Rule XIII. Deductions from Cost of Repairs Repairs to be allowed in general average shall not be subject to deductions in respect of "new for old" where old material or parts are replaced by new unless the ship is over fifteen years old in which case there shall be a deduction of one	**Rule XIII. Deductions from Cost of Repairs** Repairs to be allowed in general average shall not be subject to deductions in respect of "new for old" where old material or parts are replaced by new unless the ship is over fifteen years old in which case there shall be a	**Rule XIII. Deductions from Cost of Repairs** *a.* Repairs to be allowed in general average shall not be subject to deductions in respect of "new for old" where old material or parts are replaced by new unless the ship is over fifteen years old in which case there shall be a deduction of one

York-Antwerp Rules (1890)	York-Antwerp Rules (1924)	York-Antwerp Rules (1950)
In the case of iron or steel ships, from date of original register to the date of accident: *(Reference is requested to any of the 7th/11th editions of this work for precise details of the deductions made.)*	In the case of iron or steel ships, from date of original register to the date of accident: *(Reference is requested to any of the 7th/11th editions of this work for precise details of the deductions made.)*	The deductions to be regulated by the age of the ship from date of original register to the date of accident, except for provisions and stores, insulation, life-and similar boats, gyro compass equipment, wireless, direction finding, echo sounding and similar apparatus, machinery and boilers for which the deductions shall be regulated by the age of the particular parts to which they apply. No deduction to be made in respect of provisions, stores and gear which have not been in use. The deductions shall be made from the cost of new material or parts, including labour and establishment charges, but excluding cost of opening up. Drydock and slipway dues and costs of shifting the ship shall be allowed in full. No cleaning and painting of bottom to be allowed, if the bottom has not been painted within six months previous to the date of the accident. *(Reference is requested to any of the 7th/11th editions of this work for precise details of the deductions made.)*
Rule XIV. Temporary Repairs No deductions "new for old"' shall be made from the cost of temporary repairs of damage allowable as general average.	**Rule XIV. Temporary Repairs** Where temporary repairs are effected to a ship at a port of loading, call or refuge, for the common safety, or of damage caused by general average sacrifice, the cost of such repairs shall be admitted as general average; but where temporary repairs of accidental damage are effected merely to enable the adventure to be completed, the cost of such repairs shall be admitted as general average only up to the saving in expense which would have been incurred and allowed in general average had such repairs not been effected there. No deductions "new for old" shall be made from the cost of	**Rule XIV. Temporary Repairs** Where temporary repairs are effected to a ship at a port of loading, call or refuge, for the common safety, or of damage caused by general average sacrifice, the cost of such repairs shall be admitted as general average. Where temporary repairs of accidental damage are effected merely to enable the adventure to be completed, the cost of such repairs shall be admitted as general average without regard to the saving, if any, to other interests, but only up to the saving in expense which would have been incurred and allowed in general average if such repairs had not been effected there.

York-Antwerp Rules (1974)	York-Antwerp Rules (1994)	York-Antwerp Rules (2004)
third. The deductions shall be regulated by the age of the ship from the 31st December of the year of completion of construction to the date of the general average act, except for insulation, life and similar boats, communications and navigational apparatus and equipment, machinery and boilers for which the deductions shall be regulated by the age of the particular parts to which they apply. The deductions shall be made only from the cost of the new material or parts when finished and ready to be installed in the ship. No deduction shall be made in respect of provisions, stores, anchors and chain cables. Drydock and slipway dues and costs of shifting the ship shall be allowed in full. The costs of cleaning, painting or coating of bottom shall not be allowed in general average unless the bottom has been painted or coated within the twelve months preceding the date of the general average act in which case one half of such costs shall be allowed.	deduction of one third. The deductions shall be regulated by the age of the ship from the 31st December of the year of completion of construction to the date of the general average act, except for insulation, life and similar boats, communications and navigational apparatus and equipment, machinery and boilers for which the deductions shall be regulated by the age of the particular parts to which they apply. No deduction shall be made in respect of provisions, stores, anchors and chain cables. The deductions shall be made only from the cost of the new material or parts when finished and ready to be installed in the ship. Drydock and slipway dues and costs of shifting the ship shall be allowed in full. The costs of cleaning, painting or coating of bottom shall not be allowed in general average unless the bottom has been painted or coated within the twelve months preceding the date of the general average act in which case one half of such costs shall be allowed.	third. The deductions shall be regulated by the age of the ship from the 31st December of the year of completion of construction to the date of the general average act, except for insulation, life and similar boats, communications and navigational apparatus and equipment, machinery and boilers for which the deductions shall be regulated by the age of the particular parts to which they apply. *b.* The deductions shall be made only from the cost of the new material or parts when finished and ready to be installed in the ship. No deduction shall be made in respect of provisions, stores, anchors and chain cables. Drydock and slipway dues and costs of shifting the ship shall be allowed in full. *c.* The costs of cleaning, painting or coating of bottom shall not be allowed in general average unless the bottom has been painted or coated within the twelve months preceding the date of the general average act in which case one half of such costs shall be allowed.
Rule XIV. Temporary Repairs	**Rule XIV. Temporary Repairs**	**Rule XIV. Temporary Repairs**
Where temporary repairs are effected to a ship at a port of loading, call or refuge, for the common safety, or of damage caused by general average sacrifice, the cost of such repairs shall be admitted as general average. Where temporary repairs of accidental damage are effected in order to enable the adventure to be completed, the cost of such repairs shall be admitted as general average without regard to the saving, if any, to other interests, but only up to the saving in expense which would have been incurred and allowed in general average if such repairs had not been effected there.	Where temporary repairs are effected to a ship at a port of loading, call or refuge, for the common safety, or of damage caused by general average sacrifice, the cost of such repairs shall be admitted as general average. Where temporary repairs of accidental damage are effected in order to enable the adventure to be completed, the cost of such repairs shall be admitted as general average without regard to the saving, if any. to other interests, but only up to the saving in expense which would have been incurred and allowed in general average if such repairs had not been effected there.	*a.* Where temporary repairs are effected to a ship at a port of loading, call or refuge, for the common safety, or of damage caused by general average sacrifice, the cost of such repairs shall be *allowed* as general average. *b.* Where temporary repairs of accidental damage are effected in order to enable the adventure to be completed, the cost of such repairs shall be allowed as general average without regard to the saving, if any, to other interests, but only up to the saving in expense which would have been incurred and allowed in general average if such repairs had not been effected there. *Provided that for the purposes of this paragraph only, the*

York-Antwerp Rules (1890)	York-Antwerp Rules (1924)	York-Antwerp Rules (1950)
	temporary repairs allowable as general average.	No deductions " 'new for old" shall be made from the cost of temporary repairs allowable as general average.
Rule XV. Loss of Freight Loss of freight arising from damage to or loss of cargo shall be made good as general average, either when caused by a general average act, or when the damage to or loss of cargo is so made good.	**Rule XV. Loss of Freight** Loss of freight arising from damage to or loss of cargo shall be made good as general average, either when caused by a general average act, or when the damage to or loss of cargo is so made good. Deduction shall be made from the amount of gross freight lost, of the charges which the owner thereof would have incurred to earn such freight, but has, in consequence of the sacrifice, not incurred.	**Rule XV. Loss of Freight** Loss of freight arising from damage to or loss of cargo shall be made good as general average, either when caused by a general average act, or when the damage to or loss of cargo is so made good. Deduction shall be made from the amount of gross freight lost, of the charges which the owner thereof would have incurred to earn such freight, but has, in consequence of the sacrifice, not incurred.
Rule XVI. Amount to be made good for Cargo Lost or Damaged by Sacrifice The amount to be made good as general average for damage or loss of goods sacrificed shall be the loss which the owner of the goods has sustained thereby, based on the market values at the date of the arrival of the vessel or at the termination of the adventure.	**Rule XVI. Amount to be made good for Cargo Lost or Damaged by Sacrifice** The amount to be made good as general average for damage to or loss of goods sacrificed shall be the loss which the owner of the goods has sustained thereby, based on the market values at the date of the arrival of the vessel or at the termination of the adventure where this ends at a place other than the original destination. Where goods so damaged are sold after arrival, the loss to be made good in general average shall be calculated by applying to the sound value on the date of arrival of the vessel the percentage of loss resulting from a	**Rule XVI. Amount to be made for Cargo Lost or Damaged by Sacrifice** The amount to be made good as general average for damage to or loss of goods sacrificed shall be the loss which the owner of the goods has sustained thereby, based on the market values at the last day of discharge of the vessel or at the termination of the adventure where this ends at a place other than the original destination. Where goods so damaged are sold and the amount of the damage has not been otherwise agreed, the loss to be made good in general average shall be the difference between the net proceeds of sale and the net sound value at the last day of

York-Antwerp Rules (1974)	York-Antwerp Rules (1994)	York-Antwerp Rules (2004)
No deductions "new for old" shall be made from the cost of temporary repairs allowable as general average.	No deductions "new for old" shall be made from the cost of temporary repairs allowable as general average.	*cost of temporary repairs falling for consideration shall be limited to the extent that the cost of temporary repairs effected at the port of loading, call or refuge, together with either the cost of permanent repairs eventually effected or, if unrepaired at the time of the adjustment, the reasonable depreciation in the value of the vessel at the completion of the voyage. exceeds the cost of permanent repairs had they been effected at the port of loading, call or refuge.* *c.* No deductions "new for old" shall be made from the cost of temporary repairs allowable as general average.
Rule XV. Loss of Freight Loss of freight arising from damage to or loss of cargo shall be made good as general average, either when caused by a general average act, or when the damage to or loss of cargo is so made good. Deduction shall be made from the amount of gross freight lost, of the charges which the owner thereof would have incurred to earn such freight, but has, in consequence of the sacrifice, not incurred.	**Rule XV. Loss of Freight** Loss of freight arising from damage to or loss of cargo shall be made good as general average, either when caused by a general average act. or when the damage to or loss of cargo is so made good. Deduction shall be made from the amount of gross freight lost, of the charges which the owner thereof would have incurred to earn such freight, but has, in consequence of the sacrifice, not incurred.	**Rule XV. Loss of Freight** Loss of freight arising from damage to or loss of cargo shall be allowed as general average, either when caused by a general average act, or when the damage to or loss of cargo is so *allowed.* Deduction shall be made from the amount of gross freight lost, of the charges which the owner thereof would have incurred to earn such freight, but has, in consequence of the sacrifice, not incurred.
Rule XVI. Amount to be made good for Cargo Lost or Damaged by Sacrifice The amount to be made good as general average for damage to or loss of cargo sacrificed shall be the loss which has been sustained thereby, based on the value at the time of discharge, ascertained from the commercial invoice rendered to the receiver or if there is no such invoice from the shipped value. The value at the time of discharge shall include the cost of insurance and freight except in so far as such freight is at the risk of interests other than the cargo. Where cargo so damaged is sold and the amount of the damage has not been otherwise agreed, the	**Rule XVI. Amount to be made good for Cargo Lost or Damaged by Sacrifice** The amount to be made good as general average for damage to or loss of cargo sacrificed shall be the loss which has been sustained thereby, based on the value at the time of discharge, ascertained from the commercial invoice rendered to the receiver or if there is no such invoice from the shipped value. The value at the time of discharge shall include the cost of insurance and freight except in so far as such freight is at the risk of interests other than the cargo. Where cargo so damaged is sold and the amount of the damage has not been otherwise agreed, the	**Rule XVI. Amount to be Allowed for Cargo Lost or Damaged by Sacrifice** *a.* The amount to be allowed as general average for damage to or loss of cargo sacrificed shall be the loss which has been sustained thereby based on the value at the time of discharge, ascertained from the commercial invoice rendered to the receiver or if there is no such invoice from the shipped value. The value at the time of discharge shall include the cost of insurance and freight except insofar as such freight is at the risk of interests other than the cargo. **b.** When cargo so damaged is sold and the amount of the damage has not been otherwise agreed,

York-Antwerp Rules (1890)	York-Antwerp Rules (1924)	York-Antwerp Rules (1950)
	comparison of the proceeds with the sound value on date of sale.	discharge of the vessel or at the termination of the adventure where this ends at a place other than the original destination.
Rule XVII. Contributory Values The contribution to a general average shall be made upon the actual values of the property at the termination of the adventure, to which shall be added the amount made good as general average for property sacrificed; deduction being made from the shipowner's freight and passage-money at risk, of such port charges and crew's wages as would not have been incurred had the ship and cargo been totally lost at the date of the general average act or sacrifice, and have not been allowed as general average; deduction being also made from the value of the property of all charges incurred in respect thereof subsequently to the general average act, except such charges as are allowed in general average. Passengers' luggage and personal effects, not shipped under bill of lading, shall not contribute in general average.	**Rule XVII. Contributory Values** The contribution to a general average shall be made upon the actual net values of the property at the termination of the adventure, to which values shall be added the amount made good as general average for property sacrificed, if not already included, deduction being made from the shipowner's freight and passage-money at risk, of such charges and crew's wages as would not have been incurred in earning the freight had the ship and cargo been totally lost at the date of the general average act and have not been allowed as general average; deduction being also made from the value of the property, of all charges incurred in respect thereof subsequently to the general average act, except such charges as are allowed in general average. Passengers' luggage and personal effects not shipped under bill of lading shall not contribute in general average.	**Rule XVII. Contributory Values** The contribution to a general average shall be made upon the actual net values of the property at the termination of the adventure, to which values shall be added the amount made good as general average for property sacrificed, if not already included, deduction being made from the shipowner's freight and passage money at risk, of such charges and crew's wages as would not have been incurred in earning the freight had the ship and cargo been totally lost at the date of the general average act and have not been allowed as general average; deductions being also made from the value of the property of all charges incurred in respect thereof subsequently to the general average act, except such charges as are allowed in general average. Passengers' luggage and personal effects not shipped under bill of lading shall not contribute in general average.

York-Antwerp Rules (1974)	York-Antwerp Rules (1994)	York-Antwerp Rules (2004)
loss to be made good in general average shall be the difference between the net proceeds of sale and the net sound value as computed in the first paragraph of this Rule.	loss to be made good in general average shall be the difference between the net proceeds of sale and the net sound value as computed in the first paragraph of this Rule.	the loss to be allowed in general average shall be the difference between the net proceeds of sale and the net sound value as computed in the first paragraph of this Rule.
Rule XVII. Contributory Values	**Rule XVII. Contributory Values**	**Rule XVII. Contributory Values**
The contribution to a general average shall be made upon the actual net values of the property at the termination of the adventure except that the value of cargo shall be the value at the time of discharge, ascertained from the commercial invoice rendered to the receiver or if there is no such invoice from the shipped value. The value of the cargo shall include the cost of insurance and freight unless and insofar as such freight is at the risk of interests other than the cargo, deducting therefrom any loss or damage suffered by the cargo prior to or at the time of discharge. The value of the ship shall be assessed without taking into account the beneficial or detrimental effect of any demise or time charterparty to which the ship may be committed.	The contribution to a general average shall be made upon the actual net values of the property at the termination of the adventure except that the value of cargo shall be the value at the time of discharge, ascertained from the commercial invoice rendered to the receiver or if there is no such invoice from the shipped value. The value of the cargo shall include the cost of insurance and freight unless and insofar as such freight is at the risk of interests other than the cargo, deducting therefrom any loss or damage suffered by the cargo prior to or at the time of discharge. The value of the ship shall be assessed without taking into account the beneficial or detrimental effect of any demise or time charterparty to which the ship may be committed.	a. (i) The contribution to a general average shall be made upon the actual net values of the property at the termination of the adventure except that the value of cargo shall be the value at the time of discharge, ascertained from the commercial invoice rendered to the receiver or if there is no such invoice from the shipped value. (ii) The value of the cargo shall include the cost of insurance and freight unless and insofar as such freight is at the risk of interests other than the cargo, deducting therefrom any loss or damage suffered by the cargo prior to or at the time of discharge. (iii) The value of the ship shall be assessed without taking into account the beneficial or detrimental effect of any demise or time charterparty to which the ship may be committed.
To these values shall be added the amount made good as general average for property sacrificed, if not already included, deduction being made from the freight and passage money at risk of such charges and crew's wages as would not have been incurred in earning the freight had the ship and cargo been totally lost at the date of the general average act and have not been allowed as general average; deduction being also made from the value of the property of all extra charges incurred in respect thereof subsequently to the general average act, except such charges as are allowed in general average.	To these values shall be added the amount made good as general average for property sacrificed, if not already included, deduction being made from the freight and passage money at risk of such charges and crew's wages as would not have been incurred in earning the freight had the ship and cargo been totally lost at the date of the general average act and have not been allowed as general average; deduction being also made from the value of the property of all extra charges incurred in respect thereof subsequently to the general average act, except such charges as are allowed in general average or fall upon the ship by virtue of an award for special compensation under Art.14 of the International Convention on Salvage, 1989 or under any other provision similar in substance.	b. To these values shall be added the amount allowed as general average for property sacrificed, if not already included, deduction being made from the freight and passage money at risk of such charges and crew's wages as would not have been incurred in earning the freight had the ship and cargo been totally lost at the date of the general average act and have not been allowed as general average; deduction being also made from the value of the property of all extra charges incurred in respect thereof subsequently to the general average act, except such charges as are allowed in general average or fall upon the ship by virtue of an award for special compensation under Art.14 of the International Convention on Salvage, 1989 or under any other provision similar in substance.
Where cargo is sold short of destination, however, it shall contribute upon the actual net proceeds of sale, with the addition of any amount made good as general average. Passengers' luggage and personal effects not shipped under bill of lading shall not contribute in general average.	In the circumstances envisaged in the third paragraph of Rule G, the cargo and other property shall	c. In the circumstances envisaged in the third paragraph of Rule G, the cargo and other property shall

York-Antwerp Rules (1890)	York-Antwerp Rules (1924)	York-Antwerp Rules (1950)
Rule XVIII. Adjustment Except as provided in the foregoing rules, the adjustment shall be drawn up in accordance with the law and practice that would have governed the adjustment had the contract of affreightment not contained a clause to pay general average according to these rules.	(No corresponding rule.)	(No corresponding rule.)
	Rule XVIII. Damage to Ship The amount to be allowed as general average for damage or loss to the ship, her machinery and/or gear when repaired or replaced shall be the actual reasonable cost of repairing or replacing such damage or loss, deductions being made as above (Rule XIII) when old material is replaced by new. When not repaired, the reasonable depreciation shall be allowed, not exceeding the estimated cost of repairs. Where there is an actual or constructive total loss of the ship the amount to be allowed as general average for damage or loss to the ship caused by a general average act shall be the estimated sound value of the ship after deducting therefrom the estimated cost of repairing damage which is not general average and the proceeds of sale, if any.	**Rule XVIII. Damage to Ship** The amount to be allowed as general average for damage or loss to the ship, her machinery and/or gear when repaired or replaced shall be the actual reasonable cost of repairing or replacing such damage or loss, subject to deduction in accordance with Rule XIII. When not repaired, the reasonable depreciation shall be allowed, not exceeding the estimated cost of repairs. Where there is an actual or constructive total loss of the ship the amount to be allowed as general average for damage or loss to the ship caused by a general average act shall be the estimated sound value of the ship after deducting therefrom the estimated cost of repairing damage which is not general average and the proceeds of sale, if any.

York-Antwerp Rules (1974)	York-Antwerp Rules (1994)	York-Antwerp Rules (2004)
	contribute on the basis of its value upon delivery at original destination unless sold or otherwise disposed of short of that destination, and the ship shall contribute upon its actual net value at the time of completion of discharge of cargo.	contribute on the basis of its value upon delivery at original destination unless sold or otherwise disposed of short of that destination, and the ship shall contribute upon its actual net value at the time of completion of discharge of cargo.
	Where cargo is sold short of destination, however, it shall contribute upon the actual net proceeds of sale, with the addition of any amount made good as general average.	d. Where cargo is sold short of destination, however, it shall contribute upon the actual net proceeds of sale, with the addition of any amount *allowed* as general average.
	Mails, passengers' luggage, personal effects and accompanied private motor vehicles shall not contribute in general average.	e. Mails, passengers' luggage, personal effects and accompanied private motor vehicles shall not contribute *to* general average.
(No corresponding rule.)	(No corresponding rule.)	(No corresponding rule.)
Rule XVIII. Damage to Ship	**Rule XVIII. Damage to Ship**	**Rule XVIII. Damage to Ship**
The amount to be allowed as general average for damage or loss to the ship, her machinery and/or gear caused by a general average act shall be as follows:	The amount to be allowed as general average for damage or loss to the ship, her machinery and/or gear caused by a general average act shall be as follows:	The amount to be allowed as general average for damage or loss to the ship, her machinery and/or gear caused by a general average act shall be as follows:
(a) When repaired or replaced,	(a) When repaired or replaced,	a. When repaired or replaced,
The actual reasonable cost of repairing or replacing such damage or loss, subject to deductions in accordance with Rule XIII:	The actual reasonable cost of repairing or replacing such damage or loss, subject to deductions in accordance with Rule XIII;	The actual reasonable cost of repairing or replacing such damage or loss, subject to deductions in accordance with Rule XIII;
(b) When not repaired or replaced,	(b) When not repaired or replaced,	b. When not repaired or replaced,
The reasonable depreciation arising from such damage or loss, but not exceeding the estimated cost of repairs. But where the ship is an actual total loss or when the cost of repairs of the damage would exceed the value of the ship when repaired, the amount to be allowed as general average shall be the difference between the estimated sound value of the ship after deducting therefrom the estimated cost of repairing damage which is not general average and the value of the ship in her damaged state which may be measured by the net proceeds of sale, if any.	The reasonable depreciation arising from such damage or loss, but not exceeding the estimated cost of repairs. But where the ship is an actual total loss or when the cost of repairs of the damage would exceed the value of the ship when repaired, the amount to be allowed as general average shall be the difference between the estimated sound value of the ship after deducting therefrom the estimated cost of repairing damage which is not general average and the value of the ship in her damaged state which may be measured by the net proceeds of sale, if any.	The reasonable depreciation arising from such damage or loss, but not exceeding the estimated cost of repairs. But where the ship is an actual total loss or when the cost of repairs of the damage would exceed the value of the ship when repaired, the amount to be allowed as general average shall be the difference between the estimated sound value of the ship after deducting therefrom the estimated cost of repairing damage which is not general average and the value of the ship in her damaged state which may be measured by the net proceeds of sale, if any.

York-Antwerp Rules (1890)	York-Antwerp Rules (1924)	York-Antwerp Rules (1950)
	Rule XIX. Undeclared or Wrongfully Declared Cargo Damage or loss caused to goods loaded without the knowledge of the shipowner or his agent or to goods wilfully mis-described at time of shipment shall not be allowed as general average, but such goods shall remain liable to contribute if saved. Damage or loss caused to goods which have been wrongfully declared on shipment at a value which is lower than their real value shall be contributed for at the declared value, but such goods shall contribute upon their actual value.	**Rule XIX. Undeclared or Wrongfully Declared Cargo** Damage or loss caused to goods loaded without the knowledge of the shipowner or his agent or to goods wilfully mis-described at time of shipment shall not be allowed as general average, but such goods shall remain liable to contribute if saved. Damage or loss caused to goods which have been wrongfully declared on shipment at a value which is lower than their real value shall be contributed for at the declared value, but such goods shall contribute upon their actual value.
	Rule XX. Expenses Bearing up for Port, etc. Fuel and stores consumed and wages and maintenance of master, officers and crew incurred, during the prolongation of the voyage occasioned by a ship entering a port or place of refuge or returning to her port or place of loading shall be admitted as general average when the expenses of entering such port or place are allowable in general average in accordance with Rule X (a). Fuel and stores consumed during extra detention in a port or place of loading, call or refuge shall also be allowed in general average for the period during which wages and maintenance of master, officers and crew are allowed in terms of Rule XI, except such fuel and stores as are consumed in effecting repairs not allowable in general average.	(Corresponding provisions are to be found in Rule XI, supra.)
	Rule XXI. Provision of Funds A commission of 2 per cent on general average disbursements shall be allowed in general average, but when the funds are not provided by any of the contributing interests, the necessary cost of obtaining the funds required by means of a bottomry bond or otherwise, or the loss sustained by owners of goods sold for the purpose, shall be allowed in general average.	**Rule XX. Provision of Funds** A commission of 2 per cent on general average disbursements, other than the wages and maintenance of master, officers and crew and fuel and stores not replaced during the voyage, shall be allowed in general average, but when the funds are not provided by any of the contributing interests, the necessary cost of obtaining the funds required by means of a bottomry bond or otherwise, or the loss sustained by owners of goods sold for the purpose, shall be allowed in general average.

York-Antwerp Rules (1974)	York-Antwerp Rules (1994)	York-Antwerp Rules (2004)
Rule XIX. Undeclared or Wrongfully Declared Cargo Damage or loss caused to goods loaded without the knowledge of the shipowner or his agent or to goods wilfully mis-described at time of shipment shall not be allowed as general average, but such goods shall remain liable to contribute if saved. Damage or loss caused to goods which have been wrongfully declared on shipment at a value which is lower than their real value shall be contributed for at the declared value, but such goods shall contribute upon their actual value.	**Rule XIX. Undeclared or Wrongfully Declared Cargo** Damage or loss caused to goods loaded without the knowledge of the shipowner or his agent or to goods wilfully mis-described at time of shipment shall not be allowed as general average, but such goods shall remain liable to contribute if saved. Damage or loss caused to goods which have been wrongfully declared on shipment at a value which is lower than their real value shall be contributed for at the declared value, but such goods shall contribute upon their actual value.	**Rule XIX. Undeclared or Wrongfully Declared Cargo** *a.* Damage or loss caused to goods loaded without the knowledge of the shipowner or his agent or to goods wilfully mis-described at time of shipment shall not be allowed as general average, but such goods shall remain liable to contribute, if saved. *b.* Damage or loss caused to goods which have been wrongfully declared on shipment at a value which is lower than their real value shall be contributed for at the declared value, but such goods shall contribute upon their actual value.
(Corresponding provisions are to be found in Rule XI, supra.)	(Corresponding provisions are to be found in Rule XI, supra.)	(Corresponding provisions are to be found in Rule XI, supra.)
Rule XX. Provision of Funds A commission of 2 per cent on general average disbursements, other than the wages and maintenance of master, officers and crew and fuel and stores not replaced during the voyage, shall be allowed in general average, but when the funds are not provided by any of the contributing interests, the necessary cost of obtaining the funds required by means of a bottomry bond or otherwise, or the loss sustained by owners of goods sold for the purpose, shall be allowed in general average.	**Rule XX. Provision of Funds** A commission of 2 per cent on general average disbursements, other than the wages and maintenance of master, officers and crew and fuel and stores not replaced during the voyage, shall be allowed in general average. The capital loss sustained by the owners of goods sold for the purpose of raising funds to defray general average disbursements shall be allowed in general average.	**Rule XX. Provision of Funds** *a.* The capital loss sustained by the owners of goods sold for the purpose of raising funds to defray general average disbursements shall be allowed in general average. *b.* The cost of insuring average disbursements shall also be *allowed* in general average.

York-Antwerp Rules (1890)	York-Antwerp Rules (1924)	York-Antwerp Rules (1950)
	The cost of insuring money advanced to pay for general average disbursements shall also be allowed in general average.	The cost of insuring money advanced to pay for general average disbursements shall also be allowed in general average.
	Rule XXII. Interest on Losses made good in General Average Interest shall be allowed on expenditure, sacrifices and allowances charged to general average at the legal rate per annum prevailing at the final port of destination at which the adventure ends, or where there is no recognised legal rate, at the rate of 5 per cent per annum, until the date of the general average statement, due allowance being made for any interim reimbursement from the contributory interests or from the general average deposit fund.	**Rule XXI. Interest on Losses made good in General Average** Interest shall be allowed on expenditure, sacrifices and allowances charged to general average at the rate of 5 per cent per annum, until the date of the general average statement, due allowance being made for any interim reimbursement from the contributory interests or from the general average deposit fund.
	Rule XXIII. Treatment of Cash Deposits Where cash deposits have been collected in respect of cargo's liability for general average, salvage or special charges, such deposits shall be paid into a special account, earning interest where possible in the joint names of two trustees (one to be nominated on behalf of the shipowner and the other on behalf of the depositors) in a bank to be approved by such trustees. The sum so deposited, together with accrued interest, if any, shall be held as security for and upon trust for payment to the parties entitled thereto of the general average, salvage or special charges payable by the cargo in respect of which the deposits have been collected. The trustees shall have power to make payments on account or refunds of deposits which may be certified to in writing by the average adjuster. Such deposits and payments or refunds shall be without prejudice to the ultimate liability of the parties.	**Rule XXII. Treatment of Cash Deposits** Where cash deposits have been collected in respect of cargo's liability for general average, salvage or special charges, such deposits shall be paid without any delay into a special account in the joint names of a representative nominated on behalf of the shipowner and a representative nominated on behalf of the depositors in a bank to be approved by both. The sum so deposited, together with accrued interest, if any, shall be held as security for payment to the parties entitled thereto of the general average, salvage or special charges payable by cargo in respect to which the deposits have been collected. Payments on account or refunds of deposits may be made, if certified to in writing by the average adjuster. Such deposits and payments or refunds shall be without prejudice to the ultimate liability of the parties.

York-Antwerp Rules (1974)	York-Antwerp Rules (1994)	York-Antwerp Rules (2004)
The cost of insuring money advanced to pay for general average disbursements shall also be allowed in general average.	The cost of insuring money advanced to pay for general average disbursements shall also be allowed in general average.	
Rule XXI. Interest on Losses made good in General Average Interest shall be allowed on expenditure, sacrifices and allowances charged to general average at the rate of 7 per cent per annum, until the date of the general average statement, due allowance being made for any interim reimbursement from the contributory interests or from the general average deposit fund.	**Rule XXI. Interest on Losses made good in General Average** Interest shall be allowed on expenditure, sacrifices and allowances in general average at the rate of 7 per cent per annum, until three months after the date of issue of the general average adjustment, due allowance being made for any payment on account by the contributory interests or from the general average deposit fund.	**Rule XXI. Interest on Losses *Allowed* in General Average** *a.* Interest shall be allowed on expenditure, sacrifices and allowances in general average until three months after the date of issue of the general average adjustment, due allowance being made for any payment on account by the contributory interests or from the general average deposit fund. *b. Each year the Assembly of the Comité Maritime International shall decide the rate of interest which shall apply. This rate shall be used for calculating interest accruing during the following calendar year.*
Rule XXII. Treatment of Cash Deposits here cash deposits have been collected in respect of cargo's liability for general average, salvage or special charges, such deposits shall be paid without any delay into a special account in the joint names of a representative nominated on behalf of the shipowner and a representative nominated on behalf of the depositors in a bank to be approved by both. The sum so deposited, together with accrued interest, if any, shall be held as security for payment to the parties entitled thereto of the general average, salvage or special charges payable by cargo in respect to which the deposits have been collected. Payments on account or refunds of deposits may be made, if certified to in writing by the average adjuster. Such deposits and payments or refunds shall be without prejudice to the ultimate liability of the parties.	**Rule XXII. Treatment of Cash Deposits** Where cash deposits have been collected in respect of cargo's liability for general average, salvage or special charges, such deposits shall be paid without any delay into a special account in the joint names of a representative nominated on behalf of the shipowner and a representative nominated on behalf of the depositors in a bank to be approved by both. The sum so deposited, together with accrued interest, if any, shall be held as security for payment to the parties entitled thereto of the general average, salvage or special charges payable by cargo in respect to which the deposits have been collected. Payments on account or refunds of deposits may be made, if certified to in writing by the average adjuster. Such deposits and payments or refunds shall be without prejudice to the ultimate liability of the parties.	**Rule XXII. Treatment of Cash Deposits** Where cash deposits have been collected in respect of cargo's liability for general average, salvage or special charges such deposits shall be paid without any delay into a special account in the joint names of a representative nominated on behalf of the shipowner and a representative nominated on behalf of the depositors in a bank to be approved by both. The sum so deposited together with accrued interest, if any, shall be held as security for payment to the parties entitled thereto of the general average, salvage or special charges payable by cargo in respect *of* which the deposits have been collected. Payments on account or refunds of deposits may be made if certified to in writing by the average adjuster. Such deposits and payments or refunds shall be without prejudice to the ultimate liability of the parties.

York-Antwerp Rules (1890)	York-Antwerp Rules (1924)	York-Antwerp Rules (1950)

York-Antwerp Rules (1974)	York-Antwerp Rules (1994)	York-Antwerp Rules (2004)
		Rule XXIII. Time Bar for Contributions to General Average *a. Subject always to any mandatory rule on time limitation contained in any applicable law:* *(i) Any rights to general average contribution, including any rights to claim under general average bonds and guarantees, shall be extinguished unless an action is brought by the party claiming such contribution within a period of one year after the date upon which the general average adjustment was issued. However, in no case shall such an action be brought after six years from the date of the termination of the common maritime adventure.* *(ii) These periods may be extended if the parties so agree after the termination of the common maritime adventure.* *b. This Rule shall not apply as between the parties to the general average and their respective insurers*

APPENDIX 3

RULES OF PRACTICE

ADOPTED BY THE ASSOCIATION OF AVERAGE ADJUSTERS UP TO 2007

(Only the Rules relating to or having some bearing on General Average are shown here. The references in parentheses are to the printed Annual Reports of the Association.)

NOTE. Some of the undermentioned Rules are, as indicated, "Customs of Lloyd's", now by resolution of the Association incorporated amongst the Rules of Practice. **70.01**

The preamble to the Customs was:

> "Nothing can be called a 'Custom of Lloyd's' which is determined by a decision of the superior courts; for whatever is thus sanctioned rests on a ground surer than Custom. A 'Custom of Lloyd's' then must relate to a point on which the law is doubtful, or not yet defined, but as to which, for practical convenience, it is necessary that there should be some uniform rule. By the term is here understood the Customs of English Adjusting, whether as affecting General or Particular Average."

SECTION A—GENERAL RULES

A2 INTEREST AND COMMISSION FOR ADVANCING FUNDS

(Proposed and Accepted 1906, p.21. Confirmed 1907, p.60.) **70.02**

That, in practice, interest and commission for advancing funds are only allowable in average when, proper and necessary steps having been taken to make a collection on account, an out-of- pocket expense for interest and/or commission for advancing funds is reasonably incurred.

A3 AGENCY COMMISSION AND AGENCY

(Proposed and Accepted 1906, p.21. Confirmed 1907, p.60.) **70.03**

That, in practice, neither commission (excepting bank commission) nor any charge by way of agency or remuneration for trouble is allowed to the shipowner in average, except in respect of services rendered on behalf of cargo when such services are not involved in the contract of affreightment.

A4 Duty of Adjusters in Respect of Cost of Repairs

70.04 (Proposed and Accepted 1879, p.24. Confirmed 1880, p.21.)

That in adjusting particular average on ship or general average which includes repairs, it is the duty of the adjuster to satisfy himself that such reasonable and usual precautions have been taken to keep down the cost of repairs as a prudent shipowner would have taken if uninsured.

A5 Claims on Ship's Machinery

70.05 (Proposed and Accepted 1890, p.32. Confirmed 1891, p.32.)

That in all claims on ship's machinery for repairs, no claim for a new propeller or new shaft shall be admitted into an adjustment, unless the adjuster shall obtain and insert into his statement evidence showing what has become of the old propeller or shaft.

A6 Water Casks (Custom of Lloyd's, 1876)

70.06 Water casks or tanks carried on a ship's deck are not paid for by underwriters as general or particular average; nor are warps or other articles when improperly carried on deck.

A7 Adjustment: Policies of Insurance and Names of Underwriters

70.07 (Proposed and Accepted 1968, p.25. Confirmed 1969, p.22.)

That no adjustment shall be drawn up showing the amount of payments by or to the underwriters, unless the policies or copies of the policies of insurance or certificates of insurance, for which the statement is required, be produced to the average adjusters. Such statement shall set out sufficient details of the underwriters interested and the amounts due on the respective policies produced.

SECTION B—GENERAL AVERAGE

B1 Basis of Adjustment

70.08 (Proposed and Accepted 1889, p.60. Confirmed 1890, p.33.)
(Addition Proposed and Accepted 1899, p.29. Confirmed 1900, p.20.)

That in any adjustment of general average not made in accordance with British law it shall be prefaced on what principle or according to what law the adjustment has been made, and the reason for so adjusting the claim shall be set forth.

In all cases the adjuster shall give particulars in a prominent position in the average statement of the clause or clauses contained in the charter-party and/or bills of lading with reference to the adjustment of general average.

B9 Claims Arising out of Deficiency of Fuel

(Proposed and Accepted 1899, p.50. Confirmed 1900, p.25.) **70.09**

That in adjusting general average arising out of deficiency of fuel, the facts on which the general average is based shall be set forth in the adjustment, including the material dates and distances, and particulars of fuel supplies and consumption.

B24 Contributory Value of Ship

(Proposed and Accepted 1899, p.41. Confirmed 1900, p.20.) **70.10**

That in any adjustment of general average there shall be set forth the certificate on which the contributory value of the ship is based or, if there be no such certificate, the information adopted in lieu thereof, and any amount made good shall be specified.

B25 Contributory Value of Freight

(Original Rule of Practice 1873—Part) **70.11**
(Referred to a Special Committee 1908—Report 1909.)
(Amended 1968, p.22. Confirmed 1969, p.22.)

That in any adjustment of general average there shall be set forth the amount of the gross freight and the freight advanced, if any; also the charges and wages deducted and any amount made good.

B26 Vessel in Ballast and under Charter: Contributing Interests

(Proposed and Accepted 1945, p.53. Confirmed 1946, p.45.) **70.12**

For the purpose of ascertaining the liability of Underwriters on British policies of insurance, the following provisions shall apply:

When a vessel is proceeding in ballast to load under a voyage charter entered into by the shipowner before the general average act, the interests contributing to the general average shall be the vessel, such items of stores and equipment as belong to parties other than the owners of the vessel (e.g. bunkers, wireless installation and navigational instruments) and the freight earned under the voyage charter computed in the usual way after deduction of contingent expenses subsequent to the general average act. Failing a prior termination of the adventure, the place where the adventure shall be deemed to end and at which the values for contribution to general average shall be calculated is the final port of discharge of the cargo carried under the charter but in the event of the prior loss of the vessel and freight, or either of them, the general average shall attach to any surviving interest or interests including freight advanced at the loading port deducting therefrom contingent expenses subsequent to the general average act.

When a vessel is proceeding in ballast under a time charter alone or a time charter and a voyage charter entered into by the time charterer, the general average shall attach to the vessel and such items of stores and equipment as are indicated above. Failing a prior termination of the adventure, the adventure shall be deemed to end and the values for contribution to general average calculated at the first loading port upon the commencement of loading cargo.

When the charter to which the shipowner is a party provides for York-Antwerp Rules, the general average shall be adjusted in accordance with those Rules and British law and practice and without regard to the law and practice of any foreign port at which the adventure may terminate; and in the interpretation of Rule XI it shall be immaterial whether the extra period of detention takes place at a port of loading, call or refuge, provided that the detention is in consequence of accident, sacrifice or other extraordinary circumstance occurring whilst the vessel is in ballast.

In practice neither time charter hire, as such, nor time charterer's voyage freight shall contribute to general average.

B27 Chartered Freight (ulterior): Contribution to General Average

70.13 (Proposed and Accepted 1891, p.35, Confirmed 1892, p.27.)

That when at the time of a general average act the vessel has on board cargo shipped under charter-party or bills of lading, and is also under a separate charter to load another cargo after the cargo then in course of carriage has been discharged, the ulterior chartered freight shall not contribute to the general average.

B28 Deductions from Freight at Charterer's Risk

70.14 (Original Rule of Practice, 1873.)
(Referred to a Special Committee 1908—Report 1909.)
(Amended 1968, p.23. Confirmed 1969, p.22.)

That freight at the risk of the charterer shall be subject to no deduction for wages and charges, except in the case of charters in which the wages or charges are payable by the charterer, in which case such freight shall be governed by the same rule as freight at the risk of the shipowner.

B29 Forwarding Charges on Advanced Freight

70.15 (Original Rule of Practice, 1873.)

That in case of wreck, the cargo being forwarded to its destination, the charterer, who has paid a lump sum on account of freight, which is not to be returned in the event of the vessel being lost, shall not be liable for any portion of the forwarding freight and charges, when the same are less than the balance of freight payable to the shipowner at the port of destination under the original charter-party.

B30 Sacrifice for the Common Safety: Direct Liability of Underwriters

70.16 (Proposed and Accepted 1890), p.42. Confirmed 1891, p.34.)

That in case of general average sacrifice there is, under ordinary policies of insurance, a direct liability of an underwriter on ship for loss of or damage to ship's materials, and of an underwriter on goods or freight, for loss of or damage to goods or loss of freight so sacrificed as a general average loss; that such loss not being particular average is not taken into account in computing the memorandum percentages, and that the direct liability of an underwriter for such loss is consequently unaffected by the memorandum or any other warranty respecting particular average.

B31 Sacrifice of Ship's Stores: Direct Liability of Underwriters

(Proposed and Accepted 1821, p.50. Confirmed 1822, p.43.) **70.17**

That underwriters insuring ship's stores, bunker coal or fuel, destroyed or used as part of a general average operation, shall only be liable for those articles as a direct claim on the policy when they formed part of the property at risk at the time of the peril giving rise to the general average act.

B32 Enforcement of General Average: Lien by Shipowners

(Proposed and Accepted 1890, p.56. Confirmed 1891, p.34.) **70.18**

That in all cases where general average damage to ship is claimed direct from the underwriters on that interest, the average adjusters shall ascertain whether the shipowners have taken the necessary steps to enforce their lien for general average on the cargo, and shall insert in the average statement a note giving the result of their enquiries.

B33 Underwriter's Liability (custom of Lloyd's 1876)

If the ship or cargo be insured for more than its contributory value, the underwriter pays what is assessed on the contributory value. But where insured for less than the contributory value, the underwriter pays on the insured value; and when there has been a particular average for damage which forms a deduction from the contributory value of the ship that must be deducted from the insured value to find upon what the underwriter contributes. **70.19**

This rule does not apply to foreign adjustments, when the basis of contribution is something other than the net value of the thing insured.

(Proposed and Accepted 1922, p.56. Confirmed 1923, p.19.)

That in practice, in applying the above rule for the purpose of ascertaining the liability of underwriters for contribution to general average and salvage charges, deduction shall be made from the insured value of all losses and charges for which underwriters are liable and which have been deducted in arriving at the contributory value.

(Proposed and Accepted June 1926, p.38. Confirmed November 1926, p.7.)

In adjusting the liability of underwriters on freight for general average contribution and salvage charges, effect shall be given to Section 73 of the Marine Insurance Act, 1906, by comparing the gross and not the net amount of freight at risk with the insured value in the case of a valued policy or the insurable value in the case of an unvalued policy.

B34 The Duty of Adjusters in cases involving refunds of general average deposits or apportionment of Salvage, Collision Recoveries, or Other Funds

70.20 (Proposed and Accepted 1896, p.50. Confirmed 1897, p.34.)

That in cases of general average where deposits have been collected and it is likely that repayments will have to be made, measures be taken by the adjuster to ascertain the names of underwriters who have reimbursed their assured in respect of such deposits; that the names of any such underwriters be set forth in the adjustment as claimants of refund, if any, to which they are apparently entitled; and that on completion of the adjustment, notice be sent to all underwriters whose names are so set forth as to any refund of which they appear as claimants and as to the steps to be taken in order to obtain payment of the same.

That in cases where the names of any underwriters are not to be ascertained on completion of the adjustment, notice be sent to the Secretary of Lloyd's, to the Institute of London Underwriters, to the Liverpool Underwriters' Association, and to the Association of Underwriters of Glasgow, notifying such interests as have not been appropriated to underwriters.

And that in cases of apportionment of salvage or other funds for distribution, similar measures be taken by the adjuster to safeguard the interests of any underwriters who may be entitled to benefit under the apportionment.

B35 "Memorandum" to Statements showing Refunds in respect of General Average Deposits

(Proposed and Accepted 1904, p.50. Confirmed 1905, p.36.)

70.21 That the following memorandum shall appear at the end of statements which show refunds to be due in respect of General Average Deposits, viz:

Memorandum—Refunds of general average deposits shown in this statement should only be paid on production of the "original" deposit receipts.

B36 Interest on Deposits

70.22 (Proposed and Accepted 1923, p.32. Confirmed 1924, p.36.)

That, unless otherwise expressly provided, the interest accrued on deposits on account of salvage and/or general average and/or particular and/or other charges, or on the balance of such deposits after payments on account, if any, have been made, shall be credited to the depositor or those to whom his rights in respect of the deposits have been transferred.

B37 Apportionment of Interest on Amounts Made Good

70.23 (Proposed and Accepted 1925, p.68. Confirmed 1926, p.38.)

That in practice (in the absence of express agreement between the parties concerned) interest allowed on amounts made good shall be apportioned between assured and underwriters, taking into account the sums paid by underwriters and the dates when such payments were made, notwithstanding that by the addition of interest the underwriter may receive a larger sum than he has paid.

SECTION C—YORK-ANTWERP RULES

C1 Salvage Services Rendered under an Agreement

(Proposed and Accepted 1942, p.50. Confirmed 1943, p.39.) **70.24**
(Amended 1950, p.28. Confirmed 1951, p.38.)

Expenses for salvage services rendered by or accepted under agreement shall in practice be treated as general average provided that such expenses were incurred for the common safety within the meaning of Rule "A" of the York-Antwerp Rules 1924 or York-Antwerp Rules 1950.

C2 Commission Allowed under York-Antwerp Rules

(Proposed and Accepted 1933, p.45. Confirmed 1934, p.40.) **70.25**
(Amended 1950, 1974 and 1996.)

That the commission of 2 per cent allowed on general average disbursements under the York-Antwerp Rules shall be credited in full to the party who has authorised the expenditure and is liable for payment, except that where the funds for payment are provided in the first instance in whole or in part from the deposit funds, or by other parties to the adventure, or by underwriters, the commission on such advances shall be credited to the deposit funds or to the parties or underwriters providing the funds for payment.

C3 York-Antwerp Rules, 1924: Rules X (A) and XX

(Proposed and Accepted 1949, p.36. Confirmed 1950, p.27.) **70.26**

That, in practice, where a vessel is at any port or place in circumstances in which the wages and maintenance of crew during detention there for the purpose of repairs necessary for the safe prosecution of the voyage would be admissible in general average under Rule XI of the York-Antwerp Rules, 1924, and the vessel is necessarily removed thence to another port or place because such repairs cannot be effected at the first port or place, the provisions of Rule X (a) shall be applied to the second port or place as if it were a port or place of refuge within that Rule and the provisions of Rule XX shall be applied to the prolongation of the voyage occasioned by such removal.

C4 York-Antwerp Rules 1950, 1974 and 1994: Rule X (A)

(Proposed and Accepted 1957, p.24. Confirmed 1958, p.18.) **70.27**
(Amended 1974 and 1996.)

That in practice, in applying the second paragraph of Rule X (a), a vessel shall be deemed to be at a port or place of refuge when she is at any port or place in circumstances in which the wages and maintenance of the Master, Officers and crew incurred during any extra period of detention there would be admissible in General Average under the provisions of Rule XI.

SECTION F—GENERAL AVERAGE ADJUSTMENT UNDER ENGLISH LAW AND PRACTICE

F1 Deckload Jettison (custom of Lloyd's, amended 1890–1891)

70.28 The jettison of a deckload carried according to the usage of trade and not in violation of the contracts of affreightment is general average.

There is an exception to this rule in the case of cargoes of cotton, tallow, acids and some other goods.

F2 Damage by Water used to Extinguish Fire

70.29 (Proposed and Accepted 1873, p.20. Confirmed 1874, p.18.)

That damage done by water poured down a ship's hold to extinguish a fire be treated as general average.

F3 Extinguishing Fire on Shipboard

70.30 (Proposed and Accepted 1968, p.18. Confirmed 1969, p.22.)
(Amended 1974.)

Damage done to a ship and cargo, or either of them, by water or otherwise, including damage by beaching or scuttling a burning ship, in extinguishing a fire on board the ship, shall be made good as general average; except that no compensation shall be made for damage by smoke or heat however caused.

F4 Voluntary Stranding

70.31 (Proposed and Accepted 1968, p.20. Confirmed 1969, p.22.)
(Amended 1996.)

Where a ship is intentionally run on shore for the common safety, whether or not she might have been driven on shore, the consequent loss or damage shall be allowed as general average.

F5 Expenses Lightening a Ship when Ashore

70.32 (Custom of Lloyd's. Amended 1890–1991 and 1968–1969)

When a ship is ashore in a position of peril and, in order to float her, cargo is put into lighters, and is then at once re-shipped, the whole cost of lightering, including lighter hire and re-shipping, is general average.

F6 Sails set to force a Ship off the Ground

(Custom of Lloyd's. 1876) **70.33**

Sails damaged by being set, or kept set, to force a ship off the ground or to drive her higher up the ground for the common safety, are general average.

F7 Stranded Vessels: Damage to Engines in Getting off

(Proposed and Accepted 1890, p.64. Confirmed 1891, p.35.) **70.34**
(Amended 1906, p.15. Confirmed 1907, p.46.)

That damage caused to machinery and boilers of a stranded vessel, in endeavouring to refloat for the common safety, when the interests are in peril, be allowed in general average.

F8 Resort to Port of Refuge for General Average Repairs: Treatment of the Charges Incurred

(Proposed and Accepted 1888, p.45. Confirmed 1889, p.48.) **70.35**

That when a ship puts into a port of refuge in consequence of damage which is itself the subject of general average, and sails thence with her original cargo, or a part of it, the outward as well as the inward port charges shall be treated as general average; and when cargo is discharged for the purpose of repairing such damage, the warehouse rent and reloading of the same shall, as well as the discharge, be treated as general average. (See *Attwood v Sellar*).

F9 Resort to Port of Refuge on Account Of Particular Average Repairs: Treatment of the Charges Incurred

(Proposed and Accepted 1888, p.47. Confirmed 1889, p.49.) **70.36**

That when a ship puts into a port of refuge in consequence of damage which is itself the subject of particular average (or not of general average) and when the cargo has been discharged in consequence of such damage, the inward port charges and the cost of discharging the cargo shall be general average, the warehouse rent of cargo shall be a particular charge on cargo, and the cost of reloading and outward port charges shall be a particular charge on freight. (See *Svendsen v Wallace*).

F10 Treatment of Costs of Storage and Reloading at Port of Refuge

(Proposed and Accepted 1886, p.37. Confirmed 1887, p.36.) **70.37**

That when the cargo is discharged for the purpose of repairing, re-conditioning, or diminishing damage to ship or cargo which is itself the subject of general average, the cost of storage on it and of reloading it shall be treated as general average, equally with the cost of discharging it.

F11 Insurance on Cargo Discharged Under Average

70.38 (Proposed and Accepted 1924, p.43. Confirmed 1925, p.43.)
(Amended 1968, p.21. Confirmed 1969, p.22.)

That in practice, where the cost of insurance has been reasonably incurred by the ship-owner, or his agents, on cargo discharged under average, such cost shall be treated as part of the cost of storage.

F12 Expenses at a Port of Refuge

70.39 (Custom of Lloyd's. Amended 1890–1991)

When a ship puts into a port of refuge on account of accident and not in consequence of damage which is itself the subject of general average, then on the assumption that the ship was seaworthy at the commencement of the voyage, the Custom of Lloyd's is as follows:

(a) All cost of towage, pilotage, harbour dues, and other extraordinary
1876 expenses incurred in order to bring the ship and cargo into a place of safety, are general average. Under the term "extraordinary expenses" are not included wages or victuals of crew, coals, or engine stores, or demurrage.

(b) The cost of discharging the cargo, whether for the common
1876 safety, or to repair the ship, together with the cost of conveying it to the warehouse, is general average.

The cost of discharging the cargo on account of damage to it resulting from its own vice propre, is chargeable to the owners of the cargo.

(c) The warehouse rent, or other expenses which take the place of
1876 warehouse rent, of the cargo when so discharged, is, except as under, a special charge on the cargo.

(d) The cost of reloading the cargo, and the outward port charges
1876 incurred through leaving the port of refuge, are, when the discharge of cargo falls in general average, a special charge on freight.

(e) The expenses referred to in clause (d) are charged to the party
1876 who runs the risk of freight—that is, wholly to the charterer—if the whole freight has been prepaid; and, if part only, then in the proportion which the part prepaid bears to the whole freight.

(f) When the cargo, instead of being sent ashore, is placed on board hulk or lighters during the ship's stay in port, the hulk-hire is divided between general average, cargo, and freight, in such proportions as may place the several contributing interests in nearly the same relative positions as if the cargo has been landed and stored.

F13 Treatment of Costs of Extraordinary Discharge

(Proposed and Accepted 1886, p.37. Confirmed 1887, p.36.) **70.40**

That no distinction be drawn in practice between discharging cargo for the common safety of ship and cargo, and discharging it for the purpose of effecting at an intermediate port or ports of refuge repairs necessary for the prosecution of the voyage.

F14 Towage from a Port of Refuge

(Proposed and Accepted 1876, p.26. Confirmed 1877, p.54.) **70.41**

That if a ship be in a port of refuge at which it is practicable to repair her, and if, in order to save expense, she be towed thence to some other port, then the extra cost of such towage shall be divided in proportion to the saving of expense thereby occasioned to the several parties to the adventure.

F15 Cargo Forwarded from a Port of Refuge

(Proposed and Accepted 1876, p.26. Confirmed 1877, p.54.) **70.42**

That if a ship be in a port of refuge at which it is practicable to repair her so as to enable her to carry on the whole cargo, but, in order to save expense, the cargo, or a portion of it, be transhipped by another vessel, or otherwise forwarded, then the cost of such transhipment (up to the amount of expense saved) shall be divided in proportion to the saving of expense thereby occasioned to the several parties to the adventure.

F16 Cargo Sold at a Port of Refuge

(Proposed and Accepted 1902, p.34. Confirmed 1903, p.18.) **70.43**

That if a ship be in a port of refuge at which it is practicable to repair her so as to enable her to carry on the whole cargo, or such portion of it as is fit to be carried on, but, in order to save expense, the cargo, or a portion of it, be, with the consent of the owners of such cargo, sold at the port of refuge, then the loss by sale including loss of freight on cargo so sold (up to the amount of expense saved) shall be divided in proportion to the saving of expense thereby occasioned to the several parties to the adventure; provided always that the amount so divided shall in no case exceed the cost of transhipment and/or forwarding referred to in the preceding rule of the Association.

F17 Interpretation of the Rule Respecting Substituted Expenses

(Proposed and Accepted 1877, p.63. Confirmed 1878, p.18.) **70.44**

That for the purpose of avoiding any misinterpretation of the resolution relating to the apportionment of substituted expenses, it is declared that the saving of expense therein mentioned is limited to a saving or reduction of the actual outlay, including the crew's wages and provisions, if any, which would have been incurred at the port of refuge, if the vessel has been repaired there, and does not include supposed losses or expenses, such as interest, loss of market, demurrage, or assumed damage by discharging.

F18 Damage to Cargo, Fuel and Stores in Discharging Etc.

70.45 (Proposed and Accepted 1886, p.37. Confirmed 1887, p.36.)
(Amended 1996.)

Damage to or loss of cargo, fuel or stores, sustained in consequence of their handling, discharging, storing, reloading and stowing shall be made good as general average when, and only when the cost of those measures respectively is admitted as general average.

F19 Deductions from Cost of Repairs in Adjusting General Average

70.46 (Proposed and Accepted 1887, p.36. Confirmed 1888, p.28.)
(Referred to Special Committee 1884, p.45—Reports, Prov. 1885, p.19, Final 1886, p.16.)
(Amended 1934, p.41. Confirmed 1935, p.22.)
(Amended 1950, p.30. Confirmed 1951, p.38.)
(Amended 1974.)

Repairs to be allowed in general average shall not be subject to deductions in respect of "new for old" where old materials or parts are replaced by new unless the ship is over fifteen years old in which case there shall be a deduction of one third. The deductions shall be regulated by the age of the ship from the December 31 of the year of completion of construction to the date of the general average act, except for insulation, life and similar boats, communications and navigational apparatus and equipment, machinery and boilers for which the deductions shall be regulated by the age of the particular parts to which they apply.

The deductions shall be made only from the cost of the new material or parts when finished and ready to be installed in the ship.

No deduction shall be made in respect of provisions, stores, anchors and chain cables.

Drydock and slipway dues and costs of shifting the ship shall be allowed in full.

The costs of cleaning, painting or coating of bottom shall not be allowed in general average unless the bottom has been painted or coated within the twelve months preceding the date of the general average act in which case one half of such costs shall be allowed.

F20 Freight Sacrificed: Amount to be Made Good in General Average

70.47 (Proposed and Accepted 1894, p.56. Confirmed 1895, p.29.)

That the loss of freight to be made good in general average shall be ascertained by deducting from the amount of gross freight lost the charges which the owner thereof would have incurred to earn such freight, but has, in consequence of the sacrifice, not incurred.

F21 Basis of Contribution to General Average

70.48 (Original Rule of Practice, 1873.)

When property saved by a general average act is injured or destroyed by subsequent accident, the contributing value of that property to a general average which is less than the total contributing value, shall, when it does not reach the port of destination, be its actual net proceeds; when it does it shall be its actual net value at the port of destination on its delivery there; and in all cases any values allowed in general average shall be added to and form part of the contributing value as above.

The above rule shall not apply to adjustments made before the adventure has terminated.

F22 Contributory Value of Freight

(Original Rule of Practice 1873—Part.) **70.49**
(Referred to a Special Committee 1908—Report 1909.)
(Amended 1968, p.22. Confirmed 1969, p.22.)

That freight at the risk of the shipowner shall contribute to general average upon its gross amount, deducting such charges and crew's wages as would not have been incurred in earning the freight had the ship and cargo been totally lost at the date of the general average act and have not been allowed as general average.

UNIFORMITY RESOLUTION

1. York-Antwerp Rules 1924: Application of Rule XIV

(Passed November 1928, p.11.) **70.50**

That, in practice, in applying Rule XIV of the York-Antwerp Rules, 1924, the cost of the temporary repair of the accidental damage there referred to shall be allowed in general average up to the saving to the general average by effecting such temporary repair, without regard to the saving (if any) to other interests.

APPENDIX 4

DOCUMENTS

GENERAL AVERAGE

The documents shown are in a standard form issued or approved by Lloyd's. 80.01

Since the 1974 Rules when r.XVII was amended so that cargo values were based on the CIF invoice rather than market prices, the valuation form is less frequently used. The usual practice is for receivers to be asked to attach a copy of the CIF invoice to the signed average bond.

The wording of the average bond and guarantee is not fixed by the York-Antwerp Rules and variations may be found where adjusters and insurers have amended the wordings, either as a matter of general practice or to suit the circumstances of a particular case. It was held in the *Jute Express* [1991] 2 Lloyd's Rep. 55 that the words in the standard average bond referring to general average "which is payable" mean "and which is legally due", thus preserving the right to challenge any alleged liability for contribution. Nonetheless, to put the matter beyond doubt in other jurisdictions, the words "properly due" are used on the average guarantee and in some cases the phrase "legally and properly due" may also be used.

In many cases the adjusters will add a jurisdiction clause to the guarantee and bond wording.

In cases involving a large number of interests (and/or a relatively low percentage rate of contribution from each interest) it may be decided not to request Average Bonds from receivers who are insured, in order to reduce the cost and paper work involved in the security collection. This decision can be made on a case by case basis, but BIMCO's Documentary Committee have drafted a recommended wording for insertion into bills of leading which imports the terms of the Average Bond into the contract of coverage. The wording was drawn up in consultation with the British Association of Average Adjusters.

Salvage

80.02 The following are Corporation of Lloyd's wordings:

The International Salvage Union produces the following guarantee wordings:

LLOYD'S AVERAGE BOND

To 80.03
Owner(s) of the ....
Voyage and date ....
Port of shipment...
Port of destination/discharge..
Bill of Lading or waybill number(s) ....

Quantity and description of goods

In consideration of the delivery to us or to our order, on payment of the freight due, of the goods notes above we agree to pay the proper proportion of any salvage and/or general and/or special charges which may hereafter be ascertained to be due from the goods or the shippers or owners thereof under an adjustment prepared in accordance with the provisions of the contract of affreightment governing the carriage of the goods or, failing any such provision, in accordance with the law and practice of the place where the common maritime adventure ended and which is payable in respect of the goods by the shippers or owners thereof.

We also agree to:

(i) furnish particulars of the value of the goods, supported by a copy of the commercial invoice rendered to us or, if there is no such invoice, details of the shipped value and

(ii) make a payment on account of such sum as is duly certified by the average adjusters to be due from the goods and which is payable in respect of the goods by the shippers or owners thereof.

Date.. Signature of receiver of goods.................................
Full name and address..
....
....

VALUATION FORM

80.04 To ....

Owner(s) of the ....

Voyage and date ....

Port of shipment...

Port of destination/discharge...

Bill of Lading or waybill number(s) ....

Quantity and description of goods	Particular of Value A Invoice Value	 B Shipped Value
	(specify currency)	
Currency		

1. If the goods are insured please state the following details (if known):–
   Name and address of insurers and brokers...
   Policy or certificate number and date....... Insured value ....
2. If the goods arrived subject to loss or damage, please state nature and extent thereo ....
   ....
   ....
   and ensure that copies of supporting documents are forwarded wither direct or through the insures to the average adjusters named below.
3. If general average deposit has been paid, please state:–
   (a) Amount of the deposit.................. (b) Deposit receipt number...............
   (c) Whether you have made any claim on your insurers for reimbursement

Date ....Signature ....

Full name and address ....

....

....

Notes

1. If the goods form the subject of a commercial transaction, fill in column A with the amount of the commercial invoice rendered to you, and attach a copy of this invoice hereto.
2. If there is no commercial invoice covering the goods, state the shipped value, if known to you, in column B.
3. In either case, state the currency involved.
4. The shipowners have appointed as average adjusters .... to whom this form should be sent duly completed together with a copy of the commercial invoice.

AVERAGE GUARANTEE

Wording approved by the Association of Average Adjusters and the Institute of London Underwriters **80.05**

NOTE: This guarantee will be accepted provided that no additions, deletions or amendments are made to it.

TO: the Owners of the vessel named below and other parties to the adventure as their interest may appear.

VESSEL.................. from ....to ....
CASUALTY and DATE...

In consideration of the delivery in due course of the goods specified below to the consignees thereof without collection of a deposit, we, the undersigned insurers, hereby undertake to pay to the shipowners or to the Average Adjusters**, on behalf of the various parties to the adventure as their interests may appear, any contribution to General Average and/or Salvage and/or Special Charges which may hereafter be ascertained to be properly due in respect of the said goods.

We further agree:

(a) to make prompt payment(s) on account of such contribution as may be reasonably and properly due in respect of the said goods, as soon as the same may be certified by the said Average Adjusters**.
(b) to furnish to the said Average Adjusters** at their request all information which is available to us relative to the value and condition of the said goods.

Port of Loading	Port of Discharge	Bill of Lading	Quantity & description of goods	Insured Value	Polity/Ref No. and Premium (if known)

Signature of Insurers ....
Name and address ....
....

Telephone No....................Fax No.............................Email
Date:...

** The Average Adjusters are:

80.06

No . . .

General Average Deposit Receipt

LLOYD'S FORM

Dated at . . . .

. . . . **19** . . . .

Vessel . . . .

Depositors, Messrs. . . . .

Contributory Value (provisional) . . . .

B/L or Waybill No. . . . .

Amount of Deposit. . . . .

Description of Goods:

NOTE FOR DEPOSITORS: IF INSURED you may wish to send this receipt together with the original policy or certificate of insurance to your insurers who, subject to the policy conditions, may be prepared to refund this deposit. **IF NOT INSURED** you should notify the Average Adjusters direct of your interest and retain this receipt until the adjustment is issued when any credit balance can be claimed.

NOTE FOR INSURERS: When a repayment of this deposit has been made, advise the Average Adjusters and thus assist in final settlement.

NO DUPLICATE OF THIS RECEIPT CAN BE ISSUED.

No. . . . . .

GENERAL AVERAGE DEPOSIT RECEIPT.

LLOYD'S FORM.

Dated at . . . . 19 . . . .

Vessel . . . . from . . . . to

Nature and date of Accident. . . . .

. . . .

RECEIVED from Messrs. . . . .

the sum of. . . . .

deposit on account of General Average and or Salvage and or Charges,

being. . . . . per cent on . . . .

provisionally accepted as the contributory value of the following goods, viz.:

. . . . Marks and Nos

. . . . and Description

. . . . of Interest to be

. . . . inserted here

B/L or Waybill No. . . . .

£ . . . .

for and on behalf of the Trustue(s) or nominated representative(s)

N.B.–The refund, if any, will be made only to the bearer of, and in exchange for, this Receipt, and will be the whole balance of the deposit after satisfying the General Average and or Salvage and or Charges, without deduction or set off of any other claims of the Shipowner against the Shipper or Consignee.

The General Average will be adjusted in and the Shipowner have given the necessary instructions to Messrs. Average Adjusters

80.07

BIMCO REVISED AVERAGE BOND CLAUSE

On presentation of this bill of lading and

(i) payment of any freight due; and

(ii) provision of a satisfactory security in respect of General Average, Salvage and Special Charges,

it is agreed that, in consideration of the delivery of the cargo described on the face of this bill of lading ("the cargo") to the presenter of the bill of lading, or to order, without providing an average bond, the party or parties which present(s) this bill of lading, or their assigns, shall:

a) pay the proper proportion of any salvage and/or general average and/or special charges which may be ascertained to be properly due from the cargo or the shippers or owners thereof,

b) where appropriate, contribute to salvage and/or general average and/or special charges in accordance with an adjustment prepared pursuant to the non-separation wording contained in Rules G and XVII of the York-Antwerp Rules 1994,

c)

(i) at the time of presentation of the bill of lading, furnish a copy of the commercial cargo invoice rendered to the receiver, and;

(ii) as soon as is reasonably practicable following delivery of the cargo, notify the Carrier, their Agent or appointed average adjusters of the nature and value of any damage to or loss of the cargo.

d) following delivery of the cargo make a payment on account of such sum as is certified by the average adjusters to be properly due from the cargo and is payable in respect of such cargo by the shippers or owners thereof.

Except when the adjustment is made in accordance with the York-Antwerp Rules 2004, rights to claim under this Clause shall be extinguished, unless an action is brought by the party claiming within a period of six years from the date of issue of the general average adjustment.

80.08 LLOYD'S STANDARD FORM OF SALVAGE AGREEMENT

(Approved and Published by the Council of Lloyd's)

NO CURE – NO PAY

1. Name of the salvage Contractors: (referred to in this agreement as "the Contractors")	2. Property to be salved: The vessel: her cargo freight bunkers stores and any other property thereon but excluding the personal effects or baggage of passengers master or crew (referred to in this agreement as "the property")
3. Agreed place of safety:	4. Agreed currency of any arbitral award and security (if other than United States dollars)
5. Date of this agreement	6. Place of agreement
7. Is the Scopic Clause incorporated into this agreement? State alternative: Yes/No	
8. Person signing for and on behalf of the Contractors Signature:	9. Captain or other person signing for and on behalf of the property Signature:

A Contractors' basic obligation: The Contractors identified in Box 1 hereby agree to use their best endeavours to salve the property specified in Box 2 and to take the property to the place stated in Box 3 or to such other place as may hereafter be agreed. If no place is inserted in Box 3 and in the absence of any subsequent agreement as to the place where the property is to be taken the Contractors shall take the property to a place of safety.

B Environmental protection: While performing the salvage services the Contractors shall also use their best endeavours to prevent or minimise damage to the environment.

C Scopic Clause: Unless the word "No" in Box 7 has been deleted this agreement shall be deemed to have been made on the basis that the Scopic Clause is not incorporated and forms no part of this agreement. If the word "No" is deleted in Box 7 this shall not of itself be construed as a notice invoking the Scopic Clause within the meaning of sub-clause 2 thereof.

D **Effect of other remedies**: Subject to the provisions of the International Convention on Salvage 1989 as incorporated into English law ("the Convention") relating to special compensation and to the Scopic Clause if incorporated the Contractors services shall be rendered and accepted as salvage services upon the principle of "no cure – no pay" and any salvage remuneration to which the Contractors become entitled shall not be diminished by reason of the exception to the principle of "no cure – no pay" in the form of special compensation or remuneration payable to the Contractors under a Scopic Clause.

E **Prior services:** Any salvage services rendered by the Contractors to the property before and up to the date of this agreement shall be deemed to be covered by this agreement.

F **Duties of property owners:** Each of the owners of the property shall cooperate fully with the Contractors. In particular:

(i) the Contractors may make reasonable use of the vessel's machinery gear and equipment free of expense provided that the Contractors shall not unnecessarily damage abandon or sacrifice any property on board;

(ii) the Contractors shall be entitled to all such information as they may reasonably require relating to the vessel or the remainder of the property provided such information is relevant to the performance of the services and is capable of being provided without undue difficulty or delay;

(iii) the owners of the property shall co-operate fully with the Contractors in obtaining entry to the place of safety stated in Box 3 or agreed or determined in accordance with Clause A.

G **Rights of termination:** When there is no longer any reasonable prospect of a useful result leading to a salvage reward in accordance with Convention Articles 12 and/or 13 either the owners of the vessel or the Contractors shall be entitled to terminate the services hereunder by giving reasonable prior written notice to the other.

H **Deemed performance:** The Contractors' services shall be deemed to have been performed when the property is in a safe condition in the place of safety stated in Box 3 or agreed or determined in accordance with clause A. For the purpose of this provision the property shall be regarded as being in safe condition notwithstanding that the property (or part thereof) is damaged or in need of maintenance if (i) the Contractors are not obliged to remain in attendance to satisfy the requirements of any port or habour authority, governmental agency or similar authority and (ii) the continuation of skilled salvage services from the Contractors or other salvors is no longer necessary to avoid the property becoming lost or significantly further damaged or delayed.

I **Arbitration and the LSSA Clauses**: The Contractors' remuneration and/or special compensation shall be determined by arbitration in London in the manner prescribed by Lloyd's Standard Salvage and Arbitration Clauses ("the LSSA Clauses") and Lloyd's Procedural Rules in force at the date of this agreement. The provisions of the said LSSA Clauses and Lloyd's Procedural Rules are deemed to be incorporated in this agreement and form an integral part hereof. Any other difference arising out of this agreement or the operations hereunder shall be referred to arbitration in the same way.

J **Governing law:** This agreement and any arbitration hereunder shall be governed by English law.

K **Scope of authority:** The Master or other person signing this agreement on behalf of the property identified in Box 2 enters into this agreement as agent for the respective owners thereof and binds each (but not the one for the other or himself personally) to the due performance thereof.

L **Inducements prohibited**: No person signing this agreement or any party on whose behalf it is signed shall at any time or in any manner whatsoever offer provide make give or promise to provide or demand or take any form of inducement for entering into this agreement.

IMPORTANT NOTICES

1 **Salvage security**. As soon as possible the owners of the vessel should notify the owners of other property on board that this agreement has been made. If the Contractors are successful the owners of such property should note that it will become necessary to provide the Contractors with salvage security promptly in accordance with Clause 4 of the LSSA Clauses referred to in Clause I. The provision of General Average security does not relieve the salved interests of their separate obligation to provide salvage security to the Contractors.

2 **Incorporated provisions**. Copies of the applicable Scopic Clause, the LSSA Clauses and Lloyd's Procedural Rules in force at the date of this agreement may be obtained from (i) the Contractors or (ii) the Salvage Arbitration Branch at Lloyd's, One Lime Street, London EC3M 7HA.

3 **Awards**. The Council of Lloyd's is entitled to make available the Award, Appeal Award and Reasons on www.lloydsagency.com (the website) subject to the conditions set out in Clause 12 of the LSSA Clauses.

4 **Notification to Lloyd's**. The Contractors shall within 14 days of their engagement to render services under this agreement notify the Council of Lloyd's of their engagement and forward the signed agreement or a true copy thereof to the Council as soon as possible. The Council will not charge for such notification.

LLOYD'S STANDARD FORM OF SALVAGE AGREEMENT 80.09

(Approved and Published by the Council of Lloyd's)

LLOYD'S STANDARD SALVAGE AND ARBITRATION CLAUSES

1 Introduction

1.1 These clauses ("the LSSA Clauses") or any revision thereof which may be published with the approval of the Council of Lloyd's are incorporated into and form an integral part of every contract for the performance of salvage services undertaken on the terms of Lloyd's Standard Form of Salvage Agreement as published by the Council of Lloyd's and known as LOF 2011 (or its predecessor LOF 2000) ("the Agreement" which expression includes the LSSA clauses and Lloyd's Procedural Rules referred to in Clause 6).

1.2 All notices communications and other documents required to be sent to the Council of Lloyd's should be sent to:

Salvage Arbitration Branch
Lloyd's
One Lime Street
London EC3M 7HA
Tel: +44 (0) 20 7327 5408/5407
Fax: +44 (0) 20 7327 6827
E-mail: lloyds-salvage@lloyds.com

2 Overriding Objective

In construing the Agreement or on the making of any arbitral order or award regard shall be had to the overriding purposes of the Agreement namely:

a to seek to promote safety of life at sea and the preservation of property at sea and during the salvage operations to prevent or minimise damage to the environment;

b to ensure that its provisions are operated in good faith and that it is read and understood to operate in a reasonably businesslike manner;

c to encourage cooperation between the parties and with relevant authorities;

d to ensure that the reasonable expectations of salvors and owners of salved property are met and

e to ensure that it leads to a fair and efficient disposal of disputes between the parties whether amicably, by mediation or by arbitration within a reasonable time and at a reasonable cost.

3 Definitions

In the Agreement and unless there is an express provision to the contrary:

3.1 "Award" includes an interim or provisional Award and "Appeal Award" means any Award including any interim or provisional Award made by the Appeal Arbitrator appointed under clause 10.2.

3.2 "personal effects or baggage" as referred to in Box 2 of the Agreement means those which the passenger, Master and crew member have in their cabin or are otherwise in their possession, custody or control and shall include any private motor vehicle accompanying a passenger and any personal effects or baggage in or on such vehicle.

3.3 "Convention" means the International Convention on Salvage 1989 as enacted by section 224, Schedule II of the Merchant Shipping Act 1995 (and any amendment of either) and any term or expression in the Convention has the same meaning when used in the Agreement.

3.4 "Council" means the Council of Lloyd's

3.5 "days" means calendar days

3.6 "Owners" means the owners of the property referred to in box 2 of the Agreement

3.7 "owners of the vessel" includes the demise or bareboat charterers of that vessel.

3.8 "special compensation" refers to the compensation payable to salvors under Article 14 of the Convention.

3.9 "Scopic Clause" refers to the agreement made between (1) members of the International Salvage Union (2) the International Group of P&I Clubs and (3) certain property underwriters which first became effective on 1st August 1999 and includes any replacement or revision thereof. All references to the Scopic Clause in the Agreement shall be deemed to refer to the version of the Scopic Clause current at the date the Agreement is made.

4 Provisions as to Security, Maritime Lien and Right to Arrest

4.1 The Contractors shall immediately after the termination of the services or sooner notify the Council and where practicable the Owners of the amount for which they demand salvage security (inclusive of costs expenses and interest) from each of the respective Owners.

4.2 Where a claim is made or may be made for special compensation the owners of the vessel shall on the demand of the Contractors whenever made provide security for the Contractors' claim for special compensation provided always that such demand is made within 2 years of the date of termination of the services.

4.3 The security referred to in clauses 4.1 and 4.2. above shall be demanded and provided in the currency specified in Box 4 or in United States Dollars if no such alternative currency has been agreed.

4.4 The amount of any such security shall be reasonable in the light of the knowledge available to the Contractors at the time when the demand is made and any further facts which come to the Contractors' attention before security is provided. The arbitrator appointed under clause 5 hereof may, at any stage of the proceedings, order that the amount of security be reduced or increased as the case may be.

4.5 Unless otherwise agreed such security shall be provided (i) to the Council (ii) in a form approved by the Council and (iii) by persons firms or corporations either acceptable to the Contractors or resident in the United Kingdom and acceptable to the Council. The Council shall not be responsible for the sufficiency (whether in amount or otherwise) of any security which shall be provided nor the default or insolvency of any person firm or corporation providing the same.

4.6 The owners of the vessel including their servants and agents shall use their best endeavours to ensure that none of the property salved is released until security has been provided in respect of that property in accordance with clause 4.5.

4.7 Until security has been provided as aforesaid the Contractors shall have a maritime lien on the property salved for their remuneration.

4.8 Until security has been provided the property salved shall not without the consent in writing of the Contractors (which shall not be unreasonably withheld) be removed from the place to which it has been taken by the Contractors under clause A. Where such consent is given by the Contractors on condition that they are provided with temporary security pending completion of the voyage the Contractors' maritime lien on the property salved shall remain in force to the extent necessary to enable the Contractors to compel the provision of security in accordance with clause 4.5.

4.9 The Contractors shall not arrest or detain the property salved unless:

(i) security is not provided within 21 days after the date of the termination of the services or
(ii) they have reason to believe that the removal of the property salved is contemplated contrary to clause 4.8. or
(iii) any attempt is made to remove the property salved contrary to clause 4.8.

5 Appointment of Arbitrators

5.1 Whether or not security has been provided (and always subject to Clause 6.6 and 10.8 below) the Council shall appoint an arbitrator ("the Arbitrator") upon receipt of a written request provided that any party requesting such appointment shall if required by the Council undertake to the Council's reasonable satisfaction to pay the reasonable fees and expenses of the Council and those of the Arbitrator and the Appeal Arbitrator.

5.2 The Arbitrator, the Appeal Arbitrator and the Council may charge reasonable fees and expenses for their services whether the arbitration proceeds to a hearing or not and all such fees and expenses shall be treated as part of the costs of the arbitration.

6 Arbitration Procedure and Arbitrators Powers

6.1 The arbitration shall be conducted in accordance with the Procedural Rules approved by the Council ("Lloyd's Procedural Rules") in force at the date of the LOF agreement.

6.2 The arbitration shall take place in London unless (i) all represented parties agree to some other place for the whole or part of the arbitration and (ii) any such agreement is approved by the Arbitrator on such terms as to the payment of the Arbitrator's travel and accommodation expenses as he may see fit to impose.

6.3 The Arbitrator shall have power in his absolute discretion to include in the amount awarded to the Contractors the whole or part of any expenses reasonably incurred by the Contractors in:
(i) ascertaining demanding and obtaining the amount of security reasonably required in accordance with clause 4.5
(ii) enforcing and/or protecting by insurance or otherwise or taking reasonable steps to enforce and/or protect their lien

6.4 The Arbitrator shall have power to make but shall not be bound to make a consent award between such parties as so consent with or without full arbitral reasons

6.5 The Arbitrator shall have power to make a provisional or interim award or awards including payments on account on such terms as may be fair and just

6.6 The Arbitrator shall be entitled to satisfactory security for his reasonable fees and expenses, whether such fees and expenses have been incurred already or are reasonably anticipated. The Arbitrator shall have the power to order one or more of the parties to provide such security in a sum or sums and in a form to be determined by the Arbitrator. The said power may be exercised from time to time as the Arbitrator considers appropriate.

6.7 Awards in respect of salvage remuneration or special compensation (including payments on account) shall be made in the currency specified in Box 4 or in United States dollars if no such alternative currency has been agreed.

6.8 The Arbitrator's Award shall (subject to appeal as provided in clause 10) be final and binding on all the parties concerned whether they were represented at the arbitration or not and shall be published by the Council in London.

7 Representation of Parties

7.1 Any party to the Agreement who wishes to be heard or to adduce evidence shall appoint an agent or representative ordinarily resident in the United Kingdom to receive correspondence and notices for and on behalf of that party and shall give written notice of such appointment to the Council.

7.2 Service on such agent or representative by letter, e-mail or facsimile shall be deemed to be good service on the party which has appointed that agent or representative.

7.3 Any party who fails to appoint an agent or representative as aforesaid shall be deemed to have renounced his right to be heard or adduce evidence.

8 Interest

8.1 Unless the Arbitrator in his discretion otherwise decides the Contractors shall be entitled to interest on any sums awarded in respect of salvage remuneration or special compensation (after taking into consideration any sums already paid to the Contractors on account) from the date of termination of the services until the date on which the Award is published by the Council and at a rate to be determined by the Arbitrator.

8.2 In ordinary circumstances the Contractors' interest entitlement shall be limited to simple interest but the Arbitrator may exercise his statutory power to make an award of compound interest if the Contractors have been deprived of their salvage remuneration or special compensation for an excessive period as a result of the Owners' gross misconduct or in other exceptional circumstances.

8.3 If the sum(s) awarded to the Contractors (including the fees and expenses referred to in clause 5.2) are not paid to the Contractors or to the Council by the payment date specified in clause 11.1 the Contractors shall be entitled to additional interest on such outstanding sums from the payment date until the date payment is received by the Contractors or the Council both dates inclusive and at a rate which the Arbitrator shall in his absolute discretion determine in his Award.

9 Currency Correction

In considering what sums of money have been expended by the Contractors in rendering the services and/or in fixing the amount of the Award and/or Appeal Award the Arbitrator or Appeal Arbitrator shall to such an extent and insofar as it may be fair and just in all the circumstances give effect to the consequences of any change or changes in the relevant rates of exchange which may have occurred between the date of termination of the services and the date on which the Award or Appeal Award is made.

10 Appeals and Cross Appeals

10.1 Any party may appeal from an Award by giving written Notice of Appeal to the Council provided such notice is received by the Council no later than 21 days after the date on which the Award was published by the Council.

10.2 On receipt of a Notice of Appeal the Council shall refer the appeal to the hearing and determination of an appeal arbitrator of its choice ("the Appeal Arbitrator").

10.3 Any party who has not already given Notice of Appeal under clause 10.1 may give a Notice of Cross Appeal to the Council within 21 days of that party having been notified that the Council has received Notice of Appeal from another party.

10.4 Notice of Appeal or Cross Appeal shall be given to the Council by letter, e-mail or facsimile.

10.5 If any Notice of Appeal or Notice of Cross Appeal is withdrawn prior to the hearing of the appeal arbitration, that appeal arbitration shall nevertheless proceed for the purpose of determining any matters which remain outstanding.

10.6 The Appeal Arbitrator shall conduct the appeal arbitration in accordance with Lloyd's Procedural Rules so far as applicable to an appeal.

10.7 In addition to the powers conferred on the Arbitrator by English law and the Agreement, the Appeal Arbitrator shall have power to:

(i) admit the evidence or information which was before the Arbitrator together with the Arbitrator's Notes and Reasons for his Award, any transcript of evidence and such additional evidence or information as he may think fit;

(ii) confirm increase or reduce the sum(s) awarded by the Arbitrator and to make such order as to the payment of interest on such sum(s) as he may think fit;

(iii) confirm revoke or vary any order and/or declaratory award made by the Arbitrator;

(iv) award interest on any fees and expenses charged under clause 10.8 from the expiration of 28 days after the date of publication by the Council of the Appeal Arbitrator's Award until the date payment is received by the Council both dates inclusive.

10.8 The Appeal Arbitrator shall be entitled to satisfactory security for his reasonable fees and expenses, whether such fees and expenses have been incurred already or are reasonably anticipated. The Appeal Arbitrator shall have the power to order one or more of the parties to provide such security in a sum or sums and in a form to be determined by the Appeal Arbitrator. The said power may be exercised from time to time as the Appeal Arbitrator considers appropriate.

10.9 The Appeal Arbitrator's Award shall be published by the Council in London.

11 Provisions as to Payment

11.1 When publishing the Award the Council shall call upon the party or parties concerned to pay all sums due from them which are quantified in the Award (including the fees and expenses referred to in clause 5.2) not later than 28 days after the date of publication of the Award ("the payment date")

11.2 If the sums referred to in clause 11.1 (or any part thereof) are not paid within 56 days after the date of publication of the Award (or such longer period as the Contractors may allow) and provided the Council has not received Notice of Appeal or Notice of Cross Appeal the Council shall realise or enforce the security given to the Council under clause 4.5 by or on behalf of the defaulting party or parties subject to the Contractors' providing the Council with any indemnity the Council may require in respect of the costs the Council may incur in that regard.

11.3 In the event of an appeal and upon publication by the Council of the Appeal Award the Council shall call upon the party or parties concerned to pay the sum(s) awarded. In the event of non-payment and subject to the Contractors providing the Council with any costs indemnity required as referred to in clause 11.2 the Council shall realise or enforce the security given to the Council under clause 4.5 by or on behalf of the defaulting party.

11.4 If any sum(s) shall become payable to the Contractors in respect of salvage remuneration or special compensation (including interest and/or costs) as the result of an agreement made between the Contractors and the Owners or any of them, the Council shall, if called upon to do so and subject to the Contractors providing to the Council any costs indemnity required as referred to in clause 11.2 realise or enforce the security given to the Council under clause 4.5 by or on behalf of that party.

11.5 Where (i) no security has been provided to the Council in accordance with clause 4.5 or (ii) no Award is made by the Arbitrator or the Appeal Arbitrator (as the case may be) because the parties have been able to settle all matters in issue between them by agreement the Contractors shall be responsible for payment of the fees and expenses referred to in clause 5.2. Payment of such fees and expenses shall be made to the Council within 28 days of the Contractors or their representatives receiving the Council's invoice failing which the Council shall be entitled to interest on any sum outstanding at UK Base Rate prevailing on the date of the invoice plus 2% per annum until payment is received by the Council.

11.6 If an Award or Appeal Award directs the Contractors to pay any sum to any other party or parties including the whole or any part of the costs of the arbitration and/or appeal arbitration the Council may deduct from sums received by the Council on behalf of the Contractors the amount(s) so payable by the Contractors unless the Contractors provide the Council with satisfactory security to meet their liability.

11.7 Save as aforesaid every sum received by the Council pursuant to this clause shall be paid by the Council to the Contractors or their representatives whose receipt shall be a good discharge for it.

11.8 Without prejudice to the provisions of clause 4.5 the liability of the Council shall be limited to the amount of security provided to it.

12 Awards

12.1 The Council will ordinarily make available the Award or Appeal Award and Reasons on www.lloydsagency.com (the website) except where the Arbitrator or Appeal Arbitrator has ordered, in response to representations by any party to the Award or Appeal Award, that there is a good reason for deferring or withholding them. Any party may make such representations to the Arbitrator provided a written notice of its intention to do so is received by the Council no later than 21 days after the date on which the Award or Appeal Award was published by the Council and the representations themselves are submitted in writing to the Arbitrator or Appeal Arbitrator within 21 days of the date of the notice of intention.

12.2 Subject to any order of the Arbitrator or Appeal Arbitrator, the Award, or Appeal Award, and Reasons will be made available on the website as soon as practicable after expiry of the 21 day period referred to in clause 12.1.

12.3 In the event of an appeal being entered against an Award, the Award and Reasons shall not be made available on the website until either the Appeal Arbitrator has issued his Appeal Award or the Notice of Appeal is withdrawn subject always to any order being made in accordance with clause 12.1.

Special Provisions

These Special Provisions shall apply to salved cargo insofar as it consists of laden containers.

13 The parties agree that any correspondence or notices in respect of salved cargo which is not the subject of representation in accordance with Clause 7 of these Rules may be sent to the party or parties who have provided salvage security in respect of that property and that this shall be deemed to constitute proper notification to the owners of such property.

14 Subject to the express approval of the Arbitrator, where an agreement is reached between the Contractors and the owners of salved cargo comprising at least 75% by value of salved cargo represented in accordance with Clause 7 of these Rules, the same agreement shall be binding on the owners of all salved cargo who were not represented at the time of the said approval.

15 Subject to the express approval of the Arbitrator, any salved cargo with a value below an agreed figure may be omitted from the salved fund and excused from liability for salvage where the cost of including such cargo in the process is likely to be disproportionate to its liability for salvage.

General Provisions

16 Lloyd's documents: Any Award notice authority order or other document signed by the Chairman of Lloyd's or any person authorised by the Council for the purpose shall be deemed to have been duly made or given by the Council and shall have the same force and effect in all respects as if it had been signed by every member of the Council.

17 Contractors' personnel and subcontractors

17.1 The Contractors may claim salvage on behalf of their employees and any other servants or agents who participate in the services and shall upon request provide the Owners with a reasonably satisfactory indemnity against all claims by or liabilities to such employees servants or agents.

17.2 The Contractors may engage the services of subcontractors for the purpose of fulfilling their obligations under clauses A and B of the Agreement but the Contractors shall nevertheless remain liable to the Owners for the due performance of those obligations.

17.3 In the event that subcontractors are engaged as aforesaid the Contractors may claim salvage on behalf of the subcontractors including their employees servants or agents and shall, if called upon so to do provide the Owners with a reasonably satisfactory indemnity against all claims by or liabilities to such subcontractors their employees servants or agents.

18 Disputes under Scopic Clause

Any dispute arising out of the Scopic Clause (including as to its incorporation or invocation) or the operations thereunder shall be referred for determination to the Arbitrator appointed under clause 5 hereof whose Award shall be final and binding subject to appeal as provided in clause 10 hereof.

19 Lloyd's Publications

Any guidance published by or on behalf of the Council relating to matters such as the Convention the workings and implementation of the Agreement is for information only and forms no part of the Agreement.

LLOYD'S STANDARD FORM OF SALVAGE AGREEMENT 80.10

(Approved and Published by the Council of Lloyd's)

PROCEDURAL RULES

(pursuant to Clause I of LOF 2000)

1 Arbitrators Powers

In addition to all powers conferred by the Arbitration Act 1996 (or any amendment thereof) the Arbitrator shall have power:

a to admit such oral or documentary evidence or information as he may think fit;

b to conduct the arbitration in such manner in all respects as he may think fit subject to these Procedural Rules and any amendments thereto as may from time to time be approved by the Council of Lloyd's ("the Council");

c to make such orders as to costs, fees and expenses including those of the Council charged under clauses 5.2 and 10.8 of the Lloyd's Standard Salvage and Arbitration Clauses ("the LSSA clauses") as may be fair and just;

d to direct that the recoverable costs of the arbitration or of any part of the proceedings shall be limited to a specified amount;

e to make any orders required to ensure that the arbitration is conducted in a fair and efficient manner consistent with the aim to minimise delay and expense and to arrange such meetings and determine all applications made by the parties as may be necessary for that purpose:

f to conduct all such meetings by means of a conference telephone call if the parties agree;

g on his own initiative or on the application of a party to correct any award (whether interim provisional or final) or to make an additional award in order to rectify any mistake error or omission provided that (i) any such correction is made within 28 days of the date of publication of the relevant award by the Council (ii) any additional award required is made within 56 days of the said date of publication or, in either case, such longer period as the Arbitrator may in his discretion allow.

2 Preliminary Meeting

a Within 6 weeks of being appointed or so soon thereafter as may be reasonable in the circumstances, the Arbitrator shall convene a preliminary meeting with the represented parties for the purpose of giving directions as to the manner in which the arbitration is to be conducted.

b The Arbitrator may dispense with the requirement for a preliminary meeting if the represented parties agree a consent order for directions which the Arbitrator is willing to approve. For the purpose of obtaining such approval, the Arbitrator must be provided by the contractors or their representatives with a brief summary the case in the form of a check list, any other party providing such comments as they deem appropriate so that the Arbitrator is placed in a position to decide whether to approve the consent order.

c In determining the manner in which the arbitration is to be conducted, the Arbitrator shall have regard to:

i the interests of unrepresented parties;

ii whether some form of shortened and/or simplified procedure is appropriate including whether the arbitration may be conducted on documents only with concise written submissions;

iii the overriding objectives set out in clause 2 of the LSSA clauses.

3 Order for Directions

Unless there are special reasons, the initial order for directions shall include;–

a a date for disclosure of documents including witness statements (see Rule 4);

b a date for proof of values;

c a date by which any party must identify any issue(s) in the case which are likely to necessitate the service of pleadings;

d a date for a progress meeting or additional progress meetings unless all represented parties with reasonable notice agree that the same is unnecessary;

e unless agreed by all represented parties to be premature, a date for the hearing and estimates for the time likely to be required by the Arbitrator to read evidence in advance and for the length of the hearing;

f any other matters deemed by the Arbitrator or any party to be appropriate to be included in the initial order.

4 Disclosure of documents

Unless otherwise agreed or ordered, disclosure shall be limited to the following classes of document:

a logs and any other contemporaneous records maintained by the shipowners personnel and personnel employed by the Contractors (including any subcontractors) and their respective surveyors or consultants in attendance during all or part of the salvage services;

b working charts, photographs, video or film records;

c contemporaneous reports including telexes, facsimile messages or prints of e-mail messages;

d survey reports;

e documents relevant to the proof of:

i out of pocket expenses

ii salved values

iii the particulars and values of all relevant salving tugs or other craft and equipment

f statements of witnesses of fact or other privileged documents on which the party wishes to rely.

5 Expert Evidence

a No expert evidence shall be adduced in the arbitration without the Arbitrators permission.

b The Arbitrator shall not give such permission unless satisfied that expert evidence is reasonably necessary for the proper determination of an issue arising in the arbitration.

c No party shall be given permission to adduce evidence from more than one expert in each field requiring expert evidence save in exceptional circumstances.

d Any application for permission to adduce expert evidence must be made at the latest within 14 days after disclosure of relevant documents has been effected.

6 Mediation

The Arbitrator shall ensure that in all cases the represented parties are informed of the benefit which might be derived from the use of mediation.

7 Hearing of Arbitration

a In fixing or agreeing to a date for the hearing of an arbitration, the Arbitrator shall not unless agreed by all represented parties fix or accept a date unless the Arbitrator can allow time to read the principal evidence in advance, hear the arbitration and produce the award to the Council for publication in not more than 1 month from conclusion of the hearing.

b The date fixed for the hearing shall be maintained unless application to alter the date is made to the Arbitrator within 14 days of the completion of discovery or unless the Arbitrator in the exercise of his discretion determines at a later time that an adjournment is necessary or desirable in the interests of justice or fairness.

c Unless all parties represented in the arbitration agree otherwise the Arbitrator shall relinquish his appointment if a hearing date cannot be agreed, fixed or maintained in accordance with rule 7(a) and/or (b) above due to the Arbitrator's commitments. In that event the Council shall appoint in his stead another arbitrator who is able to meet the requirements of those rules.

8 Appeals

a All references in these Rules to the Arbitrator shall include the Arbitrator on Appeal where the circumstances so permit.

b in any case in which a party giving notice of appeal intends to contend that the Arbitrator's findings on the salved value of all or any of the salved property were erroneous, or that the Arbitrator has erred in any finding as to the person whose property was at risk, a statement of such grounds of appeal shall be given in or accompanying the notice of appeal.

c in all cases grounds of appeal or cross-appeal will be given to the Arbitrator on Appeal within 21 days of the notice of appeal or cross- appeal unless an extension of time is agreed.

d Any respondent to an appeal who intends to contend that the award of the Original Arbitrator should be affirmed on grounds other than those relied upon by the Original Arbitrator shall give notice to that effect specifying the grounds of his contention within 14 days of receipt of the grounds of appeal mentioned in (c) above unless an extension of time is agreed.

80.11 # SCOPIC CLAUSE

1. General

This SCOPIC clause is supplementary to any Lloyd's Form Salvage Agreement "No Cure–No Pay" ("Main Agreement") which incorporates the provisions of Article 14 of the International Convention on Salvage 1989 ("Article 14"). The definitions in the Main Agreement are incorporated into this SCOPIC clause. If the SCOPIC clause is inconsistent with any provisions of the Main Agreement or inconsistent with the law applicable hereto, the SCOPIC clause, once invoked under sub-clause 2 hereof, shall override such other provisions to the extent necessary to give business efficacy to the agreement. Subject to the provisions of sub-clause 4 hereof, the method of assessing Special Compensation under Convention Article 14(1) to 14(4) inclusive shall be substituted by the method of assessment set out hereinafter. If this SCOPIC clause has been incorporated into the Main Agreement the Contractor may make no claim pursuant to Article 14 except in the circumstances described in sub-clause 4 hereof. For the purposes of liens and time limits the services hereunder will be treated in the same manner as salvage.

2. Invoking the SCOPIC Clause

The Contractor shall have the option to invoke by written notice to the owners of the vessel the SCOPIC clause set out hereafter at any time of his choosing regardless of the circumstances and, in particular, regardless of whether or not there is a "threat of damage to the environment". The assessment of SCOPIC remuneration shall commence from the time the written notice is given to the owners of the vessel and services rendered before the said written notice shall not be remunerated under this SCOPIC clause at all but in accordance with Convention Article 13 as incorporated into the Main Agreement ("Article 13").

3. Security for SCOPIC Remuneration

(i) The owners of the vessel shall provide to the Contractor within 2 working days (excluding Saturdays and Sundays and holidays usually observed at Lloyd's) after receiving written notice from the contractor invoking the SCOPIC clause, a bank guarantee or P&I Club letter (hereinafter called "the Initial Security") in a form reasonably satisfactory to the Contractor providing security for his claim for SCOPIC remuneration in the sum of US$3 million, inclusive of interest and costs.

(ii) If, at any time after the provision of the Initial Security the owners of the vessel reasonably assess the SCOPIC remuneration plus interest and costs due hereunder to be less than the security in place, the owners of the vessel shall be entitled to require the Contractor to reduce the security to a reasonable sum and the Contractor shall be obliged to do so once a reasonable sum has been agreed.

(iii) If at any time after the provision of the Initial Security the Contractor reasonably assesses the SCOPIC remuneration plus interest and costs due hereunder to be greater than the security in place, the Contractor shall be entitled to require the owners of the vessel to increase the security to a reasonable sum and the owners of the vessel shall be obliged to do so once a reasonable sum has been agreed.

(iv) In the absence of agreement, any dispute concerning the proposed Guarantor, the form of the security or the amount of any reduction or increase in the security in place shall be resolved by the Arbitrator.

4. Withdrawal

If the owners of the vessel do not provide the Initial Security within the said 2 working days, the Contractor, at his option, and on giving notice to the owners of the vessel, shall be entitled to withdraw from all the provisions of the SCOPIC clause and revert to his rights under the Main Agreement including Article 14 which shall apply as if the SCOPIC clause had not existed. PROVIDED THAT this right of withdrawal may only be exercised if, at the time of giving the said notice of withdrawal the owners of the vessel have still not provided the Initial Security or any alternative security which the owners of the vessel and the Contractor may agree will be sufficient.

5. Tariff Rates.

(i) SCOPIC remuneration shall mean the total of the tariff rates of personnel; tugs and other craft; portable salvage equipment; out of pocket expenses; and bonus due.

(ii) SCOPIC remuneration in respect of all personnel; tugs and other craft; and portable salvage equipment shall be assessed on a time and materials basis in accordance with the Tariff set out in Appendix "A". This tariff will apply until reviewed and amended by the SCR Committee in accordance with Appendix B(1)(b). The tariff rates which will be used to calculate SCOPIC remuneration are those in force at the time the salvage services take place.

(iii) "Out of pocket" expenses shall mean all those monies reasonably paid by or for and on behalf of the Contractor to any third party and in particular includes the hire of men, tugs, other craft and equipment used and other expenses reasonably necessary for the operation. They will be agreed at cost, PROVIDED THAT:

(a) If the expenses relate to the hire of men, tugs, other craft and equipment from another ISU member or their affiliate(s), the amount due will be calculated on the tariff rates set out in Appendix "A" regardless of the actual cost.

(b) If men, tugs, other craft and equipment are hired from any party who is not an ISU member and the hire rate is greater than the tariff rates referred to in Appendix "A" the actual cost will be allowed in full, subject to the Special Casualty Representative ("SCR") being satisfied that in the particular circumstances of the case, it was reasonable for the Contractor to hire such items at that cost. If an SCR is not appointed or if there is a dispute, then the Arbitrator shall decide whether the expense was reasonable in all in the circumstances.

(c) Any out of pocket expense incurred during the course of the service in a currency other than US dollars shall for the purpose of the SCOPIC clause be converted to US dollars at the rate prevailing at the termination of the services.

(iv) In addition to the rates set out above and any out of pocket expenses, the Contractor shall be entitled to a standard bonus of 25% of those rates except that if the out of pocket expenses described in sub-paragraph 5(iii)(b) exceed the applicable tariff rates in Appendix "A" the Contractor shall be entitled to a bonus such that he shall receive in total

(a) The actual cost of such men, tugs, other craft and equipment plus 10% of the cost, or

(b) The tariff rate for such men, tugs, other craft and equipment plus 25% of the tariff rate whichever is the greater.

6. Article 13 Award

(i) The salvage services under the Main Agreement shall continue to be assessed in accordance with Article 13, even if the Contractor has invoked the SCOPIC clause. SCOPIC remuneration as assessed under sub-clause 5 above will be payable only by the owners of the vessel and only to the extent that it exceeds the total Article 13 Award (or, if none, any potential Article 13 Award) payable by all salved interests (including cargo, bunkers, lubricating oil and stores) before currency 1 9.2000 adjustment and before interest and costs even if the Article 13 Award or any part of it is not recovered.

(ii) In the event of the Article 13 Award or settlement being in a currency other than United States dollars it shall, for the purposes of the SCOPIC clause, be exchanged at the rate of exchange prevailing at the termination of the services under the Main Agreement.

(iii) The salvage Award under Article 13 shall not be diminished by reason of the exception to the principle of "No Cure – No Pay" in the form of SCOPIC remuneration.

7. Discount

If the SCOPIC clause is invoked under sub-clause 2 hereof and the Article 13 Award or settlement (before currency adjustment and before interest and costs) under the Main Agreement is greater than the assessed SCOPIC remuneration then, notwithstanding the actual date on which the SCOPIC remuneration provisions were invoked, the said Article 13 Award or settlement shall be discounted by 25% of the difference between the said Article 13 Award or settlement and the amount of SCOPIC remuneration that would have been assessed had the SCOPIC remuneration provisions been invoked on the first day of the services.

8. Payment of SCOPIC Remuneration

(i) The date for payment of any SCOPIC remuneration which may be due hereunder will vary according to the circumstances.

(a) If there is no potential salvage award within the meaning of Article 13 as incorporated into the Main Agreement then, subject to Appendix B(5)(c)(iv), the undisputed amount of SCOPIC remuneration due hereunder will be paid by the owners of the vessel within 1 month of the presentation of the claim. Interest on sums due will accrue from the date of termination of the services until the date of payment at the US prime rate plus 1%.

(b) If there is a claim for an Article 13 salvage award as well as a claim for SCOPIC remuneration, subject to Appendix B(5)(c)(iv), 75% of the amount by which the assessed SCOPIC remuneration exceeds the total Article 13 security demanded from ship and cargo will be paid by the owners of the vessel within 1 month and any undisputed balance paid when the Article 13 salvage award has been assessed and falls due. Interest will accrue from the date of termination of the services until the date of payment at the US prime rate plus 1%.

(ii) The Contractor hereby agrees to give an indemnity in a form acceptable to the owners of the vessel in respect of any overpayment in the event that the SCOPIC remuneration due ultimately proves to be less than the sum paid on account.

9. Termination

(i) The Contractor shall be entitled to terminate the services under the SCOPIC clause and the Main Agreement by written notice to owners of the vessel with a copy to the SCR (if any) and any Special Representative appointed if the total cost of his services to date and the services that will be needed to fulfil his obligations hereunder to the property (calculated by means of the tariff rate but before the bonus conferred by sub-clause 5(iii) hereof) will exceed the sum of:

(a) The value of the property capable of being salved; and

(b) All sums to which he will be entitled as SCOPIC remuneration

(ii) The owners of the vessel may at any time terminate the obligation to pay SCOPIC remuneration after the SCOPIC clause has been invoked under sub-clause 2 hereof provided that the Contractor shall be entitled to at least 5 clear days' notice of such termination. In the event of such termination the assessment of SCOPIC remuneration shall take into account all monies due under the tariff rates set out in Appendix A hereof including time for demobilisation to the extent that such time did reasonably exceed the 5 days' notice of termination.

(iii) The termination provisions contained in sub-clause 9(i) and 9(ii) above shall only apply if the Contractor is not restrained from demobilising his equipment by Government, Local or PortAuthorities or any other officially recognised body having jurisdiction over the area where the services are being rendered.

10. Duties of Contractor

The duties and liabilities of the Contractor shall remain the same as under the Main Agreement, namely to use his best endeavours to salve the vessel and property thereon and in so doing to prevent or minimise damage to the environment.

11. Article 18–1989 Salvage Convention

The Contractor may be deprived of the whole or part of the payment due under the SCOPIC clause to the extent that the salvage operations thereunder have become necessary or more difficult or more prolonged or the salved fund has been reduced or extinguished because of fault or neglect on its part or if the Contractor has been guilty of fraud or other dishonest conduct.

12. Special Casualty Representative ("SCR")

Once this SCOPIC clause has been invoked in accordance with sub-clause 2 hereof the owners of the vessel may at their sole option appoint an SCR to attend the salvage operation in accordance with the terms and conditions set out in Appendix B. Any SCR so appointed shall not be called upon by any of the parties hereto to give evidence relating to non-salvage issues.

13. Special Representatives

At any time after the SCOPIC clause has been invoked the Hull and Machinery underwriter (or, if more than one, the lead underwriter) and one owner or underwriter of all or part of any cargo on board the vessel may each appoint one special representative (hereinafter called respectively the "Special Hull Representative" and the "Special Cargo Representative" and collectively called the "Special Representatives") at the sole expense of the appointor to attend the casualty to observe and report upon the salvage operation on the terms and conditions set out in Appendix C hereof. Such Special Representatives shall be technical men and not practising lawyers.

14. Pollution Prevention

The assessment of SCOPIC remuneration shall include the prevention of pollution as well as the removal of pollution in the immediate vicinity of the vessel insofar as this is necessary for the proper execution of the salvage but not otherwise.

15. General Average

SCOPIC remuneration shall not be a General Average expense to the extent that it exceeds the Article 13 Award; any liability to pay such SCOPIC remuneration shall be that of the Shipowner alone and no claim whether direct, indirect, by way of indemnity or recourse or otherwise relating to SCOPIC remuneration in excess of the Article 13 Award shall be made in General Average or under the vessel's Hull and Machinery Policy by the owners of the vessel.

16. Any dispute arising out of this SCOPIC clause or the operations thereunder shall be referred to Arbitration as provided for under the Main Agreement.

80.12 APPENDIX A (SCOPIC)

1. PERSONNEL

a) The daily tariff rate, or pro rata for part thereof, for personnel reasonably engaged on the contract, including any necessary time in proceeding to and returning from the casualty, shall be as follows:

Office administration, including communications	US$1,155
Salvage Master	US$1,735
Naval Architect or Salvage Officer/Engineer	US$1,440
Assistant Salvage Officer/Engineer	US$1,155
Diving Supervisor	US$1,155
HSE qualified diver or his equivalent but excluding saturation or mixed gas divers (whose rate should be agreed with the SCR or determined by the Arbitrator)	US$1,040
Salvage Foreman	US$ 865
Riggers, Fitters, Equipment Operators	US$ 693
Specialist Advisors–Fire Fighters, Chemicals, Pollution Control	US$1,155

b) The crews of tugs, and other craft, normally aboard that tug or craft for the purpose of its customary work are included in the tariff rate for that tug or craft but when because of the nature and/or location of the services to be rendered, it is a legal requirement for an additional crew member or members to be aboard the tug or craft, the cost of such additional crew will be paid.

c) The rates for any personnel not set out above shall be agreed with the SCR or, failing agreement, be determined by the Arbitrator.

d) For the avoidance of doubt, personnel are "reasonably engaged on the contract" within the meaning of Appendix A sub-clause 1(a) hereof if, in addition to working, they are eating, sleeping or otherwise resting on site or travelling to or from the site; personnel who fall ill or are injured while reasonably engaged on the contract shall be charged for at the appropriate daily tariff rate until they are demobilised but only if it was reasonable to mobilise them in the first place.

e) SCOPIC remuneration shall cease to accrue in respect of personnel who die on site from the date of death.

2. TUGS AND OTHER CRAFT

(a) (i) Tugs, which shall include salvage tugs, harbour tugs, anchor handling tugs, coastal/ocean towing tugs, off-shore support craft, and any other work boat in excess of 500 b.h.p., shall be charged at the following rates, exclusive of fuel or lubricating oil, for each day, or pro rata for part thereof, that they are reasonably engaged in the services, including proceeding towards the casualty from the tugs location when SCOPIC is invoked or when the tugs are mobilised (whichever is the later) and from the tugs position when their involvement in the services terminates to a reasonable location having due regard to their employment immediately prior to their involvement in the services and standing by on the basis of their certificated b.h.p.:

For each b.h.p. up to 5.000 b.h.p.	US$ 2.500
For each b.h.p. between 5,001 & 12,000 b.h.p.	US$ 1.875
For each b.h.p. between 12,001 & 20,000 b.h.p.	US$ 1.250
For each b.h.p. over 20,000 b.h.p.	US$ 0.625

(ii) Any tug which has aboard certified fire fighting equipment shall, in addition to the above rates, be paid:

US$625 per day, or pro rata for part thereof, if equipped with Fi Fi 0.5

US$1,250 per day, or pro rata for part thereof, if equipped with Fi Fi 1.0 for that period in which the tug is engaged in fire fighting necessitating the use of the certified fire fighting equipment.

(iii) Any tug which is certified as "Ice Class" shall, in addition to the above, be paid US$1,250 per day, or pro rata for part thereof, when forcing or breaking ice during the course of services including proceeding to and returning from the casualty.

(iv) For the purposes of paragraph 2(a)(i) hereof tugs shall be remunerated for any reasonable delay or deviation for the purposes of taking on board essential salvage equipment, provisions or personnel which the Contractor reasonably anticipates he shall require in rendering the services which would not normally be found on vessels of the tugs size and type.

(b) Any launch or work boat of less than 500 b.h.p. shall, exclusive of fuel and lubricating oil, be charged at a rate of US$3.75 for each b.h.p.

(c) Any other craft, not falling within the above definitions, shall be charged out at a market rate for that craft, exclusive of fuel and lubricating oil. such rate to be agreed with the SCR or. failing agreement, determined by the Arbitrator.

(d) All fuel and lubricating oil consumed during the services shall be paid at cost of replacement and shall be treated as an out of pocket expense.

(e) For the avoidance of doubt, the above rates shall not include any portable salvage equipment normally aboard the tug or craft and such equipment shall be treated in the same manner as portable salvage equipment and the Contactors shall be reimbursed in respect thereof in accordance with Appendix paragraphs 3 and 4 (i) and (ii) hereof.

(f) SCOPIC remuneration shall cease to accrue in respect of tugs and other craft which become a commercial total loss from the date they stop being engaged in the services plus a reasonable period for demobilisation (if appropriate) PROVIDED that such SCOPIC remuneration in respect of demobilisation shall only be payable if the commercial total loss arises whilst engaged in the services and through no fault of the Contractors, their servants, agents or sub-contractors.

3. PORTABLE SALVAGE EQUIPMENT

(a) The daily tariff, or pro rata for part thereof, for all portable salvage equipment reasonably engaged during the services, including any time necessary for mobilisation and demobilisation, shall be as follows:

	Rate–US$.
Generators	
Up to 50 Kw	69
51 to 120 Kw	144
121 to 300 kW	230
Over 301 kW	403
Portable Inert Gas Systems	
1,000m³/hour	1,380
1.500m³/hour	1,610
Compressors	
High Pressure	115
185 Cfm	173
600 Cfm	288
1200 Cfm	480
Air Manifold	12
Blower; 1.500m³/min.	978

Pumping Equipment	
Air	
2"	86
Diesel	
2"	58
4"	104
Electrical Submersible	
2"	58
4"	173
6"	138
Hydraulic	
6"	690
8"	1,150

Hoses	**Rate–US$.**
Air Hose	
¾" per 30 metres or 120 feet	23
2" per 30 metres or 120 feet	46
Layflat	
2" per 6 metres or 20 feet	12
4" per 6 metres or 20 feet	17
6" per 6 metres or 20 feet	23
Rigid	
2" per 6 metres or 20 feet	17
4" per 6 metres or 20 feet	23
6" per 6 metres or 20 feet	29
8" per 6 metres or 20 feet	35

Fenders	
Yokohama	
1.00m, × 2.00m	86
2.50m, × 5.50m	173
3.50m, × 6.50m	288
Low Pressure inflatable	
3 metres	81
6 metres	81
9 metres	173
12 metres	288
16 metres	288

Welding & Cutting Equipment	**Rate US$.**
Bolt Gun	345
Gas Detector	115

Welding & Cutting Equipment	**Rate US$.**
Hot Tap Machine, including supporting equipment	1150
Oxy-acetylene Surface Cutting Gear	29
Underwater Cutting Gear	58
Underwater Welding Kit	58
250 Amp Welder	173
400 Amp Welder	230

Pollution Control Equipment	
Oil Boom, 24", per 10 metres	35
Oil Boom, 36", per 10 metres	115
Oil Boom, 48", per 10 metres	224

Lighting Systems	
Lighting String, per 50 feet	**29**
Light Tower	**58**
Underwater Lighting System, 1,000 watts	**86**

Winches	
Up to 20 tons, including 50 metres of wire	230

Storage Equipment	
12′ Container	29
20′ Container	46

Miscellaneous Equipment	
Air Bags, less than 5 tons lift	46
5 to 5 tons lift	230
Air Lift 4"	115
6"	230
8"	345
Air Tugger, up to 3 tons	86
Ballast/Fuel Oil Storage Bins, 50.000 litres	115
Chain Saw	23
Damage Stability Computer and Software	288
Echo Sounder, portable	29
Extension Ladder	23
Hydraulic Jack, up to 120 tons	86
Hydraulic Powerpack 75kW	86
Pressure washer water	288
Pressure washer steam	618
Rigging Package, heavy	460
Light	230
Rock, Drill	58
Splitter	460
Steel Saw	23
Tirfors, up to 5 tonnes	12
Thermal Imaging Camera	288
Tool Package, per set	201
Ventilation Package	23
VHF Radio	12
Z Boat, including outboard	
up to 14 feet	230
over 14 feet	403

Shackles	**Rate–US$.**
Up to 50 tonnes	12
51 to 120 tonnes	23
121 to 200 tonnes	35
Over 200 tonnes	58

Distribution Boards	
Up to 50 Kw	69
51 to 120 Kw	144
121 to 300 Kw	230
Over 301 Kw	403

Protective Clothing	**Rate–US$.**
Breathing Gear.	58
Hazardous Environment Suit	115

Diving Equipment	
Decompression Chamber	
2 man, including compressor	575
4 man, including compressor	805
Hot Water Diving Assembly	288
Underwater Magnets	23
Underwater Drill	23
Shallow Water Dive Spread	259

(b) Any portable salvage equipment engaged but not set out above shall be charged at a rate to be agreed with the SCR or, failing agreement, determined by the Arbitrator.

(c) The total charge (before bonus) for each item of portable salvage equipment, owned by the contractor, shall not exceed the manufacturer's recommended retail price on the last day of the services multiplied by 1.5.

(d) Compensation for any portable salvage equipment lost or destroyed during the services shall be paid provided that the total of such compensation and the daily tariff rate (before bonus) in respect of that item do not exceed the actual cost of replacing the item at the Contractors base with the most similar equivalent new item multiplied by 1.5.

(e) All consumables such as welding rods, boiler suits, small ropes etc. shall be charged at cost and shall be treated as an out of pocket expenses.

(f) The Contractor shall be entitled to remuneration at a stand-by rate of 50% of the full tariff rate plus bonus for any portable salvage equipment reasonably mobilised but not used during the salvage operation provided

  (i) It has been mobilised with the prior agreement of the owner of the vessel or its mobilisation was reasonable in the circumstances of the casualty, or

  (ii) It comprises portable salvage equipment normally aboard the tug or craft that would have been reasonably mobilised had it not already been aboard the tug or craft.

(g) SCOPIC remuneration shall cease to accrue in respect of portable salvage equipment which becomes a commercial total loss from the date it ceases to be useable plus a reasonable period for demobilisation (if appropriate) PROVIDED that such SCOPIC remuneration in respect of demobilisation shall only be payable if the commercial total loss arises while it is engaged in the services and through no fault of the Contractors, their servants, agents or sub-contractors.

4. DOWNTIME

If a tug or piece of portable salvage equipment breaks down or is damaged without fault on the part of the Contractor, his servants, agents or sub-contractors and as a direct result of performing the services it should be paid for during the repair while on site at the stand-by rate of 50% of the tariff rate plus uplift pursuant to sub-clause 5(iv) of the SCOPIC clause. If a tug or piece of portable salvage equipment breaks down or otherwise becomes inoperable without fault on the part of the Contractor, his servants, agents or subcontractors and as a direct result of performing the services and cannot be repaired on site then:

(i) If it is not used thereafter but remains on site then no SCOPIC remuneration is payable in respect of that tug or piece of portable salvage equipment from the time of the breakdown,

(ii) if it is removed from site, repaired and reasonably returned to the site for use SCOPIC remuneration at the standby rate of 50% of the tariff rate plus bonus pursuant to sub-clause 5(iv) of the SCOPIC clause shall be payable from the breakdown to the date it is returned to the site.

(iii) If it is removed from the site and not returned SCOPIC remuneration ceases from the breakdown but is, in addition, payable for the period that it takes to return it directly to base at the stand-by rate of 50% of the tariff rate plus bonus pursuant to sub-clause 5(iv) of the SCOPIC clause

80.13 SALVAGE GUARANTEE FORM I.S.U.1

To:

Dear Sirs,

"..................................." **Salvage**

Lloyd's Standard Form of Salvage Agreement dated ("the LOF")

1. In consideration of your refraining from calling for the completion of security by means of a guarantee in the form prescribed by the Council of Lloyd's in connection with your claim for salvage remuneration (but not any claim for Art. 14 Special Compensation or SCOPIC Remuneration) in respect of salvage services rendered to the "......" under the terms of the LOF we
   hereby undertake to pay to you on demand any sum or sums, together with interest and costs which may be agreed between you and the owners of the salved property or which may be awarded to you in respect of the said salved property by an arbitrator or appeal arbitrator appointed by the Council of Lloyd's under the terms of the said LOF.
2. In the event of an amicable settlement of your claim under the LOF being reached, and in the absence of any agreement as to date of payment and interest accruing thereafter, it is hereby agreed that payment of the settlement monies will be effected within 28 calendar days after the date of such settlement and, in the event of non-payment within that period, we undertake to pay, in addition to the principal sum, interest thereon at the rate of ....% per annum from and including the day after the due date for payment specified above until and including the date upon which payment is received and credited for value to your account with ....Bank, at ....
3. Any monies paid by the undersigned hereunder shall be deemed to have been paid by the undersigned as surety for the party or parties hereby guaranteed, provided that, notwithstanding anything hereinbefore contained, the liability of the undersigned as between the undersigned on the one hand and you on the other hand shall be that of a principal debtor, and the undersigned shall not be released by time being given or other indulgence shown to the party or parties hereby guaranteed or by any other act, matter or thing whereby the undersigned, if liable as a surety only, would or might have been released.
4. This undertaking shall be governed by and construed in accordance with English law and we undertake, when called upon to do so, to give irrevocable instructions to English solicitors to accept service of proceedings issued by you against us in relation to this undertaking
5. Provided always that our liability under this guarantee shall not exceed the sum of $ inclusive of interest and costs.
6. This undertaking is given in respect of ....

Signed this day of 20

By...

Authorised signatory of........................

SEE OVER FOR NOTES ON COMPLETION OF THIS GUARANTEE FORM

GUIDANCE NOTES ON THE COMPLETION OF SALVAGE GUARANTEE I.S.U.1 80.14

1. The guarantee should be addressed to the contractors named in the LOF.

2. **Paragraph 1**
Insert the general identity of the party on whose behalf the guarantee is given, e.g. m.v. "..........." her cargo, freight, bunkers and stores and any other property thereon;
or
the bunkers aboard m.v. "..........."
or
the cargo aboard m.v. ".........."

Insert the date of the LOF Agreement.

The guarantee is designed for a single guarantor. If there are two or more guarantors amend the 4th line to read "we hereby jointly and severally undertake to pay you"

3. **Paragraph 2**
Insert the appropriate rate of interest.

At the end of this paragraph insert the name of the company or firm, or the bank and account number to whom the contractors wish payment to be made. If unknown amend to read "for value to an account to be specified by you".

4. **Paragraph 5**
Insert the amount in the currency for which the guarantee is given, inclusive of interest and costs.

5. **Paragraph 6**
Insert details of the salved property on whose behalf the guarantee is given
e.g. m.v." " her cargo, freight, bunkers, stores and any other property thereon;
or
the bunkers aboard m.v. "...........";
or
the cargo aboard m.v. "...........";
or
the cargo aboard m.v. "...........", carried under Bills of Lading New York to London Nos. 1, 4, 8,9.

80.15 SALVAGE GUARANTEE FORM I.S.U.2

To:

Dear Sirs,

"........................" **Salvage**

Lloyd's Standard Form of Salvage Agreement dated . . . ("the LOF")

1. In consideration of your not causing delay to the ". . . . ." at the port or ports of . . . . by the detention or arrest of the cargo and/or other salved property described in paragraph 5 ("the Unsecured Property") for the purpose of obtaining security from the Unsecured Property in connection with your claim for salvage remuneration in respect of salvage services rendered pursuant to the LOF in accordance with the requirements of Clause 4.5 of the Lloyd's Standard Salvage and Arbitration Clauses (the "LSSA Clauses") we hereby undertake to pay to you on demand any sum or sums together with interest and costs which may either be agreed between you and the owners of the Unsecured Property or which may be awarded to you in respect thereof by an arbitrator or appeal arbitrator appointed by the Council of Lloyd's under the LOF provided always that:–
   (a) you will continue your efforts to obtain from the owners of the Unsecured Property security in accordance with your requirements such efforts to comprise:–
   (i) notifying your security requirements to the Council of Lloyd's in accordance with Clause 4.1 of the LSSA Clauses
   (ii) liaising with the owners and/or charterers of the vessel to ensure that none of the Unsecured Property is released to its owners until security has been provided to you in respect of it in accordance with Clause 4.5 of the LSSA Clauses;
   (iii) if so requested by the owners and/or charterers of the vessel taking such action as may be possible to enforce your maritime lien (the right to which is not to be affected by this agreement) against the Unsecured Property at the port or ports where it is discharged
   (b) our liability hereunder inclusive of any liability for interest and/or costs shall not exceed the sum of and we shall cease to have any liability in respect of Unsecured Property when security has been provided in respect of it in accordance with your requirement.

2. In the event of an amicable settlement of your claim under the LOF being reached, and in the absence of any agreement as to date of payment and interest accruing thereafter, it is agreed that payment of the settlement monies will be effected within 28 calendar days after the date of such settlement and, in the event of non-payment within that period, we undertake to pay, in addition to the principal sum, interest thereon at the rate of percent per annum from and including the day after the due date for payment specified above until and including the date upon which payment is received and credited for value to your account with Bank, .at . . . .

3. Any monies paid by the undersigned hereunder shall be deemed to have been paid by the undersigned as surety for the party or parties hereby guaranteed, provided that, notwithstanding anything hereinbefore contained, the liability of the undersigned as between the undersigned on the one hand and you on the other hand shall be that of a principal debtor; and the undersigned shall not be released by time being given or other indulgence shown to the party or parties hereby guaranteed or by any other act, matter or thing whereby the undersigned, if liable as a surety only, would or might have been released.

4. This undertaking shall be governed by and construed in accordance with English law and we undertake, when called upon to do so, to give irrevocable instructions to English solicitors to accept service of proceedings issued by you against us in relation to this undertaking.

5. This undertaking is given in respect of

Signed this day of 20

By...

Authorised signatory of..........................

SEE OVER FOR NOTES ON COMPLETION OF THIS GUARANTEE FORM

80.16 GUIDANCE NOTES ON THE COMPLETION OF SALVAGE GUARANTEE I.S.U.2

1. The guarantee should be addressed to the contractors named in the LOF.

2. **Paragraph 1**

   Insert the name of the salved vessel, e.g. m.v “”

   Insert the date of the LOF.

   The guarantee is designed for a single guarantor. If there are two or more guarantors amends the 6th line to read “we hereby jointly and severally undertake to pay you on demand”

3. **Paragraph 1 (b)**

   Insert the amount of the guarantee in words and figures.

4. **Paragraph 2**

   Insert the appropriate rate of interest.

   At the end of this paragraph insert the name of the company or firm, or the bank and account no to whom the contractors wish payment to be made. If unknown amend to read “for value to an account to be specified by you”.

5. **Paragraph 5**

   (a) Insert details of the salved cargo and/or other salved property on whose behalf the Guarantee is given, e.g.

   the bunkers aboard m.v. “ . . . . ”;

   or

   the cargo aboard m.v. “ . . . . ”;

   or

   the cargo aboard m.v. “. . . . . ”, carried under Bills of Lading, New York to London Nos. 1,4,8,9.

Index